Fodor's 2012

CARIBBEAN

Fodor's Travel Publications   New York, Toronto, London, Sydney, Auckland
www.fodors.com

Eugene Fodor:
The Spy Who Loved Travel

As Fodor's celebrates our 75th anniversary, we are honoring the colorful and adventurous life of Eugene Fodor, who revolutionized guidebook publishing in 1936 with his first book, *On the Continent, The Entertaining Travel Annual.*

Eugene Fodor's life seemed to leap off the pages of a great spy novel. Born in Hungary, he spoke six languages and graduated from the Sorbonne and the London School of Economics. During World War II he joined the Office of Strategic Services, the budding spy agency for the United States. He commanded the team that went behind enemy lines to liberate Prague, and recommended to Generals Eisenhower, Bradley, and Patton that Allied troops move to the capital city. After the war, Fodor worked as a spy in Austria, posing as a U.S. diplomat.

In 1949 Eugene Fodor—with the help of the CIA—established Fodor's Modern Guides. He was passionate about travel and wanted to bring his insider's knowledge of Europe to a new generation of sophisticated Americans who wanted to explore and seek out experiences beyond their borders. Among his innovations were annual updates, consulting local experts, and including cultural and historical perspectives and an emphasis on people—not just sites. As Fodor described it, "The main interest and enjoyment of foreign travel lies not only in 'the sites,' . . . but in contact with people whose customs, habits, and general outlook are different from your own."

Eugene Fodor died in 1991, but his legacy, Fodor's Travel, continues. It is now one of the world's largest and most trusted brands in travel information, covering more than 600 destinations worldwide in guidebooks, on Fodors.com, and in ebooks and iPhone apps. Technology and the accessibility of travel may be changing, but Eugene Fodor's unique storytelling skills and reporting style are behind every word of today's Fodor's guides.

Our editors and writers continue to embrace Eugene Fodor's vision of building personal relationships through travel. We invite you to join the Fodor's community at fodors.com/community and share your experiences with like-minded travelers. Tell us when we're right. Tell us when we're wrong. And share fantastic travel secrets that aren't yet in Fodor's. Together, we will continue to deepen our understanding of our world.

Happy 75th Anniversary, Fodor's! Here's to many more.

Tim Jarrell, Publisher

FODOR'S CARIBBEAN 2012

Editors: Eric B. Wechter, Douglas Stallings

Editorial Contributors: Carol M. Bareuther, John Bigley, Erica Duecy, Marlise Kast, Lynda Lohr, Elise Meyer, Susan Maccallum-Whitcomb, Vernon O'Reilly-Ramesar, Paris Permenter, Heather Rodino, Ramona Settle, Eileen Robinson Smith, Roberta Sotonoff, Julie Schwietert Collazo, Jordan Simon, Jeffrey Van Fleet, Jane E. Zarem

Production Editor: Carrie Parker
Maps & Illustrations: Mark Stroud and David Lindroth, *cartographers;* Bob Blake, Rebecca Baer, *map editors;* William Wu, *information graphics*
Design: Fabrizio La Rocca, *creative director;* Guido Caroti, Siobhan O'Hare, *art directors;* Tina Malaney, Nora Rosansky, Chie Ushio, *designers;* Melanie Marin, *senior picture editor*
Cover Photo: (Tobago): Peter Adams/Agency Jon Arnold Images/age fotostock
Production Manager: Angela L. McLean

COPYRIGHT

ISBN 978-0-679-00926-9

ISSN 1524-9174

SPECIAL SALES

This book is available at special discounts for bulk purchases for sales promotions or premiums. Special editions, including personalized covers, excerpts of existing books, and corporate imprints, can be created in large quantities for special needs. For more information, write to Special Markets/Premium Sales, 1745 Broadway, MD 6-2, New York, NY 10019, or e-mail specialmarkets@randomhouse.com.

AN IMPORTANT TIP & AN INVITATION

Although all prices, opening times, and other details in this book are based on information supplied to us at press time, changes occur all the time in the travel world, and Fodor's cannot accept responsibility for facts that become outdated or for inadvertent errors or omissions. So **always confirm information when it matters**, especially if you're making a detour to visit a specific place. Your experiences—positive and negative—matter to us. If we have missed or misstated something, **please write to us**. Share your opinion instantly through our online feedback center at fodors.com/contact-us.

PRINTED IN CHINA

10 9 8 7 6 5 4 3 2 1

CONTENTS

Fodor's Features

ABOUT
THIS BOOK

Our Ratings

At Fodor's, we spend considerable time choosing the best places in a destination so you don't have to. By default, anything we recommend in this book is worth visiting. But some sights, properties, and experiences are so great that we've recognized them with additional accolades. Orange **Fodor's Choice** stars indicate our top recommendations; black stars highlight places we deem **Highly Recommended**; and **Best Bets** call attention to top properties in various categories. Disagree with any of our choices? Care to nominate a new place? Visit our feedback center at www.fodors.com/feedback.

Hotels

Hotels have private bath, phone, TV, and air-conditioning, and do not offer meals unless we specify that in the review. We always list facilities but not whether you'll be charged an extra fee to use them.

> For expanded hotel reviews, visit **Fodors.com**

Restaurants

Unless we state otherwise, restaurants are open for lunch and dinner daily. We mention dress only when there's a specific requirement and reservations only when they're essential or not accepted—it's always best to book ahead.

Credit Cards

We assume that restaurants and hotels accept credit cards. If not, we'll note it in the review.

Budget Well

Hotel and restaurant price categories from ¢ to $$$$ are defined in the opening pages of the respective chapters. For attractions, we always give standard adult admission fees; reductions are usually available for children, students, and senior citizens.

Listings
★ Fodor's Choice
★ Highly recommended
⊠ Physical address
✛ Directions or Map coordinates
🕧 Mailing address
☎ Telephone
🖷 Fax
⊕ On the Web

✍ E-mail
🎫 Admission fee
🕓 Open/closed times
Ⓜ Metro stations
🚍 No credit cards

Hotels & Restaurants
🏨 Hotel
🛏 Number of rooms
♿ Facilities
🍽 Meal plans
✗ Restaurant
🍴 Reservations
🎩 Dress code
🚭 Smoking

Outdoors
🏌 Golf
⛺ Camping

Other
😊 Family-friendly
⇨ See also
⊠ Branch address
☞ Take note

Experience
the Caribbean

WHAT'S NEW IN THE CARIBBEAN

Tourism on the upswing—finally!

The Caribbean is more dependent on travel and tourism than almost any other region in the world. Finally—happily and thankfully—the Caribbean islands have begun to see signs of recovery from the global recession. According to the Caribbean Tourism Organization (CTO), visitor arrivals throughout the region in 2010 rose to 23.1 million, up 4.7% from 22.1 million visitors in 2009. Cruise tourism also grew—up 6% in 2010 over the prior year. The warm Caribbean breeze that wafts gently across the archipelago could very well symbolize those in the region exhaling a cautious but collective sigh of relief.

More good news—new hotel openings

Some development projects managed to be completed despite the recession. In St. Vincent, the massive Buccament Bay Resort had a soft opening of the first 70 units in September 2010; the final phase of the luxurious, 368-villa community should be complete by the time the island's new international airport opens in 2012. The new Secrets St. James, an all-inclusive adults-only resort in Montego Bay, Jamaica, is adjacent to a sister property, Secrets Wild Orchid. Some new boutique properties also made it through the financial gauntlet of the recession. In Grenada, for instance, Kalinago Beach Resort, Le Phare Bleu, and Petite Anse Hotel are three delightful additions to the island's inventory of small inns. And in Barbados, the completely rebuilt Atlantis Hotel is once again welcoming guests.

Victims of the downturn

Despite the generally bright outlook going forward, some resort properties weren't able to survive the economic downturn.

Lenders simply lost their appetite to continue financing some of the large resort developments. On Anguilla, for example, Temenos Anguilla, an unfinished resort on 275 acres with the island's only golf course (now managed by Cap Juluca), went into receivership in early 2010; completion of the development is subject to government approval of revised plans. Viceroy Anguilla Resort and Residences filed for Chapter 11 protection in March 2011; a Starwood affiliate owns the mortgage and expects to acquire the resort at auction, but it remains open. Other troubled resorts were sold and successfully reopened with new names. The Aruban Resort, for example, reopened as Tropicana Aruba Resort and Casino. The former Moon Palace Resort, an enormous 1,800-room property in Punta Cana, Dominican Republic, reopened as Hard Rock Hotel and Casino. And in the Bahamas, Emerald Bay Exuma (the former Four Seasons) reopened as Sandals Emerald Bay. One slightly sobering effect of the economy: SuperClubs renamed and rebranded its erotically themed Hedonism III resort in Jamaica as SuperFun Beach Resort, an all-inclusive resort for budget-conscious, fun-loving (but not so erotic) adults.

Air travel: New routes and added service

Several airlines have begun new routes and/or added flights to the region. American Airlines recently launched service between Dallas–Ft. Worth and Barbados; Continental Airlines now flies between Newark and Providenciales, Turks and Caicos; Caribbean Airlines services Grenada and Tobago from JFK via Trinidad; AirTran added flights between BWI and San Juan, Puerto Rico; Cayman Airways revived seasonal service from Chicago and

Washington, D.C. to the Cayman Islands; and JetBlue now flies nonstop to more than 15 Caribbean destinations. Within the region, Winair has expanded its primarily Leeward Islands service and flies twice-daily between Antigua and Dominica. New, low-cost, regional airlines have been lining up to compete with LIAT on certain interisland routes. RedJet plans to service Trinidad and Jamaica from Barbados, adding other destinations in time; Caribbean Airways is considering a new regional service; and CARICOM Airways, based in Surinam, also plans service from St. Lucia.

Newly independent Dutch islands

On October 10, 2010, with the dissolution of the Netherlands Antilles as a political entity, the islands of Curaçao and St. Maarten became independent "constituent" countries within the Kingdom of the Netherlands—similar to Aruba, which separated from the Netherlands Antilles in 1986. The islands of Bonaire, Saba, and St. Eustatius are now "special municipalities" of the Netherlands and, as of January 1, 2011, have switched their official currency to the U.S. dollar. Curaçao and St. Maarten will continue to use the Netherlands Antilles guilder as their official currency until they jointly introduce a new currency, the Caribbean guilder (CMg), expected by 2012.

Ecotourism: Going, going . . . green

The Caribbean tourism sector is increasingly buying into the logic and appeal of sustainable tourism. Noted for their environmental consciousness, Maho Bay Camps on St. John in the USVI and Cocoa Cottages on Dominica each offer ecosensitive, back-to-nature experiences. Likewise, Jamaica's ecochic Hotel Mocking Bird Hill is a bit of paradise in peaceful, natural surroundings. And St. Lucia's Fond Doux Holiday Plantation offers guests a handful of accommodations and an ecofriendly, 19th-century "plantation" experience. Island hoteliers everywhere, whether at internationally owned megaresorts or family-run boutique inns, tout their ecofriendly operations and openly encourage guests to conserve water, reuse towels, and expect fresh bed linens only every other day. By necessity, a good number of hotels and resorts recycle "gray" water for their gardens and other landscaping needs. Some have added solar panels—a no-brainer in the sunny Caribbean—and many have instituted other energy-saving and conservation measures. Green Globe and other internationally recognized programs supported by the Caribbean Alliance for Sustainable Tourism (CAST) have certified properties throughout the Caribbean.

Crime and safety

Although the threat of violent crime on most islands of the Caribbean is considered low, travelers should always take normal precautions and may find theft of unattended belongings left on the beach or in cars (even in a locked trunk) to be a problem on many islands. Lock your valuables (including your passport) in the hotel safe; don't leave them exposed or unattended. Violent crimes against tourists are rare but lately have been most prevalent after dark in parts of Trinidad and Tobago, Jamaica (especially in impoverished areas of Kingston and Montego Bay), and New Providence Island (Nassau) in the Bahamas. There are also sporadic reports of crime on St. Maarten/St. Martin. Illegal drug trafficking/smuggling/possession/consumption is not tolerated anywhere in the Caribbean, and punishment for violators can be severe.

UNITED
STATES

Miami ○

Key West ○

Nassau ○

The Bahamas

Havana ○

C u b a

Turks and
Caicos Islands

George
Town ○
*Little
Cayman*
*Cayman
Brac*

*Grand
Cayman*

Puerto Plata ○

H a i t i *Hispaniola*

Montego Bay ○
○ Ocho Rios
Port-au-Prince ○

Santo
Domingo ○

Jamaica
○ Kingston

G R E A T E R

Greater Antilles

C a r i b b e a n   *S e a*

0 _____ 200 mi

0 _____ 200 km

Cartagena ○ **COLOMBIA** Maracaibo ○

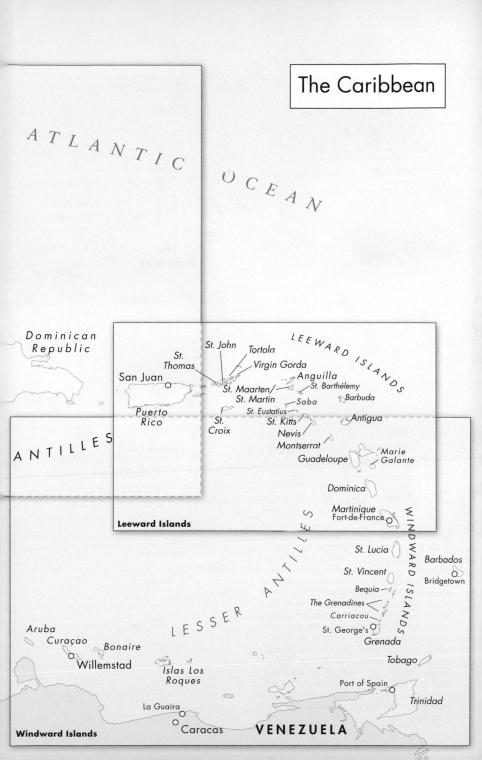

The Caribbean

ATLANTIC OCEAN

*Dominican
Republic*

San Juan

*Puerto
Rico*

St.
Thomas

St. John

Tortola

Virgin Gorda

St. Maarten/
St. Martin

St.
Croix

St. Eustatius

St. Kitts

Nevis

Montserrat

LEEWARD ISLANDS

Anguilla

St. Barthélemy

Saba

Barbuda

Antigua

Guadeloupe

Marie
Galante

Dominica

Martinique
Fort-de-France

Leeward Islands

ANTILLES

LESSER ANTILLES

LESSER ANTILLES

WINDWARD ISLANDS

St. Lucia

St. Vincent

Bequia

The Grenadines

Carriacou

St. George's

Grenada

Barbados

Bridgetown

Tobago

Aruba

Curaçao

Bonaire

Willemstad

*Islas Los
Roques*

La Guaira

Caracas

Port of Spain

Trinidad

VENEZUELA

Windward Islands

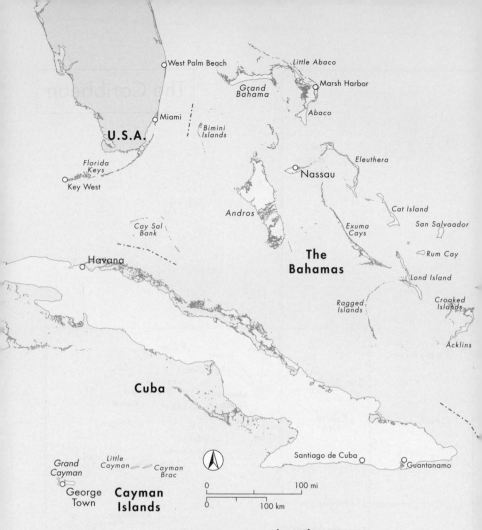

West Palm Beach

Little Abaco

Grand
Bahama

Marsh Harbor

Miami

Abaco

U.S.A.

*Bimini
Islands*

Eleuthera

*Florida
Keys*

Nassau

Cat Island

San Salvaador

Key West

Andros

*Cay Sal
Bank*

**The
Bahamas**

Rum Cay

Havana

Lond Island

Exuma
Cays

Crooked
Islands

Ragged
Islands

Cuba

Acklins

Santiago de Cuba

*Grand
Cayman*

*Little
Cayman*

*Cayman
Brac*

Guantanamo

0   100 mi

George
Town

**Cayman
Islands**

0   100 km

Jamaica

Montego
Bay

Cayman Islands
➪ Ch. 8

Vacationers appreciate the mellow civility of the islands, and Grand Cayman's exceptional Seven Mile Beach has its share of fans. Divers come to explore the pristine reefs or perhaps to swim with friendly stingrays. Go if you want a safe, family-friendly vacation spot. Don't go if you're trying to save money, because there are few real bargains here.

Negril

Ocho Rios

Black River

Kingston

Jamaica ➪ Ch. 14

Easy to reach and with resorts in every price range, Jamaica is also an easy choice for many travelers. Go to enjoy the music, food, beaches, and sense of hospitality that's made it one of the Caribbean's most popular destinations. Don't go if you can't deal with the idea that a Caribbean paradise still has problems of its own to solve.

G R E A T E R

C a r i b b e a n

THE GREATER ANTILLES

The islands closest to the United States mainland—composed of Cuba, Jamaica, Haiti, the Dominican Republic, and Puerto Rico—are also the largest in the chain that stretches in an arc from the southern coast of Florida down to Venezuela. Haiti and Cuba aren't covered in this book. The Cayman Islands, just south of Cuba, are usually included in this group.

Dominican Republic ⇨ Ch. 11
Dominicans have beautiful smiles and warm hearts and are proud of their island, which is blessed with pearl-white beaches and a vibrant, Latin culture. Go for the best-priced resorts in the Caribbean and a wide range of activities that will keep you moving day and night. Don't go if you can't go with the flow. Things don't always work here, and not everyone speaks English.

Turks and Caicos Islands ⇨ Ch. 26
Miles of white-sand beaches surround this tiny island chain, only eight of which are inhabited. The smaller islands seem to come from some long-forgotten era of Caribbean life. Go for deserted beaches and excellent diving on one of the world's largest coral reefs. Don't go for nightlife and a fast pace. And don't forget your wallet. This isn't a budget destination.

Puerto Rico ⇨ Ch. 17
San Juan is hopping day and night; beyond the city, you'll find a sunny escape and slower pace. Party in San Juan, relax on the beach, hike the rain forest, or play some of the Caribbean's best golf courses. You have the best of both worlds here, with natural and urban thrills alike. So go for both. Just don't expect to do it in utter seclusion.

WHAT'S WHERE

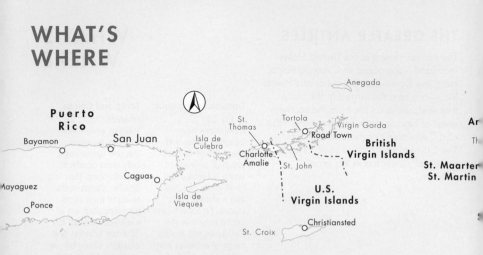

LESSER ANTILLES: THE EASTERN CARIBBEAN

The Lesser Antilles are larger in number but smaller in size than the Greater Antilles, and they make up the bulk of the Caribbean arc. Beginning with the Virgin Islands but going all the way to Grenada, the islands of the Eastern Caribbean form a barrier between the Atlantic Ocean and the Caribbean Sea. The best beaches are usually on the Caribbean side.

U.S. Virgin Islands ⇨ Ch. 27
A perfect combination of the familiar and the exotic, the U.S. Virgin Islands are a little bit of America set in an azure sea. Go to St. Croix if you like history and interesting restaurants. Go to St. John if you crave a back-to-nature experience. Go to St. Thomas if you want a shop-'til-you-drop experience and a big selection of resorts, activities, and nightlife.

British Virgin Islands ⇨ Ch. 7
The lure of the British Virgins is exclusivity and personal attention, not lavish luxury. Even the most expensive resorts are selling a state of mind rather than state-of-the-art. So go with an open mind, and your stress may very well melt away. Don't go if you expect glitz or stateside efficiency. These islands are about getting away, not getting it all.

Montserrat ⇨ Ch. 16
Montserrat has staged one of the best comebacks of the new century, returning to the tourism scene after a disastrous volcanic eruption in 1995. Go for exciting volcano eco-tourism and great diving or just to taste what the Caribbean used to be like. Don't go for splashy resorts or nightlife. You'll be happier here if you can appreciate simpler pleasures.

Anguilla ⇨ Ch. 2
With miles of brilliant beaches and a range of luxurious resorts (even a few that mere mortals can afford), Anguilla is where the rich, powerful, and famous go to chill out. Go for the fine cuisine in elegant surroundings, great snorkeling, and funky late-night music scene. Don't go for shopping and sightseeing. This island is all about relaxing and reviving.

St. Maarten/St. Martin ⇨ Ch. 23
Two nations (Dutch and French), many nationalities, one small island, a lot of development. But there are also more white, sandy beaches than days in a month. Go for the awesome restaurants, excellent shopping, and wide range of activities. Don't go if you're not willing to get out and search for the really good stuff.

St. Barthélemy ⇨ Ch. 19
If you come to St. Barths for a taste of European village life, not for a conventional full-service resort experience, you will be richly rewarded. Go for excellent dining and wine, great boutiques with the latest hip fashions, and an active, on-the-go vacation. Don't go for big resorts, and make sure your credit card is platinum-plated.

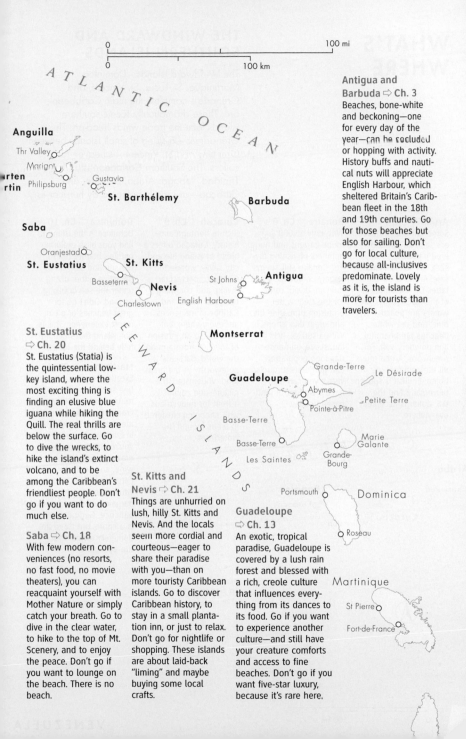

100 mi

100 km

ATLANTIC OCEAN

Anguilla

Thr Valley

Marigot

rten
rtin   Philipsburg   Gustavia

St. Barthélemy

Saba

Oranjestad

St. Eustatius   St. Kitts

Basseterre   Nevis

Charlestown   English Harbour

St Johns   Antigua

Barbuda

Montserrat

LEEWARD ISLANDS

Guadeloupe   Grande-Terre   Le Désirade

Abymes

Pointe-à-Pitre   Petite Terre

Basse-Terre

Basse-Terre   Marie
Galante

Les Saintes   Grande-
Bourg

Portsmouth   Dominica

Roseau

Martinique

St Pierre

Fort-de-France

Antigua and Barbuda ⇨ Ch. 3

Beaches, bone-white and beckoning—one for every day of the year—can be secluded or hopping with activity. History buffs and nautical nuts will appreciate English Harbour, which sheltered Britain's Caribbean fleet in the 18th and 19th centuries. Go for those beaches but also go for sailing. Don't go for local culture, because all-inclusives predominate. Lovely as it is, the island is more for tourists than travelers.

St. Eustatius ⇨ Ch. 20

St. Eustatius (Statia) is the quintessential low-key island, where the most exciting thing is finding an elusive blue iguana while hiking the Quill. The real thrills are below the surface. Go to dive the wrecks, to hike the island's extinct volcano, and to be among the Caribbean's friendliest people. Don't go if you want to do much else.

Saba ⇨ Ch. 18

With few modern conveniences (no resorts, no fast food, no movie theaters), you can reacquaint yourself with Mother Nature or simply catch your breath. Go to dive in the clear water, to hike to the top of Mt. Scenery, and to enjoy the peace. Don't go if you want to lounge on the beach. There is no beach.

St. Kitts and Nevis ⇨ Ch. 21

Things are unhurried on lush, hilly St. Kitts and Nevis. And the locals seem more cordial and courteous—eager to share their paradise with you—than on more touristy Caribbean islands. Go to discover Caribbean history, to stay in a small plantation inn, or just to relax. Don't go for nightlife or shopping. These islands are about laid-back "liming" and maybe buying some local crafts.

Guadeloupe ⇨ Ch. 13

An exotic, tropical paradise, Guadeloupe is covered by a lush rain forest and blessed with a rich, creole culture that influences everything from its dances to its food. Go if you want to experience another culture—and still have your creature comforts and access to great beaches. Don't go if you want five-star luxury, because it's rare here.

WHAT'S WHERE

THE WINDWARD AND SOUTHERN ISLANDS

The Windward Islands—Dominica, Martinique, St. Lucia, St. Vincent, and Grenada—complete the main Caribbean arc. These dramatically scenic southern islands face the trade winds head-on. The Grenadines—a string of small islands between Grenada and St. Vincent—is heaven for sailors. The Southern Caribbean islands— Trinidad, Tobago, Aruba, Bonaire, and Curaçao—are rarely bothered by hurricanes.

Aruba ⇨ Ch. 4
Some Caribbean travelers seek an undiscovered paradise, some seek the familiar and safe: Aruba is for the latter. On the smallest of the ABC islands, the waters are peacock blue, and the white beaches are beautiful and powdery soft. For Americans, Aruba offers all the comforts of home: English is spoken universally, and the U.S. dollar is accepted everywhere.

Bonaire ⇨ Ch. 6
With only 15,000 year-round citizens and huge numbers of visiting divers, Bonaire still seems largely untouched by tourism. Divers come for the clear water, profusion of marine life, and great dive shops. With a surreal, arid landscape, immense flamingo population, and gorgeous turquoise vistas, you can also have a wonderful land-based holiday.

Curaçao ⇨ Ch. 9
Rich in heritage and history, Curaçao offers a blend of island life and city savvy, wonderful weather, spectacular diving, and charming beaches. Dutch and Caribbean influences are everywhere, but there's also an infusion of touches from around the world, particularly noteworthy in the great food. Willemstad, the picturesque capital, is a treat for pedestrians, with shopping clustered in areas around the waterfront.

Dominica ⇨ Ch. 10
Dominica is the island to find your bliss exploring nature's bounty, not in the sun and surf. Go to be active, either diving under the sea or hiking on land. Don't go for great beaches or a big-resort experience. This is one island that's delightfully behind the times.

Martinique ⇨ Ch. 15
Excellent cuisine, fine service, highly touted rum, and lilting Franco-Caribbean music are the main draws in Martinique. Go if you're a Francophile drawn to fine food, wine, and sophisticated style. Don't go if you are looking for a bargain and don't have patience. Getting here is a chore, but there are definitely rewards for the persistent.

Caribbean

Sea

Aruba
○ Oranjestad

Bonaire
○ Kralendijk

Curaçao ○
Willemstad

Islas Los Roques

La Guaira

Isla La Tortuga

Caracas

| 0 | | 100 mi |
| 0 | | 100 km |

VENEZUELA

St. Kitts

LEEWARD

Nevis

Antigua

Montserrat

ISLANDS

Grande-Terre   Guadeloupe
Abymes   Le Désirade
Basse-Terre   Pointe-à-Pitre

Basse-Terre   Marie Galante
Les Saintes   Grande-
                   Bourg

Portsmouth

Dominica

Roseau

La Trinité
St Pierre
Fort-de-France

Martinique

Castries

St. Lucia

Kingstown

Bequia

St. Vincent

Bridgetown

Barbados

The Grenadines

Carriacou

Grenada
St. George's

WINDWARD   ISLANDS

Tobago

Scarborough

Port of Spain

San Fernando

Trinidad

St. Lucia ⇨ Ch. 22

One of the most green and beautiful islands in the Caribbean is, arguably, the most romantic. The scenic south and central regions are mountainous and lush, with dense rain forest, endless banana plantations, and fascinating historic sites. Along the west coast, some of the region's most interesting resorts are interspersed with dozens of delightful inns, appealing to families as well as lovers and adventurers.

St. Vincent and the Grenadines ⇨ Ch. 24

Thirty-two perfectly endowed islands and cays have no mass tourism but a lot of old-style Caribbean charm, several have not a small sense of luxury. Tourism isn't even the biggest business in lush, mountainous St. Vincent. Throughout the chain, wildlife trusts protect rare species of flora and fauna, and villa walls ensure privacy for the islands' rich and famous human visitors.

Grenada ⇨ Ch. 12

The spice business is going strong, but tourism is just as important. On the laid-back island, the only sounds are the occasional abrupt call of a cuckoo in the lush rain forest, the crash of surf in the secluded coves, and the slow beat of a big-drum dance. Resorts are mostly small and charming. St. George's, the island's capital, is often called the most beautiful city in the Caribbean.

Trinidad and Tobago ⇨ Ch. 25

Trinidad and Tobago, the most southerly Caribbean islands, are two different places. Trinidad is an effervescent mix of cultures—mostly descendants of African slaves and East Indian indentured workers—who like to party but also appreciate the island's incredibly diverse ecosystem. Little sister Tobago is laid-back and rustic, with beaches that can match any in the Caribbean.

Barbados ⇨ Ch. 5

Broad vistas, sweeping seascapes, craggy cliffs, and acre upon acre of sugarcane make up the island's varied landscape. A long, successful history of tourism has been forged from the warm, Bajan hospitality, welcoming hotels and resorts, sophisticated dining, lively nightspots, and, of course, magnificent sunny beaches.

ISLAND FINDER

To help you decide which island is best for you, we've rated each island in several areas that might influence your decision on choosing the perfect Caribbean vacation spot. Each major island covered in this book has been rated in terms of cost from $ (very inexpensive) to $$$$$ (very expensive), and since prices often vary a great deal by season, we've given you a rating for the high season (December through mid-April) and low season (mid-April through November). We've also compared each island's relative strength in several other categories that might influence your decision.

If an island has no marks in a particular column (under "Golf" for example), it means that the activity is not available on the island.

	Cost High Season	Cost Low Season
Anguilla	$$$$	$$$
Antigua	$$$	$$
Aruba	$$$	$$
Barbados	$$$$	$$$$
Bonaire	$$	$$
BVI: Tortola	$$$	$$
BVI: Virgin Gorda	$$$$$	$$$$
BVI: Anegada	$$$$	$$$
BVI: Jost Van Dyke	$$$$	$$$
Cayman Islands: Grand Cayman	$$$$	$$$
Cayman Islands: Little Cayman	$$$	$$$
Cayman Islands: Cayman Brac	$$	$$
Curaçao	$$$$	$$$
Dominica	$$	$
Dominican Republic	$$	$
Grenada	$$$	$$$
Grenada: Carriacou	$$	$
Guadeloupe	$$	$$
Jamaica	$$$	$$
Martinique	$$$	$$
Montserrat	$	$
Puerto Rico	$$$	$$
Saba	$$	$
St. Barthélemy	$$$$$	$$$$
St. Eustatius	$$	$
St. Kitts & Nevis: St. Kitts	$$$	$$
St. Kitts & Nevis: Nevis	$$$$	$$$
St. Lucia	$$$$	$$$
St. Maarten/St. Martin	$$$	$$$
SVG: St. Vincent	$$	$$
SVG: The Grenadines	$$$$	$$$
T&T: Trinidad	$$$	$$
T&T: Tobago	$$$	$$
Turks & Caicos Islands	$$$$*	$$$*
USVI: St. Thomas	$$$$	$$$
USVI: St. Croix	$$	$
USVI: St. John	$$$	$$

*   Cost for Provo (Parrot Cay $$$$$, other islands $$)

**   Provo Only

	Beautiful Beaches	Fine Dining	Shopping	Casinos	Nightlife	Diving	Golf	Ecotourism	Food for Families
	5	4	2		2	1	3	1	2
	5	5	4	3	3	2	3	3	3
	4	4	4	4	5	3	2	2	4
	3	5	3		3	2	5	2	4
	3	3	2	1		5		4	4
	2	3	2		2	3		3	3
	5	3	1			3		3	3
	5	3	1		1	3		3	3
	4	3	1			3		3	3
	5	4	5		2	4	3	2	4
						4	5	3	3
	2					4		3	3
	4	4	3	3	4	4	3		3
	1	3	3		2	5		5	3
	5	3	2	3	4	4	5		4
	4	3	2		1	3	1	4	4
	3	1	1			4		4	2
	4	2	3	3	3	3	3	5	3
	3	3	2	1	2	2	5	5	5
	4	4	3	2	3	3	3	3	2
	1	1	1		1	4		4	2
	3	4	4	4	4	3	4	5	5
		4	2		1	5		5	1
	4	5	5		2	3		4	1
	1	1	2		1	5		5	3
	3	3	3	4	3	4	4	4	5
	3	4	2		3	4	5	5	3
	3	3	2			4	1	5	3
	4	5	3	3	4	3	1	2	3
	1	2	1	1	1	4		5	3
	5	4	1		1	5	5	3	3
	3	3	2	2	5	4	4	4	3
	4	3	2		3	4	4	4	4
	5	2**	1	1	1	5	4**	4	3**
	3	4	5		2	3	4	2	4
	3	3	2	2		5	3	3	3
	5	3	2		1	3	3	4	5

CARIBBEAN LODGING

When to Reserve

School holiday periods, especially in high season, generally require advance booking at most hotels. The most popular properties book as much as a year in advance because of their high numbers of repeat clientele, many of whom request the same room every year. Many respected chain resorts, such as the Ritz-Carlton and the Four Seasons, also book well in advance during peak periods. The most difficult time to find a well-priced room is typically around the Christmas holidays and New Year's, when minimum-stay requirements of one to two weeks may be common and when room rates typically double.

But for the typical Caribbean resort, two months is usually sufficient notice. In popular mass-market destinations such as Punta Cana or Negril, you could probably find something even a couple of weeks in advance. Paradoxically, it's easier to find an acceptable room in the busiest destinations by sheer virtue of the number of rooms available at any given time. Although waiting until the last minute doesn't net as many bargains as cruises, flexibility can pay off either in a deep discount (usually at a larger resort) or a room category upgrade.

Fees and Add-Ons

Every island charges an accommodations tax, whether on private villa rentals, bed-and-breakfast stays, or megaresorts. This ranges from 7% to 15%, depending on the destination (you can find the exact surcharge listed in the individual chapters' hotel and restaurant price chart). In addition, most Caribbean hotels and resorts tack on a service fee, usually around 10%. The service fee isn't quite the same as a tip for service, and it is customary at most non-all-inclusive resorts to tip the staff. Generally, expect to pay at least 20% above and beyond the base rate for a Caribbean resort room. The latest growing trend—though it's hardly unique to the Caribbean—is the "resort fee." You can encounter this almost anywhere, though resort fees are almost universal in San Juan, Puerto Rico. The fee presumably covers costs such as housekeeping (though you might sometimes see this on your bill, too, especially for villa rentals), utilities, and use of resort facilities. Figure $5 to $50 per night, but know that this is generally restricted to larger hotels and defies generalization because it depends more on the individual resort or hotel chain than the island itself. These additional costs aren't always mentioned when you book, so be sure to inquire.

Picking the Best Room

On virtually every island, especially at beachfront lodgings, the better the beach access or ocean view, the higher the price. If you're the active type who really uses a room only to sleep, then you can save $100 or more per night by choosing a garden-, mountain-, or town-view room. But regardless of view, be sure to ask about the property's layout. For example, if you want to be close to the "action" at many larger resorts, whether you have mobility concerns or just need to satisfy your gambling or beach-gamboling itch, the trade-off might be noise, whether from screaming kids jumping in the pool or DJs pumping and thumping reggae in the bar. Likewise, saving that $100 may not be worth it if your room faces a busy thoroughfare. This is your vacation, so if you have any specific desires or dislikes, discuss them thoroughly with the reservations staff.

Types of Lodgings

Most islands offer the gamut of glitzy resorts, boutique-chic hotels, historic hostelries, family-run B&Bs, condo resorts, self-catering apartments, and private villas that are typical throughout the Caribbean.

Condos and Time-Shares: Condo resorts are increasingly popular and can offer both extra space and superior savings for families with kitchens, sofa beds, and more. In fact, they dominate the sensuous sweeps of Grand Cayman's Seven-Mile Beach and Provo's amazing Grace Bay in the Turks and Caicos. Some of these are time-share properties, but not all time-shares require you to sit through a sales pitch.

Inns and B&Bs: Historic inns come in all shapes and sizes. The old Spanish colonial capitals of Santo Domingo and San Juan have converted monasteries. Puerto Rico also offers affordable lodgings in its paradors, patterned after the Spanish system, most of them historically and/or culturally significant buildings such as old-time thermal baths or working coffee plantations. Longtime sailing and whaling destinations such as Antigua or Bequia in the Grenadines offer their own pieces of history adapted to modern comfort, and Guadeloupe and Martinique feature converted sugar plantations. St. Kitts and Nevis are also prized by Caribbean connoisseurs for their restored greathouse plantation inns, often with a resident eccentric expat owner who lives on-site and enhances your experience with amusing anecdotes and insider insights.

Private Villas: Another increasingly popular option for families or those seeking a surprising bargain: private villas. Self-catering means saving on dining out on more expensive islands, such as St. Barths (where villas usually cost much less than hotels), though a car is usually necessary except in mini-villages such as Cayman Kai on Grand Cayman. Many villas have private pools with stunning sea views and/or beachfront access. Montserrat offers exceptional value for anyone.

Resorts: Most prevalent are large resorts, including all-inclusives, usually strategically positioned on the beach. These include golf/spa resorts and name-brand chain hotels in various price categories from Ritz-Carlton to Comfort Suites. Jamaica and the Dominican Republic specialize in the all-inclusive experience. Some islands abound in cookie-cutter tour-group hotels that look like they could be plonked down anywhere, including Aruba (along one of the Caribbean's most alluring beaches) and Guadeloupe, though both also offer distinctive properties as well.

Inclusive or Not?

The AI (which stands for "all-inclusive") concept is especially prominent on islands such as Jamaica, the Dominican Republic, Antigua, and St. Lucia. For those who have only a week for vacation, the allure is obvious: a hassle-free, pay-one-price vacation including accommodations, meals, unlimited drinks, entertainment, and most activities. And you tend to get what you pay for: AIs range from hedonistic high-tech luxury to barebones beachfront bang-for-the-buck, with prices to match. It pays to do your homework: some of these resorts are intimate romantic hideaways, some emphasize sporting options, others cater to families, and still others cater to singles ready to mingle in a nonstop frat-party atmosphere.

But there are caveats. Few AIs offer *everything* for free. That sybaritic spa treatment, the scuba trip (and instruction), the sunset cruise, the tour of the nearby plantation generally won't be included. Moreover, there can be surcharges for dining in some restaurants (which must be reserved).

AI resorts appeal most to travelers who just need to get away and bask in the sun, piña colada within easy reach. They're not for more adventuresome types who seek genuine interaction with the locals and immersion in their culture, nor are they good for people who want to eat local food since most AI travelers rarely leave their resort boundaries.

CARIBBEAN LOGISTICS

Time

The Cayman Islands, Cuba, Haiti, Jamaica, and the Turks and Caicos Islands are all in the Eastern Standard Time zone. All other Caribbean islands are in the Atlantic Standard Time zone, which is one hour later than Eastern Standard. Caribbean islands don't observe daylight saving time, so during that period (March through October) Eastern Standard is one hour behind, and Atlantic Standard is the same time as Eastern Daylight Time.

Driving

Your own valid driver's license works in some countries. However, temporary local driving permits are required in several Caribbean destinations (Anguilla, Antigua, Barbados, the British Virgin Islands, Cayman Islands, Dominica, Grenada, Nevis, St. Kitts, St. Lucia, and St. Vincent and the Grenadines), which you can get at rental agencies or local police offices upon presentation of a valid license and a small fee. St. Lucia and St. Vincent and the Grenadines require a temporary permit only if you don't have an International Driving Permit (available from AAA).

Flights

Many carriers fly nonstop or direct routes to the Caribbean from major international airports in the United States, including Atlanta, Boston, Charlotte, Chicago, Dallas, Fort Lauderdale, Houston, Miami, New York, JFK), Newark, Philadelphia, Phoenix, and Washington (Dulles). If you live somewhere else in the United States, you'll probably have to make a connection to get to your Caribbean destination. It's also not uncommon to make a connection in the Caribbean, most often in San Juan, Montego Bay, Barbados, or St. Maarten.

Some flights will be on small planes operated by local or regional carriers, which may have codeshare arrangements with major airlines from the U.S. Or you can confidently book directly with the local carrier, using a major credit card, sometimes online but more often by phone.

Some smaller airlines may make multiple stops, accepting and discharging passengers and/or cargo at each small airport or airstrip along the way. This is not unusual. What is also not unusual is the sometimes erratic schedules these smaller airlines can have. Be sure to confirm your flights on interisland carriers and make sure that the carrier has a local contact telephone number for you, as you may be subject to a small carrier's whims: if no other passengers are booked on your flight, particularly if the carrier operates "scheduled charters," you'll be rescheduled onto another flight or at a different departure time (earlier or later than your original reservation) that is more convenient for the airline. If you're connecting from an interisland flight to a major airline, be sure to include a substantial buffer of time for these kinds of delays.

Typical Travel Times by Air

	New York	Miami
Puerto Rico	3½ hours	2½ hours
Jamaica	4½ hours	1½ hours
St. Lucia	4½ hours	3½ hours
Trinidad	5 hours	3½ hours
Aruba	4¾ hours	2½ hours

Airlines

Major Airlines: Air Jamaica (☎ *800/523–5585* ⊕ *www. airjamaica.com*). **American Airlines/American Eagle** (☎ *800/433–7300* or *800/223–5436* for automated flight information ⊕ *www.aa.com*). **Caribbean Airlines** (☎ *800/920–4225* ⊕ *www.caribbean-airlines.com*). **Continental Airlines** (☎ *800/231–0856* ⊕ *www.continental. com*). **Delta Airlines** (☎ *800/241–4141* ⊕ *www.delta. com*). **JetBlue** (☎ *800/538–2583* ⊕ *www.jetblue.com*). **Spirit Airlines** (☎ *800/772–7117* ⊕ *www.spiritair.com*). **United Airlines** (☎ *800/538–2929* ⊕ *www.united.com*). **US Airways** (☎ *800/622–1015* ⊕ *www.usairways.com*).

Smaller/Regional Airlines: Air Antilles Express (☎ *0890/648–648* in Guadeloupe ⊕ *www.airantilles. com*). **Air Caraïbes** (☎ *877/772–1005* ⊕ *www. aircaraibes.com*). **Air Sunshine** (☎ *800/327–8900*, *800/435–8900* in Florida ⊕ *www.airsunshine. com*). **Air Turks & Caicos** (☎ *954/323–4949* ⊕ *www. airturksandcaicos.com*). **Bahamas Air** (☎ *242/702–4140* in Nassau, *800/222–4262* in U.S. ⊕ *www2.bahamasair. com*). **Caicos Express** (☎ *649/243–0237*). **Cape Air** (☎ *866/227–3247* or *508/771–6944* ⊕ *www.flycapeair. com*). **Cayman Airways** (☎ *345/949–8200* or *800/422– 9626* ⊕ *www.caymanairways.com*). **Dutch Antilles Express** (☎ *599/461–3009* ⊕ *www.flydae.com*). **Grenadine Air Alliance (Mustique Air, SVG Air, TIA)** (☎ *246/418–1654* for shared-charter flights, *784/456–6793* for intra-Grenadines flights). **Insel Air** (☎ *800/386–4800* ⊕ *www. fly-inselair.com*). **LIAT** (☎ *866/549–5428*, *888/844–5428* within the Caribbean ⊕ *www.liatairline.com*). **Mustique Airways** (☎ *718/618–4492* in U.S., *784/458–4380* in St. Vincent ⊕ *www.mustique.com*). **Seabourne Airlines** (☎ *340/773–6442* or *866/359–8784* ⊕ *www. seaborneairlines.com*). **St. Barths Commuter** (☎ *599/546– 7698* ⊕ *www.stbarthcommuter.com*) **SVG Air** (☎ *784/ 457–5124* or *800/744–7285* ⊕ *www.svgair.com*). **Winair** (Windward Island Airways ☎ *866/466–0410* ⊕ *www. fly-winair.com*). **Windward Express Airways** (☎ *599/545– 2001* in St. Maarten ⊕ *www.windwardexpress.com*).

Ferries

Interisland ferries are an interesting and often less expensive way to travel around certain areas of the Caribbean, but they are not offered everywhere. There are a few destinations that are reached only by ferry (St. John, for example). In most cases, where service is offered, it is frequent (either daily or several times daily).

MAJOR FERRY ROUTES

Ferries connect Puerto Rico with the outlying islands of Vieques and Culebra; St. Thomas with Water Island, St. John, St. Croix, and the British Virgin Islands; St. Croix with St. Thomas; the various islands of the British Virgin Islands with each other and with the U.S. Virgin Islands; St. Martin/St. Maarten with Anguilla, St. Barths, and Saba; St. Kitts with Nevis; Antigua with Barbuda and Montserrat; Guadeloupe with La Désirade, Marie-Galante, and Les Saintes, as well as Dominica, Martinique, and St. Lucia; St. Lucia with Guadeloupe, Martinique, Dominica, and Barbados; St. Vincent with Bequia and the other islands of the Grenadines; Grenada with Carriacou and Petite Martinique; and Trinidad with Tobago; there's limited ferry service in the Turks & Caicos Islands (Provo and North Caicos, Grand Turk and Salt Cay). In most cases, service is frequent—either daily or several times daily.

RENTING A VILLA

In the Caribbean, the term villa can be used to describe anything from a traditional cottage to a luxurious architectural wonder, but what it almost always means is a stand-alone accommodation, often privately owned. Villa rentals provide some of the region's most desirable accommodations, both from a comfort and economic point of view. We recommend considering this option, especially if you're a group of friends or a family: you get a lot more space, much more privacy, and a better sense of the island than you would get at a hotel, usually at a fraction of the cost.

Factor in the ability to fix simple meals, snacks, and drinks, and the savings really add up. An additional advantage to Americans is that villa rates are generally negotiated in dollars, thus bypassing unfavorable euro fluctuations in St. Martin, St. Barths, and Martinique.

What Does It Cost?

Rental rates vary widely by island and by season. In-season rates range anywhere from $1,200 for a simple one-bedroom cottage to more than $40,000 a week for a multiroom luxury home. Many full-service resorts also offer villas of varying sizes on their property, and, although pricey, these can be an excellent choice if you want the best of both worlds—full service and facilities but also space and privacy. In many cases, renting a villa at a resort will cost less than renting three or four "normal" rooms, and you can still have a waiter deliver your 'ti punch to a beach chair or enjoy access to a high-tech fitness room.

What's Included?

Units are generally furnished nicely and have updated bathrooms and usable kitchens. They are equipped with linens, kitchen utensils, CD and DVD players,

a phone, satellite TV, and, increasingly, Wi-Fi access to the Internet. The sophistication of all of the above is factored into the price, so the more luxurious the digs, the higher the price.

Upscale rental villas generally have small, private swimming pools (rather few are beachfront), and housekeeping service a few hours daily except Sunday included in the quoted price. On some islands, including the Dominican Republic, Jamaica, and Barbados, two or even three staff members are common. Inquire about the villa's staff, and specify particular needs or expectations right from the start, including start times and specific duties such as laundry, cooking, or child care.

How Do You Rent?

Some owners rent their properties directly (⊕ www.vrbo.com), but in general, we recommend renting a villa through a reputable local agency that both manages and maintains the properties and has an office with local staff to facilitate and troubleshoot on your behalf if something goes wrong. Lavish catalogs or Web sites with detailed descriptions and photographs of each villa can help to assuage your fears about what to expect. The agent will meet you at the airport, bring you to the villa, explain and demonstrate the household systems, and even stock the kitchen with starter groceries (for a fee). Some agencies provide comprehensive concierge services and will arrange or recommend car rentals and help you find additional staff such as chefs or babysitters or yoga instructors. Some of the larger companies even host a weekly cocktail party so renters can meet each other and form a community to share local information or socialize. Specific villa-rental companies are listed and recommended throughout this guide.

Choosing a Villa

These days, your hunt will no doubt start on the Internet. A simple search for "villa rental [island name]" will get you started, and the tourist board of each island can provide a list of reputable local rental agents.

Villa-rental Web sites allow you to see pictures of the places you may wish to rent. And, via the Web site, you can talk to a knowledgeable representative who can help you sort through the listings according to your requirements. But use caution, warns Peg Walsh of St. Barths Properties: "There are a lot of Web sites and listings [from] people who say they do villa rentals, but in many cases, they don't actually know the villa they are renting." Instead, they consolidate listings from other sources. It pays to seek out reputable companies, especially for first-time renters.

Things to Think about When Searching for a Villa

How many people are you? How many bedrooms will you want? Do they have to be equal? Do they all have to be attached to the house? If you are two couples, you might want to specify that there be two master suites. If you are traveling with young children, you might not want them in a separate bedroom pavilion. Definitely confirm what types of beds are in each room; couples may prefer queens or kings while kids would be better in single beds. Those looking for a bit more privacy might prefer to be in a guesthouse or small cottage that's separate from the main house.

What location do you prefer? Do you need to be right on a beach? Do you want to walk to town? Will proximity to a particular activity such as golf or scuba diving enhance your vacation? Are you willing to rent a car to get around?

What are your requirements for electronics and appliances? Do you require satellite TV? Internet service (and if so, does it need to be Wi Fi)? Or would you be okay with something less connected? Do you need a dishwasher? A microwave? How about an outdoor gas grill, or is charcoal sufficient?

Is the villa child-friendly? Ask whether rooms have direct access to the pool area; this might not be a safe choice for younger kids who could open a sliding door and enter the pool area unsupervised. Are you comfortable at all having a pool? Most Caribbean villas don't have child-roof security gates around pools or pool alarms. If the villa has two floors, are the rooms best suited for kids on a separate floor from the master suite?

What specific issues about your destination will affect your villa choice? There are realities about personal security in many areas of the Caribbean. Evaluate the location of potential rentals in relation to known problem areas and ask if the villa has an alarm system. A surprisingly low rental rate on an otherwise expensive island might be a red flag.

Will you really be comfortable on your own? The final thing to consider is your relative hardiness and that of your traveling companions. Is this your first time in the destination? Do you relish or dread the idea of navigating local markets? Will you miss having a concierge to help arrange things for you? Do you really want to be faced with a sink full of dishes a few times a day? Will your kids be happy without a hotel full of peers? What about you?

CARIBBEAN TOP EXPERIENCES

Diving in Bonaire
(A) Nautical nuts love Bonaire for the kaleidoscopic profusion of marine life, dramatic underwater-scape, excellent environmental stewardship, and accessibility of its pyrotechnic reefs: the majority explode with color just 5–25 minutes from shore in currents mild enough for snorkeling, too.

Hiking in Dominica
(B) Morne Trois Pitons National Park, a UNESCO World Heritage Site, explains Dominica's nickname "The Nature Isle." The island is so green that you can practically see plants grow during rainfall, with mountains filigreed by waterfalls, crater lakes, and natural pools—contrasted with the blast furnace Valley of Desolation, including the world's second-largest Boiling Lake belching sulfurously.

Snorkeling the Cayman Islands
(C) Swimming at Stingray City, even wading at the adjacent sandbar, you can interact with gracefully balletic stingrays, so tame you can feed them as they nuzzle you, practically begging petlike for handouts. Numerous boats take you out for the raydiant experience. Shore diving and snorkeling excels throughout all three islands.

Shopping St. Thomas
(D) The Caribbean has colorful historic capitals known for duty-free shopping, including Curaçao's Willemstad and St. Maarten's Philipsburg, but Charlotte Amalie on St. Thomas is like an elegant bazaar, with name-brand luxury boutiques tucked away in its charming arcaded Danish alleys.

Birding in Trinidad
(E) Trinidad is noted for Carnival, calypso, oil, and asphalt production—and bountiful birdlife. More than 200 species flutter flirtatiously through the Asa Wright

Nature Centre, a glorious old plantation also home to bats and giant lizards. Flocks of scarlet ibis turn the mangroves at Caroni Bird Sanctuary into a Christmas decoration come sunset.

Whale-Watching in the Dominican Republic

(F) Samaná in the northeast D.R. is revered for shimmering water, champagne-hue strands, and superior sportfishing. But its signature aquatic activity is world-class whale-watching in season (January through March), as pods of humpbacks mate and calve, the male's signature song echoing across the water.

Eating Well in St. Martin

(G) Few places rival the French West Indies for fine food and exotic ambience. One small St. Martin fishing village, Grand Case, has become the Caribbean's Restaurant Row. More than 40 eateries line the main beachfront drag, from humble lolos (shacks serving heaping helpings of creole fare at fair prices) to Michelin-worthy haute kitchens.

Boating in the Grenadines

(H) Yachties forever debate the merits of the British Virgin Islands versus the Grenadines for calm waters, exquisite anchorages, warm islanders, boisterous beach bars (such as Basil's on Mustique), and splendid diving and snorkeling (and beachcombing) at such spots as the deserted Tobago Cays.

Viewing Colonial Architecture in Puerto Rico

(I) Old San Juan is a majestic maze of narrow cobblestone alleys opening into broad tree-shaded plazas; beautifully preserved 18th-century Spanish buildings range from stone mansions with wrought-iron balconies (now housing chic boutiques and restaurants) to the UNESCO World Heritage El Morro fortress guarding the bay.

IF YOU LIKE

Great Beaches

What makes a great beach can depend on personal preference. You might dream of sifting your toes in soft white sand with just a hint of warmth. You may love to walk along a virgin beach with nothing but the occasional palm tree. You may be charmed by that cute little crescent that's reachable by a precipitous climb down an almost-sheer rock cliff. You may want to be surrounded by a hundred pairs of beautiful limbs, all smelling slightly of coconut oil. The Caribbean can give you all these. Part of the fun of taking a tropical vacation is discovering your own favorites, which are sometimes the ones you'd least suspect. Here are a few of the beaches we like:

■ **Baie Orientale, St. Maarten/St. Martin.** Often crowded, but considered by many to be the island's most beautiful beach.

■ **The Baths, Virgin Gorda, British Virgin Islands.** Giant boulders form grottoes filled with seawater that you can explore.

■ **Eagle Beach, Aruba.** Once undeveloped, this beach on Aruba's southwestern coast is now hopping and happening.

■ **Half Moon Bay, Providenciales, Turks and Caicos Islands.** A natural ribbon of ivory sand joins two tiny, uninhabited cays.

■ **Macaroni Beach, Mustique, St. Vincent and the Grenadines.** The most famous beach on the most famous Grenadine.

■ **Negril Beach, Jamaica.** Seven miles of sand lined by bars, restaurants, and hotels in westernmost Jamaica.

■ **Seven Mile Beach, Grand Cayman, Cayman Islands.** Free of litter and peddlers, the best northern sections are a sight to behold.

■ **Shoal Bay, Anguilla.** Sand or talcum powder? You decide.

Diving and Snorkeling

Many people would rather spend their days under the sea rather than on the beach. Generally, the best conditions for diving—clear water and lots of marine life—are also good for snorkelers, though you won't see as much from the surface looking down. If you haven't been certified yet, take a resort course. After learning the basics in a pool, you can often do a short dive from shore. Here are some of the Caribbean's best dive destinations:

■ **Anegada, British Virgin Islands.** The reefs surrounding this flat coral and limestone atoll are a sailor's nightmare but a scuba diver's dream.

■ **Bonaire.** The current is mild, the reefs often begin just offshore, visibility is generally 60 feet to 100 feet, and the marine life is magnificent.

■ **Dominica.** Serious divers know that the pristine, bubbly waters around Dominica's submerged volcanic crater are among the best in the world.

■ **Little Cayman, Cayman Islands.** The drop-off at Bloody Bay Wall goes from 18 feet to more than 1,000 feet—diving doesn't get much better than this.

■ **Saba.** Beside one of the lively Caribbean reefs, the diving on Saba is some of the best in the world.

■ **St. Eustatius.** The waters here are tops for wreck diving.

■ **Tobago Cays, St. Vincent and the Grenadines.** A group of five uninhabited islands surrounds a beautiful lagoon studded with sponges, coral formations, and countless colorful fish.

■ **Turks and Caicos Islands.** The world's third-largest coral reef is visible from the air and packed with exotic marine life, dramatic wall drop-offs, colorful fans, and pristine coral formations.

Shopping

Almost as many people go to the Caribbean to shop as to lie on the beach. Whether it's jewelry in St. Maarten, fragrant spices in Grenada, high-end designer fashions in St. Bartha, or Island crafts almost anywhere, you're likely to come home with a bag full of treasures.

■ **Grenada.** Visit a historic spice plantation, tour a nutmeg-processing plant, and replenish your spice rack with nutmeg, cinnamon sticks, cocoa, and cloves at an outdoor market.

■ **Puerto Rico.** From the boutiques of Old San Juan to ateliers of the young designers elsewhere in metro San Juan to galleries scattered all over the island, there's plenty to see and buy. You may also consider picking up some of the santos created in San Germán.

■ **St. Barthélemy.** Without a doubt, the shopping here for luxury goods and fashion is the best in the Caribbean. The variety and quality are astounding. The unfavorable exchange rates mean fewer bargains for Americans, but the prices here—all duty-free—are still less than what you'd pay in Paris or St. Tropez.

■ **St. Maarten/St. Martin.** Hundreds of duty-free shops in Phillipsburg make the island the best in the Caribbean for bargain hunters, especially for high-quality jewelry and perfumes. Marigot has its fair share of nice boutiques

■ **St. Thomas, U.S. Virgin Islands.** Main Street in Charlotte Amalie is well known for numerous duty-free shops, selling everything from rum to designer fashions and gems. The Caribbean's biggest cruise port also has several malls.

Staying Active

There's much more to do in the Caribbean than simply lie on the beach, sip rum punches, or play a round of golf. Try hiking through rain forests, kayaking through mangroves, or sailing on a board through a windswept bay.

■ **Bird-Watching, Trinidad and Tobago.** So the watching part isn't so active, but hiking through the rain forests and savannahs on these sister islands will give you the opportunity to see more bird species than any other place in the Caribbean.

■ **Hiking the Quill, St. Eustatius.** The crater of Statia's extinct volcano is filled with a primeval rain forest and is a top hiking destination.

■ **Horseback Riding at Chukka Cove, Jamaica.** Headquartered at the Ocho Rios polo fields, Chukka Caribbean Adventures is now Jamaica's top soft-adventure outfitter, having added canopy tours, river rafting, and more to its excellent horseback-riding program.

■ **Kayaking Through Bahía Mosquito, Puerto Rico.** Vieques's bioluminescent bay is best experienced on a kayak tour on a moonless night, when every stroke makes the water light up.

■ **Tennis at Casa de Campo, Dominican Republic.** Casa de Campo isn't just for golfers. With 13 courts (10 lit for night play) and a staff of more than 25 pros and instructors, this is one place where you can enjoy your game, whether you're an experienced player or a beginner.

■ **Trekking to Boiling Lake, Dominica.** This bubbly, brackish cauldron is actually a flooded fumarole. A trek here is an unforgettable trip into an otherworldly place.

IF YOU WANT

To Take It Easy on Your Wallet

The Caribbean isn't all about five-star resorts. Often, you may want to save a bit of your vacation cash to eat in elegant restaurants or to shop for the perfect gift. Saving money in the Caribbean doesn't have to mean sacrificing comfort. Sometimes it just means going to a cheaper island, such as the Dominican Republic, Saba, or Dominica. But there are some unique inns and resorts in the Caribbean, where you can sleep for much less and still have a great time.

■ **Bayaleau Point Cottages, Carriacou.** Owner Dave Goldhill built four colorful gingerbread guest cottages on this peaceful Windward hillside overlooking the Grenadines, as well as a 28-foot boat to take his guests on snorkeling trips.

■ **Bay Gardens Beach Resort, St. Lucia.** One of three Bay Gardens properties in Rodney Bay known for their friendly hospitality, this family-friendly hotel has a prime location on beautiful Reduit Beach.

■ **Beachcombers Hotel, St. Vincent.** Cheryl Hornsey's family home, once a tiny B&B, has morphed into a popular, 31-room beachfront hotel overlooking the sea at Villa Beach.

■ **Bellafonte Chateau de la Mer, Bonaire.** An oceanfront room at this chic, palazzo-style hotel will remind you why you came to the Caribbean.

■ **Carringtons Inn, St. Croix, U.S. Virgin Islands.** A stay at this spacious B&B harks back to a gentler time, when people spent the winter, rather than a week, in the Caribbean.

■ **Coco Palm, St. Lucia.** Rodney Bay is a beehive of activity, and this stylish boutique hotel is definitely the honey—beautiful rooms, amenities you'd expect at pricier resorts, great restaurant, and nightly entertainment.

■ **Frangipani Hotel, Bequia.** Luxurious guest rooms, built of local stone and hardwoods, are tucked into a gentle slope filled with fragrant frangipani trees and overlook Admiralty Bay.

■ **The Horny Toad, St. Maarten/St. Martin.** A marvelous little oceanfront guesthouse with a funky name offers the island's best value for those who want to keep costs down.

■ **La Sagesse Nature Centre, Grenada.** At this secluded country inn on La Sagesse Bay, 10 mi from town, guest rooms are 30 feet from the beach and a hop, skip, and jump from surrounding nature trails.

■ **Peach and Quiet, Barbados.** This small seaside inn on the southeast coast is the sweetest deal on Barbados.

■ **Rockhouse Hotel, Jamaica.** Perched on the cliffs of Negril's West End, unique bungalows blend comfort and rustic style. Regular rooms keep costs down, but if you want to spend a bit more, the dramatic villas are worth every penny.

To Have the Perfect Honeymoon

Swaying palms, moonlight strolls on the beach, candlelit dinners: no wonder the Caribbean is a favorite honeymoon destination. Whatever you are looking for in a honeymoon—seclusion, privacy, or more active fun—you can certainly find it, and it will usually be on a perfect beach. You can be pampered or just left alone, stay up late or get up with the sun, get out and stay active or simply rest and relax. Our favorites run the gamut, so if you need a place with easy access, or if you want to really get away from it all, we have the perfect spot.

■ **Horned Dorset Primavera, Puerto Rico.** Whisk your beloved to this sunset-kissed hotel and just disappear. You may never leave your elegant oceanfront room.

When you do, the restaurant is one of the best in Puerto Rico.

■ **Palm Island, Grenadines.** Enjoy five dazzling beaches for water sports, nature trails for quiet walks, a pool with waterfall, sophisticated dining, impeccable service, exquisite accommodations—and privacy.

■ **Sandals Grande St. Lucian Spa & Beach Resort, St. Lucia.** Big, busy, and all-inclusive, this resort is a favorite of young honeymooners—particularly for its complimentary weddings.

■ **The Somerset, Turks and Caicos Islands.** Provo's most beautiful resort is more focused on your comfort than on attracting a celebrity clientele, so regular folks will still feel at home.

■ **Spice Island Beach Resort, Grenada.** Grenada's best resort has impeccable service, placing it among the Caribbean's finest small resorts.

To Eat Well

Caribbean food is a complex blend of indigenous, African, and colonial influences. Native tubers such as yuca and taro, leafy vegetables like callaloo, and herbs such as cilantro recur in most island cuisines. Africans brought plantains, yams, pigeon peas, and assorted peppers. The Spanish introduced rice, and the British brought breadfruit from the South Pacific. Here are some of our favorite Caribbean restaurants:

Banana Tree Grille, St. Thomas, U.S. Virgin Islands. The eagle's-eye view of the Charlotte Amalie harbor from this breeze-cooled restaurant is as fantastic as the food.

■ **Blue by Eric Ripert, Cayman Islands.** Grand Cayman's best restaurant is brought to you by one of New York's finest chefs.

■ **Boston Jerk Centre, Port Antonio, Jamaica.** To enjoy the best Jamaican jerk in the place where it was invented, these simple beach huts are the place to head.

■ **Brandywine Bay, Tortola (BVI).** A romantic, candlelit atmosphere coupled with stellar food makes this Tortola's best restaurant.

■ **The Cliff, Barbados.** Chef Paul Owens's mastery is the foundation of one of the finest dining experiences in the Caribbean, with prices to match.

■ **Coyaba Restaurant, Providenciales, Turks and Caicos Islands.** This posh eatery serves nostalgic favorites in a palm-fringed setting, one of the island's most romantic and inviting places to dine.

■ **Iguane Café, Guadeloupe.** Unquestionably original cuisine with influences from around the world is daring and dramatic, not to mention delicious.

■ **KoalKeel, Anguilla.** One of the island's best new restaurants mixes French and West Indian styles to excellent effect.

■ **Le Tastevin, St. Martin.** In the heart of Grand Case, Le Tastevin is on everyone's list of favorites.

■ **Le Ti St. Barth Caribbean Tavern, St. Barthélemy.** Chef-owner Carole Gruson captures the funky, sexy spirit of the island in her wildly popular hilltop hot spot.

■ **The Verandah, Trinidad.** Phyllis Vieira's free-style Caribbean cuisine is one of the best-kept secrets in Trinidad—well, we can't keep this secret any longer.

WHEN TO GO

The Caribbean high season is traditionally winter—from December 15 to April 14. During this season you're guaranteed the most entertainment at resorts and the most people with whom to enjoy it. It's also the most fashionable, the most expensive, and the most popular time to visit. You must make reservations at least two or three months in advance for the very best places (sometimes a year in advance for the most exclusive spots). Hotel prices drop 20% to 50% after April 15; airfares and cruise prices also fall. Saving money isn't the only reason to visit the Caribbean during the off-season. Temperatures are only a few degrees warmer than at other times of the year, and many islands now schedule their carnivals, music festivals, and other events during the off-season. Late August, September, October, and early November are the least crowded.

Climate

The Caribbean climate is fairly constant. The average year-round temperatures for the region are 78°F to 88°F. The temperature extremes are 65°F low, 95°F high; but, as everyone knows, it's the humidity, not the heat, that makes you suffer, especially when the two go hand in hand.

Hurricanes occasionally sweep through the Caribbean. Check the news daily and keep abreast of brewing tropical storms. The southernmost Caribbean islands (from St. Vincent to Trinidad, along with Aruba, Bonaire, and Curaçao) are generally spared the threat of hurricanes. The rainy season consists mostly of brief showers interspersed with sunshine. You can watch the clouds thicken, feel the rain, then have brilliant sunshine dry you off, all while remaining on your lounge chair. A spell of overcast days or heavy rainfall is unusual, as everyone will tell you.

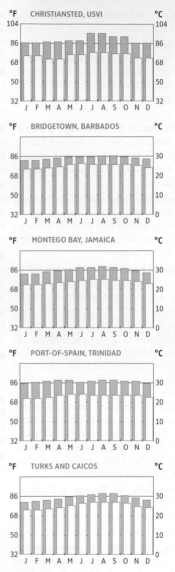

HURRICANE SEASON

The Atlantic hurricane season lasts from June 1 through November 30, but it's fairly rare to see a large storm in either June or November. Most major hurricanes occur between August and October, with the peak season in September.

Avoiding the Storms: Keep in mind that hurricanes are more rare the farther south you go. The ABC Islands (Aruba, Bonaire, and Curaçao) as well as Trinidad and Tobago are the least likely to see a direct hit by a hurricane, but all these islands have had their run-ins, so it's not a certainty that you'll avoid storms by going south. Similarly, Barbados is less likely to be adversely affected by a strong storm because it lies 100 mi farther east than the rest of the Antilles.

Airlines: Airports are usually closed during hurricanes and many flights canceled, which results in a disruption of the steady flow of tourists in and out of affected islands. If you are scheduled to fly into an area where a hurricane is expected, check with your airline regularly and often. If flights are disrupted, airlines will usually allow you to rebook at a later date, but you will not get a refund if you have booked a nonrefundable ticket, nor in most cases will you be allowed to change your ticket to a different destination; rather, you will be expected to reschedule your trip for a later date.

Hotels and Resorts: If a hurricane warning is issued and flights to your destination are disrupted, virtually every Caribbean resort will waive cancellation and change penalties and allow you to rebook your trip for a later date; some will allow you to cancel even if a hurricane threatens to strike, even if flights aren't canceled. Some will give you a refund if you have prepaid for your stay; others will expect you to

rebook your trip for a later date. Some large resort companies—including Sandals and SuperClubs—have "hurricane guarantees," but they apply only when flights have been canceled or when a hurricane is sure to strike.

Travel Insurance: If you plan to travel to the Caribbean during the hurricane season, it is wise to buy travel insurance that allows you to cancel for any reason. This kind of coverage can be expensive (up to 10% of the value of the trip), but if you have to prepay far in advance for an expensive vacation package, the peace of mind may be worth it. Just be sure to read the fine print; some policies don't kick in unless flights are canceled and the hurricane strikes, something you may not be assured of until the day you plan to travel. To get a complete cancellation policy, you must usually buy your insurance within a week of booking your trip. If you wait until after the hurricane warning is issued to purchase insurance, it will be too late.

Track Those Hurricanes: The obsessive and naturally curious keep a close eye on the Caribbean during hurricane season. You can, too. Several Web sites track hurricanes during the season, including ⊕ *weather.com*, ⊕ *www.hurricanetrack. com*, and ⊕ *www.accuweather.com*.

WEDDINGS

Destination weddings, once the exclusive domain of celebs and the superrich, are becoming more affordable in the Caribbean. Many resorts offer attractive packages that couples are taking advantage of to create their ultimate island-paradise wedding. As an added bonus, many islands and resorts provide a plethora of experienced wedding planners. So whether you picture an intimate beachfront ceremony for two or a full-blown affair, you can confidently leave the details to a professional and simply concentrate on exchanging your vows.

Finding a Wedding Planner

Hiring a planner to handle all of the logistics—from the preliminary paperwork right down to final toast—allows you to relax and truly enjoy your big day. The best of the bunch will advise you about legalities (like any residency requirements), help organize the marriage license, and hire the officiant, plus arrange for venues, flowers, music, refreshments, or anything else your heart desires. Planners typically have established relationships with local vendors, and can bundle packages with them—which can save you money. Most resorts have on-site coordinators. But there are also many independents available, including those who specialize in certain types of ceremonies—by locale, size, religious affiliation, and so on. Island tourism boards often maintain an online list of names, and a simple "Caribbean weddings" Google search will yield scores more. What's important is that you feel comfortable with your coordinator. Ask for references—and call them. Share your budget. Ask how long they've been in business, how much they charge, how often you'll meet with them, and how they select vendors. Above all, request a detailed, written list of what

they'll provide. If your vision of the dream wedding doesn't match their services, try someone else. If you can afford it, you might even want to schedule a preliminary trip to meet the planner in person.

Making It Legal

Your goal is to tie the knot, not get tied up in red tape. So it is important to be mindful of the legalities involved. Specifics vary widely, depending on the type of ceremony you want (civil ones are invariably less complicated than religious services) and the island where you choose to wed. In the Dominican Republic, for example, key documents must be submitted in Spanish: unless you enlist a translator, your wedding will be conducted in Spanish, too. On the French-speaking islands (Guadeloupe, Martinique, St. Barths, and St. Martin) language issues are further compounded by stringent residency requirements, which can make marrying there untenable.

There are, however, **standard rules** that apply throughout the islands:

■ Most places will expect you to produce a valid passport as proof of identification when applying for a marriage license (the exceptions being Puerto Rico and the U.S. Virgin Islands, where official government-issued picture ID will suffice for American citizens).

■ If you are under 18 years old, parental consent is also needed unless otherwise stated in the chart that follows.

■ If you are divorced, the original divorce or annulment decree is required.

■ If you are a widow or widower, original marriage and death certificates are required. (In certain locales, an apostille stamp confirming the authenticity of such documents must be attached.)

1

ISLAND	COSTS	WAITING PERIOD	GOOD TO KNOW
Anguilla	License $279	At least 2 business days to process license	As elsewhere in the Caribbean, special rules apply here for religious weddings. Couples marrying in church must allow extra time; some churches require prenuptial consultation and extra documentation.
Antigua	License $150; marriage officer's fee $50	None	Couples landing in Antigua after 3 pm won't have enough time to get a license from the Ministry of Justice and wed the same day. If you're really in a rush, catch an earlier flight.
Aruba	License $80 during office hours; $200 on Sat. or after hours	None, provided all documents are submitted at least one month in advance	Civil ceremonies may take place in Oranjestad's historic City Hall, on the beach, or at your venue of choice.
Barbados	License $100 plus a $12.50 stamp fee; separate magistrate and court fees for civil ceremonies	None	Couples must apply in person to the Ministry of Home Affairs in Bridgetown for a license. A letter from the person performing your ceremony must be presented at this time.
Bonaire	License $150	One partner must be on-island 7 days to establish residency; license takes 4 business days to process.	One partner must get a temporary residency permit before applying for a license. Official witnesses must do the same, but most wedding coordinators can arrange for local ones.
British Virgin Islands	License $110 for those in the territory less than 15 days before the ceremony; $50 inf in the BVI more than 15 days; registrar's fee $35 for weddings in the office and $100 at other locations	Minimum of 3 business days to process license	It is standard practice to have two witnesses at your ceremony. In BVI you also need two different witnesses present when you sign your license application.
Cayman Islands	License $200	None	When applying for a license, you must present a letter from the marriage officer who will be officiating (a list can be obtained from the deputy chief secretary's office).

Island	Costs	Waiting Period	Good to Know
Curaçao	License $197	3 days before applying for license; 14-day waiting period	Like the other Dutch Antilles, Curaçao is a stickler for paperwork, so hiring a wedding pro helps. Documents, which must be original, recent, and apostille, are to be with your planner at least 2 months in advance
Dominica	License $112; statutory declaration fee $187; registrar's fee $11 for weddings at the office and $37 at other locations	One partner must be on-island 2 days before the wedding.	Couples must sign a statutory declaration on marital status in the presence of a local lawyer. You must also complete an application form and have it witnessed by a magistrate.
Dominican Republic	Combined fees $400 for civil ceremonies in the registry office; $600 elsewhere	Notice of intended marriage must be published prior to ceremony	Both partners must provide proof of single status that has been translated into Spanish at a Dominican Consulate. All paperwork should be submitted at least 6 months in advance.
Grenada	License $2.50; registration and stamp fees $10	Couples must be on-island 3 days before applying for a license; 2 business days needed for processing.	If you are under the age of 21, parental consent (in the form of an affidavit) is required. If you've been married before, it may take a bit longer for your license to be processed.
Jamaica	License $80; marriage officer's fee $50–$250	24 hours	Accommodating laws and upscale couples-only resorts make Jamaica a top pick. Some all-inclusives even offer complimentary weddings, complete with officiant and license.
Nevis	License $80 if on-island for a minimum of 2 business days; $20 if on-island for 15 days prior	Both parties must be on-island at least 2 business days	You'll pay $20 to complete your application before a justice of the peace. If you've never been married, also be prepared to pop $20 for a notarized affidavit of single status.
Puerto Rico	License and stamp fees $30	None	Blood tests and a health license are needed (the former done within 14 days of the wedding, the latter within 10). These can be obtained from your own physician, then certified by one in Puerto Rico.

Island	Costs	Waiting Period	Good to Know
St. Eustatius	License, stamp fees, and marriage book $275	14 days after document registration	Marriages performed outside the marriage hall require 6 witnesses.
St. Kitts	License $80 if on-island for a minimum of 2 business days; $20 if on-island for 15 days prior	Both parties must be on-island a minimum of 2 business days	Thinking of a casual sunrise or sunset ceremony on the beach? Consider this: Civil weddings are performed only from 8 to 6. Church weddings may be held 6 to 6.
St. Lucia	License $125 for standard or $200 for special; registrar fees $37; marriage certificate $3	None with a special license, 3 days with a standard license	St. Lucia, a leader in the destination wedding biz, has a streamlined process that makes marrying easy. Most lodgings have enticing packages and on-site planners.
St. Maarten	Combined cost of civil ceremony, marriage book, certificate, and stamps $410	Couples must submit requests 14 days before the wedding and be on-island 7 days beforehand	It is much easier to marry in St. Maarten than in St. Martin. The French side of the island requires translated documents and a monthlong residency period for one partner.
St. Vincent and the Grenadines	License $197 for governor–general's or $15 for registrar's (including stamp fees)	1 day with Governor–General's license; 7 days with registrar's license	Blessed with camera-ready beaches, gorgeous gardens, private island resorts and historic buildings, these 32 islands boast a broader-than-average range of venues.
Trinidad and Tobago	License $51	3 days	To obtain a license both partners must be nonresidents. Documents, such as airline tickets, are required to confirm your dates of entry and onward passage.
Turks and Caicos	License $150	24 hours, but licenses may take 2–3 days to process	The marriage is registered here. To have it registered in your home country, you must make special arrangements. Parental consent needed if under 21.
U.S. Virgin Islands	Marriage application and license fee $100; officiating fee $200 if not married in court by a judge	8 days from receipt of application	Licenses must be picked up in person on weekdays, but you can shorten the wait by applying from home.

KIDS AND FAMILIES

Traveling with kids to the Caribbean is fun and easy. Many resorts, except for those that are exclusively couples-only, offer kids free promotions, special restaurant menus, and programs for tots on up to teens.

Choosing a Place to Stay

Everything from brand-name resorts to independent hotels, condominiums, and even campgrounds can offer a great family vacation. It just depends what you're looking for.

Let them entertain you. If you prefer to relax while the kids are entertained, choose a major resort with all-inclusive meal plan and kids' program. A few best bets are **Beaches Resorts** (Beaches Turks and Caicos, Beaches Negril, and Beaches Sandy Bay in Jamaica). The **Sandals** chain (Antigua, Jamaica, St. Lucia) has kids' programs to match all ages, outdoor playgrounds, gaming centers, trips for ages 12 and up such as snorkeling and scuba diving, and Sesame Street character appearances. **Hyatt Regency Aruba Beach Resort & Casino** features Camp Hyatt, where kids ages 3 to 12 can participate in a variety of activities and adventures. **Club Med Punta Cana**, in the Dominican Republic, offers a baby gym, Crayola arts-and-crafts programs, hip-hop dance instruction, Petite Chef (ages 3 to 7) cooking classes, and The Ramp, an interactive club for 14- to 17-year-olds.

DIY. If you'd prefer more of a home base from which to explore the island on your own, choose a hotel, condo, or villa near the attractions you'd most like to visit. Condos and villas provide more of an at-home atmosphere with full kitchens and separate bedrooms, and many include home entertainment systems. The **Cinnamon Bay Campground** on St. John, in the U.S. Virgin Islands, is a great kid-friendly option. Camp right on the beach in screened cottages or canvas tents. There are cooking facilities in each unit, and a cafeteria-style restaurant gives Mom the night off. Lifeguards are on duty, there are water-sports rentals, and there's plenty of white-sand beach for sand castles and swimming.

Top Attractions

The Caribbean offers an abundance of family attractions. Museums, forts, caves, zoos, and aquariums are sure to keep tots, teens, adults, and seniors happy when it's time to take a break from the sun, sand, and sea.

Momentous Museums. Many kids have read about Christopher Columbus in history books, but at **El Faro a Colón** (Columbus Lighthouse), just outside Santa Domingo in the Dominican Republic, they can visit his tomb. The huge pyramid-shaped complex has six museums that trace the history of the area from the ancient Indian days to the construction of this modern, multimillion-dollar structure. Kids will marvel over ancient maps, jewelry-studded royal crowns, and replicas of dugout canoes. For a real treat, visit at night when the 688-foot-tall lighthouse projects a cross-shaped beam of light some 44 mi into the sky. In Jamaica, teenagers may enjoy the **Bob Marley Museum**. This former home of the late great king of reggae music—painted Rastafarian red, yellow, and green—is filled with Marley's personal memorabilia. A 15-minute video presents the life story of Marley along with familiar music clips. Younger kids will love the **Anancy Family Fun & Nature Park**. Located near Negril, the park boasts three small museums—crafts-, conservation-, and heritage-oriented—along with

a nature trail, fishing pond, go-kart riding track, and miniature-golf course. The park is named for Anancy, a mischievous spider in Jamaican folk stories.

Fantastic Fortresses. A long grassy walk leads up to the 500-year-old **Castillo del Morro** (El Morro) Castle, an imposing structure in Puerto Rico's Old San Juan that looks like the Wicked Witch's scary fortress. Venture inside the thick walls and cruise the ramparts, tunnels, and dungeons. Wax mannequins model historic battle uniforms, and a video shows the history of building and defending this stronghold. Equally imposing is St. Kitts's **Brimstone Hill**, known as the Gibraltar of the West Indies. Ft. George, which sits atop the hill, is built of 7-foot-thick walls of black volcanic stone. Kids can woefully imagine being imprisoned here during a "time-out." From high atop the fort's cannon ways, kids can search the horizon for the islands of Nevis, Montserrat, Saba, St. Maarten/St. Martin, and St. Barths. It's also fun to try spotting the scampering green monkeys that play along the nature trails that wind around this 38-acre site.

Cool Caves. Don a bright yellow hard hat and ride a tramcar into Barbados's **Harrison's Cave**. Specially lighted caverns illuminate the stalactites, stalagmites, and underground waterfalls so the caves don't seem too spooky. The **Hato Caves** in Curaçao were made during the Ice Age, but today the inhabitants are not cavemen but long-nosed bats. Puerto Rico's **Rio Camuy Cave Park** tour begins with a short video and then a trolley ride right to the mouth of the cave. Though 200 feet high, the cave is only half a mile long. The walking tour is level and flat, allowing kids' eyes to roam all over without fear of stumbling.

Zany Zoos. Roam freely with the animals at the **Barbados Wildlife Reserve**. This outdoor zoo keeps kids engaged as they walk along shady pathways and spot exotic animals, reptiles, and birds in their natural habitat. There are land turtles, fine-feathered peacocks, green monkeys, parrots, and even an otter. Some species here are threatened by extinction. After exploring outside, kids can check out the walk-in aviary and the many natural history exhibits. The **Emperor Valley Zoo**, named for Trinidad's native blue butterflies, is one of the best in the Caribbean. The island's president and prime minister have houses on this site, but most intriguing for kids is the 8-acre zoo that is filled with birds and other wildlife from the region, ranging from blue and gold macaws and small red brocket deer to giant anacondas.

Awesome Aquariums. **Curaçao Sea Aquarium** boasts more than 400 species of sea life. Some of the most fascinating creatures are the sharks—hand-fed daily, to the delight of kids of all ages. Sharks are another big draw to the **Acuario National** outside Santa Domingo in the Dominican Republic. The huge creatures sometimes nap across glass-tunneled walkways where kids can check out the vibrating gills of these sleeping demons. Coral World's shark encounter is also a draw, as is a baby shark pond where park staff will let kids feel this fearsome fish's sandpaper skin.

FLAVORS OF THE
CARIBBEAN

by Charyn Pfeuffer

As an entry point to the New World, the Caribbean has a rich culinary tradition reflecting the diversity of its immigrants. This melting pot of Spanish, African, French, English, and Dutch influences has created dishes packed with fresh ingredients and bold, spicy flavors and seasonings.

Local produce is varied and includes lima beans, black-eyed peas, corn, yams, sweet potatoes, cassava, and taro. Rice and beans are ever-present staples, commonly seasoned with ingredients like curry, cilantro, soy sauce, and ginger. The spice-forward "jerk" style of marinated and rubbed meat, fish, and fowl is prevalent. Jamaica, Haiti, Guadeloupe, and other French Caribbean islands savor goat meat in dishes like goat water, a tomato-based stew, which is the official national dish of Montserrat and a speciality on St. Kitts and Nevis. Fresh-caught seafood from local waters also figures prominently into the cuisine.

Modern menus don't stray too far from tradition, opting instead for clever twists rather than reinvention, like flavoring black beans with tequila and olive oil, or serving rice spiked with coconut and ginger. No matter where your culinary curiosities take you in the islands, plan on a well-seasoned eating adventure.

(opposite) Dasheene Restaurant at Ladera Resort, St. Lucia, (top) Jerk pork, a signature Jamaican dish, (bottom) scotch bonnet peppers.

THE ISLANDS' GLOBAL FLAVORS

Island cuisine developed through waves of wars, immigration, and natives' innovations from the 15th century through the mid-19th century. Early Amerindian native peoples, the Arawaks and the Caribs, are said to have introduced the concept of spicing food with chili peppers, a preparation that remains a hallmark of Caribbean cuisine. Pepper pot stew was a staple for the Caribs, who would make the dish with *cassareep*, a savory sauce made from cassava. The stew featured wild meats (possum, wild pig, or armadillo), squash, beans, and peanuts, which were added to the cassareep and simmered in a clay pot. The dish was traditionally served to guests as a gesture of hospitality. Today's recipes substitute meats like pig trotters, cow heel, or oxtail.

Caribbean-style curried goat

After Columbus' discovery of the New World, European traders and settlers brought new fruits, vegetables, and meats. Their arrival coincided with that of African slaves en route to the Americas. Every explorer, settler, trader, and slave brought something to expand the palette of flavors. Although Caribbean cooking varies from island to island, trademark techniques and spices unite the cuisine.

SPANISH INFLUENCES

The Caribbean islands were discovered by Christopher Columbus in 1492, while he was working for the Spanish crown. When he returned to colonize the islands a year later, he brought ships laden with coconut, chickpeas, cilantro, eggplant, onions, and garlic. The Bahamas, Hispaniola, and Cuba were among Columbus' first findings, and as a result, Cuba and nearby Puerto Rico have distinctly Spanish-accented cuisine, including *paella* (a seafood- or meat-studded rice dish), *arroz con pollo* or *pilau* (chicken cooked with yellow rice), and white-bean Spanish stews.

Arroz con Pollo

FRENCH TECHNIQUE

As tobacco and sugar crops flourished and the Caribbean became a center of European trade and colonization, the French settled Martinique and Guadeloupe in 1635 and later expanded to St. Barthélemy, St. Martin, Grenada, St. Lucia, and western Hispaniola. French culinary technique meets the natural resources of the islands to create dishes like whelk (sea snail) grilled in garlic butter, fish cooked *en papillote* (baked in parchment paper), and *crabs farcis*, land crab meat that is steamed, mixed with butter, breadcrumbs, ham, chilis, and garlic, then stuffed back into the crab shells and grilled.

DUTCH INGENUITY

Beginning in the 1620s, traders from the Dutch East India Company brought Southeast Asian ingredients like soy sauce to the islands of Curaçao and St. Maarten. Dutch influence is also evident throughout Aruba and Bonaire (all have been under Dutch rule since the early 19th century), where dishes like *keshi yeni*, or "stuffed cheese," evolved from stuffing discarded rinds of Edam cheese with minced meat, olives, and capers. Another Dutch-influenced dish is *boka dushi* (Indonesian-style chicken satay), which translates to "sweet mouth" in the islands' Papiamento dialect.

Paella

Boka dushi

Roti

Jerk meat

ENGLISH IMPORTS
British settlers brought pickles, preserves, and chutneys to the Caribbean, and current-day chefs take advantage of the islands' indigenous fruits to produce these items. British influence also is evidenced by the Indian and Chinese contributions to Caribbean cuisine. British (and Dutch) colonists brought over indentured laborers from India and China to work on sugar plantations, resulting in the introduction of popular dishes like curry goat and *roti*, an Indian flatbread stuffed with vegetables or chicken curry.

AFRICAN INGREDIENTS
The African slave trade that began in the early 1600s brought foods from West Africa, including yams, okra, plantains, breadfruit, pigeon peas, and oxtail to the islands. Slave cooks often had to make do with plantation leftovers and scraps, yielding dishes like cow heel soup and pig-foot souse (a cool soup with pickled cucumber and meat), both of which are still popular today. One of the most significant African contributions to the Caribbean table is "jerking," the process of dry-rubbing meat with allspice, Scotch bonnet peppers, and other spices. Although the cooking technique originated with native Amerindians, it was the Jamaican Maroons,

Whelk

a population of runaway African slaves living in the island's mountains during the years of slavery, who developed and perfected it, resulting in the style of jerk meat familiar in restaurants today.

CARIBBEAN'S NATURAL BOUNTY

Soursop

Despite its spicy reputation, Caribbean food isn't always fiery; the focus is on enhancing and intensifying flavors with herbs and spices.

Food plays a major role in island culture, family life, and traditions, and no holiday would be complete without traditional dishes prepared from the island's natural products.

TANTALIZING TROPICAL FRUIT

Breadfruit, a versatile starch with potato-like flavor, can be served solo—baked or grilled—or added to soups and stews.

With its rich, refreshing milk, **coconut** frequently appears in soups, stews, sauces, and drinks to help temper hot, spicy flavors with its rich, refreshing milk.

The bright orange tropical fruit **guava** tastes somewhat like a tomato when it's not fully ripe, but is pleasantly sweet when mature. It is used in compotes, pastes, and jellies.

The pungent smell of **jackfruit** may be off-putting for some, but its sweet fleshy meat is popular in milkshakes.

Papaya is sweet and floral when ripe; unripe, it can be shredded and mixed with spices and citrus for a refreshing salad. It is often used in fruit salsas that are served with seafood.

The brightly flavored **passion fruit** is commonly puréed and used in sauces, drinks, and desserts.

The dark-green skinned, creamy fleshed **soursop** is known for its sweet-tart juice used in drinks, sorbets, and ice creams.

The fibrous stalks of **sugarcane**, a giant grass native to India, are rich with sugar, which can be consumed in several forms, including freshly extracted juice and processed sugar.

Tamarind is the fruit of a large tree. The sticky pulp of its pod is used in chutneys and curries to impart a slightly sweet, refreshingly sour flavor.

FARM-FRESH VEGETABLES

Cassava (also called yucca) can be used much like a potato in purées, dumplings, soups, and stews. The flour of its roots is made into tapioca.

Chayote is a versatile member of the squash and melon family, often used raw in salads or stuffed with cheese and tomatoes and baked.

Dasheen (taro) is much like a potato, but creamier. It can be

Jackfruit

sliced thinly and fried like a potato chip.

Fitweed (or French thistle) is a tropical herb related to coriander (cilantro), and is popular in Caribbean seasonings.

Pod-like **okra** is commonly used in *callaloo*, the national dish of Trinidad and Tobago. The creamy, spicy stew is made of leafy greens, okra, and crabmeat.

Green plantain is a cooking staple across the Caribbean, often sliced, pounded, dipped in a seasoned batter, and deep-fried.

The leafy green **sorrel** is typically pureed in soups

Tamarind

Chayote

Curry powder

and stews, or used in salads.

SWEET AND SAVORY SPICES

Native **allspice**, also called Jamaican pepper, is commonly added to Caribbean curries. It is the dried unripe berry of the evergreen pimento tree. Native Jamaicans once used it to preserve meats. It is an essential ingredient in jerk preparations.

Curries are intensely seasoned gravy-based dishes originating from India—they are most prevalent on the islands of Jamaica, Trinidad, and Tobago.

Native Carib people pioneered the use of **chili peppers** in the islands for hot, spicy flavoring, using primarily habaneros and Scotch bonnet peppers.

Ginger can be used raw or dried and ground into a powder that adds flavor

and heat to ginger beer, sweet potatoes, or coconut milk-based sauces.

The mix of spices in **jerk** seasoning vary, but typically include scallions, thyme, allspice, onions, and garlic.

The tiny island of Grenada is the second largest exporter of **nutmeg** in the world. It often accents sweet dishes, and is frequently added to vegetables in Dutch preparations.

ISLAND FISH AND SEAFOOD

Bonito is a medium-sized fish in the mackerel family. Atlantic bonito is moderately fatty, with a firm texture and darker color. It is served blackened, grilled (sometimes with fruit-based salsas), or Jamaican jerk style.

On many islands, including the Bahamas, **conch**—a large shellfish—are made into conch fritters, a mix of conch meat, corn meal, and spices that are deep fried and make an excellent snack.

Cascadura fish is a small fish found in the freshwater swamps of Trinidad and Tobago. It is typically served in curry with a side of rice or dumplings.

Conch salad

Flying fish are named for the wing-like fins that enable them to glide or "fly" over water. Firm in texture, it is typically served steamed or fried. Flying fish is a staple in Bajan cuisine and is found in abundance off the coast of Barbados.

Kingfish is another word for wahoo, a delicate white fish commonly fished off the coasts of St. Croix and Barbados. It's served *escabeche* style, marinated in a vinegar mixture, then fried or poached.

Land crab is found throughout the islands. Delicate in flavor, its common preparations include curried crab stewed in coconut milk, stuffed crab, and crab soup.

Mahi mahi is fished off the coast of St. Croix. With a subtle, sweet flavor, its firm, dark flesh lends itself to soy sauce glazes and Asian preparations.

Salt fish is a dish made from dried cod, often seasoned with tomatoes, onions, and thyme. Stir-fried ackee (a tropical fruit with nutty-flavored flesh) and saltfish is Jamaica's national dish.

Allspice

Salt fish

THE RISE OF RUM

The Caribbean is the world center for rum production, with many islands making their own brands and styles of rum. Dozens of rum companies operate throughout the islands. Although larger, mainstream brands like Bacardi, Captain Morgan, and Mount Gay are available on every island, you may have to look harder for the smaller brands. The best-quality rums are dark, aged rums meant for sipping, priced from $30 to $700 a bottle. For excellent sipping rum at the lower end of the spectrum, try Appleton or Rhum Barbancourt. For mixed drinks, use clear or golden-colored rums that are less expensive and pair well with fruit juices or cola. Spiced and flavored rums are also popular in cocktails. Here are some of the best rums you'll encounter at an island bar:

Appleton Estate (Jamaica) The Estate VX is an amber-colored rum with subtle brown sugar aromas and a smooth, toasted honey finish. Excellent mixer for classic cocktails.
Bacardi (Bermuda, PR) Superior is a clear, mild rum with subtle hints of vanilla and fresh fruits. It is smooth and light on the palate. Best in mixed drinks.
Captain Morgan (PR) Its Black Label Jamaica Rum is dark, rich, and smooth, with strong notes of vanilla. Sip it iced, or with a splash of water.
Clarke's Court (Grenada) The Original White is clear with a touch of sweetness

Ron Barceló

and a hint of heat, best used as a mixer.
Cruzan (VI) Less strong and sweet than most rums, the White Rum is smooth, and best suited for mixing.
Havana Club (Cuba) The Añejo 3 Años is deceiving—light in color and body and delicate in flavor. It is a nice rum to sip neat.
Mount Gay Rum (Barbados) Eclipse, the brand's flagship rum, has a golden color with a butterscotch caramel nose and sweet taste on the palate with mouth-warming flavor.
Pusser's (BVI) Self-described as "the single malt of rum," the aged 15-year variety boasts notes of cinnamon, woody spice, and citrus. A good sipping rum.

Rhum Barbancourt (Haiti) Aged 15-years, this premium dark rum is distilled twice in copper pot stills and often called the "Cognac of Rum." Sip it neat.
Ron Barceló (DR) The Añejo is dark copper in color, with a rich flavor, while the aged Imperial boasts notes of toffee on the nose, and a buttery smooth finish.
Shillingford Estates (Dominica) Its most popular product, Macoucherie Spiced is a blend of rum, the bark of the Bois Bande tree, and spices.

Mount Gay Rum

(left) Pusser's Rum, (right) Havana Club

ISLANDS' BEST BREWS

Beer in the Caribbean was largely home-made for centuries, a tradition inherited from British colonial rulers. The first commercial brewery in the islands was founded in Trinidad and Tobago in 1947.

In the islands, do what the locals do: drink local beer. Whatever brand is brewed on island is the one you'll find at every restaurant and bar. And no matter where you go in the Caribbean, there's a local island brew worth trying. Another plus: local brands are almost always cheaper than imports like Corona or Heineken. Most island beers are pale lagers, though you'll find a smattering of Dutch-style pilsners and English-style pale ales. The beers listed below are our top picks for beachside sipping:

Kalik

Banks Beer (Banks Breweries, Barbados) A straw-colored lager that is light tasting with a touch of maltiness on the nose and tongue.

Blackbeard Ale (Virgin Islands Brewing Co., Virgin Islands) This English pale ale-style beer is bright amber in color with a creamy white head. Well-crafted beer with a nice hoppy bite at the finish.

Balashi Beer (Brouwerij Nacional Balashi N.V., Aruba) Refreshingly light, this Dutch pilsner boasts mild flavor, slight sweetness, and subtle hop bitterness.

Legends Premium Lager (Banks Breweries, Barbados) One of the Caribbean's best brews, this golden yellow lager offers crisp hops and a clean finish. Distinctive toasty, malt character.

Carib Lager Beer (Carib Brewery, Trinidad and Tobago) This great beach refresher is pale yellow color with a foamy head. Fruity and sweet malty corn aromas, it is sometimes referred to as the "Corona of the Caribbean."

Kalik Gold (Commonwealth Brewery LTD., New Providence, Bahamas) Clear straw color with gentle hoppy, herbal notes, this is an easy drinking, warm weather lager.

Medalla Light (Puerto Rico) This bright gold lager is substantial for a light beer. It's a local favorite.

Red Stripe (Jamaica) The Jamaican lager pours golden yellow in color with lots of carbonation. Light bodied, crisp, and smooth.

Carib Lager Beer

Piton (St. Lucia) Light and sparkly with subtle sweetness, this pale yellow lager is pleasant enough, but barely flavored.

Presidente (Domincan Republic) Slight citrus aroma, light body, and fizziness, plus a clean finish make for easy drinking. Perfect pairing for barbecued meats.

Wadadli (Antigua Brewery Ltd., Antigua and Barbuda) A crisp, light-bodied American-style lager. Toasty malt on the nose.

Banks Beer

(left) Red Stripe,
(right) Presidente

DID YOU KNOW?

In the varied habitats of Virgin Islands National Park, approximately 144 species of birds can be seen throughout the year.

Anguilla

WORD OF MOUTH

"[W]e just prefer Anguilla because of the beaches, the people, and the food. Much more of an island vibe."

—MaryD

WELCOME TO ANGUILLA

TRANQUIL AND UPSCALE

This dry limestone isle is the most northerly of the Leeward Islands, lying between the Caribbean Sea and the Atlantic Ocean. The island is only 16 mi (26 km) long and 3 mi (5 km) wide at its widest point. A low-lying limestone island, its highest spot is 213 feet above sea level. Since there are neither streams nor rivers—only saline ponds used for salt production—water is provided by cisterns that collect rainwater, or desalinization plants.

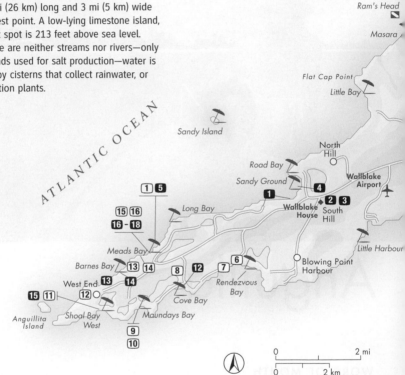

In tiny Anguilla, where fishermen have been heading out to sea for centuries in hand-made boats, the beaches are some of the Caribbean's best and least crowded. Heavy development has not spoiled the island's atmospheric corners, and independent restaurants still thrive. Resorts run the gamut from over-the-top palaces to quaint inns.

Little Scrub Island

Scrub Island

Upper Flats

Stoney Bay
Marine Park

Grouper Bowl

Island Harbour   Scilly
Shoal Bay   Cupium's Bay
                Island
Katouche   Harbour   **5**
Bay   **2 3 4**
                Island   **11** ◆ Heritage Museum Collection
        9   **10**   Harbour
                                Savannah Bay
    8
Crocus Bay

Mimi Bay
Sea Feathers Bay

6 7

The Valley   Sandy Hill Bay
The Quarter

◆ Warden's Place   Long Salt Pond

Forest Bay

KEY	
➢	Beaches
◣	Dive Sites
1	Restaurants
①	Hotels

TOP REASONS TO VISIT ANGUILLA

1 **Beautiful Beaches:** Miles of brilliant beach ensure you have a high-quality spot in which to lounge.

2 **Great Restaurants:** The dining scene offers both fine dining and delicious casual food.

3 **Fun, Low-Key Nightlife:** A funky late-night local music scene features reggae and string bands.

4 **Upscale Accommodations:** Excellent luxury resorts coddle you in comfort.

5 **Hidden Bargains:** You'll find a few relative bargains if you look hard enough.

ANGUILLA PLANNER

Logistics

Getting to Anguilla: There are no nonstop flights to Anguilla (AXA) from the United States, so you will almost always have to fly through San Juan, St. Maarten, or some other Caribbean island. You'll ordinarily be making the hop on a smaller plane. You can also take a ferry from St. Maarten.

Hassle Factor: Medium.

On the Ground: Some hotels provide transfers from the airport or ferry pier, especially the more expensive ones. For everyone else, if you don't rent a car, the taxi ride from the airport to your hotel will be less than $25 even to the West End (and considerably less if you're going to Sandy Ground).

Getting Around on the Island: It's possible to base yourself in Sandy Ground, Rendezvous Bay, Meads Bay, or Upper Shoal Bay without a car, but restaurants and resorts are quite spread out, so for the sake of convenience you may wish to rent a car for a few days or for your entire stay. If you do, prepare to drive on the left. Taxis are fairly expensive on Anguilla, another reason to consider renting a car.

Getting to Anguilla

Flights: There are no nonstop flights to Anguilla from the U.S. American Eagle flies daily from San Juan. TransAnguilla Airways offers daily flights from Antigua, St. Thomas, and St. Kitts. Windward Islands Airways flies several times a day from St. Maarten. Anguilla Air Services is a reliable charter operation. LIAT comes in from Antigua, Nevis, St. Kitts, St. Thomas, and Tortola. Cape Air has two daily flights from San Juan.

Local Airline Contacts: American Eagle (☎ 264/497–3500). **Anguilla Air Services** (☎ 264/498–5922 ⊕ www. anguillaairservices.com). **Cape Air** (☎ 866/Cape–Air or 508/771–6944 ⊕ www.capeair.net). **LIAT** (☎ 264/497–5002 ⊕ www.liatairline.com). **TransAnguilla Airways** (☎ 264/497–8690 ⊕ www.transanguilla.com). **Windward Islands Airways** (☎ 264/497–2748 ⊕ www.fly-winair.com).

Airport: Wallblake Airport (☎ 264/497–2719).

Ferries: Ferries run frequently between Anguilla and St. Martin. Boats leave from Blowing Point on Anguilla approximately every half hour from 7:30 am to 6:15 pm and from Marigot, St. Martin, every 45 minutes from 8 am to 7 pm. You pay a $20 departure tax before boarding ($5 for day-trippers), in addition to the $15 one-way fare. On very windy days the 20-minute trip can be bouncy. Remember that the drive between the Marigot ferry terminal and the airport can take up to 45 minutes with traffic. Private transfers by speedboat are sometimes offered from a dock right at the airport, at a cost of about $75 per person (arranged through your Anguilla hotel). Private ferry companies, including Shauna, run six or more round-trips a day, coinciding with major flights, from Blowing Point direct to the airport in St. Maarten. On the St. Maarten side they will bring you right to the terminal in a van, or you can just walk across the parking lot. These trips are $35 one-way or $60 round-trip (cash only). Shauna also can arrange charters.

Ferry Companies: Anguilla Ferries (☎ 264/235–6205 ⊕ www.anguillaferryandcharter.com). **Link Ferries** (☎ 264/497–2231 ⊕ www.link.ai). **Shauna Ferries** (☎ 264/772–2031).

Getting Around Anguilla

Driving: Although most of the rental cars on-island have the driver's side on the left as in North America, Anguillian roads are like those in the United Kingdom—driving is on the left side of the road. It's easy to get the hang of, but the roads can be rough, so be cautious, and observe the 30 mph (48 kph) speed limit. Roundabouts are probably the biggest driving obstacle for most. As you approach, give way to the vehicle on your right; once you're in the rotary, you have the right of way.

Car Rentals: A temporary Anguilla driver's license is required to rent a car—you can get into real trouble if you're caught driving without one. You get it for $20 (good for three months) at any of the car-rental agencies at the time you pick up your car; you'll also need your valid driver's license from home. Rental rates start at about $45 to $55 per day, plus insurance.

Car-Rental Agencies: Apex/Avis (⊠ Airport Rd. ☎ 264/497–2642 ⊕ www.avisanguilla.com). **Triple K Car Rental/Hertz** (⊠ Airport Rd. ☎ 264/497–5934).

Taxis: Taxis are fairly expensive, so if you plan to explore the island's many beaches and restaurants, it may be more cost-effective to rent a car. Taxi rates are regulated by the government, and there are fixed fares from point to point, which are listed in brochures the drivers should have handy and are also published in the local guide *What We Do in Anguilla*. It's $24 from the airport or $22 from Blowing Point Ferry to West End hotels. Posted rates are for one or two people; each additional passenger adds $5 to the total, and there is a $1 charge for each piece of luggage beyond the allotted two. You can also hire a taxi for the hourly rate of $28. Surcharges of $4–$10 apply to trips after 6 pm. You'll always find taxis at the Blowing Point Ferry landing and at the airport. You'll need to call them to pick you up from hotels and restaurants, and arrange ahead with the driver who took you if you need a taxi late at night from one of the nightclubs or bars.

Taxi Companies: Airport Taxi Stand (☎ 264/235–3828). **Blowing Point Ferry Taxi Stand** (☎ 264/497–6089).

Island Activities

Beachgoing and **fine dining** are the two of the most popular activities on Anguilla. However, if you want to be active, it's not a problem. The **diving** is good, though not excellent. You'll have many options for **day sails** and **snorkeling trips**. And there's even **horseback riding**. For **shopping**, St. Martin is a short ferry ride away.

Fast Facts

Banks and Exchange Services: Legal tender is the Eastern Caribbean (EC) dollar, but U.S. dollars are widely accepted. ATMs dispense both U.S. and EC dollars.

Electricity: 110 volts, just as in the United States.

Emergencies: As in the United States, dial 911 in any emergency.

Passport Requirements: All visitors must carry a valid passport and have a return or ongoing ticket.

Weddings: Weddings are common, but there's a huge $284 fee for a license.

ANGUILLA PLANNER

Essentials

Mail: Airmail postcards and letters cost EC$1.50 (for the first ½ ounce) to the United States. The only post office is in The Valley; it's open weekdays 8 to 3:30. There's a FedEx office near the airport. It's open weekdays 8 to 5 and Saturday 9 to 1.

Safety: Anguilla is a quiet, relatively safe island, but crime has been on the rise, and there's no sense in tempting fate by leaving your valuables unattended in your hotel room, on the beach, or in your car. Avoid remote beaches, and lock your car, hotel room, and villa. Most hotel rooms are equipped with a safe for stashing your valuables.

Taxes: The departure tax is $20 for adults and $10 for children, payable in cash, at the airport at Blowing Point Ferry Terminal. If you are staying in Anguilla, but day-tripping to St. Martin, be sure to mention it, and the rate will be only $5. A 10% accommodations tax is added to hotel bills along with a $1 per night marketing tax, along with whatever service charge the hotel adds.

Visitor Information: Anguilla Tourist Office (✉ *Coronation Ave., The Valley* ☎ *264/497-2759, 800/553-4939 from U.S.* ⊕ *www.ivisitanguilla.com*).

Essentials

Telephones: Most hotels will arrange with a local provider for a cell phone to use during your stay (or you can rent one). A prepaid, local cell gives you the best rates. Some U.S. GSM phones will work in Anguilla, some not. To call Anguilla from the United States, dial 1 plus the area code 264, then the local seven-digit number. To call the United States and Canada, dial 1, the area code, and the seven-digit number.

Tipping: Despite any service charge, it's usually expected that you will tip more—$5 per day for housekeeping, $20 for a helpful concierge, and $10 per day to beach attendants. Many restaurants include a service charge of 10% to 15% on the bill; if there's no surcharge, tip about 15%. Taxi drivers should receive 10% of the fare.

Where to Stay

Anguilla is known for its luxurious resorts and villas, but there are also a few places that mere mortals can afford (and some that are downright bargains).

Hotel and Restaurant Costs: Restaurant prices are for a main course and do not include a customary 10%–15% service charge. Hotel prices are for two people in a double room in high season and do not include 8% tax, 10%–15% service charge, or meal plans.

WHAT IT COSTS IN U.S. DOLLARS

	¢	$	$$	$$$	$$$$
Restaurants	under $8	$8–$12	$12–$20	$20–$30	over $30
Hotels	under $150	$151–$275	$276–$375	$376–$475	over $475

DID YOU KNOW?

Anguilla, about 150 miles east of Puerto Rico, has 33 beaches, each more beautiful than the next.

ANGUILLA BEACHES

You can always tell a true beach fanatic: say "Anguilla" and watch for signs of ecstasy. They say there are 33 beaches on the island's 34 square mi; we say, "Who's counting? Pack the sunscreen!"

(Above) Shoal Bay. (Opposite page bottom) Cove Bay. (Opposite page top) Shoal Bay.

Renowned for their beauty, Anguilla's 30-plus beaches are among the best in the Caribbean. You can find long, deserted stretches suitable for sunset walks, or beaches lined with lively bars and restaurants—all surrounded by crystal clear warm waters in several shades of turquoise. The sea is calmest at 2½-mi-long Rendevous Bay, where gentle breezes tempt sailors. But Shoal Bay (East) is the quintessential Caribbean beach. The white sand is so soft and abundant that it pools around your ankles. Cove Bay and Maundays Bay, both on the southeast coast, must also rank among the island's best beaches. Maundays is the location of the island's top resort, Cap Juluca, while smaller Cove Bay is just a walk away. Unlike on the French islands, topless sunbathing is not permitted.

DAZZLING WHITE

The dazzling white sand of Anguilla's famous beaches, as fine and soft as confectioners' sugar, is a result of calcareous marine algae called Halimeda, which thrive in the rich offshore sea grass beds and reefs. Its coral-like skeleton is broken down by wave action and swept ashore by swift currents where it mixes with the eroded tertiary limestone of Anguilla's surface.

NORTHEAST COAST

Captain's Bay. On the north coast just before the eastern tip of the island, this quarter-mile stretch of perfect white sand is bounded on the left by a rocky shoreline where Atlantic waves crash. If you make the tough, four-wheel-drive-only trip along the dirt road that leads to the northeastern end of the island toward Junk's Hole, you'll be rewarded with peaceful isolation. The surf here slaps the sands with a vengeance, and the undertow is strong—so wading is the safest water sport.

Island Harbour. These mostly calm waters are surrounded by a slender beach. For centuries Anguillians have ventured from these sands in colorful handmade fishing boats. It's not much of a beach for swimming or lounging, but there a several restaurants (Hibernia, Arawak Café, Côtée Mer, and Smitty's), and this is the departure point for the three-minute boat ride to Scilly Cay, where a thatched beach bar serves seafood. Just hail the restaurant's free boat and plan to spend most of the day (the all-inclusive lunch starts at $40 and is worth the price—Wednesday, Friday, and Sunday only).

NORTHWEST COAST

Sandy Island. A popular day trip for Anguilla visitors, tiny Sandy Island shelters a pretty lagoon, nestled in coral reefs about 2 mi (3 km) from Road Bay.

Most of the operators in Sandy Ground can bring you here.

★ **Fodor's Choice** **Shoal Bay.** Anchored by sea grape and coconut trees, the 2-mi (3-km) powdered-sugar strand at Shoal Bay (not to be confused with Shoal Bay West at the other end of the island) is universally considered one of the world's prettiest beaches. You can park free at any of the restaurants, including Elodia's, Uncle Ernie's, or Gwen's Reggae Grill, most of which either rent or provide chairs and umbrellas for patrons for about $20 a day per person. There is plenty of room to stretch out in relative privacy, or you can bar-hop, take a ride on Junior's Glass Bottom Boat, or arrange a wreck dive at PADI-certified Shoal Bay Scuba near Kú, where ZaZaa, the island's chicest boutique will satisfy fans of St. Barth shopping. The relatively broad beach has shallow water that is usually gentle, making this a great family beach; a coral reef not far from the shore is a wonderful snorkeling spot. Sunsets over the water are spectacular. You can even enjoy a beachside massage at Malakh, a little spa near Madeariman's.

SOUTHWEST COAST

★ **Fodor's Choice** **Cove Bay.** Follow the signs to Smokey's at the end of Cove Road, and you will find water that is brilliantly blue and sand that is as soft as sifted flour. It's just as spectacular as

Catamarans beached on beautiful Rendezvous Bay

its neighbors Rendezvous Bay and Maundays Bay. You can walk here from Cap Juluca for a change of pace, or you can arrange a horseback ride along the beach. Weekend barbecues with terrific local bands at Smokey's are an Anguillian must.

Maundays Bay. ⭐ Fodor's Choice The dazzling, mile-long platinum-white beach is especially great for swimming and long beach walks. It's no wonder that Cap Juluca, one of Anguilla's premier resorts, chose this as its location. Public parking is straight ahead at the end of the road near Cap Juluca's Pimms restaurant. You can have lunch or dinner at Cap Juluca (just be prepared for the cost), and if you dine, you can also rent chaises and umbrellas from the resort for the day. Depending on the season you can book a massage in one of the beachside tents.

Rendezvous Bay. Follow the signs to Anguilla Great House for public parking at this broad swath of pearl-white sand that is some 1½ mi (2½ km) long. The beach is lapped by calm, bluer-than-blue water and a postcard-worthy view of St. Martin. The expansive crescent

is home to three resorts; stop in for a drink or a meal at one of the hotels, or rent a chair and umbrella at one of the kiosks. Don't miss the daylong party at the tree-house Dune Preserve, where Bankie Banx, Anguilla's most famous musician, presides and where Dale Carty (of Tasty's fame) cooks delicious barbecue and fixes great salads.

Shoal Bay West. This glittering bay bordered by mangroves and sea grapes is a lovely place to spend the day. The mile-long beach is home to the dazzling Covecastles and Altamer villas. The tranquillity is sublime, with coral reefs for snorkeling not too far from shore. Punctuate your day with a meal at beachside Trattoria Tramonto. Reach the beach by taking the main road to the West End and bearing left at the fork, then continuing to the end. Note that similarly named Shoal Bay is a separate beach on a different part of the island.

Updated by
Elise Meyer

Peace, pampering, great food, and a wonderful local music scene are among the star attractions on Anguilla (pronounced ang-*gwill*-a). Beach lovers may become giddy when they first spot the island from the air; its blindingly white sand and lustrous blue-and aquamarine waters are intoxicating. And, if you like sophisticated cuisine served in casually elegant open-air settings, this may be your culinary Shangri-la.

The island's name, a reflection of its shape, is most likely a derivative of *anguille,* which is French for "eel." (French explorer Pierre Laudonnaire is credited with having given the island this name when he sailed past it in 1556.) In 1631 the Dutch built a fort here, but so far no one has been able to locate its site. English settlers from St. Kitts colonized the island in 1650, with plans to cultivate tobacco and, later, cotton and then sugar. But the thin soil and scarce water doomed these enterprises to fail. Except for a brief period of independence, when it broke from its association with St. Kitts and Nevis in the 1960s, Anguilla has remained a British colony ever since.

From the early 1800s various island federations were formed and disbanded, with Anguilla all the while simmering over its subordinate status and enforced union with St. Kitts. Anguillians twice petitioned for direct rule from Britain and twice were ignored. In 1967, when St. Kitts, Nevis, and Anguilla became an associated state, the mouse roared; citizens kicked out St. Kitts's policemen, held a self-rule referendum, and for two years conducted their own affairs. To what *Time* magazine called "a cascade of laughter around the world," a British "peacekeeping force" of 100 paratroopers from the Elite Red Devil unit parachuted onto the island, squelching Anguilla's designs for autonomy but helping a team of royal engineers stationed there to improve the port and build roads and schools. Today Anguilla elects a House of Assembly and its own leader to handle internal affairs, and a British governor is responsible for public service, the police, the judiciary, and external affairs.

The territory of Anguilla includes a few islets (or cays, pronounced "keys"), such as Scrub Island, Dog Island, Prickly Pear Cay, Sandy Island, and Sombrero Island. The 16,000 or so residents are predominantly of African descent, but there are also many of Irish background, whose ancestors came over from St. Kitts in the 1600s. Historically, because the limestone land was unfit for agriculture, attempts at enslavement never lasted long; consequently, Anguilla doesn't bear the scars of slavery found on so many other Caribbean islands. Instead, Anguillians became experts at making a living from the sea and are known for their boatbuilding and fishing skills. Tourism is the stable economy's growth industry, but the government carefully regulates expansion to protect the island's natural resources and beauty. New hotels are small, select, and casino-free; Anguilla emphasizes its high-quality service, serene surroundings, and friendly people.

EXPLORING ANGUILLA

Exploring on Anguilla is mostly about checking out the spectacular beaches and resorts. The island has only a few roads, but they have been improving significantly in recent years, and the lack of adequate signage is being addressed. Locals are happy to provide directions, but using the readily available tourist map is the best idea. Visit the Anguilla Tourist Board, centrally located on Coronation Avenue in The Valley.

The Anguilla Heritage Trail, begun in 2010, is a free, self-guided tour of 10 important historical sights that can be explored independently in any order. Wallblake House, in The Valley (see ⇨ Exploring Anguilla), is the main information center for the trail, or you can just look for the large boulders with descriptive plaques.

WHAT TO SEE

Bethel Methodist Church. Not far from Sandy Ground, this charming little church is an excellent example of skillful island stonework. It also has some colorful stained-glass windows. ⊠ South Hill ☎ No phone.

Heritage Museum Collection. Don't miss this remarkable opportunity to learn about Anguilla. Old photographs and local records and artifacts trace the island's history over four millennia, from the days of the Arawaks. The tiny museum (complete with gift shop) is painstakingly curated by Colville Petty. High points include the historical documents of the Anguilla Revolution and the albums of photographs chronicling island life, from devastating hurricanes to a visit from Queen Elizabeth in 1964. You can see examples of ancient pottery shards and stone tools along with fascinating photographs of the island in the early 20th century—many depicting the heaping and exporting of salt and the christening of schooners—and a complete set of beautiful postage stamps issued by Anguilla since 1967. ⊠ East End at Pond Ground ☎ 264/235-7440 ✉ petty@anguillanet.com ☒ $5 ⊗ Mon.–Sat. 10–5.

★ **Island Harbour.** Anguillians have been fishing for centuries in the brightly painted, simple, handcrafted fishing boats that line the shore of the harbor. It's hard to believe, but skillful pilots take these little boats out to sea as far as 50 mi or 60 mi (80 km or 100 km). Late afternoon is the best time to see the day's catch. Hail the free boat to Gorgeous Scilly Cay, a classic little restaurant offering sublime lobster and Eudoxie Wallace's knockout rum punches on Wednesday and Sunday. ⊕ *www.scillycayanguilla.com.*

Old Factory. For many years the cotton grown on Anguilla and exported to England was ginned in this beautiful historic building, now home of the Anguilla Tourist Office. Some of the original ginning machinery is intact and on display. ⊠ *The Valley* ☎ *264/497-2759* ⊠ *Free* ⊙ *Weekdays 10–noon and 1–4.*

Old Prison. The ruins of this historic jail on Anguilla's highest point— 213 feet above sea level—offer outstanding views. ⊠ *Valley Rd. at Crocus Hill.*

Sandy Ground. Almost everyone who comes to Anguilla stops by this central beach, home to several popular open-air bars and restaurants, as well as boat-rental operations. You can also tour the Pyrat rum factory, also in Sandy Ground. Finally, this is where you catch the ferry for tiny Sandy Island, just 2 mi (3 km) offshore.

Wallblake House. The only surviving plantation house in Anguilla, Wallblake House was built in 1787 by Will Blake (Wallblake is probably a corruption of his name) and has recently been thoroughly and thoughtfully restored. The place is associated with many a tale involving murder, high living, and the French invasion in 1796. On the grounds are an ancient vaulted stone cistern and an outbuilding called the Bakery (which wasn't used for making bread at all but for baking turkeys and hams). Tours are usually offered three days a week, and you can only visit on a guided tour. It's also the information center for the Anguilla Heritage Tour. ⊠ *Wallblake Rd., The Valley* ☎ *264/497-6613* ⊠ *Free* ⊙ *Mon., Wed., and Fri. Tours at 10 and 2.*

Warden's Place. This former sugar-plantation greathouse was built in the 1790s and is a fine example of island architecture. It now houses KoalKeel restaurant and a sumptuous bakery upstairs. But for many years it served as the residence of the island's chief administrator, who also doubled as the only medical practitioner. Across the street you can see the oldest dwelling on the island, originally built as slave housing. ⊠ *The Valley.*

WHERE TO EAT

Despite its small size, Anguilla has nearly 70 restaurants ranging from stylish temples of haute cuisine to classic, barefoot beachfront grills, roadside barbecue stands, food carts, and casual cafés. Many have breeze-swept terraces, where you can dine under the stars. Call ahead— in winter to make a reservation and in late summer and fall to confirm if the place you've chosen is open. Anguillian restaurant meals are leisurely events, and service is often at a relaxed pace, so settle in and enjoy. Most restaurant owners are actively and conspicuously present, especially at dinner. It's a special treat to take the time to get to know them a bit when they stop by your table to make sure that you are enjoying your meal.

WHAT TO WEAR

During the day, casual clothes are widely accepted: shorts will be fine, but don't wear bathing suits and cover-ups unless you're at a beach bar. In the evening, shorts are okay at the extremely casual eateries. Elsewhere, women wear sundresses or nice casual slacks; men will be fine in short-sleeve shirts and casual pants. Some hotel restaurants are slightly more formal, but that just means long pants for men.

$$$$
AMERICAN
Fodor'sChoice
★

✕ **Blanchard's.** This absolutely delightful restaurant, a mecca for foodies, is considered one of the best in the Caribbean. Proprietors Bob and Melinda Blanchard moved to Anguilla from Vermont in 1994 to fulfill their culinary dreams. A festive atmosphere pervades the handsome, airy white room, which is accented with floor-to-ceiling teal-blue shutters to let in the breezes, and colorful artwork by the Blanchards' son Jesse on the walls. A masterful combination of creative cuisine, an upscale atmosphere, attentive service, and an excellent wine cellar (including a selection of aged spirits) pleases the star-studded crowd. The nuanced contemporary menu is ever changing but always delightful; house classics like corn chowder, lobster cakes, and a Caribbean sampler are crowd-pleasers. For dessert, you'll remember concoctions like the key lime "pie-in-a-glass" or the justly famous "cracked coconut" long after your suntan has faded. A recent addition is a three-course prix-fixe menu that includes many of the signature dishes and is a bargain at $45. ⊠ Box 898, Meads Bay ☎ 264/497–6100 ⊕ www.blanchardsrestaurant.com ♨ Reservations essential ⊘ Closed Sun. Closed Mon. May–mid-Dec. No lunch.

$$$
CARIBBEAN

✕ **da'Vida.** Sometimes you really can have it all. Right on exquisite Crocus Bay, this resort-cum-restaurant-cum-club is a place where you could spend the whole day dining, drinking, and lounging under umbrellas on the comfortable chairs. There are kayaks and snorkeling equipment for rent, not to mention two boutiques. You can picnic at the Beach Grill (burgers, hotdogs, wraps, salads) or head inside the main building for contemporary choices like dumplings, soups, pastas, and pizzas. Lunch starts at 11, and you can get tapas and sunset drinks from about 3. At dinner, the stylish and relaxed wood interior (built by craftsmen from St. Vincent) is accented by candlelight. On the menu are such dishes as tasty seared snapper with gingered kale, coconut-crusted scallops, and Angus steaks. Go for the music on weekend nights. Owners David and Vida Lloyd, brother and sister, who also operate Lloyd's Guest House, grew up right here, and they have taken pains to get it all just right. ⊠ Box 52, Crocus Bay ☎ 264/498–5433 ⊕ www.davidaanguilla.com ⊘ Closed Mon.

$$
CARIBBEAN

✕ **English Rose.** Lunchtime finds this neighborhood hangout packed with locals: cops flirting with sassy waitresses, entrepreneurs brokering deals with politicos, schoolgirls in lime-green outfits doing their homework. The decor is not much to speak of, but this is a great place to eavesdrop or people-watch while enjoying island-tinged specialties like beer-battered shrimp, jerk-chicken Caesar salad, snapper creole, and buffalo wings. There is karaoke on Friday. ⊠ *Carter Rey Blvd., The Valley* ☎ *264/497–5353* ⊘ *Closed Sun.*

$$
FRENCH
✗ **Geraud's Patisserie.** A stunning array of absolutely delicious French pastries and breads—and universal favorites like cookies, brownies, and muffins—are produced by Le Cordon Bleu dynamo Geraud Lavest in this tiny, well-located shop. Come in the early morning for cappuccino and croissants, and pick up fixings for a wonderful lunch later (or choose from among the list of tempting daily lunch specials). During the high season (December through May), there is a terrific Sunday brunch. Geraud also does a lively offsite catering business, from intimate villa and yacht dinners to weddings. ⊠ *South Hill Plaza* ☎ *264/497–5559* ⊕ *www.anguillacakesandcatering.com* ⊘ *Closed Mon. No dinner.*

$$$$
ASIAN
Fodor'sChoice
★
✗ **Hibernia.** Some of the island's most creative dishes are served in this wood-beam cottage restaurant–art gallery overlooking the water at the far eastern end of Anguilla. Unorthodox yet delectable culinary pairings—inspired by chef-owners Raoul Rodriguez and Mary Pat's annual travels to the Far East—include chilled-tomato-and-mango soup; duck breast with passion-fruit sauce and herb-crusted gnocchi; and a crayfish casserole with jasmine rice, roasted garlic, and coconut milk. The restaurant uses local organic products whenever possible. Every visit here is an opportunity to share in Mary Pat and Raoul's passion for life, expressed through the vibrant combination of setting, art, food, unique tableware, beautiful gardens, and thoughtful hospitality. ⊠ *Box 268, Island Harbour* ☎ *264/497–4290* ⊕ *hiberniarestaurant.com* ⊘ *Closed mid-Aug.–mid-Oct. Call for seasonal hrs.*

$$$$
FRENCH
✗ **Jacala Beach Restaurant.** Right on beautiful Meads Bay, this new restaurant opened to raves in 2010. Alain the chef and Jacques the maître d' (from Malliouhana) have joined forces, and the happy result is carefully prepared and nicely presented French food served with care in a lovely open-air restaurant, accompanied with good wines. A delicious starter of feta and grilled vegetables is infused with pesto. For an entrée, you must try hand-chopped steak tartare, or seared and marinated sushi-grade tuna on a bed of delightful mashed plantain. Lighter lunchtime options include a tart cucumber-yogurt soup garnished with piquant tomato sorbet. After lunch you can digest on the beach in one of the "Fatboy" loungers. ⊠ *Meads Bay* ☎ *264/498–5888* ✉ *jacala_restaurant@me.com* ⊘ *Closed Mon. and Aug. and Sept.*

$$$–$$$$
CARIBBEAN
Fodor'sChoice
★
✗ **KoalKeel.** Dinner at KoalKeel is a unique culinary and historic treat not to be missed on Anguilla. Originally part of a sugar and cotton plantation, the restaurant, with its beautiful dining verandah, is owned and lovingly overseen by Lisa Gumbs, a descendent of the slaves once housed here. A tour of the history-rich buildings is a must. A

200-year-old rock oven is used in the on-site bakery upstairs, and with a day's notice you can enjoy a slow-roasted whole chicken from that oven. It is also used to delightful effect in touches of the East Indies on the mostly West Indies menu, like tandoori-spiced lamb, spiced vegetable samosa, and tandoori roasted shrimp spring rolls. Be sure to save room for the incredible desserts. Wine lovers take note of the exceptional 15,000-bottle wine cellar, in an underground cistern. Anguilla's savvy early risers show up here for the fresh French bread, croissants, and *pain au chocolat*, which are sold out by 9 am. ⊠ *Coronation Ave., Box 640, The Valley* ☎ *264/497–2930* ⊕ *www.koalkeel.com* ⌕ *Reservations essential* ⊘ *Closed Mon.*

$$ ✕ **Madeariman Reef Bar and Restaurant.** This casual, feet-in-the-sand bis-
FRENCH tro right on busy, beautiful Shoal Bay is open for breakfast, lunch, and dinner; the soups, salads, and simple grills here are served with a bit of French flair. Come for lunch and stay to lounge on the beach chaises or barhop between here and Uncle Ernie's barbecue next door. ⊠ *Shoal Bay East* ☎ *264/497–5750.*

$$$$ ✕ **Mango's.** One meal at Mango's and you'll understand why it's a peren-
SEAFOOD nial favorite of repeat visitors to Anguilla. Sparkling-fresh fish specialties have starring roles on the menu here. Light and healthy choices like a spicy grilled whole snapper are deliciously perfect. Save room for dessert—the warm apple tart and the coconut cheesecake are worth the splurge. There's an extensive wine list, and the Cuban cigar humidor is a luxurious touch. ⊠ *Box 682, Barnes Bay* ☎ *264/497–6479* ⊕ *www.mangosseasidegrill.com* ⌕ *Reservations essential* ⊘ *Closed Tues. No lunch.*

$$$$ ✕ **Michel Rostang at Malliouhana.** Sparkling crystal and fine china, atten-
FRENCH tive service, a wonderful 25,000-bottle wine cellar, and a spectacularly romantic, open-air room complement exceptional haute cuisine rivaling any in the French West Indies. Consulting chef Michel Rostang, renowned for his exceptional Paris bistros, revamps the menu season-ally, incorporating local ingredients in both classic and contemporary preparations. The dining patio is one of the most sublime spots in the Caribbean, if not the world. The ultimate in hedonism is sipping champagne as the setting sun triggers a laser show over the bay, before repairing to your table. ⊠ *Meads Bay* ☎ *264/497–6111* ⌕ *Reservations essential* ⊘ *Closed Sept. and Oct.*

$$ ✕ **Picante.** This casual, bright-red roadside Caribbean *taquería*, opened
MEXICAN by a young California couple, serves huge, tasty burritos with a choice
☾ of fillings, fresh warm tortilla chips with first-rate guacamole, seafood enchiladas, and tequila-lime chicken grilled under a brick. Passion-fruit margaritas are a must, and the creamy Mexican chocolate pud-ding makes a great choice for dessert. Seating is at picnic tables; the friendly proprietors cheerfully supply pillows on request. Reserva-tions are recommended. ⊠ *West End Rd., West End* ☎ *264/498–1616* ⊕ *www.picante-restaurant-anguilla.com* ⊘ *Closed Tues. and Sept. and Oct. No lunch.*

$$$ ✕ **Roy's Bayside Grille.** Some of the best grilled lobster on the island is
CARIBBEAN served up here along with burgers, fish-and-chips, and good home-style
★ cooking. Happy hour hops from 4 to 6 every day, thanks to the good rum concoctions. On Sunday you can get roast beef and Yorkshire

Straw Hat's outdoor patio on Forest Bay.

pudding, and there is free Wi-Fi. The restaurant is open daily. ✉ *Box 3, Sandy Ground* ☎ *264/497–2470* ⊕ *www.roysbaysidegrill.com* ⊘ *No lunch Mon.*

$$
BARBECUE
☺
✕ **Smokey's**. This quintessential Anguillian beach barbecue, part of the Gumbs family mini-empire of authentic and delicious eateries, is located on pretty Cove Bay. On the beach, lounges with umbrellas welcome guests. African-style hot wings, honey-coated smoked ribs, salt-fish cakes, curried chicken roti, and grilled lobsters are paired with local staple side dishes such as spiced-mayonnaise coleslaw, hand-cut sweet-potato strings, and crunchy onion rings. If your idea of the perfect summer lunch is a roadside lobster roll, be sure to try the version here, served on a home-baked roll with a hearty kick of hot sauce. The dinner menu includes crayfish tails and chicken in orange sauce. On Saturday afternoon, a popular local band enlivens the casual, laid-back atmosphere, and on Sunday the restaurant is party central for locals and visitors alike. ✉ *Cove Rd., Box 31, Cove Bay* ☎ *264/497–6582* ⊕ *www.smokeysatthecove.com.*

$$$$
ECLECTIC
☺
Fodor's Choice
★
✕ **Straw Hat**. Since this Anguilla favorite moved to the beautiful sands of Meads Bay (at the Frangipani) its many fans now enjoy lunch and dinner seven days a week on its tropical beachfront patio. Charming owners Peter and Anne Parles, the sophisticated and original food, and friendly service are the main reasons the restaurant has been in business since the late 1990s. The menu features appealing small plates like lobster spring rolls and clever "chips n'fish," which diners can share; or mix and match for the perfect meal. The curried goat here sets the bar for the island. And "fish of the day" truly means fish caught that

day. ✉ *Frangipani Beach Club, Box 1197, Meads Bay* ☎ *264/497–8300* ⊕ *www.strawhat.com* ⊙ *Closed Sept. and Oct.*

$$$
CARIBBEAN

✕ **Tasty's.** Once your eyes adjust to the quirky kiwi, lilac, and coral color scheme, you'll find that breakfast, lunch, or dinner at Tasty's is, well, very tasty. It's open all day long, so if you come off a midafternoon plane starving, head directly here—it's right near the airport. Chef-owner Dale Carty trained at Malliouhana, and his careful, confident preparation bears the mark of French culinary training, but the menu is classic Caribbean. It's worth leaving the beach at lunch for the lobster salad here. A velvety pumpkin soup garnished with roasted coconut shards is superb, as are the seared jerk tuna and the garlic-infused marinated conch salad. Yummy desserts end meals on a high note. This is one of the few restaurants that do not allow smoking, so take your Cubans elsewhere for an after-dinner puff. The popular Sunday brunch buffet features island specialties like salt-fish cakes. Dale is also the chef at Kú's beachfront restaurant. ✉ *Main Rd., South Hill* ☎ *264/497–2737* ⌖ *Reservations essential.*

$$$
ITALIAN
☾

✕ **Trattoria Tramonto and Oasis Beach Bar.** The island's only beachfront Italian restaurant features a dual (or dueling) serenade of Andrea Bocelli on the sound system and gently lapping waves a few feet away. Chef Valter Belli artfully adapts recipes from his home in Emilia-Romagna. Try the delicate lobster ravioli in truffle-cream sauce, or go for a less Italian option: kangaroo steak. For dessert, don't miss the tiramisu. Though you might wander in here for lunch after a swim, when casual dress is accepted, you'll still be treated to the same impressive menu. You can also choose from a luscious selection of champagne fruit drinks, a small but fairly priced Italian wine list, and homemade grappa. ✉ *Shoal Bay West* ☎ *264/497–8819* ⊕ *www.trattoriatramonto.com* ⌖ *Reservations essential* ⊙ *Closed Mon. and Sept. and Oct.*

$$$$
ECLECTIC
Fodor's Choice
★

✕ **Veya.** On the suavely minimalist, draped, four-sided verandah, the stylishly appointed tables glow with flickering candlelight (in white-matte, sea urchin–shaped votive holders made of porcelain). A lively lounge where chic patrons mingle and sip mojitos to the purr of soft jazz anchors the room. Inventive, sophisticated, and downright delicious, Carrie Bogar's "Cuisine of the Sun" features thoughtful but ingenious preparations of first-rate provisions. Ample portions are sharable works of art—sample Moroccan-spiced shrimp "cigars" with roast tomato–apricot chutney or Vietnamese-spiced calamari. Jerk-spiced tuna is served with a rum-coffee glaze on a juicy slab of grilled pineapple with curls of plantain crisps. Dessert is a must. Sublime warm chocolate cake with chili-roasted banana ice cream and caramelized bananas steals the show. Downstairs there is a café that serves breakfast and light lunches like salads and panini, as well as delicious bakery goodies. It opens at 6:30 am for early risers. ✉ *Box WE 8067, Sandy Ground* ☎ *264/498–8392* ⊕ *www.veya-axa.com* ⌖ *Reservations essential* ⊙ *Closed Sun. and Aug. Closed weekends June, July, Sept., and Oct. No lunch.*

$$$–$$$$
ECLECTIC

✕ **Zara's.** Chef Shamash Brooks presides at this cozy restaurant with beamed ceilings, terra-cotta floors, and colorful artwork. His kitchen turns out tasty fare that combines Caribbean and Italian flavors with panache (Rasta Pasta is a specialty). Standouts include a velvety pumpkin soup with coconut milk, crunchy calamari, lemon pasta scented with garlic, herbed rack of lamb served with a roasted applesauce, and spicy fish fillet steamed in banana leaf. ✉ *Allamanda Beach Club, Upper Shoal Bay* ☎ *264/497–3229* ◐ *No lunch.*

WHERE TO STAY

Tourism on Anguilla is a fairly recent phenomenon—most development didn't begin until the early 1980s, so most hotels and resorts are of relatively recent vintage. The lack of native topography and, indeed, vegetation, and the blindingly white expanses of beach have inspired building designs of some interest; architecture buffs might have fun trying to name some of the most surprising examples. Inspiration largely comes from the Mediterranean: the Greek Islands, Morocco, and Spain, with some Miami-style art deco thrown into the mixture.

Anguilla accommodations basically fall into two categories: grand resorts and luxury resort-villas, or low-key, simple, locally owned inns and small beachfront complexes. The former can be surprisingly expensive, the latter surprisingly reasonable. In the middle are some condo-type options, with full kitchens and multiple bedrooms, which are great for families or for longer stays. Private villa rentals are becoming more common and are increasing in number and quality every season as development on the island accelerates.

A good phone chat or email exchange with the management of any property is a good idea, as some lodgings don't have in-room TVs, a few have no air-conditioning, and units within the same complex can vary greatly in layout, accessibility, distance to the beach, and view. When calling to reserve a room, ask about special discount packages, especially in spring and summer. Most hotels include Continental breakfast in the price, and many have meal-plan options. But keep in mind that Anguilla is home to dozens of excellent restaurants before you lock yourself into an expensive meal plan that you may not be able to change. All hotels charge a 10% tax, a $1 per room/per day tourism marketing levy, and—in most cases—an additional 10% service charge.

VILLAS AND CONDOMINIUM RENTAL AGENCIES

The tourist office publishes an annual *Anguilla Travel Planner* with informative listings of available vacation apartment rentals. You can contact the **Anguilla Connection** (☎ *264/497–9852 or 800/916–3336* ⊕ *www.luxuryvillas.com*) for condo and villa listings. **Anguilla Luxury Collection** (☎ *264/497–6049* ⊕ *www.anguillaluxurycollection.com*) is operated by Sue and Robin Ricketts, longtime Anguilla real estate experts, who manage a collection of first-rate villas. They also manage a range of attractive properties in the Anguilla Affordable Collection linked through the same Web site. **myCaribbean** (☎ *877/471–2733* ⊕ *www.mycaribbean.com*) is the largest local private villa-rental company. Gayle Gurvey and her staff manage and rent more than 100 local villas, and have been in business since 2000.

The following hotel reviews have been condensed for this book. Please go to Fodors.com for expanded reviews of each property.

$
RENTAL
℃

⊡ Allamanda Beach Club. Youthful, active couples from around the globe happily fill this casual, three-story, white-stucco building hidden in a palm grove just off the beach, opting for location and price over luxury. **Pros:** front row for all Shoal Bay's action; young crowd; good restaurant. **Cons:** location requires a car; rooms are clean, but not at all fancy; beach and pool lounges are aging poorly. ⌂ *Box 662, Upper Shoal Bay Beach AI2640* 🕾 *264/497–5217* ⊕ *www.allamanda.ai* 📞 *20 units* ⌂ *In-room: a/c, kitchen. In-hotel: restaurants, pool, gym, business center, water sports* ℣❘ *No meals.*

$–$$$
HOTEL

⊡ Anacaona. Veteran Anguilla hoteliers Sue and Robin Ricketts took over Sirena, a low-key resort overlooking Meads Bay, with an eye toward creating an "affordable chic" hideaway imbued with the culture and traditions of Anguilla. **Pros:** sensitive to local culture; modern, clean, and good value; nice high-tech amenities. **Cons:** bit of a walk to beach; smallish rooms. ⌂ *Box 200, Meads Bay AI2640* 🕾 *264/497–6827 or 877/647–4736* ⊕ *www.anacaonahotel.com* 📞 *27 rooms* ⌂ *In-room: a/c, kitchen (some), no TV, Wi-Fi. In-hotel: restaurant, bar, pools* ℣❘ *Multiple meal plans.*

$$
RESORT

⊡ Anguilla Great House Beach Resort. These traditional West Indian–style bungalows strung along one of Anguilla's longest beaches evoke an old-time Caribbean feel with their cotton-candy colors, and the gentle prices and interconnected rooms appeal to families and groups of friends traveling together. **Pros:** real, old-school Caribbean; young crowd; gentle prices. **Cons:** rooms are very simple, and bathrooms are the bare basics. ✉ *Rendezvous Bay* 🕾 *264/497–6061 or 800/583–9247* ⊕ *www.anguillagreathouse.com* 📞 *31 rooms* ⌂ *In-room: a/c, no safe, Internet (some). In-hotel: restaurant, pool, gym, beach, water sports* ℣❘ *No meals.*

$–$$
B&B/INN

⊡ Arawak Beach Inn. These hexagonal two-story villas are a good choice for a funky, budget-friendly, low-key guesthouse experience. **Pros:** funky, casual crowd; friendly owners; gentle rates. **Cons:** not on the beach; isolated location makes a car a must. ⌂ *Box 1403, Island Harbour AI2640* 🕾 *264/497–4888, 877/427–2925 reservations* ⊕ *www.arawakbeach.com* 📞 *17 rooms* ⌂ *In-room: no a/c (some), kitchen (some), no TV (some), Wi-Fi. In-hotel: restaurant, bar, pool, beach, water sports* ℣❘ *No meals.*

$$$$
RESORT
℃
Fodor's Choice
★

⊡ Cap Juluca. Sybaritic and serene, this 179-acre resort wraps around breathtaking Maundays Bay. **Pros:** golf course; lots of space to stretch out on miles of talcum-soft sand; warm service; romantic atmosphere; all on-site water sports are included, even waterskiing. **Cons:** as of this writing, bathrooms are still to be updated. ⌂ *Box 240, Maundays Bay AI2640* 🕾 *264/497–6666, 888/858–5822 in U.S.* ⊕ *www.capjuluca.com* 📞 *72 rooms, 7 patio suites, 6 pool villas* ⌂ *In-room: a/c, no safe, Wi-Fi. In-hotel: golf course, restaurants, tennis courts, bar, children's programs, pool, gym, spa, beach, water sports* ℣❘ *Breakfast.*

CuisinArt Resort and Spa, Rendezvous Bay.

$$$$
RENTAL

▦ **Carimar Beach Club.** This horseshoe of bougainvillea-draped Mediterranean-style buildings on beautiful Meads Bay has the look of a Sun Belt condo. **Pros:** tennis courts; easy walk to restaurants and spa; right next door to Malliouhana; laundry facilities. **Cons:** no pool or restaurant; only bedrooms have a/c. ⊠ *Meads Bay* ⟟ *Box 327, Meads Bay AI2640* ☎ *264/497–6881 or 800/235–8667* ⊕ *www.carimar.com* ⟿ *24 apartments* ᗕ *In-room: a/c, kitchen, Internet, Wi-Fi. In-hotel: tennis courts, beach, business center, water sports* ⊘ *Closed Sept.–Oct. 15* ⊺⊙⊺ *No meals.*

$$$$
RENTAL

▦ **Covecastles Villa Resort.** Though this secluded Myron Goldfinger–designed enclave resembles a series of giant concrete baby carriages from the outside, the airy curves and angles of the skylighted interiors are comfortable, if a little dated, with the sort of oversize wicker furniture and raw-silk accessories that defined resort-chic in the late 1980s. **Pros:** secluded, large, private villas; private beach with reef for snorkeling; great service. **Cons:** beach is small and rocky; located at the far end of the island; redecoration is a bit overdue. ⟟ *Box 248, Shoal Bay West AI2640* ☎ *264/497–6801 or 800/223–1108* ⊕ *www.covecastles. com* ⟿ *16 apartments* ᗕ *In-room: a/c, no safe, Internet* ⊺⊙⊺ *No meals.*

$$$$
RESORT
☾
Fodor's Choice
★

▦ **CuisinArt Resort and Spa.** This family-friendly beachfront resort's design—gleaming white-stucco buildings, blue domes and trim, glass-block walls—blends art deco with a Greek Islands feel. **Pros:** family-friendly; great spa and sports; gorgeous beach and gardens. **Cons:** food service can be slow; pool area is noisy. ⟟ *Box 2000, Rendezvous Bay AI2640* ☎ *264/498–2000 or 800/943–3210* ⊕ *www.cuisinartresort. com* ⟿ *93 rooms, 2 penthouses, 6 villas* ᗕ *In-room: a/c, Internet. In-*

hotel: restaurants, tennis courts, bars, pool, gym, spa, beach, water sports ⊘ *Closed Sept. and Oct.* ⭕ *No meals.*

$$$$
RESORT
Frangipani Beach Club. This flamingo-pink Mediterranean-style complex on the beautiful champagne sands of Meads Bay was redone in 2008, and is under new management as of 2009. **Pros:** great beach; good location for restaurants and resort-hopping; first-rate on-site restaurant; helpful staff. **Cons:** some rooms have no view, be sure to ask. ⌂ *Box 1655, Meads Bay AI2640* ☎ *264/497–6442 or 866/780–5165* ⊕ *www. frangipaniresort.com* ⊅ *18 rooms, 7 suites* ⚭ *In-room: a/c, kitchen (some), Internet, Wi-Fi. In-hotel: restaurant, tennis court, bar, pool, laundry facilities, beach, water sports* ⊘ *Closed Sept. and Oct.* ⭕ *No meals.*

$$–$$$
RENTAL
☾
Indigo Reef. If you are looking for the antidote to the big resort developments on the island but still want attractive, modern, private villa accommodations close to the restaurants, resorts, and beautiful beaches of West End, this intimate enclave of eight small villas (with one to four bedrooms) nestled at the tip of the island could be just the thing. **Pros:** cozy, fresh, and well designed; great for groups traveling together; far from the madding crowd but still on the West End. **Cons:** the beach here is rocky and the water's rough; a/c only in bedrooms; must have car. ✉ *Indigo Reef, West End* ☎ *264/497–6144* ⊕ *www.indigoreef.com* ⊅ *8 villas* ⚭ *In-room: a/c, kitchen, no safe, Wi-Fi. In-hotel: pools, laundry facilities, some pets allowed* ⭕ *No meals.*

$$$$
RENTAL
☾
★
Inspirata Villas at Sheriva. This intimate, luxury-villa hotel opened in 2006, offering a glimpse into the future of Anguilla's high-end lodgings; now offering a high-end timeshare-style arrangement, the villas are at this writing still available for rental by the public. **Pros:** incredible staff to fulfill every wish; all the comforts of home and more; good value for large family groups. **Cons:** not on the beach; you risk being spoiled for life by the staff's attentions. ✉ *Maundays Bay Rd., West End* ☎ *264/498–9898* ⊕ *www.inspirato.com* ⊅ *20 villas* ⚭ *In-room: a/c, kitchen, Wi-Fi. In-hotel: pools, laundry service* ⭕ *No meals.*

$$–$$$
HOTEL
☾
Kú. This all-suites hotel is modeled on the barefoot chic of Miami's South Beach; the airy white apartments have lime and turquoise decorative accents, glass and chrome furniture, and balconies overlooking the beach or the pool. **Pros:** beautiful beach with tropical sunsets; the convenience of apartment living; several walkable dining options; good beds with nice linens. **Cons:** bathrooms are small and older; decor is pleasant but not luxurious and needs updating, ditto a/c. ⌂ *Box 51, Shoal Bay East AI2640* ☎ *264/497–2011 or 800/869–5827* ⊕ *www. ku-anguilla.com* ⊅ *27 suites* ⚭ *In-room: a/c, kitchen, Internet. In-hotel: restaurant, bar, pool, gym, spa, beach, water sports* ⭕ *No meals.*

$$$$
RESORT
☾
Malliouhana Hotel and Spa. European refinement in a tranquil beach setting, attentive service, fine dining, and a plethora of activities keep the international clientele returning, despite nearly universal agreement that a general refurbishment is overdue. **Pros:** huge rooms; stellar dining on a beautiful terrace over the sea; caring service; nice spa. **Cons:** the beach drops off at the edge, and the water can be rough; dated decor; shabby outdoor furniture. ⌂ *Box 173, Meads Bay AI2640* ☎ *264/497–6111 or 800/835–0796* ⊕ *www.malliouhana.com* ⊅ *34 rooms, 6 junior suites, 13 suites* ⚭ *In-room: a/c, no TV (some). In-hotel: restaurants,*

Viceroy Anguilla, Meads Bay.

tennis courts, bars, pools, gym, spa, beach, business center, water sports ⊙ *Closed Sept. and Oct.* ¶❍❙*No meals.*

$$–$$$

RENTAL

☝

★

🖼 **Paradise Cove.** This simple complex of reasonably priced one- and two-bedroom apartments compensates for its location away from the beach with two whirlpools, a large pool, and tranquil tropical gardens where you can pluck fresh guavas for breakfast. **Pros:** reasonable rates; great pool; lovely gardens. **Cons:** a bit far from the beach; decor is bland. ☍ *Box 135, The Cove AI2640* ☎ *264/497–6959 or 264/497–6603* ⊕ *www.paradise.ai* ⟿ *12 studio suites, 17 1- and 2-bedroom apartments* ☝ *In-room: a/c, kitchen (some), no safe, Wi-Fi. In-hotel: restaurant, bar, pools, gym, laundry facilities, business center* ¶❍❙*No meals.*

$$–$$$

RENTAL

☝

🖼 **Serenity Cottages.** Despite the name of this property, it comprises not cottages but rather large, fully equipped, and relatively affordable one-and two-bedroom apartments (and studios created from lockouts) in a small complex at the farthest end of glorious Shoal Bay Beach. **Pros:** big apartments; quiet end of beach; snorkeling right outside the door. **Cons:** no pool; generic decor; more condo than hotel in terms of staff; location at the end of Shoal Bay pretty much requires a car and some extra time to drive to the West End. ✉ *Box 308, Shoal Bay East* ☎ *264/497–3328* ⊕ *www.serenity.ai* ⟿ *2 1-bedroom suites, 8 2-bedroom apartments* ☝ *In-room: a/c, kitchen. In-hotel: restaurant, bar, beach, business center* ⊙ *Closed Sept.* ¶❍❙*No meals.*

$$$$

RESORT

☝

Fodor's Choice

★

🖼 **The Viceroy.** On a promontory over 3,200 feet of the gorgeous pearly sand on Meads Bay, Kelly Wurstler's haute-hip showpiece will wow the chic international-sophisticate set, especially those lucky enough to stay in one of the spacious two- to five-bedroom villas, complete with private infinity pools and hot tubs, indoor-outdoor showers, electronics

galore, and a gourmet professional kitchen stuffed with high-end equipment, not to mention a house manager to keep it all running smoothly.
Pros: state-of-the-art luxury; cutting-edge contemporary design; flexible, spacious rooms. **Cons:** international rather than Caribbean in
feel; very large resort; kind of a see-and-be-seen scene. ⊠ *Barnes Bay,
Box 8028, West End* ☎ *264/497–7000, 866/270–7798 in U.S.* ⊕ *www.
viceroyhotelsandresorts.com* ⤳ *163 suites, 3 villas* ⚭ *In-room: a/c,
kitchen (some), Wi-Fi. In-hotel: restaurants, tennis courts, bars, children's programs, pools, gym, laundry facilities, spa, beach, business
center, water sports, some pets allowed* ☉ *Closed Sept.* ❢⊙❘ *Breakfast.*

NIGHTLIFE

In late February or early March, reggae star and impresario Bankie
Banx stages Moonsplash, a three-day music festival that showcases local
and imported talent around the nights of the full moon. At the end of
July is the International Arts Festival, which hosts artists from around
the world. BET (Black Entertainment Television) sponsors the Tranquil-
ity Jazz Festival in November, attracting major musicians such as Michel
Camilo, James Moody, Bobby Watson, and Dee Dee Bridgewater.

Most hotels and many restaurants offer live entertainment in high season and on weekends, ranging from pianists and jazz combos to traditional steel and calypso bands. Check the local tourist magazines and
newspaper for listings. Friday and Saturday, Sandy Ground is the hot
spot; Wednesday and Sunday the action shifts to Shoal Bay East.

The nightlife scene here runs late into the night—the action doesn't
really start until after 11 pm. If you do not rent a car, be aware that taxis
are not readily available at night. If you plan to take a taxi back to your
hotel or villa at the end of the night, be sure to make arrangements in
advance with the driver who brings you or with your hotel concierge.

Dune Preserve. The funky Dune Preserve is the driftwood-fabricated
home of Bankie Banx, Anguilla's famous reggae star. He performs here
weekends and during the full moon. There's a dance floor and a beach
bar, and sometimes you can find a sunset beach barbecue in progress.
In high season there's a $15 cover charge. ⊠ *Box 85, Rendezvous Bay*
☎ *264/497–6219* ⊕ *www.bankiebanx.net.*

Fodor's Choice **Elvis' Beach Bar.** This is the perfect locale (it's actually a boat) to hear
★ great music and sip the best rum punch on earth. The bar is open every
day but Tuesday, and there's live music on Wednesday through Sunday
nights during the high season—as well as food until 1 am. Check to
see if there's a full-moon LunaSea party. You won't be disappointed.
⊠ *Sandy Ground* ☎ *264/772–0637.*

★ **Johnno's Beach Stop.** Things are lively at Johnno's, where there is live
music and alfresco dancing every night and on Sunday afternoon, when
just about everybody drops by. This is *the* classic Caribbean beach bar,
attracting a funky eclectic mix, from locals to movie stars. It's open
daily from 11 to 9. ⊠ *Sandy Ground* ☎ *264/497–2728.*

★ **Pumphouse.** At the Pumphouse, in the old rock-salt factory, you can
find live music most nights—plus surprisingly good pub grub, and a

mini-museum of artifacts and equipment from 19th-century salt factories. There's calypso-soca on Thursday; it's open from noon until 3 am daily, except Sunday. ⊠ *Sandy Ground* ☎ *264/497–5154* ⊕ *www. pumphouse-anguilla.com.*

SHOPPING

Anguilla is by no means a shopping destination. In fact, if your suitcase is lost, you will be hard-pressed to secure even the basics on island. If you're a hard-core shopping enthusiast, a day trip to nearby St. Martin will satisfy. Well-heeled visitors sometimes organize boat or plane charters through their hotel concierge for daylong shopping excursions to St Barth. The island's tourist publication, *What We Do in Anguilla,* has shopping tips and is available free at the airport and in shops. Pyrat rums—golden elixirs blending up to nine aged and flavored spirits—are a local specialty available at the Anguilla Rums distillery and several local shops. For upscale designer sportswear, check out the small boutiques in hotels (some are branches of larger stores in Marigot on St. Martin). Outstanding local artists sell their work in galleries, which often arrange studio tours (you can also check with the Antigua Tourist Office).

ART GALLERIES AND CRAFTS

Anguilla Arts and Crafts Center. This gallery carries island crafts, including textiles and ceramics. Of particular interest are unique ceramics by Otavia Fleming, lovely spotted-glaze items with adorable lizards climbing on them. Look for special exhibits and performances—ranging from puppetry to folk dance—sponsored by the Anguilla National Creative Arts Alliance. ⊠ *Brooks Building, The Valley* ☎ *264/729–4825.*

Cheddie's Carving Studios. Cheddie's showcases Cheddie Richardson's fanciful wood carvings and coral and stone sculptures. ⊠ *West End Rd., The Cove* ☎ *264/497–6027.*

Devonish Art Gallery. This gallery purveys the wood, stone, and clay creations of Courtney Devonish, an internationally known potter and sculptor, plus creations by his wife, Carolle, a bead artist. Also available are works by other Caribbean artists and regional antique maps. ⊠ *West End Rd., George Hill* ☎ *264/497–2949.*

★ **Hibernia Restaurant and Gallery.** Hibernia has striking pieces culled from the owners' travels, from contemporary Eastern European artworks to traditional Indo-Chinese crafts. ⊠ *Island Harbour* ☎ *264/497–4290.*

★ **Savannah Gallery.** The Savannah Gallery specializes in works by local Anguillian artists as well as other Caribbean and Central American art, including oil paintings by Marge Morani. You'll also find works by artists of the renowned Haitian St. Soleil school, as well as Guatemalan textiles, Mexican pottery, and brightly painted metalwork. ⊠ *Coronation St., Lower Valley* ☎ *264/497–2263* ⊕ *www.savannahgallery.com.*

★ **World Arts Gallery.** The peripatetic proprietors of World Arts, Nik and Christy Douglas, display a veritable United Nations of antiquities: exquisite Indonesian ikat hangings to Thai teak furnishings, Aboriginal didgeridoos to Dogon tribal masks, Yuan Dynasty jade pottery to

CLOSE UP

A Day at the Boat Races

If you want a different kind of trip to Anguilla, try for a visit during Carnival, which starts on the first Monday in August and continues for about 10 days. Colorful parades, beauty pageants, music, delicious food, arts-and-crafts shows, fireworks, and nonstop partying are just the beginning. The music starts at sunrise jam sessions—as early as 4 am—and continues well into the night. The high point? The boat races. They are the national passion and the official national sport of Anguilla.

Anguillians from around the world return home to race old-fashioned, made-on-the-island wooden boats

that have been in use on the island since the early 1800s. Similar to some of today's fastest sailboats, these are 15 to 28 feet in length and sport only a mainsail and jib on a single 25-foot mast. The sailboats have no deck, so heavy bags of sand, boulders, and sometimes even people are used as ballast. As the boats reach the finish line, the ballast—including some of the sailors—gets thrown into the water in a furious effort to win the race. Spectators line the beaches and follow the boats on foot, by car, and by even more boats. You'll have almost as much fun watching the fans as the races.

Uzbeki rugs. There is also handcrafted jewelry and handbags. ⊠ *Cove Rd., West End* ☎ *264/497–5950 or 264/497–2767.*

SPORTS AND ACTIVITIES

Anguilla's expanding sports options are enhanced by its beautiful first golf course, designed by Greg Norman to accentuate the natural terrain and maximize the stunning ocean views over Rendezvous Bay. Players say the par-72, Troon-managed course is reminiscent of Pebble Beach. Personal experience says bring a lot of golf balls! The Anguilla Tennis Academy, designed by noted architect Myron Goldfinger, operates in the Blowing Point area. The 1,000-seat stadium, equipped with pro shop and seven lighted courts, was created to attract major international matches and to provide a first-class playing option for tourists and locals.

BOATING AND SAILING

Anguilla is the perfect place to try all kinds of water sports. The major resorts offer complimentary Windsurfers, paddleboats, and water skis to their guests.

If your hotel lacks facilities, you can get in gear at **Sandy Island Enterprises** (⊠ *Sandy Ground* ☎ *264/476–6534* ⊕ *www.mysandyisland.com*), which rents Sunfish and Windsurfers and arranges fishing charters.

DIVING

Sunken wrecks; a long barrier reef; terrain encompassing walls, canyons, and hulking boulders; varied marine life, including greenback turtles and nurse sharks; and exceptionally clear water—all of these make for excellent diving. Prickly Pear Cay is a favorite spot. **Stoney Bay Marine Park,** off the northeast end of Anguilla, showcases the late-18th-century *El Buen Consejo,* a 960-ton Spanish galleon that sank here in 1772. Other good dive sites include **Grouper Bowl,** with exceptional hard-coral formations; **Ram's Head,** with caves, chutes, and tunnels; and **Upper Flats,** where you are sure to see stingrays.

Anguillian Divers (⊠ *Meads Bay* ☎ *264/497–4750* ⊕ *anguilliandiver.com*) is a full-service dive operator with a PADI five-star training center.

Shoal Bay Scuba and Watersports (☎ *264/497–4371* ⊕ *www.shoalbayscuba. com*) is in beautiful Shoal Bay. Single-tank dives start at $50, two-tank dives, $90. Daily snorkel trips at 1 pm are $25 per person.

GOLF

Temenos Golf Club (*Long Bay* ☎ *264/498–5602*), the 7,200-yard, $50 million wonder designed by superstar Greg Norman, had 13 of its 18 holes directly on the water. Now managed by Cap Juluca, the course features sweeping sea vistas and an ecologically responsible watering system of ponds and lagoons that snake through the grounds. Players thrill to the spectacular vistas of St. Maarten and blue sea at the tee box of the 390-yard starting hole. The fairway descends over 40 feet to a narrow, two-tiered green sitting precariously on the edge of a saltwater lagoon. This first hole has been called "the Caribbean's answer to the 18th at Pebble Beach." At this writing, the greens fee for a round of 18 holes during peak times was set at $225 per person. Discounted greens fees will be offered for twilight tee times.

GUIDED TOURS

A round-the-island tour by taxi takes about 2½ hours and costs $55 for one or two people, $5 for each additional passenger.

Contact the **Anguilla Tourist Office** (⊠ *Coronation Ave., The Valley* ☎ *264/497–2759 or 800/553–4939* ⊕ *www.anguilla-vacation.com*) to arrange the tour by Sir Emile Gumbs, the island's former chief minister, of the Sandy Ground area. This tour, which highlights historic and ecological sites, is on Tuesday at 10 am. The $20 fee benefits the Anguilla Archaeological Historical Society. Gumbs also organizes bird-watching expeditions that show you everything from frigate birds to turtledoves.

Bennie's Tours (⊠ *Blowing Point* ☎ *264/497–2788*) is one of the island's more reliable tour operators.

Malliouhana Travel and Tours (⊠ *The Quarter* ☎ *264/497–2431*) will create personalized package tours of the island.

The **Old Valley Tour** (☎ *264/497–2263*), created by longtime resident Frank Costin, ambles up Crocus Hill, where you'll see many of Anguilla's best-preserved historic edifices, including Ebenezer's Methodist

Church (the island's oldest), the Warden's Place, and typical turn-of-the-20th-century cottages (most housing galleries). The tour is by appointment only and offers a fascinating insight into Anguillian architecture, past and present.

HORSEBACK RIDING

The scenic Gibbons nature trails, along with any of the island's miles of beaches, are perfect places to ride, even for the novice. Ride English or Western style, or take lessons at **El Rancho Del Blues** (☎ 264/497–6164). The stable is near Anguilla Gases, across from Bennie's Tours on the Blowing Point Road. Prices start at $25 to $35 per hour ($50 for two-hour rides).

Seaside Stables (✉ *Paradise Dr., Cove Bay* ☎ 264/497–3667 ⊕ *www. seaside-stables-anguilla.com*), located in Cove Bay, offers rides and instruction, if a sunset gallop (or slow clomp) has always been your fantasy. Private rides at any time of the day are about $75, or try a full-moon ride, if the timing works, for $90; prior riding experience is not required. Choose from English, Western, or Australian saddles.

SEA EXCURSIONS

A number of boating options are available for airport transfers, day trips to offshore cays or neighboring islands, night trips to St. Martin, or just whipping through the waves en route to a picnic spot.

Chocolat (✉ *Sandy Ground* ☎ 264/497–3394) is a 35-foot catamaran available for private charter or scheduled excursions to nearby cays. Captain Rollins is a knowledgeable, affable guide. Rates for day sails with lunch are about $80 per person.

Funtime Charters (✉ *The Cove* ☎ 264/497–6511 *or 866/334–0047* ⊕ *www.funtime-charters.com*) operates five powerboats ranging in size from 32 to 38 feet.

For an underwater peek without getting wet, catch a ride ($20 per person) on **Junior's Glass Bottom Boat** (✉ *Sandy Ground* ☎ 264/235–1008 ⊕ *www.junior.ai*). Snorkel trips and instruction are available, too.

No Fear Sea Tours (✉ *The Cove* ☎ 264/235–6354 ⊕ *www.nofearseatours. com*) has three 32-foot speedboats and a 19-foot ski boat.

Picnic, swimming, and diving excursions to Prickly Pear Cay, Sandy Island, and Scilly Cay are available through **Sandy Island Enterprises** (☎ 264/476–6534).

Antigua and Barbuda

WORD OF MOUTH

"Check out the historic Nelson's Dockyard. It's very unique. They have so much to see there, including the Copper and Lumber store, which they converted into a hotel and restaurant. It has that beautiful Georgian architecture with an arched courtyard where you just step back in time."

—Knowing

WELCOME TO ANTIGUA AND BARBUDA

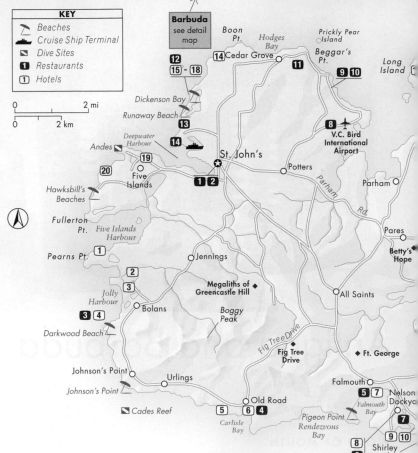

KEY

- Beaches
- Cruise Ship Terminal
- Dive Sites
- **1** Restaurants
- ① Hotels

0 — 2 mi
0 — 2 km

Barbuda
see detail
map

Boon Pt.

Hodges Bay

Prickly Pear Island

Beggar's Pt.

Long Island

12 **14** Cedar Grove **11**

15 - **18**

9 **10**

Dickenson Bay

Runaway Beach **13**

8 ✈
V.C. Bird International Airport

14 St. John's

Deepwater Harbour

Andes

19

20

Five Islands

Hawksbill's Beaches

1 **2**

Potters

Parham

Parham Rd.

Pares

Betty's Hope

Fullerton Pt.

Five Islands Harbour

Pearns Pt. **1**

Jennings

Megaliths of Greencastle Hill

Boggy Peak

All Saints

Jolly Harbour

2

3

3 **4**

Bolans

Darkwood Beach

Fig Tree Drive

Fig Tree Drive

Ft. George

Johnson's Point

Urlings

Falmouth

5 **7**

Nelson Dockyd

Falmouth Bay

7

Johnson's Point

Cades Reef

5 **6** **4**

Old Road

Carlisle Bay

Pigeon Point Rendezvous Bay

9 **10**

8 **6**

Shirley Heights

Excellent beaches—365 of them—might make you think that the island has never busied itself with anything more pressing than the pursuit of pleasure. But for much of the 18th and 19th centuries, English Harbour sheltered Britain's Caribbean fleet. These days, pleasure yachts bob where galleons once anchored.

3

A BEACH FOR EVERY DAY

At 108 square mi (280 square km), Antigua is the largest of the British Leeward Islands. Its much smaller sister island, Barbuda, is 26 mi (42 km) to the north. Together, they are an independent nation and part of the British Commonwealth. The island was under British control from 1667 until it achieved independence in 1981.

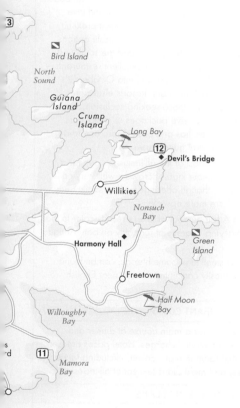

Bird Island

North Sound

Guiana Island

Crump Island

Long Bay

[12]

◆ Devil's Bridge

Willikies

Nonsuch Bay

Harmony Hall ◆

Green Island

Freetown

Half Moon Bay

Willoughby Bay

[11]

Mamora Bay

TOP REASONS TO VISIT ANTIGUA AND BARBUDA

1 Beaches Galore: So many paradisiacal beaches of every size provide a tremendous selection for an island its size.

2 Nelson's Dockyard: One of the Caribbean's best examples of historic preservation.

3 Sailing Away: With several natural anchorages and tiny islets to explore, Antigua is a major sailing center.

4 Activities Galore: Land and water sports, sights to see, and nightlife.

5 Shopping Options: A nice selection of shopping options, from duty-free goods to local artists and craftspeople (especially distinctive ceramics).

ANTIGUA AND BARBUDA PLANNER

Logistics

Getting to Antigua and Barbuda: Antigua is a Caribbean base, and several airlines fly there nonstop. You can continue on a small Winair plane to Barbuda, or there is ferry service several days a week, though it's geared for day-trippers. Good package deals are often available from resorts.

Hassle Factor: Low for Antigua, medium for Barbuda.

On the Ground: Taxis meet every flight, and drivers will offer to guide you around the island. Taxis are unmetered, but rates are posted at the airport. Drivers must carry a rate card with them. The fixed rate from the airport to St. John's is $12 (although drivers have been known to quote in Eastern Caribbean dollars), to Dickenson Bay $16, and to English Harbour $31.

If you are staying at an isolated resort or wish to sample the island's many fine restaurants, a car is a necessity, less so if you are staying at an all-inclusive with limited island excursions. It's possible to get by without a car if you are staying near St. John's or English Harbour, but taxi rates mount up quickly. A temporary driving permit is required on the island ($20), and you drive on the left.

Where to Stay

In Antigua you're almost certain to have an excellent beach regardless of where you stay. Dickenson Bay and Five Islands Peninsula suit beachcombers who want proximity to St. John's, and Jolly Harbour offers affordable options and activities galore. English Harbour and the southwest coast have the best inns and several excellent restaurants—although many close from August well into October; it's also the yachting crowd's hangout. Resorts elsewhere on the island are ideal for those seeking seclusion; some are so remote that all-inclusive packages or rental cars are mandatory. Barbuda has one posh resort, one fairly upscale hotel, and several guesthouses.

All-Inclusive Resorts: Most of the all-inclusives aim for a mainstream, package-tour kind of crowd—with varying degrees of success—though offerings such as Galley Bay and Curtain Bluff are more upscale.

Luxury Resorts: A fair number of luxury resorts cater to the well-heeled in varying degrees of formality on both Antigua and Barbuda.

Small Inns: A few small inns, some historic, can be found around Antigua, mostly concentrated in or near English Harbour.

HOTEL AND RESTAURANT COSTS

Restaurant prices are for a main course at dinner and include any taxes or service charges. Hotel prices are per night for a double room in high season, excluding taxes, service charges, and meal plans (except at all-inclusives).

WHAT IT COSTS IN U.S. DOLLARS

	¢	$	$$	$$$	$$$$
Restaurants	under $8	$8–$12	$12–$20	$20–$30	over $30
Hotels	under $150	$150–$275	$276–$375	$376–$475	over $475

Getting Here and Around

Air Travel: In addition to many nonstop flights from the United States, **LIAT** (☎ 268/480–5600 ⊕ www.liatairline. com) has daily flights to and from many other Caribbean islands.

Nonstop Flights: Atlanta (Delta, twice weekly in season), Charlotte (US Airways), Miami (American, Caribbean Airlines, Continental), New York–JFK (Caribbean), and Newark (Continental).

Airline Contacts: American Airlines/American Eagle (☎ 268/462–0950 ⊕ www.aa.com). **Caribbean Airlines** (☎ 268/480–2900 or 800/744–2225 ⊕ www. caribbean-airlines.com). **Continental Airlines** (☎ 268/462–5355 ⊕ www.continental.com). **Delta Airlines** (☎ 800/532–4777 or 268/562–5951 ⊕ www.delta. com). **US Airways** (☎ 268/480–5601 or 268/481–3801 ⊕ www.usairways.com).

Airport: V. C. Bird International Airport (✉ VNU ☎ 268/462–4672 or 268/462–0358).

Boat and Ferry Travel: Barbuda Express (☎ 268/560–7989 ⊕ www.antiguaferries.com) runs six days a week (but call for the changing schedule) from Antigua's Heritage Quay Ferry Dock. Fare is EC$110 one-way, EC$220 round-trip (day tour costs US$159).

Car Travel: The main roads are mostly in good condition, with some bumpy dirt stretches at remote locations and a few hilly areas that flood easily and become impassable for a day. Driving is on the left. To rent a car, you need a valid license and a temporary permit ($20), available through the rental agent. Costs start about $50 per day in season, with unlimited mileage, though multiday discounts are standard. Most agencies offer automatic, stick-shift, and right- and left-hand drive. Four-wheel-drive vehicles ($55 per day) will get you more places and are useful because so many roads are full of potholes.

Avis (☎ 268/462–2840). **Budget** (☎ 268/462–3009). **Dollar** (☎ 268/462–0362). **Hertz** (☎ 268/481–4440). **Thrifty** (☎ 268/462–9532).

Taxi Travel: Some cabbies may take you from St. John's to English Harbour and wait for about a half hour while you look around, for about $50. You can always call a cab from the **St. John's taxi stand** (☎ 268/462–5190, 268/460–5353 for 24-hr service).

When to Go

The high season runs from mid-December through April; after that time, you can find real bargains, for as much as 40% off the regular rates, particularly if you book an air–hotel package. A fair number of the restaurants and properties close for part of the time between August and October.

FESTIVALS AND EVENTS

The year's big event is **Antigua Sailing Week,** which draws some 300 yachts for a series of races in late April and early May. The **Back II Life Music Festival** usually overlaps.

Mid-April sees the **Antigua Classic Yacht Regatta,** a five-day event that includes a tall-ships race.

Antigua Tennis Week, usually the second week of May, has exhibition games by former greats plus a pro-am tournament.

June brings the **Antigua & Barbuda Sports Fishing Tournament** in Falmouth.

Summer Carnival runs 10 days from the end of July to early August and is one of the Caribbean's more elaborate, with eye-catching costumes and fierce music competitions.

3

ANTIGUA AND BARBUDA PLANNER

Fast Facts

Banks and Exchange Services: The local currency is the Eastern Caribbean dollar (EC$); at this writing US$1 is worth approximately EC$2.70. American dollars are readily accepted, although change is often EC dollars. Exchanging currency really isn't necessary, especially if you are staying in an all-inclusive resort. Most hotels, restaurants, and duty-free shops take major credit cards. ATMs (dispensing EC$) are available at the island's banks and at the airport.

Electricity: 110 volts, 50 cycles.

Emergency Services: Ambulance (☎ 268/462–0251 or 999). **Fire** (☎ 268/462–0044 or 911). **Police assistance** (☎ 268/462–0125).

Passport Requirements: All visitors must carry a valid passport and must have a return or ongoing ticket.

Weddings: No minimum residency or blood test is required. A license application fee is $150. You must have valid passports as proof of citizenship and, in the case of previous marriages, the original divorce or annulment decree. A marriage certificate registration fee is $40.

Essentials

Mail and Shipping: Airmail letters to North America cost EC$1.50; postcards EC75¢. The main post office is at the foot of High Street in St. John's. Note that there are no postal codes; when addressing letters to the island, you need only indicate the address and "Antigua, West Indies."

Taxes and Service Charges: The departure tax is $28, payable in cash only—either U.S. or EC currency. Hotels collect an 8½%–10½% government room tax; some restaurants will add a 7% tax. Hotels and restaurants also usually add a 10% service charge to your bill.

Telephones: GSM tri-band mobile phones from the United States and United Kingdom usually work on Antigua; you can also rent one from LIME (formerly Cable & Wireless) and APUA (Antigua Public Utilities Authority). Basic rental costs range between EC$25 and EC$50 per day.

Most hotels have direct-dial phones; other hotels can easily make connections through the switchboard. You can use the LIME Phone Card (available in $5, $10, and $20 denominations in most hotels and post offices) for local and long-distance calls. Phone-card rather than coin-operated phones work far better.

Information: APUA (✉ Cassada Gardens, St. John's ☎ 268/480–7000 or 268/727–2782). **LIME** (✉ Woods Centre, St. John's ☎ 268/480–2628 ✉ Long St., St. John's ☎ 268/480–4236 ✉ Clare Hall, St. John's ☎ 268/480–4000 ⊕ www.time4lime.com).

Tipping: Restaurants, 5% beyond the regular service charge added to your bill; taxi drivers, 10%; porters and bellmen about $1 per bag; maids $2 to $3 per night. Staff at all-inclusives aren't supposed to be tipped unless they've truly gone out of their way.

Visitor Information: Antigua & Barbuda Department of Tourism (✉ Government Complex, Queen Elizabeth Hwy., St. John's ☎ 268/462–0480 ⊕ www.antigua-barbuda. org). **Antigua & Barbuda Tourist Offices** (☎ 212/541–4117 in New York City, 305/381–6762 in Miami, 888/268–4227 ⊕ www.antigua-barbuda.org). **Antigua Hotels & Tourist Association** (✉ Newgate St., St. John's ☎ 268/462–0374 ⊕ www.antiguahotels.org). **Barbudaful.net** (⊕ www.barbudaful.net).

ANTIGUA AND BARBUDA BEACHES

Antigua and Barbuda proudly offer 365 beaches, one for every day of the year. And you could probably spend a year beach-hopping its beautiful shores—some lined with bars and sports concessions and some virtually deserted.

(Above) Half Moon Bay. (Opposite page bottom) Darkwood Beach. (Opposite page top) Jet-skiing in Dickenson Bay.

Antigua's beaches are public, and many are lined with resorts that have water-sports outfitters and beach bars. The government does a fairly good job of cleaning up seaweed and garbage. Most restaurant and bars on beaches won't charge for beach-chair rentals if you buy lunch or drinks; otherwise the going rate is $3 to $5. Access to some of the finest stretches, such as those at the Five Islands Peninsula resorts, is somewhat restricted by security gates. Sunbathing topless is strictly illegal except on one small beach at Hawksbill by Rex Resorts. When cruise ships dock in St. John's, buses drop off loads of passengers on most of the west-coast beaches. Choose such a time to visit one of the more remote east-end beaches, or take a day trip to Barbuda.

EASY, BREEZY

Most Antiguan beaches feature talcum-powdery sand right out of a brochure. Those on the windward side, such as Dutchman's Bay in the north, and Nonsuch, Long, and Half Moon bays to the east, receive brisk breezes, making them favorites of windsurfers and boarders. Blissfully undeveloped Barbuda seems like one big beach; indeed sand exceeds lobster as its primary export.

ANTIGUA

Darkwood Beach. This ½-mi (1-km) beige ribbon on the southwest coast has stunning views of Montserrat. Although popular with locals and cruise passengers on weekends, it's virtually deserted during the week. Waters are calm, but there's scant shade, no development other than Darkwood Beach Bar (and Admiral's Bar across the coastal road). *2 mi (3 km) south of Jolly Harbour and roughly ½ mi (1 km) southwest of Valley Church off main coast road.*

Dickenson Bay. Along a lengthy stretch of powder-soft white sand and exceptionally calm water you can find small and large hotels, water sports, concessions, and beachfront restaurants. There's decent snorkeling at either point. ⚓ *2 mi (3 km) northeast of St. John's, along main coast road.*

Half Moon Bay. This ½-mi (1-km) ivory crescent is a prime snorkeling and windsurfing area. On the Atlantic side, the water can be rough at times, attracting intrepid hard-core surfers and wakeboarders. The northeastern end, where a protective reef offers spectacular snorkeling, is much calmer. A tiny bar has restrooms, snacks, and beach chairs. Half Moon is a real trek, but one of Antigua's showcase beaches. ⊠ *On southeast coast, 1½ mi (2½ km) from Freetown.*

Johnson's Point/Crabbe Hill. This series of connected, deserted beaches on the southwest coast looks out toward Montserrat, Guadeloupe, and St. Kitts. Notable beach bar–restaurants include OJ's, Gibson's, and Turner's. The water is generally placid, though not good for snorkeling. ⊠ *3 mi (5 km) south of Jolly Harbour complex on main west-coast road.*

Pigeon Point. Near Falmouth Harbour lie two fine white-sand beaches. The leeward side is calmer, the windward side is rockier, and there are sensational views and snorkeling around the point. Several restaurants and bars are nearby, though Bumpkin's satisfies most on-site needs. ⊠ *Off main south-coast road, southwest of Falmouth.*

BARBUDA

★ Fodor's Choice **Pink Beach.** You can sometimes walk miles of this classic strand without encountering another footprint. The sand is soft as silk; crushed coral often imparts a rosy glint in the sun, hence its (unofficial) name. The water can be rough with a strongish undertow in spots, though it's mainly protected by the reefs that make the island a diving mecca. Hire a taxi to take you here, since none of the roads is well marked. ⊠ *1 mi (2 km) from ferry and airstrip along unmarked roads.*

By Jordan Simon

The wonder of Antigua, and especially its astonishingly undeveloped sister island, Barbuda, is that you can still play Robinson Crusoe here. Travel brochures trumpet the 365 sensuous beaches, "one for every day of the year," as locals love saying, though when the island was first developed for tourism, the unofficial count was 52 ("one for every weekend"). Either way, even longtime residents haven't combed every stretch of sand.

The island's extensive archipelago of cays and islets is what attracted the original Amerindian settlers—the Ciboney—at least 4,000 years ago. The natural environment, which is rich in marine life, flora, and fauna, has been likened to a "natural supermarket." Antigua's superior anchorages and strategic location naturally caught the attention of the colonial powers. The Dutch, French, and English waged numerous bloody battles throughout the 17th century (eradicating the remaining Arawaks and Caribs in the process), with England finally prevailing in 1667. Antigua remained under English control until achieving full independence on November 1, 1981, along with Barbuda, 26 mi (42 km) to the north.

Boats and beaches go hand in hand with hotel development, and Antigua's tourist infrastructure has mushroomed since the 1950s. Though many of its grande dames such as Curtain Bluff remain anchors, today all types of resorts line the sand, and the island offers something for everyone, from gamboling on the sand to gambling in casinos. Environmental activists have become increasingly vocal about preservation and the limiting of development, and not just because green travel rakes in the green. Antigua's allure is precisely that precarious balance and subliminal tension between its unspoiled natural beauty and its sun-sand-surf megadevelopment. And the British heritage persists, from teatime (and tee times) to fiercely contested cricket matches.

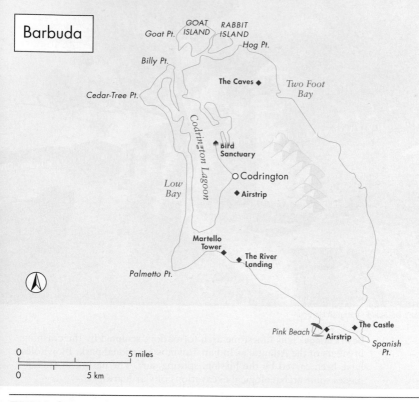

EXPLORING

ANTIGUA

Hotels provide free island maps, but you should get your bearings before heading out on the road. Street names aren't listed (except in St. John's), though *some* easy-to-spot signs lead the way to major restaurants and resorts. Locals generally give directions in terms of landmarks (turn left at the yellow house, or right at the big tree). Wear a swimsuit under your clothes—one of the sights to strike your fancy might be a secluded beach.

WHAT TO SEE

Betty's Hope. Just outside the village of Pares, a marked dirt road leads to Antigua's first sugar plantation, founded in 1650. You can tour the twin windmills, various ruins, still-functional crushing machinery, and the visitor center's exhibits (often closed) on the island's sugar era. The private trust overseeing the restoration has yet to realize its ambitious, environmentally aware plans to replant indigenous crops destroyed by the extensive sugarcane plantings. Indeed, the site is somewhat neglected, with goats grazing the grounds. ⊠ *Pares* ☎ *268/462–1469* ⊞ *$2* ⊘ *Tues.–Sat. 10–4.*

Nelson's Dockyard at English Harbour.

Devil's Bridge. This limestone arch formation, sculpted by the crashing breakers of the Atlantic at Indian Town, is a national park. Blowholes have been carved by the hissing, spitting surf. The park also encompasses some archaeological excavations of Carib artifacts.

Falmouth. This town sits on a lovely bay backed by former sugar plantations and sugar mills. The most important historic site here is St. Paul's Church, which was rebuilt on the site of a church once used by troops during the Horatio Nelson period.

Fig Tree Drive. This often muddy, rutted, steep road takes you through the rain forest, which is rich in mangoes, pineapples, and banana trees (*fig* is the Antiguan word for "banana"). The rain forest is the island's hilliest area—1,319-foot Boggy Peak (renamed Mt. Obama), to the west, is the highest point. At its crest, Elaine Francis sells seasonal local fruit juices—ginger, guava, sorrel, passion fruit—and homemade jams at a stall she dubs the Culture Shop. A few houses down (look for the orange windows) is the atelier of noted island artist Sallie Harker (shimmering seascapes and vividly hued fish incorporating gold leaf). You'll also pass several tranquil villages with charming churches and Antigua Rainforest Canopy Tours (⇨ *Zip-Lining under Sports and Activities later in this chapter)* here.

Ft. George. East of Liberta—one of the first settlements founded by freed slaves—on Monk's Hill, this fort was built from 1689 to 1720. Among the ruins are the sites for 32 cannons, water cisterns, the base of the old flagstaff, and some of the original buildings.

Harmony Hall. Northeast of Freetown (follow the signs), this art gallery–cum–restaurant is built on the foundation of a 17th-century sugar-plantation greathouse. No longer affiliated with the original Jamaican outpost, the Antigua facility is run by enterprising Italians who operate a fine restaurant and six chic, charming cottages. Its remote location is a headache, but you can allot the whole afternoon to enjoy lunch (dinner Wednesday, Friday, and Saturday), soak in the historic ambience and panoramic ocean views, browse through the exhibits, comb the beach, and perhaps even snorkel at nearby Green Island via the property's boat, *Luna.* ✉ *Brown's Mill Bay, Brown's Mill* ☏ *268/460–4120* ⊕ *www.harmonyhallantigua.com* ☉ *June–mid-Nov., daily 10–6, later Wed,, Fri., and Sat.*

Megaliths of Greencastle Hill. It's an arduous climb to these eerie rock slabs in the south-central part of the island. Some say the megaliths were set up by early inhabitants for their worship of the sun and moon or as devices for measuring time astronomically; others believe they're nothing more than unusual geological formations.

Fodor's Choice
★
Nelson's Dockyard. Antigua's most famous attraction is the world's only Georgian-era dockyard still in use, a treasure trove for history buffs and nautical nuts alike. In 1671 the governor of the Leeward Islands wrote to the Council for Foreign Plantations in London, pointing out the advantages of this landlocked harbor. By 1704 English Harbour was in regular use as a garrisoned station.

In 1784, 26-year-old Horatio Nelson sailed in on the HMS *Boreas* to serve as captain and second-in-command of the Leeward Island Station. Under him was the captain of the HMS *Pegasus,* Prince William Henry, duke of Clarence, who was later crowned King William IV. The prince acted as best man when Nelson married Fannie Nisbet on Nevis in 1787.

When the Royal Navy abandoned the station at English Harbour in 1889, it fell into a state of decay, though adventuresome yachties still lived there in near-primitive conditions. The Society of the Friends of English Harbour began restoring it in 1951; it reopened with great fanfare as Nelson's Dockyard on November 14, 1961. Within the compound are crafts shops, restaurants, and two splendidly restored 18th-century hotels, the Admiral's Inn and the Copper & Lumber Store Hotel, worth peeking into. (The latter, occupying a supply store for Nelson's Caribbean fleet, is a particularly fine example of Georgian architecture and has an interior courtyard evoking Old England.) The Dockyard is a hub for oceangoing yachts and serves as headquarters for the annual Sailing Week Regatta in late April and early May. Water taxis will ferry you between points for EC$5. The Dockyard National Park also includes serene nature trails accessing beaches, rock pools, and crumbling plantation ruins and hilltop forts.

The **Dockyard Museum,** in the original Naval Officer's House, presents ship models, mock-ups of English Harbour, displays on the people who worked there and typical ships that docked, silver regatta trophies, maps, prints, antique navigational instruments, and Nelson's very own telescope and tea caddy. ✉ *English Harbour* ☏ *268/481–5022 or 268/463–1060, 268/460–1379 for National Parks Authority* ⊕ *www. antiguamuseums.org* 🎫 *$2 suggested donation* ☉ *Daily 8–5.*

NEED A BREAK?

The restaurant at the Admiral's Inn (✉ *Nelson's Dockyard, English Harbour* ☎ *268/460–1027*) is a must for Anglophiles and mariners. Soak up the centuries at the inside bar, where 18th-century sailors reputedly carved their ships' names on the dark timbers. Most diners sit on the flagstone terrace under shady Australian gums to enjoy the views of the harbor complex and trendy new exhibition kitchen; yachts seem close enough to eavesdrop. Specialties include pumpkin soup and fresh snapper with equally fresh limes.

Parham. This sleepy village is a splendid example of a traditional colonial settlement. St. Peter's Church, built in 1840 by English architect Thomas Weekes, is an octagonal Italianate building with unusual ribbed wooden ceiling, whose facade is richly decorated with stucco and keystone work, though it suffered considerable damage during an 1843 earthquake.

Shirley Heights. This bluff affords a spectacular view of English Harbour. The heights are named for Sir Thomas Shirley, the governor who fortified the harbor in 1787. At the top is Shirley Heights Lookout, a restaurant built into the remnants of the 18th-century fortifications. Most notable for its boisterous Sunday barbecues that continue into the night with live music and dancing, it serves dependable burgers, pumpkin soup, grilled meats, and rum punches.

Not far from Shirley Heights is the **Dows Hill Interpretation Centre**, where observation platforms provide still more sensational vistas of the English Harbour area. A multimedia sound-and-light presentation on island history and culture, spotlighting lifelike figures and colorful tableaux accompanied by running commentary and music, results in a cheery, if bland, portrait of Antiguan life from Amerindian times to the present. ☎ *268/460–1379 for National Parks Authority* ☜ *EC$15* ☉ *Daily 9–5.*

St. John's. Antigua's capital, with some 45,000 inhabitants (approximately half the island's population), lies at sea level at the inland end of a sheltered northwestern bay. Although it has seen better days, a couple of notable historic sights and some good waterfront shopping areas make it worth a visit.

Signs at the **Museum of Antigua and Barbuda** say "Please touch," encouraging you to explore Antigua's past. Try your hand at the educational video games or squeeze a cassava through a *matapi* (grass sieve). Exhibits interpret the nation's history, from its geological birth to its political independence in 1981. There are fossil and coral remains from some 34 million years ago; models of a sugar plantation and a wattle-and-daub house; an Arawak canoe; and a wildly eclectic assortment of objects from cannonballs to 1920s telephone exchanges. The museum occupies the former courthouse, which dates from 1750. The superlative museum gift shop carries such unusual items as calabash purses, seed earrings, warri boards (warri being an African game brought over to the Caribbean), and lignum vitae pipes, as well as historic maps and local books (including engrossing, detailed monographs on varied subjects by the late Desmond Nicholson, a longtime resident). ✉ *Long and*

Market Sts. ☎ *268/462–1469* 🖃 *$2 suggested donation* ☾ *Sun.–Thurs. 8:30–4, Fri. 8:30–3, Sat. 10–2.* At the south gate of the **Anglican Cathedral of St. John the Divine** are figures of St. John the Baptist and St. John the Divine, said to have been taken from one of Napoléon's ships and brought to Antigua. The

WORD OF MOUTH

"We found Antigua to be a thoroughly relaxing place where you can do as little or as much as you want. It's a shame more people don't choose to visit." —Knowing

original church was built in 1681, replaced by a stone building in 1745, and destroyed by an earthquake in 1843. The present neo-baroque building dates from 1845; the parishioners had the interior completely encased in pitch pine, hoping to forestall future earthquake damage. Tombstones bear eerily eloquent testament to the colonial days. ⊠ *Between Long and Newgate Sts.* ☎ *268/461–0082.*

Shopaholics head directly for **Heritage Quay,** an ugly multimillion-dollar complex. The two-story buildings contain stores that sell duty-free goods, sportswear, down-island imports (paintings, T-shirts, straw baskets), and local crafts. There are also restaurants, a bandstand, and a casino. Cruise-ship passengers disembark here from the 500-foot-long pier. Expect heavy shilling. ⊠ *High and Thames Sts.*

Fodor's Choice **Redcliffe Quay,** at the water's edge just south of Heritage Quay, is the
★ most appealing part of St. John's. Attractively restored (and superbly re-created) buildings in a riot of cotton-candy colors house shops, restaurants, and boutiques and are linked by courtyards and landscaped walkways. At the far south end of town, where Market Street forks into Valley and All Saints roads, haggling goes on every Friday and Saturday, when locals jam the **Public Market** to buy and sell fruits, vegetables, fish, and spices. Ask before you aim a camera; your subject may expect a tip. This is old-time Caribbean shopping, a jambalaya of sights, sounds, and smells.

BARBUDA

This flat, 62-square-mi (161-square-km) coral atoll—with 17 mi (27 km) of gleaming white-sand beaches (sand is the island's main export)—is 26 mi (42 km) north of Antigua. Most of Barbuda's 1,200 people live in Codrington. Nesting terns, turtles, and frigate birds outnumber residents at least 10 to 1. Goats, guinea fowl, deer, and wild boar roam the roads, all fair game for local kitchens. A few very basic efficiencies and guesthouses exist, but most visitors stay overnight at the deluxe Coco Point Lodge (two other glam properties have closed). Pink Beach lures beachcombers, a bird sanctuary attracts ornithologists, caves and sinkholes filled with rain forest or underground pools (containing rare, even unique crustacean species) attract spelunkers, and reefs and roughly 200 offshore wrecks draw divers and snorkelers. Barbuda's sole historic ruin is the 18th-century, cylindrical, 56-foot-tall **Martello Tower,** which was probably a lighthouse built by the Spaniards before to English occupation. The **Frigate Bird Sanctuary,** a wide mangrove-filled lagoon, is home to an estimated 400 species of birds, including frigate birds with 8-foot wingspans. Your hotel can make arrangements.

As of this writing, you can no longer fly to Barbuda from Antigua save by expensive charters. It's reachable by boat, the *Barbuda Express*, although the 95-minute ride is extremely bumpy ("a chiropractor's nightmare—or fantasy," quipped one passenger).

WHERE TO EAT

Antigua's restaurants are almost a dying breed since the advent of all-inclusives. But several worthwhile hotel dining rooms and nightspots remain, especially in the English Harbour and Dickenson Bay areas. Virtually every chef incorporates local ingredients and elements of West Indian cuisine.

Most menus list prices in both EC and U.S. dollars; if not, ask which currency the menu is using. Always double-check if credit cards are accepted and if service is included. Dinner reservations are needed during high season.

WHAT TO WEAR

Perhaps because of the island's British heritage, Antiguans tend to dress more formally for dinner than dwellers on many other Caribbean islands. Wraps and shorts (no beach attire) are de rigueur for lunch, except at local hangouts.

$$
ITALIAN
✕ **Big Banana—Pizzas in Paradise.** This tiny, often crowded spot is tucked into one side of a restored 18th-century rum warehouse with broad plank floors, wood-beam ceiling, and stone archways. Cool, Benetton-style photos of locals and musicians jamming adorn the brick walls. Big Banana serves some of the island's best pizza—try the lobster or the seafood variety—as well as such tasty specials as conch salad, fresh fruit crushes, and sub sandwiches bursting at the seams. There's live entertainment some nights, and a large-screen TV for sports fans. ⊠ *Redcliffe Quay, St. John's* ☎ *268/480–6985* ⊕ *www.bigbanana-antigua.com* ☉ *Closed Sun.*

$$–$$$
CONTINENTAL
✕ **Cecilia's High Point Café.** The eponymous owner, a vivacious, striking Swedish ex-model, floats (and once in a while flirts) about the tables in this cozy beachfront Creole cottage. An equally animated cross section of Antiguan life usually packs the coveted patio tables (it's a terrific spot to eavesdrop on island gossip). The day's selections, including wine specials, are written on a blackboard. Stellar standbys run from a fried eggplant napoleon layered with tomatoes and mozzarella to mushroom ravioli nestled in spinach with a gossamer creamy pesto, but the high points are the setting and Cecilia herself. As a bonus, Wi-Fi access is free. ⊠ *Dutchman's Bay* ☎ *268/562–7070* ⊕ *www.highpointantigua.com* ⟐ *Reservations essential* ☉ *Closed Tues. and Wed. No dinner Thurs.–Sun.*

$$$–$$$$
CONTINENTAL
★
✕ **Coconut Grove.** Coconut palms grow through the roof of this open-air thatched restaurant, flickering candlelight illuminates colorful local murals, waves lap the white sand, and the warm waitstaff provides just the right level of service. Jean-François Bellanger's superbly presented

dishes fuse French culinary preparations with island ingredients. Top choices include smoked salmon with watermelon-ginger jam, sundried tomatoes, and tapenade; pan-seared snapper medallions served with roasted sweet potato in a saffron white-wine curry; Caribbean bouillabaisse with coconut milk and pumpkin aioli; and chicken stuffed with creole vegetables in mango-kiwi sauce. The kitchen can be uneven, the wine list is unimaginative and overpriced (save for the occasional $31 specials), and the buzzing happy-hour bar crowd lingering well into dinnertime can detract from the otherwise romantic atmosphere. Nonetheless, Coconut Grove straddles the line between casual beachfront boîte and elegant eatery with aplomb. ⊠ *Siboney Beach Club, Dickenson Bay* ☎ *268/462–1538* ⊕ *www.coconutgroveantigua.net* ⌦ *Reservations essential.*

$$$–$$$$
PAN-ASIAN
✕**East.** Imposing Indonesian carved doors usher you into this bold and sexy Asian fusion spot. Flames flicker in the outdoor lily pond while candles illuminate lacquered dark-wood tables with blood-red napery and oversize fuchsia-color chairs. Exquisite pan-Pacific fare (with delicious detours to the Indian subcontinent) courts perfection through simplicity and precision: prawn spring rolls with hoisin–sweet chili sauce; superlative sashimi; entrées from Thai lobster curry to tandoori chicken, to tilapia *katsudon* (lightly fried fillets served with onion *dashi* broth, egg, and rice); and green tea crème brûlée. The small main courses mandate tapas-style dining; the comprehensive wine list is pricey but offers values from intriguing lesser-known regions. ⊠ *Carlisle Bay, Old Road, St. Mary's* ☎ *268/484–0000* ⌦ *Reservations essential.*

$$–$$$
ECLECTIC
★
✕**Johnny CocoNat.** It's difficult to find a more enchanting spot for a casual meal than this open-air patio painted natty nautical blue and white overlooking the old Admiralty and boats traversing English Harbour while jazz mingles with the gentle surf. The food is music to discriminating palates, artfully presented on bright, contemporary plates, utilizing fresh local ingredients wherever possible. The subtle interplay of sweet, savory, and spicy flavors, and textures is evident in the nearly 20 creative pizzas and such standout specials as mango gazpacho, wahoo carpaccio with raspberry vinaigrette and dill foam, and four-seafood ravioli (each large square a different color, enfolding its own marine delicacy). Day and night, the lively little spot percolates with happy chatter and good strong espresso, thanks to Nat, the animated owner, who swans among the tables with irrepressible high spirits. ⊠ *Slipway, English Harbour* ☎ *268/562–5012* ⊕ *www.johnnycoconat. com* ⊘ *Closed Wed. No lunch May–Sept.*

$$$–$$$$
ITALIAN
★
✕**La Bussola.** Blend a genuinely *simpatico* welcome with lapping waves, the murmur of jazz, and expert Italian fare and you have Omar Tagliavente and family's recipe for the perfect beachfront bistro. Bleached-wood ceilings, billowing white curtains, old island photos of Antigua, boating paraphernalia, and brightly painted plates enhance the relaxed, romantic mood. The presentation is invariably pretty and Omar has a particularly facile touch with seafood; try the artichoke-shrimp pie in satiny garlic sauce, lobster-asparagus risotto, shark tartare with grapefruit nestling on a bed of arugula, mahimahi with olive "pâté" in filo, or the "fishermen's" spaghetti. The carefully considered wine

list showcases lesser-known Italian regions. Your evening ends with a complimentary grappa, Frangelico, or *limoncello* (lemon liqueur), representing northern, central, and southern Italy. La Bussola means "the compass" in Italian, and it certainly takes the right gastronomic direction. ⊠ *Runaway Bay* ☎ *268/562–1545* ⊕ *www.labussolarestaurant. net* ⚔ *Reservations essential* ⊘ *Closed Tues.*

$$–$$$ ✕ **La Mia Cucina.** Davide and Barbara Anfi's dockside charmer lives up
ITALIAN   to its homey name, "My Kitchen." The pungent scent of garlic commingles with the salt air as you enter. Barbara escorts you to your table in the semi-alfresco space punctuated by glowing hibiscus and ixora, a few nautical touches, and a tree picturesquely growing through the roof. Davide will explain the menu, proudly if shyly noting he's from "three generations of Napoli restaurateurs," adding with a wink, "but living 20 years on Antigua, though I keep trying to escape." He artfully weaves both traditions: the octopus or fish soup make splendid starters, as does the tremendous traditional *sformato di* zucchini (a light, flaky pie with tomato sauce and homemade mozzarella, which also shines in the *insalata* Caprese). He effortlessly adapts his family's Aeolian recipes to Antiguan ingredients, but the wine list is patriotically Italian, with intriguing buys from Alto Adige, Campania, and the Langhe. ⊠ *Catamaran Marina, Falmouth Harbour* ☎ *268/562–2226* ⊘ *Closed Aug.–Oct. and Sun.*

$$$–$$$$ ✕ **Le Bistro.** This Antiguan institution's peach, periwinkle, and pistachio
FRENCH   accents subtly match the tile work, jade chairs, mint china, and painted
★   lighting fixtures. Trellises divide the large space into intimate sections. Chef Patrick Gaducheau delights in blending classic regional fare with indigenous ingredients, displaying an especially deft hand with delicate sauces. The kitchen now runs smoothly after bouts of inconsistency. Opt for daily specials, such as smoked marlin carpaccio with pink peppercorns, cold carrot soup with mango chutney, fresh snapper with spinach and grapefruit in thyme-perfumed lime-butter sauce, lobster medallions in basil-accented old-rum sauce with roasted red peppers, and almost anything swaddled in puff pastry. The fine wine list hits all the right spots, geographically and varietally, without outrageous markups. Co-owner Phillipa Esposito doubles as hostess and pastry chef; her passion-fruit mousse and chocolate confections are sublime. ⊠ *Hodges Bay* ☎ *268/462–3881* ⊕ *www.antigualebistro.com* ⚔ *Reservations essential* ⊘ *Closed Mon. No lunch.*

$$$–$$$$ ✕ **Le Cap Horn.** As Piaf and Aznavour compete with croaking tree frogs
FRENCH   in a trellised, plant-filled room lighted by straw lamps, it's easy to imagine yourself in a tropical St. Tropez. From the small but select menu, begin with escargots in a lovely tomato, onion, and pepper sauce (sop it up with the marvelous home-baked bread) or the ultimate in hedonism (and expense), lobster–foie gras millefeuille; then segue into tiger shrimp swimming in gossamer vanilla-lobster sauce or duck breast wrapped with mango in rice sheet floating in rum-tamarind sauce. Gustavo Belaunde (he's Peruvian of Catalan extraction) elicits fresh, delicate, almost ethereal flavors from his ingredients; his versatility is displayed in the restaurant's other half, a pizzeria replete with wood-burning oven. Finish with wife Hélène's divine desserts or a cognac and cigar.

⊠ *English Harbour* ☎ *268/460–1194* ☽ *Closed Aug., Sept., and Thurs. Closed Wed. in low season(May–July, Oct. and Nov.). No lunch.*

$$-$$$
CARIBBEAN

✗ **Papa Zouk.** Who would have thought that two jovial globe-trotting German gents could create a classic Caribbean hangout? But the madras tablecloths, fishnets festooned with Christmas lights, painted bottles of homemade hot sauces, colorful island clientele, and lilting rhythms on the sound system justify the name (*zouk* is a sultry, musical stew of soul and calypso). Seafood is king, from Guyanese butterfish to Barbudan snapper, usually served either deep-fried or steamed with a choice of such sauces as guava pepper teriyaki or tomato-basil-coriander. Tangy Caribbean bouillabaisse with garlicky Parmesan mayonnaise and fish 'n' rum (spike it with a vinegar hot sauce) are specialties, as are the knockout rum punches. Finish dinner with a snifter of aged rum: the tiny bar holds 250 varieties from around the globe. Dine family-style in front or more intimately in back. ⊠ *Hilda Davis Dr., Gambles Terrace, St. John's* ☎ *268/464–7576* ▤ *No credit cards* ☽ *Closed May–Oct. and Sun. No lunch sometimes; call ahead for hrs.*

$$-$$$
CARIBBEAN

✗ **Russell's.** Convivial owner Russell Hodge had the brilliant idea of restoring a part of Ft. James, with its glorious views of the bay and headlands, and converting it into a semi-alfresco eatery. Potted plants, jazz on the sound system (live musicians Friday and Sunday), and red or black hurricane lamps lend a romantic aura to the beamed, stone-and-wood terrace. The limited menu—local specialties emphasizing seafood—includes fabulous chunky conch fritters and whelks in garlic butter. Russell's sister Faye co-owns Papa Zouk, and sister Valerie runs Shirley Heights Lookout; the Hodges might well be Antigua's first family of food. ⊠ *Fort James* ☎ *268/462–5479* ☽ *No lunch Sun.*

$$-$$$
ECLECTIC
★

✗ **Sheer Rocks.** This sensuous eatery, a series of tiered wood decks carved into a sheer cliff side, showcases the setting sun from the staggered, thatched dining nooks, many separated by billowing white-gauze curtains. Large white beds surround plunge pools, making it equally sybaritic for daytime lounging. The menu encompasses a tapestry of creative tapas that can be served in larger portions. Chef Alex Grimley's philosophy emphasizes simplicity, detail, and only the best ingredients to create a symphonic counterpoint of flavors and textures—subtle to lusty, crispy to creamy. Witness seared scallops with crispy pork and pumpkin puree; caramelized red onion tart with roasted beetroot, goat cheese, and fine herbs; or baked mahimahi with red-pepper pesto and aubergine cannelloni. Add a dash of sultry music, season with smashing views, complement with an admirable wine list (not to mention inventive cocktails), and you have the recipe for a tropical St. Tropez experience. ⊠ *CocoBay, Valley Church* ☎ *268/562–4510* ⌑ *Reservations essential* ☽ *Closed Tues. No dinner Sun. No lunch Mon., Wed., and Thurs.*

$$-$$$
CARIBBEAN

✗ **Sticky Wicket.** With a dining room framed by flagstone columns and a trendy, open kitchen, this is one of the classiest sports bars imaginable. Cricket is the overriding theme: sit in the posh lounge surrounded by cricket memorabilia or outside on the patio overlooking the equally handsome Stanford Cricket Ground. The menu ranges from snacks, such as near-definitive conch fritters and a fine po'boy sandwich, to standouts like shrimp Provençal or anything from the enormous rotisserie. The potent house cocktails and daily specials, not to mention the ambience, remain pure Antillean. This is a splendid respite while waiting for your flight at the airport across the road. ✉ *20 Pavilion Dr., Coolidge* ☎ *268/481–7000.*

$$$$ ✕ **The Tides.** A marine motif from food to decor distinguishes this hand-
CONTINENTAL some seaside eatery. The look subtly suggests a yacht: decks on either side, steering wheels, oars hung as artwork, and petrified driftwood mobiles, as well as antique Asian carved doors and lovely local ceramics for color. Although the kitchen isn't quite shipshape, it isn't ship-wrecked, making visits to several gastronomic ports of call from the Mediterranean to the Pacific Rim. Start with crispy duck spring rolls or seared sea scallops with mixed greens and julienne fennel splashed with passion-fruit dressing, then segue to snapper meunière with cinnamon-pumpkin puree and deep-fried leeks or Black Angus sirloin with wild mushroom sauce. More affordable, lunch emphasizes wraps and paninis, alongside more ambitious offerings like the almost-by-the-book bouillabaisse. Management also runs several charming, affordable beachfront cottages next door. ✉ *Dutchman's Bay* ☎ *268/462–8433* ⊘ *Closed Aug., Mon., and Tues.*

WHERE TO STAY

Scattered along Antigua's beaches and hillsides are exclusive, elegant hideaways; romantic restored inns; and all-inclusive hot spots for couples. Check individual lodgings for restrictions (many have minimum stays during certain high-season periods). Look also for specials on the Web or from tour packagers, since hotels' quoted rack rates are often negotiable (up to 45% off in season). There are several new condo and villa developments; although not reviewed in this edition, Sugar Ridge opened in December 2009 in the Jolly Harbour area (despite nice if smallish units, elegant setting, Aveda Spa, and fine upscale restaurant, it may suffer from the lack of beachfront). Tamarind Hills is one of several other major developments slated to open between mid-2011 and 2013. *The following reviews have been condensed for this book. Please go to Fodors.com for expanded reviews of each property.*

$ ⊡ **Admiral's Inn.** This Georgian brick edifice, originally the shipwright's
B&B/INN offices in what is now Nelson's Dockyard, has withstood acts of God
★ and war since the early 18th century. **Pros:** historic ambience; central English Harbour location; fine value; charming restaurant setting. **Cons:** occasionally noisy when yachties take over the bar; recently remodeled bathrooms are still cramped; no beach. ✉ *English Harbour* ⌂ *Box 713, St. John's* ☎ *268/460–1027* ⊕ *www.admiralsantigua.com* ⤴ *14 rooms, 1 2-bedroom apartment* ⌂ *In-room: no TV (some), Wi-Fi. In-hotel: restaurant, bar, water sports, business center* ❏ *No meals.*

$$$$ ⊡ **Blue Waters Hotel.** A well-heeled Brit crowd goes barefoot at this
RESORT swank yet understated seaside retreat. **Pros:** pomp without pretension;
★ exquisite setting; trendy minimalist decor. **Cons:** small beachfront; little steps along the hillside make it less accessible for the physically challenged; trendy minimalist decor; difficulty obtaining reservations at Vyvien's at peak times. ✉ *Boon Point, Soldiers Bay* ⌂ *Box 256,*

St. John's ☎ *268/462–0290, 800/557–6536 reservations only* ⊕ *www. bluewaters.net* ⬦ *65 rooms, 32 suites, 3 villas, 4 penthouses* ♿ *In-room: safe, Internet, Wi-Fi. In-hotel: restaurants, room service, tennis court, bars, children's programs, pools, gym, spa, beach, business center, water sports* ⊙ *Closed Sept.* ⊺⊙⊺ *All-inclusive.*

$$$$
RESORT
★
Carlisle Bay. This cosmopolitan, boutique sister property of London's trendy One Aldwych hotel daringly eschews everything faux colonial and Creole. **Pros:** luxury resort; attentive service; family-friendly. **Cons:** family-friendly; aggressively hip; lovely beach but often murky water; pricey restaurants; no elevators. ✉ *Carlisle Bay, Old Road, St. Mary's* ✒ *Box 2288, St. John's* ☎ *268/484–0000, 866/502–2855 reservations only* ⊕ *www.carlisle-bay.com* ⬦ *88 suites* ♿ *In-room: kitchen (some), Wi-Fi. In-hotel: restaurants, room service, tennis courts, bars, children's programs, pool, gym, spa, beach, business center, water sports* ⊙ *Closed late Aug.–early Oct.* ⊺⊙⊺ *Breakfast.*

$
HOTEL
★
Catamaran Hotel. The main building at the congenial cozy harborfront "Cat Club" evokes a plantation greathouse with verandahs, white columns, and hand-carved doors. **Pros:** intimacy; central location; friendly staff; children under 12 stay free. **Cons:** small beach (swimming not advised); smallish rooms; surrounding area has limited dining and nightlife options during off-season (May–November). ✉ *Falmouth Harbour* ✒ *Box 958, St. John's* ☎ *268/460–1036 or 800/223–6510* ⊕ *www.catamaran-antigua.com* ⬦ *12 rooms, 2 suites* ♿ *In-room: safe, kitchen. In-hotel: restaurant, bar, pool, beach, business center, water sports* ⊺⊙⊺ *No meals.*

$$$
RESORT
CocoBay. This healing hideaway on a hillside aims to "eliminate all potential worries" by emphasizing simple natural beauty and West Indian warmth. **Pros:** emphasis on local nature and culture; beautiful views; nice main pool and bar area; generally pleasant helpful staff. **Cons:** mediocre food; stifling on breezeless days; difficult climb for those with mobility problems; smallish beaches; bar closes early; poor bedroom lighting. ✉ *Valley Church* ✒ *Box 431, St. John's* ☎ *268/562–2400 or 866/692–6094* ⊕ *www.cocobayresort.com* ⬦ *49 rooms, 4 2-bedroom houses* ♿ *In-room: no a/c (some), safe, no TV. In-hotel: restaurants, bar, pool, gym, spa, beach, business center, water sports* ⊺⊙⊺ *All-inclusive.*

$$$$
RESORT
Fodor's Choice
★
Curtain Bluff. An incomparable beachfront setting, impeccable service, superb extras (free scuba diving and deep-sea fishing), effortless elegance: Curtain Bluff is that rare retreat that stays modern while exuding a magical timelessness. **Pros:** luxury lodging; sublime food; beautiful beaches; incredible extras. **Cons:** some find clientele standoffish; lodgings atop bluff not ideal for those with mobility problems; despite offering value, pricey by most standards; limited menu selection. ✉ *Morris Bay* ✒ *Box 288, St. John's* ☎ *268/462–8400, 888/289–9898 for reservations* ⊕ *www.curtainbluff.com* ⬦ *18 rooms, 54 suites* ♿ *In-room: safe, no TV, Wi-Fi. In-hotel: restaurants, tennis courts, bar, children's programs, pool, gym, spa, beach, business center, water sports* ⊙ *Closed early Aug.–Oct.* ⊺⊙⊺ *All-inclusive.*

$
RENTAL
★
Dickenson Bay Cottages. Lush landscaping snakes around the two-story buildings and pool at this small hillside complex, which offers

The beach at Curtain Bluff Hotel Resort.

excellent value for families. **Pros:** relatively upscale comfort at down-home prices; walking distance to Dickenson Bay dining and activities. **Cons:** hike from beach; lacks cross-breeze in many units. ⊠ *Marble Hill* ⌂ *Box 1379, St. John's* ☎ *268/462–4940* ⊕ *www. dickensonbaycottages.com* ⤴ *11 units* ⚄ *In-room: safe, kitchen, Wi-Fi. In-hotel: pool* |◎| *No meals.*

$$$$
RESORT
★

⚄ **Galley Bay.** This posh all-inclusive channels the fictional Bali H'ai (with colonial architectural flourishes) on 40 impossibly lush acres. **Pros:** luxury lodging; gorgeous beach and grounds, including new croquet lawn; impeccable maintenance; fine food by all-inclusive standards. **Cons:** some lodgings are claustrophobic and lack a view; outdoor spa can get hot; surf is often too strong for weaker swimmers; only suites have tubs; no waitstaff service on the long beach. ⊠ *Five Islands* ⌂ *Box 305, St. John's* ☎ *268/462–0302 or 866/237–1644, 800/858–4618 reservations only* ⊕ *www.galleybayresort.com* ⤴ *98 rooms* ⚄ *In-room: safe, Wi-Fi (some). In-hotel: restaurants, tennis court, bars, pools, gym, spa, beach, business center, water sports, some age restrictions* ⊙ *Closed mid-Aug.–early Sept.* |◎| *All-inclusive.*

$$–$$$
RESORT
★

⚄ **Jolly Beach Resort.** If you're looking for basic sun-sand-surf fun, this active resort—Antigua's largest—fits the bill for few bills, luring a gregarious blend of honeymooners, families, and singles. **Pros:** inexpensive; great range of activities for the price; nice beach; good food for a cheaper all-inclusive. **Cons:** many cramped, ugly rooms; overrun by tour groups; often impersonal service; lack of elevators and rambling layout make it difficult for the physically challenged. ⊠ *Jolly Harbour* ⌂ *Box 2009, Bolans Village* ☎ *268/462–0061 or 866/905–6559* ⊕ *www.jollybeachresort.com* ⤴ *461 units, 2 2-bedroom cottages, 1*

1-bedroom cottage ⚐ In-room: safe, Wi-Fi (some). In-hotel: restaurants, tennis courts, bars, children's programs, pools, gym, spa, beach, business center, water sports ⦿ All-inclusive.

$
RENTAL

▦ **Jolly Harbour Villas.** These duplex, two-bedroom villas ring the marina of a sprawling, 500-acre compound offering every conceivable facility from restaurants and shops to a casino and golf course. **Pros:** nice beach; good value; plentiful recreational, dining, and nightlife choices nearby. **Cons:** mosquito problems; reports of hidden surcharges; inability to charge most restaurants and activities to your villa; some units have 220-volt outlets requiring adapters. ✉ *Jolly Harbour ⌂ Box 1793, St. John's* ☏ *268/462–6166* ⊕ *www.jollyharbourantigua.com and hbkvillas.com/* ⇨ *150 villas ⚐ In-room: safe, kitchen. In-hotel: golf course, restaurants, tennis courts, bars, children's programs, pools, beach, business center, water sports ⦿ No meals.*

$$$$
☾
★

▦ **Jumby Bay.** This refined resort proffers all the makings of a classic Caribbean private island hideaway, right from the stylish airport limo pickup, private launch, dockside greeting, and registration at your leisure. **Pros:** isolated private island location; sterling cuisine; complimentary Caloi bicycles; free nightly movies in the screening room; thoughtful extras upon request such as cooking classes and wireless baby monitors. **Cons:** isolated private island location; jet noise occasionally disturbs the main beach. ✉ *Long Island ⌂ Box 243, St. John's* ☏ *268/462–6000* ⊕ *www.jumbybayresort.com* ⇨ *40 suites, 22 villas ⚐ In-room: safe, Wi-Fi. In-hotel: restaurants, room service, tennis courts, bars, children's programs, pools, gym, spa, beach, business center, water sports ⦿ All-inclusive.*

¢–$
B&B/INN

▦ **Ocean Inn.** Views of English Harbour, affable management, and affordability distinguish this homey inn. **Pros:** fabulous views; affable staff; inexpensive. **Cons:** rickety paths down a steep hill linking cottages; worn rooms need updating; Wi-Fi dodgy; gym is very basic and public. ✉ *English Harbour ⌂ Box 838, St. John's* ☏ *268/463–7950* ⊕ *www.theoceaninn.com* ⇨ *6 rooms, 4 with bath; 4 cottages ⚐ In-room: Wi-Fi. In-hotel: bar, pool, gym, business center ⦿ Breakfast.*

$$$$
RESORT

▦ **Sandals Grande Antigua Resort & Spa.** The sumptuous public spaces, lovely beach, glorious gardens, and plethora of facilities almost mask this once-sterling resort's impersonal atmosphere and often apathetic service. **Pros:** lovely beach; excellent spa; good dining options. **Cons:** sprawling layout; too bustling; uneven service. ✉ *Dickenson Bay ⌂ Box 147, St. John's* ☏ *268/462–0267, 888/726–3257 reservations only* ⊕ *www.sandals.com* ⇨ *100 rooms, 257 suites, 16 rondavels ⚐ In-room: safe, Wi-Fi (some). In-hotel: restaurants, room service, tennis courts, bars, pools, gym, spa, beach, business center, water sports, some age restrictions* ⌖ *3-night minimum ⦿ All-inclusive.*

$–$$
HOTEL
Fodor'sChoice
★

▦ **Siboney Beach Club.** This affordable beachfront oasis nestled in a tranquil corner of Dickenson Bay delights with intimacy and warmth, and knowledgeable Aussie owner Tony Johnson gladly acts as a de facto tourist board. **Pros:** friendly service; superb location; great value; well maintained with rooms smartly refurbished regularly. **Cons:** no TV in bedrooms; aging kitchenettes really best only for breakfast; patios lack screens, thus forcing a choice between sweltering and swatting pests

CLOSE UP

Other Lodgings to Consider on Antigua

We can't include every property deserving mention without creating an encyclopedia. Consider the following accommodations, many of which are popular with tour operators.

Antigua Yacht Club Marina & Resort (✉ *Falmouth Harbour* ☎ *268/562–3030 or 888/790–5264* ⊕ *www.aycmarina. com*) is a handsome collection of 19 hotel rooms and 24 studio and one-bedroom condos (for rent when owners are off-island), climbing a hill with stunning marina views. Accommodations are stylish if spare, with island crafts and the occasional high-tech amenity; the adjacent marina is a center of nautical hubbub with several restaurants, pubs, and shops.

Coconut Beach Club (✉ *Yepton Beach* ☎ *268/462–3239 or 800/361–4621* ⊕ *www.coconutbeachclub.com*) is on a beach overlooking the ruins of Ft. James. The food in the restaurants creative; all units feature smashing sea views, and the price is right—for now.

Grand Pineapple Beach Resort (✉ *Long Bay* ☎ *268/463–2006 or 800/327–1991* ⊕ *www. grandpineapple.com*) is a

Sandals-owned, Sandals-branded all-inclusive (formerly Allegro/Occidental) on a tranquil beach amid lush landscaping. It's in the midst of ongoing renovations, restoring its sheen. Buildings and 180 rooms feature almost edible pastel hues inside and out; the beachfront units and 500 block offer smashing east-coast views.

Hermitage Bay (✉ *Hermitage Bay* ☎ *268/562–5500* ⊕ *www. hermitagebay.com*) is a deluxe enclave of 30 beachfront and hillside cottages on a secluded, hard-to-reach but pretty stretch of sand. Affecting a look and ambience that borrow from both Carlisle Bay and Curtain Bluff, the minimalist-chic lodgings include a garden shower and private plunge pool.

Rex Halcyon Cove Beach Resort (✉ *Dickenson Bay* ☎ *268/462–9256 or 800/255–5859* ⊕ *www.rexresorts. com*) is a large, impersonal but admirably outfitted resort (from dive shop to car rental) on one of Antigua's top beaches. Buildings are a bit institutional-looking and you'll have to watch out for stampeding tour groups; however, you can usually find good package deals here.

---

on rare still days; no elevator; inconsistent Wi-Fi signal. ✉ *Dickenson Bay* ⌂ *Box 222, St. John's* ☎ *268/462–0806 or 800/533–0234* ⊕ *www. siboneybeachclub.com* ⇥ *12 suites* ⌂ *In-room: safe, kitchen, Wi-Fi. In-hotel: restaurant, bar, pool, beach, business center* ⓧ *No meals.*

$$$$
RESORT
⌂ **St. James's Club.** Management has diligently smartened the public spaces and exquisite landscaping here, taking full advantage of the peerless location straddling 100 acres on Mamora Bay. **Pros:** splendid remote location; beautiful beaches and landscaping; complimentary Wi-Fi in public areas; long-overdue ongoing upgrades improving the property; plentiful activities; additional adult pools offer more privacy. **Cons:** remote location makes a car a necessity for non-all-inclusive guests; tour groups can overrun the resort; uneven food and service; sprawling hilly layout not ideal for physically challenged. ✉ *Mamora Bay* ⌂ *Box 63, St. John's* ☎ *268/460–5000 or 800/858–4618* ⊕ *www.*

eliteislandresorts.com ⤳ *234 rooms, 72 villas (usually 17 in rental pool)* ⌂ *In-room: safe, Wi-Fi (some). In-hotel: restaurants, room service, tennis courts, bars, children's programs, pools, gym, spa, beach, business center, water sports* ¶◯¶ *All-inclusive.*

$$$$ ⊞ **Verandah Resort & Spa.** Though local activists disagree, this ecocentric
RESORT resort on Antigua's wild east coast emphasizes low-impact environmental
⌣ responsibility without sacrificing upscale contemporary conveniences.
★ **Pros:** gorgeous remote location; sprawling but cleverly centralized; good
kids' facilities with own pool. **Cons:** remote location makes a car a
necessity to explore; smallish beaches; inconsistent food and service.
🖾 *Long Bay* ⌂ *Box 54, St. Philips* ☎ *268/562–6848 or 800/858–4618,
866/237–1785 reservations only* ⊕ *www.verandahresortandspa.com*
⤳ *200 suites* ⌂ *In-room: safe, kitchen, Wi-Fi (some). In-hotel: restaurants, tennis courts, bars, children's programs, pools, gym, spa, beach, business center, water sports* ¶◯¶ *All-inclusive.*

NIGHTLIFE

Most of Antigua's evening entertainment takes place at the resorts, which occasionally present calypso singers, steel bands, limbo dancers, and folkloric groups. Check with the tourist office for up-to-date information. In addition, a cluster of clubs and bars pulsate into the night in season around English and Falmouth Harbours.

BARS

It's always a party at busy, bright trattoria **Abracadabra** (🖾 *Nelson's Dockyard, English Harbour* ☎ *268/460–2701*). Late nights often turn into a disco with live music or DJs spinning reggae and 1980s dance music, and special events run from art exhibits to masquerades to fashion shows.

Carmichael's (🖾 *Tottenham Park, across from Jolly Harbour* ☎ *268/562–7700* ⊕ *www.sugarridgeantigua.com*) is the fine-dining hilltop aerie at the Sugar Ridge residential complex. Nestle into a banquette or lounge in the infinity pool while sipping luscious libations that match the setting sun's colorful display. It's also a splendid spot for a postprandial cigar and port or single malt. You can always head downhill to sister nightspot, the bustling buzzing **Sugar Club** (by the resort entrance) for live music (jazz to funk) and DJ disco evenings.

Castaways (🖾 *Jolly Harbour* ☎ *268/562–4445*) is a boisterous beach bar–bistro with a thatched roof, kids' playground and colorful local murals that serves an inexpensive menu of tapas and pub grub along with occasional entertainment.

★ **Indigo on the Beach** (🖾 *Carlisle Bay, Old Road* ☎ *268/480–0000*) is a soigné yet relaxed spot any time of day for creative tapas, salads, grills, and burgers, but the beautiful people turn out in force come evening to pose at the fiber-optically lighted bar, or on white lounges scattered with throw pillows.

The **Inn at English Harbour Bar** (🖾 *English Harbour* ☎ *268/460–1014*), with its green leather, wood beams, fieldstone walls, 19th-century maps, steering-wheel chandeliers, petit point upholstery, and maritime prints, is uncommonly refined.

The **Mad Mongoose** (⊠ *Falmouth Harbour* ☎ 268/463–7900) is a wildly popular yachty (and singles') joint, splashed in vivid Rasta colors, with tapas and martini menus, live music Tuesday and Friday, a game room, and satellite TV.

The **Mainbrace Pub** (⊠ *Copper & Lumber Store Hotel, English Harbour* ☎ 268/460–1058) has a historic ambience and is known as a beer, darts, and fish-and-chips kind of hangout for the boating set.

★ **Shirley Heights Lookout** (⊠ *Shirley Heights* ☎ 268/460–1785) hosts Sunday-afternoon barbecues that continue into the night with reggae, soca, and steel-band music and dancing that sizzle like the ribs on the grill. Residents and visitors gather for boisterous fun, the latest gossip, and great sunsets. Most tourist groups vanish by 7 pm, when the real partying begins.

★ **Trappa's** (⊠ *Main Rd., English Harbour* ☎ 268/562–3534) is a hipster hangout set in a bamboo-walled courtyard hung with huge hibiscus paintings. It serves delectable, sizable tapas (tuna sashimi, deep-fried Brie with black-currant jelly, Thai mango chicken curry, beer-batter shrimp with garlic dip) for reasonable prices (EC$23–EC$46) into the wee hours. Live music is often on the menu.

CASINOS

There are three full casinos on Antigua, as well as several holes-in-the-wall that have mostly one-arm bandits. Hours depend on the season, so it's best to inquire upon your arrival.

Grand Bay Casino (⊠ *Dickenson Bay* ☎ 268/481–7700) is delightfully garish, from gold accents to Greco-Roman urns. More than 100 slots and video-poker machines, table games, and Texas Hold 'Em tournaments compete for guests' attention with live bands, DJs, and karaoke–trivia nights.

You can find abundant slots and gaming tables at the somewhat dilapidated, unintentionally retro (icicle chandeliers, Naugahyde seats, and 1970s soul crooners on the sound system) **King's Casino** (⊠ *Heritage Quay, St. John's* ☎ 268/462–1727). The best time to go is Friday night, which jumps with energetic karaoke competitions, live bands, and dancing.

DANCE CLUBS

The Coast (⊠ *Heritage Quay, St. John's* ☎ 268/562–6278 ⊕ *www.coast. ag*) attracts a casually swanky, over-21 mix of locals and tourists for fine island food, rollicking live bands, fire-blowing bartenders, theme nights like "Wednesday Wine and Jazz," and the latest in techno and house in a dockside setting.

Rush (⊠ *Runaway Bay* ☎ 268/480—2030 or 268/480–2031) lures mostly young, lively locals in cool club gear for disco, Latin, and reggae-soca mixes; sea views from the romantic terrace; Leah's restaurant; and the Conors Billiards Lounge (which opens earlier, with happy hours and pub grub). The nightclub itself only opens Friday, but the eateries open nightly.

SHOPPING

Antigua's duty-free shops are at Heritage Quay, one reason so many cruise ships call here. Bargains can be found on perfumes, liqueurs, and liquor (including English Harbour Antiguan rum), jewelry, china, and crystal. As for other local items, check out straw hats, baskets, batik, pottery, Susie's hot sauce, and hand-printed cotton clothing. Fine artists to look for include Gilly Gobinet, Heather Doram, Jan Farara, Jennifer Meranto, and Heike Petersen (delightful dolls and quilts). Several artists and craftspeople have banded together to form ⊕ *www.antiguanartists. com*, which lists their information, including whether they accept atelier visits by appointment.

SHOPPING AREAS

Fodor's Choice
★
Redcliffe Quay, on the waterfront at the south edge of St. John's, is by far the most appealing shopping area. Several restaurants and more than 30 boutiques, many with one-of-a-kind wares, are set around landscaped courtyards shaded by colorful trees.

Heritage Quay, in St. John's, has 35 shops—including many that are duty-free—that cater to the cruise-ship crowd, which docks almost at its doorstep. Outlets here include Benetton, the Body Shop, Sunglass Hut, Dolce & Gabbana, and Oshkosh B'Gosh. There are also shops along **St. John's, St. Mary's, High,** and **Long streets.** The tangerine-and-lilac-hue four-story **Vendor's Mall** at the intersection of Redcliffe and Thames streets gathers the pushy, pesky vendors that once clogged the narrow streets. It's jammed with stalls; air-conditioned indoor shops sell some higher-price, if not higher-quality, merchandise. On the west coast the Mediterranean-style, arcaded **Jolly Harbour Marina** holds some interesting galleries and shops, as do the marinas and main road snaking around English and Falmouth Harbours.

SPECIALTY STORES

ALCOHOL AND TOBACCO
Manuel Dias Liquor Store (⊠ *Long and Market Sts., St. John's* ☎ *268/462–0490*) has a wide selection of Caribbean rums and liqueurs.

Quin Farara (⊠ *Long St. and Corn Alley, St. John's* ☎ *268/462–3869* ⊠ *Heritage Quay, St. John's* ☎ *268/462–1737* ⊠ *Jolly Harbour* ☎ *268/462–6245*) has terrific deals on both hard liquor and wines as well as cigars.

ART
Fine Art Framing (⊠ *Redcliffe Quay, St. John's* ☎ *268/562–1019*) carries Jennifer Meranto's incomparable hand-colored black-and-white photos of Caribbean scenes; Heather Doram's exquisite, intricately woven "collage" wall hangings; and ever-changing exhibits.

★ **Harmony Hall** (✉ *Brown's Mill Bay, Brown's Mill* ☎ *268/460–4120*) remains Antigua's top exhibition venue. A large exhibit space is used for one-person shows; other rooms display works in various media, from Aussie aboriginal carvings to Antillean pottery. The sublime historic ambience, sweeping vistas, and fine Italian fare compensate for the remote location.

BOOKS AND MAGAZINES

The **Best of Books** (✉ *Lower St. Mary's St., St. John's* ☎ *268/562–3198*) is an excellent, extensive source for everything from local cookbooks and nature guides to international newspapers. Check out the books of Jamaica Kincaid, whose writing about her native Antigua has won international acclaim. You'll also find an intriguing selection of crafts and artworks.

CLOTHING

Exotic Antigua (✉ *Redcliffe Quay, St. John's* ☎ *268/562–1288*) sells everything from antique Indonesian ikat throws to crepe de chine caftans to Tommy Bahama resort wear.

★ At **Galley Boutique** (✉ *Nelson's Dockyard, English Harbour* ☎ *268/460–1525*), Janey Easton personally seeks out exclusive creations from both international (Calvin Klein, Adrienne Vittadini) and local Caribbean designers, ranging from swimwear to evening garb. She also sells handicrafts and lovely hammocks.

Jacaranda (✉ *Redcliffe Quay, St. John's* ☎ *268/462–1888*) sells batik, sarongs, and swimwear as well as Caribbean food, perfumes, soaps, and artwork.

New Gates (✉ *Redcliffe Quay, St. John's* ☎ *268/562–1627*) is a duty-free authorized dealer for such name brands as Ralph Lauren, Calvin Klein, and Tommy Hilfiger.

★ **Noreen Phillips** (✉ *Redcliffe Quay, St. John's* ☎ *268/462–3127*) creates glitzy appliquéd and beaded evening wear—inspired by the colors of the sea and sunset—in sensuous fabrics ranging from chiffon and silk to Italian lace and Indian brocade.

Sunseakers (✉ *Heritage Quay, St. John's* ☎ *268/462–3618*) racks up every conceivable bathing suit and cover-up—from bikini thongs to sarongs—by top designers.

DUTY-FREE GOODS

Abbott's (✉ *Heritage Quay, St. John's* ☎ *268/462–3108*) sells luxury items from Breitling watches to Belleek china to Kosta Boda art glass in a luxurious, air-conditioned showroom.

Lipstick (✉ *Heritage Quay, St. John's* ☎ *268/562–1130*) imports high-priced scents and cosmetics, from Clarins to Clinique and Givenchy to Guerlain.

Passions (✉ *Heritage Quay, St. John's* ☎ *268/562–5295*) gives Abbott's a run for its (and your) considerable money on luxury brands like Chanel, Hermès, and Lalique.

HANDICRAFTS

★ **Cedars Pottery** (⊠ *St. Claire Estate, Buckleys* ☎ *268/460–5293*) is the airy studio of Michael and Imogen Hunt. Michael produces a vivid line of domestic ware and Zen-simple teapots, vases, and water fountains featuring rich earth hues and sensuous lines. Imogen fashions ethereal paper-clay fish sculptures, and mask-shaped, intricately laced light fixtures and candelabras.

Eureka (⊠ *Thames St., St. John's* ☎ *268/560–3654*) spans the globe, from Azerbaijani handblown glass to Zambian weavings and carvings.

Isis (⊠ *Redcliffe Quay, St. John's* ☎ *268/462–4602*) sells island and international bric-a-brac, such as antique jewelry, hand-carved walking sticks, and glazed pottery.

The **Pottery Shop** (⊠ *Redcliffe Quay, St. John's* ☎ *268/562–1264 or 268/462–5503*) sells the work of gifted potter Sarah Fuller, whose hand-painted tiles, wind chimes, and plates and cobalt-blue glazes are striking. You can also visit her studio–gallery on Dutchman's Bay.

★ **Rhythm of Blue Gallery** (⊠ *Dockyard Dr., English Harbour* ☎ *268/562–2230*) is co-owned by Nancy Nicholson, who's renowned for her exquisite glazed and matte-finish ceramics, featuring Caribbean-pure shades, as well as her black-and-white yachting photos.

★ **Things Local** (⊠ *Nelson's Dockyard, English Harbour* ☎ *268/562–5386, 268/461–7595, or 268/770–5780*) features the wondrous wood carvings of Carl Henry, who fashions local mahogany into boats, fish, and warri boards (an African game brought over to the Caribbean).

JEWELRY

Colombian Emeralds (⊠ *Heritage Quay, St. John's* ☎ *268/462–3462*) is the largest retailer of Colombian emeralds in the world and also carries a wide variety of other gems.

Diamonds International (⊠ *Heritage Quay, St. John's* ☎ *268/481–1880*) has a huge selection of loose diamonds as well as a variety of rings, brooches, bracelets, and pendants. Several resorts have branches.

★ The **Goldsmitty** (⊠ *Redcliffe Quay, St. John's* ☎ *268/462–4601*) is Hans Smit, an expert goldsmith who turns gold, black coral, and precious and semiprecious stones into one-of-a-kind works of art.

SPORTS AND ACTIVITIES

Several all-inclusives offer day passes that permit use of all sporting facilities from tennis courts to water-sports concessions, as well as free drinks and meals. The cost begins at $50 for singles (but can be as much as $200 for couples at Sandals), and hours generally run from 8 am to 6 pm, with extensions available until 2 am. Antigua has long been famed for its cricketers (such as Viv Richards and Richie Richardson); aficionados will find one of the Caribbean's finest cricket grounds right by the airport, with major test matches running January through June.

ADVENTURE TOURS

Antigua is developing its ecotourist opportunities, and several memorable offshore experiences involve more than just snorkeling. The archipelago of islets coupled with a full mangrove swamp off the northeast coast is unique in the Caribbean.

★ **Adventure Antigua** (☎ *268/727–3261 or 268/726–6355* ⊕ *www. adventureantigua.com*) is run by enthusiastic Eli Fuller, who is knowledgeable not only about the ecosystem and geography of Antigua but also about its history and politics (his grandfather was the American consul). His thorough seven-hour excursion (Eli dubs it "re-creating my childhood explorations") includes stops at Guiana Island (for lunch and guided snorkeling; turtles, barracuda, and stingrays are common sightings), Pelican Island (more snorkeling), Bird Island (hiking to vantage points to admire the soaring ospreys and frigate and red-billed tropic birds), and Hell's Gate (a striking limestone rock formation where the more intrepid may hike and swim through sunken caves and tide pools painted with pink and maroon algae). The company also offers a fun, shorter "Xtreme amusement park ride" variation on a racing boat catering to adrenaline junkies who "feel the need for speed" that also visits Stingray City, as well as a more sedate Antigua Classic Yacht sail-and-snorkel experience that explains the rich West Indian history of boatbuilding.

★ **"Paddles" Kayak Eco Adventure** (⊠ *Seaton's Village* ☎ *268/463–1944* ⊕ *www.antiguapaddles.com*) takes you on a 3½-hour tour of serene mangroves and inlets with informative narrative about the fragile ecosystem of the swamp and reefs and the rich diversity of flora and fauna. The tour ends with a hike to sunken caves and snorkeling in the North Sound Marine Park, capped by a rum punch at the fun Creole-style clubhouse. Experienced guides double as kayaking and snorkeling instructors, making this an excellent opportunity for novices. Conrad and Jennie's brainchild is one of Antigua's better bargains.

☾ **Stingray City Antigua** (⊠ *Seaton's Village* ☎ *268/562–7297* ⊕ *www. stingraycityantigua.com*) is a carefully reproduced "natural" environment nicknamed by staffers the "retirement home," though the 30-plus stingrays, ranging from infants to seniors, are frisky. You can stroke, feed, even hold the striking gliders, as well as snorkel in deeper, protected waters. The tour guides do a marvelous job of explaining the animals' habits, from feeding to breeding, and their predators (including man).

BOATING

Antigua's circular geographic configuration makes boating easy, and its many lovely harbors and coves provide splendid anchorages. Experienced boaters will particularly enjoy Antigua's east coast, which is far more rugged and has several islets; be sure to get a good nautical map, as there are numerous minireefs that can be treacherous. If you're just looking for a couple of hours of wave hopping, stick to the Dickenson Bay or Jolly Harbour area.

Nicholson Yacht Charters (☎ *268/460–1530 or 305/433–5533* ⊕ *www. nicholson-charters.com*) are real professionals, true pioneers in Caribbean sailing, with three generations spanning 60 years of experience. A long-established island family, they can offer you anything from a 20-foot ketch to a giant schooner.

Ondeck (☎ *268/562–6696* ⊕ *www.ondeckoceanracing.com*) runs skippered charters on the likes of Farr and Beneteau out of the Antigua Yacht Club Marina in Falmouth Harbour, terrific one- and two-day sailing workshops, and eco-adventure trips to Montserrat on a racing yacht. You can even participate in official regattas. Instructors and crew are all seasoned racers.

Sunsail (☎ *268/460–2615 or 800/327–2276* ⊕ *www.sunsail.com*) has an extensive modern fleet of dinghies and 32-foot day-sailers starting at $25 per half day, $50 for a full day. It also arranges bareboat yachting, often in conjunction with hotel stays.

DIVING

Antigua is an unsung diving destination, with plentiful undersea sights to explore, from coral canyons to sea caves. Barbuda alone features roughly 200 wrecks on its treacherous reefs. The most accessible wreck is the 1890s bark *Andes,* not far out in Deep Bay, off Five Islands Peninsula. Among the favorite sites are **Green Island, Cades Reef,** and **Bird Island** (a national park). Memorable sightings include turtles, stingrays, and barracuda darting amid basalt walls, hulking boulders, and stray 17th-century anchors and cannon. One advantage is accessibility in many spots for shore divers and snorkelers. Double-tank dives run about $90.

Dive Antigua (✉ *Rex Halcyon Cove Beach Resort, Dickenson Bay* ☎ *268/462–3483* ⊕ *www.diveantigua.com*) offers certification courses and day and night dives. Advantages include the central location, knowledgeable crew, satellite technology sounding the day's best dive sites, free drinks after dives, and exceptionally priced packages. Drawbacks include generally noisy groups and inconsistent maintenance (less safety than hygiene concerns).

Dockyard Divers (✉ *Nelson's Dockyard, English Harbour* ☎ *268/460–1178* ⊕ *www.dockyard-divers.com*), owned by British ex-merchant seaman Captain A. G. "Tony" Fincham, is one of the island's most established outfits and offers diving and snorkeling trips, PADI courses, and dive packages with accommodations. They're geared to seasoned divers, but staff work patiently with novices. Tony is a wonderful source of information on the island; ask him about the "Fincham's Follies" musical extravaganza he produces for charity.

FISHING

Antigua's waters teem with game fish such as marlin, wahoo, and tuna. Most boat trips include equipment, lunch, and drinks. Figure at least $495 for a half day, $790 for a full day, for up to six people.

The 45-foot Hatteras Sportfisherman *Obsession* (☎ 268/462–2824) has top-of-the-line equipment, including an international-standard fighting chair, outriggers, and handcrafted rods.

Overdraft (☎ 268/720–4954 or 268/463–3112 ⊕ www.antiguafishing. com) is a sleek, spacious, fiberglass 40-footer outfitted with the latest techno-gadgetry and operated by Frank Hart, a professional fisherman who knows the waters intimately and regales clients with stories of his trade. He also rents the 26-foot *H2O,* a ProKat versatile enough to accommodate fly-fishing and deeper-water bay bait fishing.

GOLF

Though Antigua hardly qualifies as a duffer's delight, its two 18-hole courses offer varied layouts.

Cedar Valley Golf Club (✉ Friar's Hill ☎ 268/462–0161 ⊕ www. cedarvalleygolf.ag), northeast of St. John's, has a driving range and par-70, 6,157-yard, 18-hole course. The not terribly well-maintained terrain offers some challenges with tight hilly fairways and numerous doglegs (Hole 7 is a perfect example). The 5th hole has exceptional ocean vistas from the top of the tee, and the par-5 9th offers the trickiest design with steep slopes and swales. Greens fees are $49 ($25 for 9 holes); carts are $42 ($22 for 9 holes).

Jolly Harbour Golf Course (✉ Jolly Harbour ☎ 268/462–7771 Ext. 608) is a par-71, 6,001-yard (officially, but it's really 5,587 yards from the back tees), 18-hole course designed by Karl Litten. The flat Florida-style layout is lushly tropical, with seven lakes adding to the challenge. The 15th is the signature hole, with a sharp dogleg and long carry over two hazards. Unfortunately, fairways are often dry and patchy, drainage is poor, and the pro shop and "19th hole" are barely adequate. Greens fees are $57.50 ($97.75 including motorized cart) or $34.50/$23 for 9 holes. Visitors can participate in regular tournaments and "meet-and-greet" events.

GUIDED TOURS

Almost all taxi drivers double as guides; an island tour with one costs about $25 an hour. Every major hotel has a cabbie on call and may be able to negotiate a discount, particularly off-season. Several operators specialize in off-road four-wheel-drive adventures that provide a taste of island history and topography. **D&J Tours** (☎ 268/773–9766) offers day-trippers the chance to experience Barbuda on a round-trip flight with a beach picnic and full tour for $120. Four-wheel off-road adventures by **Island Safaris** (☎ 268/480–1225 ⊕ www.tropicaladventures-antigua. com), which also runs other land- and water-based excursions, enables you to fully appreciate the island's natural beauty, history, folklore, and cultural heritage as you zoom about the southwest part of Antigua. Hiking is involved, though it's not strenuous. Lunch and snorkeling are also included. Active adventurers will particularly enjoy the combo Land Rover–kayak outback ecotour. Prices start at $99 per adult, $60–$75 children 7–12. **Scenic Tours** (✉ Woods Mall, St. John's ☎ 268/764–3060

⊕ *www.scenictoursantigua.com*) gives affordable half- and full-day island tours, geared toward cruise passengers, that focus on such highlights as Shirley Heights and English Harbour, as well as soft adventure hikes.

HORSEBACK RIDING

Comparatively dry Antigua is best for beach rides, though you won't find anything wildly romantic and deserted à la *Black Stallion*. **Spring Hill Riding Club** (⊠ *Falmouth Harbour* ☎ *268/460–7787, 268/773–3139, or 268/460–1333* ⊕ *www.springhillridingclub.com*) specializes in equestrian lessons in show jumping and dressage but also offers $50 hour-long trail rides on the beach or through the bush past ruined forts (swimming is an additional $20); half-hour private lessons from a British Horse Society instructor are $25.

SAILING AND SNORKELING

Not a sailor yourself? Consider signing up for one of the following boat tours. Each tour provides a great opportunity to enjoy the seafaring life while someone else captains the ship.

Miguel's Holiday Adventures (☎ *268/460–9978, 268/772–3213, or 268/723–7418* ⊕ *www.pricklypearisland.com*) leaves every Tuesday, Thursday, and Saturday morning at 10 am from the Hodges Bay jetty for snorkeling, rum punches, and lunch at Prickly Pear Island, which offers both shallow- and deepwater snorkeling, as well as hiking. In this comfortable family operation, Miguel's wife, Josephine, prepares an authentic, lavish West Indian buffet including lobster, and Miguel and his son Terrence are caring instructors.

Tropical Adventures (☎ *268/480–1225* ⊕ *www.tropicaladventures-antigua.com*) operates Barbuda day trips on the catamaran *Excellence* that overflow with rum and high spirits, as do circumnavigations of Antigua. The company also operates ecokayaking tours and slightly more sedate, intimate catamaran cruises from sunset to snorkeling on the *Mystic*.

Wadadli Cats (☎ *268/462–4792* ⊕ *www.wadadlicats.com*) offers several cruises, including a circumnavigation of the island and snorkeling at Bird Island or Cades Reef, on its five sleek catamarans, including the handsome, fully outfitted *Spirit of Antigua*. Prices are fair ($95–$110) and advance direct bookers get a free T-shirt.

WINDSURFING AND KITEBOARDING

Most major hotels offer windsurfing equipment. The best areas are Nonsuch Bay and the east coast (notably Half Moon and Willoughby bays), which is slightly less protected and has a challenging juxtaposition of sudden calms and gusts.

KiteAntigua (⊠ *Jabberwock Beach* ☎ *268/720–5483 or 268/727–3983* ⊕ *www.kitesurfantigua.com*) offers lessons in the Caribbean's hot new sport, kiteboarding, where a futuristic surfboard with harness is propelled only by an inflated kite; kite-board rentals (for the certified) are also available at $30 per hour, $50 half day, $70 full day. The varied multiday lesson packages are expensive but thorough; a four-hour beginners course is $260. KiteAntigua closes from September through November, when winds aren't optimal. The center is on a stretch near the airport, but road trips to secret spots are arranged for experienced kitesurfers seeking that sometimes harrowing "high."

Patrick Scales of **Windsurfing Antigua** (⊠ *Jabberwock Beach* ☎ *268/461–9463 or 268/773–9463* ⊕ *www.windsurfantigua.net*) has long been one of Antigua's, if not the Caribbean's, finest instructors; he now offers a mobile service in high season. He provides top-flight equipment for $25 per hour ($75 per day), beginner lessons for $80, and specialty tours to Half Moon Bay and other favorite spots for experienced surfers.

ZIP-LINING

Play Tarzan and Jane at **Antigua Rainforest Canopy Tours** (⊠ *Fig Dr., Wallings* ☎ *268/562–6363* ⊕ *www.antiguarainforest.com*). You should be in fairly good condition for the ropes challenges, which require upper-body strength and stamina; there are height and weight restrictions. But anyone (vertigo or acrophobia sufferers, beware) can navigate the intentionally rickety "Indiana Jones–inspired" suspension bridges, then fly (in secure harnesses) over a rain-forest-filled valley from one towering turpentine tree to the next on lines with names like "Screamer" and "Leap of Faith." There are 21 stations, as well as a bar–café and interpretive signage. First-timers, fear not: the "rangers" are affable, amusing, and accomplished. Admission varies slightly, but is usually $85. It's open Monday–Saturday from 8 to 6.

Aruba

WORD OF MOUTH

"We usually go [to Aruba] in May, but this past year we also went there in November and found it very affordable. It's an island with beautiful beaches, exquisite dining, and wonderful, warm people. Lots to do and see, and the perfect island for romance."

—Joly226

WELCOME TO ARUBA

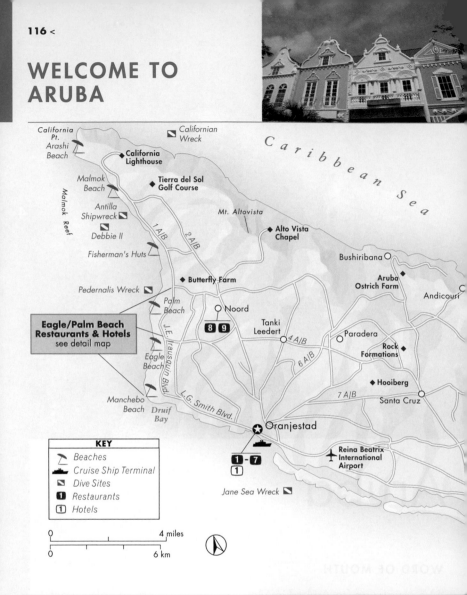

California Pt.
Arashi Beach

California Lighthouse

Californian Wreck

Caribbean Sea

Malmok Beach

Tierra del Sol Golf Course

Malmok Reef

Antilla Shipwreck

Mt. Altovista

Alto Vista Chapel

Debbie II

Bushiribana

1 A/B

2 A/B

Fisherman's Huts

Aruba Ostrich Farm

Pedernalis Wreck

Andicouri

Butterfly Farm

Palm Beach

Noord

Eagle/Palm Beach Restaurants & Hotels
see detail map

8 9

Tanki Leedert

Paradera

4 A/B

Rock Formations

6 A/B

Eagle Beach

J.E. Irausquin Blvd.

Hooiberg

7 A/B

Santa Cruz

Manchebo Beach

Druif Bay

L.G. Smith Blvd.

Oranjestad

1 - 7
1

Reina Beatrix International Airport

Jane Sea Wreck

KEY
- Beaches
- Cruise Ship Terminal
- Dive Sites
- 1 Restaurants
- 1 Hotels

0 ——————— 4 miles
0 ——————— 6 km

N

The pastel-color houses of Dutch settlers still grace the waterfront in the capital city of Oranjestad. Winds are fierce, even savage, on the north coast, where you'll find a landscape of cacti, rocky desert, and wind-bent divi-divi trees. On the west coast the steady breezes attract windsurfers to the shallow, richly colored waters.

THE A IN THE ABC ISLANDS

The A in the ABC Islands (followed by Bonaire and Curaçao), Aruba is small—only 19½ mi (31½ km) long and 6 mi (9½ km) across at its widest point. It became an independent entity within the Netherlands in 1986. The official language is Dutch, but almost every native speaks English and Spanish as well. The island's population is 104,000.

Restaurants ▼
Cuba's Cookin' **5**
El Gaucho Argentine Grill **2**
Gasparito Restaurant & Art Gallery **8**
Gostoso **4**
L. G. Smith's Steak & Chop House **1**
Marandi **3**
Matilde **4**
Papiamento **9**
Pinchos Grill & Bar **6**
Qué Pasa? **7**

Hotels ▼
Renaissance Aruba Resort & Casino .. **1**

4

ARUBA

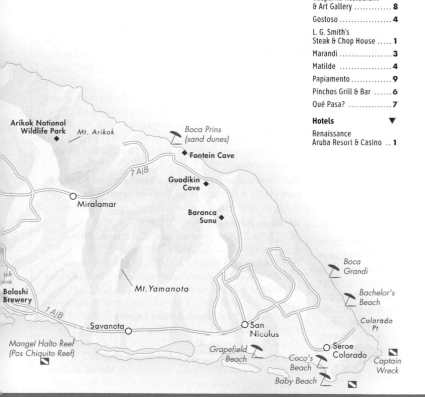

TOP REASONS TO VISIT ARUBA

1 The Nightlife: Nightlife is among the best in the Caribbean. The colorful Kukoo Kunuku party bus picks you up and pours you out at your hotel.

2 The Beaches: Powder-soft beaches and turquoise waters are legendary.

3 The Restaurants: Great restaurants offer a wide range of cuisine as good as any in the Caribbean.

4 The Casinos: Aruba's casinos will please both casual and serious gamblers.

ARUBA PLANNER

Driving Tips

International traffic signs and Dutch-style traffic signals (with an extra light for a turning lane) can be misleading if you're not used to them; use extreme caution, especially at intersections, until you grasp the rules of the road. Speed limits are rarely posted but are usually 50 mph (80 kph) in the countryside. Aside from the major highways, the island's winding roads are poorly marked. Gas prices average about $1.10 a liter (roughly ⅓ gallon), which is reasonable by Caribbean standards.

Language Tips

Everyone on the island speaks English, but the official languages are Dutch and Papiamento. Most locals speak Papiamento—a fascinating, rapid-fire mix of Spanish, Dutch, English, French, and Portuguese—in normal conversation. Here are a few helpful phrases: *bon dia* (good day), *bon nochi* (good night), *masha danki* (thank you very much).

Getting to Aruba

Hassle Factor: Low.

Nonstops: There are nonstop flights from Atlanta (Delta), Boston (American, JetBlue, US Airways), Charlotte (US Airways), Chicago (United—weekly), Fort Lauderdale (Spirit—weekly), Houston (Continental), Miami (American), Newark (Continental), New York–JFK (American, Delta, Jet-Blue), New York–LGA (Continental—weekly), Philadelphia (US Airways—twice weekly), and Washington, D.C.–Dulles (United), though not all flights are daily.

Air Travel: Many airlines fly nonstop to Aruba from several cities in North America; connections will usually be at a U.S. airport. Smaller airlines connect the Dutch islands in the Caribbean, often using Aruba as a hub. Travelers to the United States clear U.S. Customs and Immigration before leaving Aruba.

The island's state-of-the-art **Reina Beatrix International Airport** (AUA) is equipped with thorough security, many flight displays, and state-of-the-art baggage-handling systems.

American Airlines (☎ *297/582–2700 on Aruba, 800/433–7300 ⊕ www.aa.com*). **Continental Airlines** (☎ *297/588–0044 on Aruba, 800/523–3273 for U.S. and Mexico reservations, 800/231–0856 for international reservations ⊕ www.continental.com*). **Delta Airlines** (☎ *297/588–0044 on Aruba, 800/221–1212 for U.S. reservations, 800/241–4141 for international reservations ⊕ www.delta.com*). **Dutch Antilles Express** (☎ *599/717–0808 ⊕ www.flydae.com*). **JetBlue** (☎ *800/538–2583 ⊕ www.jetblue.com*). **KLM** (☎ *297/582–3546 on Aruba, 31/20–4–747–747*). **Spirit Airlines** (☎ *800/772–7117 or 586/791–7300 ⊕ www.spiritair.com*). **United Airlines** (☎ *297/588–6544 on Aruba, 800/538–2929 in North America ⊕ www.united.com*). **US Airways** (☎ *297/800–1580 on Aruba, 800/428–4322 for U.S. and Canada reservations, 800/622–1015 for international reservations ⊕ www.usairways.com*).

Getting Around Aruba	Island Activities

Getting Around Aruba

Bus Travel: Buses run hourly trips between the beach hotels and Oranjestad. The one-way fare is $1.25 ($2.25 round-trip), and exact change is preferred (so be sure to keep some U.S. change handy if you plan to pay in U.S. currency). There are also minibuses that will pick you up at the same stops for the same price; just be sure to look for the "ATA approved" sign. Buses also run down the coast from Oranjestad to San Nicolas for the same fare.

Car Travel: If you want to explore the countryside and try different beaches, then you should rent a car. Try to make reservations before arriving, and rent a four-wheel drive if you plan to explore the island's natural sights. For just getting to and around town, taxis are preferable, and you can use tour companies to arrange your activities.

To rent a car you'll need a driver's license, and you must meet the minimum age requirements of the company (Budget, for example, requires drivers to be over 25; Avis, between 23 and 70; and Hertz, over 21). A deposit of $500 (or a signed credit-card slip) is required. Rates are between $47 and $75 a day (local agencies generally have lower rates).

Contacts: Avis (⊠ Kolibristraat 14, Oranjestad ☎ 297/582–8787 ⊠ Airport ☎ 297/582–5496 ⊕ www.avis.com). **Budget** (⊠ Kolibristraat 1, Oranjestad ☎ 297/582–8600 or 800/472–3325 ⊕ www.budgetaruba.com). **Dollar** (⊠ Grendeaweg 15, Oranjestad ☎ 297/582–2783 ⊠ Airport ☎ 297/582–5651 ⊕ www.dollar.com). **Economy** (⊠ Kolibristraat 5, Oranjestad ☎ 297/582–5176 ⊕ www.economyaruba.com). **Hertz** (⊠ Sabana Blanco 35, Oranjestad, near airport ☎ 297/582–1845 ⊠ Airport ☎ 297/582–9112 ⊕ www.arubarentcar.com). **National** (⊠ Tanki Leendert 170, Noord ☎ 297/587–1967 ⊠ Airport ☎ 297/582–5451 ⊕ www.nationalcar.com). **Thrifty** (⊠ Balashi 65, Santa Cruz ☎ 297/585–5300 ⊠ Airport ☎ 297/583–5335 ⊕ www.thriftyaruba.com).

Taxis: There's a dispatch office at the airport; you can also flag down taxis on the street (look for license plates with a "TX" tag). Rates are fixed (i.e., there are no meters; the rates are set by the government and displayed on a chart), though you and the driver should agree on the fare before your ride begins. Add $2 to the fare after midnight and $3 on Sunday and holidays. An hour-long island tour costs about $45, with up to four people. Rides into town from Eagle Beach run about $10; from Palm Beach, about $11. **Airport Taxi Dispatch** (☎ 297/582–2116).

Island Activities

Soft, sandy **beaches** and turquoise waters are the biggest draws in Aruba. Beaches are often crowded, particularly the best stretches of Eagle Beach, which is the island's—and perhaps one of the Caribbean's—finest. Baby Beach, on the east end of the island, is also good.

But the island also comes alive by night and has become a true **party hot spot**. The **casinos**—though not as elaborate as those in Las Vegas—are among the best of any Caribbean island.

Restaurants are very good, though sometimes expensive.

Diving is good in Aruba, though perhaps not as spectacular as in nearby Bonaire.

Near-constant breezes and tranquil, protected waters have proven to be a boon for **windsurfers,** who have discovered that conditions on the southwestern coast are ideal for their sport.

A largely undeveloped region in Arikok National Wildlife Park is the destination of choice for those wishing to **hike** and explore some wild terrain.

4

ARUBA PLANNER

Fast Facts

Banks and Exchange Services: Arubans happily accept U.S. dollars virtually everywhere. The official currency is the Aruban florin (Afl), also called the guilder, which is made up of 100 cents. ATMs are easy to find.

Electricity: 110 volts, 50 cycles.

Emergency Services: Ambulance, Fire, and Police (☎ 911). **Dr. Horacio Oduber Hospital** (✉ L.G. Smith Blvd. 47, Manchebo Beach ☎ 297/587–4300).

Weddings: You must be over 18 and submit the appropriate documents one month in advance. Couples are required to submit birth certificates with raised seals, through the mail or in person, to Aruba's Office of the Civil Registry. They also need an apostille—a document proving they are free to marry—from their country of residence. Most major hotels have wedding coordinators, and there are other independent wedding planners on the island.

Wedding Planners Aruba Fairy Tales (✆ Box 4151, Noord ☎ 297/993–0045 ⊕ www.arubafairytales. com). **Aruba Weddings for You** (✉ Nune 92, Paradera ☎ 297/583–7638 ⊕ www. arubaweddingsforyou.com).

Essentials

Mail: If you need to send a package in a hurry, there is a Federal Express office across from the airport that offers overnight service to the United States if you get your package in before 3 pm. The **Main Post Office** (✉ 9 J.E. Irausquinplein, Oranjestad ☎ 297/582–1900) is in Oranjestad. There is also a branch office at Royal Plaza Mall, and others are scattered throughout the island.

Taxes: The airport departure tax is a hefty $37 for departures to the United States and $33.50 to other international destinations (including Bonaire and Curaçao), but the fee is usually included in your ticket price. Hotels collect 7.5% in government taxes (scheduled to rise to 9.5% in the future) on top of a typical 11% service charge, for a total of 18.5%. A 3% B.B.O. tax (turnover tax) is included in the price charged in most shops.

Telephones: You can dial international calls directly or call from the SETAR office in Oranjestad. Simply dial the seven-digit number in Aruba. AT&T customers can dial 800–8000 from special phones at the cruise dock and in the airport's arrival and departure halls. From other phones, dial 121 to contact the SETAR international operator to place a collect or calling-card call. Local calls from pay phones, which accept both local currency and phone cards, cost 25¢. Because hotel phone charges on Aruba can verge on obscene, renting a mobile phone for your stay can save you a bundle.

SETAR Offices Telekiosk Airport (✉ Arrival Hall, Reina Beatrix Airport ☎ 297/583–0525). **Teleshop Irausquinplein** (✉ J.E. Irausquinplein, Oranjestad ☎ 297/582–1871). **Teleshop Palm Beach** (✉ Next to Brickell Bay Resort, J.E. Irausquin Blvd. 370, Palm Beach ☎ 297/586–2042).

Tipping: Restaurants generally include a 10% to 15% service charge. If service isn't included, a 10% tip is standard; if it is included, it's customary to add something extra at your discretion. Taxi drivers, 10% to 15%; porters and bellhops, about $2 per bag; housekeeping, about $2 a day.

Visitor Information: Aruba Tourism Authority (☎ 954/767–6477 in Fort Lauderdale, 201/330–0800 in Weehawken, NJ, 800/862–7822 ⊕ www.aruba.com ✉ L.G. Smith Blvd. 172, Eagle Beach, Aruba ☎ 297/582–3777).

Where to Stay

Almost all of the resorts are along the island's southwest coast, along L.G. Smith and J.E. Irausquin boulevards, with the larger high-rise properties being farther away from Oranjestad. A few budget places are in Oranjestad itself. Since most hotel beaches are equally fabulous, it's the resort, rather than its location, that's going to be a bigger factor in how you enjoy your vacation.

Boutique Resorts: You'll find a few small resorts that offer more personal service, though not always the same level of luxury as the larger places. But smaller resorts are better suited to the natural sense of Aruban hospitality you'll find all over the island.

Large Resorts: These all-encompassing vacation destinations offer myriad dining options, casinos, shops, watersports centers, health clubs, and car-rental desks. The island has only a handful of all-inclusives, though these are gaining in popularity.

Time-shares: Large time-share properties are cropping up in greater numbers, luring visitors who prefer to prepare some of their own meals and have a bit more living space than you might find in the typical resort hotel room.

HOTEL AND RESTAURANT COSTS

Restaurant prices are for a main course at dinner and include any taxes or service charges. Hotel prices are per night for a double room in high season, excluding taxes, service charges, and meal plans (except at all-inclusives).

WHAT IT COSTS IN U.S. DOLLARS

	¢	$	$$	$$$	$$$$
Restaurants	under $8	$8–$12	$12–$20	$20–$30	over $30
Hotels	under $150	$150–$275	$276–$375	$376–$475	over $475

When to Go

Aruba's popularity means that hotels are usually booked solid during the high season from mid-December through mid-April or early May, so early booking is essential. During other times of the year, rate reductions can be dramatic.

Aruba doesn't really have a rainy season and rarely sees a hurricane, so you take fewer chances by coming here in late summer and fall. However, if you travel at this time, remember that hurricanes and tropical storms are not unheard of—just rare.

February or March witnesses a spectacular **Carnival,** a riot of color whirling to the tunes of steel bands and culminating in the Grand Parade, where some of the floats rival the extravagance of those in the Big Easy's Mardi Gras.

4

ARUBA BEACHES

There are few destinations that can match the glorious beach vistas of Aruba. Virtually every popular beach has a resort attached but as all beaches are public there is never a problem with access. The constant breezes are a lovely cool counterpoint to the intense sunshine.

(Above) Eagle Beach. (Opposite page bottom) Baby Beach. (Opposite page top) Fisherman's Huts.

The beaches on Aruba are legendary: white sand, turquoise waters, and virtually no litter—everyone takes the "no tira sushi" (no littering) signs very seriously, especially considering the island's $280 fine. The major public beaches, which back up to the hotels along the southwestern strip, are usually crowded. You can make the hour-long hike from the Holiday Inn to the Tamarijn without ever leaving sand. Make sure you're well protected from the sun—it scorches fast despite the cooling trade winds. Luckily, there's at least one covered bar (and often an ice-cream stand) at virtually every hotel. On the island's northeastern side, stronger winds make the waters too choppy for swimming, but the vistas are great and the terrain is wonderful for exploring.

BRING YOUR SHADES

Aruba's most popular beaches, from Druif Beach to the end of the High Rise Resort area, are wide, white, and pristine. The powdery sand is highly reflective, so you'll need your sunglasses. Beaches on the island's North Coast are much rockier and swimming is not advisable. Baby Beach on the southwestern tip of the island is a bit of a drive but the wide stretch of sugar-icing sand makes it worthwhile.

Arashi Beach. Just after Malmok Beach, this is a ½-mi (1-km) stretch of gleaming white sand. Although it was once rocky, nature—with a little help from humans—has turned it into an excellent place for sunbathing and swimming. Despite calm waters, the rocky reputation has kept most people away, making it relatively uncrowded, ⊠ *West of Malmok Beach, on west end.*

🐾 **Baby Beach**. On the island's eastern tip (near the refinery), this semicircular beach borders a placid bay that's just about as shallow as a wading pool—perfect for tots, shore divers, and terrible swimmers. Thatched shaded areas are good places to cool off. Down the road is the island's rather unusual pet cemetery. Stop by the nearby snack truck for burgers, hot dogs, beer, and soda. The road to this beach (and several others) is through San Nicolas and along the road toward Seroe Colorado. Just before reaching the beach, keep an eye out for a strange, 300-foot, natural seawall made of coral and rock that was thrown up overnight when Hurricane Ivan swept by the island in 2004. ⊠ *Near Seroe Colorado, on east end.*

Boca Prins. You'll need a four-wheel-drive vehicle to make the trek to this strip of coastline, which is famous for its backdrop of enormous vanilla sand dunes. Near the Fontein Cave and Blue Lagoon, the beach itself is about as large

as a Brazilian bikini—but with two rocky cliffs and tumultuously crashing waves, it's as romantic as Aruba gets. The water is rough and swimming is prohibited (with good reason), however. Bring a picnic, a beach blanket, and sturdy sneakers, and descend the rocks that form steps to the water's edge. ⊠ *Off 7 A/B, near Fontein Cave.*

★ **Fodor's Choice** **Eagle Beach**. On the southwestern coast, across the highway from what is quickly becoming known as Time-Share Lane, is one of the Caribbean's—if not the world's—best beaches. Not long ago it was a nearly deserted stretch of pristine sand with the occasional thatched picnic hut. Now that the resorts have been completed, this mile-plus-long beach is always hopping. The white sand is literally dazzling, and sunglasses are essential. Many of the hotels have facilities on or near the beach, and refreshments are never far away. ⊠ *J.E. Irausquin Blvd., north of Manchebo Beach.*

Fisherman's Huts (Hadicurari). Next to the Holiday Inn is a windsurfer's haven with good swimming conditions and a decent, slightly rocky, white sand beach. Take a picnic lunch (tables are available) and watch the elegant purple, aqua, and orange sails struggle in the wind. ⊠ *1 A/B, at Holiday Inn SunSpree Aruba.*

Grapefield Beach. To the southeast of San Nicolas, a sweep of blinding-white

Looking down on Palm Beach

sand in the shadow of cliffs and boulders is marked by an anchor-shape memorial dedicated to all seamen. Pick sea grapes from January to June. Swim at your own risk; the waves here can be rough. This is not a popular tourist beach so finding a quiet spot is almost guaranteed, but the downside of this is a complete lack of facilities or nearby refreshments. ✉ *Southwest of San Nicolas, on east end.*

Malmok Beach (Boca Catalina). On the northwestern shore, this small, nondescript beach borders shallow waters that stretch 300 yards from shore. There are no snack or refreshment stands here, but shade is available under the thatched umbrellas. It's the perfect place to learn to windsurf. Right off the coast here is a favorite haunt for divers and snorkelers—the wreck of the German ship *Antilla,* scuttled in 1940. ✉ *At end of J.E. Irausquin Blvd., Malmokweg.*

Manchebo Beach *(Punta Brabo).* Impressively wide, the white-sand shoreline in front of the Manchebo Beach Resort is where officials turn a blind eye to the occasional topless sunbather. This beach merges with Druif Beach, and most locals use the name Manchebo to refer to both. ✉ *J.E. Irausquin Blvd., at Manchebo Beach Resort.*

Palm Beach. This stretch runs from the Westin Aruba Resort, Spa & Casino to the Marriott Aruba Ocean Club. It's the center of Aruban tourism, offering good swimming, sailing, and other water sports. In some spots you might find a variety of shells that are great to collect, but not as much fun to step on barefoot—bring sandals. ✉ *J.E. Irausquin Blvd. between Westin Aruba Resort, Spa & Casino and Marriott Aruba Ocean Club.*

Rodger's Beach. Near Baby Beach on the island's eastern tip, this beautiful curving stretch of sand is only slightly marred by its proximity to the oil refinery at the bay's far side. Swimming conditions are excellent here. Drive around the refinery perimeter to get here. ✉ *Next to Baby Beach, on east end.*

4

By Vernon
O'Reilly-
Ramesar

Cruise ships gleam in Oranjestad Harbour, and thousands of eager tourists scavenge through souvenir stalls looking for the perfect memento. The mile-long stretch of L.G. Smith Boulevard is lined with cafés, designer stores, and signs for the latest Vegas-style shows. The countryside is dotted with colorful *cunucu* (country-style houses) and small neighborhood shops. Suddenly, the rocky desert landscape is startlingly austere.

Aruba offers an amazingly diverse experience in a small package. Tourists flock here for the sunny climate, perfect waters, and excellent beaches—so much so that the area around beautiful Eagle Beach is an almost unbroken line of hotels, restaurants, and bars. Here on the south coast, the action is nonstop both day and night, whereas the fiercely rugged north coast is a desolate and rocky landscape that has so far resisted development.

As with Bonaire and Curaçao, the island was originally populated by the Caquetio, an Amerindian people related to the Arawak. After the Spanish conquered the island in 1499, Aruba was basically left alone, since it held little agricultural or mineral appeal. The Dutch took charge of the island in 1636, and things remained relatively quiet until gold was discovered in the 1800s.

Like the trademark *watapana* (divi-divi) trees that have been forced into bonsailike angles by the constant trade winds, Aruba has always adjusted to changes in the economic climate. Mining dominated the economy until the early part of the 20th century, when the mines became unsustainable. Shortly thereafter, Aruba became home to a major oil-refining operation, which was the economic mainstay until the early 1990s, when its contribution to the local economy was eclipsed by tourism. Today, after being so resolutely dedicated to attracting visitors for so many years, Aruba's national culture and tourism industry are inextricably intertwined.

With more than a million visitors a year, Aruba is not a destination that will appeal to those trying to avoid the beaten path—but you should visit Aruba if you're looking for a pleasant climate, excellent facilities, lots of nightlife, and no surprises. The U.S. dollar is accepted everywhere, and English is spoken universally, which makes Aruba a popular spot for Americans who want an overseas trip to a place that doesn't feel foreign. In fact, Americans go through U.S. customs right at the airport in Aruba, so there are no formalities upon landing in the United States.

EXPLORING ARUBA

Aruba's wildly sculpted landscape is replete with rocky deserts, cactus clusters, secluded coves, blue vistas, and the trademark divi-divi tree. To see the island's wild, untamed beauty, you can rent a car, take a sightseeing tour, or hire a cab for $45 an hour (for up to four people). The main highways are well paved, but on the windward side (the north- and east-facing side) some roads are still a mixture of compacted dirt and stones. Although a car is fine, a four-wheel-drive vehicle will allow you to explore the unpaved interior.

Traffic is sparse, but signs leading to sights are often small and hand-lettered (this is slowly changing as the government puts up official road signs), so watch closely. Route 1A travels southbound along the western coast, and 1B is simply northbound along the same road. If you lose your way, just follow the divi-divi trees, which always lean southwest.

WHAT TO SEE

Alto Vista Chapel. Alone near the island's northwest corner sits the scenic little Alto Vista Chapel. The wind whistles through the simple mustard-color walls, eerie boulders, and looming cacti. Along the side of the road back to civilization are miniature crosses with depictions of the stations of the cross and hand-lettered signs exhorting "pray for us sinners" and the like—a simple yet powerful evocation of faith. ✛ *Follow the rough, winding dirt road that loops around the island's northern tip, or, from the hotel strip, take Palm Beach Rd. through three intersections and watch for the asphalt road to the left just past the Alto Vista Rum Shop.*

Arikok National Wildlife Park. Nearly 20% of Aruba has been designated part of this national park, which sprawls across the eastern interior and the northeast coast. The park is the keystone of the government's long-term ecotourism plan to preserve Aruba's resources and showcases the island's flora and fauna as well as ancient Arawak petroglyphs, the ruins of a gold-mining operation at Miralmar, and the remnants of Dutch peasant settlements at Masiduri. At the park's main entrance, Arikok Center houses offices, restrooms, and food facilities. All visitors must stop here upon entering so that officials can manage the traffic flow and hand out information on park rules and features. Within the confines of the park are Mt. Arikok and the 620-foot Mt. Yamanota, Aruba's highest peak.

Anyone looking for geological exotica should head for the park's caves, found on the northeastern coast. Baranca Sunu, the so-called Tunnel of Love, has a heart-shape entrance and naturally sculpted rocks farther inside that look like the Madonna, Abraham Lincoln, and even a jaguar. Fontein Cave, which was used by indigenous peoples centuries ago, is marked with ancient drawings (rangers are on hand to offer explanations). Bats are known to make appearances—don't worry, they won't bother you. Although you don't need a flashlight because the paths are well lighted, it's best to wear sneakers. ☎ 297/585–1234.

★ **Aruba Ostrich Farm.** Everything you ever wanted to know about the world's largest living birds can be found at this farm. A large *palapa* (palm-thatched roof) houses a gift shop and restaurant (popular with large bus tours), and tours of the farm are available every half hour. This operation is virtually identical to the facility in Curaçao; it's owned by the same company. ✉ *Makividiri Rd., Paradera* ☎ *297/585–9630* ⊕ *www.arubaostrichfarm.com* ✎ *$12* ☉ *Daily 9–4.*

Balashi Brewery. The factory that manufactures the excellent local beer, Balashi, offers daily tours to the public that will take you through every stage of the brewing process. It makes for a fascinating hour, and the price of the tour includes a free drink at the end. Those more interested in beer drinking than beer making might want to visit the factory any Friday from 6 to 9 for happy hour (there is live music). ✉ *Balashi 75, Balashi* ☎ *297/592–2544* ⊕ *www.balashi.com* ✎ *$6.*

Butterfly Farm. Hundreds of butterflies from around the world flutter about this spectacular garden. Guided 20- to 30-minute tours (included in the price of admission) provide an entertaining look into the life cycle of these insects, from egg to caterpillar to chrysalis to butterfly. There's a special deal offered here: after your initial visit, you can return as often as you like for free during your vacation. ✉ *J.E. Irausquin Blvd., Palm Beach* ☎ *297/586–3656* ⊕ *www.thebutterflyfarm.com* ✎ *$13* ☉ *Daily 9–4:30; last tour at 4.*

California Lighthouse. The lighthouse, built by a French architect in 1910, stands at the island's far northern end. Although you can't go inside, you can ascend the hill to the lighthouse base for some great views. In this stark landscape, you might feel as though you've just landed on the moon. The lighthouse is surrounded by huge boulders that look like extraterrestrial monsters and sand dunes embroidered with scrub that resemble undulating sea serpents.

Mt. Hooiberg. Named for its shape (*hooiberg* means "haystack" in Dutch), this 541-foot peak lies inland just past the airport. If you have the energy, climb the 562 steps to the top for an impressive view of Oranjestad (and Venezuela on clear days).

Oranjestad. Aruba's charming capital is best explored on foot. L.G. Smith Boulevard, the palm-lined thoroughfare in the center of town, runs between pastel-painted buildings, old and new, of typical Dutch design. You'll find many malls with boutiques and shops here.

The **Archaeological Museum of Aruba** has two rooms chock-full of fascinating artifacts from the indigenous Arawak people, including farm and domestic utensils dating back hundreds of years. ✉ *J.E. Irausquin Blvd. 2A, Oranjestad* ☎ *297/582–8979* ✎ *Free* ☉ *Tues.–Sun. 10–5.*

★ Learn all about aloe—its cultivation, processing, and production—at **Aruba Aloe**, Aruba's own aloe farm and factory. Guided tours lasting about a half hour will show you how the gel—revered for its skin-soothing properties—is extracted from the aloe vera plant and used in a variety of products, including after-sun creams, soaps, and shampoos. Though not the most exciting tour on the island and unlikely to keep kids entertained, it might be a good option in the event of a rainy day. You can purchase the finished goods in the gift shop. ⊠ *Pitastraat 115, Oranjestad* ☎ *297/588–3222* 🖾 *Free* ☉ *Weekdays 8:30–4, Sat. 9–noon.*

☾ One of the island's oldest edifices, **Ft. Zoutman** was built in 1796 and played an important role in skirmishes between British and Curaçao troops in 1803. The Willem III Tower, named for the Dutch monarch of that time, was added in 1868 to serve as a lighthouse. Over time, the fort has been a government office building, a police station, and a prison; now its historical museum displays Aruban artifacts in an 18th-century house. ⊠ *Zoutmanstraat, Oranjestad* ☎ *297/582–6099* 🖾 *Free* ☉ *Weekdays 8–noon and 1–4.*

★ The **Numismatic Museum** displays more than 40,000 historic coins and paper money from around the world. A few pieces were salvaged from shipwrecks in the region. Some of the coins circulated during the Roman Empire, the Byzantine Empire, and the ancient Chinese dynasties; the oldest dates to the 3rd century BC. The museum had its start as the private collection of an Aruban who dug up some old coins in his garden. It's now run by his granddaughter. ⊠ *Weststraat, Oranjestad* ☎ *297/582–8831* 🖾 *$5* ☉ *Weekdays 9–noon and 1:30–4:30.*

Rock Formations. The massive boulders at Ayo and Casibari are a mystery, as they don't match the island's geological makeup. You can climb to the top for fine views of the arid countryside. On the way you'll doubtless pass Aruba whiptail lizards—the males are cobalt blue, and the females are blue-gray with light-blue dots. The main path to Casibari has steps and handrails, and you must move through tunnels and along narrow steps and ledges to reach the top. At Ayo you can find ancient pictographs in a small cave (the entrance has iron bars to protect the drawings from vandalism). You may also encounter boulder climbers, who are increasingly drawn to Ayo's smooth surfaces. Access to Casibari is via Tanki Highway 4A; you can reach Ayo via Route 6A. Watch carefully for the turnoff signs near the center of the island on the way to the windward side.

San Nicolas. During the oil refinery heyday, Aruba's oldest village was a bustling port; now its primary purpose is tourism. *The* institution in town is Charlie's Restaurant and Bar. Stop in for a drink and advice on what to see and do in this little town. Aruba's main red-light district is here and will be fairly apparent to even the most casual observer.

WHERE TO EAT

Aruba has many fine restaurants, so you can expect outstanding meals and international cuisine. Arubans tend to eat their main meal at lunch-time, so feel free to follow suit and save money by trying the lunch menus at the better restaurants. Be sure to try such Aruban specialties as *pan bati* (a mildly sweet bread that resembles a pancake) and *keshi yena* (a baked concoction of Gouda cheese, spices, and meat or seafood in a rich brown sauce). On Sunday you may have a hard time finding a restaurant outside a hotel that's open for lunch, and many restaurants are closed for dinner on Sunday or Monday. Reservations are essential for dinner in high season.

The **Aruba Gastronomic Association** (AGA ⊕ *www.arubadining.com*) offers Dine-Around packages that involve more than 20 island restaurants. Here's how it works: you can buy tickets for three dinners ($117 per person), five dinners ($190), seven dinners ($262), or five breakfasts or lunches plus four dinners ($230). Dinners include an appetizer, an entrée, dessert, coffee or tea, and a service charge (except when a restaurant is a VIP member, in which case $38 will be deducted from your final bill instead).

4

WHAT TO WEAR

Even the finest restaurants require at most a jacket for men and a sundress for women. If you plan to eat in the open air, remember to bring along insect repellent—the mosquitoes sometimes get unruly.

$$–$$$
CUBAN
★

✕**Cuba's Cookin'**. This funky little establishment is tucked away on an innocuous street downtown. Nightly entertainment, great authentic Cuban food, and a lively crowd are the draws here. The empanadas are excellent, as is the chicken stuffed with plantains. Don't leave without trying the roast pork, which is pretty close to perfection. The signature dish is the *ropa vieja*, a sautéed flank steak served with a rich sauce (the name literally translates as "old clothes"). Service can be a bit spotty at times, depending on how busy it gets. There's always a crowd, as loyal fans and fun-seekers usually flock to the bar area. ⊠ *Wilhelminastraat 27, Oranjestad* ☎*297/588–0627* ⊕ *www.cubascookin.com* ♥ *Closed Sun. mid-Apr.–mid-Dec.*

$$$–$$$$
STEAK
♻

✕**El Gaucho Argentine Grill**. Faux-leather-bound books, tulip-top lamps, wooden chairs, and tile floors decorate this Argentina-style steak house, which has been in business since 1977. The key here is meat served in mammoth portions (think 16-ounce steaks). A welcome feature is a children's playroom, which allows adults to dine while the kids are entertained with videos and games. Be warned, though: even with the kids out of sight, the noise level can still be a bit high in this busy restaurant. ⊠ *Wilhelminastraat 80, Oranjestad* ☎*297/582–3677* ⊕ *www. elgaucho-aruba.com* ♥ *No lunch Sun.*

$$–$$$
CARIBBEAN
★

✕**Gasparito Restaurant & Art Gallery**. You can find this enchanting hideaway in a *cunucu* (country) house in Noord, not far from the hotels. Dine indoors, where works by local artists are showcased on softly lighted walls, or on the outdoor patio. Either way, the service is excellent. The Aruban specialties—pan bati, keshi yena—are feasts for the eye as well as the palate. The standout dish is the Gasparito chicken; the sauce recipe was passed down from the owner's ancestors and features seven special ingredients, including brandy, white wine, and pineapple juice. (The rest, they say, are secret.) Gasparito is an AGA Dine-Around member. ⊠ *Gasparito 3, Noord* ☎*297/586–7044* ⊕ *www.gasparito. com* ♥ *Closed Sun. No lunch.*

Cunucu Houses

Pastel houses surrounded by cacti fences adorn Aruba's flat, rugged *cunucu* ("country" in Papiamento). The features of these traditional houses were developed in response to the environment. Early settlers discovered that slanting roofs allowed the heat to rise and that small windows helped to keep in the cool air. Among the earliest building materials was *caliche,* a durable calcium carbonate substance found in the island's southeastern hills. Many houses were also built using interlocking coral rocks that didn't require mortar (this technique is no longer used, thanks to cement and concrete). Contemporary design combines some of the basic principles of the earlier homes with touches of modernization: windows, though still narrow, have been elongated; roofs are constructed of bright tiles; pretty patios have been added; and doorways and balconies present an ornamental face to the world beyond.

$$–$$$
CARIBBEAN
✕ **Gostoso.** Locals adore the magical mixture of Portuguese, Aruban, and international dishes on offer at this consistently excellent establishment. The decor walks a fine line between kitschy and cozy, but the atmosphere is relaxed and informal and outdoor seating is available. The *bacalhau* vinaigrette (dressed salted cod) is a delightful Portuguese appetizer and pairs nicely with most of the Aruban dishes on the menu. Meat lovers are sure to enjoy the Venezuelan mixed grill, which includes a 14-ounce steak and chorizo accompanied by local sides like fried plantain. ✉ *Caya Ing Roland H. Lacle 12, Oranjestad* ☎ *297/588–0053* ⊕ *www.gostosoaruba.com* ⚲ *Reservations essential* ⊘ *Closed Mon.*

$$$–$$$$
ITALIAN
✕ **Hostaria Da' Vittorio.** Part of the fun at this family-oriented spot is watching chef Vittorio Muscariello prepare authentic Italian regional specialties in the open kitchen. The staff helps you choose wines from the extensive list and recommends portions of hot and cold antipasti, risottos, and pastas. Those on a tight budget should stick to the pizza offerings. Service can be a bit dismissive during busy periods. As you leave, pick up some limoncello (lemon liqueur) or olive oil at the gourmet shop. Be aware that the decibel level of the crowd can be high. A 15% gratuity is automatically added to your bill. It's an AGA VIP member. ✉ *L.G. Smith Blvd. 380, Palm Beach* ☎ *297/586–3838.*

$$$–$$$$
STEAK
★
✕ **L.G. Smith's Steak & Chop House.** A study in teak, cream, and black, this fine steak house offers some of the best beef on the island. Subdued lighting and cascading water create a pleasant atmosphere, and the view over L.G. Smith Boulevard to the harbor makes for an exceptional dining experience. The menu features high-quality cuts of meat, all superbly prepared. The casino is steps away if you fancy a few pulls at the slots after dinner. ✉ *Renaissance Aruba Beach Resort & Casino, L.G. Smith Blvd. 82, Oranjestad* ☎ *297/523–6115* ⊕ *www.lgsmiths.com* ⊘ *No lunch.*

$$$–$$$$
ECLECTIC
Fodor'sChoice
★
✕ **Marandi.** This seaside restaurant, whose name means "on the water" in Malaysian, is simultaneously cozy and chic. Tables are tucked under a giant thatched roof by the water's edge. The restaurant relocated to a new location on a pier near the airport but seems to have lost none of

4

its charm, though the fact that it is harder to find means it is often less crowded than its previous incarnation. The grouper Marandi, stuffed with shrimp, scallops, and cheese, is a popular choice. Reservations are essential at any time, and if you're lucky, you can dine at the chef's table, which is right in the kitchen, ⊠ *Bucutiweg 50, Oranjestad* ☎ *297/582–0157* ⊕ *www.marandi-aruba.com* ⌂ *Reservations essential* ⊙ *No lunch.*

$$$–$$$$
ECLECTIC
★
✕ **Papiamento.** The Ellis family converted its 175-year-old manor into a bistro with an atmosphere that is elegant, intimate, and always romantic. You can feast in the dining room, which is filled with antiques, or outdoors on the terrace by the pool (sitting on plastic patio chairs covered in fabric). The chefs mix Continental and Caribbean cuisines to produce sumptuous seafood and meat dishes. Items cooked "on the stone" are popular as much for the drama of the sizzling stone as for the incredible aromas that envelop you when they are presented. Service is unhurried, so don't come here if you're in a rush. ⊠ *Washington 61, Noord* ☎ *297/586–4544* ⊕ *www.papiamentorestaurant.com* ⌂ *Reservations essential* ⊙ *Closed Mon. No lunch.*

WORD OF MOUTH

"Papiamento—Hands down our FAVORITE restaurant in Aruba. The historical 1879 manor house had so much character and was elegantly appointed with antiques and quirky furnishings. The food was good - my husband loved his chargrilled hot stone walla dish w/shrimp (the Mermaid entrée). I had a tasty seafood casserole, which was very creamy, and came with sweet potato puree, okra and rice on the side. Definitely get a reservation."

—catherineinbrooklyn

$$$–$$$$
FRENCH
✕ **Papillon.** Despite being inspired by Henri Charrière's escape from Devil's Island, the food here couldn't be more removed from from bread and water. The owners use the famous story as a metaphor for a culinary journey to freedom as classic French cuisine is transformed with Caribbean flair. There are whimsical prison touches throughout the restaurant and especially in the washrooms. The menu includes classics like beef bourguignonne but isn't afraid to offer more adventurous dishes such as a standout crispy duck breast served with passion fruit and chocolate. Whatever you order, you'll find the presentation is always impeccable. ⊠ *Irausquin Blvd. 348A, The Village, Palm Beach* ☎ *297/586–5400* ⊕ *www.papillonaruba.com* ⌂ *Reservations essential.*

$$$–$$$$
ECLECTIC
Fodor's Choice
★
✕ **Passions.** Every night the Amsterdam Manor Beach Resort (⇨ *below*) transforms the area of Eagle Beach in front of the hotel into a magical and romantic beach dining room. Tiki torches illuminate the white sand, and the linen-covered tables are within inches of the lapping water. Dine on imaginative dishes that are as beautiful as they are delicious. The huge tropical watermelon salad presented in a watermelon half is refreshing and whets the appetite with a soothing chili heat. Described as "reef cuisine," the main courses lean toward seafood, though meat lovers also are indulged. After dinner, relax with your toes in the sand and enjoy the best show that nature has to offer

over signature cocktails. ⊠ *J.E. Irausquin Blvd. 252, Eagle Beach* ☎ *297/527–1100* ⚔ *Reservations essential.*

$$$–$$$$
ECLECTIC
Fodor's Choice
★

✕ **Pinchos Grill & Bar.** Built on a pier, this casual spot—with only 11 tables—has one of the most romantic settings on the island. At night the restaurant glimmers from a distance as hundreds of lights reflect off the water. Guests can watch as chef Robby Peterson prepares delectable meals on the grill in his tiny kitchen. His wife and co-owner, Anabela, keeps diners comfortable and happy. The fish-cakes appetizer with a pineapple-mayonnaise dressing is a marriage made in heaven. The bar area is great for enjoying ocean breezes over an evening cocktail, and there is live entertainment every weekend. Many visitors consider a visit to Pinchos an essential part of the Aruba experience. ⊠ *L.G. Smith Blvd. 7, Oranjestad* ☎ *287/583–2666* ☾ *Closed Mon. No lunch.*

$$–$$$
ECLECTIC

✕ **Qué Pasa?** This funky eatery serves as something of an art gallery–restaurant where diners can appreciate the colorful, eclectic works of local artists while enjoying a meal or savoring a drink. The terra-cotta outdoor spaces are illuminated by strings of lights. Inside, jewel-colored walls serve as an eye-popping backdrop for numerous paintings. Despite the name, there isn't a Mexican dish on the menu, which includes everything from sashimi to rack of lamb; the fish dishes are especially good. Everything is done with Aruban flair, and the staff is helpful and friendly. Save room for one of the delightfully comforting desserts such as a banana split or a brownie with ice cream. The bar area is lively and fun. ⊠ *Wilhelminastraat 18, Oranjestad* ☎ *297/583–4888* ⊕ *www.quepasaaruba.com* ☾ *No lunch.*

WHERE TO STAY

Hotels on the island are categorized as low-rise or high-rise and are grouped in two distinct areas along L.G. Smith and J.E. Irausquin boulevards north of Oranjestad. The low-rise properties are closer to the capital, the high-rises in a swath a little farther north. Hotel rates, with the exception of those at a few all-inclusives, generally do not include meals or even breakfast. The larger resorts feel like destinations unto themselves, complete with shopping, entertainment, and casinos.

The following reviews have been abbreviated for this book. Please go to Fodors.com for expanded reviews of each property.

$$
HOTEL
Fodor's Choice
★

🏨 **Amsterdam Manor Beach Resort.** An intimate, family-run hotel with a genuinely friendly staff and an authentic Dutch-Caribbean atmosphere, this little place offers excellent value for the money. **Pros:** feels like a European village; very good family restaurant; friendly and helpful staff; minigrocery on-site; modern and airy rooms; public bus stop in front of hotel for easy access to downtown and the high-rise area. **Cons:** across the road from the beach; lacks the boutiques and attractions of a larger hotel; pool is quite small. ⊠ *J.E. Irausquin Blvd. 252, Eagle Beach* ☎ *297/527–1100 or 800/932–6509* ⊕ *www.amsterdammanor. com* ⇆ *68 rooms, 4 suites* ⚷ *In-room: safe, kitchen, Internet, Wi-Fi. In-hotel: restaurants, bars, pool, laundry facilities, business center, water sports, some pets allowed* ⦙⦶ *No meals.*

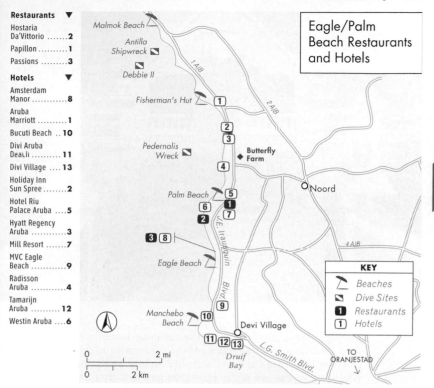

Eagle/Palm
Beach Restaurants
and Hotels

KEY

◢ Beaches

◣ Dive Sites

1 Restaurants

① Hotels

Malmok Beach

Antilla Shipwreck

Debbie II

Fisherman's Hut

Pedernalis Wreck

Butterfly Farm

Palm Beach

Noord

Eagle Beach

Manchebo Beach

Devi Village

Druif Bay

TO ORANJESTAD

4

$$$$
RESORT
Fodor's Choice
★

Aruba Marriott Resort & Stellaris Casino. The gentle sound of the surf and splashing waterfalls compete for your attention in this sprawling compound, where everything seems to run smoothly. **Pros:** large rooms; variety of excellent restaurants; great shopping; every imaginable service is conveniently on-site. **Cons:** large, impersonal resort; reception can become gridlocked in peak season. ⊠ *L.G. Smith Blvd. 101, Palm Beach* ☎ *297/586–9000 or 800/223–6388* ⊕ *www.marriott. com* ⤳ *388 rooms, 23 suites* ⌕ *In-room: safe, Internet, Wi-Fi. In-hotel: restaurants, tennis courts, bars, pool, gym, spa, beach, water sports* ❘○❘ *No meals.*

$$$$
RESORT
Fodor's Choice
★

Bucuti Beach Resort featuring Tara Suites & Spa. An extraordinary beach setting, impeccably understated service, and attention to detail help this elegant Green Globe resort easily outclass anything else on the island. **Pros:** intimate European feel; impeccable service; ecoconscious hotel; luxurious without insulating guests from island life. **Cons:** beach can get busy, as other hotels share it; little to buy at hotel; ecoconscious means that hot water is not always that hot. ⊠ *L.G. Smith Blvd. 55B, Eagle Beach* ☎ *297/583–1100* ⊕ *www.bucuti.com* ⤳ *63 rooms, 38 suites, 3 bungalows* ⌕ *In-room: safe, Wi-Fi. In-hotel: restaurant, bars, pool, laundry facilities, beach, business center* ❘○❘ *Breakfast.*

$$$$
RESORT
♻

Divi Aruba Beach Resort All Inclusive. The main advantage to staying at this resort is that it offers a variety of room types, along with the

Amsterdam Manor Beach Resort.

privilege of using the facilities of the adjoining Tamarijn Resort (⇨ *below*). **Pros:** on wonderful stretch of beach; margarita machines in lobby; common areas feel light and airy; live nightly entertainment. **Cons:** poolside area can get pretty noisy; the gourmet restaurant isn't that good; Internet access is strangely not included. ⊠ *L.G. Smith Blvd. 93, Manchebo Beach* ☎ *297/582–3300 or 800/554–2008* ⊕ *www. diviaruba.com* ⌐ *203 rooms* 🖒 *In-room: refrigerator, safe. In-hotel: restaurants, tennis court, bars, children's programs, pools, gym, beach, business center, water sports* ⌂ *3-night minimum* ⏲⃝ *All-inclusive.*

$$ 🏨 **Divi Village Golf & Beach Resort.** The newest of the midsize Divi resorts
RESORT   focuses on golf, and although it's just across the road from its sister
★   properties, the atmosphere at this all-suites version is much quieter and more refined. **Pros:** excellent golf course; spacious rooms; lushly landscaped grounds. **Cons:** bit of a hike from some rooms to the lobby; you must cross a busy road to get to the beach; atmosphere might be a bit too quiet for some tastes. ⊠ *J.E. Irausquin Blvd. 93, Oranjestad* ☎ *297/583–5000* ⊕ *www.divivillage.com* ⌐ *250 suites* 🖒 *In-room: kitchen, Internet, Wi-Fi. In-hotel: golf course, restaurants, room service, tennis courts, bars, pools* ⌂ *3-night minimum* ⏲⃝ *No meals.*

$ 🏨 **Holiday Inn SunSpree Aruba Beach Resort & Casino.** This popular, family-
RESORT   oriented package-tour resort has three seven-story buildings filled with
☺   spacious rooms lining a sugary, palm-dotted shore. **Pros:** affordable and predictable quality; great beachfront location; lots of activities for the kids. **Cons:** hallways have an institutional feel; lines at reception can make you feel you are back at the airport; restaurants are mediocre at best and service can be a problem. ⊠ *J.E. Irausquin Blvd. 230, Palm Beach* ☎ *297/586–3600 or 800/465–4329* ⊕ *www.caribbeanhi.com/*

aruba ↝ *600 rooms, 7 suites* ❧ *In-room: Wi-Fi. In-hotel: restaurants, tennis courts, bars, children's programs, pools, gym, beach, business center, water sports* ⅋⅋ *No meals.*

$$$$
RESORT
⊞ **Hotel Riu Palace Aruba.** This white wedding cake of a resort towers over Palm Beach with one 8-story and two 10-story towers. **Pros:** beautiful vistas; everything is brand-new; large and lively pool area. **Cons:** resort is large and impersonal; pool area is always crowded and very loud; the à la carte restaurants feel like sterile afterthoughts; interior decor is a bit jarring for an island destination. ✉ *J.E. Irausquin Blvd. 79, Palm Beach* ☎ *297/586–3900 or 800/345–2782* ⊕ *www.riuaruba.com* ↝ *4,419 rooms* ❧ *In-room: safe. In-hotel: restaurants, bars, pools, gym, beach, business center, water sports* ⅋⅋ *All-inclusive.*

$$$$
RESORT
☾
Fodor's Choice
★
⊞ **Hyatt Regency Aruba Beach Resort & Casino.** This 12-acre resort offers everything from a casino for adults to waterslides for kids, so it's popular with families. **Pros:** beautiful grounds; great for kids; excellent restaurants. **Cons:** small balconies for a luxury hotel; some rooms are quite a stretch from the beach. ✉ *J.E. Irausquin Blvd. 85, Palm Beach* ☎ *297/586–1234 or 800/554–9288* ⊕ *www.aruba.hyatt.com* ↝ *342 rooms, 18 suites* ❧ *In-room: safe, Internet, Wi-Fi. In-hotel: restaurants, room service, tennis courts, bars, children's programs, pool, gym, spa, beach, business center, water sports* ⅋⅋ *No meals.*

$
RESORT
☾
★
⊞ **Mill Resort & Suites.** This lovely low-rise resort is deservedly popular with travelers in the know. **Pros:** entire compound has an intimate feel; lively bar area; theme nights are fun; numerous activities to keep kids amused. **Cons:** not on the beach; pool area can be busy and noisy; rates are not quite the steal they used to be. ✉ *J.E. Irausquin Blvd. 330, Palm Beach* ☎ *297/586–7700* ⊕ *www.millresort.com* ↝ *64 studios, 128 suites* ❧ *In-room: safe, kitchen (some), Wi-Fi. In-hotel: restaurant, tennis courts, bar, pools, gym, laundry facilities, spa, business center* ⅋⅋ *No meals.*

¢
HOTEL
☾
★
⊞ **MVC Eagle Beach.** For the price and the excellent location across from Eagle Beach, this former vacation facility for the visiting families of Dutch marines is a great bargain. **Pros:** unbeatable price; popular restaurant with food at affordable prices; since the main language is Dutch, you feel that you're someplace other than South Florida here; very short walk to beach; friendly and helpful staff. **Cons:** spartan accommodations; not for those who want to be away from kids. ✉ *J.E. Irausquin Blvd. 240, Eagle Beach* ☎ *297/587–0110* ⊕ *www.mvceaglebeach.com* ↝ *16 rooms, 3 suites* ❧ *In-hotel: restaurant, tennis court, bar, pool, laundry facilities, beach* ⅋⅋ *No meals.*

$$$–$$$$
RESORT
★
⊞ **Radisson Aruba Resort & Casino.** Luxury is the key word at this 14-acre resort with lavish rooms, appointed with colonial West Indian–style furniture, including four-poster beds. **Pros:** rooms have an intimate feel; exercise junkies will love the top-notch facilities; one of the best spas on the island; free high-speed Internet in rooms. **Cons:** restaurants are good but not great; some rooms are on the small side and don't seem worth the cost; you never forget you are in a big hotel. ✉ *J.E. Irausquin Blvd. 81, Palm Beach* ☎ *297/586–6555* ⊕ *www.radisson.com* ↝ *321 rooms, 34 suites* ❧ *In-room: safe, Wi-Fi. In-hotel: restaurants, room*

4

service, tennis courts, bars, children's programs, pools, gym, spa, beach, business center, water sports ⦿*No meals.*

\$\$–\$\$\$ ⊡ **Renaissance Aruba Resort & Casino.** This downtown hotel with many
RESORT spectacular views consists of two distinct parts: the Renaissance Marina
Fodor'sChoice Hotel and the Renaissance Ocean Suites. **Pros:** right in the heart of
★ the downtown shopping district; lobby and shopping areas are always
lively; pool area offers an unmatched view of the port; access to private island with beaches. **Cons:** rooms overlooking the atrium can
be a bit claustrophobic; beach is off-site; hard to find a quiet spot;
no hotel grounds; no balconies in downtown section. ⊠*L.G. Smith
Blvd. 82, Oranjestad* ☎*297/583–6000 or 800/421–8188* ⊕*www.
renaissancearuba.com* ⤶*287 rooms, 269 suites* ♿*In-room: kitchen
(some), Internet. In-hotel: restaurants, room service, tennis court, bars,
children's programs, pools, gym, laundry facilities, spa, business center,
water sports* ⦿*No meals.*

\$\$\$\$ ⊡ **Tamarijn Aruba All-Inclusive Beach Resort.** An upscale alternative to its
RESORT sister property, the Divi Aruba *(⇨ above)*, this resort is pleasantly laid-
back for an all-inclusive. **Pros:** stunning beach; access to the Divi Aruba
All Inclusive next door; perfect for families. **Cons:** being right on the
beach can mean noise during busy periods; the linear layout means some
rooms are quite far from the lobby; Wi-Fi is an additional charge. ⊠*J.E.
Irausquin Blvd. 41, Punta Brabo* ☎*297/525–5200 or 800/554–2008*
⊕*www.tamarijnaruba.com* ⤶*236 rooms, 97 suites* ♿*In-hotel: restaurants, tennis courts, bars, pools, gym, beach, business center, water
sports* ⟳*3-night minimum* ⦿*All-inclusive.*

\$\$\$\$ ⊡ **Westin Aruba Resort, Spa & Casino.** Westin added a few extra touches to
RESORT the already tasteful rooms at the former Wyndham, including flat-screen
Fodor'sChoice TVs, and the fine restaurants that helped make this hotel a standout
★ choice in the past remain as well. **Pros:** chic and airy rooms; magnificent beachfront and pool area; comprehensive spa facilities; great restaurants. **Cons:** immediate area is congested and busy; resort lacks an
intimate feel. ⊠*J.E. Irausquin Blvd. 77, Palm Beach* ☎*297/586–4466
or 877/822–2222* ⊕*www.westinaruba.com* ⤶*481 rooms, 81 suites*
♿*In-room: safe, Wi-Fi. In-hotel: restaurants, tennis court, bars, pool,
spa, beach, business center, water sports* ⦿*No meals.*

NIGHTLIFE AND THE ARTS

NIGHTLIFE

Unlike many islands, Aruba's nightlife isn't confined to the touristy
folkloric shows at hotels. Arubans like to party. They usually start
celebrating late, and the action doesn't pick up until around midnight.

One uniquely Aruban institution is a psychedelically painted '57 Chevy
bus called the **Kukoo Kunuku** (☎*297/586–2010* ⊕*www.kukookunuku.
com*). Every night except Sunday you can find as many as 40 passengers
traveling among three bars from sundown to around midnight. The \$59
fee per passenger includes a so-so dinner, some drinks, and pickup at
your hotel. The same company operates the infamous *Tatoo* party boat,

which has a buffet, $1 drinks, live entertainment, and a lot of rowdy behavior for $49. The boat leaves at 7:15 pm on Friday from the De Palm pier near the Radisson.

BARS

Bambu (✉ *Babijn 53, Paradera* ☎ *No phone*) is a local joint that offers typical Aruban food, cheap drinks, and a lively crowd on the terrace on weekends.

Charlie's Bar (✉ *Zeppenfeldstraat 56, San Nicolas* ☎ *297/584 5086*) has been an Aruba institution since 1941. It's a bit far from most hotels, but certainly worth the trip. Expect a raucous (and, most likely, very inebriated) crowd. The food here is quite good as well, all the better for padding your stomach before the margaritas.

For specialty drinks, try **Iguana Joe's** (✉ *Royal Plaza Mall, L.G. Smith Blvd. 94, Oranjestad* ☎ *297/583–9373*). The creative reptilian-theme decor is as colorful as the cocktails.

★ With painted parrots flocking on the ceiling, **Mambo Jambo** (✉ *Royal Plaza Mall, L.G. Smith Blvd. 94, Oranjestad* ☎ *297/583–3632*) is daubed in sunset colors. Sip one of several concoctions sold nowhere else on the island, then browse for memorabilia at a shop next door.

With front-row seats to view the green flash—that ray of light that supposedly flicks through the sky as the sun sinks into the ocean—the **Palms Beach Bar** (✉ *Hyatt Regency Aruba Beach Resort & Casino, J.E. Irausquin Blvd. 85, Palm Beach* ☎ *297/586–1234*) is the perfect spot to enjoy the sunset.

CASINOS

Aruban casinos offer something for both high and low rollers, as well as live, nightly entertainment in their lounges. Die-hard gamblers might look for the largest or the most active casinos, but many simply visit the casino closest to their hotel.

★ In the casual **Alhambra Casino** (✉ *L.G. Smith Blvd. 47, Oranjestad* ☎ *297/583–5000*), a "Moorish slave" named Roger gives every gambler a hearty handshake upon entering.

The smart money is on the **Casablanca Casino** (✉ *Westin Aruba Resort, Spa & Casino, J.E. Irausquin Blvd. 77, Palm Beach* ☎ *297/586–4466*). It's quietly elegant and has a Bogart theme.

Overhead at the **Casino at the Radisson Aruba Resort** (✉ *Radisson Aruba Resort & Casino, J.E. Irausquin Blvd. 81, Palm Beach* ☎ *297/586–4045*), thousands of lights simulate shooting stars that seem destined to carry out your wishes for riches. The slots here open at noon, and table action begins at 3 pm.

The ultramodern **Copacabana Casino** (✉ *Hyatt Regency Aruba Beach Resort & Casino, J.E. Irausquin Blvd. 85, Palm Beach* ☎ *297/586–1234*) is an enormous complex with a Carnival-in-Rio theme and live entertainment.

The **Crystal Casino** (✉ *Renaissance Aruba Resort & Casino, L.G. Smith Blvd. 82, Oranjestad* ☎ *297/583–6000*) is open 24 hours a day.

The **Excelsior Casino** (✉ *Holiday Inn SunSpree Aruba Beach Resort & Casino, J.E. Irausquin Blvd. 230, Palm Beach* ☎ *297/586–7777*) has sports betting in addition to the usual slots and table games.

Royal Palm Casino (✉ *Occidental Grand Aruba, J.E. Irausquin Blvd. 250, Eagle Beach* ☎ *297/587–4665*) is one of the largest in the Caribbean. It has an expansive, sleek interior; 400 slot machines; a no-smoking slot room; and gaming tables.

Low-key gambling can be found at the waterside **Seaport Casino** (✉ *L.G. Smith Blvd. 9, Oranjestad* ☎ *297/583–6000*).

The **Stellaris Casino** (✉ *Aruba Marriott Resort, L.G. Smith Blvd. 101, Palm Beach* ☎ *297/586–9000*) is one of the island's most popular and is open 24 hours.

DANCE AND MUSIC CLUBS

★ For jazz and other types of music, try cozy **Garufa Cigar & Cocktail Lounge** (✉ *Wilhelminastraat 63, Oranjestad* ☎ *297/582–7205*), which serves as a lounge for customers awaiting a table at the nearby Gaucho Argentine Grill (you're issued a beeper so you know when your table is ready). While you wait, have a drink, enjoy some appetizers, and take in the leopard-print carpet and funky bar stools. The ambience may very well draw you back for an after-dinner cognac. There's live entertainment most nights, and the powerful smoke extractor system helps make life bearable for nonsmokers.

THE ARTS

ART GALLERIES

★ **Access** (✉ *Caya G.F. Betico Croes 16–18, Oranjestad* ☎ *297/588–7837*) showcases new and established artists; it's a major venue for Caribbean art. Located in the downtown shopping district, the gallery is home to a thriving cultural scene that includes poetry readings, chamber music concerts, and screenings of feature films and documentaries. The owner, artist Landa Henriquez, is also a bolero singer.

At **Galeria Eterno** (✉ *Emanstraat 92, Oranjestad* ☎ *297/583–9607*), you can find local and international artists at work. Be sure to stop by for concerts by classical guitarists, dance performances, visual-arts shows, and plays.

Galeria Harmonia (✉ *Zeppenfeldstraat 10, San Nicolas* ☎ *297/584–2969*), the island's largest exhibition space, has a permanent collection of works by local and international artists.

Gasparito Restaurant & Art Gallery (✉ *Gasparito 3, Noord* ☎ *297/586–7044*) features a permanent exhibition by Aruban artists.

ISLAND CULTURE

The **Bon Bini Festival,** a year-round folkloric event (the name means "welcome" in Papiamento), is held every Tuesday from 6:30 pm to 8:30 pm at Ft. Zoutman in Oranjestad. In the inner courtyard you can check out the Antillean dancers in resplendent costumes, feel the rhythms of the steel drums, browse among the stands displaying local artwork, and partake of local food and drink. Admission is usually around $3, but can be as high as $10, depending on what is on offer.

SHOPPING

"Duty-free" *is* a magical term in the Caribbean—but it's not always accurate. The duty-free shopping zone in Aruba closed several years ago, so the only true duty-free shopping is in the departure area of the airport. (Passengers bound for the United States should be sure to shop before proceeding through U.S. customs in Aruba.) Downtown stores often advertise "duty-free prices," with markdowns of up to 25%, but comparison shopping is still advisable. Major credit cards are welcome virtually everywhere, U.S. dollars are accepted almost as readily as the local currency, and traveler's checks can be cashed with proof of identity.

Aruba's souvenir and crafts stores are full of Dutch porcelains and figurines, as befits the island's heritage. Dutch cheese is a good buy, as are hand-embroidered linens and any products made from the native aloe vera plant—sunburn cream, face masks, or skin refreshers. Local arts and crafts run toward wood carvings and earthenware emblazoned with "Aruba: One Happy Island" and the like. Since there's no sales tax, the price you see on the tag is what you pay. (Note that although large stores in town and at hotels include the value-added tax of 3%, tiny shops and studios may add it separately.) Don't try to bargain. Arubans consider it rude to haggle, despite what you may hear to the contrary.

AREAS AND MALLS

Oranjestad's **Caya G.F. Betico Croes** is Aruba's chief shopping street, lined with several shops advertising "duty-free prices" (again, these are not truly duty-free), boutiques, and jewelry stores noted for the aggressiveness of their vendors on cruise-ship days.

For late-night shopping, head to the **Alhambra Casino Shopping Arcade** (⊠ *L.G. Smith Blvd. 47, Manchebo Beach*), which is open until midnight. Souvenir shops, boutiques, and fast-food outlets fill the arcade, which is attached to the popular casino. Although small, the **Aquarius Mall** (⊠ *Elleboogstraat 1, Oranjestad*) has some upscale shops. The **Holland Aruba Mall** (⊠ *Havenstraat 6, Oranjestad*) houses a collection of smart shops and eateries. **Paseo Herencia** (⊠ *L.G. Smith Blvd., Palm Beach* ☏ *297/586–6533*) is the newest mall in Aruba, just minutes away from the high-rise hotel area. It's all about style, and from the great bell tower to the nightly dancing-waters shows and the selection of restaurants, the aim here is to pull in shoppers. Offerings include Cuban cigars, the fine leather goods of Mario Hernandez, Italian denim goods at Moda & Stile, perfumes, cosmetics, and a variety of souvenir shops. Stores at the **Port of Call Marketplace** (⊠ *L.G. Smith Blvd. 17, Oranjestad*) sell fine jewelry, perfumes, low-priced liquor, batiks, crystal, leather goods, and fashionable clothing.

Right under the Renaissance Hotel, the **Renaissance Mall** (⊠ *L.G. Smith Blvd. 82, Oranjestad*) has a variety of high-end stores such as Guess,

Lacoste, and Calvin Klein that are sure to please the more discerning traveler—prices, though, are about the same or more than in the United States; the Crystal Casino is right above the mall. Five minutes from the cruise-ship terminal, the **Renaissance Marketplace** (⊠ *L.G. Smith Blvd. 82, Oranjestad*), also known as Seaport Mall, has more than 120 stores selling merchandise to meet every taste and budget; the Seaport Casino is also here.

The **Royal Plaza Mall** (⊠ *L.G. Smith Blvd. 94, Oranjestad*), across from the cruise-ship terminal, has cafés, a post office (open weekdays 8 to 3:30), and such stores as Nautica, Benetton, Tommy Hilfiger, and Gandelman Jewelers. There's also a cybercafé for those who want to send email and get their caffeine fix all in one stop.

SPECIALTY STORES

CLOTHING

Confetti (⊠ *Renaissance Mall, L.G. Smith Blvd. 82, Oranjestad* ☎ *297/583–8614*) has the hottest European and American swimsuits, cover-ups, and beach essentials.

★ **Wulfsen & Wulfsen** (⊠ *Caya G.F. Betico Croes 52, Oranjestad* ☎ *297/582–3823*) has been one of the most highly regarded clothing stores in Aruba and the Netherlands Antilles for 30 years. It carries elegant suits for men and linen cocktail dresses for women; it's also a great place to buy Bermuda shorts.

HANDICRAFTS

★ **Art & Tradition Handicrafts** (⊠ *Caya G.F. Betico Croes 30, Oranjestad* ☎ *297/583–6534* ⊠ *Royal Plaza Mall, L.G. Smith Blvd. 94, Oranjestad* ☎ *297/582–7862*) sells intriguing souvenirs. Buds from the *mopa mopa* tree are boiled to form a resin, which is colored using vegetable dyes, then stretched by hand and mouth. Tiny pieces are cut and layered to form intricate designs—these are truly unusual gifts.

The **Artistic Boutique** (⊠ *L.G. Smith Blvd. 90–92, Oranjestad* ☎ *297/588–2468* ⊠ *Holiday Inn SunSpree Aruba Beach Resort & Casino, J.E. Irausquin Blvd. 230, Palm Beach* ☎ *297/583–3383*) is known for its Giuseppe Armani figurines from Italy, usually sold at a 20% discount; Aruban hand-embroidered linens; gold and silver jewelry; and porcelain and pottery from Spain.

JEWELRY

Filling 6,000 square feet of space, **Boolchand's** (⊠ *Renaissance Mall, L.G. Smith Blvd. 82, Oranjestad* ☎ *297/583–0147*) sells jewelry and watches. It also stocks leather goods, cameras, and electronics.

If green fire is your passion, **Colombian Emeralds** (⊠ *Renaissance Mall, L.G. Smith Blvd. 82, Oranjestad* ☎ *297/583–6238*) has a dazzling array. There are also fine European watches.

Kenro Jewelers (⊠ *Renaissance Mall, L.G. Smith Blvd. 82, Oranjestad* ☎ *297/583–4847 or 297/583–3171*) has two stores in the same mall, attesting to the popularity of its stock of bracelets and necklaces from Ramon Leopard; jewelry by Arando, Micheletto, and Blumei; and various brands of watches. There are also six other locations, including some in major hotels.

PERFUMES

For perfumes, cosmetics, men's and women's clothing, and leather goods (including Bally shoes), stop in at **Aruba Trading Company** (⊠ *Caya G.F. Betico Croes 12, Oranjestad* ☎ *297/582–2602*), which has been in business since the 1930s.

A venerated name in Aruba, **J.L. Penha & Sons** (⊠ *Caya G.F. Betico Croes 11/13, Oranjestad* ☎ *297/582–4160 or 297/582–4161*) sells high-end perfumes and cosmetics. It stocks such brands as Boucheron, Cartier, Dior, and Givenchy.

★ **Little Switzerland** (⊠ *Caya G.F. Betico Croes 14, Oranjestad* ☎ *297/582–1192* ⊠ *Royal Plaza Mall, L.G. Smith Blvd. 94, Oranjestad* ☎ *297/583–4057*), the Caribbean retail giant, is the place to go for brand-name men's and women's fragrances as well as china, crystal, and fine tableware.

At **Weitnauer** (⊠ *Caya G.F. Betico Croes 29, Oranjestad* ☎ *297/582–2790*) you can find specialty Lenox items, as well as a wide range of fragrances.

SPORTS AND ACTIVITIES

On Aruba you can participate in every conceivable water sport, as well as play tennis and golf or go on a fine hike through Arikok National Wildlife Park.

BIKING

Biking is a great way to get around the island; the climate is perfect, and the trade winds help to keep you cool. **Melchor Cycle Rental** (⊠ *Bubali 106B, Noord* ☎ *297/587–1787*) rents ATVs and bikes. **Rancho Notorious** (⊠ *Boroncana, Noord* ☎ *297/586–0508* ⊕ *www.ranchonotorious.com*) organizes mountain-biking tours.

DAY SAILS

If you plan to take a cruise around the island, know that the trade winds can make the waters choppy and that catamaran rides are much smoother than those on single-hull boats. Sucking on a peppermint or ginger candy may soothe your queasy stomach; avoid boating with an empty or overly full stomach. Moonlight cruises cost about $40 per person. There are also a variety of snorkeling, dinner and dancing, and sunset party cruises to choose from, priced from $30 to $60 per person. Many of the smaller operators work out of their homes; they often offer to pick you up (and drop you off) at your hotel or meet you at a particular hotel pier.

★ **Octopus Sailing Charters** (⊠ *Sali-a Cerca 1G, Oranjestad* ☎ *297/586–4281* ⊕ *www.octopusaruba.com*) operates a trimaran that holds about 20 people. The drinks flow freely during the three-hour afternoon sail, which costs $33. Having a captain named Jethro is almost worth the price of admission in itself.

Red Sail Sports (⊠ *L.G. Smith Blvd. 17, Oranjestad* ☎ *297/583–1603, 877/733–7245 in U.S.* ⊕ *www.redsailaruba.com*) offers a number of packages aboard its four catamarans, including the 70-foot *Rumba*. The popular sunset sail includes drinks and a lively atmosphere for $45 per person; the dinner-cruise package includes a three-course meal and open bar for $95. Red Sail Sports also has locations at the Hyatt and Occidental hotels. **Tranquilo Charters Aruba** (⊠ *Sibelius St. 25, Oranjestad* ☎ *297/586–1418* ⊕ *www.visitaruba.com/tranquilo*), operated by Captain Hagedoorn, offers entertaining cruises, including a six-hour cruise to the south side of the island with lunch for $75. As strange as it sounds, the special "mom's Dutch pea soup" served with lunch is actually very good. Snorkeling equipment and free lessons are included in the package. **Wave Dancer Cruises** (⊠ *Ponton 90, Oranjestad* ☎ *297/582–5520* ⊕ *www.arubawavedancer.com*), in business since the mid-1970s, offers excellent value for the money. Sunset sails are $37, including drinks and snacks; half-day sails are $45, including snacks, lunch, and drinks. Snorkeling packages are also available.

DIVING AND SNORKELING

With visibility of up to 90 feet, the waters around Aruba are excellent for snorkeling and diving. Advanced and novice divers alike will find plenty to occupy their time, as many of the most popular sites—including some interesting shipwrecks—are found in shallow waters ranging from 30 to 60 feet. Coral reefs covered with sensuously waving sea fans and eerie giant sponge tubes attract a colorful menagerie of sea life, including gliding manta rays, curious sea turtles, shy octopuses, and fish from grunts to groupers. Marine preservation is a priority on Aruba, and regulations by the Conference on International Trade in Endangered Species make it unlawful to remove coral, conch, and other marine life from the water.

Expect snorkel gear to rent for about $20 per day and trips to cost around $45. Scuba rates are around $50 for a one-tank reef or wreck dive, $75 for a two-tank dive, and $55 for a night dive. Resort courses, which offer an introduction to scuba diving, average $65 to $80. If you want to go all the way, complete open-water certification costs around $400.

★ **De Palm Watersports** (⊠ *L.G. Smith Blvd. 142, Oranjestad* ☎ *297/582–4400 or 800/766–6016* ⊕ *www.depalm.com*) is one of the best choices for your undersea experience, and the options go beyond basic diving. You can don a helmet and walk along the ocean floor near De Palm Island, home of huge blue parrot fish. You can even do Snuba—which is like scuba diving but without the heavy air tanks—from either a boat or from an island; it costs $65. **Dive Aruba** (⊠ *Wilhelminastraat 8, Oranjestad* ☎ *297/582–7337* ⊕ *www.divearuba.com*) offers resort courses, certification courses, and trips to interesting shipwrecks. **Mermaid Sport Divers** (⊠ *Bubali 112-J, Sasaki Hwy. between low-rise and high-rise*

A bouquet of colorful reefs can be explored in the waters of Aruba.

hotels, Oranjestad ☎ *297/587–4103* ⊕ *www.scubadivers-aruba.com*) has dive packages but is not PADI certified.

Native Divers Aruba (✉ *Koyari 1, Noord* ☎ *297/586–4763* ⊕ *www.nativedivers.com*) offers all types of dives; underwater naturalist courses are taught by PADI-certified instructors. Legions of return customers are testament to the personal attention provided by owner Romeo Croes. **Red Sail Sports** (✉ *J.E. Irausquin Blvd. 83, Oranjestad* ☎ *297/586–1603, 877/733–7245 in U.S.* ⊕ *www.redsail.com*) has courses for children and others new to scuba diving. An introductory class costs about $95.

FISHING

Deep-sea catches here include barracuda, kingfish, wahoo, bonito, and tuna. November to April is the catch-and-release season for sailfish and marlin. Many skippered charter boats are available for half- or full-day sails. Packages include tackle, bait, and refreshments. Prices range from $300 to $500 for a half-day charter and from $550 to $700 for a full day.

Pelican Tours & Watersports (✉ *Pelican Pier, near Holiday Inn and Playa Linda hotels, Palm Beach* ☎ *297/586–3271* ⊕ *www.pelican-aruba.com*) is not just for the surf-and-snorkel crowd; the company will help you catch trophy-size fish. **Red Sail Sports** (✉ *J.E. Irausquin Blvd. 83, Oranjestad* ☎ *297/586–1603, 877/733–7245 in U.S.* ⊕ *www.redsail.com*) can arrange everything for your fishing trip. Captain Kenny of **Teaser Charters** (✉ *St. Vincentweg 5, Oranjestad* ☎ *297/582–5088* ⊕ *www.teasercharters.com*) runs a thrilling expedition. The expertise of the crew is matched by a commitment to sensible fishing practices, which include catch and release, and avoiding ecologically sensitive areas. The company's two boats are fully equipped, and the crew seem to have an uncanny ability to locate the best fishing spots.

GOLF

The **Aruba Golf Club** (⊠ *Golfweg 82, San Nicolas* ☎ *297/584–2006*) has a 9-hole course with 20 sand traps, five water traps, roaming goats, and lots of cacti. There are also 11 greens covered with artificial turf, making 18-hole tournaments a possibility. The clubhouse has a bar and locker rooms. Greens fees are $10 for 9 holes, $15 for 18 holes. Golf carts are available.

The **Links at Divi Aruba** (⊠ *J.E. Irausquin Blvd. 93, Oranjestad* ☎ *297/581–4653*) is a 9-hole course designed by Karl Litten and Lorie Viola. The par-36 paspalum grass course (best for seaside courses) takes you past beautiful lagoons. Amenities include a golf school with professional instruction, a swing-analysis station, a driving range, and a two-story golf clubhouse with a pro shop. Two restaurants are available: Windows on Aruba for fine dining and Mulligan's for a casual and quick lunch. Greens fees are $85 for 9 holes, $124 for 18 from December to April; guests of the Divi properties pay a reduced rate.

★ **Tierra del Sol** (⊠ *Malmokweg* ☎ *297/586–0978*), a stunning course, is on the northwest coast near the California Lighthouse. Designed by Robert Trent Jones Jr., this 18-hole championship course combines Aruba's native beauty—cacti and rock formations—with the lush greens of the world's best courses. The greens fee varies depending on the time of day (from December to March it is $159 in the morning, $124 for early afternoon, and $100 from 3 pm). The fee includes a golf cart equipped with a communications system that allows you to order drinks for your return to the clubhouse. Half-day golf clinics, a bargain at $45, are available Monday, Tuesday, and Thursday. The pro shop is one of the Caribbean's most elegant, with an extremely attentive staff.

GUIDED TOURS

De Palm Tours (⊠ *L.G. Smith Blvd. 142, Oranjestad* ☎ *297/582–4400 or 800/766–6016* ⊕ *www.depalm.com*) has a near monopoly on Aruban sightseeing; you can make reservations through its general office or at hotel tour-desk branches. The basic 3½-hour tour hits highlights of the island. Wear sneakers or hiking shoes, and bring a lightweight jacket or wrap, as the air-conditioned bus gets cold.

HIKING

Despite Aruba's arid landscape, hiking the rugged countryside will give you the best opportunities to see the island's wildlife and flora. Arikok National Wildlife Park is an excellent place to glimpse the real Aruba, free of the trappings of tourism. The heat can be oppressive, so be sure to take it easy, wear a hat, and have a bottle of water handy.

○ **Aruba Nature Sensitive Hikers** (⊠ *Pos Chiquito 13E, Savaneta* ☎ *297/587–*
★ *5017* ⊕ *naturesensitivetours.com/*) is run by Eddy Croes, a former park
ranger whose passion for the area is seemingly unbounded. Groups are
never larger than eight people, so you'll see as much detail as you can
handle. Expect frequent stops when Eddy will ask for silence so that
you can hear the sounds of the park. The hikes are done at an easy pace
and are suitable for basically anyone. A moonlight walk is available for
those looking to avoid the heat.

HORSEBACK RIDING

Ranches offer short jaunts along the beach or longer rides along trails
passing through countryside flanked by cacti, divi-divi trees, and aloe
vera plants. Ask if you can stop off at Cura di Tortuga, a natural pool
that's reputed to have restorative powers. Rides are also possible in
Arikok National Wildlife Park. Rates run from $35 for an hour-long
trip to $65 for a three-hour tour; private rides cost slightly more.

○ **De Palm Tours** (⊠ *L.G. Smith Blvd. 142, Oranjestad* ☎ *297/582–4400*
or 800/766–6016 ⊕ *www.depalm.com*) arranges horseback-riding
excursions.

Rancho del Campo (⊠ *Sombre 22E, Santa Cruz* ☎ *297/585–0290*), the
first to offer rides to Natural Pool back in 1991, leads various excursions that start at $75 per person. **Rancho Daimari** (⊠ *Palm Beach 33B,
Noord* ☎ *297/586–6284* ⊕ *www.ranchodaimari.com*) will lead your
horse to water—either at Natural Bridge or Natural Pool—in the morning or afternoon for $75 per person. The "Junior Dudes" program is
tailored to young riders. There are even ATV trips. **Rancho Notorious**
(⊠ *Boroncana, Noord* ☎ *297/586–0508* ⊕ *www.ranchonotorious.com*)
will take you on a tour of the countryside for $45, to the beach to snor-
kel for $120, or on a three-hour ride up to the California Lighthouse
for $70. The company also organizes ATV and mountain-biking trips.

SUBMARINE EXCURSIONS

Explore an underwater reef teeming with marine life without getting
wet. **Atlantis Submarines** (⊠ *Renaissance Marina, L.G. Smith Blvd. 82,
Oranjestad* ☎ *297/583–6090* ⊕ *www.atlantisadventures.com*) operates
a 65-foot air-conditioned sub, *Atlantis VI*, which takes 48 passengers
for a two-hour tour 95 to 150 feet below the surface along Barcadera
Reef ($99 per person). The company also owns the *Seaworld Explorer*,
a semisubmersible that allows you to sit and view Aruba's marine habitat from 5 feet below the surface ($44 per person). Make reservations
a day in advance.

WINDSURFING

★ The southwestern coast's tranquil waters make windsurfing conditions
ideal for both beginners and intermediates, as the winds are steady but
sudden gusts rare. Experts will find the Atlantic coast, especially around
Grapefield and Boca Grandi beaches, more challenging; winds are fierce
and often shift course without warning. Most operators also offer

complete windsurfing vacation packages. The up-and-coming sport of kitesurfing (sometimes called kite boarding) is also popular in Aruba.

Aruba Active Vacations (✉ *L.G. Smith Blvd. 486, near Fisherman's Huts, Palm Beach* ☎ *297/586–3940* ⊕ *www.aruba-active-vacations.com*) is a major windsurfing center on the island. **Pelican Adventures Tours & Watersports** (✉ *Pelican Pier, near Holiday Inn and Playa Linda hotels, Palm Beach* ☎ *297/586–3600* ⊕ *www.pelican-aruba.com*) usually has rental boards and sails on hand. **Sailboard Vacations** (✉ *L.G. Smith Blvd. 462, Malmok Beach* ☎ *297/586–2527* ⊕ *www.sailboardvacations.com*) offers complete windsurfing packages, including accommodation. Equipment can be rented for $60 a day. Trade jokes and snap photos with your fellow windsurfers at **Vela Aruba** (✉ *L.G. Smith Blvd. 101, Palm Beach* ☎ *297/586–9000 Ext. 6430* ⊕ *www.velawindsurf.com*). This is *the* place to make friends. It's a major kitesurfing center as well.

Barbados

WORD OF MOUTH

"Imagine an ideal day on a Caribbean island with beautiful beaches and as much sightseeing and activities as you desire. Add wonderful food! You're in Barbados."

—Knowing

WELCOME TO BARBADOS

Broad vistas, sweeping seascapes, craggy cliffs, and acre upon acre of sugarcane— that's Barbados. Beyond that, what draws visitors to the island is the Bajan hospitality, the welcoming hotels and resorts, the sophisticated dining, the never-ending things to see and do, the exciting nightspots, and, of course, the sunny beaches.

TOP REASONS TO VISIT BARBADOS

1 Great resorts: They run the gamut—from unpretentious to knock-your-socks-off.

2 Great Golf: Golfers can choose from of the best championship courses

3 Restaurants Galore: Great food includes everything from street-party barbecue to fine dining.

4 Wide Range of Activities: Between land and water sports, sightseeing options, and nightlife, there's always plenty to do.

5 Welcoming Locals: Bajans are friendly, welcoming, helpful, and hospitable. You'll like them; they'll like you.

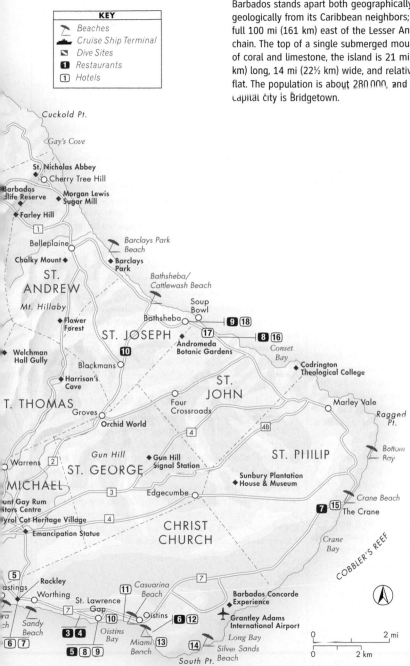

KEY

- Beaches
- Cruise Ship Terminal
- Dive Sites
- 1 Restaurants
- 1 Hotels

BARBADOS BASICS

Barbados stands apart both geographically and geologically from its Caribbean neighbors; it's a full 100 mi (161 km) east of the Lesser Antilles chain. The top of a single submerged mountain of coral and limestone, the island is 21 mi (34 km) long, 14 mi (22½ km) wide, and relatively flat. The population is about 280,000, and the capital city is Bridgetown.

Cuckold Pt.

Gay's Cove

St. Nicholas Abbey
Cherry Tree Hill
Barbados
Wildlife Reserve
Morgan Lewis
Sugar Mill
Farley Hill

1

Belleplaine
Chalky Mount
Barclays Park
Beach
Barclays
Park

ST.
ANDREW

Bathsheba/
Cattlewash Beach

Mt. Hillaby
Soup
Bowl
Bathsheba
9 18

Flower
Forest
ST. JOSEPH
17
8 16

Welchman
Hall Gully
10
Andromeda
Botanic Gardens
Conset
Bay

Blackmans
Codrington
Theological College

Harrison's
Cave
ST.
JOHN

T. THOMAS
Four
Crossroads
Marley Vale

Groves
Ragged
Pt.

Orchid World

4
4B

Warrens
2
Gun Hill
Gun Hill
Signal Station
ST. PHILIP
Bottom
Bay

ST. GEORGE

MICHAEL
3
Edgecumbe
Sunbury Plantation
House & Museum

unt Gay Rum
itors Centre
4
Crane Beach

yrol Cot Heritage Village
7 15
The Crane

Emancipation Statue

CHRIST
CHURCH
Crane
Bay

COBBLER'S REEF

5
Rockley
7

astings
Worthing
Casuarina
Beach

St. Lawrence
Gap
11
Barbados Concorde
Experience

7
10
Oistins
6 12
Grantley Adams
International Airport

ra
3 4
Oistins
Bay
Miami
Beach
13
Long Bay

ch
6 7
5 8 9
14
Silver Sands
Beach
South Pt.

Sandy
Beach

0   2 mi

0   2 km

BARBADOS PLANNER

Logistics

Getting to Barbados: Several airlines fly nonstop to Barbados, or you may have to connect in Miami or San Juan. Grantley Adams International Airport (BGI) is in Christ Church Parish on the south coast about 15 minutes from hotels situated along the south coast, 45 minutes from the west coast, and 30 minutes from Bridgetown.

Hassle Factor: Low.

On the Ground: Ground transportation is available immediately outside the customs area. Airport taxis aren't metered, but fares are regulated (about $35 to Speightstown, $25–$30 to west-coast hotels, $15–$20 to south-coast hotels). Be sure, however, to establish the fare before getting into the cab and confirm whether the price quoted is in U.S. or Barbadian dollars.

Getting Around on the Island: If you are staying in an isolated area, you may want or need to rent a car, but bus service is good, especially between Bridgetown and stops along the west and south coasts. Taxis may suffice for those travelers staying in busy resort areas.

Getting to Barbados

Nonstop Flights: You can fly nonstop to Barbados from Atlanta (Delta), Charlotte (US Airways), Miami (American), New York–JFK (American and JetBlue), and Philadelphia (US Airways).

Other Flights: American Eagle flies nonstop from San Juan, so many American Airlines customers transfer there instead of Miami. Caribbean Airlines offers connecting service from Fort Lauderdale, Miami, and New York via Port of Spain, Trinidad, but this adds at least two hours onto your flight time even in the best of circumstances and may not be the best option for most Americans. Barbados is also well connected to other Caribbean islands via LIAT. Mustique Airways and SVG Air connect Barbados to St. Vincent and the Grenadines, and many passengers use Barbados as a transit hub for points south, often spending the night each way.

Local Airline Contacts: Not all airlines flying into Barbados have local numbers. If your airline doesn't have a local contact number on the island, you will have to pay for the call. **American Airlines** (☎ 246/428–4170). **Caribbean Airlines** (☎ 246/428–1950 or 800/744–2225). **Caricom Airways** (⊕ www.caricomairways.com). **LIAT** (☎ 246/428–0986). **Mustique Airways** (☎ 246/428–1638). **Redjet** (⊕ www.flyredjet.com). **SVG Air** (☎ 784/457–5124).

Airport: Grantley Adams International Airport (BGI ☎ 246/428–7101) is a stunning, modern facility in Christ Church Parish, on the south coast. It's about 15 minutes from hotels situated along the south or east coasts, 45 minutes from the west coast, and 30 minutes from Bridgetown.

Cruise Ship Terminal: Bridgetown's Deep Water Harbour is on the northwest side of Carlisle Bay, and up to eight cruise ships at one time can dock at the cruise-ship terminal. Downtown Bridgetown is a ½-mi (1-km) walk from the pier (about 15 minutes by foot); a taxi costs about $4 each way.

Getting Around Barbados

Buses: Bus service is efficient and inexpensive. Blue buses with a yellow stripe are public, yellow buses with a blue stripe are private, and private "Zed-R" vans (so called for their ZR license plate designation) are white with a maroon stripe. All buses travel frequently along Highway 1 (St. James Road) and Highway 7 (South Coast Main Road), as well as inland routes. The fare is Bds$1.50 (75¢) for any one destination; exact change in either local or U.S. currency is appreciated. Buses run about every 20 minutes. Small signs on roadside poles that say "To City" or "Out of City," meaning the direction relative to Bridgetown, mark the bus stops. Flag down the bus with your hand, even if you're standing at the stop. Bridgetown terminals are at Fairchild Street for buses to the south and east and at Lower Green for buses to Speightstown via the west coast.

Driving: Barbados has good roads, but traffic can be heavy, particularly around Bridgetown. Drive on the left, British-style. When someone flashes headlights at you at an intersection, it means "after you." Be especially careful negotiating roundabouts (traffic circles). The speed limit is 30 mph (50 kph) in the country, 20 mph (30 kph) in town. Bridgetown actually has rush hours: 7 to 9 and 4 to 6. Park only in approved parking areas; downtown parking costs Bds75¢ to Bds$1 per hour.

Car Rentals: Most car-rental agencies require renters to be between 21 and either 70 or 75 years of age. More than 75 agencies rent cars, jeeps, or minimokes (small, open-sided vehicles). **Rates** are about $60 per day for a minimoke to $85 or more per day for a four-wheel-drive vehicle (or $225 to $400 or more per week) in high season. Most firms also offer discounted three-day rates, and many require at least a two-day rental in high season.

Car-Rental Agencies: Coconut Car Rentals (⊠ Bay St., Bridgetown, St. Michael ☎ 246/437–0291 ⊕ www. coconutcars.com). **Courtesy Rent-A-Car** (⊠ Grantley Adams International Airport, Christ Church ☎ 246/431–4160 ⊕ www.courtesyrentacar.com). **Drive-a-Matic Car Rental** (⊠ Lower Carlton, St. James ☎ 246/422–3000 ⊕ www. carhire.tv).

Taxis: Taxis operate 24 hours a day. They aren't metered but charge according to fixed rates set by the government. They carry up to three passengers, and the fare may be shared. Sample one-way fares from Bridgetown are $20 to Holetown, $25 to Speightstown, $20 to St. Lawrence Gap, and $35 to Bathsheba. Drivers can also be hired for an hourly rate of about $25–$30 for up to three people.

Island Activities

There's always something to do in Barbados, and that's the appeal to most visitors. The soft, white-sand **beaches** await your arrival whether you choose to stay in the millionaire's row of resorts on the west coast or along the more affordable south coast.

Exceptional **golf** courses lure a lot of players to the island, but the private courses—at Royal Westmoreland and Sandy Lane—aren't for anyone with a light wallet.

The island's **restaurant scene** is impressive; choose from street-party barbecue to international cuisine that rivals the finest dining on the planet.

Getting out on the water is the favored activity, whether that's on a **snorkeling** day sail, in a **mini-sub**, on a **deep-sea fishing** boat, or from a **dive boat** to explore the island's reefs and wrecks.

In season—from December through April—the conditions around the southern tip of Barbados are ideal for **windsurfing.** All year long, the pounding surf of the east coast draws **surfers** to the Bathsheba Soup Bowl, but the Independence Classic is the highlight every November.

5

BARBADOS PLANNER

Fast Facts

Banks and Exchange Services: The Barbados dollar is pegged to the U.S. dollar at the rate of Bds$1.98 to $1. The U.S. dollar is widely accepted. Barbados National Bank has a branch at Grantley Adams International Airport open daily from 8 am until the last plane lands or departs. ATMs are available 24 hours a day throughout the island. All prices quoted in this chapter are in U.S. dollars.

Electricity: 110 volts, 50 cycles, U.S. standard. Hotels generally have plug adapters and transformers available.

Emergency Services: Ambulance (☎ 511). **Fire** (☎ 311). **Police** (☎ 211 emergencies, 242/430–7100 non-emergencies). **Divers' Alert Network** (☎ 246/684–8111 or 246/684–2948).

Passport Requirements: All visitors, including U.S. and Canadian citizens, must have a valid passport and a return or ongoing ticket to enter Barbados. A birth certificate and photo ID are *not* sufficient proof of citizenship.

Weddings: There are no minimum residency requirements to get married; however, you need a license.

Essentials

Mail: An airmail letter from Barbados to the United States or Canada costs Bds$1.15 per half ounce; an airmail postcard, Bds45¢. When sending mail to Barbados, be sure to include the parish name in the address.

Taxes and Service Charges: A departure tax of $27.50 is automatically added to the price of your airfare. A 7.5% government tax is added to all hotel bills. A 10% service charge is often added to hotel bills and restaurant checks. A 15% V.A.T. is imposed on restaurant meals, admissions to attractions, and merchandise sales (other than those that are duty-free). Prices are often tax-inclusive; if not, the V.A.T. will be added to your bill.

Telephones: The area code for Barbados is 246. Local calls from private phones are free; some hotels charge a small fee. For directory assistance, dial 411. Calls from pay phones cost Bds25¢ for five minutes. Prepaid phone cards, which can be used throughout Barbados and other Caribbean islands, are sold at shops, attractions, transportation centers, and other convenient outlets.

Most U.S. cell phones will work in Barbados, though roaming charges can be expensive. Renting a cell phone or buying a local SIM card for your own unlocked phone may be a less expensive alternative if you're planning an extended stay or expect to make a lot of local calls. A cell phone can be rented for as little as $5 a day (minimum one-week rental); prepaid cards in varying denominations and top-off services are available at several locations throughout the island.

Tipping: If no service charge is added to your bill, tip waiters 10% to 15% and maids $2 per room per day. Tip bellhops and airport porters $1 per bag. Taxi drivers and tour guides appreciate a 10% tip.

Visitor Information: Barbados Tourism Authority (✉ Harbour Rd., Bridgetown, St. Michael ☎ 246/427–2623 ✉ Grantley Adams International Airport, Christ Church ☎ 246/428–5570 ✉ Cruise-ship terminal, Bridgetown, St. Michael ☎ 246/426–1718 or 800/221–9831 ⊕ www.visitbarbados.org).

Where to Stay

Most people stay either in luxurious enclaves on the fashionable west coast—north of Bridgetown—or on the action-packed south coast within easier reach of small, independent restaurants, bars, and nightclubs. A few inns on the remote southeast and east coasts offer ocean views and tranquillity, but those on the east coast don't have easy access to good swimming beaches. Prices in Barbados are sometimes twice as high in season as during the quieter months. Most hotels include no meals in their rates, but some include breakfast, and many offer a meal plan; some require you to purchase the meal plan in the high season, and a few offer all-inclusive packages.

Resorts: Great resorts run the gamut—from unpretentious to knock-your-socks-off—in terms of size, intimacy, amenities, and price. Many are well suited to families.

Small Inns: A few small, cozy inns may be found in the east and southeast regions of the island.

Villas and Condos: Families and long-term visitors may choose from a wide variety of condos (everything from busy time-share resorts to more sedate vacation complexes). Villas and villa complexes can be luxurious, simple, or something in between.

HOTEL AND RESTAURANT COSTS

Restaurant prices are for a main course at dinner and include any taxes or service charges. Hotel prices are per night for a double room in high season, excluding taxes, service charges, and meal plans (except at all-inclusives).

WHAT IT COSTS IN U.S. DOLLARS

	¢	$	$$	$$$	$$$$
Restaurants	under $8	$8–$12	$12–$20	$20–$30	over $30
Hotels	under $150	$151–$275	$276–$375	$376–$475	over $475

When to Go

Barbados is busiest in the high season, which extends from December 15 through April 15. Off-season hotel rates can be half what they are during this busy period. During the high season, too, a few hotels may require you to buy a meal plan, which is usually not required in the low season. As noted in the listings, some hotels close in September and October, the slowest months of the off-season, for annual renovations. Some restaurants may close for brief periods within that time frame, as well.

In mid-January the **Barbados Jazz Festival** is a weeklong event jammed with performances by international artists, jazz legends, and local talent.

In February the weeklong **Holetown Festival** is held at the fairgrounds to commemorate the date in 1627 when the first European settlers arrived in Barbados.

Gospelfest occurs in May, and hosts performances by gospel headliners from around the world.

Dating from the 19th century, **Crop Over,** a monthlong festival similar to Carnival that begins in July and ends on **Kadooment Day** (a national holiday), marks the end of the sugarcane harvest.

5

BARBADOS BEACHES

Geologically, Barbados is a coral-and-limestone island (not volcanic) with few rivers and, as a result, has beautiful beaches, particularly along the island's southern and southeastern coastlines.

(Above) Bathsheba, Barbados. (Opposite page bottom) Surfers at Soup Bowl, Bathsheba. (Opposite page top) Couple on beach in Barbados.

The west coast has some lovely beaches as well, but they're more susceptible to erosion after major autumn storms, if any, have taken their toll. With long stretches of open beach, crashing ocean surf, rocky cliffs, and verdant hills, the Atlantic (windward) side of Barbados is where Barbadians spend their holidays, but these beaches aren't safe for swimming. The surf and currents are too strong, even for experienced swimmers. All Bajan beaches have fine white sand, and all are open to the public. Most have access from the road, so nonguest bathers don't have to pass through hotel properties. When the surf is too high and swimming becomes dangerous, a red flag will be hoisted on the beach. A yellow flag—or a red flag at half-staff—means swim with caution. Topless sunbathing—on the beach or at the pool—is not allowed anywhere in Barbados by government regulation.

LOTS OF BEACHES

All along the south and west coasts, you'll find excellent beaches with broad swaths of white sand. The unique pink coral sand at Crane Beach and magnificent—and rather remote—Bottom Bay definitely lure romantics. Sand on the east-coast beaches is equally white, but the treacherous surf means you can only wade or stroll, not swim.

SOUTH COAST

A young, energetic crowd favors the south-coast beaches, which are broad and breezy, blessed with powdery white sand, and dotted with tall palms. The reef-protected areas with crystal-clear water are safe for swimming and snorkeling. The surf is medium to high, and the waves get bigger and the winds stronger (windsurfers take note) the farther southeast you go.

Accra Beach. This popular beach, also known as Rockley Beach, is next to the Accra Beach Hotel. Look forward to gentle surf and a lifeguard, plenty of nearby restaurants for refreshments, a children's playground, and beach stalls for renting chairs and equipment for snorkeling and other water sports. Parking is available at an on-site lot. ⊠ *Hwy. 7, Rockley, Christ Church.*

★ **Bottom Bay.** Popular for fashion and travel-industry photo shoots, Bottom Bay is the quintessential Caribbean beach. Surrounded by a coral cliff, studded with a stand of palms, and with an endless ocean view, this dreamy enclave is near the southeastern tip of the island. The waves can be too strong for swimming, but it's *the* picture-perfect place for a picnic lunch. Park at the top of the cliff and follow the steps down to the beach. ⊠ *Dover, St. Philip.*

Word of Mouth. "[C]heck out Bottom Bay. There are limestone cliffs with a

small field of palm trees and a natural looking gorgeous beach. It's featured in most of the promotional commercials for Barbados, and for a reason." —Blamona

Carlisle Bay. Adjacent to the Hilton Barbados just south of Bridgetown, this broad half circle of white sand is one of the island's best beaches—but it can become crowded on weekends and holidays. Park at Harbour Lights or at the Boatyard Bar and Bayshore Complex, both on Bay Street, where you can also rent umbrellas and beach chairs and buy refreshments. ⊠ *Aquatic Gap, Needham's Point, St. Michael.*

Word of Mouth. "Carlisle bay is calm and has the most beautiful crystal clear aqua water." —nunnles

★ **Casuarina Beach.** Stretched in front of the Almond Casuarina Resort, where St. Lawrence Gap meets the Maxwell Coast Road, this broad strand of powdery white sand is great for both sunbathing and strolling, with the surf from low to medium. Find public access and parking on Maxwell Coast Road, near the Bougainvillea Resort. ⊠ *Maxwell Coast Rd., Dover, Christ Church.*

★ **Crane Beach.** This exquisite crescent of pink sand on the southeast coast was named not for the elegant long-legged wading birds but for the crane used to haul and load cargo when this area was a busy port. Crane Beach usually has

Miami Beach.

a steady breeze and lightly rolling surf that is great for bodysurfing. A lifeguard is on duty. Changing rooms are available at The Crane resort for a small fee. Access is through the hotel and down to the beach via either a cliff-side elevator or 98 steps. ⊠ *Crane Bay, St. Philip*.

Word of Mouth. "[Crane Beach] has pink sand like baby powder. The cliffs are a sight, and you can jump off into the ocean." —kmw1211

★ **Fodor's Choice** | **Miami Beach.** Also called Enterprise Beach, this isolated spot on Enterprise Coast Road, just east of Oistins, is an underrated slice of pure white sand with cliffs on either side and crystal-clear water. You can find a palm-shaded parking area, snack carts, and chair rentals. Bring a picnic or have lunch across the road at Café Luna in Little Arches Hotel. ⊠ *Enterprise Beach Rd., Enterprise, Christ Church*.

Sandy Beach. This beach has shallow, calm waters and a picturesque lagoon, making it an ideal location for families with small kids. Park right on the main road. You can rent beach chairs and umbrellas, and plenty of places

nearby sell food and drinks. ⊠ *Hwy. 7, Worthing, Christ Church*.

Silver Sands–Silver Rock Beach. Nestled between South Point, the southernmost tip of the island, and Inch Marlow Point, Silver Sands–Silver Rock is a beautiful strand of white sand that always has a stiff breeze. That makes this beach the best in Barbados for intermediate and advanced windsurfers and, more recently, kitesurfers. ⊠ *Off Hwy. 7, Christ Church*.

EAST COAST

Be cautioned: swimming at east-coast beaches is treacherous, even for strong swimmers, and is *not* recommended. Waves are high, the bottom tends to be rocky, the currents are unpredictable, and the undertow is dangerously strong.

Barclays Park. Serious swimming is unwise at this beach, which follows the coastline in St. Andrew, but you can take a dip, wade, and play in the tide pools. A lovely shaded area with picnic tables is directly across the road. ⊠ *Ermy Bourne Hwy., north of Bathsheba, St. Andrew*.

★ **Bathsheba/Cattlewash.** Although it's not safe for swimming, the miles of untouched, windswept sand along the East Coast Road in St. Joseph Parish are great for beachcombing and wading. As you approach Bathsheba Soup Bowl, the southernmost stretch just below Tent Bay, the enormous mushroom-shape boulders and rolling surf are uniquely impressive. This is also where expert ourfers from around the world converge each November for the Independence Classic Surfing Championship. ⊠ *East Coast Rd., Bathsheba, St. Joseph.*

WEST COAST

Gentle Caribbean waves lap the west coast, and leafy mahogany trees shade its stunning coves and sandy beaches. The water is perfect for swimming and water sports. An almost unbroken chain of beaches runs between Bridgetown and Speightstown. Elegant homes and luxury hotels face much of the beachfront property in this area, dubbed Barbados's "Platinum Coast."

West-coast beaches are considerably smaller and narrower than those on the south coast. Also, prolonged stormy weather in September and October may cause sand erosion, temporarily making the beach even narrower. Even so, west-coast beaches are seldom crowded. Vendors stroll by, selling handmade baskets, hats, dolls, jewelry, even original watercolors; owners of private boats offer waterskiing, parasailing, and snorkeling excursions. There are no concession stands, but hotels and beachside restaurants welcome nonguests for terrace lunches (wear a cover-up), and you can buy picnic items at supermarkets in Holetown.

Brighton Beach. Calm as a lake, this is where you can find locals taking a quick dip on hot days. Just north of Bridgetown, Brighton Beach is also home to the Cockspur Beach Club. ⊠ *Spring Garden Hwy., Brighton, St. Michael.*

★ **Fodor's Choice** **Mullins Beach.** This lovely beach just south of Speightstown is a perfect place to spend the day. The water is safe for swimming and snorkeling, there's easy parking on the main road, and Mullins Restaurant serves snacks, meals, and drinks—and rents chairs and umbrellas. ⊠ *Hwy. 1, Mullins Bay, St. Peter.*

Paynes Bay Beach. The stretch of beach just south of Sandy Lane is lined with luxury hotels. It's a very pretty area, with plenty of beach to go around and good snorkeling. Public access is available at several locations along Highway 1; parking is limited. Grab liquid refreshments and a bite to eat at Bomba's Beach Bar. ⊠ *Hwy. 1, Paynes Bay, St. James.*

Word of Mouth. "Payne's Bay Beach . . . almost always has pretty calm water and is one of the nicest beaches on the island. You can walk the beach far north to Sandy Lane Resort and south way past Tamarind." —xkenx

5

Mullins Beach.

By Jane E. Zarem

Barbados stands apart from its neighbors in the Lesser Antilles archipelago, the chain of islands that stretches in a graceful arc from the Virgin Islands to Trinidad. Barbados is isolated in the Atlantic Ocean, 100 mi (160 km) due east of St. Lucia, its nearest neighbor.

Geologically, most of the Lesser Antilles are the peaks of a volcanic mountain range, whereas Barbados is the top of a single, relatively flat protuberance of coral and limestone—the source of building blocks for many a plantation manor. Several of those historic greathouses, in fact, have been carefully restored. Some are open to visitors.

Bridgetown, both capital city and commercial center, is on the southwest coast of pear-shape Barbados. Most of the 280,000 Bajans (Bajan, pronounced *bay*-jun, derives from the phonetic British pronunciation of Barbadian) live and work in and around Bridgetown, elsewhere in St. Michael Parish, or along the idyllic west coast or busy south coast. Others reside in tiny villages that dot the interior landscape. Broad sandy beaches, craggy cliffs, and numerous coves make up the coastline, and the interior is consumed by forested hills and gullies and acre upon acre of sugarcane.

Without question, Barbados is the "most British" island in the Caribbean. In contrast to the turbulent colonial past experienced by neighboring islands, which included repeated conflicts between France and Britain for dominance and control, British rule in Barbados carried on uninterrupted for 340 years—from the first established British settlement in 1627 until independence was granted in 1966. That's not to say, of course, that there weren't significant struggles in Barbados, as elsewhere in the Caribbean, between the British landowners and their African-born slaves and other indentured servants.

With that unfortunate period of slavery relegated to the history books, the British influence on Barbados remains strong today in local manners, attitudes, customs, and politics—tempered, of course, by the characteristically warm nature of the Bajan people. In keeping with British-born traditions, many Bajans worship at the Anglican church, afternoon tea is a ritual, cricket is the national pastime (a passion, most admit), dressing for dinner is a firmly entrenched tradition, and patrons at some bars are as likely to order a Pimm's Cup or a shandy as a rum and Coke. And yet, Barbados is hardly stuffy—this is still the Caribbean, after all.

Tourist facilities are concentrated on the west coast in St. James and St. Peter parishes (appropriately dubbed the Platinum Coast) and on the south coast in Christ Church Parish. Traveling along the west coast to historic Holetown, the site of the first British settlement, and continuing to the northern city of Speightstown, you can find posh beachfront resorts, luxurious private villas, and fine restaurants enveloped by lush gardens and tropical foliage. The trendier, more commercial south coast offers competitively priced hotels and beach resorts, and its St. Lawrence Gap area is jam-packed with shops, restaurants, and nightlife. The relatively wide-open spaces along the southeast coast are proving ripe for development, and some wonderful inns and hotels already take advantage of the intoxicatingly beautiful ocean vistas. For their own vacations, though, Bajans escape to the rugged east coast, where the Atlantic surf pounds the dramatic shoreline with unrelenting force.

All in all, Barbados is a sophisticated tropical island with a rich history, lodgings to suit every taste and pocketbook, and plenty to pique your interest both day and night—whether you're British or not!

SAFETY

Crime isn't a major problem in Barbados, but take normal precautions. Lock your room, and don't leave valuables—particularly passports, electronic equipment, and wallets—in plain sight or unattended on the beach. Use your hotel safe. For personal safety, avoid walking on the beach or on unlighted streets at night. Lock your rental car, and don't pick up hitchhikers. Using or trafficking in illegal drugs is strictly prohibited in Barbados. Any offense is punishable by a hefty fine, imprisonment, or both.

5

EXPLORING BARBADOS

The terrain changes dramatically from any one of the island's 11 parishes to the next, and so does the pace. Bridgetown, the capital, is a somewhat sophisticated city. West-coast resorts and private estates ooze luxury, whereas the small villages and vast sugar plantations found throughout central Barbados reflect the island's history. The relentless Atlantic surf shaped the cliffs of the dramatic east coast, and the northeast is called Scotland because of its hilly landscape. Along the lively south coast, the daytime hustle and bustle produce a palpable energy that continues well into the night at countless restaurants, dance clubs, and nightspots.

BRIDGETOWN

This bustling capital city is a major duty-free port with a compact shopping area. The principal thoroughfare is Broad Street, which leads west from National Heroes Square.

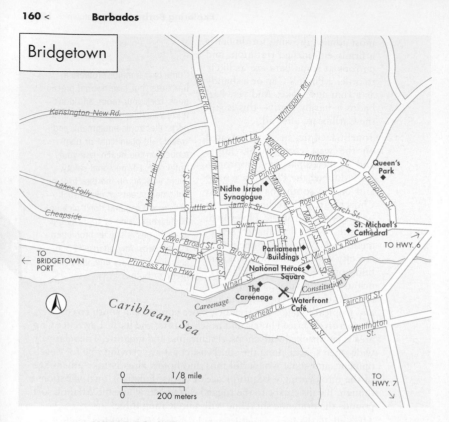

Bridgetown

Kensington New Rd.

Lakes Folly

Cheapside

Baxters Rd.

Whitepark Rd.

Lightfoot La.

Coleridge St.

Waldron

Pinfold

Pinfold St.

Queen's
Park ◆

Crumpton St.

Mason Hall St.

Reed St.

Milk Market

Suttle St.

Nidhe Israel ◆
Synagogue
James St.

Magazine La.

Roebuck St.

Church St.

Marhill St.

St. Michael's ◆
Cathedral

Swan St.

Lower Broad St.

McGregor St.

St. George St.

Broad St.

Parliament ◆
Buildings

Mary St.

St. Michael's Row

TO HWY. 6

→

Chamberlain Bridge

National Heroes ◆
Square

Princess Alice Hwy.

TO ←
BRIDGETOWN
PORT

Wharf St.

The
Careenage ✕

Constitution R.

Fairchild St.

Careenage

Waterfront
Café

Bay St.

Wellington
St.

Pierhead La.

Caribbean Sea

0   1/8 mile

0   200 meters

TO
HWY. 7
↘

WHAT TO SEE

The Careenage. Bridgetown's natural harbor and gathering place is where, in the early days, schooners were careened (turned on their sides) to be scraped of barnacles and repainted. Today the Careenage serves as a marina for pleasure yachts and excursion boats. A boardwalk skirts the north side of the Careenage; on the south side, a lovely esplanade has pathways and benches for pedestrians and a statue of Errol Barrow, the first prime minister of Barbados. The Chamberlain Bridge and the Charles Duncan O'Neal Bridge cross the Careenage.

National Heroes Square. Across Broad Street from the Parliament Buildings and bordered by High and Trafalgar streets, this triangular plaza marks the center of town. Its monument to Lord Horatio Nelson (who was in Barbados only briefly in 1777 as a 19-year-old navy lieutenant) predates Nelson's Column in London's Trafalgar Square by 36 years. Also here are a war memorial and a fountain that commemorates the advent of running water on Barbados in 1865.

Nidhe Israel Synagogue. Providing for the spiritual needs of one of the oldest Jewish congregations in the Western Hemisphere, this synagogue was formed by Jews who left Brazil in the 1620s and introduced sugarcane to Barbados. The adjoining cemetery has tombstones dating from the 1630s. The original house of worship, built in 1654, was destroyed in an 1831 hurricane, rebuilt in 1833, and restored with the assistance of the Barbados National Trust in 1987. Friday-night services are held during the winter months, but the building is open to the public year-round. Shorts are not acceptable during services but may be worn at other times. ⊠ *Synagogue La., St. Michael* ☎ *246/426–5792* ✉ *Donation requested* ⊙ *Weekdays 9–4.*

Parliament Buildings. Overlooking National Heroes Square in the center of town, these Victorian buildings were constructed around 1870 to house the British Commonwealth's third-oldest parliament. A series of stained-glass windows depicts British monarchs from James I to Victoria. ⊠ *Broad St., St. Michael* ☎ *246/427–2019* ✉ *Donations welcome* ⊙ *Tours weekdays at 11 and 2, when parliament isn't in session.*

Queen's Park. Northeast of Bridgetown, Queen's Park contains one of the island's two immense baobab trees. Brought to Barbados from Guinea, West Africa, around 1738, this tree has a girth of more than 60 feet. Queen's Park Art Gallery, managed by the National Culture Foundation, is the island's largest gallery; exhibits change monthly. Queen's Park House, the historic home of the British troop commander, has been converted into a theater, with an exhibition room on the lower floor and a restaurant. Originally called King's House, the name was changed upon Queen Victoria's succession to the throne. ⊠ *Constitution Rd., St. Michael* ☎ *246/427–2345 gallery* ✉ *Free* ⊙ *Daily 9–5.*

St. Michael's Cathedral. Although no one has proved it, George Washington is said to have worshiped here on his only trip outside the United States in 1751. The original structure was nearly a century old by then. Destroyed twice by hurricanes, it was rebuilt in 1784 and again in 1831. ⊠ *Spry St. east of National Heroes Sq., St. Michael.*

SOUTH COAST

Christ Church Parish, which is far busier and more developed than the west coast, is chockablock with condos, high- and low-rise hotels, and beach parks. It is also the location of St. Lawrence Gap, with its many places to eat, drink, shop, and party. As you move southeast, the broad, flat terrain comprises acre upon acre of cane fields, interrupted only by an occasional oil rig and a few tiny villages. Along the byways are colorful chattel houses, which were the traditional homes of tenant farmers. Historically, these typically Barbadian, ever-expandable small buildings were built so they could be dismantled and moved, as required.

WHAT TO SEE

ⓒ **Barbados Concorde Experience.** Opened to the public in April 2007, the Concorde Experience revolves around the British Airways Concorde G-BOAE (Alpha Echo, for short) that for many years flew between London and Barbados and has made its permanent home here. Besides boarding the sleek supersonic aircraft itself, you'll learn about how the technology was developed and how this plane differed from other jets. You may or may not have been able to fly the Concorde when it was still plying the Atlantic, but this is your chance to experience some unique modern history. ⊠ *Grantley Adams International Airport, Christ Church* ☎ *246/253–6257* ⊕ *www.barbadosconcorde.com* ✉ *$17.50* ⊙ *Daily 9–5.*

☺ **Barbados Museum.** This intriguing museum, established in 1933 in the
Fodor's Choice former British Military Prison (1815) in the historic Garrison area,
★ has artifacts from Arawak days (around 400 BC) and galleries that
depict 19th-century military history and everyday life. You can see
cane-harvesting tools, wedding dresses, ancient (and frightening) den-
tistry instruments, and slave sale accounts kept in spidery copperplate
handwriting. The museum's Harewood Gallery showcases the island's
flora and fauna, its Cunard Gallery has a permanent collection of 20th-
century Barbadian and Caribbean paintings and engravings, and its
Connell Gallery features European decorative arts. Additional galleries
include one with exhibits targeted to children. The Shilstone Memorial
Library houses rare West Indian documentation—archival documents,
genealogical records, photos, books, and maps—dating back to the 17th
century. The museum also has a gift shop and a café. ☒ *Hwy. 7, Garrison Savannah, St. Michael* ☎ *246/427–0201 or 246/436–1956* ⊕ *www.
barbmuse.org.bb* ☒ *$7.50* ☉ *Mon.–Sat. 9–5, Sun. 2–6.*

Codrington Theological College. An impressive stand of royal palms lines
the road leading to the coral-stone buildings and serene grounds of
Codrington College, an Anglican theological seminary opened in 1745
on a cliff overlooking Conset Bay. You're welcome to tour the buildings
and walk the nature trails. Keep in mind, though, that beachwear is not
appropriate here. ☒ *Sargeant St., Conset Bay, St. John* ☎ *246/423–1140*
⊕ *www.codrington.org* ☒ *$2.50* ☉ *Daily 10–4.*

Emancipation Statue. This powerful statue of a slave—whose raised
hands, with broken chains hanging from each wrist, evoke both con-
tempt and victory—is commonly referred to as the Bussa Statue. Bussa
was the man who, in 1816, led the first slave rebellion on Barbados.
The work of Barbadian sculptor Karl Brodhagen was erected in 1985
to commemorate the emancipation of the slaves in 1834. ☒ *St. Bar-
nabas Roundabout, intersection of ABC Hwy. and Hwy. 5, Haggatt
Hall, St. Michael.*

☺ **George Washington House.** George Washington slept here! This carefully
★ restored and refurbished 18th-century plantation house in Bush Hill
was the only place where the future first president of the United States
actually slept outside North America. Teenage George and his older
half-brother Lawrence, who was suffering from tuberculosis and seeking treatment on the island, rented this house overlooking Carlisle Bay
for two months in 1751. Opened to the public in December 2006, the
lower floor of the house and the kitchen have period furnishings; the
upper floor is a museum with both permanent and temporary exhibits
that display artifacts of 18th-century Barbadian life. The site includes
an original 1719 windmill and bathhouse, along with a stable added
to the property in the 1800s—and, of course, a gift shop and small
café. Guided tours begin with an informative 15-minute film appropriately called *George Washington in Barbados.* ☒ *Bush Hill, Garrison,
St. Michael* ☎ *246/228–5461* ⊕ *www.georgewashingtonbarbados.org*
☒ *$12.50* ☉ *Mon.–Sat. 9–4:30.*

☺ **Harry Bayley Observatory.** The Barbados Astronomical Society headquarters since 1963, the observatory has a Celestron 14-inch reflector

Sunbury Plantation House.

telescope—the only one in the eastern Caribbean. Visitors can view the moon, stars, planets, and astronomical objects that may not be visible from North America or Europe. ⊠ *Off Hwy. 6, Clapham, St. Michael* ☎ *246/426–1317 or 246/422–2394* ✉ *$5* ☉ *Fri. 8:30 pm–11:30 pm.*

Fodor's Choice **Sunbury Plantation House and Museum.** Lovingly rebuilt after a 1995 fire
★ destroyed everything but the thick flint-and-stone walls, Sunbury offers an elegant glimpse of the 18th and 19th centuries on a Barbadian sugar estate. Period furniture, old prints, and a collection of horse-drawn carriages lend an air of authenticity. A buffet luncheon is served daily in the courtyard for $30 per person. A five-course candlelight dinner is served ($100 per person, reservations required) two nights a week at the 200-year-old mahogany dining table in the Sunbury dining room. ⊠ *Off Hwy. 5, Six Cross Roads, St. Philip* ☎ *246/423–6270* ⊕ *www. barbadosgreathouse.com* ✉ *$7.50* ☉ *Daily 9:30–4:30.*

☉ **Tyrol Cot Heritage Village.** This coral-stone cottage just south of Bridgetown was constructed in 1854 and is preserved as an example of period architecture. In 1929 it became the home of Sir Grantley Adams, the first premier of Barbados and the namesake of its international airport. Part of the Barbados National Trust, the cottage is filled with antiques and memorabilia that belonged to the late Sir Grantley and Lady Adams. It's also the centerpiece of an outdoor "living museum," where artisans and craftsmen have their workshops in a cluster of traditional chattel houses. Workshops are open, crafts are for sale, and refreshments are available at the "rum shop" primarily during the winter season and when cruise ships are in port. ⊠ *Rte. 2, Codrington Hill, St. Michael* ☎ *246/424–2074 or 246/436–9033* ✉ *$7* ☉ *Weekdays 8–4.*

CENTRAL BARBADOS

On the west coast, in St. James Parish, Holetown marks the center of the Platinum Coast—so called for the vast number of luxurious resorts and mansions that face the sea. Holetown is also where Captain John Powell and the crew of the British ship *Olive Blossom* landed on May 14, 1625, to claim the island for King James I (who had actually died of a stroke seven weeks earlier). On the east coast, the crashing Atlantic surf has eroded the shoreline, forming steep cliffs and prehistoric rocks that look like giant mushrooms. Bathsheba and Cattlewash are favorite seacoast destinations for local folks on weekends and holidays. In the interior, narrow roads weave through tiny villages and along and between the ridges. The landscape is covered with tropical vegetation and is rife with fascinating caves and gullies.

WHAT TO SEE

Fodor's Choice
★
Andromeda Botanic Gardens. More than 600 beautiful and unusual plant specimens from around the world are cultivated in 6 acres of gardens nestled among streams, ponds, and rocky outcroppings overlooking the sea above the Bathsheba coastline. The gardens were created in 1954 with flowering plants collected by the late horticulturist Iris Bannochie. They're now administered by the Barbados National Trust. The Hibiscus Café serves snacks and drinks. ⊠ *Bathsheba, St. Joseph* ☎ *246/433–9384* ⊠ *$10* ⊘ *Daily 9–5.*

Chalky Mount. This tiny east-coast village is perched high in the clay-yielding hills that have supplied local potters for about 300 years. A number of working potteries are open daily to visitors. You can watch as artisans create bowls, vases, candleholders, and decorative objects—which are for sale.

Cockspur Beach Club. Just north of Bridgetown, the fun-loving Cockspur rum people encourage those taking the West Indies Rum Distillery tour to make a day of it. The beach—which has a variety of water-sports options—is adjacent to the visitor center. Lunch and drinks are available at the beachside grill. ⊠ *Black Rock, Brighton, St. Michael* ☎ *246/425–9393* ⊠ *$5* ⊘ *Weekdays 9–5.*

Fodor's Choice
★
Flower Forest. It's a treat to meander among fragrant flowering bushes, canna and ginger lilies, puffball trees, and more than 100 other species of tropical flora in a cool, tranquil forest of flowers and other plants. A ½-mi-long (1-km-long) path winds through the 50-acre grounds, a former sugar plantation; it takes about 30 to 45 minutes to follow the path, or you can wander freely for as long as you wish. Benches throughout the forest give you a place to pause and reflect. There's also a snack bar, a gift shop, and a beautiful view of Mt. Hillaby, at 1,100 feet the highest point of land on Barbados. ⊠ *Hwy. 2, Richmond Plantation, St. Joseph* ☎ *246/433–8152* ⊠ *$10* ⊘ *Daily 9–5.*

Ⓒ
Folkestone Marine Park and Visitor Centre. On land and offshore, the whole family will enjoy this park just north of Holetown. The museum and aquarium illuminate some of the island's marine life, and for some firsthand viewing, there's an underwater snorkeling trail around Dottins Reef (glass-bottom boats are available for nonswimmers). A barge

sunk in shallow water is home to myriad fish, making it a popular dive site. ⊠ *Church Point, Holetown, St. James* ☎ *246/422–2314* ▣ *Free* ☉ *Park daily 9–5, museum weekdays 9–5.*

Gun Hill Signal Station. The 360-degree view from Gun Hill, 700 feet above sea level, gave this location strategic importance to the 18th-century British army. Using lanterns and semaphore, soldiers based here could communicate with their counterparts at the Garrison on the south coast and at Grenade Hill in the north. Time moved slowly in 1868, and Captain Henry Wilkinson whiled away his off-duty hours by carving a huge lion from a single rock—which is on the hillside just below the tower. Come for a short history lesson but mainly for the view; it's so gorgeous, military invalids were once sent here to convalesce. ⊠ *Gun Hill, St. George* ☎ *246/429–1358* ▣ *$5* ☉ *Weekdays 9–5.*

Harrison's Cave. This limestone cavern, complete with stalactites, stalagmites, subterranean streams, and a 40-foot waterfall, is a rare find in the Caribbean—and one of Barbados's most popular attractions. The cave reopened in early 2010, after extensive renovations comprising a new visitor center with interpretive displays, life-size models and sculptures, a souvenir shop, improved restaurant facilities, and access for people with disabilities. Tours include a nine-minute video presentation and a 40-minute underground journey through the cavern via electric tram. Tours fill up fast, so make a reservation. ⊠ *Hwy. 2, Welchman Hall, St. Thomas* ☎ *246/438–6640* ⊕ *www.harrisonscave.com* ▣ *$30* ☉ *Wed.–Sun. 8:45–3:45 (last tour).*

Mount Gay Rum Visitors Centre. On this popular tour, you learn the colorful story behind the world's oldest rum—made in Barbados since 1703. Although the distillery is in the far north, in St. Lucy Parish, tour guides explain the rum-making procedure. Both historic and modern equipment is on display, and rows and rows of barrels are stored in this location. The 45-minute tour runs hourly (last tour begins at 3:30 weekdays; 2:30 on Saturday) and concludes with a tasting and an opportunity to buy bottles of rum and gift items—and even have lunch or cocktails, depending on the time of day. ⊠ *Spring Garden Hwy., Brandons, St. Michael* ☎ *246/425–8757* ⊕ *www.mountgayrum.com* ▣ *$7, $50 with lunch; $35 with cocktails* ☉ *Weekdays 9–5.*

Orchid World. Follow meandering pathways through tropical gardens filled with thousands of colorful orchids. You'll see Vandaceous orchids attached to fences or wire frames, Schomburgkia and Oncidiums stuck on mahogany trees, Aranda and Spathoglottis orchids growing in a grotto, and Ascocendas suspended from netting in shady enclosures. You'll find seasonal orchids, scented orchids, multicolor Vanda orchids, and more. Benches are well placed to stop for a little rest, admire the flowers, or simply take in the expansive view of the surrounding cane fields and distant hills of Sweet Vale. Snacks, cold beverages, and other refreshments are served in the café. ⊠ *Hwy. 3B, Ashbury, St. John* ☎ *246/433–0306* ▣ *$10* ☉ *Daily 9–5.*

Welchman Hall Gully. This 1½-mi-long (2-km-long) natural gully is really a collapsed limestone cavern, once part of the same underground network as Harrison's Cave. The Barbados National Trust protects the peace and quiet here, making it a beautiful place to hike past acres of labeled flowers and stands of trees. You can see and hear some interesting birds—and, with luck, a native green monkey. The tour is self-guided (although a guide can be arranged with 24 hours' notice) and takes about 30 to 45 minutes; the last tour begins at 4 pm. ⊠ *Welchman Hall, St. Thomas* ☎ *246/438–6671* ⊕ *www.welchmanhallgullybarbados.com* ⌕ *$10* ⊘ *Daily 9–4:30.*

NORTHERN BARBADOS

Speightstown, the north's commercial center and once a thriving port city, now relies on its appealing local shops and informal restaurants. Many of Speightstown's 19th-century buildings, with traditional overhanging balconies, have been or are being restored. The island's northernmost reaches, St. Peter and St. Lucy parishes, have a varied topography and are lovely to explore. Between the tiny fishing towns along the northwestern coast and the sweeping views out over the Atlantic to the east are forest and farm, moor and mountain. Most guides include a loop through this area on a daylong island tour—it's a beautiful drive.

WHAT TO SEE

Ꮯ **Animal Flower Cave.** Small sea anemones, or sea worms (resembling flowers when they open their tiny tentacles), live in small pools in this cave at the island's very northern tip. The cave itself, discovered in 1780, has a coral floor that ranges from 126,000 to 500,000 years old, according to geological estimates. The view of breaking waves from inside the cave is magnificent. ⊠ *North Point, St. Lucy* ☎ *246/439–8797* ⌕ *$7.50* ⊘ *Daily 9–4.*

Ꮯ **Barbados Wildlife Reserve.** The reserve is the habitat of herons, innumer-
★ able land turtles, screeching peacocks, shy deer, elusive green monkeys, brilliantly colored parrots (in a large walk-in aviary), a snake, and a caiman. Except for the snake and the caiman, the animals run or fly freely—so step carefully and keep your hands to yourself. Late afternoon is your best chance to catch a glimpse of a green monkey. ⊠ *Farley Hill, St. Peter* ☎ *246/422–8826* ⌕ *$12* ⊘ *Daily 10–5.*

Farley Hill. At this national park in northern St. Peter, across the road from the Barbados Wildlife Reserve, gardens and lawns, along with an avenue of towering royal palms and gigantic mahogany, whitewood, and casuarina trees, surround the imposing ruins of a plantation greathouse built by Sir Graham Briggs in 1861 to entertain royal visitors from England. Partially rebuilt for the filming of *Island in the Sun,* the classic 1957 film starring Harry Belafonte and Dorothy Dandridge, the structure was destroyed by fire in 1965. Behind the estate, there's a sweeping view of the region called Scotland for its rugged landscape. ⊠ *Farley Hill, St. Peter* ☎ *246/422–3555* ⌕ *$2 per car, pedestrians free* ⊘ *Daily 8:30–6.*

Ꮯ **Morgan Lewis Sugar Mill.** Built in 1727, the mill was operational until 1945. Today it's the only remaining windmill in Barbados with its wheelhouse and sails intact. No longer used to grind sugarcane, except for occasional demonstrations, it was donated to the Barbados National Trust in 1962 and eventually restored to its original working

St. Nicholas Abbey.

specifications in 1998 by millwrights from the United Kingdom. The surrounding acres are now used for dairy farming. ⊠ *Cherry Tree Hill, St. Andrew* ☎ *246/422–7429* ✉ *$5* ☉ *Weekdays 9–5.*

Fodor's Choice **St. Nicholas Abbey.** There's no religious connection here at all. The
★ island's oldest greathouse (circa 1650) was named after the original British owner's hometown, St. Nicholas Parish near Bristol, and Bath Abbey nearby. Its stone-and-wood architecture makes it one of only three original Jacobean-style houses still standing in the Western Hemisphere. It has Dutch gables, finials of coral stone, and beautiful grounds that include an old sugar mill. The first floor, fully furnished with period furniture and portraits of family members, is open to the public. Fascinating home movies, shot by a previous owner's father, record Bajan life in the 1930s. Behind the greathouse is a rum distillery with a 19th-century steam press. Visitors can watch the rum-making process, purchase artisanal plantation rum produced nearby (the Abbey's current production will become fully aged about 2018), and also enjoy light refreshments at the terrace café. ⊠ *Cherry Tree Hill, St. Peter* ☎ *246/422–8725* ⊕ *www.stnicholasabbey.com* ✉ *$15* ☉ *Sun.–Fri. 10–3:30.*

WHERE TO EAT

First-class restaurants and hotel dining rooms serve quite sophisticated cuisine—often prepared by chefs with international experience and rivaling that served in the world's best restaurants. Most menus include seafood: dolphin—the fish, not the mammal, and also called dorado or mahimahi—kingfish, snapper, and flying fish prepared every way imaginable. Flying fish is so popular that it has officially become a national symbol. Shellfish also abounds, as do steak, pork, and local black-belly lamb.

Local specialty dishes include *buljol* (a cold salad of pickled codfish, tomatoes, onions, sweet peppers, and celery) and *conkies* (cornmeal, coconut, pumpkin, raisins, sweet potatoes, and spices, mixed together, wrapped in a banana leaf, and steamed). *Cou-cou*, often served with steamed flying fish, is a mixture of cornmeal and okra, usually topped with a spicy creole sauce made from tomatoes, onions, and sweet peppers. Bajan-style pepper pot is a hearty stew of oxtail, beef chunks, and "any other meat" in a rich, spicy gravy and simmered overnight.

BEST BETS FOR DINING

Fodor's Choice ★
The Atlantis, Brown Sugar, Champers, the Cliff, Daphne's, Fish Pot, Pisces, the Tides

BEST VIEW
L'Azure at the Crane, the Atlantis

BEST FOR FAMILIES
Angry Annie's, Bellini's Trattoria

MOST ROMANTIC
The Mews, Lone Star

BEST FOR LOCAL BAJAN CUISINE
Cliffside at New Edgewater, Naniki, Waterfront Café

For lunch, restaurants often offer a traditional Bajan buffet of fried fish, baked chicken, salads, macaroni pie (macaroni and cheese), and a selection of steamed or stewed local roots and vegetables. Be cautious with the West Indian condiments—like the sun, they're hotter than you think. Typical Bajan drinks, besides Banks Beer and Mount Gay rum, are *falernum* (a liqueur concocted of rum, sugar, lime juice, and almond essence) and *mauby* (a nonalcoholic drink made by boiling bitter bark and spices, straining the mixture, and sweetening it). You're sure to enjoy the fresh fruit or rum punch.

WHAT TO WEAR

The dress code for dinner in Barbados is conservative, casually elegant, and, on occasion, formal—a jacket and tie for gentlemen and a cocktail dress for ladies in the fanciest restaurants and hotel dining rooms, particularly during the winter holiday season. Jeans, shorts, and T-shirts (either sleeveless or with slogans) are always frowned upon at dinner. Beach attire is appropriate only at the beach.

BRIDGETOWN

$$$
CARIBBEAN

✕ **Waterfront Café.** This friendly bistro alongside the Careenage is the perfect place to enjoy a drink, snack, or meal—and to people-watch. Locals and tourists alike gather for all-day alfresco dining on sandwiches, salads, fish, pasta, pepper-pot stew, and tasty Bajan snacks such as buljol, fish cakes, or plantation pork (plantains stuffed with spicy minced pork). The panfried flying-fish sandwich is especially popular. In the evening you can gaze through the arched windows while savoring nouvelle Caribbean cuisine, enjoying cool trade winds, and listening to live jazz. There's a special Caribbean buffet and steel-pan music on Tuesday night from 7 to 9. ⊠ *The Careenage, Bridgetown, St. Michael* ☎ *246/427–0093* ⊕ *www. waterfrontcafe.com.bb* ⊗ *Closed Sun.*

SOUTH COAST

$$$ ✗**Bellini's Trattoria.** Classic northern Italian cuisine is the specialty at
Bellini's, on the main floor of the Little Bay Hotel. The atmosphere
ITALIAN here is smart-casual. Toast the evening with a Bellini cocktail (ice-cold
sparkling wine with a splash of fruit nectar) and start your meal with
bruschetta, an individual gourmet pizza, or perhaps a homemade pasta
dish with fresh herbs and a rich sauce. Move on to the signature garlic
shrimp entrée or the popular chicken parmigiana—then top it all off
with excellent tiramisu. We recommend making your reservations early;
request a table on the Mediterranean-style verandah to enjoy one of the
most appealing dining settings on the south coast. ⊠ *Little Bay Hotel,
St. Lawrence Gap, Dover, Christ Church* ☎ 246/420–7587 ⊕ *www.
bellinisbarbados.com* ♿ *Reservations essential* ☾ *No lunch.*

$$$–$$$$ ✗**Brown Sugar.** Set back from the road in a traditional Bajan home, the
CARIBBEAN lattice-trimmed dining patios here are filled with ferns, flowers, and
water features. Brown Sugar is a popular lunch spot for local business-
Fodor'sChoice people, who come for the nearly 30 delicious local and creole dishes
★ spread out at the all-you-can-eat, four-course Bajan buffet. Here's your
chance to try local specialties such as flying fish, cou-cou, buljol, *souse*
(pickled pork, stewed for hours in broth), fish cakes, and pepper pot.
In the evening, the à la carte menu has dishes such as fried flying fish,
coconut shrimp, and plantain-crusted mahimahi; curried lamb, filet
mignon, and broiled pepper chicken; and seafood or pesto pasta. Bring
the kids—there's a special children's menu with fried chicken, fried
flying-fish fingers, and pasta dishes. Save room for the warm pawpaw
(papaya) pie or Bajan rum pudding with rum sauce. ⊠ *Bay St., Aquatic
Gap, St. Michael* ☎ 246/426–7684 ⊕ *www.brownsugarbarbados.com*
☾ *No lunch Sat.*

$$$$ ✗**Café Luna.** The sweeping view of pretty Enterprise (Miami) Beach
ECLECTIC from Café Luna, the alfresco dining deck on top of the Mediterranean-
style Little Arches Hotel, is spectacular at lunchtime and magical in
the moonlight. At lunch, sip on crisp white wine or a fruity cocktail
while you await your freshly made salad, pasta, or sandwich. At din-
ner, co-owner and executive chef Mark de Gruchy prepares contempo-
rary favorites from around the world, including fresh Scottish salmon
grilled to perfection, oven-roasted New Zealand rack of lamb, fresh sea-
food bouillabaisse, and local chicken breast with mango chutney. Sushi
is a specialty on Thursday and Friday nights. ⊠ *Little Arches Hotel,
Enterprise Beach, Oistins, Christ Church* ☎ 246/420–4689 ⊕ *www.
littlearches.com* ♿ *Reservations essential.*

$$$ ✗**Champers.** Chiryl Newman's snazzy seaside restaurant and popular
ECLECTIC watering hole is in an old Bajan home on a quiet lane just off the main
Fodor'sChoice south-coast road in Rockley. Luncheon guests—about 75% local busi-
★ nesspeople—enjoy repasts such as char-grilled beef salad, Champers fish
pie, grilled barracuda, or chicken-and-mushroom fettuccine in a creamy
chardonnay sauce. Dinner guests swoon over dishes such as the roasted
rack of lamb with spring vegetables and mint-infused jus, the sautéed
sea scallops with stir-fried vegetables and noodles with red Thai curry
sauce, and the Parmesan-crusted barracuda with whole-grain mustard
sauce. But this isn't nouvelle cuisine. The portions are hearty and the

5

food is well seasoned with Caribbean flavors, "just the way the locals like it," says Newman. The cliff-top setting overlooking Accra Beach offers diners a panoramic view of the sea and a relaxing atmosphere for daytime dining. At night, particularly at the bar, there's a definite buzz in the air. Nearly all the artwork gracing the walls is by Barbadian artists and may be purchased through the on-site gallery. ⊠ *Skeetes Hill, Rockley, Christ Church* ☎ *246/434–3464* ⊕ *www.champersbarbados. com* ⌕ *Reservations essential.*

$$$$
SEAFOOD

✕ **Josef's Restaurant.** The signature restaurant of Austrian restaurateur Josef Schwaiger, in a cliff-side Bajan dwelling surrounded by gardens, is one of the most upscale seaside dining spots on the south coast. Josef's cuisine fuses Asian culinary techniques and Caribbean flavors with fresh seafood. Dinner is prix fixe, with your choice of either a two-course ($50) or three-course ($60) option. Fruits of the sea—such as seared yellowfin tuna with mango-cilantro sauce or catch of the day with grilled vegetables and nutmeg-creamed potatoes—are prominent, and the wine list is extensive. Try shredded duck with herbed hoisin pancakes as an innovative starter, or let the free-range chicken teriyaki with stir-fry noodles tingle your taste buds. Pasta dishes assuage the vegetarian palate. ⊠ *Waverly House, St. Lawrence Gap, Dover, Christ Church* ☎ *246/420–7638* ⊕ *www.josefsinbarbados.com* ⌕ *Reservations essential* ☾ *No lunch.*

$$$$
SEAFOOD
☾

✕ **L'Azure at the Crane.** Perched on an oceanfront cliff, L'Azure is an informal luncheon spot by day that becomes elegant after dark. Enjoy seafood chowder or a light salad or sandwich while absorbing the breathtaking view. At dinner, candlelight and a soft guitar enhance a fabulous Caribbean lobster seasoned with herbs, lime juice, and garlic butter and served in its shell; if you're not in the mood for seafood, try the perfectly grilled filet mignon. The dinner menu is prix fixe (two courses, $35; three courses and a glass of wine, $50). Sunday is really special, with a Gospel Brunch at 10 am and a Bajan Buffet at 12:30 pm. ⊠ *The Crane, Crane Bay, St. Philip* ☎ *246/423–6220* ⊕ *www.thecrane. com* ⌕ *Reservations essential.*

$$$$
SEAFOOD
Fodor's Choice
★

✕ **Pisces.** For seafood lovers, this is nirvana. Prepared in every way by chef-owner Larry Rogers—from charbroiled to gently sautéed—seafood specialties may include conch strips in tempura, rich fish chowder, panfried fillets of flying fish with a toasted-almond crust and a light mango-citrus sauce, and seared prawns in a fragrant curry sauce. Landlubbers in your party can select from the chicken, beef, and pasta dishes on the menu. Whatever you choose, the herbs that flavor it and the accompanying vegetables will have come from the chef's own garden. Save room for the homemade bread pudding, yogurt-lime cheesecake, or rum-raisin ice cream. Twinkling white lights reflect on the water as you dine. ⊠ *St. Lawrence Gap, Dover, Christ Church* ☎ *246/435–6564* ⊕ *www.piscesbarbados.com* ⌕ *Reservations essential* ☾ *No lunch.*

EAST COAST

$$$
CARIBBEAN
Fodor's Choice
★

✕ **The Atlantis.** For decades, an alfresco lunch on the Atlantis deck overlooking the ocean has been a favorite of visitors touring the east coast and Bajans alike. Totally renovated and reopened in 2009 by the owners of Little Good Harbour and the Fishpot on the west coast, the revived restaurant effectively combines the atmosphere and good food that have always been the draw with an up-to-date, rather elegant dining room and a top-notch menu that focuses on local produce, seafood, and meats. The Bajan buffet lunch on Wednesday and Sunday is particularly popular; it's also well used for special occasions for local folks. At dinner, entreés include fresh fish, lobster (sometimes), roasted black-belly lamb or free-range chicken, fricassee of rabbit, and more. Or choose more traditional pepper pot, saltfish, or chicken stew with peas and rice, cou-cou, yam pie, or breadfruit mash, all of which are available at the Bajan buffet. Rotis and cutters (sandwiches) are always available, along with pasta specials, salads, soups, and fried flying fish. ✉ *Tent Bay, Bathsheba, St. Joseph* ☎ *246/433–9445* ⊕ *www.atlantishotelbarbados. com* ⤳ *Reservations essential* ☾ *No dinner Sun.*

$$$
CARIBBEAN
☾
✕ **Cliffside at New Edgewater.** The outdoor deck of this restaurant in the New Edgewater hotel provides one of the prettiest, breeziest ocean views in all Barbados and, therefore, is a good stop for lunch when touring the east coast. From noon to 3 pm, choose the Bajan buffet or select from the menu. Either way, you might enjoy fried flying fish, roast or stewed chicken, local lamb chops, rice and peas, steamed root vegetables, sautéed plantains, and salad. Afternoon tea with scones, pastries, and sandwiches is served from 3:30 to 6 pm. Dinner is also served but mostly to hotel guests and local residents, who are able to find their way home in the dark on the neighborhood's winding, often unmarked roads. ✉ *New Edgewater Hotel, Bathsheba, St. Joseph* ☎ *246/433–9900* ⊕ *www.newedgewater.com* ⤳ *Reservations essential.*

$$$
CARIBBEAN
✕ **Naniki Restaurant.** Rich wooden beams and stone tiles, clay pottery, straw mats, colorful dinnerware, and fresh flowers from the adjacent anthurium farm set the style here. Huge picture windows and outdoor porch seating allow you to enjoy the exhilarating panoramic view of surrounding fields and hills and, when making the alfresco choice, a refreshing breeze along with your lunch of exquisitely prepared Caribbean standards. Seared flying fish, grilled dorado, stewed lambi (conch), curried chicken, and jerk chicken or pork are accompanied by cou-cou, peas and rice, or salad. For dinner (by special request only), start with conch fritters or Caribbean fish soup; then try roasted Bajan black-belly lamb, grilled snapper, or shrimp garnished with tarragon. Sunday brunch is a Caribbean buffet often featuring great jazz music by some of the Caribbean's best musicians. Vegetarian dishes are always available. ✉ *Lush Life Nature Resort, Suriname, St. Joseph* ☎ *246/433–1300* ⊕ *www.lushlife.bb* ⤳ *Reservations essential.*

WEST COAST

$$$
CARIBBEAN
☾
✕ **Angry Annie's.** You can't miss this place. Outside and inside, everything's painted in cheerful Caribbean pinks, blues, greens, and yellows—and it's just steps from the main road. The food is just as lively: great barbecued "jump-up" ribs and chicken (as tasty as the roadside barbecue sold at street parties), grilled fresh fish or juicy steaks, "Rasta pasta" for vegetarians, and several spicy curries. Eat inside on gaily colored furniture or outside under the stars, or take it away with you. ✉ *1st St., Holetown, St. James* ☎ *246/432–2119* ☾ *No lunch.*

5

$$$$ ✕ **The Cliff**. Chef Paul Owens's mastery is the foundation of one of the
ECLECTIC finest dining experiences in the Caribbean, with prices to match. Steep
Fodor's Choice steps hug the cliff on which the restaurant sits to accommodate those
★ arriving by yacht, and every candlelit table has a sea view. Starter suggestions include smoked salmon ravioli with garlic sauce or grilled
portobello mushroom on greens with truffle vinaigrette; for the main
course, try Caribbean shrimp with a Thai green-curry–coconut sauce,
veal chop with a mustard-and-tarragon sauce, or red snapper fillet on
a baked-potato cake. Dessert falls into the sinful category, and service
is impeccable. The prix-fixe menu will set you back $125 per person
for a two-course meal (starter–main course or main course–dessert)
or $150 per person for a three-course meal. Reserve days or even
weeks in advance to snag a table at the front of the terrace for the
best view. ✉ *Hwy. 1, Derricks, St. James* ☎ *246/432–1922* ⊕ *www.
thecliffbarbados.com* ⚐ *Reservations essential* ☉ *Closed Sun. Apr. 15–
Dec. 15. No lunch.*

$$$$ ✕ **Daphne's**. The beachfront restaurant of the House, Daphne's is the
ITALIAN chic Caribbean outpost of the famed London eatery Daphne's of Chel-
Fodor's Choice sea. Chef Marco Festini Cromer whips up contemporary Italian cuisine.
★ Dine à la carte or choose the table d'hote menu ($55 for two courses or
$65 for three courses). Grilled mahimahi, for example, becomes "mod-
ern Italian" when combined with marsala wine, *peperonata* (stewed
peppers, tomatoes, onions, and garlic), and zucchini. Perfectly prepared
melanzane (eggplant) and zucchini parmigiana is a delicious starter,
and a half portion of risotto with porcini mushrooms, green beans,
and Parma ham is fabulously rich. Pappardelle with braised duck, red
wine, and oregano is a sublime pasta choice. Light meals, salads, and
half portions of pasta are available at lunch. The extensive wine list
features both regional Italian and fine French selections. ✉ *Paynes Bay,
St. James* ☎ *246/432–2731* ⊕ *www.daphnesbarbados.com* ⚐ *Reservations essential* ☉ *Closed Mon. in June–Nov.*

$$$$ ✕ **Fish Pot**. Just north of the little fishing village of Six Men's Bay, toward
MEDITERRANEAN the north end of the west coast of Barbados, this attractive seaside res-
Fodor's Choice taurant serves excellent Mediterranean cuisine and some of the island's
★ freshest fish. Gaze seaward through windows framed with pale-green
louvered shutters while lunching on a seafood crepe, a grilled panini,
snow-crab salad, or perhaps pasta with seafood or roasted-pepper-
and-chili tomato sauce; in the evening, the menu may include seafood
bouillabaisse; seared, herb-crusted tuna on garlic-and-spinach polenta;
sun-dried-tomato risotto tossed with vegetables; or cracker-crusted rack
of lamb with thyme jus on roasted ratatouille. Bright and cheery by day
and relaxed and cozy by night, the Fish Pot offers a tasty dining experience in a setting that's classier than its name might suggest. ✉ *Little
Good Harbour Hotel, Shermans, St. Peter* ☎ *246/439–3000* ⊕ *www.
littlegoodharbourbarbados.com* ⚐ *Reservations essential.*

$$$$ ✕ **Lone Star**. In the 1940s, this was the only commercial garage on the
CONTINENTAL west coast; today, it's a snazzy restaurant in the tiny but chic Lone Star
Hotel, where top chefs in the open-plan kitchen turn the finest local
ingredients into gastronomic delights. The menu is extensive but pricey,
even for lunch. All day, such tasty dishes as fish soup with rouille,

Caesar or Thai chicken salad, tuna tartare, rotisserie chicken, and linguine with tomato-basil sauce and feta cheese are served in the ocean-front beach bar. At sunset, the casual daytime atmosphere turns trendy. You might start with tuna tartare with mango or Thai crab cakes with peppers and lemongrass dip, followed by crispy Peking duckling, grilled fish of the day, or lamb shank with basil mashed potatoes—or choose from dozens of other tasty land, sea, and vegetarian dishes. ⊠ *Lone Star Hotel, Hwy. 1, Mount Standfast, St. James* ☎ *246/419–0599* ⊕ *www. thelonestar.com.*

$$$$ ✕ **The Mews.** Dining at the Mews is like being invited to a very chic
CONTINENTAL friend's home for dinner. This restaurant once was, in fact, a private home. The front room is now an inviting bar, and an interior courtyard is an intimate, open-air dining area. The second floor is a maze of small dining rooms and dining balconies, but you've come for the food, after all. The international cuisine is presented with contemporary flair. A plump chicken breast, for example, will be stuffed with cream cheese, smoked salmon, and herb pâté and served on a garlic-and-chive sauce. A braised lamb shank is presented on a bed of cabbage with a port-thyme jus and creamed potatoes, and fillet of mahimahi is poached in a lemongrass, ginger, and cilantro broth. The warm molten chocolate cake is a must for dessert. Some call the atmosphere avant-garde; others call it quaint. Everyone calls the food delicious. But don't stop at dinner; by about 10 pm, the bar begins to bustle. On weekends, the fun spills out into the street. ⊠ *2nd St., Holetown, St. James* ☎ *246/432–1122* ⚖ *Reservations essential* ⊗ *Closed Sun. No lunch.*

$$$$ ✕ **The Tides.** Local residents and repeat visitors agree that the Tides is one
CONTINENTAL of the island's best restaurants. Enter into a pretty courtyard and have
Fodor's Choice a cocktail at the cozy bar or the coral-stone lounge in what was once a
★ private mansion, then proceed to your seaside table. Perhaps the most intriguing feature of this stunning setting—besides the sound of waves crashing onto the shore just feet away—is the row of huge tree trunks growing right through the dining room. The food is equally dramatic. Chef Guy Beasley and his team give a contemporary twist to fresh seafood, fillet of beef, rack of lamb, and other top-of-the-line main courses by adding inspired sauces and delicate vegetables and garnishes. Save room for the sticky toffee pudding—definitely worth the calories. ⊠ *Balmore House, Hwy. 1, Holetown, St. James* ☎ *246/432–8356* ⊕ *www. tidesbarbados.com* ⚖ *Reservations essential* ⊗ *No lunch weekends.*

WHERE TO STAY

Most visitors stay on either the fashionable west coast north of Bridgetown or on the action-packed south coast. On the west coast, the beachfront resorts in St. Peter and St. James parishes are mostly luxurious, self-contained enclaves. Highway 1, a two-lane road with considerable traffic, runs past these resorts, which can make strolling to a nearby bar or restaurant a bit difficult. Along the south coast in Christ Church Parish, many hotels are clustered near the busy strip known as St. Lawrence Gap, convenient to dozens of small restaurants, bars, and nightclubs. On the much more remote east coast, a few small inns offer oceanfront views and get-away-from-it-all tranquillity.

Prices in Barbados may be twice as high in season (December 15–April 15) compared to the quieter months. Most hotels include no meals in their rates, but some include breakfast, and many offer a meal plan. Some require you to purchase a meal plan in the high season, and a few offer all-inclusive packages.

Resorts run the gamut—from unpretentious to exceedingly formal—in terms of size, intimacy, amenities, and price. Families and long-term visitors may choose from a wide variety of villas and condos. A few small, cozy inns are found along the east and southeast coasts, as well as the northwest. They can be ultraluxurious, fairly simple, or something in between.

BEST BETS FOR LODGING

Fodor's Choice★
Accra Beach Hotel and Spa, Almond Beach Club and Spa, Almond Beach Village, the Atlantis Hotel, Coral Reef Club, Hilton Barbados, Little Arches Hotel, Peach and Quiet, Sandy Lane Hotel and Golf Club, the Sandpiper, Sweetfield Manor

BEST FOR HONEYMOONERS
Cobblers Cove, Fairmont, the House, Treasure Beach

BEST FOR FAMILIES
Almond Beach Village, Almond Casuarina, Bougainvillea, Royal Westmoreland, Tamarind, Turtle Beach

Villa and condo complexes, which are continually cropping up along the south and west coasts of Barbados, may be the most economical option for families, other groups, or couples vacationing together. Nonowner vacationers rent individual units directly from the property managers, the same as reserving hotel accommodations. Units with fully equipped kitchens, two to six bedrooms, and as many baths run $200 to $2,500 per night in the off-season—double that in winter.

PRIVATE VILLAS AND CONDOS

Local real-estate agencies will arrange holiday rentals of privately owned villas and condos along the west coast in St. James and St. Peter. All villas and condos are fully furnished and equipped, including appropriate staff depending on the size of the villa or unit—which can range from one to eight bedrooms; the staff usually works six days a week. Most villas have TVs, DVDs and/or VCRs, and CD players; all properties have telephones, and some have Internet access. International telephone calls are usually blocked; plan on using your own mobile phone or a phone card or calling card. Vehicles generally are not included in the rates, but rental cars can be arranged and delivered to the villa upon request. Linens and basic supplies (e.g., bath soap, toilet tissue, dishwashing detergent) are normally included.

Units with one to six bedrooms and as many baths run $200 to $2,500 per night in summer, and double that in winter. Rates include utilities and government taxes. The only additional cost is for groceries and staff gratuities. A security deposit is required upon booking and refunded seven days after departure less any damages or unpaid miscellaneous charges.

Villa Rental Agencies **Altman Real Estate** (✉ *Hwy. 1, Derricks, St. James* ☎ *246/432–0840 or 866/360–5292* ⊕ *www.aaaltman.com*). **Bajan Services** (✉ *Newton House, Battaleys, St. Peter* ☎ *246/422–2618 or 866/978–5239* ⊕ *www.bajanservices.com*). **Island Villas** (✉ *Trents Bldg., Holetown, St. James* ☎ *246/432–4627 or 866/978–8499* ⊕ *www.island-villas.com*).

PRIVATE APARTMENT RENTAL SOURCES

Apartments are available for vacation rentals in buildings or complexes that can have as few as three or four units or as many as 30 to 40 units—or even more. Prices range from $30 to $300 per night. The **Barbados Tourism Authority** (☎ *246/427–2623* ⊕ *www.visitbarbados.org*) on Harbour Road in Bridgetown has a listing of apartments in prime resort areas on both the south and west coasts, complete with facilities offered and current rates.

The following hotel reviews have been condensed for this book. Please go to Fodors.com for expanded reviews of each property.

SOUTH COAST

$
RESORT
Fodor's Choice
★

Accra Beach Hotel and Spa. An excellent choice if you prefer a full-service resort in the middle of the busy south coast, the Accra is large, it's modern, it faces a great beach, and it's competitively priced. **Pros:** right on a great beach and, on the street side, near shopping, restaurants, and nightspots; terrific value; pleasant staff. **Cons:** standard rooms are fairly ordinary—at least opt for accommodations with a pool or ocean view. ✉ *Hwy. 7, Box 73W, Rockley, Christ Church* ☎ *246/435–8920* ⊕ *www.accrabeachhotel.com* ↩ *188 rooms, 36 suites* ⌂ *In-room: a/c, safe, Internet, Wi-Fi. In-hotel: restaurants, bars, pool, gym, spa, beach, water sports, business center* ⍥ *No meals.*

$$$$
ALL-INCLUSIVE
☾

Almond Casuarina Beach Resort. One of three all-inclusive Almond properties in Barbados, this is the only one on the south coast. Blocks of accommodations surround a lush 8-acre garden of mature bamboo, palm, and fruit trees (and a few resident green monkeys). **Pros:** great beach and beautiful garden; every amenity you could imagine; wonderful for kids. **Cons:** lots of good restaurants to try in nearby St. Lawrence Gap, but you've paid for an all-inclusive. ✉ *St. Lawrence Gap, Dover, Christ Church* ☎ *246/428–3600* ⊕ *www.almondresorts.com* ↩ *280 rooms* ⌂ *In-room: a/c, safe, Internet. In-hotel: restaurants, room service, bars, tennis court, pools, gym, spa, beach, water sports, children's programs, business center* ⍥ *All-inclusive.*

$-$$
RENTAL
☾

Bougainvillea Beach Resort. Attractive seaside town houses, with separate entrances, wrap around the pool or face the beachfront. Most importantly, the suites are huge compared with hotel suites elsewhere in this price range, are decorated in appealing Caribbean pastels, and have full kitchens. **Pros:** great for families; easy stroll to St. Lawrence Gap or to Oistins; groceries prestocked upon request. **Cons:** bathrooms could use updating; sea can be rough for swimming. ✉ *Maxwell Coast Rd., Maxwell, Christ Church* ☎ *246/418–0990* ⊕ *www.bougainvillearesort.com* ↩ *138 suites* ⌂ *In-room: a/c, Internet, Wi-Fi. In-hotel: restaurants, bars, tennis court, pools, gym, spa, beach, water sports, children's programs, business center* ⍥ *No meals.*

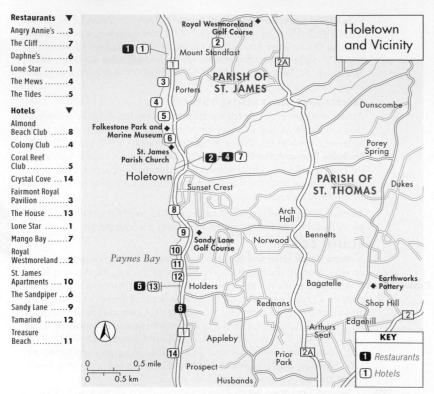

$$$–$$$$
RENTAL

The Crane. Hugging a seaside bluff on the southeast coast, the Crane is the island's oldest hotel in continuing operation. Today, the original coral-stone hotel building (1887) is the centerpiece of a luxurious, 40-acre villa complex that includes private residences, pools, restaurants, bars, and even a little village. **Pros:** enchanting view; lovely beach; fabulous suites; great restaurants. **Cons:** remote location; rental car recommended; service tends to be aloof; not all villas have laundry facilities. ⊠ *Crane Bay, St. Philip* ☎ *246/423–6220* ⊕ *www.thecrane.com* ↪ *4 rooms, 14 suites, 202 villas* ⌂ *In-room: a/c, safe, kitchen (some), Internet, Wi-Fi (some). In-hotel: restaurants, bars, tennis courts, pools, gym, spa, beach, laundry facilities (some), business center* ⑩ *No meals.*

$$
RENTAL
☺

Divi Southwinds Beach Resort. The all-suites Divi Southwinds is on 20 acres of lawn and gardens bisected by action-packed St. Lawrence Gap. The bulk of the suites are north of the Gap in a large, unspectacular, three-story building offering garden and pool views. **Pros:** beautiful beach; beach villas are the best value; close to shopping, restaurants, and nightspots. **Cons:** few water sports available and none included; some rooms aching for renovations; comparatively pricey for the value received. ⊠ *St. Lawrence Main Rd., Dover, Christ Church* ☎ *246/428–7181* ⊕ *www.divisouthwinds.com* ↪ *121 1-bedroom suites, 12 2-bedroom suites* ⌂ *In-room: a/c, kitchen. In-hotel: restaurants, bars, tennis courts, pools, gym, beach, business center* ⑩ *No meals.*

$$ 🏨 **Hilton Barbados.** Beautifully situated on the sandy Needham's Point
HOTEL peninsula, the Hilton Barbados is minutes from Bridgetown. All 350
☺ rooms and suites in this high-rise have private balconies overlooking
Fodor'sChoice either the ocean or Carlisle Bay; 77 rooms are on executive floors,
★ with a private lounge and concierge services. **Pros:** great location near
town and on a beautiful beach; excellent accommodations; lots of ser-
vices and amenities; frequent promotional deals provide real value.
Cons: huge convention hotel; attracts groups; not much island fla-
vor. ⊠ *Needham's Point, Aquatic Gap, St. Michael* 🖀 *246/426–0200*
⊕ *www.hiltoncaribbean.com* 🛏 *317 rooms, 33 suites* ♿ *In-room: a/c,
safe, Internet, Wi-Fi. In-hotel: restaurants, bars, tennis courts, pools,
gym, water sports, children's programs, business center, some pets
allowed* ⏀ *No meals.*

$$ 🏨 **Little Arches Hotel.** Just east of the fishing village of Oistins, this classy
HOTEL boutique hotel has a distinctly Mediterranean ambience and a perfect
Fodor'sChoice vantage point overlooking the sea. **Pros:** stylish accommodations; great
★ restaurant; across from fabulous Miami Beach. **Cons:** fairly remote;
rental car advised. ⊠ *Enterprise Beach Rd., Enterprise, Christ Church*
🖀 *246/420–4689* ⊕ *www.littlearches.com* 🛏 *8 rooms, 2 suites* ♿ *In-
room: a/c, safe, kitchen (some), Internet, Wi-Fi. In-hotel: restaurant,
bar, pool, business center* ⏀ *No meals.*

¢ 🏨 **Peach and Quiet.** Forgo the flashy accoutrements of a resort and,
INN instead, claim one of the stylish suites in this small seaside inn. With
Fodor'sChoice no in-room noisemakers and no children around, the only sounds you
★ will hear are the gentle surf and your own conversations. **Pros:** the
rates alone make this inn a great choice; peace and quiet; adults-only
environment; engaging owners; stargazing and nature walks are special treats. **Cons:** inn is closed half the year; remote location requires
a rental car. ⊠ *Inch Marlow Main Rd., Inch Marlow, Christ Church*
🖀 *246/428–5682* ⊕ *www.peachandquiet.com* 🛏 *22 suites* ♿ *In-room:
no a/c, no phone, safe, no TV. In-hotel: restaurant, bar, pool, some age
restrictions* ☽ *Closed May–Oct.* ⏀ *No meals.*

$$ 🏨 **The Savannah.** Convenient, comfortable, and appealing to indepen-
HOTEL dent travelers who don't need organized entertainment, the Savannah
is nevertheless perfectly situated for walks to the Garrison historic
area, the Barbados Museum, and the racetrack—and minutes from
Bridgetown by car or taxi. **Pros:** right on the beach; inviting pool;
convenient to Bridgetown and sites. **Cons:** not a good choice for kids;
rather dreary interior hallways. ⊠ *Garrison Main Rd., Hastings, Christ
Church* 🖀 *246/435–9473* ⊕ *www.gemsbarbados.com* 🛏 *90 rooms, 8
suites* ♿ *In-room: a/c, safe, Wi-Fi. In-hotel: restaurants, bars, pools,
gym, spa, beach, business center* ⏀ *Breakfast.*

$–$$ 🏨 **Silver Point Hotel.** This gated community of modern condos at Sil-
RENTAL ver Sands–Silver Rock Beach is operated as a trendy boutique hotel.
Pros: stylish suites; perfect location for windsurfers; gated community.
Cons: very remote; not within walking distance of anything except the
beach; sea can be rough for swimming; rental car recommended. ⊠ *Silver Sands–Silver Rock Beach, Christ Church* 🖀 *246/420–4416* ⊕ *www.
silverpointhotel.com* 🛏 *58 suites* ♿ *In-room: a/c, kitchen (some), Wi-Fi.*

5

In-hotel: restaurants, bar, pools, gym, spa, beach, water sports, laundry facilities, business center ⁺⁰⁺ No meals.

$-$$ · RENTAL · ☾ **South Beach Resort.** This resort is actually a time-share vacation club, but it's run like a hotel—a very cool hotel, indeed. **Pros:** beautiful bathrooms; Accra Beach is great for families; Wi-Fi everywhere. **Cons:** more hotel than resort; on-site restaurant serves only breakfast; beach is across the street. ⊠ *Main Rd., Rockley, Christ Church* ☎ *246/435–8561* ⊕ *www.southbeachbarbados.com* ⥃ *22 rooms, 25 suites* ⚉ *In-room: a/c, kitchen, Wi-Fi. In-hotel: restaurant, bar, pool, laundry facilities, business center* ⁺⁰⁺ *No meals.*

$-$$ · B&B/INN · **Fodor's**Choice · ★ **Sweetfield Manor.** George and Ann Clarke transformed a decrepit manse (circa 1900) perched on a ridge about a mile from Bridgetown—the former residence of the Dutch ambassador to Barbados—into the island's most delightful bed-and-breakfast inn. **Pros:** peaceful enclave primarily suitable for adults; inviting pool and gardens; gracious and friendly innkeepers; delicious gourmet breakfast; perfect wedding venue. **Cons:** long walk to beach; rental car advised; not the best choice for kids. ⊠ *Britton New Road, Brittons Hill, St. Michael* ☎ *246/429–8356* ⊕ *www.sweetfieldmanor.com* ⥃ *6 rooms, 4 with bath, 1 suite* ⚉ *In-room: a/c, no phone, safe, no TV, Wi-Fi (some). In-hotel: bar, pool* ⁺⁰⁺ *Breakfast.*

$$$-$$$$ · ALL-INCLUSIVE · ☾ **Turtle Beach Resort.** Families flock to Turtle Beach because it offers large, bright suites and enough all-included activities for everyone to enjoy. **Pros:** perfect for family vacations; nice pools; roomy accommodations; lots of services and amenities. **Cons:** beach is fairly narrow and congested compared with other south-coast resorts; open vent between room and hallway can be noisy at night. ⊠ *St. Lawrence Gap, Dover, Christ Church* ☎ *246/428–7131* ⊕ *www.turtlebeachresortbarbados.com* ⥃ *164 suites* ⚉ *In-room: a/c, safe, Internet. In-hotel: restaurants, bars, tennis courts, pools, gym, spa, beach, water sports, children's programs, business center* ⁺⁰⁺ *All-inclusive.*

EASTERN BARBADOS

$ · HOTEL · **Fodor's**Choice · ★ **The Atlantis Hotel.** The legendary Atlantis Hotel, a fixture on the rugged east coast for more than a century and renowned for its spectacular oceanfront location, was completely renovated and reopened in 2009 by the owners of Little Good Harbour. **Pros:** historical and modern blend works wonderfully; spectacular oceanfront location; excellent restaurant. **Cons:** oceanfront rooms have fabulous views, but the smashing waves can be noisy at night; remote location, so rental car advised; no beach for swimming. ⊠ *Tent Bay, Bathsheba, St. Joseph* ☎ *246/433–9445* ⊕ *www.atlantishotelbarbados.com* ⥃ *5 rooms, 3 suites, 2 apartments* ⚉ *In-room: a/c, Wi-Fi. In-hotel: restaurant, bar, pool, laundry facilities, business center* ⊘ *Closed Sept.* ⁺⁰⁺ *Breakfast.*

WEST COAST

$$$$ · ALL-INCLUSIVE · **Fodor's**Choice · ★ **Almond Beach Club and Spa.** Among several similar beachfront resorts south of Holetown, Almond Beach Club distinguishes itself as an adults-only environment with all-inclusive rates (only spa and salon services are extra) and reciprocal guest privileges (including shuttle service) at its enormous sister resorts, Almond Beach Village

Peach and Quiet.

and Almond Casuarina. **Pros:** adults only; intimate atmosphere; short walk to Holetown; next door to Sandy Lane Beach. **Cons:** beach erodes to almost nothing at certain times of the year—usually the result of fall storms. ⊠ *Hwy. 1, Vauxhall, St. James* ☎ *246/432–7840* ⊕ *www. almondresorts.com* ⤳ *133 rooms, 28 suites* ⚐ *In-room: a/c, safe. In-hotel: restaurants, bars, pools, gym, spa, beach, water sports, some age restrictions* ⦿ *All-inclusive.*

$$$$
ALL-INCLUSIVE
☂
Fodor's Choice
★
🏨 **Almond Beach Village.** Barbados's premier family resort is massive enough to be a popular conference venue and romantic enough to host intimate weddings. Situated on an 18th-century sugar plantation north of Speightstown, the Village's 32 acres front a mile-long, powdery beach. **Pros:** family resort with certain areas for adults only; lots to do and all included, including Bajan cooking lessons; sugar mill is a popular wedding venue. **Cons:** it's huge; more emphasis might be placed on room renovations and less on expansion. ⊠ *Hwy. 1B, Heywoods, St. Peter* ☎ *246/422–4900* ⊕ *www.almondresorts.com* ⤳ *373 rooms, 29 suites* ⚐ *In-room: a/c, safe. In-hotel: restaurants, bars, golf course, tennis courts, pools, gym, spa, beach, water sports, children's programs, laundry facilities, business center* ⦿ *All-inclusive.*

$$$$
RESORT
🏨 **Cobblers Cove Hotel.** "English Country" best describes the style of this lovely resort favored by British sophisticates. **Pros:** very classy establishment; lovely grounds; the penthouse suites are amazing; very quiet. **Cons:** too quiet for some; only bedrooms have a/c. ⊠ *Road View, Speightstown, St. Peter* ☎ *246/422–2291* ⊕ *www.cobblerscove.com* ⤳ *40 suites* ⚐ *In-room: a/c, safe, no TV, Internet, Wi-Fi. In-hotel: restaurant, bar, tennis court, pool, gym, spa, beach, water sports, children's programs, business center, some age restrictions* ⦿ *Breakfast.*

CLOSE UP

More Barbados Lodging Options

Because we would like to recommend more places to stay than space allows, here are some additional suggestions:

SOUTH COAST

$ Coconut Court Beach Hotel (⌂ *Main Rd., Hastings, Christ Church BB15156* ☎ *246/427–1655* ⊕ *www. coconut-court.com*) is popular among families who love the welcoming atmosphere and the activities for kids. The 112 beachfront apartments and efficiencies have kitchenettes.

$ Hotel PomMarine (⌂ *Barbados Community College, Marine Gardens, Hastings, Christ Church* ☎ *246/228– 0900* ⊕ *www.pommarinebarbados. com*) is staffed by students at the Hospitality Institute of Barbados Community College; the 20 rooms and one self-catering suite here are simple yet comfortable. Hastings Beach is across the street.

EAST COAST

¢–$ New Edgewater Hotel (⌂ *Bathsheba Beach, Bathsheba, St. Joseph* ☎ *246/433–9900* ⊕ *www. newedgewater.com*), a scenic outpost overlooking the stunning east coast, has a rustic, beach-house atmosphere.

¢ Round House Inn (⌂ *Tent Bay, Bathsheba, St. Joseph* ☎ *246/433– 9678* ⊕ *www.roundhousebarbados. com*) has four simple guestrooms,

each with a private deck providing an extraordinary ocean view.

$$ Sea-U Guest House (⌂ *Tent Bay, Bathsheba, St. Joseph* ☎ *246/433– 9450* ⊕ *www.seaubarbados.com*) is a tiny guesthouse with six simple studio or apartment units, each with a kitchenette, perched on a cliff overlooking the Atlantic Ocean.

WEST COAST

$$$$ Crystal Cove Hotel (⌂ *Hwy. 1, Appleby, St. James* ☎ *246/432–2683* ⊕ *www.crystalcovehotelbarbados.com*) spills down a hillside to the beach, where you can swim, sail, snorkel, water-ski, windsurf, or kayak to your heart's content—or play tennis, dip in the pool, or take advantage of the golf privileges.

$$$–$$$$ Little Good Harbour (⌂ *Hwy. 1B, Shermans, St. Peter* ☎ *246/439–3000* ⊕ *www. littlegoodharbourbarbados.com*) is a cluster of classy, spacious one-, two-, and three-bedroom, self-catering cottages overlooking a narrow strip of beach in the far north of Barbados— just beyond the fishing village of Six Men's Bay.

$$$$ Lone Star Hotel (⌂ *Hwy. 1, Holetown, St. James* ☎ *246/419–0599* ⊕ *www.thelonestar.com*), a 1940s service station transformed into a chic four-room hotel, is popular among celebs. The restaurant is also extraordinary.

$$$$
RESORT 🏨 **Colony Club Hotel.** As the signature hotel of five Elegant Hotel properties on Barbados, the Colony Club is certainly elegant—but with a quiet, friendly, understated style. **Pros:** clubby atmosphere; some rooms open directly onto the lagoon pool. **Cons:** relatively pricey; beach comes and goes, depending on storms. ⌂ *Hwy. 1, Porters, St. James* ☎ *246/422– 2335* ⊕ *www.colonyclubhotel.com* ⏎ *64 rooms, 32 junior suites* ⚭ *In-*

room: safe. In-hotel: restaurants, bars, tennis courts, pools, gym, spa, beach, water sports, business center, some age restrictions ⦾ *Breakfast.*

$$$–$$$$

RESORT

Fodor's Choice

★

⊞ **Coral Reef Club.** The upscale Coral Reef Club offers the epitome of elegance and style, along with a welcoming, informal atmosphere. Individually designed suites are in pristine coral-stone manses and cottages scattered over 12½ acres of flower-filled gardens; the public areas ramble along the waterfront. **Pros:** absolutely delightful; elegant yet informal; beautiful suites with huge verandahs; delicious dining; six computers available to guests for free Internet access. **Cons:** few room TVs (if that matters); narrow beach sometimes disappears, depending on the seasonal weather. ⊠ *Hwy. 1, Porters, St. James* ☎ *246/422–2372* ⊕ *www.coralreefbarbados.com* ⊅ *29 rooms, 57 suites, 2 villas* ⌂ *In-room: a/c, safe, no TV (some), Internet, Wi-Fi. In-hotel: restaurant, bar, tennis courts, pools, gym, spa, beach, water sports, children's programs, business center, some age restrictions* ⊙ *Closed June* ⦾ *Breakfast.*

$$$$

RESORT

⊞ **Fairmont Royal Pavilion.** Every suite in this adults-oriented resort has a view of the sea from its broad balcony or patio. From ground-floor patios, in fact, you can step directly onto the sand. **Pros:** beautiful resort; excellent service—everyone remembers your name; dining is excellent. **Cons:** dining is expensive; in fact, everything here is expensive. ⊘ *Hwy. 1, Porters, St. James BB24051* ☎ *246/422–5555* ⊕ *www.fairmont.com* ⊅ *72 suites, 1 3-bedroom villa* ⌂ *In-room: a/c, safe, Internet, Wi-Fi. In-hotel: restaurants, bars, tennis courts, pool, gym, beach, water sports, some age restrictions* ⦾ *No meals.*

$$$$

RESORT

⊞ **The House.** Privacy, luxury, and service are hallmarks of this intimate adult sanctuary next door to sister resort Tamarind. The 34 junior and one-bedroom suites wrap around a central courtyard filled with tropical trees, plants, and water features. **Pros:** trendy and stylish; privacy assured; pure relaxation. **Cons:** the resort can be a little stuffy, but you can always head next door to Tamarind for a reality check. ⊠ *Hwy. 1, Paynes Bay, St. James* ☎ *246/432–5525* ⊕ *www.thehousebarbados.com* ⊅ *34 suites* ⌂ *In-room: a/c, safe, Internet. In-hotel: restaurant, gym, beach, business center, some age restrictions* ⦾ *Breakfast.*

$$$$

ALL-INCLUSIVE

⊞ **Mango Bay.** In the heart of Holetown, this convenient boutique resort is within walking distance of shops, restaurants, nightspots, historic sites, and the public bus to either Bridgetown or Speightstown. **Pros:** nice rooms; great food; friendly staff; walk to Holetown shopping and entertainment. **Cons:** although heroic measures continue to be taken to address the problem, a natural drainage stream on the north side of the property can sometimes become odoriferous. ⊠ *2nd St., Holetown, St. James* ☎ *246/432–1384* ⊕ *www.mangobaybarbados.com* ⊅ *64 rooms, 10 suites, 2 penthouse suites* ⌂ *In-room: a/c, safe, Internet, Wi-Fi. In-hotel: restaurant, bar, pool, beach, gym, spa, water sports, business center* ⦾ *All-inclusive.*

$$$$

RESORT

⊞ **Port St. Charles.** A luxury residential marina development near historic Speightstown on the northwest tip of Barbados, Port St. Charles is a perfect choice for boating enthusiasts who either arrive on their own yacht or plan to charter one during their stay. **Pros:** a boater's dream; well-appointed units with beautiful views; friendly and safe; great restaurant. **Cons:** not the best spot for little kids. ⊠ *Hwy. 1B, Heywoods, St. Peter*

Coral Reef Club luxury cottage.

☎ 246/419–1000 ⊕ www.portstcharles.com ⇱ 31 villas ♿ In-room: a/c, kitchen, Internet. In-hotel: restaurants, bars, tennis courts, pools, gym, beach, water sports, laundry facilities, business center ⎮◯⎮ No meals.

$$$$
RESORT
☼

⌖ **Royal Westmoreland Villas.** On a ridge overlooking the sea, this villa community was the first of its kind in Barbados, built on a 500-acre estate in the mid-1990s adjoining the Royal Westmoreland Golf Club. **Pros:** nirvana for golfers; huge accommodations with every possible modern convenience; lots of activities and amenities for families; private and safe. **Cons:** very expensive; not on or close to the beach. ✉ Hwy. 2A, Westmoreland, St. James ☎ 246/422–4653 ⊕ www.royal-westmoreland.com ⇱ 5 villas ♿ In-room: a/c, kitchen. In-hotel: restaurants, bars, golf course, tennis courts, pools, gym, spa, children's programs, laundry facilities ⎮◯⎮ No meals.

$$$$
RESORT
Fodor's Choice
★

⌖ **The Sandpiper.** This little gem just north of Holetown is every bit as elegant as its sister hotel, Coral Reef Club, yet the atmosphere is more like a private hideaway. **Pros:** chic and sophisticated, the Tree Top Suites are fabulous; the bathrooms are amazing. **Cons:** beach is small—typical of west-coast beaches; hotel is small and many guests return year after year, so reservations can be hard to get. ✉ Hwy. 1, Holetown, St. James ☎ 246/422–2251 ⊕ www.sandpiperbarbados.com ⇱ 22 rooms, 25 suites ♿ In-room: a/c, safe, kitchen (some), no TV, Internet, Wi-Fi. In-hotel: restaurant, bars, tennis courts, pool, gym, beach, water sports, business center, some age restrictions ☉ Closed Sept. ⎮◯⎮ Breakfast.

$$$$
RESORT
☼
Fodor's Choice
★

⌖ **Sandy Lane Hotel and Golf Club.** Few places on Earth can compare to Sandy Lane's luxurious facilities and ultrapampering service—or to its astronomical prices. But for the few who can afford to stay here, it's an unparalleled experience. **Pros:** top of the line, cream of the crop—no debate about that; the spa is amazing. **Cons:** over the top for most mortals; very formal—you feel like dressing up just to walk through the lobby. *Hwy. 1, Paynes Bay, St. James BB24024* ☎ *246/444–2000* ⊕ *www. sandylane.com* ⤴ *96 rooms, 16 suites, 1 5-bedroom villa* ⚹ *In-room: a/c, safe, Internet, Wi-Fi. In-hotel: restaurants, bars, golf courses, tennis courts, pool, spa, beach, water sports, children's programs, business center* ⊡ *Breakfast.*

$$–$$$
RENTAL

St. James Apartment Hotel. These apartments are perfectly situated right on Paynes Bay Beach, one of the best on the west coast. The real appeal in staying in these elegant apartments is the self-catering aspect. **Pros:** save money by cooking some meals yourself; great quarters for independent travelers and long stays; great beach and sundeck; convenient to shopping and restaurants. **Cons:** no pool; no organized activities. ⊠ *Hwy. 1, Paynes Bay, St. James* ☎ *246/432–0489* ⊕ *www. the-stjames.com* ⤴ *11 apartments* ⚹ *In-room: a/c, safe, kitchen, Internet. In-hotel: beach* ⊡ *No meals.*

$$$$
RESORT
☪

Tamarind. This Mediterranean-style resort, completely renovated and modernized in 2010, sprawls along 750 feet of prime west-coast beachfront and is large enough to cater to sophisticated couples and active families while, at the same time, offering cozy privacy to honeymooners. **Pros:** central location right on Paynes Bay beach; lots of free water sports. **Cons:** some rooms could use a little TLC; uninspired buffet breakfast. ⊠ *Hwy. 1, Paynes Bay, St. James* ☎ *246/432–1332* ⊕ *www.tamarindcovehotel.com* ⤴ *58 rooms, 47 suites* ⚹ *In-room: a/c, safe, Internet. In-hotel: restaurants, bars, pools, gym, spa, beach, water sports, children's programs, business center* ⊡ *No meals.*

$$$$
HOTEL

Treasure Beach. Quiet, upscale, and intimate, this boutique all-suites hotel has a residential quality. Many guests—mostly British—are regulars, suggesting that the ambience here is well worth the price. **Pros:** cozy retreat; congenial crowd; swimming with the turtles just offshore. **Cons:** narrow beach; only bedrooms are air-conditioned; offshore turtles attract boatloads of tourists. *Hwy. 1, Paynes Bay, St. James BB24009* ☎ *246/432–1346* ⊕ *www.treasurebeachhotel.com* ⤴ *35 suites* ⚹ *In-room: a/c, safe, Wi-Fi. In-hotel: restaurant, bar, pool, gym, beach, business center, some age restrictions* ⊙ *Closed Sept. and Oct.* ⊡ *Breakfast.*

NIGHTLIFE

When the sun goes down, the people come out to "lime" (which may be anything from a "chat-up" to a full-blown "jump-up" or street party). Performances by world-renowned stars and regional groups are major events, and tickets can be hard to come by—but give it a try. Most resorts have nightly entertainment in season, and nightclubs often have live bands for listening and dancing. The busiest bars and dance clubs rage until 3 am. On Saturday nights, some clubs—especially those with live music—charge a cover of about $15.

Barbados supports the rum industry with more than 1,600 "rum shops," simple bars where men (mostly) congregate to discuss the world (or life in general), drink rum, and eat a cutter (sandwich). In more sophisticated

A local chef cooks up a fish fry at the Oistins fish market in Bridgetown.

establishments, you can find upscale rum cocktails made with the island's renowned Mount Gay and Cockspur brands—and no shortage of Barbados's own Banks Beer.

BRIDGETOWN

BARS

Boatyard. The Boatyard is a popular pub with both a DJ and live bands; from happy hour until the wee hours, the patrons are mostly local and visiting professionals. ⊠ *Bay St., Carlisle Bay, Bridgetown, St. Michael* ☎ *246/436–2622* ⊕ *www.theboatyard.com.*

Waterfront Café. Waterfront Cafe has live jazz in the evening, with a small dance floor for dancing. The location alongside the wharf is also a draw. ⊠ *The Careenage, Bridgetown, St. Michael* ☎ *246/427–0093* ⊕ *www.waterfrontcafe.com.bb.*

DANCE CLUBS

Harbour Lights. This open-air, beachfront club claims to be the "home of the party animal" and has dancing under the stars most nights to live reggae and soca music. ⊠ *Upper Bay St., Bridgetown, St. Michael* ☎ *246/436–7225* ⊕ *www.harbourlightsbarbados.com.*

SOUTH COAST

BARS

Bubba's Sports Bar. On the south coast, Bubba's offers merrymakers and sports lovers live sports on three 10-foot video screens and a dozen TVs, along with a Bajan à la carte menu and drinks at the bar. ⊠ *Main Rd., Rockley, Christ Church* ☎ *246/435–6217* ⊕ *www.bubbassportsbar. com.*

DANCE CLUBS

★ **Reggae Lounge**. This is a popular open-air nightclub where live bands or DJs play the latest Jamaican hits and old reggae favorites. ⊠ *St. Lawrence Gap, Dover, Christ Church* ☎ *246/435–6462.*

Ship Inn. The Ship Inn is a large, friendly pub with local band music every night for dancing. ⊠ *St. Lawrence Gap, Dover, Christ Church* ☎ *246/420–7447* ⊕ *www.shipinnbarbados.com.*

STREET PARTIES

♻ **Oistins Fish Fry**. Oistins is the place to be on Friday evenings, when the
Fodor's Choice south-coast fishing village becomes a convivial outdoor street fair. Bar-
★ becued chicken and a variety of fish are served right from the grill and consumed at roadside picnic tables; servings are huge, and prices are inexpensive—about $10. Drinks, music, and dancing add to the fun. ⊠ *Oistins, Christ Church.*

THEME NIGHTS

♻ **Plantation Restaurant and Garden Theater**. On Wednesday and Friday eve-
Fodor's Choice nings, the Tropical Spectacular calypso cabaret presents *Bajan Roots*
★ *and Rhythms*, a delightful extravaganza that the whole family will enjoy. The show includes steel-band music, fire eating, limbo, and dancing to the reggae, soca, and pop music sounds of popular Barbadian singer John King and the Plantation House Band. The fun begins at 6:30 pm. A Barbadian buffet dinner, unlimited drinks, transportation, and the show cost $97.50; for the show and drinks only, it's $57.50. ⊠ *St. Lawrence Main Rd., Dover, Christ Church* ☎ *246/428–5048* ⊕ *www. plantationtheatre.com.*

WEST COAST

BARS

★ **Lexy Piano Bar**. Lexy's is a cool, trendy club named for owner Alex Santoriello, a transplanted Broadway singer and actor. A changing roster of singer-pianists play sing-along standards, classic rock, R&B, and Broadway tunes. Most any night, you'll find Santoriello there. ⊠ *2nd St., Holetown, St. James* ☎ *246/432–5399* ⊕ *www.lexypianobar.com.*

SHOPPING

WHAT TO BUY

Perhaps one of the most long-lasting souvenirs to bring home from Barbados is a piece of authentic Caribbean art. The colorful flowers, quaint villages, mesmerizing seascapes, and fascinating cultural experiences and activities that are endemic to the region and familiar to visitors have been translated by local artists onto canvas and into photographs, sculpture, and other media. Gift shops and even some restaurants display local artwork for sale, but the broadest array of artwork will be found in an art gallery. Typical crafts include pottery, shell and glass art, woodcarvings, handmade dolls, watercolors, and other artwork (both originals and prints).

Although many of the private homes, greathouses, and museums in Barbados are filled with priceless antiques, you'll find few for sale—mainly British antiques and some local pieces, particularly mahogany furniture. Look especially for planters' chairs and the classic Barbadian rocking chair, as well as old prints and paintings.

DUTY-FREE SHOPPING

Duty-free luxury goods—china, crystal, cameras, porcelain, leather items, electronics, jewelry, perfume, and clothing—are found in Bridgetown's Broad Street department stores and their branches, at the Bridgetown Cruise Terminal shops (for passengers only), and in the departure lounge shops at Grantley Adams International Airport. Prices are often 30% to 40% less than at home. To buy goods at duty-free prices, you must produce your passport, immigration form, or driver's license, along with departure information (e.g., flight number and date) at the time of purchase—or you can have your purchases delivered free to the airport or harbor for pickup. Duty-free alcohol, tobacco products, and some electronic equipment *must* be delivered to you at the airport or harbor.

BRIDGETOWN

Bridgetown's **Broad Street** is the primary downtown shopping area. **DaCostas Mall,** in the historic Colonnade Building on Broad Street, has more than 25 shops that sell everything from Piaget watches to postcards; across the street, **Mall 34** has 22 shops where you can buy duty-free goods, souvenirs, and snacks. At the **cruise-ship terminal** shopping arcade, passengers can buy both duty-free goods and Barbadian-made crafts at more than 30 boutiques and a dozen vendor carts and stalls. **Pelican Craft Centre** is a cluster of workshops halfway between the cruise-ship terminal and downtown Bridgetown, where craftspeople create and sell locally made items.

HANDICRAFTS

★ **Pelican Craft Centre**. Pelican is made up of a cluster of workshops halfway between the cruise-ship terminal and downtown Bridgetown where craftspeople create and sell locally made leather goods, batik, basketry, carvings, jewelry, glass art, paintings, pottery, and other items. It's open weekdays 9 to 5 and Saturday 9 to 2, with extended hours during holidays or cruise-ship arrivals (when it's also busiest). ⊠ *Princess Alice Hwy., Bridgetown, St. Michael* ☎ *246/427–5350.*

CLOSE UP

Where de Rum Come From

For more than 300 years (from 1655 through "Black Tot Day, July 31, 1970"), a daily "tot" of rum (2 ounces) was duly administered to each sailor in the British Navy—as a health ration. At times, rum has also played a less appetizing—but equally important— role. When Admiral Horatio Nelson died in 1805 aboard ship during the Battle of Trafalgar, his body was preserved in a cask of his favorite rum until he could be properly buried.

Hardly a Caribbean island doesn't have its own locally made rum, but Barbados is truly "where de rum come from." Mount Gay, the world's oldest rum distillery, has continuously operated on Barbados since 1703, according to the original deed for the Mount Gay Estate, which itemized two stone windmills, a boiling house, seven copper pots, and a still house. The presence of rum-making equipment

on the plantation at the time suggests that the previous owners were actually producing rum in Barbados long before 1703.

Today, much of the island's interior is still planted with sugarcane—where the rum really does come from—and several greathouses, on historic sugar plantations, have been restored with period furniture and are open to the public.

To really fathom rum, however, you need to delve a little deeper than the bottom of a glass of rum punch. Mount Gay offers an interesting 45-minute tour of its main plant, followed by a tasting. You can learn about the rum-making process from cane to cocktail, hear more rum-inspired anecdotes, and have an opportunity to buy bottles of its famous Eclipse or Extra Old rum at duty-free prices. Bottoms up!

5

SOUTH COAST

The St. Lawrence Gap, like Holetown, has a **Chattel House Village,** where you can buy locally made crafts and other souvenirs. In Rockley, Christ Church, **Quayside Shopping Center** houses a small group of boutiques, restaurants, and services.

HANDICRAFTS

Best of Barbados. Best of Barbados was the brainchild of architect Jimmy Walker as a place to showcase the works of his artist wife. Now with five locations, the shops offer products that range from Jill Walker's frameable prints, housewares, and textiles to arts and crafts in both "native" style and modern designs. Everything is made or designed on Barbados. ⊠ *Quayside Centre, Rockley, Christ Church* ☎ *246/435– 6820* ⊕ *www.best-of-barbados.com.*

CENTRAL BARBADOS

ART

On the Wall Art Gallery. This gallery at Earthworks Pottery, has an array of original paintings by Barbadian artists, along with arts and crafts products (closed Sunday). An additional gallery is in dedicated space at Champers restaurant on the south coast. ⊠ *Earthworks*

Pottery, No. 2, Edgehill Heights, St. Thomas ☎ *246/425–0223* ⊕ *www.* *onthewallartgallery.com.*

HANDICRAFTS

Fodor's Choice   **Earthworks Pottery.** Earthworks is a family-owned and -operated pottery
★   workshop where you can purchase anything from a dish or knickknack
to a complete dinner service or one-of-a-kind art piece. You can find the
characteristically blue or green pottery decorating hotel rooms for sale
in gift shops throughout the island, but the biggest selection (including
some "seconds") is at Earthworks, where you also can watch the potters at work. ⊠ *No. 2, Edgehill Heights, St. Thomas* ☎ *246/425–0223*
⊕ *www.earthworks-pottery.com.*

WEST COAST

Holetown has a great **Chattel House Village,** a cluster of shops selling local
products, fashions, beachwear, and souvenirs. Also in Holetown, **Sunset
Crest Mall** has two branches of the Cave Shepherd department store, a
bank, a pharmacy, and several small shops; at **West Coast Mall,** you can
buy duty-free goods, island wear, and groceries.

CLOTHING

NORTHERN BARBADOS

ART

Gallery of Caribbean Art. This gallery is committed to promoting Caribbean
art from Cuba to Curaçao, including a number of pieces by Barbadian
artists (closed Sunday). A branch gallery is at the Hilton Barbados hotel,
Needham's Point. ⊠ *Northern Business Centre, Queen St., Speightstown,
St. Peter* ☎ *246/419–0858* ⊕ *www.artgallerycaribbean.com.*

SPORTS AND ACTIVITIES

DIVING AND SNORKELING

More than two dozen dive sites lie along the west coast between Maycocks Bay and Bridgetown and off the south coast as far as the St. Lawrence Gap. Certified divers can explore flat coral reefs and see dramatic
sea fans, huge barrel sponges, and more than 50 varieties of fish. Nine
sunken wrecks are dived regularly, and at least 10 more are accessible
to experts. Underwater visibility is generally 80 to 90 feet. The calm
waters along the west coast are also ideal for snorkeling. The marine
reserve, a stretch of protected reef between Sandy Lane and the Colony
Club, contains beautiful coral formations accessible from the beach.

On the west coast, **Bell Buoy** is a large, dome-shape reef where huge
brown coral tree forests and schools of fish delight all categories of
divers at depths ranging from 20 to 60 feet. At **Dottins Reef,** off Holetown, you can see schooling fish, barracudas, and turtles at depths of
40 to 60 feet. **Maycocks Bay,** on the northwest coast, is a particularly
enticing site; large coral reefs are separated by corridors of white sand,

and visibility is often 100 feet or more. The 165-foot freighter *Pamir* lies in 60 feet of water off Six Men's Bay; it's still intact, and you can peer through its portholes and view dozens of varieties of tropical fish. **Silver Bank** is a healthy coral reef with beautiful fish and sea fans; you may get a glimpse of the *Atlantis* submarine at 60 to 80 feet. Not to be missed is the *Stavronikita,* a scuttled Greek freighter at about 135 feet; hundreds of butterfly fish hang out around its mast, and the thin rays of sunlight filtering down through the water make fully exploring the huge ship a wonderfully eerie experience.

Farther south, **Carlisle Bay** is a natural harbor and marine park just below Bridgetown. Here you can retrieve empty bottles thrown overboard by generations of sailors and see cannons and cannonballs, anchors, and six unique shipwrecks (*Berwyn, Fox, CTrek, Eilon,* the barge *Cornwallis,* and *Bajan Queen*) lying in 25 to 60 feet of water, all close enough to visit on the same dive. The *Bajan Queen,* a cruise vessel that sank in 2002, is the island's newest wreck.

Dive shops provide a two-hour beginner's "resort" course ($75 to $85) followed by a shallow dive, or a weeklong certification course (about $400). Once you're certified, a one-tank dive runs about $50 to $60; a two-tank dive is $75 to $100. All equipment is supplied, and you can purchase multidive packages. Gear for snorkeling is available (free or for a small rental fee) from most hotels. Snorkelers can usually accompany dive trips for $25 for a one- or two-hour trip. Most dive shops have relationships with several hotels and offer special dive packages, with transportation, to hotel guests.

On the west coast, **Dive Barbados** (⊠ *Mount Standfast, St. James* ☎ *246/ 422–3133* ⊕ *www.divebarbados.net*), on the beach next to the Lone Star Hotel, offers all levels of PADI instruction, two or three reef and wreck dives daily for up to six divers each time, snorkeling with hawksbill turtles just offshore, as well as underwater camera rental and free transportation.

On the south coast, the **Dive Shop, Ltd** (⊠ *Amey's Alley, Upper Bay St., Carlisle Bay, St. Michael* ☎ *246/426–9947, 888/898–3483 in U.S., 888/575–3483 in Canada* ⊕ *www.divebds.com*), the island's oldest dive shop, offers daily reef and wreck dives, plus beginner classes, certification courses, and underwater photography instruction. Underwater cameras are available for rent.

Hightide Watersports (⊠ *Coral Reef Club, Holetown, St. James* ☎ *246/ 432–0931, 800/970–0016, or 800/513–5763* ⊕ *www.divehightide.com*) offers three dive trips—one- and two-tank dives and night reef–wreck–drift dives—daily for up to eight divers, along with PADI instruction, equipment rental, and free transportation.

FISHING

Fishing is a year-round activity in Barbados, but its prime time is January through April, when game fish are in season. Whether you're a serious deep-sea fisher looking for marlin, sailfish, tuna, and other billfish or you prefer angling in calm coastal waters where wahoo, barracuda, and other small fish reside, you can choose from a variety of half-or full-day charter trips departing from the Careenage in Bridgetown. Expect to pay $175 per person for a shared half-day charter; for a private charter, expect to pay $500 to $600 per boat for a four-hour half-day or $950 to $1,000 for an eight-hour full-day charter. Spectators who don't fish are welcome for $50 per person.

Billfisher II (☎ 246/431–0741), a 40-foot Pacemaker, accommodates up to six passengers with three fishing chairs and five rods. Captain Winston ("The Colonel") White has been fishing these waters since 1975. His full-day charters include a full lunch and guaranteed fish (or a 25% refund); all trips include drinks and transportation to and from the boat.

Blue Jay (☎ 246/429–2326 ⊕ *www.bluemarlinbarbados.com*) is a spacious, fully equipped, 45-foot Sport Fisherman with a crew that knows the water's denizens—blue marlin, sailfish, barracuda, and kingfish. Four to six people can be accommodated—it's the only charter boat on the island with four chairs. Most fishing is done by trolling. Drinks, snacks, bait, tackle, and transfers are provided.

Cannon II (☎ 246/424–6107), a 42-foot Hatteras Sport Fisherman, has three chairs and five rods and accommodates six passengers; drinks and snacks are complimentary, and lunch is served on full-day charters.

GOLF

Barbadians love golf, and golfers love Barbados. In addition to the courses listed below, Almond Beach Village has a 9-hole, par-3 executive course open only to guests. **Barbados Golf Club** (✉ *Hwy. 7, Durants, Christ Church* ☎ 246/428–8463 ⊕ *www.barbadosgolfclub.com*), the first public golf course on Barbados, is an 18-hole championship course (6,805 yards, par 72) redesigned in 2000 by golf course architect Ron Kirby. Greens fees with a cart are $125 for 18 holes; $80 for 9 holes. Unlimited three-day and seven-day golf passes are available. Several hotels offer preferential tee-time reservations and reduced rates. Club and shoe rentals are available.

Fodor's Choice ★ At the prestigious **Country Club at Sandy Lane** (✉ *Hwy. 1, Paynes Bay, St. James* ☎ 246/444–2500 ⊕ *www.sandylane.com/golf*), golfers can play on the Old Nine or on either of two 18-hole championship courses: the Tom Fazio–designed Country Club Course or the spectacular Green Monkey Course, reserved for hotel guests and club members only. Golfers have complimentary use of the club's driving range. The Country Club Restaurant and Bar, which overlooks the 18th hole, is open to the public. Greens fees in high season are $155 for 9 holes ($135 for hotel guests) or $240 for 18 holes ($205 for hotel guests). Golf carts, caddies, or trolleys are available for hire, as are clubs and shoes. Carts are equipped with GPS, which alerts you to upcoming traps and hazards, provides tips on how to play the hole, and allows you to order refreshments!

Rockley Golf and Country Club (✉ *Golf Club Rd., Worthing, Christ Church* ☎ 246/435–7873 ⊕ *www.rockleygolfclub.com*), on the southeast coast, has a challenging 9-hole course (2,800 yards, par 35) that can be played

Continued on page 196

SPORT FISHING

Marlise Kast

With its abundance of marlin, sailfish, tuna, and Mahi Mahi, the Caribbean has enough catch to beckon any angler. Crystal-blue waters, white-sand beaches, and tropical weather make this the perfect place to set sail. From Barbados and the Bahamas to Puerto Rico and the Virgin Islands, there is plenty of opportunity to cast your line.

Fishing on sailing boat, Grenadines Islands.

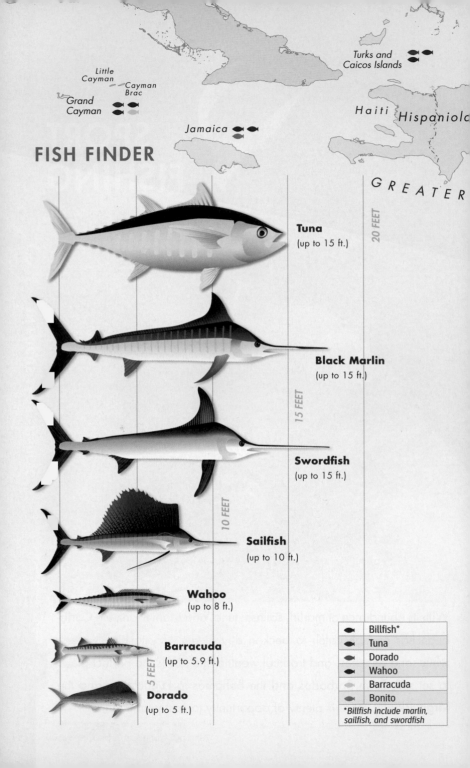

FISH FINDER

Little Cayman
Cayman Brac
Grand Cayman
Jamaica
Turks and Caicos Islands
Haiti Hispaniola

GREATER

20 FEET

Tuna
(up to 15 ft.)

Black Marlin
(up to 15 ft.)

15 FEET

Swordfish
(up to 15 ft.)

10 FEET

Sailfish
(up to 10 ft.)

Wahoo
(up to 8 ft.)

Barracuda
(up to 5.9 ft.)

5 FEET

Dorado
(up to 5 ft.)

	Billfish*
	Tuna
	Dorado
	Wahoo
	Barracuda
	Bonito

*Billfish include marlin, sailfish, and swordfish

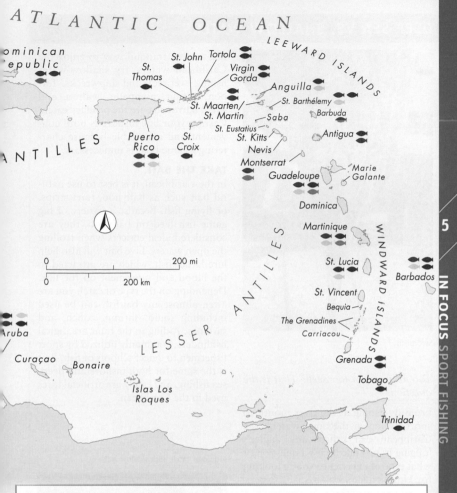

ATLANTIC OCEAN

ominican
epublic

LEEWARD ISLANDS

St. John   Tortola
St.
Thomas   Virgin
               Gorda
                              Anguilla
          St. Maarten/   St. Barthélemy
          St. Martin   Barbuda
                      Saba
                  St. Eustatius   Antigua
Puerto   St.   St. Kitts
Rico   Croix   Nevis
                  Montserrat   Marie
                    Guadeloupe   Galante

ANTILLES

Dominica

0   200 mi
0   200 km

Martinique

WINDWARD ISLANDS

St. Lucia   Barbados

St. Vincent

LESSER ANTILLES

Bequia

The Grenadines

Carriacou

Grenada

Aruba

Curaçao   Bonaire

Islas Los
Roques

Tobago

Trinidad

So many islands, so little time. Among anglers' favorites are the **Virgin Islands**, known for bluefish, wahoo, swordfish, and shark. These deep-sea fishing waters host annual tournaments where eight world records for blue marlin have been set. Equally attractive to deep-sea fishermen are the **Cayman Islands**, home to tuna, wahoo, and marlin. Bottom dwellers, such as grouper and snapper are always an easy hook in this area.

For great bonefishing, head to nearby Little Cayman at Bloody Bay. Between January and June, the **Dominican Republic** is popular with sport fishermen in search of sailfish, bonito, marlin, and wahoo. Although the bonefish-laden **Bahamas** cater to fly-fishermen, **Barbados** is a paradise for both deep-sea anglers reeling in billfish, and for coastal catchers forging for wahoo, barracuda, and smaller fish. Luring fishermen from afar, **Puerto Rico's** coast has reeled in 30+ world records, making it the fishing capital of the Caribbean.

DEEP SEA VS. SHALLOW WATERS

Swordfish

Too deep or not too deep? That is the question!

From fly-fishing at the river mouth to sport fishing in the open waters, the Caribbean can satisfy any angler's longing to reel one in. It's a question of what type of experience you're looking for. How active vs. passive of an experience do you want?

If you're feeling strong head for the deep. Any quest for catch below 30 meters (98 ft) is considered deep-sea fishing. The massive sport fish that frequent the deeper waters are magnificent specimens, and it's a thrilling experience to wrestle one from the deep. Albacore, marlin, barracuda, and tuna are the common catch, and it requires a tremendous amount of patience, strength, and effort to properly hook and land these mighty creatures.

For a more tranquil way to enjoy the Caribbean waters, try shallow-water fishing over reefs and shipwrecks. Tarpon, permit, pompano, wahoo, and small barracuda are the primary catch. Casting your line inshore is both convenient and affordable because chartering a large boat is unnecessary.

TAKE THE BAIT

In the Caribbean, it is best to use natural bait such as ballyhoo, tuna strips, or flying fish. Because a variety of big game fish feed on ballyhoo, they are considered ideal enticers when trolling the open waters. Live bait will also help lure larger fish, which are attracted to the blood and movement on the line. Depending on the type of catch you are after, almost any baitfish can be used including squid, shrimp, conch, and sardines. Aiding in the hunt are digital fishfinders, commonly utilized by sport fishermen to detect schools of fish. Bait is the same for both inshore and deep-sea fishing, and rarely are artificial lures used in the Caribbean.

A golden catch from shallow waters.

PRACTICAL INFORMATION

TYPE OF FISHING	COSTS	CHARACTERISTICS
OFFSHORE TRIPS	Start at $325 for a half-day, $625 for a full day.	Many packages include roundtrip transportation to and from your hotel, a boat crew, food, beverages, bait, gear, taxes and licenses. Tips are not included.
REEF FISHING	$300 to $600 per day; or cut the fee in half by opting for a 4-hour trip. A bonefishing guide is $250 for a half-day.	An experienced captain to steady the boat directly over the reefs is recommended. Most reefs are home to large schools of fish, but some areas are barren. Use a braided line, which is more abrasion resistant than monofiliament lines, to keep your line from snapping between the crevices.
DEEP-SEA FISHING	From $500 for a half-day to $1,500 for a full day.	The open waters are where you'll find the big catch. Most operators offer half-day and full-day charters with an experienced crew that knows where to find that trophy fish. Packages generally include your captain, crew, fishing tackle, bait, license and fees.

Private boat owners who plan on fishing for tuna, shark, swordfish and billfish in the Atlantic Ocean, (including the Gulf of Mexico and Caribbean Sea), must obtain an **Atlantic Highly Migratory Species** (HMS) permit for $16.00. Valid from the date of issue through December of that same year, permits can be ordered online through the **National Marine Fisheries Service** (⊕ www.hmspermits.noaa.gov).

MAN OVERBOARD: RULES/REGULATIONS

Although guidelines vary from island to island, it is safe to assume that a permit is required for fishing in the Caribbean. These licenses are usually included in sport fishing tours and packages, but it is best to inquire prior to booking. Because hundreds of fish can be hooked in a single day in the Caribbean waters, the catch-and-release method is vital for conservation. Throughout the entire region, spear fishing is illegal as is fishing within the boundaries of any marine park. It's advisable to utilize the services of licensed professionals.

Many of the Caribbean territories do not require a saltwater fishing license. One definite exception is the British Virgin Islands, where private charters must obtain permits for $45, valid up to one month. Fishing permits are available from the Department of Conservation and Fisheries ☎ 284/494–5681.

STAYING AFLOAT: SAFETY

Before setting sail, be sure to inform someone of your intended whereabouts as well as the time of your scheduled return. If you're fishing solo, double check all safety equipment including your means of communication, life jackets, and emergency supplies. Above all, inquire about local weather conditions and policies before booking your charter.

Deep-sea fishing boats.

as 18 from varying tee positions. Club and cart rentals are available. Greens fees are $60 for 18 holes and $50 for 9 holes.

★ The **Royal Westmoreland Golf Club** (✉ *Westmoreland, St. James* ☎ *246/ 422–4653* ⊕ *www.royal-westmoreland.com*) has a well-regarded Robert Trent Jones Jr.–designed, 18-hole championship course (6,870 yards, par 72) that meanders through the 500-acre property. This challenging course is primarily for villa renters, with a few midmorning tee times for visitors subject to availability; greens fees for villa renters or guests at hotels with golf privileges at the club are $300 for tee times before 10 am or $250 after 10 am for 18 holes and $125 after 2 pm for 9 holes. Greens fees include use of an electric cart (required); club rental is available.

GUIDED TOURS

Taxi drivers will give you a personalized tour of Barbados for about $25 per hour for up to three people. Or you can choose an overland horseback or mountain-bike journey, a 4x4 safari expedition, or a full-day bus excursion. The prices vary according to the mode of travel and the number and kind of attractions included. Ask your hotel to help you make arrangements.

Highland Adventure Centre (✉ *Cane Field, St. Thomas* ☎ *246/438–8069 or 246/438–8928*) offers beautiful horseback or mountain-bike tours for $60 per person, including transportation, guides, and refreshments. The mountain bike tour is an exhilarating 7½-mi (12-km) ride (15% uphill) through the heart of northern Barbados, ending up at Barclays Park on the east coast.

THIKING

Hilly but not mountainous, the northern interior and the east coast are ideal for hiking.

The **Barbados National Trust** (✉ *Wildey House, Wildey, St. Michael* ☎ *246/228–8027* ⊕ *www.hikebarbados.com*) sponsors free walks, called **Hike Barbados,** year-round on Sunday from 6 am to about 9 am and from 3:30 pm to 6 pm; once a month, a moonlight hike substitutes for the afternoon hike and begins at 5:30 pm (bring a flashlight). Experienced guides group you with others of similar levels of ability. Stop and Stare hikes go 5 to 6 mi (8 to 10 km); Here and There, 8 to 10 mi (13 to 16 km); and Grin and Bear, 12 to 14 mi (19 to 23 km). Wear loose clothes, sensible shoes, sunscreen, and a hat, and bring your camera and a bottle of water. Routes and locations change, but each hike is a loop, finishing in the same spot where it began. Check local newspapers, call the Trust, or check online for the full hike schedule or the scheduled meeting place on a particular Sunday.

SEA EXCURSIONS

Mini-submarine voyages are enormously popular with families and those who enjoy watching fish but don't wish to snorkel or dive. Party boats depart from Bridgetown's Deep Water Harbour for sightseeing and snorkeling or romantic sunset cruises. Prices are $75 to $85 per person for daytime cruises and $55 to $85 for three-hour sunset cruises, depending on the type of refreshments and entertainment included; transportation to and from the dock is provided. For an excursion that may be less splashy in terms of a party atmosphere—but is definitely splashier in terms of the actual experience—turtle tours allow participants to feed and swim with a resident group of hawksbill and leatherback sea turtles.

The 48-passenger **Atlantis Submarine** (⊠ *Shallow Draught, Bridgetown, St. Michael* ☎ *246/436–8929* ⊕ *www.atlantisadventures.com*) turns the Caribbean into a giant aquarium. The 45-minute underwater voyage aboard the 50-foot submarine ($104 per person, including transportation) takes you to wrecks and reefs as deep as 150 feet. Children love the adventure, but they must be at least 3 feet tall to go on board.

Five-hour daytime cruises along the west coast on the 100-foot **MV Harbour Master** (☎ *246/430–0900* ⊕ *www.tallshipscruises.com*) stop in Holetown and land at beaches along the way; evening cruises are shorter but add a buffet dinner and entertainment. Day or night you can view the briny deep from the ship's onboard 34-seat semisubmersible.

A daytime cruise on the 57-foot catamaran **Heatwave** (☎ *246/826–4447* ⊕ *www.heatwavesailingcruises.com*) includes stops along the coast for swimming and snorkeling and a barbecue lunch. The sunset cruise includes a short swim and dinner.

★ **Just Breezing Water Sports** (☎ *246/432–7645*), based in Holetown, has a 32-foot glass-bottom boat from which guests can view, snorkel, and swim with the turtles. The cruise is particularly fun for families with young children. Two trips depart daily, at 10 am and 2 pm. They cover about 6 mi of coastline along the west coast, cost $45 per adult, and last two hours each. Hotel transportation, cool drinks, snorkels, and masks are all included.

The 53-foot catamaran **Tiami** (☎ *246/430–0900* ⊕ *www.tallshipscruises.com*) offers a luncheon cruise to a secluded bay or a romantic sunset and moonlight cruise with special catering and live music.

SURFING

The best surfing is on the east coast, at Bathsheba Soup Bowl, but the water on the windward side of the island is safe only for the most experienced swimmers. Surfers also congregate at Surfer's Point, at the southern tip of Barbados near Inch Marlow, where the Atlantic Ocean meets the Caribbean Sea.

Dread or Dead Surf Shop (⊠ *Hastings Main Rd., Hastings, Christ Church* ☎ *246/228–4785* ⊕ *www.dreadordead.com*) promises to get beginners from "zero to standing up and surfing" in a single afternoon. The four-hour course—"or until you stand up or give up"—costs $75 per person and includes a board, wax, a rash guard (if necessary), a ride to and from the surf break, and an instructor; additional lessons cost $37.50. Intermediate or experienced surfers can get all the equipment and the instructor for a full day of surfing for $150.

WINDSURFING

Barbados is on the World Cup Windsurfing Circuit and is one of the prime locations in the world for windsurfing. Winds are strongest November through April at the island's southern tip, at Silver Sand–Silver Rock Beach, which is where the Barbados Windsurfing Championships are held in mid-January. Use of boards and equipment is often among the amenities included at larger hotels; equipment can usually be rented by nonguests.

More-experienced windsurfers congregate at **Silver Rock Windsurfing Club** (⊠ *Silver Sands–Silver Rock Beach, Christ Church* ☎ *246/428–2866*), where the surf ranges from 3 to 15 feet and provides an exhilarating windsurfing experience.

Bonaire

WORD OF MOUTH

"I love Bonaire. It only has 14,000 people, so it's more relaxing than Curaçao. It also has Klein Bonaire, which is a perfect day trip to an idyllic island with no development."

—heijobroek

WELCOME TO BONAIRE

At the market in Kralendijk, hagglers vie for produce brought in by boat from lusher islands. But nature holds sway over human pursuits on this scrubby, cactus-covered landfall. Divers come to explore some of the best sites this side of Australia's Great Barrier Reef. Above the water are more than 15,000 flamingos—the biggest flock in the Western Hemisphere.

TOP REASONS TO VISIT BONAIRE

1 The Diving: As locals say, you come here to dive, eat, dive, sleep, and dive.

2 The Snorkeling: You don't have to be a certified diver to appreciate Bonaire's reefs; snorkelers can see a lot of the beauty just below the surface of the water.

3 The Quiet: Visitors came to enjoy the tranquillity of the island long before they started exploring offshore.

4 The Dining: Dining is surprisingly good and varied for such a small island.

5 The Smiles: Bonaireans are friendly without a hint of the phoniness sometimes found on other tourist-dependent islands.

DIVER'S PARADISE

With just over 15,000 people, this little island (112 square mi [290 square km]) has a real, small-town atmosphere. Kralendijk, the capital, has just 3,000 inhabitants. The entire coastline—from the high-water tidemark to a depth of 200 feet—is protected as part of the Bonaire Marine Park, making it one of the best diving destinations in the Western Hemisphere.

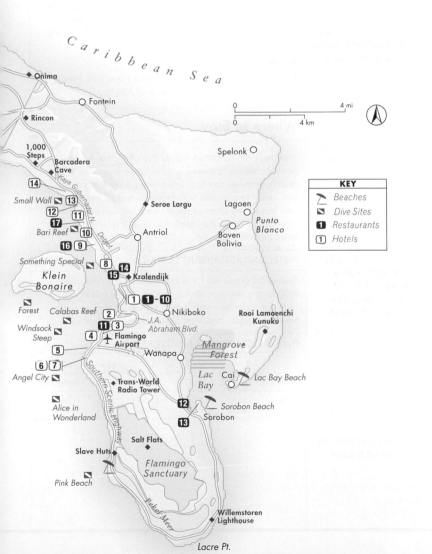

Caribbean Sea

Onima

Fontein

Rincon

1,000 Steps

Barcadera Cave

14

Small Wall 13

12 11

17

Bari Reef 10

16 9

Something Special

8

15 14

Klein Bonaire

Kralendijk

Forest Calabas Reef

2

Windsock Steep

11 3

4

5

Flamingo Airport

6 7

Angel City

Alice in Wonderland

Seroe Largu

Antriol

Spelonk

Lagoen

Punto Blanco

Boven Bolivia

1 1 - 10

Nikiboko

J.A. Abraham Blvd.

Wanapa

Rooi Lamoenchi Kunuku

Mangrove Forest

Lac Cai

Lac Bay Lac Bay Beach

12 Sorobon Beach

13 Sorobon

Trans-World Radio Tower

Salt Flats

Slave Huts

Pink Beach

Flamingo Sanctuary

Pekel Meer

Willemstoren Lighthouse

Lacre Pt.

Kaya Gubernador N.

Debrot

Southern Scenic Highway

0   4 mi
0   4 km

KEY	
〜	Beaches
◰	Dive Sites
❶	Restaurants
⑴	Hotels

BONAIRE PLANNER

Fast Facts

Banks and Exchange Services: As of January 2011 the U.S. dollar became the official currency, replacing the NAf guilder. You can find ATMs at the airport, in Kralendijk, and at Hato branches of MCB, as well as at the Sand Dollar Condominium Resort and the Plaza Resort; at the Tourism Corporation Bonaire; and at Banco di Caribe on Kaya Grandi.

Electricity: 120 AC/50 cycles. A transformer and occasionally a two-prong adapter are required. Some appliances may work slowly; hair dryers may overheat, and sensitive equipment may be damaged.

Emergency Services: Ambulance (☏ 599/717–8900). **Fire** (☏ 599/717–8000). **Police emergencies** (☏ 599/717–8000). **Scuba-diving emergencies** (☏ 599/717–8187).

Weddings: One person must apply for temporary residency. Official witnesses must also apply for residency, but most wedding coordinators can arrange for local witnesses. After the marriage, an apostille (official seal) must be placed on the marriage license and certificate. Blood tests are not required.

Logistics

Getting to Bonaire: Most flights from the United States connect in San Juan or Aruba. If you want to connect through Aruba, you'll more likely than not have to book your flight directly with an island-based airline. Bonaire's Flamingo Airport (BON) is tiny but welcoming (the KLM 747 almost dwarfs the airport when it lands).

Hassle Factor: Medium to high.

Nonstops: The only nonstops are from New York–Newark, New York–JFK, Houston, Miami, and Atlanta.

Where to Stay

Alongside the numerous lodges that offer only the basics (mostly catering to divers), you can now find some real resorts. Families can find self-catering accommodations, and many smaller inns will appeal to budget travelers. The best resorts are often on decent beaches, but these are mostly man-made. Almost all the island's resorts are clustered around Kralendijk.

HOTEL AND RESTAURANT COSTS

Restaurant prices are for a main course at dinner and include any taxes or service charges. Hotel prices are per night for a double room in high season, excluding taxes, service charges, and meal plans (except at all-inclusives).

WHAT IT COSTS IN U.S. DOLLARS

	¢	$	$$	$$$	$$$$
Restaurants	under $8	$8–$12	$12–$20	$20–$30	over $30
Hotels	under $150	$150–$275	$276–$375	$376–$475	over $475

Getting to and Around Bonaire

Air Travel: Continental Airlines offers once-weekly direct service to **Flamingo Airport** (⊠ *BON* ☎ *599/717–3800*) from Houston and Newark, Insel Air offers once-weekly service from Miami, and Delta offers direct flights weekly from Atlanta and JFK. Canadians and Americans will usually have to change planes in San Juan or Aruba. American Eagle and Dutch Antilles Express provide connecting service. KLM offers daily direct flights from Amsterdam.

American Eagle (☎ *599/717–2005 or 800/433–7300*). **Continental Airlines** (☎ *800/231–0856*). **Delta** (☎ *800/221–1212*). **Dutch Antilles Express** (☎ *599/717–0808* ⊕ *www.flydae.com*). **Insel Air** (☎ *599/737–0444* ⊕ *www.fly-inselair.com*). **KLM** (☎ *599/717–7447*).

Bike and Moped: Scooters are a great way to get around the island. Rates are about $25 per day for a one-seater and up to $35 for a deluxe two-seater. A valid driver's license and cash deposit or credit card are required. **Bonaire Motorcycle Shop** (⊠ *Kaya Grandi 64, Kralendijk* ☎ *599/717–7790*) rents Harley-Davidson motorcycles. **Rento Fun Drive** (⊠ *Kaya Grandi 47, Kralendijk* ☎ *599/717–2408*) will have you zipping about.

Car Travel: Minimum and maximum age to rent a car are 21 and 70. There's a government tax of 5% per rental; no cash deposit is needed if you pay by credit card.

Gas prices are about double those of the United States. Main roads are well paved, but during the rainy season (October and November) mud—called Bonairean snow—can be difficult to navigate. Traffic is to the right, and there's not a single traffic light.

Avis (⊠ *Flamingo Airport, Kralendijk* ☎ *599/717–5795*). **Budget** (⊠ *Flamingo Airport, Kralendijk* ☎ *599/717–7424*). **Flamingo Car Rental** (⊠ *Kaya Grandi 86, Kralendijk* ☎ *599/717–8888, 599/717–5588 at airport*). **Hertz** (⊠ *Flamingo Airport, Kralendijk* ☎ *599/717–7221*). **Island Rentals** (⊠ *Kaya Industria 31, Kralendijk* ☎ *599/717–2100*). **National** (⊠ *Kaya Nikiboko Zuid 114, Kralendijk* ☎ *599/717–7940 or 599/717–7907*).

Taxi Travel: Taxis are unmetered; fixed rates are controlled by the government. A trip from the **Airport Taxi Stand** (☎ *599/717–8100*) to your hotel is $9 to $20 for up to four passengers. From most hotels into town it costs between $9 and $13. Fares increase from 7 pm to midnight by 25% and from midnight to 6 am by 50%. Drivers will conduct half-day tours; they charge about $25 per hour for up to four passengers. **Taxi Central Dispatch** (☎ *599/717–8100*).

Essentials

Passport Requirements: U.S. citizens must carry valid passports. In addition, everyone must have a return or ongoing ticket and you are advised to confirm reservations 48 hours before departure. The maximum stay is 90 days.

Taxes: The departure tax when going to Curaçao or Aruba is $9. For all other destinations it's $35. This tax is supposed to be included in the ticket price. Hotels charge a room tax of $6.50 per person, per night in addition to the V.A.T. (value-added tax). Many hotels add a 10% to 15% service charge to your bill. A V.A.T. of 6% is tacked on to dining and lodging costs. The V.A.T. may or may not be included in your quoted room rates, so be sure to ask. It's almost always included in restaurant prices.

Telephones: The country code for Bonaire is 599; 717 is the exchange for every four-digit number on the island. Phone cards from home rarely work on Bonaire. You can try AT&T by dialing 001–800/872–2881 from public phones. To call Bonaire from the United States, dial 011–599/717 plus the local four-digit number.

6

BONAIRE BEACHES

Although most of Bonaire's charms are under-water there are a few excellent beaches. Even those beaches that are unsuitable for sunbathing can be worth a visit if only to view the intense turquoise waters that surround this little desert island.

(Above) Boca Slagbaai beach.
(Opposite page bottom)
The coast of Klein Bonaire.
(Opposite page top) Grab a
chair at Sorobon Beach.

Don't expect long stretches of glorious powdery sand. Bonaire's beaches are small, and though the water is blue (several shades of it, in fact), the sand isn't always white. Bonaire's National Parks Foundation requires all nondivers to pay a $10 annual Nature Fee to enter the water anywhere around the island (divers pay $25). The fee can be paid at most dive shops, and the receipt will also allow access to Washington–Slagbaai Park.

SALT AND PEPPER

Sorobon Beach offers white powder. Many beaches have white sand but are also peppered with broken coral and rocks, which makes strolling difficult. At the rugged Washington Slagbaai Park you'll find the black sand of Boca Cocolishi, a testament to the island's past volcanic activity. Pink Beach near Kralendijk is popular with families but offers no facilities and no shade.

Boca Slagbaai. Inside Washington–Slagbaai Park is this beach of coral fossils and rocks with interesting offshore coral gardens that are good for snorkeling. Bring scuba boots or canvas sandals to walk into the water, because the beach is rough on bare feet. The gentle surf makes it an ideal place for swimming and picnicking. ⊕ *Off main park road, in Washington–Slagbaai National Park.*

Klein Bonaire. Just a water-taxi hop across from Kralendijk, this little island offers picture-perfect white-sand beaches. The area is protected, so absolutely no development has been allowed. Make sure to pack everything before heading to the island, including water and an umbrella to hide under, because there are no refreshment stands or changing facilities, and there's almost no shade to be found. Boats leave from the Town Pier, across from the City Café, and the round-trip water-taxi ride costs roughly $20 per person.

Lac Bay Beach. Known for its festive music on Sunday nights, this open bay area with pink-tinted sand is equally dazzling by day. It's a bumpy drive (10 to 15 minutes on a dirt road) to get here, but you'll be glad when you arrive. It's a good spot for diving, snorkeling, and kayaking (as long as you bring your own), and there are public restrooms and a restaurant for your convenience. ✉ *Off Kaminda Sorobon, Lac Cai.*

Playa Funchi. This Washington–Slagbaai National Park beach is notable for the lagoon on one side, where flamingos nest, and the superb snorkeling on the other, where iridescent green parrot fish swim right up to shore. ⊕ *Off main park road, in Washington–Slagbaai National Park.*

Sorobon Beach. This is *the* windsurfing beach on Bonaire and one of the most beautiful beaches on the island, with a wide swath of soft white sand sloping gently into the intense blue waters of the sheltered cove. You can find a restaurant-bar next to the resort and windsurfing outfitters on the beach. The public beach area has restrooms and huts for shade. Take E.E.G. Boulevard south from Kralendijk to Kaya I.R. Randolf Statuuis Van Eps, and then follow this route straight on to Sorobon Beach. ✉ *Kaya I.R. Randolf Statuuis Van Eps, Sorobon Beach.*

Windsock Beach *(aka Mangrove Beach).* Near the airport (just off E.E.G. Boulevard), this pretty little spot looks out toward the north side of the island and has about 200 yards of white sand along a rocky shoreline. It's a popular dive site and swimming conditions are good. ⊕ *Off E.E.G. Blvd. near Flamingo Airport.*

6

By Vernon
O'Reilly
Ramesar

Bonaire is widely regarded as one of the best destinations in the Caribbean for shore diving, and with good reason. The dry climate and coral composition of the island mean that there's little soil runoff, allowing near-perfect visibility in the coastal waters. The islanders have exploited this advantage, and you can find local businesses that cater to virtually every diving need.

Even though tourism is the backbone of the economy here, authorities try to ensure that the booming hotel industry does not damage the environment upon which it is based. Thankfully, the fact that most visitors to Bonaire come for the natural beauty has prevented the kind of tourism that has turned neighboring islands like Aruba into commercialized tourist magnets.

Islanders are serious about conserving Bonaire's natural beauty. All the coastal waters of the island were turned into a national park in 1979, and in 1999 Bonaire purchased the 1,500-acre privately owned outlying island of Klein Bonaire to prevent unwanted development. Anyone diving around the island must purchase a one-year permit, and park rangers patrol the waters, handing out hefty fines to people who violate park rules. Spearfishing, removing coral, and even walking on coral are just some of the restricted activities. Rather than restricting legitimate divers, these rules have resulted in a pristine marine environment that makes for a supremely satisfying dive experience. Damage to the reefs caused by rare passing hurricanes is usually quickly repaired by the healthy ecosystem. Small wonder that even the license plates in Bonaire declare it a diver's paradise.

Bonaire also offers a variety of experiences above the surface to those willing to explore its 112 square mi (290 square km). The southern salt flats give an interesting glimpse into the island's economic history. Washington–Slagbaai National Park, in the north, has the island's highest peak (784 feet) and is a haven for some of the thousands of flamingos that make Bonaire their home. The near-perfect climate also makes Bonaire the ideal destination for soaking in some sun.

Although many islanders claim that the name Bonaire comes from the French for "good air," this explanation is unlikely, particularly because the island was never colonized by the French. The island was first inhabited by an Amerindian people (related to the Arawaks) called the Caquetios. Alonso de Ojeda and Amerigo Vespucci landed here in 1499 and claimed it for Spain. It seems likely that they adopted the Amerindian name for the island, which probably sounded very much like Bonaire and meant "low country." Because the Spanish found little use for the island except as a penal colony, the original inhabitants were shipped off to work on the plantations of Hispaniola, and Bonaire remained largely undeveloped. When the Dutch seized the islands of Aruba, Bonaire, and Curaçao in 1633, they started building the salt industry in Bonaire, which fueled the economy then and remains an important industry today.

> **LANGUAGE**
>
> The official language is Dutch, but the everyday language is Papiamento, a mix of Spanish, Portuguese, Dutch, English, and French, as well as African tongues. You can light up your waiter's eyes if you can say *masha danki* (thank you very much) and *pasa un bon dia* (have a nice day). English is spoken by almost everyone on the island.

The majority of the 15,000 inhabitants live in and around the capital, Kralendijk. The word almost universally applied to this diminutive city with a downtown area that can be traversed in less than three minutes is cute. Part of the BES Islands, Bonaire, Sint Eustatius, and Saba were made special municipalities of the Netherlands in late 2010. Prior to this change Bonaire was governed from neighboring Curaçao.

EXPLORING BONAIRE

Two routes, north and south from Kralendijk, the island's small capital, are possible on the 24-mi-long (39-km-long) island; either route will take from a few hours to a full day, depending on whether you stop to snorkel, swim, dive, or lounge. Those pressed for time will find that it's easy to explore the entire island in a day if stops are kept to a minimum.

KRALENDIJK

Bonaire's small, tidy capital city (population 3,000) is five minutes from the airport. The main drag, J.A. Abraham Boulevard, turns into **Kaya Grandi** in the center of town. Along it are most of the island's major stores, boutiques, and restaurants. Across Kaya Grandi, opposite the Littman jewelry store, is Kaya L.D. Gerharts, with several small supermarkets, a handful of snack shops, and some of the better restaurants. Walk down the narrow waterfront avenue called Kaya C.E.B. Hellmund, which leads straight to the **North and South piers**. In the center of town, the Harbourside Mall has chic boutiques. Along this route is **Ft. Oranje,** with its cannons. From December through April, cruise ships dock in the harbor once or twice a week. The diminutive ocher-and-white structure that looks like a tiny Greek temple is the **fish market**; local anglers no longer bring their catches here (they sell out of their homes these days), but you can find plenty of fresh produce brought over from Colombia and Venezuela. Pick up the brochure *Walking and Shopping in Kralendijk* from the tourist office to get a map and full listing of all the monuments and sights in the town.

SOUTH BONAIRE

The trail south from Kralendijk is chock-full of icons—both natural and man-made—that tell Bonaire's mini-saga. Rent a four-wheel-drive vehicle (a car will do, but during the rainy season of October through November the roads can become muddy) and head out along the Southern Scenic Route. The roads wind through dramatic desert terrain, full of organ-pipe cacti and spiny-trunk mangroves—huge stumps of saltwater trees that rise from the marshes like witches. Watch for long-haired goats, wild donkeys, and lizards of all sizes.

Rooi Lamoenchi Kunuku. Owner Ellen Herrera restored her family's homestead north of Lac Bay, in the Bonairean *kadushi* (cactus) wilderness, to educate tourists and residents about the history and tradition of authentic kunuku living and show unspoiled terrain in two daily tours. You must make an appointment in advance and expect to spend a couple of hours. ⊠ *Kaya Suiza 23, Playa Baribe* ☎ *599/717–8489* ☜ *$21* ⊘ *By appointment only.*

Salt Flats. You can't miss the salt flats—voluptuous white drifts that look like mountains of snow. Harvested once a year, the "ponds" are owned by Cargill, Inc., which has reactivated the 19th-century salt industry with great success (one reason for that success is that the ocean on this part of the island is higher than the land—which makes irrigation a snap). Keep a lookout for the three 30-foot obelisks—white, blue, and red—that were used to guide the trade boats coming to pick up the salt. Look also in the distance across the pans to the abandoned solar saltworks that's now a designated **flamingo sanctuary**. With the naked eye you might be able to make out a pink-orange haze just on the horizon; with binoculars you will see a sea of bobbing pink bodies. The sanctuary is completely protected, and no entrance is allowed (flamingos are extremely sensitive to disturbances of any kind).

Slave Huts. The salt industry's gritty history is revealed in Rode Pan, the site of two groups of tiny slave huts. The white grouping is on the right side of the road, opposite the salt flats; the second grouping, called the red slave huts (though they appear yellow), stretches across the road toward the island's southern tip. During the 19th century, slaves working the salt pans by day crawled into these huts to rest. Each Friday afternoon they walked seven hours to Rincon to weekend with their families, returning each Sunday. Only very small people will be able to enter, but walk around and poke your head in for a look.

Willemstoren Lighthouse. Bonaire's first lighthouse was built in 1837 and is now automated (but closed to visitors). Take some time to explore the beach and notice how the waves, driven by the trade winds, play a crashing symphony against the rocks. Locals stop here to collect pieces of driftwood in spectacular shapes and to build fanciful pyramids from objects that have washed ashore.

NORTH BONAIRE

The Northern Scenic Route takes you into the heart of Bonaire's natural wonders—desert gardens of towering cacti (kadushi, used to prepare soup, and the thornier *yatu*, used to build cactus fencing), tiny coastal coves, and plenty of fantastic panoramas. The road also weaves between eroded pink-and-black limestone walls and eerie rock formations with fanciful names like the Devil's Mouth and Iguana Head (you'll need a vivid imagination and sharp eye to recognize them). Brazil trees growing along the route were used by Indians to make dye (pressed from a red ring in the trunk). Inscriptions still visible in several island caves were made with this dye.

A snappy excursion with the requisite photo stops will take about 2½ hours, but if you pack your swimsuit and a hefty picnic basket (forget about finding fast food), you could spend the entire day exploring this northern sector. Head out from Kralendijk on Kaya Gobernador N. Debrot until it turns into the Northern Scenic Route. Once you pass the Radio Nederland towers, you cannot turn back to Kralendijk. The narrow road becomes one way until you get to Landhuis Karpata, and you have to follow the cross-island road to Rincon and return via the main road through the center of the island.

1,000 Steps. Directly across the road from the Radio Nederland towers on the main road north, you'll see a short yellow marker that points to the location of these limestone stairs carved right out of the cliff. If you trek down the stairs, you can discover a lovely coral beach and protected cove where you can snorkel and scuba dive. Actually, you'll count only 67 steps, but it feels like 1,000 when you walk back up carrying scuba gear.

Barcadera Cave. Once used to trap goats, this cave is one of the oldest in Bonaire; there's even a tunnel that looks intriguingly spooky. It's the first sight along the northern route; watch closely for a yellow marker on your left before you reach the towering Radio Nederland antennas. Pull off across from the entrance to the Bonaire Caribbean Club, and you can discover some stone steps that lead down into a cave full of stalactites and vegetation.

Gotomeer. This saltwater lagoon near the island's northern end is a popular flamingo hangout. Bonaire is one of the few places in the world where pink flamingos nest. The shy, spindly-leg creatures—affectionately called "pink clouds"—are magnificent birds to observe, and there are about 15,000 of them in Bonaire (more than the number of human residents). The best time to catch them at home is January to June, when they tend to their gray-plumed young. For the best view take the paved access road alongside the lagoon through the jungle of cacti to the parking and observation area on the rise overlooking the lagoon and Washington–Slagbaai National Park beyond.

Landhuis Karpata. This mustard-color building was the manor house of an aloe plantation in the 19th century. The site was named for the *karpata* (castor bean) plants that are abundant in the area—you can see them along the sides of the road as you approach. Notice the rounded outdoor oven where aloe was boiled down before the juice was exported. Although the government has built a shaded rest stop at Karpata, there's still no drink stand.

Mangazina di Rei. Built around the second-oldest stone structure on Bonaire, this cultural park a few miles before Rincon provides a fascinating insight into the island's history. The museum commands an excellent view of the surrounding countryside and contains artifacts tracing the often hard lives of the early settlers. There are numerous traditional structures built around the museum illustrating how living conditions have changed over the years. The park is usually filled with local school kids learning how to use traditional musical instruments and how to cook local foods. ⊠ *Kaya Rincon z/n, Rincon* ☎ *599/786–2101* ⊕ *www.mangazinadirei.org* ⊠ *$10 adults, $5 children under 12* ◷ *Tues.–Sat. 10–5.*

Onima. Small signposts direct the way to the Indian inscriptions found on a 3-foot limestone ledge that juts out like a partially formed cave entrance. Look up to see the red-stained designs and symbols inscribed on the limestone, said to have been the handiwork of the Arawak Indians when they inhabited the island centuries ago. The pictographs date back at least to the 15th century, and nobody has a clue what they mean. To reach Onima, pass through Rincon on the road that heads back to Kralendijk, but take the left-hand turn before Fontein.

Rincon. The island's original Spanish settlement, Rincon is where slaves brought from Africa to work the plantations and salt fields lived. Superstition and voodoo lore still have a powerful impact here, more so than in Kralendijk, where the townspeople work hard at suppressing old ways. Rincon is now a well-kept cluster of pastel cottages and 19th-century buildings that constitute Bonaire's oldest village. Watch your driving here—goats and dogs often sit right in the middle of the main drag.

Seroe Largu. Just off the main road, this spot, at 394 feet, is one of the highest on the island. A paved but narrow and twisting road leads to a magnificent daytime view of Kralendijk's rooftops and the island of Klein Bonaire. A large cross and figure of Christ stand guard at the peak, with an inscription reading *ayera* (yesterday), *awe* (today), and *semper* (always).

Washington–Slagbaai National Park. Once a plantation producing divi-divi trees (the pods were used for tanning animal skins), aloe (used for medicinal lotions), charcoal, and goats, the park is now a model of conservation. It's easy to tour the 13,500-acre tropical desert terrain on the dirt roads. As befits a wilderness sanctuary, the well-marked, rugged routes force you to drive slowly enough to appreciate the animal life and the terrain. (Think twice about coming here if it has rained recently—the mud you may encounter will be more than inconvenient.) If you're planning to hike, bring a picnic lunch, camera, sunscreen, and plenty of water. There are two routes: the long one (22 mi [35½ km]) is marked by yellow arrows, the short one (15 mi [24 km]) by green arrows. Goats and donkeys may dart across the road, and if you keep your eyes peeled, you may catch sight of large iguanas camouflaged in the shrubbery.

Bird-watchers are really in their element here. Right inside the park's gate, flamingos roost on the salt pad known as **Salina Mathijs,** and exotic parakeets dot the foot of **Mt. Brandaris,** Bonaire's highest peak, at 784 feet. Some 130 species of birds fly in and out of the shrubbery in the park. Keep your eyes open and your binoculars at hand. Swimming, snorkeling, and scuba diving are permitted, but you're asked not to frighten the animals or remove anything from the grounds. Absolutely no hunting, fishing, or camping is allowed. A useful guide to the park is available at the entrance for about $6. To get here, take the secondary road north from the town of Rincon. The Nature Fee for swimming and snorkeling also grants you free admission to this park—simply present proof of payment and some form of photo ID. ☎ 599/717–8444 ⊕ *www.washingtonparkbonaire.org* ✉ *Free with payment of scuba diving Nature Fee ($25) or $15 without* ☉ *Daily 8–5; you must enter before 3.*

WHERE TO EAT

Dining on Bonaire is far less expensive than on Aruba or Curaçao, and you can find everything from Continental to Tex-Mex to Asian fare. Many restaurants serve only dinner—only a few establishments not affiliated with hotels are open for breakfast, so check ahead.

$$–$$$
CONTINENTAL
★

✕ **Appetite.** This recent edition to the downtown dining scene is an oasis of chic. The historic house offers cozy private rooms and a large courtyard, which always seems to be buzzing. The menu encourages diners to forget the main course and order a series of starters, but such items as stewed veal cheek with crispy sweetbreads are worth the splurge. The restaurant is just a few steps away from the Tourism Corporation Bonaire office. ⊠ *Kaya Grandi 12, Kralendijk* ☎ *599/717–3595* ☉ *Closed Sun.*

$$–$$$
FRENCH
Fodor's Choice
★

✕ **Bistro de Paris.** Any restaurant that welcomes you with a free glass of Kir and a personal greeting from the owner should be taken very seriously. Patrice Ranhou has transformed an unassuming house into a lovely bistro serving the best French food on the island. The low-key decor (complete with Perrier-bottle vases) belies the extraordinary food on offer. Lamb lovers will fall to pieces over the char-grilled chops served with haricots verts and asparagus. The dinner menu is very reasonably priced, but those on an extremely tight budget should at least explore the lunch offerings or even order sandwiches to take along on a day of exploring. Those with kids and a lot of patience may want to try the novelty of the grill stone, which lets diners cook their own meal at the table. Many patrons choose to dine on the outdoor patio. ⊠ *Kaya Gobernador N. Debrot 46, Kralendijk* ☎ *599/717–7070* ☉ *Closed Sun. No lunch Sat.*

$–$$
ECLECTIC

✕ **Boudoir.** Despite the nighttime-bedroom connotation this excellent patio eatery at the Royal Palm Mall is only open for breakfast, lunch, and late-afternoon snacks. Besides having some of the best coffee on the island, Boudoir offers a range of soups, salads, sandwiches, and burgers that should please even the most discerning of diners. It's the perfect place to relax with an iced coffee and a smoked-salmon-and-capers sandwich after a day of exploring Kralendijk. ✉ *Kaya Grandi 26 F/G, Royal Palm Mall, Kralendijk* ☎ *599/717–4321.*

$$–$$$　✕ **Capriccio.** This splendid, family-run Italian eatery has plenty to boast
ITALIAN　about. The pastas are handmade daily, and fresh mozzarella is imported
★　from Italy once a week. The wine cellar includes hundreds of labels and more than thousands of bottles. You can opt for casual à la carte dining on the terrace or a romantic meal in the tonier, air-conditioned dining room. If your appetite is hearty, go for the five-course prix-fixe menu. Otherwise, choose one of the 50 regular offerings. The owners plan to relocate to a location nearby in late 2011. ✉ *Kaya Isla Riba 1, Kralendijk* ☎ *599/717–7230* ⊕ *www.emporiocapriccio.com* ⊗ *Closed Tues. No lunch weekends.*

$$–$$$　✕ **City Café/City Restaurant.** This busy waterfront eatery is also one of
ECLECTIC　the most reliable nightspots on the island, so it's always hopping day or
Fodor's Choice　night. Breakfast, lunch, and dinner are served daily at reasonable prices.
★　Seafood is always featured, as are a variety of sandwiches and salads. The pita sandwich platters are a good lunchtime choice for the budget challenged. Weekends, there's always live entertainment and dancing. This is the place to people-watch on Bonaire, as it seems everyone ends up at City Café eventually. ✉ *Hotel Rochaline, Kaya Grandi 7, Kralendijk* ☎ *599/717–8286* ⊕ *www.citybonaire.com.*

$$–$$$　✕ **Donna & Giorgio's.** Donna and her Sardinian-born husband, Giorgio,
ITALIAN　serve delicious home-style meals in this charming restaurant on the
★　main road just outside Kralendijk. With Giorgio in the kitchen, Donna and her daughter greet diners and make them feel at home. You may choose to sit in the cozy interior near the bar or outside at one of the tables on the gravel-covered terrace, which is lovely on a cloudless night; however, it's only inches from the road, so there's occasional car noise. You can always find a selection of pizzas and pastas, as well as daily specials displayed on a blackboard outside. Live music on weekends attracts a large crowd. This restaurant was up for sale at the time of writing. ✉ *Kaya Grandi 60, near entrance to Divi Flamingo, Kralendijk* ☎ *599/717–3799* ⊗ *Closed Wed. Closed Sept.*

$$$–$$$$　✕ **It Rains Fishes.** Those seeking upscale urban chic flock to this water-
ECLECTIC　front establishment where beautiful people serve beautiful food. The grilled seafood platter is superb and the ambience is unbeatable. Despite its popularity and large size, by Bonaire standards, service is impeccable and efficient. The funky bar is a popular hangout until late in the night, and live entertainment is sometimes featured. ✉ *Kaya Jan N.E. Craane 24, Kralendijk* ☎ *599/717–8780* ⊕ *www.itrainsfishesbonaire. com* ⌂ *Reservations essential* ⊗ *Closed Sun.*

$$–$$$　✕ **Kontiki Beach Club.** The dining room is a harmonious blend of terra-
ECLECTIC　cotta tile floors and rattan furnishings around a limestone half-moon bar. There's also a brick terrace for alfresco dining. Chef-owners Miriam and Martin are especially proud of their Dutch *kibbeling* (fish in a beer batter served with chili sauce). Those in the know order the Antillean fish soup, a delightful blend of fresh seafood and finely diced carrots

and cucumber. The display of local art on the walls changes constantly. It's quite far from downtown, but the view of the lagoon and intimate ambience mean it is definitely worth the drive for breakfast, lunch, or dinner. ✉ *Kaminda Sorobon 64, Lac Bay* ☎ *599/717–5369* ⊕ *www. kontikibonaire.com.*

$$–$$$
ECLECTIC
Fodor'sChoice
★
✕ **La Guernica.** This trendy eatery overlooking the boardwalk and the harbor is great for people-watching; there's outdoor seating as well as a couch-and-pillow-filled lounge area. The interior is done in hacienda style, with terra-cotta tiles, clay decorations, and comfy lounge chairs. Though many come here for the excellent tapas, those with heartier appetites can choose from a variety of seafood and meat main courses, including an excellent beef tenderloin with a blue-cheese sauce. The lunch menu offers a range of sandwiches and salads. This is *the* place to sip a cocktail and be seen. ✉ *Kaya Bonaire 4C, Kralendijk* ☎ *599/717– 5022* ⊕ *www.laguernica.com.*

$$$–$$$$
CONTINENTAL
Fodor'sChoice
★
✕ **Mona Lisa Bar & Restaurant.** Here you can find Continental, Caribbean, and Indonesian fare as well as throngs of regulars who would not dream of visiting Bonaire without a meal here. Popular bar dishes include Wiener schnitzel and fresh fish with curry sauce. The intimate stucco-and-brick dining room, presided over by a copy of the famous painting of the lady with the mystic smile, is decorated with Dutch artwork, lace curtains, and whirring ceiling fans. The colorful bar adorned with baseball-style caps is a great place for late-night schmoozing and noshing on light snacks or the catch of the day, which is served until 10 pm. There is a four-course fixed-price dinner on offer most evenings. ✉ *Kaya Grandi 15, Kralendijk* ☎ *599/717–8718* ⚏ *Reservations essential* ⊘ *Closed Sun. No lunch.*

$$–$$$
MEXICAN
✕ **Paradise Moon.** The Texan owners have picked up stakes (and steaks) and relocated from Harbour Village to the downtown waterfront. The menu still favors Tex-Mex, but there are also Asian and Continental choices. The food is reasonably priced by Bonaire standards, and portions are huge by any definition. Fans of throwing calorie caution to the wind will appreciate such Texan touches as deep-fried cheesecake and homemade apple pie floating in a sea of melted butter. ✉ *Harbour Village Marina, Kaya Debrot 71, Kralendijk* ☎ *599/717–5025* ⊕ *www. paradisebonaire.com* ⊘ *Closed Sat. No lunch.*

$$$
STEAK
✕ **Patagonia Argentinean Steakhouse** Meat lovers pack this 60-seat waterfront establishment. Though it caters largely to steak lovers with everything from top sirloin to prime rib, there's a respectable selection of seafood and other meats, too. The quality of some of the lower-price steaks can be a bit erratic, however, and the occasional use of frozen vegetables is puzzling. Portions are huge and the quality of the high-end cuts is consistently good. The restaurant's popularity can lead to lengthy wait times, but you can mosey over to the cozy bar area to pass some time. ✉ *Harbour Village Marina, Kralendijk, in lighthouse* ☎ *599/717– 7725* ⚏ *Reservations essential* ⊘ *Closed Mon. No lunch weekends.*

$$$
SEAFOOD
★
✕ **Richard's Waterfront Dining.** Animated, congenial Richard Beady and his partner, Mario, own this casually romantic waterfront restaurant. The daily menu is listed on large blackboards, and the seafood is consistently excellent. Fish soup is usually offered and is sure to please, as

6

is the grilled wahoo. Service can be erratic, depending on the level of staffing and the number of diners. ⊠ *J.A. Abraham Blvd. 60, Kralendijk* ☎ *599/717–5263* ⊕ *www.richardsofbonaire.com* ⊙ *Closed Mon. No lunch.*

$$–$$$
CONTINENTAL
Fodor'sChoice
★

✕ **Sunset Bar & Grill**. This casual restaurant at the Den Laman Condominiums offers a great variety of family-friendly options. The lunch and dinner menu includes a broad selection, ranging from seafood to pastas, and there is always a nightly themed buffet option. Given the casual atmosphere the quality of the food is excellent and the presentation is eye-popping. The open-air oceanfront setting is unbeatable and especially great at sunset. ⊠ *Kaya Gobernador N. Debrot 77, Kralendijk* ☎ *599/717–1700* ⊙ *Closed Wed.*

$$
CONTINENTAL

✕ **Wind & Surf Beach Hut Bar**. Part of Bonaire Windsurf Place—and located right on the beach—this fun eatery is one of the most casual dining experiences on the island. Tables and chairs are set directly in the sand under a straw-roof structure so that cooling winds sweep through the space. The food is simple but very good; the main offerings are sandwiches, salads, and burgers. The experience of dining with your toes in the sand is sure to leave lingering pleasant memories. The weekly barbecue on Wednesday nights with live entertainment is well worth the drive. ⊠ *Sorobon Beach* ☎ *599/717–2288* ▭ *No credit cards.*

$$$
ECLECTIC
★

✕ **Zeezicht Bar & Restaurant**. Zeezicht (pronounced zay-*zeekt* and meaning "sea view") serves three meals a day and is a Kralendijk institution. At breakfast and lunch you get basic American fare with an Antillean touch, such as a fish omelet; dinner is more Caribbean and mostly seafood, served either on the terrace overlooking the harbor or in the nautically themed, homey, rough-hewn main room. Locals are dedicated to this hangout, especially for the ceviche, conch sandwiches, and the Zeezicht special soup with conch, fish, and shrimp. The location makes it a popular spot for sunset watchers. ⊠ *Kaya J.N.E. Craane 12, Kralendijk* ☎ *599/717–8434.*

WHERE TO STAY

Although meal plans are available at most hotels, the island has many excellent—and often inexpensive—restaurants. If you're planning a dive holiday, look into the many attractive dive packages.

The following reviews have been condensed for this book. Please go to Fodors.com for expanded reviews of each property.

¢
HOTEL
Fodor'sChoice
★

⛏ **Bellafonte Chateau de la Mer**. Although it lacks the amenities of a large resort—including a pool—the intimacy and exclusivity of this elegant palazzo-style hotel near Kralendijk more than compensate. **Pros:** well-designed rooms; diving straight from hotel pier; upper rooms have excellent views; free Wi-Fi; groceries can be ordered online before arrival. **Cons:** no restaurant or bar; not close to downtown or shopping; no elevator. ⊠ *E.E.G. Blvd. 10, Belnem* ☎ *599/717–3333* ⊕ *www.bellafontebonaire.com* ⤳ *6 studios, 8 1-bedroom suites, 8 2-bedroom suites* ⌕ *In-room: kitchen (some), Wi-Fi. In-hotel: Wi-Fi, beach, diving, business center* ⏐⊙⏐ *No meals.*

¢ ▦ **Bruce Bowker's Carib Inn.** The cozy rooms and owner–dive-instructor
B&B/INN Bruce Bowker's personal touch have given his inn the highest return-
★ visitor ratio on the island. **Pros:** intimate and friendly; excellent dive
courses; Wi-Fi throughout. **Cons:** smaller size means fewer amenities
such as shopping; nondivers will find little to entertain them. ✉ *J.A.
Abraham Blvd. 46, Box 68, Kralendijk* ☎ *599/717–8819* ⊕ *www.
caribinn.com* ⇥ *10 units* & *In-room: kitchen (some), Wi-Fi. In-hotel:
pool, beach, water sports* ⦿ *No meals.*

¢–$ ▦ **Buddy Dive Resort.** Well-equipped rooms, a nicely landscaped com-
RESORT pound, and excellent dive packages keep guests coming back to this
☺ large resort. **Pros:** excellent dive shop; rooms are spacious; open-air
restaurant has one of the best ocean views on the island. **Cons:** complex can feel like a maze; room amenities vary, depending on which
side of the property they are located. ✉ *Kaya Gobernador N. Debrot
85, Box 231, Kralendijk* ☎ *599/717–5080 or 866/462–8339* ⊕ *www.
buddydive.com* ⇥ *6 rooms, 72 apartments* & *In-room: kitchen (some).
In-hotel: restaurants, bar, children's programs, pools, laundry facilities,
beach* ⦿ *No meals.*

$ ▦ **Captain Don's Habitat.** Bonaire's first hotel catering to divers remains
HOTEL a favorite, with a PADI five-star dive center offering more than 20
★ specialty courses. **Pros:** variety of accommodation types; pizzeria with
wood-burning oven; excellent diving facilities. **Cons:** little to entertain
nondivers; Wi-Fi coverage is spotty; staff can sometimes seem aloof.
✉ *Kaya Gobernador N. Debrot 113, Box 88, Kralendijk* ☎ *599/717–
8290 or 800/327–6709* ⊕ *www.habitatbonaire.com* ⇥ *24 rooms, 12
junior suites, 5 villas, 19 cottages* & *In-room: safe, kitchen (some), Wi-Fi
(except villas). In-hotel: restaurant, bar, pool, spa, beach* ⦿ *No meals.*

¢ ▦ **Coco Palm Garden & Casa Oleander.** Friends and neighbors operate this
RENTAL series of cozy cottages and villas, each fully equipped and individually
☺ decorated to the point where the hard part is choosing among them. **Pros:**
★ charming and quirky with no two rooms alike; friendly staff; quiet pool
area. **Cons:** not close to downtown or shopping; limited on-site dining
options; long walk from the villas to get to the common areas and office;
charge for using the air-conditioner. ✉ *Kaya I.R. Randolf Statuuis van
Eps 9, Belnem* ✑ *Box 216, Kralendijk* ☎ *599/717–2108 or 599/790–
9080* ⊕ *www.cocopalmgarden.org* ⇥ *19 rooms, 6 villas* & *In-room:
kitchen, no TV (some). In-hotel: pool, laundry facilities* ⦿ *No meals.*

¢ ▦ **Den Laman Condominiums.** Though the exterior of this property will
RENTAL not win any design awards, the location and beautifully finished inte-
★ riors are definitely first-class. **Pros:** excellent restaurant on-site; rooms
are chicly appointed; convenient to downtown. **Cons:** no elevator
means upper rooms can require a climb; common areas feel a little
sterile. ✉ *Kaya Gobernador N. Debrot 77, Kralendijk* ☎ *599/717–1700*
⊕ *www.denlaman.com* ⇥ *16 condos* & *In-room: safe, kitchen, Wi-Fi.
In-hotel: restaurant, bar* ⦿ *No meals.*

$ ▦ **Divi Flamingo Resort.** The brightly colored buildings of this resort are
RESORT a two-minute stroll from downtown, but the main draw is the combi-
☺ nation of a top-notch dive program and the only casino on Bonaire.
Fodor's Choice **Pros:** beautifully landscaped grounds; steps from downtown and res-
★ taurants; on-site casino. **Cons:** pool can get crowded; beach is quite

6

Pool at the Harbour Village Beach Club.

small. ⊠ *J.A. Abraham Blvd. 40, Box 143, Kralendijk* ☏ *599/717–8285 or 800/367–3484* ⊕ *www.diviflamingo.com* ↰ *129 rooms* ♿ *In-room: safe. In-hotel: restaurants, bar, pools, gym, spa, Wi-Fi, water sports* ⫯◯⫯ *No meals.*

¢ ⛉ **Golden Reef Inn.** This low-rise lemon-sherbet-hue complex offers
B&B/INN comfy rooms and a genuinely intimate feel. **Pros:** almost unbeatable price and friendly service; virtually any tour or dive can be arranged by the front office; rooms are fully self-contained; rates include all taxes; free meet-and-greet at airport; free Wi-Fi. **Cons:** grounds have little landscaping; basic dining and bar facilities; not on ocean. ⊠ *Kaya Den Haag 7, Hato* ☏ *599/717–5759* ⊕ *www.goldenreefinn.com* ↰ *4 studios, 7 1-bedrooms, 1 2-bedroom villa, 1 1-bedroom villa* ♿ *In-room: safe, kitchen, Wi-Fi. In-hotel: restaurant, bar, pool, laundry facilities* ⫯◯⫯ *Breakfast.*

$$$ ⛉ **Harbour Village Beach Club.** This snazzy enclave of ocher-color build-
HOTEL ings is the benchmark for luxury accommodations on the island. **Pros:**
☺ great for a secluded getaway; not awash with budget tourists; conve-
Fodor'sChoice nient to downtown. **Cons:** some rooms are quite far from the beach;
★ grounds can feel a bit deserted. ⊠ *Kaya Gobernador N. Debrot 71, Kralendijk* ☏ *599/717–7500 or 800/424–0004* ⊕ *www.harbourvillage. com* ↰ *40 rooms, 14 1-bedroom suites, 6 2-bedroom suites* ♿ *In-room: safe (some), Wi-Fi. In-hotel: restaurant, room service, tennis courts, bar, pool, gym, beach, water sports* ⫯◯⫯ *No meals.*

$–$$ ⛉ **Plaza Resort Bonaire.** No other property in Bonaire can match the range
RESORT of activities offered here, with everything from tennis to water sports, not to mention a gorgeous beach. **Pros:** every imaginable recreational activity is available; good shopping in hotel; beautiful grounds; most

rooms are huge. **Cons:** size of the compound can make getting around a chore; not an easy walk to downtown; Wi-Fi reception is spotty except in lobby. ☒ *J.A. Abraham Blvd. 80, Kralendijk* 🕾 *599/717–2500 or 800/766–6016* ⊕ *www.plazaresortbonaire.com* ⇆ *174 rooms, 48 villas* ⚒ *In-room: safe, kitchen (some), Internet. In-hotel: restaurants, room service, tennis courts, bars, children's programs, pool, gym, beach, water sports* ⦿ *No meals.*

¢ HOTEL ☾ ⊞ **Roomer.** This excellent, economically priced family hotel has small rooms, but they are individually decorated with tasteful splashes of color. **Pros:** very family-oriented; excellent for budget travelers; kid-friendly pool area; free Wi-Fi. **Cons:** not on the ocean; miles from downtown. ☒ *E.E.G. Blvd. 97, Belnem* 🕾 *599/717–7488* ⊕ *www.roomerbonaire.com* ⇆ *10 rooms* ⚒ *In-room: Wi-Fi. In-hotel: restaurant, bar, pool* ⦿ *No meals.*

$ RENTAL ☾ ⊞ **Sand Dollar Condominium Resort.** This condo complex has family-friendly apartments ranging from studios to three-bedrooms, each of which is individually owned and decorated for a comfortable, lived-in feeling. **Pros:** all rooms have great ocean views; well equipped for families; grocery and ATM on property. **Cons:** few rooms have phones; no beach bar; landscaping can be a bit shabby. ☒ *Kaya Gobernador N. Debrot 79, Box 262, Kralendijk* 🕾 *599/717–8738 or 800/288–4773* ⊕ *www.sanddollarbonaire.com* ⇆ *50 condos* ⚒ *In-room: no phone (some), kitchen, Wi-Fi. In-hotel: restaurant, tennis courts, bar, pool, spa* ⦿ *No meals.*

¢ RENTAL **Fodor's Choice** ★ ⊞ **Waterlands Village.** These individually owned, roomy cottages offer all the comforts of home and feature thoughtful touches such as canopy beds and the option of an private outdoor shower. **Pros:** great price for relatively upscale accommodations; lovely pool area. **Cons:** no ocean view; airport noise can be an issue from time to time; bit of a walk to downtown; hefty $95 cleaning charge per stay. ☒ *Kaya International, Kralendijk* 🕾 *599/701–5540* ⊕ *www.waterlandsvillage.com* ⇆ *24 cottages (18 for rent)* ⚒ *In-room: safe, kitchen, Wi-Fi. In-hotel: pool* ⦿ *No meals.*

¢ RENTAL ★ ⊞ **Yachtclub Apartments.** Across from Harbour Village, these apartments offer some of the best budget lodging on the island. **Pros:** reasonable price for excellent accommodations; expansive pool area is great for sunbathing; close to several good restaurants and the on-site restaurant is excellent. **Cons:** no ocean view; hotel is on the main road to Kralendijk and can get a bit dusty. ☒ *Kaya Gobernador N. Debrot 52, Kralendijk* 🕾 *599/717–7424* ⊕ *www.yachtclubapartmentsbonaire. com* ⇆ *13 apartments* ⚒ *In-room: safe, kitchen. In-hotel: restaurant* ⇆ *2-night minimum* ⦿ *No meals.*

RENTAL APARTMENTS

If you prefer do-it-yourself home-style comfort over the pampering and other services offered by a hotel, you can rent a fully furnished apartment. The **Bonaire Hotel & Tourism Association** (🕾 *800/388–5951* ⊕ *www.bonairestays.com*) has information on a variety of properties ranging from budget to upscale. **Sun Rentals** (🕾 *599/717–6130* ⊕ *www. sunrentalsbonaire.com*) offers quite a range of accommodations. You can choose among private ocean-view villas in luxurious areas like

Sabadeco, furnished oceanfront apartments (with a pool) in town, or bungalows in Lagoenhill, an inland community. The Sun Oceanfront Apartments are an excellent budget choice for families.

NIGHTLIFE

Most divers are exhausted after they finish their third, fourth, or fifth dive of the day, which may explain why there are no full-time discos on Bonaire. Strange as it may sound, the most effective approach to finding the best hot spot is to stand downtown, listen for the loudest music, and then follow your ears. Most of the time nightlife consists of sitting on a quiet beach sipping a local Amstel Bright beer. Top island performers, including the Foyan Boys, migrate from one resort to another throughout the week. You can find information in the free magazines (published once a year) *Bonaire Affair* and *Bonaire Nights*. The twice-monthly *Bonaire Update Events and Activities* pamphlet is available at most restaurants.

Carnival, generally held in February, is the usual nonstop parade of steel bands, floats, and wild costumes, albeit on a much smaller scale than on some other islands. It culminates in the ceremonial burning in effigy of King Momo, representing the spirit of debauchery.

BARS

Downtown, **City Café** (⊠ *Hotel Rochaline, Kaya Grandi 7, Kralendijk* ☎ *599/717–8286*) is a wacky hangout splashed in magenta, banana, and electric blue. Here you can find cocktails, snack food, live music on weekends, and karaoke on Wednesday nights.

The Thursday-night happy hour at **Deco Stop Bar** (⊠ *Captain Don's Habitat, Kaya Gobernador N. Debrot 113, Kralendijk* ☎ *599/717–8286*) is popular.

Karel's (⊠ *Kaya J.N.E. Craane 12, Kralendijk* ☎ *599/717–8434*) sits on stilts above the sea and is *the* place for mingling—especially Friday and Saturday nights, when there's live island and pop music.

La Guernica (⊠ *Kaya Bonaire 4C, Kralendijk* ☎ *599/717–5022*), with an ultrachic bar and comfy-couch-lined terrace, is the place to be seen on weekend nights.

CASINO

Divi Flamingo Resort (⊠ *J.A. Abraham Blvd., Kralendijk* ☎ *599/717–8285*) is the only casino on the island and operates until 4 am.

DANCE CLUBS

★ **City Café** (⊠ *Hotel Rochaline, Kaya Grandi 7, Kralendijk* ☎ *599/717–8286*) is the island's closest thing to a dance club. On weekend nights the restaurant moves the tables aside and it becomes an instant dance floor.

On Sunday afternoon at **Lac Cai** (✉ *Lac Cai*) enjoy the festive **Sunday Party**, where locals celebrate the day with live music, dancing, and food from 3 to 11. Take a taxi, especially if you plan to imbibe a few rum punches.

SHOPPING

You can get to know all the shops in Kralendijk in an hour or so, but sometimes there's no better way to enjoy some time out of the sun and sea than to go shopping (particularly if your companion is a dive fanatic and you're not). Almost all the shops are on the Kaya Grandi and adjacent streets and in tiny malls. Harbourside Mall is a pleasant, open-air mall with several fine air-conditioned shops. The most distinctive local crafts are fanciful painted pieces of driftwood and hand-painted *kunuku*, or little wilderness houses. ■**TIP→** Buy as many flamingo T-shirts as you want, but don't take home items made of goatskin or tortoiseshell; they aren't allowed into the United States. Remember, too, that it's forbidden to take sea fans, coral, conch shells, and all other forms of marine life off the island.

SPECIALTY STORES

CLOTHING

Benetton (✉ *Kaya Grandi 29, Kralendijk* ☎ *599/717–5107*) claims that its prices for men's, women's, and children's clothes are 30% lower than in New York.

Best Buddies (✉ *Kaya Grandi 32, Kralendijk* ☎ *599/717–7570*) stocks a selection of Indonesian batik shirts, pareus, and T-shirts.

At **Island Fashions** (✉ *Kaya Grandi 5, Kralendijk* ☎ *599/717–7071*) you can buy swimsuits, sunglasses, T-shirts, and costume jewelry.

DUTY-FREE GOODS

Flamingo Airport Duty Free (✉ *Flamingo Airport* ☎ *599/717–5563*) sells perfumes and cigarettes.

Perfume Palace (✉ *Harbourside Mall, Kaya Grandi 31, Kralendijk* ☎ *599/717–5288*) sells perfumes and makeup from Lancôme, Estée Lauder, Chanel, Ralph Lauren, and Clinique.

HANDICRAFTS

IanArt Gallery (✉ *Kaya Gloria 7, Kralendijk* ☎ *599/717–5246*), on the outskirts of town, sells unique paintings, prints, and art supplies; artist Janice Huckaby also hosts art classes.

Kas di Arte (✉ *Kaya J.N.E. Craane 34 , Kralendijk* ☎ *No phone* ⊙ *Closed Sun.*)features the works of local and international artists including such notables as Ronald Verhoeven.

Maharaj Gifthouse (✉ *Kaya Grandi 11, Kralendijk* ☎ *599/717–4402*) has a vast assortment of hand-painted delft blue china, local artwork, and stainless-steel and crystal items that make great gifts.

Whatever you do, make a point of visiting **Yenny's Art** (✉ *Kaya Betico Croes 6, near post office, Kralendijk* ☎ *599/717–5004*). Roam around

6

her house, which is a replica of a traditional Bonaire town complete with her handmade life-size dolls and the skeletons of all her dead pets. Lots of fun (and sometimes kitschy) souvenirs made out of driftwood, clay, and shells are all handmade by Jenny.

JEWELRY

★ **Atlantis** (✉ *Kaya Grandi 32B, Kralendijk* ☎ *599/717–7730*) carries a large range of precious and semiprecious gems. The tanzanite collection is especially beautiful. You will also find Sector, Raymond Weil, and Citizen watches, among others, all at great savings. Since gold jewelry is sold by weight here, it's an especially good buy.

Littman's (✉ *Kaya Grandi 33, Kralendijk* ☎ *599/717–8160* ✉ *Harbourside Mall, Kaya Grandi 31, Kralendijk* ☎ *599/717–2130*) is an upscale jewelry and gift shop where many items are handpicked by owner Steven Littman on his regular trips to Europe. Look for Rolex, Omega, Cartier, and Tag Heuer watches; fine gold jewelry; antique coins; nautical sculptures; resort clothing; and accessories.

SPORTS AND ACTIVITIES

BICYCLING

Bonaire is generally flat, so bicycles are an easy way to get around. Because of the heat it's essential to carry water if you're planning to cycle for any distance and especially if your plans involve exploring the deserted interior. There are more than 180 mi (290 km) of unpaved routes (as well as the many paved roads) on the island.

Cycle Bonaire (✉ *Kaya Gobernador N. Debrot 77A, Kralendijk* ☎ *599/717–2229*) rents mountain bikes and gear (trail maps, water bottles, helmets, locks, repair and first-aid kits) for $20 a day or $100 for six days; half-day and full-day guided excursions start at $60, not including bike rental.

Tropical Travel (✉ *J.A. Abraham Blvd. 80, Kralendijk* ☎ *599/717–2500 Ext. 8199*) at the Plaza Resort Bonaire offers bikes for $10 per day or $60 per week.

DAY SAILS AND SNORKELING TRIPS

Regularly scheduled sunset sails and snorkel trips are popular (prices range from $35 to $50 per person), as are private or group sails (expect to pay about $500 per day for a party of four).

Kantika de Amor Watertaxi (✉ *Kaya J.N.E. Craane 24, opposite the restaurant It Rains Fishes, Kralendijk* ☎ *599/560–7254 or 599/786–5399*) provides daily rides to Klein Bonaire and drift snorkel and evening cruises with complimentary cocktails.

The *Mushi Mushi* (☎ *599/790–5399*) is a catamaran offering a variety of two- and three-hour cruises starting at $50 per person. It departs from the Bonaire Nautico Marina in downtown Kralendijk (opposite the restaurant It Rains Fishes).

If you want to do some sailing on your own, **Tropical Travel** (⊠ *Plaza Resort Bonaire, J.A. Abraham Blvd. 80, Kralendijk* ☎ *599/717–2500 Ext. 8199* ⊕ *www.tropicaltravelbonaire.com*) offers a variety of cruise packages, with prices available on request.

The **Woodwind** (☎ *599/786–7055* ⊕ *www.woodwindbonaire.com*) is a 37-foot trimaran that offers regular sailing and snorkeling trips as well as charters. It leaves from the dock at Divi Flamingo and offers a sail-snorkel–sunset cruise for $50 per person.

DIVING AND SNORKELING

Bonaire has some of the best reef diving this side of Australia's Great Barrier Reef. It takes only 5 to 25 minutes to reach many sites, the current is usually mild, and although some reefs have sudden, steep drops, most begin just offshore and slope gently downward at a 45-degree angle. General visibility runs 60 to 100 feet, except during surges in October and November. You can see several varieties of coral: knobby-brain, giant-brain, elkhorn, staghorn, mountainous star, gorgonian, and black. You can also encounter schools of parrot fish, surgeonfish, angelfish, eel, snapper, and grouper. Beach diving is excellent just about everywhere on the leeward side, so night diving is popular. There are sites here suitable for every skill level; they're clearly marked by yellow stones on the roadside.

Bonaire, in conjunction with *Skin Diver* magazine, has also developed the **Guided Snorkeling Program.** The highly educational and entertaining program begins with a slide show on important topics, from a beginner's look at reef fish, coral, and sponges to advanced fish identification and night snorkeling. Guided snorkeling for all skill levels can be arranged through most resort dive shops. The best snorkeling spots are on the island's leeward side, where you have shore access to the reefs, and along the west side of Klein Bonaire, where the reef is better developed. All snorkelers and swimmers must pay a $10 Nature Fee, which allows access to the waters around the island and Washington–Slagbaai National Park for one calendar year. The fee can be paid at most dive shops.

Fodor's Choice In the well-policed **Bonaire Marine Park** (⊠ *Karpata* ☎ *599/717–8444* ★ ⊕ *www.bmp.org*), which encompasses the entire coastline around Bonaire and Klein Bonaire, divers take the rules seriously. Don't even *think* about (1) spearfishing; (2) dropping anchor; or (3) touching, stepping on, or collecting coral. In order to dive (as opposed to simply swim and enter the water), you must pay a fee of $25 (used to maintain the park), for which you receive a colored plastic tag (to attach to an item of scuba gear) entitling you to one calendar year of unlimited diving. Checkout dives—dives you do first with a master before going out on your own—are required, and you can arrange them through any dive shop. All dive operations offer classes in free buoyancy control, advanced buoyancy control, and photographic buoyancy control. Tags are available at all scuba facilities and from the Marine Park Headquarters.

A Bonaire diver shows off her photographic buoyancy control.

DIVE SITES

The *Guide to the Bonaire Marine Park* lists 86 dive sites (including 16 shore-dive-only and 35 boat-dive-only sites). Another fine reference book is the *Diving and Snorkeling Guide to Bonaire,* by Jerry Schnabel and Suzi Swygert. Guides associated with the various dive centers can give you more complete directions. It's difficult to recommend one site over another; to whet your appetite, here are a few of the popular sites.

★ **Angel City.** Take the trail down to the shore adjacent to the Radio Nederland tower station; dive in and swim south to Angel City, one of the shallowest and most popular sites in a two-reef complex that includes Alice in Wonderland. The boulder-size green-and-tan coral heads are home to black margates, Spanish hogfish, gray snappers, stingrays, and large purple tube sponges.

Bari Reef. Catch a glimpse of the elkhorn and fire coral, queen angelfish, and other wonders of Bari Reef, just off the Sand Dollar Condominium Resort's pier.

★ **Calabas Reef.** Off the coast of the Divi Flamingo Resort, this is the island's busiest dive site. It's replete with Christmas-tree worms, sponges, and fire coral adhering to a ship's hull. Fish life is frenzied, with the occasional octopus putting in an appearance.

Forest. You need to catch a boat to reach Forest, a dive site off the southwest coast of Klein Bonaire. Named for the abundant black-coral forests found in it, the site gets a lot of fish action, including a resident spotted eel that lives in a cave.

CLOSE UP

Bonaire Marine Park

The Bonaire Marine Park was founded in 1979 in an effort to protect the island's most precious natural resource. Covering an area of less than 700 acres, the park includes all the waters around the island from the high-water mark to the 60-meter depth. Legislation prevents collecting (or even walking on) coral, using spearguns, or removing marine life. It also means that boats may not drop anchor in most of the island's waters and that divers may not use gloves unless they're needed for ascending or descending a line.

Because the island has so zealously protected its marine environment, Bonaire offers an amazing diversity of underwater life. Turtles, rays, and fish of every imaginable color abound in the pristine waters of the park. The charge ($10 for swimmers and snorkelers, $25 for divers) for a swimming or diving tag allows unlimited use of the park for a year, and every cent goes toward the care and management of the Bonaire Marine Park. And it's money well spent, islanders and most visitors will tell you.

6

Rappel. This spectacular site is near the Karpata Ecological Center. The shore is a sheer cliff, and the lush coral growth is the habitat of some unusual varieties of marine life, including occasional orange sea horses, squid, spiny lobsters, and spotted trunkfish.

Small Wall. One of Bonaire's three complete vertical wall dives (and one of its most popular night-diving spots), Small Wall is in front of the Black Durgon Inn, near Barcadera Beach. Because the access to this site is on private property, this is usually a boat-diving site. The 60-foot wall is frequented by squid, turtles, tarpon, and barracuda and has dense hard and soft coral formations; it also allows for excellent snorkeling.

Something Special. South of the marina entrance at Harbour Village Beach Club, this spot is famous for its garden eels. They wave about from the relatively shallow sand terrace looking like long grass in a breeze.

Town Pier. Known for shielding one of Bonaire's best night dives, the pier is right in town, across from the City Café. Divers need permission from the harbormaster and must be accompanied by a local guide.

Windsock Steep. This excellent shore-dive site (from 20 to 80 feet) is in front of the small beach opposite the airport runway. It's a popular place for snorkeling. The current is moderate, the elkhorn coral profuse; you may also see angelfish and rays.

DIVE OPERATORS

Many of the dive shops listed below offer PADI and NAUI certification courses and SSI, as well as underwater photography and videography courses. Some shops are also qualified to certify dive instructors. Full certification courses cost approximately $385; open-water refresher courses run about $240; a one-tank boat dive with unlimited shore diving costs about $40; a two-tank boat dive with unlimited shore diving is about $65. As for equipment, renting a mask, fin, and snorkel costs about $12 all together; for a BC (buoyancy compensator) and regulator, expect to pay about $20. Check out children's programs like Aquakids and Ocean Classroom—or inquire about their equivalents.

Most dive shops on Bonaire offer a complete range of snorkel gear for rent and will provide beginner training; some dive operations also offer guided snorkeling and night snorkeling. The cost for a guided snorkel session is about $50 and includes slide presentations, transportation to the site, and a tour. Gear rental is approximately $10 per 24-hour period.

Bonaire Dive & Adventure (⊠ *Sand Dollar Condominium Resort, Kaya Gobernador N. Debrot 77A, Kralendijk* ☎ *599/717–2229* ⊕ *www. bonairediveandadventure.com*) is probably the best choice for first-timers who want a stress-free introduction to the sport.

Bonaire Scuba Center (⊠ *Black Durgon Inn, Kaya Gobernador N. Debrot 145, Kralendijk* ⊡ *Box 775, Morgan, NJ 08879* ☎ *599/717–5736 or 908/566–8866, 800/526–2370 for reservations in U.S.*).

Bruce Bowker's Carib Inn Dive Center (⊠ *J.A. Abraham Blvd. 46, Kralendijk* ☎ *599/717–8819* ⊕ *www.caribinn.com*).

Buddy Dive Resort (⊠ *Kaya Gobernador N. Debrot 85, Kralendijk* ☎ *599/717–5080* ⊕ *www.buddydive.com*).

Captain Don's Habitat Dive Shop (⊠ *Kaya Gobernador N. Debrot 113, Kralendijk* ☎ *599/717–8290* ⊕ *www.habitatbonaire.com*).

Dive Friends Bonaire (⊠ *Kaya Playa Lechi 24, Kralendijk* ☎ *599/717– 2929* ⊕ *www.dive-friends-bonaire.com*).

★ **Divi Dive Bonaire** (⊠ *Divi Flamingo Resort & Casino, J.A. Abraham Blvd. 40, Kralendijk* ☎ *599/717–8285* ⊕ *www.diviflamingo.com*).

★ **Larry's Shore & Wild Side Diving** (☎ *599/790–9156* ⊕ *www.larryswildsidediving. com*) is run by a former army combat diver and offers a variety of appealing options ranging from the leisurely to downright scary. This company has become an extremely popular choice, so try to book as early as possible.

Toucan Diving (⊠ *Plaza Resort Bonaire, J.A. Abraham Blvd. 80, Kralen-dijk* ☎ *599/717–2500* ⊕ *www.toucandiving.com*) offers the Aquakids program for children ages 5 to 12.

Touch the Sea with Dee Scarr (⊡ *Box 369, Kralendijk* ☎ *599/717–8529* ⊕ *www.touchthesea.com*).

Wannadive (⊠ *Hotel Rochaline, Kaya Grandi 7, next to City Café, Kralendijk* ☎ *599/717–3531* ⊕ *www.wannadivebonaire.com*).

FISHING

Multifish Charters (☎ *599/717–3648* ⊕ *www.bonairefishing.net*) has day or night reef fishing on a 44-foot Striker twin diesel; the cost for six hours is $550 (six-person maximum). An eight-hour day of deep-sea fishing costs $700 (six-person maximum), including refreshments.

Piscatur Charters (⊠ *Kaya H.J. Pop 3, Kralendijk* ☎ *599/717–8774* ⊕ *www.piscatur.com*) offers light-tackle angler reef fishing for jackfish, barracuda, and snapper. Rates are $475 for a half day. You can charter the 42-foot Sport Fisherman *Piscatur,* which carries up to six people, for $550 for a half day, $700 for a full day.

GUIDED TOURS

Achie Tours (✉ *Kaya Nikiboko Noord 33, Kralendijk* ☎ *599/717–8630*) has several half- and full-day options. **Bonaire Tours & Vacations** (✉ *Kaya Gobernador N. Debrot 79, Kralendijk* ☎ *599/717–8738* ⊕ *www. bonairetours.com*) will chauffeur you around on two-hour tours of either the island's north or south sides or on a half-day city-and-country tour ($35), which visits sights in both regions.

Or simply ask any taxi driver for an island tour (be sure to negotiate the price up front).

HORSEBACK RIDING

☺ You can take hour-long trail rides at the 166-acre **Riding Academy Club** (✉ *Near airport, east of Kralendijk* ☎ *599/560–7949 or 599/786–2094*) for $120. A guide takes you through groves of cacti where iguanas, wild goats, donkeys, and flamingos reside. Reserve one of the gentle pintos or Paso Finos a day in advance, and try to go early in the morning, when it's cool. Tours are available by reservation only and are limited to two people.

6

KAYAKING

Divers and snorkelers can use kayaks to reach otherwise inaccessible dive sites and simply tow the craft along during their dive. Nondivers can take advantage of the calm waters around the island to explore the coastline and the fascinating stands of mangrove around the Lac Bay area. The mangrove harbors myriad wildlife and acts as a hatchery for marine life. Almost all of the kayaks used are of the sit-on-top variety, which are able to negotiate shallow waters better.

Bonaire Dive & Adventure (✉ *Kaya Gobernador N. Debrot 79, Kralendijk* ☎ *599/717–8738 or 800/288–4773* ⊕ *www.bonairediveandadventure. com*) rents kayaks and also operates guided trips.

At **Jibe City** (✉ *Sorobon Beach* ☎ *599/717–5233, 800/748–8733 in U.S.* ⊕ *www.jibecity.com*), which is primarily a windsurfing outfit, kayaks go for $10 (single) and $15 (double) for the first two hours; $25 and $30, respectively, per half day (closed in September).

★ **Mangrove Info & Kayak Center** (✉ *Kaminda Lac 141, on road to Lac Cai, Lac Bay* ☎ *599/790–5353* ⊕ *www.mangrovecenter.com*) offers guided kayak tours of the mangrove forest at 9 am and 11 am daily, for $27 an hour and $46 for two hours. The center houses a unique mangrove aquarium designed to study the Lac Bay mangroves' effect on the global ecosystem as well as a photo gallery showing underwater existence within the forest like never before. The tours are pleasant even for the exercise-challenged and usually provide a great way to work on your tan. The two-hour tour includes snorkeling and is a lot more fun.

LAND SAILING

☞ Basically windsurfing on land using a sail and a three-wheeled apparatus (called a blokart), land sailing is dusty but definitely fun. **Landsailing Bonaire** (✉ *Kaya Jupiter 4, Belnem* ☎ *599/717–8122 or 599/786–8122* ⊕ *www.landsailingbonaire.com*) provides training, equipment, and safety clothing for $50 for the first hour, but most people find the $68 two-hour package more rewarding.

WINDSURFING

With near-constant breezes and calm waters, Bonaire is consistently ranked among the best places in the world for windsurfing. Lac Bay, a protected cove on the east coast, is ideal for windsurfing. The island's windsurfing companies are headquartered there on Sorobon Beach.

★ The **Bonaire Windsurf Place** (✉ *Sorobon Beach* ☎ *599/717–2288* ⊕ *www. bonairewindsurfplace.com*), commonly referred to as "the Place," rents the latest Hot Sails Maui, Starboard, and RRD equipment for $60 for a full day. A two-hour group lesson costs $45; private lessons are $75 per hour (these rates do not include equipment, which adds at least $40 to the price). Groups are generally limited to four people. Owners Elvis, Roger, and Constantine are all former windsurfing champs.

Jibe City (✉ *Sorobon Beach* ☎ *599/717–5233, 800/748–8733 in U.S.* ⊕ *www.jibecity.com*) offers lessons for $50 (includes board and sail for beginners only); board rentals start at $25 an hour, $50 for a half day. There are pickups at all the hotels at 9 am and 1 pm; ask your hotel to make arrangements.

British Virgin Islands

WORD OF MOUTH

"On Tortola, Brewers Bay is great along with Smuggler's Cove. On Virgin Gorda, Savannah Bay [has] wonderful shore snorkeling. We preferred Spring Bay over the Baths because it wasn't as crowded."

—greenie

WELCOME TO BRITISH VIRGIN ISLANDS

NATURE'S LITTLE SECRETS

Most of the 60-some islands, islets, and cays that make up the British Virgin Islands (BVI) are remarkably hilly and volcanic in origin, having exploded from the depths of the sea some 25 million years ago. The exception is Anegada, which is a flat, coral-limestone atoll. Tortola (about 10 square mi/26 square km) is the largest member of the chain.

The British Virgin Islands are mostly quiet and casual, so don't expect to party until dawn, and definitely leave the tux at home. Luxury here means getting away from it all rather than getting the trendiest state-of-the-art amenities. And the jackpot is the chance to explore the many islets and cays by sailboat.

TOP REASONS TO VISIT BRITISH VIRGIN ISLANDS

1 **The Perfect Place to Sail:** With more than 60 islands in the chain, sailors can drop anchor at a different, perfect beach every day.

2 **Low-Key Resorts:** Laid-back luxury resorts offer a full-scale retreat from your everyday life.

3 **Diving and Snorkeling:** Vibrant reefs are often just feet from the shore.

4 **Jost Van Dyke:** Your trip isn't complete until you've chilled at casual beach bars.

5 **Few Crowds:** There's no mass tourism; the farther you get from Tortola, the quieter things become.

BRITISH VIRGIN ISLANDS PLANNER

Logistics

Getting to the BVI: There are no nonstop flights to the BVI from the U.S. Most travelers connect in San Juan or St. Thomas. You can fly to Tortola, Virgin Gorda, or Anegada, but only on a small plane. There are also ferries from St. Thomas, with regular service to Tortola and Virgin Gorda.

Hassle Factor: Medium to high.

On the Ground: Although taxi service is good, you may wish to rent a car on Tortola or Virgin Gorda to explore farther afield or try many different beaches (you may need to if you are staying at an isolated resort). On Anegada it's possible to rent a car, but most people rely on taxis for transportation. Jost Van Dyke has a single road, and visitors travel on foot or by local taxi.

Getting Around on the Islands: Most people take ferries to get from island to island, though flights are possible (some are regularly scheduled, or there are plenty of charter opportunities if you are traveling in a group). Once on the ground, you'll find that taxi rates aren't set in the BVI and have to be negotiated. Your hotel or villa manager can help with expected fares.

Getting to the BVI

Air Travel: Several airlines have regularly scheduled service to either Tortola or Virgin Gorda. Although it may be cheaper to fly via Puerto Rico, the connections are better through St. Thomas. If you have seven or more people in your party, you can also charter a plane from St. Thomas or San Juan.

Airlines: Air Sunshine (☎ 800/327–8900, 800/435–8900 in Florida, 888/879–8900 in USVI, 495–8900 in BVI ⊕ www.airsunshine.com). **American Airlines/American Eagle** (☎ 800/433–7300, 340/776–2560 in St. Thomas, 340/778–2000 in St. Croix, 284/495–2559 in Tortola ⊕ www.aa.com). **Cape Air** (☎ 800/352–0714, 284/495–1440 in Tortola ⊕ www.flycapeair.com). **Fly BVI** (☎ 284/495–1747 ⊕ www.bviaircharters.com). **LIAT** (☎ 888/844–5428, 866/549–5428 in USVI, 284/495–2577 in Tortola ⊕ www.liat.com).

Airport Transfers Airport Taxi Association (☎ 284/495–1982). **Mahogany Rentals and Taxi Service** (⊠ The Valley, Virgin Gorda ☎ 284/495–5469).

Airports: Tortola (TOC), Virgin Gorda (VIJ), and Anegada (no code).

Ferries: Frequent daily ferries connect Tortola with St. Thomas (both Charlotte Amalie and Red Hook) and St. John. Ferries also link Tortola with Jost Van Dyke, Peter Island, and Virgin Gorda. Tortola has three ferry terminals—one at West End, one on Beef Island (at the airport), and one in Road Town. Schedules vary, and not all companies make daily trips.

Ferries also connect Virgin Gorda with St. Thomas (both Charlotte Amalie and Red Hook) and St. John, but not daily. All Red Hook–bound ferries stop in Cruz Bay to clear customs and immigration. Ferries to Virgin Gorda land in Spanish Town. Schedules vary by day, and not all companies make daily trips.

The BVI Tourist Board Web site ⊕ www.bvitourism.com/GettingAround/InterIslandFerries.aspx has links to all the ferry companies, and these sites are the best sources for ever-changing routes and schedules.

Getting Around the BVI

Driving: Driving in the BVI is on the left, British-style, but your car will always have its steering wheel on the left, as in the U.S. Your valid U.S. license will also do for driving in the BVI. The minimum age to rent a car is 25. Most agencies offer both four-wheel-drive vehicles and cars (often compacts). Both Tortola and Virgin Gorda have a number of car-rental agencies.

Tortola Contacts: Avis (⊠ *Opposite Police Station, Road Town* ☎ *284/494–3322* ✉ *Towers, West End* ☎ *284/495–4973*). **D&D** (⊠ *West End Rd., West End* ☎ *284/495–4765*). **Dollar** (⊠ *Long Bay Beach Resort, Long Bay* ☎ *284/495–4252 Ext. 2017* ✉ *East End* ☎ *284/494–6093*). **Hertz** (⊠ *West End* ☎ *284/495–4405* ✉ *Airport, Beef Island* ☎ *284/495–6600* ✉ *Road Town* ☎ *284/494–6228*). **Itgo Car Rental** (⊠ *Wickham's Cay I, Road Town* ☎ *284/494–2639*). **National** (⊠ *Airport, Beef Island* ☎ *284/495–2626* ✉ *Duffs Bottom, Road Town* ☎ *284/494–3197*).

Virgin Gorda Contacts: L&S Jeep Rental (⊠ *South Valley, Virgin Gorda* ☎ *284/495–5297*). **Mahogany Rentals & Taxi Service** (⊠ *Spanish Town, Virgin Gorda* ☎ *284/495–5469* ⊕ *www.mahoganycarrentalsbvi.com*). **Speedy's Car Rentals** (⊠ *The Valley, Virgin Gorda* ☎ *284/495–5240* ⊕ *www.speedysbvi.com*).

Taxis: Taxi rates aren't set in the BVI, so you should negotiate the fare with your driver before you start your trip. Fares are per destination, not per person here, so it's cheaper to travel in groups. The taxi number is always on the license plate.

Tortola Taxis: Airport Taxi Association (☎ *284/495–1982*). **BVI Taxi Association** (☎ *284/494–3942*). **Waterfront Taxi Association** (☎ *284/494–6362*). **West End Taxi Association** (☎ *284/495–4934*).

Virgin Gorda Taxis: Andy's Taxi and Jeep Rental (⊠ *The Valley, Virgin Gorda* ☎ *284/495–5252*). **Mahogany Rentals and Taxi Service** (⊠ *The Valley, Virgin Gorda* ☎ *284/495–5469*).

Island Activities

The BVI **sailing** scene is one of the best in the world, with Tortola as one of the major charter-yacht centers of the Caribbean. It's no wonder that sailing is so popular; most of the best BVI beaches are on deserted islands and are accessible only by boat. The most famous **beach** in the chain is The Baths on Virgin Gorda, which is lined with giant, round boulders that provide for great off-the-beach snorkeling. Tortola also has its share of beautiful strands, including the beaches at Cane Garden Bay. Jost Van Dyke's White Bay beach is also excellent.

The **nightlife** center of the region is actually a series of simple beach bars on Jost Van Dyke, but yachties in the know are happy to bop over for a drink and to hear Foxy Callwood sing at his eponymous bar and restaurant. **Diving**—especially the wreck of the Rhone and the the reefs around Tortola—make the BVI a major dive destination. Snorkelers appreciate the many opportunities to snorkel right off the beach, though some better shallow reefs can be reached on a day sail. And **game fishing** in these waters is also good, as participants in the summer sportfishing tournament will attest.

7

BRITISH VIRGIN ISLANDS PLANNER

Fast Facts	Essentials

Fast Facts

Banks: The currency in the BVI is the U.S. dollar, so there's never a need to change money. ATMs are common in Road Town, Tortola, and around Virgin Gorda Yacht Harbour.

Electricity: 110 volts, the same as in North America, so American appliances work just fine.

Emergencies: In an emergency, dial ☎ 999.

Passport Requirements: All travelers going to the British Virgin Islands need to have a valid passport, even if they are traveling by private yacht.

Weddings: You must apply in person for your license ($110) weekdays at the attorney general's office in Road Town, Tortola. You must wait three days to pick it up at the registrar's office in Road Town. If you plan to be married in a church, announcements (called *banns* locally) must be published for three consecutive Sundays in the church bulletin. Only the registrar or clergy can perform ceremonies. The registrar charges $35 at the office and $100 at another location. No blood test is required.

BVI Wedding Planners and Consultants (☎ 284/494–5306 ⊕ www.bviweddings. com).

Essentials

Mail: There's a post office in Road Town on Tortola and Spanish Town on Virgin Gorda. If you want to write to an establishment in the BVI, be sure to include the specific island in the address. **Rush It** (☎ 284/494–4421 in BVI) takes your packages to the USVI for quicker delivery to the mainland; it offers service on both Tortola and Virgin Gorda.

Taxes: The departure tax is $5 per person by boat and $20 per person by plane. There are separate booths at the airport and ferry terminals to collect this tax, which must be paid in cash in U.S. currency. Most hotels add a service charge ranging from 5% to 18% to the bill. A few restaurants and some shops tack on an additional 10% charge if you use a credit card. There's no sales tax in the BVI. However, there's a 7% government tax on hotel rooms.

Telephones: The area code for the BVI is 284; when you make calls from North America, you need only dial the area code and the number. To call anywhere in the BVI once you've arrived, dial all seven digits. A local call from a pay phone costs 25¢, but such phones are sometimes on the blink. An alternative is a Caribbean phone card, available in $5, $10, and $20 denominations. They're sold at most major hotels and many stores and can be used to call within the BVI, as well as all over the Caribbean, and to access **USADirect** (☎ 800/872–2881, 111 from a pay phone) from special phone-card phones. For credit card or collect long-distance calls to the United States, use a phone-card telephone or look for special USADirect phones, which are linked directly to an AT&T operator. USADirect and pay phones can be found at most hotels and in towns.

Visitor Information: BVI Tourist Board (☎ 212/563–3117, 800/835–8530 in New York ⊕ www.bvitourism.com).

Where to Stay

Pick your island carefully, because each is different, as are the logistics of getting there. **Tortola** gives you a wider choice of restaurants, shopping, and resorts. **Virgin Gorda** has fewer off-resort places to eat and shop, but the resorts themselves are often better, and the beaches are exquisite. **Anegada** is remote and better suited for divers. **Jost Van Dyke** has some classic Caribbean beach bars, along with fairly basic accommodations.

When you want to be pampered and pampered some more, select a remote, **private-island resort** reached only by ferry, or even one of the appealing outer-island resorts that are still somewhat affordable for mere mortals.

If you want to enjoy everything the BVI have to offer, **charter a sailboat** so you can drop anchor where and when you want.

The largest resort in the British Virgin Islands has 120-some rooms, and most have considerably fewer. Luxury here is more about personal service than over-the-top amenities. The best places are certainly comfortable, but they aren't showy. You'll find **villas and condos** in abundance, and they are a good option for families.

HOTEL AND RESTAURANT PRICES

Restaurant prices are for a main course at dinner and include any taxes or service charges. Hotel prices are per night for a double room in high season, excluding taxes, service charges, and meal plans (except at all-inclusives).

WHAT IT COSTS IN U.S. DOLLARS

	¢	$	$$	$$$	$$$$
Restaurants	under $8	$8–$12	$13–$20	$21–$30	over $30
Hotels	under $150	$151–$275	$276–$375	$376–$475	over $475

When to Go

High season doesn't really get into full swing until Christmas and ends sooner (usually by April 1) than on most Caribbean islands. In the off-season, rates can be a third less. Locals and yachties gather at Foxy's bar on Jost Van Dyke for the annual **St. Patrick's Day** celebration in March.

Glimpse the colorful spinnakers as sailing enthusiasts gather for the internationally known **BVI Spring Regatta and Sailing Festival,** which begins during the last week in March and continues until the first weekend in April. Tortola celebrates **Carnival** on and around August 1 to mark the anniversary of the end of slavery in 1834. A slew of activities culminating with a parade through the streets take place in Road Town. Hotels fill up fast, so make sure to reserve your room and rental car well in advance.

In August, you can also try your hand at sportfishing, as anglers compete to land the largest catch at the **BVI Sportfishing Tournament**.

BVI BEACHES

With a couple of exceptions, restful and relaxing best describe most beaches across the British Virgin Islands. If peace and quiet are your goals, avoid popular beaches such as Cane Garden Bay on Tortola and The Baths on Virgin Gorda on days when cruise ships are in port.

(Above) White Bay, Jost Van Dyke. (Opposite page bottom) Beef Island, Tortola. (Opposite page top) Spring Bay Beach, Virgin Gorda.

The best BVI beaches are on deserted islands reachable only by boats, so take a snorkeling or sailing trip at least once. Tortola's north side has several perfect palm-fringed, white-sand beaches that curl around turquoise bays and coves, but none really achieves greatness. Nearly all are accessible by car (preferably a four-wheel-drive vehicle), albeit down bumpy roads that corkscrew precipitously. Some of these beaches are lined with bars and restaurants as well as water-sports equipment stalls; others have absolutely nothing.

Anybody going to Virgin Gorda must experience swimming or snorkeling among its unique boulder formations, which can be visited at several sites along Lee Road. The most popular is The Baths, but there are several other similar places nearby that are easily reached.

THE SAND

Soft, white talcum-powder strands of sand predominate across the British Virgin Islands, but beach-goers will find an occasional patch of yellowish sand here and there. If you have to draw a line in the sand, Virgin Gorda has the best selection of beaches, but you'll find similar beaches out near the airport on Tortola.

For complete information on these beaches see individual beach sections within the chapter.

TORTOLA

Apple Bay, including nearby Little Apple Bay and Capoon's Bay, is your spot if you want to surf—although the white, sandy beach itself is narrow. If you're swimming and the waves are up, take care not to get dashed on the rocks. **Cane Garden Bay** is a silky stretch of sand with exceptionally calm, crystalline waters—except when storms at sea turn the water murky. Snorkeling is good along the edges. **Long Bay, Beef Island** has superlative scenery: the beach stretches seemingly forever, and you can catch a glimpse of Little Camanoe and Great Camanoe islands. If you walk around the bend to the right, you can see little Marina Cay and Scrub Island. Long Bay is also a good place to search for seashells. Swim out to wherever you see a dark patch for some nice snorkeling. **Long Bay West** is a stunning, mile-long stretch of white sand; have your camera ready to snap the breathtaking approach. The entire beach is open to the public. **Smuggler's Cove,** a beautiful, palm-fringed beach, is down a pothole-filled dirt road. You probably won't be alone on weekends, though, when the beach fills with snorkelers and sunbathers. There's a fine view of Jost Van Dyke from the shore.

VIRGIN GORDA

The Baths is a national park that features a stunning maze of huge granite boulders that extend into the sea. It's usually crowded midday with day-trippers. The snorkeling is good, and you're likely to see a wide variety of fish, but watch out for dinghies coming ashore from the numerous sailboats anchored offshore. **Nail Bay,** at the island's north tip, will reward you with a trio of beaches within the Nail Bay Resort complex that are ideal for snorkeling. Mountain Trunk Bay is perfect for beginners, and Nail Bay and Long Bay beaches have coral caverns just offshore. **Savannah Bay** is a wonderfully private beach close to Spanish Town. It may not always be completely deserted, but you can find a spot to yourself on this long stretch of soft, white sand. **Spring Bay Beach** is a national-park beach that gets much less traffic than the nearby Baths, and has the similarly large, imposing boulders that create interesting grottoes for swimming. The snorkeling is excellent, and the grounds include swings and picnic tables.

JOST VAN DYKE

Sandy Cay is a gleaming scimitar of white sand, with marvelous snorkeling. **White Bay** has a long stretch of white sand that is especially popular with boaters who come ashore for a libation at one of the beach bars.

Updated by
Carol M.
Bareuther and
Lynda Lohr

Once a collection of about 60 sleepy islands and cays, the British Virgin Islands—particularly the main island of Tortola—now sees huge cruise ships crowding its dock outside Road Town. Shoppers clog the downtown area, and traffic occasionally comes to a standstill. Even the second-largest island, Virgin Gorda, gets its share of smaller ships anchored off the main village of Spanish Town. Despite this explosive growth in the territory's tourism industry, it's still easy to escape the hubbub. Hotels outside Road Town usually provide a quiet oasis, and those on the other islands can be downright serene.

Each island has a different flavor. Want access to lots of restaurants and shopping? Make Tortola your choice. The largest of the BVIs, it covers 10 square mi (26 square km) and sits only a mile from St. John in the United States Virgin Islands (USVI). If you want to kick back at a small hotel or posh resort, try Virgin Gorda. Sitting nearly at the end of the chain, the 8-square-mi (21-square-km) island offers stellar beaches and a laid-back atmosphere. If you really want to get away from it all, the outermost islands, including Anegada and Jost Van Dyke, will fill the bill. Some of the smallest—Norman, Peter, Cooper, and Necker—are home to just one resort or restaurant. Others remain uninhabited specks on the horizon.

Visitors have long visited the BVI, starting with Christopher Columbus in 1493. He called the islands Las Once Mil Virgines—the 11,000 Virgins—in honor of the 11,000 virgin companions of St. Ursula, martyred in the 4th century AD. Pirates and buccaneers followed, and then came the British, who farmed the islands until slavery was abolished in 1834. The BVI are still politically tied to Britain, so the queen appoints a royal governor, but residents elect a local Legislative Council. Offshore banking and tourism share top billing in the territory's economy, but the majority of the islands' jobs are tourism-related. Despite the growth, you can usually find a welcoming smile.

TORTOLA

By Lynda Lohr

Once a sleepy backwater, Tortola is definitely busy these days, particularly when several cruise ships tie up at the Road Town dock. Passengers crowd the streets and shops, and open-air jitneys filled with cruise-ship passengers create bottlenecks on the island's byways. That said, most folks visit Tortola to relax on its deserted sands or linger over lunch at one of its many delightful restaurants. Beaches are never more than a few miles away, and the steep green hills that form Tortola's spine are fanned by gentle trade winds. The neighboring islands glimmer like emeralds in a sea of sapphire. It can be a world far removed from the hustle of modern life, but it simply doesn't compare to Virgin Gorda in terms of beautiful beaches—or even luxury resorts, for that matter.

Initially settled by Taíno Indians, Tortola saw a string of visitors over the years. Christopher Columbus sailed by in 1493 on his second voyage to the new world, and ships from Spain, Holland, and France made periodic visits about a century later. Sir Francis Drake arrived in 1595, leaving his name on the passage between Tortola and St. John. Pirates and buccaneers followed, with the British finally laying claim to the island in the late 1600s. In 1741 John Pickering became the first lieutenant governor of Tortola, and the seat of the British government moved from Virgin Gorda to Tortola. As the agrarian economy continued to grow, slaves were imported from Africa. The slave trade was abolished in 1807, but slaves in Tortola and the rest of the BVI did not gain their freedom until August 1, 1834, when the Emancipation Proclamation was read at Sunday Morning Well in Road Town. That date is celebrated every year with the island's annual Carnival.

Visitors have a choice of accommodations, but most fall into the small and smaller-still categories. Only Long Bay Resort on Tortola's North Shore qualifies as a resort, but even some of the smaller properties add an amenity or two. A couple of new hotel projects are in the works, so look for more growth in the island's hotel industry over the next decade.

EXPLORING TORTOLA

Tortola doesn't have many historic sights, but it does have lots of beautiful natural scenery. Although you could explore the island's 10 square mi (26 square km) in a few hours, opting for such a whirlwind tour would be a mistake. There's no need to live in the fast lane when you're surrounded by some of the Caribbean's most breathtaking panoramas. Also, the roads are extraordinarily steep and twisting, making driving demanding. The best strategy is to explore a bit of the island at a time. For example, you might try Road Town (the island's tiny metropolis) one morning and a drive to Cane Garden Bay and West End (a little town on, of course, the island's west end) the next afternoon. Or consider a visit to East End, a *very* tiny town exactly where its name suggests. The

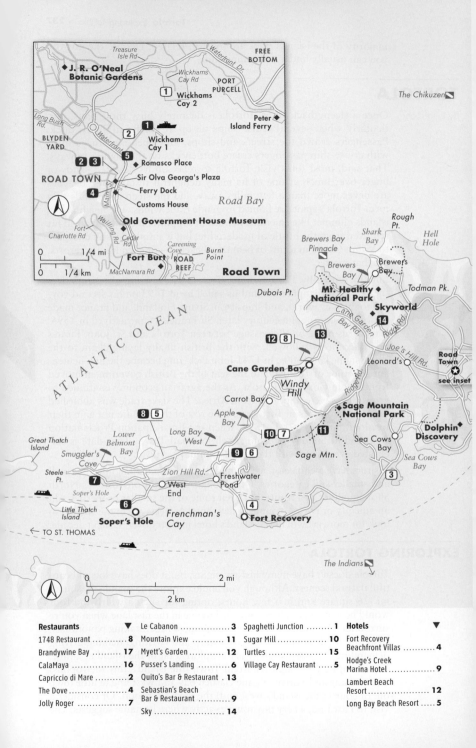

Road Town

Treasure Isle Rd
FREE BOTTOM
Waterfront Dr.
◆ J. R. O'Neal Botanic Gardens
Wickhams Cay Rd
PORT PURCELL
The Chikuzen
① Wickhams Cay 2
Long Bush Rd.
② ① Wickhams Cay 1
Peter Island Ferry ◆
BLYDEN YARD
Waterfront Dr.
② ③ ⑤ ◆ Romasco Place
ROAD TOWN
Sir Olva Georga's Plaza
④ Ferry Dock
Customs House
Road Bay
Fort Charlotte Rd
Cedar Rd
Old Government House Museum
Wailling Rd
Careening Cove
Burnt Point
Fort Burt ◆
ROAD REEF
0   1/4 mi
0   1/4 km
MacNamara Rd
Road Town

Rough Pt.
Brewers Bay Pinnacle
Shark Bay
Hell Hole
Brewers Bay
Brewers Bay
ATLANTIC OCEAN
Dubois Pt.
Mt. Healthy National Park ◆
Todman Pk.
Cane Garden Bay Rd
Skyworld ◆
⑭
⑫ ⑧ ⑬
Cane Garden Bay
Joe's Hill Rd.
Leonard's
Road Town see inset ✦
Windy Hill
Carrot Bay
Ridge Rd
⑧ ⑤
Apple Bay
Sage Mountain National Park ◆
Dolphin Discovery ◆
Great Thatch Island
Lower Belmont Bay
Long Bay West
⑩ ⑦
⑪
Sea Cows Bay
Smuggler's Cove
⑨ ⑥
Sage Mtn.
Sea Cows Bay
Steele Pt.
Zion Hill Rd.
Freshwater Pond
⑦
Soper's Hole
West End
③
Little Thatch Island
⑥
Frenchman's Cay
④ ◇ Fort Recovery
Soper's Hole
← TO ST. THOMAS
The Indians
0   2 mi
0   2 km

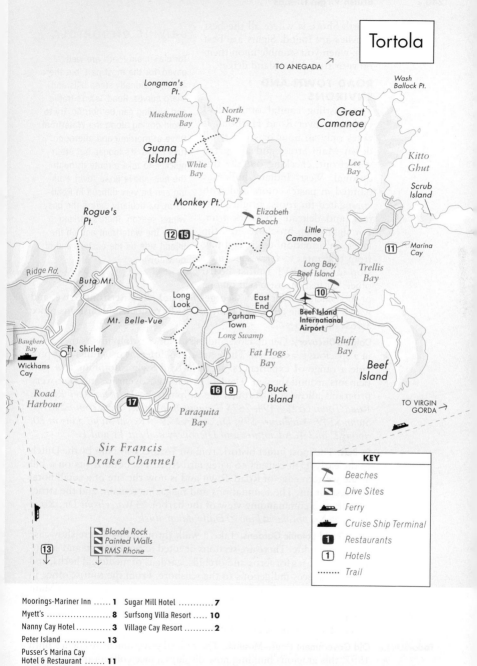

Tortola

TO ANEGADA →

Longman's Pt.

Wash Ballock Pt.

Muskmellon Bay

North Bay

Great Camanoe

Guana Island

White Bay

Lee Bay

Kitto Ghut

Scrub Island

Monkey Pt.

Rogue's Pt.

Elizabeth Beach

Little Camanoe

Marina Cay

12 **15**

11

Ridge Rd.

Buta Mt.

Long Look

Long Bay, Beef Island

Trellis Bay

Mt. Belle-Vue

East End

Parham Town

Long Swamp

10

Beef Island International Airport

Baughers Bay

Ft. Shirley

Fat Hogs Bay

Bluff Bay

Beef Island

Wickhams Cay

16 **9**

Buck Island

TO VIRGIN GORDA →

Road Harbour

17

Paraquita Bay

Sir Francis Drake Channel

13

Blonde Rock
Painted Walls
RMS Rhone

KEY

| Beaches |
| Dive Sites |
| Ferry |
| Cruise Ship Terminal |
| **1** Restaurants |
| **1** Hotels |
| .... Trail |

North Shore is where all the best beaches are found. Sights are best seen when you stumble upon them on your round-the-island drive.

ROAD TOWN AND ENVIRONS

The bustling capital of the BVI looks out over Road Harbour. It takes only an hour or so to stroll down Main Street and along the waterfront, checking out the traditional West Indian buildings painted in pastel colors and with corrugated-tin roofs, bright shutters, and delicate fretwork trim. For sightseeing brochures and the latest information on everything from taxi rates to ferry schedules, stop in at the BVI Tourist Board office. Or just choose a seat on one

> ### DRIVING ON TORTOLA
>
> Tortola's main roads are well paved, for the most part, but there are exceptionally steep hills and sharp curves. Road Town's traffic and parking can be horrific. Try to avoid driving along the Waterfront Drive at morning and afternoon rush hours. It's longer, but often quicker, to take a route through the hills above Road Town. Parking can be very difficult in Road Town, particularly during the busy winter season. There's parking along the waterfront and on the inland side on the eastern end of downtown.

of the benches in Sir Olva Georges Square, on Waterfront Drive, and watch the people come and go from the ferry dock and customs office across the street.

Dolphin Discovery. Get up close and personal with dolphins as they swim in a spacious seaside pen. There are three different programs that provide a range of experiences. In the Royal Swim, dolphins tow participants around the pen. The less expensive Adventure and Discovery programs allow you to touch the dolphins. ⊠ *Prospect Reef Resort, Road Town* ☎ *284/494–7675* ⊕ *www.dolphindiscovery.com* ⊠ *Royal Swim $149, Adventure $99, Discovery $79* ⊙ *Royal Swim daily at 10, noon, 2, and 4. Adventure and Discovery daily at 11 and 1.*

Ft. Burt. The most intact historic ruin on Tortola was built by the Dutch in the early 17th century to safeguard Road Harbour. It sits on a hill at the western edge of Road Town and is now the site of a small hotel and restaurant. The foundations and magazine remain, and the structure offers a commanding view of the harbor. ⊠ *Waterfront Dr., Road Town* ☎ *No phone* ⊠ *Free* ⊙ *Daily dawn–dusk.*

★ **J.R. O'Neal Botanic Gardens.** Take a walk through this 4-acre showcase of lush plant life. There are sections devoted to prickly cacti and succulents, hothouses for ferns and orchids, gardens of medicinal herbs, and plants and trees indigenous to the seashore. From the tourist office in Road Town, cross Waterfront Drive and walk one block over to Main Street and turn right. Keep walking until you see the high school. The gardens are on your left. ⊠ *Botanic Station, Road Town* ☎ *284/494–3904* ⊠ *$3* ⊙ *Mon.–Sat. 8:30–4:30.*

Fodor's Choice **Old Government House Museum.** The official government residence until ★ 1997, this gracious building now displays a nice collection of artifacts from Tortola's past. The rooms are filled with period furniture, hand-painted china, books signed by Queen Elizabeth II on her 1966 and

Old Government House Museum, Road Town.

1977 visits, and numerous items reflecting Tortola's seafaring legacy. ⊠ *Waterfront Dr., Road Town* 🕾 *284/494–4091* 🖃 *$3* ☉ *Weekdays 9–3, Sat. 9–1.*

WEST END

Ft. Recovery. The unrestored ruins of a 17th-century Dutch fort sit amid a profusion of tropical greenery on the grounds of Villas of Fort Recovery Estates. There's not much to see here, and there are no guided tours, but you're welcome to stop by and poke around. ⊠ *Waterfront Dr., Pockwood Pond* 🕾 *284/485–4467* 🖃 *Free.*

Soper's Hole. On this little island connected by a causeway to Tortola's western end, you can find a marina and a captivating complex of pastel West Indian–style buildings with shady balconies, shuttered windows, and gingerbread trim that house art galleries, boutiques, and restaurants. Pusser's Landing is a lively place to stop for a cold drink (many are made with Pusser's famous rum) and a sandwich and to watch the boats in the harbor. ⊠ *Soper's Hole.*

NORTH SHORE

Cane Garden Bay. Once a sleepy village, Cane Garden Bay is growing into one of Tortola's most important destinations. Stay here at a small hotel or guesthouse, or stop by for lunch, dinner, or drinks at a seaside restaurant. You can find a few small stores selling clothing and basics such as suntan lotion, and, of course, one of Tortola's most popular beaches is at your feet. The roads in and out of this area are dauntingly steep, so use caution when driving.

Mount Healthy National Park. The remains of an 18th-century sugar plantation can be seen here. The windmill structure has been restored, and you can see the ruins of a mill, a factory with boiling houses, storage areas, stables, a hospital, and many dwellings. It's a nice place to picnic. ⊠ *Ridge Rd., Todman Peak* ☎ *No phone* 🖃 *Free* ☉ *Daily dawn–dusk.*

★ **Sage Mountain National Park.** At 1,716 feet, Sage Mountain is the highest peak in the BVI. From the parking area, a trail leads you in a loop not only to the peak itself (and extraordinary views) but also to a small rain forest that is sometimes shrouded in mist. Most of the forest was cut down over the centuries to clear land for sugarcane, cotton, and other crops; to create pastureland; or simply to use the stands of timber. In 1964 this park was established to preserve what remained. Up here you can see mahogany trees, white cedars, mountain guavas, elephant-ear vines, mamey trees, and giant bullet woods, to say nothing of such birds as mountain doves and thrushes. Take a taxi from Road Town or drive up Joe's Hill Road and make a left onto Ridge Road toward Chalwell and Doty villages. The road dead-ends at the park. ⊠ *Ridge Rd., Sage Mountain* ☎ *284/494–3904* 🖃 *$3* ☉ *Daily dawn–dusk.*

★ **Skyworld.** Drive up here and climb the observation tower for a stunning 360-degree view of numerous islands and cays. On a clear day you can even see St. Croix (40 mi [64 km] away) and Anegada (20 mi [32 km] away). ⊠ *Ridge Rd., Joe's Hill* ☎ *No phone* 🖃 *Free.*

BEACHES

WEST END

Long Bay West. This beach is a stunning, mile-long stretch of white sand; have your camera ready to snap the breathtaking approach. Although Long Bay Resort sprawls along part of it, the entire beach is open to the public. The water isn't as calm here as at Cane Garden or Brewers Bay, but it's still swimmable. Rent water-sports equipment and enjoy the beachfront restaurant at the resort. Turn left at Zion Hill Road; then travel about half a mile. ⊠ *Long Bay Rd.*

Smuggler's Cove. A beautiful, palm-fringed beach, Smuggler's Cove is down a pothole-filled dirt road. After bouncing your way down, you'll feel as if you've found a hidden piece of the island. You probably won't be alone on weekends, though, when the beach fills with snorkelers and sunbathers. There's a fine view of Jost Van Dyke from the shore. The beach is popular with Long Bay Resort guests who want a change of scenery, but there are no amenities. Follow Long Bay Road past Long Bay Resort, keeping to the roads nearest the water until you reach the beach. It's about a mile past the resort. ⊠ *Long Bay Rd.*

NORTH SHORE

Apple Bay. Including nearby Little Apple Bay and Capoon's Bay, this is your spot if you want to surf—although the white, sandy beach itself is narrow. Sebastian's, a casual hotel, caters to those in search of the perfect wave. The legendary Bomba's Surfside Shack—a landmark festooned with all manner of flotsam and jetsam—serves drinks and casual food. Otherwise, there's nothing else in the way of amenities. Good waves are never a sure thing, but you're more apt to find them in January and February. If you're swimming and the waves are up, take care not to get dashed on the rocks. ✉ *North Shore Rd. at Zion Hill Rd.*

Brewers Bay. Brewers Bay is good for snorkeling, and you can find a campground with showers and bathrooms and beach bar tucked in the foliage right behind the beach. An old sugar mill and ruins of a rum distillery are off the beach along the road. The beach is easy to find, but the steep, twisting paved roads leading down the hill to it can be a bit daunting. You can actually reach the beach from either Brewers Bay Road East or Brewers Bay Road West. ✉ *Brewers Bay Rd. E off Cane Garden Bay Rd.*

Cane Garden Bay. A silky stretch of sand, Cane Garden Bay has exceptionally calm, crystalline waters—except when storms at sea turn the water murky. Snorkeling is good along the edges. Casual guesthouses, restaurants, bars, and even shops are steps from the beach in the growing village of the same name. The beach is a laid-back, even somewhat funky place to put down your towel. It's the closest beach to Road Town—one steep uphill and downhill drive—and one of the BVI's best-known anchorages (unfortunately, it can be very crowded). Water-sports shops rent equipment. ✉ *Cane Garden Bay Rd. off Ridge Rd.*

BVI FERRIES

BVI ferries can be confusing for newcomers. Ferries depart from three different places in Totola—Road Town, West End, and Beef Island—so make sure you get to the right place at the correct time. Sometimes boats bound for Jost Van Dyke, Virgin Gorda, Anegada, St. Thomas, and St. John depart minutes apart, other times the schedule is skimpy. Departures can be suddenly canceled, particularly in the summer season. To avoid being stranded, always call your ferry company on the morning of departure, and check with the locals catching a ferry if you're still not sure.

EAST END

Elizabeth Beach. Home to Lambert Beach Resort, Elizabeth Beach is a palm-lined, wide, and sandy beach with parking along its steep downhill access road. Other than at the hotel, which welcomes nonguests, there are no amenities aside from peace and quiet. Turn at the sign for Lambert Beach Resort. If you miss it, you wind up at Her Majesty's Prison. ✉ *Lambert Rd. off Ridge Rd., on eastern end of island.*

★ **Long Bay, Beef Island.** Long Bay on Beef Island has superlative scenery: the beach stretches seemingly forever, and you can catch a glimpse of Little Camanoe and Great Camanoe islands. If you walk around the bend to the right, you can see little Marina Cay and Scrub Island. Long Bay is also a good place to search for seashells. Swim out to wherever you see a dark patch for some nice snorkeling. There are no amenities, so come prepared with your own drinks and snacks. Turn left shortly after crossing the bridge to Beef Island. ✉ *Beef Island Rd., Beef Island.*

WHERE TO EAT

Local seafood is plentiful on Tortola, and although other fresh ingredients are scarce, the island's chefs are a creative lot who apply their skills to whatever the boat delivers. Contemporary American dishes with Caribbean influences are very popular, but you can find French and Italian fare as well. The more expensive restaurants have dress codes: long pants and collared shirts for men and elegant but casual resort wear for women. Prices are often a bit higher than you'd expect to pay back home and the service can sometimes be a tad on the slow side, but enjoy the chance to linger over the view.

ROAD TOWN AND ENVIRONS

$$$
ITALIAN
Fodor'sChoice
★
✕Brandywine Bay. At this restaurant in Brandywine Bay, candlelit outdoor tables have sweeping views of nearby islands. Owner Davide Pugliese prepares foods the Tuscan way: grilled with lots of fresh herbs. The remarkable menu may include duck with a mango sauce, beef carpaccio, grilled swordfish, and veal chop with ricotta and sun-dried tomatoes. The homemade mozzarella is another standout. The wine list is excellent, and the lemon tart and the tiramisu are irresistible. If you want something lighter, the lounge serves a tapas menu. ⊠ *Sir Francis Drake Hwy., east of Road Town, Brandywine Bay* 🕭 *Box 2914, East End VG1120* 🕾 *284/495–2301* 🍴 *Reservations essential* ▤ *AE, MC, V* ☯ *Closed Sun. No lunch.*

$
ITALIAN
Fodor'sChoice
★
✕Capriccio di Mare. The owners of the well-known Brandywine Bay restaurant also run this casual, authentic Italian outdoor café. Stop by for an espresso, a fresh pastry, a bowl of perfectly cooked penne, or a crispy tomato-and-mozzarella pizza. Drink specialties include a mango Bellini, an adaptation of the famous cocktail served at Harry's Bar in Venice. ⊠ *Waterfront Dr., Road Town* 🕾 *284/494–5369* 🍴 *Reservations not accepted* ☯ *Closed Sun.*

$$$
ECLECTIC
✕The Dove. Here's a two-in-one restaurant that can meet your needs regardless of the meal you're craving. When you want something more casual or just a few bites along with some drinks, head upstairs for something from the Dove's tapas menu—the sushi plate, pad thai noodles, and duck nachos are especially tasty. For more formal dining, you can eat downstairs and try some of the Dove's innovative cuisine—including five-spice duck breast served in a red-wine-and-ginger sauce, which comes with an apple-and-cabbage mixture and a sweet potato. ⊠ *Waterfront Dr., Road Town* 🕾 *284/494–0313* ☯ *Closed Sun. and Mon. No lunch.*

$$$
FRENCH
✕Le Cabanon. Birds and bougainvillea brighten the patio of this breezy French restaurant and bar, a popular gathering spot for locals and visitors alike. French onion soup and smoked salmon salad are good appetizer choices. From there, move on to the grilled tuna with wasabi sauce, sole in a brown butter sauce, or beef tenderloin with green peppercorn sauce. Save room for such tasty desserts as chocolate cake and crème brûlée, or opt for a platter of French cheeses. ⊠ *Waterfront Dr., Road Town* 🕾 *284/494–8660* ☯ *Closed Sun.*

$$
ITALIAN
★
✕Spaghetti Junction. Popular with the boating crowd, this longtime favorite serves up such West Indian dishes as stewed oxtail along with Italian favorites like penne smothered in a spicy tomato sauce, spinach-mushroom lasagna, and angel-hair pasta with shellfish. For something that combines a bit of both, try the spicy jambalaya pasta. You can also find old-fashioned favorites such as osso buco on the menu. ⊠ *Wickhams Cay I, Road Town* 🕾 *284/494–4880* ⊕ *www.spaghettijunction. net* ☯ *Closed Sun.*

$$$ ✕**Village Cay Restaurant.** Docked sailboats stretch nearly as far as the
CARIBBEAN eye can see at this busy Road Town restaurant. For lunch, try the grouper club sandwich with an ancho chili mayonnaise. Dinner offerings run to fish served a variety of ways, including West Indian–style with okra, onions, and peppers, as well as a seafood jambalaya with lobster, crayfish, shrimp, mussels, crab, and fish in a mango-passion-fruit sauce. ✉ *Wickhams Cay I, Road Town* ☎ *284/494–2771.*

WEST END

$$$ ✕**Jolly Roger Restaurant.** This casual, open-air restaurant near the ferry
ECLECTIC terminal is as popular with locals as it is with visitors. The menu ranges from burgers to rib-eye steaks to the island favorite, local lobster. Try the savory fritters filled with tender local conch and herbs for a good start to your dinner. End it with a slice of sweet key lime pie. ✉ *West End* ☎ *284/495–4559* ⊕ *www.jollyrogerbvi.com.*

$$$ ✕**Pusser's Landing.** Yachters navigate their way to this waterfront restau-
AMERICAN rant. Downstairs, from late morning to well into the evening, you can
☺ belly up to the outdoor mahogany bar or sit downstairs for sandwiches, fish-and-chips, and pizzas. At dinnertime head upstairs for a harbor view and a quiet alfresco meal of grilled steak or fresh fish. ✉ *Soper's Hole* ☎ *284/495–4554* ⊕ *www.pussers.com.*

NORTH SHORE

$$$ ✕**1748 Restaurant.** Relax over dinner in this open-air eatery at Long Bay
CONTINENTAL Beach Resort. Tables are well spaced, offering enough privacy for intimate conversations. The menu changes daily, but several dishes show up regularly. Start your meal with smoked salmon with green mussels, creamy seafood soup, or a Caesar salad. Entrées include baby back ribs in a tangy barbecue sauce served with peas and rice, plantains and corn on the cob, pan-seared red snapper with vegetables, and for vegetarians, vegetable spring rolls with lo-mein noodles. There are always at least five desserts to choose from, which might include Belgian chocolate mousse, strawberry cheesecake, or a fluffy lemon-and-coconut cake. ✉ *Long Bay Beach Resort, Long Bay* ☎ *284/495–4252* ⊕ *www. longbay.com.*

$$ ✕**Myett's Garden and Grille.** Right on the beach, this bi-level restaurant
CARIBBEAN and bar is hopping day and night. Chowder made with fresh conch is the specialty here, although the menu includes everything from vegetarian dishes to grilled shrimp, steak, and tuna. There's live entertainment every night in winter. ✉ *Cane Garden Bay* ☎ *284/495–9649.*

$$$ ✕**Quito's Bar and Restaurant.** This rustic beachside bar and restaurant
CARIBBEAN is owned and operated by island native Quito Rymer, a multitalented recording star who plays and sings solo on Tuesday and Thursday and performs with his reggae band on Friday. The menu is Caribbean, with an emphasis on fresh fish, but you should try the conch fritters or the barbecue chicken. ✉ *Cane Garden Bay* ☎ *284/495–9051* ⊕ *www. quitorymer.com* ☻ *No lunch.*

$$$ ✕**Sebastian's Beach Bar and Restaurant.** The waves practically lap at your
ECLECTIC feet at this beachfront restaurant on Tortola's North Shore. The menu emphasizes seafood—especially lobster, conch, and local fish—but you can also find dishes such as ginger chicken and filet mignon. It's a

7

perfect spot to stop for lunch on your around-the-island tour. Try the grilled dolphinfish sandwich, served on a soft roll with an oniony tartar sauce. Finish off with a cup of Sebastian's coffee spiked with home-brewed rum. ⊠ *North Coast Rd., Apple Bay* ☎ *284/494–4212* ⊕ *www. sebastiansbvi.com.*

$$$$ ✕ **Sugar Mill Restaurant.** Candles gleam, and the background music is
ECLECTIC peaceful in this romantic restaurant inside a 17th-century sugar mill.
Fodor's Choice Well-prepared selections on the à la carte menu, which changes nightly,
★ include some pasta and vegetarian entrées. Lobster bisque with basil croutons and a creamy conch chowder are good starters. Favorite entrées include fresh fish with soba noodles, shiitake mushrooms, and a scallion broth; filet mignon topped with an herb-cream sauce; butter-poached shrimp with creamy polenta; and pumpkin-and-black-bean lasagna. ⊠ *Sugar Mill Hotel, Apple Bay* ☎ *284/495–4355* ⊗ *No lunch.*

EAST END

$$$ ✕ **CalaMaya.** Casual fare is what you can find at this waterfront restau-
ECLECTIC rant. You can always order a burger or Caesar salad; the chicken wrap with sweet-and-sour sauce is a tasty alternative. For dinner, try the mahimahi with sautéed vegetables and rice. ⊠ *Hodge's Creek Marina, Blackburn Hwy.* ☎ *284/495–2126.*

$$$ ✕ **Turtles.** If you're touring the island, Turtles is a good place to stop for
ECLECTIC lunch or dinner. Sitting near the ocean at Lambert Beach Resort, this casual place provides a relaxing respite from the rigors of navigating mountain roads. At dinner you might find tiger shrimp in a curry sauce or rack of lamb with a raspberry glaze. Lunch favorites include fried shrimp, fresh tuna on a bun, and some vegetarian dishes. ⊠ *Lambert Beach Resort, Lambert Bay, East End* ☎ *284/495–2877.*

MID-ISLAND

$$$ ✕ **Mountain View.** It's worth the drive up Sage Mountain for lunch or
ECLECTIC dinner at this casual restaurant. The view is spectacular—one of the best
Fodor's Choice on Tortola. The small menu includes dishes such as veal with a ginger
★ sauce and grilled mahimahi in a lime-onion sauce. The lobster-salad sandwich is the house lunch specialty. If it's on the menu, don't pass up the fish sandwich with fries. ⊠ *Sage Mountain* ⊕ *Box 4036, Road Town VG1110* ☎ *284/495–9536.*

$$ ✕ **Sky.** The top of a mountain is the location for this casually elegant
ASIAN dining room with a menu that features sushi, sashimi, and similar dishes. You'll find the usual tuna, sea bass, and shrimp on the sushi menu, but locals like the tropical-style sushi with smoked salmon and mango. If you like some heat, try the Hurricane. If you're renting a villa in the area, the take-out menu will save you some kitchen chores. ⊠ *Ridge Rd., Joe's Hill* ☎ *284/494–3567* ⊗ *No lunch.*

WHERE TO STAY

Luxury on Tortola is more about a certain state of mind—serenity, seclusion, gentility, and a bit of Britain in the Caribbean—than about state-of-the-art amenities and fabulous facilities. Some properties, especially the vacation villas, are catching up with current trends, but others seem stuck in the 1980s. But don't let a bit of rust on the screen door or a chip in the paint on the balcony railing mar your appreciation of the ambience. You will likely spend most of your time outside, so the location, size, or price of a hotel should be more of a factor to you than the decor.

Hotels in Road Town don't have beaches, but they do have pools and are within walking distance of restaurants, bars, and shops. Accommodations outside Road Town are relatively isolated, but most face the ocean. Tortola resorts are intimate—only a handful have more than 50 rooms. Guests are treated as more than just room numbers, and many return year after year. This can make booking a room at popular resorts difficult, even off-season, despite the fact that more than half the island's visitors stay aboard their own or chartered boats.

A few hotels lack air-conditioning, relying instead on ceiling fans to capture the almost constant trade winds. Nights are cool and breezy, even in midsummer, and never reach the temperatures or humidity levels that are common in much of the United States. You may assume that all accommodations listed here have air-conditioning unless we mention otherwise. Remember that some places may be closed during the peak of hurricane season—August through October—to give their owners a much-needed break.

VILLAS

Renting a villa is growing in popularity. Vacationers like the privacy, the space to spread out, and the opportunity to cook meals. As is true everywhere, the most important thing is location. If you want to be close to the beach, opt for a villa on the North Shore. If you want to dine out in Road Town every night, a villa closer to town may be a better bet. Prices per week during the winter season run from around $2,000 for a one- or two-bedroom villa up to $10,000 for a five-room beachfront villa. Rates in summer are substantially less. Most, but not all, villas accept credit cards.

Areana Villas (⌂ *Box 263, Road Town VG1110* ☎ *284/494–5864* ⊕ *www.areanavillas.com*) represents top-of-the-line properties. Pastel-color villas with one to six bedrooms can accommodate up to 10 guests. Many have pools, whirlpool tubs, and tiled courtyards.

The St. Thomas–based **McLaughlin-Anderson Luxury Villas** (⌂ *1000 Blackbeard's Hill, Suite 3, St. Thomas, U.S. Virgin Islands 00802-6739* ☎ *340/776–0635 or 800/537–6246* ⊕ *www.mclaughlinanderson.com*) manages nearly three dozen properties around Tortola. Villas range in size from one to six bedrooms and come with full kitchens and stellar views. Most have pools. The company can hire a chef and stock your kitchen with groceries.

Smiths Gore (⌂ *Box 135, Road Town VG1110* ☎ *284/494–2446* ⊕ *www.smithsgore.com*) has properties all over the island, but many are in the Smuggler's Cove area. They range in size from two to five to bedrooms. They all have stellar views, lovely furnishings, and lush landscaping.

The following reviews have been condensed for this book. Please go to Fodors.com for expanded reviews of each property.

CLOSE UP

American or British?

Yes, the Union Jack flutters overhead in the tropical breeze, schools operate on the British system, place names have British spellings, Queen Elizabeth II appoints the governor—and the queen's picture hangs on many walls. Indeed, residents celebrate the queen's birthday every June with a public ceremony. You can overhear that charming English accent from a good handful of expats when you're lunching at Road Town restaurants, and you can buy British biscuits— which Americans call cookies—in the supermarkets.

But you can pay for your lunch and the biscuits with American money, because the U.S. dollar is legal tender here. The unusual circumstance is a matter of geography. The practice started in the mid-20th century, when BVI residents went to work in the nearby USVI. On trips home, they brought their U.S. dollars with

them. Soon, they abandoned the barter system, and in 1959, the U.S. dollar became the official form of money. Interestingly, the government sells stamps for use only in the BVI that often carry pictures of Queen Elizabeth II and other royalty with the monetary value in U.S. dollars and cents.

The American influence continued to grow when Americans began to open businesses in the BVI because they preferred its quieter ambience to the hustle and bustle of St. Thomas. Inevitably, cable and satellite TV's U.S.-based programming, along with Hollywood-made movies, further influenced life in the BVI. And most goods are shipped from St. Thomas in the USVI, meaning you can find more American-made Oreos than British-produced Peak Freens on the supermarket shelves.

ROAD TOWN AND VICINITY

$$
B&B/INN
🖬 **Moorings-Mariner Inn.** If you enjoy the camaraderie of a busy marina, this inn on the edge of Road Town may appeal to you. **Pros:** good dining options; friendly guests; excellent spot to charter boats. **Cons:** busy location; long walk to Road Town; need car to get around. ⊠ *Waterfront Dr., Box 139* ☎ *284/494–2333 or 800/535–7289* ⊕ *www. bvimarinerinnhotel.com* ➟ *32 rooms, 7 suites* ⚘ *In-room: a/c, no safe. In-hotel: restaurant, bar, pool, business center* ⦿❘ *No meals.*

$
HOTEL
🖬 **Nanny Cay Hotel.** This quiet oasis is far enough from Road Town to give it a secluded feel but close enough to make shops and restaurants convenient. **Pros:** nearby shops and restaurant; pleasant rooms; marina atmosphere. **Cons:** busy location; need car to get around. ⊠ *Nanny Cay* ⦿ *Box 281, Road Town VG1110* ☎ *284/494–2512* ⊕ *www.nannycay. com* ➟ *38 rooms* ⚘ *In-room: a/c, no safe, kitchen (some). In-hotel: restaurants, tennis court, pool, business center* ⦿❘ *No meals.*

¢–$
HOTEL
🖬 **Village Cay Resort and Marina.** If you want to be able to walk to restaurants and shops, you simply can't beat Village Cay's prime location in the heart of Road Town. **Pros:** prime location; shops and restaurants nearby; nautical ambience. **Cons:** little parking; busy street; need car to get around. ⊠ *Wickham's Cay I, Box 145* ☎ *284/494–2771* ⊕ *www. villagecayhotelandmarina.com* ➟ *17 rooms, 5 suites* ⚘ *In-room: a/c,*

no safe, kitchen (some), Internet. In-hotel: restaurant, bar, pool, spa, business center ❙◎❙ *No meals.*

WEST END

$$
RENTAL
☺
★

🏨 **Fort Recovery Beachfront Villas.** This is one of those small but special properties distinguished by friendly service and the chance to get to know your fellow guests rather than the poshness of the rooms and the upscale amenities. **Pros:** beautiful beach; spacious units; historic site. **Cons:** need car to get around; isolated location. ✉ *Waterfront Dr., Box 239 Pockwood Pond* ☎ *284/495–4467 or 800/367–8455* ⊕ *www. fortrecovery.com* ⇋ *29 suites, 1 villa* ᕲ *In-room: a/c, no safe, kitchen (some), Wi-Fi. In-hotel: pool, gym, beach, water sports, business center* ❙◎❙ *Breakfast.*

$$–$$$
RESORT

🏨 **Long Bay Beach Resort.** Long Bay Beach Resort is Tortola's only choice if you want all the resort amenities, including a beach, scads of water sports, tennis courts, and even a pitch-and-putt golf course. **Pros:** resort atmosphere; good restaurants; many activities. **Cons:** need car to get around; sometimes curt staff; uphill hike to some rooms. ✉ *Long Bay* ⌂ *Box 433, Road Town VG1130* ☎ *284/495–4252 or 800/345–0271* ⊕ *www.longbay.com* ⇋ *53 rooms, 37 suites, 26 villas* ᕲ *In-room: a/c, kitchen (some). In-hotel: restaurants, bars, tennis courts, pool, gym, spa, beach, water sports, business center* ❙◎❙ *No meals.*

$–$$
HOTEL

🏨 **Myett's.** Tucked away in a beachfront garden, this tiny hotel puts you right in the middle of Cane Garden Bay's busy hustle and bustle. **Pros:** beautiful beach; good restaurant; shops nearby. **Cons:** busy location; need car to get around. ✉ *Cane Garden Bay* ⌂ *Box 556, Cane Garden Bay VG1130* ☎ *284/495–9649* ⊕ *www.myettent.com* ⇋ *6 rooms, 4 cottages, 1 villa* ᕲ *In-room: a/c, no safe, kitchen (some). In-hotel: restaurant, spa, beach, business center* ❙◎❙ *No meals.*

$
HOTEL

🏨 **Sebastian's on the Beach.** Sitting on the island's north coast, Sebastian's definitely has a beachy feel, and that's its primary charm. **Pros:** nice beach; good restaurants; beachfront rooms. **Cons:** on busy road; some rooms nicer than others; need car to get around. ✉ *Apple Bay* ⌂ *Box 441, Road Town VG1110* ☎ *284/495–4212 or 800/336–4870* ⊕ *www. sebastiansbvi.com* ⇋ *26 rooms, 9 villas* ᕲ *In-room: a/c, no safe, no TV (some). In-hotel: restaurant, bar, beach, business center* ❙◎❙ *No meals.*

$$–$$$
HOTEL
Fodor's Choice
★

🏨 **Sugar Mill Hotel.** Though it's not a sprawling resort, the Sugar Mill Hotel has a Caribbean cachet that's hard to beat, and it's our favorite place to stay on Tortola. **Pros:** lovely rooms; excellent restaurant; nice views. **Cons:** on busy road; small beach; need car to get around. ✉ *Apple Bay* ⌂ *Box 425, Road Town VG1130* ☎ *284/495–4355 or 800/462–8834* ⊕ *www.sugarmillhotel.com* ⇋ *19 rooms, 2 suites, 1 villa, 1 cottage* ᕲ *In-room: a/c, no safe, kitchen (some), no TV (some), Wi-Fi. In-hotel: restaurants, bar, pool, beach, water sports, business center* ❙◎❙ *No meals.*

EAST END

¢–$
HOTEL

🏨 **Hodge's Creek Marina Hotel.** Sitting marina-side on the island's East End, this hotel puts you in the middle of the nautical action. **Pros:** marina atmosphere; good restaurant; some shopping. **Cons:** bland rooms; need car to get around. ✉ *Hodge's Creek* ⌂ *Box 663, Road Town VG1110*

7

Surfsong Village Resort.

☎ 284/494–5000 ⊕ *www.pennhotels.com* ➫ *33 rooms* ₺ *In-room: a/c, no safe. In-hotel: restaurant, pool, business center* ⦿ *No meals.*

$$
RESORT

🏨 **Lambert Beach Resort.** Although this isolated location on the northeast coast puts you far from Road Town, Lambert Bay is one of the island's loveliest stretches of sand and the main reason to recommend this resort. **Pros:** lovely beach; beautiful setting; good restaurant. **Cons:** bland rooms; isolated location; need car to get around. ⊠ *Lambert Bay, Box 534, East End* ☎ *284/495–2877* ⊕ *www.lambertresort.com* ➫ *38 rooms, 2 villas, 27 condos* ₺ *In-room: a/c, no safe, kitchen (some), Wi-Fi (some). In-hotel: restaurant, bar, tennis court, pool, spa, beach, water sports, business center* ⦿ *No meals.*

$$$
RESORT
Fodor's Choice
★

🏨 **Surfsong Villa Resort.** Nested in lush foliage right at the water's edge, this small resort on Beef Island provides a pleasant respite for vacationers who want a villa atmosphere with some hotel amenities. **Pros:** lovely rooms; beautiful beach; chef on call. **Cons:** need car to get around; no restaurants nearby. ⊠ *Beef Island* 🖃 *Box 606, Road Town VG1110* ☎ *284/495–1864* ⊕ *www.surfsong.net* ➫ *1 suite, 7 villas* ₺ *In-room: a/c (some), kitchen, Wi-Fi. In-hotel: beach, water sports, business center, some age restrictions* ⦿ *No meals.*

NIGHTLIFE AND THE ARTS

NIGHTLIFE

Like any other good sailing destination, Tortola has watering holes that are popular with salty and not-so-salty dogs. Many offer entertainment; check the weekly *Limin' Times* for schedules and up-to-date information. Bands change like the weather, and what's hot today can be old news tomorrow. The local beverage is the Painkiller, an innocent-tasting mixture of fruit juices and rums. It goes down smoothly but packs quite a punch, so give yourself time to recover before you order another.

Bomba's Surfside Shack. By day, you can see that Bomba's, which is covered with everything from crepe-paper leis to ancient license plates to spicy graffiti, looks like a pile of junk; by night it's one of Tortola's liveliest spots. There's a fish fry and a live band every Wednesday and Sunday. People flock here from all over on the full moon, when bands play all night long. ⊠ *Apple Bay* ☎ *284/495-4148*.

Jolly Roger. At the Jolly Roger, an ever-changing roster of local and down-island bands plays everything from rhythm and blues to reggae and rock every Friday and Saturday—and sometimes Sunday—starting at 8. ⊠ *West End* ☎ *284/495-4559*.

Fodor'sChoice **Myett's.** Local bands play at this popular spot, which has live music ★ during happy hour, and there's usually a lively dance crowd. ⊠ *Cane Garden Bay* ☎ *284/495-9649*.

Pub. At this popular watering hole, there's a happy hour from 5 to 7 every day and live music on Thursday and Friday. ⊠ *Waterfront St., Road Town* ☎ *284/494-2608*.

Pusser's Road Town Pub. Courage is what people are seeking here—John Courage by the pint. Or try Pusser's famous mixed drink, called the Painkiller, and snack on the excellent pizza. ⊠ *Waterfront St., Road Town* ☎ *284/494-3897*.

Quito's Bar and Restaurant. BVI recording star Quito Rhymer sings island ballads and love songs at his rustic beachside bar–restaurant. Solo shows are on Tuesday and Thursday at 8:30; on Friday at 9:30 Quito performs with his band. ⊠ *Cane Garden Bay* ☎ *284/495-9051*.

Sebastian's. There's often live music at Sebastian's on Thursday and Sunday evenings, and you can dance under the stars. ⊠ *Apple Bay* ☎ *284/495-4212*.

THE ARTS
Fodor'sChoice **BVI Music Festival.** Every May hordes of people head to Tortola for the ★ three-day for this popular festival to listen to reggae, gospel, blues, and salsa music by musicians from around the Caribbean and the U.S. mainland. ⊠ *Cane Garden Bay* ⊕ *www.bvimusicfestival.com*.

Performing Arts Series. Musicians from around the world take to the stage during the island's Performing Arts Series, held from October to May each year. Past artists have included Britain's premier a cappella group, Black Voices; the Leipzig String Quartet; and pianist Richard Ormand. ⊠ *H. Lavity Stoutt Community College, Paraquita Bay* ☎ *284/494-4994* ⊕ *www.hlscc.edu.vg*.

SHOPPING

The BVI aren't really a shopper's delight, but there are many shops showcasing original wares—from jams and spices to resort wear to excellent artwork.

Most of Tortola's shops are in Road Town.

SHOPPING AREAS

Many shops and boutiques are clustered along and just off Road Town's **Main Street.** You can shop in Road Town's **Wickham's Cay I** adjacent to the marina. The **Crafts Alive Market** on the Road Town waterfront is a collection of colorful West Indian–style buildings with shops that carry items made in the BVI. You might find pretty baskets or interesting pottery or perhaps a bottle of home-brewed hot sauce. An ever-growing number of art and clothing stores are opening at **Soper's Hole** in West End.

SPECIALTY STORES

ART

Allamanda Gallery. Allamanda carries photography by owner Amanda Baker. ⊠ *124 Main St., Road Town* ☎ *284/494–6680.*

Sunny Caribbee. This gallery has many paintings, prints, and watercolors by artists from around the Caribbean. ⊠ *Main St., Road Town* ☎ *284/494–2178.*

CLOTHES AND TEXTILES

Arawak. This boutique carries batik sundresses, sportswear, and resort wear for men and women. There's also a selection of children's clothing. ⊠ *On dock, Nanny Cay* ☎ *284/494–3983.*

Latitude 18°. This store sells Maui Jim, Smith, and Oakley sunglasses; Freestyle watches; and a fine collection of beach towels, sandals, Crocs, sundresses, and sarongs. ⊠ *Main St., Road Town* ☎ *284/494–6196.*

Pusser's Company Store. The Road Town Pusser's sells nautical memorabilia, ship models, and marine paintings. There's also an entire line of clothing for both men and women, handsome decorator bottles of

Pusser's rum, and gift items bearing the Pusser's logo. ⊠ *Main St. a. Waterfront Rd., Road Town* ☎ *284/494–2467.*

Zenaida's of West End. Zenaida's displays the fabric finds of Argentine Vivian Jenik Helm, who travels through South America, Africa, and India in search of batiks, hand-painted and hand-blocked fabrics, and interesting weaves that can be made into pareus (women's wraps) or wall hangings. The shop also sells unusual bags, belts, sarongs, scarves, and ethnic jewelry. ⊠ *Soper's Hole Marina, West End* ☎ *284/495–4867.*

FOOD
Ample Hamper. This store has an outstanding collection of cheeses, wines, fresh fruits, and canned goods from the United Kingdom and the United States. The staff will stock your yacht or rental villa. ⊠ *Inner Harbour Marina, Road Town* ☎ *284/494–2494* ⊠ *Frenchman's Cay Marina, West End* ☎ *284/495–4684* ⊕ *www.amplehamper.com.*

Best of British. This boutique has lots of nifty British food you won't find elsewhere. Shop here for Marmite, Vegemite, shortbread, frozen meat pies, and delightful Christmas crackers filled with surprises. ⊠ *Wickham's Cay I, Road Town* ☎ *284/494–3462.*

RiteWay. This market carries a good selection of the usual supplies, but don't expect an inventory like your hometown supermarket. RiteWay will stock villas and yachts. ⊠ *Waterfront Dr. at Pasea Estate, Road Town* ☎ *284/494–2263* ⊠ *Fleming St., Road Town* ☎ *284/494–2263* ⊕ *www.rtwbvi.com.*

GIFTS
Fodor's Choice ★ **Bamboushay.** Bamboushay sells handcrafted Tortola-made pottery in shades that reflect the sea. ⊠ *Nanny Cay Marina, Nanny Cay* ☎ *284/494–0393.*

Sunny Caribbee. In a brightly painted West Indian house, this store packages its own herbs, teas, coffees, vinegars, hot sauces, soaps, skin and suntan lotions, and exotic concoctions—Arawak Love Potion and Island Hangover Cure, for example. ⊠ *Main St., Road Town* ☎ *284/494–2178.*

JEWELRY
Colombian Emeralds International. This Caribbean chain caters to the cruise-ship crowd and is the source for duty-free emeralds and other gems in gold and silver settings. ⊠ *Wickham's Cay I, Road Town* ☎ *284/494–7477.*

Samarkand. Samarkand crafts charming gold-and-silver pendants, earrings, bracelets, and pins, many with island themes such as seashells, lizards, pelicans, and palm trees. There are also reproduction Spanish pieces of eight (old Spanish coins) that were found on sunken galleons. ⊠ *Main St., Road Town* ☎ *284/494–6415.*

STAMPS
BVI Post Office. The BVI's post office is a philatelist's dream. It has a worldwide reputation for exquisite stamps in all sorts of designs. Although the stamps carry U.S. monetary designations, they can be used for postage only in the BVI. ⊠ *Blackburn Rd., Road Town* ☎ *284/494–3701.*

7

~ORTS AND ACTIVITIES

DIVING AND SNORKELING

Clear waters and numerous reefs afford some wonderful opportunities for underwater exploration. In some spots visibility reaches 100 feet, but colorful reefs teeming with fish are often just a few feet below the sea surface. The BVI's system of marine parks means the underwater life visible through your mask will stay protected.

There are several popular dive spots around the islands. **Alice in Wonderland** is a deep dive south of Ginger Island with a wall that slopes gently from 15 feet to 100 feet. It's an area overrun with huge mushroom-shape coral, hence its name. Crabs, lobsters, and shimmering fan corals make their homes in the tunnels, ledges, and overhangs of **Blonde Rock,** a pinnacle that goes from 15 feet below the surface to 60 feet deep. It's between Dead Chest and Salt Island. When the currents aren't too strong, **Brewers Bay Pinnacle** (20 to 90 feet down) teems with sea life. At the **Indians,** near Pelican Island, colorful coral decorates canyons and grottoes created by four large, jagged pinnacles that rise 50 feet from the ocean floor. The **Painted Walls** is a shallow dive site where coral and sponges create a kaleidoscope of colors on the walls of four long gullies. It's northeast of Dead Chest.

The *Chikuzen,* sunk northwest of Brewers Bay in 1981, is a 246-foot vessel in 75 feet of water; it's home to thousands of fish, colorful corals, and big rays. In 1867 the **RMS *Rhone,*** a 310-foot royal mail steamer, split in two when it sank in a devastating hurricane. It's so well preserved that it was used as an underwater prop in the movie *The Deep.* You can see the crow's nest and bowsprit, the cargo hold in the bow, and the engine and enormous propeller shaft in the stern. Its four parts are at various depths from 30 to 80 feet. Get yourself some snorkeling gear and hop aboard a dive boat to this wreck near Salt Island (across the channel from Road Town). Every dive outfit in the BVI runs scuba and snorkel tours to this part of the BVI National Parks Trust; if you have time for only one trip, make it this one. Rates start at around $75 for a one-tank dive and $100 for a two-tank dive.

Your hotel probably has a dive company right on the premises. If not, the staff can recommend one nearby. Using your hotel's dive company makes a trip to the offshore dive and snorkel sites a breeze. Just stroll down to the dock and hop aboard. All dive companies are certified by PADI, the Professional Association of Diving Instructors, which ensures your instructors are qualified to safely take vacationers diving. The boats are also inspected to make sure they're seaworthy. If you've never dived, try a short introductory dive, often called a resort course, which teaches you enough to get you under water. In the unlikely event you get a case of the bends, a condition that can happen when you rise to the surface too fast, your dive team will whisk you to the decompression chamber at Roy L. Schneider Regional Medical Center in nearby St. Thomas.

Blue Waters Divers (✉ *Nanny Cay* ☎ *284/494–2847* ✉ *Soper's Hole, West End* ☎ *284/495–1200* ⊕ *www.bluewaterdiversbvi.com*) teaches resort, open-water, rescue, and advanced diving courses, and also makes daily dive trips. If you're chartering a sailboat, the company's boat will me your boat at Peter, Salt, Norman, or Cooper Island for a rendezvou. dive. Rates include all equipment as well as instruction. Reserve two days in advance.

FISHING

Most of the boats that take you deep-sea fishing for bluefish, wahoo, swordfish, and shark leave from nearby St. Thomas, but local anglers like to fish the shallower water for bonefish. A half day runs about $480, a full day around $850. Wading trips are $325

Call **Caribbean Fly Fishing** (⊠ *Nanny Cay* ☎ *284/494–4797* ⊕ *www. caribflyfishing.com*).

HIKING

Sage Mountain National Park attracts hikers who enjoy the quiet trails that crisscross the island's loftiest peak. There are some lovely views and the chance to see rare species that grow only at higher elevations.

SAILING

The BVI are among the world's most popular sailing destinations. They're clustered together and surrounded by calm waters, so it's fairly easy to sail from one anchorage to the next. Most of the Caribbean's biggest sailboat charter companies have operations in Tortola. If you know how to sail, you can charter a bareboat (perhaps for your entire vacation); if you're unschooled, you can hire a boat with a captain. Prices vary depending on the type and size of the boat you wish to charter. In season, a weekly charter runs from $1,500 to $35,000. Book early to make sure you get the boat that fits you best. Most of Tortola's marinas have hotels, which give you a convenient place to spend the nights before and after your charter.

If a day sail to some secluded anchorage is more your cup of tea, the BVI have numerous boats of various sizes and styles that leave from many points around Tortola. Prices start at around $80 per person for a full-day sail, including lunch and snorkeling equipment.

Aristocat Charters (⊠ *West End* ☎ *284/499–1249* ⊕ *www.aristocatcharters. com*) sets sail daily to Jost Van Dyke, the Indians, and Peter Island aboard a 48-foot catamaran.

BVI Yacht Charters (⊠ *Port Purcell, Road Town* ☎ *284/494–4289 or 888/615–4006* ⊕ *www.bviyachtcharters.com*) offers 31-foot to 52-foot sailboats for charter—with or without a captain and crew, whichever you prefer.

Catamaran Charters (⊠ *Village Cay Marina, Road Town* ☎ *284/494– 6661 or 800/262–0308* ⊕ *www.catamarans.com*) charters catamarans with or without a captain.

The **Moorings** (⊠ *Wickham's Cay II, Road Town* ☎ *284/494–2332 or 800/535–7289* ⊕ *www.moorings.com*), considered one of the world's best bareboat operations, has a large fleet of well-maintained monohulls and catamarans. Hire a captain or sail the boat yourself.

If you prefer a powerboat, call **Regency Yacht Vacations** (⊠ *Wickham's Cay I, Road Town* ☎ *284/495–1970 or 800/524–7676* ⊕ *www.*

7

regencyvacations.com) for both bareboat and captained sail and powerboat charters.

Sunsail (✉ *Wickham's Cay II, Road Town* ☎ *284/495–4740 or 800/327–2276* ⊕ *www.sunsail.com*) offers a full fleet of boats to charter with or without a captain.

Voyage Charters (✉ *Soper's Hole Marina, West End* ☎ *284/494–0740 or 888/869–2436* ⊕ *www.voyagecharters.com*) offers a variety of sailboats for charter with or without a captain and crew.

White Squall II (✉ *Village Cay Marina, Road Town* ☎ *284/494–2564* ⊕ *www.whitesquall2.com*) takes you on regularly scheduled day sails to The Baths at Virgin Gorda, Cooper, the Indians, or the Caves at Norman Island on an 80-foot schooner.

SURFING

Surfing is big on Tortola's north shore, particularly when the winter swells come in to Josiah's and Apple bays. Rent surfboards starting at $65 for a full day.

HIHO (✉ *Trellis Bay, Road Town* ☎ *284/494–7694* ⊕ *www.go-hiho. com*) has a good surfboard selection for sale or rent. The staff will give you advice on the best spots to put in your board.

WINDSURFING

Steady trade winds make windsurfing a breeze. Three of the best spots for sailboarding are Nanny Cay, Slaney Point, and Trellis Bay on Beef Island. Rates for sailboards start at about $25 an hour or $100 for a two-hour lesson.

Boardsailing BVI Watersports (✉ *Trellis Bay, Beef Island* ☎ *284/495–2447* ⊕ *www.windsurfing.vi*) rents equipment and offers private and group lessons.

SIDE TRIPS FROM TORTOLA

There are several islands that make great side trips from Tortola, including lovely Marina Cay and tony Peter's Island. Both have great accommodations, so you might want to spend the night.

The following reviews have been condensed for this book. Please go to Fodors.com for expanded reviews of each property.

MARINA CAY

Beautiful little Marina Cay is in Trellis Bay, not far from Beef Island. Sometimes you can see it and its large J-shaped coral reefs—a most dramatic sight—from the air soon after takeoff from the airport on Beef Island. Covering 8 acres, this islet is considered small even by BVI standards. On it there's a restaurant, Pusser's Store, and a six-unit hotel. Ferry service is free from the dock on Beef Island.

WHERE TO STAY

$$–$$$
HOTEL
Pusser's Marina Cay Hotel and Restaurant. If getting away from it all is your priority, this may be the place for you, because there's nothing to do on this beach-rimmed island other than swim, snorkel, and soak up the sun—there's not even a TV to distract you. **Pros:** lots of character; beautiful beaches; interesting guests. **Cons:** older property; ferry needed

Continued on page 264

TRY A YACHT CHARTER

IT'S SURPRISINGLY AFFORDABLE

Savoring a freshly brewed mug of coffee, I sat on the front deck of our chartered 43-foot catamaran and watched the morning show. Laserlike rays of sunlight streamed through a cottony cloud bank, bringing life to the emerald islands and turquoise seas. What would it have been like to sail with Columbus and chart these waters for the first time? How would it feel to cast about the deserted beaches for the perfect place to bury plundered treasure? The aroma of freshly made banana pancakes roused me from my reverie.

Once considered an outward-bound adventure or exclusive domain of the rich and famous, chartering a boat can be a surprisingly affordable and attractive vacation alternative. Perhaps you're already a sailor and want to explore beyond your own lake, river, or bay. Or maybe your idea of sailing has always been on a cruise ship, and now you're ready for a more intimate voyage. Or perhaps you've never sailed before, but you are now curious to cast off and explore a whole new world.

By Carol M. Bareuther

CREWED CHARTER

On a crewed charter, you sit back and relax while the crew provides for your every want and need. Captains are licensed by the U.S. Coast Guard or the equivalent in the British maritime system. Cooks—preferring to be called chefs—have skills that go far beyond peanut butter and jelly sandwiches. There are four meals a day, and many chefs boast certificates from culinary schools ranging from the Culinary Institute of America in New York to the Cordon Bleu in Paris.

The advantage of a crewed yacht charter, with captain and cook, is that it takes every bit of stress out of the vacation. With a captain who knows the local waters, you get to see some of the coves and anchorages that are not necessarily in the guidebooks. Your meals are prepared, cabins cleaned, beds made up every day—and turned down at night, too. Plus, you can sail and take the helm as often as you like. But at the end of the day, the captain is the one who will take responsibility for anchoring safely for the night while the chef goes below and whips up a gourmet meal.

COSTS

$4,100–$6,450 for 2 people for 5 days

$5,200–$8,200 for 2 people for 7 days

$8,200–$13,200 for 6 people for 5 days

$9,700–$16,900 for 6 people for 7 days

Prices are all-inclusive for a 50- to 55-foot yacht in high season except for 15%–20% gratuity.

PROS

■ Passengers just have to lay back and relax (unless they want to help sail)

■ Most are catamarans, offering more space than monohulls

■ You have an experienced, local hand on board if something goes wrong

■ Water toys and other extras are often included

■ Competively priced within an all-inclusive resort

CONS

■ More expensive than a bareboat, especially if you get a catamaran

■ Less privacy for your group than on a bareboat

■ Captain makes ultimate decisions about the course

■ Chance for personality conflicts: you have to get along with the captain and chef. This is where a charter yacht broker is helpful in determining what yachts and crews might be a good fit.

(top) Family sailing in the British Virgin Islands

BAREBOAT

If you'd like to bareboat, don't be intimidated. It's a myth that you must be a graduate of a sailing school in order to pilot your own charter boat. A bareboat company will ask you to fill out a resume. The company checks for prior boat-handling experience, the type of craft you've sailed (whether powerboat or sailboat), and in what type of waters. Real-life experience, meaning all those day and weekend trips close to home, count as valuable know-how. If you've done a bit of boating, you may be more qualified than you think to take out a bareboat.

Costs can be very similar for a bareboat and crewed charter, depending on the time of year and size of the boat. You'll pay the highest rates between Christmas and New Year's, when you may not be allowed to do a charter of less than a week. But there are more than 800 bareboats between the USVI and BVI, so regardless of your budget, you should be able to find something in your price range. Plus, you might save a bit by chartering an older boat from a smaller company instead of the most state-of-the-art yacht from a larger company.

COSTS	PROS	CONS
$2,800–$4,800 for a small monohull (2–3 cabins)	■ The ultimate freedom to set the yacht's course	■ Must be able to pass a sailing test
$4,800–$8,400 for a large monohull (4–5 cabins)	■ A chance to test your sailing skills	■ Those unfamiliar with the region may not find the best anchorages
$5,200–$6,400 for a small catamaran (2 cabins)	■ Usually a broader range of boats and prices to choose from	■ You have to cook for and clean up after yourself
$6,800–$13,300 for a large catamaran (4 cabins)	■ More flexibility for meals (you can always go ashore if you don't feel like cooking)	■ You have to do your own provisioning and planning for meals
Prices exclude food, beverages, fuel, and other supplies. Most bareboat rates do not include water toys, taxes, insurance, and permits.	■ You can always hire a captain for a few days	■ If something goes wrong, there isn't an experienced hand onboard

Three women rigging the sails.

WHAT TO CONSIDER

Whether bareboat or a crewed yacht, there are a few points to ponder when selecting your boat.

HOW BIG IS YOUR GROUP?

As a general rule, count on one cabin for every two people. Most people also prefer to have one head (bathroom) per cabin. A multihull, also called a catamaran, offers more space and more equal-size cabins than a monohull sailboat.

WHAT TYPE OF BOAT?

If you want to do some good old traditional sailing, where you're heeling over with the seas at your rails, monohulls are a good option. On the other hand, multihulls are more stable, easier to board, and have a big salon for families. They're also ideal if some people get seasick or aren't as gung-ho for the more traditional sailing experience. If you'd like to cover more ground, choose a motor yacht.

DO YOU HAVE A SPECIAL INTEREST?

Some crewed charter boats specialize in certain types of charters. Among these are learn-to-sail excursions, honeymoon cruises, scuba-diving adventures, and family-friendly trips. Your broker can steer you to the boats that fit your specific needs.

WHAT KIND OF EQUIPMENT DO YOU WANT ONBOARD?

Most charter boats have satellite navigation systems and autopilots, as well as regulation safety gear, dinghies with motors, and even stereos and entertainment systems. But do you want a generator or battery-drive refrigeration system? How about a/c? Do you want a satellite phone? Do you want water toys like kayaks, boogie boards, and Windsurfers?

Now that you've decided on bareboat versus crewed charter and selected your craft, all you need to do is confirm the availability of the date with the company or broker and pay a nonrefundable deposit equal to 50% of the charter price.

TO SAIL OR NOT TO SAIL?

If you're not sure whether a charter yacht vacation is right for you, consider this: would you enjoy a floating hotel room where the scenery outside your window changed according to your desires? A "yes" may entice wary companions to try chartering. A single one-week trip will have them hooked.

Two catamaran sailboats seen from behind.

CATAMARANS
Multihulls are more stable, easier to board and have a big salon for families. Seasickness is less of an issue.

MOTOR YACHT
Best if you want to cover more ground, but costs a lot more than a sailboat.

MONOHULLS
Good for more traditional and active sailing, but the movement may not appeal to non-sailors.

CHOOSING A CHARTER

Information on charters is much easier to find now than even a decade ago. Web sites for bareboat companies show photos of different types of boats—both interiors and exteriors—as well as layout schematics, lists of equipment and amenities, and sample itineraries. Many sites will allow you to book a charter directly, while others give you the option of calling a toll-free number to speak with an agent first.

There are two types of Web sites for crewed charters. If you just want some information, the **Virgin Islands Charteryacht League** (⊕ *www.vicl.org*) and the **Charter Yacht Society of the British Virgin Islands** (⊕ *www.bvicrewedyachts.com*) both help you understand what to look for in a crewed charter, from the size of the boat to the amenities. You can't reserve on these sites, but they link to the sites of brokers, who are the sales force for the charter yacht industry. Most brokers, whether they're based in the Caribbean, the United States, or Europe, attend annual charter yacht shows in St. Thomas, Tortola, and Antigua. At these shows, brokers visit the boats and meet the crews. This is what gives brokers their depth of knowledge for "matchmaking," or linking you with a boat that will meet your personality and preferences.

The charter companies also maintain Web sites. About 30% of the crewed charter yachts based out of the U.S. and British Virgin Islands can be booked directly. This saves the commission an owner has to pay to the broker. But while "going direct" might seem advantageous, there is usually little difference in pricing, and if you use a broker, he or she can help troubleshoot if something goes wrong or find a replacement boat if the boat owner has to cancel.

Timing also matters. Companies may offer last-minute specials that are available only online. These special rates—usually for specific dates, destinations, and boats—are updated weekly or even daily.

PREPARING FOR YOUR CHARTER

British Virgin Islands—anchorage in a tropical sea with breakfast on board.

PROVISIONING

Bareboaters must do their own provisioning. It's a good idea to arrange provisioning at least a week in advance.

Bobby's Market Place ⊠ *Wickham's Cay I, Road Town, Tortola* ☎ *284/494–2189* ⊕ *www.bobbysmarketplace.com*) offers packages from $18 to $28 per person per day. **Ample Hamper** (⊠ *Inner Harbour Marina, Road Town, Tortola* ☎ *284/494–2494* ⊠ *Frenchmans Cay Marina, West End, Tortola* ☎ *284/495–4684* ⊕ *www.amplehamper.com*) offers more than 1,200 items but no prearranged packages.

Provisioning packages from the charter company are usually a bit more expensive, at $30 to $35 per person per day, but they save you the hassle of planning the details. You can also shop on arrival. Both St. Thomas and Tortola have markets, though larger grocery stores may require a taxi ride. If you shop carefully, this route can still save you money. Just be sure to allow yourself a few hours after arrival to get everything done.

PLANNING

For a crewed charter, your broker will send a preference sheet for both food and your wishes for the trip. Perhaps you'd like lazy days of sleeping late, sunning, and swimming. Or you might prefer active days of sailing with stops for snorkeling and exploring ashore. If there's a special spot you'd like to visit, list it so your captain can plan the itinerary accordingly.

PACKING TIPS

Pack light for any type of charter. Bring soft-sided luggage (preferably a duffle bag) since space is limited and storage spots are usually odd shapes. Shorts, T-shirts, and swimsuits are sufficient. Bring something a bit nicer if you plan to dine ashore. Shoes are seldom required except ashore, but you might want beach shoes to protect your feet in the water. Most boats provide snorkel equipment, but always ask. Bring sunscreen, but a type that will not stain cockpit cushions and decks.

WHAT YOU'LL SEE IN THE USBVI

Cruz Bay in St. John

MAIN CHARTER BASES

The U.S. and British Virgin Islands boast more than 100 stepping-stone islands and cays within a 50-nautical-mi radius. This means easy line-of-sight navigation and island-hopping in protected waters, and it's rare that you'll spend more than a few hours moving between islands.

Tortola, in the British Virgin Islands, is the crewed charter and bareboat mecca of the Caribbean. This fact is plainly apparent from the forest of masts rising out from any marina.

The U.S. Virgin Islands fleet is based in **St. Thomas**. Direct flights from the mainland, luxurious accommodations, and duty-free shopping are drawing cards for departures from the U.S. Virgin Islands, whereas the British Virgins are closer to the prime cruising grounds.

POPULAR ANCHORAGES

On a typical weeklong charter you could set sail from Red Hook, St. Thomas, then cross Pillsbury Sound to St. John, which offers popular north-shore anchorages in Honeymoon, Trunk, or Francis bays.

But the best sailing and snorkeling always includes the British Virgin Islands (which require a valid passport or passport card). After clearing customs in West End, Tortola, many yachts hop along a series of smaller islands that run along the south side of the Sir Francis Drake Channel. But some yachts will also visit Guana Island, Great Camanoe, or Marina Cay off Tortola's more isolated east end.

The islands south of Tortola include **Norman Island,** the rumored site of Robert Lewis Stevenson's *Treasure Island*. The next island over is **Peter Island,** famous for it's posh resort and a popular anchorage for yachters. Farther east, off Salt Island, is the wreck of the **RMS Rhone**—the most magnificent dive site in the eastern Caribbean. Giant boulders form caves and grottos called The Baths at the southern end of **Virgin Gorda.**

A downwind run along Tortola's north shore ends at **Jost Van Dyke,** where that famous guitar-strumming calypsonian Foxy Callwood sings personalized ditties that make for a memorable finale.

to get here. ✉ *West side of Marina Cay ☏ Box 76, Road Town, Tortola VG1110 ☎ 284/494–2174 ⊕ www.pussers.com/t-marina-cay. aspx ⇆ 4 rooms, 2 2-bedroom villas ♿ In-room: no a/c, no safe, no TV. In-hotel: restaurant, bar, beach ⍟ Breakfast.*

PETER ISLAND

Although Peter Island is home to the resort of the same name, it's also a popular anchorage for charter boaters and a destination for Tortola vacationers. The scheduled ferry trip from Peter Island's shore-side base outside Road Town runs $15 round-trip for nonguests. The island is lush, with forested hillsides sloping seaward to meet white sandy beaches. There are no roads other than those at the resort, and there's nothing to do but relax at the lovely beach set aside for day-trippers. You're welcome to dine at the resort's restaurants.

VIRGIN GORDA FERRIES

The ferry service from the public dock in Spanish Town can be a tad erratic. Call ahead to confirm the schedule, get there early to be sure it hasn't changed, and ask at the dock whether you're getting on the right boat. The Thursday and Sunday service between Virgin Gorda and St. John is particularly prone to problems.

WHERE TO STAY

$$$$ RESORT ⛱ **Peter Island Resort.** Total pampering and the prices to match are the ticket at this luxury resort. **Pros:** lovely rooms; nice beach. **Cons:** need ferry to get here; pricey rates. ✉ *Peter Island ☏ Box 211, Road Town, Tortola VG1110 ☎ 284/495–2000 or 800/346–4451 ⊕ www. peterisland.com ⇆ 52 rooms, 3 villas ♿ In-room: a/c, no TV. In-hotel: restaurants, bar, pool, gym, spa, beach, water sports, business center ⍟ No meals, all meals.*

VIRGIN GORDA

By Lynda Lohr

Virgin Gorda, or "Fat Virgin," received its name from Christopher Columbus. The explorer envisioned the island as a pregnant woman in a languid recline, with Gorda Peak being her big belly and the boulders of The Baths her toes. Different in topography from Tortola, with its arid landscape covered with scrub brush and cactus, Virgin Gorda has a slower pace of life, too. Goats and cattle own the right-of-way, and the unpretentious friendliness of the people is winning.

EXPLORING VIRGIN GORDA

One of the most efficient ways to see Virgin Gorda is by sailboat. There are few roads, and most byways don't follow the scalloped shoreline. The main route sticks resolutely to the center of the island, linking The Baths on the southern tip with Gun Creek and Leverick Bay at North Sound. The craggy coast, scissored with grottoes and fringed by palms and boulders, has a primitive beauty. If you drive, you can hit all the sights in one day. The best plan is to explore the area near your hotel (either Spanish Town or North Sound) first, then take a day to drive to

The Baths.

the other end. Stop to climb Gorda Peak, which is in the island's center. Signage is erratic, so come prepared with a map.

THE VALLEY

The Baths. At Virgin Gorda's most celebrated sight, giant boulders are scattered about the beach and in the water. Some are almost as large as houses and form remarkable grottoes. Climb between these rocks to swim in the many placid pools. Early morning and late afternoon are the best times to visit if you want to avoid crowds. If it's privacy you crave, follow the shore northward to quieter bays—Spring Bay, the Crawl, Little Trunk, and Valley Trunk—or head south to Devil's Bay. ⊠ *Off Tower Rd., The Baths* ☎ *284/494–3904* ✆ *$3* ☾ *Daily dawn–dusk.*

Fodor's Choice ★

Copper Mine Point. Here stand a tall stone shaft silhouetted against the sky and a small stone structure that overlooks the sea. These are the ruins of a copper mine established 400 years ago and worked first by the Spanish, then by the English, until the early 20th century. The route is not well marked, so turn inland near LSL Restaurant and look for the hard-to-see sign pointing the way. ⊠ *Copper Mine Rd.* ☎ *No phone* ✆ *Free.*

Spanish Town. Virgin Gorda's peaceful main settlement, on the island's southern wing, is so tiny that it barely qualifies as a town at all. Also known as the Valley, Spanish Town has a marina, some shops, and a couple of car-rental agencies. Just north of town is the ferry slip. At the Virgin Gorda Yacht Harbour you can stroll along the dock and do a little shopping.

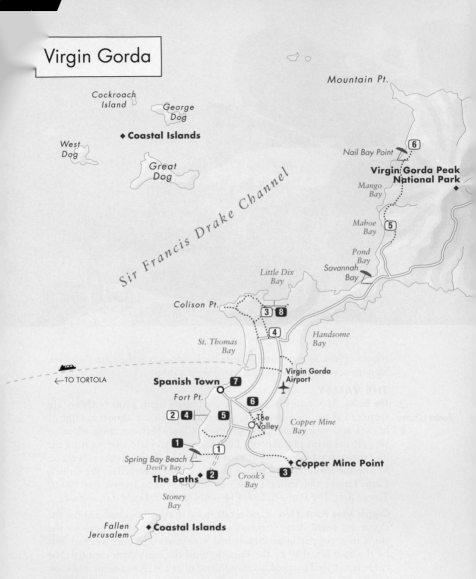

Virgin Gorda

Cockroach Island

George Dog

◆ **Coastal Islands**

West Dog

Great Dog

Mountain Pt.

Nail Bay Point　⑥

Virgin Gorda Peak National Park ◆

Mango Bay

Mahoe Bay　⑤

Sir Francis Drake Channel

Little Dix Bay

Pond Bay

Savannah Bay

Handsome Bay

Colison Pt.　③ ⑧

④

St. Thomas Bay

← TO TORTOLA

Spanish Town ❼

Fort Pt.

Virgin Gorda Airport

Copper Mine Bay

② ④　❺

The Valley

❶

Spring Bay Beach
Devil's Bay

❶

The Baths ◆　❷

◆ **Copper Mine Point**
③

Crook's Bay

Stoney Bay

Fallen Jerusalem　◆ **Coastal Islands**

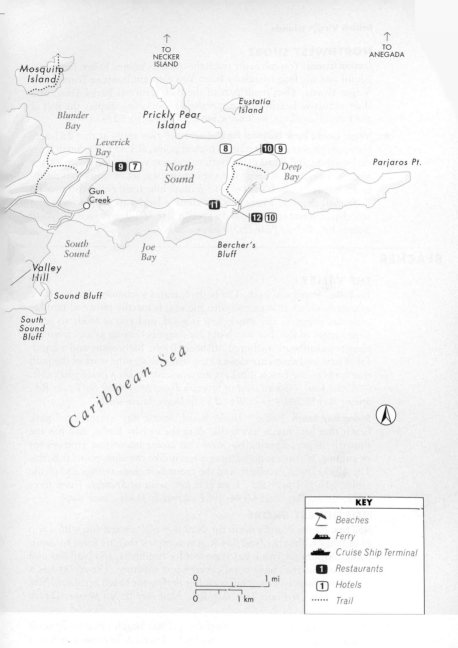

↑
TO
NECKER
ISLAND

↑
TO
ANEGADA

Mosquito
Island

Blunder
Bay

Prickly Pear
Island

Eustatia
Island

Leverick
Bay

North
Sound

Deep
Bay

Parjaros Pt.

9 7

8   **10 9**

Gun
Creek

11

12 10

South
Sound

Joe
Bay

Bercher's
Bluff

Valley
Hill

Sound Bluff

South
Sound
Bluff

Caribbean Sea

KEY

⛱ *Beaches*

🛳 *Ferry*

🚢 *Cruise Ship Terminal*

1 *Restaurants*

[1] *Hotels*

····· *Trail*

0 ——————— 1 mi

0 ——————— 1 km

NORTHWEST SHORE

Coastal Islands. You can easily reach the quaintly named Fallen Jerusalem Island and the Dog Islands by boat. You can rent boats in Tortola and Virgin Gorda. They're all part of the BVI National Parks Trust, and their seductive beaches and unparalleled snorkeling display the BVI at their beachcombing, hedonistic best. ☎ *No phone* 🖾 *Free.*

★ **Virgin Gorda Peak National Park.** There are two trails at this 265-acre park, which contains the island's highest point, at 1,359 feet. Small signs on North Sound Road mark both entrances; sometimes, however, the signs are missing, so keep your eyes open for a set of stairs that disappears into the trees. It's about a 15-minute hike from either entrance up to a small clearing, where you can climb a ladder to the platform of a wooden observation tower and a spectacular 360-degree view. ⊠ *North Sound Rd., Gorda Peak* ☎ *No phone* 🖾 *Free.*

BEACHES

THE VALLEY

The Baths. A national park, The Baths features a stunning maze of huge granite boulders that extend into the sea, is usually crowded midday with day-trippers. The snorkeling is good, and you're likely to see a wide variety of fish, but watch out for dinghies coming ashore from the numerous sailboats anchored offshore. Public bathrooms and a handful of bars and shops are close to the water and at the start of the path that leads to the beach. Lockers are available to keep belongings safe. ⊠ *About 1 mi [1½ km] west of Spanish Town ferry dock on Tower Rd., Spring Bay* ☎ *284/494–3904* 🖾 *$3* ☉ *Daily dawn–dusk.*

Spring Bay Beach. Just off Tower Road, Spring Bay is a national-park beach that gets much less traffic than the nearby Baths, and has the similarly large, imposing boulders that create interesting grottoes for swimming. It also has no admission fee, unlike the more popular Baths. The snorkeling is excellent, and the grounds include swings and picnic tables. ⊠ *Off Tower Rd., 1 mi [1½ km] west of Spanish Town ferry dock, Spring Bay* ☎ *284/494–3904* 🖾 *Free* ☉ *Daily dawn–dusk.*

NORTHWEST SHORE

Nail Bay. At the island's north tip, Nail Bay will reward you with a trio of beaches within the Nail Bay Resort complex that are ideal for snorkeling. Mountain Trunk Bay is perfect for beginners, and Nail Bay and Long Bay beaches have coral caverns just offshore. The resort has a restaurant, which is an uphill walk but perfect for beach breaks. ⊠ *Nail Bay Resort, off Plum Tree Bay Rd., Nail Bay* ☎ *No phone* 🖾 *Free* ☉ *Daily dawn–dusk.*

★ **Savannah Bay.** This is a wonderfully private beach close to Spanish Town. It may not always be completely deserted, but you can find a spot to yourself on this long stretch of soft, white sand. Bring your own mask, fins, and snorkel, as there are no facilities. The view from above is a photographer's delight. ⊠ *Off N. Sound Rd., ¾ mi [1¼ km] east of Spanish Town ferry dock, Savannah Bay* ☎ *No phone* 🖾 *Free* ☉ *Daily dawn–dusk.*

WHERE TO EAT

Dining out on Virgin Gorda is a mixed bag, with everything from hamburgers to lobster available. Most folks opt to have dinner at or near their hotel to avoid driving on Virgin Gorda's twisting roads at night. The Valley does have a handful of restaurants if you're sleeping close to town.

THE VALLEY

$$ — **AMERICAN** ✕ **Bath and Turtle.** You can sit back and relax at this informal tavern with a friendly staff—although the noise from the television can sometimes be a bit much. Well-stuffed sandwiches, homemade pizzas, pasta dishes, and daily specials such as conch soup round out the casual menu. Local musicians perform Wednesday and Sunday nights. ⊠ *Virgin Gorda Yacht Harbour, Spanish Town* ☎ *284/495–5239* ⊕ *www. bathandturtle.com.*

$$$ — **CARIBBEAN** ✕ **Chez Bamboo.** This pleasant little hideaway isn't difficult to find; look for the building with the purple-and-green latticework. Candles in the dining room and on the patio help make this a mellow place where you can enjoy a bowl of conch gumbo, something from the tapas menu, or one of the specialties such as lobster curry. For dessert, try the chocolate cake or crème brûlée. Stop by Friday night for live music. ⊠ *Across from and a little north of Virgin Gorda Yacht Harbour, Spanish Town* ☎ *284/495–5752* ⊕ *www.chezbamboo.com* ☾ *No lunch.*

$$$ — **AMERICAN** ✕ **Fischer's Cove Restaurant.** Dine seaside at this alfresco restaurant that is open to the breezes. If pumpkin soup is on the menu, give it a try for a true taste of the Caribbean. Although you can get burgers and salads at lunch, local fish (whatever is available) and a cornmeal-based fungi is a tasty alternative. For dinner, try the Caribbean lobster or grilled mahimahi with lemon and garlic. ⊠ *Lee Rd., The Valley* ☎ *284/495–5252.*

$$$$ — **CONTINENTAL** ✕ **Little Dix Bay Pavilion.** For an elegant evening, you can't do better than this—the candlelight in the open-air pavilion is enchanting, the always-changing menu sophisticated, the service attentive. Superbly prepared seafood, meat, and vegetarian entrées draw locals and visitors alike. Favorites include a Cajun pork loin with mango salsa and scallion potatoes, and mahimahi with warm chorizo and chickpea salad served with a zucchini and tomato chutney. The Monday evening buffet shines. ⊠ *Little Dix Bay Resort, Spanish Town* ☎ *284/495–5555* ☖ *Reservations essential.*

$$$ — **AMERICAN** ✕ **LSL Restaurant.** An unpretentious place along the road to The Baths, this small restaurant with pedestrian decor still manages to be a local favorite. You can always find fresh fish on the menu, but folks with a taste for other dishes won't be disappointed. Try the veal with mushrooms and herbs in a white-wine sauce or the breast of chicken with rum cream and nuts. ⊠ *Tower Rd., The Valley* ☎ *284/495–5151.*

$$$ — **AMERICAN** ✕ **Mine Shaft Café.** Perched on a hilltop that offers a view of spectacular sunsets, this restaurant near Copper Mine Point serves simple yet well-prepared food, including grilled fish, steaks, and baby back ribs. Tuesday night features an all-you-can-eat Caribbean-style barbecue. The monthly

7

full-moon parties draw a big local crowd. ⊠ *Copper Mine Point, The Valley* ☎ *284/495–5260.*

$$$ ITALIAN ✕ **The Rock Café.** Surprisingly good Italian cuisine is served among the waterfalls and giant boulders that form the famous Baths. For dinner at this open-air eatery, feast on chicken and penne in a tomato-cream sauce, spaghetti with lobster sauce, or fresh red snapper in a butter-and-caper sauce. For dessert, don't miss the chocolate mousse. ⊠ *The Valley* ☎ *284/495–5482* ⊕ *www.bvidining.com* ☉ *No lunch.*

$$$ AMERICAN ☾ ✕ **Top of the Baths.** At the entrance to The Baths, this popular restaurant starts serving at 8 am. Tables are on an outdoor terrace or in an open-air pavilion; all have stunning views of the Sir Francis Drake Channel. Hamburgers, coconut chicken sandwiches, and fish-and-chips are among the offerings at lunch. For dessert, the key lime pie is excellent. The Sunday barbecue, served from noon until 3 pm, is an island event. ⊠ *The Valley* ☎ *284/495–5497* ⊕ *www.topofthebaths.com* ☉ *No dinner.*

NORTH SOUND

$$$$ CONTINENTAL ✕ **Biras Creek Restaurant.** This hilltop restaurant at the Biras Creek Hotel has eye-popping views of North Sound. The four-course prix-fixe menu changes daily and includes several choices per course. For starters, there may be an artichoke, green bean, and wild mushroom salad topped with balsamic vinaigrette, or cream of sweet potato soup accompanied by potato straws. Entrées may include pan-seared snapper over horseradish pearl pasta. The desserts, including a lemon ricotta cheesecake with a spicy passion-fruit sauce, are to die for. Dinner ends with Biras Creek's signature offering of cheese and port. ⊠ *Biras Creek Hotel, North Sound* ☎ *284/494–3555 or 800/223–1108* ⚑ *Reservations essential.*

$$$ SEAFOOD ★ ✕ **The Clubhouse.** The Bitter End Yacht Club's open-air waterfront restaurant is a favorite rendezvous for the sailing set, so it's busy day and night. You can find lavish buffets for breakfast, lunch, and dinner, as well as an à la carte menu. Dinner selections include grilled mahimahi or tuna, local lobster, and porterhouse steak, as well as vegetarian dishes. ⊠ *Bitter End Yacht Club, North Sound* ☎ *284/494–2745* ⊕ *www.beyc. com* ⚑ *Reservations essential.*

$$$ AMERICAN ☾ ✕ **Fat Virgin's Café.** This casual beachfront eatery offers a straightforward menu of baby back ribs, chicken roti, vegetable pasta, grouper sandwiches, and fresh fish specials for lunch and dinner. You can find a good selection of Caribbean beer. ⊠ *Biras Creek Resort, North Sound* ☎ *284/495–7052.*

$$$$ AMERICAN ✕ **Restaurant at Leverick Bay.** Offering casual meals at the beach, this restaurant draws cruise ship passengers on tour as well as hotels guests and locals. The menu includes burgers, pizza, roti, chili, and fish-and-chips for lunch. At dinner, the menu includes everything from wild salmon to Kobe beef. ⊠ *Leverick Bay Resort & Marina, Leverick Bay* ☎ *284/495–7154.*

WHERE TO STAY

Whereas villas are scattered all over Virgin Gorda, hotels are centered in and around the Valley, Nail Bay, and in the North Sound area. Except for Leverick Bay Resort, which is around the point from North Sound, all hotels in North Sound are reached only by ferry.

PRIVATE VILLAS

Those craving seclusion would do well at a villa. Most have full kitchens and maid service. Prices per week in winter run from around $2,000 for a one- or two-bedroom villa up to $10,000 for a five-room beachfront villa. Rates in summer are substantially less. On Virgin Gorda a villa in the North Sound area means you can pretty much stay put at night unless you want to make the drive on narrow roads. If you opt for a spot near The Baths, it's an easier drive to town.

The St. Thomas–based **McLaughlin-Anderson Luxury Villas** (⊠ *1000 Blackbeard's Hill, Suite 3, Charlotte Amalie, U.S. Virgin Islands* ☎ *340/776–0635 or 800/537–6246* ⊕ *www.mclaughlinanderson.com*) represents about 18 properties all over Virgin Gorda. Villas range in size from two bedrooms to six bedrooms, and come with many amenities, including full kitchens, pools, and stellar views. The company can hire a chef and stock your kitchen with groceries. A seven-night minimum is required during the winter season.

Tropical Care Services (⊕ *Box 1039, The Valley VG1150* ☎ *284/495–6493* ⊕ *www.tropicalcareservices.com*) manages about a dozen properties stretching from The Baths to the Nail Bay area. Several budget properties are included among the pricier offerings. Most houses have private pools, and a few are right on the beach. A sister company at the same number, Tropical Nannies, provides babysitting services.

Virgin Gorda Villa Rentals (⊕ *Box 63, The Valley VG1150* ☎ *284/495–7421 or 800/848–7081* ⊕ *www.virgingordabvi.com*) manages more than 40 properties near Leverick Bay Resort and Mahoe Bay, so it's perfect for those who want to be close to activities. Many of the accommodations—from studios to six or more bedrooms—have private swimming pools and air-conditioning, at least in the bedrooms. All have full kitchens, are well maintained, and have spectacular views.

The following reviews have been condensed for this book. Please go to Fodors.com for expanded reviews of each property.

THE VALLEY

$–$$
HOTEL
☺
Fischer's Cove Beach Hotel. The rooms are modest, the furniture is discount-store-style, and the walls are thin, but you can't beat the location right on the beach and within walking distance of Spanish Town's shops and restaurants. **Pros:** beachfront location; budget price; good restaurant. **Cons:** very basic units; thin walls; no a/c in some rooms.

VIRGIN GORDA GROCERIES

Virgin Gorda's grocery stores barely equal convenience stores elsewhere. The selection is small and the prices are high. Many Virgin Gorda residents head to Tortola or even to St. Thomas to do their shopping. If you're coming here from another island, you might want to bring along one or two items you know you'll need.

7

✉ *Lee Rd.* ⌂ *Box 60, The Valley VG1150* ☎ *284/495–5252* ⊕ *www. fischerscove.com* ⟿ *12 rooms, 8 cottages* ⚬ *In-room: a/c (some), no safe, kitchen (some), no TV (some), Wi-Fi. In-hotel: restaurant, beach* ❖*No meals.*

$–$$
RENTAL
★
⊞**Guavaberry Spring Bay Vacation Homes.** Rambling back from the beach, these hexagonal one- and two-bedroom villas give you all the comforts of home with the striking boulder-fringed beach just minutes away. **Pros:** short walk to The Baths; easy drive to town; great beaches nearby. **Cons:** few amenities; older property; basic decor. ✉ *Tower Rd.* ⌂ *Box 20, The Valley* ☎ *284/495–5227* ⊕ *www.guavaberryspringbay. com* ⟿ *12 1-bedroom units, 6 2-bedroom units, 1 3-bedroom unit, 16 villas* ⚬ *In-room: a/c (some), no safe, kitchen, no TV (some). In-hotel: beach, business center* ⊟ *No credit cards* ❖*No meals.*

$$$$
RESORT
☻
★
⊞**Rosewood Little Dix Bay.** This laid-back luxury resort offers a gorgeous crescent of sand, plenty of activities, and good restaurants. **Pros:** convenient location; lovely grounds; near many dining options. **Cons:** expensive rates; very spread out; insular though not isolated. ⌂ *Box 70, Little Dix Bay off North Sound Rd. VG1150* ☎ *284/495–5555* ⊕ *www. littledixbay.com* ⟿ *73 rooms, 20 suites, 7 villas* ⚬ *In-room: a/c, no TV, Wi-Fi (some). In-hotel: restaurants, bars, tennis courts, pool, gym, spa, beach, water sports, children's programs, business center* ❖*No meals.*

$–$$
RENTAL
⊞**Virgin Gorda Village.** All the condos in this upscale complex a few minutes' drive from Spanish Town have at least partial ocean views. **Pros:** close to Spanish Town; lovely pool; recently built units. **Cons:** no beach; on a busy street; noisy roosters nearby. ✉ *North Sound Rd.* ⌂ *Box 26, The Valley VG1150* ☎ *284/495–5544 or 800/653–9273* ⊕ *www.virgingordavillage.com* ⟿ *30 condos* ⚬ *In-room: a/c, no safe, kitchen, Wi-Fi. In-hotel: restaurant, bar, tennis courts, pool, gym, spa* ❖*No meals.*

NORTHWEST SHORE

$$–$$$$
RENTAL
⊞**Mango Bay Resort.** Sitting seaside on Virgin Gorda's north coast, this collection of contemporary condos and villas will make you feel right at home. **Pros:** nice beach; lively location; good restaurant; small grocery store. **Cons:** construction in area; drab decor; some units have lackluster views. ✉ *Off Nail Bay Rd.* ⌂ *Box 1062, Mahoe Bay VG1150* ☎ *284/495–5672* ⊕ *www.mangobayresort.com* ⟿ *17 condos, 5 villas* ⚬ *In-room: a/c, no safe, kitchen, Wi-Fi (some). In-hotel: beach* ❖*No meals.*

$$–$$$
RESORT
★
⊞**Nail Bay Resort.** Rambling up the hill above the coast, this beachfront resort offers a wide selection of rooms and suites to fit every need. **Pros:** full kitchens; lovely beach; close to town. **Cons:** busy neighborhood; bit of a drive from main road; uphill walk from beach. ✉ *Off Nail Bay Rd.* ⌂ *Box 69, Nail Bay VG1150* ☎ *284/494–8000 or 800/871–3551* ⊕ *www.nailbay.com* ⟿ *4 rooms, 4 suites, 9 villas* ⚬ *In-room: a/c, kitchen (some). In-hotel: restaurant, bar, tennis court, pool, spa, beach, water sports, business center* ❖*No meals.*

NORTH SOUND

$$$$
RESORT
★

Biras Creek Resort. Although Biras Creek is tucked out of the way on the island's North Sound, the get-away-from-it-all feel is actually the major draw for its well-heeled clientele. **Pros:** luxurious rooms; professional staff; good dining options. **Cons:** expensive rates; isolated location; difficult for people with mobility problems. ✑ *Box 54, North Sound VG1150* ☎ *284/494–3555 or 877/883–0756* ⊕ *www.biras.com* ⤳ *31 suites* ⚄ *In-room: a/c, no TV (some), Wi-Fi. In-hotel: restaurants, bar, tennis courts, pool, spa, beach, water sports, business center* ⥷ *All meals.*

$$$$
ALL-INCLUSIVE
☺
Fodor's Choice
★

Bitter End Yacht Club. Sailing's the thing at this busy hotel and marina in the nautically inclined North Sound, and the use of everything from small sailboats to kayaks to windsurfers is included in the price. **Pros:** lots of water sports; good diving opportunities; friendly guests. **Cons:** expensive rates; isolated location; lots of stairs. ✑ *Box 46, Beef Island, Tortola VG1150* ☎ *284/494–2746 or 800/872–2392* ⊕ *www.beyc.com* ⤳ *85 rooms* ⚄ *In-room: a/c (some), no safe, no TV. In-hotel: restaurants, bar, pool, beach, water sports, children's programs, business center* ⥷ *All-inclusive.*

¢
RESORT

Leverick Bay Resort and Marina. With its colorful buildings and bustling marina, Leverick Bay is a good choice for visitors who want easy access to water-sports activities. **Pros:** lively location; good restaurant; small grocery store. **Cons:** small beach; no laundry in units; 15-minute drive to town. ⊠ *Off Leverick Bay Rd.* ✑ *Box 63, Leverick Bay VG1150* ☎ *284/495–7421 or 800/848–7081* ⊕ *www.leverickbay.com* ⤳ *13 rooms, 4 apartments* ⚄ *In-room: a/c, kitchen (some), Wi-Fi. In-hotel: restaurants, bar, tennis court, pool, spa, beach, laundry facilities, business center* ⥷ *No meals.*

$
RESORT

Saba Rock Resort. Reachable only by a free ferry or by private yacht, this resort on its own tiny cay is perfect for folks who want to mix and mingle with the sailors who drop anchor for the night. **Pros:** party atmosphere; convenient transportation; good diving nearby. **Cons:** tiny beach; isolated location; on a very small island. ✑ *Box 67, North Sound VG1150* ☎ *284/495–7711 or 284/495–9966* ⊕ *www.sabarock. com* ⤳ *7 1-bedroom suites, 1 2-bedroom suites* ⚄ *In-room: a/c, no safe, kitchen (some), Wi-Fi. In-hotel: restaurant, bar, beach, water sports* ⥷ *Breakfast.*

NIGHTLIFE

Pick up a free copy of the *Limin' Times*—available at most resorts and restaurants—for the most current local entertainment schedule.

Bath and Turtle. During high season, the Bath and Turtle is one of the liveliest spots on Virgin Gorda, hosting island bands Wednesday from 8 pm until midnight. ⊠ *Virgin Gorda Yacht Harbour, Spanish Town* ☎ *284/495–5239.*

Chez Bamboo. This is the place for calypso and reggae on Friday night. ⊠ *Across from Virgin Gorda Yacht Harbour, Spanish Town* ☎ *284/ 495–5752.*

Mine Shaft Café. The cafe has music on Tuesday and Friday. ⊠ *Copper Mine Point, The Valley* ☎ *284/495–5260.*

Restaurant at Leverick Bay. This resort's main restaurant hosts live music on Tuesday and Friday in season. ⊠ *Leverick Bay Resort & Marina, Leverick Bay* ☎ *284/495–7154.*

Rock Café. Rock Cafe has live bands nearly every night during the winter season. ⊠ *The Valley* ☎ *284/495–5177.*

SHOPPING

Most boutiques are within hotel complexes or at Virgin Gorda Yacht Harbour. Two of the best are at Biras Creek and Little Dix Bay. Other properties—the Bitter End and Leverick Bay—have small but equally select boutiques.

FOOD

Bitter End Emporium. This store at the Bitter End is the place for such edible treats as local fruits, cheeses, baked goods, and gourmet prepared food to take out. ⊠ *Bitter End Yacht Harbor, North Sound* ☎ *284/494–2746.*

Buck's Food Market. This market is the closest the island offers to a full-service supermarket and has everything from an in-store bakery and deli to fresh fish and produce departments. ⊠ *Virgin Gorda Yacht Harbour, Spanish Town* ☎ *284/495–5423* ⊠ *Gun Creek, North Sound* ☎ *284/495–7368*

Chef's Pantry. This store has the fixings for an impromptu party in your villa or on your boat—fresh seafood, specialty meats, imported cheeses, daily baked breads and pastries, and an impressive wine and spirit selection. ⊠ *Leverick Bay* ☎ *284/495–7677.*

Wine Cellar and Bakery. This bakery and liquor store sells bread, rolls, muffins, cookies, sandwiches, and sodas to go. ⊠ *Virgin Gorda Yacht Harbour, Spanish Town* ☎ *284/495–5250.*

GIFTS

Reeftique. This store carries island crafts and jewelry, clothing, and nautical odds and ends with the Bitter End logo. ⊠ *Bitter End Yacht Harbor, North Sound* ☎ *284/494–2746.*

Thee Nautical Gallery. This boutique sells attractive handcrafted jewelry, paintings, and one-of-a-kind gift items, as well as books about the Caribbean. ⊠ *Leverick Bay* ☎ *284/495–7479.*

SPORTS AND ACTIVITIES

DIVING AND SNORKELING

Where you go snorkeling and what company you pick depends on where you're staying. Many hotels have on-site dive outfitters, but if they don't, one won't be far away. If your hotel does have a dive operation, just stroll down to the dock and hop aboard—no need to drive anywhere. The dive companies are all certified by PADI. Costs vary, but count on paying about $75 for a one-tank dive and $110 for a two-tank dive. All dive operators offer introductory courses as well as certification and advanced courses. Should you get an attack of the bends, which

You can learn to sail at the Bitter End Yacht Club.

can happen when you ascend too rapidly, the nearest decompression chamber is at Roy L. Schneider Regional Medical Center in St. Thomas.

There are some terrific snorkel and dive sites off Virgin Gorda, including areas around The Baths, the North Sound, and the Dogs. The Chimney at Great Dog Island has a coral archway and canyon covered with a wide variety of sponges. At Joe's Cave, an underwater cavern on West Dog Island, huge groupers, eagle rays, and other colorful fish accompany divers as they swim. At some sites you can see 100 feet down, but divers who don't want to go that deep and snorkelers will find plenty to look at just below the surface.

The **Bitter End Yacht Club** (⊠ *North Sound* ☎ *284/494–2746* ⊕ *www.beyc. com*) offers two snorkeling trips a day.

Dive BVI (⊠ *Virgin Gorda Yacht Harbour, Spanish Town* ☎ *284/495– 5513 or 800/848–7078* ⊠ *Leverick Bay Resort and Marina, Leverick Bay* ☎ *284/495–7328* ⊕ *www.divebvi.com*) offers expert instruction, certification, and day trips.

Sunchaser Scuba (⊠ *Bitter End Yacht Club, North Sound* ☎ *284/495– 9638 or 800/932–4286* ⊕ *www.sunchaserscuba.com*) offers resort, advanced, and rescue courses.

MINIATURE GOLF

The 9-hole mini-golf course **Golf Virgin Gorda** (⊠ *Copper Mine Point, The Valley* ☎ *284/495–5260*) is next to the Mine Shaft Café, delightfully nestled between huge granite boulders.

SAILING AND BOATING

The BVI waters are calm, and terrific places to learn to sail. You can also rent sea kayaks, waterskiing equipment, dinghies, and powerboats, or take a parasailing trip.

ॐ **Bitter End Sailing and Kiteboarding School** (⊠ *Bitter End Yacht Club, North Sound* ☎ *284/494–2746* ⊕ *www.beyc.com*) offers classroom, dockside, and on-the-water lessons for sailors of all levels. Private lessons are $75 per hour.

If you just want to sit back, relax, and let the captain take the helm, choose a sailing or power yacht from **Double "D" Charters** (⊠ *Virgin Gorda Yacht Harbour, Spanish Town* ☎ *284/499–2479* ⊕ *www. doubledbvi.com*). Rates are $65 for a half-day trip and $110 for a full-day island-hopping excursion. Private full-day cruises or sails for up to eight people run $950.

If you'd rather rent a Sunfish or Hobie Wave, check out **Leverick Bay Watersports** (⊠ *Leverick Bay, North Sound* ☎ *284/495–7376* ⊕ *www. watersportsbvi.com*).

WINDSURFING

ॐ The North Sound is a good place to learn to windsurf: it's protected, so you can't be easily blown out to sea. The **Bitter End Yacht Club** (⊠ *North Sound* ☎ *284/494–2746* ⊕ *www.beyc.com*) gives lessons and rents equipment for $60 per hour for nonguests. A half-day windsurfer rental runs $80 to $100.

JOST VAN DYKE

Updated by Susanna Henighan Potter

Named after an early Dutch settler, Jost Van Dyke is a small island northwest of Tortola and is *truly* a place to get away from it all. Mountainous and lush, the 4-mi-long (6½-km-long) island—with fewer than 200 full-time residents—has one tiny resort, some rental houses and villas, a campground, a few shops, a handful of cars, and a single road. There are no banks or ATMs on the island, and many restaurants and shops accept only cash. It's a good idea to buy groceries on St. Thomas or Tortola before arriving if you're staying for a few days. Life definitely rolls along on "island time," especially during the off-season from August to November, when finding a restaurant open for dinner can be a challenge. Water conservation is encouraged, as the source is rainwater collected in basementlike cisterns. Many lodgings will ask you to follow the Caribbean golden rule: "In the land of sun and fun, we never flush for number one." Jost is one of the Caribbean's most popular anchorages, and there are a disproportionately large number of informal bars and restaurants, which have helped earn Jost its reputation as the "party island" of the BVI.

BEACHES

Sandy Cay. Just offshore, the little islet known as Sandy Cay is a gleaming scimitar of white sand, with marvelous snorkeling and an inland nature trail.

Boaters docking at Jost Van Dyke.

⚓ **White Bay.** On the south shore, west of Great Harbour, this long stretch
★ of picturesque white sand is especially popular with boaters who come
ashore for a libation at one of the beach bars.

WHERE TO EAT

Restaurants on Jost Van Dyke are informal (some serve meals family-
style at long tables) but charming. The island is a favorite charter-boat
stop, and you're bound to hear people exchanging stories about the
previous night's anchoring adventures. Most restaurants don't take reservations (but for those that do, they are usually a requirement), and
in all cases dress is casual.

$$$ ✕ **Abe's by the Sea.** Many sailors who cruise into this quiet bay come so
ECLECTIC they can dock right at this open-air eatery to enjoy the seafood, conch,
lobster, and other fresh catches. Chicken, ribs, and a Wednesday night
pig roast (in season) round out the menu, and affable owners Abe Coak-
ley and his wife, Eunicy, add a pinch and dash of hospitality that makes
a meal into a memorable evening. Casual lunches are also served, and an
adjoining market sells ice, canned goods, and other necessities. Dinner
reservations are required by 5 pm. ✉ *Little Harbour* ☎ *284/495–9329*
🍽 *Reservations essential.*

$$$ ✕ **Ali Baba's.** Lobster is the main attraction at this beach bar with a
SEAFOOD sandy floor, which is just some 20 feet from the sea. Grilled local fish,
⚓ including swordfish, kingfish, and wahoo, are specialties and caught
★ fresh daily. There's also a pig roast here on Monday night in season
and Friday night is roti night. Beware: Ali Baba's special rum punch is

delicious but potent. Dinner reservations are required by 5 pm. ⊠ *Great Harbour* ☎ *284/495–9280* ⌕ *Reservations essential.*

$$$
ECLECTIC
☯

✕**Corsairs Beach Bar and Restaurant.** On an island known for seafood, it's the pizza that draws raves at this friendly beach bar considered by some to be the "Cheers" of Jost. If pizza doesn't appeal, then choose from the reliably good, eclectic menu featuring Italian, Tex-Mex, Caribbean, and English specialties plus the island's only Thai-style lobster. Bring an appetite to breakfast, when the choices include hearty omelets and breakfast burritos. The bar is easily recognized by its signature pirate paraphernalia and a restored U.S. Army Jeep parked next to the steps-from-the-sea dining room. Live music, potent libations, and the only Jagermeister machine in the territory (it chills your shots to 28°F) keep things moving from happy hour into the night. Even if you're not hungry, this is a great hangout. ⊠ *Great Harbour* ☎ *284/495–9294* ⊕ *www.corsairsbvi.com.*

$$$$
ECLECTIC
☯

✕**Foxy's Taboo.** It's well worth the winding hilly drive or sometimes-rough sail to get to Taboo, an eatery with a sophisticated menu and a welcoming attitude. Located on Jost's mostly undeveloped East End, Taboo is less of a party bar than Foxy's in Great Harbour. At dinner you'll find specialties like wild boar, mango-tamarind chicken, and pizzas topped with everything from jalapeño peppers to prosciutto and kalamata olives. There are a dozen or more wines available by the bottle or glass, and don't miss the tiramisu for dessert. At lunchtime, even the burgers are a step up from average, and the salads are the best on the island. Coupled with a walk to the nearby Bubbly Pool (ask for a map at the bar), a visit to Taboo is a good way to while away a few hours. Dinner reservations are required by 4 pm. ⊠ *East End* ☎ *284/495–0218* ⊕ *www.foxysbar. com* ⌕ *Reservations essential* ⊗ *Closed Mon. No dinner Sun.*

$$$
ECLECTIC
☯
★

✕**Foxy's Tamarind Bar and Restaurant.** The big draw here is the owner, Foxy Callwood, a calypsonian of fame who will serenade you with lewd and laughable lyrics as you fork into burgers, grilled chicken, barbecue ribs, and lobster. Check out the pennants, postcards and weathered T-shirts that adorn every inch of the walls and ceiling of this large, two-story beach shack; they've been left by previous visitors. On Friday and Saturday nights in season Foxy hosts an all-you-can-eat Caribbean-style barbeque with grilled fresh fish, chicken and ribs, peas and rice, salad and more, followed by live music. Other nights choose from steak, fresh lobster, pork, or pasta; at lunch Foxy serves sandwiches and salads. Whether because of the sheer volume of diners or the experience of the management, Foxy's is one of the most reliable eating establishments on Jost. And, for those who care, it is also home to the only espresso on the island. You're unlikely to find Foxy performing at night, but he takes the mike many afternoons, making this a popular happy hour pit stop. ⊠ *Great Harbour* ☎ *284/495–9258* ⊕ *www.foxysbar.com.*

$$
ECLECTIC
☯
★

✕**Harris' Place.** All-you-can-eat lobster in a garlic butter sauce on Monday; freshly caught seafood on Thursday; pork, chicken, and ribs on Saturday: three good reasons to make your reservations early in the day at this quaint restaurant with the distinctive red roof and picnic tables underneath. Owner Cynthia Harris is as famous for her friendliness as she is for her food. Homemade key lime pie and expertly blended bushwackers are "to live for," as Cynthia would say, but diners also praise the fresh fish and lobster. Live music on Monday and Saturday evenings turns dinner into a party. Breakfast and lunch are served, too. ⊠ *Little Harbour* 🕾 *284/495–9302.*

$$
ECLECTIC
☺
★

✕ **One Love Bar and Grill.** It's a toss-up whether Seddy Callwood's magic tricks or the finger-lickin' ribs and johnnycakes he serves are a greater draw. The Food Network's Alton Brown sought out this beachfront eatery and featured its stewed conch on a 2008 flavor-finding trip. Try that, or one of the signature lobster quesadillas or fresh garden salads. Seddy, Foxy Callwood's son, built his bar himself and decorated it with the flotsam and jetsam he has collected over years as a fisherman. Children's toys in the corner and outside that mark this as a family-friendly place. There's live music on Thursday through Sunday afternoons in season, and Rueben Chinnery plays guitar on Saturday nights. ⊠ *White Bay* 🕾 *284/495–9829* ⊕ *www.onelovebar.com.*

$$$$
ECLECTIC

✕ **Soggy Dollar Bar.** Candles illuminate this tiny beachfront, palm-lined dining room during the evening meal, making it one of the most romantic settings on the island. Each night the chef prepares a meat, chicken, and fish entrée with a choice of side dishes, appetizers, and desserts for a fixed price. The cuisine is familiar yet sophisticated—including choices like sweet and sour glazed pork, pan-fried snapper, and coq aux vin. Don't miss the Painkiller ice cream, inspired by the Painkiller cocktail created here. Recently management has relaxed its reservations-only policy for dinner, but it is still wise to call ahead. For lunch, if you can find your way through the throngs ordering Painkillers at the bar, choose from flying-fish sandwiches, hamburgers, chicken roti, and conch fritters at the Soggy Dollar. ⊠ *Sandcastle, White Bay* 🕾 *284/495–9888* ⊕ *www.soggydollar.com.*

$$$
ECLECTIC

✕ **Sydney's Peace and Love.** Here you can find great local lobster and fish, as well as barbecue chicken and ribs with all the fixings, including peas and rice, corn, coleslaw, and potato salad. All are served on an open-air terrace or in an air-conditioned dining room at the water's edge. The find here is a sensational (by BVI standards) jukebox. The cognoscenti sail here for dinner, since there's no beach—meaning no irksome sand fleas. Breakfast and lunch are served, too. Sadly, Sydney Hendrick died in 2010, but his wife and children are carrying on. ⊠ *Little Harbour* 🕾 *284/495–9271.*

WHERE TO STAY

The following reviews have been condensed for this book. Please go to Fodors.com for expanded reviews of each property.

$–$$
HOTEL

🏠 **Sandcastle.** Sleep steps from beautiful White Bay beach at this tiny beachfront hideaway, an island favorite for more than 40 years. **Pros:** beachfront rooms; near restaurants and bars; comfy hammocks. **Cons:** some rooms lack air-conditioning; beach sometimes clogged with day-trippers; no children allowed. ⊠ *White Bay* 🕾 *284/495–9888* ⊕ *www. soggydollar.com* ⇄ *2 rooms, 4 1-bedroom cottages* ⚒ *In-room: a/c (some), no safe, no TV. In-hotel: restaurant, bar, beach, some age restrictions* ⎇ *No meals.*

7

$–$$ ⌨ **White Bay Villas and Seaside Cottages.** Beautiful views and friendly
RENTAL   staff keep guests coming back to these hilltop one- to three-bedroom
☺   air-conditioned villas and cottages. **Pros:** incredible views; full kitchens;
★   friendly staff. **Cons:** 10- to 15-minute walk to White Bay and Great
Harbour's restaurants and beaches; rental cars recommended. ✉ *White
Bay* 🖂 *Box 3368, Annapolis, MD 21403* ☎ *410/571–6692 or 800/778–
8066* ⊕ *www.jostvandyke.com* ➷*7 villas, 3 cottages* ⚒ *In-room: a/c,
no safe, kitchen, Wi-Fi. In-hotel: beach (some).*

NIGHTLIFE

★   Jost Van Dyke is the most happening place to go barhopping in the BVI,
so much so that it is an all-day enterprise for some. In fact, yachties
will sail over just to have a few drinks. All the spots are easy to find,
clustered in three general locations: Great Harbour, White Bay, and
Little Harbour (⇨ *see Where to Eat, above*). On the Great Harbour
side you can find Foxy's, Corsairs, and Ali Baba's; on the White Bay
side are the One Love Bar and Grill and the Soggy Dollar Bar, where
legend has it the famous Painkiller was first concocted; and in Little
Harbour are Harris' Place, Sydney's Peace and Love, and Abe's By The
Sea. If you can't make it to Jost Van Dyke, you can have a Painkiller at
almost any bar in the BVI.

SPORTS AND ACTIVITIES

Abe and Eunicy Rentals (✉ *Little Harbour* ☎ *284/495–9329*) offers three
types of vehicles—two-door Suzukis ($65 a day), four-door auto-
matic Jeeps ($75 a day), and four-door automatic Monteros ($85 a
day)—that will allow you to explore by land, or a fiberglass dinghy
with a 15-horsepower engine ($60 a day) or inflatable dinghy with a
25-horsepower engine, radio, and CD player ($100 a day) for travel-
ing around by sea. There's pickup and drop-off service from anywhere
on the island.

JVD Scuba and BVI Eco-Tours (✉ *Great Harbour* ☎ *284/495–0271* ⊕ *www.
bvi-ecotours.com*) lets you see the undersea world around the island
with a dive master Colin Aldridge. One of the most impressive dives in
the area is off the north coast of Little Jost Van Dyke. Here you can find
the Twin Towers: a pair of rock formations rising an impressive 90 feet.
A one-tank dive costs $70, two-tank dive $110, and four-hour beginner
course $120. Colin also offers day-trips to Sandy Cay and Sandy Spit,
excursions to The Baths on Virgin Gorda, and also custom outings.

Paradise Jeep Rentals (✉ *Great Harbour* ☎ *284/495–9477*) offers the
ideal vehicles to tackle Jost Van Dyke's steep, winding roads. Even
though Jost is a relatively small island, you really need to be in shape
to walk from one bay to the next. This outfit rents four-door Suzukis
for $65 per day and Grand Vitaras for $80. It's next to the Fire Station
in Great Harbour. Reservations are a must.

ANEGADA

Updated
by Susanna
Henighan
Potter

Anegada lies low on the horizon about 14 mi (22½ km) north of Virgin Gorda. Unlike the hilly volcanic islands in the chain, this is a flat coral-and-limestone atoll. Nine miles (14 km) long and 2 mi (3 km) wide, the island rises no more than 28 feet above sea level. In fact, by the time you're able to see it, you may have run your boat onto a reef. (More than 300 captains unfamiliar with the waters have done so since exploration days; note that bareboat charters don't allow their vessels to head here without a trained skipper.) Although the reefs are a sailor's nightmare, they (and the shipwrecks they've caused) are a scuba diver's dream. Snorkeling, especially in the waters around Loblolly Bay on the North Shore, is a transcendent experience. You can float in shallow, calm water just a few feet from shore and see one coral formation after another, each shimmering with a rainbow of colorful fish. Many local captains are happy to take visitors out bonefishing. Such watery pleasures are complemented by ever-so-fine, ever-so-white sand (the northern and western shores have long stretches of the stuff) and the occasional beach bar (stop in for burgers, local lobster, or a frosty beer). The island's population of about 180 lives primarily in a small south-side village called the Settlement, which has two grocery stores, a bakery, and a general store. There are no banks or ATMs on Anegada, and many restaurants and shops take only cash.

WHERE TO EAT

There are between 6 and 10 restaurants open at any one time, depending on the season and on whim. Check when you're on the island. Fresh fish and lobster are the specialties of the island. The going rate for a lobster dinner is $50, and it's almost always the most expensive thing on any restaurant menu.

$$$$
SEAFOOD

✕ **Anegada Reef Hotel Restaurant.** Seasoned yachters gather here nightly to share tales of the high seas; the open-air bar is the most lively on the island. Dinner is by candlelight under the stars and always includes famous Anegada lobster, steaks, and succulent baby back ribs—all prepared on the large grill by the little open-air bar. The ferry dock is right next door, so expect a crowd shortly after it arrives. Dinner reservations are required by 4 pm. Breakfast favorites include lobster omelets and rum-soaked French toast' at lunch the Reef serves salads and sandwiches. ⊠ *Anegada Reef Hotel, Setting Point* ☎ *284/495–8002* ⚐ *Reservations essential.*

$$$
AMERICAN
★

✕ **Big Bamboo.** This beachfront bar and restaurant tucked among sea grape trees at famous Loblolly Bay is the island's most popular destination for lunch. After you've polished off a plate of succulent Anegada lobster, barbeque chicken or fresh fish, you can spend the afternoon on the beach, where the snorkeling is excellent and the view near perfection. Fruity drinks from the cabana bar and ice cream from the freezer will round out your day. Dinner is by request only. If your heart is set on lobster, it's a good idea to call in the morning or day before to put in your request. ⊠ *Loblolly Bay West* ☎ *284/495–2019* ⚐ *Reservations essential.*

Anegada has miles of beautiful, white-sand beaches.

$$$$
SEAFOOD
✕ **Cow Wreck Bar and Grill.** Named for the cow bones that once washed up on shore, this wiggle-your-toes-in-the-sand beachside eatery on the north shore is a fun place to watch the antics of surfers and kite-boarders skidding across the bay. Tuck into conch ceviche or the popular hot wings for lunch. The homemade coconut pie is a winner. Pack your snorkel gear and explore the pristine reef just a few strokes from the shore before you eat. Dinner is served by request; reservations required by 4 pm. ✉ *Loblolly Bay East* ☎ *284/495–8047* ⊕ *www.cowwreckbeach.com* ⌕ *Reservations essential.*

$$$$
SEAFOOD
☕
✕ **Neptune's Treasure.** The owners, the Soares family, have lived on the island for more than half a century, and the Soares men catch, cook, and serve the seafood at this homey bar and restaurant a short distance from Setting Point. The fresh lobster, swordfish, tuna and mahimahi are all delicious. Homemade bread, a symphony of sides, and made-from-scratch desserts (including key lime pie and chocolate brownies), round out your meal. Dinner is by candlelight at the water's edge, often with classic jazz playing softly in the background. If you've tired of seafood, Neptune's has a nice variety of alternatives including vegetarian pasta, pork loin, and orange chicken. The view is spectacular at sunset. Breakfast is also served. Dinner reservations are essential by 4 pm. ✉ *Benders Bay* ☎ *284/495–9439* ⊕ *www.neptunestreasure.com* ⌕ *Reservations essential* ⊘ *No lunch.*

$$$$
SEAFOOD
✕ **Pomato Point Restaurant.** This relaxed restaurant and bar sits on one of the best beaches on the island and enjoys Anegada's most dramatic sunset views. Entrées include lobster, stewed conch, and freshly caught seafood. It's open for lunch daily; call by 4 pm for dinner reservations. Be sure to take a look at owner Wilfred Creque's displays of

island artifacts, including shards of Arawak pottery and 17th-century coins, cannonballs, and bottles. These are housed in a little one-room museum adjacent to the dining room. ⊠ *Pomato Point* ☎ *284/495–8038* ⚠ *Reservations essential* ⊙ *Closed Sept.*

WHERE TO STAY

The following reviews have been condensed for this book. Please go to Fodors.com for expanded reviews of each property.

$$ ⛱ **Anegada Reef Hotel.** Head here if you want to bunk in comfortable
HOTEL lodging near Anegada's most popular anchorage. **Pros:** everything you need is nearby; nice sunsets. **Cons:** basic rooms; no beach; often a party atmosphere at the bar. ⊠ *Setting Point* ☎ *284/495–8002* ⊕ *www.anegadareef.com* 🛏 *20 rooms* ⚐ *In-room: a/c, no safe, no TV. In-hotel: restaurant, bar, beach* ⓘ◯ *No meals.*

¢ ⛱ **Neptune's Treasure.** Basic waterfront rooms with simple but squeaky-
B&B/INN clean furnishings and lovely views of the ocean are the hallmark of this
ᗣ family-owned guesthouse. **Pros:** waterfront property; run by a family full of tales of the island; nice sunset views. **Cons:** simple rooms; no kitchens; no beach. ⊠ *Between Pomato and Setting points* ☎ *284/495–9439* ⊕ *www.neptunestreasure.com* 🛏 *9 rooms, 2 cottages* ⚐ *In-room: a/c, no safe, no TV. In-hotel: restaurant* ⓘ◯ *No meals.*

SPORTS AND THE OUTDOORS

Anegada Reef Hotel. Call the Anegada Reef to arrange bonefishing and sportfishing outings with seasoned local guides. ☎ *284/495–8002* ⊕ *www.anegadareef.com.*

Danny Vanterpool. Danny offers half-, three-quarter-, and full-day bone-fishing excursions around Anegada. Cost ranges from $300 to $500. ☎ *284/441–6334* ⊕ *bonesrus@dannysbonefishing.com.*

OTHER BRITISH VIRGIN ISLANDS

The following reviews have been condensed for this book. Please go to Fodors.com for expanded reviews of each property.

COOPER ISLAND

This small, hilly island on the south side of the Sir Francis Drake Channel, about 8 mi (13 km) from Road Town, Tortola, is popular with the charter-boat crowd. There are no paved roads (which doesn't really matter, as there aren't any cars), but you can find a beach restaurant, a casual hotel, a few houses (some are available for rent), and great snorkeling at the south end of Manchioneel Bay.

WHERE TO STAY

$ ⛱ **Cooper Island Beach Club.** Diving is a focus at this small resort, but folks
RESORT who want to simply swim, snorkel, or relax can also feel right at home.
Fodor's Choice **Pros:** lots of quiet; the Caribbean as it used to be. **Cons:** small rooms;
★ modest furnishings; island accessible only by ferry. ⊠ *Manchioneel Bay,*

Cooper Island ⌂ Box 859, Road Town, Tortola VG1110 ☎ 284/495–9084 or 800/542–4624 ⊕ www.cooper-island.com ⇨ 12 rooms ⚹ In-room: no a/c, no safe, no TV. In-hotel: restaurant, bar, beach, water sports ⦿ No meals, all meals.

GUANA ISLAND

Guana Island sits off Tortola's northeast coast. Sailors often drop anchor at one of the island's bays for a day of snorkeling and sunning. The island is a designated wildlife sanctuary, and scientists often come here to study its flora and fauna. It's home to a back-to-nature resort that offers few activities other than relaxation. Unless you're a hotel guest or a sailor, there's no easy way to get here.

WHERE TO STAY

$$$$
RESORT
Fodor's Choice
★

⌂ **Guana Island Resort.** Guana Island is a nature lover's paradise, and it's a good resort if you want to stroll the hillsides, snorkel around the reefs, swim at its seven beaches, and still enjoy some degree of comfort. **Pros:** secluded feel; lovely grounds. **Cons:** very expensive; need boat to get here. ⌂ *Guana Island ⌂ 67 Irving Pl., 12th fl., New York, NY 10003 ☎ 284/494–2354 or 800/544–8262 ⊕ www.guana.com ⇨ 15 rooms, 1 1-bedroom villa, 1 2-bedroom villa, 1 3-bedroom villa ⚹ In-room: a/c (some), no safe, no TV (some). In-hotel: restaurant, beach, water sports, business center ⦿ All meals.*

NORMAN ISLAND

This uninhabited island is the supposed setting for Robert Louis Stevenson's *Treasure Island*. The famed caves at Treasure Point are popular with day-sailors and powerboaters. If you land ashore at the island's main anchorage in the Bight, you can find a small beach bar and behind it a trail that winds up the hillside and reaches a peak with a fantastic view of the Sir Francis Drake Channel to the north.

$$
SEAFOOD

✗ **Willy T.** The ship, a former Baltic trader and today a floating bar and restaurant anchored to the north of the Bight, serves lunch and dinner in a party-hearty atmosphere. Try the conch fritters for starters. For lunch and dinner, British-style fish-and-chips, West Indian roti sandwiches, and the teriyaki chicken are winners. ⌂ *The Bight ☎ 284/496–8603 ⊕ www.williamthornton.com ⚹ Reservations essential.*

Cayman Islands

WORD OF MOUTH

"Sting Ray city is a must! Try to book through the Ritz-Carlton. The boats are nice, and they only take a small group, so you are not crammed together with 100 people. . . . The restaurants on the Island are fabulous. The Wharf is great as well and is perfect for a sunset dinner, and then you can feed the tarpons off the deck."

—Travelcrazy45

WELCOME TO CAYMAN ISLANDS

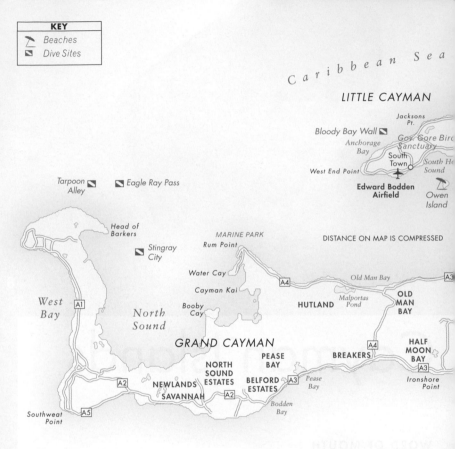

KEY
- Beaches
- Dive Sites

Caribbean Sea

LITTLE CAYMAN

Jacksons Pt.

Bloody Bay Wall

Anchorage Bay

Gov. Gore Bird Sanctuary

South Town

West End Point

South He Sound

Edward Bodden Airfield

Owen Island

Tarpoon Alley

Eagle Ray Pass

Head of Barkers

MARINE PARK
Rum Point

Stingray City

Water Cay

DISTANCE ON MAP IS COMPRESSED

Old Man Bay

A4

A3

Cayman Kai

West Bay

A1

North Sound

Booby Cay

HUTLAND

Malportas Pond

OLD MAN BAY

GRAND CAYMAN

PEASE BAY

BREAKERS

A4

HALF MOON BAY

NORTH SOUND ESTATES

BELFORD ESTATES

A3

Pease Bay

A3

Ironshore Point

A2

NEWLANDS

SAVANNAH

A2

Bodden Bay

Southweat Point

A5

Grand Cayman may be the world's largest offshore finance hub, but other offshore activities have put the Caymans on the map. Pristine waters, breathtaking coral formations, and plentiful and exotic marine creatures beckon divers from around the world. Other vacationers are drawn by the islands' mellow civility.

FUN ON AND OFF SHORE

Grand Cayman, which is 22 mi (36 km) long and 8 mi (13 km) wide, is the largest of the three low-lying islands that make up this British colony. Its sister islands (Little Cayman and Cayman Brac) are almost 90 mi (149 km) north and east. The Cayman Trough between the Cayman Islands and Jamaica is the deepest part of the Caribbean.

TOP REASONS TO VISIT CAYMAN ISLANDS

1 Diving: Underwater visibility is among the best in the Caribbean, and reefs are healthy.

2 Safety and Comfort: With no panhandlers, little crime, and top-notch accommodations, it's an easy place to vacation.

3 Dining Scene: The cosmopolitan population extends to the varied dining scene, from Italian to Indian.

4 Fabulous Snorkeling: A snorkeling trip to Stingray City is an experience you'll always remember.

5 Beaches: Grand Cayman's Seven Mile Beach is one of the best sandy beaches.

CAYMAN ISLANDS PLANNER

Logistics

Getting to the Cayman Islands: There are plenty of nonstop flights to Grand Cayman (GCM) from the United States. Most people hop over to the Brac and Little Cayman (LYB) on a small plane from Grand Cayman; a weekly nonstop from the Brac to Miami may be reinstated. Flights land at Owen Roberts Airport (Grand Cayman), Gerrard Smith Airport (Cayman Brac), or Edward Bodden Airstrip (Little Cayman).

Hassle Factor: Low for Grand Cayman; medium for Little Cayman and Cayman Brac.

On the Ground: In Grand Cayman you must take a taxi or rent a car at the airport since most hotels are not permitted to offer airport shuttles. Hotel pickup is more readily available on Cayman Brac and Little Cayman.

Getting Around: It's possible to get by without a car on Grand Cayman if you are staying in the Seven Mile Beach area, where you could walk, take a local bus, or ride a bike. If you want to explore the rest of the island—or if you are staying elsewhere—you'll need a car. Though less necessary on Cayman Brac or Little Cayman, cars are available on both islands.

Getting to and Around the Cayman Islands

Airports: Owen Roberts Airport (GCM ⊠ Grand Cayman ☎ 345/943–7070). **Gerrard Smith International Airport** (CYB ⊠ Cayman Brac ☎ 345/948–1222). **Edward Bodden Airstrip** (LYB ⊠ Little Cayman ☎ 345/948–0021).

Nonstop Flights: You can fly nonstop to Grand Cayman from Atlanta (Delta), Boston (US Airways, once weekly), Charlotte (US Airways), Chicago (Cayman Airways, twice weekly), Detroit (Delta, once weekly), Fort Lauderdale (Cayman Airways), Houston (Continental, once weekly), Miami (American, Cayman Airways), Minneapolis (Delta, once weekly), New York–JFK (Cayman Airways), New York–Newark (Continental, once weekly), Philadelphia (US Airways, once weekly), Tampa (Cayman Airways), and Washington, DC (Cayman Airways, twice weekly, and United).

Flights to the Sister Islands: Almost all nonstop air service is to Grand Cayman, with connecting flights on Cayman Airways Express to Cayman Brac and Little Cayman on a small propeller plane; there's also interisland charter-only service on Island Air. There is a once-weekly nonstop on Cayman Airways between Miami and Cayman Brac.

Local Airline Contacts: Most airlines flying into the Cayman Islands have local information numbers. If your airline doesn't have a local contact number on the island, you will be able to access the airline's toll-free number, but you may have to pay for the call. **American Airlines/American Eagle** (☎ 345/949–0666). **Cayman Airways** (☎ 345/949–2311). **Continental** (☎ 345/916–5545). **Delta** (☎ 345/945–8430). **Island Air** (☎ 345/949–5252). **US Airways** (☎ 345/949–7488).

Taxis: On Grand Cayman, taxis operate 24 hours a day; if you anticipate a late night, however, make pickup arrangements in advance. You generally cannot hail a taxi on the street except occasionally in George Town. Fares are not metered but set and are not cheap, but basic fares include as many as three passengers. Taxis are scarcer on the Sister Islands; rates are also fixed and fairly prohibitive. Your hotel will provide recommended drivers.

Getting Around the Cayman Islands

Buses: On Grand Cayman, bus service—consisting of minivans marked "Omni Bus"—is efficient, inexpensive, and plentiful, running roughly every 15 minutes in the Seven Mile Beach area and George Town with fares from CI$1.50 to CI$2.

Driving: Driving is easy on Grand Cayman, but there can be considerable traffic, especially during rush hour. One major road circumnavigates most of the island. Driving is on the left, British-style, and there are roundabouts. Speed limits are 30 mph (50 kph) in the country, 20 mph (30 kph) in town. There's much less traffic on Cayman Brac and even less on Little Cayman. Gas is expensive.

Car Rentals: You'll need a valid driver's license and a credit card to rent a car. Most agencies require renters to be between 21 and 70, though some require you to be 25. If you are over 75, you must have a certified doctor's note attesting to your ability. A local driver's permit, which costs $7.50, is obtained through the rental agencies. Rates can be expensive (from $40 to $95 per day) but usually include insurance.

Car-Rental Agencies (Grand Cayman): Ace Hertz (☎ 345/949–2280 or 800/654–3131 ⊕ www. acerentacarltd.com). **Andy's Rent a Car** (☎ 345/949–8111 ⊕ www.andys.ky). **Avis** (☎ 345/949–2468 ⊕ www.aviscayman.com). **Budget** (☎ 345/949–5605 or 800/527–0700 ⊕ www.budgetcayman.com). **Coconut Car Rentals** (☎ 345/949–4037, 345/949–7703, or 800/941–4562 ⊕ www.coconutcarrentals.com). **Dollar** (☎ 345/949–4790 ⊕ www.dollarlac.com). **Economy** (☎ 345/949–9550 ⊕ www.economycarrental.com.ky). **Thrifty** (☎ 345/949–6640 or 800/367–2277 ⊕ www. thrifty.com).

Car-Rental Agencies (Cayman Brac): B&S Motor Ventures (☎ 345/948–1646 ⊕ www.bandsmv.com). **CB Rent-a-Car** (☎ 345/948–2424 or 345/948–2847 ⊕ www. cbrentacar.com). **Four D's Car Rental** (☎ 345/948–1599).

Car-Rental Agencies (Little Cayman): McLaughlin Rentals (☎ 345/948–1000).

Island Activities

Diving is a major draw to all three of the Cayman Islands; the Bloody Bay Wall, off the coast of Little Cayman, is one of the Caribbean's top dive destinations, but there are many sites convenient to Grand Cayman, where shore diving is also good.

One of the most popular activities on Grand Cayman is a dive or snorkeling trip to **Stingray City**; petting and feeding the amazing creatures is a highlight of many Caribbean trips. There's good off-the-beach snorkeling in West Bay Cemetery, at Rum Point, and at Smith's Cove in Grand Cayman.

On land, Grand Cayman has the most to offer, with plenty of tours and activities, including **semisubmersible tours** of the bay for those who want to see under the waves without getting wet.

Grand Cayman's **Seven Mile Beach** is one of the Caribbean's finest long stretches of sand. Little Cayman has the best beaches of the Sister Islands, especially Owen Island and Point of Sand.

Rock climbers have discovered the Brac's limestone bluff.

8

CAYMAN ISLANDS PLANNER

Fast Facts

Banks and Exchange Services: You should not need to change money in Grand Cayman, since U.S. dollars are readily accepted. ATMs generally offer the option of U.S. or Cayman dollars. The Cayman dollar is pegged to the U.S. dollar at the rate of CI$1.25 to $1. Be sure you know which currency is being quoted when making a purchase.

Electricity: Electricity is reliable and is the same as in the United States (110 volts/60 cycles).

Emergency Services: Cayman Hyperbaric (⊠ Hospital Rd., George Town, Grand Cayman ☎ 345/949–2989). Emergency Services (☎ 911).

Passport Requirements: All visitors must have a valid passport and a return or ongoing ticket to enter the Cayman Islands. A birth certificate and photo ID are *not* sufficient proof of citizenship.

Weddings: Getting married in the Cayman Islands is a breeze. Documentation can be prepared ahead of time or in one day while on the island. There's no on-island waiting period. Larger resorts have on-site wedding coordinators.

Essentials

Mail: Sending a postcard to the United States, Canada, other parts of the Caribbean, or Central America costs CI25¢. An airmail letter is CI75¢ per half ounce. When addressing letters to the Cayman Islands, be sure to include the new postal codes that have been introduced.

Safety: Crime isn't a major problem in the Cayman Islands, but it is always a good idea to take general precautions such as locking your room, using your hotel safe, and avoiding walking on the beach or on unlighted streets at night.

Taxes: At the airport, each adult passenger leaving Grand Cayman must pay a departure tax of $25 (CI$20), payable in cash. It isn't usually added to airfare—check with your carrier. A 10% government tax is added to all hotel bills. A 10% service charge is often added to hotel bills and restaurant checks in lieu of a tip.

Telephones: The area code for the Cayman Islands is 345. To make local calls (on or between any of the three islands), dial the seven-digit number. Many international cell phones work in the Cayman Islands, though roaming charges can be significant. Mobile phone rental is available from LIME and Digicel, the two major providers; you can stay connected for as little as CI$5 per day plus the cost of a calling card (denominations range from CI$10 to CI$100). International per-minute rates usually range from CI35¢ to CI60¢.

Tipping: At large hotels a service charge is generally included; smaller establishments and some villas and condos leave tipping up to you. Although tipping is customary at restaurants, note that some automatically include 15% on the bill—so check the tab carefully. Taxi drivers expect a 10% to 15% tip.

Visitor Information: There's a tourism office at the airport in Grand Cayman. **Cayman Islands Department of Tourism** (☎ 305/599–9033 in Miami, 312/263–1750 in Chicago, 212/889–9009 in New York City, 713/461–1317 in Houston, 877/422–9626 ⊕ www.caymanislands.ky).

Where to Stay

Grand Cayman draws the bulk of Cayman Island visitors. It's expensive during the high season but offers the widest range of resorts, restaurants, and activities both in and out of the water. Most resorts are on or near Seven Mile Beach, but a few are north in the West Bay Area, near Rum Point, or on the quiet East End. Both Little Cayman and Cayman Brac are more geared toward serving the needs of divers, who make up the majority of visitors. Beaches on the Sister Islands, as they are called, don't measure up (literally) to Grand Cayman's Seven Mile Beach. The smaller islands are cheaper than Grand Cayman, but with the extra cost of transportation, the overall savings are minimized.

Grand Cayman: Grand Cayman has plenty of medium-size resorts as well as the Ritz-Carlton, a large seven-story resort on Seven Mile Beach. The island also has a wide range of condos and villas, many in resortlike compounds on or near Seven Mile Beach and the Cayman Kai area. There are even a few small guesthouses for budget-minded visitors.

The Sister Islands: Cayman Brac has mostly intimate resorts and family-run inns. Little Cayman has a mix of small resorts and condos, most appealing to divers.

HOTEL AND RESTAURANT COSTS

Restaurant prices are for a main course excluding 10% tax and tip. Hotel prices are for two people in a double room in high season, excluding 10% tax, 10%–15% service charge, and meal plans (except at all-inclusives).

WHAT IT COSTS IN U.S. DOLLARS

	¢	$	$$	$$$	$$$$
Restaurants	under $8	$8–$12	$12–$20	$20–$30	over $30
Hotels	under $150	$151–$275	$276–$375	$376–$475	over $475

When to Go

High season begins in mid-December and continues through early to mid-April. During the low season, you can often get a substantial discount of as much as 40%.

Grand Cayman has three major events. The **Batabano Carnival** in May (or the first week after Easter) is the Cayman Islands' answer to Mardi Gras, though it happens after instead of before Lent.

Pirates Week, Grand Cayman's big fall festival, is in early November. It's a Carnival-like celebration, when visitors and locals dress up as pirates and wenches; music, fireworks, parades, street dances, and competitions take place island-wide.

January's **Taste of Cayman Food & Wine Festival** is a multiday affair with demos, classes, lectures, and tastings. Top toque Eric Ripert headlines **Cayman Cookout** the same month, luring fellow celeb chefs and winemakers for demonstrations to decadent dinners.

During April's **Cayman Islands International Fishing Tournament**, anglers can enjoy plenty of action and win big prizes.

8

CAYMAN ISLANDS BEACHES

Limestone, coral, shells, water, and wind collaborated to fashion the Cayman Islands beaches. It's a classic example of the interaction between geology and marine biology.

(Above) A beach lounger at the Ritz-Carlton, Grand Cayman. (Opposite page bottom) Horseback riding at Barkers. (Opposite page top) Snorkelers at Stingray Sandbar.

Most of the beaches in Cayman, especially on Grand and Little Cayman, resemble powdered ivory. A few, including those on Cayman Brac, are more dramatic, a mix of fine beige sand and rugged rocky "ironshore," which often signals the healthiest reefs and best snorkeling. The islands are limestone outcroppings, the thrusting summits of a submarine mountain range called the Cayman Ridge. Grand Cayman's beaches range from cramped, untrammeled coves to long stretches basking like a cat in the sun, lined with bustling bars and water-sports concessions. There are some sandy beaches on Cayman Brac, especially along the southwest coast, but these beaches are also lined with turtle grass. Little Cayman has some spectacular white-sand beaches. All beaches are public, though access can be restricted by resorts. Remember that the Cayman Islands is a conservative place: nudity is strictly forbidden and punishable by a hefty fine and/or prison time.

CORAL SAND

On most limestone-coral-based islands around the world, the hue and texture of the sand are derived from various micro-skeletons, like the coral-like *foraminifera* and the calcareous algae Halimeda (a genus embracing a dozen species), which flourish in offshore reefs and sea grass beds. These form the powdery, pearly sand on Seven Mile Beach and Rum Point, as well as Point of Sand on Little Cayman.

GRAND CAYMAN

East End Beaches. Just drive along and look for any sandy beach, park your car, and enjoy a stroll. The vanilla-hue stretch at Colliers Bay, by the Reef and Morritts resorts, is a good clean one with superior snorkeling. ⊠ *Queen's Hwy., East End.*

Rum Point. This North Sound beach has hammocks slung in towering casuarina trees, picnic tables, the Wreck Bar and Grill for dining, a well-stocked shop for seaworthy sundries, and Red Sail Sports, which offers various water sports and boats to explore Stingray City. The barrier reef ensures safe snorkeling and soft sand. The bottom remains shallow for a long way from shore, but it's littered with small coral heads, so kids shouldn't wrestle in the water here. The Wreck is ablaze with color—yellow with navy-blue trim and lime-and-mango picnic tables—as if trying to upstage the snorkeling just offshore; an ultracasual hangout turns out outstanding pub grub from fish-and-chips to wings, as well as lethal mudslide cocktails. Showers are available. ⊠ *Rum Point, North Side.*

★ **Fodor's Choice** **Seven Mile Beach.** Grand Cayman's west coast is dominated by the famous Seven Mile Beach—actually a 6½-mi-long (10-km-long) expanse of powdery white sand overseeing lapis water stippled with a rainbow of parasails and kayaks. The

width of the beach varies with the season; toward the south end it narrows and disappears altogether south of the Marriott, leaving only rock and ironshore. It starts to broaden into its normal silky softness anywhere between Tarquyn Manor and the Reef Grill at Royal Palms. Free of litter and pesky peddlers, it's an unspoiled (though often crowded) environment. At the public beach toward the north end you can find chairs for rent ($10 for the day, including a beverage), a playground, water toys aplenty, two beach bars, restrooms, and showers. The best snorkeling is at either end, by the Marriott and Treasure Island or off the northern section called Cemetery Reef Beach. ⊠ *West Bay Rd., Seven Mile Beach.*

Smith's Cove. South of the Grand Old House, this tiny but popular protected swimming and snorkeling spot makes a wonderful beach wedding location. The bottom drops off quickly enough to allow you to swim and play close to shore. Although slightly rocky, there's little debris and few coral heads, plenty of shade, picnic tables, restrooms, and parking. Surfers will find some decent swells just to the south. Local scuttlebutt calls it a place for dalliances during work hours; it's also a romantic sunset spot. ⊠ *Off S. Church St., George Town.*

8

Looking ou at Owen Island, Little Cayman, at sunset.

South Sound Cemetery Beach. A narrow, sandy driveway takes you past the small cemetery to a perfect beach. The dock here is primarily used by dive boats during winter storms. You can walk in either direction; the sand is talcum-soft and clean, the water calm and clear (though local surfers take advantage of occasional small reef breaks; if wading, wear reef shoes since the bottom is somewhat rocky and dotted with sea urchins). You'll definitely find fewer crowds. ⊠ *S. Sound Rd., Prospect.*

CAYMAN BRAC

The island has several sandy beaches, mostly along the southwest coast. In addition to the hotel beaches, where everyone is welcome, there is a public beach with good access to the reef; it's well marked on tourist maps. The north-coast beaches, predominantly rocky ironshore, offer excellent snorkeling.

LITTLE CAYMAN

★ **Fodor's Choice** **Owen Island.** This private, forested island can be reached by rowboat, kayak, or an ambitious 200-yard swim. Anyone is welcome to come across and enjoy the deserted beaches and excellent snorkeling. Nudity is forbidden as "idle and disorderly" in the Cayman Islands, though that doesn't always stop skinny-dippers (who may not realize they can be seen quite easily from shore on the strands facing Little Cayman).

★ **Fodor's Choice** **Point of Sand.** Stretching over a mile on the easternmost point of the island, this secluded beach is great for wading, shell collecting, and snorkeling. On a clear day you can see 7 mi (11 km) across to Cayman Brac. It serves as a green- and loggerhead turtle nesting site in spring, and a mosaic of coral gardens blooms just offshore. It's magical, especially at moonrise, when it earns its nickname, Lovers' Beach. There's a *palapa* (thatch-roof shelter) for shade but no facilities. The current can be strong, so watch the kids.

By Jordan
Simon

This British Overseas Territory, which consists of Grand Cayman, smaller Cayman Brac, and Little Cayman, is one of the Caribbean's most popular destinations, particularly among Americans, who have become homeowners and constant visitors. The island's extensive array of banks also draws travelers. There are relatively few signs of the devastation caused by Hurricane Ivan in 2004, and Cayman Brac has almost completely recovered from Hurricane Paloma in November 2008.

8

Columbus is said to have sighted the islands in 1503 and dubbed them Las Tortugas after seeing so many turtles in the sea. The name was later changed to Cayman, referring to the caiman crocodiles that once roamed the islands. The Cayman Islands remained largely uninhabited until the late 1600s, when England seized them and Jamaica from Spain. Emigrants from England, Holland, Spain, and France arrived, as did refugees from the Spanish Inquisition and deserters from Oliver Cromwell's army in Jamaica; many brought slaves with them as well. The Cayman Islands' caves and coves were also perfect hideouts for the likes of Blackbeard, Sir Henry Morgan, and other pirates out to plunder Spanish galleons. Many ships fell afoul of the reefs surrounding the islands, often with the help of Caymanians, who lured vessels to shore with beacon fires.

Today's Cayman Islands are seasoned with suburban prosperity (particularly Grand Cayman, where residents joke that the national flower is the satellite dish) and stuffed with crowds (the hotels that line the famed Seven Mile Beach are often full, even in the slow summer season). Most of the 52,000 Cayman Islanders live on Grand Cayman, where the cost of living is at least 20% higher than in the United States, but you won't be hassled by panhandlers or fear walking around on a dark evening (the crime rate is very low). Add political and economic stability to the mix, and you have a fine island recipe indeed.

GRAND CAYMAN

Grand Cayman has long been known for two offshore activities: banking (the new piracy, as locals joke) and scuba diving. With 296 banks, the capital, George Town, is relatively modern and usually bustles with activity, but never more so than when two to seven cruise ships are docked in the harbor, an increasingly common occurrence. Accountants in business clothes join thousands of vacationers in their tropical togs, jostling for tables at lunch. When they're not mingling in the myriad shops or getting pampered and pummeled in spas, vacationers delve into sparkling waters to snorkel and dive; increasingly, couples come to be married, or at least to enjoy their honeymoon.

The effects of recent devastating hurricanes, such as Omar in October 2008 and Paloma in November 2008 are visible only in the mangrove swamps and interior savannah. There is a lot of new construction and plenty of traffic, so check with a local to plan driving time. It can take 45 minutes during rush hours to go 8 mi (13 km).

EXPLORING GRAND CAYMAN

The historic capital of George Town, on the southeast corner of Grand Cayman, is easy to explore on foot. If you're a shopper, you can spend days here; otherwise, an hour will suffice for a tour of the downtown area. To see the rest of the island, rent a car or scooter or take a guided tour. The portion of the island called West Bay is noted for its jumble of neighborhoods and a few attractions. When traffic is heavy, it's about a half hour to West Bay from George Town, but the opening of a new bypass road that runs parallel to West Bay Road has made the journey easier. The less-developed East End has natural attractions from blowholes to botanical gardens, as well as the remains of the island's original settlements. Plan at least 45 minutes for the drive out from George Town (more during rush hours). You need a day to explore the entire island—including a stop at a beach for a picnic or swim.

WHAT TO SEE
GEORGE TOWN
Begin exploring the capital by strolling along the waterfront Harbour Drive to **Elmslie Memorial United Church,** named after the first Presbyterian missionary to serve in Cayman. Its vaulted ceiling, wooden arches, and sedate nave reflect the religious nature of island residents. In front of the court building, in the center of town, names of influential Caymanians are inscribed on the **Wall of History,** which commemorates the islands' quincentennial in 2003. Across the street is the **Cayman Islands Legislative Assembly Building,** next door to the **1919 Peace Memorial Building**. In the middle of the financial district is the **General Post Office,** built in 1939. Let the kids pet the big blue iguana statues.

Cayman Islands National Museum. Built in 1833, the historically significant clapboard home of the national museum has had several different incarnations over the years, serving as courthouse, jail, post office, and dance hall. It features an ongoing archaeological excavation of the Old Gaol and excellent 3-D bathymetric displays, murals, dioramas, and

Boatswain's Beach, Grand Cayman.

videos that illustrate local geology, flora and fauna, and island history. The first floor focuses on natural history, including a microcosm of Cayman ecosystems, from beaches to dry woodlands and swamps, and offers such interactive elements as a simulated sub. Upstairs, the cultural exhibit features renovated murals, video history reenactments, and 3-D back panels in display cases holding thousands of artifacts ranging from a 14-foot catboat with animatronic captain to old coins and rare documents painting a portrait of daily life and past industries such as shipbuilding and turtling, stressing Caymanians' resilience when they had little contact with the outside world. There are also temporary exhibits focusing on aspects of Caymanian culture, a local art collection, and interactive displays for kids. ⊠ *Harbour Dr., George Town* ☎ *345/949–8368* ⊕ *www.museum.ky* ⊠ *$5* ⊘ *Weekdays 9–5, Sat. 10–2.*

★ **National Gallery**. A worthy nonprofit organization, the museum was established in 1996 to display and promote the range of Caymanian artists and craftspeople, both established and grassroots. The gallery coordinates a wealth of first-rate outreach programs for everyone from infants to inmates. It usually mounts six major exhibitions a year, including three large-scale retrospectives or thematic shows and multimedia installations. Director Natalie Coleman also brings in international shows that somehow relate to the island, often inviting local artists for stimulating dialogue. The gallery hosts public slide shows, a lunchtime lecture series running in conjunction with current exhibits, Art Flix (video presentations on art history, introduced with a short lecture and followed by a discussion led by curators or artists), and a CineClub (movie night). The gallery has also developed an Artist Trail

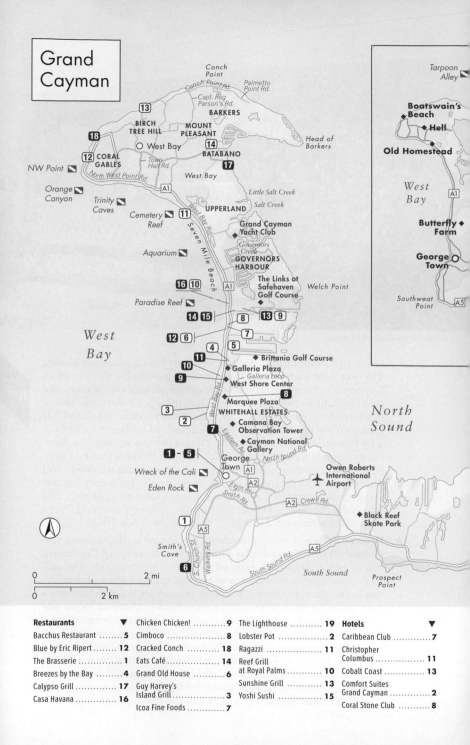

Grand Cayman

Conch Point
Palmetto Point Rd.
Conch Point Rd.
Capt. Reg Parson's Rd.

BARKERS

13

BIRCH TREE HILL

18

○ West Bay

MOUNT PLEASANT

12 **CORAL GABLES**

Head of Barkers

14 **BATABANO**

17

Town Hall Rd.

NW Point

West Bay

North West Point Rd.

A1

Orange Canyon

Trinity Caves

Little Salt Creek
Salt Creek

UPPERLAND

Cemetery Reef

11

West Bay Rd.

Grand Cayman Yacht Club

Governors Creek

GOVERNORS HARBOUR

Aquarium

Seven Mile Beach

The Links at Safehaven Golf Course

Welch Point

16 **10**

A1

Paradise Reef

14 **15**

8 **13** **9**

12 **6**

7

4 **5**

Brittania Golf Course

10 **11**

Galleria Plaza

9

Galleria Loop

West Shore Center

8

Marquee Plaza

West Bay Rd.

WHITEHALL ESTATES

West Bay

3

2

7

Camana Bay Observation Tower

North Sound

Cayman National Gallery

1 - 5

Eastern Av.

George Town

North Sound Rd.

Wreck of the Cali

A1

A2

Owen Roberts International Airport

Eden Rock

Elgin Av.

Smith Rd.

A2

Crewe Rd.

Black Reef Skate Park

1

A5

Smith's Cove

S. Church St.

Walkers Rd.

6

South Sound Rd.

A5

South Sound

Prospect Point

0   2 mi

0   2 km

Tarpoon Alley

Boatswain's Beach

◆ **Hell**

Old Homestead

West Bay

A1

Butterfly Farm ◆

George Town

Southweat Point

A5

Restaurants ▼		**Hotels** ▼
Bacchus Restaurant **5**	Chicken Chicken! **9**	Caribbean Club **7**
Blue by Eric Ripert **12**	Cimboco **8**	Christopher
The Brasserie **1**	Cracked Conch **18**	Columbus **11**
Breezes by the Bay **4**	Eats Café **14**	Cobalt Coast **13**
Calypso Grill **17**	Grand Old House **6**	Comfort Suites
Casa Havana **16**	Guy Harvey's	Grand Cayman **2**
	Island Grill **3**	Coral Stone Club **8**
	Icoa Fine Foods **7**	
	The Lighthouse **19**	
	Lobster Pot **2**	
	Ragazzi **11**	
	Reef Grill	
	at Royal Palms **10**	
	Sunshine Grill **13**	
	Yoshi Sushi **15**	

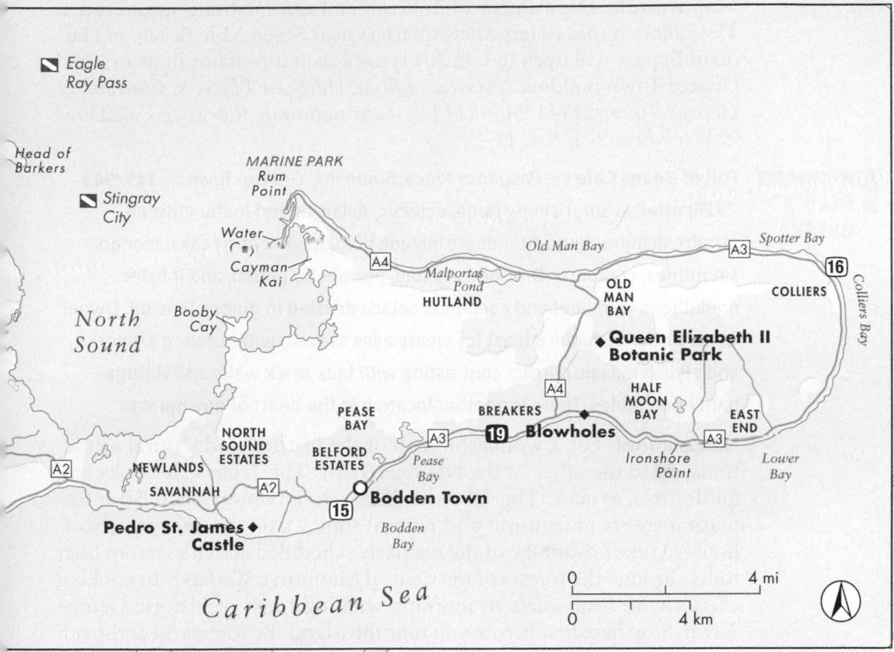

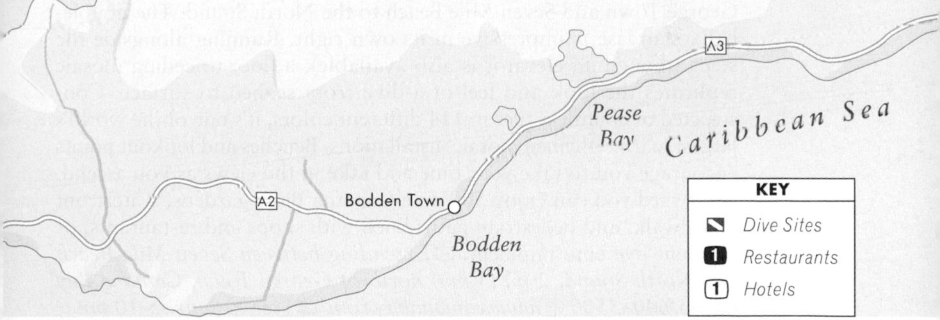

Eagle
Ray Pass

Head of
Barkers

MARINE PARK
Rum
Point

Stingray
City

Water
Cayman
Kai

North
Sound

Booby
Cay

Old Man Bay

Spotter Bay

A4

Malportas
Pond

HUTLAND

OLD
MAN
BAY

COLLIERS

16

Colliers Bay

Queen Elizabeth II
Botanic Park

A4

HALF
MOON
BAY

BREAKERS

19 Blowholes

EAST
END

PEASE
BAY

A3

A3

NORTH
SOUND
ESTATES

Pease
Bay

Ironshore
Point

Lower
Bay

A2

NEWLANDS

BELFORD
ESTATES

SAVANNAH

A2

15 Bodden Town

Bodden
Bay

Pedro St. James
Castle

Caribbean Sea

0   4 mi

0   4 km

Pease
Bay

Caribbean Sea

A2   Bodden Town

Bodden
Bay

A3

KEY

Dive Sites

1 Restaurants

1 Hotels

Map with the Department of Tourism and can facilitate studio tours. The gallery hopes its large new quarters near Seven Mile Beach on Harquail Bypass will open in late 2011; until then it remains in its original George Town building. ⊠ *Ground floor, Harbour Place, S. Church St., George Town* ☎ *345/945–8111* ⊕ *www.nationalgallery.org.ky* ⊒ *Free* ☯ *Weekdays 9–5, Sat. 11–2.*

NEED A BREAK?

Full of Beans Cafe (⊠ *Pasadora Place, Smith Rd., George Town* ☎ *345/943–2326*) offers a surprisingly large, eclectic, Asian-tinged menu utilizing ultrafresh ingredients. Standouts include homemade carrot cake, mango smoothies, cranberry-Brie-pecan salad, portobello panini, and lobster medallions with beet and cucumber salads drizzled in ginger-lime oil. Owner Cindy Butler fashions a feast for weary eyes as well, with rotating artworks and stylish mosaic mirrors contrasting with faux-brick walls and vintage hardwood tables. There is another location in the heart of downtown.

National Trust. For a wonderful map of the historic and natural attractions, go to the office of the National Trust. The Trust sells books and guides to Cayman. The fabulous Web site has more than 50 information sheets on cultural and natural topics from iguanas to schoolhouses. Take advantage of the regularly scheduled activities, from boat tours through the forests of the Central Mangrove Wetlands to cooking classes with local chefs to morning walking tours of historic George Town. Stop here first before you tour the island. Be forewarned: though the office is walkable from George Town, it's an often-hot 20-minute walk from downtown. ⊠ *Dart Park, 558 S. Church St., George Town* ☎ *345/749–1121* ⊕ *nationaltrust.org.ky* ☯ *Weekdays 9–5:30.*

SEVEN MILE BEACH

☾ ★ **Camana Bay Observation Tower.** This 75-foot structure provides striking 360-degree panoramas of otherwise flat Grand Cayman, sweeping from George Town and Seven Mile Beach to the North Sound. The double-helix staircase is impressive in its own right. Running alongside the steps (though an elevator is also available), a floor-to-ceiling mosaic replicates the look and feel of a dive from seabed to surface. Constructed of countless tiles in 114 different colors, it's one of the world's largest marine-themed mosaic installations. Benches and lookout points encourage you to take your time and take in the views as you ascend. Afterward you can enjoy 500-acre Camana Bay's gardens, waterfront boardwalk, and pedestrian paths lined with shops and restaurants, or frequent live entertainment. ⊠ *Extending between Seven Mile Beach and North Sound, 2 mi (3 km) north of George Town, Camana Bay* ☎ *345/640–3500* ⊕ *www.camanabay.com* ⊒ *Free* ☯ *Sunrise–10 pm.*

WEST BAY

☾ **Fodor's Choice** ★ **Boatswain's Beach.** Cayman's premier attraction, the Turtle Farm, has been rebranded and transformed into a marine theme park. The expanded complex now has several souvenir shops and restaurants. Still, the turtles remain a central attraction, and you can tour ponds in the original research–breeding facility with thousands in various stages of growth, some up to 600 pounds and more than 70 years old. Turtles can be picked up from the tanks, a real treat for children and adults as the little creatures flap their fins and splash the water. Four areas—three aquatic and one dry—cover 23 acres; different-color bracelets determine access (the steep full-pass admission includes snorkeling gear). The park helps promote conservation, encouraging interaction (a Tidal Pool houses invertebrates such as starfish and crabs) and observation. Animal Program Events include Keeper Talks, where you might feed birds or iguanas, and biologists speaking about conservation and their importance to the ecosystem. The freshwater **Breaker's Lagoon**, replete with cascades plunging over moss-carpeted rocks evoking Cayman Brac, is the islands' largest pool. The saltwater **Boatswain's Lagoon**, replicating all the Cayman Islands and the Trench, teems with 14,000 denizens of the deep milling about a cannily designed synthetic reef. You can snorkel here (lessons and guided tours are available). Both lagoons have underwater 4-inch-thick acrylic panels that look directly into **Predator Reef**, home to six brown sharks, four nurse sharks, and other predatory fish such as tarpons, eels, and jacks. These predators can also be viewed from terra (or terror, as one guide jokes) firma. Make sure you check out feeding times! The free-flight **Aviary**, designed by consultants from Disney's Animal Kingdom, is a riot of color and noise as feathered friends represent the entire Caribbean basin, doubling as a rehabilitation center for Cayman Wildlife and Rescue. A winding interpretive **nature trail** culminates in the Blue Hole, a collapsed cave once filled with water. Audio tours are available with different focuses, from butterflies to bush medicine. The last stop is the living museum, **Cayman Street**, complete with facades duplicating different types of vernacular architecture; an herb and fruit garden; porch-side artisans, musicians, and storytellers; model catboats; live cooking on an old-fashioned caboose (outside kitchen) oven; and interactive craft demonstrations from painting mahogany to thatch weaving. ✉ *825 Northwest Point Rd., Box 812, West Bay* 📞 *345/949-3894* ⊕ *www.boatswainsbeach.ky* 📧 *Comprehensive ticket $45, Turtle Farm only $30* ⊙ *Daily 8:30–4:30.*

Hell. Quite literally the tourist trap from Hell, especially when overrun by cruise-ship passengers, this attraction does offer free admission, fun photo ops, and sublime surrealism. Its name refers to the quarter-acre of menacing shards of charred brimstone thrusting up like vengeful spirits (actually blackened and "sculpted" by acid-secreting algae and fungi over millennia). The eerie lunarscape is now cordoned off, but you can prove you had a helluva time by taking a photo from the observation deck. The attractions are the small post office and a gift shop where you can get cards and letters postmarked from Hell, not to mention wonderfully silly postcards titled "When Hell Freezes Over" (depicting bathing beauties on the beach), "The Devil Made Me Do It" bumper stickers, Scotch bonnet–based Hell sauce, and "The coolest shop in Hell" T-shirts. Ivan Farrington, the owner of the Devil's Hang-Out store, cavorts in a devil's costume (horn, cape, and tails), regaling you with demonically bad jokes. ✉ *Hell Rd., West Bay* 📞 *345/949-3358* 📧 *Free* ⊙ *Daily 9–6.*

NORTH SIDE

Fodor'sChoice
★

Queen Elizabeth II Botanic Park. This 65-acre wilderness preserve show-cases a wide range of indigenous and nonindigenous tropical vegeta-tion, approximately 2,000 species in total. Splendid sections include numerous water features from limpid lily ponds to cascades; a Heritage Garden with a traditional cottage and "caboose" (outside kitchen) that includes crops that might have been planted on Cayman a century ago; and a Floral Colour Garden arranged by color, the walkway wander-ing through sections of pink, red, orange, yellow, white, blue, mauve, lavender, and purple. A 2-acre lake and adjacent wetlands includes three islets that provide a habitat and breeding ground for native birds just as showy as the floral displays: green herons, black-necked stilts, American coots, blue-winged teal, cattle egrets, and rare West Indian whistling ducks. The nearly mile-long Woodland Trail encompasses every Cayman ecosystem from wetland to cactus thicket, buttonwood swamp to lofty woodland with imposing mahogany trees. You'll encounter birds, lizards, turtles, agoutis, and more, but the park's star residents are the protected endemic blue iguanas, found only in Grand Cayman. The world's most endangered iguana, they're the focus of the National Trust's Blue Iguana Recovery Program, a captive breeding and reintroduction facility. This section of the park is usually closed to the general public, though released "blue dragons" hang out in the vicinity. The Trust conducts 90-minute behind-the-scenes safaris Monday–Saturday at 11 am for $30. ⊠ 367 Botanic Rd. ⊄ Box 203, North Side, Grand Cayman ☎ 345/947–9462 ⊕ www.botanic-park.ky ⊠ $10 ⊙ Apr.–Sept., daily 9–6:30; Oct.–Mar., daily 9–5:30; last admission 1 hr before closing.

EAST END

☾ **Blowholes.** When the easterly trade winds blow hard, crashing waves force water into caverns and send impressive geysers shooting up as much as 20 feet through the ironshore. The blowholes were partially filled during Hurricane Ivan in 2004, so the water must be rough to recapture their former elemental drama. ⊠ Frank Sound Rd., roughly 10 mi (16 km) east of Bodden Town, near East End.

Bodden Town. In the island's original south-shore capital you can find an old cemetery on the shore side of the road. Graves with A-frame struc-tures are said to contain the remains of pirates. There are also the ruins of a fort and a wall erected by slaves in the 19th century. The National Trust runs tours of the restored 1840s Mission House. A curio shop serves as the entrance to what's called the Pirate's Caves ($8), partially underground natural formations that are more hokey (decked out with fake treasure chests and mannequins in pirate garb, with an outdoor petting zoo) than spooky.

Cayman Islands Brewery. This brewery occupies the former Stingray facil-ity; free tours are available, but you must call ahead to ensure someone is available to squire you around. Caybrew is a full-bodied yet light lager with a crisp hop finish. The guide will explain the iconic imagery of the bottle and label, and the nearly three-week process: seven days' fermentation, 10 days' lagering (storage), and one day in the bottling tank. The brewery's ecofriendly features are also championed: local farmers receive the spent grains used to produce the beer to serve as cattle feed at no charge, while waste liquid is channeled into one of the Caribbean's most advanced water-treatment systems. Then enjoy your complimentary tasting with the knowledge that you're helping the local environment and economy. ⊠ *366 Shamrock Rd., Red Bay* ☎ *345/947–6699* ⊕ *www.cib.ky* ⊠ *Free* ⊙ *Weekdays 9–5, Sat. 10–5.*

⊙ **Pedro St. James Castle.** Built in 1780, the greathouse is Cayman's oldest

Fodor's Choice stone structure and the only remaining late-18th-century residence on

★ the island. In its capacity as courthouse and jail, it was the birthplace of Caymanian democracy, where in December 1831 the first elected parliament was organized and in 1835 the Slavery Abolition Act signed. The structure still has original or historically accurate replicas of sweeping verandahs, mahogany floors, rough-hewn wide-beam ceilings, outside louvers, stone and oxblood- or mustard-color lime-wash-painted walls, brass fixtures, and Georgian furnishings (from tea caddies to canopy beds to commodes). Paying obsessive attention to detail, the curators even fill glasses with faux wine. The mini-museum also includes a hodgepodge of displays from slave emancipation to old stamps. The buildings are surrounded by 8 acres of natural parks and woodlands. You can stroll through landscaping of native Caymanian flora and experience one of the most spectacular views on the island from atop the dramatic Great Pedro Bluff. First watch the impressive multimedia theater show, complete with smoking pots, misting rains, and two film screens where the story of Pedro's Castle is presented on the hour. The poignant Hurricane Ivan Memorial outside uses text, images, and symbols to represent important aspects of that horrific 2004 natural disaster. ⊠ *Pedro Castle Rd., Box 305, Savannah* ☎ *345/947–3329* ⊕ *www. pedrostjames.ky* ⊠ *$10* ⊙ *Daily 9–5.*

Wreck of the Ten Sails Park. This lonely, lovely park on Grand Cayman's windswept eastern tip commemorates the island's most (in)famous shipwreck. On February 8, 1794, the *Cordelia,* heading a convoy of 58 square-rigged merchant vessels en route from Jamaica to England, foundered on one of the treacherous East End reefs. Its warning cannon fire was tragically misconstrued as a call to band more closely together due to imminent pirate attack, and nine more ships ran aground. The local sailors, who knew those rough seas, demonstrated great bravery in rescuing all 400-odd seamen. Popular legend claims (romantically but inaccurately) that King George III granted the islands an eternal tax exemption. Queen Elizabeth II dedicated the park's plaque in 1994. Interpretive signs document the historic details. The ironically peaceful headland provides magnificent views of the reef (including more recent shipwrecks); bird-watching is superb from here half a mile south along the coast to the Lighthouse Park, perched on a craggy bluff. ⊠ *Gun Bay, East End* ☎ *345/949–0121 (National Trust)* ⊠ *Free* ⊙ *Daily.*

WHERE TO EAT

Despite its small size, comparative geographic isolation, and British colonial trappings, Grand Cayman offers a smorgasbord of gastronomic goodies. With more than 100 eateries, something should suit and sate every palate and pocketbook (factoring in the fast-food franchises

8

sweeping the islandscape like tumbleweed, and stands dispensing local specialties). The term *melting pot* describes both the majority of menus and the multicultural population. The sheer range of dining options from Middle Eastern to Mexican reflects the island's cosmopolitan clientele. Imported ingredients make up their own United Nations, with chefs sourcing salmon from Norway, foie gras from Périgord, and lamb from New Zealand. Wine lists can be equally global in scope. And don't be surprised to find both Czech and Chilean staffers at a remote East End restaurant. As one restaurateur quipped, "Cayman is the ultimate culture-shock absorber."

BEST BETS FOR DINING

Fodor's Choice ★
Blue by Eric Ripert, Casa Havana

BEST VIEW
Cracked Conch, Reef Grill at Royal Palms

MOST ROMANTIC
Bacchus, Grand Old House

BEST FOR LOCAL CUISINE
Chicken! Chicken!, Cimboco, Eats Café

HOT SPOTS
Guy Harvey's Island Grill, ICOA Fine Foods, Ragazzi, Yoshi Sushi

Prices are about 25% more than those in a major U.S. city. Many restaurants add a 10% to 15% service charge to the bill; be sure to check before leaving a tip. Alcohol with your meal can send the tab skyrocketing. Buy liquor duty-free before you leave the airport and enjoy a cocktail or nightcap from the comfort of your room or balcony. Cayman customs limits you to two bottles per person. You should make reservations at all but the most casual places, particularly during the high season. Note that many bars offer fine fare (and many eateries have hip, hopping bar scenes).

WHAT TO WEAR

Grand Cayman dining is casual (shorts are okay, but *not* beachwear and tank tops). Mosquitoes can be pesky when you are dining outdoors, especially at sunset, so plan ahead or ask for repellent. Winter can be chilly enough to warrant a light sweater.

GEORGE TOWN AND ENVIRONS

$$$$ ✕**Bacchus Restaurant and Wine Bar.** This cozy oenophile's den may offer
SEAFOOD   a lineup of 350-plus wines spanning Australia to Austria, but it's utterly unstuffy (conveyed by murals of reveling diners and quotes stenciled everywhere, such as "What I like to drink most is wine that belongs to others"—Diogenes). Chef–owner Keith Griffin promises "no sunsets, no fish feeding, it's all about the food." In other words, no gimmickry, though his constantly changing menu is a mischievous mélange of influences and ingredients. Accents alone, from compotes to coulis, include chili-caramel dip (for crispy sesame-coconut shrimp), mustard-olive crust (for rack of lamb with Cabernet-cranberry sauce and bacon-jalapeño mashed potatoes), and coconut-lime dressing (for tea-cured yellowfin tuna ceviche with toasted sesame-wakame salad). He'll fearlessly blacken, spice-rub, grill, deglaze, braise, stir-fry, barbecue, smoke, and poach, often delighting in unorthodox pairings that titillate every set of taste buds. Best of all, Griffin believes in sharing, with lavish happy

CLOSE UP

Eat Like a Local

Caymanian cuisine evolved from whatever could be coaxed from the sea and eked out from the poor, porous soil. Farmers cultivated carb-rich crops that could remain fresh without refrigeration and furnish energy for the heavy labor typical of islanders' hardscrabble existence. Hence pumpkins, coconuts, plantains, breadfruit, sweet potatoes, yams, and other "provisions" (root vegetables) became staple ingredients. Turtle (now farm-raised), the traditional specialty, can be served in soup or stew and as a steak. Conch, the meat of a large pink mollusk, is prepared in stews, chowders, fritters, and panfried (cracked). Fish—including snapper, tuna, wahoo, grouper, and marlin—is served baked, broiled, steamed, or "Cayman-style," as an *escoveitch* (panfried with peppers, onions, and tomatoes).

Rundown is another classic: fish (marinated with fresh lime juice, scallions, and fiery Scotch bonnet peppers) is steamed in coconut milk with breadfruit, pumpkin dumplings, and/or cassava. Fish tea boils and bubbles similar ingredients for hours—even days—until it thickens into gravy. The traditional dessert, heavy cake, earned

its name because excluding scarce flour and eggs made it incredibly dense: coconut, sugar, spices, and butter are boiled, mixed with seasonal binders (cassava, yam, pumpkin), and baked.

Jamaican influence is seen in oxtail, goat stew, jerk chicken and pork, salt cod, and ackee (a red tree fruit resembling scrambled eggs in flavor and texture when cooked), and *manish* water—a lusty goat-head stew with garlic, thyme, scallion, green banana (i.e., plaintain), yam, potato, and other tubers.

Aspiring Anthony Bourdains should seek out roadside vans, huts, kiosks, and stalls dishing out unfamiliar grub that might unnerve wannabe *Survivor* contestants. They offer authentic fare at very fair prices, with main dish and heaping helpings of sides costing less than CI$10. If you thought Mickey D's special sauce or Coke were secret formulas, try prying prized recipes handed down for generations from these islanders.

Bodden Town's jerk emporia are generally considered the best.

8

hour specials and all-you-can-eat-and-drink champagne-and-lobster Tuesday and Thursday for CI$49.95 per person; and three-course dinners (including two wine pairings) Monday, Wednesday, and Saturday for CI$39.95; not to mention fondue and steak nights. ⊠ *19 Fort St., George Town* ☎ *345/949–5747* ⊕ *www.bacchus.ky* ⤳ *Reservations essential* ⊘ *Closed Sun.*

$$$$
ECLECTIC
✕ **The Brasserie.** Actuaries, bankers, and CEOs frequent this contemporary throwback to a colonial country club for lunch and "attitude adjustment" happy hours for cocktails and complimentary canapés. Inviting fusion cuisine, emphasizing local ingredients whenever possible (the restaurant even has its own boat), includes terrific bar tapas like the "Mini Argentinian" (skirt steak, house-made chorizo, chimichurri sauce), or melted Brie with white truffle–and–mango marmalade. Several evenings, you can get a five- or eight-course market-driven

"Random Acts of Cooking" blind tasting. Dishes deftly balance flavors and textures without sensory overload: this is serious food with a sense of playfulness. Save room for desserts, from an artisanal cheese plate to an ice-cream-and-sorbet tasting menu to elaborate architectural confections. Lunch is more reasonably priced but equally creative; the adjacent Market excels at takeout, and the wine list is well considered. ⊠ *171 Elgin Ave., Cricket Sq., George Town* ☎ *345/945–1815* ⊕ *www. brasseriecayman.com* ⚱ *Reservations essential* ⊘ *Closed weekends.*

$$
CARIBBEAN

✕ **Breezes by the Bay.** There isn't a bad seat in the house at this nonstop feel-good fiesta festooned with tiny paper lanterns, Christmas lights, ship murals, and Mardi Gras beads (you're "lei'd" upon entering). Wraparound balconies take in a dazzling panorama from South Sound to Seven Mile Beach. It's a joyous nonstop happy hour all day every day, especially at Countdown to Sunset. Signs promise "the good kind of hurricanes," referring to the 23-ounce signature "category 15" cocktails with fresh garnishes; rum aficionados will find 48 varieties (flights available). Equally fresh food at bargain prices, including homemade baked goods and ice creams, isn't an afterthought. Chunky, velvety conch chowder served in a bread bowl or near-definitive conch fritters are meals in themselves. Hefty sandwiches are slathered with yummy jerk mayo or garlicky aioli. Signature standouts include meltingly moist whole fish escoveitch, curry chicken, popcorn shrimp, and jerk-glazed pork chops. ⊠ *Harbor Dr., George Town* ☎ *345/943–8439* ⊕ *www. breezesbythebay.com.*

$$$$
CONTINENTAL

✕ **Grand Old House.** Built in 1908 as the Petra Plantation House and transformed into the island's first upscale establishment decades ago, this grande dame is that rare restaurant that genuinely transports diners to a gracious era of bygone grandeur sans pretension. The interior rooms, awash in crystal and mahogany, recall its plantation-house origins. Classical and jazz pianists enhance the period ambience, but outside, hundreds of sparkling lights adorn the gazebos to compete with the starry sky. Rumors of a charming blond ghost trailing white chiffon complete the picture: this is a place to propose or let someone down easily. You'll find such expertly executed classics as butter-poached lobster with truffle risotto and chardonnay cream or beef tenderloin with a choice of five sauces, but the increasingly innovative menu has adopted Asian and even Southwestern influences. Pistachio-and-herb-crusted chicken is spiced by apple mole, while seared yellowfin tuna is served with bok choy and shiitake mushrooms. The subtle yet complex flavor interactions, stellar service, and encyclopedic if stratospherically priced wine list ensure legendary landmark status. ⊠ *648 S. Church St., George Town* ☎ *345/949–9333* ⊕ *www.grandoldhouse.com* ⚱ *Reservations essential* ⊘ *Closed Sept. No lunch weekends.*

$$$$
SEAFOOD

✕ **Guy Harvey's Island Grill.** This stylish, sporty, upstairs bistro celebrates the sea, from decor to cuisine. You half expect to find Hemingway regaling fellow barflies in the clubby interior with mahogany furnishings, ship's lanterns, porthole windows, whirring ceiling fans, and Harvey's action-packed marine art. The cool blues echo the sea and sky on display from the inviting balcony. Seafood is carefully chosen to exclude overexploited and threatened species. Seasonally changing dishes are peppered with Caribbean influences but pureed through the French chef's formal training. Hence, silken lobster bisque is served with puff pastry, scallops Rockefeller with spinach and béarnaise sauce, and the signature crab cakes with roasted-red-pepper aioli. You can select your fish baked, pan-sautéed, or grilled with any of eight sauces. Carnivores needn't despair, with rack of lamb in balsamic glaze or an intensely flavored New York strip with red wine–and-mushroom sauce (frites optional). Many specialties are cheaper at lunch. ⊠ *Aquaworld Duty-Free Mall, 55 S. Church St., George Town* ☎ *345/946–9000* ⊕ *www.harveysgrill.com.*

$$$$

SEAFOOD

✕ **Lobster Pot.** The nondescript building belies the lovely marine-motif decor and luscious seafood at the intimate, second-story restaurant overlooking the harbor. No surprise that fish seem to jump from the plate. Enjoy lobster prepared a half-dozen ways along with reasonably priced wine, which you can sample by the glass (particularly fine Austrian selections) in the cozy bar. The two musts are the Cayman Trio (lobster tail, grilled mahimahi, and garlic shrimp), and the Pot (lobster, giant prawns, and crab), but the kitchen can happily provide reduced-oil and -fat alternatives to most dishes. The balcony offers a breathtaking view of the sunset tarpon feeding. Lobster is market price and can be as much as $60; other entrées are less expensive. ⊠ *245 N. Church St., George Town* ☎ *345/949–2736* ⊕ *www.lobsterpot.ky* ☉ *No lunch weekends.*

SEVEN MILE BEACH

$$$$

SEAFOOD

Fodor'sChoice

★

✕ **Blue by Eric Ripert.** *Top Chef* judge Eric Ripert consulted on every aspect of the first outpost bearing his name, from decor to dishware. His trademark ethereal seafood (executed by his handpicked brigade), flawless but not fawning service, swish setting, and soothing sophistication sans pretension make this one of the Caribbean's finest restaurants. Choose from a regular three-course or the chef's hedonistic tasting menu (with or without wine pairing). Many dishes are clever improvisational riffs on the mother restaurant (New York's celebrated Le Bernardin), using the island's natural bounty (the tribute to the great Bernardin tuna foie gras adds Cayman sea salt). The sensuous counterpoint of flavors, textures, even colors is unimpeachable, as in sautéed kingklip with avocado-coconut cream, sunflower sprouts, and lime sauce *vierge*; sautéed ocean yellowtail in bourbon-lime–guajillo-pepper broth with mango-jalapeño salad; or melt-in-your-mouth chocolate mousse with caramelized banana, mango-saffron sauce, and cocoa sorbet. The vast wine list offers big names but also showcases hot new regions and lesser-known varietals that offer quality and comparative value. ⊠ *Ritz-Carlton Grand Cayman, West Bay Rd., Seven Mile Beach* ☎ *345/943–9000* 🍴 *Reservations essential* ☉ *Closed Sun. and Mon. No lunch.*

$$$$

ECLECTIC

Fodor'sChoice

★

✕ **Casa Havana.** This refined eatery glamorously channels prerevolution Cuba with crystal chandeliers, mahogany furnishings, burgundy walls, gold damask curtains, exquisite art naïf and still-life paintings, and picture windows. Lloyd Kremer's artfully prepared and presented Asian-Cuban cuisine adds Eastern flair to Floribbean fare, with sophisticated flavor and texture counterpoints. The velvety "Thai" lobster bisque is the gustatory equivalent of a Victoria's Secret silk negligee. Other stunning

8

starters include caramelized black cod with fava puree, wildflower honey-glazed prosciutto and miso carrots; and rooibos smoked eel and chorizo with pasilla pepper, wakame, and seasonal greens in sake-orange emulsion. The must-eat entrée is macadamia-nut-crusted sea bass floating in shiitake tea with white truffle essence. Standard items are reinvented: goosing "surf and turf" (prawns and sausage) with miso-mustard emulsion and capsicum foam or transforming a velouté with garam masala. Incredible island-inspired desserts include key lime cheesecake with island fruit coulis and melba sauce. Wine Master dinners pair several courses with wines (Marchese di Barolo to Gosset champagne), often introduced by the guest winemakers or owners from as far afield as Tuscany, Australia, Napa, and Chile. ⊠ *Westin Casuarina, West Bay Rd., Seven Mile Beach* ☎ *345/945–3800 Ext. 6017* ⊕ *www.westincasuarina.net* ⚑ *Reservations essential* ⊘ *No lunch Mon.–Sat.*

$–$$
CARIBBEAN
☺

✕ **Chicken! Chicken!** Devotees would probably award four exclamation points to the marvelously moist chicken, slow-roasted on a hardwood open-hearth rotisserie. Most customers grab takeout, but the decor is appealing for a fast-food joint; the clever interior replicates an old-time Cayman cottage. Bright smiles and home cooking completely from scratch enhance the authentic vibe. Hearty but (mostly) healthful heaping helpings of sides include scrumptious Cayman-style corn bread, honey-rum beans, jicama coleslaw, and spinach-pesto pasta. ⊠ *West Shore Centre, West Bay Rd., Seven Mile Beach* ☎ *345/945–2290.*

$$
ECLECTIC
★

✕ **Cimboco.** This animated celebration of all things fun, funky, and Caribbean is saturated in psychedelic colors: orange, lemon, and lavender walls; cobalt glass fixtures; paintings of musicians in fevered Fauvist hues; a mosaic of flames dancing up the exhibition kitchen's huge wood-burning oven. History buffs may be interested to know that the *Cimboco* was the first motorized sailing ship built in Cayman (in 1927) and for 20 years the main connection–lifeline to the outside world; National Archive photographs and old newspapers invest the space with still more character. Everything from breads (superlative bruschetta and jalapeño corn bread) to ice creams is made from scratch. Artisanal pizzas betray a (Wolfgang) Puck-ish sensibility with such toppings as balsamic-roasted eggplant, pine nuts, pesto, and feta; or curried chicken with pineapple and spinach. Signature items include banana-leaf-roasted snapper, fire-roasted bacon-wrapped shrimp, and mahimahi ceviche salad, but the daily specials are also inspired. The popular breakfast and brunch are equally creative. Amazingly good desserts start with a moist, intensely rich brownie. The small but well-considered wine list features more than a dozen by the glass. ⊠ *The Marquee, West Bay Rd. at Harquail Bypass, Seven Mile Beach* ☎ *345/947–2782* ⊕ *www.cimboco.com.*

$$–$$$
ECLECTIC

✕ **Eats Café.** This happy, hopping hangout is more eclectic and stylish than any diner, with dramatic decor (crimson booths and walls, flat-screen TVs lining the counter, pendant steel lamps, an exhibition kitchen, gigantic flower paintings, and Andy Warhol reproductions) and vast menu (Cajun to Chinese), including smashing breakfasts. The 15 burgers alone (Rasta Mon Jerkya to Cajun Peppercorn to I'm Sooo Bleu, as well as fish and veggie versions) could satisfy almost any craving, but you could also get a Caesar salad or sushi, Philly cheese steak, or chicken chimichangas. It's noisy, busy, buzzing, and hip—but not aggressively so. ⊠ *Falls Plaza, West Bay Rd., Seven Mile Beach* ☏ *345/943–3287* ⊕ *www.eats.ky.*

$ ✕ **Icoa Fine Foods**. Icoa, the goddess of water worshipped by the indigenous people of Venezuela's Paria peninsula, was renowned for her exceptional beauty and alluring perfume; innovative Dutch chef Jurgen Wevers crafts food that likewise stimulates all the senses, drawing his own adoring acolytes. The minimalist space (Cubist- and Constructivist-inspired art, IKEA-style simple lines, ornate mosaic floor, and lots of stark Starck-like white) allows his cutting-edge cuisine to take center stage. Taste buds tango to such dishes as local yellowfin tuna pastrami with organic quinoa, avocado crème, kalamata olive cake, and pine nuts; and maple duck rillette paired with maple duck consommé. Fresh-baked breads make a meal in themselves. Desserts are remarkable (you can also buy handcrafted chocolates infused with fresh key limes, passion fruit, pineapple, and Cayman honey). ⊠ *9–11 Seven Mile Shops, West Bay Rd., Seven Mile Beach* ☏ *345/945–1915* ⊕ *www.icoacafe. com* ☽ *No dinner.*

ECLECTIC

$$$ ✕ **Ragazzi**. The name means "good buddies," and this strip-mall jewel offers simpatico ambience indeed, always percolating with conversation and good strong espresso. The airy space is convivial: blond woods, periwinkle walls and columns, and handsome artworks of beach scenes, sailboats, and palm trees (against a striking yellow sky) with the scenes extended onto the frame. Chef Adriano Usini turns out magnificent, meticulously prepared standards (the antipasto alone is worth a visit, as are the homemade breadsticks and focaccia, and definitive carpaccio and insalata Caprese). The shellfish linguine (shrimp, scallops, and mussels in a light, silken tomato sauce, with cherry-tomato skins pulled back and crisped) and gnocchi in four-cheese sauce with brandy and pistachios will please any pasta perfectionist. Two dozen first-rate pizzas emerge from the wood-burning oven, and meat and seafood mains are beautifully done, never overcooked. The wine list is notable (400-odd choices) for a casual eatery, showcasing great range and affordability even on high-ticket, hard-to-find heavy hitters such as Biondi Santi Brunello, Jermann Pinot Grigio, and Giacosa Barbaresco; the affable, knowledgeable staff will gladly suggest pairings, including unusual finds. ⊠ *Buckingham Sq., West Bay Rd., Seven Mile Beach* ☏ *345/945–3484* ⊕ *www.ragazzi.ky.*

ITALIAN

8

$$$ ✕ **Reef Grill at Royal Palms**. This class act appeals to a casually suave crowd, many of them regulars, who appreciate its consistent quality, attentive yet unobtrusive service, soothing seaside setting, top-notch entertainment, and surprisingly reasonable prices. The space is cannily divided into four areas, each with its own look and feel. Co-owner–chef George Dahlstrom gives his perfectly prepared, familiar items just enough twist to satisfy jaded palates: calamari is fried in arborio rice batter with lemon aioli; toasted, sesame-crusted, seared tuna kicks with kimchi; melt-in-your-mouth braised short ribs, now one of the lighter "small plates" (think mega-tapas), come with peppercorn poutine (fries covered with cheese curds and gravy); and sea scallops are pan-seared with a roasted corn–smoked bacon mash. Dance the calories off to

SEAFOOD

the estimable reggae, calypso, and soca sounds of Coco Red, and then adjourn to the cozy lounge for an aged rum or single malt. It's equally enticing at lunch, when it exudes a soigné beach bar ambience. ⊠ 537 *West Bay Rd., Seven Mile Beach* ☎ 345/945–6358⊕ *www.reefgrill.com* ⊙ *No dinner Sun. May–Nov.*

$$
CARIBBEAN
☺

✕ **Sunshine Grill.** This cheerful, cherished locals' secret serves haute comfort food at bargain-basement prices. Even the chattel-style poolside building, painted a delectable lemon with lime shutters, whets the appetite. Sunshine ranks high in the island's greatest burger debate, and the jerk chicken egg rolls and fabulous fish tacos elevate pub grub to an art form. Wash it down with one of the many signature libations, like the Painkiller. Take advantage of affordably priced nightly dinner specials such as Thai chili salmon, red snapper amandine, and Cuban pork loin with *sofrito* (a dip of cilantro, garlic, onions, tomatoes, and oregano). Don't miss Thursday's all-you-can-eat Caribbean barbecue buffet. ⊠ *Sunshine Suites, West Bay Rd., Seven Mile Beach* ☎ 345/949–3000.

$$$
JAPANESE
★

✕ **Yoshi Sushi.** The superlative sushi's fresh—and the clientele sometimes even fresher—at this modish, modern locals' lair. Scarlet cushions, cherry pendant blown-glass lamps, leather-and-bamboo accents, and maroon walls help create a sensuous, even charged vibe in the main room. The backlighted bar sees its share of carefree customers trying to manipulate their chopsticks after a few kamikaze sake bomber missions (plunging hot cups of sake into frosty Kirin beer). Savvy diners literally leave themselves in Yoshi's hands (the rolls and nightly special sushi "pizzas" are particularly creative), and the raw-phobic can choose from fine cooked items, from beef tataki to tempura to teriyaki. The congenial staff recommends intriguing sake and beer pairings, though the wine list and martini selection are also admirable for an Asian eatery. ⊠ *Falls Plaza, West Bay Rd., Seven Mile Beach* ☎ 345/943–9674 ⊕ *www.eats.ky* ⚑ *Reservations essential.*

WEST BAY

$$$$
ECLECTIC

✕ **Calypso Grill.** Shack chic describes this inviting split-level space splashed in Dr. Seuss primary colors that contrast with brick walls, hardwood furnishings, terra-cotta floors, trompe l'oeil shutters, and (real) French doors opening onto sweeping North Sound views. If the interior is like stepping into a Caribbean painting, the outdoor deck serenely surveying frigate birds watchfully circling fishing boats is a Winslow Homer canvas brought to life. George Fowler's menu rightly emphasizes fish hauled in at the adjacent dock, so fresh (and never overcooked) that it almost literally jumps from the plate. You'll never go wrong with the unvarnished catch of the day grilled, blackened, or sautéed. Though this is seafood's turf, landlubbers can savor a veal chop with morel-marsala sauce or a proper rack of lamb. End with the sticky toffee pudding. ⊠ *Morgan's Harbour, West Bay* ☎ 345/949–3948 ⊕ *www.calypsogrillcayman.com* ⚑ *Reservations essential* ⊙ *Closed Mon.*

$$$$
ECLECTIC

✕ **Cracked Conch.** This longtime institution, rebuilt after Hurricane Ivan, effortlessly blends upscale and down-home. The interior gleams from the elaborate light-and-water sculpture at the gorgeous mosaic-and-mahogany entrance bar to the plush booths with subtly embedded lighting. You can drink in the remarkable water views through large shutters, but for maximum impact, dine on the multitiered patio. New-fangled variations on old-fashioned cuisine include honey-jerk-glazed tuna with cucumber relish, crispy calamari with cardamom-marinated carrots and chipotle sauce, and wahoo tartare in saffron-tomato broth. Sample stellar signature items include the definitive conch chowder or ceviche, short rib ravioli with truffles and Parmesan foam, and mahimahi poached with dark-rum–butter sauce, turmeric, wilted spinach, and tomato

chutney. Desserts delight, from a gossamer vanilla crème brûlée with pineapple-bergamot salsa to a miraculously moist guava-glazed bread-and-butter pudding. Locals flock to Sunday brunch or Monday's all-you-can-eat barbecue bash, or they just hang out at the wildly decorated dockside Macabuca tiki bar (fab sunsets, sunset-hued libations), which lives up to its mellow name, indigenous Taíno for "What does it matter?" ⊠ *Northwest Point Rd., West Bay* ☎ *345/945–5217* ⊕ *www.crackedconch.com.ky.*

EAST END

$$$$

SEAFOOD

✕ **The Lighthouse.** The nonworking, conical, white-stucco lighthouse surrounded by fluttering flags serves as a beacon for hungry East End explorers. The interior replicates a yacht: polished hardwood floors, ship's lanterns, mosaic hurricane lamps, steering wheels, marine artworks, portholes, and waiters in crew's garb with chevrons. Most tables afford sweeping sea vistas, but prize romantic seating is on the little deck. Ship-shape starters include Miss Nell's red conch chowder (she lives in the pink house behind the restaurant) or flash-fried calamari with shaved onions and sweet chili dip. Photo-shoot-worthy entrées (such as spice-rubbed salmon with roasted corn salsa and plantains drizzled with red pepper coulis) sing with color and flavor. Carnivores can devour braised veal shank with almond polenta or porcini-dusted chicken breast with rosemary-Marsala sauce. Vegetarians will delight in the curries, tofu stir-fries, and pastas. Save room for desserts, including the tropical cheesecake. The comprehensive wine list extends to a superb postprandial selection of liqueurs, aged rums, ports, and grappas. The gift shop offers lovely jewelry and handmade ceramic lighthouses. ⊠ *Oceanside, Breakers, East End* ☎ *345/947–2047* ⊕ *www.lighthouse.ky.*

WHERE TO STAY

Brace yourself for resort prices—there are few accommodations in the lower price ranges. You'll find no big all-inclusive resorts on Grand Cayman (though the Reef Resort now offers an optional AI plan to its guests), and very few offer a meal plan other than breakfast. Parking is always free at island hotels and resorts. Although the island has several resorts (mostly along Seven Mile Beach), the majority of accommodations are vacation rentals, and these are scattered throughout the island. Some of the condo complexes even offer resort-style amenities.

GUESTHOUSES

They may be some distance from the beach and short on style and facilities, but the island's guesthouses offer rock-bottom prices, a friendly atmosphere, and your best shot at getting to know the locals. Rooms are clean and simple, and most have private baths.

VILLAS AND CONDOMINIUMS

Most condo complexes are very similar, with telephones, satellite TV, air-conditioning, living and dining areas, patios, and parking. Differences are amenities, proximity to town and beach, and the views. As with resorts, rates are higher in winter, and there may be a three- or seven-night minimum. There are dozens of large private villas available on the beach, especially on the North Side near Cayman Kai. A growing trend: "green" condos.

Several of the condo and villa rental companies have Web sites where you can see pictures of the privately owned units and villas they represent.

Cayman Villas (☎ 800/235–5888 or 345/945–4144 ⊕ *www.caymanvillas. com*) represents villas and condos on Grand and Little Cayman.

Grand Cayman Villas (☎ 877/426–8455 ⊕ *www.grandcaymanvillas.net*) was started by Virginia resident Jim Leavitt, who carries listings for dozens of fine properties island-wide.

Island Hideaways (☎ 800/832–2302 ⊕ *www.islandhideaways.com*) rents villas all over the Caribbean, including some in the Cayman Islands.

Wimco (☎ 866/850–6140 ⊕ *www.wimco.com*), or the West Indies Management Company, is synonymous with quality throughout the world, especially the Caribbean.

The following hotel reviews have been condensed for this book. Please go to Fodors.com for expanded reviews of each property.

GEORGE TOWN AND ENVIRONS

$–$$

HOTEL

🏨 **Sunset House.** This amiable seaside dive-oriented resort is on the ironshore south of George Town, close enough for a short trip to stores and restaurants yet far enough to feel secluded. **Pros:** great shore diving and dive shop; lively bar scene; fun international clientele. **Cons:** often indifferent service; somewhat run-down; no real swimming beach. ✉ *390 S. Church St., Box 479GT, George Town* ☎ *345/949–7111 or 800/854–4767* ⊕ *www.sunsethouse.com* ⇆ *58 rooms, 2 suites* △ *In-room: a/c, kitchen (some), no safe, Wi-Fi (some). In-hotel: restaurant, bar, pool, laundry facilities, business center* ❍| *No meals.*

SEVEN MILE BEACH

$$$$

RENTAL

Fodor's Choice

★

🏨 **Caribbean Club.** Sleek but not slick, this gleaming boutique facility completely reinvented itself post-Ivan, including a striking lobby filled with aquariums, a stunning infinity pool, and the aggressively contemporary trattoria, Luca. **Pros:** luxurious, high-tech facilities beyond the typical apartment complex; trendy Italian restaurant on-site; service on the beach. **Cons:** stratospheric prices; though families are welcome, they may find it rather imposing; smaller balconies on top floor (albeit amazing views). ⊠ *871 West Bay Rd., Box 30135, Seven Mile Beach* ☎ *345/623–4500 or 800/941–1126* ⊕ *www.caribclub.com* ◁ *37 3-bedroom condos* ⟳ *In-room: a/c, kitchen, no safe, Wi-Fi. In-hotel: restaurant, bar, pool, gym, beach, laundry facilities* ⦿ *No meals.*

\$\$ 🖫 **Christopher Columbus.** This enduring favorite is quite a discovery for families, sitting on the peaceful northern end of Seven Mile Beach. Though snorkeling is superb right offshore, the CC's beach is free of rocks; the parrot-green lawn fronting the sand is so perfectly maintained you could play croquet. **Pros:** excellent snorkeling from a fine stretch of beach; great value; free Wi-Fi. **Con:** car really needed; often overrun by families

RENTAL

⟳

BEST BETS FOR LODGING

Fodor's Choice ★
Caribbean Club, Lighthouse Point, Pirates Point, Reef Resort, Ritz-Carlton, Southern Cross Club

BEST BEACHFRONT
Coral Stone Club, Lacovia Condominiums, Reef Resort, Westin Casuarina

BEST FOR DIVERS
Brac Reef Beach Resort, Cayman Breakers, Cobalt Coast, Little Cayman Beach Resort

BEST FOR ROMANCE
Shangri-La B&B, Turtle Nest Inn, Walton's Mango Manor

during holiday seasons and summer; top floors feature splendid vistas but difficult access for physically challenged. ⊠ *2013 West Bay Rd., Seven Mile Beach* ☎ *345/945–4354 or 866/311–5231* ⊕ *www. christophercolumbuscondos.com* ◁ *30 2- and 3-bedroom condos* ⟳ *In-room: kitchen, no safe, Internet, Wi-Fi. In-hotel: tennis courts, pool, beach, laundry facilities* ⦿ *No meals.*

\$–\$\$ 🖫 **Comfort Suites Grand Cayman.** This no-frills, all-suites hotel has an

HOTEL ideal location on West Bay Road, next door to the Marriott and near numerous shops, restaurants, and bars. **Pros:** affordable; nice complimentary extras like continental breakfast and Wi-Fi; fun youngish crowd. **Cons:** nearly a block from the beach; new condominium blocks sea views; no balconies; bar closes early. ⊠ *West Bay Rd., George Town* ☎ *345/945–7300 or 800/517–4000* ⊕ *www.caymancomfort.com* ◁ *108 suites* ⟳ *In-room: a/c, kitchen, Internet, Wi-Fi. In-hotel: restaurant, bar, pool, gym, laundry facilities* ⦿ *Breakfast.*

\$\$\$\$ 🖫 **Coral Stone Club.** This exclusive enclave shines in the shadow of the

RENTAL Ritz-Carlton by offering understated barefoot luxury and huge three-

★ bedroom condos. **Pros:** largest ratio of beach and pool space to guests; walking distance to several restaurants and shops; stellar service; excellent off-season deals. **Cons:** expensive in high season; Ritz-Carlton guests sometimes wander over from their packed section of sand trying to poach beach space. ⊠ *West Bay Rd., Box 30105, Seven Mile Beach* ☎ *345/945–5820 or 888/927–2322* ⊕ *www.coralstoneclub.com* ◁ *35 3-bedroom condos* ⟳ *In-room: a/c, kitchen, no safe, Wi-Fi. In-hotel: tennis court, pool, gym, beach* ⦿ *No meals.*

\$\$\$–\$\$\$\$ 🖫 **Grand Cayman Beach Suites.** The former Hyatt all-suites section, now

RESORT locally run, offers a terrific beachfront location and trendy eateries.

8

Shaded beach loungers at the Ritz-Carlton, Grand Cayman.

Pros: fine beach; superior dining and water-sports facilities; free use of gym (unusual on Grand Cayman); supermarkets and restaurants within walking distance. **Cons:** most entrances face the street, making it noisy on weekends; several units need refurbishment; music often blaring around the pool. ⊠ *West Bay Rd., Box 1588, Seven Mile Beach* ☎ *345/949–1234* ⊕ *www.grand-cayman-beach-suites.com* ⇘ *53 suites* ⚲ *In-room: a/c, kitchen, Wi-Fi. In-hotel: restaurants, bars, pools, gym, spa, beach, water sports, children's programs* ⊗ *No meals.*

$$$–$$$$
RESORT

⊞ **Grand Cayman Marriott Beach Resort.** The soaring, stylish, if impersonal marble lobby (with exquisite art glass, spectacular blown-up underwater photos, and fun elements such as red British-style telephone boxes) sets the tone for this bustling beachfront property. **Pros:** lively bars and restaurants; good snorkeling and water sports; convenient to both George Town and Seven Mile Beach. **Cons:** often overrun by tour groups and conventioneers; narrowest section of Seven Mile Beach; pool and bar often noisy late. ⊠ *389 West Bay Rd., Box 30371, Seven Mile Beach* ☎ *345/949–0088 or 800/223–6388* ⊕ *www.marriott.com* ⇘ *273 rooms, 22 suites* ⚲ *In-room: a/c, Wi-Fi. In-hotel: restaurants, bars, pool, gym, spa, beach, water sports, laundry facilities, children's programs, business center* ⊗ *No meals.*

$$$–$$$$
RENTAL
★

⊞ **Lacovia Condominiums.** The carefully manicured courtyard of this handsome arcaded Mediterranean Revival property could easily be mistaken for a peaceful park. **Pros:** central location; exquisite gardens; extensive beach. **Cons:** rear courtyard rooms can be noisy from traffic and partying from West Bay Road; pool fairly small (though most people prefer the beach). ⊠ *697 West Bay Rd., Box 32309, Seven Mile Beach* ☎ *345/949–7599* ⊕ *www.lacovia.com* ⇘ *35 1-, 2-, and*

3-bedroom condos ⚒ In-room: a/c, kitchen, no safe, Internet. In-hotel: tennis court, pool, gym, beach, laundry facilities ⛉ No meals.

$$$$
RESORT
🏊
Fodor's Choice
★

🏨 **Ritz-Carlton Grand Cayman.** Posh and pampering without pretension, the Ritz-Carlton offers unparalleled luxury and service infused with a welcome sense of place, including works by top local artists and craftspeople. **Pros:** exemplary service; exceptional facilities with many complimentary extras; marvelous local artworks including a corridor-length gallery with rotating exhibits. **Cons:** annoyingly high per-night resort fee; somewhat sprawling with a confusing layout; long walk to beach (over an interior bridge) from most rooms. ⊠ *West Bay Rd.Seven Mile Beach ⌂ Box 34328, Seven Mile Beach, Grand Cayman KY1-1209* ☎ *345/943–9000* ⊕ *www.ritzcarlton.com* ⇆ *329 rooms, 12 suites, 24 condos ⚒ In-room: a/c, kitchen (some), Internet, Wi-Fi. In-hotel: restaurants, bar, pools, golf course, gym, spa, children's programs, laundry facilities ⛉ Breakfast.*

$
HOTEL

🏨 **Sunshine Suites Resort.** This friendly, all-suites hotel is an impeccably clean money saver. The slightly musty rooms were refurbished in early 2009; they lack balconies, patios, or even views, and both windows and bathrooms are tiny, but each has a complete kitchen, flat-screen TV, and free Wi-Fi (laptops can be rented). **Pros:** good value and deals; cheerful staff; rocking little restaurant; thoughtful free extras. **Cons:** poor views; not on the beach; slightly musty. ⊠ *1465 Esterley Tibbetts Hwy., off West Bay Rd., Box 30095, Seven Mile Beach* ☎ *345/949–3000 or 877/786–1110* ⊕ *www.sunshinesuites.com* ⇆ *130 suites ⚒ In-room: kitchen, no safe, Internet, Wi-Fi. In-hotel: restaurant, bar, pool, laundry facilities, business center ⛉ Breakfast.*

$$$–$$$$
RESORT
🏊
★

🏨 **Westin Casuarina Resort and Spa.** The Westin has something to offer everyone, from conventioneers to honeymooners to families, not to mention an excellent location. **Pros:** terrific children's programs; superb beach (the largest resort stretch at 800 feet); sterling dining. **Con:** occasionally bustling and impersonal when large groups book. ⊠ *West Bay Rd., Box 30620, Seven Mile Beach* ☎ *345/945–3800* ⊕ *www.westincasuarina.net* ⇆ *339 rooms, 8 suites ⚒ In-room: a/c, Internet, Wi-Fi. In-hotel: restaurants, bars, pool, gym, spa, beach, water sports, children's programs, business center ⛉ No meals.*

WEST BAY

$$
RESORT
★

🏨 **Cobalt Coast Resort and Suites.** This small ecofriendly hotel is perfect for divers who want a sparkling, spacious room or suite right on the ironshore far, far from the madding crowds and who don't want to pay high prices. **Pros:** superb dive outfit; friendly service and clientele; free Wi-Fi. **Cons:** poky golden-sand beach; unattractive concrete pool area; remote location, so a car (included in some packages) is necessary. ⊠ *18-A Sea Fan Dr., West Bay* ☎ *345/946–5656 or 888/946–5656* ⊕ *www.cobaltcoast.com* ⇆ *7 rooms, 14 suites ⚒ In-room: a/c, kitchen (some), Wi-Fi. In-hotel: restaurant, bar, pool, laundry facilities ⛉ Breakfast.*

$$$–$$$$
RESORT
Fodor's Choice
★

🏨 **Lighthouse Point.** For travelers who want to "live lightly on the planet," leading scuba operator DiveTech's stunning new development takes the lead, from sustainable wood interiors and recycled concrete to an ecosensitive gray-water system, energy-saving appliances and lights, and Cayman's first wind turbine generator. **Pros:** ecofriendly; fantastic

8

shore diving (and state-of-the-art dive shop); creative and often recycled upscale look. **Cons:** no real beach; car necessary; bit difficult for physically challenged to navigate. ⊠ *571 N.W. Point Rd., West Bay* ☎ *345/949–1700* ⊕ *www.lighthouse-point-cayman.com* ⤳ *9 2-bedroom apartments* & *In-room: a/c, no safe (some), kitchen, Internet, Wi-Fi. In-hotel: restaurant, bar, water sports, laundry facilities* ⟟⊙⟟ *No meals.*

¢–$
B&B/INN
★

🏠 **Shangri-La B&B.** Accomplished pianist George Davidson and wife Eileen built this lavish lakeside retreat and truly make guests feel at home, along with dogs Roxie and Stella. **Pros:** use of kitchen; elegant decor. **Cons:** rental car necessary; not on the beach. ⊠ *1 Sticky Toffee La., West Bay* ☎ *345/526–1170* ⊕ *www.shangrilabandb.com* ⤳ *6 rooms, 1 apartment* & *In-room: a/c, no safe (some), Wi-Fi. In-hotel: pool, laundry facilities* ⟟⊙⟟ *Breakfast.*

EAST END

$$–$$$
RESORT
Fodor's Choice
★

🏠 **Reef Resort.** This exceedingly well-run time-share property (don't worry: no aggressive hawking!) seductively straddles a 600-foot beach on the less hectic East End. **Pros:** romantically remote; glorious beach; enthusiastic staff (including a crackerjack wedding coordinator); great packages. **Cons:** remote; few dining options within easy driving distance; sprawling layout. ⊠ *Queen's Hwy., Box 20865 SMB, East End* ☎ *345/947–3100 or 888/232–0541* ⊕ *www.thereef.com.ky* ⤳ *152 suites* & *In-room: a/c, kitchen (some), Wi-Fi. In-hotel: restaurants, bar, tennis court, pools, gym, spa, beach, water sports, laundry facilities, business center* ⟟⊙⟟ *No meals.*

¢–$$
RENTAL
★

🏠 **Turtle Nest Inn and Condos.** This affordable, intimate, Mediterranean-style seaside inn has roomy one-bedroom apartments and a pool overlooking a narrow beach with good snorkeling. **Pros:** wonderful snorkeling; thoughtful extras; caring staff; free Wi-Fi. **Cons:** car necessary; occasional rocks and debris on beach; ground-floor room views slightly obscured by palms; road noise in back rooms. ⊠ *166 Bodden Town Rd., Box 187, Bodden Town* ☎ *345/947–8665* ⊕ *www. turtlenestinn.net* ⤳ *8 apartments, 10 2-bedroom condos* & *In-room: a/c, kitchen, no safe, Wi-Fi. In-hotel: pool, beach, water sports, laundry facilities* ⟟⊙⟟ *No meals.*

NIGHTLIFE

Grand Cayman nightlife is surprisingly good for such a quiet-seeming island. Check the Friday edition of the *Caymanian Compass* for listings of music, movies, theater, and other entertainment. Bars are open during evening hours until 1 am, and clubs are generally open from 10 pm until 3 am, but none may serve liquor after midnight on Saturday and none can offer dancing on Sunday. Competition is fierce between Grand Cayman's many bars and restaurants. In addition to entertainment (fish feeding to fire-eating), even upscale joints host happy hours offering free hors d'oeuvres and/or drinks.

GEORGE TOWN AND ENVIRONS

Rackam's Pub and Restaurant. A Cayman mosaic of fishermen to Who's-the-Hugo-Boss financiers savors sensational sunsets followed by exuberantly pirouetting tarpon feeding at the open-air, marine-theme happenin' bar built on a jetty jutting into the harbor (boaters, even snorkelers cruise right up the ladder for drinks while anglers leave their catch on ice) that has complimentary snacks on Friday and serves pub fare at fair prices until midnight. ⊠ *N. Church St., George Town* ☎ *345/945–3860* ⊕ *www.rackamswaterfront.ky.*

SEVEN MILE BEACH

★ **Aqua Beach Bar.** This place feels like a country bar gone (coco)nuts: palm trees burst through thatching; art naïf portraits of musicians explode in neon reds, yellows, blues, and greens; private tiki huts provide intimacy; and neon beer signs illuminate the wood paneling. Fairly good Tex-Mex fare is dished out late. There's a variety of live bands, open-mike nights, and theme nights, such as Thursday acoustic jams. Also, there are plenty of daily drink-and-eat specials such as Sunday's NASCAR Bud buckets and the CI$18 all-you-can-eat-and-drink barbecue. ⊠ *426 West Bay Rd., Seven Mile Beach* ☎ *345/949–8498.*

★ **Bamboo Lounge.** Come here for the quiet, refined, but theatrically designed bar with sublime sushi (and other Asian standbys) and luscious libations (with suggestive names like Foreplay and Love Potion #69) abetted by an extensive wine and sake list. You can roll what you eat during Master Sushi Chef O.G.'s cooking demonstrations at 5:30 most weeknights. The musical menu runs from jazz (luring couples conducting affairs both personal and professional) to Wednesday's "Bamboozled" nights, when younger soigné singles sweat elegantly on the minuscule dance floor. ⊠ *Grand Cayman Beach Suites, West Bay Rd., Seven Mile Beach* ☎ *345/947–8744* ⊕ *www.grand-cayman-beach-suites.com.*

★ **Calico Jack's.** For a casual drink, visit this friendly outdoor beach bar at the north end of the public beach with a DJ on Saturday and open-mike night on Tuesday, bands many Friday nights, and riotous parties during the full moon when even Ritz-Carlton guests let their hair and inhibitions down. ⊠ *West Bay Rd., Seven Mile Beach* ☎ *345/945–7850.*

Coconut Joe's. You can sit at the bar or swing under a century-old poinciana tree and watch the traffic go by. There are murals of apes everywhere, from gorillas doing shots to a baboon in basketball uniform (in keeping with management's facetious suggestion that you attract your server's attention by pounding your chest while screeching and scratching yourself). It's particularly popular with the younger tourism- and hospitality-industry crowds (ply them with beers for some hair- and eyebrow-raising backstage stories). Friday really swings with DJs and free happy-hour munchies. ⊠ *Across from Comfort Suites, West Bay Rd., Seven Mile Beach* ☎ *345/943–5637.*

Jet. For a rowdy time, zoom into this new, late-night, yup-scaled, slim-hipper-than-thou version of previous tenant Next Level that delivers a dancing high, spinning everything from retro remixes to hip-hop for Jessica Alba wannabes poured into spandex and Gap poster-boy

8

slackers (potential hell for anyone over 30 years old or 20% body fat). ⊠ *West Bay Rd., opposite Marriott, Seven Mile Beach* ☎ *345/324–0221* ⊕ *www.jet.ky.*

Legendz. A sports bar with a clubby, retro feel (Marilyn Monroe and Frank Sinatra photos channel the glamour days), it's the usual testosterone test drive with plentiful scoring of both types. Good luck wrestling a spot at the bar for Pay-Per-View and major live sporting events (though 10 TVs, including two 6-by-8 foot, high-resolution screens broadcast to every corner). It doubles as an entertainment venue, booking local bands, stand-up comics, and leading island DJs. ⊠ *Falls Centre, West Bay Rd., Seven Mile Beach* ☎ *No phone.*

Lone Star Bar and Grill. The bar and restaurant proudly calls itself Cayman's top dive (and indeed, locals from dive masters to dentists get down and occasionally dirty over kick-ass margaritas). The noisy bar glorifies sports, Texas, T&A, and the boob tube, from murals of Cowboys cheerleaders to an amazing sports memorabilia collection (including items signed by both Bushes), and 10 big-screen TVs tuned to different events. ⊠ *West Bay Rd., Seven Mile Beach* ☎ *345/945–5175.*

★ **"O" Bar.** "O" Bar is a trendy black-and-crimson, industrial-style dance club with mixed music and juggling, flame-throwing bartenders—practically local celebs—flipping cocktails with cojones every night. It's as close to a stand-and-pose milieu as you'll find on Cayman, with the occasional fashion fascist parading in Prada. An upper-level private loft is available by reservation. ⊠ *Queen's Court, West Bay Rd., Seven Mile Beach* ☎ *345/943–6227* ⊕ *www.obar.ky.*

★ **Silver Palm Lounge.** The Silver Palm drips with cash and cachet. One section faithfully replicates a classic English country library (perfect for civilized, proper afternoon tea or a pre- or postdinner champagne or single malt). Then there's the sexy, überhip, black-clad Taikun lounge, with hardwood wainscoting, carved bamboo, marble floors, lacquer tables, and model (in both senses) waitstaff. Also on tap: fab cocktails, including specialty martinis (the Silver Palm cosmopolitan is a winner—Ketel One citron, triple sec, a squeeze of fresh lime juice, and a splash of cranberry topped off with Moët champagne); pages of wines by the glass; an impressive list of cigars, cognacs, and aged rums; and marvelous sushi and creative tapas. Everyone's chic-by-jowl after 10 pm, especially on funked-out DJ Fridays, when Arab sheiks mingle with American CEOs, and tonsorially challenged agent-types wear trophy wives (and mistresses) on their arms like Rolexes: it puts the sin in scintillating. ⊠ *Ritz-Carlton, West Bay Rd., Seven Mile Beach* ☎ *345/943–9000.*

The Wharf. You can dance near the water to mellow music on Saturday evenings; when there's a wedding reception in the pavilion, the crashing surf and candles twinkling as if competing with the stars bathe the proceedings in an almost Gatsby-esque glow. For something less sedate, Roger and Sarah conduct sizzling salsa dancing and lessons on Tuesday, while Fridays morph into a wild 1970s disco night. The stunning seaside setting on tiered decks compensates for often undistinguished food and service. The Ports of Call bar is a splendid place for sunset fanciers, and tarpon feeding off the deck is a nightly 9 pm spectacle. ⊠ *West Bay Rd., George Town* ☎ *345/949–2231.*

EAST END

Rusty Pelican. This spot draws an eclectic group of dive masters, expats, honeymooners, and mingling singles. The knockout, colorful cocktails pack quite a punch, making the sunset last for hours. The bar dialogue is entertainment enough, but Andrew Bacon's occasionally ribald musical games enhance the vivacity. Don't miss local legend, country-calypsonian Barefoot Man, when he plays "upstairs" at Pelican's Reef—he's to Cayman what Jimmy Buffett is to Key West. ⊠ *Reef Resort, Colliers, East End* 📱 *345/947–3100* ⊕ *www.thereef.com.ky.*

SHOPPING

On Grand Cayman the good news is that there's no sales tax *and* there's plenty of duty-free merchandise. Locally made items to watch for include woven mats, baskets, jewelry made of a marblelike stone called Caymanite (from the cliffs of Cayman Brac), and authentic sunken treasure, though the latter is never cheap. In addition, there are several noteworthy local artists, some of whose atelier–homes double as galleries, such as Al Ebanks, Horacio Esteban, and Luelan Bodden. Unique items include Cayman sea salt and luxury bath salts (solar harvested in an ecologically sensitive manner), and Tortuga rum and rum cakes. Cigar lovers take note: some shops carry famed Cuban brands, but you must enjoy them on the island; bringing them back to the United States is illegal.

Although you can find black-coral products in Grand Cayman, they're controversial. Most of the coral sold here comes from Belize and Honduras; Cayman Islands marine law prohibits the removal of live coral from its own sea (although most of it has been taken illegally). Black coral grows at a very slow rate (3 inches every 10 years) and is an endangered species. Consider buying other products instead.

GEORGE TOWN AND ENVIRONS

ART GALLERIES

★ **Al Ebanks Studio Gallery.** This gallery shows the eponymous artist's versatile, always provocative work in various media. Since you're walking into his home as well as atelier, everything is on display. Clever movable panels maximize space "like Art Murphy beds." His work, while inspired by his home, could never be labeled traditional Caribbean art, exhibiting vigorous movement through abstract swirls of color and textural contrasts. Though non-representational (save for his equally intriguing sculpture and ceramics), the focal subject from carnivals to iguanas is always subtly apparent. Ask him about the Native Sons art movement he co-founded. ⊠ *186B Shedden Rd., George Town* 📱 *345/927–5365 or 345/949–0693.*

★ **Cathy Church's Underwater Photo Centre and Gallery.** Come see a collection of the acclaimed underwater shutterbug's spectacular color and limited-edition black-and-white underwater photos. Have Cathy autograph her latest coffee-table book and regale you with anecdotes of her globe-trotting adventures. The store also carries the latest marine camera equipment, and she'll schedule private underwater photography instruction as well on her own dive boat outfitted with special graphics-oriented computers to critique your work. She also does wedding photography, both above and underwater. ⊠ *S. Church St., George Town* ☏ *345/949–7415.*

★ **Guy Harvey's Gallery and Shoppe.** This is where world-renowned marine biologist, conservationist, and artist Guy Harvey showcases his aquatic-inspired action-packed art in nearly every conceivable medium, logo tableware, and sportswear (even logo soccer balls and Zippos). The soaring, two-story 4,000-square-foot space is almost more theme park than store, with monitors playing his sportfishing videos, wood floors inlaid with tile duplicating rippling water, dangling catboats "attacked" by lifelike shark models, and life-size murals honoring such classics as Hemingway's *Old Man and the Sea.* Original paintings, sculpture, and drawings are expensive, but there's something (tile art, prints, lithographs, and photos) in most price ranges. ⊠ *49 S. Church St., George Town* ☏ *345/943–4891.*

FOODSTUFFS

There are seven modern, U.S.-style supermarkets for groceries (three of them have full-service pharmacies) on Grand Cayman. The biggest difference you'll find between these and supermarkets on the mainland is in the prices, which are about 25% to 30% more than at home.

Tortuga Rum Company. This company bakes, then vacuum-seals, more than 10,000 of its world-famous rum cakes daily, adhering to the original "secret" century-old recipe. There are seven flavors, from banana to Blue Mountain coffee. The 12-year-old rum, blended from private stock though actually distilled in Guyana, is a connoisseur's delight for after-dinner sipping. You can buy a fresh rum cake at the airport on the way home at the same prices as at the factory store. ⊠ *N. Sound Rd., Industrial Park, George Town* ☏ *345/949–7701* ⊕ *www.tortugarumcakes.com.*

JEWELRY

★ **Bernard Passman.** The black-coral creations of Bernard Passman have won the approval of the British royal family, who chose him to create a wedding present for Prince Charles and Princess Diana. His fabulous flatware and fanciful candelabras would stand out in the Addams Family manse. He even creates three-dimensional bas-relief scenes with cavorting dolphins, as well as mermaids with glittering gold gilt tails and golfers (each movement of the swing depicted by a dozen clubs in 18K gold). ⊠ *Cardinal Ave., George Town* ☏ *345/949–0123.*

MALLS AND SHOPPING CENTERS

★ **Kirk Freeport Plaza.** This downtown shopping center, home to the Kirk Freeport flagship department store, is ground zero for couture; it's also known for its boutiques selling fine watches and jewelry, china, crystal, leather, perfumes, and cosmetics. *Cardinal Ave., George Town.*

Landmark. Stores in the Landmark sell perfumes, treasure coins, and upscale beachwear; Breezes by the Bay restaurant is upstairs. ⊠ *Harbour Dr., George Town.*

SEVEN MILE BEACH

FOODSTUFFS

There are seven modern, U.S.-style supermarkets for groceries (three of them have full-service pharmacies) on Grand Cayman.

JEWELRY

★ **Mitzi's Fine Jewelry.** Mitzi's is a treasure trove of salvaged 18th-century coins, silver, Caymanite pieces, and black coral; the store also carries Italian porcelain and the Carrera y Carrera line of jewelry and sculptures. Self-taught, vivacious proprietor Mitzi Callan, who specializes in handmade pieces, is usually on hand to help. ⊠ *5 Bay Harbour Centre, West Bay Rd., Seven Mile Beach* ☎ *345/945–5014.*

★ **24K-Mon Jewelers.** This store sells works of art from many jewelers, including Wyland, Merry-Lee Rae, and Stephen Douglas, as well as designs courtesy of owner-goldsmith Gale Tibbetts and her friends, incorporating everything from Swarovski crystals to Spanish doubloons. The adjacent gallery is one of the few commercial outlets for local artists such as Miguel Powery. ⊠ *Buckingham Sq., Seven Mile Beach* ☎ *345/949–1499* ⊕ *www.24k-monjewelers.com.*

MALLS AND SHOPPING CENTERS

The Strand Shopping Centre. This mall has branches of Tortuga Rum and Blackbeard's Liquor, and banks galore—the better to withdraw cash for shops with cachet like Polo Ralph Lauren and another Kirk Freeport (this branch particularly noteworthy for china and crystal, from Kosta Boda to Baccarat, as well as a second La Parfumerie). ⊠ *West Bay Rd., Seven Mile Beach.*

EAST END

FOODSTUFFS

There are seven modern, U.S.-style supermarkets for groceries (three of them have full-service pharmacies) on Grand Cayman.

SPORTS AND ACTIVITIES

BIRD-WATCHING

Silver Thatch Tours (☎ *345/925–7401* ✎ *silvert@hotmail.com*) is run by Geddes Hislop, who knows his birds and his island (though he's Trinidadian by birth). He specializes in customizable five-hour natural and historic heritage tours that culminate at the Queen Elizabeth II Botanic Park's nature trail and lake or other prime birding spots. The cost is $45 per hour for one to four people. Serious birders leave at the crack of dawn, but you can choose the time and leave at the crack of noon instead. The cost includes guide service, pickup and return transport, and refreshments such as local drinks (a great excuse for discourse on herbal medicinal folklore); tours must be arranged in advance.

DIVING

One of the world's leading dive destinations, Grand Cayman's dramatic underwater topography features plunging walls, soaring skyscraper pinnacles, grottoes, arches, swim-throughs adorned with vibrant sponges, coral-encrusted caverns, and canyons patrolled by Lilliputian grunts to gargantuan groupers, hammerheads to hawksbill turtles.

There are more than 200 pristine dive sites, many less than half a mile from land and easily accessible, including wreck, wall, and shore options. Add exceptional visibility from 80 to 150 feet and calm, current-free water at a constant bathlike 80°F. Cayman is serious about conservation, with Marine Park, Replenishment, and Environmental Park Zones and stringently enforced laws to protect the fragile, endangered marine environment (fines of up to $500,000 and a year in prison are the price for damaging living coral, which can take years to regrow). Most boats use biodegradable cleansers and environmentally friendly drinking cups; moorings at popular sites prevent coral and sponge damage caused by continual anchoring, and diving with gloves is prohibited to reduce the temptation to touch.

CAYMAN DIVE DEVELOPMENTS

The Cayman Islands government acquired the 251-foot, decommissioned U.S. Navy ship USS *Kittiwake*. Once sunk, it will become an exciting new dive attraction.

The **Cayman Dive 365** (⊕ *www. divecayman.ky/dive365*) initiative is part of a commitment to protect reefs from environmental overuse. New dive sites will be introduced while certain existing sites are "retired" to be rested and refreshed. Visitors are encouraged to sponsor and name a new dive site from the list of selected coordinates.

Pristine clear water, breathtaking coral formations, and plentiful marine life mark the **North Wall**—a world-renowned dive area along the North Side of Grand Cayman. **Trinity Caves,** in West Bay, is a deep dive with numerous canyons starting at about 60 feet and sloping to the wall at 130 feet. The South Side is the deepest, its wall starting 80 feet deep before plummeting, though its shallows offer a lovely labyrinth of caverns and tunnels in such sites as Japanese Gardens. The less-visited, virgin East End is less varied geographically beyond the magnificent Ironshore Caves and Babylon Hanging Gardens ("trees" of black coral plunging 100 feet) but teems with "Swiss-cheese" swim-throughs and exotic life in such renowned gathering spots as the Maze.

Most dive operators offer scuba trips to **Stingray City** in the North Sound. Widely considered the best 12-foot dive in the world, it's a must-see for adventurous souls. Here dozens of stingrays congregate—tame enough to suction squid from your outstretched palm. You can stand in 3 feet of water at **Stingray Sandbar** as the gentle stingrays glide around your legs looking for a handout. Don't worry—these stingrays are so used to thousands of tourist encounters that they pose no danger. The experience is often a highlight of a Grand Cayman trip.

If someone tells you that the minnows are in at **Eden Rock,** drop everything and dive here (on South Church Street, south of George Town). The schools swarm around you as you glide through the grottoes, forming quivering curtains of liquid silver as shafts of sunlight pierce the sandy bottom. The grottoes themselves are safe—not complex caves—and the entries and exits are clearly visible at all times. Snorkelers can enjoy the outside of the grottoes as the reef rises and falls from 10 to 30 feet deep. Avoid carrying fish food unless you know how not to get

Learn to Dive

Diving is an exciting experience that does not have to be strenuous or stressful. Almost anyone can enjoy scuba, and it's easy to test the waters via a three-hour resort course costing $100 to $120. After a quick rundown of dos and don'ts, you stand in the shallow end of a pool, learning how to use the mask and fins and breathe underwater with a regulator. The instructor then explains some basic safety skills, and before you know it, you're in the drink. The instructor hovers as you float above the reef, watching fish react to you. Don't worry—there are no dangerous fish in Cayman, and they don't bite (as long as you're not "chumming," or handling fish food). You can see corals and sponges, maybe even a turtle or ray. It's an amazing world that you can enter with very little effort.

The resort course permits only shallow, instructor-guided dives in Cayman's calm, clear waters. The next step is full open-water certification (generally three or four days, including several dives, for around $450, less as part of a hotel package). This earns you a C-card, your passport to the underwater world anywhere you travel. From there, addicts will discover dozens of specialty courses. The leading teaching organizations, both with their adherents, are PADI (Professional Association of Dive Instructors) and NAUI (National Association of Underwater Instructors), affectionately nicknamed "Pay and Dive Immediately" and "Not Another Underwater Idiot" (those are the polite versions in scuba's colorful slang). Worry not: Cayman's instructors are among the world's best. And the water conditions just might spoil you.

8

bitten by eager yellowtail snappers. The waters around Grand Cayman are varied, so if the water looks rough where you are, there's usually a side of the island that's wonderfully calm.

Other good shore-entry snorkeling spots include **West Bay Cemetery,** north of Seven Mile Beach, and the reef-protected shallows of the island's **north and south coasts.** Ask for directions to the shallow wreck of the *Cali* in the George Town harbor area; there are several places to enter the water, including a ladder at Rackam's Pub. Among the wreckage you'll recognize the winch and, of course, lots of friendly fish.

DIVE OPERATORS

As one of the Caribbean's top diving destinations, Grand Cayman is blessed with many top-notch dive operations offering diving, instruction, and equipment for sale and rent. A single-tank boat dive averages $70, a two-tank dive about $100. Snorkel-equipment rental is about $15 a day. Divers are required to be certified and possess a C-card. If you're getting certified, to save time during your limited holiday, you can start the book and pool work at home and finish the open-water portion in warm, clear Cayman waters. Certifying agencies offer this referral service all around the world.

Strict marine-protection laws prohibit you from taking any marine life from many areas around the island.

Diving at one of the Cayman Islands' famous coral reefs.

Ambassador Divers (✉ *Comfort Suites, West Bay Rd., Seven Mile Beach* ☎ *345/743–5513* ⊕ *www.ambassadordivers.com*) is an on-call, guided scuba-diving operation offering dive trips to parties of two to eight persons. Co-owner Jason Washington's favorite spots include the excellent dive sites on the West Side and South and North Wall. Ambassador offers three boats, a 28-foot custom Parker (maximum six divers), another 28-foot completely custom overhauled boat, and a 26-footer primarily for snorkeling. They are available around the clock, and interested divers can be picked up from their hotels or condos. The price for a two-tank boat dive is $105 ($90 for two or more days).

Cayman Aggressor IV (☎ *985/385–2628, 345/949–5551, or 800/348– 2628* ⊕ *www.aggressor.com*), a 110-foot live-aboard dive boat refitted in 2007, offers one-week cruises for divers who want to get serious bottom time, as many as five dives daily. Nine staterooms with en suite bathrooms sleep 18. The fresh food is basic but bountiful (three meals, two in-between snacks), and the crew offers a great mix of diving, especially when weather allows the crossing to Little Cayman. Digital photography and video courses are also offered (there's an E-6 film-processing lab aboard) as well as Nitrox certification. The price is $2,495 to $2,895 double occupancy for the week.

♻ **DiveTech** (✉ *Cobalt Coast Resort & Suites, 18-A Sea Fan Dr., West* **FodorsChoice** *Bay* ☎ *345/946–5658 or 888/946–5656* ⊕ *www.divetech.com* ✉ *Light-* ★ *house Point, near Boatswain's Beach, 571 N.W. Point Rd., West Bay* ☎ *345/949–1700*) has opportunities for shore diving at its two north-coast locations, which provide loads of interesting creatures, a mini-wall, and the North Wall. With quick access to West Bay, the boats are quite comfortable. Technical training (a specialty of owner Nancy Easterbrook) is unparalleled, and the company offers good, personable service as well as the latest gadgetry such as underwater DPV scooters. They even mix their own gases, and there are multiple dive instructors for different specialties, with everything from extended cross-training Ranger packages to Dive and Art workshop weeks, popular photography–video seminars with Courtney Platt, deep diving, less disruptive free diving, search and recovery, stingray interaction, reef awareness, and underwater naturalist. Snorkel and diving programs are available year-round for children ages eight and up, SASY (supplied-air snorkeling, which keeps the unit on a personal flotation device) for five and up. Excellent multiday discounts are a bonus.

Don Foster's Dive Cayman Islands (⊠ *218 S. Church St., George Town* ☎ *345/949–5679 or 345/945–5132* ⊕ *www.donfosters.com*) has a pool with a shower as well as snorkeling along the ironshore at Casuarina Point, easily accessed starting at 20 feet, extending to depths of 55 feet. There's an underwater photo center, and there are night dives and Stingray City trips with divers and snorkelers in the same boat (perfect for families). Specialties include Nitrox courses and Underwater Naturalist guided dives. Rates are competitive, and there's free shuttle pickup–drop-off along Seven Mile Beach. If you go out with Don, he might recount stories of his wild times as a drummer in the islands, but all the crews are personable and efficient. The drawback is larger boats and groups.

Eden Rock Diving Center (⊠ *124 S. Church St., George Town* ☎ *345/949–7243* ⊕ *www.edenrockdive.com*), south of George Town, provides easy access to Eden Rock and Devil's Grotto. It features full equipment rental, lockers, shower facilities, and a full range of PADI courses from a helpful, cheerful staff. Costs for guided shore dives and two-tank dives on its Pro 42 jet boat are slightly cheaper than most outfits, without sacrificing quality or comfort.

★ **Indigo Divers** (⊠ *Box 30445, Seven Mile Beach* ☎ *345/946–7279 or 345/525–3932* ⊕ *www.indigodivers.com*) is a full-service PADI teaching facility specializing in exclusive guided dives from its 28-foot Sea Ray Bow Rider or 32-foot Donzi Express Cruiser. Comfort and safety are paramount, and the attention to detail is superior. Luxury transfers in a Chevy Avalanche are included, and the boat is stocked with goodies like fresh fruit and homemade cookies. Captain Chris Alpers has impeccable credentials: a licensed U.S. Coast Guard captain, PADI master scuba diver trainer, and Cayman Islands Marine Park officer. Katie Alpers specializes in wreck, DPV, dry suit, boat, and deep diving, but her primary role is resident videographer, and she edits superlative DVDs of your adventures, complete with music and titles. They guarantee a maximum of six divers. The individual attention is a bit pricier, but the larger your group, the more you save.

Fodor's Choice ★ **Ocean Frontiers** (⊠ *Compass Point* ⊠ *346 Austin Connelly Dr., East End* ☎ *345/947–7500 or 800/348–6096* ⊕ *www.oceanfrontiers.com*) is an excellent ecocentric operation, offering friendly small-group diving and a technical training facility, exploring the less trammeled, trafficked

8

East End. The company provides valet service, personalized attention, a complimentary courtesy shuttle, and an emphasis on green initiatives and specialized diving, including unguided computer, Technical, Nitrox Instructor, and cave diving for advanced participants. But even beginners and rusty divers (there's a wonderful Skills Review and Tune-Up course) won't feel over their heads. Special touches include hot chocolate and homemade muffins on night dives; the owner, Steve, is an ordained minister and will conduct weddings in full face masks.

Red Sail Sports (☎ 345/949–8745, 345/623–5965, or 877/506–6368 ⊕ www.redsailcayman.com) offers daily trips from most of the major hotels. Dives are often run as guided tours, a perfect option for beginners. If you're experienced and your air lasts a long time, consult the boat captain to see if he requires that you come up with the group (determined by the first person who runs low on air). There is a full range of kids' dive options for ages 5 to 15. The company also operates Stingray City tours, dinner and sunset sails, and just about every major water sport from Wave Runners to windsurfing.

Sunset Divers (✉ Sunset House, 390 S. Church St., George Town ☎ 345/949–7111 or 800/854–4767 ⊕ www.sunsethouse.com), a full-service PADI teaching facility at the George Town hostelry catering to the scuba set, has great shore diving and five dive boats to hit all sides of the island. Divers can be independent on their boats as long as they abide by the maximum time and depth standards. Instruction and packages are comparatively inexpensive. Though the company is not directly affiliated with acclaimed underwater shutterbug Cathy Church (whose shop is also at the hotel), she'll often work with the instructors on special courses.

FISHING

If you enjoy action fishing, Cayman waters have plenty to offer. Experienced, knowledgeable local captains charter boats with top-of-the-line equipment, bait, ice, and often lunch included in the price (usually $500 to $750 per half day, $800 to $1,500 for a full day). Options include deep-sea, reef, bone, tarpon, light-tackle, and fly-fishing. June and July are good all-around months for fishing for blue marlin, yellow- and blackfin tuna, dolphinfish, and bonefish. Bonefish have a second season in the winter months, along with wahoo and skipjack tuna.

Black Princess Charters (☎ 345/916–6319 or 345/949–0400 ⊕ www. fishgrandcayman.com), owned by Captain Chuckie Ebanks, is fully equipped for deep-sea and reef fishing as well as snorkel trips on his fully equipped and supplied eponymous 40-foot Sea Ray. His rates are comparatively reasonable, and he can arrange clean, inexpensive local accommodations.

★ Captain Ronald Ebanks of **R&M Fly Shop and Charters** (☎ 345/947–3146 or 345/946–0214 ⊕ www.flyfishgrandcayman.com) is arguably the island's most knowledgeable fly-fishing guide, with more than 10 years' experience in Cayman and Scotland. He also runs light-tackle trips on a 24-foot Robalo. Everyone from beginners—even children—to experienced casters will enjoy and learn from the trip; free transfers are included. Captain Ronald even ties his own flies (he'll show you how).

★ **Sea Star Charters** (☎345/949–1016), aka Clinton's Watersports, is run by Clinton Ebanks, a fine and very friendly Caymanian who will do whatever it takes to make sure that you have a wonderful time on his two 25- and 31-foot cabin cruisers (and from the 35-foot trimaran used primarily for snorkeling cruises), enjoying light-tackle, bone-, and bottom-fishing. He's a good choice for beginners and offers a nice cultural experience as well as sailing charters and snorkeling with complimentary transportation and equipment. Only cash and traveler's checks are accepted.

GOLF

The **Britannia** (✉ *West Bay Rd., Seven Mile Beach* ☎ *345/745–4653 or 345/949–3406* ⊕ *www.britannia-golf.com*) golf course, next to the Grand Cayman Beach Suites, was designed by Jack Nicklaus. The course is really three in one—a 9-hole, par-70 regulation course; an 18-hole, par-57 executive course; and a Cayman course played with a Cayman ball that travels about half the distance of a regulation ball. Signature tough holes include 3 and 10; beware tricky winds on 7 through 11. Green fees are $100 for 9 holes, $150 for 18 ($75/$100 during the off-season), including the cart. Amenities include a full pro shop and the Britannia Golf Grille (with particularly good breakfasts and local fare).

Formerly the Links at Safehaven, the par-71, 6,605-yard, 18-hole **North Sound Club** (✉ *Off West Bay Rd., Seven Mile Beach* ☎ *345/947–4653* ⊕ *www.northsoundclub.com*) is infamous among duffers for its strong gusts, giving the ball unexpected loft or backspin. Roy Case factored the wind into his design, which incorporates lots of looming water and sand traps; the handsome setting features many mature mahogany and silver thatch trees. Wear shorts at least 14 inches long (15 inches for women); no T-shirts are allowed, only collared shirts. Green fees change seasonally; in winter it's $175 ($105 for 9 holes) including cart. There are twilight and walking discounts (though carts are recommended), fine pro shop, and open-air bar with large-screen TVs.

GUIDED TOURS

Taxi drivers will give you a personalized tour of Grand Cayman for about $25 per hour for up to three people. Or you can choose a fascinating helicopter ride, a horseback or mountain-bike journey, a 4x4 safari expedition, or a full-day bus excursion. Ask your hotel to help you make arrangements.

Costs and itineraries for island tours are about the same regardless of the tour operator. Half-day tours average $35 to $45 a person and generally include a visit to Hell and the Turtle Farm at Boatswain's Beach aquatic park in West Bay, as well as shopping downtown. Full-day tours ($60 to $80 per person) add lunch, a visit to Bodden Town (the first settlement), and the East End, where you stop at the Queen Elizabeth II Botanic Park, blowholes (if the waves are high) on the ironshore, and the site of the wreck of the *Ten Sails* (not the wreck itself—just the site). The pirate graves in Bodden Town were destroyed during Hurricane Ivan in 2008, and the blowholes were partially filled. As you can tell, land tours here are low-key. Children under 12 often receive discounts.

A.A. Transportation Services (⊠ *Grand Cayman* ☎ *345/926–8294 or 345/938–8294* ⊕ *www.burtons.ky*) offers taxis and tour buses—ask for Burton Ebanks.

Cayman Safari (⊠ *Grand Cayman* ☎ *345/925–3001 or 866/389–8559* ⊕ *www.caymansafari.com*) hits the usual sights but emphasizes inter- action with locals, so you learn about craft traditions, folklore, and herbal medicines.

Majestic Tours (⊠ *Grand Cayman* ☎ *345/949–7773* ⊕ *www.majestic- tours.com*) caters mostly to cruise-ship and incentive groups but also offers similar options to individuals and can customize tours; it's par- ticularly good for West Bay, including Boatswain's Beach and Hell.

McCurley Tours (⊠ *Grand Cayman* ☎ *345/947–9626 or 345/916–0925*) is owned by B.A. McCurley, a free-spirited, freewheeling Midwesterner who's lived in Cayman since the mid-1980s and knows everything and everyone on the East End. Not only is she encyclopedic and flexible, but she also offers car rentals and transfers for travelers staying on the North Side or East End; don't be surprised if she tells you what to order at lunch, especially if it's off the menu.

Tropicana Tours (⊠ *Grand Cayman* ☎ *345/949–0944* ⊕ *www.tropicana- tours.com*) offers several excellent Cayman highlights itineraries on its larger buses, including Stingray City stops, as well as reef runner adventures across the North Sound through the mangrove swamps.

HIKING

★ The National Trust's internationally significant **Mastic Trail** (⊠ *Frank Sound Rd., entrance by fire station at botanic park, Breakers, East End* ☎ *345/749–1121, 345/749–1124 for guide reservations* ⊕ *www. nationaltrust.org.ky*), used in the 1800s as the only direct path to and from the North Side, is a rugged 2-mi (3-km) slash through 776 dense acres of woodlands, black mangrove swamps, savannah, agricultural remnants, and ancient rock formations. It embraces more than 700 species, including Cayman's largest remaining contiguous ancient for- est (one of the heavily deforested Caribbean's last examples). A com- fortable walk depends on weather—winter is better because it's drier, though flowering plants such as the banana orchid set the trail ablaze in summer. Call the National Trust to determine suitability and to book a guide for $30; tours are run daily from 9 to 5 by appointment only, regularly on Wednesday at 9 am (sometimes earlier in summer). Or walk on the wild side with a $5 guidebook that provides information on the ecosystems you traverse, the endemic wildlife you might encounter, seasonal changes, poisonous plants to avoid, and folkloric uses of vari- ous flora. The trip takes about three hours.

HORSEBACK RIDING

Coral Stone Stables (☎ *345/916–4799* ⊕ *www.csstables.com*) offers 90-minute leisurely horseback rides along the white-sand beaches at Bodden Town and inland trails at Savannah; complimentary photos are included. Your guide is Nolan Stewart, whose ranch contains 20 horses, chickens, and "randy" roosters. Nolan offers a nonstop narra- tive on flora, fauna, and history. He's an entertaining, endless font of local information, some of it unprintable. Rides are $80; swim rides cost $120.

Ⓒ **Pampered Ponies** (☎ 345/945–2262 or 345/916–2540 ⊕ www.ponies.ky) offers what is called "the ultimate tanning machine": horses walking, trotting, and cantering along the beaches. You can do either private tours or a variety of guided trips, including sunset, moonlight, and swim rides along the uninhabited beach from Conch Point to Morgan's Harbour on the north tip beyond West Bay.

KAYAKING

Ⓒ **Cayman Kayaks** (☎ 345/746–3249 or 345/926–4467 ⊕ www.
★ caymankayaks.com) explores Grand Cayman's protected mangrove wetlands, providing an absorbing discussion of the indigenous animals (including a mesmerizing stop at a gently pulsing, nonstinging Cassiopeia jellyfish pond) and plants, the effects of hurricanes, and conservation efforts. Even beginners will find the tours easy (the guides dub it low-impact aerobics), and the sit-on-top tandem kayaks are quite stable and comfortable. The Bio Bay tour involves more strenuous paddling, but the underwater light show is magical as millions of bio-luminescent microorganisms called dinoflagellates glow like fireflies when disturbed. It runs only on moonless nights for full effect and books well in advance. All tours depart from Kaibo Beach Bar in Cayman Kai; costs run from $44 to $59 (some tours offer kids' and group discounts).

SEA EXCURSIONS

The most impressive sights in the Cayman Islands are on and underwater, and several submarines, semisubmersibles, glass-bottom boats, and Jules Verne–like contraptions allow you to see these wonders without getting your feet wet. Sunset sails, dinner cruises, and other theme (dance, booze, pirate) cruises are available from $30 to $60 per person.

Ⓒ **Atlantis Submarines** (☎ 345/949–7700 or 800/887–8571 ⊕ www.
★ atlantisadventures.com) takes 48 passengers safely and comfortably along the Cayman Wall down to 100 feet. You peep through panoramic portholes as good-natured guides keep up a humorous but informative patter. A guide dons scuba gear to feed fish, who form a whirling frenzy of color rivaling anything by Picasso. At night, the 10,000-watt lights show the kaleidoscopic underwater colors and nocturnal stealth predators more brilliantly than during the day. Try to sit toward the front so you can watch the pilot's nimble maneuverings and the depth gauge. If that literally in-depth tour seems daunting, get up close and personal on the *Seaworld Observatory* semisubmersible (glorified glass-bottom boat), which just cruises the harbor (including glimpses of the *Cali* and *Balboa* shipwrecks). The cost is $99 for the submarine, $49 for the semisubmersible. There are frequent online booking discounts.

Ⓒ Scientists often call our oceans just as mysterious as deep space, and
Fodor's Choice **Deep See Cayman** (☎ 345/926–3343 ⊕ www.deepseecayman.com) pro-
★ vides spellbinding proof. Its personable owner was pilot for Paul Allen's *Octopus*, one of the world's largest yachts, helped film David Attenborough's compelling *Blue Planet*, and currently works with Scripps on underwater research with his little toy, a remotely operated underwater robot that plumbs the Cayman Trench's depths down to 2,400

feet while you comfortably watch the real time high-definition images it transmits aboard a luxury yacht, the *Deep Seeker*. Some wrecks have gradually sunk to those depths, but the real prize is otherworldly, oddly shaped creatures straight out of sci-fi. The two-hour excursions depart from the West Bay dock several times daily (including a night tour), with an eight-person maximum, costing a reasonable $74 ($5 discount for advance online booking). Gary will even let kids particularly adept with joysticks from video-game mastery navigate the Little Tyche (another robot and an appropriate name, given the eager would-be pilots).

The **Jolly Roger** (☎ 345/945–7245 ⊕ *www.jollyrogercayman.com*) is a two-thirds-size replica of Christopher Columbus's 17th-century Spanish galleon *Niña*; the company also owns the *Valhalla*, a wooden Norwegian brig built in 1934 that holds more than 100 passengers. On the afternoon snorkel cruise, play Captain Jack Sparrow while experiencing swashbuckling pirate antics, including a trial, sword fight, and walking the plank; the kids can fire the cannon, help hoist the main sail, and scrub the decks (it's guaranteed that they will love it even if they loathe doing chores at home). The evening options (sunset and dinner sails) are more standard booze cruises, less appropriate for the kiddies. Food is more appropriate to the brig, and it's more yo-ho-hokum than remotely authentic, but it's fun. Prices range from $40 to $60.

Sea Trek (☎ 345/949–0008 ⊕ *www.seatrekcayman.com*) offers helmet diving, permitting you to walk and breathe 26 feet underwater—without getting your hair wet—for an hour. No training or even swimming ability is required, and you can wear glasses. Guides give a thorough safety briefing, and a sophisticated system of compressors and cylinders provides triple the amount of air necessary for normal breathing while a safety diver program ensures four distinct levels of backup. The result at near-zero gravity resembles an exhilarating moonwalk. The minimum age is eight. The cost is $89 to $99 per person (the latter for an "Ultimate Stingray City" excursion).

SKATING AND SKATEBOARDING

Black Pearl Skate and Surf Park (✉ *Red Bay Rd., Grand Harbour* ☎ 345/947–4161 or 345/925–8576 ⊕ *www.blackpearl.ky*), a great skating park (skateboards, in-line skates), is the size of a football field (at 52,000 square feet the world's second-largest such facility) with stairs, half pipe, rails, 20-foot vert ramp, and flow course offering innumerable lies. International professional skaters such as Tony Hawk, Ryan Sheckler, and Mark Appleyard have practiced their kickflips, tailslides, wheelies, and grinds. The park also has one of only three Waveloch standing wave–surf machines in the world, which generates adjustable 11-foot swells. You can arrange lessons or rent anything you need at the adjacent skate–surf shop. The outdoor patio of the surprisingly elegant Brick House restaurant (terrific pizzas and playground) is the perfect vantage point for the rad performances local daredevils mount Friday and Saturday nights.

Fodor's Choice ★

A group of stingrays patrolling the grassy shallows of Grand Cayman.

SNORKELING

Stingray Sandbar is the most popular snorkeling destination by far, and dozens of boats head that way several times a day. It's a not-to-be-missed experience that you will remember for years to come. The area is always less crowded if you can go on a day when there aren't too many cruise ships in port.

SNORKELING OPERATORS

Bayside Watersports (☎ *345/949–3200* ⊕ *www.baysidewatersports. com*) offers half-day snorkeling trips, North Sound beach lunch excursions, Stingray City and dinner cruises, and full-day deep-sea fishing. The company operates several popular boats out of West Bay's Morgan's Harbour. Full-day trips include lunch and conch diving in season (November–April).

☾ **Red Sail Sports** (☎ *345/949–8745, 345/623–5965, or 877/506–6368* ⊕ *www.redsailcayman.com*) offers Stingray City, sunset, and evening sails (including dinner in winter) on its luxurious 65-foot catamarans, the *Spirits of Cayman, Poseidon, Calypso,* and *Ppalu.* It often carries large groups; although the service may not be personal, it will be efficient. In addition to the large cats, a glass-bottom boat takes passengers to Stingray City/Sandbar and nearby coral reefs. The cost ranges from $40 to $99 (the latter for a Stingray City in-depth excursion).

CAYMAN BRAC

Cayman Brac is named for its most distinctive feature, a rugged limestone bluff ("brac" in Gaelic) that runs up the center of the 12-mi (19-km) island, pocked with caves and culminating in a sheer 140-foot cliff at its eastern end. The Brac, 89 mi (143 km) northeast of Grand Cayman, is accessible via Cayman Airways. It's a splendid serene destination for eco-enthusiasts, offering world-class birding, scuba diving, bonefishing in the shallows or light-tackle and deep-sea angling, hiking, spelunking, and rock climbing. With only 1,800 residents—they call themselves Brackers—the island has the feel and easy pace of a small town. Brackers are known for their friendly attitude toward visitors, so it's easy to strike up a conversation. Locals wave at passing and might invite you home for a traditional rundown (a thick, sultry fish stew) and storytelling, usually about the sea, the turtle schooners, and the great hurricane of 1932 (when the caves offered shelter to islanders). Brackers are as calm and peaceful as their island is rugged, violently sculpted by sea and wind. Unfortunately, the Brac sustained a direct 145-mph hit from Hurricane Paloma in November 2008; nearly 90% of the buildings were damaged, the majority severely, and many trees were downed. Most accommodations, restaurants, shops, recreational options, and sightseeing attractions damaged by the hurricane were up and running by 2010.

EXPLORING CAYMAN BRAC

★ **Cayman Brac Museum.** Here you'll find a diverse, well-displayed collection of historic Bracker implements from scary dental pliers to pistols to pottery. A meticulously crafted scale model of the Caymanian catboat *Alsons* has pride of place. The front room faithfully reconstructs the Customs, Treasury, bank, and post office as they would have looked decades ago. Permanent exhibits include those on the 1932 hurricane, turtling, shipbuilding, and typical old-time home life, including a child's bedroom; the back room hosts rotating exhibits such as one on herbal folk medicine. ⊠ *Old Government Administration Bldg., Stake Bay* ☎ *345/948–2622 or 345/244–4446* ☞ *Free* ⊙ *Weekdays 9–noon and 1–4, Sat. 9–noon.*

★ **Parrot Preserve.** The likeliest place to spot the endangered Cayman Brac parrot—and other indigenous and migratory birds—is along this National Trust hiking trail off Major Donald Drive, aka Lighthouse Road. Prime time is early morning or late afternoon; most of the day they're camouflaged by trees, earning them the moniker "stealth parrot." The loop trail incorporates part of a path the Brackers used in olden days to cross the bluff to reach their provision grounds on the south shore or to gather coconuts, once a major export crop. It passes through several types of terrain: old farmland under grass and native trees from mango to mahogany unusually mixed with orchids and cacti. Wear sturdy shoes, as the terrain is rocky, uneven, and occasionally rough. The 6-mi (10-km) gravel road continues to the lighthouse at the bluff's eastern end, where there's an astonishing view from atop the cliff to the open ocean—the best place to watch the sunrise. ⊠ *Lighthouse Rd., Tibbetts Turn, ½ mi (1 km) south of town* ☎ *345/948–0319* ☞ *Free* ⊙ *Daily sunrise–sunset.*

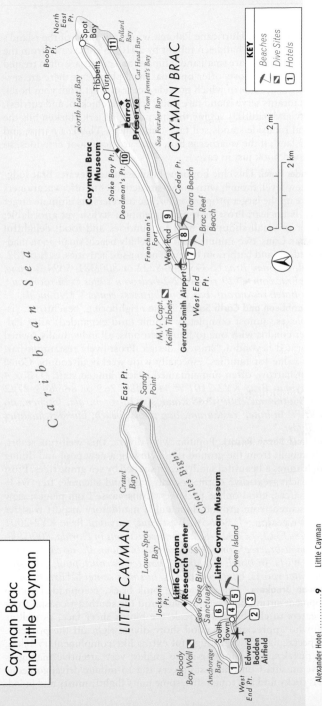

Cayman Brac and Little Cayman

KEY
/ Beaches
/ Dive Sites
1 Hotels

Caribbean Sea

LITTLE CAYMAN

West End Pt.
Edward Bodden Airfield
Anchorage Bay
Bloody Bay Wall
Jacksons Pt.
Lower Spot Bay
Little Cayman Research Center
Gov. Gore Bird Sanctuary
Owen Island
South Town
Little Cayman Museum
Crawl Bay
Charles Bight
East Pt.
Sandy Point

CAYMAN BRAC

West End Pt.
West End
Gerrard-Smith Airport
M.V. Capt. Keith Tibbetts
Frenchman's Fort
Deadman's Pt.
Stake Bay Pt.
Cayman Brac Museum
Parrot Preserve
Tibbetts Turn
Spot Bay
North East Pt.
Booby Pt.
Pollard Bay
Cat Head Bay
North East Bay
Tom Jennett's Bay
Sea Feather Bay
Cedar Pt.
Tiara Beach
Brac Reef Beach

0   2 km
0   2 mi

WHERE TO STAY

In November 2008, Hurricane Paloma wiped out most of the island's larger properties. All had been rebuilt by 2010, in some cases from the ground up. Lodgings are small and intimate, and guests are often treated like family. Most resorts offer optional meal plans, but there are several restaurants, some of which provide free transport from your hotel. Most restaurants serve island fare (local seafood, chicken, and curries). On Friday and Saturday nights the spicy scent of jerk chicken fills the air; several roadside stands sell take-out dinners. This is a nature and outdoor island; if the weather is bad, there are no indoor activities, so bring a good book just in case.

$
HOTEL
★
Alexander Hotel. This chic boutique business hotel elevates Brac lodging to a new level, though with no on-site activities to offer vacationers who make up the larger proportion of Brac travelers, its ultimate target audience is unclear. **Pros:** high-tech amenities; stylish yet affordable; next door to small shopping mall for sundries and food; delightful alfresco bar. **Cons:** two-minute walk to a pebbly beach; small pool; inadequate bedside and bathroom lighting; no on-site activities. ⊠ *Box 132, West End, Cayman Brac* ☎ *345/948–8222 or 800/381–5094* ⊕ *www. alexanderbrac.com* ⇄ *29 rooms, 2 2-bedroom suites* ♿ *In-room: a/c, Wi-Fi. In-hotel: restaurant, bar, pool, business center* ⦿ *No meals.*

$
RESORT
Brac Caribbean and Carib Sands. These neighboring, beachfront, sister complexes, almost completely rebuilt (and expanded) after Paloma, offer condos with one to four bedrooms, all individually owned and decorated beyond a "starter" design. **Pros:** lively restaurant-bar; excellent value for families, especially with weekly discounts. **Cons:** pretty but narrow, often unmaintained beach; limited staff. ⌂ *Box 4 SPO, Cayman Brac KY2-2101* ☎ *345/948–2265 or 866/843–2722* ⊕ *www.866thebrac.com* ⇄ *65 condos* ♿ *In-room: a/c, kitchen, no safe, Wi-Fi. In-hotel: restaurant, bar, pools, beach, laundry facilities* ⦿ *Breakfast.*

¢–$
RESORT
★
Brac Reef Beach Resort. Popular with divers, this well-run resort, entirely rebuilt from the ground up (including a new pool and dining room), features a beautiful sandy beach shaded by sea grape trees. **Pros:** lovely beach; great dive outfit; friendly staff and clientele; free Wi-Fi in public areas; good online packages. **Cons:** noise from planes; view often obscured from ground-floor units; mandatory airport transfer of $20 per person. ⌂ *Box 56, West End, Cayman Brac KY2-2001* ☎ *345/948–1323, 727/323–8727 for reservations in Florida, 800/594–0843* ⊕ *www.bracreef.com* ⇄ *40 rooms* ♿ *In-room: a/c, no safe (some), Internet, Wi-Fi. In-hotel: restaurants, bar, tennis court, pool, gym, spa, beach, water sports, laundry facilities, business center* ⦿ *Breakfast.*

$
RENTAL
★
Cayman Breakers. This attractive, pink-brick, colonnaded condo development sitting between the bluff and the southeast coastal ironshore caters to climbers, who scale the bluff's sheer face, as well as divers, who appreciate the good shore diving right off the property. **Pros:** spectacular views; thoughtful extras like complimentary bikes, jigsaw puzzles, and climbing-route guides; very attentive managers who live on-site. **Cons:** nearest grocery is a 15-minute drive; gorgeous beach is rocky and has rough surf; some units slightly musty and faded.

Box 202 SPO, Cayman Brac KY2-2101 345/948–1463 *www. caybreakers.com* 26 2-bedroom condos *In-room: a/c, kitchen, no safe, Wi-Fi. In-hotel: pool, beach, laundry facilities* No meals.

¢ **Walton's Mango Manor.** This beautifully restored traditional West
INN/B&B Indian home has five rooms (all with bath), accented with lovely antique
★ furnishings, nautical gadgets, maps, model catboats, and bric-a-brac
from the Waltons' world travels. **Pros:** true Caymanian hospitality;
beautiful grounds; excellent snorkeling; free Wi Fi access. **Cons:** poky
beach across the street; car required. *Box 56 SPO, Stake Bay, Cayman Brac KY2-2101* 345/948–0518, 321/226–0440 from U.S., or
888/866–5809 *www.waltonsmangomanor.com* 5 rooms, 1 2-bed-
room cottage *In-room: kitchen (some), no TV (some), no safe, Internet (some), Wi-Fi. In-hotel: beach* Breakfast.

SPORTS AND THE OUTDOORS

DIVING AND SNORKELING

Cayman Brac's waters are celebrated for their rich diversity of sea life,
from hammerhead and reef sharks to stingrays to sea horses. Divers
and snorkelers alike will find towering coral heads, impressive walls,
and fascinating wrecks. The snorkeling off the **north coast** is spectacular,
particularly at West End, where coral formations close to shore attract
all kinds of critters. The walls feature remarkable topography with
natural gullies, caves, and fissures blanketed with Technicolor sponges,
black coral, gorgonians, and sea fans. Some of the famed sites are the
West Chute, Cemetery Wall, Airport Wall, and Garden Eel Wall. The
South Wall is a wonderland of sheer drop-offs carved with a maze of
vertical swim-throughs, tunnels, arches, and grottoes that divers nickname Cayman's Grand Canyon. Notable sites include Anchor Wall,
Rock Monster Chimney, and the Wilderness. Many fish have colonized
the 330-foot MV *Capt. Keith Tibbetts,* a Russian frigate—now broken
in two—that was deliberately scuttled within swimming distance of
the northwest shore. An artist named Foots has created an amazing
underwater Atlantis off Radar Reef. The island's two dive operators
offer scuba and snorkel training and PADI certification.

★ **Reef Divers** (*Brac Reef Beach Resort, West End* 345/948–1642 or
345/948–1323 *www.bracreef.com*) offers five boats and enthusiastic,
experienced staff. Certified divers can purchase à la carte dive packages
even if they aren't guests of the hotel.

HIKING

Free printed guides to the Brac's many heritage and nature trails can be
obtained from the **Brac Tourism Office** (*West End Community Park,
west of airport, Cayman Brac* 345/948–1649); you can also get the
guides at the airport or at your hotel. Traditional routes across the bluff
have been cleared and marked; trailheads are identified with signs along
the road. It's safe to hike on your own, though some trails are fairly hard
going (wear light hiking boots) and others could be better maintained.

For those who prefer less-strenuous walking, **Christopher Columbus Gardens** (*Ashton Reid Dr. [Bluff Rd.], just north of Ashton Rutty Centre*)
has easy trails and boardwalks. The park showcases the unique natural

8

CLOSE UP

Sculpting Cayman

A sculptor named Foots dreamed since childhood of creating his own version of Plato's lost city of Atlantis. He's fulfilling that dream by creating and then sinking huge concrete sculptures in 45 feet of water off the north shore of Cayman Brac. The result is an astounding dive site and artificial reef with more than 100 sculptures covering several acres. The story starts at the Archway of Atlantis (each of the two bases weighs 21,000 pounds). The Elders' Way, lined with 5-foot temple columns, leads to the Inner Circle of Light, where there is a sundial large enough to sit in. Each Elder is modeled after an actual person who has contributed to the Cayman Islands. Foots is doing this almost entirely on his own and has made an incredible donation to the divers of the Brac. He plans to add a new phase every six months so that the story will go on for a long time before the project is finished.

flora and features of the bluff, including two cave mouths. This is a peaceful spot dotted with gazebos and wooden bridges that traverses several ecosystems from cacti to mahogany trees.

The **Sister Islands District Administration** (☎ *345/948–2222 Ext. 4420*) arranges free, government-sponsored, guided nature and cultural tours with trained local guides. Options include the Parrot Reserve, nature trails, wetlands, Lighthouse/Bluff View, caving, birding, and heritage sites. You just supply the wheels and spirit of adventure.

ROCK CLIMBING

If you are experienced and like dangling from ropes 140 feet above a churning sea, the Brac rocks. Ropes and safety gear cannot be rented on the island—you need to bring your own. Through the years, climbers have attached permanent titanium bolts to the **bluff** face, creating some 40 exotic challenging routes that lure the international climbing community. The Cayman Breakers condo complex has route maps and descriptions (⇨ *Cayman Breakers in Where to Stay*).

SPELUNKING

If you plan to explore Cayman Brac's caves, wear good sneakers or hiking shoes, as some paths are steep and rocky and some cave entrances are reachable only by ladders. **Peter's Cave** offers a stunning aerial view of the northeastern community of Spot Bay. **Great Cave**, at the island's southeast end, has numerous chambers and photogenic ocean views. In **Bat Cave** you may see bats hanging from the ceiling (try not to disturb them). **Rebecca's Cave** houses the grave site of a 17-month-old child who died during the horrific hurricane of 1932.

LITTLE CAYMAN

The smallest, most tranquil of the three Cayman Islands, Little Cayman has a full-time population of only 170, most of whom work in the tourism industry. This 12-square-mi (31-square-km) island is still unspoiled and has only a sand-sealed airstrip, no official terminal building, and few vehicles. The speed limit remains 25 mph (40 kph), as no one is in a hurry to go anywhere. In fact, the island's iguanas use roads more regularly than residents; signs created by local artists read "Iguanas Have the Right of Way." With little commercial development, the island beckons ecotourists who seek wildlife encounters, not urban wildlife. It's probably best known for its spectacular diving on world-renowned Bloody Bay Wall and adjacent Jackson Marine Park. The ravishing reefs and plummeting walls encircling the island teem with more than 500 different species of fish and more than 150 kinds of coral. Fly, lake, and deep-sea fishing are also popular, as well as snorkeling, kayaking, cycling, and hiking. And the island's certainly for the birds. The National Trust Booby Pond Nature Reserve is a designated wetland of international importance, which protects around 20,000 red-footed boobies, the Western Hemisphere's largest colony. It's just one of many superlative spots to witness avian aerial acrobatics. Pristine wetlands, secluded beaches, unspoiled tropical wilderness, mangrove swamps, lagoons, bejeweled coral reefs: Little Cayman practically redefines "escape." Yet aficionados appreciate that the low-key lifestyle doesn't mean sacrificing the high-tech amenities, and some of the resorts cater to a quietly wealthy yet unpretentious crowd.

EXPLORING LITTLE CAYMAN

Little Cayman Museum. The museum displays relics and artifacts, including a new wing devoted to maritime memorabilia, that provide a good overview of this tiny island's history and heritage. ⊠ *Across from Booby Pond Nature Reserve, Blossom Village* ☎ *No phone at museum; 345/948–1033 for Little Cayman Beach Resort* ☑ *Free* ☉ *Thurs. and Fri. 3–5, by appointment only.*

Fodor's Choice **Little Cayman National Trust.** This traditional Caymanian cottage overlooks the Booby Pond Nature Reserve; telescopes on the breezy second-floor deck permit close-up views of their markings and nests, as well as the other feathered friends. Inside you'll find shell collections, panels and dioramas discussing endemic reptiles, and diagrams on the growth and life span of red-footed boobies, frigate birds, egrets, and other island "residents." The shop sells exquisite jewelry made from Caymanite and spider-crab shells, extraordinary duck decoys and carvings of purple gallinules and black-necked stilts by local artist John Mulak, and great books on history, ornithology, and geology. Thanks to chairperson Debbi Truchan's baking skill, this is *the* spot for cappuccino, herb tea, cinnamon buns, and scrumptious homemade ice cream (guava, rum raisin, lemongrass, ginger)—a fantastic place to mingle with residents and visitors. ⊠ *Blossom Village* ☎ *No phone* ⊕ *www.nationaltrust.org. ky* ☉ *Mon.–Sat. 9–noon and 2–6.*

★ **Little Cayman Research Center.** Near the Jackson Point Bloody Bay Marine Park reserve, this vital research center supports visiting students and researchers, with a long list of projects studying the biodiversity, human impact, reef health, and ocean ecosystem of Little Cayman. Its situation is unique in that reefs this unspoiled are usually far less accessible; the

National Oceanic and Atmospheric Administration awarded it one of 16 monitoring stations worldwide. Tours explain the center's mission and ecosensitive design (including Peter's Potty, an off-the-grid bathroom facility using compostable toilets that recycle fertilizer into gray water for the gardens); sometimes you'll get a peek at the upstairs functional wet labs and dormitories. The Dive with a Researcher program (where you actually help survey and assess environmental impact and ecosystem health, depending on that week's focus) is hugely popular. ⊠ *North Side* ☎ *345/926–2789 or 345/948–1094* ⊕ *www.reefresearch. org* ⊗ *By appointment only.*

WHERE TO STAY

Accommodations are mostly in small lodges, many of which offer meal and dive packages. The meal packages are a good idea; the chefs in most places create wonderful meals.

$$$–$$$$
RENTAL
⛶ **The Club.** These ultramodern, luxurious, three-bedroom condos are Little Cayman's newest (from 2002) and nicest units, though only five are usually included in the rental pool. **Pros:** luxurious digs; lovely beach. **Cons:** housekeeping not included; rear guest bedrooms dark and somewhat cramped; handsome but heavy old-fashioned decor. ⌂ *Box 51, South Hole Sound, Blossom Village KY3-2501* ☎ *345/948–1033, 727/323–8727, or 800/327–3835* ⊕ *www.theclubatlittlecayman.com* ⇆ *8 condos* ☖ *In-room: a/c, kitchen, no safe, Wi-Fi. In-hotel: pool, beach, laundry facilities* �'◎' *No meals.*

$$–$$$
RENTAL
⛶ **Conch Club.** The handsome oceanfront development grafts Caribbean-style gingerbread onto New England maritime architecture with gables and dormers. **Pros:** splendid views; gorgeous beach; complimentary airport transfers; beachfront hot tub. **Cons:** long walk to nearby restaurants; dated decor; housekeeping surcharge. ⌂ *Box 51, Blossom Village KY3-2501* ☎ *345/948–1026 or 345/925—2875* ⊕ *www. conchclubcondos.com* ⇆ *18 2-bedroom condos, 2 3-bedroom condos* ☖ *In-room: a/c, kitchen, no safe, Wi-Fi. In-hotel: pools, spa, laundry facilities, business center* �'◎' *No meals.*

$$$
RESORT
⟳
★
⛶ **Little Cayman Beach Resort.** This two-story hotel, the island's largest, offers the most options for fun-seekers and modern facilities yet a boutique vibe. **Pros:** extensive facilities; fun crowd; state-of-the-art technology; glorious LED-lighted pool. **Cons:** less intimate feel than other island resorts; tiny patios; fee to rent bikes. ⌂ *Box 51, Blossom Village KY3-2501* ☎ *345/948–1033 or 800/327–3835* ⊕ *www.littlecayman. com* ⇆ *40 rooms* ☖ *In-room: a/c, kitchen (some), Wi-Fi. In-hotel: restaurant, bar, tennis court, pool, gym, spa, beach, water sports, business center* �'◎' *Multiple meal plans.*

$
RENTAL
⛶ **Paradise Villas.** The cozy, sunny, one-bedroom units have beachfront terraces and hammocks and are simply but immaculately appointed with rattan furnishings, marine artwork, painted driftwood, and bright abstract fabrics. **Pros:** good value; friendly staff; frequent online-only deals in addition to good dive packages. **Cons:** noisy some weekend nights in season; poky beach; now a (minimal) charge for bike use; dive shop no longer on-site (though the contracted operation runs

smoothly). ⌂ *Box 48, South Hole Sound KY3-2501* ☎ *345/948–0001 or 877/322–9626* ⊕ *www.paradisevillas.com* ⇥ *12 1-bedroom villas* ⌂ *In-room: a/c, kitchen, no safe, Wi-Fi. In-hotel: pool, beach* ⊘ *Closed mid-Sept.–late Oct.* ⦿ *No meals.*

$$$–$$$$
RESORT
Fodor'sChoice
★

⛳ **Pirates Point Resort.** The large repeat clientele attests that everything from the comfortable rooms to the fine cuisine lives up to the billing at this hideaway nestled between sea grape and casuarina pines on a sparkling sweep of palapa-dotted sand. **Pros:** fabulous food; fantastic beach; dynamic dive program; fun-loving staff and owner. **Cons:** everyone respects honeymooners' privacy, but this isn't a resort for antisocial types; tasteful rooms are fairly spare; occasional Internet problems. ⌂ *Box 43, Preston Bay, Little Cayman KY3-2501* ☎ *345/948–1010* ⊕ *www.piratespointresort.com* ⇥ *11 rooms* ⌂ *In-room: a/c, no TV, no safe. In-hotel: restaurant, bar, gym, beach, water sports, business center, some age restrictions* ⊘ *Closed Sept.–mid-Oct.* ⦿ *All meals.*

$$$$
RESORT
Fodor'sChoice
★

⛳ **Southern Cross Club.** Little Cayman's first resort was cofounded in the 1950s as a private fishing club by the CEO of Sears-Roebuck and CFO of General Motors, and its focus is still on fishing and diving. **Pros:** barefoot luxury; complimentary use of kayaks and snorkel gear; splendiferous beach; international staff regales you with globe-trotting exploits. **Cons:** not child-friendly (though families can rent a separate cottage). ⌂ *Box 44, South Hole Sound, Little Cayman KY3-2501* ☎ *345/948–1099 or 800/899–2582* ⊕ *www.southerncrossclub.com* ⇥ *11 rooms, 3 suites, 1 2-bedroom cottage* ⌂ *In-room: a/c, no TV, no safe, Wi-Fi. In-hotel: restaurant, bar, gym, spa, beach, water sports, business center, some age restrictions* ⊘ *Closed mid-Sept.–mid-Oct.* ⦿ *All meals.*

SPORTS AND ACTIVITIES

BIRD-WATCHING

★ **Booby Pond Nature Reserve** is home for 20,000 red-footed boobies (the largest colony in the Western Hemisphere) and Cayman's only breeding colony of magnificent frigate (or man-of-war) birds; other sightings include the near-threatened West Indian whistling duck and vitelline warbler. The RAMSAR Convention, an international treaty for wetland conservation, designated the reserve a wetland of global significance. Near the airport, the sanctuary is open to the public, and has a gift shop and reading library.

DIVING AND SNORKELING

Expect to pay around $95 for a two-tank boat dive and $25–$30 for a snorkeling trip. The island is small and susceptible to wind, so itineraries can change like a sudden gust.

Fodor'sChoice
★

Bloody Bay Wall (the beach was site of a spectacular 17th-century sea battle) was in fact declared one of the world's top three dive sites by no less than the *maîtres* Jacques and Philippe Cousteau and forms part of a protected marine reserve. It plunges dramatically from 18 to 6,000 feet, with a series of staggeringly beautiful drop-offs and remarkable visibility. Even snorkelers who are strong swimmers can access the edge from shore, swimming among shimmering silver curtains of minnows, jacks, bonefish, and more. The critters are amazingly friendly, including

Jerry the Grouper, whom dive masters joke is a representative for the Cayman Islands Department of Tourism.

Conch Club Divers (☎ 345/948–1026 ⊕ www.conchclubcondos.com) is a personable, experienced outfit that often customizes trips on its 42-foot *Sea-esta.*

Pirate's Point Dive Resort (☎ 345/948–1010 ⊕ www.piratespointresort. com) has fully outfitted 42-foot Newtons with dive masters who excel at finding odd and rare creatures, and encourage computer diving so you can stay down longer.

Reef Divers (☎ 345/948–1033) at Little Cayman Beach Resort also offers a full-service photo and video center; their custom boats' state-of-the-art outfitting includes AEDs (defibrillators).

The **Southern Cross Club** (☎ 345/948–1099 or 800/899–2582 ⊕ www. southerncrossclub.com) limits each of its boats to 12 divers and has its own dock. It's particularly good with specialty courses and mandates computer diving.

FISHING

Bloody Bay is equally celebrated for fishing and diving, and the flats and shallows including South Hole Sound Lagoon across from Owen Island, Tarpon Lake, and the Charles Bight Rosetta Flats offer phenomenal light-tackle and fly-fishing action: surprisingly large tarpon, small bonefish, and permit (a large fish related to pompano) weighing up to 35 pounds. Superior deep-sea fishing is available right offshore for game fish including blue marlin, dolphin, wahoo, tuna, and barracuda.

The **Southern Cross Club** (☎ 345/948–1099 or 800/899–2582 ⊕ www. southerncrossclub.com) offers light-tackle and deep-sea fishing trips.

Curaçao

WORD OF MOUTH

"I can say again that Curacao is one of the most beautiful islands in the Carribean. My next trip is problably going to be Curacao again."

—Zachstickler

WELCOME TO CURAÇAO

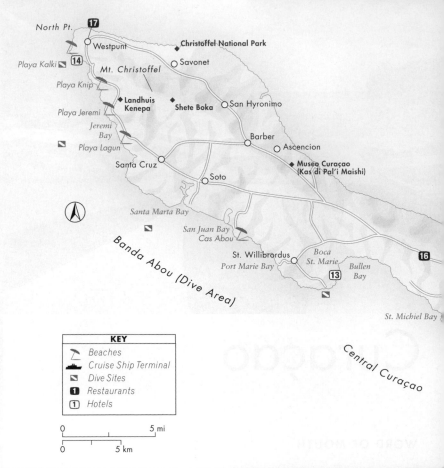

North Pt. **17**

Westpunt

Playa Kalki **14**

♦ Christoffel National Park

○ Savonet

Mt. Christoffel

Playa Knip

♦ **Landhuis Kenepa**

♦ **Shete Boka**

○ San Hyronimo

Playa Jeremi

Jeremi Bay

Playa Lagun

Barber ○

○ Ascencion

Santa Cruz

♦ **Museo Curaçao (Kas di Pal'i Maishi)**

○ Soto

Santa Marta Bay

San Juan Bay
Cas Abou

Banda Abou (Dive Area)

St. Willibrordus
Port Marie Bay

Boca St. Marie

Bullen Bay

13

16

St. Michiel Bay

Central Curaçao

KEY	
⟍	Beaches
⚓	Cruise Ship Terminal
◪	Dive Sites
1	Restaurants
①	Hotels

0 ———————— 5 mi
0 ———————— 5 km

Willemstad's fancifully hued, strikingly gabled town houses glimmer across Santa Anna Bay, and vendors at the Floating Market sell tropical fruit from their schooners. Curaçao's diverse population mixes Latin, European, and African ancestries. Religious tolerance is a hallmark here. All people are welcome in Curaçao, and even tourists feel the warmth.

AN ISLAND REBORN AND REDISCOVERED

The largest and most populous of the Netherlands Antilles is 38 mi (61 km) long and no more than 7½ mi (12 km) wide. Its capital, Willemstad, has been restored and revived over the past few years and is a recognized UNESCO World Heritage Site. The colorful waterfront town houses are unique to the island.

CURAÇAO

9

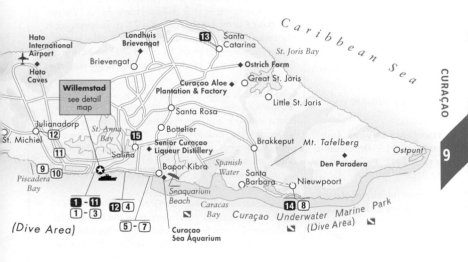

TOP REASONS TO VISIT CURAÇAO

1 Below the Belt: Because it sits below the hurricane belt, the weather in Curaçao is almost always alluring, even during the off-season.

2 Carnival: Curaçao's biggest party draws an increasingly large crowd.

3 Culture: The island's cultural diversity is reflected in the good food from many different cultures.

4 History You Can See: Striking architecture and fascinating historic sights give you something to see when you're not shopping or sunning on the charming beaches.

CURAÇAO PLANNER

Fast Facts

Addresses: In street addresses that do not specify a house number, the *z/n* is a Dutch abbreviation for *zonder nummer* (no number).

Banks and Exchange Services: U.S. dollars are accepted nearly everywhere. Currency in Curaçao is the florin (also called the guilder) and is indicated by *fl* or *NAf* on price tags. The official rate of exchange at this writing was NAf 1.77 to US$1. The currency is expected to be changed to the Caribbean guilder in 2012.

Electricity: 110–130 volts/50 cycles.

Emergency Services: Ambulance (☎ *912*). **On-call doctors** (☎ *1111*). **Police and fire** (☎ *911*).

Passport Requirements: Valid passport required. All visitors must be able to show an ongoing or return ticket as well as have proof of sufficient funds to support their stay on the island.

Weddings: You and your partner must be living outside the Netherlands Antilles; you must report to the Office of the Registrar at least three days before your marriage. You'll need a birth certificate; passport; evidence that you are single; or evidence that you are divorced or a widow or widower.

Essentials

Mail: There are post offices in Punda, Otrobanda, and Groot Kwartier on Schottegatweg (Ring Road), as well as small branches at the Curaçao World Trade Center and the airport. Some hotels sell stamps and have letter drops; you can also buy stamps at some bookstores. An airmail letter to the United States, Canada, or Europe costs NAf 2.85, a postcard NAf 1.49.

Taxes and Service Charges: The departure tax is $32.50 (including flights to Aruba), and the departure tax to other Netherlands Antilles islands is $8. This must be paid in cash, either florins or U.S. dollars. Hotels add a 12% service charge to the bill and collect a 7% government room tax; restaurants typically add 10% to 15%. Most goods and services purchased on the island will also have a 5% OB tax (a goods-and-services tax) added to the purchase price.

Telephones: To place a local call on the island, dial the seven-digit local number. Pay phones charge NAf 0.50 for a local call—far less than the typical hotel charge. Whether for local or long-distance calling, it's common to use prepaid phone cards, which are widely available around the island, as many pay phones do not accept coins. To call Curaçao direct from the United States, dial 011–5999 plus the number in Curaçao.

International roaming for most GSM mobile phones is available in Curaçao. Local companies are UTS (United Telecommunication Services) and Digicel. You can also rent a mobile phone or buy a prepaid SIM card for your own phone.

Tipping: Service is usually included, but if you find the staff exemplary, you can add another 5% to 10% to the bill. Porters and bellhops, about $1 a bag; housekeeping, $2 to $3 per day; taxi, about 10%.

Visitor Information: Curaçao Tourist Board (✉ *Pietermaai 19, Punda, Willemstad* ☎ *5999/434–8200* ✉ *Hato International Airport* ☎ *5999/868–1341* ⊕ *www.curacao.com*).

Getting to and Around Curaçao

Logistics: Most travelers will make a connection in San Juan, Montego Bay, or Aruba. To connect through Aruba, you'll likely have to book your flight on a tiny island-hopper directly with the island-based airline. **Hato International Airport** (✉ CUR ☎ 5999/839–1410) has car-rental facilities, duty-free shops, and restaurants.

Hassle Factor: Medium to high.

Air Travel: Nonstops are available on American Airlines, Delta, and Continental; you can also connect on American (via San Juan) or Air Jamaica (via Montego Bay). **Dutch Antilles Express** (☎ 5999/717–0808 ⊕ www.flydae.com) offers connecting service from Aruba, Caracas, Santo Domingo, and St. Maarten.

Air Jamaica (☎ 800/523–5585 or 5999/888–2300). **American Airlines** (☎ 5999/869–5707). **Continental Airlines** (☎ 800/231–0856 or 5999/839–1196).

Car Travel: Many of the larger hotels have free shuttles into Willemstad, or you can take a quick, cheap taxi ride; hotels in Willemstad usually provide a free beach shuttle, so it's possible to get by without a car. If you're planning to do country driving or rough it through Christoffel National Park, a four-wheel-drive vehicle is best. All you need is a valid driver's license. You can rent a car from any of the major car agencies at the airport or have one delivered free to your hotel. Rates are about $40–$45 a day for a compact car to $60–$75 for a four-door sedan or four-wheel-drive vehicle; add 5% tax and optional daily insurance.

Avis (☎ 5999/839–1500 or 800/228–0668). **Budget** (☎ 5999/868–3466 or 800/472–3325). **Hertz** (☎ 5999/888–0188). **National Car Rental** (☎ 5999/869–4433). **Thrifty** (☎ 5999/461–3089).

Taxi Travel: Fares from the airport to Willemstad and the nearby beach hotels run about $18 to $22, and those to hotels at the island's western end about $38 to $44. The government-approved rates, which do not include waiting time, can be found in a brochure called "Taxi Tariff Guide," available at the airport, hotels, cruise-ship terminals, and the tourist board. Rates are for up to four passengers. There's a 25% surcharge after 11 pm. Taxis are readily available at hotels and at taxi stands at the airport, in Punda, and in Otrobanda; in other cases, call **Central Dispatch** (☎ 5999/869–0752).

When to Go

High season in Curaçao mirrors that in much of the Caribbean: basically from mid-December through mid-April. In the off-season, rates will be reduced at least 25% and often more. Hurricanes and severe tropical storms are rare—though still possible—in Curaçao, which means the island has good weather almost year-round.

FESTIVALS AND EVENTS

The year's big event is **Carnival,** which concludes on Ash Wednesday; it's among the Caribbean's best parties and is beginning to draw visitors in larger numbers.

The **Curaçao International Jazz Festival** is held in May.

The **Curaçao North Sea Jazz Festival** occurs in early September and features international stars of jazz and pop. Past performers include John Legend, Simply Red, and George Benson.

The **Heiniken Regatta Curaçao** features exciting boat races and musical events in November.

The **African Diaspora Film Festival** runs for a week in late June and early July, presenting films by black independent filmmakers from around the world.

9

CURAÇAO PLANNER

Island Activities

The island has many good **beaches,** not to mention clear blue water; however, a lot of the beaches on the southeast coast (even the hotel beaches) are a bit rocky. The softer, whiter beaches are on the west coast.

Excellent **diving** has always been a draw in Curaçao, and a fair percentage of travelers are drawn by the teeming reefs and good shore-diving possibilities.

Day sails are the most popular way to enjoy the water if you don't dive, and all of them offer opportunities for good snorkeling.

Both sides of Willemstad— Punda and the revitalized Otrobanda—offer the shore-bound plenty to occupy their time, making it well worth your while to check out the **local sights** and do some **shopping.**

Do stop for a bite to eat at one of the many great **restaurants.**

By night, you can gamble in a few **casinos** or check out some of the lively **bars** and dance clubs.

Where to Stay

Resort development is concentrated around the capital, Willemstad, so most resorts are within easy reach of town, by shuttle or by foot. As the island becomes more developed, visitors have more options, and there are a few resorts farther removed as well, but it's the amenities that should drive your decision more than location. Choose the type of lodging that best appeals to your interests and style. Those spending a bit more time gravitate to villas and bungalows.

Resorts: Most of Curaçao's larger hotels are midsize resorts of 200 to 300 rooms, and many of them are within easy striking distance of town. The island offers a full range of resorts from the intimate and luxurious to historic properties—few other destinations offer a downtown hotel with a saltwater infinity pool complete with palm-lined beach.

Dive Resorts: Most of the resorts catering to divers are smaller operations of fewer than 100 rooms (often much smaller). Although some of these are in and around Willemstad, there are also a few on the secluded west end of the island, and that's where shore diving is best.

Villas and Bungalows: Though they are marketed primarily to European travelers who have more time to spend on the island, self-catering accommodations are an option for anyone who has at least a week to spend in Curaçao.

HOTEL AND RESTAURANT COSTS

Restaurant prices are for a main course at dinner and include any taxes or service charges. Hotel prices are per night for a double room in high season, excluding taxes, service charges, and meal plans (except at all-inclusives).

WHAT IT COSTS IN U.S. DOLLARS

	¢	$	$$	$$$	$$$$
Restaurants	under $8	$8–$12	$12–$20	$20–$30	over $30
Hotels	under $150	$150–$275	$276–$375	$376–$475	over $475

CURAÇAO BEACHES

Beautiful beaches are not hard to find on Curaçao. The island boasts more than three dozen beaches, with many of the best ones on the western side. The more popular beaches offer a wide range of facilities and excellent restaurants.

(Above) Snorkeling Playa Knip. (Opposite page bottom) Windsurfers on Seaquarium Beach. (Opposite page top) Cas Abao Beach.

Beaches in Curaçao range from small inlets shielded by craggy cliffs to longer expanses of sparkling sand. Beaches along the southeast coast tend to be rocky in the shallow water (wear reef shoes—some resorts lend them out for free); the west side has more stretches of smooth sand at the shoreline. Exploring the beaches away from the hotels is a perfect way to soak up the island's character. Whether you're seeking a lovers' hideaway, a special snorkeling adventure, or a great spot to wow the kids, you're not likely to be disappointed. There are snack bars and restrooms on many of the larger beaches, but it's at the smaller ones with no facilities where you might find utter tranquillity, especially during the week. Most spots with entry fees offer lounge chairs for rent at an additional cost, typically $2 to $3 per chair.

THE SCOOP

The most popular beaches on the west and south sides of the island have beautiful, powdery white sand. Those seeking solitude and inspiration can find beaches of all sizes on the north and east coasts. The rugged and windswept nature of these coasts means that the white sand will usually be liberally sprinkled with pebbles, which can make sunbathing uncomfortable and walking difficult.

EAST END

☙ **Seaquarium Beach.** This 1,600-foot stretch of sandy beach is divided into separate sections, each uniquely defined by a seaside resort or restaurant as its central draw. By day, no matter where you choose to enter the palm-shaded beach, you can find lounge chairs in the sand, thatched shelters, and restrooms. The sections at Mambo and Kontiki beaches also have showers. The island's largest water-sports center (Ocean Encounters at Lions Dive) caters to nearby hotel guests and walk-ins. Mambo Beach is always a hot spot and quite a scene on weekends, especially during the much-touted Sunday-night fiesta that's become a fixture of the island's nightlife. The ubiquitous beach mattress is also the preferred method of seating for the Tuesday-night movies at Mambo Beach (check the *K-Pasa* guide for listings—typically B-films or old classics—and reserve your spot with a shirt or a towel). At Kontiki Beach, you can find a spa, a hair braider, and a restaurant that serves refreshing piña colada ice cream. Unless you're a guest of a resort on the beach, the entrance fee to any section is $3 until 5 pm, then free. After 11 pm, you must be 18 or older to access the beach. ✉ *Bapor Kibra z/n, about 1 mi (1½ km) east of downtown Willemstad.*

WEST END

☙ **Cas Abao.** This white-sand gem has the brightest blue water in Curaçao, a treat for swimmers, snorkelers, and sunbathers alike. You can take respite beneath the hut-shaded snack bar. The restrooms and showers are immaculate. The only drawback is the weekend crowds, especially Sunday, when local families descend in droves; come on a weekday for more privacy. You can rent beach chairs, paddleboats, and snorkeling and diving gear. The entry fee is $3, and the beach is open from 8 to 6. Turn off Westpunt Highway at the junction onto Weg Naar Santa Cruz; follow until the turnoff for Cas Abao, and then drive along the winding country road for about 10 minutes to the beach. ✉ *West of St. Willibrordus, about 3 mi (5 km) off Weg Naar Santa Cruz.*

Playa Jeremi. No snack bar, no dive shop, no facilities, no fee—in fact, there's nothing but sheer natural beauty. Though the beach is sandy, there are rocky patches, so barefoot visitors should exercise care. The parking area is offset from the beach and vehicle break-ins are common. Quite a bit of development is planned for this beach, so have a look before it's too late. ✉ *Off Weg Naar Santa Cruz, west of Lagun.*

Playa Kalki. Noted for its spectacular snorkeling, this beach is at the western tip of the island. Sunbathers may find the narrow and rocky beach less than

9

Looking down at the splendid cove of Playa Lagun

ideal. The Ocean Encounters dive shop is here. ⊠ *Westpunt, near Jaanchi's.*

🐢 **Playa Knip.** Two protected coves offer crystal-clear turquoise waters. Big (Groot) Knip is an expanse of alluring white sand, perfect for swimming and snorkeling. You can rent beach chairs and hang out under the *palapas* (thatch-roof shelters) or cool off with ice cream at the snack bar. There are restrooms here but no showers. It's particularly crowded on Sunday and school holidays. Just up the road, also in a protected cove, Little (Kleine) Knip is a charmer, too, with picnic tables and palapas. Steer clear of the poisonous manchineel trees. There's no fee for these beaches. ⊠ *Banda Abou, just east of Westpunt.*

🐢 **Playa Lagun.** This northwestern cove is caught between gray cliffs, which dramatically frame the Caribbean blue. Cognoscenti know this as one of the best places to snorkel—even for kids—because of the calm, shallow water. It's also a haven for fishing boats and canoes. There's a small dive shop on the beach, a snack bar (open weekends), and restrooms, but there's no fee. ⊠ *Banda Abou, west of Santa Cruz.*

🐢 **Playa Porto Mari.** Calm, clear water and a long stretch of white sand are the hallmarks of this beach. Without the commercial bustle of Seaquarium Beach, it's one of the best for all-around fun, and it therefore draws throngs of local families and tourists on the weekends. A decent bar and restaurant, well-kept showers, changing facilities, and restrooms are all on-site; a nature trail is nearby. The double coral reef—explore one, swim past it, explore another—is a special feature that makes this spot popular with snorkelers and divers. The entrance fee (including one free beverage) is $2 on weekdays, $3 on Sunday and holidays. From Willemstad, drive west on Westpunt Highway for 4 mi (7 km); turn left onto Willibrordus Road at the Porto Mari billboard, and then drive 3 mi (5 km) until you see a large church; follow signs on the winding dirt road to the beach. ⊠ *Off Willibrordus Rd.*

Updated
by Vernon
O'Reilly
Ramesar

The sun smiles down on Curaçao, which sits on the outer fringe of the so-called hurricane belt. Gentle trade winds help keep temperatures generally in the 80s. Water sports — including outstanding reef diving—attract enthusiasts from all over the world. Curaçao claims 38 beaches—some long stretches of silky sand, most smaller coves suitable for picture postcards. In the countryside, the dollhouse look of planta-tion houses, or *landhuizen* (literally, "land houses"), makes a cheerful contrast to stark cacti and austere shrubbery.

The sprawling city of Willemstad is the island's capital. Its historic downtown and the natural harbor (*Schottegat*) around which it's built are included on UNESCO's World Heritage List, a coveted distinction reserved for the likes of the Palace of Versailles and the Taj Mahal. The "face" of Willemstad delights like a kaleidoscope—rows of sprightly painted town houses with gabled roofs sit perched alongside the steely blue Santa Anna Bay. Local lore has it that in the 1800s, the governor claimed he suffered from migraines and blamed the glare from the sun's reflection off the then-white structures. To alleviate the problem, he ordered the facades painted in colors.

Curaçao was discovered by Alonzo de Ojeda (a lieutenant of Columbus) in 1499. The first Spanish settlers arrived in 1527. In 1634 the Dutch came via the Netherlands West Indies Company. Eight years later Peter Stuyvesant began his rule as governor (in 1647, Stuyvesant became gov-ernor of New Amsterdam, which later became New York). Twelve Jew-ish families arrived in Curaçao from Amsterdam in 1651, and by 1732 a synagogue had been built; the present structure is the oldest synagogue in continuous use in the Western Hemisphere. Over the years the city built fortresses to defend against French and British invasions—the standing ramparts now house restaurants and hotels. The Dutch claim to Curaçao was recognized in 1815 by the Treaty of Paris. From 1954 through 2006, Curaçao was the seat of government of the Netherlands Antilles, a group

9

of islands under the umbrella of the Kingdom of the Netherlands. In October 2010, Curaçao's island council granted the territory autonomy (the same status Aruba attained in 1986).

Tourism is on a fast track to surpassing harbor-related activities as the island's primary source of income, with a corresponding surge in hotel development in recent years. The government pumped millions of dollars into the opening of a new airport in 2006, and has committed more funds to an expansion plan to accommodate future growth. The opening of a massive pier has boosted cruise-ship passengers to record numbers. In addition, the government and private sources have invested substantially in the restoration of the island's graceful colonial buildings.

Today, Curaçao's population derives from nearly 60 nationalities—an exuberant mix of Latin, European, and African roots speaking a Babel of tongues—resulting in superb restaurants and a flourishing cultural scene. Although Dutch is the official language, Papiamento is the vernacular of all the Netherlands Antilles and the preferred choice for communication among the locals. English and Spanish are also widely spoken. The island, like its Dutch settlers, is known for its religious tolerance, and tourists are warmly welcomed.

EXPLORING CURAÇAO

WILLEMSTAD

What does the capital of Curaçao have in common with New York City? Broadway, for one thing. Here it's called Breedestraat, but the origin is the same. Dutch settlers came here in the 1630s, about the same time they sailed through the Verazzano Narrows to Manhattan, bringing with them original red-tile roofs, first used on the trade ships as ballast and later incorporated into the architecture of Willemstad.

The city is cut in two by Santa Anna Bay. On one side is the Punda—crammed with shops, restaurants, monuments, and markets—and on the other is Otrobanda (literally, the "other side"), with lots of narrow, winding streets full of private homes notable for their picturesque gables and Dutch-influenced designs. In recent years the ongoing regeneration of Otrobanda has been apparent, marked by a surge in development of new hotels, restaurants, and shops; the rebirth, concentrated near the waterfront, was spearheaded by the creation of the elaborate Kura Hulanda complex.

There are three ways to cross the bay: by car over the Juliana Bridge; by foot over the Queen Emma pontoon bridge; or by free ferry, which runs when the pontoon bridge is swung open for passing ships. All the major hotels outside town offer free shuttle service to town once or twice daily. Shuttles coming from the Otrobanda side leave you at Riffort. From here it's a short walk north to the foot of the pontoon bridge. Shuttles coming from the Punda side leave you near the main entrance to Ft. Amsterdam.

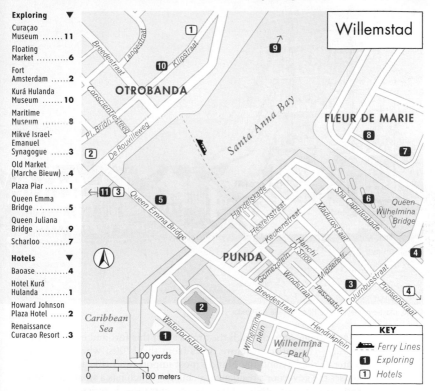

WHAT TO SEE

Curaçao Museum. Housed in an 1853 plantation house, this small museum is filled with artifacts, paintings, and antiques that trace the island's history. This is also a venue for visiting art exhibitions. ✉ *V. Leeuwenhoekstraat z/n, Otrobanda, Willemstad* ☎ *5999/462–6051* ✆ *Free* ⊙ *Weekdays 8:30–4:30, Sun. 10–4.*

★ **Floating Market.** Each morning dozens of Venezuelan schooners laden with tropical fruits and vegetables arrive at this bustling market on the Punda side of the city. Mangoes, papayas, and exotic vegetables vie for space with freshly caught fish and herbs and spices. The buying is best at 6:30 am—too early for many people on vacation—but there's plenty of action through the afternoon. Any produce bought here should be thoroughly washed or peeled before being eaten. ✉ *Sha Caprileskade, Punda, Willemstad.*

NEED A BREAK?

For a cooling break from your explorations, **Old Vienna Terrace Café** (✉ *Handelskade 6 C, Punda, Willemstad* ☎ *5999/736–1086*) serves scrumptious homemade ice cream. Indulge your sweet tooth with such flavors as green apple, mango, and rum plum. There's also a full menu of light bites and outdoor seating along the harbor.

A daring, mast-eye view of the Handelskade in Punda.

Ft. Amsterdam. Step through the archway of this fort and enter another century. The entire structure dates from the 1700s, when it was the center of the city and the island's most important fortification. Now it houses the governor's residence, a church (which has a small museum), and government offices. Outside the entrance, a series of majestic gnarled *wayaka* trees are fancifully carved with human forms—the work of local artist Mac Alberto. ⊠ *Foot of Queen Emma Bridge, Punda, Willemstad* ☎ *5999/461–1139* ✍ *Fort free, church museum $2* ☾ *Weekdays 9:30–1, Sun. service at 10.*

Fodor's Choice **Kura Hulanda Museum.** This fascinating anthropological museum reveals
★ the island's diverse roots. Housed in a restored 18th-century village, the museum is built around a former mercantile square (Kura Hulanda means "Holland courtyard"), where the Dutch once sold slaves. An exhibit on the transatlantic slave trade includes a gut-wrenching replica of a slave-ship hold. Other sections feature relics from West African empires, examples of pre-Columbian gold, and Antillean art. The complex is the brainchild of Dutch philanthropist Jacob Gelt Dekker, and the museum grew from his personal collection of artifacts. ⊠ *Klipstraat 9, Otrobanda, Willemstad* ☎ *5999/462–1400* ⊕ *www.kurahulanda. com/museum* ✍ *$9* ☾ *Thurs.–Sat. 10–5.*

Maritime Museum. The museum—designed to resemble the interior of a ship—gives you a sense of Curaçao's maritime history, using model ships, historic maps, nautical charts, navigational equipment, and audiovisual displays. Topics explored in the exhibits include the development of Willemstad as a trading city, Curaçao's role as a contraband hub, the remains of *De Alphen* (a Dutch marine freighter that exploded and sank in St. Anna Bay in 1778 and was excavated in 1984), the slave trade, the development of steam navigation, and the role of the Dutch navy on the island. The museum also offers a two-hour guided tour (Wednesday and Saturday, 2 pm) on its "water bus" through Curaçao's harbor—a route familiar to traders, smugglers, and pirates. The museum is wheelchair accessible. ⊠ *Van der Brandhofstraat 7, Scharloo, Willemstad* ☎ *5999/465–2327* ⊕ *www.curacaomaritime.com* ✉ *Museum $10, museum and harbor tour $15* ☉ *Tues.–Sat. 9–4.*

★ **Mikvé Israel-Emanuel Synagogue.** The temple, the oldest in continuous use in the Western Hemisphere, is one of Curaçao's most important sights and draws thousands of visitors a year. The synagogue was dedicated in 1732 by the Jewish community, which had already grown from the original 12 families who came from Amsterdam in 1651. They were later joined by Jews from Portugal and Spain fleeing persecution from the Inquisition. White sand covers the synagogue floor for two symbolic reasons: a remembrance of the 40 years Jews spent wandering the desert, and a re-creation of the sand used by secret Jews, or *conversos,* to muffle sounds from their houses of worship during the Inquisition. The **Jewish Cultural Museum** (☎ *5999/461–1633*), in back of the synagogue, displays antiques—including a set of circumcision instruments—and artifacts from around the world. Many of the objects are used in the synagogue, making it a "living" museum. English and Hebrew services are held Friday at 6:30 pm and Saturday at 10 am. Men who attend should wear a jacket and tie. Yarmulkes are provided to men for services and tours. ⊠ *Hanchi Snoa 29, Punda, Willemstad* ☎ *5999/461–1067* ⊕ *www.snoa.com* ✉ *$6; donations also accepted* ☉ *Weekdays 9–4:30.*

Old Market *(Marche Bieuw).* Local cooks prepare hearty Antillean lunches in coal pots at this covered market behind the post office. Enjoy such Curaçaoan specialties as *funchi* (polenta), goat stew, fried fish, or stewed okra. Prices range from $5 to $11. ⊠ *De Ruyterkade, Punda, Willemstad.*

Plaza Piar. This plaza is dedicated to Manuel Piar, a native Curaçaoan who fought for the independence of Venezuela under the liberator Simón Bolívar. On one side of the plaza is the Waterfort, built in the late 1820s to help defend the old city. The original cannons are still positioned in the battlements. The foundation, however, now forms the walls of the Howard Johnson Plaza Hotel Curaçao & Casino. ⊠ *Willemstad.*

Queen Emma Bridge. Affectionately called the Swinging Old Lady by the locals, this bridge connects the two sides of Willemstad—Punda and Otrobanda—across the Santa Anna Bay. The bridge swings open at least 30 times a day to allow passage of ships to and from the sea. The original bridge, built in 1888, was the brainchild of the American consul Leonard Burlington Smith, who made a mint off the tolls he charged for using it: 2¢ per person for those wearing shoes, free to those crossing barefoot. Today it's free to everyone. The bridge was dismantled and completely repaired and restored in 2005. ⊠ *Willemstad.*

Queen Juliana Bridge. This 1,625-foot-long bridge stands 200 feet above the water, and it's the highest bridge in the Caribbean. It's the crossing for

9

motor traffic between Punda and Otrobanda and affords breathtaking views (and photo ops) of the city, day and night. ⊠ *Willemstad*.

Scharloo. The Wilhelmina Drawbridge connects Punda with the once-flourishing district of Scharloo, where the early Jewish merchants built stately homes. The architecture along Scharlooweg (much of it from the 17th century) is magnificent, and, happily, many of the colonial mansions that had become dilapidated have been meticulously renovated. The area closest to Kleine Werf is a red-light district and fairly run-down, but the rest is well worth a visit. ⊠ *Willemstad*.

ELSEWHERE ON CURAÇAO

The Weg Maar Santa Cruz through the village of Soto winds to the island's northwest tip through landscape that Georgia O'Keeffe might have painted: towering cacti, flamboyant dried shrubbery, and aluminum-roof houses. Throughout this *cunucu,* or countryside, you can see fishermen hauling nets, women pounding cornmeal, and an occasional donkey blocking traffic. Land houses—large plantation houses from centuries past—dot the countryside. To explore the island's eastern side from Willemstad, take the coastal road called Martin Luther King Boulevard about 2 mi (3 km) to Bapor Kibra. This is where you can find the Sea Aquarium and the Dolphin Academy. Farther east is a nature park at Caracas Bay and the upscale Spanish Water neighborhood and marina. To the far northeast is Groot St. Joris, home of Curaçao's aloe plantation and one of the largest ostrich-breeding farms outside Africa.

WHAT TO SEE

★ **Christoffel National Park.** The 1,239-foot Mt. Christoffel, Curaçao's highest peak, is at the center of this 4,450-acre garden and wildlife preserve. The exhilarating climb up—a challenge to anyone who hasn't grown up scaling the Alps—takes about two hours for a reasonably fit person. On a clear day, the panoramic view from the peak stretches to the mountain ranges of Venezuela.

Through the park are eight hiking trails and a 20-mi (32-km) network of driving trails (use heavy-treaded tires if you wish to explore the unpaved stretches). All these routes traverse hilly fields full of prickly pear cacti, divi-divi trees, bushy-haired palms, and exotic flowers. Guided nature walks, horseback rides, and jeep tours can be arranged through the main park office. If you're going without a guide, first study the *Excursion Guide to Christoffel Park,* sold at the visitor center. It outlines the various routes and identifies the indigenous flora and fauna. Start out early, as by 10 am the park starts to feel like a sauna.

Watch for goats and small animals that might cross your path, and consider yourself lucky if you see any of the elusive white-tailed deer. Every day at 4 pm, guides lead 15-minute expeditions to track the protected herd. Birds are abundant, and experts lead the way twice daily. White-tailed hawks may be seen along the green hiking route, white orchids along the yellow hiking route. There are also ancient Indian drawings and caves where you might hear the rustling of bat wings or spot scuttling, nonpoisonous scorpions.

Plantation-house in Christoffel National Park with Mt. Christoffel in the distance.

Horseback tours are conducted from Rancho Alfin, which is in the park. Reservations are required. Additionally, most island sports outfitters offer some kind of activity in the park, such as kayaking, specialized hiking tours, and drive-through tours (⇨ *Sports and Activities, below*). ✉ *Savonet* ☎ *5999/864–0363 for information and tour reservations, 5999/462–6262 for jeep tours, 5999/864–0535 for horseback tours* 💲 *$10* ⊙ *Mon.–Sat. 8–4, Sun. 6–3; last admission 90 min before closing.*

Curaçao Aloe Plantation & Factory. Drop in for a fascinating tour that takes you through the various stages of production of aloe vera, renowned for its healing powers. You'll get a look at everything from the fields to the final products. At the gift shop, you can buy CurAloe products, including homemade goodies like soap, pure aloe gel, and pure aloe juice, as well as sunscreen and other skin-care products. The plantation is on the way to the Ostrich Farm and run by the same owner. Tours begin throughout the day. ✉ *Weg Naar Groot St. Joris z/n, Groot St. Joris* ☎ *5999/767–5577* ⊕ *www.aloecuracao.com* 💲 *$6* ⊙ *Mon.–Sat. 9–4; last tour at 3.*

Curaçao Sea Aquarium. You don't have to get your feet wet to see the island's underwater treasures. The aquarium has about 40 saltwater tanks filled with more than 400 varieties of marine life. A restaurant, a snack bar, two photo centers, and souvenir shops are on-site.

At the **Dolphin Academy** (☎ *5999/465–8900* ⊕ *www.dolphin-academy. com*), you can watch a fanciful dolphin show (included with Sea Aquarium admission). For up-close interactions, you may choose from several special programs (extra charges apply and reservations are essential) to encounter the dolphins in shallow water, or to swim, snorkel, or dive with them. ⊠ *Seaquarium Beach, Bapor Kibra z/n* ☎ *5999/461–6666* ⊕ *www. curacao-sea-aquarium.com* ☞ *Aquarium $19; Dolphin Academy $79– $169* ⊙ *Aquarium daily 8:30–5:30, Dolphin Academy daily 8:30–4:30.*

★ **Den Paradera**. Dazzle your senses at this organic herb garden, where guides will explain the origins of traditional folk medicines used to treat everything from stomach ulcers to diabetes. Owner Dinah Veeris is a renowned expert and author in the field. The kitchen is a factory of sorts where three busy people turn homegrown plants like cactus, aloe vera, and calabash into homemade body- and skin-care products like shampoos, ointments, and oils—all for sale at the gift shop. Reservations are essential for guided tours. ⊠ *Seru Grandi Kavel 105A, Banda Riba* ☎ *5999/767–5608* ☞ *$7 with guided tour* ⊙ *Mon.–Sat. 9–6.*

★ **Hato Caves**. Stalactites and stalagmites form striking shapes in these 200,000-year-old caves. Hidden lighting adds to the dramatic effect. Indians who used the caves for shelter left petroglyphs about 1,500 years ago. More recently, slaves who escaped from nearby plantations used the caves as a hideaway. Hour-long guided tours wind down to the pools in various chambers. Keep in mind that there are 49 steps to climb up to the entrance and the occasional bat might not be to everyone's taste. To reach the caves, head northwest toward the airport, take a right onto Gosieweg, follow the loop right onto Schottegatweg, take another right onto Jan Norduynweg and a final right onto Rooseveltweg, and follow signs. ⊠ *Rooseveltweg z/n, Hato* ☎ *5999/868–0379* ☞ *$8* ⊙ *Daily 10–4.*

Landhuis Kenepa. With the island's largest slave population, this plantation was the site of a revolt in 1795 that spurred the abolition of slavery on the island. The renovated plantation house near the island's western tip is filled with period furnishings and clothing. ⊠ *Weg Naar Santa Cruz, Knip* ☎ *5999/864–0244* ☞ *$2* ⊙ *Weekdays 9–4, weekends 10–4.*

Museo Curaçao *(Kas di Pal'i Maishi)*. The thatch-roof cottage is filled with antique furniture, farm implements, and clothing typical of 19th-century colonial life. Out back is a small farm and vegetable garden. Look closely at the fence—it's made of living cacti. There's also a snack bar. A festival featuring live music and local crafts takes place here on the first Sunday of each month. ⊠ *Dokterstuin 27, on road to Westpunt from Willemstad, Westpunt* ☎ *5999/864–2497* ☞ *$2* ⊙ *Tues.–Fri. 9–4, weekends 9–5.*

ⓒ **Ostrich Farm**. If you (and the kids) are ready to stick your neck out
★ for an adventure, visit one of the largest ostrich farms outside Africa. Every hour, guided tours show the creatures' complete development from egg to mature bird. Kids enjoy the chance to hold an egg, stroke a day-old chick, and sit atop an ostrich for an unusual photo op. At the **Restaurant Zambezi** you can sample local ostrich specialties and other African dishes (reservations are recommended; closed Monday, no dinner Tuesday). The gift shop sells handicrafts made in southern Africa, including leather goods and wood carvings, as well as products made by local artisans. ⊠ *Groot St. Joris* ☎ *5999/747–2777* ⊕ *www. ostrichfarm.net* ☞ *$11* ⊙ *Tues.–Sun. 9–5.*

Senior Curaçao Liqueur Distillery. The famed Curaçao liqueur, made from the peels of the bitter Laraha orange, is produced at this mansion, which dates to the 1800s. Don't expect a massive factory—it's just a small showroom in an open-air foyer. There are no guides, but delightful old hand-painted posters explain the distillation process, and you can watch workers filling the bottles by hand. Assorted flavors are available to sample for free. If you're interested in buying—the orange-flavor chocolate liqueur is delicious over ice cream—you can choose from a complete selection in enticing packaging, including miniature Dutch ceramic houses. ⊠ *Landhuis Chobolobo, Saliña* ☎ *5999/461–3526* 🖃 *Free* ☉ *Weekdays 8–noon and 1–5.*

★ **Shete Boka.** The name of this park means "Seven Inlets" in Papiamento. Indeed, the sea has carved out seven magnificent grottoes, the largest of which is Boka Tabla, where you can watch and listen to the waves crashing against the rocks beneath a limestone overhang. Boka Pistol is also spectacular, with thunderous waves smashing into the rocks and jetting up into towering plumes of spray, often leaving rainbows lingering in the mist. Several of the surrounding caverns serve as turtle nesting places; you might also spot flocks of parakeets emerge in formation, hawks soar and dip, and gulls dive-bomb for their lunch. ⊠ *Westpunt Hwy., just past village center, Soto* 🖃 *$1.50* ☉ *Daily 9–5.*

WHERE TO EAT

Dine beneath the boughs of magnificent old trees, on the terraces of restored mansions and plantation houses, or on the ramparts of 18th-century forts. Curaçaoans partake of generally outstanding fare, with representation from a remarkable smattering of ethnicities. Outdoor or open-air sheltered dining is commonplace; note that most restaurants offer a smoking section or permit smoking throughout. Fine dining tends to be pricey, mostly because of the high cost of importing products to the island. For cheap eats with a local flair, drop by the Old Market for lunch, or stop at one of the snack bars or snack trucks you can find all over the island (have some guilders handy—many of them won't have change for dollars).

WHAT TO WEAR

Dress in restaurants is almost always casual (though beachwear isn't acceptable). Some of the resort dining rooms and more elegant restaurants require that men wear jackets, especially in high season; ask when you make reservations.

$$$$
ECLECTIC
✕ **Angelica's Kitchen.** For an immersive, hands-on experience with the cuisine of the island you might want to try this unusual Otrobanda establishment. Self-taught cook Angelica Schoop puts guests in an apron and walks them through the process of creating their own meal in her fully equipped kitchen. Dishes may include anything from plantain soup to funchi. After the cooking is done, guests head to the back porch and enjoy the fruits of their labor. The minimum group size is 10 people, so gather up a few friends and prepare for four hours of culinary fun. Less adventurous folks can just cross the road and enjoy fine pastries

and champagne at Angelica's Delights or join her on a culinary walking tour of the city. ⊠ *Hoogstraat 49, Otrobanda* ☎ *5999/562–3699* ⊕ *www.angelicas-kitchen.com* ⌕ *Reservations essential.*

¢–$
CAFÉ

✕ **Awa di Playa.** Formerly a fisherman's hangout, the ramshackle shed-like structure located on an ocean inlet gives way to an equally ramshackle interior and some of the best local lunches anywhere on the island. There's no menu—the waiter will tell you what's available and you can watch it being cooked in the tiny kitchen. The presentation isn't fancy and the occasional fly makes an appearance, but the food is honest and delicious. ⊠ *Behind Hook's Hut and Hilton, Piscadera Bay, Willemstad* ☎ *5999/462–6939* ▭ *No credit cards* ⊙ *No dinner.*

$$$$
CONTINENTAL
Fodor's Choice
★

✕ **Bistro Le Clochard.** Built into a 19th-century fort, this romantic gem anchors the entrance to the 21st-century Riffort Village complex, the waterside terrace offering an enchanting view of the floating bridge and harbor. Switzerland and France are the key influences in the sublime preparations. The signature dish is La Potence—a spike-covered metal ball resembling a medieval weapon. It's brought to your table sizzling hot and covered with bits of sizzling tenderloin and sausage, served with various dipping sauces. Though more gimmicky fun than fine dining, it makes for a popular photo opportunity. The cheese fondue definitely keeps diners coming back. Game lovers can have their fill from the seasonal menu. No matter what, leave room for the sumptuous Toblerone chocolate mousse. ⊠ *Harborside Terr., Riffort Village, Otrobanda, Willemstad* ☎ *5999/462–5666* ⊕ *www.bistroleclochard. com* ⌕ *Reservations essential.*

$$–$$$
CONTINENTAL
★

✕ **Blues.** Jutting out onto a pier over the ocean, this jazzy spot is an alluring place for dinner. The small menu is surprisingly comprehensive with a special emphasis on seafood. The fish, mussel, and shrimp ceviche is a popular and refreshing appetizer. For meat lovers, the Spare Ribs New Orleans Style holds a spot at the top of the charts. Live music on Thursday and Saturday evening includes seductive vocalists and top-notch musicians. If you'd rather be removed from the scene, you can arrange for a cozy dinner on the beach; whether it's a table for two or for a larger group, you'll be nestled in the sand on colorful oversize pillows. There's also a terrific prix-fixe tapas buffet on Friday. ⊠ *Avila Hotel, Penstraat 130, Punda, Willemstad* ☎ *5999/461–4377* ⊕ *www. avilahotel.com* ⊙ *Closed Mon. No lunch.*

$$$–$$$$
CONTINENTAL
★

✕ **Fort Nassau Restaurant.** On a hill above Willemstad, this elegant restaurant is built into an 18th-century fort with a 360-degree view. For the best perspective, sit beside the huge bay windows in the air-conditioned interior; the terrace has a pleasant breeze and is generally more popular with diners, but the view is not quite optimal. Among the highlights of the diverse menu is the medley of Caribbean seafood with mahimahi, shrimp, and grilled octopus. Scrumptious desserts will leave you feeling sated. ⊠ *Schottegatweg 82, near Juliana Bridge, Otrobanda, Willemstad* ☎ *5999/461–3450 or 5999/461–3086* ⊕ *www.fortnassau.com* ⌕ *Reservations essential* ⊙ *No lunch weekends.*

$$–$$$
ECLECTIC

✕ **Gouverneur de Rouville Restaurant & Café.** Dine on the verandah of a restored 19th-century Dutch mansion overlooking the Santa Anna Bay and the resplendent Punda skyline. Though often busy and popular with tourists, the ambience makes it worth a visit. Intriguing soup options include Cuban banana soup and Curaçao-style fish soup. *Keshi yena* (seasoned meat wrapped in cheese and then baked) and spareribs are among the savory entrées. After dinner, you can stick around for live music at the bar, which stays open until 1 am. The restaurant is also popular for lunch and attracts crowds when cruise ships dock. ⊠ *De Rouvilleweg 9, Otrobanda, Willemstad* ☎ *5999/462–5999* ⊕ *www. de-gouverneur.com.*

$$–$$$
CARIBBEAN

✕ **Jaanchi's Restaurant.** Over the years this has become something of a road marker on Curaçao's beaten tourist path, with prices to match. You'll be greeted by the owner, Jaanchi himself, a self-described "walking, talking menu," who will recite your choices of dishes for lunch. Jaanchi's iguana soup, touted in folklore as an aphrodisiac, is famous on the island. It's quite a sight when so-called sugar-thief birds flock to feeders outside the restaurant when the owner periodically fills them with sugar. Although predominantly a lunch spot, the restaurant will accommodate groups of four or more for dinner by prior arrangement. ⊠ *Westpunt 15, Westpunt* ☎ *5999/864–0126.*

$$$–$$$$
ASIAN
★

✕ **Jaipur.** The subtle lighting and sound of the nearby waterfall seem to make the food even more sublime at this outdoor Pan-Asian restaurant—with distinct Indian and Thai influences—that's part of the expansive Kura Hulanda complex. The samosas filled with ground lamb make a great starter, and the tandoori mixed platter—with chicken, shrimp, and lamb kebobs—is a treat. The Thursday-night Asian buffet is a feast for the senses. ⊠ *Langestraat 8, Otrobanda, Willemstad* ☎ *5999/461–3482* ۩ *Closed Tues. and Wed. No lunch.*

$$
SEAFOOD
۩

✕ **La Bahia Seafood & Steakhouse.** As you dine on a sheltered terrace with a remarkable view of the harbor front, you're so close to the passing ships that it seems you can almost touch them. The menu runs the gamut from burgers and pastas to keshi yena and other local specialties. Even if the food doesn't appeal, this is a great spot to relax with a cup of coffee or a cocktail after a day of exploring. It is a short walk from the Queen Emma Bridge. ⊠ *Otrobanda Hotel & Casino, Breedestraat, Otrobanda, Willemstad* ☎ *5999/462–7400* ⊕ *www.otrobandahotel.com.*

$$$$
STEAK

✕ **L'aldea Steakhouse.** A long drive from downtown hotels along sometimes bumpy roads leads to this Brazilian steak house with a decidedly Mayan theme. Clashing motifs are quickly forgotten as you enter the lush interior filled with stone carvings and greenery. The price of dinner includes the largest salad bar on the island and a nonstop procession of servers at your table, carving a delectable selection of grilled meats until told to stop. Each table has three buttons—to hail the waiter, manager, and request the check. It isn't cheap but the service and fare are top-notch. ⊠ *Sta. Catharina #66, Willemstad* ☎ *5999/767–6777* ⊕ *www.laldeacur.com* ᕚ *Reservations essential* ۩ *Closed Mon. No lunch weekdays.*

$$–$$$
CARIBBEAN
★

✕ **Landhuis Daniel.** Many of the tasty meals served here have their roots in the restaurant's garden. Fruits, vegetables, and herbs are organically grown at this landmark plantation house—dating from 1711—and used unsparingly in the menu, which changes according to seasonal crop yield. The chef draws on creole, French, and Mediterranean influences

9

for his creations. One option is the prix-fixe "surprise menu"—just tell your waiter your preference for meat, fish, or vegetarian, and any dislikes. There's also a small inn here. ⊠ Weg Naar, Westpunt ☎ 5999/864–8400 ⊕ www.landhuisdaniel.com.

$$-$$$
ITALIAN

✕ **La Pergola.** Built into the Waterfort Arches, this restaurant and its outdoor terrace are part of an adjoining strip of eateries in a coveted spot perched over the Caribbean. Listen to the rippling waves crash against the rocks as you sip wine and enjoy creative variations on homemade pastas and pizza. The pretty dining room looks like the interior of a Tuscan villa, with its arched, stuccoed ceiling, copper pots adorning the walls, and huge picture windows. The menu changes frequently, so there is usually something new to choose should you make multiple visits. ⊠ Waterfort Archesboog 12, Punda, Willemstad ☎ 5999/461–3482.

$$-$$$
CONTINENTAL

Moon Beach Club, Lounge & Restaurant. When it comes to chic, no other place on the island can beat this beachfront eatery. A nondescript facade leads past a lighted infinity pool flanked by small cabanalike private booths. You continue to a semicovered dining room open to the eponymous moon. Choose to dine or drink around the pool or relax to the sound of the waves in the crisp white dining room. The menu features mainly European dishes but retains an eclectic flourish with a few Asian options. The seared tuna steak served on Dutch potato-salad appetizer may sound odd, but it's heaven on a plate and is large enough to be a main course. ⊠ Pietermaait 152, Willemstad ☎ 5999/461–7713.

$$-$$$
SEAFOOD

✕ **Scampi's.** Part of the Waterfort dining complex, this family-friendly eatery offers great basic food right next door to the decidedly more upscale eateries that share its waterfront location. The food is simple but well made, and better yet, very affordable. There is a good selection of fresh seafood and steaks at surprisingly reasonable prices, and kids can choose from their own menu. ⊠ Waterfortstraat 41–42, Punda ☎ 5999/465–0769.

$$$-$$$$
CONTINENTAL
★

✕ **Sculpture Garden.** Named after the sculpture garden at the Kura Hulanda Hotel in which it's located, this is one of the most romantic choices on the island. Among the stellar dishes is the Chilean sea bass served with a lemongrass and ginger sauce. Dining alfresco beneath ficus trees creates a memorable experience. Depending on how busy it is, the service can range from attentive to downright slow. The extensive wine list is noteworthy. ⊠ Kura Hulanda, Langestraat 8, Otrobanda, Willemstad ☎ 5999/434–7700 ⚌ Reservations essential ⊘ Closed Sun. and Mon. No lunch.

$$$
AMERICAN

✕ **Shor.** Despite its setting in the swanky Hyatt Regency, this airy seafood grill overlooking the ocean is surprisingly relaxed. Appetizers range from a simple but exquisite gravlax salmon salad to a huge serving of bubbling crab dip served with bread that can easily feed two. The main grill courses require a bit of pleasing deliberation as both meat and seafood offerings are fully customizable, with choices of seasoning, sauce, and side. Although the restaurant is quite a drive if you're not staying at the Hyatt, the ambience and excellent food are worth it. ⊠ Hyatt Regency Curaçao, Santa Barbara Plantation, Nieuwpoort ☎ 5999/840–1234 ⊕ www.curacao.hyatt.com.

$$$
INDONESIAN

✕ **Tempo Doeloe.** The hillside location, Balinese decor, and authentic Indonesian cuisine draw both visitors and locals to this sprawling establishment.

Although dishes may be ordered individually, the excess of either the full rijstaffel or more manageable—though without seafood—small rijstaffel is an experience not easily forgotten. Call ahead to request a table with a view. ⊠ *La Vista Resort, Piscaderaweg, Willemstad* ☎ *5999/461–2881* ⊕ *www.tempodoeloe.an* ⚞ *Reservations essential.*

WHERE TO STAY

You'll generally find that hotels at all price levels provide friendly, prompt, detail-oriented service; however, the finer points of service are in some cases still in nascent stages. Many of the large-scale resorts east and west of Willemstad proper have lovely beaches and provide a free shuttle to the city, 5 to 10 minutes away, but you'll find utmost seclusion at hotels on the island's southwestern end, a 30- to 45-minute drive from town. Most hotels in town provide beach shuttles.

The following reviews have been condensed for this book. Please go to Fodors.com for full reviews of each property.

$$–$$$
RESORT
Fodor's Choice
★

Avila Hotel. The right blend of old-world touches, modern amenities, alluring beachfront, and attentive staff makes this resort the place of choice for the visiting Dutch royalty (well, all guests actually). **Pros:** wide variety of room types and decor; old world charm; excellent restaurants; choice of upscale shops on-site. **Cons:** bit of a walk to the city; because it caters to a largely European clientele most rooms only have 220 outlets. ⊠ *Penstraat 130, Willemstad* ☎ *5999/461–4377 or 800/747–8162* ⊕ *www.avilahotel.com* ⇱ *154 rooms, 11 suites* ⚞ *In-room: safe, kitchen (some), Internet (some). In-hotel: restaurants, tennis court, bars, pool, spa, beach, business center* ¶◎¶ *No meals.*

$$$–$$$$
RESORT
Fodor's Choice
★

Baoase. No other resort on Curaçao can match this Balinese-inspired gem for understated elegance and attention to detail. **Pros:** beautiful landscaping; complete privacy and quiet. **Cons:** lacks some of the distractions of a larger resort; bit far from downtown shopping. ⊠ *Winterswijkstraat 2, Willemstad* ☎ *5999/461–1799* ⊕ *www.baoase.com* ⇱ *5 3-bedroom villas, 2 2-bedroom villas, 1 4-bedroom villa, 1 3-bedroom master villa (includes maid and butler), 3 1-bedroom suites* ⚞ *In-room: a/c, safe, kitchen (in villas), Wi-Fi (some). In-hotel: restaurant, room service, bar, pools, gym, beach, water sports, business center, parking* ¶◎¶ *No meals*

$–$$
RENTAL

Blue Bay Village. This property is a 10-minute drive from Willemstad but offers a quiet setting, beautiful villas, thoughtfully decorated rooms, and the perfect location for golf lovers. **Pros:** spacious units are ideal for families; ideal location for golfers; far from the madding crowd; on-site restaurant is quite good for basic family meals. **Cons:** a bit isolated so a car is absolutely necessary; no nightlife in the area. ⊠ *Landhuis Blauw z/n, Willemstad* ☎ *5999/888–8800* ⇱ *48 apartments, 36 3-bedroom villas* ⚞ *In-room: safe, kitchen, Wi-Fi. In-hotel: golf course, restaurant, bar, pool* ¶◎¶ *No meals.*

$$–$$$
RESORT
☙

Breezes Curaçao Resort, Spa & Casino. You might enjoy the conviviality at the island's only all-inclusive, but unless you venture off the lushly landscaped grounds, you won't get much taste of the real Curaçao; on the other hand, you won't have much reason to leave. **Pros:** ample distractions for the whole family; beautiful landscaping; great price

9

for families. **Cons:** some rooms are in need of refurbishing; free drinks mean the pool area is always crowded. ⊠ *Martin Luther King Blvd. 78, Willemstad* ☎ *5999/736–7888 or 800/467–8737* ⊕ *www.breezes.com* ➷ *285 rooms, 54 suites* ⚿ *In-room: safe. In-hotel: restaurants, tennis courts, bars, children's programs, pools, gym, spa, beach, business center, water sports* ♺ *3-night minimum* |◯| *All-inclusive.*

$–$$$
RESORT
🆑
Fodor's Choice
★

⛏ **Curaçao Marriott Beach Resort & Emerald Casino.** The cream of the crop of Curaçao's resorts beckons you to live it up from the moment you arrive. **Pros:** no need to leave the compound for anything but sightseeing; excellent beach location; first-class fitness center; five-star PADI dive shop. **Cons:** feels big and impersonal; pool area can get very busy. ⊡ *Box 6003, Piscadera Bay, Willemstad* ☎ *5999/736–8800* ⊕ *www. curacaomarriott.com* ➷ *237 rooms, 10 suites* ⚿ *In-room: safe, Internet, Wi-Fi. In-hotel: restaurants, room service, bars, children's programs, pool, gym, spa, beach, business center, water sports* |◯| *No meals.*

$
HOTEL

⛏ **Floris Suite Hotel.** Dutch interior designer Jan des Bouvrie has used warm mahogany shades offset by cool, sleek stainless-steel adornments in the suites of this modernist hotel, all of which have a balcony or porch and a full kitchen. **ros:** great for a quiet escape; beautifully designed rooms and public spaces. **Cons:** rather cold feel to the decor; bit of a hike to decent shopping and restaurants. ⊠ *J.F. Kennedy Blvd., Box 6246, Piscadera Bay* ☎ *5999/462–6111* ⊕ *www.florissuitehotel.com* ➷ *72 suites* ⚿ *In-room: kitchen, Internet, Wi-Fi. In-hotel: restaurant, room service, tennis court, bar, pool, gym, business center* |◯| *No meals.*

$
RESORT

⛏ **Habitat Curaçao.** R & R and R—rest, relaxation, and round-the-clock shore diving—are what you can look forward to at this resort, which is near a wildlife preserve in a secluded area blanketed by foliage. **Pros:** excellent diving facilities; full-service spa. **Cons:** far from downtown; a car is essential; restaurant is best avoided; mosquitoes can be a problem even in the rooms. ⊠ *Coral Estates, Rif St. Marie* ☎ *5999/864–8800 or 800/327–6709* ⊕ *www.habitatcuracaoresort.com* ➷ *56 suites, 19 2-bedroom villas* ⚿ *In-room: safe, kitchen (some), Wi-Fi (some). In-hotel: restaurant, bar, pool, spa, beach, business center* |◯| *No meals.*

$
RESORT
🆑
★

⛏ **Hilton Curaçao.** Two beautiful beaches of pillowy white sand beyond the open-air lobby make this resort a jewel in its price range. **Pros:** gorgeous beachfront; close to great shopping and off-site restaurants; friendly staff. **Cons:** hallways are a bit bland; rooms could be in a Hilton anywhere on the planet. ⊠ *J.F. Kennedy Blvd., Box 2133, Piscadera Bay* ☎ *5999/462–5000* ⊕ *www.hiltoncaribbean.com/curacao* ➷ *196 rooms, 12 suites* ⚿ *In-room: safe, Internet, Wi-Fi. In-hotel: restaurants, room service, tennis courts, bars, children's programs, pools, gym, spa, beach, business center, water sports* |◯| *No meals.*

$–$$
HOTEL
Fodor's Choice
★

⛏ **Hotel Kura Hulanda Spa & Casino.** Guest rooms here are tucked in restored 18th-century houses built along pebble-stone alleyways that diverge from a central courtyard. **Pros:** unique historic feel; top-notch restaurants; incredible museum on compound; downtown shopping just steps away; free Internet access in rooms. **Cons:** no beach nearby; getting around the compound can be like negotiating a maze. ⊠ *Langestraat 8, Otrobanda, Willemstad* ☎ *5999/434–7700* ⊕ *www.kurahulanda.com* ➷ *82 rooms,*

12 suites & In-room: safe, Internet, Wi-Fi (some). In-hotel: restaurants, room service, bars, pools, gym, spa, business center, parking ¦○¦ No meals.

¢   ⊞ **Howard Johnson Plaza Hotel & Casino.** Everything the city has to offer is at
HOTEL   your doorstep at this colorful hotel on the main square of Otrobanda, an especially coveted location during the holidays and Carnival. **Pros:** in the heart of downtown with easy access to Punda; excellent price for a downtown location; some rooms have great views of Punda and Queen Emma Bridge. **Cons:** no beach; downtown noise can sometimes be a problem. ⊠ *Brionplein, Otrobanda, Willemstad* ☎ *5999/462–7800* ⊕ *www.hojo-curacao.com* ⇌ *70 rooms & In-room: safe, Internet. In-hotel: restaurant, room service, bar, pool, business center, parking ¦○¦ No meals.*

$$$ ⊞ **Hyatt Regency Curaçao.** Miles away from any other property, Cura-
RESORT   çao's new luxury resort is ideal for a self-contained getaway. **Pros:**
☺   Camp Arawak kids program that runs from 9 am to 9 pm is a boon for parents; gorgeous location miles away from the hustle and bustle of downtown; elegant public areas; impeccable service throughout the property. **Cons:** long drive or expensive taxi ride away from everything; feels a bit sterile even by large resort standards. ⊠ *Santa Barbara Plantation, Nieuwpoort* ☎ *5999/840–1234* ⊕ *www.curacao.hyatt.com* ⇌ *335 rooms, 15 suites & In-room: a/c, safe, Internet, Wi-Fi. In-hotel: restaurants, room service, bars, golf course, tennis courts, pools, gym, spa, beach, water sports, children's programs, business center, parking.*

¢   ⊞ **Lagun Blou Dive & Beach Resort.** Travelers on a budget will love this
HOTEL   family-owned and -run hotel that combines a great view with an inti-
☺   mate setting. **Pros:** relaxed atmosphere; family run; intimate setting; bargain for families. **Cons:** far from shopping and restaurants; lacks the amenities of a big resort. ⊠ *Seaquarium Beach, Bapor Kibra z/n* ☎ *5999/864–0557* ⊕ *www.lagunblou.nl* ⇌ *13 rooms, 8 bungalows & In-room: safe, kitchen, no TV, Wi-Fi. In-hotel: pool, laundry facilities, beach ¦○¦ No meals.*

$ ⊞ **Lions Dive & Beach Resort**. Divers are lured by the first-rate program
RESORT   here, but this low-key resort has a lot to offer nondivers as well. **Pros:**
☺   ideal for diving; beautiful private beach and access to Seaquarium Beach; family-friendly, Olympic length pool. **Cons:** beach can get busy; kids everywhere. ⊠ *Seaquarium Beach, Bapor Kibra z/n* ☎ *5999/434–8888* ⊕ *www.lionsdive.com* ⇌ *102 rooms, 10 suites, 1 penthouse & In-room: safe, Internet, Wi-Fi. In-hotel: restaurants, bar, pools, spa, beach, business center, water sports ¦○¦ No meals.*

$$$ ⊞ **Lodge Kura Hulanda & Beach Club**. On the island's remote western
RESORT   tip, this sprawling resort with tranquil gardens will make you feel far
Fodor'sChoice   removed from the daily grind. Rooms in two-story villas offer plush
★   comforts, including grand porches (many overlooking the ocean), large televisions, and luxurious bathrooms. **Pros:** perfect for a complete escape; unparalleled ocean views; beautifully appointed rooms; free Wi-Fi. **Cons:** a bit quiet for some tastes; miles away from everything; although there's a shuttle, a rental car is necessary if you want to explore the island. ⊠ *Playa Kalki 1, Westpunt* ☎ *5999/839–3600* ⊕ *www.kurahulanda.com* ⇌ *42 rooms, 32 suites, 3 3-bedroom villas & In-room: safe, kitchen (some), Internet, Wi-Fi. In-hotel: restaurants, tennis court, bar, pool, gym, beach, water sports ¦○¦ No meals.*

9

$-$$ ⊡ **Renaissance Curaçao Resort & Casino.** The four gabled buildings of this
RESORT   new downtown resort are painted in colors that seem to mirror those of
Fodor'sChoice   Punda across the harbor and fit in perfectly with the historic surround-
★   ings. **Pros:** coolest beach in town; every amenity imaginable; walking
distance to all the attractions of both Otrobanda and Punda; exceptionally helpful staff. **Cons:** Rif Fort area is a major tourist draw and can
get busy; room and common-area color scheme is not exactly calming.
⊠ *The Rif Fort, Box 2178, Otrobanda, Willemstad* ☎ *5999/435–5000*
⊕ *www.renaissancecuracao.com* ⊅ *223 rooms, 14 suites* ⌂ *In-room:
safe, Internet, Wi-Fi. In-hotel: restaurants, room service, tennis courts,
bars, pools, gym, beach, business center, water sports* �ABGHNo meals.

VILLAS

⟳   Villa and bungalow rentals are especially popular with divers and European visitors and are generally good options for large groups or longer
stays. The Curaçao Tourist Board (⊕ *www.curacao.com*) has a complete
list of rental apartments, villas, and bungalows on its Web site. The
128 villas at **Livingstone Jan Thiel Resort** (⊠ *Jan Thiel* ☎ *5999/747–0332*
⊕ *www.janthielresort.com*) surround a swimming pool in a low-rise
complex that offers a minimarket on-site, free access to the beach across
the street, Wi-Fi in the open-air lobby, and a playground and special
programs for kids. Festive decor includes a large painted mural at the
entrance and beaded shades on tabletop candleholders at the poolside
restaurant. Reasonable rates even in high season make this an appealing
choice for those looking for self-catering facilities.

⟳   The bungalows at **Papagayo Beach Resort** (⊠ *Jan Thiel* ☎ *5999/747–4333*
⊕ *www.papagayo-beach.com*) give you a unique option: on a whim
you can open up a full wall so that your wraparound wooden terrace
becomes part of your living space. Suddenly you're as close as it gets to
living outdoors. These well-designed and nicely furnished homes include
two bedrooms, a full kitchen with dishwasher, and bathroom (showers
only). The restaurant menu changes seasonally; the pool bar is a cozy
place to meet your neighbors. There's no beachfront, but you get free
access to the beach across the street. Special programs and entertainment for kids are offered during school vacation periods.

NIGHTLIFE

Friday is a big night out, with rollicking happy hours and live music at
many bars and hotels. And although it might sound surprising, Sunday-
night revelry into the wee hours is an island tradition. Pick up a copy
of the weekly free entertainment listings, *K-Pasa*, available at most
restaurants and hotels. The Web site **Kikotakiko** (⊕ *www.kikotakiko.
com*) lists all the current happenings around the island.

Fodor'sChoice   Outrageous costumes, blowout parades, pulsating Tumba rhythms,
★   miniprocessions known as jump-ups, and frenetic energy characterize **Carnival.** The season lasts longer here than on many other islands:
the revelries begin at New Year's and continue until midnight the day
before Ash Wednesday. One highlight is the Tumba Festival (dates vary),
a four-day musical event featuring fierce competition between local

musicians for the honor of having their piece selected as the official road march during parades. For the Grand Parade, space is rented along the route and people mark their territory by building wooden stands, some lavishly decorated and furnished.

BARS

Wednesday-night jam sessions are hot at **De Gouverneur** (⊠ *De Rouvilleweg 9, Otrobanda, Willemstad* ☎ *5999/462–5999*). **Fort Waakzaamheid Tavern** (⊠ *Seru Domi z/n, Otrobanda* ☎ *5999/462–3633*)—the name means "Fort Alertness"—is a pleasant place for a cocktail day or night, complete with a panoramic view of the island. **Grand Café de Heeren** (⊠ *Zuikertuintjeweg, Bloempot* ☎ *5999/736–0491*) is a great spot to grab a locally brewed Amstel Bright and meet a happy blend of tourists and transplanted Dutch locals. By day **Hook's Hut** (⊠ *Next to Hilton Curaçao, Piscadera Bay* ☎ *5999/462–6575*) is a beach hangout for locals and tourists stationed at the nearby hotels. The daily happy hour from 5 to 6 kicks off a lively nighttime scene. The outdoor pool table is in terrible shape, but it's one of the few bar tables around.

With giant green leaves and thatched roofs giving each table ultimate seclusion, **Kontiki Beach Club** (⊠ *Seaquarium Beach, Bapor Kibra z/n* ☎ *5999/465–1589*) is a great spot to tuck away and have a drink with your companion if you want to feel alone yet part of the action.

Moon (⊠ *Pietermaai 152, Willemstad* ☎ *5999/461–7713*) attracts a hip, young crowd most evenings enjoying the sounds of the ocean over martinis or fruity cocktails. Those seeking a more intimate experience grab one of the many cabanas around the infinity pool.

The seaside outdoor deck at the **Waterfort Arches** (⊠ *Waterfortstraat Boog 1, Punda, Willemstad* ☎ *5999/465–0769*) comprises a connecting strip of several bars and restaurants that have live entertainment on various nights of the week. There's never a dull moment at **Wet & Wild Beach Club** (⊠ *Seaquarium Beach, Bapor Kibra z/n* ☎ *5999/561–2477*), where the name speaks for itself every weekend. Friday happy hour features free barbecue; on Saturday a DJ or live band jams until it's too late to care about the time. On Sunday things get charged, starting with happy hour at 6; the fiesta goes on past midnight.

CASINOS

The following hotels have casinos that are open daily: Breezes Curaçao, the Curaçao Marriott Beach Resort & Emerald Casino, the Hilton Curaçao, the Hotel Kura Hulanda Spa & Casino, the Holiday Beach Hotel & Casino, Howard Johnson Plaza Hotel & Casino, and the Otrobanda Hotel & Casino. Even the biggest of these rooms offer only a few card games, and some are limited to slot machines. As for ambience, only the casino at the Marriott—which features pleasant live entertainment some nights—even approaches the class of a Bond-like establishment. A few Texas Hold 'Em tables are available here, but games start up only when enough players express interest. The Veneto Casino at the Holiday Beach Resort is the largest on the island, and

9

the only one with sports betting—you can watch the live action on TV. Unfortunately, the casino is dreary. Around the island, slot machines open earlier than table games, between 10 am and 1 pm. Most of the rooms have penny and nickel slots in addition to the higher-priced machines. Tables generally open at 3 pm or 4 pm. Casinos close about 1 am or 2 am weekdays; some stay open until 4 am on weekend nights.

DANCE AND MUSIC CLUBS

★ Live jazz electrifies the pier at **Blues** (⊠ *Avila Hotel, Penstraat 130, Punda, Willemstad* ☎ *5999/461–4377*) on Thursday—*the* night to go—and Saturday. The dance floor at the **Emerald Lounge** (⊠ *Curaçao Marriott Beach Resort, Piscadera Bay* ☎ *5999/736–8800*) comes alive on weekends, and is especially steamy on Friday salsa nights. **Mambo Beach** (⊠ *Seaquarium Beach, Bapor Kibra z/n* ☎ *5999/461–8999*), an open-air bar and restaurant, draws a hip, young crowd that dances the night away under the stars. On Sunday, come in time for happy hour and warm up for the nightlong party with some beach volleyball.

SHOPPING

From Dutch classics like embroidered linens, delft earthenware, cheeses, and clogs to local artwork and handicrafts, shopping in Curaçao can turn up some fun finds. But don't expect major bargains on watches, jewelry, or electronics; Willemstad is not a duty-free port (the few establishments that claim to be "duty-free" are simply absorbing the cost of some or all of the tax rather than passing it on to consumers); however, if you come prepared with some comparison prices, you might still dig up some good deals.

SHOPPING AREAS

Willemstad's **Punda** is a treat for pedestrians, with most shops concentrated within a bustling area of about six blocks, giving you plenty of opportunity for people-watching to boot. Closed to traffic, Heerenstraat and Gomezplein are pedestrian malls covered with pink inlaid bricks. Other major shopping streets are Breedestraat and Madurostraat. Here you can find jewelry, cosmetics, perfumes, luggage, and linens—and no shortage of trinkets and souvenirs. Savvy shoppers don't skip town without a stop across the bay to **Otrobanda**, where the Riffort Village Shopping Mall houses a variety of retailers. It's worth noting that many of the bargain-price designer labels found in smaller clothing shops are just knockoffs from Latin America. The Renaissance Mall right next to Riffort has retailers such as Guess and Tiffany & Co. next to local shops offering a range of jewelry and fashion.

There are also some retail shops in the Kura Hulanda complex.

SPECIALTY STORES

ART GALLERIES

Gallery Alma Blou (⊠ *Frater Radulphusweg 4, Welgelegen* ☎ *5999/462–8896*) presents works by top local artists; you can find shimmering landscapes, dazzling photographs, ceramics, even African-inspired Carnival masks. **Gallery Eighty-Six** (⊠ *Scharlooweg 76, Punda, Willemstad* ☎ *5999/461–3417*) represents the work of local and Caribbean artists. The **Hortence Brouwn Gallery** (⊠ *Kaya Tapa Konchi 12, Brievengat* ☎ *5999/737–2193*) sells sculpted human forms (sometimes abstract) in bronze, concrete, marble, and limestone. At the **Nena Sanchez Gallery** (⊠ *Bloempot Shopping Mall, Schottegatweg Oost 17, Bloempot* ☎ *5999/738–2377*), you can find this local artist's cheerful paintings in characteristically bright yellows, reds, greens, pinks, and blues. Her work depicting marine life and island scenes is available in various forms, including posters, mouse pads, and picture frames.

CIGARS

A sweet aroma permeates **Cigar Emporium** (⊠ *Gomezplein, Punda, Willemstad* ☎ *5999/465–3955*), where you can find the largest selection of Cuban cigars on the island, including H. Upmann, Romeo y Julieta, and Montecristo. Visit the climate-controlled cedar cigar room. However, remember that Cuban cigars cannot be taken back to the United States legally.

CLOTHING

Bamali (⊠ *Breedestraat, Punda, Willemstad* ☎ *5999/461–2258*) sells funky, fabulous women's apparel, including Indonesian batik clothing; charming jewelry made of beads, shells, gemstones, and silver; handbags of leather and other fabrics; and lots of other unique accessories. Custom-made clothing is available here, too. Get suited up for the beach at the **Bikini Shop** (⊠ *Seaquarium Beach, Bapor Kibra z/n* ☎ *5999/461–7343*), where you can find women's bathing suits (Vix, Becca, La Goufe) and accessories like cover-ups, flip-flops, and sunglasses. You can find a large selection of Calvin Klein apparel at **Casa Janina** (⊠ *Madurostraat 13, Punda, Willemstad* ☎ *5999/461–1371*), which also carries Levi's jeans. **Mayura** (⊠ *Breedestraat 8, Punda, Willemstad* ☎ *5999/461–7277*) has T-shirts galore, plus souvenirs like Curaçao-theme towels and key chains. **Tommy Hilfiger** (⊠ *Breedestraat 20–21, Punda, Willemstad* ☎ *5999/465–9963*) carries the full designer line for men, women, and children. You can find a large selection of smart men's and women's wear at **Wulfsen & Wulfsen** (⊠ *Wilhelminaplein 1, Punda, Willemstad* ☎ *5999/461–2302*), from European and American designers like Gant, Kenneth Cole, and Passport.

FOOD

Centrum Supermarket (⊠ *Weg Naar Bullenbaai z/n, Piscadera* ☎ *5999/869–6222*) is one of the better markets in terms of variety and quality. A bakery is on the premises, too. **Plaza's Gourmet & Fresh Mart** (⊠ *Zuikertuintjeweg, Santa Rosa* ☎ *5999/737–0188*), in the upscale Zuikertuin Mall, is a relatively small market selling a variety of gourmet items in addition to the basics.

9

GIFTS

Boolchand's (⊠ *Heerenstraat 4B, Punda, Willemstad* ☎ *5999/461–6233*) sells electronics, jewelry, Swarovski crystal, Swiss watches, and cameras behind a facade of red-and-white checkered tiles. **Julius L. Penha & Sons** (⊠ *Heerenstraat 1, Punda, Willemstad* ☎ *5999/461–2266*), near the Pontoon Bridge, sells French perfumes and cosmetics, clothing, and accessories in a baroque-style building dating from 1708. At **Little Switzerland** (⊠ *Breedestraat 44, Punda, Willemstad* ☎ *5999/461–2111*) you can find jewelry, watches, crystal, china, and leather goods at significant savings.

HANDICRAFTS

Caribbean Handcraft Inc. (⊠ *Kaya Kakina 8, Jan Thiel* ☎ *5999/767–1171*) offers an elaborate assortment of locally handcrafted souvenirs. It's worth visiting just for the spectacular hilltop view. **Landhuis Groot Santa Martha** (⊠ *Santa Martha Bay* ☎ *5999/864–1323 or 5999/864–2969*) is where artisans with disabilities make ceramic vases, dolls, leather goods, and other products. There's a $3 entrance fee, and it's closed weekends.

JEWELRY

Clarisa (⊠ *Gomezplein 10, Punda, Willemstad* ☎ *5999/461–2006*) specializes in cultured pearls and also carries European gold jewelry and watches. **Different Design** (⊠ *Gomezplein 7, Punda, Willemstad* ☎ *5999/465–2944*) offers gorgeous custom-made pendants and rings of precious gems and gold. **Freeport** (⊠ *Heerenstraat 13, Punda, Willemstad* ☎ *5999/461–9500*) has a fine selection of watches and jewelry (lines include Movado, David Yurman, and Maurice Lacroix). **Gandelman** (⊠ *Breedestraat 35, Punda, Willemstad* ☎ *5999/461–1854*) has watches by Cartier and Rolex, leather goods by Prima Classe, and Baccarat and Daum crystal. **Pieters Jewelers** (⊠ *Gomezplein, Punda, Willemstad* ☎ *5999/465–4774*) carries watches, including Seiko, Tissot, and Swatch, as well as gold jewelry, gemstones, and glassware.

LINENS

New Amsterdam (⊠ *Gomezplein 14, Punda, Willemstad* ☎ *5999/461–2437* ⊠ *Breedestraat 29, Punda, Willemstad* ☎ *5999/461–3239*) is the place to price hand-embroidered tablecloths, napkins, and pillowcases, as well as blue delft.

PERFUMES AND COSMETICS

The **Yellow House** (⊠ *Breedestraat 23, Punda, Willemstad* ☎ *5999/461–3222*) offers a vast selection of perfumes at low prices.

SPORTS AND ACTIVITIES

☾ For the full gamut of activities in one spot, nature buffs (especially birdwatchers), families, and adventure seekers may want to visit **Caracas Bay Peninsula** (☎ *5999/747–0777*). Things to do here include hiking, mountain biking, canoeing, kayaking, windsurfing, jet skiing, and snorkeling. There's a fully equipped dive shop, a restaurant, and a bar on premises. Admission to the scenic area is $5; activities cost extra.

ATVS AND SCOOTERS

Hit the road in rugged style behind the wheel of an all-terrain vehicle with **Eric's ATV Adventures** (⊠ *Kaya Serafin 63, Willemstad* ☎ *5999/524–7418*). All you need for a guided tour of the countryside is a regular driver's license. If you're 10 or older, you can ride as a passenger in the backseat. Helmets and goggles are provided.

Strap on a helmet for an adventurous, guided excursion around the island's most popular sites with **Curaçao Buggy Adventures** (⊠ *Breezes Cura-çao, Martin Luther King Blvd. 8, Willemstad* ☎ *5999/523–8618* ⊕ *www. curacaobuggyadventures.com*). Visit caves and forts, stop for a swim or snorkel; you can even design your own tour if you're a group of four or more people. Three-hour beach buggy trips are $140 per couple, and the fee includes safety equipment, insurance, gas, a guide, and pickup at your hotel. There is also a five-hour buggy tour for $275 per couple, which includes lunch. Experience isn't required, but cyclists will have an easier time maneuvering a scooter. You'll get some instruction and the chance to race around a practice course before you go. Children under 16 may ride as passengers. Wear sneakers, sunglasses, and sunscreen; bring a swimsuit, insect repellent, and a camera—and you're off!

BIKING

So you wanna bike Curaçao? **Wanna Bike Curaçao** (☎ *5999/527–3720* ⊕ *www.wannabike.com*) has the fix: kick into gear and head out for a guided mountain-bike tour through the Caracas Bay peninsula and the salt ponds at the Jan Thiel Lagoon. Although you should be fit to take on the challenge, mountain-bike experience is not required. Tour prices vary, depending on skill level and duration, and cover the bike, helmet, water, refreshments, park entrance fee, and guide—but don't forget to bring a camera.

DIVING AND SNORKELING

The **Curaçao Underwater Marine Park** includes almost a third of the island's southern diving waters. Scuba divers and snorkelers can enjoy more than 12½ mi (20 km) of protected reefs and shores, with normal visibility from 60 to 150 feet. With water temperatures ranging from 75°F to 82°F (24°C to 28°C), wet suits are generally unnecessary. No coral collecting, spearfishing, or littering is allowed. An exciting wreck to explore is the SS *Oranje Nassau,* which ran aground in 1906. The other two main diving areas are Banda Abou, along the southwest coast between Westpunt and St. Marie, and along central Curaçao, which stretches between Bullen Bay to the Breezes Curaçao resort. The north coast—where conditions are dangerously rough—is not recommended for diving.

Introductory scuba resort courses run about $75 for one dive and $140 for two dives. Open-water certification courses run about $425 for the five-dive version. Virtually every operator charges $40 to $55 for a single-tank dive and $70 to $85 for a two-tank dive. One day of unlimited shore diving runs about $22 to $25. Snorkel gear commonly rents for $10 to $16 per day.

Diveversity at Habitat (✉ *Habitat Curaçao, Coral Estates, Rif St. Marie* ☏ *5999/864–8304* ⊕ *www.habitatcuracaoresort.com*) offers everything from introductory dives to advanced open-water courses. You are free to dive any time of the night or day, because the abundance of marine life at the house reef makes for easily accessible shore dives right from the resort. In addition, two-tank boat dives are scheduled twice daily.

Ⓒ **Ocean Encounters** (✉ *Lions Dive & Beach Resort, Seaquarium Beach,*
★ *Bapor Kibra z/n* ☏ *5999/461–8131* ⊕ *www.oceanencounters.com*) is the largest dive operator on the island. Its operations cover the popular east-coast dive sites, including the *Superior Producer* wreck, where barracudas hang out, and a tugboat wreck. West-end hot spots—including the renowned Mushroom Forest and Watamula dive sites—are accessible from the company's outlet at Westpunt. Ocean Encounters offers a vast menu of scheduled shore and boat dives and packages, as well as certified PADI instruction. In July, the dive center sponsors a kids' sea camp in conjunction with the Sea Aquarium.

FISHING

Let's Fish (✉ *Caracasbaaiweg 407N, Caracas Bay* ☏ *5999/561–1812 or 5999/747–4489* ⊕ *www.letsfish.net*), a 50-foot, fully rigged fishing boat, can accommodate groups of up to 11 people on half-day or full-day fishing trips to Klein Curaçao or Banda Abou in search of dolphinfish, marlin, wahoo, and more. With seven fishing vessels among the 14 yachts (and their captains) under his purview, Captain J.R. Van Hutten, nicknamed Captain Jaro, of **Pro Marine Yacht Services** (✉ *Warawaraweg 7, Van Engelen* ☏ *5999/560–2081* ⊕ *www.curacaoboating.com*), is *the* man to see about deep-sea fishing excursions and other fishing trips or parties. Some deals offer free pickup at your hotel. Most boats keep your catch, so check in advance if you want it. You can book the 54-foot yacht *War Eagle,* captained by Jaro himself, and head out in search of marlin, barracuda, mahimahi, and wahoo.

GOLF

In the mood to hit the greens? Try the links at **Blue Bay Curaçao Golf & Beach Resort** (✉ *Landhuis Blauw, Blue Bay z/n* ☏ *5999/868–1755* ⊕ *www.bluebaygolf.com*). This 18-hole, par-72 course beckons experts and novices alike. Facilities include a golf shop, locker rooms, and a snack bar. Greens fees range from $90 to $140 in high season, and you can rent carts, clubs, and shoes. If you'd like to drive your game to a new level, take a lesson from the house pro ($45 for a half hour).

The **Old Quarry Golf Course** (✉ *Santa Barbara Plantation, Porta Blancu, Nieuwpoort z/n* ☏ *5999/840–1234* ⊕ *www.santabarbaraplantation. com*) belies its name, as it's actually a lush, 18-hole, par-72 course designed by Pete Dye with some incredible vistas. There are a full range of facilities, and with the Hyatt Regency nearby, drinks and fine dining are mere steps away. Greens fees range from $60 to $150 in high season, and you can rent carts, clubs, and shoes.

GUIDED TOURS

Most tour operators have pickups at the major hotels, but if your hotel is outside the standard zone, there may be an additional charge of around $5. Tours are available in several languages, including English.

The so-called Trolley Train visits historic sites in Willemstad on a 1½-hour guided tour, one of the most popular run by **Atlantis Adventures** (⊠ *Hilton Curaçao, J.F. Kennedy Blvd., Box 2133, Piscadera Bay* ☎ *5999/461–0011* ⊕ *www.atlantisadventures.com*). This tour begins at Ft. Amsterdam, and there's no hotel pickup.

Dutch Dream Adventures (☎ *5999/461–9393* ⊕ *www.dutchdreamcuracao. com*) targets the action seeker with guided canoe and kayak safaris, mountain-bike excursions through Christoffel National Park for groups of 10 or more, or custom-designed tours to suit your group's interests. Although it's aimed primarily at incentive and convention travelers, **Explore Curaçao** (⊠ *Cas Coraweg 84, Willemstad* ☎ *5999/747–7714* ⊕ *www.explore-international.com*) can arrange any activities on the island, from airport transfers to island adventure tours. **Peter Trips** (☎ *5999/561–5368 or 5999/465–2703* ⊕ *www.petertrips.com*) offers full-day island tours departing from the hotels Tuesday, Wednesday, Friday, and Sunday at 9 am, with visits to many points of interest, including Ft. Amsterdam, Spanish Water, Scharloo, and Ft. Nassau. The cost is $50, and lunch is included. East-side half-day tours and a beach trip are offered Monday for $25 and $45, respectively. Among the favorites at **Taber Tours** (⊠ *Kaya Schilling 170, Willemstad* ☎ *5999/868–7012* ⊕ *www.tabertours.com*) is the Christoffel National Park–Cas Abou Beach combo: start the day with a guided hike up Mt. Christoffel followed by a tour of the park, and wind up at the beach to relax or snorkel. **Yellow Tourism Solutions** (⊠ *Curaçao Marriott Beach Resort, Piscadera Bay* ☎ *5999/462–6262* ⊕ *www.tourism-curacao.com*) offers a full range of half- and full-day tours, whether you want to check out town, beaches, or historical sites, or head out with a group for horseback riding, diving, or snorkeling. The company's Yellow Jeep Safari takes you to Christoffel National Park aboard a bright yellow Land Rover, driven by a guide who will take you off the beaten (and paved) path, deep into the park's natural terrain.

WALKING TOURS

When making reservations for any tour, mention that you speak English. Walking tours of historic Otrobanda, focusing on the unique architecture of this old section of town, are led by architect **Anko van der Woude** (☎ *5999/461–3554*) every Thursday (reservations are suggested), leaving from the central clock at Brionplein at 5:15 pm. The Talk of the Town tour with **Eveline van Arkel** (☎ *5999/747–4349 or 5999/562–1861*) will take you through historical Punda to visit sites including Ft. Amsterdam, the restored Ft. Church, the Queen Emma pontoon bridge, and the Mikvé Israel-Emanuel Synagogue (call for reservations; English tours are on Tuesday at 9:30 am). **Gigi** (☎ *5999/697–0290*) leads expert tours of Punda focusing on Jewish heritage, including an insider's look at the synagogue.

9

SEA EXCURSIONS

Many sailboats and motorboats offer sunset cruises and daylong snorkel and picnic trips to Klein Curaçao, the uninhabited island between Curaçao and Bonaire, and other destinations. Prices are around $75 to $90 for a half-day trip (including food and drinks). The half-day lunch and snorkel trip on the *Jonalisa* (☎ 5999/560–1887 ⊕ *www.bountyadventures.com*), a 54-foot catamaran, features sailing, snorkeling, and swimming. It includes an open bar and barbecue lunch. One option aboard the 120-foot Dutch sailing ketch *Insulinde* (☎ 5999/560–1340 ⊕ *www.insulinde.com*) is a snorkeling-and–scenic tour combo, capped off by a return cruise into the sunset, for $50. The *Mermaid* (☎ 5999/560–1530 ⊕ *www.mermaidboattrips.com*) is a 66-foot motor yacht that carries up to 60 people to Klein Curaçao three times a week. A buffet lunch, beer, and soft drinks are provided at the boat's exclusive beach house, which has picnic tables, shade huts, and facilities. The 76-foot *Miss Ann* (☎ 5999/767–1579 ⊕ *www.missannboattrips.com*) motorboat offers snorkeling or diving, moonlight, and party trips for up to 100 people. For a unique vantage point, soak up the local marine life on a 1½-hour-long tour of the coral reefs aboard the glass-bottom, semisubmersible *Seaworld Explorer* (☎ 5999/461–0011 ⊕ *www.atlantisadventures.com*).

WATER SPORTS

Caribbean Sea Sports (✉ *Curaçao Marriott Beach Resort, Piscadera Bay* ☎ 5999/462–2620 ⊕ *www.caribseasports.com*) runs a tight ship when it comes to all sorts of water sports, including kayaking, windsurfing, banana boats, tube rides, diving, and snorkeling. Captain "Goodlife" at **Let's Go Watersports** (✉ *Santa Cruz Beach 1, Santa Cruz* ☎ 5999/520–1147 or 5999/864–0438) will help you plan kayaking and other boat outings so you can live it up on the water and snorkel in some special spots. He also grills up a tasty lunch at the dock.

Dominica

WORD OF MOUTH

"The most exciting thing for me was going up in the mountains and taking a ride through the jungle. We booked this through the cruise ship. We then got off and walked along the jungle floor, to a huge steel bridge and back on to ride OVER THE TREE TOPS. It was completely exhilarating) . . ."

—ParrotMom

WELCOME TO DOMINICA

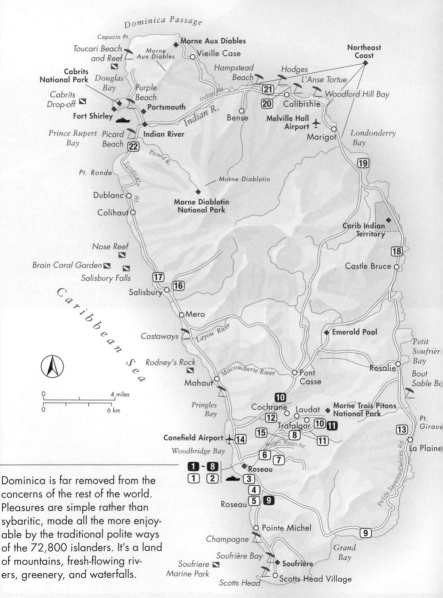

Dominica is far removed from the concerns of the rest of the world. Pleasures are simple rather than sybaritic, made all the more enjoyable by the traditional polite ways of the 72,800 islanders. It's a land of mountains, fresh-flowing rivers, greenery, and waterfalls.

THE NATURE ISLAND

The island is 29 mi (47 km) long and 16 mi (26 km) wide, with approximately 72,800 citizens. Because it was a British colony (achieving independence in 1978), you may wonder about the prevalence of French names. Although the English first claimed Dominica in 1627, the French controlled it from 1632 until 1759, when it passed back into English hands.

KEY

➤ *Beaches*
⚓ *Cruise Ship Terminal*
◪ *Dive Sites*
❶ *Restaurants*
① *Hotels*

DOMINICA

10

TOP REASONS TO VISIT DOMINICA

1 **Fewer Crowds:** Dominica is a delightful respite from the more crowded, commercial islands.

2 **Unspoiled Nature:** The island's natural environment is the major draw.

3 **Great Dives:** Diving pristine reefs full of colorful sea life or in bubbly, volcanic water is amazing.

4 **Natural Spas:** Dominica has an abundance of natural sulfur pools, some of which have become makeshift spas.

DOMINICA PLANNER

Fast Facts

Banks and Exchange Services: The official currency is the Eastern Caribbean dollar (EC$). The exchange rate hovers around EC$2.66 to the US$1. U.S. dollars and major credit cards are widely accepted. You can find ATMs in all the banks in Roseau and airports as well as some in larger villages such as Portsmouth. They dispense EC dollars only and accept international bank cards.

Electricity: 220–240 volts, AC/50 cycles. North American appliances require an adapter and transformer; however, many establishments provide these and often have dual-voltage fittings.

General Emergencies: Ambulance, police, and fire (☎ 999).

Passport Requirements: Valid passport plus a return or onward ticket.

Weddings: Two days' minimum residency. Valid passport, original birth certificate and divorce decree or death certificate for the former spouse (if applicable) is required. The parties must sign a statutory declaration on marital status, which must be obtained and sworn in Dominica in the presence of a local lawyer. At least two witnesses must be present at the ceremony.

Essentials

Mail: First-class letters to North America cost EC95¢; postcards are EC55¢. The general post office is opposite the ferry terminal in Roseau. Dominica is often confused with the Dominican Republic, so when addressing letters to the island, be sure to write The Commonwealth of Dominica, Eastern Caribbean. Dominica currently does not have a postal code.

Taxes and Service Charges: The departure-embarkation tax is EC$55 or about $21.50, payable in cash only at the airport at the time of departure from the island. Hotels collect a 15% government hotel occupancy tax and restaurants a 15% government V.A.T. (value-added tax).

Telephones: All pay phones are equipped for local and overseas dialing, accepting EC coins, credit cards, or phone cards, which you can buy at many island stores and at the airports. To call Dominica from the U.S. dial the area code (767) and the local access code (44), followed by the five-digit local number. On the island, dial only the seven-digit number that follows the area code.

Where to Stay

There are few upscale options in Dominica and absolutely no large resorts. Most accommodations are in small lodges and guesthouses.

Hotel and Restaurant Costs: Except for those not open for dinner, restaurant prices quoted are for a main course dinner and do not include any taxes or service charges. Hotel prices are per night for a double room in high season, excluding taxes, service charges, and meal plans (except at all-inclusives).

WHAT IT COSTS IN U.S. DOLLARS					
	¢	$	$$	$$$	$$$$
Restaurants	under $8	$8–$12	$12–$20	$20–$30	over $30
Hotels	under $150	$150–$275	$276–$375	$376–$475	over $475

Getting to and Around Dominica

Logistics: There are no nonstops from the U.S., so you'll have to transfer in Antigua, Barbados, Martinique, San Juan, or St. Lucia. There is also a ferry (90 minutes) from Guadeloupe or Martinique. **Canefield Airport** (✉ DCF ☎ 767/449–1199) is served by only a few small Caribbean-based airlines. **Melville Hall Airport** (✉ DOM ☎ 767/445–7100), where most flights arrive, is 75 minutes from Roseau.

Hassle Factor: High

Airline Information: American/American Eagle (☎ 767/446–0628 or 800/433–7300 ⊕ www.aa.com). **Conviasa** (☎ 767/448–2181 or 767/255–1148 ⊕ www.conviasa.aero). **LIAT** (☎ 767/440–2452, 767/445–7242 for baggage inquiries ⊕ www.liatairline. com). **Winair** (☎ 767/448–2181 or 767/255–1148 ⊕ www.fly-winair.com).

Boat and Ferry Travel: Express des Isles (☎ 767/448–2181 ⊕ www.express-des-iles.com) has regularly scheduled interisland jet catamaran ferry service connecting Dominica to Guadeloupe, Martinique, and St. Lucia. Generally, the ferry arrives and departs at the Roseau Ferry Terminal on Monday, Wednesday, Friday, Saturday, and Sunday from Guadeloupe; it continues south to Martinique, as well as St. Lucia, on specific days. The round-trip crossing costs €66.50 to Martinique, takes approximately 90 minutes, and offers superb views of the other islands.

Car Travel: Unless you are staying in Roseau or doing extensive guided tours, a car may be a necessity. Cabs can be very expensive. Daily car-rental rates begin at about $30 per day (weekly and long-term rates can be negotiated). A refundable $500 to $1,500 deposit or credit card confirmation is required at the time of pickup. You'll need to buy a visitor's driving permit for $12 (EC$30) at one of the airports or at the Traffic Division office on High Street in Roseau or at vehicle-rental offices. Gasoline stations are all over the island; at this writing, gas costs about $4.50 per gallon. Driving in Dominica is on the left side, though you can rent vehicles with a steering wheel on either the left or the right.

Best Deal Car Rental (✉ 15 Hanover St., Roseau ☎ 767/449–9204). **Budget Rent-A-Car** (✉ Canefield Industrial Site, Canefield ☎ 767/449–2080, 800/527–0700 in U.S. ⊕ www.budget.com). **Courtesy Car Rentals** (✉ 10 Winston La., Goodwill ☎ 767/448–7763 ⊕ www. avirtualdominica.com/courtesycarrental). **Island Car Rentals** (✉ Goodwill Rd., Goodwill ☎ 767/255–6844 ⊕ www. islandcar.dm).

Taxis

Taxis and minibuses are available at the airports and in Roseau as well as at most hotels and guesthouses. Rates are fixed by the government (from Melville Hall Airport to Roseau, the fare is $72), but if you share a taxi with other passengers going in the same direction, you can negotiate a special price (as little as $25.50 per person from Melville airport to Roseau). Taxi drivers also offer tours anywhere on the island beginning at $25 to $30 an hour for up to four people; a four- to five-hour island tour costs approximately $150. It's best to get a recommendation from your hotel. You can recognize a taxi or minibus by the H, HA, and HB plates; simply flag them down or make your way to the nearest bus stop. **Dominica Taxi Association** (☎ 767/449–8533) is a reputable company. **Nature Island Taxi Association** (☎ 767/440–1679) is a recommended company.

Visitor Information

Discover Dominica Authority (Dominica Tourist Office ⊕ www.discoverdominica.com ☎ 767/448–2045, 866/522–4057 in U.S.).

10

DOMINICA BEACHES

Most of Dominica's beaches are in the north and east; they are windswept, dramatic, and uncrowded, lending themselves more to relaxing than swimming. That is because many have undercurrents.

(Above) Pointe Baptiste. (Opposite page bottom) Champagne Beach. (Opposite page top) Hampstead Beach.

However, slightly farther north there are beautiful secluded beaches and coves. Although northeast-coast beaches offer excellent shallow swimming, their wind-tossed beauty can be dangerous; there are sometimes strong currents with the whipped-cream waves. From these beaches you can see the islands of Marie-Galante and Les Saintes and parts of Guadeloupe. On the southwest coast, beaches are fewer and mostly made of black sand and rounded volcanic rocks. Swimming off these rocky shores has its pleasures, too: the water is usually as flat as a lake, deep and blue, and especially good for snorkeling. In general, the west coast is more for scuba diving and snorkeling than for beachgoing.

VOLCANIC SAND

As a volcanic island, Dominica offers many powder-fine black-sand beaches. On the far north you'll find white- or brown-sand beaches with coves often speckled with volcanic sand. The beaches of the southwest coast are mostly black sand and volcanic rock.

☾**Champagne.** On the west coast, just south of the village of Pointe Michel, this stony beach is hailed as one of the best spots for swimming, snorkeling, and diving but not for sunning. It gets its name from volcanic vents that constantly puff steam into the sea, which makes you feel as if you are swimming in warm champagne. A boardwalk leads to the beach from Soufrière/Scotts Head Marine Reserve. ⊠ *1 mi (1½ km) south of Pointe Michel.*

☾**Hampstead Beach.** This isolated gold-with-speckled-black-sand shoreline on the northeast coast actually encompasses three bays. It is divided into two beaches. The Red River meets the sea at Hampstead Beach I. In *Pirates of the Caribbean: Dead Man's Chest,* Johnny Depp is chased by natives here. The palm tree–lined Hampstead Beach II is on the sheltered and calm Batibou Bay. Come here to relax, suntan, and swim. A 4x4 is the preferred mode of transportation to get here or be prepared hike in from the road. Both beaches ooze with charm and are worth the effort. There are no facilities, so it is BYOBC (bring your own beach chair). ⊠ *Off Indian Rd., west of Calibishie.*

L'Anse Tortue. On the northeast coast, this isolated, golden-sand beach with dabs of black is also known as Turtle Bay. It is a favorite for egg-laying turtles and for those who want seclusion

without having to drive all the way out to Hampstead Beach. It sits on a cove just past Woodford Hill, an easy, although sometimes steep, walk down from the road. There is no sign marking the trail or the beach, but it starts just across the road from a brown-building snack shop sporting Fanta signs. ⊠ *East of Calibishie.*

Mero Beach. The silver-gray stretch of beach on the west coast is just outside the village of Mero. It's the closest beach to Roseau, so the entire community comes to party here on Sunday. It's good for sunbathing and swimming. ⊠ *Mero.*

☾**Pointe Baptiste.** Extravagantly shaped red-sandstone boulders surround this beautiful golden-sand beach. Access is a 15-minute walk, entering through private property (Pointe Baptiste Guest House or Red Rock Haven), so the beach is quiet and unpopulated. Relax, take a dip, climb the incredible rock formations, or grab a snack at the Escape Beach Bar & Grill. ⊠ *Calibishie.*

Scotts Head. At the southernmost tip of the island, a small landmass is connected to the mainland by a narrow stretch of stony beach. It's a fantastic spot for snorkeling. Lunch at one of the village restaurants where you'll always find fresh-caught red snapper and mahimahi. ⊠ *Scotts Head Village.*

10

THE ORIGINAL CARIBBEANS

Blame Christopher Columbus: his logs give accounts of the "gentle, laughing" Arawak and the "ferocious, cannibalistic" Carib, both typecasts that pigeonholed the Caribbean's two indigenous peoples and persist to this day. Historians have had to wade through a lot of colonial romanticism to get at the truth.

Archaeologists have determined that the first Amerindian migration to the islands took place around 1000 BC from northern South America. "War and Peace" could describe the divergence between the agrarian Arawak and the more militant Carib. The Arawak—the umbrella term encompassed many smaller groups, most notably the Taíno people on the larger islands—were easily subjugated by Spanish explorers; the Carib, less so, but eventually they succumbed, too. Warfare and disease—the indigenous peoples had never encountered smallpox until the Europeans' arrival—caused populations of both groups to dwindle to a few thousand by the end of the 18th century.

TODAY'S INDIGENOUS PEOPLES

Common wisdom holds that the Arawak are extinct and the Carib subsist today only in Dominica's Carib Territory. Neither is exactly true. A few thousand Arawak people survive, but in northern South America. Most Puerto Ricans and Arubans can also claim Arawak ancestry. The enclave in Dominica, established in 1903, has its own governing body for a population of 3,000, but smaller Carib communities live in Trinidad and St. Vincent. Descendants of Carib intermarriage with African slaves—the so-called "Black Caribs"—live on as Central America's Garífuna people.

Language. Carib warfare resulted in the capture of many Arawak women. As a result, early Spanish arrivals were puzzled by what appeared to be gender-specific languages, with men speaking the Carib Kalinago language, and women, one of several Arawakan tongues. Historians debate the notion of a persistent gender-communication divide between what the British would later call Island Carib and Island Arawak. The languages gave several of the islands their names: Bequia ("cloud"), Canouan ("turtle"), Carriacou ("reef"), Saba ("rock"), and Tobago ("tobacco"). The English words "barbecue," "hurricane," and "potato" have their roots in indigenous Caribbean languages, too.

Religion. The Carib adopted many of the tenets of Arawak religion, essentially a system of animism and ancestor worship. Shamans held the keys to unlocking contact with the spirit world, thus occupying esteemed roles in their communities. Tobacco played a prominent role in worship ceremonies. (*Tabaco* is yet another Amerindian word that found its way into English.) Petroglyphs, rock carvings dedicated to objects of indigenous veneration, can be seen today in Puerto Rico, St. Kitts, St. John, and Grenada.

Innovations. With the construction of their *canoas*—source of the word "canoe"—indigenous Caribbean peoples

were able to establish interisland transport. (The Arawak used their vessels for trade; the Carib, for warfare.) And the next time you laze in a hammock, acknowledge the Arawak. *Hamacas* were a regular fixture in their homes.

Women. Carib and Arawak women participated in surprisingly egalitarian societies. Women were eligible to be a community's *cacique* (chief) and frequently served on its ruling council. Society did, however, ascribe gender roles: men went off to war while women tended agriculture and domestic chores.

Food. Fishing was a major source of nourishment for the Carib and Arawak. Perhaps no food is more identified with Caribbean indigenous peoples than the cassava or yuca, a starchy tuber and a major source of carbohydrates, with one major god even being the patron of this important crop.

Cannibalism? What of the charges of cannibalism among the Carib people? Columbus wrote that he saw the practice, but most historians side with today's Carib descendants who insist it never went on. They suggest that Spanish explorers had religious and economic motives to perpetuate the myth of cannibalism. Conversion to Christianity and even slavery would have to be better than such "barbarism" in their eyes.

—Jeffrey Van Fleet

Updated
by Roberta
Sotonoff

In Dominica, Mother Nature comes to you. Her beauty reveals itself in underwater silence as you swim in volcanic bubbles while millions of colors dash by, or perhaps in its magnificent steep, narrow stretches of red mud and lush forests on your climb up a mountain volcano. Any way you choose to experience Dominica, her big and small wonders will awe you.

With this bountiful natural abundance, there's also a lot of active watching—flying birds and butterflies, turtles hatching, plus jumping dolphins and breaching whales. Even when you're not looking, something is sure to capture your gaze. The sensory overload isn't just visual. Your soul may be soothed by the refreshing smell of clean river water and cleaner air, your taste buds will be tantalized by the freshest fruits and vegetables, and your skin will be caressed by the purest natural soaps.

Wedged between the two French islands of Guadeloupe and Martinique, Dominica (pronounced dom-in-*ee*-ka) is as close to the Garden of Eden as you're likely to get. Wild orchids, anthurium lilies, ferns, heliconia, and myriad fruit trees sprout profusely. Much of the interior is still covered by luxuriant rain forest and remains inaccessible by road. Here everything grows more intensely: greener, brighter, and bigger. A natural fortress, the island protected the Caribs (the region's original inhabitants) against European colonization. The rugged northeast is still reserved as home to the last survivors of the Caribs, along with their traditions and mythology.

Dominica—with a population of approximately 72,800—did eventually become a British colony. It attained independence in November 1978 and has a seat in the United Nations as the central Caribbean's only natural World Heritage Site. Its capital is Roseau (pronounced rose-*oh*); the official language is English, although most locals communicate with each other in Creole; roads are driven on the left; family and place-names are a mélange of English, Carib, and French; and the religion is predominantly Catholic. It's a conservative society. Unlike neighboring Martinique and Guadeloupe, Dominica frowns on topless bathing, and swimsuits should never be worn on the street. The economy is still heavily dependent on agriculture.

With fewer than 80,000 overnight visitors annually, Dominica is a little-known destination with no major hotel chains, but the island's forestry service has preserved more national forests, marine reserves, and parks, per capita, than almost anywhere on Earth.

Dominica is an ideal place to be active—hike, bike, trek, kayak, dive, snorkel, or sail in marine reserves. Explore the rain forests, waterfalls, and geothermal springs or search for one of the many resident whale and dolphin species. Discover Dominica's vibrant Carib culture. To experience Dominica is really to know Earth as it was created.

EXPLORING DOMINICA

Despite the small size of this island, it can take a couple of hours to travel between the popular destinations. Many sights are isolated and difficult to find; you may be better off taking an organized excursion. If you do go it alone, drive carefully; roads can be narrow and winding. Plan at least eight hours to see the highlights. To fully experience the island, set aside about five days so you can enjoy the water and take some hikes.

WHAT TO SEE

☾ **Cabrits National Park.** Along with Brimstone Hill in St. Kitts, Shirley Heights in Antigua, and Ft. Charlotte in St. Vincent, the Cabrits National Park's Ft. Shirley ruins are among the most significant historic sites in the Caribbean. Just north of the town of Portsmouth, this 1,300-acre park includes a marine park and herbaceous swamps, which are home to several species of rare birds and plants. At the heart of the park is the Ft. Shirley military complex. Built by the British between 1770 and 1815, it once comprised 50 major structures, including storehouses that were also quarters for 700 men. With the help of the Royal Navy (which sends sailors ashore to work on the site each time a ship is in port) and local volunteers, historian Dr. Lennox Honychurch restored the fort and its surroundings, incorporating a small museum that highlights the natural and historic aspects of the park and an open canteen-style restaurant. ⊠ *Portsmouth* ☎ *No phone* ⊡ *$2* ☉ *Museum open daily 9–4.*

☾ **Carib Indian Territory.** In 1903, after centuries of conflict, the Caribbean's
★ first settlers, the Kalinago (more popularly known as the Caribs), were granted approximately 3,700 acres of land on the island's northeast coast. Here a hardened lava formation, **L'Escalier Tête Chien** (Snake's Staircase), runs down into the Atlantic. The name is derived from a snake whose head resembles that of a dog. The ocean alongside Carib Territory is particularly fierce. The shore is full of countless coves and inlets. According to Carib legend, every night the nearby Londonderry Islets transform into grand canoes to take the spirits of the dead out to sea.

A chief administers the Carib Territory on which about 3,000 natives reside. The reservation's Catholic church in Salybia has a canoe as its altar, which was designed by Dr. Lennox Honychurch, a local historian, author, and artist.

The Kalinago resemble native South Americans and are mostly farmers and fishermen. Others are entrepreneurs who have opened restaurants, guesthouses, and little shops that offer exquisite baskets and handcrafted items. Craftspeople have retained their knowledge of basket weaving, wood carving, and canoe building through generations. They fashion long, elegant canoes from the trunk of a single *gommier* tree. You might catch canoe builders at work at **Kalinago Barana Autê** (✉ *Crayfish River, Carib Territory* ☎ *767/445–7979* ⊕ *www.kalinagobaranaaute. com* ✉ *Basic package is about $10* ☽ *Daily 9–5*), the Carib Territory's place to learn about Kalinago customs, history, and culture. A guided, 45-minute tour explores the village, stopping along the way to see some traditional dances and to learn about plants, dugout canoes, basket weaving, and cassava bread making. The path offers wonderful viewpoints of the Atlantic and a chance to glimpse Isukulati Falls.

🐾 **Emerald Pool.** Quite possibly the most visited nature attraction on the island, this emerald-green pool fed by a 50-foot waterfall is an easy trip to make. To reach this spot in the vast Morne Trois Pitons National Park, you follow a trail that starts at the side of the road near the reception center (it's an easy 20-minute walk). Along the way, there are lookout points with views of the windward (Atlantic) coast and the forested interior. If you don't want a crowd, check whether there are cruise ships in port before going out, as this spot is popular with cruise-ship tour groups.

🐾 **Indian River.** The mouth of the Indian River, which flows into the ocean at Portsmouth, was once a Carib Indian settlement. A rowboat ride down this river, which was featured in *Pirates of the Caribbean: Dead Man's Chest,* is both relaxing and educational. The river is lined with trees whose buttress roots spread up to 20 feet. Clear, brackish water is a playground for young barracudas and crayfish. Except for singing yellow warblers, flitting hummingbirds, or wing-flapping egrets, there is an eerie silence. To arrange such a trip, stop by the visitor center in Portsmouth and ask for one of the "Indian River boys," of the Portsmouth Indian River Tour Guides Association. Most boat trips take you up as far as Rahjah's Jungle Bar. You can usually do an optional guided walking tour of the swamplands and the remnants of one of Dominica's oldest plantations. Tours last one to three hours, for roughly $20 per person, but the actual price depends on your guide.

Morne Aux Diables. This peak soars 2,826 feet above sea level and slopes down to Toucari and Douglas bays and long stretches of dark-sand beach on the north side of the island. To reach it, take the road along the Caribbean coast. It twists by coconut, cocoa, and banana groves, past fern-festooned embankments, over rivers, and into villages where brightly painted shanties are almost as colorful as all the flora and fauna.

🐾 **Morne Diablotin National Park.** Here Dominica's highest mountain, Morne Diablotin, soars 4,747 feet. The peak takes its name from a bird known in English as the black-capped petrel. Now extinct on the island, it was prized by hunters in the 18th century. Dominica is still a major birding destination with many exotic—and endangered—species such as the green-and-purple Sisserou parrot (*Amazona imperialis*) and the Jaco, or red-neck, parrot (*Amazona arausiaca*). Before this national park was established, its Syndicate Nature Trail was aided by some 6,000 school-children—each donated 25¢ to protect the area's habitat. The west-coast

Emerald Pool, one of Dominica's most popular natural attractions.

road (at the bend near Dublanc) runs through three types of forest and leads to the park. The trail offers a casual walk; just bring a sweater and binoculars. But the five- to eight-hour hike up Morne Diablotin is no walk in the park. You will need a guide, sturdy hiking shoes, warm clothing, and a backpack with refreshments and a change of clothes (including socks). All should be wrapped in plastic to keep them dry.

A good guide for Morne Diablotin is local ornithology expert **Bertrand Jno Baptiste** (☎ 767/446–6358 or 767/448–6358).

★ **Morne Trois Pitons National Park.** A UNESCO World Heritage Site, this 17,000-acre swath of lush, mountainous land in the south-central interior (covering 9% of Dominica) is the island's crown jewel. Named after one of the highest (4,600 feet) mountains on the island, it contains the island's famous "boiling lake," majestic waterfalls, and cool mountain lakes. There are four types of vegetation zones here. Ferns grow 30 feet tall, wild orchids sprout from trees, sunlight leaks through green canopies, and a gentle mist rises over the jungle floor. A system of trails has been developed in the park, and the Division of Forestry and Wildlife works hard to maintain them—with no help from the excessive rainfall and the profusion of vegetation that seems to grow right before your eyes. Access to the park is possible from most points, though the easiest approaches are via the small mountaintop villages of Laudat (pronounced lau-*dah*) and Cochrane.

About 5 mi (8 km) out of Roseau, the Wotten Waven Road branches off toward Sulphur Springs, where you can see the belching, sputtering, and gurgling releases of volcanic hot springs. At the base of Morne Micotrin you can find two crater lakes: the first, at 2,500 feet above sea level, is **Freshwater Lake.** According to a local legend, it's haunted by a vindictive mermaid and a monstrous serpent. Farther on is **Boeri Lake,** fringed with greenery and with purple hyacinths floating on its surface.

★ The undisputed highlight of the park is the **Boiling Lake.** Reputedly the world's largest such lake, it's a cauldron of gurgling gray-blue water, 70 yards wide and of unknown depth, with water temperatures from 180°F to 197°F. Although generally believed to be a volcanic crater, the lake is actually a flooded fumarole—a crack through which gases escape from the molten lava below. As many visitors discovered in late 2004, the "lake" can sometimes dry up, though it fills again within a few months and, shortly after that, once more starts to boil. It has returned to its pre-2004 levels. The two- to four-hour (one way) hike up to the lake is challenging (on a very rainy day, be prepared to slip and slide the whole way up and back). You'll need attire appropriate for a strenuous hike, and a guide is a must. Most guided trips start early (no later than 8:30 am) for this all-day, 7-mi (11-km) round-trip trek.

On your way to Boiling Lake you pass through the **Valley of Desolation,** a sight that definitely lives up to its name. Harsh sulfuric fumes have destroyed virtually all the vegetation in what must once have been a lush forested area. Small hot and cold streams with water of various colors—black, purple, red, orange—web the valley. Stay on the trail to avoid breaking through the crust that covers the hot lava. During this hike you'll pass rivers where you can refresh yourself with a dip (a particular treat is a soak in a hot-water stream on the way back). At the beginning of the Valley of Desolation trail is the **TiTou Gorge,** where you can swim in the pool or relax in the hot-water springs along one side. If you're a strong swimmer, you can head up the gorge to a cave (it's about a five-minute swim) that has a magnificent waterfall; a crack in the cave about 50 feet above permits a stream of sunlight to penetrate the cavern.

Also in the national park are some of the island's most spectacular waterfalls. The 45-minute hike to **Sari Sari Falls,** accessible through the east-coast village of La Plaine, can be hair-raising. But the sight of water cascading some 150 feet into a large pool is awesome. So large are these falls that you feel the spray from hundreds of yards away. Just beyond the village of Trafalgar and up a short hill is the reception facility, where you can purchase passes to the national park and find guides to take you on a rain-forest trek to the twin **Trafalgar Falls;** the 125-foot-high waterfall is called the Father, and the wider, 95-foot-high one, the Mother. If you like a little challenge, let your guide take you to the riverbed and the cool pools at the base of the falls (check whether there's a cruise ship in port before setting out; this sight is popular with the tour operators). You need a guide for the arduous 75-minute hike to **Middleham Falls.** It's best if you start at Laudat (the turnoff for the trailhead is just before the village); the trip is much longer from Cochrane Village. The trail takes you to another spectacular waterfall, where water cascades 100 feet over boulders and vegetation and then into an ice-cold pool (a swim here is absolutely exhilarating). Guides for these hikes are available at the trailheads; still, it's best to arrange a tour before even setting out.

Northeast Coast. Steep cliffs, dramatic reefs, and rivers that swirl down through forests of mangroves and fields of coconut define this section of Dominica. The road along the Atlantic, with its red cliffs, whipped-cream waves, and windswept trees, crosses the Hatton Garden River before entering the village of Marigot. In the northeastern region there are numerous estates—old family holdings planted with fruit trees. Beyond Marigot and the Melville Hall Airport is the beautiful Londonderry Estate. The beach here is inspiring, with driftwood strewn about its velvety black sands, which part halfway where the Londonderry River spills into the Atlantic (swimming isn't advised because of strong currents, but a river bath here is a memorable treat). Farther along the coast, beyond the village of Wesley (which has a gas station and a shop that sells wonderful bread) and past Eden Estate, there are still more beautiful beaches and coves. The swimming is excellent at Woodford Hill Bay, Hodges Beach, Hampstead Estate, Batibou Bay, and L'Anse Tortue (Turtle Bay), where you might glimpse a turtle plodding on the beach to lay her eggs. At the charming community of Calibishie you'll find beach bars and restaurants, as well as laid-back villas and guesthouses. At Bense, a village in the interior just past Calibishie, you can take a connector road to Chaudiere, a beautiful swimming spot in a valley; the only crowd you're likely to encounter is a group of young villagers frolicking in the 15-foot-deep pool and diving off the 25-foot-high rocks.

Portsmouth. In 1782 Portsmouth was the site of the Battle of Les Saintes, a naval engagement between the French and the English. The English won the battle but lost the much tougher fight against malaria-carrying mosquitoes that bred in the nearby swamps. Once intended to be the capital of Dominica, thanks to its superb harbor on Prince Rupert Bay, it saw as many as 400 ships in port at one time in its heyday, but on account of those swamps, Roseau, not Portsmouth, is the capital today. Maritime traditions are continued here by the yachting set, and a 2-mi (3-km) stretch of sandy beach fringed with coconut trees runs to the Picard Estate area.

Roseau. Although it's one of the smallest capitals in the Caribbean, Roseau has the highest concentration of inhabitants of any town in the eastern Caribbean. Caribbean vernacular architecture and a bustling marketplace transport visitors back in time. Although you can walk the entire town in about an hour, you'll get a much better feel for the place on a leisurely stroll.

For some years now, the Society for Historical Architectural Preservation and Enhancement (SHAPE) has organized programs and projects to preserve the city's architectural heritage. Several interesting buildings have already been restored. **Lilac House,** on Kennedy Avenue, has three types of gingerbread fretwork, latticed verandah railings, and heavy hurricane shutters. The **J. W. Edwards Building,** at the corner of Old and King George V streets, has a stone base and a wooden second-floor gallery. The **Old Market Plaza** is the center of Roseau's historic district, which was laid out by the French on a radial plan rather than a grid, so streets such as Hanover, King George V, and Old radiate from this area. South of the marketplace is the Fort Young Hotel, built as a British fort in the 18th century; the nearby statehouse, public library, and Anglican cathedral are also worth a visit. New developments at the bay front on Dame M. E. Charles Boulevard have brightened up the waterfront.

The 40-acre **Botanical Gardens,** founded in 1891 as an annex of London's Kew Gardens, is a great place to relax, stroll, or watch a cricket match. In addition to the extensive collection of tropical plants and trees, there's also a parrot aviary. At the Forestry Division office, which is also on the garden grounds, you can find numerous publications on the island's flora, fauna, and national parks. The forestry officers are particularly knowledgeable on these subjects and can also recommend good hiking guides. ⊠ *Valley Rd.* ☎ *767/448–2401 Ext. 3417* ⊕ *www. da-academy.org/dagardens.html* 🖭 *Free* ۞ *Daily 6 am–7 pm.*

The old post office now houses the **Dominica Museum.** This labor of love by local writer and historian Dr. Lennox Honychurch contains furnishings, documents, prints, and maps that date back hundreds of years; you can also find an entire Carib hut as well as Carib canoes, baskets, and other artifacts. ⊠ *Dame M. E. Charles Blvd., opposite cruise-ship berth* ☎ *767/448–2401* 🖭 *$3* ۞ *Weekdays 9–4, Sat. 9–2; closed Sun. except when a cruise ship is in port.*

Soufrière. Tourism is quietly mingling with the laid-back lifestyle of the residents of this gently sunbaked village in the southwest, near one of the island's two marine reserves. Although it was first settled by French lumbermen in the 17th century, it's mainly fishermen you'll find here today. In the village sits one of the island's prettiest churches, a historic 18th-century Catholic church built of volcanic stone; the ruins of the L. Rose Lime Oil factory; Sulphur Springs, with its hot mineral baths to the east; and the best diving and snorkeling on the island is within the **Soufrière/Scotts Head Marine Reserve.** To the west is Bois Cotlette (a historic plantation house) and to the south the Scotts Head Peninsula—at the island's southern tip—which separates the Caribbean from the Atlantic. So if there isn't enough treasure here to satisfy you, there's always the rain forest waiting to be challenged.

WHERE TO EAT

You can expect an abundance of vegetables, fruits, and root crops to appear on menus around the island. Dominica's economy, after all, is based on agriculture. Sweet ripe plantains, *kushkush* (corn meal), yams, breadfruit, dasheen (also called taro), fresh fish, and chicken prepared at least a dozen different ways are all staples. The local drink is a spiced rum steeped with herbs such as anisette (called nanny) and *pweve* (lemongrass). Dominican cuisine is also famous for its use of local game, such as the *manicou* (a small opossum) and the agouti (a large indigenous rodent), but you'll have to be an intrepid diner to go that route. At the time of this writing, the government had banned mountain chicken (a euphemism for a large frog called *crapaud*) because of problems with disease.

WHAT TO WEAR

Most Dominicans dress nicely but practically when eating out—for dinner it's shirts and trousers for men and modest dresses for women. During the day, nice shorts are acceptable at most places; beach attire is frowned upon unless you're eating on the beach.

$-$$
FRENCH

✕**Cocorico**. It's hard to miss the umbrella-shaded chairs and tables at this Parisian-style café on a prominent bay-front corner in Roseau. Breakfast crepes, croissants, baguette sandwiches, and piping-hot café au lait are available beginning at 8:30 am. Throughout the day you can relax indoors or out and enjoy any of the extensive menu selections with the perfect glass of wine, and you can even surf the Internet on its computers. In the cellar downstairs, the Cocorico wine store has a reasonably priced selection from more than eight countries plus a wide assortment of pâtés and cheeses, crepes, sausages, cigars, French bread, and chocolates. ⊠ *Bay Front at Kennedy Ave., Roseau* ☎ *767/449–8686* ⊕ *www.natureisle.com/cocorico/* ⊙ *Closed Sun. unless ship is in port, then 10–4.*

¢
CAFÉ

✕**Cornerhouse Café**. This Internet café offers an eclectic menu to sustain you while surfing: bagels with an assortment of toppings, delicious soups, vegetarian dishes, Mexican, fish, sandwiches, salads, cakes, and coffee. Computers are rented by the half hour (US$3); relax on soft chairs and flip through books and magazines while you wait. ⊠ *Old and King George V Sts., Roseau* ☎ *767/449–9000* ▬ *No credit cards* ⊙ *Closed Sun.*

$$$
CARIBBEAN

✕**Crystal Terrace Restaurant & Bar**. You can find classic local food with a very elegant twist at this restaurant in the Evergreen Hotel. Selections range from starters like fresh soup or salad dressed with local produce to authentic creole and international main courses and, when in season, tasty crab backs. Breakfast, lunch, and Thursday-evening barbecue are also on the menu. Reservations are advised. ⊠ *Evergreen Hotel, Castle Comfort* ☎ *767/448–3288.*

$$
GRILL

✕**Garage Bar & Grill**. This former garage has become the only true grill on the island. It boasts "cool drinks, great food." The menu includes prime steaks, pasta, and seafood as well as creole food and jerk chicken. The former digs are not forgotten, evidenced by the bar stools that are anchored by old tires, and a selection of vittles like the 4x4 (ribs) and 6 Cylinders (spicy chicken wings). In early evening, it is a very happening place with the locals. Breakfast, lunch, and dinner are served. ⊠ *15 Hanover St. at Kennedy Ave., Roseau* ☎ *767/448–5433.*

$$
CARIBBEAN

✕**Gulyave**. This popular restaurant in a quaint Caribbean town house also has a shop downstairs serving a scrumptious selection of sweet and savory pastries, tarts, and cakes. These yummy morsels can also be ordered upstairs, along with breakfast and a Caribbean buffet for lunch. Choose to dine either in the airy dining room or on the sunny, narrow balcony perched above Roseau's colorful streets—the perfect spot to indulge in one of the fresh-squeezed tropical juices. ⊠ *15 Cork St., Roseau* ☎ *767/448–2930* ⊙ *Closed Sun. No dinner.*

$-$$$
CARIBBEAN

Fodor's Choice
★

✕**La Robe Creole**. A cut-stone building only steps away from the Old Market Plaza houses one of Dominica's best restaurants. In a cozy dining room with wood rafters, ladder-back chairs, and colorful madras tablecloths, you can dine on a meal selected from an eclectic à la carte menu. Local favorites are callaloo soup, *titiree* (fish balls made from a

10

type of fish called titiree), creole-style wings, vegetarian items, and crab backs and river crayfish when in season. The restaurant makes its own delicious mango chutney and plantain chips, called *Irie Itals*, which you can buy in local shops. ⊠ *3 Victoria St., Roseau* ☎ *767/448–2896 or 767/448–4436* ☼ *Closed Sun. Closed Sept. and part of Oct.*

$ ✕ **Miranda's Corner.** Just past Springfield on the way to Pont Casse, you'll
CARIBBEAN begin to see hills full of flowers. At a big bend, a sign on a tree reads "Miranda's Corner," referring to a bar, rum shop, and diner all in one. Here Miranda Alfred is at home, serving everyone from Italian tourists to banana farmers. Many of her ingredients are grown in her adjacent garden. The specialties are numerous, including titiree (when it's fresh and in season) and tropical juices. All are prepared with a potion of passion and a fistful of flavor. Miranda's is open for breakfast, lunch, and dinner and is a great pit stop if you are in the area; call ahead to make sure it's open. ⊠ *Mount Joy, Springfield* ☎ *767/449–2509.*

¢–$ ✕ **Pearl's Cuisine.** In a Creole town house in central Roseau, chef Pearl,
CARIBBEAN with her robust and infectious character, prepares some of the island's best local cuisine, such as callaloo soup, fresh fish, and rabbit. Her menu changes daily, but she offers such local delicacies as *sousse* (pickled pigs' feet), blood pudding, and rotis. When sitting down, ask for a table on the open-air gallery that overlooks Roseau and prepare for an abundant portion, but make sure you leave space for dessert. If you're on the go, enjoy a quick meal from the daily, varied menu in the ground-floor snack bar. You're spoiled for choice when it comes to the fresh fruit juices. ⊠ *50 King George V St., Roseau* ☎ *767/448–8707* ☼ *Closed Sun. No dinner.*

$–$$ ✕ **Port of Call Restaurant & Bar.** This haunt of middle-aged barristers and
CARIBBEAN laid-back locals is ideally located, just around the corner from the bay front in downtown Roseau. This breezy restaurant with a soothing gray-and-white color scheme occupies a traditional stone building and is open from 10 am to 10 pm for breakfast, lunch, and dinner. The layout is such that you can have your privacy and a relaxing meal. Management here is always ready to meet your needs for home-style local shrimp, chicken, or fish, à la carte dishes such as a hamburger and fries, or your favorite libation. ⊠ *3 Kennedy Ave., Roseau* ☎ *767/448–2910.*

$$$–$$$$ ✕ **Rainforest Restaurant at Papillote.** Savor a lethal rum punch while loung-
CARIBBEAN ing in a hot mineral bath in the Papillote Wilderness Retreat gardens. Then try the bracing callaloo soup, dasheen puffs, fish "rain forest" (marinated with papaya and wrapped in banana leaves), or the succulent freshwater prawns. This handsome Caribbean restaurant has quite possibly one of the best views in the region. Dine at an altitude cool enough to demand a throw blanket and inspire after-dinner conversation. ⊠ *Papillote Wilderness Retreat, Trafalgar Falls Rd., Trafalgar* ☎ *767/448–2287* ⊕ *www.papillote.dm* ⌖ *Reservations essential* ☼ *Closed Sept. and Oct.*

$$–$$$ ✕ **Waterfront Restaurant.** At the southern end of Roseau's bay front, this
ECLECTIC elegant and romantic restaurant overlooks the Caribbean coastline. You
☺ can dine outdoors on the wraparound verandah while listening to the
Fodor's Choice sounds of the sea or indoors in the air-conditioned formal dining room.
★ Executive chef Floyd Bell's menu incorporates spa-vegetarian choices

alongside the traditional international and local dishes. Tropical desserts include cheesecake and guava tart. The menu dips into a wide range of cuisines, from creole specialties like callaloo soup to beef, lamb, duck, and even skewered shrimp with a Thai sauce. No matter what your choice, it will be served by a friendly and efficient waitstaff. The bar's happy-hour steel band adds a nice touch. Waterfront Restaurant is closed in September and early October, but meals are served in the Marquis Restaurant, which has a regular Monday-night buffet. ⊠ *Fort Young Hotel, Victoria St., Roseau* ☎ *767/448–5000* ⊕ *www.fortyounghotel.com.*

WHERE TO STAY

Many properties offer packages with dives, hikes, tours, and meal plans included, along with all the usual amenities. Some advertise winter rates with a discount for either summer or longer stays.

The following reviews have been condensed for this book. Please go to Fodors.com for full reviews of each property.

¢–$ 🏨 **Anchorage Hotel.** Adventure seekers of every age come to this lodge
HOTEL for diving, whale-watching, or other tours led by the in-house tour
☺ company. **Pros:** a fine range of water activities; wheelchair accessible; upstairs rooms have balconies; small meeting room. **Cons:** no-frills accommodations. ⊠ *Castle Comfort* ☐ *Box 34, Roseau* ☎ *767/448–2638* ⊕ *www.anchoragehotel.dm* ↘ *32 rooms* △ *In-room: Internet, Wi-Fi. In-hotel: restaurant, bar, pool, business center* ¶⊙¶ *No meals.*

$ 🏨 **Beau Rive.** Owner Mark Steele puts Zen-like elegance and creative
B&B/INN soul into every detail of this secluded bed-and-breakfast. **Pros:** lovely
★ rooms; very good food; all rooms have awesome ocean views. **Cons:** ocean is too rough for swimming; no TVs, room phones, or a/c. ⊠ *Between Castle Bruce and Sineku* ☐ *Box 2424, Roseau* ☎ *767/445–8992* ⊕ *www.beaurive.com* ↘ *10 rooms* △ *In-room: no a/c, no phone, no TV. In-hotel: bar, pool, business center, some age restrictions* ↗ *2-night minimum* ☉ *Closed Aug. and Sept.* ¶⊙¶ *Breakfast.*

¢ 🏨 **Calibishie Lodges.** Close to one of Dominica's most picturesque seaside
RENTAL villages, the six self-contained one-bedroom units here emerge from
☺ behind terraced lemongrass. **Pros:** plenty of charm; people-pleasing
★ owners; meal plans available; 20 minutes from Melville airport. **Cons:** at least an hour's drive from Roseau; no a/c. ⊠ *Calibishie Main Rd., Calibishie* ☎ *767/445–8537* ⊕ *www.calibishie-lodges.com* ↘ *6 apartments* △ *In-room: no a/c, safe, kitchen, Wi-Fi. In-hotel: restaurant, bar, pool.*

¢ 🏨 **Castle Comfort Lodge.** The boats anchored just off the pier, the telltale
HOTEL dive log, and the guests in the hot tub with mask imprints on their foreheads give it all away—this is the best dive lodge in Dominica. **Pros:** a favorite retreat for divers; good location. **Cons:** rooms are very basic. ⊠ *Castle Comfort* ☐ *Box 63, Roseau* ☎ *767/448–2188 or 767/448–2062, 646/502–6800 in U.S.* ⊕ *www.castlecomfortdivelodge. com* ↘ *14 rooms* △ *In-room: Wi-Fi. In-hotel: restaurant, bar, pool* ☉ *Closed Sept.* ¶⊙¶ *Breakfast.*

¢ 🏨 **Cocoa Cottage.** This ecosensitive, hand-constructed wood-and-stone
B&B/INN lodge has a cozy tree-house feel, and, though very basic, is comfortable. **Pros:** immersive tropical mountain experience; artistic vibe. **Cons:** a bit far

10

removed. ✉ *Trafalgar* 🏠 *Box 288, Roseau* ☎ *767/448–0412* ⊕ *www. cocoacottages.com* ⬦ *6 rooms* ⌂ *In-room: no a/c, no phone, no TV. In-hotel: restaurant, bar* ⧄ *Breakfast.*

¢   ⬚ **Crescent Moon Cabins.** In a hidden
RENTAL   valley where waterfalls and a river
☼   run rampant, this small, family-run,
★   forest resort is so deep in the bush, you might genuinely believe you're camping—except you have the benefit of basic yet ecofriendly facilities with balconies and hammocks. **Pros:** one-of-a-kind property; excellent food. **Cons:** facilities are about two steps above camping; road here is difficult to navigate. ✉ *Sylvania* 🏠 *Box 2400, Roseau* ☎ *767/449–3449* ⊕ *www.crescentmooncabins. com* ⬦ *4 cabins,* ⌂ *In-room: no a/c, no phone, no TV. In-hotel: pool* ⊙ *Closed Aug. and Sept.* ⬦ *2-night minimum* ⧄ *Breakfast.*

¢–$ ⬚ **Evergreen Hotel.** This family-run, modern, oceanfront inn is a non-
HOTEL   diver's oasis in diver-friendly Castle Comfort. Located 1 mi (1½ km)
☼   south of Roseau, it has spacious waterfront rooms with large showers and balconies—many with ocean views. **Pros:** friendly staff; pleasant surroundings; just 1 mi (1½ km) from Roseau. **Cons:** one of the few places in the area that doesn't have diving facilities. ✉ *Castle Comfort* 🏠 *Box 309, Roseau* ☎ *767/448–3288* ⊕ *www.avirtualdominica.com/ evergreen.htm* ⬦ *16 rooms, 1 cottage* ⌂ *In-hotel: restaurant, bar, pool, business center* ⧄ *Breakfast.*

¢–$ ⬚ **Fort Young Hotel.** Sitting on the edge of a cliff just to the south of
HOTEL   Roseau, this hotel has ample-size rooms and balconies with either a
Fodor's Choice   limited or full ocean view. **Pros:** cosmopolitan vibe; friendly staff. **Cons:**
★   can get crowded during the Friday-night happy hour. ✉ *Victoria St., Box 519, Roseau* ☎ *767/448–5000* ⊕ *www.fortyounghotel.com* ⬦ *70 rooms, 3 suites* ⌂ *In-room: Internet (some), Wi-Fi. In-hotel: restaurants, bars, pool, spa* ⧄ *No meals.*

¢   ⬚ **Garraway Hotel.** A bay-front, city-style hotel on the western edge of
HOTEL   Roseau offers lovely vistas from the higher floors such as of the town's
☼   quaint architecture, the ocean, or the imposing mountains. **Pros:** spacious rooms; well located in the heart of Roseau; free Ethernet. **Cons:** rooms are a bit sparse; lower-level rooms do not have good views. ✉ *Place Heritage, 1 Dame Eugenia Charles Blvd., Box 789, Roseau* ☎ *767/449–8800* ⊕ *www.garrawayhotel.com* ⬦ *20 rooms, 10 suites* ⌂ *In-hotel: restaurant, bar* ⧄ *No meals.*

¢   ⬚ **Hummingbird Inn.** The ocean vistas, lushly fragrant garden, and natu-
B&B/INN   rally sensuous atmosphere at this hillside retreat provide a romantic setting for honeymooners and, needless to say, hummingbirds. **Pros:**

BEST BETS FOR LODGING

BEST FOR ROMANCE
Silks

Red Rock Haven, Beau Rive

BEST BEACHFRONT
Red Rock Haven

BEST POOL
Fort Young

BEST SERVICE
Fort Young

Calibishie Lodges

BEST FOR KIDS
Calibishie Lodges

Fort Young

Fort Young Hotel.

gorgeous view; if you are into lizards, this is a sanctuary for the rare *iguana delicatissima*. **Cons:** very basic rooms; a charge for in-room TV; road to the property has a very steep turn and is challenging after it rains; no a/c. ⊠ *Rockaway, Canfield* ☎ *Box 1901, Roseau* ☎ *767/449–1042* ⊕ *www.thehummingbirdinn.com* ☞ *9 rooms, 1 suite* ☖ *In-room: no a/c, kitchen (some). In-hotel: restaurant, bar* ⦿ *Breakfast.*

¢ ⛬ **Itassi Cottages.** You forget how close these three cottages are to RENTAL   Roseau as you swing on your hammock overlooking the ocean. **Pros:** ☽   very friendly atmosphere; great bang for your buck; weekly and monthly rates available. **Cons:** simple (but comfortable) accommodations. ⊠ *Morne Bruce* ☎ *Box 319, Roseau* ☎ *767/448–4313* ⊕ *www. avirtualdominica.com/itassi* ☞ *3 cottages* ☖ *In-room: no a/c, kitchen. In-hotel: laundry facilities* ⦿ *No meals.*

$$ ⛬ **Jungle Bay Resort & Spa.** Sweeping views of the untamed Atlantic sur-RESORT   round this resort, which sits on 55 acres of the only developed section of ★   the island's southeast. **Pros:** perfect for active vacationers; lovely rooms; outdoor showers; basic plan includes breakfast; tours of the island offered. **Cons:** facility is remote; water is too rough for swimming; a long trek to many of the rooms; not wheelchair accessible. ⊠ *Point Mulatre* ☎ *Box 2352, Roseau* ☎ *767/446–1789* ⊕ *www.junglebaydominica.com* ☞ *35 cottages* ☖ *In-room: no a/c, no phone, no TV. In-hotel: restaurant, bars, pool, spa, some age restrictions* ☉ *Closed Sept. and Oct.* ⦿ *Breakfast.*

¢ ⛬ **Papillote Wilderness Retreat.** This family-friendly, recently updated and B&B/INN   welcoming destination in the middle of a tropical forest has a mind-☽   boggling collection of rare and indigenous plants on its botanic trail. **Pros:** lovely grounds; location inside Morne Trois Pitons National Park and close to Trafalgar Falls. **Cons:** a rental car is needed to get to

CLOSE UP

A Place to Get Soaked

Wotten Waven is no thriving metropolis. In fact, the hamlet at the north end of the Roseau Valley is minuscule. But don't miss it. Hidden in its bush are sulfur-enriched, burping waters, fumaroles, and cascades. A few local entrepreneurs have made it a spa destination. Now, if you're thinking big-time pampering, think again. It is strictly BYOT (bring your own towel). There are four outdoor "spas." Each is unique. **Rainforest Shangri-La Resort**, with its steam and hot springs, is hand-hewed and ecofriendly. **Tia's Bamboo Cottages** are perched on a hill. The springs are at the bottom by the river. Don't want to dip? Well, the owner's

preteen daughters at **Ti Kwen Glo Cho** will take you on a tour down a flower-border path to lush gardens, a small menagerie of native wildlife, and a waterfall. Ti Kwen Glo Cho's state-of-the-art spa consists of four old-fashioned claw-foot bathtubs. Mineral water is jerry-rigged into them via a series of bamboo poles. **Screw's Sulphur Spa** is the most posh. It offers mud packs and wraps plus six pools, each a different temperature and a different depth. Screw, and that is his name, doesn't let you leave without giving you fresh juice or fruit. Dominica's spas are a far reach from the Golden Door, but then again, that is their charm.

most places from here. ⊠ *Trafalgar Falls Rd., Trafalgar* ⌂ *Box 2287, Roseau* ☎ *767/448–2287* ⊕ *www.papillote.dm* ⋑ *3 rooms, 4 suites* ⌂ *In-room: no phone, no TV. In-hotel: restaurant, bar* ⊘ *Closed Sept. and Oct.* ℐⓄ *No meals.*

$
RENTAL
Ⓒ

⊞ **Picard Beach Cottages.** Eighteen cottages, on the grounds of an old 6-acre coconut plantation and its lovely landscaped gardens, are just steps away from Dominica's longest grayish-sand beach. **Pros:** has some spa facilities; nice beach; free Wi-Fi. **Cons:** property is not well lighted and can be difficult to navigate at night without a flashlight; this part of the island can get pretty buggy. ⊠ *Prince Rupert Bay*☎ *767/445–5131, 888/790–5264 toll–free reservations* ⊕ *picardbeachcottages.dm* ⋑ *18 1-bedroom cottages* ⌂ *In-room: kitchen (some). In-hotel: spa, beach* ℐⓄ *No meals.*

$
HOTEL

⊞ **Rainforest Shangri-La Resort.** Fitness and nature take the spotlight at this pristine retreat set 1,000 feet above sea level. **Pros:** fitness and wellness focus; yoga; Tai Chi. **Cons:** rooms are a bit sparse; in-room food is discouraged; not wheelchair accessible. ⊠ *Wotten Waven* ⌂ *Box 1592, Roseau* ☎ *767/440–5093* ⊕ *rainforestshangrila.com/reservations.html* ⋑ *3 rooms, 3 bungalows* ⌂ *In-room: no a/c, no phone, no TV. In-hotel: restaurant, room service, pool* ℐⓄ *No meals.*

$$$
HOTEL
Ⓒ

⊞ **Red Rock Haven.** Perched above the secluded Pointe Baptiste Beach and tucked away amid lush landscape, are posh accommodations accented with wood, stone, bamboo, a laddered loft for the kids, and elegant bathrooms. **Pros:** modern and lovely accommodations. **Cons:** a bit pricey; steep paths so difficult for people with mobility problems; car rental necessary. ⊠ *Calibishie* ☎ *767/445–7997* ⊕ *www.redrockhaven.com* ⋑ *3 1-bedroom suites, 1 2-bedroom villa* ⌂ *In-room: no a/c, no phone,* *kitchen (villa only), no TV, Wi-Fi. In-hotel: restaurant, room service, bar, pools (villa only)* ¡○¡ *Breakfast.*

¢
HOTEL
☺
Roseau Valley Hotel. With tile floors and cheerful decor, this little hotel is quite inviting. Some rooms have TVs and terraces, and others have a shared balcony and TV access. **Pros:** reasonable and pleasant. **Cons:** a 2-mi (3-km) walk to Roseau but there is local bus service. ✉ *2 mi (3 km) east of Roseau, Box 1876, Roseau* ☎ *767/449–8176* ☞ *10 rooms* ⌂ *In-room: kitchen (some), no TV (some), Wi-Fi. In-hotel: restaurant, bar* ¡○¡ *Breakfast.*

$
HOTEL
Fodor's Choice
★
Silks Hotel. French taste transformed this 17th-century mansion and former rum distillery into the most posh hotel on the island. **Pros:** probably the most luxurious lodgings on the island; close to the airport. **Cons:** more than an hour's drive from Roseau. ✉ *Hatton Garden, Marigot* ☎ *767/445–8846* ⊕ *www.silkshotel.com* ☞ *5 rooms* ⌂ *In-room: no phone, safe, Internet (some), Wi-Fi (some). In-hotel: restaurant, pool, business center, bar* ☉ *Closed Sept.–Oct. 15* ¡○¡ *Breakfast.*

¢-$
HOTEL
☺
Sunset Bay Club. Sunset is a simple but comfortable beachfront hotel on a stretch of Dominica's spectacular west coast. **Pros:** gardens and views are beautiful; great food; kid friendly. **Cons:** rooms are basic. ✉ *Batalie Beach, Coulibistrie* ☎ *767/446–6522* ⊕ *www.sunsetbayclub.com* ☞ *12 rooms, 1 suite* ⌂ *In-room: no a/c, no phone, safe. In-hotel: restaurant, bar, pool, spa, beach* ¡○¡ *Breakfast.*

¢-$
B&B/INN
☺
Tamarind Tree Hotel & Restaurant. The warmth and friendliness of owners Annette and Stefan Loerner-Peyer are this small inn's most valuable asset. **Pros:** extremely friendly owners; good food; very child friendly; one of the owners is a certified tour guide. **Cons:** no-frills rooms. ✉ *Salisbury* ✆ *Box 754, Roseau* ☎ *767/446–7395 or 767/449–7007* ⊕ *www.tamarindtreedominica.com* ☞ *12 rooms* ⌂ *In-room: a/c (some), Wi-Fi. In-hotel: restaurant, bar, pool* ☉ *Closed Sept.* ¡○¡ *Breakfast.*

¢
RENTAL
Tia's Bamboo Cottages. Tia himself built these charming but rustic cabins, which sit on the side of a hill, amid a picturesque, natural setting. **Pros:** proximity to river and natural springs; extremely helpful staff. **Cons:** cottages are very sparse. ✉ *Wotton Waven, in Roseau Valley* ☎ *767/225–4823* ☞ *3 cottages* ⌂ *In-hotel: restaurant, bar, pools* ▭ *No credit cards* ☉ *Closed June* ¡○¡ *No meals.*

¢
B&B/INN
★
Zandoli Inn. Overlooking a 111-foot cliff on the southeast Atlantic coast, this small inn has an amazing view—both water and then mountains. **Pros:** drop-dead vistas; full-service bar and restaurant. **Cons:** steep walk to the beach, which is not the best place to take a plunge. ✉ *Roche Cassée, Stowe* ✆ *Box 2099, Roseau* ☎ *767/446–3161* ⊕ *www.zandoli.com* ☞ *5 rooms* ⌂ *In-room: no a/c, no phone, no TV. In-hotel: bar, pool, some age restrictions* ¡○¡ *No meals.*

10

NIGHTLIFE AND THE ARTS

The friendly, intimate atmosphere and colorful patrons at the numerous bars and hangouts will keep you entertained for hours. If you're looking for jazz, calypso, reggae, steel band, soca (a variation of calypso), cadence-zouk, or jing ping—a type of folk music featuring the accordion, the *quage* (a kind of washboard instrument), drums, and a "boom boom" (a percussion instrument)—you're guaranteed to find it. Wednesday through Saturday nights are really lively, and during Carnival, Independence, and summer celebrations, things can be intense. Indeed, Dominica's Carnival, the pre-Lenten festival, is the most spontaneous in the Caribbean. Other big cultural events include Emancipation celebrations hosted by the National Cultural Council each August.

Fodor's Choice ★ The annual **World Creole Music Festival** (⊕ *www.wcmfdominica.com*) in late October or early November also packs in the action, with three days and nights of pulsating rhythm and music. Creole music enthusiasts come from all over the world to listen to the likes of Kassav, Aswad, and Tabou Combo. Throughout the year, however, most larger hotels have some form of live evening entertainment.

NIGHTLIFE

Once Friday afternoon rolls around, you can sense the mood change. Local bars crank up the music, and each village and community has its own particular nightly entertainment. If by this point in your trip you have made friends with some locals, they will be only too happy to take you to the current hot spot.

Every Friday night from 6 to 8 **Balas Bar & Courtyard** (⊠ *Fort Young Hotel, Victoria St., Roseau* ☎ *767/448–5000*) has a very happening rum-punch happy hour with a live band and drink specials. **Garage Bar & Grill** (⊠ *15 Hanover St., Roseau* ☎ *767/448–5433*) is lively, very popular with locals, and stays open until the last person leaves the bar. **Melvina's Champagne Bar & Restaurant** (⊠ *Champagne Hwy., Pointe Michel* ☎ *767/235–6072*) is a popular hangout for locals and tourists, especially on Friday and Saturday nights. **Symes Zee's** (⊠ *34 King George V St., Roseau* ☎ *767/448–2494*) draws a crowd on Thursday night from 10 until the wee hours of the morning, when there's a jazz-blues-reggae band. There's no cover, and the food, drinks, and cigars are reasonably priced.

THE ARTS

Arawak House of Culture (⊠ *Kennedy Ave. near Government Headquarters, Roseau*), managed by Harry Sealy at the Cultural Division, is Dominica's main performing-arts theater. A number of productions are staged here throughout the year, including plays, recitals, and dance performances.

The **Old Mill Cultural Center** (⊠ *Canefield* ☎ *767/449–1804*) is one of Dominica's historic landmarks. The Old Mill was the island's first sugarcane processing mill and rum distillery. Today, it's a place to learn about Dominica's traditions. Performances and events—including art exhibits and cultural programs—take place here throughout the year.

SHOPPING

Dominicans produce distinctive handicrafts, with various communities specializing in their specific products. The crafts of the Carib Indians include traditional baskets made of dyed *larouma* reeds and water-proofed with tightly woven *balizier* leaves. These are sold in the Carib Indian Territory and Kalinago Barana Autê as well as in Roseau's shops. Vertivert straw rugs, screw-pine tableware, *fwije* (the trunk of the forest tree fern), and wood carvings are just some examples. Also notable are local herbs, spices, condiments, and herb teas. Café Dominique, the local equivalent of Jamaican Blue Mountain coffee, is an excellent buy, as are the Dominican rums Macoucherie and Soca. Proof that the old ways live on in Dominica can be found in the number of herbal remedies available. One stimulating memento of your visit is rum steeped with *bois bandé* (scientific name *Richeria grandis*), a tree whose bark is reputed to have aphrodisiacal properties. It's sold at shops, vendors' stalls, and supermarkets. The charismatic roadside vendors can be found all over the island bearing trays laden with local and imported souvenirs, T-shirts, and trinkets. Duty-free shopping is also available in specific stores around Roseau.

Dominican farmers island-wide bring their best crops to the Roseau Market, at the end of Dame Eugenia Boulevard and Lange Lane, every Friday and Saturday from 6 am to 1 pm. It may well be the largest farmers' market in the Caribbean. They start setting up on Friday night, and often customers begin their shopping then. Vendors are usually out on roadsides when there are cruise ships in port.

MAJOR SHOPPING AREAS

One of the easiest places to pick up a souvenir is the Old Market Plaza, just behind the Dominica Museum, in Roseau. Slaves were once sold here, but today handcrafted jewelry, T-shirts, spices, souvenirs, batik, and trays, plus lacquered and woven bamboo boxes are available from a group of vendors in open-air booths set up on the cobblestones. They are usually busiest when there's a cruise ship berthed across the street. On these days you can also find a vast number of vendors along the bay front.

10

SPECIALTY STORES

ART

Most artists work from their home studios, and it often takes the right contact to find them. You can usually see the work of the island's artists at the Old Mill Cultural Center (⇨ *Nightlife and the Arts, above*). The tree-house studio and café at **Indigo** (✉ *Bournes* ☎ *767/445–3486*) sells works by in-house artists Clem and Marie Frederick and also serves fresh sugarcane juice or bush teas.

CLOTHING

There's such a wide selection when it comes to clothing stores in Roseau that it really is best to walk around and explore for yourself. However, for classic Caribbean and international designer clothing, there are several reliable boutiques to try. **Ego Boutique** (⊠ 9 *Hillsborough St., Roseau* ☎ 767/448–2336) carries an extensive selection of designer clothing and exquisite crafts and home accessories from around the world.

GIFTS AND SOUVENIRS

As cruise-ship visits have increased in frequency, duty-free shops are cropping up, including some name-brand stores, mostly within Roseau's bay front.

Baroon International (⊠ *Kennedy Ave. at Old St., Roseau* ☎ 767/449–2888) sells unusual jewelry from Asia, the United States, and other Caribbean islands. It also features pieces that are assembled in the store, as well as personal accessories, souvenirs, and special gifts.

Jeweller's International (⊠ *Fort Young Hotel, Victoria St., Roseau* ☎ 767/440–3319) carries perfumes, crystals, liquor, and other gift items such as gold and silver jewelry and baubles with emeralds, diamonds, and other gems.

For high-quality leather goods and other personal accessories, try **Land** (⊠ *Bay Front, Roseau* ☎ 767/448–3394) at the Duty-Free Emporium next to the Royal Bank.

Pirates (⊠ 6 *Long La., Roseau* ☎ 767/449–9774 ⊙ *Weekdays 8:30–5, Sat. 8:30–2*) is the place for booze, Cuban cigars, cheese, watches, and souvenirs.

Whitchurch Duty-Free (⊠ *Fort Young Hotel, Victoria St., Roseau* ☎ 767/448–7177 or 767/448–2181) has a large assortment of items, including perfumes, leather goods, and designer sunglasses.

HANDICRAFTS

Kalinago Barana Autê (⊠ *Salybia, Carib Territory* ☎ 767/445–7979 ⊕ *www.kalinagobaranaaute.com* ⊙ *Daily 9–5*) sells handicrafts including carvings, pottery, and lovely handwoven baskets, which you can watch the women weave.

Papillote Wilderness Retreat (⊠ *Trafalgar* ☎ 767/448–2287) has an intimate gift shop with local handcrafted goods and particularly outstanding wood carvings by Louis Desire.

SPORTS AND ACTIVITIES

ADVENTURE PARKS

☾ The **Rainforest** Adventures Dominica (⊠ *Laudat* ☎ 767/448–8775, *767/440–3266, 866/759–8726 in U.S.* ⊕ *www.rfat.com*) gives you a bird's-eye view of a pristine forest aboard an open, eight-person gondola. For 90 minutes to two hours, you slowly skim the treetop canopy while a guide provides scientific information about the flora and fauna. At the top there is an optional walking tour that is worth the steps. The cost is $64. Transportation and lunch are extra. This is a popular attraction for cruise-ship passengers, so try to reserve ahead.

☾ **Wacky Rollers** (⊠ *Front St., Roseau* ⊄ *Box 900, Roseau* ☎ 767/440–4386 ⊕ *www.wackyrollers.com*) will make you feel as if you are training for the marines as you swing on a Tarzan-style rope and grab onto a vertical rope ladder, rappel across zip lines, and traverse suspended log bridges, a net bridge, and four monkey bridges (rope loops). It costs $50 (May–Oct. 15) $65 (Oct. 16–Apr.) for the adult course and should take from 1½ to 3½ hours to conquer the 28 "games." There is also an abbreviated kids' course for $25 (May–Oct. 15) and $35 (Oct. 16–Apr.). Wacky Rollers also organizes adventure tours around the island plus kayak and tubing trips. Although the office is in Roseau, the park itself is in Hillsborough Estate, about 20 to 25 minutes north of Roseau.

BIKING

Cyclists find Dominica's rugged terrain to be an exhilarating challenge, and there are routes suitable for all levels of bikers. **Nature Island Dive** (⊠ *Soufrière* ☎ *767/449–8181* ⊕ *www.natureislanddive.com*) has a fleet of bikes in good condition. You can rent a mountain bike for $30, but if you prefer a knowledgeable guide to lead you through specific areas, the cost ranges from $65 for a half day to $96 for a full day, which includes lunch, snacks, and drinks.

DIVING AND SNORKELING

Fodor's Choice
★

Not only is Dominica considered one of the top 10 dive destinations in the world by *Skin Diver* and *Rodale's Scuba Diving* magazines, but it has won many other awards for its underwater sites. They are truly memorable. The west coast of the island has awesome sites, but the best are those in the southwest—within and around **Soufrière/Scotts Head Marine Reserve.** This bay is a submerged volcanic crater. The Dominica Watersports Association has worked along with the Fisheries Division for years to establish this reserve and has set stringent regulations to prevent the degradation of the ecosystem. Within ½ mi (¾ km) of the shore, there are vertical drops from 800 feet to more than 1,500 feet, with visibility frequently extending to 100 feet. Shoals of boga fish, Creole wrasse, and blue cromis are common, and you might even see a spotted moray eel or a honeycomb cowfish. Crinoids (rare elsewhere) are also abundant here, as are giant barrel sponges. There is a $2 fee per person to dive, snorkel, or kayak in the reserve. Other noteworthy dive sites include **Salisbury Falls, Nose Reef, Brain Coral Garden,** and—even farther north—**Cabrits Drop-Off** and **Toucari Reef.** The conditions for underwater photography, particularly macrophotography, are unparalleled. Rates start at about $55 for a single-tank dive and about $90 for a two-tank dive or from about $75 for a resort course with one open-water dive. All scuba-diving operators also offer snorkeling. Equipment rents for $10 to $25 a day; trips with gear range from $15 to $35. A 10% tax is not included.

The **Anchorage Dive & Whale Watch Center** (⊠ *Anchorage Hotel, Castle Comfort* ☎ *767/448–2638* ⊕ *www.anchoragehotel.dm*) has two dive boats that can take you out day or night. It also offers PADI instruction (all skill levels), snorkeling and whale-watching trips, and shore diving. It has many of the same trips as Dive Dominica.

10

A diver pauses to admire a lavender stovepipe sponge (aplysina archeri).

Cabrits Dive Center (⊠ *Portsmouth* ☎ *767/445–3010* ⊕ *www.cabritsdive. com*) is the only PADI five-star dive center in Dominica. Nitrox courses are also available for $250. Since Cabrits is the sole operator on the northwest coast, its dive boats have the pristine reefs almost to themselves, unlike other operations, whose underwater territories may overlap.

Dive Dominica (⊠ *Castle Comfort Lodge, Castle Comfort* ☎ *767/448– 2188, 646/502–6800 in U.S.* ⊕ *www.divedominica.com*), one of the island's dive pioneers, conducts NAUI, PADI, and SSI courses as well as Nitrox certification courses. With four boats, it offers diving, snorkeling, and whale-watching trips and packages including accommodation at the Castle Comfort Lodge. Its trips are similar to Anchorage's.

Fort Young Dive Centre (⊠ *Fort Young Hotel, Victoria St., Roseau* ☎ *767/448–5000 Ext. 333* ⊕ *fortyounghotel.com/diving.cfm#diving*) conducts snorkeling, diving, and whale-watching trips that depart from the hotel's private dock.

Irie Safari (⊠ *Soufrière/Scotts Head Marine Reserve, Soufrière* ☎ *767/440–5085*) takes snorkelers to Champagne and the nearby tall grasses where turtles like to hang out.

Nature Island Dive (⊠ *Soufrière* ☎ *767/449–8181* ⊕ *www.natureislanddive. com*) is run by an enthusiastic crew who offer diving, snorkeling, kayaking, and mountain biking as well as resort and full PADI courses. Some of the island's best dive sites are right outside its door.

FISHING

Contact the **Anchorage Hotel** (⊠ *Castle Comfort* ☎ *767/448–2638*) for information about fishing excursions. Fees are $550 for a half-day trip and $800 for a full day.

GUIDED TOURS

Since Dominica is such a nature-centered destination, there's no shortage of certified guides, as well as numerous tour and taxi companies. Ask the staff at your hotel for a recommendation. Generally tours start off in the Roseau area, but most operators will arrange convenient pickups. Prices range between $35 and $75 per person, depending on the duration, amenities provided, and number of people on the excursion. **Dominica Tours** (☎ *767/448–2638* ⊕ *www.experience-dominica.com*) is one of the island's largest tour companies, offering a range of hikes and bird-watching trips. **Ken's Hinterland Adventure Tours & Taxi Service** (⊠ *Fort Young Hotel, Victoria St., Roseau* ☎ *767/448–4850, 767/448 -1660, or 866/880–0508* ⊕ *www.khattstours.com*) offers a range of island tours and guided hikes, including some oriented specifically for families with children.

HIKING

★ Dominica's majestic mountains, clear rivers, and lush vegetation conspire to create adventurous hiking trails. The island is crisscrossed by ancient footpaths of the Arawak and Carib Indians and of the Nègres Maroons, escaped slaves who established camps in the mountains. Existing trails range from easygoing to arduous. To make the most of your excursion, you'll need sturdy hiking boots, insect repellent, a change of clothes (kept dry), and a guide. Hikes and tours run $25 to $50 per person, depending on destinations and duration. Some of the natural attractions within the island's national parks require visitors to purchase a site pass. These are sold for varying numbers of visits. A single-entry site pass costs $5, and a week pass $12.

Local bird and forestry expert **Bertrand Jno Baptiste** (☎ *767/446–6358 or 767/245–4768*) leads hikes up Morne Diablotin and along the Syndicate Nature Trail; if he's not available, ask him to recommend another guide. Hiking guides can be arranged through the **Discover Dominica Authority** (⊠ *Kennedy Ave., 1st Floor Financial CentreRoseau* ☎ *767/448–2045* ⊕ *www.discoverdominica.com*).

The **Forestry Division** (⊠ *Dominica Botanical Gardens, between Bath Rd. and Valley Rd., Roseau* ☎ *767/266–3817*) is responsible for the management of forests and wildlife and has numerous publications on Dominica as well as a wealth of information on reputable guides.

10

WHALE-WATCHING

☖ Dominica records the highest species counts of resident cetaceans in the
Fodor'sChoice southern Caribbean region, so it's not surprising that tour companies
★ claim 90% sighting success for their excursions. Humpback whales, false killer whales, minke, and orcas are all occasionally seen, as are

several species of dolphin. But the resident sperm whales (they calve in Dominica's 3,000-foot-deep waters) are truly the stars of the show. During your 3½-hour expedition, which costs about $50 plus tax, you may be asked to assist in recording sightings, data that can be shared with local and international organizations. Although there are resident whale and dolphin populations, more species can be observed from November through February. Turtle-watching trips are also popular.

The **Anchorage Dive & Whale Watch Center** (⊠ *Anchorage Hotel, Castle Comfort* ☎ *767/448–2638* ⊕ *www.anchoragehotel.dm*) offers whale-watching trips.

Dive Dominica (⊠ *Castle Comfort Lodge, Castle Comfort* ☎ *767/448–2188* ⊕ *www.divedominica.com*) is a major whale-watching operator.

Dominican Republic

WORD OF MOUTH

"The Punta Cana area lends itself more to those looking for the type of vacation where the resort has everything and one never has to go outside the gates. Note the nearest city, Higuey, is about a 40-minute drive away. Beyond the resorts is mostly empty country-side. You can literally walk for miles along the beach. . . ."

—Steelersfan

WELCOME TO DOMINICAN REPUBLIC

Cofresí Beach
Luperón Beach
Montecristi
Guayubin
Puerto Plata
Mt. Isabel de Torres
Gregorie Luperón International Airport

20
8 **16** **19** Playa Dorada
7
Sosúa **14** **15**
13
Cabarete Beach
1 - **6**
8 - **12**
Cabarete
Cabrera
Cabo Francés Viejo
Laguna Grí-Grí
Playa Grande
Bahía Escocesa
7 **6**
Las Terrenas
Nagua

9 Santiago
Moca
La Vega Vieja
San Francisco de Macorís

Pico Duarte

HAITI

HISPANIOLA

← TO HAITI

Jarabacoa

Bahía de Samaná
Sabana de la Mar

Los Haitises National Park

San Juan

Monte Plata

Lago Enriquillo
Neiba
Duvergé
Barahona
Bahoruco Beach

Azua
San Cristóbal
Bani
Pto. Palenque

Las Américas International Airport

Boca Chica
Juan Dolio

Santo Domingo
see detail map

Bahía de Ocoa

Caribbean Sea

0 — 50 miles
0 — 75 km

Oviedo
Cabo Beata

Like the merengue seen on all the dance floors in Santo Domingo, the Dominican Republic is charismatic yet sensuous, energetic yet elegant. The charm of the people adds special warmth: a gracious wave of greeting here, a hand-rolled cigar tapped with a flourish there. Dazzling smiles just about everywhere will quickly beguile you.

LA ISLA ESPAÑOLA

The Dominican Republic covers the eastern two-thirds of the island of Hispaniola (Haiti covers the other third). At 18,765 square mi (48,730 square km), it's the second-largest Caribbean country (only Cuba is larger), and with more than 8.8 million people, the second-most-populous country, too. It was explored by Columbus on his 1492 voyage to the New World.

Restaurants ▼
Ali's Surf Camp **1**
Cabahá **6**
Castle Club **5**
El Mambo Social Club . .**10**
EZE **2**
Il Pasticcio **9**
Lucia ....,, ...**8**
Mares Restaurant **7**
Miró **3**
Restaurant at Natura Cabana **4**

Hotels ▼
Barcelo Puerto Plata . .**19**
Blue Bay Villa Dorada **17**
Casa Colonial **16**
Casa de Campo **1**
Coyamar **7**
Dreams La Romana **2**
Gran Ventana Beach Resort **18**
Hotel Casa Valeria **15**

Hotel El Magnifico **12**
Iberostar Costa Dorada **20**
Iberostar Hacienda Dominicus ...**3**
Natura Cabana **9**
Ocean Point ......,, ..**0**
Península House **6**
Sea Horse Ranch **13**
Velero Beach Resort ...**11**
Victorian House **14**
Villa Serena **5**
Villa Taina **10**
Viva Wyndham Dominicus Palace **4**

KEY	
↘	Beaches
◤	Dive Sites
1	Restaurants
⒈	Hotels

TOP REASONS TO VISIT DOMINICAN REPUBLIC

1 **Great Beaches.** There are some 1,000 mi of excellent, beaches, some of which are pearl-white.

2 **Great Value.** You'll find the best-value all-inclusive resorts in the Caribbean here.

3 **Myriad Water Sports.** Every imaginable activity—world-class golf, horseback riding, white-water rafting, surfing, diving, windsurfing, and more—is available here.

4 **Friendly People.** The genuine hospitality of the people and their love of norteamericanos.

5 **Happening Nightlife.** The Dominicans love to party, dance, drink, and have a good time at happening bars and clubs.

DOMINICAN REPUBLIC PLANNER

Logistics	Getting to the Dominican Republic

Logistics

Getting to the Dominican Republic: The D.R. has six major international airports. Plan your air travel carefully so you don't end up flying into Punta Cana when you are staying at Casa de Campo, a two-hour-plus drive. Travel between the island's many developed tourism zones can be arduous and expensive, with few domestic flights available.

Hassle Factor: Low for popular destinations. High for off-the-beaten-path places.

Getting Around on the Island: Most travelers to the Dominican Republic take guided tours or participate in organized excursions. Independent travel is easier if you rent a car, but car rentals are expensive and signage bad (and some working knowledge of Spanish is strongly advisable). For longer distances, buses are the best alternative, but locally taxis are widely available in all major resort areas.

On the Ground: Most travelers book packages that include airport transfers. Otherwise, you'll have to take a local taxi, which can be quite expensive.

Getting to the Dominican Republic

Nonstop Flights: Atlanta (Delta, Airtran), Boston (JetBlue), Charlotte (US Airways), Fort Lauderdale (Spirit), Miami (American), New York–JFK (American, JetBlue), New York–Newark (Continental, JetBlue), Philadelphia (US Airways). Some flights connect in San Juan or Miami.

Airlines: Air Antilles Express (☎ 809/621–8888). **Air Caraïbes** (☎ 809/621–8888). **AirTran Airways** (☎ 809/959–3014). **American Airlines/American Eagle** (☎ 809/200–5151 in Santo Domingo, toll-free elsewhere in D.R.). **Continental** (☎ 809/262–1060). **Delta** (☎ 809/200–9191). **JetBlue** (☎ 809/200–9898). **LIAT** (☎ 809/621–8888). **Spirit** (☎ 809/381–4111). **US Airways** (☎ 809/540–0505).

Charter Airlines: Aerodomca (✉ La Isabela International Dr. Joaquin Balaguer, Higüero ☎ 809/567–1195). **Air Century** (✉ La Isabela International Dr. Joaquin Balaguer, Higüero ☎ 809/566–0888 ⊕ www.aircentury.com). **DominicanShuttles.com** (✉ Las Américas ☎ 809/738–3014 or 809/481–0707 ⊕ www.DominicanShuttles.com). **Helidosa Helicopters** (✉ Punta Cana ☎ 809/688–0744 ✉ Puerto Plata ☎ 809/320–2009 ⊕ www.helidosa.com).

Airports and Transfers: If you book a package through a travel agent, your airport transfer fee will almost certainly be included. **DominicanShuttles.com** (✉ Las Américas ☎ 809/738–3014 or 809/481–0707 ⊕ www.DominicanShuttles.com) offers car service from Las Américas to most major destinations in the D.R. If you book independently, you will have to take a taxi, rent a car, or hire a private driver-guide like **Dre Broeders** (☎ 809/399–5766).

Airports: Cibao International Airport (STI) in Santiago; **El Catey International Airport** (AZS) in Catey, Samaná; **Gregorio Luperon International Airport** (POP) in Puerto Plata; **La Isabella International Dr. Joaquin Balaguer** (DHG) in Higüero; **La Romana/Casa de Campo International Airport** (LRM) in La Romana; **Las Américas International Airport** (SDQ) in Santo Domingo; and **Punta Cana International Airport** (PUJ) in Punta Cana.

11

Getting Around the Dominican Republic

Bus Travel: Privately owned buses are the cheapest way to get around the country (for example, one-way bus fare from Santo Domingo to Puerto Plata is about $8). The companies make regular runs to Santiago, Puerto Plata, Punta Cana, and other destinations from Santo Domingo. Frequent service from Santo Domingo to the town of La Romana is provided by Express Bus, leaving every hour on the hour from 5 am to 9 pm. However, there's no office and no phone, though a ticket taker will take your $4 just before departure. Travel time is about 1¾ hours. Once in town, you can take a taxi from the bus stop to your resort.

Metro Buses (☎ 809/566–7126 in Santo Domingo, 809/586–6062 in Puerto Plata, 809/587–4711 in Santiago) deluxe buses have a more upscale clientele. **Caribe Tours** (☎ 809/221–4422) is favored by locals and families. Buses are often filled to capacity, and the bus music can be loud.

Linea Gladys (☎ 809/539–2134, 809/565–1223 in Santo Domingo) is a small bus line that will get you from the capital to Constanza. (The fare is about $9.)

Espreso Bavaro (☎ 809/682–9670) buses depart from Plaza Los Girasoles at Avenida Máximo Gómez at Juan Sánchez Ruiz; the buses are not the best, but only cost $5. If you're going to one of the Punta Cana resorts, you get off at the stop before the last and take a cab waiting at the taxi stand.

Driving: Driving in the D.R. can be a harrowing and expensive experience; we don't recommend that the typical vacationer rent a car. It's best if you don't drive outside the major cities at night. If you must, use extreme caution, especially on narrow, unlighted mountain roads.

Major Car-rental Agencies: The major agencies can be found in most of the island's airports. **Avis** (⊕ www.avis.com). **Budget** (☎ 800/472–3325 ⊕ www.budget.com). **Europcar** (✉ Las Américas Airport ☎ 809/549–0942 ✉ Gregorio Luperon International Airport, Puerto Plata ☎ 809/586–7979 ✉ Punta Cana International Airport, Bavaro, Punta Cana ☎ 809/686–2861). **Hertz** (☎ 800/654–3001 ⊕ www.hertz.com).

Local Car-rental Agencies: MC Auto Rental Car (✉ Las Américas Airport ☎ 809/549–8911 ⊕ www.mccarrental.com). **McBeal** (✉ Santo Domingo ☎ 809/688–6518). **Nelly Rent-a-Car** (✉ Las Américas Airport ☎ 809/530–0036, 800/526–6684 in U.S.).

Driving Tips

Driving in the D.R. can be a harrowing and expensive experience; we don't recommend that the typical vacationer rent a car. It's best if you don't even drive outside the major cities at night. If you must, use extreme caution, especially on narrow, unlighted mountain roads.

Taxi Travel

Hotel taxis are the best option. Carry small bills; drivers rarely have change. Recommendable radio-taxi companies in Santo Domingo are Tecni-Taxi (which also operates in Puerto Plata) and Apolo. **Tecni-Taxi** (☎ 809/567–2010, 809/566–7272 in Santo Domingo, 809/320–7621 in Puerto Plata) charges RD$240 per hour but will offer hourly rates only before 6 pm. **Apolo Taxi** (☎ 809/537–0000, 809/537–1245 for a limo, which must be booked far in advance) charges RD$280 per hour, day or night. **Taxi-Cabarete** (☎ 809/571–0767 in Cabarete) is a recommended operator in Cabrete.

Taxi-Queen (☎ 809/570–0000, 809/233–3333 in Santiago) works with the Santiago hotels; its prices are especially reasonable. The going rate for a taxi between Sosúa and Cabarete is $12. **Taxi-Tourismo** (☎ 809/829–3007 in Santiago) services the Cibao Airport in Santiago, charges $80 to Sosúa and $90 to Cabarete, and has larger vehicles, mostly SUVs and minivans.

DOMINICAN REPUBLIC PLANNER

Fast Facts	Essentials

Fast Facts

Banks and Exchange Services: Currency is the Dominican peso (written RD$). At this writing, the exchange rate is approximately RD$36 to US$1. You will not need to change money unless you plan to travel independently around the D.R. Banco Popular has many locations throughout the country, with ATMs that accept international cards.

Electricity: 110–120 volts/60 cycles, the same as in the U.S.

Emergency Services: Ambulance and Fire (📞 911). **Police** (📞 809/586-2804 in Puerto Plata, 711 in Santo Domingo, 809/571-2233 in Sosúa).

Passport Requirements: All U.S. citizens must carry a valid passport. Additionally, all visitors must have a valid tourist card, which costs $10 (purchased on arrival in cash with U.S. currency only).

Weddings: No residency requirements. Blood tests are not mandatory. Original birth certificates and passports are required. Divorce certificates and proof that the bride and groom are single must be stamped by the Dominican Consulate. Documents must be submitted two weeks prior to wedding and translated into Spanish.

Essentials

Health: Never drink tap water in the D.R. (look for a hotel or restaurant that has earned an *H* for food-service hygiene or that has a Crystal America certification). Don't buy from the street vendors. Use mosquito repellant to protect yourself from mosquito-borne illnesses; long sleeves and long pants also help.

Mail: Airmail postage to North America for a letter or postcard is RD$40; letters may take more than two weeks to reach their destination or never make it. If you need to send a package home, it's more reliable to use FedEx or DHL, though they cost a small fortune.

Safety: Violent crime is rare. Nevertheless, poverty is everywhere in the D.R., and petty theft, pick-pocketing, and purse snatching are a concern. Pay attention, especially when leaving a bank or casino. Take hotel-recommended taxis at night. Don't be alarmed by the armed security guards at clubs and restaurants; it's a precautionary measure.

Taxes: Americans must purchase a $10 tourist card upon arrival (payable in U.S. dollars only); the departure tax of $20 is almost always included in the price of your airline ticket. The government tax (IBIS) is a whopping 16% and is added to almost everything—bills at restaurants, hotels, sports activities, rental cars, and even many items at the supermarkets.

Telephones: To call the D.R. from the United States, dial 1–809, and the local number. From the D.R. you also need dial only 1–809, then the number. To make a local call, you must dial 809 plus the seven-digit number (dial 1–809 if you are calling a cell phone). Directory assistance is 1411.

Tipping: A 10% service charge is included in all hotel and restaurant bills. In restaurants, the bill will say *propino incluido* or simply *servis*. Even then it's still expected that you will tip an extra 5% to 10% if the service was good. Hotel maids typically get $1–$2 per day; taxi drivers, 10%; skycaps and hotel porters, $1 per bag.

Where to Stay

A hotel in **Santo Domingo** allows you to enjoy the capital's great restaurants, nightlife, and historical sights, but most travelers visit the busy, overwhelming city as a day trip.

Boca Chica and **Juan Dolio** offer some of the island's cheapest—but most mediocre—all-inclusives, along with crowded beaches.

La Romana has Casa de Campo as well as a few resorts on other, better beaches, like on Bayahibe Bay; the region is within reasonable striking distance of Santo Domingo for those needing a taste of history to go with their *plátanos* (plantains).

The isolated, though beautiful, **Barahona** region offers a respite from development and overcrowding but is more than a three-hour drive from Santo Domingo.

Punta Cana reigns supreme for its many reasonably priced and now luxurious all-inclusives; it's better for those looking for a resort-based vacation than for the adventurous.

Samaná is somewhat isolated, less developed, and more bohemian. It is easier to reach now, with more flights arriving into the new El Catey International Airport, 25 mi (40 km) west of Samaná, and the new two-lane toll highway from Santo Domingo, with drive time just about two hours.

Playa Dorada, the D.R.'s original resort area, is still a complex of decent all-inclusives with a well-rated golf course, but more-independent-minded travelers (and all windsurfers) may prefer **Sosúa** and **Cabarete,** where you'll still find a few charming independent inns and small resorts.

HOTEL AND RESTAURANT PRICES

Restaurant prices are for a main course at dinner and include any taxes or service charges. Hotel prices are per night for a double room in high season, excluding taxes, service charges, and meal plans (except at all-inclusives).

WHAT IT COSTS IN U.S. DOLLARS

	¢	$	$$	$$$	$$$$
Restaurants	under $8	$8–$12	$12–$20	$20–$30	over $30
Hotels	under $150	$151–$275	$276–$375	$376–$475	over $475

When to Go

The D.R. is busy year-round. During the somewhat quieter summer season, Europeans keep rates high from mid-June through August. However, in late spring (after Easter until early June) and early fall (September to October—peak rainy season, with hurricanes a threat) you can get good deals.

Unlike on many islands, where rain showers are usually passing thing, the rains In the D.R. can linger, especially from June through November.

One of the largest cultural events in the country is the annual **Jazz Festival** in November, which draws enthusiasts from all over the world to the North Coast.

Carnival celebrations are held in Santiago and La Vega during the week before Lent.

The **Festival del Merengue** electrifies Santo Domingo in late July and early August.

Visitor Information: Dominican Republic Tourist Office (☎ 212/588–1012 in New York City, 305/444–4592 in Miami, 888/374–6361 ⊕ www. godominicanrepublic.com). **Oficina de Turismo (Tourist Office)** (✉ Jose del Carmen Ariza 46, Puerto Plata ☎ 809/586–3676). **Secretary of Tourism** (✉ Secretaria de Estado de Turismo, Edificios Gubernamentales, Av. México, at corner of Av. 30 de Marzo, Gazcue, Santo Domingo ☎ 809/221–4660).

11

DOMINICAN REPUBLIC BEACHES

Its beaches are what put the D.R. on the touristic sonar. The east coast beaches (near Punta Cana, Juanillo, Bavaro), which are washed by the Caribbean, rival any in the Antilles—possibly the world. The government partnered with the hospitality industry and beautified many beaches not as naturally endowed. Think cosmetic surgery. Think hundreds of millions of dollars.

(Above) Kitesurfing the waters of Punta Cana. (Opposite page bottom) Kiteboarding the waves of Cabrete. (Opposite page top) Looking down on Cabrete Beach.

The Dominican Republic has more than 1,000 mi (1,600 km) of beaches, including the Caribbean's longest stretch of white sand: Punta Cana–Bavaro. Many beaches are accessible to the public (in theory, all beaches in this country, from the high-water mark down, are open to everyone) and may tempt you to stop for a swim. That's part of the uninhibited joy of this country. Do be careful, though: some have dangerously strong currents, which may be the reason why they are undeveloped.

WHAT'S YOUR PREFERENCE?

Is white sand a must? Then you are talking the Punta Cana region. If you can go nearly white, say, a light taupe, then it's the southeast coast. Bayahibe, with its half-crescent beaches, is a charmer. Juan Dolio's Villas de Mar beach has been reborn with tons of white sand trucked in. The amber sands of Playa Dorada and Cabarete have also been enhanced with truckloads of white sand.

Playa Bahoruco. This isolated, gorgeous stretch of virgin beach goes on for miles in either direction, with rugged cliffs dropping to golden sand and warm, blue water. It's a wild, undeveloped Caribbean beach, but many sections are pebbly, so you need surf shoes for swimming. In nearby San Rafael, are beach shacks where you can buy meals of fresh fish, even whole sea bass in coconut sauce. ⊠ *Carretera La Costa, Km 17, 8 mi (13 km) south of Barahona.*

Playa Boca Chica. You can walk far out into the gin-clear waters protected by coral reefs. Unfortunately, some areas are cluttered with plastic furniture, pizza stands, and cottages. If you're staying in the capital, this is the closest good beach. Grab lunch at one of the larger beachfront restaurants like El Pelicano or nearby, the trendy waterfront restaurants Boca Marina or Neptuno's Club. ⊠ *Autopista Las Americas, 21 mi (34 km) east of Santo Domingo, Boca Chica.*

Playa Cabarete. Follow the coastal road east from Playa Dorada to find this beach, which has strong waves and ideal, steady winds (from 15 to 20 knots), making it an integral part of the international windsurfing circuit. Segments are strips of golden sand punctuated only by palm trees. In the most commercial area, restaurants and bars are back-to-back, spilling onto the sand. The informal scene is young and fun,

with expats and tourists from every imaginable country. ⊠ *Sosúa–Cabarete road, Cabarete.*

Playa Dorada. On the north's Amber Coast, this is one of the D.R.'s most established resort areas. Each hotel has its own slice of the beach, which is soft beige sand, with lots of reefs for snorkeling. Gran Ventana Beach Resort, which is on a point, marks the end of the major hotel development. The Atlantic waters are great for windsurfing, waterskiing, and fishing. ⊠ *Off Autopista Luperon, 10 mins east of Puerto Plata, Playa Dorada.*

Playa Grande. On the North Coast, between the towns of Río San Juan and Cabrera, is this long stretch of powdery sand. The public entrance is about a mile after Playa Grande Golf Course, at Km 9. Here, the beach is on a lovely cove, with towering cliffs on both sides. A few beach shacks fry up fresh fish and keep the beer on ice. An outcropping separates this beach from Playa Precioso. During the week you'll have little company, but on Sunday afternoons the locals are here in full force. ⊠ *Carretera Río San Juan–Cabrera, Km 11.*

Playa Las Terrenas. On the north coast of the Samaná Peninsula, tall palms list toward the sea, and the beach is extensive and postcard perfect, with crystalline waters and soft, golden sand. There's plenty of color—vivid blues, greens, and yellows—as well as colorful characters.

A beach on Isla Saona island, a national park just off the tip of the southeastern coast

To the west is Playa El Cosón, opposite Cayo Ballena, a great whale-watching spot (from January to April). Samaná has some of the country's best beaches and drop-dead scenery, the rough roads notwithstanding. ⊠ *Carretera Las Terrenas, Las Terrenas.*

Playa Sosúa. Sosúa Bay is a gorgeous, natural harbor with coral reefs and dive sites, about a 20-minute drive from Puerto Plata. Swimming is delightful, except after a heavy rain when litter floats in. From the beach you can see mountains in the background, the cliffs that surround the bay, and seemingly miles of coastline. Snorkeling from the beach is good, but the best spots are farther offshore, closer to the reefs. (Don't bother going to Three Rocks.) Unfortunately, the backdrop is a string of tents where hawkers push souvenirs, snacks, drinks, and water-sports equipment rentals. Lounge chairs can usually be had for RD$75. ⊠ *Carretera Puerto Plata–Sosúa, Sosúa.*

Punta Cana. The area encompasses Cabeza de Torres, Playa Bavaro, and continues all the way around the peninsula to Playa de Uvero Alto. Each hotel has its own strip of sand with rows of chaise longues, and you can call in advance for a day pass. The stretch between Club Med and the Puntacana Resort and Club is one of the most beautiful. Playa El Cortecito is more how life used to be, with fishermen bringing in their catch. The public beach at Macao is no longer a good option, having been taken over by four-wheeler excursions. A rough road leads to more-deserted stretches in the Uvero Alto area, but outside of the resorts there are few services. ⊠ *Off Autopista Las Americas, east of Higüey, Punta Cana.*

By Eileen Robinson Smith

Dominicans will extend a gracious welcome, saying, "This is your home!" and indeed are happy to share their beautiful island bathed by the Atlantic Ocean to the north and the Caribbean Sea to the south. Among its most precious assets are 1,000 mi (1,600 km) of gorgeous beaches studded with coconut palms and sands ranging from pearl white to golden brown to volcanic black. The Caribbean sun kisses this exotic land, which averages 82°F year-round. It's a fertile country blessed with resources, particularly cocoa, coffee, rum, tobacco, and sugarcane.

A land of contrasts, the Dominican Republic has mountain landscapes, brown rivers with white-water rapids, rain forests full of wild orchids, and fences of multicolor bougainvillea. Indigenous species from crocodiles to the green cockatoo, symbol of the island, live in these habitats. Bird-watchers, take note: there are 29 endemic species flying around here.

The contrasts don't stop with nature. You can see signs of wealth, for the upper strata of society lives well indeed. In the capital, the movers and shakers ride in chauffeur-driven silver Mercedes. On the country roads you'll be amazed that four people with sacks of groceries and a stalk of bananas can fit on a smoky old *motoconcho* (motorbike-taxi). This is a land of *mestizos* who are a centuries-old mix of native Indians, Spanish colonists, and African slaves, plus every other nationality that has settled here, from Italian to Arabic.

Accommodations offer a remarkable range—surfers' camps, exclusive boutique hotels, and amazing megaresorts that have brought the all-inclusive hotel to the next level of luxury. Trendy restaurants, art galleries, boutique hotels, and late-night clubs help make Santo Domingo a superb urban vacation destination. Regrettably, most Dominican towns and cities are neither quaint nor particularly pretty, and poverty still prevails. However, the standard of living has really come up along with the growth of North American tourism. Food prices are higher than they have been, which means prices at all-inclusive resorts are up; however, a vacation in the D.R. can still be a relative bargain. Even the new, small boutique hotels are still well priced for the Caribbean.

Christopher Columbus first claimed the island for Spain on his first New World voyage in 1492 and wrecked

> **LANGUAGE**
>
> Spanish is spoken in the D.R. Most staff at major tourist attractions and front-desk personnel in most major hotels speak English. Outside the popular tourist establishments, English is spoken less frequently.

his flagship, the *Santa Maria,* on its Atlantic shore on Christmas Eve; later, his brother Bartolomeo founded Santo Domingo de Guzmán (1496), the first city in the New World. With some 300 examples of Spanish colonial architecture, the Zona Colonial was declared a World Heritage Site by UNESCO in 1990. A throbbing microcosm, there are 100 square blocks of history, very much alive more than five centuries later.

The vibrant lifestyle of this sun-drenched Latin-Caribbean country, where Spanish is the national language and where the people are hospitable and good-natured, makes the Dominican Republic a different cultural experience. If you pick up the rhythm of life here, as freewheeling as the island's trademark merengue, this can be a beguiling tourist destination.

Islanders have an affinity for all things American: the people, language (more and more speak English), electronic products, fashions, and lifestyle. A great Dominican dream is to go to the States as a baseball player (shortstop or a pitcher) and become the next Sammy Sosa, then return to be a philanthropist in one's own hometown.

EXPLORING THE DOMINICAN REPUBLIC

SANTO DOMINGO

Parque Independencia separates the old city from modern Santo Domingo, a sprawling, noisy city with a population of close to 2 million. In the making is a new ethnic neighborhood, a Chinatown to resemble San Francisco's. This predominately Asian neighborhood is just north of the Zona Colonial on Calles Mella and Duarte. Chinese businesses, particularly restaurants, already exist, and a museum and a plaza honoring Confucius are planned.

Note: Hours and admission charges to sites are erratic.

Fodor'sChoice   Spanish civilization in the New World began in Santo Domingo's
    ★   12-block **Zona Colonial.** As you stroll its narrow streets, it's easy to imagine this old city as it was when the likes of Columbus, Cortés, and Ponce de León walked the cobblestones, pirates sailed in and out, and colonists were settling. Tourist brochures tout that "history comes alive here"—a surprisingly truthful statement. Every Thursday to Sunday night at 8:30, a typical folkloric show is staged at Parque Colón and

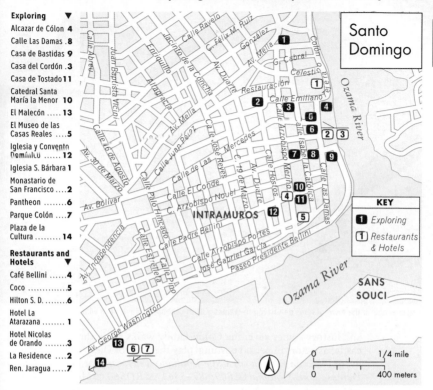

Plaza España. During the Christmas holidays an artisans' fair and live music concerts take place. Ask about other cultural events.

A fun horse-and-carriage ride throughout the Zone costs $25 for an hour. The steeds are no thoroughbreds, but they clip right along, though any commentary will be in Spanish. You can also negotiate to use them as a taxi, say, to go down to the Malecón. The drivers usually hang out in front of the Hostal Nicolas de Ovando. You can get a free walking-tour map and brochures in English at the Secretaria de Estado de Turismo office at Parque Colón (Columbus Park), where you may be approached by freelance, English-speaking guides, who will want to make it all come alive for you. They'll work enthusiastically for $20 an hour for four people. Wear comfortable shoes.

WHAT TO SEE

Alcazar de Colón. The castle of Don Diego Colón, built in 1517, has 40-inch-thick coral-limestone walls. The Renaissance-style structure, with its balustrade and double row of arches, has strong Moorish, Gothic, and Isabelline influences. The 22 rooms are furnished in a style to which the viceroy of the island would have been accustomed—right down to the dishes and the viceregal shaving mug. Multilingual audio guides can be rented for RD$50 and are strongly recommended Costumed docents appear on Saturday morning and on Saturday night,

The architecture in the town of Altos de Chavón re-creates a 16th-century Mediterranean village.

and history comes alive: the Colón family walks again throughout the castle, as actors in period costume play the roles of Diego and his family. ✉ *Plaza de España off Calle Emiliano Tejera at foot of Calle Las Damas, Zona Colonial* ☎ *809/687–5361* 🎫 *RD$60* ☉ *Mon.–Sat. 9–5 and 8 pm–midnight, Sun. 9–4. Closed if no cruise ship in port.*

★ **Calle Las Damas.** The Ladies Street was named after the elegant ladies of the court who, in the Spanish tradition, promenaded in the evening. Here you can see a sundial dating from 1753 and the Casa de los Jesuitas, which houses a fine research library for colonial history as well as the **Institute for Hispanic Culture**; admission is free, and it's open weekdays from 8 to 4:30. If you follow the street going toward the Malecón, you will pass a picturesque alley fronted by a wrought-iron gate that has perfectly maintained colonial structures that are owned by the Catholic Church.

Casa de Bastidas. There's a lovely inner courtyard here with tropical plants and galleries for temporary exhibitions. ✉ *Calle Las Damas off Calle El Conde, Zona Colonial* ☎ *No phone* 🎫 *Free* ☉ *Tues.–Sun. 9–5.*

Casa del Cordón. This structure, built in 1503, is the Western Hemisphere's oldest surviving stone house. Columbus's son Diego Colón, viceroy of the colony, and his wife lived here until the alcazar was finished. It was in this house, too, that Sir Francis Drake was paid a ransom to prevent him from totally destroying the city. ✉ *Calle Emiliano Tejera at Calle Isabel la Católica, within Banco Popular, Zona Colonial* ☎ *809/544–8915* 🎫 *Free* ☉ *Weekdays 9–4.*

Casa de Tostado. The house was built in the early 16th century and was the residence of writer Don Francisco Tostado. Note its unique

QUIET TIME

It's *tranquila* in the Zona Colonial at siesta time. Most Dominicans have never given up the habit of taking a siesta after their main midday meal, a vestige of their Spanish heritage. You will be able to hear the distinctive flutter of pigeons' wings as they peck for crumbs among the dramatic ruins of the Bari Hospital. The little old tailor in his ancient shop closes the narrow doors from the inside.

The coconut boys and the frying empanada men; the barbers in their gossipy, 1950s-vintage shops; the old women sitting on their white balconies adorned with fuchsia bougainvillea: they'll all be awake soon, but for now you can't help but love the stillness.

twin Gothic windows. It houses the Museo de la Familia Dominicana (Museum of the Dominican Family), which has exhibits on well-heeled 19th-century Dominican society. The house, garden, and antiquities have all been restored. ⊠ *Calle Padre Bellini 22, near Calle Arzobispo Meriño, Zona Colonial* ☎ *809/689–5000* ☑ *RD$40* ☉ *Mon.–Sat. 9–4.*

Catedral Santa María la Menor. The coral-limestone facade of the first cathedral in the New World towers over the south side of the Parque Colón. Spanish workmen began building the cathedral in 1514, but left to search for gold in Mexico. The church was finally finished in 1540. Its facade is composed of architectural elements from the late Gothic to the lavish plateresque style. Inside, the high altar is made of hammered silver. At this writing, a museum is being built for the cathedral's treasures. ⊠ *Calle Arzobispo Meriño, Zona Colonial* ☎ *809/689–1920* ☑ *Free* ☉ *Mon.–Sat. 9–4; Sun. Masses begin at 6 am.*

El Malecón. Avenida George Washington, better known as the Malecón, runs along the Caribbean and has tall palms, cafés, high-rise hotels, and sea breezes.

★ **El Museo de las Casas Reales.** This is a remarkable museum that helps you understand the New World that was discovered by Columbus and the ensuing history of exploration and colonization in the 16th century. Exhibits include everything from Taíno archaeological finds to colonial artifacts, coins salvaged from wrecks of Spanish galleons, authentic colonial furnishings, and a collection of weapons. Additionally, the building in which the collection is housed is one of the most handsome colonial edifices remaining in Santo Domingo and has undergone a careful and complete restoration. Built in the Renaissance style, it was the seat of Spanish government and housed the governor's office as well as the Royal Court. It has beautiful windows done in the plateresque style. An art gallery with rotating art shows is also resident. As a popular upscale wedding venue, it is truly magical when candlelighted by night. ⊠ *Calle Las Damas, right before Plaza de Espana, Zona Colonial* ☎ *809/682–4202* ☑ *RD$50* ☉ *Tues.–Sun. 9–5.*

Iglesia Santa Bárbara. This combination church and fortress, the only one of its kind in Santo Domingo, was completed in 1562. It is now open only for masses. ✉ *Av. Mella, between Calle Isabel la Católica and Calle Arzobispo Meriño, Zona Colonial* ☎ *809/682–3307* 🖬 *Free* ⊘ *Mon.–Sat. 6 am– 6:45 pm, Sun. 8 am–10 am.*

Monasterio de San Francisco. Constructed between 1512 and 1544, the San Francisco Monastery contained the church, convent, and hospital of the Franciscan order. Sir Francis Drake's demolition squad significantly damaged the building in 1586, and in 1673 an earthquake nearly finished the job, but when it's floodlighted at night, the eerie ruins are dramatic indeed. The Spanish government has donated money to turn this into a beautiful cultural center, but we are still waiting. On designated Sunday nights, the music plays and it is an old-fashioned block party. Zone residents mingle with expats and tourists, who are snapping pictures of the octogenarians dancing the meringue and bachata. Nice! ✉ *Calle Hostos at Calle Emiliano, Zona Colonial* ☎ *809/687–4722.*

Pantheon Nacional. The National Pantheon (circa 1714) was once a Jesuit monastery and later a theater. The real curiosity here is the military guard who stays as still as the statues, despite the schoolchildren who try to make him flinch. ✉ *Calle Las Damas, near Calle de Las Mercedes, Zona Colonial* ☎ *809/689–6010* 🖬 *Free* ⊘ *Mon.–Sat. 8 am–9 pm.*

Plaza de la Cultura. Landscaped lawns, modern sculptures, and sleek buildings make up the Plaza de la Cultura. There are several museums and a theater here.

The works of 20th-century Dominican and foreign artists are displayed in the **Museo de Arte Moderno** (☎ *809/687–2153*). Native sons include Elvis Aviles, an abstract painter whose works have a lot of texture. His art combines Spanish influences with Taíno Indian and other Dominican symbols. Tony Capellan is one of the best-known artists, representing the D.R. in major international exhibitions.

The **Museo del Hombre Dominicano** (☎ *809/687–3622*) traces the migrations of Indians from South America through the Caribbean islands.

The **Teatro Nacional** (☎ *809/687–3191*) stages fascinating performances in Spanish only, but don't let that stop you. When in Rome, you would go to an Italian opera, right? ✉ *Plaza de la Cultura, Gazcue* 🖬 *Museo de Arte Moderno RD$50, Museo del Hombre Dominicano RD$75* ⊘ *Tues.–Sun. 10–5.*

SOUTHEAST COAST

Las Américas Highway (built by the dictator Rafael Trujillo so his son could race his sports cars) runs east along the coast from Santo Domingo to La Romana—a two-hour drive. Midway are the well-established beach resorts like Juan Dolio, and Sammy Sosa's hometown, San Pedro de Macorís. East of La Romana are Punta Cana and Bavaro, glorious beaches on the sunrise side of the island. Along the way is Higüey, an undistinguished city notable only for its giant concrete cathedral and shrine (someone had a vision of the Virgin Mary here), which resembles a pinched McDonald's arch.

 Altos de Chavón. This re-creation of a 16th-century Mediterranean village sits on a bluff overlooking the Río Chavón, about 3 mi (5 km)

east of the main facilities of Casa de Campo. There are cobblestone streets lined with lanterns, wrought-iron balconies, wooden shutters, courtyards swathed with bougain-villea, and **Iglesia St. Stanislaus,** the romantic setting for many a Casa de Campo wedding. More than a museum piece, this village is a place where artists live, work, and play. Dominican and international

> **FLAT TIRE**
>
> Blowout? A *gomero* can make a flat tire round! There are many such fellows, because the rough roads are rubber-eaters. You will see their signs on the highways and if stranded in a town, just ask: *¿Donde esta un gomero?*

painters, sculptors, and artisans come here to teach sculpture, pottery, silk-screen printing, weaving, dance, and music at the school, which is affiliated with New York's Parsons School of Design. They work in their studios and crafts shops selling their finished wares. The village also has a new sports bar, a trendy dance club (Onno's of Cabarete), an amber museum, an archaeological museum, a chic new cigar lounge, a designer jewelry store, boutiques, and restaurants.

A 5,000-seat **amphitheater** (☎ *809/523–2424 for Kandela tickets* ⊕ *www.kandela.com.do*) features *Kandela,* a spectacular musical extravaganza showcasing the island's sensuous Afro-Caribbean dance moves, music, and culture. Concerts and celebrity performances by such singers as Julio Iglesias, his son Enrique, Sting, Andrea Bocelli, Il Divo, and the Pet Shop Boys share the amphitheater's schedule of events. Show dates vary to coincide with cruise-ship arrivals (usually Mon.); the price is $35 for adults, $15 for children up to 12 years old. Many people make dinner reservations at **La Piazzetta** (⊠ *Altos de Chavon* ☎ *809/523–3333*), the high-end Italian restaurant in Altos that belongs to Casa de Campo, before curtain call, as it is right near the amphi-theater. It is known for its antipasto selections, homemade pasta, and authentic regional dishes; its rustic ambience with ceramic tiles and cobblestone terrace is enlivened by strolling musicians.

Isla Saona. Off the east coast of Hispaniola lies this island, now a national park inhabited by sea turtles, pigeons, and other wildlife. Caves here were once used by Indians. The beaches are beautiful, and legend has it that Columbus once strayed here. Getting here, on catamarans and other excursion boats, is half the fun, but know that it can be a crowd scene. Vendors are allowed to bother visitors, and there are a number of beach shacks serving lunch and drinks. If you go from a resort, like Viva, it will have its own designated area and the hotel will transport the catered lunch by boat. The largest island in the national park, it is no longer as pristine as a national park should be, but of all the excursions, it is one of the better ones.

San Pedro de Macorís. The national sport and the national drink are both well represented in this city, an hour or so east of Santo Domingo. Some of the country's best baseball games are played in Tetelo Var-gas Stadium. Many Dominican baseball stars have their roots here, including George Bell, Tony Fernandez, Jose Río, and Sammy Sosa. The Macorís Rum distillery is on the eastern edge of the city. From 1913 through the 1920s this was a very important town—a cultural center—and mansions from that era are being restored by the Office of Cultural Patrimony, as are some remaining vestiges of 16th-century architecture and the town's cathedral, which has a pretense to Gothic architecture, even gargoyles. There is a nice promenade (the Malecón) along the port, and by night the beer and rum kiosks come alive. The Dominicans, Europeans, and now North Americans, who take self-catering apartments or condos in Juan Dolio, frequent San Pedro since it has the closest *supermercados* (Jumbo, Iberia—which also has a big pharmacy) and other small businesses.

SAMANÁ

In 1824 a sailing vessel called the *Turtle Dove*, carrying several hundred escaped American slaves, was blown ashore in the spot now occupied by **Santa Barbara de Samaná.** The survivors settled and prospered, and today their descendants number several thousand. The churches here are mostly Protestant; the worshippers live in villages called Bethesda, Northeast, and Philadelphia; and the language spoken is an odd 19th-century form of English mixed with Spanish.

Sportfishing in the Samaná area is considered among the best in the world. In addition, about 3,000 humpback whales winter off the coast of the Samaná Peninsula from December to March. Major whale-watching expeditions have been organized and boost the region's economy without scaring away the world's largest mammals. Postcard-perfect **Playa Las Terrenas** is a remote stretch of gorgeous, pristine Atlantic beaches on the North Coast, attracting surfers and windsurfers, the young and offbeat. There's a strong French influence here, with modest seafood restaurants, a dusty but burgeoning main street in the town, a small airfield, a couple of all-inclusive resorts, and several congenial smaller hotels right on the beach. If you're happy just hanging out, drinking rum, and soaking up the sun, this is the place.

A new highway (with tolls) connects Samaná to Santo Domingo; it's about a 2½-hour ride. El Catey International Airport, 45 minutes away from the town of Samaná, has mainly charter flights so far. Things, they are a-changing.

NORTH COAST

The Autopista Duarte ultimately leads (via a three- to four-hour drive) from Santo Domingo to the North Coast, sometimes called the Amber Coast because of its large, rich amber deposits. The coastal area around Puerto Plata, notably Playa Dorada, is a region of well-established, all-inclusive resorts and developments; the North Coast has more than 70 mi (110 km) of beaches, with condominiums and villas going up fast. The farther east you go from Puerto Plata and Sosúa, the prettier and less spoiled the scenery becomes. The autopista runs past Cabarete, a village that's a popular windsurfing haunt, and Playa Grande, which has a miraculously unspoiled white-sand beach.

Mt. Isabel de Torres. Southwest of Puerto Plata, this mountain soars 2,600 feet above sea level and is notable for its huge statue of Christ. Up there also are botanical gardens that, despite efforts, still are not memorable. You can choose to hire a knowledgeable English-speaking guide for $5 a person. A cable car takes you to the top for a spectacular view. Know that they usually wait until the cars are filled to capacity before going up—which makes them cozy; and should the electricity happen to go off, there is no backup generator. You should visit in the morning, preferably by 9 am; by afternoon, the cloud cover rolls in, and you can see practically nothing. Also be advised that the vendors are particularly tenacious. ⊠ *Off Autopista Duarte, follow signs* ☎ *No phone* ⊠ *Cable car RD$250* ☉ *Thurs.–Tues. 9–5.*

Puerto Plata. Although it has been sleeping for decades, this was a dynamic city in its heyday, and it is coming back. You can get a feeling for this past in the magnificent Victorian gazebo in the central **Parque Independencia.** Recently painted a crisp white, the park looks postcard pretty, with gleaming new statuary. On Puerto Plata's own Malecón, which has had a multimillion-dollar refurbishment, the **Fortaleza de San Felipe** protected the city from many a pirate attack and was later used as a political prison. Nearby, a new amphitheater is in the planning stages. The nearby **lighthouse** has been restored. Big changes are in store in this town, which is just realizing what it needs to do to become a tourist destination. The Office of Cultural Patrimony, which has done an admirable job of pulling the Zona Colonial from the darkness, is at work. Simultaneously, a group of private business owners and investors have developed a long-term plan for beautifying this city, which has hundreds of classic wooden gingerbread buildings. Mansions, including Casa Olivores and the Tapounet Family home, are being restored; a Victorian mansion on Calle Jose del Carmen is now a gallery and coffee shop. Architect Sara Garcia is redesigning the family home of Independence hero Gregory Luperon to create a museum for national heroes.

Change is afoot in the Playa Dorada hotel complex (7 mi [11 km] from town): several of the lower-priced all-inclusives, like Viva Wyndham's, have closed, and like Dorado Club, are reverting to short-term apartments. These apartments cater to independent travelers, who often fly in on JetBlue, rent cars, and, armed with maps, come into the city and spend time and money here.

The **Museo de Ambar Dominicano** (*Dominican Amber Museum*) is in a lovely old galleried mansion. It both displays and sells the D.R.'s national stone, semiprecious, translucent amber, which is actually fossilized pine resin that dates from about 50 million years ago, give or take a few millennia. Shops on the museum's first floor sell amber, souvenirs, and ceramics. Dominican amber is considered to be the finest in the world. If you buy from street vendors for a low price, you're probably buying plastic. ⊠ *Calle Duarte 61* ☎ *809/586–2848* ⊠ *RD$15* ☉ *Mon.–Sat. 9–5.*

Ocean World Adventure Park is a multimillion-dollar aquatic park in Cofresi with marine and wildlife interactive programs, including dolphin and sea lion shows and encounters, a tropical reef aquarium, stingrays, shark tanks, a rain forest, and a Tiger Grotto inhabited by Bengal tigers. Looking out to the sea, the buffet lunch is delightful but not included in the entrance fee. You don't have to come on a tour, but you must make advance reservations if you want to participate in one of the swims or encounters. The Royal Swim program (60 minutes) gives you the opportunity to swim and interact with dolphins. If you are brave enough for a shark and stingray encounter ($70), you can feed and touch them in the shark lagoon. If you're staying in the Puerto Plata or Cabarete area, ask at your hotel for tour schedules. Children must be at least age six for the dolphin swim, and a photo lab and video service can capture the moment. A private beach, locker room, splashy marina, Las Vegas–style casino, and fine-dining restaurant make for a fascinating mix. If you are staying at the nearby Lifestyle resorts, or the Be Live Carey (formerly Sun Village) transportation is free, and transfers from Sosúa or Cabarete are only $5. (⇨ *Casinos and Boating*). ⊠ *Off the autopista to Santiago at Cofresi sign, Cofresi* ☎ *809/291–1000 or 809/291–1111* ⊕ *www.oceanworld.net* ⊠ *$55, with many supplements for additional activities and encounters* ⊙ *Daily 9–5.*

Sosúa. This small community was settled during World War II by 600 Austrian and German Jews. After the war many of them returned to Europe or went to the United States, and most who remained married Dominicans. Only a few Jewish families reside in the community today, and there's only the original one-room wooden synagogue.

Sosúa is called Puerto Plata's little sister and consists of two communities—El Batey, the modern hotel development, and Los Charamicos, the old quarter—separated by a cove and one of the island's prettiest beaches. The sand is soft and white, the water crystal clear and calm. The walkway above the beach is packed with tents filled with souvenirs, pizzas, and even clothing for sale. The town had developed a reputation for prostitution, but much is being done to eliminate that and to clean up the more garish elements. Upscale condos and hotels are springing up, and the up-and-coming Dominican families are coming back to the big houses on the bay.

Museo Judio Sosúa chronicles the immigration and settlement of the Jewish refugees in the 1940s. This is a fascinating place, and depending on the docent, you may hear that the Jewish settlers experienced a certain amount of prejudice here when they arrived. The adjacent small wooden synagogue is the wedding spot for many Jewish couples from abroad. ⊠ *Calle Dr. Rosen at David Stern* ☎ *809/571–1386* ⊠ *RD$75* ⊙ *Weekdays 9–1 and 2–4.*

CIBAO VALLEY

The heavily trafficked four-lane highway north from Santo Domingo, known as the Autopista Duarte, cuts through the banana plantations, rice and tobacco fields, and royal poinciana trees of the Cibao Valley. Along the road are stands where a few pesos buy pineapples, mangoes, avocados, *chicharrones* (fried pork rinds), and fresh-fruit drinks.

Jarabacoa. Nature lovers should consider a trip to Jarabacoa, in the mountainous region known rather wistfully as the Dominican Alps. There's little to do in the town itself but eat and rest up for excursions on foot, horseback, or by motorbike taxi to the surrounding waterfalls

Hand-rolling cigars in the Cibao Valley.

and forests—quite incongruous in such a tropical country. Other activities include adventure tours, particularly white-water rafting or canoe trips, jeep safaris, and paragliding. Accommodations in the area are rustic but homey.

La Vega Vieja. Founded in 1495 by Columbus, La Vega is the site of one of the oldest settlements in the New World. You may find the tour of the ruins of the original settlement, Old La Vega, rewarding. About 3 mi (5 km) north of La Vega is Santo Cerro (Holy Mount), site of a miraculous apparition of the Virgin and therefore many local pilgrimages. The Convent of La Merced is here, and the views of the Cibao Valley are breathtaking. The town's remarkable Concepción de la Vega Church was constructed in 1992 to commemorate the 500th anniversary of the discovery of America. The unusual modern Gothic style—all curvaceous concrete columns, arches, and buttresses—is striking.

La Vega is also celebrated for its Carnival, featuring haunting devil masks. These papier-mâché creations are intricate, fanciful gargoyles painted in surreal colors; spiked horns and real cows' teeth lend an eerie authenticity. Several artisans work in dark, cramped studios throughout the area; their skills have been passed down for generations.

Santiago. The second city of the D.R., where many past presidents were born, sits about 90 mi (145 km) northwest of Santo Domingo and is about an hour's drive from Puerto Plata and 90 minutes from Cabarete via the scenic mountain road. An original route from centuries past, the four-lane highway between Santiago and Puerto Plata is dotted with sugar mills. The Office of Cultural Patrimony is overseeing their restoration. Although an industrial center, Santiago has a surprisingly charming, provincial feel; the women of Santiago are considered among the country's most beautiful. High on a plateau is an impressive monument honoring the restoration of the republic. Traditional yet progressive, Santiago is still relatively new to the tourist scene but already has several thriving restaurants and new hotels. It's definitely worth setting aside some time to explore the city. Colonial-style buildings—with wrought-iron details and tiled porticoes—date from as far back as the 1500s. Others are from the Victorian era, with the requisite gingerbread latticework and fanciful colors, and recent construction is nouveau Victorian. Santiago is the cigar-making center; the Fuente factory is here, though its cigars can be bought on the island only in special designated cigar stores and clubs. (If you see them for sale on the streets, they are counterfeit.)

Fodor'sChoice ★ You can gain an appreciation for the art and skill of Dominican cigar making by taking a tour of **E. León Jimenes Tabacalera** (✉ *Av. 27 de Febrero, Villa Progresso* ☎ *809/563–1111 or 809/535–5555*). A free tour takes approximately 90 minutes, and the factory is open daily from 9 to 5. Without question, the **Centro León** is a world-class cultural center for the Dominican arts. A postmodern building with an interior space full of light from a crystal dome, the center includes several attractions, including a multimedia biodiversity show, a museum dedicated to the history of the D.R., a simulated local market, a dramatic showcase of Dominican art and sculpture, galleries for special exhibits, a sculpture garden, an aviary, classrooms, a museum gift shop, and a replica of the León family's first cigar factory, where a dozen cigar rollers turn out handmade cigars (weekdays 8–4:30) and where cigars are sold. There's even a first-rate cafeteria. ✉ *Av. 27 de Febrero 146, Villa Progresso* ☎ *809/582–2315* ⊕ *www.centroleon.org.do* 💲 *RD$70, guides in English RD$180* ☉ *Exhibitions Tues.–Sun. 10–7, public areas daily 10–7.*

SOUTHWEST

Barahona. The drive west from Santo Domingo zigs and zags through small towns, passing coco and banana plantations until you get on the Carretera Azua, a fine highway with mountain views and fences of bougainvillea hiding fields of peppers and flowers. The city of Barahona is 120 mi (193 km) southwest of Santo Domingo, and about 3½ hours by car. It is the least cosmopolitan of the country's midsize cities, yet it is a college town. There is a Malecón (seafront promenade), which comes alive on weekends, where you can find popular seafood restaurants. It is west of the city, in the country, where simple pleasures and hostelries can be found. You can swim in the cascades of icy mountain rivers that flow down to beaches like San Rafael, just past Bahoruco, or submerge in hot thermal springs surrounded by dense foliage, *llanai* vines, and fruit trees. The Barahona region can be a tropical Garden of Eden.

CLOSE UP

Driving Yourself Happy in the D.R.

There is no course in Dominican culture more revealing than a drive from the north coast to the capital. Observe the smiles of entire families mounted on small motorbikes, driving, neither on the left side nor the right side, but on the *best* side of the road (hole-wise). Note the gua-gua, the public minibus, stopping to board or discharge passengers, neither on the left side nor the right side, but on the *shady* side of the road.

People sit on the road playing dominoes, waving joyfully at all who careen by, inches away. Imagine rounding a curve lined with verdant pastoral hillsides and suddenly realizing that your lane is six inches deep in almond husks (curing from the heat of the asphalt). With an intercity bus hurtling toward you at 100 klicks

(kph), options are to marry the bus, plunge into the drainage ditch, or skate across the nuts. Leaching vast quantities of adrenalin, you realize this passage truly tests the efficacy of your organic deodorant.

Finally, the approach to the capital expands the colorful, chaotic panorama to a multilane highway, with miniskirted girls walking astride the dotted lines hawking sweets, puppies, or cell-phone accessories (as talking without a headset is a serious crime hereabouts). As journeys go, this is one that roundly requires go-with-the-flow adaptability. With a strong sense of adventure, and humor, you just may enjoy this frightening, exhilarating, folkloric pilgrimage.

—Sunny Blueskyes

WHERE TO EAT

The island's culinary repertoire includes Spanish, Italian, Middle Eastern, Indian, Japanese, and *nueva cocina Dominicana* (contemporary Dominican cuisine). If seafood is on the menu, it's bound to be fresh. The dining scene in Santo Domingo is the best in the country and probably offers as fine a selection of restaurants as you will find anywhere in the Caribbean. Keep in mind that the touristy restaurants, such as those in the Colonial Zone, with mediocre fare and just-okay service, are becoming more and more costly, whereas the few fine-dining options here have lowered some of their prices—for example, La Residence now offers a daily chef's menu with three courses for about $22. Or you can order two generous appetizers for, say, $15. You will have caring service and be sequestered in luxe surroundings away from the tourist hustle. Know that *capitaleños* (residents of Santo Domingo) dress for dinner and dine late. The crowds pick up after 9:30 pm.

WHAT TO WEAR
In resort areas, shorts and bathing suits under beach wraps are usually (but not always) acceptable at breakfast and lunch. For dinner, long pants, skirts, and collared shirts are the norm. Restaurants tend to be more formal in Santo Domingo, both at lunch and at dinner, with trousers required for men and dresses suggested for women. Ties aren't required anywhere, but jackets are (even at the midday meal) in some of the finer establishments.

SANTO DOMINGO

$$ ✕ **Café Bellini.** This café has always
ITALIAN had a panache far and above its
counterparts, for the Italian own-
ers also have the adjacent furniture
design center. The modern, wicker-
weave barrel chairs and the contem-
porary art and light fixtures are all
achingly hip. It has recently had a
renovation and looks refreshed. The
menu is the same at lunch and din-
ner. The democratic pricing usually
offers pasta dishes, such as the trio
of raviolis (spinach, beet, and pump-
kin), for about $10, which works for
those on a slim budget. Also, know
that an amuse-bouche, perhaps a
tomato bruschetta, can usually suf-
fice as an appetizer. The addition of

grilled portobellos to a classic arugula-and-shaved-Parmesan salad is
brilliant. Main courses of meat or seafood are accompanied by pasta or
grilled vegetables and potato. You can enjoy French and Italian liquors
here (like pastis and grappa); dessert might be dark-chocolate mousse
and fresh mango sorbet. Service is laudable, as is the music. ✉ *Arzo-
bispo Merino, corner of Padre Bellini, Zona Colonial* ☎ *809/686–3387*
⚐ *Reservations essential* ☾ *Closed Sun. No lunch Mon.*

$$$ ✕ **La Residence.** This fine-dining enclave has always had the setting—
FRENCH Spanish colonial architecture, with pillars and archways overlooking a
★ courtyard—and an esoteric lunch-dinner menu. It has a French Certified Master Chef, Denis Schetrit (there are only 300 such designated
chefs in the world), who serves classic yet innovative cuisine. He bows
to more recent culinary trends while cleverly using local produce and
offering many moderately priced choices. The three-course, daily Menu
del Chef is less than $28, including tax. It could be brochettes of spit-
roasted duck, chicken au poivre, or vegetable risotto. You could start
with a salad of panfried young squid and segue way to a luscious French
pastry. You also get an amuse-bouche and excellent bread service. Veer
from the daily specials menu and prices can certainly go higher, but they
are still fair; even the grilled fillet and braised oxtail with foie gras sauce
and wild mushrooms is reasonable. Anything that chef Denis prepares is
heaven on a plate. Diners are serenaded by musicians and it's romantico;
service is now consistently good. ✉ *Hostal Nicolas de Ovando, Calle
Las Damas, Zona Colonial* ☎ *809/685–9955.*

PUNTA CANA

$$$$ ✕ **Blue Marlin.** Located in the Secrets Sanctuary Cap Cana (⇨ *Where
SEAFOOD to Stay*), Blue Marlin enjoys a setting like something from a fantasy
island. The pier that terminates in this dual-*palapa* (thatch-roof) restaurant could be in the South Pacific. Actually, it sits right over the

Caribbean's gentle waters and has a small fleet of fishing boats that harvest those waters daily. Fish specialties have been gleaned from around the world—France, Mexico, Peru, Spain, and New Orleans, with many dishes from the Pacific Rim. Grilled Caribbean lobster is the headliner on Wednesday night's "Lobster Festival" buffet. The most popular choices are the catches of the day, prepared as you like it (for example, mahimahi fillets steamed with ginger and soy, and baked whole red snapper) with sauce options. Salads are creative and clear the palate; appetizers are among the best offerings. Traditional sandwiches (not fish), burgers, sushi, and pizzas—some in the gourmet genre—are lunch faves. Nonhotel guests are welcome (no children) but must make reservations to pass through the security gates. ⊠ *Secrets Sanctuary Cap Cana Golf and Spa, Cap Cana, Playa Juanillo* ☎ *809/562–9191* ⚑ *Reservations essential.*

$$$$
MEDITERRANEAN
Fodor's Choice
★

✕ **La Yola.** Dining on a deck, gentle breeze blowing, over the Puntacana Marina, you feel as if you were actually aboard a *yola* (a small fishing boat). Using thatched cane for overhead shelter, and the sea as a backdrop, this restaurant has an utterly gratifying, open-air dining ambience. The cuisine features Mediterranean and Caribbean influences, and attentive service enhances an exceptional experience. Seafood and fish dominate the creative menu (you'll also find beef and chicken selections). For an appetizer, the spicy tuna tartare with guacamole relish starts you off with a pleasing burst of flavor and satisfying texture. Main plates, including the catch of the day—usually red snapper, grouper, or mahimahi—are artfully prepared and presented. Baked Chilean sea bass with clam-and-cherry-tomato risotto is a savory special, but costs as much as the lobster—$45. For a more frugal alternative, have a side of lobster risotto for $7 and an ample appetizer. ⊠ *Puntacana Resort and Club, Punta Cana* ☎ *809/959–2262 Ext. 8002* ⚑ *Reservations essential* ☉ *Closed Tues.*

$$
SEAFOOD
★

✕ **Playa Blanca.** Smack on a white-sand beach, shaded by coco palms, the dining area is sheltered by a large palapa. There's white on white—gauzy white fabric, contemporary tableware, the Euro-style chairs. Hedonistic are the Balinese sun beds in the sand. The sounds are best described as chill-out music, but speedier! Start with a perfectly executed cocktail—a lime or mango daiquiri, or hit it hard with a caipirinha. The food is savvy, but simplistic—you basically opt to have the fresh fish fried or grilled. Next you choose a sauce. The orange-and-ginger glaze is lovely. A mixed grill could include calamari, mussels, shrimp, and fish. There's Caribbean lobster and, on special occasions, sancocho. New is the separate beach menu with finger food like bite-size Dominican empanadas and some creative sandwiches and mini burgers. In high season, live music is a daily occurrence; in low season, there's a DJ on Sunday and holidays. ⊠ *Playa Blanca, Punta Cana* ☎ *809/959–7529.*

NORTH COAST

The Cabarete area in particular—where all-inclusive resorts don't yet totally dominate the scene—has some fun, original restaurants, but these are often small places, so it's important that you make reservations in advance. Expat residents complain that the prices in this town have moved past the good-value-for-money mark. Also, more and more restaurants are insisting on cash only, be it pesos, dollars, or euros. Costa Dorada and Playa Dorada each have a lovely fine-dining option, listed below.

$ ✗ **Ali's Surf Camp.** You sit at long
AMERICAN tables with a disparate group of
CASUAL strangers from at least three different countries, surrounded by bullrushes poking up from a lagoon. (Many are kiters in residence at the adjacent surf camp, considered Cabarete's best.) You can have a good feed for around $10 to $15. Try grilled, sweet barbecued ribs with fries and a Dominican salad, or the house special, *churrasco* (grilled skirt steak, Argentinean-style). There's always a shooter of mamajuana, an herbal liqueur. The German owner, Ali, changes offerings often. For lunch try the Austrian schnitzel burger. Breakfast offerings are limited. It may simply be pancakes, and there's fresh-squeezed juice—if you do the squeezing. The palapa roof gives the terrace shelter, but you'd best douse yourself with mosquito repellent. You can call to make reservations, and you should during holidays or if you have a large group. ✉ *Procab Cabarete, Cabarete* ☎ *809/571–0733* ▭ *No credit cards.*

$ ✗ **Cabahá.** The hip decor at this diminutive café illustrates the same
CAFÉ good taste as the music, top-shelf liquor, fresh-fruit drinks, and healthful fare. The fresh mango juice with añejo rum and triple sec may be the best cocktail you'll have in the D.R.—unless you try the special-recipe mojitos with crushed ice. Breakfast can be anything from fresh smoothies to muesli to omelets to crêpes. Organic salads and sandwiches, such as smoked salmon and cream cheese on dark bread, are on the lunch menu. *Picaderas* (finger foods) and fish ceviche are on offer for dinner, but you can also get entrée-size portions of such items as duck, filet mignon, and coconut fish. Most everything is healthful and low-calorie, and there are no fried foods on the menu. New owners have kept much of the restaurant's original menu, including the perfect hummus with a drizzle of house-made pepper oil. They have redecorated and added more quality wines (mainly French and Italian) available by the glass and bottle, expanded the cocktail menu, and added more innovative sandwiches. ✉ *Paseo Don Chiche 14, across from Fred's, Cabarete* ☎ *809/571–9222* ⊕ *www.cabaha.com* ▭ *No credit cards* ☾ *Closed Tues.*

$$$$ ✗ **Castle Club.** A man's home is his castle. In this one, Doug Beers pre-
CARIBBEAN pares creative lunches and dinners for guests who traverse the rocky driveway to enjoy this one-of-a-kind experience. His wife, Marguerite, is the gracious hostess, who shows patrons her expansive mountain home and the artwork strategically positioned between the many open-air arches. Served on antique lace tablecloths strewn with bougainvillea,

---

KITESURFING IN PLAYA BLANCA

A new activity has come to gorgeous Playa Blanca at Puntacana Resort. Kitesurfers now dance on the steady trade winds since the first IKO kite school has opened in Punta Cana (it's a sister club of pioneer Kite Club Cabarete). Beginners are bolstered with confidence by having certified instructors, while pros come from around the world for the competitions. For more information, check out the kitesurfing school's Web site ⊕ *www.kiteclubpuntacana.com.*

the well-orchestrated dinner might consist of canapés, carrot-ginger soup, Thai salad, grouper with a ginger–passion fruit sauce, fiesta rice, cold lemon soufflé, and coffee. After dinner, Doug lights a fire in the great room and offers guests a liqueur to warm their interiors. Drinks are not included and a tip is optional. You must make reservations in advance, since this meal is cooked in the owner's private residence. Now, with the addition of a classically trained, multilingual chef, the Beerses cater weddings and cocktail parties and will deliver or do parties in villas, too. ⊠ *Mocha Rd. between Jamao and Los Brazos, 20 mins from Cabarete* ☎ *809/357–8334, 809/223–0601, or 809/223–0601* ⚓ *Reservations essential* ⊟ *No credit cards.*

$ ✕ **EZE Bar and Restaurant.** This beach restaurant has a loyal following from
AMERICAN   breakfast to dinner, from wallet-watchin' windsurfers to wealthy *capitaleño* families. Menu names reflect the jargon of the surfers who frequent the place, including Bluebird's Salad (chicken tenders over mixed greens with a sweet chili salsa), the EZE Club Dude (curried grilled chicken), and the Rocker (grilled, marinated beef with onions, peppers, tomato, and tzatziki on a soft pita). Frosty, tropical cocktails are excellent, and you can get an energy kick from yogurt-and-mango smoothies. The blenders also churn out healthful, organic-veggie elixirs. Conversely, if you need a bacon-cheeseburger fix, this be the place. Dinner is priced similarly to lunch, with more-refined specials, like calamari or even lobster. There are some *nueva criolla* (contemporary takes on local creole dishes) specialties, and the kitchen stays open late, often until midnight. The new manager is a personable Italian named Tomas. There have been some menu changes, but most everything remains the same. ⊠ *Cabarete Beach in front of Carib Wind Center, Cabarete* ☎ *809/601–8809* ⊟ *No credit cards.*

$$$ ✕ **Lucia.** New life has been breathed into Lucia by innovative chef Angel
CONTINENTAL   Mejia. His menu is comprehensive and contemporary. The setting is as
★   artistic as a gallery, with orchids galore, crisp white linens, and attentive waiters in white guayabera shirts. Carnivores with more basic tastes can order an Angus fillet off the "simple" menu. Foodies will be delighted by the tamarind lamb. Choose a bottle from the extensive wine list that features many Italian vintages. The molten-chocolate volcano with vanilla ice cream is the dessert of choice. For a *digestivo*, be daring with a Brunello grappa or a local Brugal Unico rum, and look out to the orchids clinging to the trees and the tropical mangrove garden. It is the good life at Lucia. ⊠ *Casa Colonial, Playa Dorada* ☎ *809/320–3232.*

$$–$$$ ✕ **Mare's Restaurant and Pool Lounge.** If rock baby lobsters flambéed with
ECLECTIC   Ricard, then dashed with curry, and tossed with fresh mangoes sounds
★   like it's from food heaven, it is. Begin with fresh foie gras over yucca cake drizzled with a mix of brandy, honey, vinegar, hoisin sauce, and a hit of spicy dark chocolate and chives. Too rich for your blood? Then have a spicy tuna roll with passion fruit sauce. This contemporary home-cum-restaurant has a bar at the swimming pool so you can swim first and then sip a digestif afterward. Prominent chef-owner Rafael Vasquez has a limitless imagination that can even accommodate you with heart-healthy dishes. ⊠ *Francisco J Peynado 6, Puerto Plata* ☎ *809/261–3330* ⊕ *www.maresrestaurant.com* ☽ *No lunch. No dinner Sun.–Tues.*

$-$$ ✕ **Miró Gallery and Restaurant.** A new Peruvian-Japanese chef in 2010
ASIAN   has rejoined the kitchen staff, bringing an Asian emphasis to Miró's
menu, which now includes ceviche, yakitori, and sushi. Miró has always
offered eclectic global cuisine, and the menu still reflects the interests
of the owner Lydia Wazana, who is prominent in the local arts scene.
It still includes some Italian favorites such as *zarzuela*, an Italian seafood stew, and lobster with porcini-cream sauce. Lunch is now served
on weekends; a $3.95 Japanese-style bento-box lunch is the hot ticket.
Take a table on the beach and listen to the gentle jazz. Miró sponsors
special music events, too. ⊠ *Cabarete Beach, Cabarete* ☎ *809/853–6848
or 809/571–9709* ☉ *No lunch Mon.–Thurs.*

$$$ ✕ **Restaurant at Natura Cabana.** Seafood is at the heart of the menu here,
SEAFOOD   and appropriately so, for diners listen to the sounds of the waves crash-
★   ing on coral rock as they fork the catch of the day with a buttery
pistachio sauce. It all tastes so fresh. A new chef in 2010 has brought
a repertoire gleaned from his Latin–Mediterranean roots. Start with
one of his unexpected pairings, like a poached quail egg with potato
foam and prosciutto powder, drizzled with truffle oil. Segue to a freshly
made pasta like *srozzapreti* ("strangled priest") with tomato sauce and
shrimp flambéed in cognac. For dessert enjoy a house-made sorbet,
say pineapple-prosecco, wth watermelon cubes, passion fruit juice, and
mint. The wines are French, Italian, Spanish, and Chilean (go for the
reservas). Tables are set with geometric plates and oversized wine gob-
lets. Service is warm, caring, and efficient, the international music atmo-
spheric. ⊠ *Natura Cabana, Perla Marina, Cabarete* ☎ *809/858–5822
or 809/571–1507* ⌕ *Reservations essential.*

SANTIAGO

The D.R.'s second city, Santiago, has always been a lovely, provincial
place; the draw nowadays is the wonderful art gallery and museum, Cen-
tro León. Most people come from the Puerto Plata area as day-trippers,
but a few spend the night, especially if they fly in directly from New York.
From Sosúa and Cabarete, it's about a 1½-hour drive on the scenic high-
way that passes through mountain villages; from Puerto Plata it's about
one hour, from Santo Domingo 2½ hours. Those who come for the day
can at least enjoy lunch in one of Santiago's great restaurants.

$-$$ ✕ **Il Pasticcio.** Everyone from college students to cigar kings, presidents
ITALIAN   and politicos, movie producers and stars, packs this eccentrically deco-
★   rated culinary landmark. Tourists take photos of the bathrooms, with
their ornate mirrors and Romanesque plaster sinks. Chef-owner Paolo
makes this bungalow a personality palace. (You will see either his yellow or pink Vespa on display. He takes turns driving them to the market.) A living art gallery, it is where the artists, poets, and intelligentsia
hang. His mouthwatering creations are authentic and fresh. Try the
great antipasto selections, or commence with the pasticcio salad, which
might have smoked salmon, mozzarella, anchovies, capers, and baby
arugula. Paolo couples fresh pastas with unexpected sauces, like gnoc-
chi with puttanesca. Even the bread service comes with three sauces:
one is like pesto, there's a *pomodoro* (tomato sauce), and the best is a

creamy anchovy sauce. They can all be had on pasta, too. Finish with a shot of *limoncello* (lemon liqueur) and the best tiramisu outside Italy. Value for the peso is remarkable. ⊠ *Calle 3, No. 5, at Av. Del Llano, Cerros de Gurabo* ☎ *809/582–6061* ⊘ *Closed Mon.*

SAMANÁ

$$ ✕ **El Mambo Social Club.** If the name makes you sing: "Hey mambo, ECLECTIC mambo Italiano . . ." well, get over it. Yes, there are billiard tables in the front room, and the bar is a popular place to hang for island characters. Latin dance night is certainly salsa-social, but the only things authentically Italian are the maitre'd and some pasta dishes. Owner Alex Rodriguez is from Spain, and he and his partner make this a personality palace. Slide into a comfy banquette in the dining area and you'll understand what local expats know, that this is a fine-dining enclave. Just a New York minute from the beach, the fresh fish and particularly the *mariscos* (shellfish) are wise choices. The ceviche is with shrimp and mango, red tuna stars as an appetizer or a main, and salads get creative with goat cheese and cashews. The churrasco would be a standout even in Argentina. Expect the town's best chocolate fondant, and pair it with a tropical sorbet. ⊠ *Av. 27 de Febrero, Las Terrenas* ☎ *809/240–5312 or 809/877–8374* ⊘ *Closed Tues. No lunch.*

WHERE TO STAY

The Dominican Republic has the largest hotel inventory (at this writing some 70,000 rooms, with even more under construction) in the Caribbean and draws large numbers of stateside visitors. Surfers can still find digs for $25 a night in Cabarete, and the new generation of luxurious all-inclusives in Punta Cana and Uvero Alto is simply incredible.

Santo Domingo properties generally base their tariffs on the European Plan (no meals)—though many include breakfast—and maintain the same room rates year-round. Beach resorts have high winter rates, with prices reduced for the shoulder seasons of late spring and early fall (summer has become another strong season). All-inclusives dominate in Punta Cana. Cabarete was a stronghold of the small inn, but it does have all-inclusives. Villa rentals are gaining in popularity all over the island, particularly in Cabarete and the Cabrera area.

During your stay your patience may be tested at times, particularly at all-inclusives. Even in the touristic zones, the D.R. still has vestiges of a third-world country. The nodding in and out of the electricity is one annoyance, and sometimes the *plantas* (generators) either don't kick in or wheeze and hiss from age. Service lapses and the language barrier can also be frustrating. But when an employee sincerely says, "How can I serve you, missus?" followed by, "It's a pleasure to help you. Have a happy day!" you're pleasantly reminded of the genuine hospitality of the locals. You gotta love it!

The following reviews have been condensed for this book. Please go to Fodors.com for full reviews of each property.

SANTO DOMINGO

The seaside capital of the country is in the middle of the island's south coast. In Santo Domingo, most of the better hotels are on or near the Malecón, with several small, desirable properties in the trendy Colonial Zone, allowing you to feel part of that magical environment. The capital is where you'll find some of the most sophisticated hotels and restaurants, not to mention nightlife. However, such an urban vacation is best coupled with a beach stay elsewhere on the island.

¢   **⊞ Coco Boutique Hotel.** Behind the
B&B/INN   soft, Caribbean-turquoise facade,
★   you'll find a most untypical B&B, with earth tones and white almost everywhere—the reception and lounge, the stark wooden staircase, the grillwork on the French doors.

> ### BEST BETS FOR LODGING
>
> **BEST FOR ROMANCE**
> Peninsula House
>
> Excellence Punta Cana
>
> **BEST POOL**
> Casa Colonial Beach and Spa
>
> Dreams Punta Cana Resort and Spa
>
> **BEST SERVICE**
> Hilton Santo Domingo
>
> Tortuga Bay Villas
>
> **BEST FOR KIDS**
> Club Med Punta Cana
>
> Casa de Campo

Pros: amazingly quiet for the Zona Colonial; opposite the Plaza Pellerano Castro; rooftop terrace with Balinese sun beds and restaurant serving lunch and dinner. **Cons:** not steeped in creature comforts; bathrooms are small, as is one upstairs room. ⊠ *Arzobispo Porte 7, corner of Las Damas, Zona Colonial* ☎ *809/685–8467* ⊕ *www.cocoboutiquehotel. com* ⌁*5 rooms* ⚭ *In-room: a/c, no phone, no TV, no safe, Wi-Fi. In-hotel: bar, parking* ❑ *Breakfast.*

¢–$ **⊞ Hilton Santo Domingo** This has become *the* address on the Malecón
HOTEL   for businesspeople, convention attendees, and leisure travelers. **Pros:**
★   Sunday brunch is one of the city's top tickets; best service in Santo Domingo. **Cons:** little about the property is authentically Dominican; hotel can feel large and impersonal. ⊠ *Av. George Washington 500, Gazcue* ☎ *809/685–0000* ⊕ *hiltoncaribbean.com/santodomingo* ⌁*228 rooms, 32 suites* ⚭ *In-room: a/c, Internet, Wi-Fi. In-hotel: restaurants, bars, pool, gym, spa, business center* ❑ *No meals.*

¢–$$ **⊞ Hostal Nicolas de Ovando.** Listed as a World Heritage Site, this luxury
HOTEL   hotel, sculpted from the residence of the first governor of the Americas,
Fodor's Choice   is the best thing to happen in the Zone since Diego Columbus's palace
★   was finished in 1517. **Pros:** lavish breakfast buffet; beautifully restored historic section. **Cons:** can be pricey; no executive floor. ⊠ *Calle Las Damas, Zona Colonial* ☎ *809/685–9955 or 800/763–4835* ⊕ *www. sofitel.com* ⌁*97 rooms, 3 junior suites, 4 suites* ⚭ *In-room: a/c, Wi-Fi. In-hotel: restaurant, bars, pool, gym, business center, parking, some pets allowed* ❑ *Breakfast.*

¢   **⊞ Hotel La Atarazana.** A white wrought-iron gate opens to a small foyer
HOTEL   with a large mirror and long stems of tropical flowers at this artisti-
★   cally renovated town house. **Pros:** superior service; excellent location near Plaza España but not on a touristy block; rooftop terrace offers

views, sunny and shaded sitting areas. **Cons:** no luxurious creature comforts except in-room cable TV and Wi-Fi; some back rooms are petite (but quieter than those in front). ⊠ *Vicente Celestino Duarte #19, next door to police station, Zona Colonial* ☎ *809/688–3693* ⊕ *www. hotel-atarazana.com* ⇨ *7 rooms* ⅙ *In-room: no a/c (some), no phone, no safe, Wi-Fi. In-hotel: bar, business center* ¶ *Breakfast.*

¢

HOTEL

🏨 **Hotel Villa Colonial.** Owner Lionel Biseau has kept as much of the original structure here as feasible, including the second-floor verandah, the columns, and the patterned tile floors so distinctive of the Zone circa 1920. **Pros:** stylin' breakfast room and bar overlooking the petite pool; all rooms have Wi-Fi; low rates make this an exceptional value. **Cons:** staff has limited English; hotel takes no credit cards; no sign out front. ⊠ *Calle Sanchez 157, near Padre Bellini, Zona Colonial* ☎ *809/221–1049* ⊕ *www.villacolonial.net* ⇨ *13 rooms* ⅙ *In-room: a/c, no phone, no safe, Wi-Fi. In-hotel: bar, pool* ⊟ *No credit cards* ¶ *Breakfast.*

¢–$

RESORT

🏨 **Renaissance Jaragua Hotel and Casino.** This sprawling pink oasis is perennially popular, particularly with Americans, for its beautiful grounds and huge free-form pool. **Pros:** hotel is busy and lively; hotel will match any discount Internet rate; offers an optional all-inclusive plan (rare in Santo Domingo). **Cons:** can be a bit too busy at times; nothing understated about the decor; some rooms outdated. ⊠ *Av. George Washington 367, Gazcue* ☎ *809/221–2222* ⊕ *www.marriott. com* ⇨ *292 rooms, 8 suites* ⅙ *In-room: a/c, kitchen, Internet (some). In-hotel: restaurants, bars, tennis courts, pool, gym, spa, business center* ¶ *No meals.*

SOUTHEAST COAST

La Romana is on the southeast coast, about a two-hour drive from Santo Domingo and the same distance southwest of Punta Cana. An international airport here has nonstop service from the United States. Casa de Campo's Marina Chavón, with its Mediterranean design and impressive yacht club and villa complex, is as fine a marina facility as can be found anywhere. The shops and restaurants are a big draw for all tourists to the area, as is Altos de Chavón, the re-created 16th-century Mediterranean town on the grounds of Casa de Campo. The resorts in nearby Bayahibe Bay, which has an idyllic, horseshoe-shaped beach and a real fishing village, have always been popular with capitaleños and Europeans. But North Americans are also checking in here and leaving satisfied. Often, when guests want to party down, they buy an inexpensive night pass to the Viva Wyndhams, allowing them entry to the resort's discos along with dinner and drinks. The actual town of La Romana is not pretty or quaint, although it has a lovely central park and a couple of recommendable restaurants, and is a real slice of Dominican life. ■**TIP→ One way to sample the wares at Casa de Campo if you can't afford to stay there is to buy the resort's day pass ($75 for adults, $45 for children 4–12 years). It will give you a place in the sun at Minitas Beach, towels, nonmotorized water sports, lunch at the Beach Club by Le Cirque, and entrance to Altos de Chavon.**

$$$$ ALL-INCLUSIVE ★ **Casa de Campo.** The country's most illustrious resort, which set the benchmark for luxury travel in the Caribbean decades ago, has entered a new era with the dramatic renovation of its public spaces and the total redecoration of its rooms and suites. **Pros:** excellent golf and tennis; the Beach Club by Le Cirque and La Casita in the marina are on the meal plan; the pampering Excel Service at the villas. **Cons:** not the largest beach; expensive food if not on the inclusive supplement; a bit too sprawling. *Box 140, La Romana 809/523–3333 or 305/856–7083 www.casadecampo.com.do 165 rooms, 50 villas In-room: a/c, kitchen (some), Internet. In-hotel: restaurants, bars, golf courses, tennis courts, pools, gym, spa, beach, water sports, children's programs Multiple meal plans.*

$$ ALL-INCLUSIVE Fodor's Choice ★ **Dreams La Romana Resort and Spa.** With its whimsical Victorian fretwork, the former Sunscape Casa del Mar sits on an exceptional, palm-fringed ribbon of white sand protected by a coral reef that offers great snorkeling from the beach. **Pros:** caring and efficient staff; top-shelf liquors available at the lobby bar for no extra charge; free Wi-Fi in main lobby and in-room at club level. **Cons:** large and busy property usually feels overly full; lines and seating in the buffet can be problematic. *Bayahibe Bay, Bayahibe 809/221–8880 www.dreamsresorts.com/drelr 751 rooms, 34 suites In-room: a/c, Wi-Fi (some). In-hotel: restaurants, bars, tennis courts, pools, gym, beach, water sports, children's programs, business center, parking All-inclusive.*

$$ ALL-INCLUSIVE ★ **Iberostar Hacienda Dominicus.** Iberostar has one of the best success rates in the all-inclusive world; this resort's idyllic beach with its lighthouse bar doesn't hurt, either. **Pros:** fun resort; gorgeous beach; family-friendly. **Cons:** room decor is a bit outdated; always packed; reservations at à la carte restaurants not always available and must be made very early in the morning. *Playa Bayahibe, Bayahibe 809/688–3600 or 888/923–2722 www.iberostar.com 460 rooms, 38 junior suites In-room: a/c. In-hotel: restaurants, bars, tennis courts, pools, gym, spa, beach, water sports, children's programs, business center All-inclusive.*

$ ALL-INCLUSIVE **Viva Wyndham Dominicus Palace.** Some Americans may prefer this classier sister to the nearby Viva Wyndham Dominicus Beach resort with its reputation for strong animation programs, its sports, and its fun atmosphere. **Pros:** absolutely fabulous blue-flag beach and dive center; fun Italian crowd in high season; several of the restaurants, like Atlantis, are first-rate. **Cons:** always busy; no interior transportation even though resort grounds are sprawling; reservations needed for à la carte restaurants. *Playa Bayahibe, Bayahibe 809/686–5658 www.vivaresorts.com 330 rooms In-room: a/c, Wi-Fi (some). In-hotel: restaurants, bars, tennis courts, pools, gym, spa, beach, water sports, children's programs, business center All-inclusive.*

PUNTA CANA

The easternmost coast of the island has 35 mi (56 km) of incredible beach punctuated by coco palms; add to that a host of all-inclusive resorts, an atmospheric thatch-roof airport, and many more direct flights than any other D.R. resort area, and it's easy to see why this region—despite having some 24,000 hotel rooms (more than on most other Caribbean islands)—is often sold out. It has become the Cancun of the D.R. You can usually get a room during hurricane season (late August–October), but booking far in advance for other months is advisable. That said, the global economic downturn has slowed tourism even here, and rooms are not as in demand. Deals, usually found on Web sites, can really knock down prices. Look for resorts with spas, which offer a soothing atmosphere away from the madding crowd, and a litany of both therapeutic and fun body treatments.

The region commonly referred to as Punta Cana actually encompasses the beaches and villages of Juanillo, Punta Cana, Bavaro, Cabeza de Toro, El Cortecito, Arena Gorda, Macao, and Uvero Alto, which hug an unbroken stretch of the eastern coastline; however, Uvero Alto, the farthest developed resort area to the north, lies an hour from the Punta Cana airport.

$$–$$$
ALL-INCLUSIVE
☺
★
🏨 **Club Med Punta Cana.** Never better, Punta Cana's first all-inclusive has a shiny new face after a $34 million renovation that infused spark and savvy into a tried-and-true resort. **Pros:** inspiring, fun staff; themed weeks for music, dance, and sports; special events like a Wine and Food Festival. **Cons:** good but limited dining options; Wi-Fi only in public spaces and it costs from $5 per hour to $50 per week; in-room Internet (free) available in Tiara suites only. ⊠ *Provincia La Altagracia, apartado postal 106, Punta Cana* ☎ *809/686–5500 or 800/258–2633* ⊕ *www.clubmed. com* ➥ *553 rooms, 32 family suites* ⚭ *In-room: a/c, Internet (some). In-hotel: restaurants, bars, tennis courts, pools, gym, spa, beach, water sports, children's programs, business center* ¶⊚¶ *All-inclusive.*

$$$$
ALL-INCLUSIVE
☺
🏨 **Dreams Palm Beach Punta Cana.** The glorious Dreams–AMResorts brand bespeaks luxury and this location is both family-oriented and American-friendly—and has estatelike grounds and chic, contemporary guest rooms. **Pros:** great fitness room with cardio training; staff tend to speak pretty good English; excellent room service. **Cons:** singles may feel left out with all the families; romantic couples may prefer an adults-only scenario; some service and Wi-Fi lapses. ⊠ *Box 68, Cabeza de Toro, Higüey* ☎ *809/552–6000 or 866/237–3267* ⊕ *www.dreamsresorts.com* ➥ *325 rooms* ⚭ *In-room: a/c, Internet (some), Wi-Fi (some). In-hotel: restaurants, tennis courts, pools, gym, spa, beach, water sports, children's programs, business center, parking* ¶⊚¶ *All-inclusive.*

$$$
ALL-INCLUSIVE
☺
🏨 **Dreams Punta Cana Resort and Spa.** This is a fun and active resort, which is especially good if you are traveling with kids, but there are enough upscale amenities to appeal to adults as well. **Pros:** simply, this is a beautiful, friendly, feel-good place; great nightly entertainment. **Cons:** you have to be early (or clever) to be guaranteed a raft in the pool; some service lapses; Wi-Fi is expensive. ⊠ *Playa de Uvero Alto, Uvero Alto* ☎ *809/682–0404 or 866/237–3267* ⊕ *www.dreamspuntacana.com.do* ➥ *592 rooms, 28 suites* ⚭ *In-room: a/c, Wi-Fi (some). In-hotel: restaurants, bars, tennis courts, pool, gym, spa, beach, water sports, children's programs, business center, parking* ¶⊚¶ *All-inclusive.*

$$$$
ALL-INCLUSIVE
Fodor's Choice
★
🏨 **Excellence Punta Cana.** A sumptuous lovers' lair, this adults-only all-inclusive is particularly appealing to honeymooners or wedding parties. **Pros:** adults-only getaway; gorgeous setting for weddings; waiter service at pool and beach; all bars have international brands of liquor. **Cons:** distant from shopping, other restaurants, and airport; always

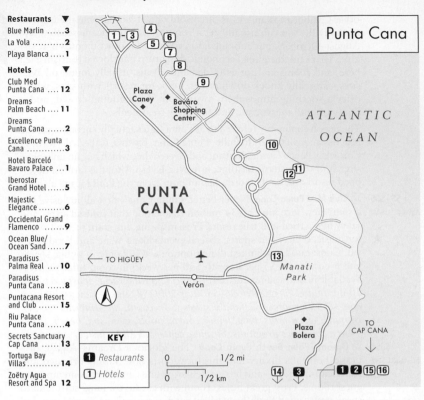

seems to be full and can feel crowded at times. ⊠ *Uvero Alto, Higüey* ☎ *809/685–9880* ⊕ *www.excellence-resorts.com* ⇒ *452 suites* ⅍ *In-room: a/c. In-hotel: restaurants, bars, tennis courts, pools, gym, spa, beach, water sports, business center* ⅋⊙⅋ *All-inclusive.*

$
ALL-INCLUSIVE

⊡ **Hotel Barceló Bávaro Palace Deluxe.** The recent transformation of the entire Punta Cana Barceló complex is astounding, but the standout offering is the Palace Deluxe. **Pros:** excellent bedding; automated lighting; everything is new and state-of-the-art. **Cons:** Palace Deluxe does not have its own pool; still a megaresort experience. ⊠ *Carretera Bavero Km 1, Box 3177, Playa Bavaro, Higüey* ☎ *809/686–5797* ⊕ *www. barcelo.com* ⇒ *472 junior suites* ⅍ *In-room: a/c, Wi-Fi. In-hotel: restaurants, golf courses, tennis courts, pools, gym, spa, beach, water sports, business center, parking* ⅋⊙⅋ *All-inclusive.*

$$$$
ALL-INCLUSIVE

⊡ **Iberostar Grand Hotel.** Iberostar's first adults-only resort in Punta Cana (for those 18 and over) is a knockout. **Pros:** impressive collection of designer restaurants with outstanding cuisine; a stellar honeymoon destination; free in-room Wi-Fi. **Cons:** hasn't really developed a personality yet; resort can seem particularly quiet, even for an adults-only place. ⊠ *Playa Bavaro* ☎ *809/221–6500 or 888/774–0040* ⊕ *www.iberostar. com* ⇒ *260 suites, 13 grand suites, 1 presidential suite* ⅍ *In-room: a/c. In-hotel: restaurants, golf course, tennis courts, pools, gym, spa, business center, parking, some age restrictions* ⅋⊙⅋ *All-inclusive.*

Excellence Punta Cana.

\$\$\$ **Majestic Elegance.** This elegant "M" property's mission is to fulfill the
ALL-INCLUSIVE demands of a clientele that desires a high-end menu of facilities and
services. **Pros:** staff is nonintrusive; premium liquors at all bars and à
la carte restaurants. **Cons:** large size can make it impersonal; buffeteria
lacks personality. ⊠ *Playa Bavaro, Bavaro* ☎ *809/221–9898* ⊕ *www.
majestic-resorts.com* ↝ *537 junior suites, 59 suites* ⚷ *In-room: a/c,
Internet, Wi-Fi. In-hotel: restaurants, tennis courts, pools, gym, spa,
beach, children's programs, business center, parking* ⎮⊙⎮ *All-inclusive.*

\$\$–\$\$\$ **Occidental Grand Flamenco Punta Cana.** You'll find plenty of choices for
ALL-INCLUSIVE food and fun at this gigantic resort, which is likely to appeal to families,
meeting and wedding groups and night owls. **Pros:** nightlife is excellent;
cuisine and service at Royal Club are exceptional; fun for the whole family. **Cons:** no room service for standard rooms; several restaurants have
dated decor. ⊠ *Bavaro* ☎ *809/221–8787* ⊕ *www.occidentalhotels.com*
↝ *801 rooms, 51 junior suites/suites* ⚷ *In-room: a/c. In-hotel: restaurants, room service (some), bars, tennis courts, pools, gym, spa, beach,
water sports, children's programs, business center* ⎮⊙⎮ *All-inclusive.*

\$–\$\$ **Ocean Blue/Ocean Sand Golf and Beach Resort.** Although the pub-
ALL-INCLUSIVE lic areas of this moderately priced megaresort, designed like a small
town, are still attractive, the standard rooms are starting to look a little
worn and could definitely use a face-lift, though the expansive pools
and recreational activities are still highlights. **Pros:** free trolley every
10–15 minutes; free Wi-Fi in the lobby; 24-hour all-inclusive including
international liquors and disco. **Cons:** Internet access is spotty, even in
premium sections (and no Wi-Fi in rooms); some drab interiors; food
even at the gourmet room not as good as it once was. ⊠ *Playa Arena
Gorda, Bavaro* ☎ *809/476–2326* ⊕ *www.oceanhotels.net* ↝ *436 junior*

suites, 272 suites ☼ *In-room: a/c. In-hotel: restaurants, bars, golf, tennis courts, pools, gym, spa, beach, water sports, children's programs, business center* ⁏⊙⁏ *All-inclusive.*

$$$$
ALL-INCLUSIVE
☾
Fodor's Choice
★

▦ **Paradisus Palma Real Resort.** One of Punta Cana's luxury all-inclusives—and a member of the Leading Hotels of the World—is one of the region's most beautiful resorts. **Pros:** personalized attention; enticing and professional spa; complimentary golf. **Cons:** Internet access costs extra (and Wi-Fi only in public areas); service can be sketchy even within the Royal level; the restaurants and nightlife are far from the accommodations and there is no shuttle service; even the Reserve rooms do not have sea views. ✉ *Bavaro* ☎ *809/688–5000 or 800/688–5000* ⊕ *www. solmelia.com* ➾ *554 suites* ☼ *In-room: a/c, Internet. In-hotel: restaurants, bars, tennis courts, pools, gym, spa, beach, water sports, children's programs* ⁏⊙⁏ *All-inclusive.*

$
ALL-INCLUSIVE
☾
★

▦ **Paradisus Punta Cana.** Big-league improvements have been made in recent years at this seasoned tropical getaway as it has struggled to keep pace with the newer competition. **Pros:** some impressive architecture and decor; management has service right on; the Reserve is an ultraresort. **Cons:** the resort is very family-oriented and not recommended for solo travelers; older rooms show signs of wear; as the Reserve is geared to families, a full dining room can be noisy. ✉ *3542 Playa de Bavaro, Bávaro* ⊕ *www.paradisuspuntacana.solmelia.com* ➾ *500 suites, 192 royal suites* ☼ *In-room: a/c. In-hotel: restaurants, bars, golf course, tennis courts, pool, gym, spa, beach, water sports, children's programs, business center* ⁏⊙⁏ *All-inclusive.*

¢–$
RESORT
☾
★

▦ **Puntacana Resort and Club.** A plethora of amenities—not to mention meticulously kept grounds, 5 mi (8 km) of white-sand beach, and world-class golf—await guests at this charismatic resort, which spearheaded the area's tourism industry and has kept pace with the times. **Pros:** expansive and beautiful grounds; spectacular golf and spa; one of the area's most gorgeous, unspoiled beaches. **Cons:** limited nightlife on-site; some elements are dated now; low season can mean low occupancy. ✉ *Puntacana Resort and Club, Punta Cana* ☎ *809/959–2262 or 888/442–2262* ⊕ *www.puntacana.com* ➾ *175 rooms, 16 junior suites, 11 suites, 38 casitas* ☼ *In-room: a/c. In-hotel: restaurants, bars, golf courses, tennis courts, pools, gym, spa, beach, water sports, children's programs, business center* ⁏⊙⁏ *Breakfast.*

$
ALL-INCLUSIVE

▦ **Riu Palace Punta Cana.** On a moonlit night, this megaresort decorated with Arabian-style domes looks like a fairy-tale palace. **Pros:** the live music at the wrought-iron gazebo in the plaza is inviting; the grand hotel elements are dazzling. **Cons:** the resort can be alienating to solo travelers; the spa is disappointing on many levels; resort stays very busy with the crowd made up mainly of seniors and Germans. ✉ *Playa Arena Gorda, Bavaro* ☎ *809/687–4242* ⊕ *www.riu.com* ➾ *572 junior suites, 28 suites* ☼ *In-room: a/c. In-hotel: restaurants, bars, tennis courts, pools, gym, spa, beach, water sports, children's programs, business center* ⁏⊙⁏ *All-inclusive.*

$$$$
ALL-INCLUSIVE
Fodor's Choice
★

▦ **Secrets Sanctuary Cap Cana Resort and Spa.** The first hotel to be built within the gates of Cap Cana, this exclusive property has been relaunched as a luxury, adults-only Secrets resort; there have been changes, but they are nearly all positive. **Pros:** gorgeous beach; top-notch golf; large fun

Secrets Sanctuary Cap Cana Resort and Spa

quotient. **Cons:** continuing development all around at Cap Cana; some guests hide from the overly aggressive entertainment team. ⊠ *Playa Juanillo, Cap Cana* ☎ *809/562–9191 or 800/836–9618* ⊕ *secretsresorts. com/sanctuary* ↩ *115 junior suites, 27 suites, 33 villas* ⌂ *In-room: a/c, kitchen (some), Internet. In-hotel: restaurants, bars, golf courses, tennis courts, pools, gym, spa, beach, water sports* ¶⊙¶ *All-inclusive.*

$$$$
RESORT
Fodor'sChoice
★

🖼 **Tortuga Bay Villas.** Shuttered French windows opening to grand vistas of the sea and a cotton-white private beach are hallmarks of this luxury-villa enclave within the grounds of Puntacana Resort and Club. **Pros:** exceptional, personal attention; gorgeous sprawling grounds; outstanding golf; VIP check-in at airport. **Cons:** little nightlife; too isolated for singles; its Bamboo restaurant is expensive and the food isn't always successful. ⊠ *Puntacana Resort and Club, Punta Cana* ☎ *809/959–8229 or 888/442–2262* ⊕ *www.puntacana.com* ↩ *15 1- to 4-bedroom villas* ⌂ *In-room: a/c, kitchen, Internet. In-hotel: restaurants, room service, bars, golf courses, tennis courts, pools, gym, spa, beach, water sports, children's programs, business center* ¶⊙¶ *Breakfast.*

$$$$
ALL-INCLUSIVE
★

🖼 **Zoëtry Agua Resort and Spa.** At this serene all-inclusive oceanfront resort, rustic luxury, natural beauty, and high architectural style blend seamlessly. **Pros:** superlative spa; serene, rustic location; rates include free international calls and laundry service. **Cons:** remote location; mosquitoes; limited nightlife opportunities. ⊠ *Playa Uvero Alto* ☎ *809/468–0000* ⊕ *www.zoetryresorts.com* ↩ *38 junior suites, 2 suites, 5 villas* ⌂ *In-room: a/c, Wi-Fi. In-hotel: restaurants, bars, tennis court, pools, gym, spa, beach, water sports, children's programs, business center* ¶⊙¶ *All-inclusive.*

CLOSE UP

Cap Cana

One of the most ambitious new development projects in the Dominican Republic, Cap Cana is a resort and villa complex spread out over 30,000 acres—a 3½-mi stretch—of precious beach on bluffs 200 feet above sea level and about 10 minutes south of the Punta Cana airport. An exclusive gated community, it comprises luxury hotels, deluxe residential units, golf courses, a casino, a marina and a deep-sea fishing fleet, beach club, spas, and more to come.

The flagship hotel, the Sanctuary Cap Cana Golf and Spa, opened in 2008, but it has since become Secrets Sanctuary Resort and Spa, having been relaunched by AMResorts as an unlimited-luxury, adults-only resort.

The pioneer of the golf courses, Punta Espada opened in 2006 and has since been chosen as the site of the Cap Cana Championship, a PGA Champions Tour event, for three consecutive years. A second Nicklaus-designed course, Las Iguanas, is still under construction at this writing.

Overlooking the golf course and the sea from its hilltop vantage point, Golden Bear Resort and Spa is made up of luxurious, contemporary condominiums (studios to two-bedrooms), which are now managed by Coral Hospitalities, and marketed under its XELITER brand.

Marina Cap Cana is being built in three phases; it's destined to be the Caribbean's largest marina, with 1,000 slips capable of docking yachts of up to 250 feet. At this writing, Phase One, 100 slips, is complete. The marina will have a port authority and customs (now on call), restaurants (four are up and running), shops, and soon nightclubs. A casino is also open.

Other resort and condo developments (including a Ritz-Carlton and a Donald Trump project) are on hold. However, Las Canas City, a year-round residential community now has an international school as well as professional offices.

Yet, among the real treasures of Cap Cana is the biodiversity represented in its flora and fauna, some of which can be observed along the so-called Great Ecological Trail. A 9-mi (15-km) hike begins where an endangered cotoperí fruit tree, endemic to the area, marks the trailhead, which leads to grottoes, wet forests, and a pond of shimmering blue water.

SAMANÁ

Samaná is the name of both the peninsula that curves around the eponymous bay and of the largest town. Las Terrenas is at least a 2½-hour drive from Cabarete. Conveniently, El Catey Airport (AZS) is served regularly by American Eagle from San Juan; otherwise, Takeoff Destination Service offers regular flights from several D.R. airports. The nearest major international airport is Puerto Plata's International Gregorio Luperon, more than a three-hour-drive away (⇨ *By Air under Transportation in Dominican Republic Essentials*).

¢
HOTEL
★
Coyamar. If you don't mind going without air-conditioning and other creature comforts, it's hard not to like the hyper-relaxed atmosphere of this small, family-run hotel on Playa Bonita. **Pros:** hands-on owners;

green hotel; great value. **Cons:** fluorescent lights are dim; resort badly needs renovation of dated decor and facilities; no a/c. ✉ *Playa Bonita 1, Las Terrenas* ☎ *809/240–5130* ⊕ *www.coyamar.com* ⤷ *10 rooms* ⚘ *In-room: no a/c, no phone, no TV, Internet, Wi-Fi. In-hotel: restaurant, bar, pool, beach, some pets allowed* ⍾⊘ *Breakfast.*

$$$$
B&B/INN
Fodor's Choice
★

 ⌂ **Peninsula House.** The gorgeous Victorian-style plantation house with wraparound verandahs overlooks miles of coconut palms down to the ocean, and it's one of the best B&Bs in the Caribbean. **Pros:** quiet and remote; impeccable guest attention; special promotions during summer and fall. **Cons:** the fun son, Tomas, no longer there; you might be afraid of breaking a treasure; high-priced, but that's the only real drawback we can find. ✉ *Camino Cosón, Las Terrenas* ☎ *809/962–7447 or 809/882–7712* ⊕ *www.thepeninsulahouse.com* ⤷ *6 rooms* ⚘ *In-room: a/c, Wi-Fi. In-hotel: bar, pool, spa, some age restrictions* ⍾⊘ *Breakfast.*

$
HOTEL
★

 ⌂ **Villa Serena.** The best hotel choice in the eastern corner of the peninsula, Villa Serena makes a wonderful, relaxed vacation in Samaná a breeze. **Pros:** private beachfront; quiet and secluded property; fine staff. **Cons:** dated decor; really rough road from Samaná (city); Wi-Fi in lobby is sporadic. ✉ *Las Galeras* ☎ *809/538–0000* ⊕ *www.villaserena. com* ⤷ *21 rooms* ⚘ *In-room: no a/c (some), no phone, no TV, Wi-Fi. In-hotel: restaurants, bar, pool, beach, water sports* ⍾⊘ *Breakfast.*

NORTH COAST

The northern coast of the island, with mountains on one side, is also called the Amber Coast because of the large quantities of amber found in the area. The sands on its 75 mi (121 km) of beach are also golden. Major resort areas are Playa Dorada, Cabarete, and Sosúa. Plan to fly into Puerto Plata's Gregorio Luperon International Airport.

$
ALL-INCLUSIVE

 ⌂ **Barcelo Puerto Plata.** Barcelo Hotels has rescued and resuscitated the landmark property in Playa Dorada that had been the Flamenco. **Pros:** the buffet, Italian, and Brazilian restaurants are all top-notch; kids' mini-disco and adults-only disco are both on the beach; aqua-gym in pool complex shaded by gardens. **Cons:** some elements still look dated; staff not consistently accommodating; house wine poor. ✉ *Playa Dorada, Puerto Plata* ☎ *809/320–5084* ⊕ *www.barcelo.com* ⤷ *531 rooms, 52 suites* ⚘ *In-room: a/c, Wi-Fi. In-hotel: restaurants, bars, tennis courts, pools, beach, water sports, business center* ⍾⊘ *All-inclusive.*

$
ALL-INCLUSIVE

 ⌂ **Blue Bay Villa Doradas.** The stunning grand entrance (a Sara Garcia design) at this adults-only resort with its slender white pillars uses white fabric to shelter the lobby from tropical rainfalls. **Pros:** great spa; handsome beach club and stellar beachfront; yoga and golf classes included. **Cons:** standard and standard-plus rooms are not luxurious; rooms near the stage can be noisy until 11 pm; there is a cost for the safe and a very high cost for Wi-Fi. ✉ *Playa Dorada, Puerto Plata* ☎ *809/320–3000, 809/320–1600 for reservations* ⊕ *www.bluebayresorts.com* ⤷ *245 rooms, 4 suites* ⚘ *In-room: a/c, Wi-Fi. In-hotel: restaurants, bars, tennis courts, pools, gym, spa, beach, water sports, business center* ⍾⊘ *All-inclusive.*

$$–$$$
HOTEL
Fodor's Choice
★

Casa Colonial Beach and Spa. Rivals say "over the top" isn't superlative enough to describe this exquisite, all-suites boutique hotel designed by Sara Garcia, the first in the D.R. to join the lofty Small Luxury Hotels of the World. **Pros:** luxury boutique experience; glorious spa; exquisite gourmet restaurant. **Cons:** can feel empty during the low season; service not as sharp as you would expect (and not all staffers speak English well). ⊠ *Playa Dorada, Puerto Plata* ☎ *809/320–3232* ⊕ *www.casacolonialhotel.com* ⌂ *50 suites* ⚭ *In-room: a/c, no safe, Internet, Wi-Fi. In-hotel: restaurants, bar, pool, gym, spa, beach* ✺ *No meals.*

$–$$
ALL-INCLUSIVE
☺

Gran Ventana Beach Resort. This resort is characterized by a sophisticated style that sets it apart from the nearby competition. **Pros:** consistently good food and service for this price point; plenty of activities for the whole family. **Cons:** feels busy year-round; the buffet is particularly good. ⊠ *Playa Dorada, Puerto Plata* ☎ *809/320–2111* ⊕ *www.vhhr.com* ⌂ *499 rooms, 2 suites, 1 penthouse* ⚭ *In-room: a/c. In-hotel: restaurants, bars, tennis court, pools, gym, beach, water sports, children's programs, business center* ✺ *All-inclusive.*

¢
HOTEL

Hotel Casa Valeria. In a sweeping hacienda design—reminiscent of Mexico—this salmon-color adobe, housing both a hotel and a restaurant, is a standout in this quiet neighborhood. **Pros:** the owners offer discount airport transfers (must be arranged through hotel); rooms have cable TV; mini-refrigerators are stocked with 16 beverages. **Cons:** no resort amenities or services; no ocean views. ⊠ *Calle Dr. Rosen 28, El Batey, Sosúa* ☎ *809/571–3536* ⊕ *www.hotelcasavaleria.com* ⌂ *9 rooms, 2 apartments* ⚭ *In-room: a/c, no phone, kitchen (some), Wi-Fi. In-hotel: restaurant, pool* ✺ *No meals.*

$–$$
HOTEL

Hotel El Magnifico. You'll find a healthy dose of unexpected luxury at this stellar boutique condo-hotel just a gravel driveway from the dusty, noisy highway into town. **Pros:** the spaces are large, so you never feel crowded here; the interior decor is *très chic*; children under 15 stay free. **Cons:** steep spiral staircases and no elevators; no restaurant or bar; no in-room phones and no way to communicate with reception unless you have a cell phone or rent one here. ⊠ *Calle del Cementario, Cabarete* ☎ *809/571–0868* ⊕ *www.hotelmagnifico.com* ⌂ *7 rooms, 10 1-bedrooms, 6 2-bedrooms, 1 3-bedroom, 6 2-bedroom penthouses* ⚭ *In-room: a/c, no phone, no safe, kitchen (some), Wi-Fi. In-hotel: pool, beach* ✺ *No meals.*

TRAVEL TIP

If you are going to the North Coast, check out airfares to Cibao International Airport in Santiago, which has numerous direct flights from New York, Newark, and Miami. JetBlue has rates as low as $150 one-way. The flight arrives around 4:30 am, but now that the spiffy Garden Court by the Hodelpa Hotel Group has opened five minutes from the airport, you can bunk there, spend the morning at Centro León, and take a bus or taxi to the North Coast towns of Puerto Plata, Sosúa, and Cabarete. Since JetBlue prices by segments, you could fly out of another destination without penalty.

$–$$
ALL-INCLUSIVE
★

Iberostar Costa Dorada. This resort will dazzle you with its sprawling lobby, its hardwood benches and sculptures, and its curvaceous pool with a central Jacuzzi encircled by Roman pillars. **Pros:** good management makes for a happy staff and a fun resort; blue-flag beach; top-shelf liquor in the lobby bar. **Cons:** popularity translates to high-occupancy year-round; rooms need to be renovated; pool can be very noisy. ⊠ *Playa Costa Dorada, Carretera Luperon, Km 4, Marapica* ☎ *809/320–1000 or 888/923–2722* ⊕ *www.iberostar.com* ⇆ *498 rooms, 18 junior suites* ⌂ *In-room: a/c. In-hotel: restaurants, bars, tennis courts, pools, gym, spa, beach, water sports, children's programs, business center* ⦿ *All-inclusive.*

$
HOTEL
★

Natura Cabana. This oceanfront ecoparadise offers accommodations in thatch-roof cabanas, such as the Africana, a sophisticated structure made from bamboo, artistic brick, and stonework. **Pros:** good restaurants; caring owner; great spa. **Cons:** car is almost a requirement; outside of town (a one-hour walk by the beach); no a/c but sea breezes. ⊠ *Playa Perla Marina, Cabarete* ☎ *809/571–1507* ⊕ *www.naturacabana.com* ⇆ *11 bungalows* ⌂ *In-room: no a/c, no phone, no safe, kitchen (some), Wi-Fi, no TV. In-hotel: restaurants, bar, pool, spa, beach* ⦿ *Breakfast.*

$
RENTAL

Ocean Point. Enjoy the good life at this stellar condo complex as you sit at the pool, shaded by a golden market umbrella, and watch the parade of multicolor surf-kites over the big blue ocean. **Pros:** gorgeous views; high-quality building materials; elevators. **Cons:** a 20-minute beach walk to most restaurants; in some units the furnishings look dated; no breakfast or meals available on-site (one small, good, and inexpensive restaurant next door, at the Kite Club Grill, serves breakfast and lunch). ⊠ *Kite Beach, Carretera Principal, Cabarete* ☎ *809/571–0030* ⊕ *www.oceanpointdr.com* ⇆ *28 2-bedroom condos, 10 4-bedroom penthouses* ⌂ *In-room: a/c, Internet, Wi-Fi. In-hotel: pool, beach, laundry facilities* ⦿ *No meals.*

$$$$
RESORT
★

Sea Horse Ranch. This luxury residential resort is democratic, with tiered rates that make it affordable for families who love that it is a safe haven for children; the celebrities and bigwigs who come here love that privacy is paramount. **Pros:** one of the most organized, well-managed villa enclaves in the country; potent security makes your vacation worry-free; location close to Puerto Plata and the airport; all villas have free Wi-Fi and DSL. **Cons:** not much sense of place (you could be in an upscale neighborhood in Florida or Southern California). ⊠ *Cabarete* ☎ *809/571–3880 or 800/635–0991* ⊕ *www.sea-horse-ranch.com* ⇆ *75 villas* ⌂ *In-room: a/c, no safe (some), kitchen, Wi-Fi. In-hotel: restaurant, bar, tennis courts, pool, beach* ⦿ *No meals.*

¢
RESORT
★

Velero Beach Resort. This well-managed hotel and residential enclave with its own beachfront and manicured gardens studded with cacti, orchids, and pottery is a favorite among well-heeled Dominicans, hip Americans, and international guests. **Pros:** blenders, microwaves, and DVDs in the junior suites and above; new, draped, Balinese sun beds at the pool are wonderful; Velero is blossoming into a wedding and honeymoon venue. **Cons:** no elevators—it's a climb up the spiral staircases to the third floor; standard rooms are not spacious. ⊠ *Calle la Punta 1,*

Cabarete ☎ *809/571–9727* ⊕ *www.velerobeach.com* ➳ *22 2-bedroom suites, 7 penthouses* ⚠ *In-room: a/c, kitchen (some), Wi-Fi (some). In-hotel: restaurant, pool, beach, business center* |◯| *No meals.*

$ ⬚ **Victorian House.** Roosting on a cliff above breathtaking Sosúa Bay, this
HOTEL   boutique hotel is a delightful replica of a Victorian gingerbread house.
Pros: bi-level penthouses are outstanding; consistently good service; small hotel that still offers tie-in meal plan with a nearby sister property. **Cons:** lack of elevators can be hard if you're on a higher floor; latest renovation not entirely successful. ✉ *Calle Dr. Alejo Martinez 1, El Batey, Sosúa* ☎ *809/571–4000* ➳ *32 rooms, 7 junior suites, 8 suites, 3 penthouses* ⚠ *In-room: a/c, kitchen (some). In-hotel: restaurants, bars, pools, gym, beach, water sports, children's programs, laundry facilities, business center* |◯| *No meals.*

¢   ⬚ **Villa Taina.** Smack amid the action, steps down from the main drag, this
B&B/INN   small, German-owned inn encapsulates the original spirit of Cabarete.
Pros: great location; efficient and caring owner. **Cons:** small pool; noise of town can be heard in the buildings closest to the street; standard rooms are on the small side. ✉ *Calle Principal, Cabarete* ☎ *809/571–0722* ⊕ *www.villataina.com* ➳ *56 rooms, 1 apartment* ⚠ *In-room: a/c, no safe, Internet. In-hotel: restaurant, bar, pool, beach, water sports* |◯| *Breakfast.*

NIGHTLIFE

Santo Domingo's nightlife is vast and ever changing. Check with the concierges and hip capitaleños. At this writing, there is still a curfew for clubs and bars; they must close at midnight during the week, and 2 am on Friday and Saturday nights. There are some exceptions to the latter, primarily those clubs and casinos in hotels. Sadly, the curfew has put some clubs out of business, but it has cut down on the crime and late-night noise, particularly in the Zone. Some clubs are now pushing the envelope and staying open until 3, but they do get in trouble with the authorities when caught, and you probably don't want to be there then.

Dancing is as much a part of the culture here as eating and drinking. As in other Latin countries, after dinner it's not a question of *whether* people will go dancing but *where* they'll go. Move with the rhythm of the merengue and the pulsing beat of salsa (adopted from neighboring Puerto Rico). Among the young, the word is that there's no better place to party in the Caribbean than Santo Domingo. Almost every resort in Puerto Plata and Punta Cana has live entertainment, dancing, or both.

The action can heat up—and the island does have casinos—but gambling in the Dominican Republic here is more a sideline than a raison d'être. Most casinos are in the larger hotels of Santo Domingo, with a couple in Playa Dorada and elsewhere on the north coast, plus many more in Punta Cana. All offer slot machines, blackjack, craps, and roulette and are generally open daily from 3 pm to 4 am, the exception being those in Santo Domingo, which, for now, must close at midnight (2 am on Friday and Saturday). You must be 18 to enter, and jackets are required at the chic casinos in the capital.

SANTO DOMINGO

BARS AND CLUBS

Guácara Taína. This club is a landmark, for it is the only *disco* a cave formerly inhabited by Taíno Indians and, well, bats. (Sa Domingo has a network of natural caves within its city limits.) you descend, you see hundreds of heads bobbing and bodies gyrating among the stalactites: it's a unique sight. Banquettes and seating are carved into the limestone walls ornamented with Taíno pictographs. Alas, the fashionable crowd deserted it maybe 15 years ago, leaving it to the *turistas* and, increasingly, groups of cruise-ship passengers. Cover charge is $10 and includes one drink and Latin music you want to dance to. It's open Thursday–Sunday 9 pm–2 am. ✉ *Av. Mirador del Sur 655* ☎ *809/533–0671.*

LED. This disco is in a hotel, so it is able to stay open later than the other clubs, and that in itself is what has made this a favorite of the young and well-to-do party set who take their music *loud*. Many a graduation is celebrated here until the wee small hours of the *mañana*. ✉ *Hispaniola Hotel and Casino, Av. Abraham Lincoln at Av. Independencia, Gazcue* ☎ *809/476–7733.*

Marrakesh Café and Bar. This is where a sophisticated after-work crowd gathers for American and international music and *Casablanca* style. Complimentary tapas come to the table, and you can get top-shelf liquors. ✉ *Hotel Santo Domingo, Av. Abraham Lincoln at Av. Independencia, Gazcue* ☎ *809/221–1511.*

★ **Wine Tasting Room at El Catador.** This avant-garde wine bar and wine store was created by the major wine distributor El Catador. Cushy leather armchairs and hardwood floors help create a clubby atmosphere. There's a well-chosen selection of hors d'oeuvres, canapés, and tapas, both hot and chilled. Check out its calendar, as the events here include well-priced, prix-fixe dinners paired with wine on designated nights. You will want to buy one of the 500 bottles of wine from around the wine-making world. It's open until 11 pm on weekdays, but only until 6 on Saturday. If you opt to buy a bottle, you have to do it by 10:15 (or 5:15) so as to finish up by closing time. ✉ *Calle Jose Brea Péna 43, Avaristo Morales, Piantini* ☎ *809/540–1644.*

CASINOS

In Santo Domingo, several upscale hotels have casinos: Barceló Gran Hotel Lina and Spa; Mélia Santo Domingo Hotel and Casino; Hispaniola Hotel and Casino (attracts a younger crowd); Renaissance Jaragua Hotel and Casino; and the Hilton Santo Domingo. In Bayahibe, the Dominicus Diamante Casino, which reopened in 2010, is a class act.

Atlantis World Casino. Adjacent to the Intercontinental Hotel, Atlantis is one of the newest and most American-friendly, with slots that accept dollars. Although there's no charge to enter the gaming room, the table minimums are higher than most, so the casino attracts a more upscale crowd until closing time, which doesn't come until 6 am. ✉ *Av. George Washington 218, Gazcue* ☎ *809/688–8080.*

Dominican Republic Jazz Festival

It's shades of Havana in the 1950s, of New York's Harlem in the 1920s, with bearded jazz musicians in berets playing among *cubanos* with white Panama hats and guayabera shirts. It's a fusion of African percussion and drums—bongos and congos, backed up by marimbas and maracas, sexy songbirds and their piano men. It's rotund tuba players and sweat-stained black shirts as trumpet and sax players blow it out.

In November, the town of Cabarete is transformed into a music venue when the biggest names in Latin jazz hit the North Coast, including such legends as Chuck Mangione, Sade, Carlos Santana, Mongo Santa Maria, Chucho Valdés, and Arturo Sandoval. And on one night, the festivities move to Santiago's Centro León.

As hot as salsa, the pulsating tropical sounds draw thousands of aficionados, from poor students to black-tie patrons of the arts, who come for the music, the energy, the art exhibits, the educational workshops, the sun, and the sea. This is one five-star event that is democratic—most tickets cost about $15, and beach concerts are free.

Sizzling hot nights inevitably climax in impromptu jam sessions at such venues as Miró Restaurant in Cabarete. In short, the D.R. Jazz Fest is one of the best parties of the year.

Resorts book up early, especially those that are hotbeds of jazz activity. Check out the festival's Web site for more information: ⊕ *www. drjazzfestival.com.*

Majestic Casino. This is the newest of the Malecón casinos, and it is on a par with its Las Vegas counterparts. You'll find 20 gaming tables (even baccarat), a VIP salon, 200 video slots, live music (national and international talent), an upscale restaurant, and more. ⊠ *Hilton Santo Domingo, 1st Level, Av. George Washington, Gazcue* ☎ *809/685–0000.*

SOUTHEAST COAST

BARS AND CLUBS

Victory Club Piano Bar. A piano bar in a faux lighthouse at the very end of the marina's boardwalk, Victory Club is like a vacation fantasy. Yes, drinks are expensive, but at least you don't have to pay just to sit down in the Italian designer chairs and black leather couches. In the salon-lounge is artwork, a muted plasma TV, and wondrous vistas of the sea and moored yachts. The bar, which is shaped like a boat with a starry backdrop, has all of the fashionable drinks and wine choices—mostly Italian—and top-shelf champagnes. Food is served late—Italian-style light bites as well as pasta dishes and also some desserts and ice creams. It's only open on weekends in low season but seven nights in high season, closing at midnight. It is a good Saturday-night destination whenever there is a piano player. ⊠ *Casa de Campo Marina, Paseo del Mar 10, La Romana* ☎ *809/523–2264.*

Continued on page 454

PIRATES
IN THE
CARIBBEAN

Susan MacCallum Whitcomb & Julie Collazo Schwietert

Peg legs, parrots, and an easy-to-imitate "ahoy matey" lexicon: these are requisite elements in any pirate tale, but so are avarice and episodes of unspeakable violence. The combination is clearly compelling. Our fascination with pirates knows no bounds.

The true history of piracy has largely been obscured by competing pop-culture images. On one hand, there is the archetypal opportunist—fearsome, filthy, and foul-mouthed. On the other is the lovable scallywag epitomized by Captain Jack Sparrow in Disney's *Pirates of the Caribbean* franchise. Actual pirates, however, usually fell somewhere between these two extremes.

They could be uneducated men with limited life choices or crewmen from legitimate commercial and exploratory vessels left unemployed in the wake of changing political agendas. In either case, the piratical career path offered tempting benefits. Making a fast doubloon was only the beginning. Piracy also promised adventure plus egalitarian camaraderie—a kind of social equality unlikely to be found elsewhere during that class-conscious period.

Life aboard ship was governed by majority, as opposed to autocratic, rule. Pirates moreover, adhered to the Pirate's Code (a sort of "honor among thieves" arrangement). On the ships, at least, the common good took precedence.

X MARKS THE SPOT

Movie *Pirates of the Caribbean*.

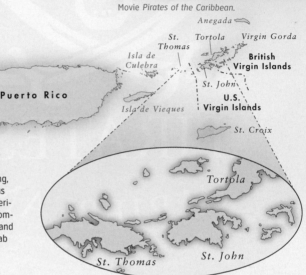

The Caribbean offered easy pickings for pirates because Spanish imperialists had already done the heavy lifting, extracting gems and precious metals from their South American colonies. Pirates from competing powers (namely England and France) could simply grab the spoils as Spanish ships island-hopped homeward.

Jamaica
Calico Jack Rackham, his lover Anne Bonny, and Mary Read were ultimately captured in **Bloody Bay** near Negril. Reportedly the male crew members were too busy drinking rum to mount a proper defense.

Dominican Republic
The centuries-old Spanish architecture in Santo Domingo's **Zona Colonial** is so well-preserved you can almost picture the area populated with

Santo Domingo, Dominican Republic

tankard-toting buccaneers and corset-clad wenches.

Puerto Rico
Massive fortifications, like **Castillo San Felipe del Morro** in Old San Juan, show just how far the Spanish were prepared to go to protect their assets from seagoing attackers, whether authorized or otherwise.

British Virgin Islands
Sir Francis Drake Channel, Jost Van Dyke, and Great Thatch Island were named for pirates or privateers. Ditto for **Norman Island**, which reputedly inspired the setting for R.L. Stevenson's *Treasure Island*.

St. Thomas
A strategic location, protected anchorages, plus easy-to-hide-in inlets made the U.S. Virgin Islands an ideal habitat for plunderers. High points like

Drake's Seat and Blackbeard's Castle were used to survey the terrain.

Anguilla
Underwater heritage preserves let divers explore vessels that sailed during piracy's Golden Age. **Stoney Ground Marine Park** contains a Spanish galleon wrecked in 1772, plus cannons, anchors, and other artifacts.

Stoney Ground Marine Park

Pirate ship arrives for Pirates Week, the Cayman Islands.

Peppered Pickled Pirate Party, Nevis.

Castillo de San Felipe del Morro, Puerto Rico.

Anguilla

St. Maarten
St. Martin

St. Barthélemy

Saba

Barbuda

St. Eustatius   St. Kitts

Nevis

Antigua

Montserrat

Guadeloupe

Marie Galante

Dominica

Martinique

St. Lucia

St. Vincent

PIRATES OF THE CARIBBEAN

Dominica
Convoys of booty-filled Spanish ships often stopped at this lush island. Pirates followed—and so did Hollywood. Key scenes for the second and third *Pirates of the Caribbean* movies were shot here.

St. Vincent
Sequences for the first three *Pirates of the Caribbean* installments were filmed on location here. The meticulously detailed cluster of buildings built to represent Port Royal can be seen at **Wallilabou Bay**.

PIRATE PARTIES

Cayman Islands
In mid-November, islanders celebrate their piratical past with an 11-day festival featuring treasure hunts, mock trials, and other themed events. The highlight is an invasion of **George Town** staged by *faux* pirates.

Nevis
Taking a page from the Cayman Islands book, Nevis introduced the weeklong **Peppered Pickled Pirate Party**. Held twice during the last week of October and November, it celebrates William Kidd and Black Bart with an "invasion," regattas, cooking and cocktail competitions, treasure hunts, and more

St. Barthélémy
Logically enough, Frenchman Daniel Montbars used this French island as his home base. Legend has it some of his treasure remains hidden in the beachfront caves around **Anse du Gouverneur**.

St. Lucia
Now a peaceful national park, **Pigeon Island** (on St. Lucia's northern tip) was once the hideout of François Le Clerc. This peg-legged pirate orchestrated attacks from his hilly vantage point in the late 16th century.

TIMELINE

1523 First Spanish treasure ships seized

1577 Francis Drake begins circumnavigating the globe

1604 James I revok— Letters of Marqu—

1500

1550

1600

1492 onward exploitation of New World resources

1585–1604 Anglo-Spanish War

FAMOUS PIRATES

Years after they wreaked havoc on the high seas, history still remembers some of the most notorious pirates of the Caribbean.

SIR FRANCIS DRAKE

Drake was a busy fellow. The first Englishman to circumnavigate the globe, he popularized tobacco, led slave-trading expeditions, helped destroy the Spanish Armada, and still had time to terrorize treasure-laden ships with Queen Elizabeth's blessing. Drake led his country's fleet in epic encounters throughout the Caribbean.

HENRY MORGAN

Captain Morgan led a colorful life before lending his name to a ubiquitous brand of rum. Leaving Wales for the West Indies as a young man, he successfully segued from debauched buccaneer to semi-respectable privateer and, after dodging piracy charges in England, ended up

Captin Morgan

Edward "Blackbeard" Teach

as the Lieutenant Governor of Jamaica.

BLACKBEARD

Born Edward Teach, Blackbeard was notable for his business savvy (which included making profit-sharing deals with politicos) as well as his fiendish looks. His signature beard was braided and often laced with lit fuses to terrify enemies. Alas, in 1718 Blackbeard's head was severed in a dramatic showdown with Lt. Robert Maynard of the Royal Navy. It

was mounted on Maynard's ship as a warning to others.

WILLIAM KIDD

Life was a roller-coaster ride for the legendary Captain Kidd. Kidd was a retired privateer living in New York when he accepted a commission to hunt pirates and then became one himself with the encouragement of a mutinous crew. He was executed in London in 1701, but hopefuls still hunt for the treasure he supposedly left buried.

PIRATES, PRIVATEERS, AND BUCCANEERS

The "pirate" label is generally applied to sailors engaging in any type of maritime marauding. Yet there are variations on the theme.

Privateers such as Sir Francis Drake were licensed looters, their escapades were authorized by a royal Letter of Marque, which issued private commissions for strategic naval operations. Privateers were sanctioned to attack only specific enemy ships, with the goodies gained benefitting their government. Since this rogue diplomacy was intended to challenge Spain's

dominance in the Americas, many privateers felt they were protecting national interests. Hence, they were pirates… but patriotic.

Buccaneers, conversely, were a motley crew. The word, originally reserved for pirates from Hispaniola (the island shared by Haiti and the Dominican Republic), eventually included anyone from

Sir Francis Drake

1655 Jamaica established as privateer base

1674 Henry Morgan knighted

1650

1700

1750

11

1618–1648
Thirty Years War

1689–1697
King William's War

1701–1714
War of Spanish Succession

IN FOCUS PIRATES IN THE CARIBBEAN

William Kidd

Calico Jack Rackman

Anne Bonny

BLACK BART ROBERTS

Though not the most famous pirate, he is often considered the most successful. He racked up impressive credits, plundering some 400 ships between 1719 and 1722. A snappy dresser who was fashionably attired even in battle, he was also a strict disciplinarian. Roberts quashed onboard gambling and banned music on Sunday.

DANIEL MONTBARS

Montbars proved Brits didn't hold a monopoly on bad behavior. French lineage aside, he differed from his 17th-century peers in that he was affluent and educated. His manners needed polishing, though. Violent outbursts (disemboweling Spaniards was a favorite sport) earned Montbars the nickname "The Exterminator."

CALICO JACK RACKHAM

An Englishman who ascended from mate to captain, Rackham, secured his legend by adding women to his crew. Workwise, his favorite tactic was attacking small vessels close to shore. Such boldness led to an inglorious end. Rackham was hung then tarred, feathered, and displayed in a cage in Port Royal, Jamaica.

ANNE BONNY AND MARY READ

Thought to be unlucky, female pirates were rare. Yet the comely Bonny and cross-dressing Read were respected by their shipmates… and feared by their victims. Captured together in 1720, they were sentenced to death. Both, however, escaped the noose by claiming to be pregnant.

the "Boys Gone Wild" school. Coming from diverse ethnic backgrounds, many buccaneers were fugitive slaves, escaped criminals, or other social outcasts who became plunderers by choice or force. Operating solely in their own interests and typically lacking a strategy or social order, they were the bottom feeders.

Political shifts could turn privateers into pirates (James I's decision to revoke Letters of Marque was a case in point). Desperation or moral degeneration could just as easily turn pirates into buccaneers.

PIRATE FLAGS

Flashy flags were to pirates what coats of arms were to royal families: visible signs of group identity. Each crew flew its own, depending on what attributes the captain wanted to emphasize or the degree of menace he wanted to convey.
The most recognizable is the "Jolly Roger": an iconic white-on-black skull cradled by crossbones.

CASINOS

On the North Coast, Holiday Village Golden Beach in Playa Dorada and Occidental Allegro Playa Dorada both have popular American-style casinos. Coral Puerto Plata (the former Breezes) in Cabarete has its Casino Carnival, which had a glamorous redo. East of Cabarete's downtown is Ocean Sands Casino and Club. The long-awaited mega-casino, Sosúa Bay Grand Casino in the impressive Sosúa Bay Center, is now open, and over on Cofresi Beach, there's the whimsical Ocean World Casino.

El Casino Diamante Dominicus Bayahibe. Across from the Iberostar, El Casino Diamante opened after a couple of bumpy years in early 2010. This brightly lit hotspot in Bayahibe has high, arched ceilings. Gamblers can try their luck at one of 23 table games, 60 slots, or at the sports book. There's Bubaraba, a sensuous disco; a classy sports bar with a hand-painted mural; and an inexpensive, casual restaurant that looks expensive. (It's open daily from 9 pm to 5 am.) A nightly, continuous shuttle service (using both a bus and golf carts) runs from all major Dominicus- and Bayahibe-area resorts. The casino is open daily, from 6 pm to 4 am. ✉ *Calle Juan Ponce de Leon, Plaza Montecarlo at Dominicus Americanus* ☎ *809/833–0574* ⊕ *www.casinosdiamante. com/bayahibe.*

PUNTA CANA

BARS AND CLUBS

★ **Montecristo.** A trendy spot, Montecristo evolves from a bar to a pulsating disco as the night goes on. The head bartender makes great mixed drinks with a flourish, and the manager is generally accessible to guests—tourists and locals alike. A big video screen serves as the backdrop for the dance floor, which mixes up DJ-spun international club music with merengue, *bachata* (a typical Dominican dance form), and salsa rhythms—and sometimes live music. The club has arrangements with several local hotels for transporting groups. There's no cover charge here, and there's special pricing for various sponsored drinks on different nights. ✉ *Palma Real Shopping Village, Carretera Cortecito-Bavaro, Bávaro* ☎ *809/552–8999.*

Pacha. A favorite among locals and still one of the best resort-based dance spots, Pacha plays more merengue and bachata than most of the other clubs. Drinks here are cheaper, too. For a beer, expect to pay about 80 pesos (or about $2.50); the price can be double in some of the other clubs. Cover charges apply when live bands perform; otherwise it's free to enter, and nonresort guests are welcome. The doors don't open until 11 pm, but they stay open until 4 am. ✉ *Av. Estados Unidos, at Riu complex, between Riu Palaca Macao and Riu Palace Bavaro, Bávaro.*

NORTH COAST

BARS AND CLUBS

Celuisina Tropicale. Celuisina Tropicale doesn't crank up until after midnight, but it keeps rolling until 4 am. Locals and tourists dance hiphop together. ✉ *Playa Nacho Resort, Playa Dorada* ☎ *809/320–6226.*

Deja Voodoo. This is Sosúa's most upscale bar. Melanie, a hip French-Canadian, is once again the proprietress, and she is intent on maintaining the two-story lounge and dance club's good level (and decibel) of music. Each night has a different theme, be it karaoke or Latin; locally well-known blues and jazz players perform often. On weekends it might be a mix of live bands or a DJ. Good news: there is no cover charge, and if you start drinking early—from 1 pm to 8 pm—you will enjoy discounted prices. ✉ *Pedro Clisante corner of Calle Arzeno, last building in Sosúa Bay complex, Sosúa* ☎ *No phone.*

Hemingway's Café. Hemingway's has long been the rockin' spot for the young and young at heart who love to party. There's rock or reggae by DJs or live bands, but only big-name merengue bands elicit a cover charge. On Saturday night there's a Latin fiesta, and on Thursday the mike is taken over by karaoke singers. The kitchen closes at 2 am and serves American-style fun food and good burgers, with fajitas a specialty. ✉ *Playa Dorada Plaza, Puerto Plata* ☎ *809/320–2230.*

Lax. Lax is a perennially popular, open-air bar that really comes alive by night. You can sit in the sand in lounge chairs or jump into the action inside under the palapa, where a DJ will be spinning madly or a live band will be rockin'. There's good grazing chow, too, and special theme nights like Thai (not bad, either); one night even offers an incredible, African fire-eating show. Drinks come from the blenders and in pitchers, but be patient: getting one can take time when the bar backs up. As it is next to a small hotel, it now can stay open until 3 am but must turn down the decibel from midnight to close. ✉ *Cabarete Beach, Cabarete* ☎ *809/915–4842.*

Onno's Bar. This remains a serious party place. It is usually wall-to-wall and back-to-back as the young and fit pack the dance floor and groove to techno sounds while other multinational youth sit at the tables in the sand. It's easier to get served at the beach bar than the main one, and as you chill, people will pass by, introduce themselves, converse, and then move on. It's fun and friendly, although on Friday and Saturday nights, when it stays open until 3 am, the scene can get rowdy. ✉ *Cabarete Beach, Cabarete* ☎ *809/571–0461.*

CASINOS

Ocean World Casino. Ocean World's extravagant casino was constructed within the Ocean World complex that includes the adventure park, and it rivals its counterparts in Las Vegas even though it's not as large. The whimsical decor and furnishings are from a fantasy world, and windows offer sea views. The Octopus Bar overlooks the spiffy new marina and its flotilla of yachts. A nocturnal tour of the Ocean World complex can include a sunset happy hour at the Lighthouse Lounge, dinner at Poseidón, and then a Las Vegas–style review, *Bravissimo,* which is a flurry of beautiful dancing girls and guys with incredible voices. If you want the night to continue even later, there's the Lighthouse Disco. ✉ *3 mi [5 km] west of Puerto Plata, Cofresi* ☎ *809/291–1111* ⊕ *www.oceanworld.net.*

SHOPPING

Cigars continue to be the hottest commodity coming out of the D.R. Many exquisite hand-wrapped smokes come from the island's rich Cibao Valley, and Fuente Cigars—handmade in Santiago—are highly prized. Only reputable cigar shops sell the real thing, and many you will see sold on the street are fakes. You can also buy and enjoy Cuban cigars here, but they can't be brought back to the United States legally. Dominican rum and coffee are also good buys. Mamajuana, an herbal liqueur, is said to be the Dominican answer to Viagra. The D.R. is the homeland of designer Oscar de la Renta, and you may want to stop at the chic shops that carry his creations. La Vega is famous for its *diablos cajuelos* (devil masks), which are worn during Carnival. Look also for the delicate, faceless ceramic figurines that symbolize Dominican culture.

Though locally crafted products are often of a high caliber (and very affordable), expect to pay hundreds of dollars for designer jewelry made of amber and larimar. Larimar—a semiprecious stone the color of the Caribbean Sea—is found on the D.R.'s south coast. Prices vary according to the stone's hue and category, AAA being the highest. Amber has been mined extensively between Puerto Plata and Santiago. A fossilization of resin from a prehistoric pine tree, it often encases ancient animal and plant life, from leaves to spiders to tiny lizards. Beware of fakes, which are especially prevalent in street stalls. A reputable dealer can show you how to tell the difference between real larimar and amber and imitations.

Bargaining is both a game and a social activity in the D.R., especially with street vendors and at the stalls in El Mercado Modelo. Vendors are disappointed and perplexed if you don't haggle. They're also tenacious, so unless you really plan to buy, don't even stop to look.

SANTO DOMINGO

SHOPPING AREAS AND MALLS
Acropolis Mall, between Avenida Winston Churchill and Calle Rafael Augusto Sanchez, has become a favorite shopping arena for the young and/or hip capitaleños. Stores like Zara and Mango (both from Spain) have today's look without breaking budget.

One of the main shopping streets in the Zone is **Calle El Conde,** a pedestrian thoroughfare. With the advent of so many restorations, the dull and dusty stores with dated merchandise are giving way to some hip, new shops. However, many of the offerings, including local designer shops, are still of a caliber and cost that the Dominicans can afford. Some of the best shops are on **Calle Duarte,** north of the Colonial Zone, between Calle Mella and Avenida de Las Américas. **El Mercado Modelo,** a covered market, borders Calle Mella in the Colonial Zone; vendors here sell a dizzying selection of Dominican crafts.

The **Malecón Center,** the latest complex, adjacent to the classy Hilton Santo Domingo, will eventually house 170 shops, boutiques, and services plus several movie theaters. In the tower above are luxury apartments and Sammy Sosa, in one of the penthouses.

Piantini is a swanky residential neighborhood that has an increasing number of fashionable shops and clothing boutiques. Its borders run from Avenida Winston Churchill to Avenida Lope de Vega and from Calle Jose Amado Soler to Avenida 27 de Febrero.

Plaza Central. This is a major shopping center with high-end shops, including a Jenny Polanco shop (an upscale Dominican designer who has incredible white linen outfits, artistic jewelry, purses, and more). ⊠ *Avs. Winston Churchill and 27 de Febrero, Piantini* ☎ *809/541–5929.*

RECOMMENDED STORES

Casa Jardin. This is the garden studio of abstract painter Ada Balacer. Works by other women artists are also shown; look for pieces by Yolarda Naranjo, known for her modern work that integrates everything from fiberglass, hair, rocks, and wood to baby dresses. ⊠ *Balacer Gustavo Medjía Ricart 15, Naco, Santo Domingo* ☎ *809/565–7978.*

Casa Virginia. One of the D.R.'s leading department stores was founded in 1945 by the mother of the present Virginia, who took it to the next level, adding a great day spa. What a novel idea for ladies who love to shop *and* to spa. The store is stocked mostly with high-end designer clothing (including a Jenny Polanco department), fashion finds, and Italian jewelry, but also some tasteful yet moderately priced gifts. ⊠ *Corner Av. Roberto Pastoriza 255, Piantini* ☎ *809/566–1535 or 809/566–4000.*

★ **Cigar Club.** This upscale club sells a variety of fine cigars, and it is one of the few places in the country where you can buy authentic Arturo Fuentes cigars. The club has a walk-in humidor as well as a lounge with a full bar, where you can enjoy fine wines, an aged rum, and Dominican coffee. Possibly you will get to hear the owner play the piano. The club has recently had a tasteful redecoration. It's open weekdays from 9 am to midnight, until 3 on Saturday. ⊠ *Av. 27 Febrero 211, Naco, Santo Domingo* ☎ *809/683–2770.*

Cigar King. Cigar King keeps Dominican and Cuban cigars in a temperature-controlled cedar room. ⊠ *Calle Conde 208, Baguero Bldg., Zona Colonial, Santo Domingo* ☎ *809/686–4987.*

Galería de Arte Mariano Eckert. This gallery focuses on the work of Eckert, an older Dominican artist who's known for his still lifes. ⊠ *Av. Winston Churchill and Calle Luis F. Tomen, 3rd fl., Evaristo Morales, Santo Domingo* ☎ *809/541–7109.*

Galería de Arte Nader. Galeria de Arte Nader showcases top Dominican artists in various media. The gallery staff is well known in Miami and New York and works with Sotheby's. ⊠ *Rafael Augusto Sanchez 22, between Ensanche Piantini and Plaza Andalucia II, Piantini, Santo Domingo* ☎ *809/687–6674 or 809/544–0878.*

Jorge Caridad. Because of their Taíno, African, and European heritage, artisans creating modern Dominican art forms are using seeds, fiber, bones, coconut skin, cow horns, and African motifs. A good selection is found at Jorge Caridad. ⊠ *Arzobispo Merino, corner of General Cabral, Zona Colonial, Santo Domingo.*

L'ile Au Tresor. This jewelry store has a *Pirates of the Caribbean* theme, but, that aside, it's fun and owned by a talented Frenchman, Patrick Joyas, who has some of the most attractive and creative designer pieces in native larimar, amber, and even conch. If you have never bought any of these lovely stones because the settings are usually cheesy, or if exquisite, too pricey, then this is your chance. His innovative custom work, with sterling or gold, can be done in 48 hours. His prices for the quality are kept moderate by the basement location and a shop that is not glamorous. ⊠ *Conde Plaza, lower floor, Calle Conde, across from Mercure Hotel, Zona Colonial, Santo Domingo* ☎ *809/688–8751.*

Lyle O. Reitzel Art Contemporaneo. The Reitzel gallery has, since 1995, specialized in contemporary art and showcases mainly Latin artists, from Mexico, South America, and Spain, and some of the most controversial Dominican visionaries. ⊠ *Plaza Andalucia II, Piantini, Santo Domingo* ☎ *809/227–8361.*

Nuovo Rinascimento. The exquisite store is replete with contemporary furniture and antiques, has beautiful Venetian linens and towels. Shipping can be arranged. The wooden hacienda doors open to a wonderful world of white sculptures and an inner courtyard with a lily-pad-dotted pool. Adjacent is Café Bellini, offering authentic Italian cuisine in a striking contemporary setting. ⊠ *Plazoleta Padre Billini, Zona Colonial, Santo Domingo* ☎ *809/686–3387.*

Plaza Toledo Bettye's Galeria. This gallery sells a fascinating array of artwork, including Haitian voodoo banners, metal sculptures, even souvenirs, chandeliers, and estate jewelry; the American expat owner, Bettye Marshall, has a great eye and can also rent you a room in one of her B&Bs. ⊠ *Isabel la Católica 163, Zona Colonial, Santo Domingo* ☎ *809/688–7649.*

SOUTHEAST COAST

SHOPPING AREAS AND MALLS

Altos de Chavón. This re-creation of a 16th-century Mediterranean village is on the grounds of the Casa de Campo resort, where you can find art galleries, boutiques, and souvenir shops grouped around a cobbled square. At the Altos de Chavón Art Studios you can find ceramics, weaving, and screen prints made by local artists. Extra special is Casa Montecristo, a chic cigar lounge, which also offers a tour with cigar history and trivia.

The Casa de Campo Marina. Casa de Campo's top-ranked marina is home to shops and international boutiques, galleries, and jewelers scattered amid restaurants, an ice-cream parlor, bars, banks, beauty salons, and a yacht club. It's a great place to spend some time shopping, sightseeing, and staring at the extravagant yachts. The chic shopping scene at the marina includes Bleu Marine, Fiori Coleccion (leather), Mediterraneo (women's fashions from designers like Gucci and Versace), Everett Designs (high-end larimar and amber jewelry, even authentic Spanish coins). Art Arena sells local artisan jewelry and gifts. Dominican designer Jenny Polanco sells clothes, purses, and jewelry in the Bibi Leon boutique, which is known for its tropical-themed home accessories. There's also a marvelous Italian antiques shop, Nuovo Rinascimento, and the Club de Cigarro (Fumo). By the way, the Nacional supermercado at the marina has not only groceries but sundries, postcards, and snacks.

PUNTA CANA

SHOPPING AREAS AND MALLS

Fodor's Choice
★

Galerías at Puntacana Village. This shopping center lies within a still-blossoming shopping, dining, and residential complex built on the road to the airport. It was built to house employees of Puntacana Resort and Club, but now it's also a tourist draw. The village houses a church, a school, and three banks (with ATMs) as well as Western Union. The commercial square also has several restaurants and bars, a bagel shop, pizzeria, ice-cream parlor, and American-style fast-food chains. There are also a hair salon and shops selling everything from clothing to sundries. An art gallery sells locally crafted items, including an exquisite wooden chess set with giant pieces carved to resemble classical musicians on one side and Dominican pop stars on the other. Free transportation is provided to guests at Puntacana Resort and Club and Tortuga Bay Villas. ⊠ *Puntacana Resort and Club, Punta Cana.*

Fodor's Choice
★

Palma Real Shopping Village. A standout among the region's shopping centers, Palma Real Shopping Village is a swanky, partially enclosed mall. Fountains and tropical plants infuse life into the bright and airy interior areas beneath the blue-tile roof. Music pipes through the stone-floor plaza in the center, where seating is available and security is tight. Upscale retail shops, which sell beachwear, clothing, skin-care products, and jewelry, line the walls. Several restaurants give visitors welcome dining alternatives beyond the gates of their resorts. There are two banks, ATMs, and a money-exchange outlet. Stores are open 10–10, but the restaurants stay open later. Shuttle buses run to and from many of the hotels, with pick-ups every two hours. Punta Cana's first movie theater is now open and showing first-run films. ⊠ *Bávaro* ☎ *809/552–8725* ⊕ *www.palmarealshoppingvillage.com.*

Plaza Higüeyana. This artisan market, which draws busloads of tourists, is on the right-hand side of the road just outside the town of Higüey. Here you can browse through racks and shelves full of souvenirs, like mamajuana, rum, T-shirts, jewelry, crafts, and ceramics. Inside the market, you can take a free tour of the **Museo Vivo Del Tabaco**, where you can see how tobacco is planted, harvested, and rolled into cigars. Near the entrance to the museum, you can also purchase hand-rolled cigars. ⊠ *Carretera Higüey–La Otra Banda, at east end of Higüey* ☎ *809/551–1128 for museum only* ⊙ *Daily 9–noon and 2–5.*

Plaza Uvero Alto. You won't find brand-name shops at this shopping center, but it's a convenient shopping center for the hotels in the remote Uvero Alto area, with a bank and outdoor ATM, money exchange, Internet café, small pharmacy, gift shops, and two minimarkets (one in the front, the other tucked away in the back row of booths) that sell sundries such as suntan lotion and deodorant at prices that are much cheaper than in the hotels. Behind the first row of enclosed stores, peruse the colorful kiosks full of handicrafts, paintings, ceramics, and other gift items; most shopkeepers here, although very friendly, don't speak much English, so knowing even a few words of Spanish will come in handy. ⊠ *Carretera Uvero Alto, Playa Uvero Alto.*

RECOMMENDED STORES

Harrisons. This store doesn't sell trinkets but rather high-end jewelry, most likely at better prices than in your hometown. For quality larimar and amber with well-designed settings, many in platinum, this is it. Branches can be found in many other tourist destinations, including several North Shore locations. ⊠ *Palma Real Shopping Village, Bávaro* ☎ *809/552–8721.*

La Tabaquería Cigar Club. Near the airport, La Tabaqueria Cigar Club is a haven for cigar lovers, who can watch the handmade production process or relax at the bar with a drink. Fine Dominican and Cuban cigars are for sale, as are humidors and related accessories, from 9 am to 9 pm daily. You can call the store to arrange transportation. ⊠ *La Plaza Bolera, Suite 10A, Punta Cana* ☎ *809/959–0040.*

Tesoro Caribeño. This store has a fine selection of amber and larimar jewelry and other stones amid the colorful shelves full of souvenirs and crafts. Unique pieces are crafted by the same designers who create jewelry for the Harrison's chain, but are sold at generally lower prices. The owner speaks fluent English. ⊠ *Plaza Uvero Alto, Local 5, Playa Uvero Alto* ☎ *No phone.*

NORTH COAST

SHOPPING AREAS AND MALLS

In Puerto Plata you can find enough interesting stores to both quell your shopping urge and pick up a few funky gifts, like mamajuana, the Dominican herbal liqueur. A popular shopping street for costume jewelry and souvenirs is **Calle Beller.**

Discount Plaza (⊠ *Playa Dorada Plaza, Calle Duarte at Av. 30 de Marzo, Puerto Plata* ☎ *809/320–6645*) is the local equivalent of Walmart, though on a small scale. The clothes you can find here are of the same caliber—bathing suits, flip-flops, baseball caps, and the like. You can choose from a pretty good selection of toiletries if you have forgotten anything, as well as rum. There are also cheap Dominican souvenirs. You can buy phone cards here, as well as make long-distance calls in private booths and exchange currency.

RECOMMENDED STORES

Harrisons. This store doesn't sell trinkets but rather high-end jewelry, most likely at better prices than in your hometown. For quality larimar and amber with well-designed settings, many in platinum, this is it. Branches can be found in many other tourist destinations, including Cabarete and Sosúa. ⊠ *Playa Dorada Plaza, Puerto Plata* ☎ *809/586–3933.*

Miró Gallery and Restaurant. At Miró, you can find rotating exhibitions of contemporary art with an emphasis on Latino artists and photographers, especially from the Dominican Republic and Cuba. Opening soirees are social events. ⊠ *Cabarete Beach, Cabarete* ☎ *809/571–0888.*

SPORTS AND ACTIVITIES

Although there's hardly a shortage of activities here, the resorts have virtually cornered the market on sports, including every conceivable water sport. In some cases, facilities may be available only to guests of the resorts.

BIKING AND HIKING

Pedaling is easy on pancake-flat beaches, but there are also some steep hills in the D.R. Several resorts rent bikes to guests and nonguests alike.

NORTH COAST

Iguana Mama (⊠ *Calle Principal 74, Cabarete* ☎ *809/571–0908 or 809/571–0228* ⊕ *www.iguanamama.com*) has traditional and mountain bikes, and will take you on guided rides on the flats or test your mettle on the steep grades in the mountains. Their "Cascading" tour takes you to 27 waterfalls on a full-day trip that includes climbing up and jumping off various waterfalls. Downhill bike rides, which include a taxi up to the foothills, breakfast, and lunch, cost $99 for a full-day trip, $65 for a half-day trip. Advanced rides, on and off roads, are $40 to $50. Guided hikes cost $35 to $70. In addition, this well-established, safety-oriented company offers horseback riding on the beach and in the countryside for $40 for two hours, canyoning, ecotours, and a lots of other adventure sports.

BOATING

Sailing conditions are ideal, with constant trade winds. Favorite excursions include day trips to Catalina and Saona islands—both in the La Romana area—and sunset cruises on the Caribbean. Prices for crewed sailboats of 26 feet and longer, with a capacity of 4 to 12 people, are priced according to size and duration, from a low of $200 a day to the norm of $700 a day. Examples of other prices, taken from the new fleet at Cap Cana Marina, are as follows: Sportfishermen from 47 to 51 feet accommodating up to eight people (crewed with all equipment, snacks, and beverages with sandwiches on all day trips), $1,800 for four hours, $2,500 for eight hours; a 62-foot custom, luxury power-sail catamaran, $1,650 for two hours (everything included for Cap Cana guests); a 56-foot Sea Ray Sedan Bridge motor yacht, $2,000 for two hours, $2,500 for four hours, $3,500 for eight hours (everything included); and a luxury 90-foot custom motor yacht, ideal for an incentive group, $3,500 for two hours, $5,000 for four hours, $8,500 for eight hours.

SOUTHEAST COAST

Casa de Campo Marina (⊠ *Casa de Campo, Calle Barlovento 3, La Romana* ☎ *809/523–8646* ⊕ *www.casadecampo.com.do*) has much going on, from sailing to motor yachting and socializing at the Casa de Campo Yacht Club. A first for the marina was hosting the Rolex FARR 40 World's Championship 2010, held in April. One of the world's most important annual sailing events, this was the first time it came to the Caribbean.

PUNTA CANA

Marina Cap Cana (⊠ *Cap Cana,, Juanillo* ☎ *809/695–5539* ⊕ *www. capcana.com/site/index.php/en/activity/marina*) on the Mona Passage on the southeastern edge of the Dominican Republic, offers a superb port for sportfishing during the summer season, when the grounds are renowned for an abundance of blue marlin and white marlin. Currently, 89 wet slips are available for vessels of 30 feet to 130 feet. All have cable TV, water, and Wi-Fi. A thousand slips are planned, some with capacity for yachts over 150 feet long. Slip rentals are available; anglers participating in any of three seasonal fishing tournaments get discount dockage rates. For deep-sea fishing, 48' and 51' Riviera Sportfish may be chartered (four- or eight-hour excursions for marlin, wahoo, tuna, snapper, grouper, etc.). There's also a designated fishing area for snook, tarpon, barracuda, and jack, with guides and equipment available. The marina hosts festivities and cocktail parties during the height of the fishing season.

NORTH COAST

★ **Carib Wind Center** (⊠ *Cabarete* ☎ *809/571–0640* ⊕ *www.caribwind. com*) is a renowned windsurfing center (known for decades as Carib BIC Center) that also rents Lasers, 17-foot catamarans, bodyboards, and sea kayaks. It has an Olympic Laser training center with a former racing instructor. Experts—even champions—come to train here.

Ocean World Marina (⊠ *Cofresí, 3 mi [5 km] west of Puerto Plata* ☎ *809/970–3373 or 809/291–1111* ⊕ *www.oceanworldmarina.com*) is a state-of-the art marina strategically positioned between the heavily traveled Florida-Bahamas region and the Puerto Rico–eastern Caribbean region. It has filled a large 300-mi (480-km) void on the North Coast where no full-service marina previously existed. The 35-acre complex has 120 slips that accommodate sailboats of up to 200 feet. It is a port of entry with its own immigration and customs office, concierge, laundry and shower facilities, duty-free shop, food and liquor store, car-rental service (even hourly rentals), and marina store with fishing supplies, as well as an entertainment clubhouse, nightclub, and casino.

DIVING

Ancient sunken galleons, undersea gardens, and offshore reefs are among the lures here. Most divers head to the north shore. In the waters off Sosúa alone you can find a dozen dive sites (for all levels of ability) with such catchy names as Three Rocks (a deep, 163-foot dive), Airport Wall (98 feet), and Pyramids (50 feet). Some 10 dive schools are represented on Sosúa Beach; resorts have dive shops on-site or can arrange trips for you.

SAMANÁ

In 1979 three atolls disappeared after a seaquake off Las Terrenas, providing an opportunity for truly memorable dives. Also just offshore from Las Terrenas are the Islas Las Ballenas (The Whale Islands), a cluster of four little islands with good snorkeling. A coral reef is off Playa Jackson, a beach accessible only by boat.

Las Terrenas Divers (⌧ *At hotel Bahía Las Ballenas, Playa Bonita, Las Terrenas* ☎ *809/889–2422* ⊕ *www.lt-divers.com*) offers diving lessons and trips. A dive is $38; daily diving-equipment rentals are $10. Learn-to-dive programs are $80. It is closed Sunday.

NORTH COAST

Northern Coast Aquasports (⌧ *Sosúa* ☎ *809/571–1028* ⊕ *www.northerncoastdiving.com*) is a five-star, Gold Palm PADI dive center; it's also the only National Geographic diver-certification site in the Dominican Republic. Professionalism is apparent in the initial classroom and pool practice, as well as in the selection of legendary dive sites around beautiful Sosúa Bay, where you can explore the reefs, walls, wrecks, and swim-throughs, from 25 to 130 feet. Successful completion of a three-day course and $350 earns you a PADI Open Water Certification card. Classrooms have air-conditioning and DVDs. On Friday night the British owners host a curry supper and beer party for their clients, and there are also eight self-catering apartments nearby that can be rented for a moderate cost.

FISHING

Big-game fishing is big in Punta Cana, with blue and white marlin, wahoo, sailfish, dorado, and mahimahi among the most common catches in these waters. Several fishing tournaments are held every summer. The Puntacana Resort and Club has hosted the ESPN Xtreme Billfishing Tournament every year since 2003. Blue marlin tournaments are held at the La Mona Channel in Cabeza de Toro. Several tour operators offer organized deep-sea fishing excursions.

PUNTA CANA

At **Puntacana Marina** (⌧ *Puntacana Resort and Club, Punta Cana* ☎ *809/959–2262 Ext. 8004* ⊕ *www.puntacana.com*), on the southern end of the resort, half-day, deep-sea fishing excursions are available for US$95 per person, with a minimum of two people, $70 for observers. For a Bertram 33-footer to go after tuna, marlin, dorado, and wahoo, it's $575 for four hours. It costs the same to charter a 45-foot Sportfisherman. Also, ask about the *yolas*, simple fishing boats with outboards.

GOLF

This island has earned a reputation as a golf destination, and deservedly so. The D.R. has some of the best courses in the Caribbean, designed by top golf architects; among these leading designers are Pete Dye, P.B. Dye, Jack Nicklaus, Robert Trent Jones, Gary Player,

Tom Fazio, Nick Faldo, Tom Watson, and Severiano Ballesteros. The Dominican Republic was voted Golf Destination of the Year by the International Association of Golf Tour Operators (IAGTO) during its IAGTO Awards 2009 celebrations in Spain. IAGTO operators control more than 80% of golf holiday packages sold worldwide. Criteria for choosing the winner included customer satisfaction, quality of courses and accommodations, value for money, support from suppliers and tourist boards, and professional conduct. Most courses charge higher rates during the winter high season; some, but not all, reduce their rates between April and October, so be sure to ask. Also, some have cheaper rates in the afternoon (mornings are cooler). And guests of certain hotels get better prices.

LA ROMANA

Fodor's Choice   The famed 18-hole Teeth of the Dog course at **Casa de Campo** (✉ *La*
★   *Romana* ☎ *809/523–3333, 809/523–8115 golf director* ⊕ *www. casadecampo.com.do*), with seven holes on the sea, is often ranked as the number one course in the Caribbean, and is among the top courses in the world. In 2010 it was awarded a gold medal in the resorts category. Greens fees are $225 per round for each nonguest, and $160 for guests, as well as $25 (plus tip) for a mandatory caddy. Pete Dye has designed this and two other globally acclaimed courses here: Dye Fore, with 18 holes close to Altos de Chavón, hugs a cliff that looks over the sea, a river, and the stunning marina ($225 for nonguests, $160 guests); the Links is an 18-hole inland course ($150 and $130). Avid golfers should inquire about the resort's various golf packages. Resort guests must reserve tee times for all courses at least one day in advance, nonguests earlier. Jim McLean, a leading golf instructor, offers high-quality instruction. Lessons are available to individuals and groups in half days and full days.

Los Marlins Championship Golf Course (✉ *Autovia del Este, Km 55, Juan Dolio* ☎ *809/526–1359*) is an 18-hole, 6,400-yard, par-72 course designed by Charles Ankrom. Guests of the adjacent Embassy Suites pay $45 for 18 holes including cart, $22 for 9 holes; nonguests pay $70 for 18 holes, $40 for 9. Golfers get 10% off at the Metro Country Club. A Fuentes Cigar Club, one of the few such clubs in the country, is on the second floor. Kids and moms can be seen on the 18-hole miniature golf range when the dads are playing the 18-hole course. The tennis courts are lighted at night. ■TIP➔ If you're playing golf at Los Marlins, plan on taking your lunch at the adjacent Metro Country Club. You can sit in the air-conditioned dining room or outside on the terrace. Some of the menu items, particularly the starters, are especially good, and the mains are reasonably priced.

PUNTA CANA

Barceló Bávaro Golf (✉ *Bávaro* ☎ *809/686–5797*) is an 18-hole, par-72 course integrated within the Barceló Bávaro Beach Golf and Casino Resort complex, which is open to its own guests and those of other hotels. The course, with numerous water obstacles, was designed by Juan Manuel Gordillo, and was the first in the Bávaro area. The rate for those not staying at Bávaro is $130, which includes greens fees, golf cart, and a day pass to the resort, where you can get food and beverages for the day. Complete renovations have been finished by designer P. B. Dye.

Challenging and reasonably priced, **Catalonia Caribe Golf Club** (✉ *Catalonia Bávaro Resort, Cabeza de Toro, Bávaro* ☎ *809/321–7058* ⊕ *www.cataloniabavaro.com*) is an 18-hole, par-72 course spread out on greens surrounded by five lakes and an abundance of shady palms. Alberto Sola was the designer. Greens fees are $120, including golf cart.

Named for the coconut plantation on which it was built, **Cocotal Golf Course** (✉ *Bávaro* ☎ *809/687–4653* ⊕ *www.cocotalgolf.com*), designed by Spaniard José "Pepe" Gancedo, has 18 championship holes and 9 regular holes. It's a challenging par-72 course in a residential community dotted with palm trees and lakes. It also has a driving range, clubhouse, pro shop, and golf academy. Greens fees are $149 for 18 holes for nonmembers who are not guests at one of Punta Cana's Sol Meliá properties including the cart. The cost is $65 for 9 holes, excluding cart.

★ **La Cana Golf Course** (✉ *Puntacana Resort and Club, Puntacana* ☎ *809/959–4653* ⊕ *www.puntacana.com*) is a breathtaking 18-hole championship course designed by P.B. Dye, with spectacular ocean views—four holes play right along the water. For resort guests, greens fees are $75 for 9 holes, $125 for 18 holes, with cart included; for nonguests, fees are $102 for 9 holes, $165 for 18 holes, and that includes a golf cart, water, and tees, but not the caddie ($20–$30). Reserve two weeks in advance from November through April. Lessons and clinics are offered at the resort. Puntacana Resort also has a course by Tom Fazio (Corales Golf Course) and an inland course that is under construction at this writing.

Fodor'sChoice
★ **Punta Espada Golf Course** (✉ *Cap Cana, Carretera Juanillo, Playa Juanillo* ☎ *809/688–5587*) is a par-72 Jack Nicklaus signature golf course with striking bluffs, lush foliage, and winding waterways. There's a Caribbean view from all the holes, and eight of them play right along the ocean. It's the first of three Jack Nicklaus signature courses planned at Cap Cana, and the site of an annual, internationally televised PGA Champions Tour event. The top-notch golf club has concierge services, a restaurant, the Hole 19 bar, a pro shop, a members' trophy gallery, a library, lockers, an equipment repair shop, and a meeting room. Greens fees are $395, which includes golf cart, caddy, tees, water, and practice on the driving range. The course is closed Tuesday for maintenance.

NORTH COAST

Golf Digest has named **Playa Dorada Golf Club** (✉ *Playa Dorada, Puerto Plata, next door to Victoria Resort* ☎ *809/320–3472* ⊕ *www.playadoradagolf.com*) one of the top 100 courses outside the United States. It's open to guests of all the hotels in the area. Greens fees for 9 holes are $58, 18 holes $87; caddies are mandatory for foursomes and will cost about $15 for 18 holes, $8 for 9; carts are optional, at $20 and $15, for 18 or 9 holes, respectively. Guests at certain hotels in the Playa Dorada complex, particularly the Victoria Golf and Beach Resort, get discounts.

GUIDED TOURS

Visitors to the Dominican Republic will have a plethora of excursions to choose from, but many options are not wonderful and are over-priced. Wait until you arrive before booking anything. As far as the group excursions, "interview" fellow guests to find out if their tour was worth the money and effort. Often the full-day excursions are too long and leave too early. Best are half-day trips—particularly boat excursions. Horseback riding can sound appealing, as the trails usually include some stretches of beach, but do not envision superior horseflesh, tack, instruction, or even guides who can speak English. And whatever, just enjoy! Clients traveling on a tour-company package tend to book excursions with the same company, or through the company affiliated with their resort.

SANTO DOMINGO

Private tours are a good option in Santo Domingo, but you will have to pay approximately $125 a day for a guide—more if the tour guide works with a driver. Your hotel concierge can best arrange these for you, and he or she will know the best English-speaking guides. Be sure you hire a guide who is licensed by the government.

LA ROMANA

In La Romana, **Tropical Tours** (✉ *Casa de Campo, La Romana* ☎ *809/556–5801* ⊕ *tropicaltoursromana.com.do*) has prices that are even less expensive than some nonpros and the cruise-ship excursions. Its Santo Domingo city tours are $300 for up to four people. (A rental car at Casa costs $90 and driving is risky.) Vans are new or nearly so, and well maintained. Also, most staff speaks English as well as other languages.

PUNTA CANA

Amstar DMC–Apple Vacations (✉ *Carretera Bavaro, Bavaro* ☎ *809/221–6626* ⊕ *www.amstardmc.com*) is well managed and reliable.

Go Golf (☎ *809/688–2978* ⊕ *www.golfreservationcenter.com*) specializes in golf packages, tailored to clients seeking to make golf part of their getaway—whether it's the primary focus or a onetime outing; they will help arrange tee times, golf instruction, and transport to courses.

NORTH COAST

In Playa Dorada the norm is to tour with the company from which you bought your vacation package. But a good local one is **Hotel Beds** (✉ *Puerto Plata* ☎ *No phone* ⊕ *www.hotelbeds.com*), which will also take individual travelers, when space is available. The city tours include stops in nearby Puerto Plata, with a stop at the authentic Amber Museum, and the seaside town of Sosúa, with its historic Jewish settlement, plus a nice luncheon for about $45. The day trip to Cayo El Paraiso ($80–$149) begins with lunch and drinks at a substantial, open-air restaurant in a little village. A motorboat then speeds you off to an idyllic white sandbar of a beach. A VIP lunch and sportfishing boat is an option.

HORSEBACK RIDING

11

SOUTHEAST COAST

The 250-acre **Equestrian Center at Casa de Campo** (⊠ *La Romana* ☎ *809/ 523–3333* ⊕ *www.casadecampo.com.do*) has something for both Western and English riders—a dude ranch, a rodeo arena (where Casa's trademark "Donkey Polo" is played), guided trail rides, and jumping and riding lessons. Guided rides run about $56 an hour, $88 for two hours; lessons cost $65 an hour, and jumping lessons are $88 an hour or $55 a half hour. There are early morning and sunset trail rides, too. Handsome, old-fashioned carriages are available for hire as well.

Guavaberry Equestrian Center (⊠ *Guavaberry Golf and Country Club, Autovía del Este, Km 55, Juan Dolio* ☎ *809/333–4653*) has a clean stable, good stock, and English and Western saddles. Delightful hour-plus trail rides throughout the extensive grounds of the resort cost $25; free transportation is provided from all Juan Dolio hotels.

PUNTA CANA

Rancho Punta Cana (⊠ *Puntacana Resort and Club, Punta Cana* ☎ *809/ 959–2714* ⊕ *www.puntacana.com*) is across from the main entrance of the resort. A one-hour trail ride winds along the beach, the golf course, and through tropical forests. The two-hour jungle trail ride has a stopover at a lagoon fed by a natural spring, so wear your swimsuit under your long pants. You can also do a three-hour full-moon excursion or take riding lessons. The stock are Paso Fino horses.

SAMANÁ

Rancho Cedric (⊠ *Playa Las Terrenas, behind Hotel Las Cayenas, Las Terrenas* ☎ *809/847–4849*) offers rides on Playa Bonita for $18 and Playa Cosón or Las Terrenas for $45. **Club Hippique Las Terrenas** (☎ *829/ 962–4259*) has mountain and beach excursions.

NORTH COAST

The **Sea Horse Ranch Equestrian Center** (⊠ *Cabarete* ☎ *809/571–3880 or 809/571–4462*) is a professional, well-staffed operation. The competition ring is built to international regulations, and there is a large schooling ring. The Dominican Equestrian Federation sanctions an annual invitational jumping event. Lessons, including dressage instruction, start at $35 an hour, and endurance rides are $30 for 90 minutes, $50 for three hours, including drinks and snacks—but make reservations. The most popular ride includes stretches of beach and a bridle path across a neighboring farm's pasture that's full of wildflowers and butterflies. Feel free to tie your horse to a palm tree and jump into the waves.

WIND- AND KITESURFING

FodorśChoice
★

Between June and October, Cabarete Beach has what many consider to be optimal windsurfing conditions: wind speeds at 20 to 25 knots (they come from the side shore) and 3- to 10-foot Atlantic waves. The Professional Boardsurfers Association has included Cabarete in its international windsurfing slalom competition. The novice is also welcome to learn and train on wider boards with light sails.

Carib Wind Center (⊠ *Cabarete* ☎ *809/571–0640* ⊕ *www.caribwind. com*) carries a number of brands, including many Olympic Laser boards. Equipment and instruction are offered, and lessons are generally $30 to $35 an hour; boards rent for $20 an hour. A gem of a windsurfing club, this family-owned business has many repeat clients and is open year-round. In the complex is its beach bar, EZE, as well as a retail shop. It has all the paraphernalia for surfing and a good variety of sunglasses, including Maui Jim's, and some of the best bikinis, cute miniskirts, and dresses in town.

Kitexcite (⊠ *Kite Beach Hotel, Kite Beach, Cabarete* ☎ *809/571–9509, 809/913–0827, or 809/914–9745* ⊕ *www.kiteclub.com*) operates a large school. (Fuel up at the adjacent Kite Club Grill.)

Grenada

WITH CARRIACOU

WORD OF MOUTH

"Grenada is a stunning, breathtaking island that will steal your heart for a lifetime . . . at least that is what has happened to me. It has everything that you are looking for, and you will still likely find things you never imagined. You can't go wrong with Grenada. I have not."

—caribheart

WELCOME TO GRENADA

THE SPICE ISLAND

A relatively small island, Grenada is 21 mi (34 km) long and 12 mi (19 km) wide; much of the interior is a lush rain forest. It's a major producer of nutmeg, cinnamon, mace, cocoa, and other spices and flavorings. Carriacou—23 mi (37 km) north of Grenada—is just 13 square mi (34 square km). Tiny Petite Martinique is 2 mi (3 km) farther north.

22 Sauteur Bay

David Bay

Carib's Leap

Sauteurs

Morne Fendue

14

St. Mark Bay

Victoria

Gouyave Nutmeg ◆ Processing Coop

Gouyave

Mt. St. Catherine

◆ Dougaldston Spice Estate

Gouyave Bay

▲ Mt. Granby

Concord Falls ◆

▲ Mt. Qua Qua

Black Bay Pt.

Flamingo Bay

Halifax Harbour

◆ Grand Étang National Park and Forest Reserve

Marq

Annandale Falls ◆

▲ Mt. Lebanon

Molinère Reef

Molinère Pt.

Constantine

▲ Mt. Sinai

Pomme Rose

Grand Mal Bay

St. George's

De la Grenade ◆ Industries

St. David's

Bianca C

St. George's Harbour

1

1 2

Laura Herb and Spice Garden

0   5 mi

0   5 km

Boss Reef

Belmont

Westerhall Estate

La Sagesse Beach

3 - 6
2 - 8

Grand Anse Beach

Grand Anse

Morne Rouge Bay

Morne Rouge Beach

9 10

19

13 21

La Sagesse Bay

Magazine Beach

St. George's U.

12 20

Pink Gin Beach
Pt. Salines

15   L'Anse aux Épines

Westerhall Bay

8 14

11 18

Maurice Bishop International Airport

9 10
16 17

Prickly Bay

7 11 - 13

These days, the people on the Isle of Spice busy themselves cultivating nutmeg, cloves, and other spices. Vestiges of Grenada's briefly turbulent past have all but disappeared. Renowned for its natural beauty, its fragrant air, and its friendly people, Grenada has lovely beaches and plenty of outdoor and cultural activities.

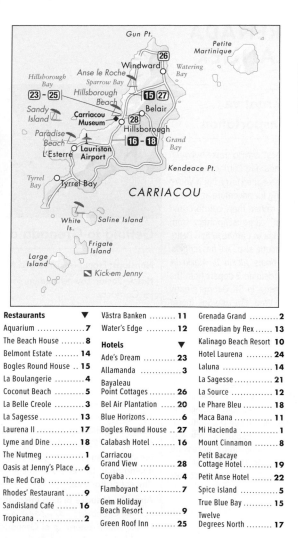

KEY

- Beaches
- Cruise Ship Terminal
- Dive Sites
- 1 Restaurants
- 1 Hotels

TOP REASONS TO VISIT GRENADA

1 The Aroma: The scent of spices fills the air, perfumes the soap, improves the drinks, and even flavors the ice cream.

2 Nature Abounds: Spot monkeys in the mountains, watch birds in the rain forest, join fish in the sea, and build sand castles on the beach.

3 Local Hospitality: Grenadians go out of their way to make you feel welcome.

4 A Great Getaway: With no megaresorts, you really can get away from it all.

GRENADA PLANNER

Alternative Transportation

The best way to travel between Grenada and Carriacou is by air or high-speed ferry; but if you're looking for adventure and economy rather than comfort and speed, cargo schooners from Grenada to Carriacou and Petite Martinique also take passengers. Mail boats *Alexia II, Alexia III,* and *Adelaide B* depart from the Carenage in St. George's early Tues., Wed., Fri., and Sat. mornings for the four-hour voyage to Carriacou; the return trip to Grenada departs Carriacou on Mon., Wed., Thurs., and Sun. mornings. The fare between Grenada and Carriacou on these schooners is $10 each way. The *Adelaide B* continues on from Carriacou to Petite Martinique (1½-hour trip); the fare is about $5 each way. Reservations aren't necessary, but get to the wharf at daybreak to be sure you don't miss the boat.

Water taxis are available along the Esplanade, near the port area. For about $8 (EC$20) a motorboat will transport you on an exciting cruise between St. George's and the jetty at Grand Anse Beach. Water taxis are privately owned, unregulated, and don't follow any particular schedule—so make arrangements for a pickup time if you expect a return trip.

Getting to Grenada and Carriacou

Nonstops: From New York and Miami.

Hassle Factor: Low to medium for Grenada, medium–high for Carriacou.

Air Travel: American Airlines/American Eagle (☏ 473/444–2121 or 800/744–0006) flies nonstop between Grenada and Miami. All other flights require a connection in San Juan or elsewhere in the Caribbean. **Caribbean Airlines** (☏ 800/744–2225) provides twice-weekly nonstop service from New York. **Delta Air Lines** (☏ 800/241–4141) provides twice-weekly nonstop service from New York. **LIAT** (☏ 888/844–5428) offers frequent scheduled service linking Grenada with more than two dozen neighboring islands. **SVG Air** (☏ 473/444–3549, 800/744–7285, 473/443–8519 in Carriacou) flies between Grenada and Carriacou, with some flights continuing on to Union Island to connect with flights to St. Vincent or Barbados.

Airports: Maurice Bishop International Airport (✉ *Point Salines Grenada* ☏ 473/444–4101) at Point Salines, on the southwestern tip of Grenada, is a modern facility suitable for the largest jets. Best of all, it's no more than a 10-minute drive from most hotels and resorts. On Carriacou, five minutes south of Hillsborough, **Lauriston Airport** (✉ *Carriacou* ☏ 473/443–6306) has a lighted landing strip suitable for small planes, with a small building for ticket sales and shelter. On Grenada, taxis are always available for transportation between the airport and hotels. Fares to St. George's are $25; to the hotels of Grand Anse and L'Anse aux Épines, $15. Rides taken between 6 pm and 6 am incur a $4 surcharge. At Carriacou's airport, taxis meet every plane; the fare to Hillsborough is $6.

Getting Around Grenada and Carriacou

Driving: Most of Grenada's 650 mi (1,050 km) of paved roads are kept in fairly good condition—albeit steep, curving, and narrow beyond the Grand Anse area. Driving is on the left, British-style. Gas stations are in St. George's, Grand Anse, Grenville, Gouyave, and Sauteurs.

Some rental agencies impose a minimum age of 21 to rent a car. Rental cars (including four-wheel-drive vehicles) cost $55 to $75 a day or $285 to $375 a week with unlimited mileage. In high season there may be a three-day minimum rental. Rental agencies offer free pickup and drop-off at either the airport or your hotel. A temporary driving permit, available through the rental agency, costs $12.

On Grenada: David's Car Rentals (☎ 473/444–3399 ⊕ www.davidscars.com). **Indigo Car Rentals** (☎ 473/439–3300 ⊕ www.indigocarsgrenada.com). **McIntyre Bros. Ltd.** (☎ 473/444–3944 ⊕ www.caribbeanhorizons.com). **Y & R Car Rentals** (☎ 473/444–4448 ⊕ www.y-r.com).

On Carriacou: Barba's Auto Rentals (☎ 473/443–7454 or 473/407–5156).

Ferries: The high-speed ferry **Osprey Express** (☎ 473/440–8126 ⊕ www.ospreylines.com) makes two round-trip voyages daily from Grenada to Carriacou and on to Petite Martinique. The fare for the 90-minute trip from Grenada to Carriacou is $31 each way. For the 15-minute trip from Carriacou to Petite Martinique, the fare is $24 round-trip. The boat leaves Grenada from the Carenage in St. George's.

Taxis: On Grenada, taxis are plentiful, and rates are set. The trip between Point Salines Airport and Grand Anse or L'Anse aux Epines costs $15; between Grand Anse and St. George's, $15; and between Point Salines and St. George's, $25. A $4 surcharge is added for rides taken between 6 pm and 6 am. Taxis can be hired at an hourly rate of $25 as well.

In Carriacou the taxi fare from Lauriston Airport to Hillsborough is $6; from Hillsborough to Belair, the fare is $4; to Prospect, $6; and to Tyrrel Bay or Windward, $8.

Island Activities

Grenada's **beaches** are beautiful, and Grand Anse is among the Caribbean's finest.

It may be hard to pull yourself away from the beach, but be sure to spend a day or two exploring Grenada's lush **scenery.**

The capital city of **St. George's** has a busy harbor, interesting shops, and several historic sites.

A visit to a **spice plantation** and a **nutmeg-processing plant** or, if you're adventurous, a guided **hike** in the rain forest, up a mountainside, or to a hidden waterfall is a highlight of most trips.

Little **Carriacou** has a few nice beaches, the best of which is on Sandy Island, which is just offshore from the major town, Hillsborough.

Sailing, particularly to the Grenadines, a small chain of islands north of Carriacou, is exceptional.

Diving, fishing, and **snorkeling** opportunities are also good on both islands.

12

GRENADA PLANNER

Fast Facts

Banks and Exchange Services: Grenada uses the Eastern Caribbean dollar (EC$). The official exchange rate is fixed at EC$2.67 to US$1; taxis, shops, and hotels sometimes have slightly lower rates (EC$2.50 to EC$2.60). You can exchange money at banks and hotels, but U.S. paper currency and major credit cards are widely accepted.

Electricity: Current on Grenada is 220 volts/50 cycles. U.S. standard appliances (110 volts) require a transformer and adapter plug. For dual-voltage computers or appliances, you'll still need an adapter plug; some hotels will lend adapters.

Passport Requirements: To enter Grenada, visitors must produce a valid passport; a return or onward ticket is also required.

Weddings: Three days' residency is required to get a marriage license; no blood test is necessary.

Essentials

Mail: Airmail rates for letters to the United States are EC$1 for a half-ounce letter or postcard. When addressing a letter to Grenada, simply write "Grenada, West Indies" after the local address. International courier services (FedEx, DHL, and UPS) are also available at the post office.

Taxes and Service Charges: The departure tax of $20 (EC$50) for adults and $10 (EC$25) for children ages 5–11 is incorporated into the price paid for airfare, eliminating the need to pay at the airport when departing the country. Grenada has a 10% V.A.T. (value-added tax), which is either added to or included in hotel and restaurant bills, as well as retail sales. In addition, a 10% service charge is often added to hotel and restaurant bills.

Telephones: The area code is 473. Prepaid phone cards, which can be used in special card phones throughout the Caribbean for local or international calls, are sold in denominations of EC$20 ($7.50), EC$30 ($12), EC$50 ($20), and EC$75 ($28) at shops, attractions, transportation centers, and other convenient outlets. You can place direct-dial calls from Grenada to anywhere in the world using pay phones, card phones, most hotel room phones, and some mobile phones. For international calls using a major credit card, dial 111; to place a collect call or use | a calling card, dial 800/225–5872 from any telephone.

Tipping: If there is no service charge, then tip 10%; if a service charge has been included, additional tipping is discretionary. Bellhops, $1 per bag; housekeeping, $1 or $2 per night; taxi drivers and tour guides, 10% of the fare or fee.

Visitor Information: Grenada Board of Tourism (☎ *561/588–8176 in Lake Worth, FL, 800/927–9554* ⊕ *www.grenadagrenadines.com*). **Grenada Hotel & Tourism Association** (☎ *473/444–1353* ⊕ *www.gogrenada. gd/*). **Grenada Board of Tourism** (✉ *Burns Point, St. George's* ☎ *473/440–2001 or 473/440–2279* ✉ *Maurice Bishop International Airport, Point Salines, St. George* ☎ *473/444–4140* ✉ *Main St., Hillsborough, Carriacou* ☎ *473/443–7948*).

When to Go

The high season stretches from December 15 to April 15. In the off-season, prices at Grenada resorts may be discounted by up to 40%. In September and early October, some hotels close for annual maintenance and renovations. There are fewer seasonal changes on Carriacou, where the small hotels and guesthouses are all relatively inexpensive anyway.

Where to Stay

Grenada's tourist accommodations are, for the most part, in the southwest part of the island—primarily on or near Grand Anse Beach or overlooking small bays along the island's southern coast. Carriacou is a small island, and several of its guesthouses are in or around Hillsborough.

Guesthouses: Mi Hacienda, a small guesthouse on Grenada, is a gem. Small guesthouses predominate on Carriacou, where no property has more than 25 rooms.

Luxury Resorts: Grenada has a handful of luxurious inns and resorts. Spice Island Beach Resort is, arguably, the best resort on the island and one of the finest boutique resorts in the Caribbean.

Modest Resorts and Apartment Complexes: Most resorts and hotels on Grenada are small, and many are modest; but that is part of their charm.

HOTEL AND RESTAURANT COSTS

Restaurant prices are for a main course at dinner and include any taxes or service charges. Hotel prices are per night for a double room in high season, excluding taxes, service charges, and meal plans (except at all-inclusives).

WHAT IT COSTS IN U.S. DOLLARS

	¢	$	$$	$$$	$$$$
Restaurants	under $8	$8–$12	$12–$20	$20–$30	over $30
Hotels	under $150	$150–$275	$276–$375	$376–$475	over $475

Festivals and Events

12

The **Spice Island Billfish Tournament** is held in late January.

The **Grenada Sailing Festival** happens in late January or early February and includes six days of races and regattas.

The Grenada **International Triathlon** is in late April or early May.

Grenada's **Carnival** is a month-long celebration culminating in the second week of August.

The **Carriacou Carnival** in mid-February is the small island's biggest celebration.

The **Carriacou Maroon Music Festival**, celebrated in April, involves the cooking and eating of lots of local dishes, accompanied by big drum music.

The **Carriacou Regatta** draws yachts from around the Caribbean during the first weekend in August.

The Big Drum Dance is the highlight of the **Carriacou Parang Festival**, a musical and cultural celebration held in mid-December.

GRENADA AND CARRIACOU BEACHES

Grenada's best beaches are found all along the island's southwest coastline, which is also where you'll find most of the tourist facilities. Carriacou has lovely beaches that are an easy walk for day-trippers who arrive by ferry, but the deserted islands just offshore are the most memorable.

(Above) Grande Anse Beach. (Opposite page bottom) La Sagesse Beach. (Opposite page top) Sandy Island.

Grenada has some 80 mi (130 km) of coastline, 65 bays, and 45 beaches—many in little coves. The best beaches are just south of St. George's, facing the Caribbean, where most resorts are also clustered. Nude or topless bathing is against the law if you are in view of others.

On Carriacou, you'll find beaches within walking distance of the ferry jetty in Hillsborough—miles of soft, white sand that slopes gently down to the warm (average 83°F), calm sea. Carriacou's best beach experience, though, is a day spent swimming, snorkeling, and picnicking on one of the otherwise uninhabited islands just offshore.

BLACK AND WHITE

Grenada has primarily white-sand beaches with a few black-sand beaches. Grand Anse Beach has 2 mi (3 km) of white sand. Morne Rouge, nearby, is a perfect semicircle of white sand.

Paradise Beach on Carriacou has lovely white sand. Sandy Island and White Island require a water taxi from Hillsborough, but the powdery sand and crystal-clear water make the effort worthwhile.

12

GRENADA

Bathway Beach. A broad strip of sand with a natural reef that protects swimmers from the rough Atlantic surf on Grenada's far northern shore, this Levera National Park beach has changing rooms at the park headquarters. ⊠ *Levera, St. Patrick.*

⭐ **Fodor's Choice** **Grand Anse Beach.** In the southwest, about 3 mi (5 km) south of St. George's, Grenada's loveliest and most popular beach is a gleaming 2-mi (3-km) semicircle of white sand lapped by clear, gentle surf. Sea grape trees and coconut palms provide shady escapes from the sun. Brilliant rainbows frequently spill into the sea from the high green mountains that frame St. George's Harbour to the north. The Grand Anse Craft & Spice Market is at the midpoint of the beach. ⊠ *Grand Anse, St. George.*

La Sagesse Beach. Along the southeast coast, at La Sagesse Nature Centre, this is a lovely, quiet refuge with a strip of powdery white sand. Plan a full day of nature walks, with lunch at the small inn adjacent to the beach. ⊠ *La Sagesse, St. David.*

Magazine Beach. Near the international airport in Point Salines, Magazine Beach is a magnificent strip of pure white sand that stretches from the Aquarium Restaurant at its southern end to the Grenadian by Rex Resort. Never crowded, it's

excellent for swimming and sunbathing; the surf ranges from gentle to spectacular. Cool drinks, light refreshments, or a full lunch are available at the Aquarium. Access to the beach is next to the restaurant or next to the hotel. ⊠ *Point Salines, St. George.*

Morne Rouge Beach. One mile (1½ km) south of Grand Anse Bay, this ½-mi-long (¾-km-long) sheltered crescent has a gentle surf, excellent for swimming. Light meals are available nearby. ⊠ *Morne Rouge, St. George.*

CARRIACOU

Hillsborough Beach. Day-trippers can take a dip at this strip of sand adjacent to the jetty. The beach extends far in each direction, so there's plenty of room to swim without interference from the boat traffic. The best part of the beach is at the northern end along the Esplanade. ⊠ *Hillsborough.*

Paradise Beach. This long, narrow stretch between Hillsborough and Tyrrel Bay has calm, clear, inviting water and a snack bar, toilets, showers, and a souvenir shop. ⊠ *L'Esterre.*

White Island. On this deserted island off Carriacou's southern coast, a beautiful white sandy beach and calm Caribbean waters await you. Arrange transportation from Belmont, on the south shore, for about $25 to $30 (EC$70) round-trip. ⊠ *Manchineel Bay.*

By Jane E. Zarem

On February 7, 2010, the people on this lush, green isle happily celebrated the nation's 36th year of independence. The divisive political events leading to the intervention by U.S. troops in October 1983 are fading from memory. Grenada has developed a healthy tourism sector and a modern infrastructure, including welcoming hotels and resorts, good roads, up-to-date technology, and reliable utilities.

The nation of Grenada actually consists of three islands: Grenada, the largest, with a population of 90,000; Carriacou (*car*-ree-a-coo), north of Grenada, with a population of about 9,000; and Petite Martinique, with a population of only 900. Carriacou and Petite Martinique are popular for day trips, fishing adventures, or diving and snorkeling excursions, but most of the tourist activity is on Grenada. People interested in a really quiet, get-away-from-it-all vacation will, however, appreciate the simple pleasures of Carriacou during an extended stay.

The island of Grenada itself has 45 beaches and countless secluded coves. Crisscrossed by nature trails and laced with spice plantations, its mountainous interior is mostly consumed by a natural rain forest preserve. St. George's is one of the most picturesque capital cities in the Caribbean, and Grand Anse is one of the region's finest beaches.

Although he never set foot on the island, Christopher Columbus sighted Grenada in 1498 and named it Concepción. Spanish sailors following in his wake renamed it Granada, after the city in the hills of their homeland. Adapted to Grenade by French colonists, the transformation to Grenada was completed by the British in the 18th century.

Throughout the 17th century, Grenada was the scene of many bloody battles between indigenous Carib Indians and the French. Rather than surrender to the Europeans after losing their last battle in 1651, the Caribs committed mass suicide by leaping off a cliff—now called Carib's Leap or Leapers Hill—in Sauteurs, at the island's northern tip. The French were later overwhelmed by the British in 1762, the beginning of a seesaw of power between the two nations. By the Treaty of Versailles in 1783, Grenada was granted to the British, and almost immediately, thousands of African slaves were brought in to work the sugar plantations. Slavery in Grenada actually began with the French colonization in 1650; it was finally abolished in 1834.

Forts that the French began to construct to protect St. George's Harbour during their colonization of Grenada were later completed and used by the British during theirs. Today, Ft. George and Ft. Frederick are two of the most visited sites in St. George's. Besides their historical interest, the two locations have magnificent views of the harbor, the capital city itself, and the distant mountains and countryside. Interestingly, not a single shot was fired from either fort for more than two centuries. Then in 1983, Prime Minister Maurice Bishop and several of his supporters were murdered at Ft. George by political foes who had split off from Bishop's political party. That event triggered the request from Grenada's governor general and the heads of state of neighboring islands for U.S. troops to intervene, which they did on October 25, 1983.

From that time forward, Grenada's popularity as a vacation destination has increased each year, notwithstanding the temporary effects of Hurricane Ivan in 2004, as travelers continue to seek friendly, exotic islands to visit. Nearly all hotels, resorts, and restaurants in Grenada are family-owned and run (mostly by Grenadians); their guests often become good friends. All Grenadians, in fact, have a well-deserved reputation for their friendliness, hospitality, and entrepreneurial spirit. You can be sure you'll be "enjoyin' it" when you visit Grenada.

EXPLORING GRENADA AND CARRIACOU

GRENADA

Grenada is divided into six parishes, including one named St. George that includes the communities of Grand Anse, Morne Rouge, True Blue, L'Anse aux Épines, and the capital city of St. George's. Note: removing bark from trees, taking wildlife from the forest, and removing coral from the sea are all against the law.

WHAT TO SEE

Annandale Falls. This is a lovely, cool spot for swimming and picnicking. A mountain stream cascades 40 feet into a pool surrounded by exotic vines. A paved path leads to the bottom of the falls, and a trail leads to the top. ✉ *Main interior road, 15 mins northeast of St. George's, St. George* ☎ *473/440–2452* 🎫 *$1* ⏲ *Daily 9–5.*

Carib's Leap. At Sauteurs (the French word for "leapers"), on the island's northernmost tip, Carib's Leap (or Leapers Hill) is the 100-foot vertical cliff from which the last of the indigenous Carib Indians flung themselves into the sea in 1651. After losing several bloody battles with European colonists, they chose to kill themselves rather than surrender to the French. A commemorative display recounts the event. ✉ *Sauteurs, St. Patrick.*

★ **Concord Falls.** About 8 mi (13 km) north of St. George's, a turnoff from the West Coast Road leads to Concord Falls—actually three separate waterfalls. The first is at the end of the road; when the currents aren't too strong, you can take a dip under the cascade. Reaching the two other waterfalls requires an hour's hike into the forest reserve. The third and most spectacular waterfall, at Fountainbleu, thunders 65 feet over huge boulders and creates a small pool. It's smart to hire a guide. The path is clear, but slippery boulders toward the end can be treacherous without assistance. ⊠ *Off West Coast Rd., St. John* 🚻 *Changing room $2* ☉ *Daily 9–5.*

De La Grenade Industries. In the suburb of St. Paul's, five minutes east of St. George's, this company produces syrups, jams, jellies, and a liqueur from nutmeg and other homegrown fruits and spices. The liqueur "recipe" is a 19th-century secret formula. Sybil La Grenade founded the company in 1960 as a cottage industry. Since her tragic death in a car accident in 1991, the company has been overseen by her daughter, Cécile, a U.S.–trained food technologist. You're welcome to watch the manufacturing process and stroll around the adjacent herb and spice gardens. ⊠ *Morne Délice, St. Paul* 🕿 *473/440–3241* ⊕ *www. delagrenade.com* 🖭 *$1* ☉ *Weekdays 8–5, Sat. 9–12:30.*

Ⓒ **Dougaldston Spice Estate.** Just south of Gouyave, this historic plantation, now primarily a living museum, still grows and processes spices the old-fashioned way. You can see cocoa, nutmeg, mace, cloves, and other spices laid out on giant racks to dry in the sun. A worker will be glad to explain the process (and will appreciate a small donation). You can buy spices for about $2 a bag. ⊠ *Gouyave, St. John* 🕿 *No phone* 🖭 *Free* ☉ *Weekdays 9–4.*

Ⓒ **Gouyave Nutmeg Processing Cooperative.** Touring the nutmeg-processing
★ co-op, in the center of the west-coast fishing village of Gouyave (pronounced *gwahv*), is a fragrant, fascinating way to spend half an hour. You can learn all about nutmeg and its uses, see the nutmegs laid out in bins, and watch the workers sort them by hand and pack them into burlap bags for shipping worldwide. The three-story plant turned out 3 million pounds of Grenada's most famous export each year before Hurricane Ivan's devastating effect on the crop in 2004, when most of the nutmeg trees were destroyed. Locals estimate it will be 2014 before the nutmeg industry returns to that level. It took about a year to source a large amount of new plants, and nutmeg trees take between 7 and 10 years to produce at economically viable levels. ⊠ *Gouyave, St. John* 🕿 *473/444–8337* 🖭 *$1* ☉ *Weekdays 10–1 and 2–4.*

Ⓒ **Grand Anse.** A residential and commercial area about 5 mi (8 km) south of downtown St. George's, Grand Anse is named for the world-renowned beach it surrounds. Grenada's tourist facilities—resorts, restaurants, some shopping, and most nightlife—are concentrated in this general area. **Grand Anse Beach** is a 2-mi (3-km) crescent of sand, shaded by coconut palms and sea grape trees, with gentle turquoise surf. A public entrance is at Camerhogne Park, just a few steps from the main road. Water taxis carry passengers between the Esplanade in St. George's and a jetty on the beach. **St. George's University,** which for years held classes at its enviable beachfront location in Grand Anse, has a sprawling campus in True Blue, a nearby residential community. ⊠ *Grand Anse, St. George.*

Grand Étang National Park & Forest Reserve. Deep in the mountainous interior of Grenada is a bird sanctuary and forest reserve with miles of hiking trails, lookouts, and fishing streams. **Grand Étang Lake** is a 36-acre expanse of cobalt-blue water that fills the crater of an extinct volcano 1,740 feet above sea level. Although legend has it the lake is bottomless, maximum soundings are recorded at 18 feet. The informative **Grand Étang Forest Center** has displays on the local wildlife and vegetation. A forest manager is on hand to answer questions. A small snack bar and souvenir stands are nearby. ⊠ *Main interior road, between Grenville and St. George's, St. Andrew* ☎ *473/440–6160* ⊠ *$1* ⊗ *Daily 8:30–4.*

Grenville Cooperative Nutmeg Association. Like its counterpart in Gouyave, this nutmeg-processing plant is open to the public for guided tours. You can see and learn about the entire process of receiving, drying, sorting, and packing nutmegs. ⊠ *Grenville, St. Andrew* ☎ *473/442–7241* ⊠ *$1* ⊗ *Weekdays 10–1 and 2–4.*

Laura Herb & Spice Garden. The 6½-acre gardens are part of an old plantation in the village of Laura, in St. David Parish, just 6 mi (10 km) east of Grand Anse. On the 20-minute tour, you will learn all about Grenada's indigenous spices and herbs—including cocoa, clove, nutmeg, pimiento, cinnamon, turmeric, and tonka beans (similar to vanilla)—and how they're used for flavoring and for medicinal purposes. ⊠ *Laura, St. David* ☎ *473/443–2604* ⊠ *$2* ⊗ *Weekdays 8–4.*

Levera National Park & Bird Sanctuary. This portion of Grenada's protected parkland encompasses 450 acres at the northeastern tip of the island, where the Caribbean Sea meets the Atlantic Ocean. A natural reef protects swimmers from the rough Atlantic surf at Bathway Beach. Thick mangroves provide food and protection for nesting seabirds and seldom-seen parrots. The first islets of the Grenadines are visible from the beach. Entrance and use of the beaches and grounds are free. ⊠ *Levera, St. Patrick* ⊠ *Free* ⊗ *Daily dawn–dusk.*

Pearl's Airport. Just north of Grenville, on the east coast, is the island's original airport, which was replaced in 1984 by Point Salines International Airport (now Maurice Bishop International Airport). Deteriorating Cuban and Soviet planes sit at the end of the old runway, abandoned after the 1983 intervention, when Cuban "advisers" helping to construct the airport at Point Salines were summarily removed from the island. There's a good view north to the Grenadines and a small beach nearby. ⊠ *Grenville, St. Andrew.*

River Antoine Rum Distillery. At this rustic operation, kept open primarily as a museum, a limited quantity of Rivers rum is produced by the same methods used since the distillery opened in 1785. The process begins with the crushing of sugarcane from adjacent fields. The result is a potent overproof rum, sold only in Grenada, that will knock your socks off. ⊠ *River Antoine Estate, St. Patrick* ☎ *473/442–7109* ⊠ *$2* ⊗ *Guided tours daily 9–4.*

St. George's. Grenada's capital is a bustling West Indian city, most of which remains unchanged from colonial days. Narrow streets lined with shops wind up, down, and across steep hills. Brick warehouses and small shops cling to the waterfront, and pastel-painted homes rise from the waterfront and disappear into steep green hills.

Picturesque **St. George's Harbour,** a submerged volcanic crater, is arguably the prettiest harbor in the Caribbean and the center of town. Schooners, ferries, and tour boats tie up along the seawall or at the small dinghy dock. The **Carenage** (pronounced car-a-*nahzh*), which surrounds horseshoe-shape St. George's Harbour, is the capital's main thoroughfare. Warehouses, shops, and restaurants line the waterfront. The *Christ of the Deep* statue that sits on the pedestrian plaza at the center of the Carenage was presented to Grenada by Costa Cruise Line in remembrance of its ship *Bianca C,* which burned and sank in the harbor in 1961 and is now a favorite dive site.

The **Grenada National Museum** (✉ *Young and Monckton Sts.* ☎ 473/440–3725 ✆ *$1* ◷ *Weekdays 9–4:30, Sat. 10–1*), a block from the Carenage, is built on the foundation of a French army barracks and prison that was originally built in 1704. The small museum has exhibitions of news items, photos, and proclamations relating to the 1983 intervention, along with the childhood bathtub of Empress Joséphine (who was born on Martinique), and other memorabilia.

Ft. George (✉ *Church St.*) is high on the hill at the entrance to St. George's Harbour. It's Grenada's oldest fort—built by the French in 1705 to protect the harbor. No shots were ever fired here until October 1983, when Prime Minister Maurice Bishop and some of his followers were assassinated in the courtyard. The fort now houses police headquarters but is open to the public daily; admission is free. The 360-degree view of the capital city, St. George's Harbour, and the open sea is spectacular.

An engineering feat for its time, the 340-foot-long **Sendall Tunnel** was built in 1895 and named for an early governor. It separates the harbor side of St. George's from the Esplanade on the bay side of town, where you can find the markets (produce, meat, and fish), the Cruise Ship Terminal, the Esplanade Mall, and the public bus station.

Don't miss St. George's **Market Square** (✉ *Granby St.*), a block from the Cruise Ship Terminal. It's open every weekday morning but really comes alive on Saturday from 8 to noon. Vendors sell baskets, spices, brooms, clothing, knickknacks, coconut water, and heaps of fresh produce. A continuing renovation project is increasingly providing permanent cover for the vendors. Historically, Market Square is where parades begin and political rallies take place.

St. George's Methodist Church (✉ *Green St. near Herbert Blaize St.*) was built in 1820 and is the oldest original church in the city. It was damaged in Hurricane Ivan in 2004 but has been completely refurbished.

The Gothic tower of **St. George's Roman Catholic Church** (✉ *Church St.*) dates from 1818, but the current structure was built in 1884; the tower is the city's most visible landmark. The destruction Hurricane Ivan inflicted on the building in 2004 has been repaired.

Overlooking the city of St. George's and the inland side of the harbor, historic **Ft. Frederick** (✉ *Richmond Hill*) provides a panoramic view of two-thirds of Grenada. The fort was started by the French and completed in 1791 by the British; it was also the headquarters of the People's Revolutionary Government during the 1983 coup. Today you can get a bird's-eye view of much of Grenada from here.

Westerhall Estate. Back in the late 1800s, cocoa, sugarcane, coconuts (the oil used for soap), and limes (the oil used for perfumes) were produced on the 951-acre Westerhall Estate (called Bacaye back then). More recently, Westerhall has concentrated its efforts on making rum. The Westerhall Estate tour includes an explanation of the ruins and sugar-processing machinery on the grounds, along with a small museum comprising the eclectic collection of the late Grenadian journalist Dr. Alistair Hughes (1919–2005). Particularly interesting items on display in the museum include old rum bottles and labels, Carib artifacts, a number of vintage sewing machines, a World War I Maxim machine gun, and a 1915 Willys Overland automobile. ✉ *Westerhall, St. David* ☎ 473/443–5477 ✍ $4 ⊙ *Mon., Wed., and Fri. 9–3.*

CARRIACOU

Carriacou, the land of many reefs, is a hilly island and has neither lakes nor rivers, so its drinking water comes from rainwater caught in cisterns and purified with bleach. It gets quite arid during the dry season (January through May). Nevertheless, pigeon peas, corn, and fruit are grown here, and the climate seems to suit the mahogany trees used for furniture making and the white cedar critical to the boatbuilding industry that has made Carriacou famous.

Hillsborough is Carriacou's main town. Just offshore, Sandy Island is one of the nicest beaches around (although recent storms and the gradually rising sea have taken their toll on this tiny spit of land). Almost anyone with a boat can give you a ride out to Sandy Island for a small fee (about $10 round-trip), and you can leave your cares on the dock. Rolling hills cut a wide swath through the middle of Carriacou, from Gun Point in the north to Tyrrel Bay in the south.

Interestingly, tiny Carriacou has several distinct cultures. Hillsborough is decidedly English; the southern region, around L'Esterre, reflects French roots; and the northern town of Windward has Scottish ties. African culture is the overarching influence.

WHAT TO SEE

Belair. For a wonderful bird's-eye view of Hillsborough and Carriacou's entire west coast, drive to Belair, 700 feet above sea level, in the north-central part of the island. On the way, you'll pass by the photogenic ruins of an old sugar mill and the Princess Royal Hospital.

Carriacou Museum. Housed in a building that once held a cotton gin and just one block from the waterfront, the museum has exhibitions of Amerindian, European, and African artifacts, a collection of watercolors by native folk artist Canute Caliste, and a small gift shop with

The lookout from Belair with Hillsborough and Carriacou's west coast below.

local items. ✉ *Paterson St., Hillsborough* ☎ *473/443–8288* 🎫 *$2* ⊙ *Weekdays 9:30–4, Sat. 10–4.*

Tyrrel Bay. Tyrrel Bay is a large protected harbor in southwest Carriacou. The bay is almost always full of sailboats, powerboats, and working boats—coming, going, or bobbing at their moorings. A few shops and snack bars face the waterfront.

🔄 **Windward**. The small town of Windward, on the northeast coast, is a boatbuilding community. At certain times of year, primarily during school vacations, you may encounter a work in progress along the roadside, where Grenada's Ministry of Culture has set up a training ground for interested youngsters to learn skills from seasoned boatbuilders. Originally constructed for interisland commerce, the boats are now built primarily for fishing and pleasure sailing.

PETITE MARTINIQUE

Petite Martinique, 10 minutes north of Carriacou by boat, is tiny and residential, with a guesthouse or two but no tourist facilities or attractions—just peace and quiet. Meander along the beachfront and watch the boatbuilders at work. If by chance there's a boat launching, sailboat race, wedding, holiday, or cultural festival taking place while you're there, you're in for a treat. The music is infectious, the food bountiful, and the spirit lively.

WHERE TO EAT

12

Grenada grows everything from lettuce and tomatoes to citrus, mangoes, papaya (called paw paw here), callaloo (similar to spinach), dasheen (a root vegetable), christophenes (like squash), breadfruit—the list is endless. And all restaurants prepare dishes with local produce and season them with the many spices grown here. Be sure to try the local flavors of ice cream: soursop, guava, rum raisin, coconut (the best), or nutmeg.

Soups—especially pumpkin and callaloo—are divine and often start a meal. Pepper pot is a savory stew of pork, oxtail, vegetables, and spices. *Oildown,* the national dish, is salted meat, breadfruit, onions, carrots, celery, dasheen, and dumplings all boiled in coconut milk until the liquid is absorbed and the savory mixture becomes "oily." A roti—curried chicken, beef, or vegetables wrapped in pastry and baked—is similar to a turnover and more popular in Grenada than a sandwich.

Fresh seafood of all kinds, including lobster, is plentiful. Conch, known here as *lambi,* often appears curried or in a stew. Crab back, though, is not seafood—it's land crab. Most Grenadian restaurants serve seafood and at least some local dishes.

Rum punches are ubiquitous and always topped with grated nutmeg. Clarke's Court and Westerhall are local rums. Carib, the local beer, is refreshing, light, and quite good. If you prefer a nonalcoholic drink, opt for fruit punch—a delicious mixture of freshly blended tropical fruit.

WHAT TO WEAR

Dining in Grenada is casual. At dinner, collared shirts and long pants are appropriate for men (even the fanciest restaurants don't require jacket and tie), and sundresses or slacks are fine for women. Beachwear and other revealing attire should be reserved for the beach.

GRENADA

$-$$
SEAFOOD
🔄
Fodor's Choice
★

✕ **Aquarium Restaurant.** As the name suggests, fresh seafood is the specialty here. Many guests spend the day at the adjacent beach (you can rent kayaks or snorkeling gear) and then break for a cool drink or satisfying lunch—a salad, sandwich or burger, fresh fish, or pasta—served on the waterfront deck. Lush plants and palms surround the dining room, and a waterfall adds romance in the evening. The dinner menu always includes fresh fish, grilled lobster, and specialties such as callaloo cannelloni. On Sunday there's a beach barbecue. Also, the Aquarium is convenient to the airport and, if you plan carefully, perfect for a preflight meal. ⊠ *LaSource Rd., Point Salines, St. George* ✆ *Box 496, St. George's* ☎ *473/444–1410* ⊕ *www.aquarium-grenada.com* ⚑ *Reservations essential* ☉ *Closed Mon.*

$$-$$$
ECLECTIC
★

✕ **Beach House.** At this colorful restaurant a short walk down the beach from Laluna resort or accessed from the airport road, the gleaming white sand and sea views are the perfect backdrop for a salad or pasta luncheon on the deck. At dinner, excellent entrées—rack of lamb, blackened fish, or prime rib—and superb wines give new meaning to the term beach party. A kids' menu is available, too. ⊠ *Airport Rd., Point Salines, St. George* ☎ *473/444–4455* ⚑ *Reservations essential* ☉ *Closed Sun.*

$$
CARIBBEAN
☺
★

✗**Belmont Estate.** Luncheon is served! If you're visiting the northern reaches of Grenada island, plan to stop for lunch at Belmont Estate, a 400-year-old working nutmeg and cocoa plantation. Settle into the breezy open-air dining room, which overlooks enormous trays of nutmeg, cocoa, and mace drying in the sunshine. A waiter will offer some refreshing local juice and a choice of callaloo or pumpkin soup. Then head to the buffet and help yourself to salad, rice, stewed chicken, beef curry, stewed fish, and vegetables. Dessert may be homemade ice cream, ginger cake, or another delicious confection. Afterward, feel free to take a tour of the museum, cocoa fermentary, sugarcane garden, and old cemetery. Farm animals (and a couple of monkeys) roam the property, and there's often folk music and dancing on the lawn. ⊠ *Belmont, St. Patrick* ☎ *473/442–9524* ⊕ *www.belmontestate.net* ۞ *Closed Sat. No dinner.*

$$
CARIBBEAN

✗**Coconut Beach Restaurant.** Take local seafood, add butter, wine, and Grenadian spices, and you have excellent French-creole cuisine. Throw in a beautiful location on Grand Anse Beach, and this West Indian cottage becomes a perfect alfresco spot. Lobster is a specialty, as lobster thermidor or perhaps wrapped in a crepe, dipped in garlic butter, or added to pasta. Homemade coconut pie is a winner for dessert. Dine "wet or fine," at a table on the beach or inside. On Wednesday and Sunday nights in season, dinner is a beach barbecue with live music. ⊠ *Grand Anse, St. George* ☎ *473/444–4644* ⊕ *www.coconutbeachgrenada.com* ۞ *Closed Tues.*

$$$$
CARIBBEAN
★

✗**La Belle Creole.** The marriage of contemporary and West Indian cuisines and a splendid view of distant St. George's are the delights of this romantic hillside restaurant at the Blue Horizons Garden Resort. The always-changing five-course table d'hôte menu is based on original recipes from the owner's mother, a pioneer in incorporating local products into "foreign" dishes. Try, for instance, Grenadian caviar (roe of the white sea urchin), lobster-egg flan, callaloo quiche, creole fish, baked chicken roulade, or ginger pork chops—with homemade mango cheesecake for dessert. The inspired cuisine, romantic setting, and gracious service are impressive. ⊠ *Blue Horizons Garden Resort, Morne Rouge Rd., Grand Anse, St. George* ☎ *473/444–4316 or 473/444–4592* ⊕ *www.grenadabluehorizons.com* ◬ *Reservations essential.*

¢–$
CAFÉ
☺

✗**La Boulangerie.** This combination French bakery and Italian pizzeria, convenient to the hotels at Grand Anse, is a great place for an inexpensive breakfast or light meal—to eat in, take out, or have delivered. You'll find freshly baked croissants and Danish pastry, focaccia and baguette sandwiches, homemade pizza and pasta, fresh-squeezed juice or house wine, coffee and espresso, and homemade gelato. ⊠ *Le Marquis Complex, Grand Anse, St. George* ☎ *473/444–1131.*

$
SEAFOOD

✗**La Sagesse Nature Centre.** The perfect spot to soothe a frazzled soul, La Sagesse's open-air seafood restaurant is on a secluded cove in a nature preserve about 30 minutes from Grand Anse. Combine your lunch or dinner with a nature walk or a day at the beach. Linger over sandwiches, salads, or lobster for lunch. Lambi, smoked marlin, tuna steak, and a daily vegetarian entrée may be joined on the dinner menu by specials such as chicken française. Transportation is available. ⊠ *La Sagesse, St. David* ☎ *473/444–6458* ⊕ *www.lasagesse.com* ◬ *Reservations essential.*

12

$–$$
CARIBBEAN
✕ **The Nutmeg.** West Indian specialties, fresh seafood, great hamburgers, and a waterfront view make the Nutmeg a favorite with locals and visitors alike. It's upstairs on the Carenage (above Sea Change bookstore), with large, open windows from which you can watch the harbor activity as you eat. Try the callaloo soup, curried lambi, fresh seafood, or a steak—or just stop by for a roti and a rum punch. ⊠ *The Carenage, St. George's, St. George* ☎ 473/440–2539.

$$–$$$
SEAFOOD
★
✕ **Oasis at Jenny's Place.** Steps from the sand at the north end of Grand Anse Beach, the open-air restaurant at Jenny's Place specializes in pan-seared catch of the day—perhaps served with a tamarind sauce—and other enticing dishes created by celebrated chef Roxanne Russell (of Bogles Round House in Carriacou). Sunday lunch features a lobster special. For a light waterside lunch anytime, try the fresh Greek salad, a slice of nutmeg cheesecake, and a glass of wine. ⊠ *Grand Anse, St. George* ☎ 473/440–2539 ⊕ *www.jennysplacegrenada.com* ☖ *Reservations essential.*

$$–$$$
SEAFOOD
✕ **The Red Crab.** West Indian basics such as curried lambi and garlic shrimp—and old-fashioned international favorites such as lobster Newburg, Coquilles St. Jacques, and Wiener schnitzel—keep the regulars coming back to the Red Crab, which has served lunch and dinner to locals and expats alike for decades. Seafood, particularly lobster, and steak (imported from the United States) are staples of the menu; hot garlic bread comes with every order. Eat inside or outside on the front patio, and enjoy live music Monday and Friday evenings in season. ⊠ *Near Calabash Hotel, L'Anse aux Épines, St. George* ☎ 473/444–4424 ☖ *Reservations essential* ⊙ *Closed Sun.*

$$$
ECLECTIC
★
✕ **Rhodes' Restaurant.** The open-air restaurant at the Calabash Hotel, named for acclaimed British chef Gary Rhodes, is surrounded by palms, flowering plants, and twinkling lights. Past menus have featured citrus-cured salmon with a lime, fennel, and paw paw (papaya) salad as a starter, followed by grilled swordfish steak with Caribbean paella risotto or fillet of beef on a roast potato cake with whole-grain-mustard cream. The passion-fruit panna cotta, light as a soufflé, is nothing short of divine. ⊠ *Calabash Hotel, L'Anse aux Épines, St. George* ☎ 473/444–4334 ⊕ *www.calabashhotel.com* ☖ *Reservations essential* ⊙ *No lunch.*

¢–$
CARIBBEAN
✕ **Tropicana.** The chef–owner here hails from Trinidad and specializes in both Chinese and West Indian cuisine. Local businesspeople seem to be the best customers for the extensive menu of Chinese food, the tantalizing aroma of barbecued chicken notwithstanding. Eat in or take out—it's open from 7:30 am to midnight. Tropicana is right at the Lagoon Road traffic circle, overlooking the marina. ⊠ *Lagoon Rd., St. George's* ☎ 473/440–1586 ⊕ *www.tropicanainn.com.*

$$$$
ECLECTIC
★
✕ **Västra Banken at Le Phare Bleu.** Fine dining is served aboard this historic lightship, brought to Grenada in 2006 and the centerpiece of Le Phare Bleu Marina Hotel. The chef uses local ingredients to create contemporary cuisine served in a setting that is both nautical and romantic. Try the seafood ravioli or the callaloo and crab soufflé appetizer, followed by roasted rack of lamb or seared swordfish. The warm home-baked breads are wonderful, but the chocolate plate dessert takes the cake. ⊠ *Le Phare Bleu Marina Hotel, Petite Calivigny Bay, St. David*

☎ 473/443–3443 ⊕ www.lepharebleu.com ⚐ Reservations essential ⊘ No lunch. Closed Sun.

$$–$$$
ECLECTIC
✕ **Water's Edge.** At this Bel Air Plantation restaurant overlooking pristine St. David's Harbour, the dining experience is as exquisite as the view is mesmerizing. (The napkins are even folded into the shape of binoculars.) Tables are set on the covered verandah or on the garden patio. The extensive menu includes fish and lobster from the surrounding waters, fresh produce from nearby farms and the resort's own gardens, and imported meats—all delicately flavored with local herbs and spices. ⊠ Bel Air Plantation, Corinth, St. David ☎ 473/443–2822 ⚐ Reservations essential.

CARRIACOU

$$$–$$$$
CARIBBEAN
Fodor's Choice
★
✕ **Bogles Round House.** The Round House restaurant is, in fact, in a small round structure built with a concrete-filled tree trunk as its central support and a long bench that was once the jawbone of a whale. It's surrounded by gardens and a handful of cottages for rent. Chef Roxanne Russell is celebrated for her elegant style of Caribbean cuisine. Her three-course, prix-fixe menu, which changes according to market availability, may include such starters as fish cakes and cream of callaloo soup and such entrées as rack of lamb au jus and grilled lobster with garlic butter—there's always a vegetarian dish, too. Pasta and pizza are available for kids upon request. Desserts are all homemade, including the ice cream. ⊠ Sparrow Bay, Bogles ☎ 473/443–7841 ⊕ www.boglesroundhouse.com ⚐ Reservations essential ⊘ Closed Tues. and Wed.

$
CARIBBEAN
✕ **Laurena II.** As you approach this popular restaurant and bar, just a few giant steps from the ferry wharf, the unmistakable scent of authentic Jamaican jerk chicken and pork greets you. That's the specialty (and personal favorite) of chef Purgeon Reece, who hails from Negril, although his menu also includes other local and regional dishes such as curried goat, baked chicken, or grilled fish with rice and peas. Daily specials are posted on a street-side blackboard. Laurena is definitely a casual spot, the best bet for a delicious lunch, and a good place to catch the local vibe. ⊠ Main St., Hillsborough ☎ 473/443–8333 ⊕ www.hotellaurena.com ⊘ Closed Mon.

$$$$
ECLECTIC
✕ **Lyme and Dine.** Claudia and Werner "Max" Nagel, who also operate Carriacou Silver Diving, serve breakfast and a three-course dinner at their cottage on Main Street in a lovely, informal garden setting. The menu changes daily, depending on what's fresh at the market, and runs the gamut from grilled or smoked fish or lambi fritters to roast pork, schnitzels, or even Italian cuisine—all accompanied by an excellent selection of wines. Call ahead for the menu. ⊠ Main St., Hillsborough ☎ 473/444–6458 ⊕ www.lymeanddine.com ⚐ Reservations essential ⊘ No lunch.

WHERE TO STAY

Lodging options range from simply furnished, inexpensive apartments to elegant suites or villas just steps from the sea. Hotels tend to be small and intimate, with friendly management and attentive staff. All guest rooms are equipped with air-conditioning, an in-room TV, and telephone unless indicated otherwise. During the off-season (April 15 to December 15), prices may be discounted up to 40%.

VILLA COMMUNITIES

As is the case throughout the eastern Caribbean, villa communities are sprouting up like crocuses in spring—everywhere and in profusion. Grenada is one of the last

BEST BETS FOR LODGING

BEST FOR ROMANCE
Laluna

Petite Anse Hotel

Spice Island Beach Resort

BEST BEACHFRONT
Coyaba Beach Resort

Grenada Grand Beach Resort

Kalinago

La Sagesse Nature Centre

Laluna

Spice Island Beach Resort

12

islands to join the party, but properties are opening here quickly. Mount Cinnamon on Grand Anse Beach opened in April 2007. Bacolet Bay Resort & Spa is an extensive villa development under way in St. David's, on the (so far) remote southern coast of Grenada, and Port Louis is a brand-new marina village on the drawing boards—a $500 million project that, when complete in the next few years, will transform the lagoon and St. George's Harbour areas in the capital city. All these developments are investment properties, in which individually owned villas will be made available to nonowner guests through management companies.

PRIVATE VILLAS

Villas and private homes are available for rent for a week or longer. The minimum staff includes a maid and a laundress, but a cook, housekeeper, gardener, and others can be arranged.

In Grenada, many rental properties are in and around L'Anse aux Épines, a beautiful residential peninsula that juts into the sea. In-season rates range from about $1,600 a week for a two-bedroom home with a pool to $8,000 a week for a six-bedroom home on the beach. In Carriacou, in-season rates range from $65 per day for a small cottage or in-town apartment suitable for two people to $185 per day for a villa that accommodates up to six people in the countryside, with panoramic views and a swimming pool.

Altman Real Estate (Grenada) (⊠ Le Marquis Shopping Complex, Grand Anse ☎ 473/435–2081 ⊕ www.realestategrenada.com). **Down Island Villa Rentals** (⊠ Craigston, Carriacou ☎ 473/443–8182 ⊕ www.islandvillas.com). **Villas of Grenada** (⌂ Box 218, St. George's ☎ 473/444–1896 ⊕ www.villasofgrenada.com).

The following reviews have been condensed for this book. Please go to Fodors.com for expanded reviews of each property.

GRENADA

¢ ⊞ **Allamanda Beach Resort.** Right on Grand Anse Beach, this small
HOTEL hotel has some rooms with whirlpool baths; many rooms also have
☾ connecting doors, making it a good choice for families. **ros:** location,
location, location; great value. **Cons:** rooms are modest; don't expect
luxury at this price. ⊠ *Grand Anse, St. George* ☍ *Box 27, St. George's*
☎ *473/444–0095* ⊕ *www.allamandaresort.com* ↩ *50 rooms* ♿ *In-
room: safe, Wi-Fi. In-hotel: restaurant, room service, tennis court, bar,
pool, gym, spa, beach, water sports, business center* ⎟⊙⎟ *No meals.*

$$–$$$$ ⊞ **Bel Air Plantation.** On an 18-acre peninsula on Grenada's southeastern
RESORT coast, Bel Air's colorful gingerbread cottages dot a verdant hillside on
★ St. David's Harbour. **Pros:** beautifully decorated cottages; private; great
pool; excellent restaurant. **Cons:** be prepared to walk up and down the
hillside; far from town—far from anything, in fact. ⊠ *St. David's Point,
Corinth, St. David* ☍ *Box 857, LB 125, St. George's* ☎ *473/444–6305*
⊕ *www.belairplantation.com* ↩ *11 cottages* ♿ *In-room: safe, kitchen.
In-hotel: restaurant, room service, bars, pool, business center, water
sports* ⎟⊙⎟ *No meals.*

$ ⊞ **Blue Horizons Garden Resort.** A short walk (300 yards) from Grand
RESORT Anse Beach, "Blue" is especially popular among divers, nature lov-
☾ ers, and family vacationers. **ros:** spacious accommodations; excellent
★ value; good dive and hiking packages. **Cons:** not directly on the beach.
⊠ *Morne Rouge Rd., Grand Anse, St. George* ☍ *Box 41, St. George's*
☎ *473/444–4316 or 473/444–4592* ⊕ *www.grenadabluehorizons.com*
↩ *26 suites, 6 studios* ♿ *In-room: safe, kitchen, room service, Internet,
Wi-Fi. In-hotel: restaurant, bars, pool, business center* ⎟⊙⎟ *No meals.*

$$$$ ⊞ **Calabash Hotel.** The elegant suites here are in 10 two-story cottages
RESORT distributed in a horseshoe around 8 acres of lawn and gardens that
★ hug a curved beach on Prickly Bay (L'Anse aux Épines). **Pros:** excellent
service; love those treats; breakfast on the verandah. **Cons:** pricey; taxi
or rental car required to get around. ⊠ *L'Anse aux Épines, St. George*
☍ *Box 382, St. George's* ☎ *473/444–4334* ⊕ *www.calabashhotel.com*
↩ *30 suites* ♿ *In-room: safe, kitchen (some), Internet, Wi-Fi. In-hotel:
restaurant, room service, tennis court, bars, pool, gym, spa, beach,
business center, water sports, some age restrictions (Jan. 15–Mar. 15)*
☽ *Closed Aug. 15–Oct. 15* ⎟⊙⎟ *Breakfast.*

$$–$$$$ ⊞ **Coyaba Beach Resort.** Coyaba, which means "heaven" in the Arawak
RESORT language, is one of a handful of hotels directly on beautiful Grand Anse
Beach. **ros:** excellent beachfront location; spacious grounds; swim-up
pool bar. **Cons:** rooms are attractive but not extraordinary. ⊠ *Grand
Anse, St. George* ☍ *Box 336, St. George's* ☎ *473/444–4129* ⊕ *www.
coyaba.com* ↩ *80 rooms* ♿ *In-room: safe, Wi-Fi. In-hotel: restaurants,
room service, tennis court, bars, pool, gym, spa, beach, business center,
water sports* ⎟⊙⎟ *No meals.*

$ ⊞ **Flamboyant Hotel & Villas.** Built on a steep hillside, the rooms at
HOTEL this venerable, Grenadian-owned hotel have private verandahs with
☾ panoramic views of Grand Anse Bay. **Pros:** comparatively inexpensive; great views; nightlife at the Owl bar. **Cons:** decidedly *un*flamboyant rooms; lots of stairs. ⊠ *Grand Anse, St. George* ☍ *Box 214, St.
George's* ☎ *473/444–4247* ⊕ *www.flamboyant.com* ↩ *38 rooms, 27*

12

suites, 2 cottages ⚖ In-room: safe, kitchen (some), Internet. In-hotel: restaurants, room service, bar, pool, gym, beach, business center, water sports ⦿No meals.

¢–$
HOTEL

Gem Holiday Beach Resort. Owner Miriam Bedeau and her family operate this no-frills hotel on pretty Morne Rouge Beach. **Pros:** friendly, family-run hotel on a beautiful beach; excellent restaurant; popular bar, nightclub on-site. **Cons:** air-conditioning only in bedrooms ⊠ *Morne Rouge, St. George ⬡ Box 58, St. George's ☎ 473/444–2288 ⊕ www. gembeachresort.com ⇨ 15 1-bedroom apartments, 5 2-bedroom apartments ⚖ In-room: kitchen, Wi-Fi. In-hotel: restaurant, room service, bars, pool, beach, business center, water sports ⦿No meals.*

$–$$
RESORT
☼

Grenada Grand Beach Resort. On 20 landscaped acres along a broad section of beautiful Grand Anse Beach, this resort offers comfortable rooms and extensive amenities. **Pros:** huge hotel full of amenities; fabulous pools; beautiful beachfront location. **Cons:** rooms are comfortable but not extraordinary; popular meeting venue. ⊠ *Grand Anse, St. George ⬡ Box 441, St. George's ☎ 473/444–4371 ⊕ www. grenadagrand.com ⇨ 238 rooms, 2 suites ⚖ In-room: safe, Wi-Fi. In-hotel: restaurants, room service, tennis courts, bars, pools, gym, beach, business center, water sports, children's programs ⦿Breakfast.*

$
RESORT
☼

Grenadian by Rex Resorts. This massive, Palladian-style, beachfront resort on Tamarind Bay, favored particularly by Europeans, is minutes from the airport. **Pros:** large play area for kids; excellent beach. **Cons:** rooms are unremarkable; quite a hike from room to beach to lobby; meals are comparatively expensive. ⊠ *Tamarind Bay, Point Salines, St. George ☎ 473/444–3333 ⊕ www.rexresorts.com ⇨ 202 rooms, 10 suites ⚖ In-room: no a/c (some), safe (some), no TV (some), Internet, Wi-Fi. In-hotel: restaurants, room service, tennis courts, bars, children's programs, pool, gym, beach, water sports, business center ⦿No meals.*

$
HOTEL
☼

Kalinago Beach Resort. A contemporary beachfront hotel adjacent to Gem Holiday Resort (same owner), Kalinago's stylish suites all have a patio or deck with a view of the ocean and exquisite Morne Rouge Beach. **Pros:** modern rooms; great beach; personalized attention **Cons:** walk to nearby Grand Anse requires negotiating a steep hill; a rental car is a good idea. ⊠ *Morne Rouge, St. George ⬡ Box 58, St. George's ☎ 473/444–5254 ⊕ www.kalinagobeachresort.com ⇨ 29 rooms ⚖ In-room: safe, Internet, Wi-Fi. In-hotel: restaurant, room service, bar, pool, beach, laundry facilities, business center ⦿No meals.*

$$$$
RESORT
Fodor'sChoice
★

Laluna. You may think you've landed on an island in the South Pacific, but this upscale enclave is hidden away on a remote, pristine beach near Grenada's Quarantine Point. **Pros:** nifty cottages; great restaurant; fabulous beach; attentive staff. **Cons:** the long, bumpy, dirt access road; total seclusion could seem confining. ⊠ *Morne Rouge, St. George ⬡ Box 1500, St. George's ☎ 473/439–0001 or 866/452–5862 ⊕ www. laluna.com ⇨ 16 cottages ⚖ In-room: safe, Wi-Fi. In-hotel: restaurant, room service, bar, pool, gym, spa, beach, business center, water sports, some age restrictions (mid-Dec.–mid-Apr., except Christmas and Easter) ⦿No meals.*

$
INN

La Sagesse Nature Centre. Secluded on La Sagesse Bay—10 mi (16 km) east of the airport (about a 30-minute drive)—the grounds here include a country inn, restaurant, and beach bar, along with a salt-pond bird sanctuary, thick mangroves, nature trails, and ½ mi (¾ km) of palm tree–shaded beach. **Pros:** rather charming; beautiful beach; excellent restaurant. **Cons:** remote; you'll need a car to get anywhere else; no Internet access. ✉ *La Sagesse, St. David* ☎ *Box 44, St. George's* 🖀 *473/444–6458* ⊕ *www.lasagesse.com* ⇨ *9 rooms, 3 suites* ⚬ *In-room: no a/c (some), no phone, no TV. In-hotel: restaurant, bar, beach, water sports* ⦿ *No meals.*

$$$$
RESORT
★
🖀 **La Source.** Everything you could possibly want on an adults-only luxury vacation is included in the rates at this sparkling property. **Pros:** loads of activities and daily spa treatments included in the rates; congenial adult atmosphere. **Cons:** newshounds must get their TV fix in the lounge; not a good choice for anyone with walking difficulties. ✉ *Pink Gin Beach, Point Salines, St. George* ☎ *Box 852, St. George's* 🖀 *473/444–2556* ⊕ *www.theamazingholiday.com* ⇨ *91 rooms, 9 suites* ⚬ *In-room: safe, no TV. In-hotel: golf course, restaurants, room service, tennis courts, bars, pools, gym, spa, beach, business center, water sports, some age restrictions* ⦿ *All-inclusive.*

$$
RENTAL
☾
🖀 **Le Phare Bleu Marina & Holiday Resort.** Spacious, self-catering seaside accommodations at family-friendly Le Phare Bleu (The Blue Lighthouse) are perfectly situated for those who arrive by boat or who like to be around boats. **ros:** boater's delight; casual atmosphere; family-friendly; minimart on-site. **Cons:** somewhat isolated; rental car advised. ✉ *Petite Calivigny Bay, St. George* 🖀 *473/443–3443* ⊕ *www.lepharebleu.com* ⇨ *9 cottages, 4 apartments, 1 villa* ⚬ *In-room: kitchen, Wi-Fi. In-hotel: restaurants, room service, bars, pool, beach, water sports* ⦿ *Breakfast.*

$$$$
RENTAL
Fodor's Choice
★
🖀 **Maca Bana Villas.** Clustered on a 2-acre hillside overlooking mile-long Magazine Beach, each of Maca Bana's seven villas offers a breathtaking view—of the white sand below, out to sea, up the coastline to pretty St. George's Harbour, and beyond to the cloud-capped mountains. **ros:** roomy villas with huge kitchens; enormous decks with amazing views; excellent restaurant; fabulous beach. **Cons:** steep hill down to the restaurant and beach; tiny pool. ✉ *Magazine Beach, Point Salines, St. George* 🖀🖀 *473/439–5355* ⊕ *www.macabana.com* ⇨ *2 1-bedroom villas, 5 2-bedroom villas* ⚬ *In-room: safe, kitchen, Wi-Fi. In-hotel: restaurant, bar, pool, laundry facilities, spa, beach* ⦿ *No meals.*

¢–$
B&B
🖀 **Mi Hacienda.** Owner Merle McEwen designed this magnificent boutique hotel herself and had it built on a narrow street near the Grenada Golf & Country Club. She then filled her "hacienda" with family heirlooms, antiques collected from far and wide, and stylish furniture covered in snowy white slipcovers. **Pros:** home-away-from-home atmosphere; stylish and elegant yet comfortable; million-dollar view. **Cons:** hidden away in a maze of residential streets; no phones; TV in sitting room. ✉ *Belmont, St. George's* 🖀 *473/439–2799* ⊕ *www.mihacienda.gd* ⇨ *14 rooms, 2 apartments* ⚬ *In-room: no phone, kitchen (some), no TV. In-hotel: restaurant, room service, bar, pool, spa, business center* ⦿ *Breakfast.*

$$$–$$$$
VILLA RESORT
☾
🖀 **Mount Cinnamon.** Beautifully situated on a hillside that rises above Grand Anse Beach, Mount Cinnamon comprises spacious, self-contained villas with one, two, or three bedrooms, full kitchens, Bose entertainment systems, cable TV, and such convenient extras as washers and

dryers. **Pros:** excellent location on Grand Anse Beach; good choice for families. **Cons:** villas are on a steep hill, but golf-cart transport to restaurant or beach is available. ⊠ *Grand Anse, St. George* ☎ *Box 3858, St. George's* ☏ *473/439–0000* ⊕ *www.mountcinnamongrenada.com* ⇔ *21 units* ⚲ *In-room: safe, kitchen, Internet, Wi-Fi. In-hotel: restaurants, tennis court, bars, children's programs (holiday periods only), pool, laundry facilities, spa, beach, business center, water sports, some pets allowed* ⊗*Breakfast.*

$
RENTAL
☻

🖾 **Petit Bacaye Cottage Hotel.** Hidden along the coast in St. David's, about a half-hour drive east of Grand Anse and the hustle and bustle of St. George's, Petit Bacaye is a tiny oasis of pure serenity. **Pros:** idyllically private, quiet spot; airport shuttle service; perfect for a wedding or honeymoon. **Cons:** remote (you'll need a car); access driveway is steep and scary for drivers; no Internet access. ⊠ *Westerhall, St. David* ☏ *473/443–2902* ⊕ *www.petitbacaye.com* ⇔ *5 cottages* ⚲ *In-room: no a/c, no phone, kitchen, no TV. In-hotel: restaurant, room service, bar, beach* ☞ *7-day min stay* ⊘ *Closed Aug. and Sept.* ⊗*No meals.*

$-$$
HOTEL
★

🖾 **Petite Anse Hotel.** Philip and Annie Clift built their delightful beachfront hotel at the northern tip of Grenada, surrounded by beautiful gardens on one side and an unobstructed view of the southern Grenadines on the other. **Pros:** romantic setting; secluded palm-studded beach; fabulous views of the Grenadines. **Cons:** rather remote; rental car advised. ⊠ *Sauteurs, St. Patrick* ☏ *473/442–5252* ⊕ *www.petiteanse.com* ⇔ *2 rooms, 9 cottages* ⚲ *In-room: no phone, safe, no TV, Wi-Fi. In-hotel: restaurant, room service, bar, pool, beach, business center* ⊗*Breakfast.*

$$$$
RESORT
☻
Fodor's Choice
★

🖾 **Spice Island Beach Resort.** Presenting the most luxurious resort experience in Grenada, the service at "Spice" is always personalized and impeccable. **Pros:** elegant and luxurious yet family-friendly and casual; perfect beachfront location; excellent service; nonsmoking resort. **Cons:** the elegant, table d'hôte dining experience every night, although included, may seem limiting during long stays or for families with kids. ⊠ *Grand Anse, St. George* ☎ *Box 6, St. George's* ☏ *473/444–4258* ⊕*www.spiceislandbeachresort.com* ⇔ *64 suites* ⚲ *In-room: safe, Internet. In-hotel: restaurants, room service, tennis court, bar, children's programs, pool, gym, spa, beach, business center, water sports* ⊗*Some meals.*

$-$$
RESORT
☻

🖾 **True Blue Bay Resort & Villas.** The lawns and gardens at this family-run resort, a former indigo plantation, slope down to True Blue Bay. **Pros:** nice accommodations at reasonable prices; complimentary shuttle to Grand Anse Beach. **Cons:** no beach for swimming; rental car recommended. ⊠ *Old Mill Ave., True Blue, St. George* ☎ *Box 1414, St. George's* ☏ *473/443–8783 or 866/325–8322* ⊕*www.truebluebay.com* ⇔ *33 rooms, 5 villa suites* ⚲ *In-room: safe, kitchen, Wi-Fi. In-hotel: restaurant, room service, bar, pools, gym, spa, business center, water sports* ⊗*Breakfast.*

$-$$
INN

🖾 **Twelve Degrees North.** Named for the latitude at which the inn sits, this small, secluded property on 3 acres of hillside has one- and two-bedroom self-contained suites, all of which face the sea—and face west, providing beautiful sunset views from the balcony or patio. **Pros:** private getaway; personalized service; excellent snorkeling off the dock. **Cons:** beach not suitable for swimming because of reef; showers only; no

Internet of any kind. ⊠ *L'Anse aux Épines, St. George* ☎ *Box 241, St. George's* ☎ *473/444–4580* ⊕ *www.twelvedegreesnorth.com* ⇝ *8 suites* ⚭ *In-room: no a/c, no phone, kitchen, no TV. In-hotel: tennis court, pool, beach, water sports, some age restrictions* ⑉ *No meals.*

CARRIACOU

¢   **Ade's Dream Guest House.** By the jetty in Hillsborough, Ade's (add-ees)
HOTEL   is a convenient—and popular—place to rest your weary head after a
day snorkeling at Sandy Island or scuba diving at some of Grenada's
best dive spots. ros: steps from the jetty; convenient for an overnight
on Carriacou. **Cons:** basic accommodations. ⊠ *Main St., Hillsborough*
☎ *473/443–7317* ⊕ *www.adesdream.com* ⇝ *23 rooms* ⚭ *In-room: safe,
kitchen (some), Internet, Wi-Fi. In-hotel: restaurant, bar, laundry facilities, business center* ⑉ *No meals.*

¢   **Bayaleau Point Cottages.** Four colorful gingerbread cottages were lov-
VILLA RESORT   ingly built, one by one, by owner Dave Goldhill, an expat American
☼   who has lived on Carriacou for 30 years and opened Bayaleau (bee-
ah-loo) in 1992. **Pros:** ideal for small groups or whole families (up to
16 people); swinging in your hammock is an "active" sport; beautiful
Grenadines view. **Cons:** way off the beaten path; rental car advised.
⊠ *Bayaleau, Windward* ☎ *473/443–7984* ⊕ *www.carriacoucottages.
com* ⇝ *4 cottages* ⚭ *In-room: no a/c, no phone, kitchen, no TV, Wi-Fi.
In-hotel: restaurant, beach, water sports* ⑉ *No meals.*

¢   **Bogles Round House.** Pick your flavor: Lime, Mango, or Plum—Lime
RESORT   cottage is the largest of the three, with room for three or four people;
★   Mango and Plum sleep two comfortably and a third person, if needed.
Pros: the price; the restaurant; the ambience. **Cons:** no a/c; no communication with the outside world (although that may be a "pro" for some).
⊠ *Sparrow Bay, Bogles* ☎ *473/443–7841* ⊕ *www.boglesroundhouse.com*
⇝ *3 cottages* ⚭ *In-room: no a/c, no phone, kitchen, no TV. In-hotel: restaurant, bar, laundry facilities, beach, business center, water sports, some
pets allowed* ⊘ *Closed May* ⑉ *Breakfast.*

¢   **Carriacou Grand View Hotel.** The view is lovely, particularly at sun-
HOTEL   set, from this perch high above Hillsborough Harbour. **Pros:** truly a
grand view; friendly atmosphere; popular restaurant. **Cons:** accommodations are basic. ⊠ *Beausejour* ☎☎ *473/443–6348* ⊕ *www.
carriacougrandview.com* ⇝ *7 rooms, 7 suites* ⚭ *In-room: no a/c (some),
kitchen. In-hotel: restaurant, bar, pool, business center* ⑉ *No meals.*

¢   **Green Roof Inn.** You're guaranteed beautiful views of Hillsbor-
INN   ough Bay and the offshore cays at this perfect venue for a scuba-
diving, snorkeling, or beachcombing vacation. **Pros:** great water view;
homey atmosphere; close to town. **Cons:** rooms are small; showers
only. ⊠ *Hillsborough Bay, Hillsborough* ☎ *473/443–6399* ⊕ *www.
greenroofinn.com* ⇝ *5 rooms, 1 cottage* ⚭ *In-room: no a/c, no phone,
kitchen (some), no TV, Wi-Fi. In-hotel: restaurant, bar, beach, business
center* ⑉ *Breakfast.*

¢   **Hotel Laurena.** Certainly large by Carriacou standards, the fam-
HOTEL   ily-owned, family-operated Hotel Laurena is within walking dis-
☼   tance of downtown Hillsborough, the ferry wharf, shops, and some
beaches. **Pros:** convenient to town; accommodations are large. **Cons:**

not particularly attractive views; no beach or pool. ✉ *Hillsborough, Carriacou* ☎ *473/443–8759* ⊕ *www.hotellaurena.com* ⇆ *20 rooms, 6 apartments* ⅔ *In-room: safe, kitchen (some), Internet, Wi-Fi. In-hotel: restaurant, room service, bar, gym* ❧ *Breakfast.*

NIGHTLIFE

Grenada's nightlife is centered on the resort hotels and a handful of nightspots. During the winter season some hotels have a steel band or other local entertainment several nights a week.

BARS

Banana's Sports Bar (✉ *True Blue, St. George* ☎ *473/444–4662*) is a casual restaurant and nightspot popular among the students at nearby St. George's University. There's happy hour every evening from 5 to 7 pm. Latin dance classes begin at 6:30 pm on Tuesday and Thursday nights. On Saturday night there's live entertainment beginning at 8 pm. Sunday and Monday are reserved for sports, with major events shown on big-screen TVs.

DANCE CLUBS

Fantazia 2001 (✉ *Morne Rouge, St. George* ☎ *473/444–2288*) is a popular nightspot; disco, soca, reggae, and international pop music are played from 9:30 pm until the wee hours on weekends. There's a small cover charge of EC$10 to EC$20. **Karma** (✉ *The Carenage, St. George's* ☎ *473/409–2582*) is a spacious (10,000-square-foot), first-class entertainment facility with a stage and a dozen plasma TV screens. The club features karaoke on Wednesday night, "student night" on Thursday, video DJ entertainment on Friday, and special parties and headliner concerts on Saturday night. The nightclub entrance fee is EC$25; admission for special events runs EC$50 and up. **The Owl** (✉ *Flamboyant Hotel, Grand Anse, St. George* ☎ *473/444–4247*), open nightly until 3 am, features karaoke on Thursday and Friday nights and two happy hours (4–7 and 11–midnight) every night.

THEME NIGHTS

☺ ★ **Gouyave Fish Friday** (✉ *St. Francis and St. Dominic Sts., Gouyave, St. John* ☎ *473/444–8430 or 473/444–9490* ⊕ *www.gogouyave.com*) celebrates the deep sea fishing heritage of the coastal town of Gouyave, about 45 minutes north of St. George's, every Friday night starting at 4 pm and continuing until 1 am. Street vendors sell freshly caught fish, lobster, and other seafood cooked on open fires, as well as your favorite beverages. Local music and cultural performances make Friday night in Gouyave an entertaining family event.

SHOPPING

Grenada is truly a nation of entrepreneurs, from physical businesses with employees and processing operations to self-employed vendors (about one-third of the population) who personally sell their handicrafts in the markets. Bargaining is not appropriate in shops and isn't customary with vendors.

Some of the unique, locally made goods to look for in gift shops and supermarkets are chocolate candy bars, nutmeg jam and syrup, spice-scented soaps and body oils, pain-relief spray, and fruit- and herb-flavored wine, rum, and liqueur.

Grenada's best souvenirs or gifts for friends back home are spice baskets filled with cinnamon, nutmeg, mace, bay leaves, cloves, turmeric, and ginger. You can buy them for as little as $5 to $10 in practically every shop, at the open-air produce market at **Market Square** in St. George's, at the vendor stalls along the Esplanade near the port, and at the Vendor's Craft & Spice Market on Grand Anse Beach. Vendors also sell handmade fabric dolls, coral jewelry, seashells, and hats and baskets handwoven from green palm fronds.

Here's some local terminology you should know. If someone asks if you'd like a "sweetie," you're being offered a candy. When you buy spices, you may be offered "saffron" and "vanilla." The saffron is really turmeric, a ground yellow root rather than the fragile pistils of crocus flowers; the vanilla is an essence made from locally grown tonka beans, a close substitute but not the real thing. No one is trying to pull the wool over your eyes; these are common local terms.

AREAS AND MALLS

In St. George's, on the north side of the harbor, **Young Street** is a main shopping thoroughfare; it rises steeply uphill from the Carenage, and then descends just as steeply to the market area. On Melville Street, near the Cruise Ship Terminal and Market Square, the **Esplanade Mall** has shops that offer duty-free jewelry, electronics, liquor, and gift items, as well as local crafts. On Lagoon Road in Belmont, just south of St. George's Harbor, the **Grenada Craft Center** houses several shops with handmade art and craft items; some items are made in workshops on-site.

In Grand Anse, a short walk from the resorts, the **Excel Plaza** has shops and services to interest locals and tourists alike, including a full-service health club and a three-screen movie theater. **Grand Anse Shopping Centre** has a supermarket and liquor store, a clothing store, a fast-food restaurant, a pharmacy, an art gallery, and several small gift shops. **Le Marquis Complex** has restaurants, shops, an art gallery, and tourist services. **South City Plaza Mall,** adjacent to the Grand Anse vendor's market, has 35 shops, some that sell duty-free goods, as well as banking facilities and a hotel. **Spiceland Mall** has a modern supermarket with a liquor section, clothing and shoe boutiques for men and women, housewares stores, a wineshop, gift shops, a food court, a bank, and a video-game arcade.

SPECIALTY STORES

ART

Art Grenada (✉ *Grand Anse Shopping Centre, Suite 7, Grand Anse, St. George* ☎ *473/444–2317*) sells paintings, drawings, and watercolors exclusively by Grenadian artists, among them Canute Caliste, Lyndon Bedeau, and Susan Mains. Exhibitions change monthly, and you can have your purchases shipped.

12

BOOKS

A colorful souvenir picture book, a book on island culture and history, a charming local story for kids, a thick novel for the beach, or a paperback for the trip home—all are good reasons to drop into a bookstore. **Sea Change** (⊠ *The Carenage, St. George's* ☎ *473/440–3402*) overlooks the waterfront.

DUTY-FREE GOODS

Duty-free shops at the airport sell liquor at impressive discounts of up to 50%, as well as perfumes, crafts, and Grenadian syrups, jams, and hot sauces. You can shop duty-free at some shops in town, but you must show your passport and outbound ticket to benefit from the duty-free prices. **Gitten's** (⊠ *Halifax St., St. George's, St. George* ☎ *473/440–2165* ⊠ *Grand Anse Main Rd., Grand Anse, St. George* ☎ *473/444–4954* ⊠ *Maurice Bishop International Airport, Point Salines, St. George* ☎ *473/444–2549*) carries perfume and cosmetics at its three shops.

FOODS

De La Grenade Industries (⊠ *Morne Délice, St. Paul* ☎ *473/440–3241*) makes nutmeg and guava jams and jellies, nutmeg syrup, nutmeg liqueur (from a 200-year-old family recipe), and a dozen other kinds of delicious jellies, marmalades, and condiments that are sold at the processing plant and in food stores and gift shops throughout Grenada. **Grenada Chocolate Company** (⊠ *Hermitage, St. Patrick* ☎ *473/442–0050* ⊕ *www. grenadachocolate.com*) makes organic chocolate bars and Smilo cocoa powder from cocoa beans grown at nearby Belmont Estate. Employees at the small factory use antique machinery to roast the beans and mix and temper the chocolate. Then the rich, dark chocolate is molded and wrapped by hand. The candy bars sell in supermarkets and gift shops for about $5 each.

★ The open-air **Market Square** (⊠ *Foot of Young St., St. George's*) is a bustling produce market that's open mornings; Saturday is the best—and busiest—time to stock up on fresh fruit to enjoy during your stay. But it's also a particularly good place to buy island-grown spices, perhaps the best such market in the entire Caribbean. Crafts, leather goods, and decorative objects are also sold. **Marketing & National Importing Board** (⊠ *Young St., St. George's, St. George* ☎ *473/440–1791*) stocks fresh fruits and vegetables, spices, hot sauces, and local syrups and jams at lower prices than you can find in most gift shops.

GIFTS

Arawak Islands (⊠ *Frequente Industrial Park, Point Salines, St. George* ☎ *473/444–3577* ⊕ *www.arawak-islands.com*) produces spice-scented soaps, body oils, perfumes, insect repellents, balms, beeswax candles, and incense made by hand. Shoppers are welcome at the plant, where you can view the manufacturing process, and the company's products and gift baskets are sold in most gift shops. **Imagine** (⊠ *Grand Anse Shopping Centre, Grand Anse, St. George* ☎ *473/444–4028*) specializes in straw work, ceramics, island fashions, and batik fabrics. **Pssst Boutique** (⊠ *Spiceland Mall, Grand Anse, St. George* ☎ *473/439–0787*) will catch your eye; it's chock-full of unusual costume jewelry, colorful island clothing, and fascinating gift items for the home.

Although it may not seem like much of a gift, a bottle of **Nut-Med Pain Relieving Spray** makes a neat souvenir for anyone with aches and pains. The brainchild of agronomist Denis Noel, whose handful of employees prepare and package the remedy in a facility behind his home in St. Patrick, Nut-Med spray is made from nutmeg oil, wintergreen or peppermint scent, and "a few other ingredients." It sells like hotcakes in supermarkets and gift shops throughout Grenada for about $12 a bottle.

HANDICRAFTS

★ At **Art Fabrik** (✉ *Young St., St. George's* ☎ *473/440–0568* ⊕ *www. artfabrikgrenada.com*), you'll find batik fabric created by hand in the next-door studio and sold either by the yard or fashioned into dresses, shirts, shorts, hats, and scarves. **Tikal** (✉ *Young St., St. George's* ☎ *473/440–2310*) is known for its regional artwork, jewelry, batik items, and fashions. The **Vendor's Craft & Spice Market at Grand Anse** (✉ *Grand Anse, St. George* ☎ *473/444–3780*), managed by the Grenada Board of Tourism, has 82 booths for vendors who sell arts, crafts, spices, music tapes, clothing, produce, and refreshments. It's open daily from 7 to 7.

★ **Veronica's Vision** (✉ *Concord, St. John* ☎ *473/439–9006* ⊕ *www. grenadaspicecloth.com*), housed in a former nutmeg receiving station, sells colorful silk-screened lengths of fabric, along with handmade totes, bags, women's dresses, men's shirts and ties, T-shirts, scarves, belts, cushions, and more. The fabrics and other products are all designed and created by artist Jessie-Ann Jessamy—the colors and themes celebrate the isle of spice—and hand-printed in her next-door workshop, located on the main road at the turn-off to Concord Falls.

SPORTS AND ACTIVITIES

BOATING AND SAILING

★ As the "Gateway to the Grenadines," Grenada attracts significant numbers of seasoned sailors to its waters. Large marinas are located at Port Louis along the Lagoon in St. George's, at Prickly Bay and True Blue on Grenada's south coast, at Petite Calivigny Bay and St. David's in southeast Grenada, and at Tyrrel Bay in Carriacou. You can charter a yacht, with or without crew, for weeklong sailing vacations through the Grenadines or along the coast of Venezuela. Scenic day sails along Grenada's coast cost about $145 per person (with a minimum of four passengers), including lunch or snacks and open bar; a charter will cost $400 to $1,000 per day (with a five-day minimum), depending on the boat, for up to six people.

Carib Cats (☎ *473/444–3222*) departs from the Lagoon in St. George's for a full-day sail along the southwest coast, a half-day snorkel cruise to Molinère Bay, or a two-hour sunset cruise along the west coast. **Footloose Yacht Charters** (☎ *473/440–7949* ⊕ *www.grenadasailing.com*) operates from the Lagoon in St. George's and has both sailing and motor yachts available for day trips around Grenada or longer charters to the Grenadines. **Horizon Yacht Charters** (☎ 473/439–1000 ⊕ *www. horizonyachtcharters.com*), at True Blue Bay Resort, will arrange bareboat or crewed charters, as well as day sails or five-day trips to the Grenadines. The **Moorings** (☎ 800/535–7289 ⊕ *www.moorings.com*) is based at Port Louis Marina in St. George's and offers bareboat or crewed charters on its custom-built 35-foot to 51-foot catamarans and monohulls. The diverse itinerary options include one-way charters to the company's bases in either Canouan or St. Lucia.

12

DIVING AND SNORKELING

★ You can see hundreds of varieties of fish and some 40 species of coral at more than a dozen sites off Grenada's southwest coast—only 15 to 20 minutes by boat—and another couple of dozen sites around Carriacou's reefs and neighboring islets. Depths vary from 20 to 120 feet, and visibility varies from 30 to 100 feet.

Off Grenada: A spectacular dive is *Bianca C,* a 600-foot cruise ship that caught fire in 1961, sank to 100 feet, and is now encrusted with coral and serves as a habitat for giant turtles, spotted eagle rays, barracuda, and jacks. **Boss Reef** extends 5 mi (8 km) from St. George's Harbour to Point Salines, with a depth ranging from 20 to 90 feet. **Flamingo Bay** has a wall that drops to 90 feet and is teeming with fish, sponges, sea horses, sea fans, and coral. **Molinère Reef** slopes from about 20 feet below the surface to a wall that drops to 65 feet. Molinère is also the location of the Underwater Sculpture Park, a rather odd artificial reef consisting of more than 55 life-size figures that were sculpted by artist and scuba instructor Jason Taylor and placed on the sea bottom. It's a good dive for beginners, and advanced divers can continue farther out to view the wreck of the *Buccaneer,* a 42-foot sloop.

Off Carriacou: There's an active underwater volcano known as **Kick-em Jenny,** with plentiful coral and marine life in the vicinity and, usually, visibility up to 100 feet, though you can't dive down 500 feet to reach the actual volcano. **Sandy Island,** in Hillsborough Bay, is especially good for night diving and has fish that feed off its extensive reefs 70 feet deep. For experienced divers, **Twin Sisters of Isle de Rhonde** is one of the most spectacular dives in the Grenadines, with walls and drop-offs of up to 185 feet and an underwater cave.

Most dive operators take snorkelers along on dive trips or have special snorkeling adventures. The best snorkeling in Grenada is at Molinère Point, north of St. George's; in Carriacou, Sandy Island is magnificent and just a few hundred yards offshore. Snorkeling trips cost about $35 per person.

The PADI-certified dive operators offer scuba and snorkeling trips to reefs and wrecks, including night dives and special excursions to the *Bianca C.* They also offer resort courses for beginning divers and certification instruction for more experienced divers. It costs about $50 to $55 for a one-tank dive, $95 for a two-tank dive, $60 for trips to the *Bianca C,* $130 to dive Isle de Rhonde, and $65 to $70 for night dives. Discounted five- and 10-dive packages are usually offered. Resort courses cost about $100, and open-water certification runs from $265 to $460.

GRENADA DIVE OPERATORS

Aquanauts Grenada (✉ *Spice Island Beach Resort, Grand Anse Beach, Grand Anse, St. George* ☎ *473/444–1126, 888/446–9235 in U.S.* ✉ *True Blue Bay Resort, True Blue, St. George* ☎ *473/439–2500* ⊕ *www.aquanautsgrenada.com*) has a multilingual staff, so instruction is available in English, German, Dutch, French, and Spanish. Two-tank dive trips, accommodating no more than eight divers, are offered each morning to both the Caribbean and Atlantic sides of Grenada. **Dive Grenada** (✉ *Flamboyant Hotel, Morne Rouge, St. George* ☎ *473/444–1092* ⊕ *www.divegrenada.com*) offers dive trips twice daily (at 10 am and 2 pm), specializing in diving the *Bianca C.* **EcoDive** (✉ *Coyaba Beach Resort, Grand Anse, St. George* ☎ *473/444–7777* ⊕ *www.ecodiveandtrek.com*) offers two dive trips daily, both drift and wreck dives, as well as weekly trips to dive Isle de Rhonde. The company also runs Grenada's marine-conservation and education center, which conducts coral-reef monitoring and **ScubaTech Grenada** (✉ *Calabash Hotel, L'Anse aux Épines, St. George* ☎ *473/439–4346* ⊕ *www.scubatech-grenada.com*) has two full-time diving instructors and, in addition to daily dive trips, offers the complete range of PADI programs, from discover scuba, which allows novices to learn the basics and dive for the length of their vacation, to dive master, the highest level a diver can achieve.

CARRIACOU DIVE OPERATORS

Arawak Divers (✉ *Tyrrel Bay* ☎ *473/443–6906* ⊕ *www.arawak.de*) has its own jetty at Tyrrel Bay; it takes small groups on daily dive trips and night dives, offers courses in German and English, and provides pickup service from yachts. **Carriacou Silver Diving** (✉ *Main St., Hillsborough* ☎ *473/443–7882* ⊕ *www.scubamax.com*) accommodates up to 12 divers on one of its dive boats and up to six on another. The center operates two guided single-tank dives daily as well as individually scheduled excursions. For the folks who operate **Lumbadive** (✉ *Tyrrel Bay* ☎ *473/443–8566* ⊕ *www.lumbadive.com*), the goal is to share their enthusiasm for safe, exciting scuba-diving adventures with both new and experienced divers. Lumbadive offers open-water diving courses that range from discover to dive master.

FISHING

Deep-sea fishing around Grenada is excellent, with marlin, sailfish, yellowfin tuna, and dolphinfish topping the list of good catches. You can arrange sportfishing trips that accommodate up to five people starting at $475 for a half day and $700 for a full day. **True Blue Sportfishing** (☎ *473/444–2048* ⊕ *www.yesaye.com*) offers big-game charters on its 31-foot *Yes Aye*. It has an enclosed cabin, a fighting chair, and professional tackle. British-born Captain Gary Clifford, who has been fishing since the age of six has run the company since 1998. Refreshments and courtesy transport are included.

Take an exciting safari-style tour of Grenada on an Adventure Jeep Tour.

GOLF

Determined golfers might want to try the 9-hole course at the **Grenada Golf & Country Club** (☎ *473/444–4128*), about halfway between St. George's and Grand Anse. Greens fees are $16 (or $24 to play the course twice), and club rental is available; your hotel can make arrangements for you. Popular with local businessmen, this course is convenient to most hotels and is the only public course on the island.

GUIDED TOURS

Guided tours offer the sights of St. George's, Grand Étang National Park & Forest Reserve, spice plantations and nutmeg-processing centers, rain-forest hikes and treks to waterfalls, snorkeling trips to local islands, and day trips to Carriacou. A full-day sightseeing tour costs $70 to $75 per person, including lunch; a half-day tour, $45 to $55; a guided hike to Concord or Mt. Qua Qua, $55 to $60 per person. Grenada taxi drivers will conduct island sightseeing tours for $150 per day or $25 to $35 per hour for up to four people. Carriacou minibus drivers will take up to four people on a 2½-hour island tour for $60, and $20 per hour thereafter.

On **Adventure Jeep Tour** (☎ *473/444–5337* ⊕ *www.adventuregrenada. com*) you ride in the back of a Land Rover, safari fashion, along scenic coastal roads, trek in the rain forest, lunch at a plantation, take a swim, and skirt the capital. **Caribbean Horizons** (☎ *473/444–1555* ⊕ *www.caribbeanhorizons.com*) offers personalized tours of historic and natural island sites, market and garden tours, and excursions to

Carriacou. Denis Henry of **Henry's Safari Tours** (☎ 473/444–5313 ⊕ *www. henrysafari.com*) knows Grenada like the back of his hand. He leads adventurous hikes and four-wheel-drive-vehicle nature safaris, or you can design your own tour. **Mandoo Tours** (☎☎ 473/440–1428 ⊕ *www. grenadatours.com*) offers half- and full-day tours following northern, southern, or eastern routes, as well as hikes to Concord Falls and the mountains. **Sunsation Tours** (☎ 473/444–1594 ⊕ *www.grenadasunsation. com*), whose guides speak English, German, and French, offers customized and private island tours to all the usual sites and "as far off the beaten track as you want to go." From garden tours or a challenging hike to a day sail on a catamaran, it's all possible.

HIKING

Fodor's Choice
★

Mountain trails wind through **Grand Étang National Park & Forest Reserve** (☎ 473/440–6160); if you're lucky, you may spot a Mona monkey or some exotic birds on your hike. There are trails for all levels—from a self-guided nature trail around Grand Étang Lake to a demanding one through the bush to the peak of Mt. Qua Qua (2,373 feet) or a real trek up Mt. St. Catherine (2,757 feet). Long pants and hiking shoes are recommended. The cost is $25 per person for a four-hour guided hike up Mt. Qua Qua, $20 each for two or more, or $15 each for three or more; the Mt. St. Catherine hike starts at $35 per person. **Eco-Trek** (☎ 473/444–7777 ⊕ *www.ecodiveandtrek.com*) takes small groups on day trips to the heart of the rain forest, where you'll find hidden waterfalls and hot-spring pools. **Henry's Safari Tours** (☎ 473/444–5313 ⊕ *www.henrysafari.com*) offers personalized hiking excursions through rich agricultural land and rain forest to Upper Concord Falls, to the summit of Mt. Qua Qua and other fascinating spots. **Telfor Bedeau, Hiking Guide** (☎ 473/442–6200), affectionately referred to locally as the Indiana Jones of Grenada, is a national treasure. He first began hiking at age 23. That was in 1962. Over the years he has walked up, down, or across nearly every mountain, trail, and pathway on the island. In 2005 he hit the incredible milestone of having hiked 10,000 mi (16,000 km) throughout Grenada. Even as a septuagenarian, his experience and knowledge make him an excellent guide, whether it's an easy walk with novices or the most strenuous hike with experts.

Guadeloupe

WORD OF MOUTH

"We stayed near Pigeon on Basse Terre. It's on the western half of the island and is mountainous. The east side is flat and has the more sandy beaches. We enjoyed the west side because of all the possibilities for activities. Tons of hiking, snorkeling, diving, canyoning etc."

—wug

WELCOME TO GUADELOUPE

Guadeloupe Passage

La Pointe
la Grande
Vigie

Plage de la Chapelle á
Anse Laborde

Anse Bertrand   N8   Campêche
N6
Port Louis   N8
Les Mangles   Gro
Beauport   N6   Cap
N6   N6
Petit-Canal   D1

Anse du
Vieux Fort   Ilet à Fajou   Anse du Canal   GRAND
Pte.   Vieux-Bourg
Allègre   Grand   Morne-à-
La   Cul-de-Sac   l'Eau   N
Grande-Anse   10   11   9   Marin   Jabrun
10   Ste-Rose   du Sud   Jabrun
12   Abymes   du Nord
Deshaies   N2
N2   Lamentin   Airport
Pointe-Noire   Destrelan   N1   Pointe-à-Pitre
BASSE   N1   Bas-du-   Fort Fleur
Anse   Cascade   Fort   d'Epée
Caraïbe   aux   1   Plag
Mahaut   La   Ecrevisses   D23   Ilet du   Carave
Traversée   Les   Vernou   Gosier
Ilet de Pigeon   Mamelles   Petit-
Pigeon Island   Pigeon   Bourg   1 2
Malendure   Parc National   2 3
Bouillante   8   de la Guadeloupe   Goyave   Aquarium de
Marigot   TERRE   la Guadeloupe
N2   La Soufrière   Ste-Marie
Vieux-Habitants   N1
Le Musée   Capesterre-
Volcanologique   Belle-Eau
Matouba   Anse
Plage de   St-Claude   Chutes du   Chapelle
Rocroy   Carbet   St-Sauveur
Gourbeyre   Bananier
D11   N1
Basse-Terre   D6   Trois-Rivières
D6   13
Anse   Vieux
Turlet   Fort
9 - 11   Iles des Saintes
14 - 18   (Les Saintes)
Les Pompierres
Terre-de-Haut
Terre-de-Bas   Anse Crawen
La Coche   Grand Ilet

Caribbean Sea

KEY

⚓	Beaches
🚢	Cruise Ship Terminal
🏴	Dive Sites
1	Restaurants
1	Hotels
⛴	Ferry

A heady blend of Afro-Caribbean customs, French style, and tropical delights, butterfly-shape Guadeloupe is actually two islands divided by a narrow channel: smaller, flatter, and drier Grande-Terre (Large Land) and wetter and more mountainous Basse-Terre (Low Land). Sheltered by palms, the beaches are beguiling, and the waterfront sidewalk cafés are a bit like the Riviera.

13

THE BUTTERFLY ISLAND

Guadeloupe, annexed by France in 1674, is not really a single island but rather an archipelago. The largest parts of the chain are Basse-Terre and Grande-Terre, which together are shaped somewhat like a large butterfly. The "out" islands are the Îles des Saintes, La Désirade, and Marie-Galante.

ATLANTIC OCEAN

Anse de la savane Brûlée

Baie du Nord Ouest

Plage le Moule

N7
D101 Le Moule

D114

TERRE

St. François Airport
St-François

Ste-Anne

Plage du Helleux

Anse de la Gourde
Anse à la Baie
Pointe Tarare
Anse Kahouanne
Pointe des Châteaux

Porte d'Enfer
La Désirade
Grande-Anse

Îles de la Petite Terre

0 —— 10 miles
0 —— 15 km

Anse de Vieux Fort
Grosse Pte.
Vieux Fort
Gueule Grande Gouffre

Anse.Carot
Baie de St. Louis
Saint Louis
Marie-Galante

Plage de Folle Anse

Châteaux Murat
Grand-Bourg
Pte.Des Basses
Marie-Galante
Capesterre
Petite-Anse
Aérodrome de Marie-Galante
D203

TOP REASONS TO VISIT GUADELOUPE

1 Creole Flavors: Guadeloupe's restaurants and hotel dining rooms highlight the island's fine creole cuisine.

2 Small Inns: Also called *relais,* and *gites* (apartments) these intimate accommodations give you a genuine island experience.

3 Adventure Sports: Parc National has plenty of activities to keep the adrenaline pumping.

4 La Désirade: Remote and affordable, this friendly island provides an escape-from-it-all experience.

GUADELOUPE PLANNER

Island Activities

Guadeloupe's **beaches** can be outstanding, but few resorts are on the island's best, which are mostly along the southern shore of Grande-Terre and the out islands.

Visitors come instead for good **diving,** and the chance to **hike** and explore in Basse-Terre's wild national park.

Good **water sports** make up for sometimes mediocre hotel beaches; windsurfing, sailing, fishing, and jet-skiing are all fun. **Biking** isn't limited to the annual race.

Enjoy dining at one of Guadeloupe's fine restaurants serving **creole cuisine** or a **Franco–Caribbean fusion.**

Although **shopping** isn't the best, night owls will find fun bars and clubs, and a lively music scene.

On the **smaller islands**—Marie-Galante, La Désirade, and Les Saintes—relaxing, sunbathing, and soaking up some old-time Caribbean atmosphere usually rank among the top activities.

Guadeloupe has become a pioneer in certain sectors like ecotourism, from canyoning to hiking to the volcano, every manner of boating excursion, major diving activity, and attractions such as Jardin Botanique.

Getting to Guadeloupe

Hassle Factor: Medium for Guadeloupe; high for the smaller islands.

Nonstops: You can fly nonstop from Orlando (Air France, seasonal).

Air Travel: Air Antilles Express (☏ 0890/64–86–48 ⊕ www.airantilles.com) has service to Martinique, St. Martin, and St. Barth. **Air Caraïbes** (☏ 0820/83–58–35 or 0590/82–47–00) connects the island to St. Maarten, Martinique, the Dominican Republic, and Havana, Cuba. **Air France** (☏ 0590/21–13–03 or 0820–820–820) has connections in San Juan. You can also connect in San Juan with **American Airlines** (☏ 0590/21–11–80 or 0811/30–73–00). **LIAT** (☏ 0590/21–13–93) services several other Caribbean islands like Barbados

Some travelers prefer the regularly scheduled ferry service from Dominica, St. Lucia, and Martinique, but the extra travel time certainly increases the hassle factor. The smaller out islands are harder to reach; even with regular ferries you will almost always need to spend some time on Guadeloupe both coming and going.

Airports and Transfers: Aéroport International Pôle Caraïbes (PTP) (☏ 0590/21–14–72 or 0590/21–14–00), usually called the Pointe-à-Pitre Airport, is one of the largest and most modern in the Caribbean. Excellent signage makes it very manageable. It has shops, restaurants, and car-rental agencies. There is a tourism information booth in the terminal with bilingual staffers, an ATM, and a currency exchange. Ask your resort if airport transfers can be arranged, as they are almost always cheaper than taking a taxi. Taxi fare to Pointe-à-Pitre is about €25; to Gosier resorts is about €30, to Ste-Anne €60, and to St-François it's more than €70. Cabs meet flights at the airport if you decide not to rent a car.

Getting Around Guadeloupe

Car Travel: If you're based in Gosier or at a large resort, you'll probably need a car for a day or two of sightseeing. Your valid driver's license will suffice for up to 20 days. Count on spending between €48 and €70 a day for a small car with standard transmission. Automatics are more expensive (about €75 per day in high season) and must be reserved in advance. **Europcar** (☎ 0590/21-13-52), like most companies, charges a €20 drop-off fee for the airport, even if you pick the car up there. Europcar employees speak English and are professional; convertibles go for €113 per day.

Contacts: Avis (☎ 0590/21-13-54). **Budget** (☎ 0590/21-13-49). **Hertz** (☎ 0590/21-13-46) has some automatics and convertibles. **Jumbo Car** (☎ 0590/21-13-50). **Rent A Car** (☎ 0590/21-13-62). **Sixt** (☎ 0590/21-13-44).

Ferry Travel: Ferry schedules and fares often change, so phone ahead to confirm. **Brudey Frères Transport Maritime** (☎ 0590/90-04-48 in Pointe-à-Pitre, 0590/92-69-74 in Trois-Rivières, 0590/92-69-74 in St-François, 0590/97-77-82 in Marie-Galante) travels between Terre-de-Haut, Les Saintes, and Trois-Rivières on Basse-Terre with some service from Pointe-à-Pitre. **Comatrile** (☎ 0690/50-05-09 [port], 0590/22-26-31) travels from St-François on Grande-Terre to La Désirade and to Marie-Galante and Les Saintes. Both Comatrile and Express des Isles operate ferries between Terre-de-Haut and Marie-Galante. **C.T.M. DEHER** (☎ 0590/92-06-39 or 0590/99-50-68 ⊕ www. ctmdeher.com) plies the waters between Trois-Rivieres and Terre-de-Haut. **Express des Isles** (☎ 0825/35-90-00 or 0590/91-98-53 ⊕ www.express-des-iles.com) runs ferries to Marie Galante, Les Saintes, from Pointe-à-Pitre. Longer trips to other islands like Dominica and Martinique cost about €60 to €69 and take between three and four hours.

Taxi Travel: Taxis are metered and fairly pricey. Fares jump by 40% between 7 pm and 7 am and on Sunday and holidays. Call **Narcisse Taxi** (☎ 0590/94-55-95) for an English-speaking, professional taxi driver and tour guide with a minivan. If your French is in order, call **Radio Cabs** (☎ 0590/82-00-00 or 0590/20-74-74). **Clement Vealere** (☎ 0690/35-18-02) is a recommended English-speaking taxi driver. **Michel Pain** (☎ 0690/76-25-32) will meet you at the ferry and take you where you want or give you a fun tour of the island of Desirade.

Driving Tips

Driving around Grande-Terre is relatively easy. Basse-Terre requires more skill to navigate the hairpin bends in the mountains and around the eastern shore; at night the roads are unlighted and treacherous.

Returning your rental to the airport can be stressful because it's easy to get lost. Allow for an extra hour. Conscientiously follow every sign that has a picture of a plane. You must return the car to the old (former) airport and wait for a shuttle to bring you back to the new airport. An alternative is to return it in Gosier and put that €20 toward a stress-free taxi ride. Return your vehicle with the same amount of gas or you'll be charged an exorbitant rate.

Guadeloupeans are fast and often impatient drivers and they tailgate.

Round-abouts (*rond-pointes*) are everywhere. You should use your turn signal to indicate your direction, even if no one else does, and proceed cautiously. Avoid morning and evening rush hours, which start and end early, especially around Pointe-à-Pitre. If you're lost, don't stop to ask people standing on the side of the road; they are waiting for a lift and will jump in. Try to find a gas station. Chances are the attendants speak more Creole than French. Inside, the manager or other customers will speak French and maybe some English. *"Je suis perdue!"* (I am lost!) is a good phrase to know.

13

GUADELOUPE PLANNER

Fast Facts

Banks and Exchange Services: Few places accept U.S. dollars, so plan on exchanging for euros. You must exchange cash at your hotel or a *bureau de change*. One favorite company is Change Caraïbe, with branches near the tourist office and market in Pointe-à-Pitre. It's easier to use your ATM card to get euros. Make sure you have a four-digit PIN. ATMs, particularly those in smaller towns, don't always accept foreign bank cards. There are just two ATMs on the main island, one at the ferry dock and the other next to the mayor's (Maire) office. Come with a cash reserve, for it's not unusual for the machines to run out of euros or to malfunction during electrical blackouts.

Electricity: 220 volts/50 cycles. North American electronics and laptops require an adapter and a converter.

Emergency Services: Ambulance (☎ 15). **Fire** (☎ 18). **Police emergencies** (☎ 17). **SAMU** (☎ 0590/89–11–00) is a medical service to see a doctor fast.

Passport Requirements: You must have a valid passport as well as a return or ongoing ticket to enter Guadeloupe.

Weddings: A long residency requirement makes weddings prohibitive.

Essentials

Mail: Postcards cost €0.85 to the US€1 to Canada; letters up to 20 grams are €0.85 to the US€1 to Canada. If sending mail to Guadeloupe, be sure to include the name of the specific island in the archipelago (e.g., Grande-Terre, Basse-Terre), as well as the postal code, then "Guadeloupe" followed by "French West Indies."

Taxes and Service Charges: The *taxe de séjour* (room tax), which by hotel, is usually €1 but never exceeds €1.80 per person per day. Most hotel prices include a 10% to 15% service charge in their rates; if not, it'll be added to your bill. A 15% service charge is included in all restaurant prices, as are taxes.

Telephones: If you need to make many calls outside your hotel, purchase a *télécarte* at the post office or other outlet. These can be used in special phone booths to make cheaper local and international calls. Some hotels charge a connection fee if you use a card from your room phone. It's difficult, but not impossible, to place collect or credit-card calls to the U.S.

To make on-island calls, dial 0590 (0690 if it is a cellular) and then the six-digit phone number. To call Guadeloupe from the United States, dial 00–590–590, then the local number. For cell phone numbers, dial 00–590–690, then the local number. If you're in one of the other islands in the French West Indies, dial 0590 and then the local number.

Tipping: Restaurants are required to include a 15% service charge in the menu price. No additional gratuity is necessary (although it's appreciated if service is particularly good). Tip skycaps and porters about €1 a bag, cab drivers 10% of the fare (if they work for a cab company, rather than have their own taxi), and housekeeping €1 per night.

Visitor Information: Comité du Tourisme des Iles de Guadeloupe (✉ 5 sq. de la Banque, Pointe-à-Pitre ☎ 0590/82–09–30 ⊕ www.lesilesdeguadeloupe.com). **French Government Tourist Office** (☎ 514/288–1904 for public information line, 310/271–6665 in Los Angeles ⊕ www.franceguide.com). **Office du Tourisme de Marie-Galante** (✉ Rue du Port, BP 15, Grand-Bourg, Marie-Galante ☎ 0590/97–56–51). **Office du Tourisme de Terre de Haut** (✉ 39 rue de la Grande Anse, Terre de Haut ☎ 0590/99–58–60 ⊕ www.omtlessaintes.fr).

Where to Stay

Guadeloupe is actually an archipelago of large and small islands. Grande-Terre has the big package hotels that are concentrated primarily in four or five communities on the south coast, whereas wilder Basse-Terre has more locally owned hotels. More distant and much quieter are the Iles des Saintes, Marie-Galante, and la Désirade, in that order. On each of these smaller islands tourism is only a part of the economy and development is light, and any of them will give you a sense of what the Caribbean used to be.

Relais and Gites: These small inns offer a more personal—and authentic—kind of Caribbean experience.

Resorts: You can certainly opt for a big, splashy resort with all the amenities. Many of the island's large chain hotels cater to French package groups, yet an increasing number of them are being renovated to the degree that they will appeal more to the expectations of Americans.

Villas: Private villas are another option—particularly for families—but the language barrier is often a deterrent to Americans. Best to go through one of the rental agencies recommended here.

HOTEL AND RESTAURANT COSTS

Restaurant prices are for a main course at dinner and include V.A.T. (value-added tax) and service charge. Hotel prices are per night for a double room in high season and do not include taxes, service charges, and meal plans (except at Club Med). Many do include a full buffet breakfast.

WHAT IT COSTS IN EUROS

	¢	$	$$	$$$	$$$$
Restaurants	under €8	€8–€12	€12–€20	€20–€30	over €30
Hotels	under €150	€150–€275	€276–€375	€376–€475	over €475

When to Go

The tourism industry thrives during the high season, which lasts from mid-November through May, and then the island is quiet the rest of the year. Prices decline 25% to 40% in the off-season.

13

FESTIVALS AND EVENTS

Carnival is an annual highlight, starting in February and continuing until Ash Wednesday; the celebration finishes with a parade and a huge street party à la Mardi Gras.

June's **Creole Blues Festival** on Marie-Galante is gaining in fame and beginning to ensure that the small island's hotels fill up. Most partygoers day-trip for the event.

In August, the **Tour Cycliste de la Guadeloupe,** which runs over 800 mi (1,290 km) of both Grande-Terre and Basse-Terre, is the Caribbean's answer to the Tour de France.

Le Route du Rhum is the largest solitary, transatlantic sailboat race, with its starting line in Saint-Malo, France and its finish line in Pointe-à-Pitre (PAP). It culminates in Guadeloupe on alternate years. In 2010, 89 skippers began the race, traversing 3,510 sea miles alone. A craftsmen village is set up at la Place de la Victoire (PAP), and festivities characterize the race, with crowds waiting to welcome the brave sailors.

GUADELOUPE BEACHES

Guadeloupe is an archipelago of five paradises surrounded by both the Caribbean and the Atlantic. Its beaches run the spectrum from white to black and everything in between.

(Above) La Grande Anse, overlooking Les Saintes' islands. (Opposite page bottom) Club Med Beach at Plage Caravalle. (Opposite page top) La Grande Anse.

There are idyllic beaches, long stretches of unspoiled beach shaded by coconut palms, with soft warm sand. Admittedly, hotels beaches are generally narrow, although well maintained. Some hotels allow nonguests who patronize their restaurants to use their beach facilities. The popular public beaches tend to be cluttered with campers-turned-cafés and cars parked in impromptu lots on the sand. Sunday is the big day, but these same (free) beaches are often quiet during the week.

On the southern coast of Grande-Terre, from Ste-Anne to Pointe des Châteaux, you can find stretches of soft white sand and some sparsely visited stretches. The Atlantic waters on the northeast coast are too rough for swimming. Along the western shore of Basse-Terre signposts indicate small beaches. The sand starts turning gray in Malendure; it becomes volcanic black farther south. There's only one official nude beach, Pointe Tarare, but topless bathing is common.

SAND IN A BOTTLE

Guadeloupe's sand profile is literally encapsulated in one of its popular souvenirs—an airtight glass cylinder displaying variegated stratum of sand. St-François is the lightest, followed by the blond of Ste-Anne. Next down is the golden sands of Gosier and Moule. Malendure presents dark-gray, volcanic sand that farther along the coast is black. North of Basse-Terre, Deshaies has both black and nearly white sand.

GRANDE-TERRE

L'Autre Bord. The waves on this Atlantic beach give the long expanse of sand a wild look. The beach, which is protected by an extensive coral reef, is a magnet for surfers and windsurfers. You can stroll on the seaside promenade fringed by flamboyant trees. ⊠ *Le Moule.*

Plage Caravelle. Just southwest of Ste-Anne is one of Grande-Terre's longest and prettiest stretches of sand, the occasional dilapidated shack notwithstanding. Protected by reefs, it's also a fine snorkeling spot. Club med occupies one end of this beach, and nonguests can enjoy its beach and water sports, as well as lunch and drinks, by buying a day pass. You can also have lunch on the terrace of La Toubana Hotel & Spa, then descend the stairs to the beach or enjoy lunch at its beach restaurant, wildly popular on Sunday. ⊠ *Rte. N4, southwest of Ste-Anne.*

Plage de la Chapelle à Anse-Bertrand. If you want a delightful day trip to the northern tip of Grande-Terre, aim for this spot, one of the loveliest white-sand beaches, whose gentle midafternoon waves are popular with families. When the tide rolls in, it's equally popular with surfers. Several little terrace restaurants at the far end of the beach sate your appetite, but you might want to bring your own shade, because none rent chaise longues. ⊠ *4 mi (6½ km) south of La Pointe de la Grand Vigie.*

Pointe Tarare. This secluded strip just before the tip of Pointe des Châteaux is the island's only nude beach. Small bar–cafés are in the parking area, but it's still best to bring some water, snacks, and beach chairs, as there's no place to rent them. What you do have is one of the coast's most dramatic landscapes; looming above are rugged cliffs topped by a huge crucifix. When approaching St-François Marina, go in the direction of Pointe des Châteaux at the roundabout and drive for about 10 minutes. ⊠ *Rte. N4, southeast of St-François.*

BASSE-TERRE

La Grande-Anse. One of Guadeloupe's widest beaches has soft beige sand sheltered by palms. To the west it's a round verdant mountain. It has a large parking area and some food stands, but no other facilities. The beach can be overrun on Sunday, not to mention littered. Right after the parking lot, you can see signage for the creole restaurant Le Karacoli; if you have lunch there (it's not inexpensive), you can *sieste* on the chaise longues. ⊠ *Rte. N6, north of Deshaies.*

Malendure. Across from Pigeon Island and the Jacques Cousteau Underwater Park, this long, gray, volcanic beach on the Caribbean's calm waters has restrooms, a few beach shacks offering cold drinks and snacks, and a huge parking lot. There might be some litter, but the beach is cleaned regularly. Don't

Les Pompierres

come here for solitude, as the beach is a launch point for many dive boats. The snorkeling here is good. Le Rocher de Malendure, a fine seafood restaurant, is perched on a cliff over the bay. ⊠ *Rte. N6, Bouillante.*

ILES DES SAINTES

Pompierres. This beach is particularly popular with families with small children, as there's a gradual slope, no drop-off, and a long stretch of shallow water. The calm water makes for a good snorkel. To get here, go to the seamen's church near the main plaza, and then head in the direction of Marigot. Continue until you see Le Salako Snack Bar and some scurrying chickens, and—voilà!—you'll spy a palm-fringed, half-moon stretch of tawny sand. The curve of the beach is called the Bridge of Stone and you can walk it—carefully—taking a dip in the crater that fills with water from the Atlantic. Morning sun is best; then return to Salako for some grilled fresh fish and a cold one. ⊠ *Terre-de-Haut.*

LA DÉSIRADE

Le Soufleur Plage. To reach one of La Désirade's longest and best beaches from the ferry dock, face town and follow the main road to the right. It's about 15 minutes by car or motor scooter (about €20 a day). White sand, calm waters, and snacks and cold drinks from the beach restaurant await, but there are no chaises, so BYO beach towel. ⊠ *Dpmt. Rd. 207, Le Soufleur.*

MARIE-GALANTE

Anse de Vieux Fort. This gorgeous Marie-Galante beach stretches alongside crystal-clear waters that border a large body of freshwater that is ideal for canoeing. Explore the nearby mangrove swamp on hiking trails. The beaches in this area are wide and favored by couples for the solitude. Bring your own everything to this virgin territory. ⊠ *Rte. D205, just past Pointe Fleur d'Épée, Vieux Fort.*

Petite-Anse. This long, golden beach on Marie-Galante is punctuated with sea grape trees. It's idyllic during the week, but on weekends the crowds of locals and urban refugees from the main island arrive. Le Touloulou's great creole seafood restaurant provides the only facilities. ⊠ *6½ mi (10 km) north of Grand-Bourg via rte. D203, Petite-Anse.*

DID YOU KNOW?

There are numerous hiking trails that climb La Soufrière volcano, and some of them can be pretty treacherous. Go with a guide and you can safely take in breathtaking sights, such as the views from Piton Dolomieu.

EATING AND DRINKING WELL IN THE FRENCH WEST INDIES

Creole cuisine, a sultry mélange of African, European, Arawak, even Asian traditions, reflects the islands' turbulent territorial tugs-of-war.

(Above) Lobster Barbecue. (Opposite page bottom) 'Ti Punch. (Opposite page top) Accras—Salt Cod Fritters.

Deceptively simple yet robustly flavored, authentic "Kweyol" cuisine demands patience: continual macerating and marinating, then seasoning as the food simmers. Many dishes developed in response to economic necessities, recycling leftovers and incorporating ingredients such as starches (both hardy and impervious to spoilage). The indigenous Arawaks provided tubers like tannia and yucca; lemongrass and capsicum for seasoning; arrowroot for thickening; and *roucou* (annatto, a yellowish-reddish seed) for coloring. The Africans imported plantains, pigeon peas, potatoes, and peppers. The French and British introduced tomatoes, onions, and less perishable salt cod. East Indian indentured servants brought cumin, cardamom and coriander, notably used in *colombo*, a meat (try *cabri*, goat), poultry, or seafood dish that detonates the palate. Wash it down with fresh local juices from pulpy papaya to puckering passion fruit or the fine rums. Bon appétit!

'TI PUNCH

The primary ingredient in this aperitif is 100-proof rum—no wonder the first belt is called the *pete-pied* (take-off). It's occasionally fruit-infused, muddled with fresh lime and simple cane syrup. Novices might want to request the lighter (weight) *ti-bete*. Another concoction worth sampling is the classic *planteur* (rum with fruit juices and spices); finish dinner with a *rhum vieux* (aged, cognac-quality rum) or *shrubb*, an orange- and spice-tinged rum-based liqueur. An excellent rhum vieux is Reimonenq's Ste. Rose.

Blaff. This typical method of preparation is usually used for firm, flaky, white fish such as mahimahi or grouper. The fish is poached in a seasoned broth, often a classic court-bouillon (a quick stock perfumed with fresh herbs). The broth is then doctored with lime, onion, garlic, cilantro, chilies, and other ingredients to create the incendiary "condiment" *sauce chien* (whose etymology is obscure, but may indeed have been named "dog's sauce" because it would render even canines edible).

Cod. France contributed many basic ingredients over time to economize, notably dried salt cod which required no refrigeration and became a staple in creole cooking. *Accras de morue*, fluffy cod fritters, grace every menu. Other popular traditional dishes include *chiquetaille*, shredded cod usually served with a spicy vinaigrette, and *ferocé* (saltfish mixed with avocado and peppers, deep-fried in manioc flour). *Tinnain morue*, grilled cod and bananas believed to energize, still jump-starts many locals' days.

Crayfish. This spiky freshwater crustacean, both wild, and, increasingly, farmed, is usually served whole with a variety of sauces. It goes by many names in the French West Indies, including the more Gallic *écrevisse*, patois *z'habitant* or *crebiche*, and *ouassou* (generally larger). A favorite preparation is stewed

with *dombrés* (manioc dumplings served pancake-style); you may also see it *étouffée* (stewed with vegetables, served over rice), underscoring the similarity to Cajun cuisine (alongside such dishes as *boudin*, blood sausage).

Poulet Boucané. "Buccaneer's chicken" is smoked slowly over burnt sugarcane (a centuries-old warning signal that pirates were coming) in a closed, chimney-topped barbecue. *Boucanage* is also a French preservation technique, "drying" seasoned meats and poultry on a wood fire (in this case using sugarcane husks). Roughly similar to Jamaica's jerk, it mingles smokiness, sweetness, and spiciness; the marinade typically is a variant of the combustible sauce chien, though milder versions might combine vinegar, lime, garlic, and clove.

Tripe. Another old-fashioned method of economizing was the use of internal organs, offal, which eventually became appropriated by haute cuisine. Tripe (small intestines) is particularly popular. The classic dish is *bébélé*, a stew of tripe, green bananas, tubers (usually breaded as croquettes or *domblés*), and gourds like *giraumon* (similar to pumpkin).

—Jordan Simon

By Eileen Robinson Smith

Sail the waters around the Isles of Guadeloupe and you'll observe nuances in the ocean's color palette as you glide through the gin-clear sea. Things look better from the bow of a sailboat, from the storybook islands of Les Saintes to towns not as postcard pretty. This Caribbean coastline is dramatic with white and golden beaches, rocky promontories, and rugged cliffs that span the horizon.

Although Guadeloupe is thought of as one island, it is several, each with its own personality. "The mainland" consists of the two largest islands in the Guadeloupe archipelago: Basse-Terre and Grande-Terre, which look something like a butterfly. The outer islands—Les Saintes, Marie-Galante, and La Désirade—are finally being acknowledged as wonderfully unique, unspoiled travel destinations. Tourism officials are now wisely marketing their country as a plural, Les Iles de Guadeloupe. See which one is your place in the sun. *Vive les vacances!*

It's no wonder that in 1493 Christopher Columbus welcomed the sight of this emerald paradise, where fresh, sweet water flows in cascades. And it's understandable why France annexed it in 1674 and why the British schemed to wrench it from them. In 1749 Guadeloupe mirrored what was happening in the motherland. It, too, was an island divided, between royalists and revolutionaries.

Surprisingly, the resident British sided with the royalists, so Victor Hugues was sent to banish the Brits. While here, he sent to the guillotine more than 300 loyal-to-the-royal planters and freed the slaves, thus all but destroying the plantocracy. An old saying of the French Caribbean refers to *les grands seigneurs de la Martinique et les bonnes gens de la Guadeloupe* (the lords of Martinique and the bourgeoisie of Guadeloupe), and that still rings true. You'll find more aristocratic descendants of the original French planters on Martinique (known as *békés*) and also more "expensive" people, both living and vacationing there. That mass beheading is one of the prime reasons. Ironically, Napoléon—who ultimately ousted the royals—also ousted Hugues and reestablished slavery. It wasn't until 1848 that an Alsatian, Victor Schoelcher, abolished it for good.

Guadeloupe became one of France's *départements d'outremer* in 1946, meaning that it's a dependent of France. It was designated a region in 1983, making it a part of France, albeit a distant part. This brought many benefits to the islanders, from their fine highway systems to the French social services and educational system, as well as a high standard of living. Certain tensions still exist, though the anticolonial resentment harbored by the older generations is dying out. Guadeloupe's young people realize the importance of tourism to the island's future, and you'll find them welcoming, smiling, and practicing the English and tourism skills they learn in school. Some *français* is indispensable, though you may receive a bewildering response in Creole.

Guadeloupe is a little bit of France, but far from the Metropole. Instead, the culture of this tropical paradise is more Afro-influenced. Savor the earthier pleasures here, exemplified by the wonderful potpourri of whole spices whose heady aromas flood the outdoor markets.

LANGUAGE

The official language is French, though most of the islanders also speak Creole, a lyrical patois that you won't be able to understand. Often, their French has a heavy Creole accent. Most of the staff in hotels knows some English as do some taxi drivers, but communicating is decidedly more difficult in the countryside. Arm yourself with a phrase book, a dictionary, patience, and a sense of humor.

ETIQUETTE

Guadeloupeans are deeply religious and traditional, particularly the older generations. Revealing shorts or swimwear away from the beach may be considered indecorous by some, and you should ask before taking a picture of any islander. The children, however, will probably flash you one of their happy smiles. Observe the courtesy of saying *bonjour* or *bonsoir* when you enter or leave a place or before asking someone a question or directions.

EXPLORING GUADELOUPE

To see each "wing" of the butterfly, you'll need to budget at least one day. They are connected by a bridge, and Grande-Terre has pretty villages along its south coast and the spectacular Pointe des Châteaux. You can see the main sights in Pointe-à-Pitre in a half day. Touring the rugged, mountainous Basse-Terre is a challenge. If time is a problem, head straight to the west coast; you could easily spend a day traveling its length, stopping for sightseeing, lunch, and a swim. You can make day trips to the islands, but an overnight or more works best. Leave your heavy luggage in the baggage room of your "mainland" hotel.

GRANDE-TERRE

☾ **Aquarium de la Guadeloupe.** Unique in the Antilles, this aquarium in the marina near Pointe-à-Pitre is a good place to spend an hour. The well-planned facility has an assortment of tropical fish, crabs, lobsters, moray eels, coffer fish, and some live coral. It's also a fascinating turtle rescue center and a spectacular shark tank. ⊠ *Pl. Créole off rte. N4, Pointe-à-Pitre* ☎ *0590/90–92–38* ⊠ *€10* ⊙ *Daily 9–7.*

Ft. Fleur d'Épée. The main attraction in Bas-du-Fort is this 18th-century fortress, which hunkers down on a hillside behind a deep moat. It was the scene of hard-fought battles between the French and the English in 1794. You can explore its well-preserved dungeons and battlements and take in a sweeping view of Iles des Saintes and Marie-Galante. ⊠ *Bas-du-Fort* ☎ *0590/90–94–61* ⊠ *€6* ⊙ *Mon. 10–5, Tues.–Sun. 9–5.*

■ **TIP→** You may find that you adore the tropical ice-cream flavors like mangue (mango) and coco (coconut). You may not realize that cacahuète translates to "peanut" and is addictive!

Gosier. Taking its name from the brown pelicans that nest on the islet of Gosier and along the south coast of Grande-Terre, Gosier was still a tiny village in the 1950s, a simple stopping place between Pointe-à-Pitre and Ste-Anne. However, it grew rapidly in the 1960s, when the beauty of the southern coastline began to bring tourists in ever-increasing numbers. Today Gosier is one of Guadeloupe's premier tourist areas while at the same time serving as a chic suburb of Pointe-à-Pitre. People sit at sidewalk cafés reading *Le Monde* as others flip-flop their way to the beach. The town has several hotels, nightclubs, and shops, a casino, and a long stretch of sand.

Le Moule. On the Atlantic coast, and once the capital city of Guadeloupe, this port city of 24,000 has had more than its share of troubles: it was bombarded by the British in 1794 and 1809 and by a hurricane in 1928. An important tourist center in past decades, it's experiencing a comeback. A large East Indian population, which originally came to cut cane, lives here. Canopies of flamboyant trees hang over the narrow streets, where colorful vegetable and fish markets do a brisk business. The town hall, with graceful balustrades, and a small 19th-century neoclassical church are on the main square. Le Moule's beach, protected by a reef, is perfect for windsurfing.

Morne-à-l'Eau. This agricultural town of about 16,000 people has an amphitheater-shape cemetery, with black-and-white-checkerboard tombs, elaborate epitaphs, and multicolor (plastic) flowers. On All Saints' Day (November 1), it's the scene of a moving (and photogenic) candlelight service.

Musee du Costume et Tradition. This museum is a labor of love by its creators, and seeing the dress of black, white, and *métisseé* (brown) societies is a fascinating way to visualize the island's tumultuous history. Items that you will remember: madras headdresses; baptism outfits; embroidered maternity dresses; colonial pith helmets and other various chapeaux as well as the doll collection. Make sure to go out back and visit the replica of a Guadeloupean case circa 1920. The museum is petite and privately owned; the founding owner is a retired English teacher and she can act as your guide. Call before you go for directions and to make certain that a school group is not there. ☒ *1 Perinette, Centre de Gosier* ☏ *0590/83–21–70 or 0690/50–98–16* ☒ *€9* ☉ *Tues.–Sun. 9–6. Closed Mon and often for lunch breaks.*

Pointe-à-Pitre. Although not the capital, this is the island's largest city, a commercial and industrial hub in the southwest of Grande-Terre. The Isles of Guadeloupe have 450,000 inhabitants, 99.6% of whom live in the cities. Pointe-à-Pitre is bustling, noisy, and hot—a place of honking horns and traffic jams and cars on sidewalks for want of a parking place. By day its pulse is fast, but at night, when its streets are almost deserted, you don't want to be there.

The city has suffered severe damage over the years from earthquakes, fires, and hurricanes. In recent years it took heavy hits by Hurricanes Frederick (1979), David (1980), and Hugo (1989). On one side of rue Frébault you can see the remaining French colonial structures; on the other, the modern city. Some of the downtown area has been rejuvenated. The Centre St-John Perse has transformed old warehouses into a cruise-terminal complex that consists of the spartan Hotel St-John, restaurants, shops, and the port authority headquarters. An impressive terminal serves the ferries that depart for Iles des Saintes, Marie-Galante, Dominica, Martinique, and St. Lucia.

The heart of the old city is Place de la Victoire; surrounded by wooden buildings with balconies and shutters (including the tourism office) and by sidewalk cafés, it was named in honor of Victor Hugues's 1794 victory over the British. During the French Revolution, Hugues ordered the guillotine set up here so that the public could witness the bloody end of 300 recalcitrant royalists.

Even more colorful is the bustling marketplace, between rues St-John Perse, Frébault, Schoelcher, and Peynier. It's a cacophonous place, where housewives bargain for spices, herbs (and herbal remedies), and a bright assortment of papayas, breadfruits, christophenes, and tomatoes. For fans of French ecclesiastical architecture, there's the imposing **Cathédrale de St-Pierre et St-Paul** (☒ *Rue Alexandre Isaac at rue de l'Eglise*), built in 1807. Although battered by hurricanes, it has fine stained-glass windows and Creole-style balconies and is reinforced with pillars and ribs that look like leftovers from the Eiffel Tower. Anyone with an interest in French literature and culture (not your average sightseer) won't want to miss the **Musée St-John Perse**, which is dedicated to Guadeloupe's most famous son and one of the giants of world literature, Alexis Léger, better known as St-John Perse, winner of the Nobel Prize for literature in 1960. Some of his finest poems are inspired by the history and landscape—particularly the sea—of his beloved Guadeloupe. The museum contains a collection of his poetry and some of his personal belongings. Before you go, look for his birthplace at 54 rue Achille René-Boisneuf. ☒ *At rues Noizières and Achille René-Boisneuf* ☏ *0590/90–01–92* ☒ *€2.50* ☉ *Thurs.–Tues. 8:30–12:30 and 2:30–5:30.*

Musée Schoelcher celebrates Victor Schoelcher, a high-minded abolitionist from Alsace who fought against slavery in the French West Indies in the 19th century. The museum contains many of his personal effects, and exhibits trace his life and work. ⊠ *24 rue Peynier* ☎ *0590/82–08–04* 🖃 *€3* ☉ *Weekdays 9–5.*

Pointe des Châteaux. The island's easternmost point offers a breathtaking view of the Atlantic crashing against huge rocks, carving them into shapes resembling pyramids. There are spectacular views of Guadeloupe's southern and eastern coasts and the island of La Désirade. In high season, the dramatic scene is marred by a parking lot filled with tour buses and makeshift bars and snack stands, but if you are spending hours at the beach, you will need the sustenance. On weekends locals come in numbers to walk their dogs, surf, or look for romance. But change is afoot, and the *sauvage* beach is slated to become gentrified. The landmark crucifix (circa 1954), a symbol of protection for those at sea as well as a navigational site, has been restored.

NEED A BREAK? If you don't want to take time for a two-hour French lunch, watch for gas stations such as **Shell Boutique, Total Boutique,** and **Esso Tigermart,** which sell food. The VITO station on the left going into St-François has good pizza for €8, roast chicken, and paninis, as well as tables and chairs. A Total "fillin' station" might have barbecue ribs, chicken, and turkey.

Port Louis. This fishing village of about 7,000 people is best known for Le Soufleur Plage. It was once one of the island's prettiest, but it has become a little shabby. Although the beach is crowded on weekends, it's blissfully quiet during the week. The sand is fringed by flamboyant trees, and there are also spectacular views of Basse-Terre.

Ste-Anne. In the 18th century this town, 8 mi (13 km) east of Gosier, was a sugar-exporting center. Sand has replaced sugar as the town's most valuable asset. La Caravelle and the other beaches are among the best in Guadeloupe. On a more spiritual note, Ste-Anne has a lovely cemetery with stark-white tombs.

★ **St-François.** This was once a simple little village, primarily involved with fishing and harvesting tomatoes. The fish and tomatoes are still here, as are the old Creole houses and the lively market with recommendable food stalls in the centre ville, but increasingly, the St-François marina district is overtaking Gosier as Guadeloupe's most fashionable tourist resort area. La Cocoteraie, one of the island's ritziest hotels, is just off l'avenue de l'Europe, which runs between the marina and the rolling fairways and water obstacles of the 18-hole Robert Trent Jones–designed municipal golf course. On the marina side, a string of shops, hotels, bars, and restaurants caters to tourists.

NEED A BREAK? Match, a *supermarche* on l'avenue de l'Europe/St-François Marina, has esoteric cheeses and baked goods such as pie-size, tropical-fruit tarts. Other supermarkets to look for throughout the island that have good deli or bakery departments are those in the Leader Price and Carrefour chains.

BASSE-TERRE

Basse-Terre (which translates as "low land") is by far the highest and wildest of the two wings of the Guadeloupe butterfly, with the peak of the Soufrière volcano topping off at nearly 4,811 feet. Basse-Terre, where you can find the island's national park, is an ecotourist's treasure, with lush, equatorial plant life and adventurous opportunities for hikers and mountain bikers on the old *traces*, routes that porters once took across the mountains. You can still find numerous fishing villages and banana plantations, stretching as far as the eye can see. The northwest coast, between Bouillante and Grande-Anse, is magnificent; the road twists and turns up steep hills smothered in vegetation and then drops down and skirts deep-blue bays and colorful seaside towns. Constantly changing light, towering clouds, and frequent rainbows only add to the beauty.

Basse-Terre. Because Pointe-à-Pitre is so much bigger, few people suspect that this little town of 15,000 is the capital and administrative center of Guadeloupe. But if you have any doubts, walk up the hill to the state-of-the-art Théâtre Nationale, where some of France's finest theater and opera companies perform. Paid for by the French government, it's a sign that Basse-Terre is reinventing itself. Founded in 1640, it has endured not only foreign attacks and hurricanes but sputtering threats from La Soufrière as well. The last major eruption was in the 16th century, though the volcano seemed active enough to warrant evacuating more than 70,000 people in 1975.

☺ The **Jardin Botanique**, or Botanical Garden, is an exquisitely tasteful
★ 10-acre park populated with parrots and flamingos. A circuitous walking trail takes you by ponds with floating lily pads, cactus gardens, and every kind of tropical flower and plant, including orchids galore. A panoramic restaurant with surprisingly good meals and a snack bar are housed in terraced gingerbread buildings, one overlooking a waterfall, the other the mountains. The garden has a children's park and nature-oriented playthings in the shop. A local juice and a snack is offered to visitors. ⊠ *Deshaies* ☎ *0590/28-43-02* ⊠ *€14* ⊘ *Daily 9–5:30.*

Bouillante. The name means "boiling," and so it's no surprise that hot springs were discovered here. However, the biggest attraction is scuba diving on nearby Pigeon Island, which is accessed by boat from Plage de Malendure. There's a small information kiosk on the beach at Plage de Malendure that can help you with diving and snorkeling arrangements.

Cascade aux Ecrevisses. Within the Parc National de la Guadeloupe, Crayfish Falls is one of the island's loveliest (and most popular) spots. There's a marked trail (walk carefully—the rocks can be slippery) leading to this splendid waterfall, which dashes down into the Corossol River—a good place for a dip. Come early, though; otherwise you definitely won't have it to yourself.

Chutes du Carbet. You can reach three of the Carbet Falls (one drops from 65 feet, the second from 360 feet, the third from 410 feet) via a long, steep path from the village of Habituée. On the way up you pass the Grand Étang (Great Pond), a volcanic lake surrounded by interesting plant life. For horror fans there's also the curiously named Étang

Zombi, a pond believed to house evil spirits. If there have been heavy rains, *don't even think about it.*

Ilet de Pigeon. This tiny, rocky island a few hundred yards off the coast is the site of the Jacques Cousteau Underwater Park, the island's best scuba and snorkeling site. Although the reefs here are good, they don't rank among the top Caribbean dive spots. Several companies conduct diving trips to the reserve, and it's on the itinerary of some sailing and snorkeling trips (⇨ *Diving and Sea Excursions sections in Sports and Activities*).

Fodor's Choice **La Bonifierie/Ti café.** When it comes to the island's coffee and chocolate ★ experiences, this place takes the gold. Within the attractive complex with fieldstone and wooden colonial houses, there's a display case for the truffles, chocolate candies, and confections. They are created from 100% local products, from cacao to tropical fruits. The French *chocolatiere* produces what may be *the* best chocolate, from the dark to the white, south of Paris. Call ahead and ask to be part of a group that is taught how to make candy bars and then enjoys a Franco-Caribbean buffet with tastings of island rum. The sophisticated courtyard café has a contemporary menu. The beef, like the coffee, is grown on the plantation and triggers a chemical reaction for the chocolate desserts. ⊠ *Rte. de Morin, St. Claude* ☎ *0590/80–06–05* 🖃 *Free* ⊙ *Tues.–Sun. 9–4.*

Les Mamelles. Two mountains—Mamelle de Petit-Bourg, at 2,350 feet, and Mamelle de Pigeon, at 2,500 feet—rise in the Parc National de la Guadeloupe. *Mamelle* means "breast," and when you see the mountains, you can understand why they are so named. Trails ranging from easy to arduous lace up into the surrounding mountains. There's a glorious view from the lookout point 1,969 feet up Mamelle de Pigeon. If you're a climber, plan to spend several hours exploring this area. Hark! If there have been heavy rainfalls, cancel your plans.

★ **Parc National de la Guadeloupe.** This 74,100-acre park has been recognized by UNESCO as a Biosphere Reserve. Before going, pick up a *Guide to the National Park* from the tourist office; it rates the hiking trails according to difficulty, and most are quite difficult indeed. Most mountain trails are in the southern half. The park is bisected by the route de la Traversée, a 16-mi (26-km) paved road lined with masses of tree ferns, shrubs, flowers, tall trees, and green plantains. It's the ideal point of entry. Wear rubber-soled shoes and take along a swimsuit, a sweater, and perhaps food for a picnic. Try to get an early start to stay ahead of the hordes of cruise-ship passengers making a day of it. Check on the weather; if Basse-Terre has had a lot of rain, give it up. In the past, after intense rainfall, rockslides have closed the road for months. ⊠ *Administrative Headquarters, rte. de la Traversée, St-Claude* ☎ *0590/80–86–00* ⊕ *www.guadeloupe-parcnational.com* 🖃 *Free* ⊙ *Weekdays 8–5:30.*

Pointe-Noire. Pointe-Noire is a good jumping-off point from which to explore Basse-Terre's little-visited northwest coast. A road skirts magnificent cliffs and tiny coves, dances in and out of thick stands of mahogany and gommier trees, and weaves through unspoiled fishing villages with boats and ramshackle houses as brightly colored as a child's finger painting. This town has two small museums devoted to local products. **La**

Maison du Bois (☎ 0590/98–16–09) offers a glimpse into the traditional use of wood on the island. Superbly crafted musical instruments and furnishings are for sale. There are even dance demonstrations and a restaurant. It's open Tuesday to Sunday from 9:30 to 5:30 and charges €2 admission.

Ste-Rose. In addition to a sulfur bath, there are two good beaches (Amandiers and Clugny) and several interesting small museums in Ste-Rose. **Domaine de Séverin** (☎ 0590/28–91–86), free and open daily from 8:30 to 5, is a historic rum distillery with a working waterwheel. A simple open-air dining room has a good menu. A petite train traverses the plantation from 9:30 to 10·45 and again from 3:30 to 5:30 from Sunday to Friday; this scenic tour costs €6. A gift shop sells rum, spices, and hot sauces.

★ **Vieux-Habitants.** This was the island's first colony, established in 1635. Beaches, a restored coffee plantation, and the oldest church on the island (1666) make this village worth a stop. From the riverfront **Musée du Café/Café Chaulet** (☎ 0590/98–54–96), dedicated to the art of coffee making, the tantalizing aroma of freshly ground beans reaches the highway. Plaques and photos tell of the island's coffee history. The shop sells excellent coffee and rum punches and jewelry made from natural materials. New is the "resident" chocolatier, a young French woman who hand-makes bonbons and festive holiday candies. You will even see the coffee cars—emblazoned Volkswagon Beetles. Admission is €6. It's open daily 9 to 5.

> **ZEE DRAINAGE DITCHES**
>
> Whether you're driving a car or walking on an unlighted street at night, be aware that there are drainage ditches on the side of the road meant to catch the run-off after a rain. As parking is at a premium, you will see cars straddling the ditches. Don't do it.

13

ILES DES SAINTES

The eight-island archipelago of Iles des Saintes, often referred to as Les Saintes, dots the waters off the southern coast of Guadeloupe. The islands are Terre-de-Haut, Terre-de-Bas, Ilet à Cabrit, Grand Ilet, La Redonde, La Coche, Le Pâté, and Les Augustins. Columbus discovered them on November 4, 1493, and christened them Los Santos (Les Saintes in French) for All Saints' Day.

Only Terre-de-Haut and Terre-de-Bas are inhabited, with a combined population of little more than 3,000. Many of the Saintois are fair-haired, blue-eyed descendants of Breton and Norman sailors. Unless they are in the tourism industry, they tend to be taciturn and standoffish. Fishing still is their main source of income, and they take pride in their work. The shores are lined with their boats and *filets bleus* (blue nets dotted with orange buoys).

DID YOU KNOW?

For generations, the Saintois fishermen wore hats called *salakos*, which look like large, inverted saucers, patterned after a hat said to have been brought here by a seafarer from China. You're now more likely to see the younger fishermen in visors and French sunglasses piloting boats with

powerful motors rather than the traditional small sailboats of their prede-
cessors. A fun, three-day event in late May celebrates the fishing industry
and its hardy fishermen (⊕ *www.omtlessaintes.fr*).

★ **Terre-de-Haut.** With 5 square mi (13 square km) and a population of
about 1,500, Terre-de-Haut is the largest and most developed of Les
Saintes. Its "big city" is Bourg, with one main street lined with bistros,
cafés, and shops. Clutching the hillside are trim white houses with
bright red or blue doors, balconies, and gingerbread frills.

Terre-de-Haut's ragged coastline is scalloped with lovely coves and
beaches, including the semi-nude beach at Anse Crawen. The beautiful
bay, complete with a "sugarloaf" mountain, has been called a mini Rio.
There are precious few vehicles or taxis on island, so you'll often find
yourself walking, despite the hilly terrain. Or you can add to the din and
rent a motorbike. Take your time on these rutted roads, as around any
bend there might be a herd of goats chomping on a fallen palm frond.
Two traffic lights have brought a small amount of order to the motorbike
hordes. When aggressively soliciting you, the scooter agencies will not tell
you that it is prohibited to scoot in town from 9 to noon and from 2 to 4.

This island makes a great day trip, but you can really get a feel for Les
Saintes if you stay overnight. It's not unlike St. Barth, but for a fraction
of the price. Note: most shops and restaurants close for two hours in
the afternoon.

■**TIP**➜ A wonderful introduction to the island as well as a travel keepsake,
is the coffee-table book Carnet de Route-Les Saintes on sale in shops for €20.

Fort Napoléon. This museum is noted for its exhaustive exhibit of the
greatest sea battles ever fought. You can also visit the well-preserved
barracks and prison cells, or admire the botanical gardens, which specialize in cacti. ■**TIP**➜ This is a hill climb, and if you decide to walk, allow
30 minutes from the village, wear comfortable footwear, and bring water.
You will be rewarded with outstanding views of the bay and neighboring
islands. ⊠ *Grand Bourg* ☎ *0590/37–99–59* ⊠ *€4* ☉ *Daily 9–noon.*

▌**NEED A BREAK?**	To reward yourself for making the trek to the fort, have a waffle cone at **Tropico Gelato,** on rue Jean Calot. This artisanal shop has such tempting tropical flavors as cinnamon and mango, as well as mint, apricot and a dozen more. Its sidewalk café is the "waiting room" for the ferry, where you can also take a small quiche or panini to go.

OTHER ISLANDS

La Désirade. *Desirable* is the operative word here. This small, safe, somewhat remote island is an absolute find for those who prefer a road less
traveled, who want their beaches long and white, and who don't mind
that accommodations are simple if the price is right. The Désirade popu-
lace (all 1,700 of them) welcome tourism, and these dear hearts have a
warm, old-fashioned sense of community.

According to legend, the "desired land" was so named by the crew of
Christopher Columbus, whose tongues were dry for want of fresh water

when they spied the island; alas, it was the season for drought. The 8-square-mi (21-square-km) island, 5 mi (8 km) east of St-François, is a chalky plateau, with an arid climate, perennial sunshine, cacti, and iguanas. You may even see two male iguanas locked in a prehistoric-looking battle. Rent a four-wheel-drive to climb the zigzag road that leads to the Grande Montagne. Make a photo stop at the diminutive white chapel, which offers a panorama of the sea below. Afraid that you might zig instead of zag down the precipice? Then take a fun, informative van tour that you join near the tourist office at the harbor. The ruins of the original settlement—a leper colony—are on the tour.

Only one road runs around the perimeter of the island, and if you're interested in visiting one of the many gorgeous beaches shaded by coco palms and sea grape trees, you can do that on a scooter. Driving is safer here than most anywhere.

NEED A BREAK?

La Désirade has a few cute and casual spots to grab a bite to eat. The goats and their kids that you pass on your island tour may end up in a curry at **Chez Nounoune** (⊠ *La Providence, La Désirade* ☎ *0590/20–03–59*).

If you're on the beach, you might want to stop by **La Payotte** (⊠ *Plage de Beauséjour, La Désirade* ☎ *0590/20–01–29*) for the fresh catch, conch, or lobster, or the French owner's famous chicken with a sauce of *noix de cajou* (cashews). Mind you, avoid it when there is a tour group on the island. Also, there are six rooms in an attractive Creole house for rent (€50–€90).

★ **Marie-Galante**. This island resonates with history. Columbus sighted this 60-square-mi (155-square-km) island on November 3, 1493, named it after his flagship, the *Maria Galanda*, and sailed on. It's dotted with ruined 19th-century sugar mills, and sugar is still its major product. Honey and 59% rum are its other favored harvests. You should make it a point to see one of the distilleries. With its rolling hills of green cane still worked by oxen and men with broad-brim straw hats, it's like traveling back in time to when all of Guadeloupe was still a giant farm.

Although it's only an hour by high-speed ferry from Pointe-à-Pitre, the country folk here are still sweet and shy, and crime is a rarity. You can see swarms of yellow butterflies, and maybe a marriage carriage festooned with flowers, pulled by two white oxen. A daughter of the sea, Marie-Galante has some of the archipelago's most gorgeous, uncrowded beaches. Take time to explore the dramatic coast. You can find soaring cliffs—such as the Gueule Grand Gouffre (Mouth of the Giant Chasm) and Les Galeries (where the sea has sculpted a natural arcade)—and enormous sun-dappled grottos, such as Le Trou à Diable, whose underground river can be explored with a guide. Port Louis, the island's "second city," is the new hip spot. The ferry dock is in Port Louis, and it's also on the charts for yachts and regattas. After sunset, the no-see-ums and mosquitoes can be a real irritation, so always be armed with repellent. The **Château Murat** (⊠ *Rte. de Capesterre, Grand-Bourg, Marie-Galante* ☎ *0590/97–94–41*) is a restored 18th-century sugar plantation and rum distillery housing exhibits on the history of rum making and sugarcane production and an admirable *ecomusée,* whose displays celebrate local crafts and customs. Just a mile from town, it's open daily from 9:15 to 5; admission is free. If time allows just one distillery, choose the most modern, nonpolluting **Domaine de Bellevue** (⊠ *Section Bellvue, Capesterre* ☎ *0590/97–47–11* ✆ *Free* ☉ *9:30–1*). Free tastings are just one inviting element here. There are award-winning, pure rums (50%–59%); excellent tropical liqueurs and punches; coffee-table books; and local organic products. Down from the windmill is a fascinating ecoboutique with everything made from such as calabash gourds.

Le Moulin de Bézard (⊠ *Chemin de Nesmond, off D202, Marie-Galante*) is the only rebuilt windmill in the Caribbean. There are two gift shops and a café housed in reproductions of slave quarters with wattle walls. Admission is €4; it's open daily from 10 to 2.

Père Labat (⊠ *Section Poisson, Grand-Bourg, Marie-Galante* ☎ *0590/ 97–03–79*) produces rum that is considered some of the finest in the Caribbean, and its atelier turns out lovely pottery. Admission is free, and it's open daily from 7 to noon.

WHERE TO EAT

Creole cooking is the result of a fusion of influences: African, European, Indian, and Caribbean. It's colorful, spicy, and made up primarily of local seafood and vegetables (including squashlike christophenes), root vegetables, and plantains, always with a healthy dose of pepper sauce. Favorite appetizers include *accras* (salted codfish fritters), *boudin* (highly seasoned blood sausage), and *crabes farcis* (stuffed land crabs). *Langouste* (lobster), *lambi* (conch), *chatrou* (octopus), and *ouassous* (crayfish) are considered delicacies. *Souchy* (Tahitian-style ceviche), raw fish that is "cooked" when marinated in lime juice or similar marinades, is best at seafront restaurants. *Moules et frites* (mussels in broth served with fries) can be found at cafés in Gosier and Bas du Fort Marina. Also in the marina is Rôtisseur des Isles, with aromatic roasted meats, a salad bar, and classic French desserts. Many of the most contemporary gastronomic restaurants are in Jarry, a commercial area near Pointe-à-Pitre. All restaurants and bars are smoke-free, as decreed by French law.

Diverse culinary options range from pizza and crepes to Indian cuisine. For a quick and inexpensive meal, visit a *boulangerie,* where you can buy luscious French pastries and simple baguette sandwiches. Look for the recommendable chain Délifrance, too. Good news: menu prices seem high but include tax and service (which is split among the entire staff). If service is to your liking, be generous and leave some extra euros, and they will think of Americans as "the good guys." In most restaurants in Guadeloupe (as throughout the Caribbean), lobster is the most expensive item on the menu. It can easily top €40 and often comes as part of a prix-fixe menu; *price ranges for the restaurants listed in this chapter do not include lobster for this reason.*

Looking out over Marie-Galante.

WHAT TO WEAR

Dining is casual at lunch, but beach attire is a no-no except at the more laid-back marina and beach eateries. Dinner is slightly more formal. Long pants, collared shirts, and skirts or dresses are appreciated, although not required. Guadeloupean ladies like to "dress," particularly on weekends, so don't arrive in flip-flops—they'll be in heels.

GRANDE-TERRE

$ ✕**Caraïbes Café**. This sidewalk café straight out of Paris is the "in"
CAFÉ   place for lunch and also a spot for a quick breakfast, a fresh juice cocktail—try *corossel* (a tropical fruit) and mango juices, a cappuccino, *un coupe* (a sundae), or a pastis while you people-watch and listen to French crooners. The *formule* (fixed-price menu) is always the best deal. Service is fast and friendly and can even be in English. ⊠ *Pl. de la Victoire, Pointe-à-Pitre* ☎ *0590/82–92–23* ⊙ *Closed Sun. No dinner.*

$$$–$$$$ ✕**Iguane Café**. Iguanas are indeed the theme here, and you can spy them
CAFÉ   in unexpected places—juxtaposed with antique cherubs and driftwood
Fodor's Choice   mirrors. The new salon seating for cocktails has a residential feel, with
★   basket-weave rattan furniture and hot-pink accent pillows. Unquestionably original cuisine with Asian, Indian, and African influences is chef Sylvain Serouart's trademark. Some "bistronomique" creations are served on slate plates. The menu is always evolving, yet some innovations don't always taste quite as good as they look. A sure thing is the foie gras with vintage rum and a compote of papaya and tamarind. If it's available, move on to the fishermen's casserole filled with tuna, red snapper, scallops, shrimp, and mussels. Desserts are little marvels,

such as the perfect dark-chocolate ganache—even better when it's one of a trio. If you come on a Saturday night, you may get live entertainment, too, for your money (and, yes, Iguane is pricey). A three-course lobster menu is €51, and a lavish menu degustation costs €79. ⊠ *Rte. de La Pointe des Châteaux, ½ mi (¾ km) from airport, St-François* ☎ *0590/88–61–37* ⊕ *www. iguane-cafe.com* ⊘ *Closed Mon. No lunch Tues.–Sat.*

> **COMPETITIONS DES BOEUFS TIRANTS**
>
> The annual ox-pulling competitions on Marie-Galante go on for two weeks in November. Oxen were used for the sugar mills and still power the agriculture. Where else will you see this in your lifetime?

$$$
FRENCH
✗ **La Toubana Restaurant** *(Le Gran Bleu)*. Fresh lobsters, which swim in the canals that beautify the deck, draw many diners. The new chef prepares an impressive foie gras duo—a sauté and a torchon—paired with onion and fig compotes. The French cuisine gets a delicious Caribbean infusion, as in the fillet of *daurade* (fish) with vanilla sauce or the passion fruit tart with meringue. The inside dining room, although open-air, has deep leather chairs, and, on occasion, a piano player and live music by pop-rock vocalists. You can listen whether you just "take a pot" (drink) or have dinner. Lunch patrons dine on the terrace near the infinity pool. With feet dangling in the water and an exotic cocktail in hand, you can watch the sea churn below. ⊠ *La Toubana Hotel & Spa, B. P. 63-Fonds Thezan, Ste-Anne* ☎ *0590/88–25–57.*

$$$
FRENCH
★
✗ **La Vieille Tour Restaurant.** This historic sugar mill is the backdrop for the artistic creations here, which preserve great French cuisine, yet bow to more recent culinary trends and cleverly use local produce. Desserts are dazzling, with lots of towers, sauces, and glacés. A classic like panna cotta with raspberries is the centerpiece in passion fruit soup. Each evening there is a menu du jour, a three-course dinner with two choices for each, moderately priced at €50. An appetizer and a main or a main course and a dessert can be had for €40. On the à la carte menu, any starter is €15; any main is €28, be it lobster, duck confit, or rack of lamb. The menu changes daily now and you may be treated to sea scallops flamed in vintage rum and topped with blood-orange butter. That is gastronomic elegance. ⊠ *Auberge de la Vieille Tour, Rte. 1 Montauban 97, Gosier* ☎ *0590/84–23–23* ⚘ *Reservations essential* ⊘ *Closed Wed. and Sun. in low season (but this can vary). No lunch.*

$$–$$$
INDIAN
★
✗ **Les Portes des Indes.** Dining here is truly a departure: the open-air pergola, the blue gates, the pungent aromas, and the bust of Ganesha. Within the paisley-covered menu you can find authentic creole dishes alongside such innovations as boneless chicken with crème fraîche, almonds, and raisins. Children may fill up on the addictive Indian cheese bread and be too stuffed for *kulfi,* Indian ice cream topped with ginger confit. The welcome here is always warm and the service dignified. Consistently good, its perennial popularity means that on weekends you really should make reservations. ⊠ *Desvarieux, St-François* ☎ *0590/21–30–87* ⊘ *Closed mid-Sept.–mid-Oct. and Mon. No lunch Tues.–Sat. No dinner Sun.*

13

CLOSE UP

More than Basic Creole Cooking

The young chefs coming out of the Lycee d'Hotellerie et du Tourisme de Guadeloupe are taught how to refine local dishes and to value regional products such as indigenous spices, coffee, chocolate, and rum. Preparing typical holiday feasts and (East) Indian buffets (the island has a large Indian population) are all part of the curriculum. Hygiene and food security are stressed. Many graduates go to France to work under veteran chefs and then return to their island. Seasoned French chefs are in place, too, such as Frederic Marcelli, a French-Italian chef with experience in multistarred French and Belgian restaurants. As executive chef at Creole Beach Hotel & Spa, he says, "I hope to bring new techniques and organization, while keeping the creole cooking style and elevating it to a new level."

Jean Michel Moco, a Guadeloupe chef and graduate of the Lycee, started working in 1989, at age 17. Part of a kitchen team working at reviving forgotten, old-time recipes and

enhancing them with New World techniques and presentations, he says, "I believe that the new creole movement will spread throughout the Antilles." Examples of some of the new recipes are smoked local fish with avocado mousse, mango tatin with cardamom, and luscious chutneys.

Anchoring the movement are "the ladies," the many female chefs who continue to serve the flavorful cuisine that is their heritage. If while exploring the island you see a restaurant named Chez (usually a woman's name), chances are it serves creole food. Another clue is if it says "Creole Specialties and Grillades." In Gosier, at Poucet, on Route de la Riviera, the highway to St-François, is an unexpected culinary experience. Riviera Boucherie Restaurant is a butcher shop with a front display case of piglets with ears and eyes; tripe; splayed, heads-on turkeys; and even horsemeat. Lunch and dinner is served here, with grilled steak an educated choice, and on Saturday, curried goat.

$$–$$$
SEAFOOD

✕ **Zawag.** This secret hideaway has a dramatic view of the churning sea below and the sounds of crashing waves against the coral rock upon which it sits. Its interior architecture is all hardwood with matching furniture and white linen napkins. Primarily a grill, the simplicity is reflected in the food offerings. Kids are particularly fascinated when the lobster net is dipped into the tank and the thrashing begins. The fish of the night is fresh from the waters below, often accompanied by creole or tropical-fruit sauces. Creole dishes and sides are being gently contemporized by the French chef and offered as nightly specials. ⊠ *La Creole Beach Hotel & Spa, Pointe de la Verdure, Gosier* ☎ *0590/90–46–66* ⚐ *Reservations essential* ⊙ *Closed Sun., depending on season.*

BASSE-TERRE

$$–$$$
FRENCH
★

✕ **Le Rocher de Malendure.** Guests first climb the worn yellow stairs for the panoramic sea views, but return again and again for the food. If you arrive before noon, when the divers pull in, you might snag one of the primo tables in a gazebo that literally hangs over the Caribbean.

STILL WATERS

Guadeloupe has some of the best-tasting mountain water in the Caribbean isles, but you'll rarely see anyone drinking it out of the tap (*robinet*). Some say that is because the city pipes are rusty, others that they can taste the chlorine. At restaurants, the server will usually ask if you want a bottle of water, and if so, what kind: *plat?* (pronounced plah, meaning "still"). Say "*Oui, Capes*" to request the main island brand.

You'll pay €3 to €4 for a big bottle (1½ liter), half the price of Evian. In your hotel minibar, a small bottle may cost that much. Stop at a gas station, minimart, or supermarche and buy the big ones for anywhere from €0.70 to €1.50. Or join the new movement to help save the environment by not using plastic bottles, and at restaurants ask for *une carafe d'eau du robinet*. Is it safe? Guadeloupe sells water to all the big ships.

Begin with a perfectly executed mojito. With fish just off the boat, don't hesitate to try the sushi *antillaise* or grilled crayfish and lobster from the pool. ⊠ *Bord de Mer, Malendure de Pigeon, Bouillante* ☎ *0590/98–70–84* ⊗ *Closed Wed. and Sept.–early Oct.*

ILES DES SAINTES

$-$$ ✕**Couleurs du Monde.** New arrivals from the ferries and those waiting
CAFÉ to depart are immediately attracted to this second-floor, waterfront café–cum–art gallery. Under the green canopy, it's shades of Greenwich Village with books and newspapers, teas and coffees, wine, and icy rum cocktails. Contemporary art, primarily from Didier Spindler, lines the walls, there for the buying, and some fab glassware adorns the table. International tapas are the main food source and include sushi and smoked-fish plates, smoked duck salad, and so on, but there is a full menu in place. Seashells are affixed to the menus to keep them from blowin' in the sea breeze. The catch of the day with an exotic sauce is a wise choice. Although the restaurant stays open, lunch service is from noon to 3 pm. After sunset there are aperitifs, and although reservations are requested for dinner, the friendly, accommodating staff will take walk-ins. Finish off with the house-made Punch du Monde. ⊠ *Main dock, Terre-de-Haut* ☎ *0590/92–70–98* ⊗ *Closed Tues., Wed., and Sept.–mid-Oct.*

$$-$$$ ✕**L'Auberge les Petits Saints aux Anarcadiers Restaurant.** This hotel–res-
ECLECTIC taurant showcases many cuisines: French, Mediterranean, and creole. Chef Vincent Malbec and the new owners, Mireille and Pierre, insist on top-grade prime rib and superior quality duck for the confit with pineapple sauce. The fresh grilled lobster here is famous and is priced per gram. Vincent is remarkably inventive with lambi and the local vegetables. Contemporary dinnerware brought from France complements the updated menu and presentation. And as is fashionable in France, you can order a sampling of appetizers that includes the island's smoked fish and tartares. Fresh fish is always a good choice especially with curry sauce. For the finale, there is a generous selection of house-made desserts, like the profiteroles stuffed with coconut and vanilla gelato, made

in the village. Service is on the verandah, where the night sounds of the tropics vie with jazz and sexy French *musique.* A separate children's menu is offered as well. ✉ *L'Auberge les Petits Saints aux Anarcadiers, La Savane, Terre-de-Haut* ☎ *0590/99–50–99* ⚓ *Reservations essential* ⊙ *Closed Mon. No lunch.*

$$$ ✕ **ti Kaz.** This small, convivial waterfront restaurant has a lot to rec

CONTEMPORARY ommend—it's artsy, with contemporary originals, hanging plants, hip music, and a talented chef-owner, Philippe Dade Brochettes are the popular items, due to their dramatic presentation. Metal skewers of beef, lamb, and shrimp or ouassous are hooked to what looks like a hangmen's scaffold, and are accompanied by two sauces—chien and passion fruit—plus authentic *pomme frites. Le choucroute de la mer* has fish, scallops, and mussels in a bath of white wine. The pouffed marvel—a mango soufflé with raspberry coulis—must be ordered in advance. ✉ *Rue Benoit Cassin, Terre-de-Haut* ☎ *0590/99–57–63* ⊙ *No dinner Tues.; closed Wed.*

MARIE-GALANTE

It's not gastronomic, but L'Ornata has the bay-front location if you're catching the ferry and don't want to chance missing it. Grab a cold one or a rich, tropical sundae. It serves three squares a day (cheap) and will have breakfast when you disembark.

$$$ ✕ **Chez Henri.** This hip place on the water, flanked by the town pier, is

CARIBBEAN named for its passionate chef–owner, Henri Vergerolle. An island character, he spent much of his life in France and returned to create this restaurant–cum–cultural center. Begin with a rum and fresh-squeezed juice. Smoked fish can be a component of a salad or an appetizer; interestingly, the creole omelet is an app, too. It's quite an original, with breadfruit and sweet potatoes. Another innovation is the fish of the day with a Caribe sauce. Kick back and listen to African blues (sometimes live) and view the latest art or sculpture exhibits. ✉ *8 rue des Caraïbes, St. Louis, Marie Galante* ☎ *0590/97–04–57* ⊕ *www.chezhenri.net* ⊙ *Closed Mon. No lunch Tues.–Thurs. during low season (Sept.–early Oct.).*

$$ ✕ **Le Touloulou.** On the curve of Plage de Petite-Anse, this ultracasual eat-

SEAFOOD ery has tables in the sand. *Merci* to Hurricane Dean, a major renovation has it born again. Chef José Viator serves the freshest seafood; his standout dish just might be fricassee of conch or octopus with breadfruit. Set menus start at €20-something and often include a shrimp-and-fish curry duo. La Pergola's, the circular bar, has the best in rum cocktails to sip while contemplating the sun's descent. At night the anteroom is a disco, with theme nights on Friday and Saturday. ✉ *Plage de Petite-Anse, Capesterre* ☎ *0590/97–32–63* ⊕ *www.letouloulou.com* ⊙ *Closed Mon. and mid-Sept.–mid-Oct. No dinner Sun.*

$$$ ✕ **Sun7Beach.** Sit with your feet in the sand and an icy Desperados Red

SEAFOOD (beer) in your hand and watch the sunsets turn the sky pink. Drinks and their prices are *veddy* potable here. Segue into dinner at this whimsical, colorful beach bar–restaurant that also has two simple bungalows (€40). By day or night there are creative burgers and inventive pizzas. Chef Gilbert, a Marie-Galantais, has fresh lobsters for €28 and

13

three-course prix fixes from €20 to €25. And the bilingual French manageress, Claire, will even let you take a kayak out. ⊠ *Rte. du Capesterre, Grand-Bourg* ☎ *0590/97-87-58.*

LA DÉSIRADE

$-$$ ✕ **Oualiri Breeze Restaurant.** With tables smack in the sand, on the cov-
ECLECTIC ered terrace, and under a conical tent, this beachfront eatery lays out a
☾ bountiful creole buffet on Friday nights and for Sunday brunch. Both are accompanied by live entertainment. You can always grab a continental breakfast, lunch, or dinner, and customize your own €15.50 prix fixe. Seafood is the obvious specialty, particularly creole fricassees of lambi and chatrou. Sidle up to the fieldstone bar for a perfect planter's punch, and between courses, jump into the sea. Children have their own menus and love that this is also a *glacier* (ice-cream shop) with a litany of flavors; drizzle your scoops with cajou syrup. P.S.: You can check your email here. Also, the affable, English-speaking owner, Theodore Compper, will pick you up at the dock or airport. ⊠ *Plage Beau Sejour, Beau Sejour, Le Désirade* ☎ *0590/20-20-08 or 0690/71-24-76* ⊕ *www. rendezvouskarukera.com.*

WHERE TO STAY

Most of the island's resort hotels are on Grande-Terre: Gosier, St-François, and Bas-du-Fort are generally considered major resort areas, as is Ste-Anne. With each passing year, the hotels here improve. The Swedish-owned Langley Hotel Fort Royal has breathed new life into the north of Basse-Terre, the closest area of that island to Pointe-à-Pitre and Grande-Terre.

Often, hotel rates include a generous buffet breakfast; ask whether this is included in your rate quote. Many smaller properties do not accept American Express. As dictated by French law, all public spaces in hotels are no-smoking, but hotel rooms are considered private, and properties can chose to offer smoking rooms.

The following reviews have been condensed for this book. Please go to Fodors.com for full reviews of each property.

GRANDE-TERRE

$$$ 🏨 **Auberge de la Vieille Tour.** An island classic fashioned around a historic
HOTEL sugar mill, this hotel consistently renews itself. **ros:** most rooms have
Fodor'sChoice great views; breakfast (included) is a highlight; the gourmet restaurant
★ is one of the island's best. **Cons:** expensive; exteriors of some sections are unattractive 1960s-style; it is a hill climb back from breakfast, the pool, and the beach. ⊠ *Rte. de Montauban, Gosier* ☎ *0590/84-23-23* ⊕ *www.mgallery.com* ⇝ *70 rooms, 32 deluxe rooms, 1 suite* ⚭ *In-room: safe, Wi-Fi. In-hotel: restaurants, room service, tennis courts, bars, pool, beach, business center, parking* ⍟ *Full breakfast.*

La Toubana Hotel & Spa.

$$–$$$ 🏨 **Club Med La Caravelle.** Facing one of the island's best white-sand
RESORT   beaches, La Caravelle, one of the oldest resorts in the Caribbean, is
☙   noted for its water sports. **Pros:** Internet café; exceptional boutique;
★   good service from the international G.O.s. **Cons:** Club Med experi-
          ence is not to everyone's taste; older standard rooms are small; kid-
          friendly atmosphere not for everyone. ⊠ *Quartier Caravelle, Ste-Anne*
          ☎ *0590/85–49–50 or 800/258–2633* ⊕ *www.clubmed.us* ⊅ *299 rooms,*
          45 suites ⚒ *In-room: safe, Wi-Fi. In-hotel: restaurants, tennis courts,*
          bars, children's programs, pool, beach, business center, water sports,
          parking ⟦⊙⟧ *All-inclusive.*

$ 🏨 **Eden Palm.** Set away from the tourist zones, this resort is brimming
RESORT   with sophisticated French style. **ros:** known for its entertainment; staff
          is efficient and genuinely caring; lovely Balinese poolside beds. **Cons:**
          you can't see the beach; beds take up a lot of the guest-room space.
          ⊠ *Lieu dit Le Helleux, Ste-Anne* ☎ *0590/88–48–48* ⊕ *www.edenpalm.*
          com ⊅ *57 rooms, 21 suites* ⚒ *In-room: safe. In-hotel: restaurant, room*
          service, tennis court, bar, pool, gym, business center, parking, some pets
          allowed ⟦⊙⟧ *Breakfast.*

¢–$ 🏨 **Hotel Amaudo.** This *hotel de charme* is a small *madam-et-monsieur*
HOTEL   operation, the mom 'n' pop being the sophisticated French managers.
          ros: a moderate price tag for unobstructed sea views; safe (mechanized
          security gate). **Cons:** you need a car, as it is not in the tourist zone of
          St-François; no bar, restaurant or activities; could be too quiet and
          peaceful. ⊠ *Anse à la Barque, St-François* ☎ *0590/88–87–00* ⊕ *www.*
          amaudo.fr ⊅ *10 rooms* ⚒ *In-room: safe, Wi-Fi. In-hotel: pool, laundry*
          facilities, beach, business center, parking ⟦⊙⟧ *Breakfast.*

$$–$$$ ⬛ **La Cocoteraie.** This boutique hotel, with its lobby of basket-weave rat-
HOTEL tan furnishings, decorative masks, and walls of burnt orange is a study
in refinement. **Pros:** by a calm lagoon; sophisticated clientele; great,
international crowd at the Indigo Bar. **Cons:** generic, white-plastic furniture on terraces; aqua tiles segue abruptly to red tiles. ⊠ *Av. de l'Europe,
St-François* ☎ *0590/88–79–81* ⊕ *www.lacocoteraie.com* ↩ *50 suites*
⛅ *In-room: safe. In-hotel: restaurant, room service, tennis courts, bar,
pool, gym, beach, business center, parking* ⊘ *Closed Aug. 24–Oct. 21*
†⊙† *Breakfast.*

$ ⬛ **La Créole Beach Hotel.** This 10-acre complex has a contemporary, col-
RESORT orful lobby, cosmopolitan bar, and the oversize rooms and ocean-view
★ suites at Les Palms resemble those on a teak-appointed yacht. **Pros:**
excellent management and long-term staff; exceptionally good buffets
(also upgraded by the French chef); lovely tropical gardens. **Cons:** guest
rooms vary in quality; some rooms quite a hike from lobby; beach is
nice but small. ⊠ *Pointe de la Verdure, Box 61, Gosier* ☎ *0590/90–46–
46* 🖷 *0590/90–46–66* ⊕ *www.deshotelsetdesiles.com* ↩ *353 rooms, 15
junior suites, 6 suites, 13 apartments* ⛅ *In-room: safe, kitchen (some),
Wi-Fi (some). In-hotel: restaurants, bar, pool, beach, business center,
water sports, parking* †⊙† *No meals.*

$$ ⬛ **La Toubana Hôtel & Spa.** Few hotels on Guadeloupe command such
RESORT a panoramic view of the sea—spanning four islands, no less. **Pros:** a
Fodor'sChoice special place with sophisticated style; glass-enclosed cocktail lounge–
★ library has remarkable views; restaurant continues to evolve and to
earn praise; meal plans are available. **Cons:** the little beach is down the
hill by a paved path that's very steep; bedrooms are small by Ameri-
can standards. ⬧ *B.P. 63-Fonds Thezan, Ste-Anne* ☎ *0590/88–25–57*
⊕ *www.toubana.com* ↩ *32 bungalows, 1 suite* ⛅ *In-room: kitchen.
In-hotel: restaurants, tennis court, pool, spa, business center, parking*
†⊙† *Breakfast.*

BASSE-TERRE

$ ⬛ **Caraib Bay Hotel.** This complex of colorful duplex bungalows may not
RENTAL initially impress, but its admirable customer-satisfaction award backed
☾ up by the buzz on the street makes you want to book in. **Pros:** homey
feel with multilingual library; moderate prices; innovative bar and fla-
vorful creole specialties by night. **Cons:** good, long beach, but it's down
and across the highway; not luxe. ⊠ *Allée du Cour, Ziotte, Deshaies*
☎ *0590/28–41–71* ⊕ *www.caraib-bay-hotel.com* ↩ *56 rooms, 3 villas*
⛅ *In-room: no phone, kitchen, no TV. In-hotel: restaurant, room ser-
vice, bar, pool, business center, parking* †⊙† *Breakfast.*

¢ ⬛ **Langley Hotel Fort Royal.** The island's new Swedish connection is a
RESORT major redo of a 1970s seafront high-rise with the addition of conical
☾ bungalows (14 beachfront). **Pros:** nearly all is nearly new; nonguests can
sample the fun by paying €10 for a beach chaise or enjoying the sail and
surf club; free Internet. **Cons:** not all hotel rooms have a sea view; beach
has eroded and needs sand; large and somewhat impersonal. ⊠ *Petit Bas
Vent, Deshaies* ☎ *0590/68–76–70* ⊕ *www.fortroyal.eu* ↩ *142 rooms, 7
suites, 82 bungalows* ⛅ *In-room: safe, Internet, Wi-Fi. In-hotel: restau-*

Le Jardin de Malanga.

rant, tennis courts, bars, children's programs, pool, laundry facilities, beach, business center, water sports, parking ⫶◎⫶ *Breakfast.*

$
HOTEL
Fodor's Choice
★

⫶▦⫶ **Le Jardin de Malanga.** At this former coffee plantation, trees laden with fruit are like the temptations of the Garden of Eden. **Pros:** a romantic hideaway with history and character; superior cuisine (half-board is recommendable); signage and Web site directions greatly improved. **Cons:** still not easy to find and best navigated by day; no TV; the nearest beach is 20 minutes away by car. ⊠ *Hermitage, Trois-Rivières* ☎ *0590/92–67–57* ⊕ *www.deshotelsetdesiles.com* ⇥ *9 rooms, 1 suite* ⚲ *In-room: no TV, Wi-Fi (some). In-hotel: restaurant, room service, pool, business center, parking* ⫶◎⫶ *Breakfast.*

$$
RENTAL

⫶▦⫶ **Tainos Cottages.** Now *this* is a story: a globe-trotting Frenchman designed seven teakwood cottages resembling Guadeloupean *cases* from the 1920s, had them constructed in Indonesia, and imported the cottages to a site overlooking Plage de Grande-Anse. **Pros:** summer rates drop by half; get a discount by booking online; great long beach with no other commercial development. **Cons:** insects, particularly mosquitoes, are a drawback (but they use American mosquito traps that kill them outside the room); most rooms are open-air. ⊠ *Plage de Grande-Anse, Deshaies* ☎ *0590/28–44–42* 🖷 *0590/21–30–20* ⊕ *www.tainoscottages. com* ⇥ *7 bungalows* ⚲ *In-room: no a/c, no phone, safe, no TV. In-hotel: restaurant, bar, pool, beach, business center, parking* ⫶◎⫶ *Breakfast.*

ILES DES SAINTES

¢ ⌐⌐ **L'Auberge les Petits Saints aux Anarcadiers.** Fashionably eccentric, fun cou-
B&B/INN ples, hip families, and serious Caribbeanophiles gravitate to this charis-
★ matic inn. **Pros:** cool vibe, reminiscent of the island guesthouses of the
1970s; village just down the hill; free Wi-Fi **Cons:** do not expect luxury,
though improvements continue. ⊠ *La Savane, Terre-de-Haut* ☎ *0590/99–*
50–99 ⊕ *www.petitssaints.com* ☞ *4 bungalows, 4 suites, 2 rooms* ♿ *In-*
room: Wi-Fi (some). In-hotel: restaurant, bar, pool ⦵ *Breakfast.*

¢ ⌐⌐ **Lô Bleu Hôtel.** The French owners—he a banker, she a medical doctor—
HOTEL came for a cocktail at the waterfront restaurant and ended up buying
the place (and painting it sunset orange with marine-blue trim). **Pros:**
smack on the bay; large front rooms with sea view and balconies; hip
music; family-friendly with baby monitors and some bunk beds. **Cons:** no
beautiful grounds; no resort amenities. ⊠ *Fond de Curé, Terre-de-Haut*
☎ *0590/92–40–00 or 0690/63–80–36* ⊕ *www.lobleuhotel.com* ☞ *10*
rooms ♿ *In-hotel: restaurant, bar, beach, business center* ⦵ *Breakfast.*

¢ ⌐⌐ **Paradis Saintois.** You'll feel like the king of the hill as you rock your-
RENTAL self to sleep in your hammock while gazing down on the Caribbean
below. **Pros:** good fun quotient (even petanque); super managers. **Cons:**
no phones or TVs in rooms; a hike up the hill from town (15 minutes).
⊠ *211 Rte. des Pres Cassin, B. P. I., Terre-de-Haut* ☎ *0590/99–56–16*
🖶 *0590/99–56–11* ⊕ *www.ParadisSaintois.com* ☞ *5 apartments, 3*
studios, 1 room ♿ *In-room: no a/c (some), no phone, kitchen, no TV*
(some). In-hotel: pool, laundry service, bicycles, some pets allowed
☞ *3-night min.* ⦵ *No meals.*

MARIE-GALANTE

Accommodations here run the gamut from inexpensive, locally owned
beachfront bungalows to complexes with international owners.

¢ ⌐⌐ **Kawann Beach Hotel.** Marie Galante's only full-service hotel (formerly
HOTEL La Cohoba) has reopened with a battery of sustainable tourism and
it's attracting ecoconscious travelers. **Pros:** new professional French
manager; ecoshop Atelier Nature; the pool with center island. **Cons:**
accommodations still need new soft furnishings and décor, which should
come shortly; cannot see beach from the rooms or pool. ⊠ *Folle Anse*
near St. Louis ☎ *0590/97–50–50* ☞ *100 suites* ♿ *In-room: safe (some),*
kitchen. In-hotel: business center, parking ⦵ *Breakfast.*

OTHER LODGING CHOICES

MARIE-GALANTE

Le Touloulou (⊠ *Plage de Petite-Anse, Capesterre* ☎ *0590/97–32–63*
⊕ *www.letouloulou.com*) has four simple stucco bungalows with kitchenettes. You can roll out of your terrace hammock onto the beach.
The good creole seafood restaurant (⇨ *Where to Eat, Marie-Galante*
above) is a happening place, with atmospheric music from the beach
bar vying with the slapping of the waves. The disco adjacent to the
restaurant warms up to hot at night. **Le Village de Canada** (⊠ *Section*
Canada ☎ *0690/50–55–50* ⊕ *www.villagedecanada.com*) has studios,

bungalows, and apartments, some with sea views; there's a pool, and many guests are Canadian. **Residence Passiflora** (⊠ *Le Haute des Basses-Grand-Bourg* ☎ *0590/97–50–48* ⊕ *www.residence-passiflora.com*) is composed of two deluxe villas perched on a hillside overlooking the sea. The decor is chic French, the ambience fosters romance, and it's close to town. Meals can now be taken if desired. **Village de Menard** (⊠ *Section Canada* ☎ *0590/97–09–45* ⊕ *www.villagedemenard.com*) consists of squeaky-clean, colorful but not stylin' bungalows and studios with a pool in a pastoral setting. This is "out there," yet it is close to two great beaches and has a restaurant.

LA DÉSIRADE

Even more remote than Marie-Galante, tiny La Désirade has a few simple guesthouses. **Amour D'Oliver** (☎ *0590/81–40–52 or 0690/69–66–45*) is small and immaculate, but you'll likely want a car if you stay here. There's no beach, but there's a pool and a barbecue for grilling. **Club Caravelle** (☎ *0590/20–04–00* ⊕ *www.desirade-islands.com*) is inland, but some of the apartments have two floors and sea views. The best views are from the terrace restaurant. **Oualiri Beach Hotel** (☎ *0590/20–20–08 or 0690/71–24–76* ☎ *0590/85–51–51* ⊕ *www.im-caraibes.com/oualiri*), a feet-in-the-sand bed-and-breakfast, has sling-back chairs on the beach. Amenities such as air-conditioning, cable TV, phones, and in-room Wi-Fi have updated this simple six-room inn. A pioneer from the 1930s, the hotel retains some of its original French windows and doors, patterned tile floors, and fieldstone bar. The beachfront creole restaurant is one of the island's best and the only one with live entertainment. Oualiri's owner, Theodore, a tourism veteran in Guadeloupe for decades, also has villas and apartments in St-François for short-term rental.

VILLAS

French Caribbean International (☎ *800/322–22–23, 805/967–9850 in U.S.* ⊕ *www.frenchcaribbean.com*) handles hotel arrangements and private villa rentals, from charming cottages in Basse-Terre ($130 to $350 a night) to deluxe sea-view villas in Grande-Terre ($2,600 to $7,000 per week), all with pools. With decades of experience in the French Caribbean, including Les Saites and Marie-Galante, the company has a reputation for honesty and professionalism.

The progressive **Nouvelles Antilles** (☎ *0590/85–00–00* ⊕ *www.nouvellesantilles.com*), based in St-François, acts as an agent for some 30 villas around the islands, mostly luxurious. In addition, the first online travel agency dedicated to the French West Indies can book your villa or hotel accommodations, flight, rental car, and sports activities, and create a well-priced package. It deals with all the Guadeloupe isles, Martinique, St. Barth, and St. Martin, too, and can customize a multi-destination package for groups up to 15.

BASSE-TERRE

$$
RENTAL

Aquarelle's Villas. In a securely gated community on Basse-Terre's north coast, these 15 homes have private pools on their sundecks, and five have direct sea views. **Pros:** villas are spacious; the beach has a raw, dramatic beauty. **Cons:** beach has no chaise longues; it is a fair walk to the swimmable end. ⊠ *1 Domaine de Nogent, Ste-Rose* ☎ *0590/68–65–23* 🖷 *0590/68–38–23* ⊕ *www.aquarelles-villas.com* ➷ *15 2- to 5-bedroom homes* ⚭ *In-room: no a/c (some), safe. In-hotel: business center, pool, laundry facilities, some pets allowed* ⊙ *Closed Sept. 18–Oct. 1* ⁙❙*No meals.*

¢　🎦 **Le Neem.** These three attractive gites, or suites, have spicy names—
RENTAL　Vanille, Safron, and Canela (cinnamon), and that is the order of preference. **Pros:** fine beach just across the street; gites are newly built (2009); owning couple are caring, and wife, Ancette, speaks *Anglais.* **Cons:** no space between suites; no views; no hotel amenities. ⊠ *Rte. de la Pointe des Chateaux, St-François* ⊕ *www.leneem.fr* ➷ *3 suites* ⁙❙*Breakfast.*

ILES DES SAINTES

¢　🎦 **Residence Anse Caraibe.** This large residence, perched on a hill five
RENTAL　minutes from town, houses six apartments, from a studio to a three-bedroom flat. **Pros:** English-speaking French manager (Catherine Voglimacci), who can even arrange transportation on the mainland; two apartments open onto spacious, private terraces that look to the bay; all can be rented by the night (three-night minimum in high season, two in low season) or week(s). **Cons:** no phones; steep hill; no cushy, creature comforts. ⊠ *Emmanuel Laurent St., Terre de Haut* ⊕ *www. grandbaie.com* ➷ *4 studio apartments, 1 2-bedroom apartment, 1 3-bedroom apartment* ⚭ *In-room: no phone. In-hotel: laundry facilities* ⁙❙*No meals.*

$$　🎦 **Villa Dao.** Ideally located smack on the bay and a five-minute walk
RENTAL　from the center of the town, this premium four-bedroom house has a high-tech kitchen, and each of the master bedrooms (two with water views) are artfully decorated with reds and greens and fanciful objets d'art. **Pros:** living room can be totally opened to the sea or secured by a push-button wall; a luxurious, hip guest cottage is ideal for teenagers or children and their nannies. **Cons:** manager does not speak English but translates and answers emails in English; doesn't have the full services and amenities of a boutique hotel; no telephones (but Wi-Fi). ⊠ *88–90 rue B Cassin, Terre de Haut* ⊕ *www.villasantilles.com* ➷ *4 bedrooms, 4 baths* ⚭ *In-room: no phone, safe, Wi-Fi. In-hotel: pool, laundry facilities, beach, business center* ⁙❙*No meals.*

NIGHTLIFE

Guadeloupeans maintain that the beguine began here, and, for sure, the beguine and mazurkas were heavily influenced by the European quadrille and orchestrated melodies. Their merging together is the origin of West Indian music, and it gave birth to zouk (music with an African-influenced Caribbean rhythm) at the beginning of the 1980s. Still the rage here, it has spread not only to France but to other European countries. Many resorts have dinner dancing or offer regularly scheduled entertainment by steel bands and folkloric groups.

The island's performing arts scene is centered on the **Centre des Arts** (⊠ *Pl. des Martyrs de la Liberté, Pointe-à-Pitre, Grande-Terre* ☎ *0590/82–79–78*), where each season is more exciting than the last. Here you'll find exceptional jazz and blues concerts, musical comedies, and even art exhibitions. Hip-hop artists, break-dancers, and classical musicians have all performed here. Prices are democratic. Ask for the special deals.

BARS AND NIGHTCLUBS

Club Med (⊠ *Quartier Caravelle, Ste-Anne, Grande-Terre* ☎ *0590/85–49–50*) sells night passes (6 pm–2 am) that include all cocktails, dinner with wine, and a show in the theater, followed by admission to the disco. Passes cost €65; go on Friday (€75) for the gala dinner and the most creative show. It's a super option for single women, who will feel comfortable and safe at the disco, where there are plenty of fun staffers (G.O.s) willing to be dance partners.

Something is always happening at the **Creole Beach Hotel** (⊠ *Pointe de la Verdure, Gosier, Grande-Terre* ☎ *0590/90–46–46*). The entertainment is often bands playing beguine and zouk, or a piano man, all of which are very danceable. The group of native dancers and the tom-tom drummers are amazing.

★ Nightly entertainment (in high season) at **Auberge de la Vieille Tour** (⊠ *Rte. de Montauban, Gosier, Grande-Terre* ☎ *0590/84–23–23*) ranges from the talented piano man to jazz combos (Friday and Saturday only in low season). The atmospheric piano bar with its planter's chairs and whirring fan blades is as memorable as Rick's Café in *Casablanca*. Accras and munchies generally arrive with your cocktails. New is the extensive menu of rums that gives their history and even offers flights.

The jazzed up **Eden Palm Theater** (⊠ *Eden Palm Hotel, Lieu-dit le Helleux, Ste-Anne, Grande-Terre* ☎ *0590/88–48–48*) presents a Cuban-influenced Caribbean musical review on Saturday nights. The spectacle—like nothing else on the island—has plumage, imaginative costumes, a super sound system, and a bevy of dancers. The cost is €70 for dinner and show and is a good value for the money. The multicourse dinner is refined, Franco-Caribbean cuisine, the service both caring and professional. The fast-moving, grand spectacle is celebratory. Holidays, like New Year's Eve, are major happenings here.

Hemingway Restaurant & Lounge (⊠ *Domaine Pointe Batterie, Deshaies* ☎ *0590/28–57–17*) is the buzzword that is becoming synonymous with live music, dancing, and nightlife. It is another indicator that northern Basse-Terre is on a roll. A typical lineup is as follows: Friday night, "jazz fever"; Saturday, a tropical show with emcee and orchestra; Sunday, a buffet lunch and stellar live music with dancing on the dock overlooking the bay. Bring a swimsuit and snorkel.

Hot spot **Zoo Rock Café** (⊠ *La Marina Gosier, Gosier* ☎ *0590/90–77–77* ⊕ *www.zoorockcafe.com*) is a bar, a *rhumerie* (rum distillery), a restaurant, and a café where live music concerts happen. Theme nights are a house party, be it Havana night or Halloween; the crowd is young and mostly French from the Metropole.

CASINOS

Both of the island's casinos are on Grande-Terre and have American-style roulette, blackjack, and stud poker. The legal age for gambling is 18, and French law dictates that everyone show a passport, or for locals, a driver's license. Jacket and tie aren't required, but "proper attire" means no shorts, T-shirts, jeans, flip-flops, or sneakers.

Casino de Gosier (✉ *Gosier, Grande-Terre* ☎ *0590/84–79–69*) has a bar; a well-priced buffet restaurant is open for lunch and dinner (closed Sunday and Monday). The higher-stakes gambling is behind a closed door—you'll have to change €100 into chips to be part of that action. However, the blackjack limit is €5 and roulette just €2. It's open daily from 9 pm; slot machines open at 10 am and shut down at 3 am. It is showing signs of age, but locals love it and jam the parking lot on weekends. The bar can really crank up on Saturday nights or holidays, with sexy island girls in brief silver lamé costumes dispensing free champagne. Local bands can add to the energy. **Casino de St-François** (✉ *In front of golf course near Centre Commercial, St-François, Grande-Terre* ☎ *0590/88–41–31*), although petite, has a contemporary élan that makes you want to dress up and come on out. There's a dramatic water installation, leather furniture, and a small, appealing restaurant, Le Joker (à la carte, or €25 prix fixe with wine), with a piano bar and a stage for performers, which also doubles as a disco on Friday and Saturday. The lighting, installed by Martinique's MPA architectural firm, can project one or multiple colors, depending on the desired mood. It is truly a handsome showplace, and there are some 85 slots, as well as American roulette and gaming tables (stud poker, blackjack, etc.), English-speaking management (sometimes), and a parking lot. A calendar of events includes such celebrations as Oktoberfest and dance lessons.

DISCOS

Night owls should note that carousing here isn't cheap. On the weekend and when there's live music, most discos charge a cover of at least €10, which might go up to as much as €20. Your cover usually includes a drink, and other drinks cost about €12 each.

Le Cheyenne (✉ *Rte. de Montauban, Gosier, Grande-Terre* ☎ *0590/90–01–01* ⊕ *www.lecheyenne.com*) is a dramatic, Native American–theme disco that continues to draw the crowds. Look for the sculpture of a Cheyenne chief over the grand entrance. It's open every night and on weekends; there's a cover charge when the basement disco is open. With two separate sections, one caters to the young crowd—heavy on the techno—and the other is for the ageless. It has an attractive restaurant named Bora Bora that was originally designed for Pacific Rim cuisine. It has gone over to creole, with an emphasis on seafood, and serves from 8 pm until midnight, until 2 am on *le weekend*. New is the Ed Hardy by Christian Audigier Boutique, open every night. Models—gals and guys—walk the runway wearing sexy swimwear and beach togs for the stellar fashion shows. The crowds are loving it!

SHOPPING

The island has a lot of desirable French products, from designer fashions for women and men and sensual lingerie to French china and liqueurs. As for local handicrafts, you can find attractive wood carvings, madras table linens, island dolls dressed in madras, woven straw baskets and hats, and *salakos*—fishermen's hats made of split bamboo, some covered in madras—which make great wall decorations. Of course, the favorite Guadeloupean souvenir is rum. Look for *rhum vieux*, the top of the line. For foodies, the market ladies sell aromatic fresh spices, crisscrossed with cinnamon sticks, in little baskets lined with madras.

AREAS AND MALLS

Grande-Terre's largest shopping mall, **Destrelland**, has more than 70 stores and is just minutes from the airport, which is a shopping destination in its own right. In **Pointe-à-Pitre** you can enjoy browsing in the street stalls around the harbor quay and at the two markets (the best is the Marché de Frébault). The town's main shopping streets are rue Schoelcher, rue de Nozières, and the lively rue Frébault. At the St-John Perse Cruise Terminal there's an attractive mall with about two dozen shops. **Bas-du-Fort**'s two shopping areas are the Cora Shopping Center and the marina, where there are 20 or so shops and quite a few restaurants. In **St-François** there are more than a dozen shops surrounding the marina, some selling French lingerie, swimsuits, and fashions. A supermarket has particularly good prices on French wines and cheeses, and if you pick up a fresh baguette, you'll have a picnic. (Then you can go get lost at a secluded beach.)

SPECIALTY STORES

ART
Pascal Foy (✉ *Rte. à Pompierres, Terre-de-Haut, Iles des Saintes* ☎ *0590/ 99–52–29*) produces stunning homages to traditional Creole architecture: paintings of houses that incorporate collage make marvelous wall hangings. As his fame has grown, his media attention has expanded, so prices have risen. You are more likely to find his mother manning the shop nowadays.

CLOTHING
Côté Plage (✉ *Pl. du Marché, Pointe-à-Pitre, Grande-Terre* ☎ *No phone*) sells bikinis, sundresses, and straw beach totes in addition to T-shirts and other ideal island necessities. There's also a line of simple jewelry—turtles, geckos, and sea horses—made of sand and resin. Across from the market, **Dody** (✉ *31 rue Frébault, Pointe-à-Pitre, Grande-Terre* ☎ *0590/82–18–59*) is the place to go if you want white eyelet (blouses, skirts, dresses, even bustiers). The shop has a high-quality designer line, but you will pay €100 to €300 for a single piece. There's lots of madras, too, which is especially cute in children's clothing. **Le Gall** (✉ *La Marina–La Coursive, St-François, Grande-Terre* ☎ *No phone*) handles a line of fashionable resort wear for women and children, designed by French painter Jean Claude Le Gall, that has hand-painted figures like turtles and dolphins on high-quality cotton knits. There are several other branches of this French favorite across the island, at the Bas-du-Fort Marina and even on Les Saintes. A gift from this store is considered prestigious in the Motherland.

13

Basse-Terre Market.

COSMETICS AND PERFUME

L'Artisan Parfumeur (⊠ *Centre St-John Perse, Pointe-à-Pitre, Grande-Terre* ☎ *0590/83–80–25*) sells top French and American brands as well as tropical scents.

Au Bonheur des Dames (⊠ *49 rue Frébault, Pointe-à-Pitre, Grande-Terre* ☎ *0590/82–00–30*) sells several different lines of cosmetics and skin-care products in addition to its own perfumes. **L'Atelier du Savon** (⊠ *Terre-de-Haut, Iles des Saintes* ☎ *No phone*) makes all of its soaps from vegetable products, with scents including marine spice and mandarin orange. Beautifully packaged gift baskets include bath salts and aromatic oils. You never know when the sign: "Closed today, we are making soap," will go up. **Phoenicia** (⊠ *Bas-du-Fort, Grande-Terre* ☎ *0590/90–85–56* ⊠ *8 rue Frébault, Pointe-à-Pitre, Grande-Terre* ☎ *0590/83–50–36* ⊠ *121 bis rue Frébault, Pointe-à-Pitre, Grande-Terre* ☎ *0590/82–25–75*) sells mainly French perfumes. **Vendôme** (⊠ *8–10 rue Frébault, Pointe-à-Pitre, Grande-Terre* ☎ *0590/83–42–84*) is Guadeloupe's exclusive purveyor of Stendhal and Germaine Monteil cosmetics.

HANDICRAFTS

The **Centre Artisanat** (⊠ *Ste-Anne, Grande-Terre* ☎ *No phone*) offers a wide selection of local crafts, including art composed of shells, wood, and stone. One of the outlets sells authentic Panama hats.

★ **Madras Bijoux** (⊠ *115 rue Nozières, Pointe-à-Pitre, Grande-Terre* ☎ *0590/82–88–03*) specializes in replicas of authentic Creole jewelry; it also creates custom designs and does repairs. At **Maogany Artisanat** (⊠ *Terre-de-Haut, Iles des Saintes* ☎ *090/99–55–69 or 0690/50–48–44*), the shop resembles a yacht. Artist and designer Yves Cohen, an island pioneer since 1976, has left the island for Brazil. The new owner continues to carry his batiks and clothing in luminescent seashell shades, which he continues to supply—long distance. Hand-loomed silk fabrics are embellished with gold thread; others are translucent, such as his sensual women's collection. Ladies love *pareos* (wraparound fabric for skirts) the colors of the sea, from pale green to deep turquoise, as well as the new jewelry collection. For men, there are authentic Panama hats and buccaneer shirts. Stylin' additions are the several lines of women's clothing by French designers. The shop is closed on Monday in the low season.

LIQUOR AND TOBACCO
The airport duty-free stores have a good selection of rum and tobacco. **Délice Shop** (✉ *45 rue Achille René-Boisneuf, Pointe-à-Pitre, Grande-Terre* ☎ *0590/82–98–24*) is the spot for island rum and edibles from France—from cheese to chocolate.

SPORTS AND ACTIVITIES

BIKING

The French are mad about *le cyclisme*. If you rent a bicycle, expect to be asked to leave a deposit, but the amount seems to vary; normally you can use a credit card to secure your rental. On Terre-de-Haut, there are a number of shops to the immediate left and right of the ferry dock; the farther from the dock they are, the lower the rates. And you can usually negotiate the price down—a little.

On Grande-Terre, **Eli Sport** (✉ *Rond Point de Grand-Camp, Grand Camp, Grande-Terre* ☎ *0590/90–37–50*) can set you up with a *vélo tout terrain,* or all-terrain bike. There are no children's bikes, however. The price is right at €10 a day, but reserve as far in advance as possible, or you may find yourself walking instead. **Vert Intense** (✉ *Basse-Terre, Basse-Terre* ☎ *0590/99–34–73 or 0690/55–40–47* ⊕ *www.vert-intense. com*) is your main Basse-Terre sports connection. The company is known for hiking excursions but also puts together bike excursions. Try to make a reservation four days in advance.

BOATING AND SAILING

Generally speaking, most of the towns and cities of Guadeloupe are not beautiful; however, the craggy coastline and the waters of variegated blues and greens are gorgeous. If you plan to sail these waters, you should be aware that the winds and currents tend to be strong. There are excellent, well-equipped marinas in Pointe-à-Pitre, Bas-du-Fort, Deshaies, St-François, and Gourbeyre. You can rent a yacht (bareboat or crewed) from several companies. To make a bareboat charter, companies will evaluate your navigational and seamanship skills. If you do not pass, you must hire a skipper or be left on dry land.

Antilles Sail (✉ *Bas-du-Fort Marina, Pointe-à-Pitre* ☎ *0590/90–16–81* ⊕ *www.antilles-sail.com*) is a charter operation specializing in large, commodious catamarans from 40 to 62 feet, which can accommodate eight guests. For those who don't qualify to captain their own ship, or for those who want to just relax and be pampered, a skipper and crew can be hired. Provisioning and meal service can be arranged and VIP, dive, and other packages are available. The fleet also contains monohulls from 35 to 55 feet, which are used mainly for bareboating. Antilles Sail can actually arrange flights, lands stays, and your complete vacation package.

The giant yacht-rental company **Sunsail** (✉ *Bas-du-Fort Marina, Pointe-à-Pitre, Grande-Terre* ☎ *0590/90–92–02 or 410/280–2553, 207/253–5400 in U.S.* ⊕ *www.sunsail.com*) has a base on Guadeloupe. Although it's primarily a bareboat operation, you can hire skippers by the week if you have limited experience, or you can get expert instruction in sailing techniques and the local waters. Windsurfers, kayaks, and kite boards can be rented, too, but these must be reserved in advance.

DIVING

The main diving area at the **Cousteau Underwater Park,** just off Basse-Terre near Pigeon Island, offers routine dives to 60 feet. The numerous glass-bottom boats and other crafts make the site feel like a marine parking lot; however, the underwater sights are spectacular. Guides and instructors are certified under the French CMAS (some also have PADI, but none have NAUI). Most operators offer two-hour dives three times per day for about €45 to €50 per dive; three-dive packages are €120 to €145. Hotels and dive operators usually rent snorkeling gear.

Plaisir Plongee Karokera (PPK) (✉ *Plage de Malendure, Basse-Terre* ☎ *0590/98–82–43*) has a good reputation and is well established among those who dive off Pigeon Island. One dive boat departs three times daily and charges €30 a dive. A second dive boat goes to Les Saintes, with two dives, one at a wreck, the other at a reef. The €85 price includes lunch. English-speaking dive masters are PADI certified. Show your Fodor's guide and ask for a discount.

☾ **Les Heures Saines** (✉ *Le Rocher de Malendure, Plage de Malendure, Bouillante, Basse-Terre* ☎ *0590/98–86–63* ⊕ *www.heures-saines.gp*) is the premier operator for dives in the Cousteau Underwater Park. Trips to Les Saintes offer one or two dives for average and advanced divers, with plenty of time for lunch and sightseeing. Wreck, night, and Nitrox diving are also available. The instructors, many of them English speakers, are excellent with children. The company also offers winter whale- and dolphin-watching trips with marine biologists as guides. These tours, aboard a 60-foot catamaran, cost €55, less for children.

☾ With more than 10 years of experience, dive master Cedric Phalipon of **Pisquettes Club de Plongée Des Saintes** (✉ *Le Mouillage, Terre-de-Haut, Iles des Saintes* ☎ *0590/99–88–80* ⊕ *www.pisquettes.com*) knows all the best sites. He gives excellent lessons, in English. Equipment is replaced frequently and is of a high caliber. Small tanks are available for kids, who are taken buddy diving. There are two PADI instructors and an open-water, advanced PADI certificate is offered. Sec Pate is a famous underwater mountain, off the island's coast, in open seas. Les Saintes is known for its underwater hills, caves, canyons, and wall dives. Divers can see sponges of varied colors and gorgeous underwater trees that sway.

FISHING

Not far offshore from Pigeon-Bouillante, in Basse-Terre, is a bounty of big-game fish such as bonito, dolphinfish, captain fish, barracuda, kingfish, and tuna. You can also thrill to the challenge of the big billfish like marlin and swordfish. Anglers have been known to come back with as many as three blue marlins in a single day. For Ernest Hemingway wannabes, this is it. To reap this harvest, you'll need to charter one of the high-tech sportfishing machines with flying bridges, competent skippers, and mates. The price is $430 to $600 a day, with lunch and drinks included. The boats can accommodate up to six passengers.

With a pair of state-of-the-art boats with covered fly bridges, **Centre de Peche Sportive** (⊠ *Malendure de Pigeon, Bouillante, Basse-Terre* ☎ *0590/98–70–84*) is known for success in showing anglers where to pull in the big billfish. The per-day rate is €500, and you do get your money's worth; the boat often doesn't come back until sunset, after a fine lunch and cold bevs. You can also go night fishing for swordfish, and the crew will cut the bills and fins off your catch. The company is affiliated with the restaurant Le Rocher de Malendure, which has two simple oceanfront bungalows on the cliffs—a real value for the money. **Michel** (⊠ *Les Galbas, Ste-Anne, Basse-Terre* ☎ *0690/55–21–35*) is a reliable big-fishing charter outfit that can usually pick anglers up at their hotel and allows them to charge its €150 to their hotel bill. The mates will be happy to take your picture with your catch of the day.

GUIDED TOURS

With **Le Haras de Saint-François** (⊠ *Chemin de la Princesse, St-François, Grande-Terre* ☎ *0690/39–90–00*) you can take a four-wheeler quad off road and onto the beach for two hours with a fun guide for €60. **Marius Voyages** (⊠ *Main St., Ste-Anne, Grande-Terre* ☎ *0590/88–19–80*) offers excursions to the southern and northern coasts of Basse-Terre; the latter includes a visit to the botanical gardens and a glass-bottom boat ride to Pigeon Island. Excursions are by land, sea, and air—catamaran cruises to helicopter tours. Also, it provides transport to the ferries for Marie-Galante and Les Saintes; you can even get to Martinique or Dominica for a couple of nights. Best of all, the company offers airport transfers to hotels in Ste-Anne and St-François at prices that beat taxi prices and can eliminate the need for a rental car.

GOLF

Golf Municipal St-François (⊠ *St-François, Grande-Terre* ☎ *0590/88–41–87*), across from La Cocoteraie hotel, is an 18-hole, par-71, Robert Trent Jones–designed course (1973). The long-awaited renovation of all 18 holes, from fairways to greens and bunkers, at a cost of €4.5

million, officially debuted in December 2010. A new clubhouse is slated for 2012. The course has an English-speaking pro, a clubhouse, a pro shop, and electric carts for rent. The greens fees are still just €25 for 9 holes, €40 for 18 holes. Carts rent for €25 for 9 holes, €35 for 18; chariots (pull carts) rent for €4 for 9, €6 for 18. There are no caddies. Clubs can be rented for about €25. The course is open daily from 7:30 am to 6 pm. It's best to reserve tee times a day or two in advance. La Cocoteraie and BWA CHIK Hotel & Golf guests enjoy a 20% discount. Directly across from the golf course, the former **Golf Marine Hotel** has been transformed into a boutique hotel, renamed BWA CHIK Hotel & Golf, with surprisingly low rates. Recycled wood is used in the rooms and public spaces, which are decorated with contemporary wood sculpture. It's focus is on golfers, boaters, and sophisticated travelers. (☎ *0590/88–60–60* ⊕ *www.deshotelsetdesiles.com*).

HIKING

Fodor's Choice With hundreds of trails and countless rivers and waterfalls, the **Parc**
★ **National de la Guadeloupe** on Basse-Terre is the main draw for hikers. Some of the trails should be attempted only with an experienced guide. All tend to be muddy, so wear a good pair of boots. Know that even the young and fit can find these outings arduous; the unfit may find them painful. Start off slowly, with a shorter hike, and then go for the gusto. All water sports—even canoeing and kayaking—are forbidden in the center of the park. Scientists are studying the impact of these activities on the park's ecosystem. It will retain its prestigious award for ongoing sustainable tourism development, given by the EUROPARC Federation, until the year 2012.

Les Heures Saines (✉ *Le Rocher de Malendure, Plage de Malendure, Bouillante, Basse-Terre* ☎ *0590/98–86–63* ⊕ *www.heures-saines.gp*), a professional operation that has distinguished itself at sea, has now come ashore to offer freshwater canyoning in a river outside the national park as well as hikes to La Randonnée and the volcano. There are three different canyoning circuits, including one called the Trail of the Three Waterfalls that lasts six to seven hours. On the Bivouac trip you spend 24 reality-show-like hours in the forest. For many of these excursions, you have to wait for a group to be assembled. Book as far in advance as you can. Rates range from €45 to €115, and €28 to €50 for ages 8 to 14.

Vert Intense (✉ *Rte. de la Soufrière, Mourne Houel, Basse-Terre* ☎ *0590/ 99–34–73 or 0690/55–40–47* ⊕ *www.vert-intense.com*) organizes fascinating hikes in the national park and to the volcano. You move from steaming hot springs to an icy waterfall in the same hike. Guides are patient and safety-conscious, and can bring you to heights that you never thought you could reach, including the top of Le Soufrière. The volcano hike costs only €30 but must be booked four days in advance. A mixed-adventure package spanning three days costs €225. The two-day bivouac and other adventures can be extreme sport, so before you decide to play Indiana Jones, know what is expected. The French-speaking guides, who also know some English and Spanish, can take you to other tropical forests and rivers, where the sport of canyoning can still be practiced. If you are just one or two people, the company can team you up with a group.

HORSEBACK RIDING

A 50-horse stable, **Le Haras de Saint-François** (✉ *Chemin de la Princesse, St-François, Grande-Terre* ☎ *0690/39–90–00*) has English lessons and Western trail rides for two hours (€50) or three hours (€60). The latter will take you to the beach, where you can go bareback into the sea.

13

KAYAKING AND OTHER WATER SPORTS

Centre Nautique (✉ *Creole Beach Hotel & Spa, Pointe de la Verdure, Gosier, Grande-Terre* ☎ *0590/90–46–59*), on the watefront, rents sea kayaks for €10 an hour and Hobie Cats for €40 an hour, and can arrange fishing, catamaran, kayaking, diving, and motorboat excursions. It runs water taxis to the Islet du Gosier (€10) and to the outdoor market in Pointe-à-Pitre for €15. There are PADI instructors for the dive segment of the operation, and certifications are possible. Jet Ski rentals include a guide, and range from a half hour for €65 to €230 for five hours including lunch. **Jouez dans l'eau** (water games) (✉ *Main St., to left of main dock, Terre-de-Haut, Les Saintes* ☎ *0690/65–79–81* ⊕ *www.clearbluecaraibes.fr*) is great for underwater exploration without ever getting your hair wet. Rent a transparent kayak, which allows paddlers to see the myriad colors of one of the world's most beautiful bays. This creative company is still new to the island, and you can expect good, informative, 90-minute tours with an audio guide for commentary on coral reefs and sea life. The English version is coming soon. The cost is €20 per person, with special family and group rates available.

SEA EXCURSIONS

☾ **Evasion Tropicale** (✉ *Le Rocher de Malendure, Pigeon-Bouillante, Basse-Terre* ☎ *0590/92–74–24 or 0690/57–19–44* ⊕ *www.evasiontropicale.org*) operates daylong whale-watching cruises. With the help of the onboard sonar, humpback whales are easy to find from December through March. Trips on the 51-foot motor sailer cost €60 per person, but every passenger must also buy an annual membership in the Association for Study and Census of Turtles, Marine and Mammals of the Caribbean for €25.

Attracting an upscale clientele, **Paradoxe** (✉ *St-François Marina, St-François, Grande-Terre* ☎ *0590/85–41–73*) is a top-of-the-line catamaran that sails to Marie-Galante (anchoring at the idyllic beach, Anse Canot) for €95. It only sails to Les Saintes if the whole boat is booked by a group. (The off-season price can be significantly discounted.) It's not your typical booze cruise. Bottles of rum aboard? Sure, but passengers are more likely to be in it for the marine experience and the stopover on nature preserve Petit Terre. The music is soothing and the lunch tasty, with cheesy bread, fresh fish, barbecue chicken, ribs, and vegetarian dishes.

⚠ CAUTION: Rendezvous before departure for these sails can be as early as 7:15. No skipper can completely guarantee calm waters. Free-flowing rum can take its toll, and it will also rain at some point. And the Cats usually don't return until 5:30. Keep that all in mind, especially if you have children.

WIND- AND KITESURFING

Ⓒ Most beachfront hotels can help you arrange lessons and rentals. **LCS** (✉ *Ste-Anne Lagoon, Ste-Anne, Grande-Terre* ☎ *0590/88–15–17* ⊕ *www.lookasurf.com*), in business since the early 1980s, specializes in lessons for adults and children six and older. Instructors are certified by the French National Federation of Sailing. The company organizes offshore competitions and also runs a retail surf shop.

Windsurfing buffs congregate at the **UCPA Hotel Club** (✉ *Terre-de-Haut, Iles des Saintes* ☎ *0590/99–54–94 in-town reservations, 0590/99–56–34* ⊕ *www.ucpa.com*), where for moderate weekly rates (beginning at €805 or €115 a day) they sleep in hostel-style quarters, eat three meals a day, and do a lot of windsurfing. Lessons and boards (also available to nonguests) are included in the package, as are bikes to pedal to the lagoon. A sister club on Terre-de-Haut has a water-sports center in the middle of town, though the hotel itself is out on isolated Baie de Marigot. There is a lot of action at *le centre* UCPA, where island visitors rent windsurfing equipment for €25, or take a lesson for €30, and take kitesurfing lessons for €60, €20 if part of a group. Kayaks and dive tanks are available, too.

Jamaica

WORD OF MOUTH

"Believe me, I tell all our friends how beautiful Jamaica is. I really can't say enough about the beaches, the good times we've had, and the easy flight!."

—Knowing

WELCOME TO JAMAICA

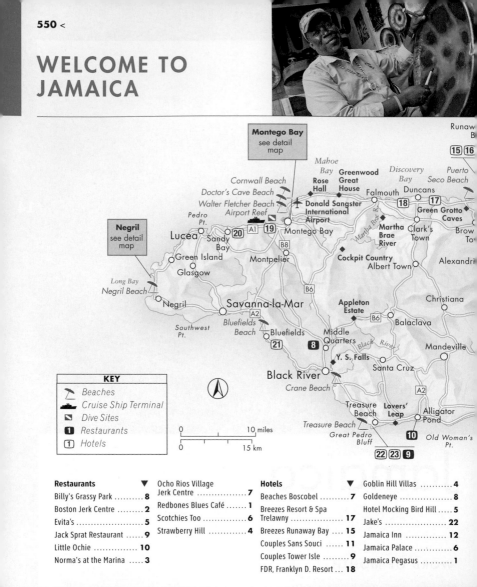

KEY

- ⌇ Beaches
- ⛴ Cruise Ship Terminal
- ⬎ Dive Sites
- **1** Restaurants
- **1** Hotels

0 — 10 miles
0 — 15 km

Restaurants ▼

Billy's Grassy Park	**8**
Boston Jerk Centre	**2**
Evita's	**5**
Jack Sprat Restaurant	**9**
Little Ochie	**10**
Norma's at the Marina	**3**
Ocho Rios Village Jerk Centre	**7**
Redbones Blues Café	**1**
Scotchies Too	**6**
Strawberry Hill	**4**

Hotels ▼

Beaches Boscobel	**7**
Breezes Resort & Spa Trelawny	**17**
Breezes Runaway Bay	**15**
Couples Sans Souci	**11**
Couples Tower Isle	**9**
FDR, Franklyn D. Resort	**18**
Goblin Hill Villas	**4**
Goldeneye	**8**
Hotel Mocking Bird Hill	**5**
Jake's	**22**
Jamaica Inn	**12**
Jamaica Palace	**6**
Jamaica Pegasus	**1**

Chances are you will never fully understand Jamaica in all its delightful complexity, but you will probably have a good time trying. You can party in Negril, shop in Montego Bay, or simply relax at one of the island's many all-inclusive resorts, but you'll also discover culture and delicious island cuisine.

OUT OF MANY, ONE PEOPLE

The third-largest island in the Caribbean (after Cuba and Hispaniola), Jamaica is 146 mi (242 km) long and is slightly smaller than the state of Connecticut. It has a population of 2.7 million. With about 800,000 people, the capital, Kingston, is the largest English-speaking city south of Miami (in the Western Hemisphere, at least). The highest point is Blue Mountain Peak at 7,402 feet.

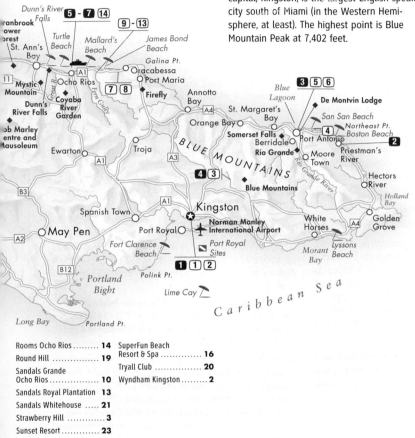

TOP REASONS TO VISIT JAMAICA

1 **All-Inclusive Resorts:** The all-inclusive resort was invented here.

2 **Great Golf:** Golfers will be delighted by the many wonderful courses.

3 **Fun for the Kids:** Every conceivable activity, great beaches, and many child-friendly resorts appeal to families.

4 **Negril Beach:** It's simply one of the Caribbean's best.

5 **Unique Culture:** Jamaica has rich cultural traditions—particularly local music, art, and cuisine.

JAMAICA PLANNER

Logistics

Getting to Jamaica: Donald Sangster International Airport (MBJ), in Montego Bay, is the most efficient point of entry for travelers destined for MoBay, Ocho Rios, Runaway Bay, the South Coast, and Negril. Norman Manley International Airport (KIN), in Kingston, is the best arrival point for travelers headed to the capital or to Port Antonio.

Hassle Factor: Low–high, depending on your distance from MoBay.

On the Ground: Most all-inclusive resorts include transfers. If transfers are not included for your trip, you can get shared-van service from the airport in Montego Bay to your final destination. You can rent a car at either airport.

Getting Around on the Island: Most travelers to Jamaica take guided tours on trips outside their resorts. The average traveler will not want to rent a car. Rentals are possible but are difficult to arrange on arrival and expensive, so make a reservation before your trip. In most places, a taxi may suffice for occasional trips around town, but your resort may have a free shuttle, so ask. In isolated areas (Port Antonio, for instance), a taxi isn't practical.

Getting to Jamaica

Nonstop Flights: You can fly to Jamaica from Atlanta (Air Tran, Delta), Boston (JetBlue, US Airways), Charlotte (US Airways), Chicago (American), Dallas (American), Detroit (US Airways), Fort Lauderdale (Air Jamaica, Spirit), Houston (Continental), Las Vegas (American), Los Angeles (American), Miami (American), New York–JFK (Air Jamaica, American, JetBlue), New York–Newark (Continental), Orlando (JetBlue), Philadelphia (Air Jamaica, US Airways), Phoenix (US Airways), San Diego (American), or Tampa (American). Most flights come into Montego Bay, but some nonstops go to Kingston.

Local Airline Contacts: Air Jamaica (☎ 888/359–2475, 876/952–4300 in Montego Bay). **Air Tran** (☎ 800/247–8726). **American Airlines** (☎ 800/744–0006). **Cayman Airways** (☎ 876/924–8650 in Kingston, 876/924–8809 in Montego Bay). **Continental Airlines** (☎ 800/231–0856, 876/952–5530 in Montego Bay). **Delta Airlines** (☎ 800/221–1212). **JetBlue** (☎ 800/963–3014). **United Airlines** (☎ 800/538–2929 or 800/864–8331). **US Airways** (☎ 876/940–0171).

International Airports: Donald Sangster International Airport (MBJ ⊠ Montego Bay ☎ 876/952–3124 ⊕ www.mbjairport.com). **Norman Manley International Airport** (KIN ⊠ Kingston ☎ 876/924–8452 ⊕ www.nmia.aero).

Domestic Air Service: If you need to continue to a smaller airport on Jamaica from your international flight, there are a couple of options. **Island Hoppers** (☎ 876/974–1285 ⊕ www.jamaicahelicopterservices.com) offers charter helicopter service to and from Ocho Rios. **Tim Air** (☎ 876/952–2516 in Montego Bay ⊕ www.timair.com) offers charter service between Montego Bay's Sangster International Airport and airports in Port Antonio, Ocho Rios, Runaway Bay, Kingston, and Negril.

Domestic Airports: Jamaica's minor domestic airports accommodate only charters at this writing. **Ian Fleming International Airport** (⊠ 8 mi [14 km] east of Ocho Rios, Oracabessa ☎ 876/975–3101). **Negril Aerodrome** (⊠ Negril ☎ 876/957–5016).

Getting Around Jamaica

Buses: Knutsford Express (☏ *876/971–1822* ⊕ *www. knutsfordexpress.com*), an air-conditioned bus, offers scheduled service between Montego Bay, Ocho Rios, and Kingston. For about $25, the bus company offers service from Montego Bay to Kingston three times daily. Service is also available from Montego Bay to Ocho Rios and Ocho Rios to Kingston for about $15. Pickups and drop-offs are not at the airports, however; service leaves from downtown locations.

Driving: Driving in Jamaica can be an extremely frustrating chore. You must constantly be on guard—for enormous potholes, people and animals darting out into the street, and aggressive drivers. Local drivers are quick to pass other cars—and sometimes two cars will pass simultaneously. Gas stations are open daily but accept cash only. Gas costs roughly double the price found in the United States. Driving in Jamaica is on the left, British-style.

Car Rentals: To rent a car, you must be at least 23 years old, have a valid driver's license (from any country), and have a valid credit card. You may be required to post a security deposit of several hundred dollars before taking possession of your car; ask about it when you make the reservation. Rates average $70 to $120 a day after the addition of the compulsory insurance, which you must usually purchase even if your credit card offers it.

Car-Rental Agencies: Budget (☏ *876/924–8762 in Kingston, 876/952–3838 in Montego Bay* ⊕ *www. budgetjamaica.com*). **Fiesta Car Rentals** (☏ *876/926– 0133* ⊕ *www.fiestacarrentals.com*). **Hertz** (☏ *876/924– 8028 in Kingston, 876/979–0438 in Montego Bay* ⊕ *www.hertz.com*). **Island Car Rentals** (☏ *876/924–8075 in Kingston, 876/952–7225 in Montego Bay* ⊕ *www. islandcarrentals.com*).

Taxis: Some but not all of Jamaica's taxis are metered. If you accept a driver's offer of his services as a tour guide, be sure to agree on a price before the vehicle is put into gear. (Note that a one-day tour should run about $150 to $180, in U.S. dollars, depending on distance traveled.) All licensed taxis display red Public Passenger Vehicle (PPV) plates. Your hotel concierge can call a taxi for you, or you can flag one down on the street. Rates are per car, not per passenger, and 25% is added to the metered rate between midnight and 5 am. Licensed minivans are also available and bear the red PPV plates. JUTA is the largest taxi franchise, with offices in all resort areas.

Island Activities

Negril has the island's best **beaches,** but there are also good beaches in the southwest and in Montego Bay. Despite the conservative culture of Jamaica, nude sunbathing is common at some resorts.

Tour operators will pick you up from your resort for a wide range of **activities.** Although diving isn't a top activity, dive operators work from all of the island's major resort areas.

Jamaica has some spectacular **golf courses,** the best of which are near Montego Bay.

You can go **rafting** on the slow, lazy Rio Grande, Martha Brae, or Great River.

Tour operators are coming up with new activities all the time. **Chukka Caribbean Adventures** operates ATV courses, canopy tours, river tubing, horseback riding, and even a dogsledding adventure.

But many people seem to be drawn to Jamaica for the music—particularly **reggae,** which originated on the island. **Bob Marley,** one of reggae's most famous stars, is an island legend, and a pilgrimage to the places that were meaningful to him is often on the tourist's agenda.

14

JAMAICA PLANNER

Fast Facts	Essentials

Fast Facts

Banks and Exchange Services: The official currency is the Jamaican dollar, but few Americans bother to exchange money, since U.S. dollars are widely accepted. Some ATMs in Jamaica don't accept American ATM cards, and others will accept American ATM cards and dispense U.S. dollars. Major credit cards are widely accepted, although cash is required at gas stations, in markets, and in many small stores.

Electricity: As in North America, the current in Jamaica is 110 volts but only 50 cycles, with outlets that take two flat prongs. Some hotels provide 220-volt plugs as well as special shaver outlets.

Emergency Services: Ambulance and Fire Emergencies (☏ 110). **Police Emergencies & Air Rescue** (☏ 119). **Scuba-Diving Emergencies** (✉ St. Ann's Bay Hospital, St. Ann's Bay ☏ 876/972–2272).

Passports: All visitors must have a valid passport. A birth certificate and photo ID are not sufficient proof of citizenship.

Weddings: A 24-hour waiting period is required; many resorts offer free weddings.

Essentials

Mail: Postcards may be mailed anywhere in the world for J$50. Letters cost J$60 to the United States and Canada. However, mail is unreliable and very slow.

Taxes: Almost all airline ticket prices include the $20 departure tax; otherwise, it must be paid in cash. A value-added tax of 16.5% is included in the cost of most goods and services; there is no longer a separate hotel-occupancy tax.

Telephones: Cellular service is expanding throughout Jamaica, especially in Kingston and in the resort areas. GSM cell phones equipped with tri-band or world-roaming service will find coverage throughout much of the coastal region. Cellular service averages about $1.50 to $2 per minute on the island. Rates for local calls start about 14¢ per minute, and incoming calls are free. Outgoing international calls to the United States start at about 30¢ per minute. Prepaid SIM cards cost about $60 and usually include a $20 airtime credit; they're a more economical option for travelers planning to make a large number of local calls. Cellular-phone rentals are also available starting at about $20 per week.

Most hotels offer direct-dial telephone services with a substantial service change; local businesses provide fax services for a fee. Pay phones and calling cards are available.

To dial Jamaica from the United States, just dial 1 + area code 876. Some U.S. phone companies provide only limited credit-card calls from Jamaica because they've been victims of fraud. The best option is to purchase Jamaican phone cards, sold in most stores across the island.

Tipping: Most hotels and restaurants add a 10% service charge to your bill. When a service charge isn't included, a 10% to 20% tip is expected. Tips of 10% to 20% are customary for taxi drivers as well. However, many all-inclusives have a strict no-tipping policy.

Visitor Information: Jamaica Tourist Board (☏ 305/665–0557 in Miami, 876/929–9200 in Kingston, 876/952–4425 in Montego Bay ⊕ www.visitjamaica.com).

Where to Stay

Montego Bay has the largest concentration of resorts on the island; **Negril** is a more relaxed haven on the west coast. Both offer a mix of large and small resorts, plus good nightlife. **Runaway Bay** and **Ocho Rios** are more than an hour east of MoBay. **Port Antonio,** a sleepy, laid-back haven, has a few resorts and a quiet atmosphere and is usually accessed by a short flight or long drive from Kingston. The **South Coast** has a few small resorts, uncrowded beaches, and only one large resort. Few vacationers choose to stay in the capital, **Kingston,** but the surrounding area also includes the **Blue Mountains,** home of the luxe Strawberry Hill resort.

All-inclusive Resorts: Jamaica was the birthplace of the Caribbean all-inclusive resort, which is still the most popular vacation option here. Several of these are open only to couples.

Small Hotels: Particularly in Negril, you'll find smaller, more unique hotels and inns that aren't part of the big chains; they range in price from budget to luxury. The Island Outpost company operates several upscale boutique resorts all over Jamaica.

Villas: Jamaica is home to an increasing number of villas aimed at travelers looking for a home-away-from-home experience. Discovery Bay, near Runaway Bay, is a top location for many high-end villas. Many have a one-week minimum stay.

HOTEL AND RESTAURANT PRICES

Restaurant prices are for a main course at dinner and include any taxes or service charges. Hotel prices are per night for a double room in high season, excluding taxes, service charges, and meal plans (except at all-inclusives).

When to Go

High season in Jamaica runs roughly from mid-December through mid-April. From May through mid-December, you can save from 20% to as much as 40% on rates, more if you use value-oriented travel packagers. There are several annual events in Jamaica that draw huge numbers of visitors.

14

Jamaica Jazz & Blues Festival is in Montego Bay each January.

In Ocho Rios, the biggest event of the year is the **Jamaica Ocho Rios International Jazz Festival** held each June.

Reggae Sumfest is usually sometime between mid-July and early August.

The Port Antonio **International Marlin Tournament** is held every October.

The largest islandwide festival is **Carnival,** which is held in Kingston, Ocho Rios, and MoBay every March and April and in Negril every May.

WHAT IT COSTS IN U.S. DOLLARS					
	¢	$	$$	$$$	$$$$
Restaurants	under $8	$8–$12	$12–$20	$20–$30	over $30
Hotels*	under $80	$80–$150	$150–$250	$250–$350	over $350
Hotels	under $150	$150–$275	$276–$375	$376–$475	over $475

JAMAICA BEACHES

As the Caribbean's third-largest island, Jamaica has no shortage of beaches, ranging from the North Coast's tourist-filled stretches of sand lined by exclusive resorts to the nearly deserted beaches of the South Coast, where beach action often means a fisherman cleaning his catch.

(Above) The beach at Sandals Whitehouse, on the South Shore. (Opposite page bottom) Doctor's Cave Beach, Montego Bay. (Opposite page top) Dunn's River Falls, Ocho Rios.

North- and west-coast beaches tend to be busy, well supplied with amenities, and blessed with large expanses of sand. Both Negril (and its lovely Seven Mile Beach) and Montego Bay (which has both Doctor's Cave and Half Moon Bay) are renowned for their beaches, and both have many resorts directly on the beach to choose from. Beaches on the South Coast are generally less crowded but are smaller, with fewer services. The best South Coast beaches are in the Treasure Beach area near Calabash Bay. Kingston-area beaches are generally congested; ask your hotel concierge before heading out to any of them. Some of the best beaches are private, owned by the resorts and accessible only to resort guests or travelers who have purchased a day pass to gain access to the facilities.

BEST BEACHES?

Most of Jamaica's beaches are coral based, creating a medium-coarse, light-color sand. In general, the best Jamaican beach sand is on the north and west sides of the island. The softest and most beautiful beaches are in Negril, on the island's west coast, and in the Montego Bay area. Those on the South Coast are narrower and wilder, with coarser, darker sand.

While hotel beaches are generally private and restricted to guests of the property, other beaches are public and are open to all kinds of vendors, who have a reputation of being rather aggressive. At resort areas, even if the beach area is considered private, the area below the high-water mark is always public, so vendors will roam longer beaches looking for business. In most cases, a simple "no thanks" will do, but. . . .

MONTEGO BAY

★ **Doctor's Cave Beach.** Montego Bay's tourist scene has its roots right on the Hip Strip, the bustling entertainment district along Gloucester Avenue. Here a sea cave's waters were said to be curative and drew many travelers to bathe in them. Though the cave was destroyed by a hurricane generations ago, the beach is always busy and has a perpetual spring-break feel. It's the best beach in Jamaica outside one of the more developed resorts, thanks to its plantation-style clubhouse with changing rooms, showers, gift shops, a bar, a grill, and even a cybercafé. There's a $5 fee for admission; beach chairs and umbrellas are also for rent. Its location within the Montego Bay Marine Park—where there are protected corals and marine life—makes it a good spot for snorkeling. More active travelers can opt for parasailing, glass-bottom boat rides, or jet skiing. ⊠ *Gloucester Ave., Montego Bay* ☎ *876/952–2566.*

Walter Fletcher Beach. Though not as pretty as Doctor's Cave Beach, or as tidy, Walter Fletcher Beach is home to Aquasol Theme Park, which offers a large beach (with lifeguards and security), water trampolines, Jet Skis, Wave Runners, glass-bottom boats, snorkeling, tennis, go-kart racing, a disco at night, a bar, and a grill. The park is open daily from 10 to 10; admission is $5, with à la carte pricing for most activities. Near the center of town, the beach has protection from the surf on a windy day. This means you can find unusually fine swimming here; the calm waters make it a good bet for children. ⊠ *Gloucester Ave., Montego Bay* ☎ *876/979–9447.*

RUNAWAY BAY

Puerto Seco Beach. This public beach looks out on Discovery Bay, the location where, according to tradition, Christopher Columbus first came ashore on this island. The explorer sailed in search of freshwater but found none, naming the stretch of sand Puerto Seco, or "dry port." Today the beach is anything but dry; concession stands sell Red Stripe beer and local food, including jerk and patties, to a primarily local beach crowd. ⊠ *Discovery Bay, 5 mi (8 km) west of Runaway Bay.*

OCHO RIOS

Dunn's River Falls Beach. You'll find a crowd (especially if there's a cruise ship in town) at the small beach at the foot of

The Blue Lagoon, Port Antonio.

the falls. Although tiny—especially considering the crowds that pack the falls—it's got a great view, as well as a beach bar and grill. Look up from the sands for a spectacular view of the cascading water, whose roar drowns out the sea as you approach. ⊠ *Rte. A1 between St. Ann's Bay and Ocho Rios.*

James Bond Beach. Another alternative near Ocho Rios—if you don't mind the drive—is in the community of Oracabessa. This beach, on the estate of James Bond's creator, the late Ian Fleming, is owned by former Island Records producer Chris Blackwell, so it's no surprise that it often rocks with live music performances on the bandstand. Guests of the Goldeneye resort enjoy it for free; visitors must pay $5 per person. The beach is open daily except Monday from 9:30 to 6. ⊠ *Oracabessa* ☎ *876/726–1630.*

Turtle Beach. One of the busiest beaches in Ocho Rios is usually lively, and has a mix of both residents and visitors. It's next to the Sunset Jamaica Grande and looks out over the cruise port. ⊠ *Main St.*

PORT ANTONIO

Blue Lagoon. Though the beach is small, the large lagoon has to be seen to be believed. The cool, spring-fed waters cry out to swimmers and are a real contrast to the warmer sea waters. Floating docks encourage you to sun a little, or you can lie out on the small beach. Just how deep is the Blue Lagoon? You might hear it's bottomless (Jacques Cousteau verified that it is not), but the lagoon has been measured at a depth of 180 feet. At present, tour operators offer admission as part of their Port Antonio tours, and freelance operators at the gates sometimes offer entry but, for current (and official) conditions, call the Jamaica Tourist Board. ⊠ *9 mi (13 km) east of Port Antonio, 1 mi (2 km) east of San San Beach.*

Boston Beach. Considered the birthplace of Jamaica's famous jerk-style cooking, it's the beach where some locals visit just to buy dinner. You can get peppery jerk pork at any of the shacks spewing scented smoke along the beach. While you're there, you'll also find a small beach perfect for an after-lunch dip, although these waters are occasionally rough and much more popular for surfing. ⊠ *11 mi (18 km) east of Port Antonio.*

★**Frenchman's Cove.** This beautiful, somewhat secluded beach is petite perfection. Protected by two outcroppings that form the cove, the inlet's calm waters are a favorite with families. A small stream trickles into the cove. You'll find a bar and restaurant serving fried chicken right on the beach. If this stretch of sand looks a little familiar, it just might be because you've seen it in the movies; it has starred in *Club Paradise, Treasure Island* (the Charlton Heston version), and *The Mighty Quinn*. If you are not a guest of Frenchman's Cove, admission is $4.50 ($2.50 for children). ⊠ *Rte. A4, 5 mi (8 km) east of Port Antonio.*

San San Beach. This small beach ($5 admission fee) has beautiful blue water. Just offshore, Monkey Island is a good place to snorkel (and, sometimes, surf). ⊠ *5 mi (8 km) east of Port Antonio.*

THE SOUTH COAST

If you're looking for something off the main tourist routes, head for Jamaica's largely undeveloped southwest coast. Because the population in this region is sparse, these isolated beaches are some of the island's safest, with hasslers practically nonexistent. You should, however, use common sense; never leave valuables unattended on the beach.

Treasure Beach. The most atmospheric beach in the southwest is in the community of Treasure Beach, which comprises four long stretches of sand as well as many small coves. Though it isn't as pretty as those to the west or north—it has more rocks and darker sand—the idea that you might be discovering a bit of the "real" Jamaica more than makes up for the small negatives. Both locals and visitors use the beaches here, though you're just as likely to find it completely deserted save a friendly beach dog. ⊠ *Treasure Beach township.*

NEGRIL

★ **Fodor's Choice** **Negril Beach.** Stretching for 7 mi (11 km), the long, white-sand beach in Negril is arguably Jamaica's finest. It starts with the white sands of Bloody Bay north of town and continues along Long Bay all the way to the cliffs on the southern edge of town. Some stretches remain undeveloped, but these are increasingly few. Along the main stretch of beach, the sand is public to the high-water mark, so a nonstop line of visitors and vendors parade from end to end. The walk is sprinkled with many good beach bars and open-air restaurants, some of which charge a small fee to use their beach facilities. Bloody Bay is lined with large all-inclusive resorts, and these sections are mostly private. Jamaica's best-known nude beach, at Hedonism II, is always among the busiest; only resort guests or day-pass holders may sun here. ⊠ *Norman Manley Blvd.*

Word of Mouth. "Negril, hands down [is our favorite beach in Jamaica]. Friendly. Clear water. White sand beaches. miles of that. <sigh> wish I was there now."—lynzdee

Negril Beach.

EATING AND DRINKING WELL IN JAMAICA

"We love to marinate our food longer even when using the same ingredients. Our food is also a bit hotter yet aromatic and pungent." — Jacqui Sinclair, Jamaican chef and food writer.

(Above) Lobster at Evita's Italian Restaurant. (Opposite page bottom) A bounty of native Jamaican fruits. (Opposite page top) Fresh seafood, a part of many memorable Jamaican meals.

Jamaica's national motto, "Out of Many, One Country," serves equally well to describe its multicultural, melting-pot cuisine: a savvy, savory fusion of African, Asian, Arawak-Taíno, and European influences, ingredients, techniques, and traditions. Even the humble patty blends African peppers, Chinese soy sauce, and Cornish pasties. Sizzling Scotch bonnet peppers are indigenous, as are pimento—from which allspice is produced (Jamaica produces 80% of the world's supply), and the liberally used native ginger is stronger in Jamaica than elsewhere. Aspiring Anthony Bourdains should try beachfront or roadside vans, kiosks, and shacks dishing out darkly bubbling grub from cow foot to curried goat that might unnerve *Survivor* contestants. They offer authentic fare like succulent slow-cooked jerk with heaping helpings of rice 'n' peas (beans) and provisions (tubers like yam and cassava). —Jordan Simon

THE JERK TRAIL

In May 2009, citing the international popularity of jerk cuisine, Jamaica's Ministry of Tourism introduced the Culinary Jerk Trail, spanning the island from Negril through MoBay and Ocho Rios to Kingston and Port Antonio. The attraction features 10 of the hottest jerk spots where diners can interact with chefs and learn the origins behind jerk cooking. For more information, go to ⊕ *www.visitjamaica. com/jerk.*

JERK

Arguably Jamaica's most famous export after reggae, jerk supposedly originated with the Maroons, freed descendants of slaves who settled the island's most remote, inhospitable areas. Meat (usually chicken or pork) is marinated for hours in a fiery blend of peppers, pimento, scallion, and thyme, then cooked over an outdoor pit lined with pimento wood. Low, slow heating retains the natural juices while infusing the meat with the flavor of the wood and spices and ensures that the meat lasts in the tropical heat.

SALTFISH AND ACKEE

The British brought salt cod with them as a cheap, long-lasting foodstuff for sailors and slaves alike. Ackee, a red tree fruit introduced to Jamaica from western Africa via Britain, is actually poisonous in its natural state. Once the pear-shaped fruit's tough, toxic, ruddy membrane is removed, however, the boiled, yellowish, pulpy arils surprisingly resemble scrambled eggs in taste and texture.

EXOTICA

Local menus traditionally feature pickled pigs' trotters or souse. Goat figures in incendiary curries, as well as "mannish water," a lusty soup—believed to be an aphrodisiac, traditionally served on wedding nights—including the head and brains slow-cooked with various seasonings and tubers. Oxtail is a

culinary constant from Italy to Indonesia. Jamaicans serve it stewed, braised, or in soup; inventive chefs might toss it with pasta in rum-cream sauce.

SEAFOOD ESCOVEITCH

Freshly caught fish—including snapper, tuna, wahoo, grouper, and marlin—is often served as *escoveitch* aka *escoveech* (stewed or sautéed, sometimes in coconut milk, with peppers, onions, chayote, carrots, Scotch bonnet peppers, and tomatoes). Despite the linguistic and gastronomic similarity to ceviche and *escabeche*, escoveitch is rarely served cold, though it is usually marinated in vinegar and lime juice before it is cooked.

PROVISIONS

Farmers traditionally cultivated carb-rich crops that could furnish energy for islanders' hardscrabble heavy labor without requiring refrigeration. Pumpkins, coconuts, plantains, breadfruit, sweet potatoes, cassava, yams, and other "provisions" (root and gourd vegetables) became staples, sometimes replacing expensive imported ingredients (chayote was used in mock-apple crumble). Most homeowners still have kitchen gardens; Olympic champion Usain Bolt credits yams from his native Trelawny Parish for his speed. Today, even sophisticated chefs creatively return to their "grow what you eat" locavore roots.

By Paris
Permenter and
John Bigley

Jamaicans define enthusiasm. Whether the topic is ackee or dominoes, politics or Carnival, the spirit of this island comes out in every interaction. Although the island is well known for its tropical beauty, reggae music, and cuisine, you may find that your interactions with local residents are what you truly remember.

The island is rich in beauty, but a quick look around reveals widespread poverty and a land where the disparity between the lives of the resort guests and the resort employees is often staggering. Where vacationers opt to make their Jamaican home away from home depends on factors ranging from the length of their vacation to personal interests. With its direct air connections to many cities in the United States, Montego Bay (or MoBay) is favored by Americans taking short trips; many properties are just minutes from the airport. Ocho Rios (often just "Ochi"), 90 minutes east of the airport, is a lush destination that's favored by honeymooners for its tropical beauty and myriad couples-only resorts. Ocho Rios is also a popular cruise port and where you can find one of the island's most recognizable attractions: the stair-step Dunn's River Falls, which invites travelers to climb in daisy-chain fashion, hand-in-hand behind a sure-footed guide.

East of Ocho Rios, Port Antonio is considered the most beautiful, untouched area of Jamaica, a hideaway for the rich and famous since Errol Flynn first lived here.

More than an hour west of MoBay lies Negril, once a hippie haven and now a growing destination that still hangs on to its laid-back roots despite the addition of several expansive all-inclusive resorts in recent years.

The South Coast is more attractive to those travelers looking for funky fun in small, one-of-a-kind resorts and an atmosphere that encourages them to get out and mingle in the community, whether that means a game of dominoes in a local rum shop or a bicycle trip to buy the day's catch from a local fisherman. The beaches here don't have the white-sand beauty of their northern cousins, but this area is uncrowded and still mostly undiscovered.

Jamaica's capital city, Kingston, is a sharp contrast to the beach destinations. The largest English-speaking city in the Western Hemisphere south of Miami (with some 800,000 residents), this sprawling metropolis is primarily visited by business travelers or by those who want to learn more about the cultural side of Jamaica, thanks to its numerous galleries, theaters, and cultural programs. If you really want to understand Jamaica, you can't ignore Kingston.

> ### WORD OF MOUTH
>
> "The people of Jamaica were such warm people, and I got the feeling that they did want visitors to love Jamaica in the same way that they did. That was genuine and not because they wanted to sell me something or because they wanted a tip. It was a warmth that added to the beauty of the island."—writealiving

Some of the island's earliest residents were the Arawak Indians, who arrived from South America around 650 AD and named the island Xaymaca, or "land of wood and water." Centuries later, the Arawaks welcomed Christopher Columbus on his second voyage to the New World. Later when the Spanish arrived, the peaceful inhabitants were executed or taken as slaves.

The Spanish maintained control of the island until 1655, when the English arrived. Soon, slavery increased as sugar became a booming industry. In 1834, slavery was abolished, but the sugar as well as banana industries continued. Jamaica's plantation owners looked for another source of labor. From 1838 to 1917, more than 30,000 Indians immigrated here, followed by about 5,000 Asians as well as immigrants from the Middle East, primarily from what is now Lebanon.

In the early 1900s, the boats that took the banana crop off the island began returning with travelers. By 1960, the tourism industry had become Jamaica's most important form of income. In 1962, Jamaica became an independent nation.

Although 95% of the population traces its bloodlines to Africa, Jamaica is a stockpot of cultures, including those of other Caribbean islands, Great Britain, the Middle East, India, China, Germany, Portugal, and South America. The third-largest island in the Caribbean (after Cuba and Hispaniola), Jamaica enjoys a considerable self-sufficiency based on tourism, agriculture, and mining.

EXPLORING JAMAICA

Touring Jamaica can be both thrilling and frustrating. Rugged (albeit beautiful) terrain and winding (often potholed) roads make for slow going. *Always* check conditions before you set off to explore the island by car, but especially in the rainy season from June through October, when roads can easily be washed out. Primary roads that loop around and across the island are two-lane routes but are not particularly well marked. Numbered addresses are seldom used outside major townships, locals drive aggressively, and people and animals seem to have a knack for appearing on the street out of nowhere. That said, Jamaica's

Safety in Jamaica

CLOSE UP

Crime in Jamaica is, unfortunately, a persistent problem, so don't let the beauty of the island cause you to abandon the caution you would practice in any unfamiliar place. Many of the headlines are grabbed by murders in Kingston, often gang-related; violent crimes are, for the most part, largely a problem for residents who live in the city. Visitors should be extremely cautious about visiting many of the neighborhoods in Kingston that are outside the business district of New Kingston.

Property crime is an islandwide problem. Use your in-room safe and be sure to lock all doors—including balconies—when you leave your room or villa. Traveler's checks are a good idea in Jamaica, being safer than cash (just keep a record of the check numbers in a secure place so they can be replaced if necessary). Never leave your car unlocked, and never leave valuables inside it, even when it is locked. Ignore efforts, however persistent, to sell you ganja (marijuana), which is illegal across the island.

scenery shouldn't be missed. To be safe and avoid frustration, stick to guided tours and licensed taxis.

If you're staying in Kingston or Port Antonio, set aside at least one day for the capital's highlights and another for a guided excursion to the Blue Mountains. You can find at least three days' worth of activity right along MoBay's boundaries; you should also consider a day trip to Negril or Ocho Rios. If you're based in Ocho Rios, be sure to visit Dunn's River Falls; you may also want to stop by Firefly or Bob Marley's birthplace, Nine Mile. If Negril is your hub, take in the South Coast, including Y.S. Falls and the Black River.

NORTH COAST

MONTEGO BAY

Today many explorations of MoBay are conducted from a reclining chair—frothy drink in hand—on Doctor's Cave Beach. As home of the north-shore airport, Montego Bay is the first taste most visitors have of the island. It's the second-largest city in Jamaica and has a busy cruise pier west of town. Travelers from around the world come and go in this bustling community year-round. The name Montego is derived from *manteca* ("lard" in Spanish). The Spanish first named this Bahía de Manteca, or Lard Bay. Why? The Spanish once shipped hogs from this port city. Jamaican tourism began here in 1924, when the first resort opened at Doctor's Cave Beach so that health seekers could "take the waters." If you can pull yourself away from the water's edge, you'll find some interesting colonial sights in the surrounding area.

★ **Greenwood Great House.** Unlike Rose Hall, Greenwood has no spooky legend to titillate, but it's much better than Rose Hall at evoking life on a sugar plantation. The Barrett family, from whom the English poet Elizabeth Barrett Browning descended, once owned all the land from Rose Hall to Falmouth; on their vast holdings they built this and several other greathouses. (The poet's father, Edward Moulton Barrett, "the Tyrant of Wimpole Street," was born at nearby Cinnamon Hill, later the estate of country singer Johnny Cash.) Highlights of Greenwood include oil paintings of the Barretts, china made for the family by Wedgwood, a library filled with rare books from as early as 1697, fine antique furniture, and a collection of exotic musical instruments. There's a pub on-site as well. It's 15 mi (24 km) east of Montego Bay. ⊠ *Greenwood* ☎ *876/953–1077* ⊕ *www.greenwoodgreathouse.com* ⊐ *$14* ⊘ *Daily 9–6 (last tour at 5).*

Fodor'sChoice
★

Rose Hall. In the 1700s it may well have been the greatest of greathouses in the West Indies. Today it's popular less for its architecture than for the legend surrounding its second mistress, Annie Palmer. As the story goes, Annie was born in 1802 in England to an English mother and Irish father. When she was 10, her family moved to Haiti, and soon her parents died of yellow fever. Annie was adopted by a Haitian voodoo priestess and soon became skilled in the practice of voodoo. Annie moved to Jamaica, married, and built Rose Hall, an enormous plantation spanning 6,600 acres with more than 2,000 slaves. There's a pub on-site. It's across the highway from the Rose Hall Resort & Country Club, A Hilton Resort. ⊠ *North Coast Hwy., St. James* ✦ *15 mi (24 km) east of Montego Bay* ☎ *876/953–2323* ⊐ *$20* ⊘ *Daily 9:15–5:15.*

OFF THE BEATEN PATH

Martha Brae River. This gentle waterway about 25 mi (40 km) southeast of Montego Bay takes its name from an Arawak woman who killed herself because she refused to reveal the whereabouts of a local gold mine. According to legend, she agreed to take her Spanish inquisitors there and, on reaching the river, used magic to change its course, drowning herself and the greedy Spaniards with her. Her *duppy* (ghost) is said to guard the mine's entrance. Rafting on this river is a very popular activity.

COCKPIT COUNTRY

Fifteen miles (24 km) inland from MoBay is one of the most untouched areas in the West Indies: a terrain of pitfalls and potholes carved by nature in limestone. For nearly a century after 1655 it was known as the Land of Look Behind, because British soldiers nervously rode their horses through here on the lookout for the guerrilla freedom fighters known as Maroons. Former slaves who refused to surrender to the invading English, the Maroons eventually won their independence. Today their descendants live in this area, untaxed and virtually ungoverned by outside authorities. Most visitors to the area stop in Accompong, a small community in St. Elizabeth Parish. You can stroll through town, take in the historic structures, and learn more about the Maroons—considered Jamaica's greatest herbalists.

OCHO RIOS

Although Ocho Rios isn't near eight rivers as its name would seem to indicate, it does have a seemingly endless series of cascades that sparkle from limestone rocks along the coast. (The name Ocho Rios came about because the English misunderstood the Spanish *las chorreras*— "the waterfalls.") The town itself isn't very attractive and can be traffic-clogged, but the area has several worthwhile attractions, including the very popular and touristic Dunn's River Falls. A few steps from the main road in Ocho Rios are some of the most charming inns and oceanfront restaurants in the Caribbean. Lying on the sand of what seems to be your very own cove or swinging gently in a hammock while sipping a tropical drink, you'll soon forget the traffic that's just a stroll away. The original "defenders" stationed at the Old Fort, built in 1777, spent much of their time sacking and plundering as far afield as St. Augustine, Florida, and sharing their booty with the local plantation owners who financed their missions. Discovery Bay, 15 mi (24 km) west, is where Columbus landed and where there's a small museum with such artifacts as ships' bells and cannons and iron pots used for boiling sugarcane. Don't miss a drive through Fern Gully, a natural canopy of vegetation filtered by sunlight. (Jamaica has the world's largest number of fern species, more than 570.) To reach the stretch of road called Fern Gully, take the A3 highway south of Ocho Rios.

★ **Bob Marley Centre and Mausoleum.** Travelers with an interest in Bob Marley won't want to miss Nine Mile, the community where the reggae legend was born and is buried. Today his former home is a shrine to his music and values. Tucked behind a tall fence, the site is marked with green and gold flags. Tours are led by Rastafarians, who take visitors through the house and point out the single bed that Marley wrote about in "Is This Love." Visitors also step inside the mausoleum where the singer is interred with his guitar. The site includes a restaurant and gift shop. Visitors from Ocho Rios can arrange transport by taxi, but the round-trip fare is about $175; a less expensive option is the Chukka Bob Marley Jeep Safari ($74, 4½ hours, ages 18 and older), a guided tour with Chukka Caribbean. We strongly recommend a guided tour here since the hustlers that meet you outside the Bob Marley Centre are some of the most aggressive in Jamaica. ✉ *Rhoden Hall, Nine Mile* ☎ *876/843–0498* ⊕ *www.bobmarleymovement.com* 🖃 *$15* ⏱ *Daily 9–4.*

★ **Coyaba River Garden & Museum and Mahoe Waterfalls.** Jamaica's national motto is "Out of Many, One People," and here you can see exhibits on the many cultural influences that have contributed to the creation of the one. The museum covers the island's history from the time of the Arawak Indians up to the present day. A guided 45-minute tour through the lush 3-acre garden, which is 1½ mi (2½ km) south of Ocho Rios, introduces you to the flora and fauna of the island. The complex includes a crafts and gift shop and a snack bar. ✉ *Shaw Park Estate, Shaw Park Ridge Rd., Ocho Rios* ☎ *876/974–6235* ⊕ *www. coyabagardens.com* 🖃 *$10* ⏱ *Daily 8–5.*

★ **Cranbrook Flower Forest and River Head Adventure Trail.** You can enjoy the north-coast rivers and flowers without the crowds at this botanical reserve filled with blooming orchids, ginger, and ferns. This park is the private creation of Ivan Linton, who has pampered the plants of this former plantation since the early 1980s. Today Linton proudly points out the birds-of-paradise, croton, ginger, heliconia, and begonias as if they were his dear children. The grounds are perfect for a picnic followed by a hike alongside shady Laughlin's Great River. The path climbs high into the hills to a waterfall paradise. Donkey rides, picnicking, croquet, wading, and volleyball are also available here. The complex has

Climbing Dunn's River Falls, Ocho Rios.

a snack shop and restrooms. ⊠ *5 mi (8 km) east of Runaway Bay, 1 mi (2 km) off North Coast Hwy.* ☎ *876/610–6509* ⊕ *www.cranbrookff. com* ✉ *$10* ⊙ *Daily 9–5.*

Fodor's Choice
★ **Dunn's River Falls.** One of Jamaica's most popular attractions is an eye-catching sight: 600 feet of cold, clear mountain water splashing over a series of stone steps to the warm Caribbean. The best way to enjoy the falls is to climb the slippery steps: don a swimsuit, take the hand of the person ahead of you, and trust that the chain of hands and bodies leads to an experienced guide. The leaders of the climbs are personable fellows who reel off bits of local lore while telling you where to step; you can hire a guide's service for a tip of a few dollars. After the climb, you exit through a crowded market, another reminder that this is one of Jamaica's top tourist attractions. If you can, try to schedule a visit on a day when no cruise ships are in port. ⚠ Always climb with a licensed guide at Dunn's River Falls. Freelance guides might be a little cheaper, but the experienced guides can tell you just where to plant each footstep—helping you prevent a fall. ⊠ *Off Rte. A1, between St. Ann's Bay and Ocho Rios, Ocho Rios* ☎ *876/974–4767* ⊕ *www.dunnsriverfallsja.com* ✉ *$15* ⊙ *Daily 8:30–5 (last entry 4 pm).*

★ **Firefly.** About 20 mi (32 km) east of Ocho Rios near Port Maria, Firefly was once Sir Noël Coward's vacation home and is now maintained by the Jamaican National Heritage Trust. Although the setting is Eden-like, the house is surprisingly spartan, considering that he often entertained jet-setters and royalty. He wrote *High Spirits, Quadrille,* and other plays here, and his simple grave is on the grounds next to a small stage where his works are occasionally performed. Recordings of Coward singing about "mad dogs and Englishmen" echo over the lawns. Tours include a walk through the house and grounds where Coward is buried. The view from the house's hilltop perch is one of the best on the north coast, making Firefly well worth the price of admission. ⊠ *Port Maria* ☎ *876/725–0920* ✉ *$10* ⊙ *Mon.–Thurs. and Sat. 9–5.*

Mystic Mountain. This is Ocho Rios' newest attraction, covering 100 acres of mountainside rain forest near Dunn's River Falls. Visitors board the Rainforest Sky Explorer, a chairlift that soars through and over the pristine rain forest to the apex of Mystic Mountain. On top, there is a restaurant with spectacular views of Ocho Rios, arts-and-crafts shops, and the attraction's signature tours, the Rainforest Bobsled Jamaica ride and the Rainforest Zipline Tranopy ride. Custom-designed bobsleds, inspired by Jamaica's Olympic bobsled team, run downhill on steel rails with speed controlled by the driver, using simple push-pull levers. Couples can run their bobsleds in tandem. The zipline tours streak through lush rain forest under the care of an expert guide who points out items of interest. The entire facility was built using environmentally friendly techniques and materials so as to leave the native rain forest undisturbed. ⊠ *North Coast Hwy., Ocho Rios* ☎ *876/974–3990* ⊕ *www.rainforestadventure.com* ✉ *$42 (tram only), $62 (tram and bobsled), $104 (tram and zipline), $124 (tram, bobsled, and zipline)* ⊙ *Sun.–Thurs. 7:30–5, Fri. and Sat. 7:30 am–10 pm.*

RUNAWAY BAY

Green Grotto Caves. A good choice for rainy days, these caves offer 45-minute guided tours that include a look at a subterranean lake. The cave has a long history as a hiding place for everyone from fearsome pirates to runaway slaves to the Spanish governor (he was on the run from the British at the time). It's a good destination if you want to see one of Jamaica's caves without going too far off the beaten path. You'll feel like a spelunker, since you must wear a hard hat throughout the tour. ⊠ *North Coast Hwy., 2 mi (3 km) east of Discovery Bay* ☎ *876/973–2841* ⊕ *www.greengrottocavesja.com* ✉ *$20* ⊙ *Daily 9–4.*

NORTHEAST COAST

PORT ANTONIO

The first Port Antonio tourists arrived in the early 20th century seeking a respite from New York winters. In time, the area became fashionable among a fast-moving crowd that included everyone from Rudyard Kipling to Bette Davis; today, celebs such as Tom Cruise, Eddie Murphy, Brooke Shields, and Denzel Washington dodge the limelight with a getaway in this quiet haven. Although the action has moved elsewhere, the area can still weave a spell. Robin Moore wrote *The French Connection* here, and Broadway's tall and talented Tommy Tune found inspiration for the musical *Nine* while being pampered at Trident. Today Port Antonio is one of Jamaica's quietest getaways, primarily preferred by long-staying Europeans. Even with the recent improvement of the North Coast Highway from Ocho Rios to Port Antonio, tourism remains slow here, and several attractions have shuttered their doors because of low tourism numbers. Port Antonio has also long been a center for some of the Caribbean's finest deep-sea fishing. Dolphin (the delectable fish, not the lovable mammal) is the likely catch here, along with tuna, kingfish, and wahoo. In October the weeklong Blue Marlin Tournament attracts anglers from around the world. By the time they've all had their fill of beer, it's the fish stories—rather than the fish—that carry the day.

★ **Boston Beach.** A short drive east of Port Antonio is Boston Beach, a don't-miss destination for lovers of jerk pork. The recipe may have originated with the Arawak, the island's original inhabitants, but modern jerk was perfected by the Maroons. Eating almost nothing but wild hog preserved over smoking coals enabled these former slaves to survive years of fierce guerrilla warfare with the English. Jerk resurfaced in the 1930s, and the spicy barbecue drew diners from around the island. Today a handful of small jerk stands, collectively known as the Boston Jerk Centre, offers fiery flavors cooled by some *festival* bread (similar to a southern hush puppy) and a cold Red Stripe. ⊠ *Rte. A4, east of Port Antonio, Port Antonio.*

DeMontevin Lodge. On Titchfield Hill, the DeMontevin Lodge is owned by the Mullings family. The late Gladys Mullings was Errol Flynn's cook, and you can still sample her recipes here. The lodge, and a number of structures on nearby Musgrave Street, is built in a traditional seaside style that's reminiscent of New England. ⊠ *19 Fort George St., Port Antonio* ☎ *876/993–2604.*

Rio Grande. Jamaica's river-rafting operations began here, on an 8-mi-long (13-km-long), swift, green waterway from Berrydale to Rafter's Rest. (Beyond that, the Rio Grande flows into the Caribbean at St. Margaret's Bay.) The trip of about three hours is made on bamboo rafts pushed along by a guide who is likely to be quite a character. You can pack a picnic lunch to enjoy on the raft or on the riverbank; wherever you lunch, a Red Stripe vendor is likely to appear. A restaurant, a bar, and several souvenir shops can be found at Rafter's Rest. ⊠ *Rte. A4, 5 mi (8 km) west of Port Antonio.*

★ **Somerset Falls.** On the Daniels River, these falls are in a veritable botanical garden. A concrete walk to the falls takes you past the ruins of a Spanish aqueduct and Genesis Falls before reaching Hidden Falls. At Hidden Falls, you board a boat and travel beneath the tumbling water; more daring travelers can swim in a whirlpool or jump off the falls into a pool of water. A bar and restaurant specializing in local seafood is a great place to catch your breath. ⊠ *Rte. A4, 13 mi (21 km) west of Port Antonio* ☎ *876/913–0046* ⊕ *www.somersetfallsjamaica.com* ⊠ *$12* ⊗ *Daily 9–5.*

14

SOUTHEAST

KINGSTON

Few leisure travelers—particularly Americans—take the time to visit Kingston, because it's not reachable on a day trip from anywhere on the island besides Ocho Rios or the Blue Mountains. It's also a tough city to love. It's big and, all too often, bad, with gang-controlled neighborhoods that are known to erupt into violence, especially near election time.

However, if you've seen other parts of the island and yearn to know more about the heart and soul of Jamaica, Kingston is worth a visit despite big-city security concerns. The government and business center is also a cultural capital, home to numerous dance troupes, theaters, and museums. Indeed, Kingston seems to reflect more of the true Jamaica—a wonderful cultural mix—than do the sunny havens of the north coast. As one Jamaican put it, "You don't really know Jamaica until you know Kingston." It's also home to the University of the West Indies, one of the Caribbean's largest universities. In March 2007 Kingston played host to cricket's World Cup, serving as the site of the opening ceremonies and drawing the attention of the world to the island.

Kingston sprawls in every direction. To the west, coming in from Spanish Town, lie some of the city's worst slums, in the neighborhoods of Six Miles and Riverton City. Farther south, Spanish Town Road skirts through a high-crime district that many Kingstonians avoid. In the heart of the business district, along the water, the pace is more peaceful, with a lovely walk and parks on Ocean Boulevard. Also here is the Jamaica Convention Centre, home of the U.N. body that creates all laws for the world's seas. From the waterfront you can look across Kingston Harbour to the Palisadoes Peninsula. This narrow strip is where you can find Norman Manley International Airport and, farther west, Port Royal, the island's former capital, which was destroyed by an earthquake in 1692. Downtown Kingston is considered unsafe, particularly at night, so be careful whenever you go.

Most travelers head to New Kingston, north of downtown. This is home to hotels and offices as well as several historic sites. New Kingston is bordered by Old Hope Road on the east and Half Way Tree Road (which changes to Constant Spring Road) on the west. The area is sliced by Hope Road, a major thoroughfare that connects this region with the University of the West Indies, about 15 minutes east of New Kingston.

North of New Kingston, the city gives way to steep hills and magnificent homes. East of here, the views are even grander as the road winds into the Blue Mountains. Hope Road, just after the University of the West Indies, becomes Gordon Town Road and starts twisting up through the mountains—it's a route that leaves no room for error.

★ **Bob Marley Museum.** At the height of his career, Bob Marley purchased a house on Kingston's Hope Road and added a recording studio—painted Rastafarian red, yellow, and green, of course. It now houses this museum, the capital's best-known tourist site. The guided tour takes you through rooms wallpapered with magazine and newspaper articles that chronicle his rise to stardom. The tour includes a 20-minute biographical film on Marley's career; there's also a reference library if you want to learn more. A striking mural by Jah Bobby, *The Journey of Superstar Bob Marley,* depicts the hero's life from its beginnings, in a womb shaped like a coconut, to enshrinement in the hearts of the Jamaican people. ⊠ *56 Hope Rd., Kingston* ☎ *876/927–9152* ⊕ *www. bobmarley-foundation.com* ⊠ *$20* ⊙ *Mon.–Sat. 9:30–4.*

Devon House. Built in 1881 as the mansion of the island's first black millionaire, then bought and restored by the government in the 1960s,

Devon House is filled with period furnishings, such as Venetian-crystal chandeliers and period reproductions. You can visit the two-story mansion (built with a South American gold miner's fortune) only on a guided tour. On the grounds you can find some of the island's best crafts shops, as well as one of the few mahogany trees to have survived Kingston's ambitious but not always careful development. ⊠ *26 Hope Rd., Kingston* ☎ *876/929–6602* ✆ *House tour $8* ☉ *House Mon. Thurs. 9:30–4:30, Fri. and Sat 9·30 4.*

★ **National Gallery.** The artists represented at the National Gallery may not be household names, but their paintings are sensitive and moving. You can find works by such Jamaican masters as painter John Dunkley and sculptor Edna Manley. Among other highlights from the 1920s through 1980s are works by the artist Kapo, a self-taught painter who specialized in religious images. The gallery's exhibition program introduces visitors to the work of contemporary Jamaican artists through events such as The National Biennial and the National Visual Arts Competition and Exhibition, which are staged annually each July and August, respectively. Guided tours are offered for $28 and must be booked in advance of your visit. ⊠ *12 Ocean Blvd., near waterfront, Kingston* ☎ *876/922–1561* ⊕ *www.natgalja.org.jm* ✆ *$2.80* ☉ *Tues.–Thurs. 10–4:30, Fri. 10–4, Sat. 10–3.*

Port Royal. Just south of Kingston, Port Royal was called "the wickedest city in Christendom" until an earthquake tumbled much of it into the sea in 1692. The spirits of Henry Morgan and other buccaneers add energy to what remains. The proudest possession of St. Peter's Church, rebuilt in 1726 to replace Christ's Church, is a silver communion set said to have been donated by Morgan himself (who probably obtained it during a raid on Panama).

A ferry from the square in downtown Kingston goes to Port Royal at least twice a day, but most visitors arrive by road, continuing past the airport to this small community. If you drive out to Port Royal from Kingston, you pass several other sights, including remains of old forts virtually overgrown with vegetation, an old naval cemetery (which has some intriguing headstones), and a monument commemorating Jamaica's first coconut tree, planted in 1863 (there's no tree there now, just plenty of cactus and scrub brush). You can no longer down rum in Port Royal's legendary 40 taverns, but two small pubs remain in operation.

You can explore the remnants of **Fort Charles**, once the city's largest garrison. Built in 1662, this is the oldest surviving structure from the British occupation. On the grounds you can find an old artillery store-house, called Giddy House, which gained its name after being tilted by the earthquake of 1907. Locals say its slant makes you dizzy. The Fort Charles Maritime Museum is housed in what was once the headquarters for the British Royal Navy. Admiral Horatio Nelson served as a naval lieutenant here in 1779. The museum features a re-creation of Nelson's private quarters, as well as other artifacts from the era, including models of various sailing vessels. ⊠ *12 Long La., Port Royal* ☎ *876/967–8438* ✆ *$5* ☉ *Weekdays 9–5.*

14

BLUE MOUNTAINS

★ **Blue Mountains.** Best known as the source of Blue Mountain coffee, these mountains rising out of the lush jungle north of Kingston are a favorite destination with adventure travelers, as well as hikers, birders, and anyone looking to see what lies beyond the beach. You can find guided tours to the mountains from the Ocho Rios and Port Antonio areas, as well as from Kingston. Unless you're traveling with a local, don't try to go on your own; the roads wind and dip without warning, and hand-lettered signs blow away, leaving you without a clue as to which way to go. It's best to hire a taxi (look for red PPV license plates to identify a licensed cab) or book a guided tour.

The site of Jamaica's government-owned coffee plant, the small town of Mavis Bank is northeast of Kingston on the main road to Blue Mountain Peak. An hour-long guided tour of **Mavis Bank Coffee Factory** takes you through the processing of coffee, from planting to distribution. Inquire about tours when you arrive at the main office. ✉ *Gordon Town Rd., Mavis Bank* ☎ *876/977–8528* ⊕ *www.jablumonline.com* 🖾 *$8* ⊙ *Weekdays 9–2.*

SOUTHWEST COAST

★ **Appleton Estate.** Before the rise of tourism as Jamaica's main industry, the island was highly prized for its sugarcane production. Vast fortunes were made here during colonial times, and many of the island's historic greathouses remain as reminders of that time. Much of the sugarcane was processed into molasses, the main ingredient in the production of rum. Appleton Estate, still one of the Caribbean's premier rum distillers, offers guided tours illustrating the history of rum making in the region. After a lively discussion of the days when sugarcane was crushed by donkey power, the tours move on to a behind-the-scenes tour of the modern facility. After the tour, samples flow freely, and every visitor receives a complimentary bottle of rum. There's a good restaurant here serving genuine Jamaican dishes. ✉ *Hwy. B6, Siloah* ☎ *876/963–9215* ⊕ *www.appletonrum.com* 🖾 *$18* ⊙ *Mon.– Sat. 9–3:30.*

Lovers' Leap. As legend has it, two slaves who were in love chose to jump off this 1,700-foot cliff rather than be recaptured by their master. Today it's a favorite stop with travelers, who enjoy a drink at the bar (try the lover's punch) and a view of the coastline. Tours of local cacti are available, and a small farm demonstrates the dry-farming technique used in this area. ✉ *Yardley Chase, Treasure Beach* ☎ *876/365–6577* 🖾 *$1.50* ⊙ *Daily 9–5.*

★ **Y.S. Falls.** A quiet alternative to Dunn's River Falls in Ocho Rios, the falls are part of a cattle and thoroughbred horse farm and are reached via motorized jitney. If you aren't staying on the South Coast, companies in Negril offer half-day excursions. The last tour of the day begins at 3:30. ✉ *North of A2, just past town of Middle Quarters* ☎ *876/997–6360* ⊕ *www.ysfalls.com* 🖾 *$15.50* ⊙ *Tues.–Sun. 9:30–4:30.*

EN ROUTE   Although the constant roar of speeding trucks keeps the site from being idyllic, **Bamboo Avenue,** the section of Route A1 between Middle

Quarters and Lacovia, is an often-photographed stretch of highway that's completely canopied with tall bamboo. Roadside vendors sell chilled coconuts, cracking them with machetes to reveal the jelly inside.

WEST COAST

NEGRIL

In the 18th century, English ships assembled here in convoys for dangerous ocean crossings. The infamous pirate Calico Jack and his crew were captured right here while they guzzled rum. All but two of them were hanged on the spot; Mary Read and Anne Bonney were pregnant at the time, so their executions were delayed.

On the winding coast road 55 mi (89 km) southwest of MoBay, Negril was once Jamaica's best-kept secret, but it has shed some of its bohemian, ramshackle atmosphere for the attractions and activities traditionally associated with MoBay. One thing that hasn't changed about this west-coast center (whose only true claim to fame is a 7-mi [11-km] beach) is a casual approach to life. As you wander from lunch in the sun to shopping in the sun to sports in the sun, you'll find that swimsuits and cover-ups are common attire.

Negril stretches along the coast south from horseshoe-shaped Bloody Bay (named when it was a whale-processing center) along the calm waters of Long Bay to the lighthouse. Nearby, divers spiral downward off 50-foot-high cliffs into the deep green depths as the sun turns into a ball of fire and sets the clouds ablaze with color. Sunset is also the time when Norman Manley Boulevard, which intersects West End Road, comes to life with bustling bistros and ear-splitting discos.

⊙ ★ **Kool Runnings Waterpark.** Billing itself as "The Greatest Chill under the Sun," this park makes a good beach alternative on days when the sea is rough or for travelers not staying at beachfront properties. Admission to the park includes 10 waterslides and a ¼-mi lazy-river float ride; a go-kart track and bungee trampoline each have a separate charge. The park's newest attraction is the Kool Swamp Adventure, a 20-minute guided boat tour of the Great Morass (additional cost of $7). Kids less than 48 inches tall can't use some slides so a discounted rate ($19) is charged. ⊠ *Norman Manley Blvd.* ☎ *876/957–5418* ⊕ *www. koolrunnings.com* ⊴ *$28* ⊙ *Early Oct.–mid-May, Wed. and weekends 11–6; late May–early Sept., Tues.–Sun. 11–7.*

WHERE TO EAT

It would be a shame to travel to the heart of this complex culture without having at least one typical island meal. Probably the most famous Jamaican dish is jerk pork—the ultimate island barbecue. The pork (purists cook a whole pig) is covered with a paste of Scotch bonnet peppers, pimento berries (also known as allspice), and other herbs, and cooked slowly over a coal fire. Many aficionados believe the best jerk comes from Boston Beach, near Port Antonio. Jerk chicken and fish are also seen on many menus. The ever-so-traditional rice and peas, also known as "coat of arms," is similar to the *moros y cristianos* of Spanish-speaking islands:

white rice cooked with red kidney beans, coconut milk, scallions, and seasonings.

The island's most famous soup—the fiery pepper pot—is a spicy mixture of salt pork, salt beef, okra, and the island green known as callaloo. Patties (spicy meat pies) elevate street food to new heights. Although patties actually originated in Haiti, Jamaicans excel at making them. Curried goat is another island standout: young goat is cooked with spices and is more tender and has a gentler flavor than the lamb for which it was substituted by immigrants from India. Salted fish was once the best that islanders could do between catches. Out of necessity, a breakfast staple (and the national dish of Jamaica) was invented. It joins seasonings with saltfish and ackee, a red fruit that grows on trees throughout the island. When cooked in this dish, ackee reminds most people of scrambled eggs.

There are fine restaurants in all the resort areas, many in the resorts themselves, though the Kingston area has the widest selection. Many restaurants outside the hotels in MoBay and Ocho Rios will provide complimentary transportation.

WHAT TO WEAR

Dinner dress is usually casual chic (or just plain casual at many local hangouts, especially in Negril). There are a few exceptions in Kingston and at the top resorts; some require semiformal wear (no shorts; collared shirts for men) in the evening during high season. People tend to dress up for dinner; men might be more comfortable in nice slacks, women in a sundress.

> **BEST BETS FOR DINING**
>
> **Fodor's Choice ★**
> Boston Jerk Centre, Evita's Italian Restaurant, Pork Pit, Redbones Blues Café, Scotchies Too, Strawberry Hill, Three Palms Restaurant
>
> **BEST LOCAL FOOD**
> Boston Jerk Centre, Pork Pit, Scotchies, Scotchies Too
>
> **BEST FOR A SPECIAL OCCASION**
> Strawberry Hill, Three Palms Restaurant

MONTEGO BAY

$$ ✕ **The Groovy Grouper Beach Bar and Grill.** Located on Doctor's Cave
JAMAICAN Beach at the Beach Club, this casual eatery may be a tourist favorite because of its location, but it offers a menu of genuine Jamaican and other Caribbean dishes. Sit outside beneath the thatched roof and start with Jamaican fish tea (a local soup) or conch fritters, and then move on to a grouper burger, fish and *bammy* (fried cassava bread), escoveitch fish (fish topped with a vinegar and Scotch bonnet pepper mixture), or the signature dish, an 8-ounce grouper fillet dusted with jerk spices. Steaks and burgers round out the menu options. ✉ *Gloucester Ave.* ☎ *876/952–8287.*

$$$ ✕ **Marguerites Seafood By the Sea.** At this romantic seaside restaurant,
SEAFOOD flambé is the operative word. Lobster, shrimp, fish, and several desserts are prepared in dancing flames as you sip an exotic cocktail. The

CLOSE UP

Barbecue, Jamaica-Style

Modern jerk originated in the 1930s along Boston Beach, east of Port Antonio. Here, the first wayside stands sprang up on the side of the road, offering fiery jerk served in a casual atmosphere. Today, jerk stands are everywhere on the island, but many aficionados still return to Boston Beach for the "real thing," which is sold by the pound.

The practice of jerking meat was first recorded in 1698 by a French priest, who wrote of a jerk pit made with four forked sticks with crosspieces covered with a grill made of sticks. On the grill was placed a whole pig, stuffed with lime juice, salt, pimento, and spices that helped preserve the meat in the hot climate.

Today, jerk is still cooked in a pit that contains a fire made from pimento wood. The meat, which is primarily pork but can also be chicken, goat, or fish, is marinated with jerk sauce. Every cook has his own favorite recipe, but most include allspice (pimento berries), cloves, garlic, onion, ginger, cinnamon, thyme, and peppers. Commercial jerk sauces are also available. Once the jerk is cooked to perfection, it's served up with side dishes such as breadfruit, rice and peas, and a bread called festival.

14

Caesar salad, prepared table-side, is also a treat. ⊠ *Gloucester Ave.* ☎ *876/952–4777* ⚓ *Reservations essential* ☺ *No lunch.*

$–$$
CARIBBEAN
✕ **The Native.** Shaded by a large poinciana tree and overlooking Gloucester Avenue, this open-air stone terrace serves Jamaican and international dishes. To go native, start with smoked marlin, move on to the *boonoonoonoos* platter (a sampler of local dishes), and round out with coconut pie or *duckanoo* (a sweet dumpling of cornmeal, coconut, and banana wrapped in a banana leaf and steamed). Live entertainment and candlelit tables make this a romantic choice for dinner on weekends. ⊠ *29 Gloucester Ave.* ☎ *876/979–2769.*

$$
SEAFOOD
✕ **Pier 1.** After tropical drinks at the deck bar, you'll be ready to dig into the international variations on fresh seafood; the best are the grilled lobster and any preparation of island snapper. Several party cruises leave from the marina here, and on Friday night the restaurant is mobbed by locals who come to dance. ⊠ *Off Howard Cooke Blvd.* ☎ *876/952–2452.*

¢
JAMAICAN
Fodor's Choice
★
✕ **Pork Pit.** A favorite with many MoBay locals, this no-frills eatery serves Jamaican specialties including some fiery jerk—note that it's spiced to local tastes, not watered down for tourist palates. Many get their food to go, but you can also find picnic tables just outside. ⊠ *27 Gloucester Ave.* ☎ *876/940–3008.*

$$
BRITISH
✕ **The Royal Stocks.** In Half Moon's Shopping Village, this pub brings a slice of jolly old England to Jamaica, from its dark decor to its menu featuring shepherd's pie, bangers and mash, and plenty of fish-and-chips. Umbrella-shaded tables out in the courtyard are the most popular, except on the hottest of days, when visitors retreat to the dark-panel pub. ⊠ *Half Moon Shopping Village, N. Coast Rd., 7 mi (11 km) east of Montego Bay* ☎ *876/953–9770.*

¢   **✗Scotchies**. Many call this open-air jerk eatery the best in Jamaica, but
JAMAICAN   Scotchies Too in Ocho Rios certainly makes it a tough decision. Like
★   its sister restaurant, Scotchies serves up genuine jerk—chicken, pork,
fish, sausage, and more—with fiery sauce and delectable side dishes,
including festival (similar to a Southern hush puppy) and rice and peas.
This restaurant is a favorite with Montego Bay residents; on a typical
day, you're likely to see a slap-the-table game of dominoes. ⊠ *North
Coast Hwy., across from Holiday Inn SunSpree, 10 mi (16 km) east of
Montego Bay* ☎ *876/953–3340.876/953–3340*

$$$$ **✗Sugar Mill**. Seafood is served with flair at this terrace restaurant on
ECLECTIC   the Half Moon golf course. Taking a cue from the diverse cultures that
★   season the Caribbean kitchen, Sugar Mill's chefs have fused the region's
many culinary influences to create a mélange of tastes that can accu-
rately be deemed Caribbean-fusion. Recipes and methods from Europe,
Asia, Africa, and the Americas are joined together in a "melting pot"
to create new exotic flavors to tempt the appetite and awaken the palate. Live music and a well-stocked wine cellar round out the experience. ⊠ *Half Moon, N. Coast Rd., 7 mi (11 km) east of Montego Bay*
☎ *876/953–2228* ⚑ *Reservations essential.*

$$$$ **✗Three Palms Restaurant**. This fine-dining enclave serves Jamaican as
JAMAICAN   well as Continental cuisine with a gourmet twist all presided over by
Fodor's Choice   executive chef Michael Dannecker. Born and trained in the culinary
★   arts in his native Switzerland, Dannecker was named Chef of the Year
in 2010 by the Culinary Federation of Jamaica. At Three Palms, he has
revamped the menus to include more dishes combining local ingredients with modern flair. Menu highlights include thyme-spiked chicken
breast served on sautéed callaloo and pumpkin mash; fillet of snapper
with Ting and ginger broth served with jasmine rice; and chicken satay
glazed with Appleton Rum. Located within Cinnamon Hill's Ocean
Course Clubhouse, the restaurant includes both indoor and alfresco
dining options with scenic views of the countryside. ⊠ *Hilton Rose
Hall Resort & Spa, North Coast Hwy., St. James* ✛ *15 mi (24 km)
east of Montego Bay* ☎ *876/953–2650* ⊕ *www.RoseHallResort.com*
⚑ *Reservations essential* ☾ *No lunch.*

OCHO RIOS

$$ **✗Evita's Italian Restaurant**. Evita's commands a wonderful view of Ocho
ECLECTIC   Rios and the sea from its outdoor verandah dining area. Just about
Fodor's Choice   every celebrity who has visited Ocho Rios has dined at this hilltop
★   restaurant, and Evita has the pictures to prove it. Guests feel like stars
themselves, with attentive waitstaff helping to guide them through a
list of about 30 kinds of pasta, ranging from lasagna Rastafari (vegetar-
ian) and fiery jerk spaghetti to *Ravioli Eccellenza* (jumbo cheese ravioli
tossed in baby-shrimp tomato-Alfredo sauce and laced with Sambuca).
Kids under 12 eat for half price, and light eaters will appreciate half
portions. The restaurant offers free transportation from area hotels.
⊠ *Mantalent Inn, Eden Bower Rd., Ocho Rios* ⌁ *Box 118, Ocho Rios,
Jamaica* ☎ *876/974–2333.*

¢   **✗Ocho Rios Village Jerk Centre**. This blue-canopied, open-air eatery is
JAMAICAN   a good place to park yourself for frosty Red Stripe beer and fiery jerk

Fresh shrimp offered at a colorful roadside stand.

pork, chicken, or seafood. Milder barbecued meats, also sold by weight (typically, a quarter or half pound makes a good serving), turn up on the fresh-daily chalkboard menu posted on the wall. It's lively at lunch, especially when passengers from cruise ships swamp the place. ✉ *Da Costa Dr., Ocho Rios* ☎ *876/974-2549.*

¢ ✕ **Scotchies Too.** The Ocho Rios branch of the longtime Montego Bay
CARIBBEAN favorite has already been lauded by international chefs for its excellent
Fodor's Choice jerk. The open-air eatery offers plates of jerk chicken, sausage, fish,
★ pork, and ribs, all accompanied by festival, bammy, and some fire-breathing hot sauce. Be sure to step over to the kitchen to watch the preparation of the jerk over the pits. ✉ *North Coast Hwy., Drax Hall, Ocho Rios* ☎ *876/794-9457.*

PORT ANTONIO

¢ ✕ **Boston Jerk Centre.** Actually a collection of about half a dozen open-air
JAMAICAN stands, this supercasual eatery is a culinary capital in Jamaica thanks
Fodor's Choice to its popular jerk pits. Stroll up to the open pits, fired by pimento logs
★ and topped with a piece of corrugated roofing metal, locally known as zinc, and order meat by the quarter, half, or full pound; chicken, pork, goat, and fish are top options. Side dishes are few but generally include festival and rice and peas. ✉ *Boston Beach on Rte. A4, Port Antonio, east of Port Antonio* ☎ *No phone* 🗀 *No credit cards.*

$$ ✕ **Norma's at the Marina.** Another showcase for the culinary talents of the
JAMAICAN late Jamaican celebrity-chef Norma Shirley (her other establishments
★ are in Kingston and Negril), this seaside restaurant serves gourmet dishes with a Jamaican twist. Start with an appetizer of smoked marlin

or grilled, deviled, ocean-crab back, then move on to entrées such as grilled shrimp in Jamaican herbs and mango salsa or pork riblets with local seasonings. ⊠ *Errol Flynn Marina, Ken Wright Dr., Port Antonio* ☎ *876/993–9510* ⊘ *Closed Mon.*

KINGSTON

$$ ✕ **Redbones Blues Café.** In a colonial-era residence, this restaurant lets
JAMAICAN you choose between tables in two dining rooms, outdoors on the ter-
Fodor'sChoice race, or in the courtyard. The menu was created by the late Norma
★ Shirley (of Norma's fame), so look for interesting dishes like chicken breast stuffed with callaloo and jerk cheddar, or guava-glazed lamb chops. Open for lunch on weekdays, the café really comes alive during dinner, when meals are accompanied by live jazz or events ranging from fashion shows to poetry readings. ⊠ *21 Braemar Ave., Kingston* ☎ *876/978–8262* ⚱ *Reservations essential* ⊘ *Closed Sun. No lunch Sat.*

$$$ ✕ **Strawberry Hill.** A favorite with Kingstonians for its elegant Sunday
JAMAICAN brunch, Strawberry Hill is well worth the drive from the city. The open-
Fodor'sChoice air terrace has a spectacular view of Kingston and the countryside.
★ Entrées range from grilled snapper with a balsamic reduction to a variety of jerked meats, including a lamb rack with a guava glaze. ⊠ *Strawberry Hill, New Castle Rd., Irishtown, St. Andrew* ☎ *876/944–8400* ⚱ *Reservations essential.*

SOUTHWEST COAST

¢ ✕ **Billy's Grassy Park.** A true side-of-the-road stop on the South Coast
JAMAICAN Highway, Billy's Grassy Park serves fiery Jamaican food, includ-
★ ing scorching peppered shrimp caught just behind the kitchen. Dining's mostly a grab-and-go affair, although stands next door provide local desserts like fresh coconut jelly to cool the burn. ⊠ *A2, about 30 mins east of Whitehouse, Middlequarters* ☎ *876/366–4182* ▬ *No credit cards.*

$$ ✕ **Jack Sprat Restaurant.** It's no surprise that this restaurant shares its
ECLECTIC home resort's bohemian style (it's the beachside dining spot at Jake's).
★ From the casual outdoor tables to the late-night dance-hall rhythm, it's a place to come and hang loose. Jerk crab joins favorites like pizzas and jerk chicken on the menu, all followed by house-made ice cream. ⊠ *Jake's, Calabash Bay, Treasure Beach* ☎ *876/965–3583.*

$–$$ ✕ **Little Ochie.** This casual beachside eatery is a favorite with locals and
JAMAICAN travelers, favored for its genuine Jamaican dishes like fish tea, escoveitch
★ fish, peppered shrimp, jerk chicken, seapuss (octopus), and more. Most of the seafood is brought in by fishermen just yards away. For those staying in Treasure Beach, a favorite way to reach Little Ochie is by boat. ⊠ *About 7 mi (11 km) south of A2, Alligator Pond* ☎ *876/382–3375* ⊕ *www.littleochie.com.*

NEGRIL

$$
SEAFOOD

✕**Cosmo's Seafood Restaurant and Bar.** Owner Cosmo Brown has made this seaside open-air bistro a pleasant place to spend the afternoon—and maybe stay on for dinner. Fish is the main attraction, and the conch soup—a house specialty—is a meal in itself. You can also find lobster (grilled or curried), fish-and-chips, and the catch of the morning. Customers often drop cover-ups to take a dip before coffee and dessert and return to lounge in chairs scattered under almond and sea grape trees (there's an entrance fee of $3.50 for the beach). ⊠ *Norman Manley Blvd., Negril* ☎ *876/957–4330 or 876/957–4784.*

$
ECLECTIC

✕**Kuyaba on the Beach.** This charming thatch-roof eatery has an international menu—including curried conch, kingfish steak, grilled lamb with sautéed mushrooms, and several pasta dishes—plus a lively ambience, especially at the bar. There's a crafts shop on the premises, and chaise longues line the beach; come prepared to spend some time, and don't forget a towel and bathing suit. ⊠ *Norman Manley Blvd., Negril* ☎ *876/957–4318.*

$$$
FRENCH
Fodor's Choice
★

✕**Le Vendome.** At the middle-of-the-road Charela Inn, you might expect this place to be a simple eatery featuring standard beach fare. Le Vendome is fine dining at its best—with the added attraction of a beachside location. From fine wines to crusty bread baked fresh daily, this restaurant serves French cuisine with a hint of Jamaica (don't be surprised to see a dusting of jerk spice or ginger). The restaurant features a different five-course gourmet dinner every evening, but you can always order à la carte, and there are always dishes such as filet mignon in wine-and-mushroom sauce, duck à l'orange, and shrimp in garlic sauce. On Thursday nights, the restaurant offers live jazz, blues, and reggae, while Sunday nights showcase folkloric music with Rastafarian drummers. Shows start at 7:30 pm. ⊠ *Norman Manley Blvd., Negril* ☎ *876/957–4277* ⊕ *www.charela.com* ⌕ *Reservations essential.*

$$
CARIBBEAN
★

✕**Norma's on the Beach.** Although it's in the modest boutique hotel Sea Splash, make no mistake: this is Jamaican dining at some of its finest. Norma is the late Norma Shirley, one of Jamaica's best-known culinary artists, often called the Julia Child of the Caribbean. Opt for terrace or candlelit dining. The dressed-up Jamaican fare is prepared with a creative flair. Try callaloo-stuffed chicken breast or jerk-chicken pasta. ⊠ *Sea Splash Hotel, Norman Manley Blvd., Negril* ☎ *876/957–4041.*

$$–$$$
CARIBBEAN
★

✕**Rick's Cafe.** It's hard to keep a good café–tourist attraction down, even when a force like Hurricane Ivan blew through in 2004, sending much of the establishment into the sea. By 2005, Rick's had been rebuilt and was bigger than ever, with two floors of dining options along with poolside cabanas for rent—as well as the cliff diving and sunset views the restaurant has been known for since 1974. Menu options range from escoveitch shrimp to jerk chicken skewers to steak. ⊠ *West End Rd., Negril* ☎ *876/957–0380* ⊕ *www.rickscafejamaica.com.*

14

WHERE TO STAY

Jamaica was the birthplace of the Caribbean all-inclusive resort, a concept that started in Ocho Rios and has spread throughout the island, now comprising the lion's share of hotel rooms. Package prices usually include airport transfers, accommodations, three meals a day, snacks, all bar drinks (often including premium liquors) and soft drinks, a full menu of sports options (including scuba diving and golf at high-end establishments), nightly entertainment, and all gratuities and taxes. At most all-inclusive resorts, the only surcharges are for such luxuries as spa and beauty treatments, telephone calls, tours, vow-renewal ceremonies, and weddings (though even weddings are often included at high-end establishments).

> ## BEST BETS FOR LODGING
>
> **Fodor's** Choice★
> Breezes Grand Negril, Breezes Runaway Bay, the Caves, Half Moon, Hotel Mockingbird Hill, Jake's, Jamaica Inn, Rockhouse, Sandals Royal Caribbean, Sandals Royal Plantation Ocho Rios, Sandals Whitehouse, Strawberry Hill
>
> ## BEST FAMILY RESORTS
> Beaches Boscobel, Franklyn D Resort, Holiday Inn SunSpree, Hilton Rose Hall Resort and Spa, Sunset Beach Resort
>
> ## BEST FOR ROMANCE
> Couples Swept Away Negril, Couples Tower Isle

The all-inclusive market is especially strong with couples and honeymooners. To maintain a romantic atmosphere (no Marco Polo games by the pool), some resorts have minimum age requirements ranging from 12 to 18. Other properties court families with tempting supervised kids' programs, family-friendly entertainment, and in-room amenities especially for young travelers.

The following reviews have been condensed for this book. Please go to Fodors.com for expanded reviews of each property.

MONTEGO BAY

MoBay has miles of hotels, villas, apartments, and duty-free shops. Although without much cultural stimulus, it presents a comfortable island backdrop for the many conventions it hosts. And it has the added advantage of being the closest resort area to the island's main airport.

¢–$
ALL-INCLUSIVE
Breezes Resort and Spa Trelawny. This all-inclusive resort (formerly Starfish Trelawny) is operated by SuperClubs and is a favorite with families. **Pros:** good value; excellent children's program; numerous activities. **Cons:** high-rise balconies can be scary with small children; may not have much appeal for guests not traveling with children. ⊠ *North Coast Hwy., Box 54, Falmouth* ☎ *876/954–2450* ⊕ *www.superclubs. com* ⤳ *350 rooms* ⚬ *In-room: a/c, Internet, Wi-Fi (some). In-hotel: restaurants, tennis courts, bars, children's programs, pools, gym, spa, water sports* ⚏ *3-night minimum* ❏ *All-inclusive.*

$–$$$
RESORT
Coyaba Beach Resort and Club. Privately owned and operated, this intimate property offers a relaxing, welcoming ambience. **Pros:** quiet atmosphere of an inn; excellent restaurants; good-size private beach.

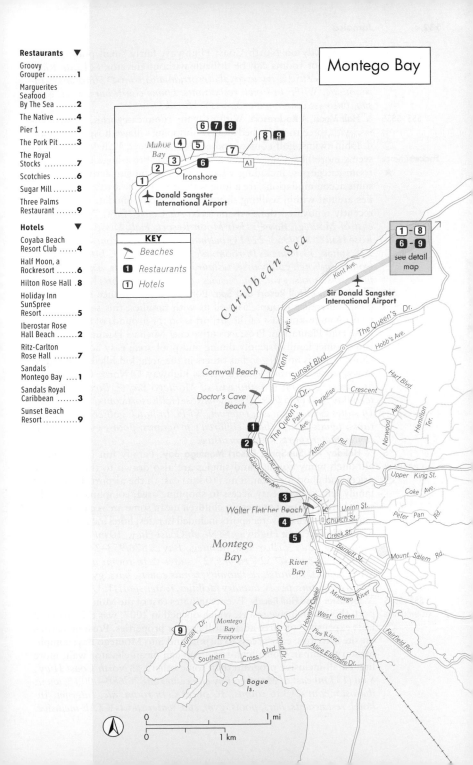

Montego Bay

KEY

⬎ *Beaches*

1 *Restaurants*

① *Hotels*

Caribbean Sea

Sir Donald Sangster
International Airport

Mahoe
Bay

Ironshore

Donald Sangster
International Airport

A1

Kent Ave.

Kent Ave.

Sunset Blvd.

The Queen's Dr.

Hobb's Ave.

Cornwall Beach

Hart Blvd.

Doctor's Cave
Beach

The Queen's Park Ave.

Paradise Dr.

Crescent

Norwood Ave.

Hamilton Ter.

Albion Rd.

Upper King St.

Coke Ave.

Corniche Rd.

Gloucester Ave.

Fort

Union St.

Peter Pan Rd.

Walter Fletcher Beach

Church St.

Creek St.

Barnett St.

Mount Salem Rd.

Montego
Bay

River Bay

Montego River

Blvd.

Howard Cooke

West Green

Pies River

Fairfield Rd.

Montego
Bay Freeport

Sunset Dr.

Coconut Dr.

Alice Eldemire Dr.

Southern Cross Blvd.

Bogue
Is.

0   1 mi
0   1 km

Cons: directly on North Coast Highway; fairly small pool: getting to third-floor rooms can be difficult without elevator. ⊠ *Little River* ☎ *876/953–9150* ⊕ *www.coyabaresortjamaica.com* ⊸ *50 rooms* ♿ *In-room: a/c, Wi-Fi. In-hotel: restaurants, tennis court, bars, pool, gym, spa, business center, water sports* ⏐◎⏐ *Breakfast.*

$$$–$$$$
RESORT
🕙
Fodor's Choice
★

🛏️ **Half Moon, A Rockresort.** With its many room categories, massive villas (with three to seven bedrooms), shopping village, hospital, school, dolphin swims, golf course, and equestrian center, Half Moon almost seems more like a town than a mere resort. **Pros:** huge beach; many room categories, including villas; numerous on-site activities. **Cons:** some accommodations are a long walk from public areas; some activities are not within walking distance; some accommodations are more recently renovated than others. ⊠ *North Coast Hwy., 7 mi (11 km) east of Montego Bay* ⊘ *Half Moon Resort, Half Moon Post Office, Rose Hall* ☎ *876/953–2211* ⊕ *halfmoon.rockresorts.com* ⊸ *45 rooms, 158 suites, 33 villas* ♿ *In-room: a/c, kitchen (some), Internet, Wi-Fi (some). In-hotel: golf course, restaurants, tennis courts, bars, children's programs, pools, gym, spa, business center, water sports* ⏐◎⏐ *No meals.*

$$$
ALL-INCLUSIVE
🕙

🛏️ **Hilton Rose Hall Resort and Spa.** Popular with romance-minded couples, conference groups, as well as with families, this self-contained resort 4 mi (6 km) east of the airport is on the grounds of the 400-acre Rose Hall Plantation. **Pros:** executive chef Michael Dannecker's excellent cuisine; family-friendly dining and pool area; easy access to golf. **Cons:** beach is not as good as others in the area; kid-filled pool can be noisy; some activities located across highway. ⊠ *North Coast Hwy., St. James* ✛ *15 mi (24 km) east of Montego Bay* ⊘ *Box 999, Montego Bay* ☎ *876/953–2650* ⊕ *www.RoseHallResort.com* ⊸ *488 rooms, 14 suites* ♿ *In-room: a/c, Internet, Wi-Fi. In-hotel: golf course, restaurants, tennis courts, bars, children's programs, pools, gym, business center, water sports* ⏐◎⏐ *All-inclusive.*

$
ALL-INCLUSIVE
🕙

🛏️ **Holiday Inn SunSpree Resort Montego Bay.** Family fun is tops here, although many couples and singles are also drawn to the moderate prices and good location, 6 mi (10 km) east of the airport. **Pros:** good family atmosphere; easy access to shopping area; complimentary self-serve laundry. **Cons:** numerous children mean some areas can be noisy; only nonmotorized water sports included in rates; hotel located directly beside North Coast Highway. ⊠ *North Coast Hwy., 10 mi (16 km) east of Montego Bay* ⊘ *Box 480, Montego Bay* ☎ *876/953–2485* ⊕ *www.caribbeanhi.com* ⊸ *524 rooms, 27 suites* ♿ *In-room: a/c, Internet, Wi-Fi (some). In-hotel: restaurants, tennis courts, bars, gym, spa, children's programs, pools, laundry facilities, water sports* ⏐◎⏐ *All-inclusive.*

$$$–$$$$
ALL-INCLUSIVE
🕙

🛏️ **Iberostar Rose Hall Beach.** Twenty minutes east of the Montego Bay airport, this all-inclusive resort, which opened in 2007, was the first (and least expensive) of three adjacent Ibersotar properties. **Pros:** numerous on-site activities; easy access to airport and into Montego Bay; complimentary minibar. **Cons:** high-rise setup can mean elevator wait; more limited all-inclusive program than some others. ⊠ *North Coast Hwy., 8 mi (13 km) east of Montego Bay city center* ☎ *876/680–0000* ⊕ *www.iberostar.com* ⊸ *336 rooms, 36 suites* ♿ *In-room: a/c, Internet. In-hotel: restaurants, bars, pools, gym, spa, water sports* ⏐◎⏐ *All-inclusive.*

Sandals Royal Caribbean Resort & Private Island, Montego Bay.

$$$–$$$$
RESORT

🏨 **Ritz-Carlton Golf & Spa Resort, Rose Hall.** A favorite with conference groups, golfers, and anyone demanding the highbrow service for which the chain is known, this expansive resort lies across the road from the historic Rose Hall estate. **Pros:** excellent meeting and business-travel facilities; great golf; good children's program. **Cons:** generic decor gives no sense of Jamaica; beach is particularly small and disappointing; somewhat formal for a family-friendly resort. ✉ *1 Ritz Carlton Dr., St. James, 15 mi (24 km) east of Montego Bay* ☎ *876/953–2800* ⊕ *www.ritzcarlton.com* 🛏 *427 rooms* ♿ *In-room: a/c, Wi-Fi. In-hotel: golf course, restaurants, tennis courts, bars, children's programs, pool, gym, spa, business center, water sports* 🍽 *No meals.*

$$$$
RESORT

🏨 **Round Hill Hotel and Villas.** A favorite of celebrities thanks to its private and elegant villas, this peaceful resort 8 mi (13 km) west of MoBay also offers 36 traditional hotel rooms in the Pineapple House. **Pros:** personal service; stylish accommodations; quiet atmosphere. **Cons:** somewhat remote location; costly; some villas do not have pools. ✉ *North Coast Hwy., 8 mi (13 km) west of Montego Bay* ☎ *876/956–7050* ⊕ *www.roundhill.com* 🛏 *36 rooms, 27 villas* ♿ *In-room: a/c, kitchen (some), no TV (some), Wi-Fi. In-hotel: restaurants, tennis courts, bar, children's programs, pool, gym, laundry facilities, spa, business center, water sports* 🍽 *No meals.*

$$$$
ALL-INCLUSIVE
Fodor'sChoice
★

🏨 **Sandals Royal Caribbean Resort and Private Island.** This elegant resort 4 mi (6 km) east of the airport—the most upscale of the three Sandals properties in MoBay—consists of Jamaican-style buildings arranged in a semicircle around attractive gardens. **Pros:** numerous room categories; offshore dining; complimentary airport shuttle and shuttle to other Sandals resorts in Montego Bay. **Cons:** some guests might feel the resort is too quiet; smaller beach than Sandals Montego Bay; couples-only policy means some guests can't stay here. ⊠ *North Coast Hwy., 6 mi (9 km) east of Montego Bay city center* ⌖ *Box 167, Montego Bay* ☎ *876/953–2231* ⊕ *www.sandals.com* ⇥ *176 rooms, 14 suites* ⌂ *In-room: a/c, Internet, Wi-Fi. In-hotel: restaurants, room service (some), tennis courts, bars, pools, gym, laundry facilities, spa, business center, water sports, some age restrictions* ⌁ *2-night minimum* ⍥ *All-inclusive.*

$$$–$$$$ ⊞ **Sunset Beach Resort and Spa.** Often packed with charter groups, this
ALL-INCLUSIVE expansive resort is a very good value if you don't mind mass tourism.
☺ **Pros:** excellent beaches; good restaurants; numerous on-site activities. **Cons:** can be crowded; high-rise setup means lines for the elevator; somewhat remote location if you want to explore Montego Bay. ⊠ *5 mi (8 km) west of Montego Bay on Rte. A1, Freeport* ☎ *876/979–8800* ⊕ *www.sunsetbeachresort.com* ⇥ *430 rooms, 15 suites* ⌂ *In-room: a/c, Internet, Wi-Fi. In-hotel: restaurants, tennis courts, bars, children's programs, pools, gym, spa, business center, water sports* ⍥ *All-inclusive.*

$$$$ ⊞ **Tryall Club.** Well known among golfers, Tryall is west of MoBay. **Pros:**
RESORT excellent golf; villa experience with the conveniences of a resort; good family program. **Cons:** nonmember guests must become temporary members of Tryall Club for $100 per person per week fee; shared public facilities; somewhat formal atmosphere. ⊠ *North Coast Hwy., Sandy Bay, 15 mi (24 km) west of Montego Bay* ☎ *876/956–5660* ⊕ *www. tryallclub.com* ⇥ *56 villas* ⌂ *In-room: a/c, no safe, kitchen. In-hotel: golf course, restaurant, tennis courts, bars, children's programs, pool, gym, spa, water sports* ⍥ *No meals.*

OCHO RIOS

Ocho Rios lies on the north coast, halfway between Port Antonio and MoBay. Rivers, waterfalls, fern-shaded roads, and tropical lushness fill this fertile region. It's a favorite with honeymooners as well as Jamaicans who like to escape crowded Kingston for the weekend. The area's resorts, hotels, and villas are all a short drive from the frenetic, traffic-clogged downtown, which has a crafts market, boutiques, duty-free shops, restaurants, and several scenic attractions. The community lies 67 mi (111 km) east of Montego Bay, a drive that takes just under two hours thanks to an improved highway.

$$$$ ⊞ **Beaches Boscobel Resort and Golf Club.** Although this resort is for any-
ALL-INCLUSIVE one—including singles and couples—it's best suited for families, whose
☺ children enjoy supervised activities in one of five kids' clubs divided by age, from infants to teens. **Pros:** excellent children's program; numerous dining options; good options for adults, including spa. **Cons:** long drive from the airport; beach is a long walk (or an elevator ride) from the rooms; resort is distant from Ocho Rios attractions. ⊠ *North Coast Hwy., Box 63, St. Ann's Bay* ☎ *876/975–7777* ⊕ *www.beaches.com* ⇥ *123 rooms, 100 suites* ⌂ *In-room: a/c, Internet, Wi-Fi. In-hotel: restaurants, tennis courts, bars, children's programs, pools, gym, laundry facilities, spa, business center, water sports* ⌁ *2-night minimum* ⍥ *All-inclusive.*

$$$$
ALL-INCLUSIVE

▣ **Couples Sans Souci Resort and Spa.** This classy all-inclusive encourages its guests to check their cares at the entrance and indulge in some soul-nurturing pampering. **Pros:** excellent spa; Free weddings and expansive all-inclusive package; complimentary round-trip airport shuttle from MBJ airport. **Cons:** no reciprocal privileges with Couples Tower Isle; some rooms are very isolated and a long walk from public areas; beaches are not as good as others in area. ⊠ *North Coast Hwy, 2 mi (3 km) east of Ocho Rios, Mammee Bay* ⬚ *Box 103, St. Mary* ☎ *876/994–1206* ⊕ *www.couples.com* ⇆ *150 suites* ♿ *In-room: a/c, Wi-Fi (some). In-hotel: restaurants, tennis courts, bars, pools, gym, spa, water sports, some age restrictions* ⟲ *3-night minimum* ⍟*All-inclusive.*

$$$$
ALL-INCLUSIVE

▣ **Couples Tower Isle.** Renovations in 2004 and 2008 spiffed up the guest rooms of Jamaica's first all-inclusive resort. **Pros:** free weddings; excellent beach facilities; excellent spa. **Cons:** long distance from Montego Bay airport; does not include reciprocal privileges with Couples Sans Souci. ⊠ *Tower Isle, 5 mi (8 km) east of Ocho Rios on A1, Box 330, St. Mary* ☎ *876/975–4271* ⊕ *www.couples.com* ⇆ *200 rooms, 17 suites* ♿ *In-room: a/c, Wi-Fi (some). In-hotel: restaurants, tennis courts, bars, pools, gym, spa, water sports, some age restrictions* ⟲ *3-night minimum* ⍟*All-inclusive.*

$$$–$$$$
RENTAL
★

▣ **Goldeneye Hotel and Resort.** Whether you're a James Bond buff or just a fan of luxury getaways, this exclusive address 20 minutes east of Ocho Rios holds special appeal. Once the home of Bond author Ian Fleming, the estate is now one of the unique Island Outpost properties. **Pros:** unique and spacious accommodations; fitness program lead by Iona Wynter, Jamaican Olympic tri-athlete; plenty of privacy. **Cons:** remote location; limited dining options; may be too quiet for some travelers. ⊠ *North Coast Hwy., Oracabessa* ⬚ *Orcabessa Bay, St. Mary* ☎ *876/975–3354* ⊕ *www.goldeneye.com* ⇆ *1 house, 4 villas, 13 cottages, 6 suites* ♿ *In-room: no a/c (some), kitchen, Wi-Fi. In-hotel: restaurant, bar, pool (some), spa, water sports* ⍟*No meals.*

$$$$
ALL-INCLUSIVE
Fodor's Choice
★

▣ **Jamaica Inn.** Start a conversation about elegant Jamaican resorts, and this quietly sophisticated hotel will surely be mentioned. **Pros:** elegant accommodations; exceptional service; good spa. **Cons:** some travelers may feel it's too quiet; too traditional and stiff for some visitors; no in-room TV. ⊠ *North Coast Hwy., 2 mi (3 km) east of Ocho Rios* ⬚ *Box 1, Ocho Rios, St. Ann* ☎ *876/974–2514* ⊕ *www.jamaicainn.com* ⇆ *51 suites* ♿ *In-room: a/c, no safe, no TV, Internet (some), Wi-Fi (some). In-hotel: restaurant, bar, pool, gym, spa, business center, water sports, some age restrictions* ⍟*All-inclusive.*

¢–$
HOTEL

▣ **Rooms Ocho Rios.** Adjacent to Sunset Jamaica Grande Resort, this SuperClubs–owned hotel, as its name suggests, has a room-only plan (only Continental breakfast is included). **Pros:** good value; good beach; good location from which to explore Ocho Rios. **Cons:** small pool area; limited on-site dining options; limited activities. ⊠ *Main St., Ocho Rios* ⬚ *Box 280, Ocho Rios, St. Ann* ☎ *876/974–6632* ⊕ *www.roomsresorts.com* ⇆ *99 rooms* ♿ *In-room: a/c, Internet, Wi-Fi. In-hotel: restaurant, bar, pool, gym, laundry facilities, business center, water sports* ⍟*Breakfast.*

14

Other Sandals Resorts on Jamaica

CLOSE UP

The Sandals company has the most hotels of any company in Jamaica. Sandals resorts are open only to couples and are all-inclusive in their pricing. *In addition to our favorites, which are reviewed in full in this chapter, the following resorts are also available.*

Sandals Grande Ocho Rios Beach and Villa Resort (⊠ *North Coast Hwy., Box 771, Ocho Rios* ☎ *876/974–5691* ⊕ *www.sandals.com* ☞ *285 rooms, 244 villas*) is the largest resort in the Sandals chain. It includes the "Manor" side with greathouse and villas and the "Riviera" side with easy beach access. Villas, some fairly far from the public areas, have private pools; some villas have as many as

four individual guest suites, each with its own kitchen and living area, that share a single pool.

Sandals Montego Bay (⊠ *N. Kent Ave., 1½ mi (2½ km) east of Montego Bay city center, Montego Bay* ☎ *876/952–5510* ⊕ *www.sandals. com* ☞ *251 rooms*) is minutes from the airport on the largest stretch of beach in MoBay. The "Almond" block of rooms and extensive beach are the resort's best features.

Sandals Negril Beach Resort and Spa (⊠ *Norman Manley Blvd., Negril* ☎ *876/957–5216* ⊕ *www.sandals. com* ☞ *137 rooms, 86 suites*) is at the top of Seven Mile Beach; in 2007, a block of Negril's first swim-up rooms was added.

$$$$ **⚟ Sandals Royal Plantation Ocho Rios.** In October 2010, Royal Plantation
RESORT (which has been owned by Sandals since February 2000 but operated as
Fodor'sChoice a separate resort) joined the Sandals family of resorts, albeit without the
★ all-inclusive trappings of its sisters. **Pros:** accommodations are expansive and stylish; good dining; room service offered. **Cons:** guest rooms and beach are on different levels; small pool; small beach. ⊠ *Main St., Ocho Rios* ⚟ *Box 2, Ocho Rios, St. Ann* ☎ *876/974–5601* ⊕ *www. sandals.com* ☞ *74 suites, 1 villa* ⚟ *In-room: a/c, Internet, Wi-Fi. In-hotel: restaurants, tennis courts, bars, pools, gym, laundry facilities, spa, business center, water sports, some age restrictions* ☞ *2-night minimum* ⚟ *No meals.*

RUNAWAY BAY

The smallest of the resort areas, Runaway Bay, 50 mi (80 km) east of Montego Bay and about 12 mi (19 km) west of Ocho Rios, has a handful of modern hotels, a few all-inclusive resorts, and an 18-hole golf course.

$–$$ **⚟ Breezes Runaway Bay.** This moderately priced SuperClubs resort,
ALL-INCLUSIVE which underwent an extensive renovation and expansion in 2007,
Fodor'sChoice emphasizes an active, sports-oriented vacation—including golf (at the
★ resort's own course), a circus workshop, tennis, and an array of water sports. **Pros:** extensive sports and water sports options; complimentary airport shuttle; low-rise room blocks mean easy beach access. **Cons:** some public areas can feel crowded; small spa; some restaurants are too small to accommodate demand. ⊠ *North Coast Hwy., Runaway Bay* ⚟ *Box 58, Main St., Runaway Bay, St. Ann* ☎ *876/973–6099* ⊕ *www.*

NUDE BEACHES

It is perhaps ironic that Jamaica, one of the most conservative, religious islands in the Caribbean, has many opportunities for naturists to let it all hang out.

TAKING IT OFF

Breezes Rio Bueno gives you an opportunity to go nude, with an entire section of the resort set aside for nudists. In most places in Jamaica, letting it all hang out comes at a premium of up to 20% above the regular rates. Other clothing-optional beaches are found at Hedonism II, SuperFun Beach Resort (formerly Hedonism III),

Breezes Grand Resort and Spa Negril, Couples Negril, Couples Tower Isle, Couples Sans Souci, and Sunset Beach Resort and Spa.

KEEPING IT ON

If you'd rather enjoy the beach in your swimsuit, remember that most of Jamaica's resorts cater to the traditional beachgoer (and all public beaches require swimsuits by law). "Clothing-optional" means you're free to keep your swimsuit (or as much of it) on as you like. Only beaches deemed "nude" actually have a dress code that requires a birthday suit.

14

superclubs.com ⇱ *266 rooms, 20 suites* ⌂ *In-room: a/c, Wi-Fi. In-hotel: golf course, restaurants, tennis courts, bars, pools, gym, spa, business center, water sports, some age restrictions* ☞ *3-night minimum* ⊠ *All-inclusive.*

$$$$
ALL-INCLUSIVE
☺

▦ **FDR, Franklyn D Resort.** A favorite for families with very young children, this relaxed resort goes a step beyond the usual supervised kids' programs, assigning you a professional caregiver who will assist you throughout your stay. **Pros:** good supervised kids' programs; nanny program especially good for young families; spacious accommodations. **Cons:** not appealing to travelers without children; small pool area; rooms need updating. ⊠ *Main Rd., Box 201, Runaway Bay* ☎ *876/973–6987* ⊕ *www.fdrholidays.com* ⇱ *78 suites* ⌂ *In-room: a/c, kitchen (some), Wi-Fi. In-hotel: restaurants, tennis court, bars, children's programs, pool, gym, spa, laundry facilities, water sports, business center.* ⊠ *All inclusive.*

$-$$
ALL-INCLUSIVE

▦ **SuperFun Beach Resort and Spa.** Freshly renamed—but still part of the SuperClub resorts—Superfun is an adults-only resort for travelers looking for fun that includes a waterslide (through the disco, no less). **Pros:** upscale swim-up guest rooms; round-the-clock activities. **Cons:** spring-break-for-adults–type atmosphere; beach is not as good as others in area; not for travelers looking for a quiet getaway. ⊠ *Main Rd., Runaway Bay* ☐ *Box 250, Runaway Bay, St. Ann* ☎ *876/973–4100* ⊕ *www.superclubs.com* ⇱ *210 rooms, 15 suites* ⌂ *In-room: a/c. In-hotel: restaurants, tennis courts, bars, pools, gym, spa, business center, water sports, some age restrictions* ☞ *3-night minimum* ⊠ *All-inclusive.*

PORT ANTONIO

There's a genuine alternative to the hectic tourist scene in Jamaica's bustling resorts Montego Bay and Ocho Rios: Port Antonio. This quiet community is on Jamaica's east end, 133 mi (220 km) west of Montego Bay, and is favored by those looking to get away from it all. Don't look for mixology classes or limbo dances here; this end of Jamaica is quiet and relaxed. The fun is usually found outdoors, followed by a fine evening meal. The area's must-do activities include rafting Jamaica's own Rio Grande, exploring the Nonsuch Caves, and having lunch or a drink at the Jamaica Palace.

$–$$
RENTAL

☷ Goblin Hill Villas at San San. This lush, 12-acre estate atop a hill over-looking San San Bay is best suited for travelers looking for a home-away-from-home atmosphere, not a bustling resort. **Pros:** good for guests who would like a villa experience but with the facilities of a hotel; nice bay views from villa terraces and balconies; spacious accom-modations. **Cons:** long walk to beach; shared lawn and public areas with other villas at complex; some rooms in villas have no a/c. ⊠ *3 mi (5 km) east of Port Antonio on A4, San San* ☎ *876/925–8108* ⊕ *www. goblinhill.com* ⇆ *28 villas* ⚭ *In-room: a/c, no phone, no safe, kitchen. In-hotel: tennis courts, bar, pool* ⍾○⍾ *No meals.*

$$–$$$
HOTEL
Fodor's Choice
★

☷ Hotel Mocking Bird Hill. With only 10 rooms, some overlooking the sea and all with views of lush hillsides, Mocking Bird Hill is much more like a cozy bed-and-breakfast than a hotel. **Pros:** numerous ecotourism options; environmentally conscious; excellent dining. **Cons:** limited on-site din-ing; no a/c (rooms do have fans); somewhat remote location. ⊠ *North Coast Hwy., Point Ann, Box 254, Port Antonio* ⌖ *Drapers Heights, Box 254, Port Antonio* ☎ *876/993–7267 or 876/619–1216* ⊕ *www. hotelmockingbirdhill.com* ⇆ *10 rooms* ⚭ *In-room: no a/c, no phone, no TV. In-hotel: restaurant, bar, pool, business center* ⍾○⍾ *No meals.*

$–$$
HOTEL

☷ Jamaica Palace. The Jamaica Palace might be distinctive for its Jamaica-shaped swimming pool and surrounding black-and-white pool terrace—but that's just the beginning of the unusual aspects of this Port Antonio hotel. **Pros:** uniquely decorated public areas; large poolside area with plenty of seating; good on-site dining options. **Cons:** no beach; basic guest rooms; somewhat remote location. ⊠ *5 mi (8 km) east of Port Antonio on A4, Port Antonio* ☎ *876/993–7720* ⊕ *www.jamaica-palacehotel.com* ⇆ *34 rooms, 46 suites* ⚭ *In-room: a/c, Internet. In-hotel: restaurants, bars, pool, business center* ⍾○⍾ *No meals.*

KINGSTON

Visited by few vacationers but a frequent destination for business trav-elers and visitors with a deep interest in Jamaica heritage and culture, the sprawling city of Kingston is home to some of the island's finest business hotels. Skirting the city are the Blue Mountains, a completely different world from the urban frenzy of the capital city.

¢–$
HOTEL

☷ Jamaica Pegasus. In the heart of the financial district, this 17-story high-rise was renovated in 2009. **Pros:** good business travel facilities; good pool area; easy access to New Kingston business district. **Cons:** limited leisure activities; 17 floors of guest rooms can mean a wait for an elevator. ⊠ *81 Knutsford Blvd., Box 333, Kingston* ☎ *876/926–3690* ⊕ *www.jamaicapegasus.com* ↩ *300 rooms, 19 suites* ⚥ *In-room: a/c, Internet, Wi-Fi. In-hotel: restaurants, tennis courts, bars, pool, gym, spa, business center* ¶◉¶ *No meals.*

$$$$
HOTEL
ALL-INCLUSIVE
Fodor's Choice
★

🖼 **Strawberry Hill**. A 45-minute drive from Kingston—but worlds apart in terms of atmosphere—this exclusive resort was developed by Chris Blackwell, former head of Island Records (the late Bob Marley's label). **Pros:** stylish accommodations with great mountain views; cool retreat from the heat; best spa in Jamaica. **Cons:** remote location a distance from the beaches; limited on-site dining options; too quiet for some guests. ⊠ *New Castle Rd., Irishtown, St. Andrew* ☎ *876/944–8400* ⊕ *www.islandoutpost.com* ↩ *12 cottages* ⚥ *In-room: no a/c, kitchen, Wi-Fi. In-hotel: restaurant, bar, pool, spa* ¶◉¶ *Multiple meal plans.*

$–$$
HOTEL

🖼 **Wyndham Kingston Jamaica**. This stately hotel's tall tower has long been a familiar part of the Kingston skyline. **Pros:** good variety of restaurants; central location; nightly entertainment on-site. **Cons:** limited leisure activities; limited amenities in most rooms; no balconies in some Tower rooms. ⊠ *77 Knutsford Blvd., Box 112, Kingston* ☎ *876/926– 5430* ⊕ *www.wyndham.com* ↩ *303 rooms, 13 suites* ⚥ *In-room: a/c, kitchen (some), Internet, Wi-Fi. In-hotel: restaurants, bars, pool, gym, spa, business center* ¶◉¶ *No meals.*

14

SOUTHWEST COAST

In the 1970s, Negril was Jamaica's most relaxed place to hang out. Today that distinction is held by the South Coast, a long stretch of coastline ranging from Whitehouse to Treasure Beach. Here local residents wave to cars, and travelers spend their days exploring local communities and their nights in local restaurants. The best way to reach the South Coast is from Montego Bay, driving overland, a journey of 90 minutes to two hours, depending on the destination.

$$–$$$
HOTEL
Fodor's Choice
★

🖼 **Jake's**. The laid-back, neighborly feel of the South Coast is epitomized by Jake's, a relaxed place that's fun, funky, and friendly. **Pros:** unique accommodations; infused with South Coast friendliness; personalized service. **Cons:** some rooms can be cramped when housebound during rainy periods; no a/c in some rooms. ⊠ *Calabash Bay, Treasure Beach, St. Elizabeth* ☎ *876/965–3000* ⊕ *www.islandoutpost.com/jakes* ↩ *31 cottages, 3 villas* ⚥ *In-room: no a/c (some), no phone, kitchen (some), no TV (some), Wi-Fi. In-hotel: restaurants, room service (some), pool, water sports* ¶◉¶ *No meals.*

$$$$
ALL-INCLUSIVE
Fodor's Choice
★

🖼 **Sandals Whitehouse European Village and Spa**. The newest Sandals resort in Jamaica and the first major resort on the South Coast, this property is one of the most upscale properties in the chain. **Pros:** great beach with no vendors; numerous dining options and an extensive all-inclusive package that includes airport shuttle; stylish accommodations in all room classes. **Cons:** some travelers won't like Disney-ish re-creation of European styles; dining at other Sandals is available as part of package, but there is no transportation to other properties because of distance; Whitehouse area can be bug-ridden and hot. ⊠ *Whitehouse* ✍ *Box 500, Whitehouse, Westmoreland* ☎ *876/957–5216* ⊕ *www.sandals.com* ↩ *304 rooms,*

54 *suites ♿ In-room: a/c, Internet, Wi-Fi. In-hotel: restaurants, tennis courts, bars, pools, gym, laundry facilities, spa, business center, water sports, some age restrictions ☞ 2-night minimum ❄ All-inclusive.*

$–$$
HOTEL

⊞ **Sunset Resort and Villas.** Next door to Jake's, this resort lacks the style of its attention-getting neighbor, but it still offers a friendly getaway that's lovingly owner-managed. **Pros:** friendly staff; rooms are comfortably large; good location on Calabash Bay. **Cons:** decor is dated and fussy; remote location; limited dining choices. ✉ *Calabash Bay, Treasure Beach* 🕾 *876/965–0143* ⊕ *www.sunsetresort.com* ☎ *14 rooms ♿ In-room: a/c, no phone, no safe, kitchen (some), Wi-Fi. In-hotel: restaurant, pool, laundry service* ❄ *No meals.*

NEGRIL

Some 50 mi (80 km) west of MoBay, Negril was once a hippie hangout, favored for its inexpensive mom-and-pop hotels and laid-back atmosphere. Today there's still a bohemian flair, but the town's one of the fastest-growing tourism communities in Jamaica, with several large all-inclusives along Bloody Bay, northeast of town. The main strip of Negril Beach and the cliffs are still favored by vacationers who like to get out and explore.

$–$$
ALL-INCLUSIVE
Fodor'sChoice
★

⊞ **Breezes Grand Resort and Spa Negril.** Fancy touches at this resort are balanced by an expansive clothing-optional beach (including its own hot tub, bar, and grill), giving you one of Jamaica's best resorts, where it's fun to dress for dinner but equally good to strip down for a day of fun in the sun. **Pros:** excellent beaches; super-inclusive package, including complimentary room service for select rooms; elegant setting. **Cons:** some rooms need updating; central public area lacks view; clothing-optional pool is small. ✉ *Norman Manley Blvd., Box 88, Negril* 🕾 *876/957–5010* ⊕ *www.superclubs.com* ☎ *210 suites ♿ In-room: a/c, Internet. In-hotel: restaurants, room service (some), tennis courts, bars, pools, gym, spa, business center, water sports, some age restrictions ☞ 3-night minimum* ❄ *All-inclusive.*

$$$–$$$$
ALL-INCLUSIVE
Fodor'sChoice
★

⊞ **The Caves.** Although encompassing just 2 tiny acres, this petite resort packs a lot of punch in its cliff-side location, drawing the Hollywood set as well as travelers looking for boutique-style pampering. **Pros:** stylish and unique accommodations; personal service including nightly turndown service; quiet atmosphere. **Cons:** limited on-site dining options; may be too quiet for some travelers; no beach (on cliffs). ✉ *Lighthouse Rd., Negril* ⌖ *Box 3113, Lighthouse Rd., Negril* 🕾 *876/618–1081* ⊕ *www.islandoutpost.com* ☎ *13 rooms, 1 4-bedroom villa ♿ In-room: a/c, no safe, Wi-Fi. In-hotel: restaurant, pool, spa, water sports, some age restrictions* ❄ *All-inclusive.*

$
B&B/INN

⊞ **Charela Inn.** Directly on Negril Beach, this quiet hotel is understated but elegant in a simple way and has a widely praised French-Jamaican restaurant. **Pros:** great dining; good beach location; good value for families. **Cons:** dated room decor; some guest rooms are small; facilities are not luxurious. ✉ *Norman Manley Blvd., Box 3033, Negril* 🕾 *876/957–4648* ⊕ *www.charela.com* ☎ *49 rooms ♿ In-room: a/c, Wi-Fi (some) In-hotel: restaurant, bar, pool ☞ 5-night minimum* ❄ *No meals.*

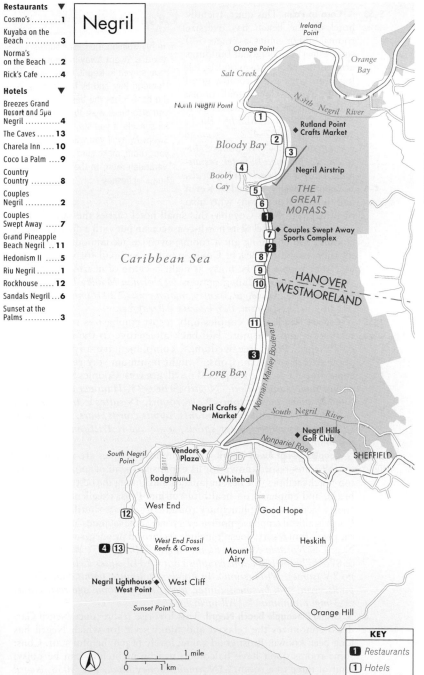

Negril

Ireland
Point

Orange Point

Orange
Bay

Salt Creek

North Negril River

North Negril Point

Rutland Point
Crafts Market

Bloody Bay

Negril Airstrip

Booby
Cay

THE
GREAT
MORASS

Caribbean Sea

Couples Swept Away
Sports Complex

HANOVER
WESTMORELAND

Long Bay

Norman Manley Boulevard

Negril Crafts
Market

South Negril River

Negril Hills
Golf Club

Vendors
Plaza

Nonpariel Road

SHEFFIELD

South Negril
Point

Rodground

Whitehall

West End

Good Hope

Heskith

West End Fossil
Reefs & Caves

Mount
Airy

Negril Lighthouse
West Point

West Cliff

Sunset Point

Orange Hill

14

KEY

1 *Restaurants*

1 *Hotels*

0   1 mile
0   1 km

$–$$ HOTEL   🏨 **Coco La Palm**. This quiet, friendly hotel on the beach has oversize rooms (junior suites average 540 square feet) in octagonal buildings around the pool. **Pros:** good beach location; large guest rooms; good on-site dining. **Cons:** small pools; dated room decor; few ocean-view rooms. ✉ *Norman Manley Blvd., Negril* ☎ *876/957–4227* ⊕ *www.cocolapalm.com* ➴ *76 rooms* ⚘ *In-room: a/c, Internet. In-hotel: restaurants, bar, pools, beach* ⊘ *No meals.*

> ## WORD OF MOUTH
>
> "In my opinion the best Couples resort is Swept Away in Negril. I have stayed in Negril, Ocho, and Montego Bay, and by far Negril is the best. It has the best beaches and also faces west for beautiful sunsets. If you stay at Couples Swept Away, if you want a TV in your room, make sure to get a 'verandah room' in the new section." —chesney

¢–$ B&B/INN   🏨 **Country Country**. Owned by Kevin and Joanne Robertson, who also own Montego Bay's Coyaba, this small hotel carries the same home-away-from-home feel of its north-coast cousin but with a distinct Negril charm. **Pros:** charming guest rooms; oversize accommodations; good location on Negril Beach. **Cons:** may be too small for some travelers; some rooms can be noisy at night because of nearby Margaritaville; limited on-site dining options. ✉ *Norman Manley Blvd., Negril* ☎ *876/957–4273* ⊕ *www.countryjamaica.com* ➴ *20 rooms* ⚘ *In-room: a/c. In-hotel: restaurant, bar, beach* ⊘ *Breakfast.*

$$$$ ALL-INCLUSIVE   🏨 **Couples Negril**. This couples-only resort emphasizes romance and relaxation and is a more laid-back alternative to the nearby Sandals Negril. **Pros:** free weddings; complimentary airport shuttle; good stretch of beach. **Cons:** 3-night minimum stay restrictive for some; doesn't include reciprocal privileges with Couples Swept Away. ✉ *Norman Manley Blvd., Negril* ✆ *Box 35, Hanover* ☎ *876/957–5960* ⊕ *www.couples.com* ➴ *216 rooms, 18 suites* ⚘ *In-room: a/c, Wi-Fi (some). In-hotel: restaurants, tennis courts, bars, pools, gym, spa, business center, water sports, some age restrictions* ✆ *3-night minimum* ⊘ *All-inclusive.*

$$$$ ALL-INCLUSIVE   🏨 **Couples Swept Away Negril**. Sports-minded couples are welcomed to this all-suites resort known for its expansive menu of sports offerings, top-notch facilities (the best in Jamaica and among the best in the Caribbean), and emphasis on healthful cuisine. **Pros:** excellent fitness and sports facilities; complimentary round-trip airport shuttle; great spa. **Cons:** healthful emphasis not for everyone; some facilities located across the road from resort; doesn't include reciprocal privileges with Couples Negril. ✉ *Norman Manley Blvd., Negril* ✆ *Box 3077, Westmoreland* ☎ *876/957–4061* ⊕ *www.couples.com* ➴ *312 suites* ⚘ *In-room: a/c, no TV (some), Wi-Fi (some). In-hotel: restaurants, tennis courts, bars, pools, gym, spa, business center, water sports, some age restrictions* ✆ *3-night minimum* ⊘ *All-inclusive.*

$ ALL-INCLUSIVE   🏨 **Grand Pineapple Beach Negril**. This low-rise resort (once Negril Gardens) epitomizes the relaxed and funky style for which Negril has long been known. **Pros:** good value; lovely beach; helpful staff. **Cons:** some rooms don't have balconies; nearby nightclubs can be noisy; limit of three to a room. ✉ *Norman Manley Blvd., Box 3058, Negril*

☎ 876/957–4408 ⊕ *www.grandpineapple.com* ➘ *65 rooms* ⚓ *In-room: a/c, Internet. In-hotel: restaurant, bars, pool, spa, water sports, laundry facilities, business center* ☞ *2-night minimum* ⎮◯⎮ *All-inclusive.*

$–$$
ALL-INCLUSIVE

⊞ Hedonism II. Promising a perpetual spring break for adults who are drawn to the legendary party atmosphere, this resort gets a lot of repeat business. **Pros:** good beaches; more economical than some adult all-inclusives; numerous activities, including squash. **Cons:** spring-break atmosphere not for everyone; nude beach and pool frequently over-crowded; rooms remain fairly basic. ⊠ *Norman Manley Blvd., Rutland Point, Box 25, Negril* ☎ *876/957–5200* ⊕ *www.superclubs.com* ➘ *280 rooms* ⚓ *In-room: a/c. In-hotel: restaurants, tennis courts, bars, pools, gym, spa, business center, water sports, some age restrictions* ☞ *3-night minimum* ⎮◯⎮ *All-inclusive.*

$$–$$$
ALL-INCLUSIVE
🜂

⊞ Riu Negril. North of Negril on Bloody Bay, this large resort has a expansive, sandy beachfront. **Pros:** economical all-inclusive; family travelers find plenty for children on-site; good on-site dining. **Cons:** pools and public areas can be overcrowded with families; limited gym amenities; long walk from attractions of Negril Beach. ⊠ *Norman Manley Blvd., Negril* ☎ *876/957–5700* ⊕ *www.riu.com* ➘ *402 rooms, 18 junior suites* ⚓ *In-room: a/c, Wi-Fi. In-hotel: restaurants, tennis courts, bars, children's programs, pools, gym, laundry facilities, spa, business center, water sports* ⎮◯⎮ *All-inclusive.*

$
HOTEL
Fodor's Choice
★

⊞ Rockhouse. With a spectacular cliff-side location like that of the Caves—but with some viable options for avoiding the high price tag—the small and trendy Rockhouse delivers both resort comforts and funky style. **Pros:** excellent dining; unique accommodations; beautiful pool area. **Cons:** no beach; may be too quiet for some visitors; traditional rooms are not nearly as nice as the villas. ⊠ *West End Rd., Box 3024, Negril* ☎ *876/957–4373* ⊕ *www.rockhousehotel.com* ➘ *14 rooms, 20 villas* ⚓ *In-room: a/c, no TV. In-hotel: restaurants, bars, pool, spa, water sports, some age restrictions* ⎮◯⎮ *No meals.*

$$$–$$$$
ALL-INCLUSIVE

⊞ Sunset at the Palms Resort and Spa, Negril. A sister property of the Sunset Resorts in Montego Bay and Ocho Rios—but far different in scale and atmosphere—this relaxed all-inclusive is a favorite with ecotourists thanks to its emphasis on environmentally sustainable tourism. **Pros:** environmentally conscious hotel; beautiful grounds; unique accommodations. **Cons:** beach is across street; eco-emphasis not for everyone; not within walking distance of many Negril Beach attractions and restaurants. ⊠ *Norman Manley Blvd., Box 118, Negril* ☎ *876/957–5350* ⊕ *www. sunsetatthepalms.com* ➘ *65 rooms* ⚓ *In-room: a/c, Internet. In-hotel: restaurants, tennis court, bars, pool, gym, spa, water sports* ⎮◯⎮ *All-inclusive.*

NIGHTLIFE

Nightlife includes both on-property shows at the all-inclusive resorts and nightclubs ranging from indoor clubs to beach bashes. For starters, there's reggae, popularized by the late Bob Marley and the Wailers and performed today by son Ziggy Marley, Jimmy Tosh (the late Peter Tosh's son), Gregory Isaacs, Jimmy Cliff, and many others. If your experience of Caribbean music has been limited to steel drums and Harry

Belafonte, then the political, racial, and religious messages of reggae may set you on your ear; listen closely and you just might hear the heartbeat of the people. Dancehall is another island favorite, as is soca.

For the most part, the liveliest late-night happenings throughout Jamaica are in the major resort hotels, with the widest variety of spots probably in Montego Bay. Some of the all-inclusives offer a dinner-and-disco pass from about $50 to $100; to buy a pass, call ahead the afternoon before to check availability and be sure to bring a photo ID with you. Pick up a copy of the *Daily Gleaner,* the *Jamaica Observer,* or the *Star* (available at newsstands throughout the island) for listings on who's playing when and where. In Negril, trucks with loudspeakers travel through the streets in the afternoon announcing the hot spot for the evening.

MONTEGO BAY

ANNUAL EVENTS

Fodor'sChoice ★ **Jamaica Jazz and Blues Festival.** In January, Montego Bay is packed with music fans for this event held at the Rose Hall Aqueduct. ☎ 876/953–8282 ⊕ *jamaicajazzandblues.com.*

Fodor'sChoice ★ **Red Stripe Reggae Sumfest.** Those who know and love reggae should visit Montego Bay between mid-July and August for this weeklong concert—at the Bob Marley Performing Arts Center in the Freeport area—which attracts such big-name performers as Third World and Ziggy Marley and the Melody Makers. Tickets are sold for each night's performances or by multi-event passes. ⊕ *www.reggaesumfest.com.*

DANCE AND MUSIC CLUBS

Blue Beat. This club moves to a jazz groove every night. Saturday brings live shows; other nights feature a DJ. Every night the club is popular as a sophisticated spot for a nightcap. ⊠ *Gloucester Ave., Montego Bay* ☎ *876/952–4777.*

★ **Margaritaville Caribbean Bar and Grill.** With its location right on what's deemed Montego Bay's Hip Strip, the colorful bar and restaurant boasts a spring-break crowd during the season and a fun-loving atmosphere any night of the year; there is also a location at the Montego Bay airport, not to mention popular locations in both Negril and Ocho Rios. ⊠ *Gloucester Ave., Montego Bay* ☎ *876/952–4777.*

The Twisted Kilt Lounge. The Hip Strip is home to Jamaica's first Irish pub. Especially popular with sports lovers for its big-screen TVs, this waterfront nightspot also serves fish-and-chips and pub grub. ⊠ *Gloucester Ave., Montego Bay* ☎ *876/952–9488.*

OCHO RIOS

ANNUAL EVENTS

Jamaica Ocho Rios International Jazz Festival. In Ocho Rios, the biggest event of the year is held each June. The festival, which started in 1991 as a one-day concert, now spans 14 days and draws many top names. ☎ *876/927–3544* ⊕ *www.ochoriosjazz.com.*

DANCE AND MUSIC CLUBS
Margaritaville Caribbean Bar and Grill. One of the most popular nonresort nightspots in Ocho Rios is this chain, which is right on the beach. It's also a popular stop for cruise-ship visitors. ⊠ *Island Village, Turtle River Rd., Ocho Rios* ☎ *876/675–8800.*

PORT ANTONIO

DANCE AND MUSIC CLUBS
Roof Club. In Port Antonio, the hottest nightlife in town is not at the hotels, but at local joints like this one. Open Thursday to Sunday night, the second-floor club plays dancehall hits. ⊠ *11 West St., Port Antonio* ☎ *876/715–5281.*

14

NEGRIL

DANCE AND MUSIC CLUBS
★ **Alfred's Ocean Palace.** You can find Negril's best live music at this club, which offers live performances right on the beach. ⊠ *Norman Manley Blvd., Negril* ☎ *876/957–4735.*

★ **Hedonism II.** The sexy, always-packed disco at is the wildest dance spot on the island; Tuesday (pajama night) and Thursday (toga night) are tops. For nonguests, night passes are $89 and include meals, drinks, and use of the facilities from 6 pm to 2 am; bring a photo ID to obtain a pass, but you should call ahead for a reservation. ⊠ *Norman Manley Blvd., Negril* ☎ *876/957–5200.*

Margaritaville Caribbean Bar and Grill. You'll find a branch of the popular burger-and-nightspot chain in Negril. ⊠ *Norman Manley Blvd., Negril* ☎ *876/957–4467.*

SHOPPING

Shopping is not really one of Jamaica's high points, though you will certainly be able to find things to buy. Good choices include Jamaican crafts, which range from artwork to batik fabrics to baskets. Wood carvings are one of the top purchases; the finest carvings are made from the Jamaican national tree, lignum vitae, or tree of life, a dense wood that requires a talented carver to transform the hard, blond wood into dolphins, heads, or fish. Bargaining is expected with crafts vendors. Naturally, Jamaican rum is another top souvenir—there's no shortage of opportunities to buy it at gift shops and liquor stores—as is Tia Maria, the Jamaican-made coffee liqueur. Coffee (both Blue Mountain and the less expensive High Mountain) is sold at every gift shop on the island as well. The cheapest prices are found at the local grocery stores, where you can buy coffee beans or ground coffee.

You can find Jamaican and even some Haitian paintings in galleries around the island. There are many other locally made goods available in the crafts markets in Montego Bay, Negril, and Ocho Rios. Reggae CDs that are locally recorded may be found nowhere else but Jamaica. Finally, liquor and tobacco products can be good buys; Cuban cigars can be purchased and smoked in Jamaica but may not be legally brought into the United States at this writing.

MONTEGO BAY

AREAS AND MALLS

In MoBay the crafts market on **Market Street** is a compendium of stalls, each selling much the same thing. Come prepared to haggle over prices and to be given the hard sell; if you're in the right mood, though, the whole experience can be a lot of fun and a peek into Jamaican commerce away from the resorts. Montego Bay is also home to some traditional shopping malls where prices are set; you can shop in air-conditioned comfort. **Holiday Inn Shopping Centre** is one of the best. It's directly across the street from the Holiday Inn and has jewelry, clothing, and crafts stores. The most serious shopping in town is at **Half Moon Village,** east of Half Moon resort. The bright yellow buildings are filled with the finest and most expensive wares money can buy, but the park benches and outdoor pub here make the mall a fun stop for window-shoppers as well. East of Half Moon, the **Shoppes at Rose Hall** is the region's newest and most upscale shopping with numerous duty-free shops with fine jewelry, watches, and perfumes. The island's largest shopping center is found at Montego Bay's expanded **Sangster International Airport;** shops selling everything from liquor to coffee to handicrafts are located beyond security.

OCHO RIOS

AREAS AND MALLS

Ocho Rios has several malls, and they are less hectic than the one in MoBay. Shopping centers include **Pineapple Place, Ocean Village, Taj Mahal,** and **Coconut Grove.** A fun mall that also serves as an entertainment center is **Island Village,** near the cruise port. The open-air mall includes Reggae Xplosion, shops selling Jamaican handicrafts, duty-free goods and clothing, a Margaritaville restaurant, and a small beach area with a water trampoline and water sports.

KINGSTON

AREAS AND MALLS

A shopping tour of the Kingston area should include **Devon House,** the place to find things old and new made in Jamaica. The greathouse is now a museum with antiques and furniture reproductions; boutiques and an ice-cream shop—try one of the tropical flavors (mango, guava, pineapple, and passion fruit)—fill what were once stables.

NEGRIL

AREAS AND MALLS

With the laid-back atmosphere of Negril, it's no surprise that most shopping involves straw hats, baskets, and T-shirts, all plentiful at the **Rutland Point** crafts market on the north edge of town or at the old crafts market in town. For more serious shopping, head to **Time Square,** known for its luxury goods ranging from jewelry to cigars to watches. The gated shopping area has air-conditioned stores with high-dollar items.

SPORTS AND ACTIVITIES

The tourist board licenses all recreational activity operators and outfitters, which should assure you of fair business practices as long as you deal with companies that display its decals.

BIRD-WATCHING

Jamaica is a major bird-watching destination, thanks to its various natural habitats. The island is home to more than 200 species, some seen only seasonally or in particular parts of the island. Many bird-watchers flock here for the chance to see the vervain hummingbird (the world's second-smallest bird, larger only than Cuba's bee hummingbird) or the Jamaican tody (which nests underground).

MONTEGO BAY

★ **Rocklands Bird Sanctuary.** A great place to spot birds is the sanctuary, which is south of Montego Bay. The station was the home of the late Lisa Salmon, one of Jamaica's first amateur ornithologists. Here you can sit quietly and feed birds—including the doctor bird (also known as the streamer-tail hummingbird), recognizable by its long tail—from your hand. A visit costs $15. ⊠ *Anchovy* ☎ *876/952–2009.*

DIVING AND SNORKELING

Jamaica isn't a major dive destination, but you can find a few rich underwater regions, especially off the north coast. MoBay, known for its wall dives, has **Airport Reef** at its southwestern edge. The site is known for its coral caves, tunnels, and canyons. The first marine park in Jamaica, the **Montego Bay Marine Park,** was established to protect the natural resources of the bay; a quick look at the area and it's easy to see the treasures that lie beneath the surface. The north coast is on the edge of the Cayman Trench, so it boasts a wide array of marine life.

Thanks to a marine area protected since 1966, the Ocho Rios region is also a popular diving destination. Through the years, the protected area grew into the **Ocho Rios Marine Park,** stretching from Mammee Bay and Drax Hall to the west to Frankfort Point on the east. Top dive sites in the area include **Jack's Hall,** a 40-foot dive dotted with all types of coral; **Top of the Mountain,** a 60-foot dive near Dunn's River Falls with many coral heads and gorgonians; and the **Wreck of the** *Katryn,* a 50-foot dive to a deliberately sunk 140-foot former minesweeper.

With its murkier waters, the southern side of the island isn't as popular for diving, especially near Kingston. **Port Royal,** which is near the airport, is filled with sunken ships that are home to many different varieties of tropical fish, although a special permit is required to dive some sites here. Prices range from $45 to $80 for a one-tank dive. All the large resorts have dive shops, and the all-inclusive places sometimes include scuba diving in their rates. To dive, you need to show a certification card, though it's possible to get a small taste of scuba diving and do a shallow dive—usually from shore—after taking a one-day resort diving course, which almost every resort with a dive shop offers. A couple of places stand out.

FALMOUTH

Scuba Jamaica. This company offers serious scuba facilities for dedicated divers. The PADI and NAUI operation also offers Nitrox diving and instruction as well as instruction in underwater photography, night diving, and open-water diving. There's a pickup service for the Montego Bay, Runaway Bay, Discovery Bay, and Ocho Rios areas. Along with the Falmouth location, Scuba Jamaica is also found at the Franklyn D Resort in Runaway Bay and at Travellers Resort in Negril. ⊠ *N-Resort, North Coast Hwy., Falmouth* ☎ *876/617–2500, 876/973–4591 in Runaway Bay, 876/957–3039 in Negril* ⊕ *www.scuba-jamaica.com*).

NEGRIL

Negril Scuba Centre. This dive shop has three locations in Negril and one in the community of Green River at Rhodes Hall Plantation. Along with the Marin's main Negril Beach Club location, you'll find dive operations at Sunset at the Palms and Negril Escape Resort and Spa resorts. ⊠ *Negril Beach Club, Norman Manley Blvd., Negril* ☎ *876/383–9533, 876/823–6300 for Sunset at the Palms, 876/957–0392 for Negril Escape Resort and Spa* ⊕ *www.negrilscuba.com.*

NEGRIL

Dolphin Cove Negril. The newest dolphin-swim program in Jamaica is related to the one outside Ocho Rios. (⊠ *North Coast Hwy., Lucea* ☎ *876/974–5335* ⊕ *www.dolphincovejamaica.com.*

FISHING

Port Antonio makes deep-sea-fishing headlines with its annual Blue Marlin Tournament in October, and MoBay and Ocho Rios have devotees who exchange tales (tall and otherwise) about sailfish, yellowfin tuna, wahoo, dolphinfish, and bonito. Licenses aren't required, and you can arrange to charter a boat at your hotel. A chartered boat (with captain, crew, and equipment) costs about $500 to $900 for a half day or $900 to $1,500 for a full-day excursion, depending on the size of the boat.

FALMOUTH

Glistening Waters Marina. This marina offers charter trips from the Falmouth area. Thirty boats moored at the Glistening Waters Marina offer deep-sea fishing charters; the marina also has nighttime boat tours for a look at the lagoon, whose iridescence is caused by microscopic dinoflagellates that become luminescent when they move. ⊠ *North Coast Hwy., Falmouth* ☎ *876/954–3229.*

Continued on page 604

REGGAE

Julie Schwietert Collazo
& Eric Wechter

There's an undeniable, universal appeal to reggae music. Its feel-good beat and impassioned lyrics resonate with listeners across the globe, but experiencing reggae in the country of its birth is the best way to enjoy the music.

Widely considered to be Jamaica's seminal music form, reggae was born out of other genres, including ska and rocksteady, and is relatively young compared to other Jamaican musical styles. In fact, the history of Jamaican music is as long as the history of the island itself. Reggae's origins are firmly rooted in traditions of African music, and its lyrics are inspired by Jamaicans' fervid resistance to colonialism and imperialism. Reggae can be distinguished from earlier music forms by its comparatively faster beat, its experimental tendencies, and a more prominent role for the guitar. Reggae is also more "ragged"—both in sound and in concept. That is it's both more earthy and down to earth, or folkloric. Lyrically, reggae is rife with social themes, primarily those that explore the plight of the working classes.

BUILDING A BEAT

Sly Dunbar, touring with Peter Tosh, 1979

Robbie Shakespeare, on tour with Peter Tosh, 1978

Pioneering reggae musicians, such as drummer **Sly Dunbar** and bassist **Robbie Shakespeare**, shaped the genre by distilling what they viewed as the best elements of ska and rocksteady. Reggae is not complex in terms of chord structure or rhythmic variation. There may be only one to three chords in a typical reggae song, and the danceable feel is propelled most commonly by a rhythm—or "riddim"—called the "drop beat" or "one drop." The bass drum emphasizes the third beat in a four-beat cycle, creating an anchor, or a pull, that the guitar and bass play on top of. For a more propulsive feel, the drummer may equally emphasize all four beats in each measure. Layered on top of this repetitive, solid foundation are socially conscious lyrics, which often preach resistance to the establishment or beseech listeners to love one another.

REGGAE AND RASTA

Reggae is a musical genre of, by, and for the people, and the influence of Rastafarianism has expanded its folk appeal. Rasta became pervasive in Jamaica in the 1950s, when resistance to colonialism peaked. Rasta, combining spiritual, political, and social concerns, had its origins in the crowning of **Haile Selassie I** as the emperor of Ethiopia in 1930. Selassie, the only black man to head an independent African nation at the time, became a vital figure and symbol of freedom for Africans in the diaspora. Greatly inspired by Selassie, Jamaicans integrated his empowering messages into many aspects of their culture. Musically, the Rasta influence is felt in reggae in two ways. The lyrics often advocate the idea of returning to Africa, and minor chords and a simple "riddim" structure characterize the songs. In the words of music historian Lloyd Bradley, Rastas were the "underclass of the underclass," and by 1959 more than one in every 25 Jamaicans identified with Rastafarianism. One of them was Bob Marley.

Haile Selassie I of Ethiopia

BOB MARLEY

Bob Marley is reggae's oracle, a visionary who introduced the world to the music of Jamaica and the struggles of its people. A stirring performer with a preternatural talent for connecting with audiences, Marley revealed the oppression of his countrymen and their indomitable spirit through his songs of hope, freedom, and redemption. His legacy extends far beyond reggae, influencing generations of artists across multiple genres.

Born in February 1945, Robert Nesta Marley left his home in rural St. Ann's Parish, Jamaica, at 14 to pursue a music career in Kingston. In 1963 Marley joined with singers Peter Tosh and Bunny Livingston to form the group the Wailers, and they began recording singles with a renowned local producer. After a series of stops and starts and a strengthened devotion to the teachings of the Rastafari faith, Bob Marley and the Wailers released *Catch a Fire* in 1973. It was their first release outside of Jamaica, and nearly instantly it became an international success. Mar-

ley's global popularity and acclaim grew with albums like *Burnin'* and *Natty Dread*. As Marley's stardom increased abroad, his influence at home became transcendent. Regarded by many of his countrymen as a prophet, Marley, whose songs of freedom and revolution reverberated throughout Jamaica, was perceived as threat in some corridors. In December 1976, he was wounded in an assassination attempt. Marley left Jamaica for more than a year and in 1977 released his biggest record thus far, *Exodus,* which included the hits "Jammin" and "One Love/People Get Ready." By 1980, Marley was poised to reach even greater heights with an extensive U.S. tour, but while jogging in New York he suddenly collapsed. Cancer had silently invaded his brain and lungs. He died in May, 1981, at age 36. Marley's spirit and music endure in the hearts and minds of fans worldwide. His greatest hits collection, *Legend,* is the top-selling reggae album of all time.

Bob Marley at Reggae Sunsplash

COMMUNING WITH THE SPIRIT

Bob Marley Museum, Kingston

Whether you're a serious enthusiast or have just a passing curiosity, Jamaica offers visitors plenty of opportunities to experience the music and culture of reggae.

Zion Bus Line Tour to Nine Mile. Marley fans won't want to miss this bus pilgrimage to the reggae icon's birthplace and final resting place. With the sounds of familiar reggae tunes thumping through the bus speakers, the guided tour takes you through the mountains to the small town of Nine Mile. The half-day tour includes a visit to Marley's house, a stop at Mount Zion (a rock where Marley meditated) and the opportunity to view Marley's mausoleum. The tour leaves from Ocho Rios. On the return trip from Nine Mile, the group stops at the Jerk Center for an authentic Jamaican lunch.

Reggae Sumfest in Montego Bay. This week-long reggae festival is held each July. In addition to featuring musical line-ups of the most popular reggae, dance hall, R&B, and hip hop acts, the Sumfest offers traditional Jamaican food and local crafts. Recent festivals have featured local favorite Tarrus Riley, as well as international performers, like LL Cool J and Mary J. Blige.

DID YOU KNOW?

The first appearance of the word *reggae* is widely attributed to the 1968 single by the Maytals called "Do the Reggay."

Burning Spear   Jimmy Cliff   The Congos

At **Reggae Yard & Island Life** (☎ 876/675–8795) in Ocho Rios you'll find an extensive selection of reggae CDs as well as other types of Caribbean music.

Bob Marley Museum in Kingston (☎ 876/927–9152). If the Zion Bus Tour only whets your appetite for Marley, visit the Bob Marley Museum for a glimpse at another chapter of his life. Housed inside the former headquarters of Marley's label, Tuff Gong Records, it is also the site of the failed attempt on Marley's life that inspired his song, "Ambush."

And, of course, your Jamaican reggae experience would not be complete without catching some live bands. Local acts play at **Bourbon Beach** (☎ 876/957–4405) in Negril on Monday, Thursday, and Saturday nights. Also in Negril is **Rick's Cafe** (☎ 876/957–0380), which features an in-house reggae band nightly.

REGGAE LINGO

Dancehall. A modern style that introduces elements of electronic dance music and improvised singing or rapping by DJs to raw reggae tracks.

Dub. A form of reggae characterized by the use of remixes of previously recorded material.

One-drop rhythm. The definitive beat of reggae characterized by a steady "drop" of the bass drum on the strong beat in each measure.

Ragamuffin (ragga). Similar to dancehall, ragga combines electronic dance music, hip-hop, and R&B with reggae for a more contemporary, club feel.

Riddim. The rhythmic foundation for nearly all reggae styles, characterized by a repetitive, driving drum and bass feel.

Rocksteady. A style of reggae that followed ska, rocksteady is marked by a slower tempo.

Ska. Precursor to reggae that combines traditional Caribbean rhythms, jazz, and calypso

RECOMMENDED LISTENING

Bob Marley
Uprising, Legend, Exodus, Burnin', Catch a Fire

Peter Tosh
Legalize It

Toots and the Maytals
Funky Kingston

Jimmy Cliff
The Harder They Come

Burning Spear
Marcus Garvey

Alton Ellis
Alton Ellis Sings Rock and Soul

The Congos
The Heart of the Congos

GOLF

Golfers appreciate both the beauty and the challenges offered by Jamaica's courses. Caddies are almost always mandatory throughout the island, and rates are $15 to $45 per round of golf. Cart rentals are available at most courses; costs are $20 to $40. Some of the best courses in the country are found near MoBay. Many resorts have their own courses (including several of the Sandals and SuperClubs resorts) and allow both guests and nonguests to play; there is generally a charge for nonguests at these courses.

MONTEGO BAY

★ **Golf at Half Moon.** This Robert Trent Jones–designed 18-hole course is the home of the Red Stripe Pro Am. Green fees are $105 for guests, $150 for nonguests with twilight packages ranging from $75 to $90. In 2005 the course received an upgrade from Jones protégé Roger Rulewich and once again draws international attention. The course is also home of the Half Moon Golf Academy, which offers one-day sessions, multiday retreats, and hour-long private sessions. ⊠ *Half Moon Resort, North Coast Hwy., 7 mi (11 km) east of Montego Bay* ☎ *876/953–2560* ⊕ *halfmoon.rockresorts.com/activities/golf.asp*.

Hilton Rose Hall Resort and Spa. This course 4 mi (6 km) east of the airport hosts several invitational tournaments. Green fees run $149 7–10 am, $119 10 am–1:30 pm, and $99 for a twilight round at the 18-hole championship **Cinnamon Hill Ocean Course.** The course was designed by Robert von Hagge and Rick Baril and is adjacent to historic Cinnamon Hill estate. Rates include green fees, cart, caddie, and tax, and apply to both guests and nonguests. ⊠ *North Coast Hwy., St. James ⊹ 15 mi (24 km) east of Montego Bay* ☎ *876/953–2650.*

★ **Ritz-Carlton Golf and Spa Resort, Rose Hall.** One of the nicest courses in Montego Bay, if not Jamaica, is the **White Witch** course at the Ritz-Carlton. The green fees at this 18-hole championship course are $175 for resort guests, $185 for nonguests, and $109 for a twilight round. Designed by Robert von Hagge and Rick Baril, it is literally on the grounds of historic Rose Hall Great House. ⊠ *1 Ritz Carlton Dr., Rose Hall, St. James* ☎ *876/518–0174 or 876/684–5174.*

Fodor's Choice ★ **Tryall Club.** Probably the best-known golf course in Jamaica is the course at this resort 15 mi (24 km) west of Montego Bay. The 18-hole championship course is on the site of a 19th-century sugar plantation. The famous 7th hole tees off between the stone pillars of a historic aqueduct; the adjacent waterwheel has been the subject of many photos. The course was designed by Ralph Plummer and is an official PGA tour–approved course, having hosted events such as the Johnnie Walker World Championship. Green fees are $70 for guests, $110 for nonguests. ⊠ *North Coast Hwy., Sandy Bay* ☎ *876/956–5681* ⊕ *www.tryallclub.com.*

OCHO RIOS

Sandals Golf and Country Club. The golf course in Ocho Rios is 700 feet above sea level (green fees are $100 for 18 holes or $70 for 9 holes for nonguests; free for guests). ⊠ *5 mi (8 km) southeast of Ocho Rios, turn south at White River and continue 4 mi (6 km), Ocho Rios* ☎ *876/975–0119.*

RUNAWAY BAY AND VICINITY

SuperClubs Golf Club at Runaway. This 18-hole course in Runaway Bay has hosted many championship events (green fees are $80 for nonguests; guests play for free) and is also home to an extensive golf academy. ✉ *North Coast Hwy., Runaway Bay* ☎ *876/973–7319.*

NEGRIL

Negril Hills Golf Club. Great golf, rolling hills, and a rolling "liquor-mobile" go hand in hand at the 18-hole golf course, the only one in Negril (it's east of town). Green fees are $28.75 for 9 holes or $57.50 for 18 holes. ✉ *Sheffield Rd., Negril* ☎ *876/957–4638* ⊕ *www.negril-hillsgolfclub.com.*

GUIDED TOURS

Because most vacationers don't rent cars for both safety and cost reasons, guided tours are a popular option if you want to take a break from the beach and explore. Check with your hotel concierge for information on half- and full-day tours that offer pickup at your resort. Jamaica's size and slow roads mean that you can't expect to see the entire island on any one trip; even a full-day tour will concentrate on just one part of the island. Most of the tours are similar in both content and price. If you're in Montego Bay, tours often include one of the plantation houses in the area. Several Negril-based companies offer tours to Y.S. Falls on the South Coast. Tours from Ocho Rios might include any of the area's top attractions, including Dunn's River Falls or Kingston. In almost all cases, you'll arrange your tour through the tour desk of your resort. However, a few of these tours are quite unique, including the following.

OCHO RIOS

Zion Bus Tour. This tour will appeal to reggae buffs visiting the Ocho Rios who want to visit Bob Marley's boyhood home. Travelers ride a country-style bus painted in bright colors to the island's interior and the village of Nine Mile. The tour includes a look at the simple home where Marley was born and is now buried. The tour ($84 including a lunch stop at a local jerk stand) lasts for five hours and is limited to guests age 18 and above. ✉ *Chukka Caribbean Adventures, Llandovery, St. Ann's Bay* ☎ *876/972–2506* ⊕ *www.chukkacaribbean.com.*

MANDEVILLE

Countrystyle Peace Village. This company allows visitors to the South Coast, Mandeville, and Kingston to experience more of the real Jamaica. Tours offers unique, personalized tours of island communities. You're linked with community residents based on your interests; tours can include anything from bird-watching in Mandeville to nightlife in Kingston. ✉ *62 Ward Ave., Mandeville* ☎ *876/962–7758 or 876/488–7207* ⊕ *www.countrystylecommunitytourism.com.*

HORSEBACK RIDING

RUNAWAY BAY

Braco Stables. In the Braco area near Trelawny, between Montego Bay and Ocho Rios, this stable offers guided rides, including a bareback romp in the sea. Two estate rides are offered a day for $70, and riders are matched to horses based on riding ability. The trip also includes an optional barbecue lunch. Experienced riders can also opt for a mountain ride ($84) for a more rugged two-hour tour. ⊠ *Duncans* 🕾 *876/954–0185* ⊕ *www.bracostables.com.*

OCHO RIOS

Annandale Plantation. Riders with an interest in history can combine both loves on a horseback tour at this old plantation. The 600-acre plantation is high above Ocho Rios and today serves as a working farm, although in its glory days it hosted dignitaries such as the Queen Mother. ⊠ *4 mi (6 km) southwest of Ocho Rios, near town of Epworth* 🕾 *876/974–2323* ⊕ *tourwise.org.*

Fodor's Choice   **Chukka Caribbean Adventures.** Ocho Rios has excellent horseback riding, ★ but the best of the operations is Chukka Caribbean's Ocho Rios stable. You don't have to be an experienced rider to enjoy its tours; horses are well trained and Chukka provides attentive guides to assist all riders along the way. The company's 2½-hour beach ride ($74, $52 for children) is a highlight of many trips to Jamaica. ⊠ *Llandovery, St. Ann's Bay* 🕾 *876/972–2506* ⊕ *www.chukkacaribbean.com.*

Hooves. This stable offers several guided tours, including a popular 2½-hour beach ride ($65 from Ocho Rios, $70 from Runaway Bay) for riders age 12 and up. The trip begins with a visit to the Seville Great House Museum before making its way to the beach for a ride. Hooves is home to many rescue horses that have been rehabilitated. ⊠ *Windsor Rd., St. Ann's Bay* 🕾 *876/972–0905* ⊕ *www.hoovesjamaica.com.*

Prospect Plantation. The plantation offers a 3½-hour ride for ages eight and older. The price ($70) includes use of helmets; advance reservations are required. For the adventurous, Prospect Plantation also offers guided camel rides. ⊠ *Rte. A1, about 3 mi (5 km) east of Ocho Rios* 🕾 *876/994–1058* ⊕ *www.prospectplantationtours.com.*

MOUNTAIN BIKING

Jamaica's hilly terrain creates a challenge for mountain bikers, though there are easier rides, especially near the beaches and on the western end of the island. Heavy, unpredictable traffic on the North Coast Highway makes it off-limits for bikers, but smaller country roads and winding trails weave a network through the countryside.

OCHO RIOS

Blue Mountain Bicycle Tours. This company takes travelers on guided rides in the spectacular Blue Mountains. The all-day excursion starts high and glides downhill, so all levels of riders can enjoy the tour. The trip ends with a dip in a waterfall; the package price includes transportation from Ocho Rios or Kingston, brunch, lunch, and all equipment. ⊠ *121 Main St., Ocho Rios* 🕾 *876/974–7075* ⊕ *www.bmtoursja.com.*

Rafting on the Rio Grande, near Port Antonio.

RIVER BOATING AND RAFTING

Jamaica's many rivers mean a multitude of freshwater experiences, from mild to wild. Jamaica's first tourist activity off the beaches was relaxing rafting trips aboard bamboo rafts poled by local boatmen. Recently, soft-adventure enthusiasts have also been able to opt for white-water action as well with guided tours through several operators.

Fodor's Choice
★

Bamboo rafting in Jamaica originated on the **Rio Grande,** a river in the Port Antonio area. Jamaicans had long used the bamboo rafts to transport bananas downriver; decades ago actor and Port Antonio resident Errol Flynn saw the rafts and thought they'd make a good tourist attraction, and local entrepreneurs quickly rose to the occasion. Today the slow rides are a favorite with romantic travelers and anyone looking to get off the beach for a few hours. The popularity of the Rio Grande's trips spawned similar trips down the **Martha Brae River,** about 25 mi (40 km) from MoBay. Near Ocho Rios, the **Great River** has lazy river rafting as well as energetic kayaking.

MONTEGO BAY

Jamaica Tours Limited. This big tour company conducts raft trips down the River Lethe, approximately 12 mi (19 km) southwest of MoBay (a 50-minute trip); the four-hour excursion costs about $54 per person, includes lunch, and takes you through unspoiled hill country. Bookings can also be made through hotel tour desks. ⊠ *Providence Dr., Montego Bay* ☎ *876/953–3700* ⊕ *www.jamaicatoursltd.com.*

River Raft Ltd. This company leads trips down the Martha Brae River, about 25 mi (40 km) from most hotels in MoBay. The cost is

$45 per person for the 1½-hour river run, including transportation from your hotel. ⊠ *66 Claude Clarke Ave., Montego Bay* ☎ *876/952–0889* ⊕ *www.jamaicarafting.com.*

OCHO RIOS

Caliche Rainforest. If you're looking for a more rugged adventure, then consider a white-water rafting trip with this company. Two tours, both offered in inflatable rafts, traverse the waters of the Great River. The Grade II Rainforest Rafting Tour ($80) glides along with stops for a swim; ages four and up can participate. The Canyon White Water Rafting tour ($90) traverses rapids up to Grade IV; travelers must be at least 14. In most cases you will be picked up at your hotel in Montego Bay, Ocho Rios, or Port Antonio, and the tour price includes the transfer cost. ☎ *876/940–1745* ⊕ *www.whitewaterraftingmontegobay.com.*

Chukka Caribbean Adventures. The big activity outfitter offers the Chukka River Tubing Safari on the White River, an easy trip that doesn't require any previous tubing experience. This tour allows you to travel in your very own tube through gentle rapids. This tour lasts for three hours and costs $63 for adults and $45 for children. ⊠ *Llandovery, St. Ann's Bay* ☎ *876/972–2506* ⊕ *www.chukkacaribbean.com.*

SOUTHWEST JAMAICA

South Coast Safaris Ltd. This company takes visitors on slow boat cruises ($17) up the river to see the birds and other animals, including crocodiles. ⊠ *1 Crane St., Black River* ☎ *876/965–2513.*

Martinique

WORD OF MOUTH

"Martinique is beautiful, historically interesting, has the French flair, easy to get around because, being a department of France, has very good, well-marked roads."

—xkenx

WELCOME TO MARTINIQUE

PARIS IN THE TROPICS

The largest of the Windward Islands, Martinique is 425 square mi (1,101 square km). The southern part of the island is all rolling hills and sugarcane fields; it's also where you'll find the best beaches and most development. In the north are craggy cliffs, lush vegetation, and one of the Caribbean's largest volcanoes, Mont Pelée.

Restaurants ▼	Hotels ▼
Chez Les Pecheurs 4	Bakoua 13
Fleur de Sel 9	Bignomia #2 12
Le Bélem 8	Cap Est Lagoon 7
La Table de Mamy Nounou 6	Club Med 10
Le Brédas 3	Engoulevent 2
Le Petitbonum 5	Hotel Cap Macabou 9
Le Plein Soleil 7	Hotel Villas St. Pierre ... 8
Mille Et Une Brindilles ... 1	Karibea St-Luce 11
Soup Bar 2	La Caravelle 5
	La Suite Villa 14
	La Valmenière 1
	Le Domaine St. Aubin ... 4
	Le Plein Soleil 6
	Squash Hotel 3

0 ——————— 5 mi
0 ——————— 5 km

KEY
➘ *Beaches*
1 *Restaurants*
① *Hotels*

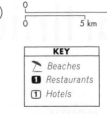

Joie de vivre is the credo in this French enclave, which is often characterized as a Caribbean suburb of Paris. Exotic fruit grows on the volcanoes' forested flanks amid a profusion of wild orchids and hibiscus. The sheer lushness of it all inspired the tropical paintings of onetime resident Paul Gauguin.

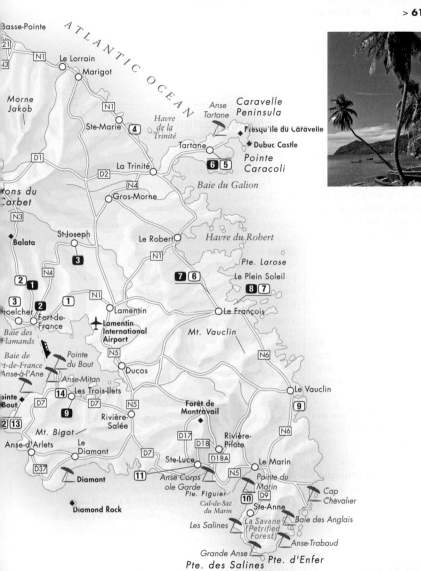

Map labels:

ATLANTIC OCEAN

Basse-Pointe
21
43
N1
Le Lorrain
Marigot

Morne Jakob

N1
Ste-Marie 4
Havre de la Trinité

Anse Tartane
Caravelle Peninsula
Presqu'île du Caravelle
Dubuc Castle
Tartane
Pointe Caracoli
6 5
Baie du Galion

D1
La Trinité
D2
N4
Gros-Morne
N3
Balata
St-Joseph
Le Robert
Havre du Robert
N1
Pte. Larose
Le Plein Soleil
7 6
3
8 7
N4
2 1
3 2
Schoelcher
Fort-de-France
N1
Lamentin
Le François
Baie des Flamands
Lamentin International Airport
Mt. Vauclin
Baie de Fort-de-France
N5
Anse-à-l'Ane
Pointe du Bout
Ducos
N6
Anse-Mitan
14
Les Trois-Îlets
D7
Le Vauclin
Pointe Bout
D7
9
Rivière-Salée
N5
Forêt de Montravail
9
2 13
Mt. Bigot
N6
Anse-d'Arlets
Le Diamant
D17
Rivière-Pilote
D7
D18
Ste-Luce
D18A
Le Marin
D37
Diamant
11
Anse Corps ole Garde
N5
Pointe du Marin
Pte. Figuier
10
D9
Cap Chevalier
Diamond Rock
Cul-de-Sac du Marin
Ste-Anne
Baie des Anglais
Les Salines
La Savane (Petrified Forest)
Anse-Trabaud
Grande Anse
Pte. des Salines
Pte. d'Enfer

TOP REASONS TO VISIT MARTINIQUE

1 The Romance: A magical sensuality infuses everything; it will awaken dormant desires and fuel existing fires.

2 Beautiful Beaches: A full roster of beautiful beaches will let you enjoy sun and sand.

3 The French Connection: Excellent French food, not to mention music and fashion, makes the island a paradise for Francophiles.

4 Range of Accommodations: Hospitable, stylish small hotels abound; big resorts, too. Or play expat in a private, luxe villa.

5 Inviting Waters: The sea, Caribbean; the ocean, Atlantic—experience the water in a kayak or on a sailboat. Even a ferry works.

MARTINIQUE PLANNER

When to Go	Getting to Martinique
High season runs from mid-November through May, and the island can be quiet the rest of the year, with some hotels closing down for months, particularly in September and October. Those places that remain open offer significant discounts.	**Hassle Factor:** Medium to high.

When to Go

High season runs from mid-November through May, and the island can be quiet the rest of the year, with some hotels closing down for months, particularly in September and October. Those places that remain open offer significant discounts.

Martinique's **Carnival** begins in February and runs until Lent, not unlike Mardi Gras in New Orleans.

About 20 days into Lent there's a mini-Carnival called **Mi-carême**; this one-day hiatus from abstinence includes a rash of parties and dances before sober times return until Easter.

Early August sees the **Tour des Yoles Rondes** point-to-point yawl race.

In odd-numbered years, the early-December **Martinique's Jazz Festival** draws a wide range of international talent, including such top performers as Branford Marsalis.

Getting to Martinique

Hassle Factor: Medium to high.

Ferries: Express des Îles (☎ 0825/35–90–00 or 0596/63–12–11 ⊕ www.express-des-iles.com) connects Martinique with Dominica, Guadeloupe, and St. Lucia. Any of these trips costs about €79 one-way. The crossings generally take between three and four hours and if the waters are choppy it can be a rough passage. French films (sometimes R-types) played on flat screens help pass the time. Most of these services are daily, with extra departures on weekends, and can be crowded. Boats depart from the new terminal in Fort-de-France, which has the same type of luggage scales used at the airport; overweight charges are now enforced.

Weather permitting, *vedettes* (ferries) operate daily between Quai d'Esnambuc in Fort-de-France and the marinas in Pointe du Bout, Anse-Mitan, and Anse-à-l'Ane and are the best way to go into the capital. Any of these trips takes about 20 min. Ferries depart every 30 min on weekdays; longer waits in the low season. Round-trip tickets cost €6.50.

Contacts: Vedettes Madinina (☎ 0596/63–06–46).

Nonstops: No nonstop flights to Martinique from the U.S.

Many travelers fly American Airlines and connect in San Juan to one of two daily flights on **American Eagle** (☎ 0590/21–13–66 in Guadeloupe). **Air Antilles Express** (☎ 0890/64–86–48 or 0596/42–16–71 ⊕ www.airantilles.com) flies from Guadeloupe, St. Maarten, and St. Barth. **Air Caraïbes** (☎ 0820/82–64–51 ⊕ www.aircaraibes.com) flies from Guadeloupe, St. Maarten, St. Barth, and Santo Domingo.(This airline offers substantial discounts for seniors.) **Air France** (☎ 0820/82–08–20 or 0892/68–29–72) is another connection option in San Juan. **LIAT** (☎ 0596/42–16–11, 0590/21–13–93 in Guadeloupe, 888/844–5428 in U.S. ⊕ www.liatairline.com) connects Martinique with the English-speaking "down islands." It code-shares with Air Caraïbes. The latter is one airline that offers substantial senior discounts.

Airport: Martinique AiméCésaire Airport (✉ FDF ☎ 0596/42–16–00) is in the commercial area of Lamentin, a 15-min taxi ride from Fort-de-France and some 40 min from Les Trois-Ilets Peninsula. A public bus to Fort-de-France costs €1.

Getting Around Martinique

Driving: The main highways, about 175 mi (280 km) of well-paved and well-marked roads, are excellent, but only in a few areas are they lighted at night. Many hotels are on roads that are barely passable, so get wherever you're going by nightfall or you could lose your way. Then tell a stranger, *"Je suis perdu!"* ("I am lost!"). It elicits sympathy. If they say, *"Suivez-moi!"*—that's "Follow me!"—stay glued to their bumper. Finally, drive defensively; although Martinicans are polite and lovely people, they drive with aggressive abandon.

Martinique, especially Fort-de-France and environs, is plagued with heavy traffic; if you must drive into Fort-de-France, do it on a weekend. Absolutely avoid the Lamentin Airport area and Fort-de-France during weekday rush hours, roughly 7 to 10 am and 4 to 7:30 pm, and on Sunday night. Even the smaller towns such as La Trinité have rush hours. Watch, too, for *dos d'ânes* (literally, donkey backs), speed bumps that are hard to spot—particularly at night. Gas is costly, some $6 per gallon. Be aware that the French gendarmes set up roadblocks, often on Sunday, to stop speeders, drunk drivers, and just to check papers.

Car Rentals: Europcar (☎ 0596/42–42–42) will deliver the car to you and pick it up later, and its rates are usually among the lowest. In Ste-Anne, and particularly if you're staying at Club Med, small **Euro Soleil Car** (☎ 0596/76–93–34) has exceptionally good prices. Of the many agencies, **JumboCar** (☎ 0596/42–22–22 or 0820/22–02–30) is the most likely to cut a deal, but few of its staffers speak English.

Major Agencies: Avis (☎ 0596/42–11–00). **Budget** (☎ 0596/42–04–04). **Hertz** (☎ 0596/51–01–01).

Taxis: Taxis, which are metered, are expensive, though you can try bargaining by offering to pay a flat rate to your destination. **J. Peloponese Taxis** (☎ 0696/25–61–02) provides luxury service in new Mercedes-Benz cars. Drivers of **M. Martial Mercedes Taxis** (☎ 0596/64–20–24, 0696/45–69–07 mobile) speak English, Spanish, and German as well as French. At **Taxi de Place** (☎ 0696/31–91–05) you will find some English-speaking drivers, lots of courtesy, and new SUVs.

Island Activities

Martinique has plenty of **beaches** for relaxing, including some nice white-sand beaches south of Fort-de-France. Anse Corps de Garde in Ste-Luce and Les Saline in Ste-Anne are among the nicest.

You'll get a better taste of the island if you take part in the myriad outdoor activities. Martinique is a major **sailing** center; **windsurfing** is also popular, as is **deep-sea fishing**. On land are **canopy tours, mountain-biking** excursions, and **horseback riding**.

Shoppers will enjoy inexpensive French wines and the fresh-from-France fashions available in Fort-de-France's boutiques. Locally made jewelry and baskets can also be good buys.

Most hotels have entertainment during the high season, but there are also plenty of **nightspots** for dancing, though the crowds tend to be younger (and mostly local).

Enjoying fine **French and creole cuisine** is also at the top of many people's lists; the island has many wonderful restaurants. Travelers looking to save on high euro prices may find relative bargains on the many prix-fixe menus (some of which include wine).

15

MARTINIQUE PLANNER

Fast Facts

Banks and Exchange Services: The euro is the official currency in Martinique. U.S. dollars are accepted in some hotels but generally at an unfavorable rate. You can usually get the best rate by withdrawing euros from ATMs, which you'll find at the airport and at branches of the Crédit Agricole bank. Major credit cards are accepted by most hotels and restaurants, but some establishments accept neither credit cards nor traveler's checks, particularly once you get away from Fort-de-France and Pointe du Bout. Many establishments don't accept American Express in any case.

Electricity: 220-volt outlets. North American appliances require a converter and adapter.

Emergency Services: Ambulance (☎ *0596/70–36–48* or *0596/71–59–48*). **Fire** (☎ *18*). **Police** (☎ *17*).

Passport Requirements: All visitors must have a valid passport and a return or ongoing ticket. A birth certificate and picture ID are *not* sufficient.

Weddings: Martinique has a long residency requirement, so it's not really feasible to plan a wedding on the island. It is, however, a most romantic honeymoon destination.

Essentials

Mail: Airmail letters to the United States cost €0.95 for up to 20 grams and €1 to Canada; postcards cost €0.85, €0.95 to Canada. Stamps can be purchased from post offices, tobacco shops, and newsstands. Letters to Martinique should include the name of the business, street (if available), town, and postal code, as well as "Martinique, French West Indies." Mail is extremely slow, both ways.

Taxes and Service Charges: A resort tax varies from city to city. Each has its own tax, with most between €0.76 and €1.25 per person per day; the maximum is €2.25. Rates quoted by hotels usually include a 10% service charge.

Telephones: There are no coin-operated phone booths. Public phones use a *télécarte*, which you can buy at post offices, *café-tabacs* (cafés with storefronts), hotels, and *bureaux de change* (currency-exchange offices). To place a local or interisland call you have to dial all 10 numbers, beginning with 0596 and then the six-digit number. To call Martinique from the United States, dial 011–596–596 plus the local six-digit number (yes, you must dial 596 *twice*). To call the United States from Martinique, dial 001, then the area code, then the local number.

Tipping: All restaurants include a 15% service charge in their menu prices. You can always add to this if you feel that service was particularly good.

Visitor Information: Martinique Promotion Bureau (✉ *825 3rd Ave., 29th fl., New York* ☎ *212/838–6887 in New York* ⊕ *www.martinique.org*).

Comité Martiniquais du Tourisme (✉ *Immeuble le Beaupre, Pointe de Jaham, Schoelcher, Fort-de-France* ☎ *0596/61–61–77* ⊕ *www.martiniquetourisme.com*). **Office du Tourisme de Fort-de-France** (✉ *76 rue Lazare Carnot, Fort-de-France* ☎ *0596/60–27–73* ⊕ *www.tourismefdf.com*).

Where to Stay

Martinique's accommodations range from tiny inns called *relais créoles*, boutique hotels, and private villas, to splashy tourist resorts and restored plantation houses. Several hotels are clustered in Point du Bout on Les Trois-Ilets Peninsula, which is connected to Fort-de-France by ferry. Other clusters are in Ste-Luce, and Le François has become known for its boutique properties. Hotels and relais can be found all over the island. Since Martinique is the largest of the Windward Islands, this can mean a substantial drive to your hotel after a long flight or ferry trip. You may want to stay closer to the airport on your first night.

Large Resorts: There are only a few deluxe properties on the island. Those that lack megastar ratings offer an equally appealing mixture of charisma, hospitality, and French style. Larger hotels often have the busy, slightly frenetic feel that the French seem to like.

Relais Créoles: Small, individually owned inns are still available on Martinique, though they may be far removed from the resort clusters.

Villas: Groups and large families can save money by renting a villa, but the language barrier can be problematic, and often you will need a car.

HOTEL AND RESTAURANT COSTS

Restaurant prices are for a main course at dinner and include any taxes or service charges. Hotel prices are per night for a double room in high season, including most taxes but not service charges and meal plans. (Club Med is the only all-inclusive reviewed.)

WHAT IT COSTS IN EUROS

	¢	$	$$	$$$	$$$$
Restaurants	under €8	€8–€12	€12–€20	€20–€30	over €30
Hotels	under €150	€150–€275	€276–€375	€376–€475	over €475

Travel Tips

Taxi Tips: Taxis in Martinique are expensive. From the airport to Fort-de-France you'll pay at least €35; from the airport to Pointe du Bout, about €50; and to Tartane, about €60. A 40% surcharge is levied between 7 pm and 6 am and on Sunday. If you arrive at night, depending on where your hotel is, it may be cheaper (although not safer) to rent a car from the airport and keep it for 24 hours than to take a taxi to your hotel.

Renting a Car: Be prepared for a manual shift, steep mountainous roads, and heavy traffic. Prices are about €70 per day or €330 per week (unlimited mileage), substantially more for an automatic, which is rare. Usually, you won't find them unless you book in advance.

Alternative Transportation: Locals take *collectifs* (white vans holding up to 10 passengers) that cost just a few euros and depart from Pointe Simon, on the waterfront in Fort-de-France, to all parts of the island. Don't be shy; the difference can be €3 and, say, €60 for a taxi to reach the same destination. Drivers don't usually speak English and there's no a/c. A new bus company, **Bus Mozaik** (⊕ *www.aquelleheure. fr/bus.htm*), with fares from €1.20 and a/c, has stops within the city, and services Lamentin, the Fort-de-France suburbs like Schoelcher, and as far into the interior of the island as St. Joseph. The tourist offices can help with maps and information.

15

MARTINIQUE BEACHES

Take to the beach in Martinique. A Caribbean vacation can be a rough ride on Atlantic surf or a swim in calm Caribbean waters as tranquil as a blue lagoon. Experience the white sandbars known as Josephine's Baths, where Napoléon's Joséphine would bathe.

(Above) Anse Corps de Garde. (Opposite page bottom) Les Salines. (Opposite page top) Diamant Beach.

All of Martinique's beaches are open to the public, but hotels charge a fee for nonguests to use changing rooms and other facilities. There are no official nudist beaches, but topless bathing is prevalent, as is the case on most French islands. Unless you're an expert swimmer, steer clear of the Atlantic waters, except in the area of Cap Chevalier (Cape Knight) and the Presqu'île du Caravelle (Caravelle Peninsula). The white-sand beaches are south of Fort-de-France; to the north, the beaches are silvery-black volcanic sand. Some of the most pleasant strips of sand are around Ste-Anne, Ste-Luce, and Havre du Robert. And one wonders how, some 15 minutes from Le François harbor, the white sandbars that form Josephine's Baths were created in the middle of the sea.

SHIFTY SANDS

Martinique's sand often belies its environment. The long tawny stretches of beach in Carbet and the neighboring town of St-Pierre, where the infamous volcano Mont Pelée is located, are *not* volcanic black sand. The famous black-sand beach of Diamant is nowhere near Mont Pelée. It is, however, across from Diamond Rock, a volcanic outcropping.

Anse Corps de Garde. On the southern Caribbean coast, this is one of the island's best long stretches of white sand. The public beach has picnic tables, restrooms, sea grape trees, and crowds, particularly on weekends, when you can find plenty of wandering food vendors The water is calm, with just enough wave action to remind you it's the sea. From Fort-de-France, exit to the right before you get to the town of Ste-Luce. You first see signs for the Karibea Hotels and then one for Corps de Garde, which is on the right. At the stop sign take a left. ⊠ *Ste-Luce.*

Anse-Mitan. This is not the French Riviera, though there are often yachts moored offshore. This long stretch of beach can be particularly fun on Sunday. Small, family-owned seaside restaurants are half hidden among palm trees and are footsteps from the lapping waves. Nearly all offer grilled lobster and some form of music, perhaps a zouk band. Inexpensive waterfront hotels line the clean, golden beach, which has excellent snorkeling just offshore. Chaise longues are available for rent from hotels for about €6. When you get to Pointe du Bout, take a left at the yellow office of Budget Rent-A-Car, then the next left up a hill, and park near the little white church. ⊠ *Pointe du Bout, Les Trois-Ilets.*

Anse Tartane. This patch of sand is on the wild side of the Presqu'île du Caravelle. It's what the French call a *sauvage* (virgin) beach, and the only people you are likely to see are brave surfers who ride the high waves or some local families. The surf school here has taught many kids the ropes. Résidence Oceane looks down on all of this action but doesn't have a restaurant. Turn right before you get to La Trinité, and follow the route de Château past the Caravelle hotel. Instead of following the signs to Résidence Oceane, veer left and go downhill when you see the ocean. The road runs right beside the beach. There are several bays and *pointes* here, but if you keep heading to the right, you can reach the surf school. ⊠ *Tartane.*

Diamant Beach. The island's longest beach has a splendid view of Diamond Rock, but the Atlantic waters are rough, with lots of wave action. Often the beach is deserted, especially midweek, which is more reason to swim with prudence. Happily, it's a great place for picnicking and beachcombing; there are shade trees aplenty, and parking is abundant and free. The hospitable, family-run Diamant les Bains hotel is a good lunch spot; if you eat lunch there, the management may let you wash off in the pool overlooking the beach. From Les Trois-Ilets, go in the direction of Rivière Salée, taking the secondary road to the east,

15

Les Salines

toward Le Diamant. A coastal route, it leads to the beach. ⊠ *Le Diamant.*

Les Salines. A short drive south of Ste-Anne brings you to a mile-long (1.5-km) cove lined with soft white sand and coconut palms. The beach is awash with families and children during holidays and on weekends but quiet during the week. The far end—away from the makeshift souvenir shops—is most appealing. The calm waters are safe for swimming, even for the kids. You can't rent chaise longues, but there are showers. Food vendors roam the sand. From Le Marin, take the coastal road toward Ste-Anne. You will see signs for Les Salines. If you see the sign for Pointe du Marin, you have gone too far. ⊠ *Ste-Anne.*

☾ **Pointe du Bout.** The beaches here are small, man-made, and lined with resorts, including the Hotel Bakoua. Each little strip is associated with its resident hotel, and security guards and closed gates make access difficult. However, if you take a left across from the main pedestrian entrance to the marina—after the taxi stand—then go left again, you will reach the beach for Hotel Bakoua, which has especially nice facilities and several options for lunch and drinks. If things are quiet—particularly during the week—one of the beach boys may rent you a chaise; otherwise, just plop your beach towel down, face forward, and enjoy the delightful view of the Fort-de-France skyline. The water is dead calm and quite shallow, but it eventually drops off if you swim out a bit. ⊠ *Pointe du Bout, Les Trois-Ilets.*

Pointe du Marin. Stretching north from Ste-Anne, this is a good windsurfing and waterskiing spot. It's also a popular family beach, with restaurants, campsites, and clean facilities available for a small fee. Club Med is on the northern edge, and you can purchase a day pass. From Le Marin, take the coastal road to Ste-Anne. Make a right before town, toward Domaine de Belfond. You can see signs for Pointe du Marin. ⊠ *Marin.*

By Eileen Robinson Smith

Numerous scattered ruins and other historical monuments reflect the richness of Martinique's sugarcane plantocracy, *rhum,* and the legacy of slavery. Called the Rum Capital of the World, it is widely considered the best gourmet island in the Caribbean. It stirs the passions with its distinctive brand of culinary offerings. If you believe in magic, Martinique has it, along with a sensuality that fosters romance. It has become known as the island of *revenants,* those who always return. *Et pourquoi non?*

15

Martinique is simply one of the most enchanting destinations in the Western Hemisphere. Francophiles adore this French island, for its gastromony, its *musique* and élan, and the availability of the finest French products, from Chanel fashions to Limoges china. It is endowed with physical beauty, as varied as white-sand beaches and tropical rain forests. The volcano Mont Pelée looms over the harbor town of St-Pierre, known as the Pompeii of the Caribbean. The recent additions to the island's tourism product include dynamic changes in its largest city, Fort-de-France, enhanced attractions, new restaurants and clubs. Martinicans will be glad you came and you will be greeted with warm smiles and politesse.

Christopher Columbus first sighted this gorgeous island in 1502, when it was inhabited by the fierce Caraïbes, who had terrorized the peace-loving Arawaks. The Arawaks called their home Madinina (the Isle of Flowers), and for good reason. Exotic wild orchids, frangipani, anthurium, jade vines, flamingo flowers, and hundreds of vivid varieties of hibiscus still thrive here.

The island reflects its rich cultural history. In colonial days, Martinique was the administrative, social, and cultural center of the French Antilles, a rich, aristocratic island famous for its beautiful women. The island even gave birth to an empress, Napoléon's Joséphine. It saw the full flowering of a plantocracy, with servants and soirees, wine cellars and snobbery.

Martinique is the largest stronghold of the *békés*—the descendants of the original French planters—and they are still the privileged class on any of the French-Caribbean islands. Numbering around 4,000, many control Martinique's most profitable businesses from banana plantations and rum distilleries to car dealerships. The island's economy depends on *les bananes* (bananas), *l'ananas* (pineapples), cane sugar, rum, and fishing. The elite dress in designer outfits straight off the Paris runways. In general, the islanders have style. In the airport waiting room, you can almost always tell the Martiniquaises by their fashionable clothes.

Of the island's 400,000 inhabitants, 100,000 live in Fort-de-France and its environs. It has 34 separate municipalities. Though the actual number of French residents from the Metropole (France) does not exceed 15% of the total population, Martinique is a part of France, an overseas *département* to be exact, and French is the official language, though the vast majority of the residents also speak Creole.

Thousands are employed in government jobs offering more paid holidays than most Americans can imagine. Martinicans enjoy their time off, celebrating everything from *le fin de la semaine* (the weekend) to Indian feast days, sailboat races, and Carnival. Their joie de vivre is infectious. Once you experience it, you'll be back.

EXPLORING MARTINIQUE

The northern part of the island will appeal to nature lovers, hikers, and mountain climbers. The drive from Fort-de-France to St-Pierre is particularly impressive, as is the one across the island, via Morne Rouge, from the Caribbean to the Atlantic. This is Martinique's wild side—a place of waterfalls, rain forest, and mountains. The highlight is Mont Pelée. The south is the more developed half of the island, where the resorts and restaurants are located, as well as the beaches.

SOUTH OF FORT-DE-FRANCE

Diamond Rock. This volcanic mound is 1 mi (1.5 km) offshore from the small, friendly village of Le Diamant and is one of the island's best diving spots. In 1804, during the squabbles over possession of the island between the French and the English, the latter commandeered the rock, armed it with cannons, and proceeded to use it as a strategic battery. The British held the rock for nearly a year and a half, attacking any French ships that came along. The French got wind that the British were getting cabin fever on their isolated island and arranged for barrels of rum to float up on the rock. The French easily overpowered the inebriated sailors, ending one of the most curious engagements in naval history.

Forêt de Montravail. A few miles north of Ste-Luce, this tropical rain forest is ideal for a short hike. Look for the interesting group of Carib rock drawings.

Lamentin. There's nothing pretty about Lamentin; the international airport is its most notable landmark. The rest of the town is a sprawling industrial and commercial zone. But many people come here for shopping in the big, fancy shopping mall, with a Carrefour supermarket as its anchor. La Galleria, a second megamall of roughly 100 shops and boutiques, offers everything from pâté de foie gras and Camembert to CDs and sunglasses.

Le François. With some 16,000 inhabitants, this is the main city on the Atlantic coast. Many of the old wooden buildings remain and are juxtaposed with concrete structures The classic West Indian cemetery, with its black-and-white tiles, is still here, and a marina is at the end of town. Two of Martinique's best hotels are in this area, as well as some of the most upscale residences. Le François is also noted for its snorkeling. Offshore are the privately owned Ilets de l'Impératrice. The islands received that name because, according to legend, this is where Empress Joséphine came to bathe in the shallow basins known as *les fonds blanc* because of their white-sand bottoms. Group boat tours leave from the harbor and include lunch and drinks. Prices vary *(⇨ Sports and Activities)*. You can also haggle with a fisherman to take you out for a while on his boat. There's a fine bay 6 mi (10 km) farther along the coast where you can swim and go kayaking. The town itself is rather lackluster but authentic, and you'll find a number of different shops and supermarkets, owned by truly lovely, helpful residents.

★ **Habitation Clément.** Get a glimpse into Martinique's colonial past, into the elegance and privilege of plantation society. Visitors are now given a multilingual audio headset, which explains highlights of the self-guided tour, such as the animal mill. Signage further educates guests on everything from the rum-making process to the tropical flora and fauna of the botanical garden. The Palm Grove, with an avenue of palms and park benches, is delightful. It was all built with the wealth generated by its rum distillery, and its 18th-century splendor has been lovingly preserved. The plantation's Creole house illustrates the adaption to life in the tropics up through the 20th century. Fascinating ancient maps, an early French typewriter, a crank-up telephone, and decades-old photos of the Clements and Hayots (béké families), are juxtaposed with some of the most avant-garde Afro-Caribbean art from Martinique and neighboring Caribbean islands. Enjoy the free tastings at the bar of the retail shop. Consider the Canne Bleu, Grappe Blanche, or one of the aged rums, some bottled as early as 1952. ⊠ *Domaine de l'Acajou, Le François* ☎ *0596/54–62–07* ⊕ *www.habitation-clement.fr* ⊠ €9 ⊗ *Oct.–Aug., daily 9–5.*

NEED A BREAK? Should you need a fast French lunch break in Le François, try **Le Grand Trianon Boulangerie Patisserie** near the new Carrefour Supermarket. Crisp baguettes and luscious pastries with ice cream are sold, and prix-fixe lunches with sandwiches or salads are offered.

Le Marin. The yachting capital of Martinique is also known for its colorful August carnival and its Jesuit church, circa 1766. From Le Marin a narrow road leads to picturesque Cap Chevalier, about 1 mi (1.5 km) from town. Most of the buildings are white and very European. The marina is lively, and there are waterfront restaurants and clubs.

Diamond Rock.

Le Vauclin. The return of the fishermen at noon is the big event in this important fishing port on the Atlantic. There's also the 18th-century Chapel of the Holy Virgin. Nearby is the highest point in the south, Mont Vauclin (1,654 feet). A hike to the top rewards you with one of the best views on the island.

Les Trois-Ilets. Named after the three rocky islands nearby, this lovely little village (population 3,000) has unusual brick-and-wood buildings roofed with antique tiles. It's known for its pottery, straw, and woodwork but above all as the birthplace of Napoléon's empress, Joséphine. In the square, where there's also a market and a fine *mairie* (town hall), you can visit the simple church where she was baptized Marie-Joseph Tascher de la Pagerie. The Martinicans have always been enormously proud of Joséphine, even though her husband reintroduced slavery on the island and most historians consider her to have been rather shallow.

★ A stone building that held the kitchen of the estate where Joséphine grew up houses the **Musée de la Pagerie.** It contains an assortment of memorabilia pertaining to her life and rather unfortunate loves, including a marriage certificate and a love letter written straight from the heart by Napoléon in 1796. The main house blew down in the hurricane of 1766, when she was 3, and the family lived for years above the sugarcane factory—a hot, odoriferous, and fly-ridden existence. At 16 she was wed (an arranged marriage because her father was a gambling man in need of money) to Alexandre de Beauharnais. After he was assassinated during the Revolution, she married Napoléon. ⊠ *Les Trois-Ilets* ☎ *0596/68–33–06* 🎫 *€5* ☻ *Tues.–Fri. 9–5, weekends 9:30– noon and 3–5.*

Down a dirt road, a Martinican has called up the past with **La Savane des Esclaves** (*the Savannah of the Slaves*), a re-created slave village. This labor of love was created by Gilbert Larose, who has a fascination with the lives of his ancestors. This is an in-depth look at that major element in Martinique's history and culture, with food tastings and artisan demonstrations. Saturday from 9 am to noon is Tradition Morning, with elaborate tastings, demonstrations, and traditional dance lessons. ✉ *Quartier La Ferme* ☎ 0696/22–79–05 💲€5, Sat. morning €20 ⏰ *Daily 10–noon and 2–5.*

NEED A BREAK? Just steps down the hill from the church in Les Trois-Ilets, a simple patisserie, recognized by its awning, brews fresh coffee and bakes wonders such as éclairs with chocolate custard interiors. Sit at a table or take it to go.

Pointe du Bout. This tourist area has a marina and several resort hotels, among them the deluxe Hotel Bakoua (formerly a Sofitel and now a member of MGallery, a collection of unique, historic hotels). The ferry to Fort-de-France leaves from here. A cluster of boutiques, ice-cream parlors, and rental-car agencies forms the hub from which restaurants and hotels of varying caliber radiate, but it's a pretty quiet place in the low season. The beach at Anse-Mitan, which is a little west of Pointe du Bout proper, is one of the best on the island. There are also several small restaurants and inexpensive guesthouses here.

Ste-Anne. A lovely white-sand beach and a Catholic church are the highlights of this town on the island's southern tip. A bevy of small, inexpensive cafés offer seafood and creole dishes, pizza parlors, produce markets, and barbecue joints—it's fun and lively. To the south of Ste-Anne is Pointe des Salines, the southernmost tip of the island and site of Martinique's best beach.

Ste-Luce. This quaint fishing village has a sleepy main street with tourist shops and markets, and you can see some cool types taking a Pernod. Many young, single people live in this town. From the sidewalk cafés there are panoramic sea views of St. Lucia. Nearby are excellent beaches and several resorts. To the east is Pointe Figuier, an excellent spot for scuba diving.

FORT-DE-FRANCE

With its historic fort and superb location beneath the towering Pitons du Carbet on the Baie des Flamands, Martinique's capital—home to about one-quarter of the island's 400,000 inhabitants—should be a grand place. It hasn't been for decades but it's now coming up fast. An ambitious redevelopment project, still under way, hopes to make it one of the most attractive cities in the Caribbean. The plan includes the renovation of the park La Savane, the construction of a spectacular waterfront promenade (completed), and coming soon, the Pointe Simon Business and Tourist Center, which will have a 100-room hotel and luxury apartment building. The striking new 215,000-square-foot Cour Perrinon Mall houses a Carrefour supermarket, a bookstore, perfume shops, designer boutiques, a French bakery, and a café-brasserie. Across from the newly renovated theater, renamed for the island's famed poet, Aimé Césaire, the mall

15

DON'T MISS NOTRE DAME

Trois-Ilets is French for "three islands" and indeed, there are three islets in the Bay of Le François. Many tourists follow the route to Les Trois-Ilets, a designated region of Martinique, because it leads to the hotels, restaurants, and beaches of the touristic zone known as Pointe du Bout. Many miss out by not taking the sharp right turn off the route at the signs that say "Village" and "Le Post" (post office), which leads to **Notre Dame de la Bonne Deliverance**. The centuries-old church designed after those in rural France in the 1700s has a steeple that looks nearly new in contrast to its aged stucco facade, and a clock face the villagers rely on. Inside, a domed ceiling meant to replicate the heavens is an ethereal blue. The church, like the island, has lived through devastating fires and hurricanes. Les Trois-Ilets' main street is named the avenue de l'Impératrice Joséphine. In November, the church's adjacent *cimetière* (cemetery) comes alive with islanders honoring their dead on La Toussaint—All Saints' Day. Notre Dame de la Bonne Deliverance is a sight tourists should not miss. Remember, take a sharp right.

This was the hometown of Joséphine, Napoléon's bride. That this small island birthed an empress continues to be a huge source of pride for Martinicans. In 2008, the island's golf course was renamed for her (⇨ *Sports and Activities*). Also, Le Spa Joséphine opened at the Hotel Carayou (⊕ *www.spa-josephine.com*). Wouldn't Napoléon have liked a four-handed couples massage?

is bordered by rue Perrinon. Alas, the Martinique Tourism Office, formerly on the waterfront, is still in its temporary quarters in the suburb of Schoelcher, so it's not readily accessible to the carless. There is a small office of Tourism de Fort-de-France at 76 rue Lazare Carnot. It has some brochures in English and helpful, English-speaking staffers. They can organize English-language tours with advance notice. Walking tours are scheduled for Wednesday and Friday at 9 am. They take in a number of historic sites in about an hour and 45 minutes and cost €12. Another Point d'Information Touristique is near the cathedral, at the junction of rues Antoine Siger and Victor Schoelcher.

The new Stewards Urbaine, easily recognized by their red caps and uniforms, are able to answer most visitor questions and give directions. These young gals and garçons are multilingual and knowledgeable. When a large cruise ship is in port, they are out in force, positioned in heavily trafficked tourist zones and at the front entrance of Lafayette's department store.

The most pleasant districts of Fort-de-France—Didier, Bellevue, and Schoelcher—are up on the hillside, and you need a car (or a taxi) to reach them. But if you try to drive here, you may find yourself trapped in gridlock in the warren of narrow streets downtown. Parking is difficult, and it's best to try for one of the garages or—as a second choice—outdoor public parking areas. Come armed with some euro coins for this purpose. A taxi or ferry from Pointe du Bout may be a better alternative. Even if your hotel isn't there, you can drive to the marina and park nearby.

There are some fine shops with Parisian wares (at Parisian prices) in which to buy French lingerie, St. Laurent or Cacharel, and sexy stiletto heels. Near the harbor is a lively indoor marketplace (grand marché), where produce and spices are sold. In La Savane the street vendors sell everything from jewelry to human hairpieces. A playground on the Malecon, which now has a half-mile wooden boardwalk, has swings, trampolines, benches, and even *pétanque* grounds.

The urban beach between the Malecon and the fort, La Française, has been cleaned up; white sand was brought in, and because of all the revitalization, Club Med, Holland America, Royal Caribbean, and Silversea are just a few of the cruise lines that pull into this port.

Fort-de-France is patrolled by about 20 civilians, on foot and on bikes, easily recognized by their blue-and-orange uniforms. They complement the presence of the police. Alas, the heat and exhaust fumes still exist, so by day, dress to stay cool and rehydrate often. There are some piano bars, hot jazz venues, new late-night restaurants, and younger-crowd bars like Le Gossip—a restaurant, boutique, and art gallery that hosts fashion shows, poetry readings, wine tastings and even speed dating. New also is Le Foyaal (⊕ *www.lefoyaal.com*), a tri-level restaurant complex featuring a bar, brasserie-patissiere, and Le Césaire, a gastronomic restaurant, that serves until midnight.

If you plan to go into the city at night, it's still best to go with a group, even better if you can go with a group of Martinicans.

Bibliothèque Schoelcher. This wildly elaborate Romanesque public library was named after Victor Schoelcher, who led the fight to free the slaves in the French West Indies in the 19th century. The eye-popping structure was built for the 1889 Paris Exposition, after which it was dismantled, shipped to Martinique, and reassembled piece by ornate piece. ⊠ *At rue de la Liberté, which runs along west side of La Savane* ☎ *0596/70–26–67* ⊠ *Free* ☉ *Mon. 1–5:30, Tues.–Fri. 8:30–5:30, Sat. 8:30–noon.*

La Savane. The heart of Fort-de-France, La Savane is a 12½-acre park filled with trees, fountains, and benches. It was a popular gathering place and the scene of promenades, parades, and impromptu soccer matches; and it has now been beautifully renovated to its former glory. Its urban decay has been eradicated. This urban park has undergone a massive revitalization, completed in late 2010. It is a focal point of the city again, with entertainment and shopping and a pedestrian mall. Attractive wooden stands have been constructed along the edge of the park that house a tourism information office, public restrooms, arts and crafts vendors, a crepe stand, and an ice-cream parlor (⇨ *see Fort-de-France above*). Diagonally across from La Savane, you can catch the ferries for the 20-minute run across the bay to Pointe du Bout and the beaches at Anse-Mitan and Anse-à-l'Ane. It's relatively cheap as well as stress-free—much safer, more pleasant, and faster than by car.

The most imposing historic site in Fort-de-France is **Ft. St-Louis**, which runs along the east side of La Savane. It is no longer open to the public, as it is now functioning as a military installation.

★ **Le Musée Régional d'Histoire et d'Ethnographie.** This museum is a learning experience that is best undertaken at the beginning of your vacation,

Anglers sitting on a dock in Fort de France harbor.

so you can better understand the history, background, and people of the island. Housed in an elaborate former residence (circa 1888) with balconies and fretwork, it has everything from displays of the garish gold jewelry that prostitutes wore after emancipation to reconstructed rooms of a home of proper, middle-class Martinicans. There's even a display of Creole headdresses with details of how they were tied to indicate if a woman was single, married, or otherwise occupied. ⊠ *10 bd. Général de Gaulle* ☎ *0596/72–81–87* ⊠ *€3* ☉ *Mon. and Wed.–Fri. 8:30–5, Tues. 2–5, Sat. 8:30–noon.*

■ **TIP→** Admission to the above and to all regional museums is free the last Saturday of the month.

Parc Floral Aimé Cesaire The Galerie de Biologie et de Géologie in this park in the northeastern corner of the city center will acquaint you with the island's exotic flora. There's also an aquarium. The park contains the island's official cultural center, where there are sometimes free evening concerts. ⊠ *Pl. José-Marti, Sermac* ☎ *0596/71–66–25* ⊠ *Grounds free, aquarium €5.60, gallery €2* ☉ *Park daily dawn–10 pm; aquarium daily 9–7; gallery Tues.–Fri. 9:30–12:30 and 3:30–5:30, Sat. 9–1 and 3–5.*

Rue Victor Schoelcher. Stores sell Paris fashions and French perfume, china, crystal, and liqueurs, as well as local handicrafts along this street running through the center of the capital's primary shopping district, a six-block area bounded by rue de la République, rue de la Liberté, rue Victor Severe, and rue Victor Hugo.

Schoelcher. Pronounced shell-*share*, this upscale suburb of Fort-de-France is home to the University of the French West Indies and Guyana, as well as Martinique's largest convention center, Madiana.

St-Louis Cathedral. The Romanesque cathedral with its lovely stained-glass windows was built in 1878, the sixth church on this site (the others were destroyed by fires, hurricanes, and earthquakes). ✉ *Rue Victor Schoelcher.*

NORTH OF FORT-DE-FRANCE

Ajoupa-Bouillon. This flower-filled 17th century village amid pineapple fields is the jumping-off point for several sights. The Saut Babin, a 40-foot waterfall, is a half-hour walk from Ajoupa-Bouillon. The Gorges de la Falaise is a river gorge where you can swim.

☺ **Aqualand.** This U.S.-style water park is a great place for families to have a wet, happy day. The large wave pool is well tended; little ones love it, as they do the pirate's galleon in their own watery playground. Older kids may prefer to get their thrill from the slides, including the hairpin turns of the Giant Slalom, the Colorado slide, and the Black Hole, which winds around in total darkness. In the best French tradition, the fast-food options are top-notch, including crepes, salads, and even beer. Inquire about catching a weekend Somatour shuttle boat. Nouvelles Frontieres organizes tours that include the park. Phone first during the low season; it shuts down for months, but is normally open from April to September. ✉ *Rte. des Pitons, Carbet* ☎ *0596/78–40–00* ⊕ *www.aqualand-martinique.fr* ✎ *€17.50* ☉ *Apr.–Sept., daily 10–6.*

Balata. This quiet little town has two sights worth visiting. Built in 1923 to commemorate those Martinicans who fought and died in World War I, **Balata Church** is an exact replica of Paris's Sacré-Coeur Basilica. The **Jardin de Balata** (*Balata Gardens*) has thousands of varieties of tropical flowers and plants. There are shaded benches from which to take in the mountain views and a plantation-style house furnished with period furniture. An aerial path gives visitors an astounding, bird's-eye view of the gardens and surrounding hills, from wooden walkways suspended 50 feet in the air. You can order anthuriums and other tropical flowers to be delivered to the airport from the habitation's mesmerizing flower boutique. Just 15 minutes from Fort-de-France, in the direction St-Pierre, this worthy site explains why Martinique is called the Island of Flowers. ✉ *Rte. de Balata, Balata* ☎ *0596/64–48–73* ⊕ *www.jardindebalata.com* ✎ *€12.50* ☉ *Daily 9–5.*

Basse-Pointe. On the route to this village on the Atlantic coast at the island's northern end you pass many banana and pineapple plantations. Just south of Basse-Pointe is a **Hindu temple** built by descendants of the East Indians who settled in this area in the 19th century. The view of Mont Pelée from the temple is amazing.

Bellefontaine. This colorful fishing village has pastel houses on the hillsides and beautifully painted *gommiers* (fishing boats) bobbing in the water. Look for the restaurant built in the shape of a boat.

Dubuc Castle. At the eastern tip of the Presqu'île du Caravelle are the ruins of this castle, once the home of the Dubuc de Rivery family, who owned the peninsula in the 18th century. According to legend, young Aimée Dubuc de Rivery was captured by Barbary pirates, sold to the

15

Making Nice in Martinique

Martinique is a polite society. Doors will open to you and you will win the favor of the Martinicans if you demonstrate proper French manners. Preface questions, particularly if asking directions, with *Bonjour* or *Bonsoir*, followed by *Excusez-moi*. Even friends greet each other with a *bonjour* rather than the equivalent of *hi* or *hello*. When finished, say, *"Merci beaucoup. Bonne journée"* ("Thank you very much. Have a good day") or *"Bonne nuit"* ("Good night"). Bone up on your French, and bring your phrase book with you, please (*s' il vous plait*, or when written, *s.v.p.*).

INTRODUCTIONS
You will likely be introduced as Madame Smith rather than *mademoiselle*, even if you are single, if you are over 30. When introduced say, *"Enchanté"* ("Enchanted"). Nice, no?

Do not call someone by their first name, especially someone who is older, until they tell you to. When they call you by your Christian name, you have carte blanche. U.S. southerners will have no difficulty remembering to say *"Merci, madame"* (not *ma'am*) and *"No merci, monsieur."* When and if you are speaking French, use the formal *vous* for *you*, not the familiar *tu*.

The French islanders will kiss each other on both cheeks if they know the other person and often if they do not. If they realize that you are not French, they will most likely extend their hand for a handshake. And yes, the older gentlemen still kiss a lady's hand, although it will likely be a mock-kiss, not touching skin. Oh, and when at a restaurant, don't ever embarrass yourself by asking for a doggie bag. You will be considered gauche.

Ottoman Empire, became a favorite of the sultan, and gave birth to Mahmud II. You can park your car right after the turnoff for Résidence Oceane and walk the dirt road to the ruins. The castle is rubble; hikers go for the dramatic ocean views, raw nature, and birdlife.

Le Morne Rouge. This town sits on the southern slopes of the volcano that destroyed it in 1902. Today it's a popular resort spot and offers hikers some fantastic mountain scenery. From Le Morne Rouge you can start the climb up the 4,600-foot **Mont Pelée.** But don't try scaling this volcano without a guide unless you want to get buried alive under pumice stones. Instead, drive up to L'Auberge de la Montagne Pelée, which has had a name change and a total renovation of accommodations. (Ask for a room with a view!) From the parking lot it's 1 mi (1.5 km) up a well-marked trail to the summit. Bring a hooded sweatshirt, because there's often a mist that makes the air damp and chilly. From the summit follow the route de la Trace (Route N3), which winds south of Le Morne Rouge to St-Pierre. It's steep and winding, but that didn't stop the *porteuses* of old: balancing a tray, these women would carry up to 100 pounds of provisions on their heads for the 15-hour trek to the Atlantic coast.

Le Prêcheur. This quaint village, the last on the northern Caribbean coast, is surrounded by volcanic hot springs. It was the childhood home of Françoise d'Aubigné, who later became the Marquise de Maintenon and

Le Morne Rouge.

the second wife of Louis XIV. At her request, the Sun King donated a handsome bronze bell, which still hangs outside the church. The Tomb of the Carib Indians commemorates a sadder event. It's a formation of limestone cliffs, from which the last of the Caraïbes are said to have flung themselves to avoid capture by the marquise's forebears.

Macouba. Named after the Carib word for "fish," this village was a prosperous tobacco town in the 17th century. Today its cliff-top location affords magnificent views of the sea, the mountains, and—on clear days—the neighboring island of Dominica. (Do not confuse it with Cap Macabou, which is near Le Vauclin.)

Macouba is the starting point for a spectacular drive, the 6-mi (10-km) **Route to Grand' Rivière** (☎ *0596/55–72–74*) on the northernmost point. This is Martinique at its greenest: groves of giant bamboo, cliffs hung with curtains of vines, and human-size tree ferns that seem to grow as you watch them. Literally at the end of the road is Grand' Rivière, a colorful, sprawling fishing village at the foot of high cliffs. The Syndicat d'Initiative Riverain, the local tourism office in Macouba, can arrange hiking and boating excursions.

Musée Gauguin. Martinique was a brief stop in Paul Gauguin's wanderings, but a decisive moment in the evolution of his art. He arrived from Panama in 1887 with friend and fellow painter Charles Laval and, having pawned his watch at the docks, rented a wooden shack on a hill above Carbet. Dazzled by the tropical colors and vegetation, Gauguin developed a style, his Martinique period that directly anticipated his Tahitian paintings. Disappointingly, this modest museum has only reproductions and some original letters and documents relating

The town of St-Pierre beneath the 4,600-foot Mont Pelée.

to the painter. Also remembered here is the writer Lafcadio Hearn. In his endearing book *Two Years in the West Indies* he provides the most extensive description of the island before St-Pierre was buried in ash and lava. ⊠ *Anse-Turin, Carbet* ☏ *0596/78–22–66* ⊠ *€6* ۞ *Daily 9–5:30.*

Neisson Distillery. The Mercedes of Martinique rum brewers is a small, family-run operation whose rum is produced from pure sugarcane juice rather than molasses. It's open for tours and tastings, and the shop sells *rhum extra-vieux* (vintage rum) that truly rivals cognac. ⊠ *Carbet* ☏ *0596/78–07–90* ⊕ *www.neisson.com* ⊠ *Free* ۞ *Daily 9–4.*

Presqu'île du Caravelle. Much of the Caravelle Peninsula, which juts 8 mi (13 km) into the Atlantic Ocean, is under the protection of the Regional Nature Reserve and offers places for trekking, swimming, and sailing. This is also the site of Anse-Spoutourne, an open-air sports and leisure center operated by the reserve. The town of Tartane has a popular surfing beach with brisk Atlantic breezes.

Ste-Marie. The winding, hilly route to this town of some 20,000 offers breathtaking views of the rugged Atlantic coastline. Ste-Marie is the commercial capital of the island's north. Look for a picturesque mid-19th-century church here. The **Musée du Rhum**, operated by the St. James Rum Distillery, is housed in a graceful, galleried Creole house. Guided tours can take in the plantation and the displays of the tools of the trade, the art gallery, and include a visit and tasting at the distillery. You can opt to take a little red train tour for €3. This venue is known for its "happenings," from beauty contests to the largest, la Fete du Rhum, in December. It can be a somewhat wild scene when a dozen or more tour buses pull in, though. It's closed during harvest, so call ahead. ✉ *Ste-Marie* ☎ *0596/69–30–02* 🎫 *Free* ⊙ *Weekdays 9–5, weekends 9–1.*

One man survived the volcano's eruption. His name was Cyparis, and he was a prisoner in an underground cell in the town's jail, locked up for public drunkenness. Later, he went on the road with the Barnum & Bailey Circus as a sideshow attraction.

St-Pierre. The rise and fall of St-Pierre is one of the most remarkable stories in the Caribbean. Martinique's modern history began here in 1635. By the turn of the 20th century St-Pierre was a flourishing city of 30,000, known as the Paris of the West Indies. As many as 30 ships at a time stood at anchor. By 1902 it was the most modern town in the Caribbean, with electricity, phones, and a tram. On May 8, 1902, two thunderous explosions rent the air. As the nearby volcano erupted, Mont Pelée split in half, belching forth a cloud of burning ash, poisonous gas, and lava that raced down the mountain at 250 mph. At 3,600°F, it instantly vaporized everything in its path; 30,000 people were killed in two minutes.

The **Cyparis Express,** a small tourist train, will take you around to the main sights with running narrative (in French) for a half hour on Saturday, an hour on weekdays, for €10 (€5 for children).

An Office du Tourisme is on the *moderne* seafront promenade. Stroll the main streets and check the blackboards at the sidewalk cafés before deciding where to lunch. At night some places have live music. Like stage sets for a dramatic opera, there are the ruins of the island's first church (built in 1640), the imposing theater, and the toppled statues. This city, situated on its naturally beautiful harbor and with its narrow, winding streets, has the feel of a European seaside hill town. With every footstep you touch a page of history. Although many of the historic buildings need work, stark modernism has not invaded this burg. As much potential as it has, this is one town in Martinique where real estate is cheap—for obvious reasons.

✪ ★ For those interested in the eruption of 1902, the **Musée Vulcanologique Frank Perret** is a must. Established in 1933 by Frank Perret, a noted American volcanologist, who came down to study the volcano. The museum houses photographs of the old town, documents, and a number of relics—some gruesome—excavated from the ruins, including molten glass, melted iron, and contorted clocks stopped at 8 am. An English-speaking guide is often available. ✉ *Rue Victor Hugo* ☎ *0596/78–15–16* 🎫 *€3* ⊙ *Daily 9–5.*

If you want to know more about volcanoes, earthquakes, and hurricanes, check out **Le Centre de Découverte des Sciences de la Terre.** Housed in a sleek building that looks like a dramatic white box, this earth-science museum has high-tech exhibits and interesting films. Watch the documentary on the volcanoes in the Antilles, highlighting the eruption of the nearby Mont Pelée. This site has fascinating summer programs on Wednesday on dance, cuisine, and ecotourism. ✉ *Habitation Perinelle* ☎ *0596/52–82–42* ⊕ *www.cdst.cg972.fr* 🎫 *€5* ⊙ *Tues.–Sun. 9–4:30, 9–5:30 in July and Aug.*

15

★ An excursion to **Depaz Distillery** is one of the island's nicest treats. Established in 1651, for four centuries it has sat at the foot of the volcano. Following a devastating eruption in 1902, the fields of blue cane were replanted and in time, the rum making began all over again. A self-guided tour includes the workers' gingerbread cottages, and sometimes there will be an exhibit of art and sculpture made from wooden casks and parts of distillery machinery. The tasting room sells its rums, including golden and aged rum and distinctive liqueurs made from orange, ginger, and basil, among others, that can add creativity to your cooking. The plantation's greathouse, or chateau, has opened for public tours for the first time. The former master's house contains a precious collection of colonial-era artifacts, archival documents, Creole period clothing, and antique furniture. The guided tour and movie tells the history of the Depaz family and their rum, and of Martinique's plantation society; it costs €3. A recommendable restaurant, Le Moulin a Canne, serves creole specialties and—you guessed it—Depaz rum to wash it down. ■TIP→ Shutters are locked and the staff leaves exactly at 5 pm, so plan on being there by at least 4. ⊠ *Mont Pelée Plantation* ☎ *0596/78–13–14* ⊕ *www.depazrhum.com* ⊠ *Free (for the distillery)* ☉ *Weekdays 10–5, Sat. 9–4.*

WHERE TO EAT

Martinique cuisine is a fusion of African and French and is certainly more international and sophisticated than that of its immediate island neighbors. The influx of young chefs, who favor a contemporary, less caloric approach, has brought exciting innovations to the table. This haute-nouvelle creole cuisine emphasizes local products, predominantly starchy tubers such as plantains, white yams, yucca, and island sweet potatoes, as well as vegetables such as breadfruit, christophene, and taro leaves. Many creole dishes have been Francofied, transformed into mousselines, terrines, and gratins topped with creamy sauces. And then there's the bountiful harvest of the sea—*lambi* (conch), *langouste* (clawless local lobsters), and dozens of species of fish predominate, but you can also find *crevisses* (freshwater crayfish, which are as luscious as jumbo prawns).

Some local creole specialties are *accras* (cod or vegetable fritters), which are the signature appetizer of Martinique, *crabes farcis* (stuffed land crab), and *feroce* (avocado stuffed with saltfish and farina). You can fire up fish and any other dish with a hit of hot *chien* (dog) sauce. Not to worry—it's made from onions, shallots, hot peppers, oil, and vinegar. To cool your jets, have a 'ti punch—four parts white rum and one part sugarcane syrup.

Supermarkets often have snack bars that serve sandwiches, as do the bakeries and larger gas stations such as Esso and Total. Supermarkets, such as Carrefour, have good deli sections and sell French wines for significantly less than at home. Another French chain, Le Baguet Shop, has locations in most tourist areas. Travelers on a budget will find creperies and pizzerias, even an African pizza place in Le François. And there may be times when you just want to drive in to Mickey D's—however, brace yourself for the price hike.

In Fort-de-France's city market, ladies serve up creole prix-fixe meals that can include accras, fricassee of octopus and conch, chicken in coconut milk, or grilled whole fish. As for euro sticker shock, the consolation is that although menu prices may seem steep, they include tax and service. Prix-fixe menus, sometimes with wine, can help keep costs in line.

WHAT TO WEAR

For dinner, casual resort wear is appropriate. Generally, men do not wear jackets and ties, as they did in decades past, but they do wear collared shirts. Women typically wear light cotton sundresses, short or long. At dinnertime, beach attire is too casual for most restaurants. Know that both the French ladies and the Martiniquais often "dress." They have an admirable French style, and almost always wear high heels.

Nice shorts are okay for lunch, depending on the venue, but jeans and shorts aren't acceptable at dinner. Keep in mind that in Martinique lunch is usually a wonderful three-course, two-hour affair.

15

SOUTH OF FORT-DE-FRANCE

$$$

CARIBBEAN

✗ **Fleur de Sel.** Everything comes together here—the cuisine, the ambience, *le musique,* the location, and the service. Situated in a 19th-century *maison bourgeoise,* it has new owners, Belinda and Raphael Fischer, who have taken it up a notch. Characterized by contemporary, global techniques, the kitchen uses local ingredients imaginatively, like the profiterole of lambi (conch) with island spices and mussels atop curly greens. It's an appetizer that could be a main, and no one will frown. Not inexpensive but generous in size, most mains have origins in Alscace, like Raphael, such as choucroute Marinere, shellfish on cabbage confit with Riesling sauce. ⌂ *27 ave. de l'Impératrice Josephine, Trois-Ilets* ☎ *0596/68–42–11* ⊘ *No lunch. Closed Sun.*

$$$–$$$$

FRENCH

★

✗ **Le Bélem.** To really experience this place, start with a cocktail in the superchic bar lined with old black-and-white photographs of the island; a simple 'ti punch gets an elaborate presentation. Le Bélem is the special-occasion restaurant for the well-heeled who enjoy innovative cuisine served in a contemporary setting. Alas, it is not inexpensive, but the complimentary amuse-bouche (single, bite size hors d'oeuvres) may save you an appetizer, although the lobster ravioli is luscious. *Terrine de foie gras,* with apples caramelized in vanilla butter enhanced by a reduction of port and balsamic vinegar, is heaven on a plate. The menu changes seasonally and features such creations as linguine with truffles, scallops, cream, and a shellfish reduction dramatically presented by a bevy of servers. Lunch at Campeche, the beach restaurant, although less glamorous, is still decidedly a treat, and provides a more affordable alternative. ⌂ *Cap Est Lagoon Resort & Spa, Quartier Cap Est, Le François* ☎ *0596/54–80–80* ⚓ *Reservations essential* ⊘ *No lunch. Closed Sun., Mon., Wed., and Thurs.*

$$$

FRENCH

Fodor'sChoice

★

✗ **Le Plein Soleil Restaurant.** Perennially popular with the chic set, Le Plein Soleil has a smashing contemporary, Creole look. But it's the inventive, beautifully executed menu that cements its well-deserved reputation. The young Martinican chef, Nathanael Ducteil, continues to draw applause for his use of the latest techniques from France coupled with remarkable twists on local products. Take a long and leisurely lunch (€35) on the terrace, which has a hilltop sea view; by night the mood is romantic, the service fine, the music heady. Soups are like a mixed-media collage. A velouté can be the canvas for a *raviole* of foie gras or pineapple, a slice of duck breast, or even a skewer of fish. The evening's three-course table d'hôte (€45) could have a lobster medallion flambéed with vintage rum or a thick tuna steak roasted with lemon confit and stacked on mushroom risotto. A memorable finale is the original basil custard topped with a red berry coulis. At dinner, guests can now choose from five different appetizers, main courses, and desserts. ⊠ *Hôtel Le Plein Soleil, Villa Lagon Sarc, Pointe Thalèmont, Le François* ☎ *0596/38–07–77* ⚓ *Reservations essential* ◷ *No dinner Sun. No lunch Mon., Tues., and Thurs.*

FORT-DE-FRANCE AND POINTS NORTH

$–$$
SEAFOOD

✕ **Chez Les Pecheurs.** This is the kind of beach restaurant you search for but seldom find. It began when owner Palmont still made his living by fishing. Now Palmont's pink-and-blue boat is the best one bobbin'. People come for the fisherman's platter, the catch of the day (which could be tuna or a white fish) with a special red sauce, ripe tomatoes, and perfect red beans and rice. Fresh "crayfish on the barbie" can usually be had Thursday through Saturday. Bottles of Neisson rum are plunked in front of a table of, say, French doctors taking a time-out from their medical conference. On Friday night and Sunday, local bands play, and on Saturday a DJ gets everyone up and dancing in the sand. ⊠ *Le Bord de Mer, Carbet* ☎ *0596/76–98–39 or 0696/23–95–59.*

$$–$$$
FRENCH
★

✕ **La Table de Mamy Nounou.** If you looked at the business card for this dining room, you'd expect a creole menu served by an elderly island lady. Not! It's owned by a French family. The elegant Madame Mahler will greet you; her husband, Jean-Paul, presides as chef, and her son, Bastian, eloquently describes the menu in the King's English. Sip an aperitif while listening to the mesmerizing music and admiring the view from the lounge decorated with fascinating African antiques. The chef is outdoing himself again this year, as the à la carte menu becomes more inventive, definitely au courant, with additions like the foie gras crème brûlée. An amuse-bouche arrives before outstanding appetizers. A member of Euro-toques, a group of European chefs who are dedicated to wholesome food, chef Jean-Paul wisely keeps on the menu perennial favorites such as the crawfish (*z'habitants*) in a sauce flamed with vintage rum; octopus (chatrou) with various preparations; and fish, shrimp, and scallops with a cinnamon-cider sauce. Even the sides here are special, like the pineapple tarte tatin with eggplant caviar. Finish with the *moelleux au chocolat* (a rich chocolate pudding) with caramel sauce, or sample a trio of desserts, which might include gingerbread ice cream. Lunch is served outdoors on the terrace and has a similar menu but is less expensive, and includes some salads. ⊠ *Anse L'Etang, Tartane, La Trinité* ☎ *0596/58–07–32* ◷ *Closed Tues. May–Dec. 14. Closed Sept. and 3 wks in June.*

$$$–$$$$
CARIBBEAN

✕ **Le Brédas.** This culinary experience necessitates a trip into the interior, down winding roads where the dense foliage is jungle-like. It's best

CLOSE UP

A How-To for Dining in Martinique

Dining in Martinique is a delightful culinary experience, but as with driving here, it is best to get some directions before you head out. First of all, as in France, entrées are appetizers; the main courses will usually be labeled as follows: *poissons* (fish); *viandes* (meat); or *principal plats* (literally, main courses). You will notice that the appetizers are almost as expensive as the mains—and if the appetizer is foie gras, you'll pay just as much as for a main course, but it is oh so worth it.

Entrecôte is a sirloin steak, usually cut too thin. A filet mignon is a rarity, but you will see *filet mignon*

du porc, which is pork tenderloin. *Ecrivesses* (known also as *ouassous* or *z'habitants*) are incredible freshwater crayfish. Don't be alarmed when they are served with their heads on. Similarly, if a fish dish does not specify fillet, you will be looking into its eyes while carving flesh from its bones.

Every respectable restaurant has an admirable wine *carte,* and the offerings will be almost completely French, with few half bottles. Wines by the glass are often swill and best avoided.

Finally, don't ever embarrass yourself by asking for a doggie bag: you will be considered gauche!

15

navigated, at least the first time, by day; come for lunch, but return for a memorable dinner. Martinican chef Jean-Charles Brédas is well-known, having worked the better restaurants in Martinique and Manhattan. His lovely wife, Marie-Julie, is a gracious hostess. The tasteful decor includes taupe linen runners on large tables speckled with colored-glass bits; the ceramic plates are the creations of an esteemed local potter, Victor Anicet. The foie gras is perfectly executed, especially when it's served with green bananas caramelized with rum and pineapple. (This appetizer, his signature dish, is a whopping €33.) One laudable main *plat* is the robust and tender beef marinated in cocoa, orange, and cardamom. The terrace dining room of this century-old house is covered by a peaked white awning. Chef Bredas' mission is to preserve the ancient *saveurs* (flavors), giving traditional island dishes and French classics a contemporary twist. A special-occasion restaurant, its holiday meals are celebratory, down to the roast suckling pigs. Note: if there is not a sufficient number of reservations for dinner, then they will not serve, but will call all those who reserved to cancel. ⊠ *Entrée Presqu'île, St. Joseph* ☎ *0596/57–65–52* ⚭ *Reservations essential* ⊗ *No dinner Sun. and Mon. No lunch Sat.*

$$-$$$ ✕ **Le Petitbonum.** Billed as an artisan restaurant, it's a marriage of French
SEAFOOD island funkiness and Miami's So' Beach. It's a one-of-a-kind in Martinique (if you don't count its sister restaurant in Fort-de-France). So is charismatic owner Guy Ferdinand, a tall Martinican with curly, blond-streaked hair who has made this a destination restaurant in the north coast's tiny town of Carbet. Smack on the beach, it's an ideal stopover if you're visiting nearby St-Pierre. Remember to wear your swimsuit. Kick off your shoes and order a perfect mojito. You can lounge on coral rubber chaises, shaded by umbrellas, and be sprayed intermittently with

a gentle, cool mist. (Guy first experienced this in South Beach.) The appetizers—escargots, foie gras with a pear-and-banana chutney—are decadently rich for a feet-in-the-sand restaurant. For mains there is fresh tuna with a soy-sesame sauce; the signature dish is jumbo crayfish in a vanilla cream sauce flambeed with rhum vieux. Desserts such as the pineapple crumble, tiramisu, or chocolate cake are special. But what you will remember is the mood and the music, which is live on Saturday night. ✉ *Le Coin, Le Bord de Mer, Carbet* 📞 *0596/78–04–34.*

$$
CAFÉ
★
✕ **Mille & Une Brindilles.** At this trendy salon you can order anything from a glass of wine to an aromatic pot of tea in flavors like vanilla or mango. You'll find a litany of tapenades, olive cakes, and flans on the prix-fixe menu. Fred, the bubbly Parisian who is both chef and proprietress, is the queen of terrines, and she makes a delicious tart (like Roquefort and pear) or pâté out of any vegetable or fish. The Saturday brunch (€22) is a very social occasion. The best-ever desserts, such as the Amadéus—as appealing as the classical music that plays—and *moelleux au chocolat,* are what you would want served at your last meal on Earth. Look for the sign on the left side, for the place is easy to miss. ✉ *27 rte. de Didier, Didier, Fort-de-France* 📞 *0596/71–75–61* ▭ *No credit cards* ⊗ *Closed Sun. and Wed. No dinner.*

$
ECLECTIC
✕ **Soup Bar du Centre Ville.** A sign reading "No Opium Smoking" is just one of the details that make this artsy eatery so much fun. This is one place that the island's colorful characters will tell you about if they think you're hip. Wild-looking art decorates one wall; on the other is a surfboard, signed by its American owner, who added "Thanks for the Soup." The list of soups is extensive, and includes local specialties such as soupe *z'habitant* (crawfish), a flavorful puree of green vegetables with pigs' tails added for flavor. Because a German owns the place, you can also get goulash and cold cream-of-cucumber soup. No matter what you order, the price is right: a huge bowl with some rolls ranges from €7 to €10. This place is a venue for art exhibits and live music. And yes, there is German beer. Doors open at 4 pm and there's now a petite sidewalk patio. ✉ *120 rue Martine, Fort-de-France* 📞 *0596/60–48–96* ⊗ *Closed Sun. No lunch.*

WHERE TO STAY

Larger hotels usually include a big buffet breakfast of eggs, fresh fruit, cheese, yogurt, croissants, baguettes, jam, and café au lait. Smaller *relais* (inns) often have open-air, terrace kitchenettes. At almost all properties, you can request smoking or no-smoking rooms; the new French law banning smoking in public places went into effect in January 2008. Alas, hotel rooms are considered private. Most hotels do not have elevators and many are built on hillsides, so if you have issues with stairs or with climbing paths, be sure to ask about that.

VILLAS AND CONDOMINIUMS

If you're staying a week or longer, you can often save money by renting a villa or apartment with a kitchen where you can prepare your own meals. The more upscale rentals come with French-speaking maids and cooks. Don't forget to add the cost of a car rental to your vacation budget. **French Caribbean International** (📞 *800/322–2223, 805/967–9850 U.S.*

office ⊕ *www.frenchcaribbean.com*), an English-speaking reservation service operated for decades by Gerard Hill, can help you with both villa rentals and hotel rooms. **Nouvelles Antilles** (☎ *0590/85–00–00* ⊕ *www. nouvellesantilles.com*), a progressive operation based in St-François, acts as an agent for some 30 villas around the islands, mostly luxurious. In addition, the first online travel agency dedicated to the French West Indies can book your flight, rental car, and sports activities, and create a well priced package. It deals with all the Guadeloupe isles, St. Barth, and St. Maarten, in addition to Martinique, and can customize a multidestination package for groups up to 15. At the **Villa Rental Service** (☎ *0596/71– 56–11*) an English-speaking staffer can help you find a home, a villa, or an apartment to rent for a week or a month. Most properties are in the southern part of the island near good beaches. Also, the tourism office (⊕ *www.martinique.org*) now assists with villa rentals.

The following reviews have been condensed for this book. Please go to Fodors.com for expanded reviews of each property.

15

SOUTH OF FORT-DE-FRANCE

$$$$
RESORT
Fodor'sChoice
★

⊡ **Cap Est Lagoon Resort & Spa.** A member of the Relais and Châteaux group, Martinique's most exclusive resort has brought back the wealthy international set. **Pros:** large central pool; island's most contemporary bar–lounge but with a Martinican feel; property has been well maintained. **Cons:** not a whole lot to do; somewhat isolated; beach is not expansive. ⊠ *Quartier Cap Est, Le François* ☎ *0596/54–80–80 or 800/735–2478* ⊕ *www.capest.com* ⌐ *50 suites* ⌂ *In-room: Internet, Wi-Fi. In-hotel: restaurants, room service, tennis court, bars, pool, gym, spa, beach, business center, water sports* ☾ *Closed Aug. 31–Oct. 10* ⦿ *Breakfast.*

$$$–$$$$
RENTAL
★

⊡ **Club Med Buccaneer's Creek.** One of the French chain's most upscale villages, this flagship is part of Club Med's strategy of meeting the more refined needs of global travelers. **Pros:** still seems nearly new; Club Med energy is contagious; even waterskiing is included. **Cons:** annual membership is $60 for each adult; some first-timers just don't fancy the Club Med style. ⊠ *Pointe Marin, Ste-Anne* ☎ *0596/76–72–72* ⊕ *www. clubmed.us* ⌐ *249 rooms, 44 suites* ⌂ *In-room: safe, Wi-Fi. In-hotel: restaurants, tennis courts, bar, pool, gym, spa, beach, business center, water sports, parking* ⦿ *All-inclusive.*

$$$–$$$$
RESORT
★

⊡ **Hotel Bakoua.** Wrought-iron gates open to arguably one of Martinique's best resorts, what French guests call a "human hotel," where you can cocoon. **Pros:** the Bakoua exudes vintage Caribbean charisma; it's a classy classic. **Cons:** constructed in stages, so some rooms show age whereas others are fresh; facades are not all pretty. ⊠ *Pointe du Bout, Les Trois-Ilets* ☎ *0596/66–02–02* ⊕ *www.mgallery.com* ⌐ *133 rooms, 6 suites* ⌂ *In-room: safe, Wi-Fi. In-hotel: restaurants, tennis courts, bars, pool, beach, business center, water sports, parking* ⦿ *Breakfast.*

¢
HOTEL
☾

⊡ **Hotel Cap Macabou.** Constructed of handsome native hardwoods and designed in a Creole style, a large number of these 40 rooms and four suites have terraces with panoramas of the Atlantic Ocean. **Pros:** key staff speak English; all is clean and new. **Cons:** it's a hard five minutes down a dirt road; not a good swimming beach; not much happens in Le Vauclin.

✉ *Petit Macabou, Le Vauclin* ☎ *0596/74–24–24* 🌐 *www.capmacabou.com* ⇨ *45 rooms, 2 suites* ♢ *In-room: safe. In-hotel: restaurant, room service, bar, pool, laundry facilities, spa, parking* 🍴 *No meals.*

$ RESORT **Karibea Sainte Luce Resort.** This complex of three once-independent hotels, which share facilities, is on a nice stretch of beach and offers rooms at the right price. **Pros:** larger loggia rooms in Amandiers are best for Americans yet cost just 7% more; can walk the beach to town or take shuttle for €4 round-trip; you can use amenities at all three hotels. **Cons:** best with a rental car; no chaises on beach; getting down-at-the-heels. ✉ *Quartier Désert, Ste-Luce* ☎ *0596/62–12–00, 0596/62–11–91 for reservations* 🌐 *www.karibea.com* ⇨ *116 rooms (Amandiers), 108 junior suites (Amyris), 75 apartments (Caribia)* ♢ *In-room: safe, kitchen (some), Wi-Fi. In-hotel: restaurants, tennis court, bars, children's programs, pools, beach, business center, water sports, parking* 🍴 *Breakfast.*

$$ HOTEL **La Suite Villa.** This hilltop boutique property gives Les Trois-Ilets a new, art-infused glamour quotient. **Pros:** inimitable, whimsical style with a profusion of Caribbean colors; entertaining and artistic owners; the upbeat social scene. **Cons:** greathouse has three floors and no elevator; no beach; more English-speaking staff would be helpful. ✉ *Rte. du Fort d'Alet, Les Trois-Ilets* ☎ *0596/63–57–30* 🌐 *www.la-suite-villa.com* ⇨ *6 suites, 9 villas (6 2-bedrooms, 3 3-bedrooms)* ♢ *In-room: safe, kitchen (some), Wi-Fi. In-hotel: restaurant, room service (some), bar, pool, parking* 🍴 *Breakfast.*

$–$$ HOTEL Fodor's Choice ★ **Le Plein Soleil.** Long one of our favorites, this heavenly hideaway has been featured so frequently in French, international, and American media that it has become a celebrity hotel. **Pros:** stimulating client mix; owner Jean Christophe is on-site and accessible; sophisticated and artistic ambience is unique in Martinique. **Cons:** rough road (particularly in rainy season); somewhat remote hilltop location; smallest rooms have small bathrooms. ✉ *Villa Lagon Sarc, Pointe Thalèmont, Le François* ☎ *0596/38–07–77* 🌐 *www.hotelpleinsoleil.fr* ⇨ *16 bungalows* ♢ *In-room: safe, kitchens (some), Wi-Fi. In-hotel: restaurant, bar, room service, pool, business center, parking* 🍴 *Breakfast.*

FORT-DE-FRANCE AND POINTS NORTH

$ RENTAL **Bignomia #2.** This cliff-side apartment is on the waterfront within the upmarket complex Les Hauts Creole, just steps from the Hotel Bakoua. **Pros:** contemporary kitchen and bath; superlative ocean views; location. **Cons:** bedrooms could have more style and cushy, creature comforts; only one bathroom. ✉ *Les Hauts Creole, Pointe du Boute, Les Trois-Ilets* 🌐 *katieholidayhomes.pagesperso-orange.fr/index.html* ⇨ *2 bedrooms, 1 bath* ♢ *In-room: no phone, kitchen. In-hotel: laundry facilities, beach, parking* ▭ *No credit cards* 🍴 *No meals.*

$ B&B/INN **Engoulevent.** This small B&B in a suburban home, about 10 minutes from Fort-de-France has deluxe suites with contemporary decor, as well as up-to-date amenities like Wi-Fi. **Pros:** rooms are stellar; unique on the island; free in-room Wi-Fi. **Cons:** not all the benefits of a hotel; best with a car. ✉ *22 rte. de l'Union Didier, Fort-de-France* ☎ *0596/64–96–00* ⇨ *5 suites* ♢ *In-room: safe, Internet, Wi-Fi. In-hotel: pool, gym, parking* 🍴 *Breakfast.*

¢   📷 **Hotel Villa St. Pierre.** A simple, modern decor typifies this modest
HOTEL   bay-front property that is somewhere between a hôtel de charme and
a French business hotel. **Pros:** caring managers Maryse and Andre;
downtown location. **Cons:** little English spoken; not luxurious. ✉ *108
rue Bonille, St-Pierre* ☎ *0596/78–68–45* ⊕ *www.hotel-villastpierre.com*
🛏 *9 rooms* ♿ *In-room: Internet. In-hotel: restaurant, room service, bar,
beach* ⊙ *Breakfast.*

¢   📷 **La Caravelle.** The energetic Mahler family has transformed this simple
HOTEL   hotel with their artwork from Africa, where patriarch Jean-Paul worked
for several decades as a hotel manager. **Pros:** caring service; interesting international family; gourmet cuisine. **Cons:** no pool; still a simple
French hotel. ✉ *Anse L'Etang, Tartane, La Trinité* ☎ *0596/58–07–32*
⊕ *www.hotel-la-caravelle-martinique.com* 🛏 *14 studios, 1 apartment*
♿ *In-room: kitchen. In-hotel: restaurant* ⊙ *No meals.*

$ 📷 **La Valmenière Hôtel.** This high-rise, perched on a hillside overlooking
HOTEL   Fort-de-France, is the closest to the airport (5 mi [8 km]) and is ideal
for first- or last-night stays. **Pros:** always alive and active; excellent restaurant; suites have balconies. **Cons:** primarily a business hotel; rooms
are large but simplistic; lacks panache. ✉ *Av. des Arawaks, Fort-de-
France* ☎ *0596/75–75–75* ⊕ *www.karibea.com* 🛏 *116 rooms, 4 suites*
♿ *In-room: safe, Wi-Fi. In-hotel: restaurant, room service, bar, pool,
business center* ⊙ *No meals.*

$ 📷 **Le Domaine Saint Aubin.** This former estate is perched on a verdant
HOTEL   hilltop with a breathtaking view overlooking the Atlantic. **Pros:** you
can daydream yourself into a more gracious era; hip owners are scintillating company; wheelchair-accessible rooms and even pool. **Cons:**
somewhat remote location requires a car; original rooms are not stylish. ✉ *Petite Rivière Salée, off rte. 1, La Trinité* ☎ *0596/69–34–77 or
0696/40–99–59* ⊕ *www.ledomainesaintaubin.com* 🛏 *30 rooms, 6
2-bedroom apartments* ♿ *In-room: no TV, Wi-Fi. In-hotel: restaurant,
pool, parking* ⊙ *Breakfast.*

$ 📷 **Squash Hôtel.** This well-run business hotel is ideally located if you
HOTEL   need to sleep close to the airport (15 minutes away) or want to explore
Fort-de-France (10 minutes). **Pros:** key staffers speak English; close
to city but with suburban quiet; always good Franco-Caribbean cuisine and usually a *menu du jour.* **Cons:** not a handsome facade; few
resort amenities. ✉ *3 bd. de la Marne, Fort-de-France* ☎ *0596/72–80–
80* ⊕ *www.karibea.com* 🛏 *105 rooms, 2 suites, 1 business suite* ♿ *In-
room: safe, Wi-Fi. In-hotel: restaurant, bar, pool, gym, business center*
⊙ *Breakfast.*

NIGHTLIFE AND THE ARTS

There are lively discos and nightclubs in Martinique, but a good deal of
the fun is to be had by befriending Martinicans, French residents, and
other expats and hope they will invite you clubbing or to their private
parties. As for casinos, French law requires everyone to show a passport
or license; the legal gambling age is 18.

15

CASINOS

On the outskirts of Fort-de-France, the classy **Casino Batelière Plaza** (✉ *Schoelcher* ☎ *0596/61–73–23*) is built in a striking nouveau-plantation-house style. It has both slot machines and table games. Slots open at 10 am, but table games don't start until after 8 pm. There's live entertainment on weekends from 8–midnight. It's open Sunday night, when most places are shut tight, except the buffet restaurant (€14), which is open only Tuesday–Saturday. ■ TIP→ You may see billboards that say: CASINO or even GEANTE CASINO, with directionals. Do not follow them if you are looking for a gambling casino. CASINO is the name of a supermarket chain. GEANTE means a megasupermarket.

The interior of this new casino in a major tourist zone, **Casino Trois-Ilets** (✉ *Turn right off rte. de Trois-Ilets to rte. de Pointe du Bout and it's on right, Trois-Ilets* ☎ *0596/66–00–30*) was designed with a French Quarter ambience and houses 70 slot machines, blackjack, U.S. roulette, and craps (Friday and Saturday). The casino is open daily 10 am to 3 am; the moderately priced fine-dining restaurant is open Sunday night, too. On weekends, jazz is the sound—live Caribbean, Creole, and standard. The music is good, but no one is dancing. The restaurant is in the middle of the floor rather than in its own space. Although it was highly anticipated, this casino does not have a strong spirit or fun quotient. Consequently, its appeal is more for locals than tourists looking for that "magic."

DANCE CLUBS

Your hotel or the tourist office can put you in touch with the current "in" places. It's also wise to check on opening and closing times and cover charges. Several free tourist publications that can be found at hotels tell of the latest happenings at the clubs. For the most part, the discos draw a mixed crowd—Martinicans and tourists, and although a younger crowd is the norm, people of all ages go dancing here.

The **Coconuts Club** (✉ *Quartier Laugier, Riviére-Salée* ☎ *0596/68–20–49*) houses a restaurant, bar–lounge, and disco. The motto here is "Life is a party!"

Crazy Nights (✉ *Ste-Luce* ☎ *0596/68–56–68*) remains popular because it's all about having one crazy time. With upward of 1,000 partying people, your chances are good. Live concerts are frequent, but dancing and hip-swinging are the priorities.

L'Amphore (✉ *Pointe du Bout, Les Trois-Ilets* ☎ *0596/66–03–09 or 0696/80–79–40*) is a hot bar and club where the young and restless dance to funk, soul, tribal, house, techno, and disco, as well as international music from the '70s and '80s. The dress code is strict: no shorts, bandanas, or sandals. Follow the road to Anse-Mitan; the club is on the left before the little church. The VIP room is bottle-service only during peak season or holidays. Halloween is a big time. The club is open weekends only during the low season and more often during the high season, when there's usually a cover. There are some theme nights, and Soir Plage (beach night) is always a hit. Sand is brought in, and people come in bikinis and so on.

Le Top 50 (✉ *Zone Artisanale, La Trinité* ☎ *0596/58–61–43*) is one of the few nightspots in the area where tourists, surfers, and locals all come together to party.

FOLKLORIC PERFORMANCES

Most leading hotels offer nightly entertainment in season, including the marvelous **Grands Ballets de Martinique,** one of the finest folkloric dance troupes in the Caribbean. Consisting of a bevy of musicians and dancers dressed in traditional costume, the ballet revives the Martinique of yesteryear through dance rhythms such as the beguine and the mazurka. They appear on Wednesday at the Hotel Carayou in Les Trois-Ilets in a dinner performance coupled with an authentic creole buffet.

At the Amyris Hotel, the **Ballet Exotica,** comprising male and female dancers in Creole costumes, perform the island's traditional dances on Friday night. It costs €28 and includes a buffet dinner. Nonhotel guests should make reservations, as seating is limited. In addition, many restaurants offer live entertainment, usually on weekends. Similarly, Les Amandiers, one of the three hotel sisters within the Karibea St. Luce Resort, features Ballet Exotica on Friday nights along with a creole buffet. Reservations for these theme nights should be made in advance, particularly for nonhotel guests.

15

MUSIC CLUBS

Jazz musicians, like their music, tend to be informal and independent. They rarely hold regular gigs. Zouk mixes Caribbean rhythm and an Occidental tempo with Creole lyrics. Jacob Devarieux is the leading exponent of this style, and he occasionally performs on the island. Otherwise, you're likely to hear one of his followers.

Calebasse Café (✉ *19 bd. Allègre, Le Marin* ☎ *0596/74–69–27*) pleases a diverse—though mostly older—crowd. Jazz is the norm, and there's often a talented local singer. Funky and hip, the interior is a bit rough but civilized. On Saturday night, if you don't make a reservation you will not have a seat. The food here isn't wonderful, but if you have the conch tart and the grilled lobster, you'll leave satisfied and avoid the cover charge. There's sometimes a beach party; it's closed Monday.

At **Club Med Buccaneer's Creek** (✉ *Pointe du Marin, Ste-Anne* ☎ *0596/76–83–36*), you can buy a night pass that, at €93, might seem expensive; it is, but it includes an impressive buffet dinner and a show in the theater. Friday costs more, €118. It's the best night, called the gala, with the elaborate food and the best show, which might be a Brazilian spectacle. Entertainment changes based on a two-week cycle; for example, Sunday there might be Celtic dancers. Following the show, it's on to dancing at the disco until 2 if you can hang. Single women feel comfortable here, and they find willing and very able dance partners, especially the G.O.s. The pass system allows you to decide whether it is your next vacation. Or plan on spending one overnight here; for a couple, the price difference is not that great.

Traditional Madras Costumes in Martinique.

Hotel Bakoua (✉ *Pointe du Bout, Les Trois-Ilets* ☎ *0596/66–02–02*) has nightly entertainment, from talented piano men to vocalists and jazz combos; the quality of the entertainment is known island-wide. The stage has moved to the alfresco Chateaubriand restaurant where drinks are served at your table. If you miss the bar, you can go to Le Gommier and order a tropical cocktail there first. There's a litany of island rums, from white to amber and rhum vieux.

Hotel Cap Macabou (✉ *Petit Macabou, Le Vauclin* ☎ *0596/74–24–24* ⊕ *www.capmacabou.com*) in Vauclin has "dancing dinners" and theme nights on Friday and Saturday. On Sunday, there's a midday buffet with dancing to a band—you can even bring your bathing suit. The first and third Friday of each month, there's a salsa soiree with Latin music and a buffet.

La Marine (✉ *Marina Pointe du Bout, Les Trois-Ilets* ☎ *0596/66–02–32*) is an animated bar and restaurant with live entertainment, mainly on weekends.

La Villa Créole (✉ *Anse Mitan* ☎ *0596/66–05–53*) is a restaurant whose Martinican owner, Guy Bruere-Dawson, has been singing and strumming the guitar since the 1980s—in five languages, everything from François Cabrel to Elton John, some Italian and Creole ballads, even original ditties. Other singers perform, too, on Friday and Saturday nights. To see the show, you must order dinner; lobster is traditionally the best option. There's also a small dance floor, and a few tables are outside the open-air restaurant. If patrons aren't using them for dinner, you can just drink and more or less hear the music.

SHOPPING

★ French fragrances, designer scarves and sunglasses, fine china and crystal, leather goods, wine (amazingly inexpensive at supermarkets), and liquor are all good buys in Fort-de-France. Purchases are further sweetened by the 20% discount on luxury items when paid for with certain credit cards. Among the items produced on the island, look for *bijoux creole* (local jewelry, such as hoop earrings and heavy bead necklaces), white and dark rum, and handcrafted straw goods, pottery, and tapestries.

AREAS AND MALLS

The area around the cathedral in Fort-de-France has a number of small shops that carry luxury goods. Of particular note are the shops on rue Victor Hugo, rue Moreau de Jones, rue Antoine Siger, and rue Lamartine. The **Galleries Lafayette** department store on rue Schoelcher in downtown Fort-de-France sells everything from perfume to pâté. On the outskirts of Fort-de-France, the **Centre Commercial de Cluny, Centre Commercial de Dillon, Centre Commercial de Bellevue,** and **Centre Commercial la Rond Point** are among the major shopping malls.

You can find more than 100 thriving businesses—from shops and department stores to restaurants, pizzerias, fast-food outlets, a superb supermarket, and the Galleria Hotel—at **La Galleria** in Lamentin. In Pointe du Bout there are a number of appealing tourist shops and boutiques, both in and around **Village Créole**, which alone has 26, plus seven restaurants–bars.

SPECIALTY STORES

CHINA AND CRYSTAL

Cadet Daniel (⊠ *72 rue Antoine Siger, Fort-de-France* ☎ *0596/71–41–48*) sells Lalique, Limoges, and Baccarat.

Roger Albert (⊠ *7 rue Victor Hugo, Fort-de-France* ☎ *0596/71–71–71*) carries designer crystal.

■TIP→ So you want to look French, oui? Yes, buy French designer resort wear, but the secret is a cool, sexy French haircut. Both ladies and men vie for appointments at **Hair du Temps** (⊠ *Arcade La Pagerie, Point du Bout, Les Trois-Ilets* ☎ *0596/66–02–51*). Note that haircut prices seem quite reasonable but do not include a blow-dry—that's extra, as are hairspray and mousse—€6 extra for whichever you choose.

CLOTHING

Bisous Sucrés (⊠ *Village Créole, Pointe du Bout, Les Trois-Ilets* ☎ *0596/74–77–04*) offers a unique children's collection, including jewelry, madras dollies, and teeny underwear.

Coté Plage Sarl (⊠ *Village Créole, Pointe du Bout, Les Trois-Ilets* ☎ *0596/66–13–00*) stocks French sailor jerseys in creative colors, youthful straw purses in bold hues, fun teenage jewelry, and ladies' bathing suits.

15

Lynx Optique (✉ *20 rue Lamartine, Fort-de-France* ☎ *0596/71–38–48*) has the latest designer sunglasses from Chanel, Gucci, Dior, Cartier, and Versace. And if you need a pair of prescription lenses, they can take care of that, too.

Mounia (✉ *Rue Perrinon near old House of Justice, Fort-de-France* ☎ *0596/73–77–27*), owned by a former Yves St. Laurent model, carries the top French designers for women and men. It will have you opening your wallet wide. Hope for a *solde* (sale).

HANDICRAFTS

The work of **Antan Lontan** (✉ *213 rte. de Balata, Fort-de-France* ☎ *0596/64–52–72*) has to be seen. Sculptures, busts, statuettes, and artistic lamps portray the Creole women and the story of the Martiniquaise culture.

Art et Nature (✉ *Ste-Luce* ☎ *0596/62–59–19*) carries Joel Gilbert's unique wood paintings, daubed with 20 to 30 shades of earth and sand.

Artisanat & Poterie des Trois-Ilets (✉ *Les Trois-Ilets* ☎ *0596/68–18–01*) allows you to watch the creation of Arawak- and Carib-style pots, vases, and jars.

Atelier Céramique (✉ *Le Diamant* ☎ *0596/76–42–65*) displays the ceramics, paintings, and miscellaneous souvenirs of owners and talented artists David and Jeannine England, members of the island's small British expat community.

★ **Bois Nature** (✉ *La Semair, Le Robert* ☎ *0596/65–77–65*) is all about mood and mystique. The gift items begin with scented soap, massage oil, aromatherapy sprays, and perfumes. Then there are wind chimes, mosquito netting, and sun hats made of coconut fiber. The big stuff includes natural wood-frame mirrors and furniture à la Louis XV.

Domaine Château Gaillard (✉ *Rte. des Trois-Ilets, Les Trois-Ilets* ☎ *0596/68–15–68*), a large two-story shopping complex, sells both handicrafts and tropical floral compositions at its nursery. You can find pottery, jewelry, toys, paintings, and gifts. Coffee and chocolate are also for sale, and there is a small museum chronicling both island products. Antique Creole hats and madras items are on display, too. A petite train for the kids is there for the touring. A boutique with Wi-Fi helps keep you connected. The restaurant Tropical Grill is doing a fine job, from the food and ambience to the service and the level of English. It's a good place to lunch (🕑 *Noon–2:30*), and if you are staying nearby, check it out for dinner. Specials include the French fave: mussels with fries. There is even a heliport, and **Héli Blue** (☎ *0596/66–10–80*) gives 'copter tours of the island that are a high-five.

Galerie de Sophen (✉ *Pointe du Bout, Les Trois-Ilets* ☎ *0596/66–13–64*), across from the Village Créole, is a combination of Sophie and Henry, both in name and content. This art gallery showcases the work (originals and limited prints) of a French couple who live aboard their sailboat and paint the beauty of the sea and the island, from exotic birds to banana trucks.

At **Galerie Jecy** (✉ *Pointe du Bout Marina, Les Trois-Ilets* ☎ *0596/66–04–98*), owner Stephanie designs fanciful, colorful metalwork that is artistic enough to be called sculpture; her island themes include starfish, octopus, geckos, and impressive billfish. She also sells more portable souvenirs such as colorful wooden napkin rings, fruit plates, and trivets.

JEWELRY

At **Thomas de Rogatis** (✉ *22 rue Antoine Siger, Fort-de-France* ☎ *0596/70–29–11*), authentic bijoux Creole jewelry, popularized after the abolition of slavery and seen in many museums, is for sale.

PERFUME

Roger Albert (✉ *7 rue Victor Hugo, Fort-de-France* ☎ *0596/71–71–71*) stocks such popular scents as those by Dior, Chanel, and Guerlain.

SPORTS AND ACTIVITIES

BICYCLING

Mountain biking is popular in mainland France, and now it has reached Martinique. You can rent a VTT (Vélo Tout Terrain), a bike specially designed with 18 speeds to handle all terrains, for €15 with helmet, delivery, and pickup from your hotel, although it requires a €150 credit card deposit. **V.T. Tilt** (✉ *Les Trois-Ilets* ☎ *0596/66–01–01*) has an English-speaking owner who loves to put together groups for fun tours, either half day or full day, which include lunch. They can be beach, river, or mountain rides; tours of plantations or horse ranches; and historic, adventure, or nature experiences. Just know that the French pedal hard.

15

BOATING AND SAILING

You can rent Hobie Cats, Sunfish, and Sailfish by the hour from most hotel beach shacks. As for larger crafts, bareboat charters can be had for $1,900 to $7,000 a week, depending on the season and the size of the craft. The Windward Islands are a joy for experienced sailors, but the channels between islands are often windy and have high waves. You must have a sailing license or be able to prove your nautical prowess, though you can always hire a skipper and crew. Before setting out, you can get itinerary suggestions; the safe ports in Martinique are many. If you charter for a week, you can go south to St. Lucia or Grenada or north to Dominica, Guadeloupe, and Les Saintes. One-way sailing to St. Martin or Antigua is a popular choice.

⚠ Don't even consider striking out on the rough Atlantic side of the island unless you're an experienced sailor. The Caribbean side is much calmer— more like a vast lagoon.

Punch Croisières (✉ *Bd. Allègre, Le Marin* ☎ *0596/74–89–18* ⊕ *www. punch-croisieres.com*) is a local, French-owned charter company with a fleet of 15 sailboats, 13 of which are catamarans from 38 to 57 feet; they go out bareboat or crewed, and you can take a boat to a neighboring island.

Sunsail (✉ *Le Marin* ☎ *0596/74–77–61; 888/350–3568 in U.S.* ⊕ *www. sunsail.com*) is one of the largest yacht-charter companies in the world. Although it's primarily a bareboat operation, those with limited experience can hire skippers by the week. Ocean kayaks can be rented, too, and must be reserved in advance. It carries 384 catamarans. Check the site for discount deals even in winter.

Windward Island Cruising Company (⊠ *Le Marin* ☎ *0596/74–31–14* ⊕ *www.sailing-adventure.com*) has sailboats from 30 to 70 feet, catamarans and motor yachts, for bareboat or crewed charters.

■ TIP➜ Located on the west coast, Anse-d'Arlets is a delightful fishing village with a historic church and wooden gingerbread houses. It is yacht-friendly and has several sheltered coves; charter boats usually anchor on Grand Anse or Petite Anse. Ti Sable is a waterfront restaurant that has a fun scene. Sunday brunch is a big event, with a good and moderately priced buffet.

CANOPY TOURS

Canopy tours—also known as tree-topping tours—are relatively new to Martinique. Even younger kids can join in the fun on some courses. However, if your body parts—particularly knees and elbows—are not as supple as they once were, or if you're afraid of heights, stay back at the hotel pool. The "tour" consists of a series of wooden ladders and bridges suspended from the trees, connected with zip lines. Participants are secured in harnesses and ropes that are hitched to them like dog leashes. You connect to a cable and then fly and bellow like Tarzan until you get to the other side. Advance reservations are usually required.

Mangofil (⊠ *Rte. de Trois-Ilets near Le Potterie, Les Trois-Ilets* ☎ *0596/68–08–08*) is a professionally run operation overseen by Frenchmen who managed a similar park in France. All of the platforms, ladders, and stations were installed by members of a special union in France that specializes in such work. Safety is key here, but there's also a lot of fun. The cost is €25 per person for adults, €17 for children, depending on height. It's open Wednesday–Sunday 9–3.

CANYONING

Bureau de la Randonnée et du Canyoning (⊠ *Joliment, Morne Vert* ☎ *0596/55–04–79* or *0696/24–32–25* ⊕ *www.bureau-rando-martinique.com*) employs professionals with diplomas in *volcanisme* (volcanoes), *randonnée* (hiking), and canyoning, which is the sport of traversing rivers and streams using your body as a toboggan. For this adrenaline rush, you must be fit and able to hike in the forest for hours. These tropical adventures can take you to the Presqu'île du Caravelle, through canals, to Mont Pelée, even to the borders of the craters. Price depends on the destination and the duration.

DAY SAILS

The catamaran **Kata Mambo** (⊠ *Pointe du Bout Marina, Les Trois-Ilets* ☎ *0696/81–90–08* or *0596/66–11–83* ⊕ *www.katamambo.com*) offers a variety of options for half-day (€42) or full-day (€76, €84 for lobster lunch) sails to St-Pierre and visits to Depaz Distillery. For €76, you also

Kayaking is a popular resort activity on Martinique.

get a 4x4 adventure through sugarcane and banana plantations. The full-day trip includes unlimited rum libations and a good multicourse lunch (half lobsters are €10 extra) with wine. This is a fun day, and although there's no guarantee, chances are you'll have dolphin encounters. The fact that it's been in the biz since the early 1990s attests to its professionalism.

La Belle Kréole (✉ *Baie du Simon, Le François* ☎ *0596/54–96–46 or 0696/ 29–93–13* ⊕ *www.baignoiredejosephine.com*) runs one of the most fun excursion boats to les fonds blanc, also known as Empress Joséphine's baths. You can experience the unique Martinican custom of drinking 'ti punch and smoking cigarettes in waist-deep water. The price of the day trip depends on what you choose to eat and includes lunch, which is taken on the remote Isle de Thierry. There's planter's punch and dancing to Martinican CDs. Yes, it is touristy. There is a two-hour excursion to the baths.

Les Ballades du Delphis (✉ *La Marina du François, Le François* ☎ *0696/90– 90–36* ⊕ *www.catadelphis.com*) is a catamaran experience that is delightfully civilized rather than a hyped-up booze cruise. It takes in the famous fond blancs or Joséphine's baths and the Baie du Robert and I'let Chancel to see the sea iguanas and ruins. And yes, you will be served planter's punch, accras, and a healthful lunch—quite a full day for €75. Recently inaugurated are nocturnal cruises "by the light of the silvery moon." These romantic cruises, (maximum 12 persons) are slated for three nights before the full moon and three nights after. For an idyllic travel memory, guests are serenaded by a violinist as they sup on lobster and sip champagne.

DIVING AND SNORKELING

Martinique's underwater world is decorated with multicolor coral, crustaceans, turtles, and sea horses. Expect to pay €40 to €45 for a single dive; a package of three dives is around €110.

Okeanos Club (✉ Pierre & Vacances, Ste-Luce ☎ 0596/62–52–36 ⊕ www. okeanos-club.com) has a morning trip close to shore; in the afternoon the boats go farther into open water. Lessons (including those for kids 8 to 12) with a PADI-certified instructor can be conducted in English. It's always a fun experience. The dive shop looks out to Diamant Rock, which has wonderful underwater caves and is one of the preferred dives on the island.

Planète Bleue (✉ *Pointe du Bout Marina, Les Trois-Ilets* ☎ *0596/66–08– 79*) has a big up-to-date dive boat, hand-painted with tropical fish and waves, so it's impossible to miss. The English-speaking international crew is proud to have been in business since the early 1990s. The company hits 20 sites, including the Citadel and Salomon's Pool. A boat goes out mornings and afternoons. Thursday is a full day on the north coast, with breakfast, lunch, and all drinks included. Half-day dives include gear and a 'ti punch. Sunday is a day of rest, except for the first one in the month, when it's off to Diamant Rock.

FISHING

Deep-sea fishing expeditions in these waters hunt down tuna, barracuda, dolphinfish, kingfish, and bonito, and the big ones—white and blue marlins. You can hire boats from the bigger marinas, particularly in Pointe du Bout, Le Marin, and Le François; most hotels arrange these Hemingway-esque trysts, but will often charge a premium. If you call several days in advance, companies can also put you together with other anglers to keep costs down. The **Centre de Peche** (✉ *Port de Plaisance, bd. Allègre, Le Marin* ☎ *0596/76–24–20 or 0696/28–80–58* ⊕ *www.sailfish-marlin.com*), a fully loaded Davis 47-foot fishing boat, is a sportfisherman's dream. It goes out with a minimum of five anglers for €195 per person for a half day, or €390 per person for a full day, including lunch. Nonanglers can come for the ride for €95 and €190, respectively. Captain Yves speaks English fluently and is a fun guy.

GOLF

The 18-hole Le **Golf de l'Impératrice Josephine** (✉ *Les Trois-Ilets* ☎ *0596/ 68–32–81*) has been renamed in honor of Empress Joséphine Napoléon, whose birthplace, La Pagerie, adjoins this 150-acre track of rolling hills. However, the course is 100% American in design. It is a par-71 Robert Trent Jones course with an English-speaking pro, pro shop, bar, and restaurant. The club offers special greens fees to cruise-ship passengers. Normal greens fees are €23 for 9 holes (after 3 pm) and €43 for 18; a cart costs another €23 for 9, €39 for 18. For those who don't mind walking while admiring the Caribbean view between the palm trees, club trolleys are €6. There are no caddies.

GUIDED TOURS

Your hotel front desk can help arrange a personalized island tour with an English-speaking driver. It's also possible to hire a taxi for the day or half day; there are set rates for certain itineraries, and if you share the ride with others, the per-person price will be whittled down.

HIKING

Two-thirds of Martinique is designated as protected land. Trails, all 31 of them, are well marked and maintained. At the beginning of each, a notice is posted advising on the level of difficulty, the duration of a hike, and any interesting facts. The **Parc Naturel Régional de la Martinique** (✉ 9 *bd. Général de Gaulle, Fort-de-France* ☎ *0596/73–19–30*) organizes inexpensive guided excursions year-round. If there have been heavy rains, though, give it up. The tangle of ferns, bamboo trees, and vines is dramatic, but during rainy season, the wet, muddy trails will temper your enthusiasm.

HORSEBACK RIDING

🕙 Horseback-riding excursions can traverse scenic beaches, palm-shaded forests, sugarcane fields, and a variety of other tropical landscapes. Trained guides often include running commentaries on the history, flora, and fauna of the island.

At **Black Horse Ranch** (✉ *Les Trois-Ilets* ☎ *0596/68–37–80*), one-hour trail rides (€35) go into the countryside and across waving cane fields; two hours on the trail (€40) bring riders near a river. Only Western saddles are used for adults; children can ride English. Semiprivate lessons in French or English are €40 a person, less for kids if they can join a group.

Some guides are English-speaking at **Ranch de Caps** (✉ *Cap Macré, Le Marin* ☎ *0596/74–70–65 or 0696/23–18–18*), where you can take a half-day ride (Western) on the wild southern beaches and across the countryside for €48. Rides go out in the morning (8:30 to noon) and afternoon (1:30 to 5) every day but Monday. If you can manage a full day in the saddle, it costs €80. A real treat is the full-moon ride, but it needs to accrue a group to orchestrate that. Most of the mounts are Anglo-Arabs. Riders are encouraged to help cool and wash their horses at day's end. Reserve in advance. Riders of all levels are welcomed.

Ranch Jack (✉ *Anse-d'Arlets* ☎ *0596/68–37–69 or 0696/92–26–58* ✍ *ranch.jack@wanadoo.fr*) has trail rides (English-style) across some beautiful country for €36 for two hours; half-day excursions for €54 (€62 with transfers from nearby hotels) go through the fields and forests to the beach. Short rides can range from €16 to €25. The lessons for kids are recommendable.

15

KAYAKING

Ecofriendly travelers will love skimming the shallow bay while paddling to bird and iguana reserves. Rent colorful fiberglass kayaks to explore the crystalline Havre du Robert, with its shallow pools (called fonds blanc), petite beaches, and islets such as Iguana Island. You'll receive one of the island's warmest welcomes at **Les Kayaks du Robert** (⊠ *Pointe Savane, Le Robert* ☎ *0596/65–33–89*). After a memorable half-day paddle through shallow lagoons and mangrove swamps chasing color-ful fish, you can enjoy a complimentary planter's punch, all for €15 per person; a full day is €23. There are no longer guided group trips.

WINDSURFING

At **Bliss** (⊠ *Anse Bonneville Trinité near Résidence Oceane, Tartane* ☎ *0596/58–00–96* ⊕ *www.surfmartinique.com*), individual (€30) or group (€20) lessons are given to newcomers ages five and up. English and Spanish are spoken. Surf- and bodyboards (with fins) can also be rented for three hours for €14 or €24 for the day.

Montserrat

WORD OF MOUTH

"Montserrat is certainly for those who don't need a lot of entertainment and yet there is more than enough if you just know where to look. It makes the journey so much more interesting. and so much more to share."

—Lindawojcik

WELCOME TO MONTSERRAT

Although the Soufrière Hills volcano continues to rumble, the island is otherwise as peaceful as the Caribbean gets—almost a throwback to another time, with the occasional modern convenience (and convenience store) thrown in. Montserrat draws ecotourists, divers, and those who simply want to experience the Caribbean as it once was.

Restaurants ▼	Hotels ▼
Gourmet Gardens 5	Erindell Villa 4
Olveston House 3	Gingerbread Hill 2
Royal Palm Club 2	Grand View Bed & Breakfast 5
Tina's 1	Olveston House 3
Ziggy's 4	Tropical Mansion 1

KEY

➘ Beaches
◥ Dive Sites
❶ Restaurants
① Hotels

TOP 4 REASONS TO VISIT MONTSERRAT

❶ Geology: Volcano lovers will experience a landscape that's been pretty much left alone for more than a decade.

❷ Diving: The diving is one of the Caribbean's unsung secrets, as the underwater terrain has also remained largely undisturbed.

❸ Peace and Quiet: You'll find tranquillity in abundance; if you want to lie back and relax, this is the place for you.

❹ Peace of Mind: There's virtually no crime, and you won't find a friendlier place in the Caribbean.

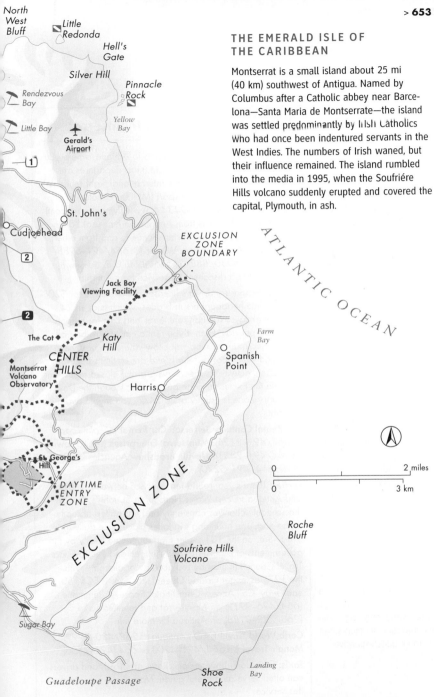

THE EMERALD ISLE OF
THE CARIBBEAN

Montserrat is a small island about 25 mi (40 km) southwest of Antigua. Named by Columbus after a Catholic abbey near Barcelona—Santa Maria de Montserrate—the island was settled predominantly by Irish Catholics who had once been indentured servants in the West Indies. The numbers of Irish waned, but their influence remained. The island rumbled into the media in 1995, when the Soufriére Hills volcano suddenly erupted and covered the capital, Plymouth, in ash.

16

MONTSERRAT

North West Bluff

Little Redonda

Hell's Gate

Silver Hill

Pinnacle Rock

Rendezvous Bay

Yellow Bay

Little Bay

Gerald's Airport

1

St. John's

Cudjoehead

EXCLUSION ZONE BOUNDARY

2

ATLANTIC OCEAN

Jack Boy Viewing Facility

2

The Cot

Katy Hill

Farm Bay

CENTER HILLS

Spanish Point

Montserrat Volcano Observatory

Harris

St. George's Hill

DAYTIME ENTRY ZONE

EXCLUSION ZONE

Roche Bluff

Soufrière Hills Volcano

0   2 miles

0   3 km

Sugar Bay

Guadeloupe Passage

Shoe Rock

Landing Bay

MONTSERRAT PLANNER

Logistics

Getting to Montserrat: There are no nonstop flights to Montserrat from North America. You can transfer on either Antigua or St. Maarten for a FlyMontserrat flight. You can also take a ferry from Antigua.

Hassle Factor: Medium to High.

Getting Around the Island: The fixed taxi fare from the airport ranges from $6 (for Tropical Mansion) to $26 (to the Olveston/Salem area villas). Though you can take taxis, you'll best appreciate Montserrat's quiet beauty if you rent a car and do some exploring on your own. Rates start at around $35 a day, but gas is expensive, so be sure to budget for that.

One main road runs from the north, down each side of the island, with little unnamed side roads streaming inland. Most addresses don't have street names or house numbers. Driving is on the left; the well-paved Main road zigs, zags, climbs, and plummets precipitously, and many equally winding side roads are pocked with potholes. There are no traffic lights but a few zebra pedestrian crossings; beware wandering pigs and goats. Gasoline in Montserrat tends to be quite expensive.

Getting to and Around Montserrat

Air Travel: There are nonstop flights to Antigua, where you can transfer to FlyMontserrat flight (most departures are scheduled to coincide with the international flight schedule) into the John A. Osborne Airport (MNI) in Geralds. **Fly-Montserrat** (☎ 664/491–3434 ⊕ www.flymontserrat.com) offers twice-daily flights from Antigua on nine-seat Britten Norman Islanders, and charter service to and from other destinations. At this writing, **Winair** (☎ 664/491–6988 or 664/491–6030, 888/255–6889 in U.S. ⊕ www.flywinair.com) had discontinued service from Antigua.

Driving: Temporary driver's licenses are available for $20 at the police headquarters in Brades, which is open 24 hours weekdays. You can rent jeeps and cars for roughly $30–$50 per day. Even if you rent a car, you're best off hiring a local guide, who will know where the best views are—and which parts of the island are off-limits because of volcanic activity. Respect the signs and closed gates that indicate the Exclusion Zone boundaries; though the Daytime Entry Zone is usually open 24/7, you should avoid it at night.

Car Rental Contacts: Jefferson Car Rental (✉ Palm Loop ☎ 664/491–2126). **Montserrat Enterprises** (✉ Old Towne ☎ 664/491–2431). **Neville Bradshaw Agencies** (✉ Olveston ☎ 664/491–5270).

Ferries: There's year-round ferry service between Little Bay and Antigua's Deep Water Harbour in St. John's, though the schedule changes constantly and has halted abruptly in the past. The hour-long trip takes place once daily Wed.–Sat. on the 101-seater Fjortoft, owned jointly by the governments of Montserrat and Antigua and the Barbuda Travel Council (it may be replaced by or alternate with the 127-passenger Caribe Queen). The fare is EC$150 each way. Call Access Coordinator Roosevelt Jemmotte (664/496–9912) on Montserrat and Jennifer Burke (268/722–8188) on Antigua for more info. **Carib World Travel** (✉ On Antigua ☎ 268/480–2999). **Monair Travel** (☎ 664/491–4200 or 664/491–2533).

Taxis: Taxis don't have meters. Rates are fixed, and drivers can often serve as a useful guide. Many have set rates for this service.

Weddings

Getting married on Montserrat is relatively easy. No blood test required. For adults 18 years and over, the minimum residency is three days. Apply for a special or Governor's marriage license at the **Department of Administration** (✉ Box 292, Government Headquarters, Brades ☎ 664/491 2365) either via mail or in person between 8 am and 4 pm weekdays. Bring valid passports as proof of citizenship and, in the case of previous marriages, the original divorce or annulment decree; widows or widowers should present the original marriage and death certificates. Given the lack of on-island wedding planners and difficulty in transportation, most visitors choose to get married on Antigua and then take a honeymoon trip to Montserrat, and that's a good idea because it will certainly allow you to spend some quiet time together.

Where to Stay

With a few small guesthouses, villas, and one small hotel, Montserrat has no large-scale development. The island's best hotel, Vue Point, is likely permanently closed at this writing because of continued volcanic activity.

Hotel and Restaurant Costs: Restaurant prices are for a main course at dinner and include any taxes or service charges. Hotel prices are per night for a double room in high season, excluding taxes, service charges, and meal plans (except at all-inclusives).

What to Wear: Dress is informal even at dinner, though skimpy attire is frowned upon by the comparatively conservative islanders. Long pants are preferred, albeit not required, for men in the evening.

WHAT IT COSTS IN DOLLARS

	¢	$	$$	$$$	$$$$
Restaurants	under $8	$8–$12	$12–$20	$20–$30	over $30
Hotels	under $80	$80–$150	$150–$250	$250–$350	over $350

When to Go

The year's big event is **St. Patrick's Day,** which ushers in a week of festivities, highlighted by musical concerts and masquerades à la Carnival. **Tourism Week,** usually late September or early October, encourages village competitions in music, dance, crafts, and food.

Late October's **Police, Fire, Search, and Rescue Services Community Week** also explodes with sound and color, as jump-ups, concerts, and barbecues lure hundreds of revelers. Mid-December into the New Year sees **Christmas festival celebrations,** from Calypso competitions to pageants and parades.

Island Activities

Many people come to Montserrat for **ecotourism,** including volcano viewing; the Soufrère Hills Volcano is one of the biggest draws, especially for day-trippers coming over from Antigua. For those willing to spend a bit more time on the island, there's surprisingly varied **diving** in amazingly pristine waters. **Hiking** through unspoiled rain forest is another attraction. The showcase beach is **Rendezvous Bay,** a cliff-shadowed cove accessible only by boat or vigorous hike. But you may come just to **relax** in a part of the Caribbean that feels as if it was picked up straight from the 1950s.

16

MONTSERRAT PLANNER

Fast Facts

Banks and Exchange Services: Local currency is the Eastern Caribbean dollar (EC$). US$1 is worth approximately EC$2.70. American dollars are readily accepted, although you usually receive change in EC$. If you decide to change money, you will get a slightly better exchange rate if you change your money in a bank than at your hotel (the exchange is sometimes rounded down to EC$2.50 in simpler transactions). Major credit cards are widely accepted. ATMs (dispensing EC$) are available at the Royal Bank of Canada and the Bank of Montserrat.

Electricity: 220 volts, 50 to 60 cycles, but most lodgings also use 110 volts, permitting use of small North American appliances like electric shavers. Outlets may be either two- or three-pronged, so bring an adapter.

Emergency Services: Ambulance (🕾 *411* or *664/491–2802*). **Fire** (🕾 *911*). **Police** (🕾 *999*). **Glendon Hospital** (✉ *St. John's* 🕾 *664/491–2552* or *664/491–7404*).

Passport Requirements: All visitors need a valid passport. All visitors must present a return or ongoing ticket.

Essentials

Mail: Airmail letters to North America and the United Kingdom cost EC$3; postcards, EC$2.25. The main post office is in the Government House in Brades. Note that there are no postal codes; when addressing letters to the island, you need only indicate the address and "Montserrat, West Indies."

Taxes and Service Charges: The departure–airport-security tax is $21—cash only. Day-trippers from Antigua spending less than 24 hours on Montserrat pay only an EC$10 "security charge" and no departure tax on Antigua. Hotels collect a 10% government room tax, guesthouses and villas 7%. Hotels and restaurants also usually add a 10% service charge to your bill.

Telephones: To place a local call, simply dial the local seven-digit number. To call Montserrat from the United States, dial 1 + 664 + the local seven-digit number. To call the United States and Canada, dial 1 + the area code + the seven-digit number. LIME phone cards are available at most hotels and post offices if you want to make an international call. LIME provides the island's cell-phone service

Tipping: In restaurants, it's customary to leave 5% beyond the regular service charge added to your bill if you're pleased with the service. Taxi drivers expect a 10% tip; porters and bellmen, about $1 per bag; maids are not often tipped, but if you do, leave $2 to $3 per night.

Visitor Information: The **Montserrat Tourist Board** (✉ *7 Farara Pl., Bldgs. B & C, Brades* 🕾 *664/491–2230* ✉ *Montserrat Government Office, 180 King's Cross Rd., London, U.K.* 🕾 *0207/031–0317* ⊕ *www.visitmontserrat. com*) keeps track of accommodations, restaurants, activities, car-rental agencies, and tours available on the island and will prove to be an invaluable resource if you decide to plan a trip to Montserrat.

By Jordan Simon

Aficionados have always regarded Montserrat as an idyllic, fairy-tale island. But in 1995, Grimm turned grim when the Soufrière Hills volcano erupted, literally throwing the island into the fire. The frilly Victorian gingerbreads of the capital, Plymouth, were buried, much of the tourism infrastructure was wiped out, and more than half the original 11,000 residents departed and have not been able to return.

Though the volcano still belches (plumes of ash are visible from as far as Antigua), plucky locals joke that new beachfront is being created. The volcano itself is an ecotourism spot, drawing travelers curious to see the awesome devastation. Ironically, other fringe benefits exist. Volcanic deposits enriched the already fertile soil; locals claim their fruit and vegetable crops have increased and improved. The slightly warmer waters have attracted even more-varied marine life for divers and snorkelers to appreciate, along with new underwater rock formations.

Although an "Exclusion Zone" covers half the island, the rest is safe; in fact, the zone was slightly retracted after the volcano's lava dome partially collapsed during a pyroclastic flow in July 2003. Seismologists and vulcanologists conduct regular risk analyses and simulation studies; as a result, the Daytime Exclusion Zone shrank after a May 2006 collapse, and then expanded again after activity in early 2008, January 2009, and fall 2009. Borders retracted slightly in early 2010 and 2011, opening parts of Old Towne and Isles Bay. Visitors expecting mass devastation are in for a surprise; Montserrat ranks among the region's most pristine, serene destinations, its luxuriant vegetation and jagged green hills justifying the moniker Emerald Isle.

Though Christopher Columbus named the island in 1493 (after the hillside Santa Maria de Montserrate monastery outside Barcelona), most locals are descended from 17th-century Irish Catholic settlers escaping English persecution. They routed the resident Caribs (who themselves had "evicted" the indigenous Saladoids and Arawaks) and eventually imported slaves to work the plantations. The Gaelic influence lingers in place and family names, folklore, jigs, and even a wispy brogue.

The island's captivating beauty, low profile, and difficult access made it a hip destination in the 1970s and '80s. Sir George Martin (The Beatles' manager) founded Air Studios in 1979, luring icons such as Eric Clapton, Sir Paul McCartney, and Stevie Wonder to record. Destroyed by Hurricane Hugo in 1989, it was never rebuilt. But locals and expats alike still like a good band. The combined Carnival and Christmas festivities go on for nearly a month, when the island is awash with color, from calypso competitions to parades and pageants.

Other than the volcano, the steamiest activities are the fiercely contested domino games outside rum shops. That may soon change. The government speaks optimistically of building a new golf course, developing spa facilities to offer volcanic mud baths, even running tours—pending safety assessments—of Plymouth as a haunting Caribbean answer to Pompeii. An airport was constructed, partly in the hope of recapturing the villa crowd that once frequented the island. But these developments—as well as debates over the new capital and threatened lawsuits against the British government for restricting access and utility service to homesites—will simmer for quite some time. One thing won't change: the people, whether native-born or expat, are among the warmest anywhere. Chat them up, and don't be surprised if you're invited to a family dinner or beach picnic.

EXPLORING MONTSERRAT

Though the more fertile—and historic—southern half of Montserrat was destroyed by the volcano, emerald hills still reward explorers. Hiking and biking are the best ways to experience this island's unspoiled rain forest, glistening black-sand beaches, and lookouts over the devastation.

The Cot. A fairly strenuous Centre Hills trail leads to one of Montserrat's few remaining historic sites—the ruins of the once-influential Sturges family's summer cottage—as well as a banana plantation. Its Duck Pond Hill perch, farther up the trail, dramatically overlooks the coastline, Garibaldi Hill, Old Towne, abandoned villages, and Plymouth.

Jack Boy Viewing Facility. This vantage point—replete with telescope, barbecue grill and tables for picnickers, landscaped grounds, and washrooms—provides bird's-eye views of the old W. H. Bramble airport and eastern villages damaged by pyroclastic flows. ⊠ *Jack Boy Hill.*

★ **Montserrat National Trust.** The MNT's Natural History Centre aims to conserve and enhance the island's natural beauty and cultural heritage. The center has permanent and rotating exhibits on Arawak canoe building, colonial sugar and lime production (the term limey was first applied here to English sailors trying to avoid scurvy), indigenous marine life, West Indian cricket, the annual Calabash Festival, and the history of Sir George Martin's Air Studios, which once lured top musicians from Dire Straits to Stevie Wonder and Paul McCartney. Eventually one archival exhibit will screen videos of Montserrat's oral history related by its oldest inhabitants. The lovingly tended botanical gardens in back make for a pleasant stroll. It may occupy new headquarters in Little Bay by 2012; funding has been slow. ⊠ *Main road, Olveston* ☎ *664/491–3086* ⊕ *www.montserratnationaltrust.ms* ✉ *$2 suggested donation* ☉ *Weekdays 10–4.*

Montserrat Volcano Observatory. The island's must-see sight occupies capacious, strikingly postmodern quarters with stunning vistas of the Soufrière Hills volcano—a lunarscape encircled by brilliant green—and Plymouth in the distance. Unfortunately, the MVO staff no longer offers tours that explain monitoring techniques on sophisticated computerized equipment in riveting detail. But you can see graphic photos, artifacts like rock and ash, and diagrams that describe the various pyroclastic surge deposits. The Interpretation Center screens a high-impact film with IMAX footage, and interactive kiosks include working seismometers (kids can jump up and down to manufacture vibrations), and other real-time monitoring instruments. ⊠ *Flemings* ☎ *664/491–5647* ⊕ *www.mvo.ms* ✉ *Observatory free, tours $4* ☉ *Weekdays 8:30–4:30. Self-guided tours Mon.–Thurs. 10:15–4.*

NEED A BREAK?

D&D Bar and Grocery (⊠ *Flemings* ☎ *664/491–9730*) is an unprepossessing shack, just downhill off the first right turn from the MVO. Owner Dawn Davis mastered mixology while working at Nisbet Plantation on Nevis, and she proudly offers more than 30 libations at her Lilliputian bar (and accepts challenges). She also bakes sublime bread and serves delectable, cheap, local fare—souse, fishwater (fish soup), macaroni pie, baked chicken—on weekdays, and just heavenly fried chicken for Saturday lunch.

Plymouth. Montserrat's former capital has been off-limits to general tourists because of volcanic activity since the May 2006 dome collapse. Before that, the adventuresome could stroll its streets, albeit at their own risk; check with the police department to see if the situation has changed again. Once one of the Caribbean's loveliest towns, facing the vividly hued sea, it now resembles a dust-covered lunarscape, with elegant Georgian buildings buried beneath several feet of ash, mud, and rubble (though rain is slowly washing layers away). Entry is officially possible only with a police escort (lest you fall through a rickety roof), but can be arranged with the police headquarters in Brades or through the Montserrat Tourist Board only when approved by the Volcano Observatory. A hazard allowance of EC$150 is charged per individual or group. ⊠ *Plymouth* ☎ *664/491–2230 for Montserrat Tourist Board* ✉ *Police escort EC$150* ☉ *Daily during daylight hrs with police escort.*

Runaway Ghaut. Montserrat's *ghauts* (pronounced guts) are deep ravines that carry rainwater down from the mountains to the sea. This natural spring, a short, well-marked walk into the hilly bush outside Woodlands, was the site of bloody colonial skirmishes between the British and French. The legend is more interesting than the trail: "Those that drink its water clear they spellbound are, and the Montserrat they must obey." If you don't want to hike or picnic, a drink from the roadside faucet should ensure that you return to Montserrat in your lifetime. ⊠ *Main road, just south of Woodlands.*

16

St. George's Hill. The only access to this incredible vantage point over the devastation is across the Belham Valley, through a once-beautiful golf course now totally covered by volcanic mudflow. This, too, was removed from the Daytime Entry Zone because of increased volcanic activity, but could be reinstated at any time. If it's accessible on your visit, be aware that routes aren't signposted on the rough road, which is often impassable after heavy rains, so it's best to hire an experienced guide. You'll drive through Cork Hill and Weekes, villages for the most part spookily intact (there's no way to provide utilities, though some enterprising souls are slowly installing solar power and water cisterns). Close to the summit, the equally eerie, abandoned, stark-white wind-generator project and the giant satellite dishes of the Gem and Antilles radio stations resemble abstract-art installations awaiting completion by Christo. At the top, Ft. St. George contains sparse ruins, including a few cannons, but the overwhelming sight is the panorama of destruction, an unrelenting swath of gray offset by vivid emerald fields and the turquoise Caribbean. ⊠ *St. George's Hill* ☉ *Daylight hrs when open.*

BEACHES

Montserrat's beaches are public and, with one exception, composed of soft, light- to dark-gray volcanic sand.

Little Bay. Boats chug in and out of the port at the northern end of this otherwise comely crescent with calm waters, which is being built up as the island's official capital. Several beach bars—Green Monkey, Pont's (fine cheap local lunch Tuesday–Sunday), Soca Cabana, Seaside and Sylvia's—provide cool shade and cooler drinks. Carlton's Fish Net Bar in the Festival Village specializes in barbecued stuffed trunkfish (a shellfish delicacy). You may see locals casting lines for their own dinner. ⊠ *Approximately 1½ mi (2½ km) north of Brades off main road; look for turnoffs to Little Bay.*

★ **Rendezvous Bay.** The island's sole white-sand beach is a perfect cove tucked under a forested cliff whose calm, unspoiled waters are ideal for swimming and offer remarkable snorkeling. It's accessible only via the sea or a steep trail that runs over the bluff to adjacent Little Bay (you can also negotiate boat rides from the fishermen who congregate there). There are no facilities or shade, but its very remoteness and pristine reef teeming with marine life lend it exceptional charm. ⊠ *Rendezvous Bay.*

Woodlands. The only drawback to this secluded strand is the occasionally rough surf (children should be closely monitored). The breezy but covered picnic area on the cliff is one of the best vantage points to watch migratory humpback whales in spring and nesting green and hawksbill turtles in early fall. From here, you can hike north, then down across a wooden bridge to even less trammeled Bunkum Bay, which has a friendly guesthouse and beach bar. ⊠ *At turnoff just outside Woodlands village.*

Luck of the Irish

Montserrat's first European settlers were persecuted English and Irish Catholics brought from Protestant St. Kitts by Englishman Thomas Warner in 1632. Seventeen years later, Oliver Cromwell sentenced many Irish political prisoners to work in the island's lucrative sugarcane fields. A 1678 census recorded that more than half the islanders were Irish. Their influence lingers today, starting with the shamrock passport stamp. The national flag bears a crest of the legendary Irish figure of Erin with a harp, and the names of both towns (Galway, Bunkum) and inhabitants (Maloney, Frith) hark back to Eire. The national dish, goat water, recalls a traditional Irish stew, and the rollicking *Bam-chick-a-lay* wouldn't be out of place in *Riverdance*. Montserrat is the only country outside Ireland where St. Patrick's Day is a public holiday; March 17 ushers in a week of celebrations across the island, the wearing of the green assuming a distinctly Caribbean beat with live calypso, reggae, and iron band music. Indeed, Montserrat's true African heritage is just as pronounced: many newborns are still given "jumbie" nicknames to fool those evil spirits, and the related jumbie dances, designed to propitiate or ward them off, are lusty and vibrant. The two traditions happily merge in the engaging people, such as Rootsman (aka Murphy), proprietor of the eponymous Carr's Bay bar, who fervently discusses his homemade herbal remedies in a lyrical, lilting brogue.

16

WHERE TO EAT

Restaurants are casual affairs indeed, ranging from glorified rum shops to hotel dining rooms. Most serve classic Caribbean fare, including such specialties as goat water (a thick stew of goat meat, tubers, and vegetables that seems to have been bubbling for days), the increasingly hard-to-find mountain chicken (giant frogs), *saal-fish kiac* (codfish fritters), home-brewed ginger beer, and freshly made juices from soursop, mango, blackberry (different from the North American species), guava, tamarind, papaya, and gooseberry.

$$–$$$ ✕ **Gourmet Gardens.** This tranquil, secluded spot—a classic gingerbread
ECLECTIC chattel-house replica echoing the adjacent historic buildings of the former Olveston estate—fulfills more than half the name's promise. There are few more delightful experiences than relaxing on Mariet's verandah amid a virtual botanical garden or beneath the huge, shady tamarind tree. Lunches are excellent value, but Sunday brunch is the winner (scrumptious eggs Benedict). "Gourmet" is a slight exaggeration, but the all-homemade global menu more than satisfies most palates and wallets. Specialties include stroganoff, chicken cordon bleu, Wiener schnitzel, shrimp stir-fry, and any dessert (try the chocolate mousse or cheesecake). ✉ *Olveston* ☎ *664/491–7859* ⚑ *Reservations essential* ▬ *No credit cards.*

$$–$$$ ✕ **Olveston House.** Five different rums power the knockout Olveston
ECLECTIC Rum Punch, but it's also the animated chatter of island locals, expats, and international guests that generates its own potent buzz. Picture

windows overlook the handsome verandah and gardens at this popular eatery. Chef Margaret Wilson creatively uses whatever ingredients are available. You might luck into fresh wahoo in orange-ginger sauce, scrumptious garlic shrimp, lasagna, pork tenderloin glazed with homemade preserves, or flaky, flavorful chicken-and-mushroom, pork, and steak-and-kidney pies that elevate traditional English pub grub to an art form. And the sublime sticky toffee pudding, mango-ginger crumble, and pear tart justify Margaret's declaration, "I'd rather make desserts than clean the house," though daughter Sarah's lush, luscious cheesecakes (mango, chocolate hazelnut) are also winners. The sailing etchings, period cabinets with mismatched china, and serenading tree frogs create the ambience of dining at someone's country estate, Caribbean-style. Friday Pub Nights and Sunday classic English brunch are casual and cheap, with no reservations required. ⊠ *Olveston* ☎ *664/491–5210 or 664/495–5210* ⊛ *www.olvestonhouse.com* ⚲ *Reservations essential* ⊗ *Closed Jan., Mon., and dinner Sun.*

$$$–$$$$ ✕ **Royal Palm Club.** This gem feels like an update on a colonial Maugham
ECLECTIC   tale, down to the eccentric expats, rumors of royal visits, and wildly
★   eclectic yet elegant decor. Though it technically operates as a "private membership club," anyone can call for reservations. The gingerbread-trim house, swallowed up in elaborate gardens, reputedly hosted Queen Elizabeth II and Princess Margaret during their 1962 trip. The interior features a marvelous mosaic bar (casual wine-and-pasta or pizza dinners are served here and at the downstairs poolside bar), stone walls, hardwood floors, stained glass, Turkish throw rugs, Indonesian kites, and 17th-century French sideboards. The enclosed patio, doubling as the main dining room, enchants with sweeping Caribbean views and fluttering butterflies. There are special evenings, such as the all-you-can-eat Italian and Chinese buffets and Tuesday film screenings. Four-course set-dinner menu choices might include garlic shrimp over linguine in a light Parmesan-cream sauce or slow-roasted pork tenderloin in orange-marmalade sauce. The peripatetic co-owners include the delightful Trevor Stephenson, who will regale you with his "lifestyles of the poor and infamous" anecdotes. ⊠ *Woodlands* ☎ *664/491–2671* ⚲ *Reservations essential* ▬ *No credit cards* ⊗ *Closed Mon. No lunch Tues.– Sat; no dinner Sun.*

$$ ✕ **Tina's.** This pretty, seafoam-green-and-white wooden building is gar-
CARIBBEAN   landed year-round with Christmas lights, a harbinger of the good vibes within. It's the best place to eavesdrop on island gossip, as government functionaries file in for lunch (at least when day-trippers don't take over). Dine either in a trim room or on a breezy verandah (admittedly sans view). Occasionally you'll find old-time dishes like souse, but the menu is generally more upscale: specialties include velvety pumpkin soup, proper escargots, and tender lobster in sultry creole sauce or (even better) tangy garlic sauce; entrées are served with heaping helpings of salads and sides. Fine desserts (moist carrot cake, cheesecake, and wonderfully textured coconut pie) end the meal, and surprisingly good take-out pizza is available. ⊠ *Brades* ☎ *664/491–3538* ▬ *No credit cards* ⊗ *Closed Sun.*

$$$–$$$$ ✕ **Ziggy's.** Vivacious owners John and Marcia Punter literally hacked
ECLECTIC Montserrat's most elegant eatery from the rain forest. They poured a
concrete floor and dressed it with a billowing, white, rectangular tent,
pergolas, palm fronds, potted plants, hardwood chairs, jade hurricane
shutters, bronze sculpted candlesticks, and colorful Moroccan-inspired
table settings: the ultimate in shack chic. The menu (posted on a black-
board) changes daily, but always offers one red meat, one white meat,
and one seafood entrée. Generally well-executed dishes lean more toward
bistro fare (emphasizing beef entrecote or goat cheese soufflé over such
island staples as chicken and fish, though specials like oxtail ravioli hap-
pily marry both culinary traditions); the signature butterfly shrimp usually
precede entrées. A decent wine list enhances the meal; save room for the
Chocolate Sludge. Though the schedule is erratic (reconfirm reservations),
the location hard to find, and the service too relaxed, the ambience is
appealingly serene and upscale. ⊠ *Mahogany La., Woodlands* ☎ *664/491–
8282* ⊕ *www.ziggysrestaurant.com* ⚄ *Reservations essential* ⊗ *No lunch.*

WHERE TO STAY

16

Currently, the island primarily offers villas (housekeepers and cooks
can be arranged) or guesthouses, the latter often incorporating meals
in the rate by request (ask if the 7% tax and 10% service charge are
included); and there is one small hotel. Note that inns rarely have air-
conditioning, relying instead on hillside breezes.

PRIVATE VILLA RENTALS

In the pre-volcano (and pre–Hurricane Hugo) days, when an interna-
tional roster of celebrity musicians (Elton to Eric, the Rolling Stones
to Sting) recorded at Sir George Martin's Air Studios, Montserrat was
a favored spot for many rich and famous Britons (and the occasional
American) to vacation. Today you can luxuriate in one of the hand-
some villas they called home when visiting and do so for comparatively
affordable rates.

The leading villa rental company in Montserrat is **Tradewinds Real Estate**
(⊠ *Main Rd., Olveston* ☎ *664/491–2004* ⊕ *www.tradewindsmontserrat.
com*). Many of its 20-plus deluxe properties, ranging from one to four
bedrooms, have plunge pools, amazing water vistas, and ultramodern
conveniences from DVD players and Internet access to gourmet kitch-
ens. Recommended properties with beach access and/or strategic hillside
locations include Mango Falls, Woodlands Estate (a restored arrow-
root factory), Cythera, Mango Pointe (owned by the former drummer
of The Turtles), and Villa Pimenta. Caring owner Susan Edgecombe
really tries to match guest to villa, remaining available throughout your
stay to make any additional arrangements and offer touring and activity
suggestions; she'll keep you updated back home with her informative
newsletter. Rates run from $700 to $2,800 per week in high season.

Another recommended option, in business since 1962, is **Montserrat
Enterprises** (▢ *Box 58, Bishop's View Rd., Old Towne* ☎ *664/491–2431*
⊕ *www.montserratenterprises.com*). Its inventory is generally smaller,
but most of its properties offer splendid views and amenities.

HOTELS AND INNS

The following reviews have been condensed for this book. Please go to Fodors.com for expanded reviews of each property.

¢

B&B/INN

★

Erindell Villa Guesthouse. This tranquil rain-forest retreat is a photo album in the making, overflowing with character and characters. **Pros:** engaging owners; beautiful landscaping; fun makeshift entertainment; abundant freebies. **Cons:** hike to beach; occasionally raucous fun makeshift entertainment; occasional ash dustings. ⊠ *Gros Michel Dr., Woodlands* ☎ *664/491–3655* ⊕ *www.erindellvilla.com* ⟋ *2 rooms* ⌂ *In-room: no a/c, Wi-Fi. In-hotel: restaurant, pool, business center* ⊟ *No credit cards* ⫶◯⫶ *Breakfast.*

¢–$

HOTEL

★

Gingerbread Hill. This secluded mountainside retreat offers remarkable value, splendid views, utter tranquillity, and exquisite grounds, where in-season you can pluck your breakfast straight from the mango, banana, citrus, papaya, and coconut trees. **Pros:** environmentally conscious; superb value; fascinating owners; delightful menagerie, including birds; constant refurbishment; access to washer/dryer. **Cons:** car necessary; no beachfront; perhaps too "granola" for some. ⌂ *Box 246, St. Peter's* ☎ *664/491–5812 or 813/774–5270* ⊕ *www.volcano-island.com* ⟋ *2 rooms, 2 villas, 1 cottage* ⌂ *In-room: no a/c, kitchen (some), no TV (some), Wi-Fi. In-hotel: laundry facilities, business center* ⫶◯⫶ *No meals.*

$

B&B/INN

Grand View Bed & Breakfast. This welcoming inn's basement holds a radio station, but contented guests send the most powerful signal thanks to energetic dynamo Theresa Silcott, who prides herself on being Montserrat's top hostess. **Pros:** splendid sweeping views; delightful gardens; congenial hostess; excellent local food (ask about medicinal folklore) by reservation. **Cons:** no pool or beachfront; very basic if clean rooms. ⊠ *Baker Hill* ☎ *664/491–2284* ⊕ *www.mnigrandview. com* ⟋ *2 suites, 5 rooms* ⌂ *In-room: no a/c (some), kitchen (some), no TV (some), Wi-Fi. In-hotel: restaurant, bar, business center, parking* ⊟ *No credit cards* ⫶◯⫶ *Breakfast.*

$

HOTEL

★

Olveston House. This 1950s villa, rented to island hotelier Carol Osborne by Beatles producer Sir George Martin, brims with history (including the owner's fabled AIR Studios where Sting, Elton John, Eric Clapton, and Paul McCartney recorded). **Pros:** incredible value; gorgeous pool; glorious views of the glowing Soufrière; invigorating blend of locals, expats, and guests at the bar and dining room. **Cons:** no beach; occasional dusting of ash; Wi-Fi spotty. ⊠ *Olveston* ☎ *664/491–5210 or 664/495–5210* ⊕ *www.olvestonhouse.com* ⟋ *6 rooms* ⌂ *In-room: no a/c (some), safe (some), no TV (some), Wi-Fi. In-hotel: restaurant, tennis court, bar, pool, parking* ☉ *Closed Jan.* ⫶◯⫶ *Breakfast.*

$

HOTEL

Tropical Mansion Suites. Despite the grandiose name, this is little more than a motel with neocolonial architectural pretensions and clean, spacious rooms. **Pros:** currently the island's only full-service lodging; centrally located. **Cons:** far from beaches; extra charge for air-conditioning; mediocre and comparatively pricey food. ⌂ *Main Rd., Box 404, Sweeney's* ☎ *664/491–8767* ⊕ *www.tropicalmansion.com* ⟋ *17 rooms, 1 suite* ⌂ *In-room: no a/c (some), kitchen (some), Wi-Fi. In-hotel: restaurant, bar, pool, business center* ⫶◯⫶ *Breakfast.*

NIGHTLIFE AND THE ARTS

Although Montserrat is better known for another kind of wildlife, Friday-night revelers lime in roadside rum shops scattered around the island, often spilling out on the street as part of the informal evening culture. There's no closing time, and many bars serve yummy, authentic local food. Little Bay is being developed as the island capital (the government will remain in Brades), in season the Hot Spot is a collection of a dozen watering holes between the "town" and Cultural Center; Festival Village is another gathering of bars. **Club Paradise** ($\boxtimes$ *Hilltop, Fogarty Hill* ☎ *664/496–4152 or 664/496–1842* 🔲*EC$10* ☉ *Open Fri.–Sun.*) is a surprisingly hip, retro-'70s nightspot, right down to the fog machine, strobe lights, and disco balls. The beat is decidedly au courant, with DJs spinning the latest soca to techno, as well as golden oldies. There's a splendid breezy patio and an intriguing mural of local scenes that curls around the bar. In season, artist **Harriet Pease** (☎ *664/491–7156*) runs a rollicking "Rumshop Tour" of three to four truly local watering holes where you can lime, drink, and play spirited dominoes.

Garry Moore's Wide Awake Bar ($\boxtimes$ *Salem* ☎ *664/491–7156*) is a perennial favorite that doesn't close as long as customers are thirsty. Don't be afraid to wake Garry to pay your tab: he often naps at the bar (when he isn't complaining—mostly humorously—about a plumber's hard life and long hours). **Howe's Rum Shop** ($\boxtimes$ *St. John's* ☎ *664/491–3008*) is the best spot for shooting pool and the breeze; get here early for luscious fried and barbecued chicken, liberally daubed with mouth- and eye-watering homemade sauces and seasonings. **Soca Cabana** ($\boxtimes$ *Little Bay* ☎ *664/492–1677* ⊕ *www.socacabana.com* 🔲 *Admission varies* ☉ *Open for lunch daily, live music and dinner Wed., Fri., and Sat. nights; dinner Sun.*) offers live Caribbean beats, as the name implies. But expat owner Tom Walker is passionate about the island's musical heritage, including the halcyon days of Air Studios. He salvaged the "Bar of the Stars" from Sir George Martin's celebrated recording space. It's a delightful liming spot, with the bamboo bar and whitewashed patio accented in mint and turquoise overlooking the beach. Seemingly half the island descends on the hotspot Sunday for meals, music, and merriment.

Lydia, the owner of the newly refurbished **Treasure Spot** ($\boxtimes$ *Cudjoe Head* ☎ *664/493–2003*), often books the island's up-and-coming musicians (usually One Man Band but also Pops Morris, Hero, and Basil—reggae and soca artists beginning to develop a reputation outside Montserrat) to play weekends.

Eight years in development, the impressive, colonnaded **Montserrat Cultural Centre** ($\boxtimes$ *Little Bay* ☎ *664/491–4242 or 664/491–4700* ⊕ *www. montserratculturalcentre.com*) and its 500-seat, state-of-the-art Sir George Martin Auditorium present craft demonstrations, folkloric and fashion shows, pageants, movies (with popcorn and hot dogs), and the occasional dance and theatrical performance. During intermission, check out the Wall of Fame (bronzed handprints of musicians who recorded or performed on Montserrat, such as Sir Paul McCartney, Sir Elton John, and Mark Knopfler). Check with the tourist board or local newspaper listings for the current schedule.

16

SHOPPING

Montserrat offers a variety of local crafts and does a brisk trade in vulcanology mementos (many shops sell not only postcards and striking photographs but also small bottles of gray ash capped by colorful, homemade cloth).

David Lea (✉ *Gingerbread Hill, St. Peter's* ☎ 664/491–5812 ⊕ *www. volcano-island.com*) has chronicled Montserrat's volcanic movements in a fascinating eight-part video–DVD series, *The Price of Paradise*, each entry a compelling glimpse into the geological and social devastation— and regeneration. These, as well as rollicking local-music CDs by his son and other musicians, are available at his studio. **Luv's Cotton Store** (✉ *Salem* ☎ 664/491–3906) is the best source for sportswear made from sea island cotton, celebrated for its softness and high quality. Also occupying the National Trust building, the **Montserrat Philatelic Bureau** (✉ *Salem* ☎ 664/491–2042 or 664/491–2996 ⊕ *www.montserratstampbureau. com*) sells a wealth of unusual stamps, including handsome first-day covers. **Oriole Gift Shop** (✉ *Salem* ☎ 664/491–3086), run by the Montserrat National Trust, is an excellent source for books on Montserrat (look for the *Montserrat Cookbook* and works by the island's former acting governor, Sir Howard Fergus), as well as trail maps, handicrafts (wonderful dolls, hand-painted boxes, and calabash purses) and locally made food products. **Woolcock's Craft & Photo Gallery** (✉ *BBC Bldg., Brades* ☎ 664/491–2025) promotes the work of local artists such as Donaldson Romeo and sells spectacular photos of the volcano as well as of indigenous birds and other wildlife.

SPORTS AND ACTIVITIES

BIKING

Mountain biking is making a comeback, with a wide network of trails through the lush Centre Hills. Bikes are also a wonderful way to explore the island and enjoy the lovely coastal vistas along the main road. Eco-centric expats David and Clover Lea rent state-of-the-art equipment from Cygnal and Mongoose ($15 to $20 per day) out of **Gingerbread Hill** (✉ *St. Peter's* ☎ 664/491–5812).

DIVING

More than 30 practically pristine dive sites surround Montserrat. The even more bountiful marine life has had time to recover from the predations of human activities, and the pyroclastic flows formed boulders, pinnacles, ledges, and walls that anchor new coral reefs. **Carr's Bay** is a favorite for shore dives, with arrow crabs, basket stars, turtles, and shimmering blue tang darting about hulking boulders and a small, colorful cave; night dives are particularly memorable as millions of bioluminescent microorganisms glow when disturbed. The shallow reefs surrounding **Woodlands Bay** feature varied underwater topography, including a small, colorful cave and thousands of banded coral shrimp, copper sweepers, sergeant majors, four-eyed butterfly fish, jackknife, attenuated trumpetfish, and turtles. **Rendezvous Bay** may be the finest spot for both snorkeling and diving, thanks to a sheltered reef and lack of ash or silt. You come face-to-face with spotted morays, porcupine fish, snake eels, octopuses, and more. You can even hang out with thousands of (harmless) fruit bats in partly submerged caves. Other top dive sites include **Lime Kiln Bay** and **Bunkum Bay**, as well as the spectacular submarine rock formations around **Little Redonda** and the **Pinnacles** off the rougher, more challenging northeastern shores.

The **Green Monkey Dive Shop** (⊠ *Little Bay* ☎ *664/491–2628* ⊕ *www. divemontserrat.com*) offers PADI certification, snorkeling trips, and a variety of dives. Scuba Master Troy Depperman customizes trips for clients' interests and skill levels. The most intriguing regular option is Dive Redonda, a tour of the island "Kingdom of Redonda" 15 mi (24 km) northwest of Montserrat. The 45-minute boat ride offers scintillating views of the coast and Soufrière Hills volcano. Once there, underwater attractions include leviathan southern stingrays, morays, turtles, nurse sharks, and barracudas cruising around 6-foot barrel sponges and darting in and out of the caves and coral-encrusted barge at the "World's End" on the island's northernmost point. It also runs nature hikes, coastal kayak tours (and rentals), and ecotours.

Ⓒ Andrew Myers and Emmy Aston of **Scuba Montserrat** (⊠ *Little Bay* ☎ *664/496–7807* ⊕ *www.scubamontserrat.com*) provide experienced PADI certification; lengthy shore, boat, and kayak dives; snorkeling excursions (including a stop at a very cool bat cave); specialty courses from drift diving to digital underwater photography; and down the road the possibility of helping regenerate volcano-damaged sites. They're particularly family focused, stocking underwater Frisbees, torpedoes, and specialized children's gear.

FISHING

Deep-sea fishing (wahoo, bonito, shark, marlin, and yellowfin tuna) is superb, since the waters aren't disturbed by leviathan cruise ships. Affable **Danny Sweeney** (⊠ *Olveston* ☎ *664/491–5645*) has won several regional tournaments, including Montserrat's Open Fishing Competition. Half-day charters (up to four people) are $300. Though schools of game fish amazingly cavort just 2 to 3 mi (3 to 5 km) offshore, Danny's depth sounder picks up action in deeper waters. An extra bonus on the open sea is the gripping views of the volcanic devastation.

GUIDED TOURS

Joe "Fergus" Phillip, who operates **Avalon Tours** (⊠ *Manjack* ☎ *664/491– 3432 or 664/492–1565* ✉ *joephillip@live.com*) often emails updates on Montserrat to visitors. Reuben Furlonge of **Furlonge Taxi & Tours** (⊠ *Gerald's* ☎ *664/491–4376 or 664/492–2790*) is another hardy helpful local (and a "goat water specialist"; you may be stopped along the way by locals inquiring if he's made a batch). All are friendly, knowledgeable, and reliable taxi and tour drivers.

HIKING

Montserrat's lush, untrammeled rain forest teeming with exotic flora, fauna, and birdlife is best experienced on foot. The tourist office provides lists of hiking trails, from easy to arduous. The most dramatic routes are gradually being upgraded as part of the Montserrat Tourism Development Project; in addition to improving their definition, the government will also be building viewing platforms and providing interpretative information at strategic points. Still, if you're not experienced or fit, go with a guide; always wear sturdy shoes and bring water. Most marked trails run through the biologically diverse, scenic Centre Hills region, offering stirring lookouts over the volcano's barren flanks, surrounding greenery, and ash-covered villages in the Exclusion Zone. The rain forest is home to many regionally endemic wildlife species (tree frogs, dwarf geckos, anoles, mountain chicken—actually a type of frog—and the half-snake-half-lizard galliwasp), as well as most of the 34 resident birds, from red-billed tropic birds to the rare national bird, the Montserrat oriole, with its distinctive orange-and-black plumage. The Silver Hills in the north are vastly different, with dry and deciduous forests and open plains blanketing a defunct, heavily faulted and eroded volcano; views here might provide a glimpse of how southern Montserrat will look millions of years from now.

Scriber Tours (☎ 664/491–2546, 664/491–3412, or 664/492–2943) is run by James "Scriber" Daley ("a describer since I was little"), an employee of the Agricultural Department legendary for his uncanny birdcalls. He leads nature hikes through the rain forest for $20 to $40; he'll hire additional guides if there are more than 10 people per group, ensuring personal attention. Scriber also explains indigenous flora, from 42 fern species (kids love when he "tattoos" them with silver fern leaves) to others prized for medicinal properties (you might collect the makings of bush tea for back pain or menstrual cramps). He also conducts a memorable, if brief, evening mountain-chicken tour, distributing flashlights to find the foot-long frogs.

HORSEBACK RIDING

Mountainous, pristine Montserrat is a natural for equine enthusiasts. **Zekie's Tours** (✉ Frith's, Salem ☎ 664/491–2765) offers two- to three-hour walking tours for all ages (6 and up) and levels of experience. Terrain and scenery range run mild to wild, from Old Road beach rides and Swimming with the Horses to the eerily desolate Belham Valley volcanic landscape ride. Prices range from $50 to $125. Experienced riders can rent horses ($30 per hour); lessons cost $25 per hour (private), $8 per person for groups up to four.

Puerto Rico

WORD OF MOUTH

"My husband and I just returned from celebrating our belated 10-year anniversary in Puerto Rico. We did not know what to expect but wanted somewhere with consistently nice weather and a direct flight from Washington, D.C. We absolutely loved it—the weather was perfect and it was a great mix of beach and urban for us."

—MILLERSU

WELCOME TO PUERTO RICO

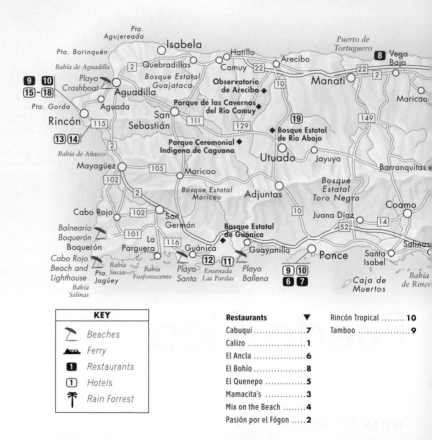

KEY	
Beaches	
Ferry	
1 Restaurants	
1 Hotels	
Rain Forrest	

Restaurants ▼		Rincón Tropical **10**
Cabuqui **7**	Tamboo **9**
Calizo **1**	
El Ancla **6**	
El Bohío **8**	
El Quenepo **5**	
Mamacita's **3**	
Mix on the Beach **4**	
Pasión por el Fógon **2**	

Mother Spain is always a presence here—on a sun-dappled cobblestone street, in the shade of a colonial cathedral or fort. Yet multifaceted Puerto Rico pulses with New World energy. The rhythms of the streets are of Afro-Latin salsa and Bomba. And the U.S. flag flaps in the salty breezes wherever you go.

SPANISH AMERICAN

Puerto Rico is 110 mi (177 km) long and 35 mi (56 km) wide. With a population of almost 4 million, it's among the biggest Caribbean islands. The first Spanish governor was Juan Ponce de León in 1508; he founded Old San Juan in 1521. The United States won the island in the Spanish-American war in 1898 and made it a commonwealth in 1952.

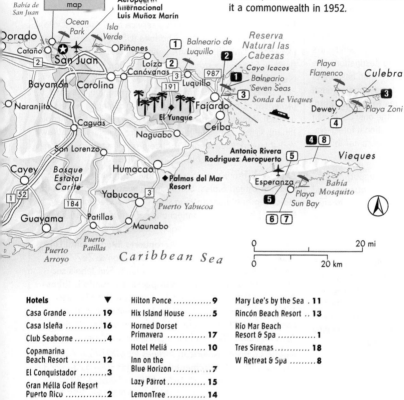

Hotels ▼	Hilton Ponce 9	Mary Lee's by the Sea . 11
Casa Grande 19	Hix Island House 5	Rincón Beach Resort .. 13
Casa Isleña 16	Horned Dorset	Río Mar Beach
Club Seaborne 4	Primavera 17	Resort & Spa 1
Copamarina	Hotel Meliá 10	Tres Sirenas 18
Beach Resort 12	Inn on the	W Retreat & Spa 8
El Conquistador 3	Blue Horizon 7	
Gran Mélia Golf Resort	Lazy Parrot 15	
Puerto Rico 2	LemonTree 14	
Hacienda Tamarindo 6		

TOP REASONS TO VISIT PUERTO RICO

1 The Nightlife: Happening clubs and discos make San Juan one of the Caribbean's nightlife capitals, rivaling even Miami.

2 The Food: Great restaurants run the gamut from elegant places in San Juan to simple spots serving delicious *comida criolla*.

3 The Beaches: Both developed and wild, beaches here suit the needs of surfers, sunbathers, and families.

4 The Nature: Nature abounds, from the underground Río Camuy to El Yunque, the only Caribbean national forest.

PUERTO RICO PLANNER

Island Activities

Because of its size, Puerto Rico supports virtually any activity you might imagine. The west coast is one of the Caribbean's major **surfing** destinations; the north-central region has one of the world's largest underground river systems for **spelunking**; El Yunque is the only Caribbean entry in the national forest system and a mecca for **hikers** and **mountain bikers**.

Large resorts support several excellent **golf courses** and **tennis** facilities, and the surrounding waters are good for **fishing** and **diving**.

Puerto Rico is also lined with several excellent **beaches**, including a few on Vieques that are only now open to the public after many years. The tiny island of Culebra also has some of Puerto Rico's most beautiful white-sand beaches.

The island is dotted with interesting **historical sights**, and San Juan itself is one of the oldest cities in the Western Hemisphere. San Juan is also one of the most vibrant cities, with excellent **restaurants**, happening **nightclubs**, and great **shopping**.

Getting to Puerto Rico

Hassle Factor: Low.

Nonstops: San Juan has nonstop service from Atlanta (Delta), Boston (American, JetBlue), Charlotte (US Airways), Chicago (American, United), Dallas (American), Fort Lauderdale (JetBlue, Spirit), Houston (Continental), Miami (American), New York–Newark (Continental), New York–JFK (American, Delta, JetBlue), Orlando (JetBlue, Spirit), Philadelphia (American, United, US Airways), and Washington–Dulles (United). Aguadilla has nonstop service from Fort Lauderdale (Spirit), Orlando (JetBlue), New York–JFK (JetBlue), and New York–Newark (Continental). Ponce has nonstop service from Orlando (JetBlue) and New York–JFK (JetBlue).

Air Travel: There are dozens of daily flights to Puerto Rico from the United States. San Juan's international airport is a major regional hub, so many travelers headed elsewhere in the Caribbean make connections here. Fares to San Juan are among the most reasonably priced to the region.

The island's main airport is **Aeropuerto Internacional Luis Muñoz Marín (SJU)** (⊠ *Isla Verde, San Juan* ☎ *787/791–3840*), 20 minutes east of Old San Juan. San Juan's secondary airport is the small **Aeropuerto Fernando L. Ribas Dominicci (SIG)** (⊠ *Isla Grande, San Juan* ☎ *787/729–8711*), also called Isla Grande. From either airport you can catch flights to Culebra, Vieques, and other destinations on Puerto Rico and throughout the Caribbean.

Airline Contacts: American Airlines (☎ *800/433–7300* ⊕ *www.aa.com*). **Continental Airlines** (☎ *800/523–3273* ⊕ *www.continental.com*). **Delta Airlines** (☎ *800/221–1212* ⊕ *www.delta.com*). **JetBlue** (☎ *800/538–2583* ⊕ *www.jetblue.com*). **Spirit Airlines** (☎ *800/772–7117* ⊕ *www.spiritair.com*). **United Airlines** (☎ *800/864–8331* ⊕ *www.united.com*). **US Airways** (☎ *800/428–4322* ⊕ *www.usairways.com*).

Regional Airlines Air Flamenco (☎ *787/724–1818* ⊕ *www.airflamenco.net*). **Cape Air** (☎ *866/227–3247* ⊕ *www.capeair.net*). **Seaborne Airlines** (☎ *866/359–8784* ⊕ *www.seaborneairlines.com*). **Vieques Air Link** (☎ *787/741–8331* or *888/901–9247* ⊕ *www.viequesairlink.com*).

Getting Around Puerto Rico

Boat and Ferry Travel: The **Autoridad de Transporte Marítimo** (☎ 800/981–2005 or 787/860–2005 ⊕ www.atm.gobierno.pr) runs ferries from Fajardo to Culebra and Vieques from the ferry terminal in Fajardo. Advance reservations are not accepted. Seating is limited, so get to the terminal at least an hour before the scheduled departure. Even still, you may have to wait for the next ferry, due to high passenger volume.

The Fajardo–Vieques ferry departs from Vieques weekdays at 9:30 am, 1 pm, 4:30 pm, and 8 pm, returning at 6:30 am, 11 am, 3 pm, and 6 pm. On weekends ferries depart from Fajardo at 9 am, 3 pm, and 6 pm and leave Vieques at 6:30 am, 1 pm, and 4:30 pm. Tickets for the 90-minute journey are $2 each way. The Fajardo–Culebra ferry leaves Culebra daily at 9 am, 3 pm, and 7 pm, returning at 6:30 am, 1 pm, and 5 pm. On weekends ferries depart from Fajardo at 4 am, 4 pm, and 6 pm and leave Culebra at 7 am and 6 pm. The 90-minute trip is $2.25.

Car Travel: In San Juan it's more trouble than it's worth to rent a car. Elsewhere a car is probably a necessity. A valid driver's license from your country of origin can be used in Puerto Rico for three months. Rates start as low as $25 a day. Several well-marked multilane highways link population centers. Distances are posted in kilometers, whereas speed limits are posted in miles per hour. Road signs are in Spanish.

International Agencies Avis (☎ 800/331–1212 ⊕ www.avis.com). **Hertz** (☎ 800/654–3131 ⊕ www.hertz.com). **National** (☎ 877/222–9058 ⊕ www.nationalcar.com). **Thrifty** (☎ 800/847–4389 ⊕ www.thrifty.com).

Local Agencies Charlie Car Rental (☎ 787/728–2418 or 800/289–1227 ⊕ www.charliecars.com). **Vias** (☎ 787/791–4120 ⊕ www.viascarrental.com).

Taxis: The Puerto Rico Tourism Company has instituted a well-organized taxi program. White taxis with the "taxi turístico" logo run from the airport or the cruise-ship piers to Isla Verde, Condado/Ocean Park, and Old San Juan, with fixed "zone" rates ranging from $10 to $19. If you take a cab going somewhere outside the fixed zones, insist on setting the meter. City tours start at $30 per hour. In other towns, you can flag down cabs on the street, but it's easier to have your hotel call one for you. Either way, make sure the driver is clear on whether he or she will charge a flat rate or use a meter to determine the fare. In most places, the cabs are metered.

Ground Transportation

Before arriving, check with your hotel about transfers: some hotels and resorts provide transport from the airport—free or for a fee—to their guests; some larger resorts run regular shuttles. Otherwise, your best bets are *taxis turísticos* (tourist taxis). Uniformed officials at the airport can help you make arrangements. They will give you a slip with your exact fare to hand to the driver. Rates are based on your destination. A taxi turístico to Isla Verde costs $10. It's $15 to Condado and $19 to Old San Juan. There's a $1 charge for each bag handled by the driver.

Language

Puerto Rico is officially bilingual, but Spanish dominates, particularly outside the tourist areas of San Juan. Although English is widely spoken, you'll probably want to take a Spanish phrase book along on your travels about the Island.

17

PUERTO RICO PLANNER

Fast Facts

Banks and Money: The U.S. dollar is the official currency. Major credit cards are widely accepted, ATMs are readily available and reliable in the cities and less frequently in rural areas. Look to local banks such as Banco Popular and First Bank.

Electricity: 110 volts/60 cycles.

Emergencies: Dial 911. The **San Juan Tourist Zone Police** (☎ 787/726–7020, 787/726–7015 for Condado, 787/728–4770, 787/726–2981 for Isla Verde) are particularly helpful to visitors.

Passport Requirements: U.S. citizens don't need passports. You will not pass through immigration, but there is an agriculture inspection before you check in for your flight home.

Weddings: You must get an application from the **Demographic Registry Office** (✉ Box 11854, Fernandez Juncos Station, San Juan 00910 ☎ 787/767–9120). No special residency requirements. Medical certificates from a local doctor are required. If applicable, a divorce decree or death certificate must be produced. Blood tests are required and must be done within 10 days of the ceremony.

Essentials

Mail: Puerto Rico uses the **U.S. Postal Service** (✉ 100 Paseo Colón, Old San Juan, San Juan ✉ 113 Calle Garrido Morales, Fajardo ✉ 93 Calle Atocha, Ponce) and all addresses on the island carry zip codes. Major post-office branches can be found in most major cities and towns.

Safety: San Juan, like any other big city, has its share of petty crime, so guard your wallet or purse on the city streets. Don't leave anything unattended on the beach. Leave your valuables in the hotel safe, and stick to the fenced-in beach areas of your hotel. Always lock your car and stash valuables and luggage out of sight. Avoid deserted beaches at night.

Taxes: Accommodations incur a tax: for hotels with casinos it's 11%, for other hotels it's 9%, and for government-approved paradores it's 7%. Ask your hotel before booking. The tax, in addition to the standard 5% to 12% service charge or resort fee applied by most hotels, can add a hefty 20% or more to your bill. There's a 7% (6% state plus 1% municipal) sales tax in Puerto Rico.

Telephones: Most U.S. mobile phone users will not pay roaming charges in Puerto Rico; confirm with your company. Area codes are 787 and 939. Toll-free numbers (prefix 800, 888, or 877) are widely used, and many can be accessed from North America (and vice versa). To make a local call in Puerto Rico you must dial 1, the area code, and the seven-digit number. For international calls, dial 011, the country code, the city code, and the number. Dial 00 for an international long-distance operator. Phone cards are widely available (most drugstores carry them).

Tipping: Tips are expected, and appreciated, by restaurant waitstaff (15% to 20% if a service charge isn't included), hotel porters ($1 per bag), maids ($1 to $2 a day), and taxi drivers (15% to 18%).

Visitor Information: The **Puerto Rico Tourism Company** (☎ 787/721–2400 or 800/866–7827 ⊕ www.seepuertorico.com) has offices at the airports in San Juan and Aguadilla, as well as downtown offices in Old San Juan, Cabo Rojo, and Ponce.

Where to Stay

If you want easy access to shopping, dining, and nightlife, then you should stay in San Juan, which also has decent—though by no means the island's best—beaches. Most of the other large, deluxe resorts are along the northeast coast. There are also a few resorts along the southern coast. Rincón, in the west, has a concentration of resorts and great surfing. Other small inns and hotels are around the island in the interior, including a few around El Yunque. Look to Vieques and Culebra if you want to find excellent beaches and little development. Many larger resorts in Puerto Rico charge resort fees, which are uncommon elsewhere in the Caribbean.

Big Hotels: San Juan's beaches are lined with large-scale hotels that include happening restaurants and splashy casinos. Most are spread out along Condado and Isla Verde beaches.

Paradores: Small inns (many offering home-style comida criolla cooking) are spread out around the island, though they are rarely on the beach.

Upscale Beach Resorts: All over the island—but particularly along the north coast—large tourist resorts offer all the amenities along with a hefty dose of isolation. Just be prepared for expensive food and few nearby off-resort dining opportunities.

HOTEL AND RESTAURANT COSTS

Restaurant prices are for a main course at dinner and include any taxes or service charges. Hotel prices are per night for a double room in high season, excluding taxes, service charges, and meal plans (except at all-inclusives).

WHAT IT COSTS IN U.S. DOLLARS

	¢	$	$$	$$$	$$$$
Restaurants	under $8	$8–$12	$12–$20	$20–$30	over $30
Hotels	under $150	$150–$275	$276–$375	$376–$475	over $475

When to Go

San Juan in particular is very expensive—many would say overpriced—during the busy tourist season from mid-December through mid-April; during the off-season, you can get good deals all over the island, with discounts of up to 40% off high-season rates.

FESTIVALS AND EVENTS

Weeklong **patron saints'** festivals happen throughout the year all over the island, so you can almost always find a celebration going on somewhere in Puerto Rico.

The annual **Fiestas de la Calle San Sebastián** feature several nights of live music as well as food festivals and cabezudos parades, where folk legends are caricatured in oversize masks.

The pre-Lenten **Carnival** is celebrated in Puerto Rico, as it is on so many islands. Ponce's celebration is the most famous, but several towns and regions have parades, music competitions, beauty pageants, and other parties.

Easter week sees spring breakers and Puerto Ricans filling up every beach.

The **Pablo Casals Festival of Classical Music** in early June is a popular event in San Juan itself.

17

PUERTO RICO BEACHES

With 365 different beaches in Puerto Rico, choosing where to spread out your towel might seem like a daunting task. The decision is easier now that four have been designated with a Blue Flag.

(Above) Playa Luquillo. (Opposite page bottom) Playa Luquillo. (Opposite page top) Playa Flamenco.

Playa Flamenco, on the island of Culebra, made the cut. After all, it's rated one of the world's best beaches. More surprisingly, two of the beaches are in San Juan: Balneario Escambrón, in Puerta de Tierra, and Balneario Carolina, in Isla Verde. The fourth is Luquillo's Balneario Monserrate (Playa Luquillo). This means that three of Puerto Rico's finest beaches are within an hour's drive of the capital. In total the government maintains 13 *balnearios* (public beaches). They're gated and equipped with dressing rooms, lifeguards, parking, and, in some cases, picnic tables, playgrounds, and camping facilities.

BLUE FLAG

Chosen by the Foundation for Environmental Education, a nonprofit agency, Blue Flag beaches have to meet 27 criteria, focusing on water quality, the presence of a trained staff, and the availability of facilities such as water fountains and restrooms.

SAN JUAN

The city's beaches can get crowded, especially on weekends. There's free access to all of them, but parking can be an issue in the peak sun hours—arriving early or in the late afternoon is a safer bet.

Balneario de Carolina. When people talk of a "beautiful Isla Verde beach," this is the one they're talking about. A government-maintained beach, this *balneario* east of Isla Verde is so close to the airport that the leaves rustle when planes take off. The long stretch of sand, which runs parallel to Avenida Los Gobernadores, is shaded by palms and almond trees. There's plenty of room to spread out and lots of amenities: lifeguards, restrooms, changing facilities, picnic tables, and barbecue grills. ⊠ *Carolina* 🅿 *Parking $3* ⊘ *Daily 8–5.*

Balneario de Escambrón. In Puerta de Tierra, this government-run beach is just off Avenida Muñoz Rivera. The patch of honey-color sand is shaded by coconut palms and has surf that's generally gentle. Favored by families, it has lifeguards, bathhouses, bathrooms, and restaurants. ⊠ *Puerta de Tierra* 🅿 *Parking $4.28* ⊘ *Daily 6 am–7 pm.*

EASTERN PUERTO RICO

A long stretch of powdery sand near the Reserva Natural Las Cabezas de San Juan, **Balneario Seven Seas** may turn out to be the best surprise of your trip.

Facilities include picnic tables, changing areas, restrooms, and showers. Many restaurants are just outside the gates. Its calm, clear waters are perfect for swimming. ⊠ *Rte. 987, Las Croabas.*

★ **Fodor's Choice** Just off Route 3, gentle **Playa Luquillo** (or Balneario La Monserrate) is a magnet for families. It's well equipped with restrooms, showers, lifeguards, guarded parking, food stands, picnic areas, and even cocktail kiosks. Lounge chairs and umbrellas are available to rent. Its most distinctive facility is the Mar Sin Barreras (Sea Without Barriers), a low-sloped ramp leading into the water that allows wheelchair users to take a dip. The beach is open daily. Admission is $2 per car, $3 for minivans. ⊠ *Off Rte. 3.*

VIEQUES AND CULEBRA

Playa Caracas. Located on former U.S. Navy land on the eastern end of Vieques, this tiny yet beautiful beach is reached via a well-maintained dirt road. The water is crystal clear, and its location in Bahía Corcho means that it is sheltered from waves. ⊠ *Off Rte. 997, east of Playa Media Luna.*

★ **Fodor's Choice** **Playa Flamenco.** Consistently ranked one of the most beautiful in the world. Snow-white sands, turquoise waters, and lush hills that rise on all sides make it feel miles away from civilization. During the week it's pleasantly uncrowded; on weekends

17

Cresting a wave at "Domes" Beach in Rincón.

it fills up fast with day-trippers from the mainland. It's the only beach on Culebra with amenities such as camping, restrooms, showers, and kiosks selling simple fare. ✉ *Rte. 251, west of airport* ☎ *787/742–0700 Daily dawn–dusk.*

Playa Sun Bay. The 1-mi-long (1½-km-long) white sands skirt a crescent-shaped bay. You'll find food kiosks, picnic tables, and changing facilities. It gets packed on holidays and weekends. On weekdays, when the crowds are thin, you might see wild horses grazing among the palm trees. Parking is $3, but often no one is at the gate to take your money. ✉ *Rte. 997, east of Esperanza* ☎ *787/741–8198.*

SOUTHERN PUERTO RICO

Caja de Muertos *(Coffin Island).* This island a few miles off the coast has the best beaches in the Ponce area and is, perhaps, the second-best spot in southern Puerto Rico for snorkeling, after La Parguera. Ask one of the many boatmen at La Guancha to take you out for about $30 round-trip. ✉ *Boats leave from La Guancha, at end of Rte. 14, Ponce.*

WESTERN PUERTO RICO

Balneario de Rincón. Swimmers can enjoy the tranquil waters at this beach. The beautiful facility has a playground, changing areas, restrooms, and a clubhouse. It's within walking distance of the center of town. Parking is $2. ✉ *Rte. 115.*

Playa Crashboat. Here you'll find the colorful fishing boats that are portrayed on postcards all over the island. The sand is soft and sugary, and the water's smooth as glass. Named after rescue boats used when Ramey Air Force Base was in operation, there are picnic huts, showers, parking, and restrooms. There's a food stand run by locals where the catch of the day is served with cold beer. ✉ *End of Rte. 458, off Rte. 107.*

EATING AND DRINKING WELL IN PUERTO RICO

More chefs and restaurateurs are developing menus in the line of a Nuevo Latino cuisine. However, even the most modern chefs here include traditional ingredients as they update old favorites.

Standard meats like chicken, pork, and lamb are given an added zest by sauces made from such tropical fruits as tamarind, mango, or guava. Puerto Rican cooking uses a lot of local vegetables: plantains are cooked a hundred different ways, and yams and other root vegetables are served baked, fried, stuffed, boiled, and mashed. Rice and beans are accompaniments to almost every dish. *Sofrito*—a garlic, onion, sweet pepper, cilantro, oregano, and tomato puree—is used as a base for practically everything. *Arroz con pollo* (chicken with rice), pernil (roasted pork shoulder), *sancocho* (beef or chicken and tuber soup), and *encebollado* (steak and onions) are all typical plates. Also look for fritters served along highways and beaches. You may find *empanadillas* (stuffed fried turnovers), *sorullitos* (cheese-stuffed corn sticks), and *bacalaítos* (codfish fritters).

BLACK GOLD

Cultivated at high altitudes in cool, moist air and mineral-rich soil, the island's coffee beans (called cherries) are black and aromatic. The dominant bean is the *arabica*, known as the richest and most flavorful among the coffee varieties. A lengthy ripening process acts as a sort of "prebrew," imbuing the bean with a rich flavor and a slightly sweet aftertaste. Look for local brands: Yauco Selecto, Rioja, Yaucono, Café Rico, Crema, Adjuntas, Coqui, and Alto Grande Super Premium. Alto Grande, guaranteed to have been grown at high altitudes, has gained the most fame off the island.

Cocina Criolla: *Cocina criolla*—literally, creole cooking—is an aggregate of Caribbean cuisines, sharing basic ingredients common to Cuban, Dominican, and even Brazilian culinary traditions. Conventional wisdom says that the secret of the cocina criolla depends on the use of sofrito, achiote (the inedible fruit of a small Caribbean shrub whose seeds are sometimes ground as a spice or simmered in oil to release their color), lard, and the *caldero* (cooking pot).

Indigenous Fruits and Vegetables: Tropical fruits often wind up at the table in the form of delicious juices. A local favorite is pineapple juice from crops grown in the north of the island. Coconut, mango, papaya, lime, and tamarind are other local favorites. Puerto Rico is home to terrific lesser-known fruits; these include the *caimito* (also called a star apple), *quenepa* (a Spanish lime with a yellow sweet-tart pulp surrounded by a tight, thin skin), and *zapote* (a plum-size fruit that tastes like peach, avocado, and vanilla). The Plaza del Mercado in Santurce is a good place to look for the unusual.

Local Seafood: The freshest seafood is to be found on the northern and western coasts, where seaside shacks and kiosks serve up red snapper, conch, crab, and spiny lobster in traditional recipes. Fried fish is also popular, served with *mojo isleño*, a sauce made with olives, onions, pimientos, capers, tomatoes, and vinegar.

Plantains and Mofongo: *Plátanos*, or plantains, are related to bananas but are larger and starchier. They are served mostly as side dishes and may be eaten green or ripe. They can be fried, baked, boiled, or roasted and served either whole or in slices. Of all the delicious plantain preparations, one of the tastiest is also the simplest—*mofongo*. Green plantains are mashed with a wooden *pilón*, mixed with garlic, pork fat, and other flavorings and fried in a pan. Served plain, it's often a side dish. But when it's stuffed with chicken, beef, or some other meat, *mofongo* becomes one of Puerto Rico's signature entrées.

Rice: Rice is omnipresent, and most often it's served with *habichuelas* (beans). Rice stuck to the pot, known as *pegao,* is the most highly prized, full of all the ingredients that have sunk to the bottom.

Rum: Although rum was first exported in 1897, it took a bit longer for it to become the massive industry it is today. The Bacardí family set up shop near San Juan in 1959. The company's product, lighter-bodied than those produced by most other distilleries, gained favor around the world. Today Puerto Rico produces more than 35 million gallons of rum a year. You might say it's the national drink.

Updated by Heather Rodino Sunrise and sunset are both worth waiting for when you're in Puerto Rico. The pinks and yellows that hang in the early-morning sky are just as compelling as the sinewy reds and purples that blend into the twilight. It's easy to compare them, as Puerto Rico is small enough that you can easily have breakfast in Fajardo, looking eastward over the boats headed to Vieques and Culebra, then settle down for a lobster dinner in Rincón as the sun is sinking into the inky-blue water.

Known as the Island of Enchantment, Puerto Rico conjures a powerful spell. Here, traffic actually leads you to a "Road to Paradise," whether you're looking for a pleasurable, sunny escape from the confines of urbanity or a rich supply of stimulation to quench your cultural and entertainment thirst. On the island you have the best of both worlds, natural and urban thrills alike, and although city life is frenetic enough to make you forget you're surrounded by azure waters and warm sand, traveling a few miles inland or down the coast can easily make you forget you're surrounded by development.

Puerto Rico was populated primarily by Taíno Indians when Columbus landed in 1493. In 1508 Ponce de León established a settlement and became the first governor; in 1521 he founded what is known as Old San Juan. For centuries, while Africans worked on the coastal sugarcane fields, the French, Dutch, and English tried unsuccessfully to wrest the island from Spain. In 1898, as a result of the Spanish-American War, Spain ceded the island to the United States. In 1917 Puerto Ricans became U.S. citizens, and in 1952 Puerto Rico became a semiautonomous commonwealth.

Since the 1950s, Puerto Rico has developed exponentially, as witnessed in the urban sprawl, burgeoning traffic, and growing population (estimated at nearly 4 million); yet *en la isla* (on the island) a strong Latin sense of community and family prevails. Puertorriqueños are fiercely proud of their unique blend of heritages.

Music is another source of Puerto Rican pride. Like wildflowers, *velloneras* (jukeboxes) pop up almost everywhere, and when one is playing, somebody will be either singing or dancing along—or both. Cars often vibrate with *reggaetón,* a hard, monotonous beat with lyrics that express social malaise. Salsa, a fusion of West African percussion, jazz, and other Latin beats, is the trademark dance. Although it may look difficult to master, it's all achieved by just loosening your hips. You may choose to let your inhibitions go by doing some clubbing *a la vida loca* made famous by pop star Ricky Martin. Nightlife options are on par with any cosmopolitan city—and then some.

By day you can drink in the culture of the old world; one of the richest visual experiences in Puerto Rico is Old San Juan. Originally built as a fortress by the Spaniards in the early 1500s, the Old City has myriad attractions that include restored 16th-century buildings and 200-year-old houses with balustraded balconies of filigreed wrought iron that overlook narrow cobblestone streets. Spanish traditions are also apparent in the countryside festivals celebrated in honor of small-town patron saints. For quiet relaxation or experiences off the beaten track, visit coffee plantations, colonial towns, or outlying islets where nightlife is virtually nonexistent.

And you don't come to a Caribbean island without taking in some of the glorious sunshine and natural wonders. In the coastal areas, the sun mildly toasts your body, and you're immediately healed by soft waves and cool breezes. In the misty mountains, you can wonder at the flickering night flies and the star-studded sky while the *coquís* (tiny local frogs) sing their legendary sweet lullaby. On a moonless night, watch the warm ocean turn into luminescent aqua-blue speckles on your skin. Then there are the island's many acres of golf courses, numerous tennis courts, rain forests, and dozens of beaches that offer every imaginable water sport.

17

EXPLORING PUERTO RICO

OLD SAN JUAN

Old San Juan, the original city founded in 1521, contains carefully preserved examples of 16th- and 17th-century Spanish colonial architecture. More than 400 buildings have been beautifully restored. Graceful wrought-iron balconies with lush hanging plants extend over narrow streets paved with *adoquines* (blue-gray stones originally used as ballast on Spanish ships). The Old City is partially enclosed by walls that date from 1633 and once completely surrounded it. Designated a U.S. National Historic Zone in 1950, Old San Juan is chockablock with shops, open-air cafés, homes, tree-shaded squares, monuments, and people. You can get an overview on a morning's stroll (bear in mind that this "stroll" includes some steep climbs). However, if you plan to immerse yourself in history or to shop, you'll need a couple of days.

TOP ATTRACTIONS

Ⓒ **Castillo San Cristóbal.** This huge stone fortress, built between 1634 and 1785, guarded the city from land attacks from the east. The largest Spanish fortification in the New World, San Cristóbal was known in the 17th and 18th centuries as the Gibraltar of the West Indies. Five freestanding structures divided by dry moats are connected by tunnels. You're free to explore the gun turrets (with cannon in situ), officers' quarters, re-created 18th-century barracks, and gloomy passageways. Along with El Morro, San Cristóbal is a National Historic Site administered by the U.S. Park Service; it's a World Heritage Site as well. Rangers conduct tours in Spanish and English. ⊠ *Calle Norzagaray at Av. Muñoz Rivera, Old San Juan* ☎ *787/729–6777* ⊕ *www.nps.gov/saju* ⊐ *$3, $5 includes admission to El Morro* ☉ *Daily 9–6.*

Ⓒ **Castillo San Felipe del Morro** (*El Morro*). On a rocky promontory at the
Fodor'sChoice northwestern tip of the Old City is El Morro ("the promontory"), a
★ fortress built by the Spaniards between 1539 and 1786. Rising 140 feet above the sea, the massive six-level fortress was built to protect the harbor entrance. It is a labyrinth of cannon batteries, ramps, barracks, turrets, towers, and tunnels. Built to protect the port, El Morro has a commanding view of the harbor. You're free to wander throughout. The cannon emplacement walls and the dank secret passageways are a wonder of engineering. The fort's small but enlightening museum displays ancient Spanish guns and other armaments, military uniforms, and blueprints for Spanish forts in the Americas, although Castillo San Cristóbal has more extensive and impressive exhibits. There's also a gift shop. The fort is a National Historic Site administered by the U.S. Park Service; it's a World Heritage Site as well. Various tours and a video are available in English. ⊠ *Calle del Morro, Old San Juan* ☎ *787/729–6960* ⊕ *www.nps.gov/saju* ⊐ *$3, $5 includes admission to Castillo San Cristóbal* ☉ *Daily 9–6.*

★ **La Fortaleza.** Sitting atop the fortified city walls overlooking the harbor, the Fortaleza was built between 1533 and 1540 as a fortress—and not a very good one. It was attacked numerous times and was occupied twice, by the British in 1598 and the Dutch in 1625. When El Morro and the city's other fortifications were finished, the Fortaleza instead became the governor's palace. Numerous changes have been made to the original primitive structure over the past four centuries, resulting in the current eclectic yet eye-pleasing collection of marble and mahogany, medieval towers, and stained-glass galleries. It is still the official residence of the island's governor and is the Western Hemisphere's oldest executive mansion in continual use. Guided tours are conducted several times a day in English and Spanish; both include a short video presentation. Call ahead to make a reservation, as the tour schedule will depend on the official functions occurring that day. The tours begin near the main gate in a yellow building called the Real Audiencia, housing the Oficina Estatal de Preservación Histórica. ⊠ *Western end of Calle Fortaleza, Old San Juan* ☎ *787/721–7000 Ext. 2211* ⊕ *www.fortaleza.gobierno.pr* ⊐ *$3* ☉ *Weekdays.*

WORTH NOTING

Alcaldía. San Juan's city hall was built between 1602 and 1789. In 1841, extensive alterations were made so that it would resemble the city hall in Madrid, with arcades, towers, balconies, and an inner courtyard.

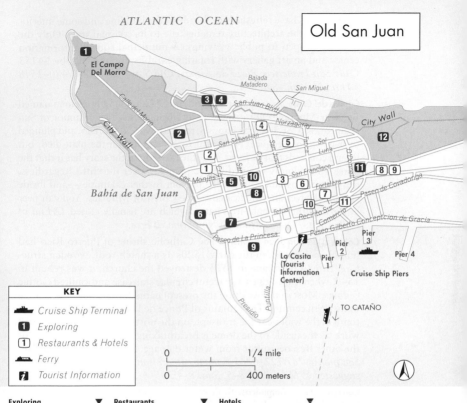

Old San Juan

ATLANTIC OCEAN

El Campo Del Morro

Bahía de San Juan

La Casita (Tourist Information Center)

Cruise Ship Piers

TO CATAÑO

KEY

- 🚢 Cruise Ship Terminal
- 1️⃣ Exploring
- ① Restaurants & Hotels
- ⛴ Ferry
- 🛈 Tourist Information

0 ————————— 1/4 mile
0 ————————— 400 meters

Renovations have refreshed the facade of the building and some interior rooms, but the architecture remains true to its colonial style. Only the patios are open to public viewings. A municipal tourist information center and an art gallery with rotating exhibits are in the lobby. ⊠ 153 *Calle San Francisco, Plaza de Armas, Old San Juan* ☎ 787/480–2548 🖃 *Free* ⊙ *Mon.–Sat. 8–4.*

Capilla del Cristo. According to legend, in 1753 a young horseman named Baltazar Montañez got carried away during festivities in honor of San Juan Bautista (St. John the Baptist), raced down Calle Cristo, and plunged over its steep precipice. Historical records maintain the man died, but legend contends that he lived. (Another version of the story has it that the horse miraculously stopped before plunging over the cliff.) Regardless, this chapel was built—in part to prevent further calamities—and inside is a small silver altar dedicated to the Christ of Miracles. You can peer in through the wrought-iron gates, which are usually closed. ⊠ *End of Calle Cristo, Old San Juan* ☎ *No phone* 🖃 *Free.*

Catedral de San Juan Bautista. The Catholic shrine of Puerto Rico had humble beginnings in the early 1520s as a thatch-roof, wooden structure. After a hurricane in 1525 destroyed the church, it was rebuilt in 1540, when it was given a graceful circular staircase and vaulted Gothic ceilings. Most of the work on the present cathedral, however, was done in the 19th century. The remains of Ponce de León are behind a marble tomb in the wall near the transept, on the north side. The trompe l'oeil work on the inside of the dome is breathtaking. Unfortunately, many of the other frescoes suffer from water damage. ⊠ *151 Calle Cristo, Old San Juan* ☎ *787/722–0861* ⊕ *www.catedralsanjuan.com* 🖃 *$1 donation suggested* ⊙ *Mon.–Sat. 8–5, Sun. 8–4:30.*

Convento de los Dominicos. Built by Dominican friars in 1523, this convent—the oldest in Puerto Rico—often served as a shelter during Carib Indian attacks and, more recently, as headquarters for the Antilles command of the U.S. Army. Now home to some offices of the Institute of Puerto Rican Culture, the beautifully restored building contains the Galería Nacional, displaying santos (traditional wood carvings); artwork by José Campeche and Francisco Oller, two of the island's most important painters; as well as twentieth-century Puerto Rican art. The institute also maintains a book and music shop on the premises. Classical concerts are held here occasionally. ⊠ *98 Calle Norzagaray, Old San Juan* ☎ *787/721–6866* 🖃 *$3* ⊙ *Mon.–Sat. 9–noon and 1–5.*

Museo de las Américas. On the second floor of the imposing former military barracks, Cuartel de Ballajá, the museum's permanent exhibit, Las Artes Populares en las Américas, focuses on the popular art and folk art of Latin America, including religious figures, musical instruments, basketwork, costumes, and farming and other implements. There's also a room showcasing the African influence on the island's culture. It's a small exhibit, worth a look if you're visiting other nearby attractions. ⊠ *Calle Norzagaray and Calle del Morro, Old San Juan* ☎ *787/724–5052* ⊕ *www.museolasamericas.org* 🖃 *$3* ⊙ *Tues., Wed., and weekends 10–4, Thurs. and Fri. 9–4.*

Museo de Nuestra Raíz Africana. The Institute of Puerto Rican Culture created this museum to help Puerto Ricans understand African influences in island culture. On display over two floors are African musical instruments, documents relating to the slave trade, and a list of African words that have made it into popular Puerto Rican culture. ⊠ *101 Calle San Sebastián, Plaza de San José, Old San Juan ☎ 787/724-4294 ⊕ www.icp.gobierno.pr ☜ Free ⊙ Tues.–Sat. 8–4:30.*

Paseo de la Princesa. Built in the mid-19th century to honor the Spanish princess of Asturias, this street with a broad pedestrian walkway is spruced up with flowers, trees, benches, and street lamps and unfurls westward from Plaza del Inmigrante along the base of the fortified city walls. It leads to the Fuente Raíces, a striking fountain depicting the various ethnic groups of Puerto Rico. Take a seat and watch the boats zip across the water. Beyond the fountain is the beginning of Paseo del Morro, a well-paved shoreline path that hugs Old San Juan's walls and leads past the city gate at Calle San Juan and continues to the tip of the headland, beneath El Morro.

Plaza de Armas. The Old City's original main square was once used as military drilling grounds. Bordered by Calles San Francisco, Rafael Cordero, San José, and Cruz, it has a fountain with 19th-century statues representing the four seasons as well as a bandstand and a small café. The Alcaldía commands the north side. This is one of the most popular meeting places in Old San Juan, so you're likely to encounter everything from artists sketching caricatures to street-food carts and hundreds of pigeons waiting for handouts.

Plaza de Colón. A statue of Christopher Columbus—the tallest in the Americas—stands atop a soaring column and fountain in this bustling Old San Juan square catercorner to Castillo San Cristóbal. Originally called St. James Square, it was renamed in 1893 to honor the 400th anniversary of Columbus's arrival in Puerto Rico. Bronze plaques on the statue's base relate various episodes in the life of the great explorer.

17

GREATER SAN JUAN

Taxis, buses, *públicos* (shared vans), or a rental car are needed to reach the points of interest in "new" San Juan. Avenida Muñoz Rivera, Avenida Ponce de León, and Avenida Fernández Juncos are the main thoroughfares that cross Puerta de Tierra, east of Old San Juan, to the business and tourist districts of Santurce, Condado, Ocean Park, and Isla Verde. Dos Hermanos Bridge connects Puerta de Tierra with Miramar, Condado, and Isla Grande. Isla Grande Airport, from which you can take short hops, is on the bay side of the bridge. On the other side, the Condado Lagoon is bordered by Avenida Ashford, which threads past the high-rise Condado hotels and Avenida Baldorioty de Castro Expreso, which barrels east to the airport and beyond. Due south of the lagoon is Miramar, a residential area with fashionable turn-of-the-20th-century homes and a few hotels and restaurants. Isla Verde, with its glittering beachfront hotels, casinos, discos, and public beach, is to the east, near the airport.

Hear your footsteps echo throughout Castillo San Felipe's vast network of tunnels, designed to amplify the sounds of approaching enemies.

WHAT TO SEE

El Capitolio. The white-marble Capitol, a fine example of Italian Renaissance style, dates from 1929. The grand rotunda, which can be seen from all over San Juan, was completed in the late 1990s. Fronted by eight Corinthian columns, it's a very dignified home for the commonwealth's constitution. Although the Senate and the House of Representatives have offices in the more modern buildings on either side, the Capitol is where the legislators meet. You can also watch the legislature on Monday and Thursday when it is in session from January to June and from August to November—note that the action is in Spanish. Guided tours, which range between 30 and 60 minutes, include visits to the rotunda, the congressional chambers, and other parts of the building. Appointments are highly recommended. ⊠ *Av. Muñoz Rivera, Puerta de Tierra* ☎ *787/724–2030 Ext. 4609, 4610, or 4611* ⊕ *www. oslpr.org* ☞ *Free* ☉ *Daily 8:30–5.*

★ **Museo de Arte Contemporáneo de Puerto Rico.** This Georgian-style structure, once a public school, displays a dynamic range of works by both established and up-and-coming Latin American artists. Many of the works on display have strong political messages, including pointed commentaries on Puerto Rico's status as a commonwealth. Only a small part of the more than 900 works in the permanent collection is on display at any time, but it might be anything from an exhibit of ceramics to a screening of videos. ⊠ *1220 Av. Ponce de León, at Av. R.H. Todd, Santurce* ☎ *787/977–4030* ⊕ *www.museocontemporaneopr.org* ☞ *Free* ☉ *Tues.–Sat. 10–4, Sun. noon–4.*

Continued on page 692

WALKING OLD SAN JUAN

Old San Juan is Puerto Rico's quintessential colonial neighborhood. Narrow streets and plazas are still enclosed by thick fortress walls, and bougainvillea bowers spill over exquisite facades. A walk along streets paved with slate-blue cobblestones leads past colonial mansions, ancient churches, and intriguing museums and galleries. Vivacious restaurants and bars that teem with life young and old are always nearby, making it easy to refuel and reinvigorate anytime during your stroll. *by Christopher P. Baker*

left, strolling down Calle del Cristo; top right, a view from El Morro; bottom right, dancers in front of Castillo San Cristóbal

A STROLL THROUGH OLD SAN JUAN

La Fortaleza

Castillo San Felipe del Morro (El Morro)

El Campo del Morro **6**

Calle del Morro

La Muralla (City Wall)

Bajada Matadero

San Juan Blvd.

Plaza del Quinto Centenario **7**

Museo de San Juan

Norzagaray

Museo de las Américas

Iglesia de San José

Museo de Pablo Casals

San Sebastián

Instituto Puertorriqueño de Cultura **5**

San Sebastián

4

Museo de Nuestra Raíz Africana

Plaza de San José

Sol

Cruz

San Justo

Case Blanca

El Gran Convento

Catedral de San Juan Bautista

Luna

San Francisco

Plazuela de la Rogativa

Las Monjas

Museo Felisa Rincón de Gautier

Museo del Niño

Calle del Cristo

San José

Calle Fortaleza

Puerta de San Juan **2**

La Fortaleza

Museo de la Casa del Libro

La Muralla

Parque de las Palomas **3**

Tetuán

Plaza de las Inmigrantes **1**

Bahía de San Juan

Paseo de la Princesa

Capilla del Cristo

Fuente Raíces

Puerto Rico Tourism Company Headquarters

This walk is best done in the morning to avoid the afternoon heat and cruise-ship crowds. The route is 2 mi (3 km); it will take half a day at a leisurely pace, with plenty of stops along the way.

❶ Start at Plaza del Inmigrante. This cobbled square facing the cruise port has impressive neoclassical and art deco buildings. From here, the **Paseo de la Princesa** promenade unfurls west beneath the ancient city wall, **La Muralla**. Artisans set up stalls under the palms on weekends. Midway along the brick-paved walkway, stop to admire the **Fuente Ra-**

Puerta de San Juan

ices monument and fountain: dolphins cavort at the feet of figures representing Puerto Rico's indigenous, Spanish, and African peoples.

❷ Pass through the Puerta de San Juan. This fortified entrance in La Muralla was built in 1520 and still retains its massive wooden gates, creaky on their ancient hinges. Immediately beyond, turn left and ascend to **Plazuela de la Rogativa**, a tiny plaza where a contemporary statue recalls

the torch-lit procession that thwarted an English invasion in 1797. The harbor views are fantastic. Then, walk east one block to reach the **Catedral de San Juan Bautista**, the neoclassical 19th-century cathedral containing the mausoleum of Ponce de León.

❸ Head south on Calle del Cristo. Sloping gradually, this lovely cobbled street is lined with beautifully restored colonial mansions housing cafés, galleries, and boutiques. Pass-

Castillo San Cristóbal | Calle del Cristo | Catedral de San Juan Bautista

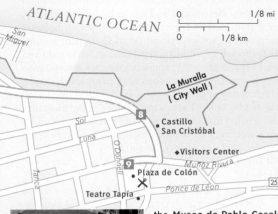

ATLANTIC OCEAN

San Miguel

0 ___ 1/8 mi
0 ___ 1/8 km

La Muralla (City Wall)

Sol

Luna

O'Donnell

Tanca

8 Castillo San Cristóbal

◆ Visitors Center

Muñoz Rivera

9 Plaza de Colón

Ponce de Léon

25

Teatro Tapia

Castillo San Felipe del Morro

ing Calle Fortaleza, note **La Fortaleza**, the official residence of the Puerto Rican Governor at the end of the street. Calle del Cristo ends at **Capilla del Cristo**, a chapel adorned within by silver *milagros* (token requests).

❹ **Return via Calle del Cristo and continue to Plaza de San José.** Catercorner to the cathedral you'll find **El Gran Convento**, a former convent turned hotel, with an excellent restaurant, tapas bar, and café. At **Plaza de San José** visit

the **Museo de Pablo Casals**, dedicated to the Spanish cellist, and the **Iglesia de San José**, a simple church dating from 1532.

❺ **Walk west on Calle San Sebastián.** This narrow street with colonial mansions painted in vibrant pastels ends at the gleaming white **Casa Blanca.** The oldest continually occupied residence in the Americas was originally the home of Ponce de León. Today it's a delightful museum furnished with period pieces. The garden is a tranquil spot for contemplation.

❻ **Follow Calle del Morro north.** One block from Casa Blanca you'll emerge upon a broad grassy headland—the Campo del Morro—popular with kite-flying families. It's skewered by an arrow-straight gravel path that aims at the imposing **Castillo San Felipe del Morro (El**

Morro), guarding the harbor entrance. Allow one-hour to roam the small museum, turrets, labyrinthine tunnels, and six levels of ramparts soaring 140 feet above the ocean.

❼ **Retrace your steps and turn left on Calle Norzagaray.** This street runs atop the Atlantic shoreline, offering sweeping ocean vistas. On your right you'll pass the **Plaza del Quinto Centenario**, pinned by an impressive statue: the *Tótem Telúrico*. Beyond, stroll past the Convento de los Dominicos to reach the **Museo de San Juan.** Housed in a former market, it traces the city's history and displays works by Puerto Rico's master painters.

❽ **Continue east to Castillo San Cristóbal.** Spanning 27 acres, this multitiered fortress was completed in 1771 with mighty bulwarks that protected the city from eastern attack by land. It features superb historical exhibits and reenactments by soldiers in period costumes.

❾ **Exit the castle, turn south and walk one block to Plaza de Colón.** This leafy square is lined with excellent cafés and restaurants where you can rest your feet and enjoy a great meal.

☺ **Museo de Arte de Puerto Rico.** One of the biggest museums in the Caribbean, this 130,000-square-foot building was once known as San Juan **Fodor's** Choice Municipal Hospital. The beautiful neoclassical building, dating from ★ the 1920s, proved to be too small to house the museum's permanent collection of Puerto Rican art dating from the 17th century to the present. The solution was to build a new east wing, which is dominated by a five-story-tall stained-glass window, the work of local artist Eric Tabales.

The collection starts with works from the colonial era, most of them commissioned for churches. Here you'll find works by José Campeche, the island's first great painter. His *Immaculate Conception,* finished in 1794, is a masterpiece. (A major exhibition of Campeche's work runs until May 2012, though an additional admission fee is required to view it.) Also well represented is Francisco Oller y Cestero, who was the first to move beyond religious subjects to paint local scenes. His influence is still felt today. A gallery on the third floor is filled with works by artists inspired by Oller. There's much more to the museum, including a beautiful garden filled with a variety of native flora and a 400-seat theater that's worth seeing for its remarkable hand-crocheted lace curtain. ⊠ *299 Av. José De Diego, Santurce* ☎ *787/977–6277* ⊕ *www.mapr.org* ⊠ *$6; free Wed. 2–8* ⊙ *Tues. and Thurs.–Sat. 10–5, Wed. 10–8, Sun. 11–6.*

Museo de Historia, Antropología y Arte. The Universidad de Puerto Rico's *Museum of History, Anthropology and Art* has archaeological and historical exhibits that deal with the Native American influence on the island and the Caribbean, the colonial era, and the history of slavery. Art displays are occasionally mounted; the museum's prize exhibit is the painting *El Velorio* (*"The Wake"*), by the 19th-century artist Francisco Oller. ⊠ *Av. Ponce de León, Río Piedras* ☎ *787/763–3939* ⊕ *www.uprrp.edu* ⊠ *Free Mon., Tues., Thurs., and Fri. 9–4:30, Wed. 9–8:30, Sun. 11–4:30.*

SAN JUAN ENVIRONS

Casa Bacardí Visitor Center. Exiled from Cuba, the Bacardí family built a small rum distillery here in the 1950s. Today it's the world's largest, with the capacity to produce more than 100,000 gallons of spirits a day and 21 million cases a year. You can hop on a little tram to take an approximately 45-minute tour of the visitor center, though you can no longer visit the distillery itself. Yes, you'll be offered a free sample. If you don't want to drive, you can reach the factory by taking the ferry from Pier 2 for 75¢ each way and then a *público* (public van service) from the ferry pier to the factory for about $2 or $3 per person. ⊠ *Rd. 165, Rte. 888, Km 2.6, Cataño* ☎ *787/788–1500 or 787/788–8400* ⊕ *www.casabacardi. org* ⊠ *Free Mon.–Sat. 9–6, last tour at 4:30; Sun. 10–5, last tour at 3:45.*

Ruinas de Caparra. In 1508, Ponce de León established the island's first settlement here. The Caparra Ruins—a few crumbling walls—are what remains of an ancient fort. The small **Museo de la Conquista y Colonización de Puerto Rico** (Museum of the Conquest and Colonization of Puerto Rico) contains historical documents, exhibits, and excavated artifacts, though you can see the museum's contents in less time than it takes to say the name. Both the ruins and the museum are maintained by the Puerto Rican Institute of Culture. ⊠ *Rte. 2, Km 6.4, Guaynabo* ☎ *787/781–4795* ⊕ *www.icp.gobierno.pr* ☒ *Free* ☺ *Weekdays 8–4:30.*

EASTERN PUERTO RICO

ⓒ **El Yunque.** More than 28,000 acres of verdant foliage and rare wild-
Fodor's Choice life make up El Yunque, the only tropical rain forest within the U.S.
★ National Forest system. El Yunque's odd name is believed to be derived from the Taíno word *yuké* (good spirit), although some people say it comes directly from *yunque*, the Spanish word for "anvil," because some of the forest's peaks have flattened tops. More than 100 billion gallons of precipitation fall here annually, spawning rushing streams and cascades, 240 tree species, and oversize impatiens and ferns. In the evening, millions of inch-long coquís (tree frogs) begin their calls. El Yunque is also home to the *cotorra*, Puerto Rico's endangered green parrot, as well as 96 other types of birds.

The forest's 13 hiking trails are well maintained; many of them are easy to walk and less than a mile long. Before you begin exploring, check out the high-tech interactive displays—explaining rain forests in general and El Yunque in particular—at **El Portal Rainforest Center** (⊠ *Rte. 191, Km 4.3* ☎ *787/888–1880* ⊕ *www.fs.fed.us/r8/caribbean*), the informa-tion center near the northern entrance. This is also a good place to pick up a map of the park and talk to rangers about weather conditions or which trails are open. You can stock up on water, snacks, film, and souvenirs at the small gift shop. The center is open daily from 9 to 5; admission is $4. The park itself, which is free, is open daily 7:30 to 6.

Fajardo. Founded in 1772, Fajardo has historical notoriety as a port where pirates stocked up on supplies. It later developed into a fishing community and an area where sugarcane flourished. (There are still cane fields on the city's fringes.) Today it's a hub for the yachts that use its marinas; the divers who head to its good offshore sites; and the day-trippers who travel by catamaran, ferry, or plane to the out-islands of Culebra and Vieques. With the most-significant docking facilities on the island's eastern side, Fajardo is often congested and difficult to navigate.

Fajardo is the gateway to the 316-acre **Reserva Natural Las Cabezas de San Juan** (⊠ *Rte. 987, Km 6* ☎ *787/722–5882 weekdays, 787/860–2560 weekends* ⊕ *www.fideicomiso.org*), a natural preserve where you can wander down boardwalks through seven ecosystems, including lagoons, mangrove swamps, and dry-forest areas. It's a half-hour hike to mangrove-lined Laguna Grande, which at night glows with biolumi-nescent microorganisms. Call ahead for mandatory guided tours, which are given Wednesday to Sunday at 9:30, 10, 10:30 in Spanish and at 2 pm in English by request. Admission is $8.

17

VIEQUES AND CULEBRA

Culebra. Culebra is known around the world for its curvaceous coast-line. Playa Flamenco, the tiny island's most famous stretch of sand, is considered one of the two or three best beaches in the world. If

Playa Flamenco gets too crowded, as it often does around Easter and Christmas, there are many other beaches that will be nearly deserted. There's archaeological evidence that Taíno and Carib peoples lived on Culebra long before the arrival of the Spanish in the late 15th century. The Spanish didn't bother laying claim to it until 1886; its dearth of freshwater made it an unattractive location for a settlement. Although the island now has modern conveniences, its pace seems little changed from a century ago. There's only one town, Dewey, named after U.S. Admiral George Dewey. When the sun goes down, Culebra winds down as well. But during the day it's a delightful place to stake out a spot on Playa Flamenco or Playa Soni and read, swim, or search for shells. So what causes stress on the island? Nada.

Fodor'sChoice
★ **Vieques.** This island off Puerto Rico's east coast is famed for its Playa Sun Bay, a gorgeous stretch of sand with picnic facilities and shade trees. In May 2003, the U.S. Navy withdrew from its military operations and turned over two-thirds of Vieques to the local government, which is transforming it into the Vieques National Wildlife Refuge. Vieques has two communities—Isabel Segunda, where the ferries dock, and the smaller Esperanza. Both have restaurants and hotels that will surprise you with their sophistication.

Fodor'sChoice
★ In addition to great beaches, Vieques has a special bioluminescent bay, an attraction that draws visitors from all over the world. **Puerto Mosquito Bay** is best experienced on moonless nights, when millions of bioluminescent organisms glow when disturbed—it's like swimming in a cloud of fireflies. If you're on the island, this is a not-to-be-missed experience. Several local companies lead trips to the bay, either by kayak or by nonpolluting electric boats.

SOUTHERN PUERTO RICO

Fodor'sChoice
★ **Bosque Estatal de Guánica.** A United Nations Biosphere Reserve, the Guánica State Forest is a great place for hiking expeditions. It's an outstanding example of a tropical dry coastal forest, with some 700 species of plants ranging from the prickly pear cactus to the gumbo limbo tree. It's also one of the best places on the island for bird-watching, as there are more than 100 types of bird, including the pearly-eyed thrasher, the lizard cuckoo, and the nightjar. One of the most popular hikes is the Ballena Trail, which begins at the ranger station on Route 334. This easy 1.2-mi (2-km) walk, which follows a partially paved road, takes you past a mahogany plantation to a dry plain covered with stunted cactus. A sign reading "Guayacán Centenario" leads you to an extraordinary guayacán tree with a trunk that measures 6 feet across. ⊠ *Rte. 334, 333, or 325*☎ *787/821–5706* 🎫 *Free* ☉ *Weekdays 6:30–5, weekends 8:30–5.*

Ponce. The island's second-largest urban area, Ponce shines in 19th-century style with pink-marble-bordered sidewalks, painted trolleys, and horse-drawn carriages. Stroll around the main square, the Plaza de las Delicias, with its perfectly pruned India-laurel fig trees, graceful fountains, gardens, and park benches. View the Catedral de Nuestra Señora de la Guadalupe (Our Lady of Guadalupe Cathedral), perhaps even attend the 6 am Mass, and walk down Calles Isabel and Cristina to see turn-of-the-20th-century wooden houses with wrought-iron balconies. The **Castillo Serrallés** is a splendid Spanish Revival mansion on Vigía Hill. This former residence of the owners of the Don Q rum distillery has been restored with a mix of original furnishings and antiques that recalls the era of the sugar barons. A short film details the history of the sugar and rum industries; tours are given every half hour in English and Spanish. You can also just stroll through the lovely gardens for a reduced admission fee. The 100-foot-tall concrete cross (La Cruceta del Vigía) behind the museum has a windowed elevator, which you can ascend for views of Ponce. ⊠ *17 El Vigía, El Vigía* ☎ *787/259–1774* ⊕ *home.coqui.net/castserr* ✉ *$8.50, $12.80 includes admission to Cruceta El Vigía* ⊙ *Thurs.–Sun. 9:30–5:30, last tour 5:30.*

At the **Centro Ceremonial Indígena de Tibes,** you can find pre-Taíno ruins and burials dating from AD 300 to 700. Some archaeologists, noting the symmetrical arrangement of stone pillars, surmise that the cemetery may have been of great religious significance. Be sure to visit the small museum before taking a walking tour of the site. ⊠ *Tibes Indian Ceremonial Center, Rte. 503, Km 2.8, Barrio Tibes* ☎ *787/840–2255 or 787/840–5685* ⊕ *ponce.inter.edu/tibes/tibes.html* ✉ *$3* ⊙ *Tues.–Sun. 8–4:30.*

ⓒ **Fodor's Choice** ★ Just outside Ponce, **Hacienda Buena Vista** is a 19th-century coffee plantation. It's a technological marvel—water from the nearby Río Canas was funneled into narrow brick channels that could be diverted to perform any number of tasks, including turning the waterwheel. (Seeing the two-story-tall wheel slowly begin to turn is thrilling, especially for kids.) Nearby is the two-story manor house, filled with furniture that gives a sense of what it was like to live on a coffee plantation nearly 150 years ago. The tours are by reservation only, so make sure to call several days ahead. After seeing the plantation, you can buy coffee beans and other souvenirs at the gift shop. Allow yourself an hour to travel the winding road from Ponce. ⊠ *Rte. 123, Km 16.8, Sector Corral Viejo* ☎ *787/722–5882 weekdays, 787/284–7020 weekends* ✉ *$8* ⊙ *Wed.–Sun., by reservation only. English tours at 1:30 by request.*

Fodor's Choice ★ **Museo de Arte de Ponce.** This building—designed by Edward Durrell Stone, who also designed the original Museum of Modern Art in New York City and the Kennedy Center in Washington, D.C.—is easily identified by the hexagonal galleries on the second story. It underwent a major, multiyear renovation before reopening in late 2010 and has one of the best art collections in Latin America, which is why residents of San Juan frequently make the trip down to Ponce. The 4,500-piece collection includes works by famous Puerto Rican artists such as Francisco Oller, represented by a lovely landscape called *Hacienda Aurora*. There are plenty of European works on display as well, including paintings by Peter Paul Rubens and Thomas Gainsborough. The highlight of the European collection is the Pre-Raphaelite paintings, particularly the mesmerizing *Flaming June*, by Frederick Leighton, which has become the museum's unofficial symbol. ⊠ *2325 Av. Las Américas, Sector Santa María* ☎ *787/840–1510* ⊕ *www.museoarteponce.org* ✉ *$6* ⊙ *Wed.–Mon. 10–6.*

17

A superlative example of early-20th-century architecture, the **Museo de la Historia de Ponce** vividly re-creates Ponce's history through 10 rooms of exhibits, providing fascinating glimpses into the worlds of culture, high finance, and journalism in the 19th century. The descriptions are mostly in Spanish, but English-speaking tour guides are happy to translate, and displays of clothing from different eras still are interesting to see. ⊠ *51–53 Calle Isabel, Ponce Centro* ☎ *787/844–7042* ✉ *Free Tues.–Sun. 8–4.*

ⓒ
Fodor's Choice
★

You haven't seen a firehouse until you've seen the **Parque de Bombas,** a structure built in 1882 for an exposition and converted to a firehouse the following year. Today it's a museum tracing the history—and glorious feats—of Ponce's fire brigade. ⊠ *Plaza de las Delicias, Ponce Centro* ☎ *787/284–3338* ✉ *Free* ◔ *Daily 9–5.*

San Germán. Around San Germán's (population 39,000) two main squares—Plazuela Santo Domingo and Plaza Francisco Mariano Quiñones (named for an abolitionist)—are buildings done in every conceivable style of architecture found on the island, including Mission, Victorian, Creole, and Spanish colonial. The city's tourist office offers a free, guided trolley tour. Students and professors from the Inter-American University often fill the center's bars and cafés.

WESTERN AND CENTRAL PUERTO RICO

The Puerto Rico Tourism Company calls the western side of the island Porta del Sol and maintains a separate Web site to highlight travel options in the region.

Bosque Estatal de Río Abajo. In the middle of karst country—a region of limestone deposits that is peppered with fissures, caves, and underground streams—the Río Abajo State Forest spans some 5,000 acres and includes huge bamboo stands, mahogany, and silk-cotton trees. Walking trails wind through the forest, which is one of the habitats of the rare Puerto Rican parrot. An information office is near the entrance, and a recreation area with picnic tables is farther down the road. ⊠ *Rte. 621, Km 4.4* ☎ *787/880–6557* ✉ *Free* ◔ *Daily dawn–dusk.*

Cabo Rojo. Named for the pinkish cliffs that surround it, Cabo Rojo was founded in 1771 as a port for merchant vessels—and for the smugglers and pirates who inevitably accompanied oceangoing trade. Today the region is known as a family resort destination, and many small, inexpensive hotels line its shores. Seaside settlements such as Puerto Real and Joyuda—the latter has a strip of more than 30 seafood restaurants overlooking the water—are found along the coast. Although you can hike in wildlife refuges at the outskirts of the town of Cabo Rojo, there aren't any area outfitters, so be sure to bring along water, sunscreen, and all other necessary supplies. The neoclassical Cabo Rojo Lighthouse marks the southwesternmost tip of the island.

Mayagüez. With a population of slightly more than 100,000, this is the largest city on Puerto Rico's west coast. Although bypassed by the mania for restoration that has spruced up Ponce and Old San Juan, Mayagüez is graced by some lovely turn-of-the-20th-century architecture, such as the landmark art deco Teatro Yagüez and the Plaza de Colón.

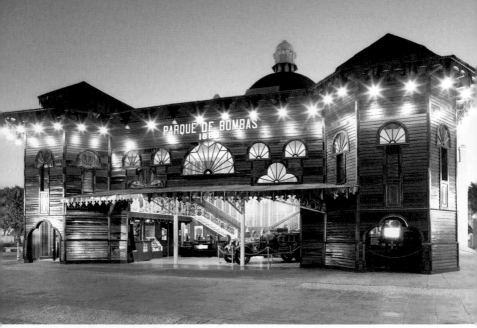

Today it's a museum, but for more than 100 years Parque de Bombas served as Ponce's main firehouse.

☾ Puerto Rico's only zoo, the 35-acre **Zoológico de Puerto Rico**, is just north of downtown. After $13 million in renovations, it's looking pretty spiffy. New on the scene is a 45-foot-tall aviary, which allows you to walk through a rain forest environment as tropical birds fly freely above your head. There's also a new butterfly park where you can let brilliant blue morphos land on your hand, and an arthropodarium where you can get up close and personal with spiders and their kin. There is a $3 charge for parking. ✉ *Rte. 108, north of Rte. 65* ☎ *787/834–8110* ⊕ *www.parquesnacionalespr.com* ✉ *$10* ⊙ *Wed.–Sun. 8:30–4.*

Fodor's Choice **Observatorio de Arecibo.** Hidden among pine-covered hills is the world's
★ largest radar–radio telescope. Operated by the National Astronomy and Ionosphere Center of Cornell University, the 20-acre dish lies in a 563-foot-deep sinkhole in the karst landscape. If the 600-ton platform hovering eerily over the dish looks familiar, it may be because it can be glimpsed in scenes from the movie *Contact*. (And yes, the dish has been used to search for extraterrestrial life.) You can view the telescope from an observation deck and explore two levels of interactive exhibits on planetary systems, meteors, and weather phenomena in the visitor center. ✉ *End of Rte. 625, Km 3.0* ☎ *787/878–2612* ⊕ *www.naic.edu* ✉ *$6* ⊙ *Dec. 15–Jan. 15, June, and July, daily 9–4; Jan. 16–May and Aug.–Dec. 14, Wed.–Sun. 9–4.*

☾ **Parque de las Cavernas del Río Camuy** contains one of the world's larg-
Fodor's Choice est cave networks. After watching an introductory film, a tram takes
★ you down a trail shaded by bamboo and banana trees to Cueva Clara, where the stalactites and stalagmites turn the entrance into a toothy grin. Hour-long audio tours in English and Spanish lead you on foot

through the 180-foot-high cave, which is teeming with wildlife. (Tour guides are available to answer questions.) You're likely to see the blue-eyed river clams and long-legged tarantulas. More elusive are the bats that make their home here. They don't come out until dark, but you can feel the heat they generate at the cave's entrance. The visit ends with a tram ride to the Tres Pueblos sinkhole, where you can see the third-longest underground river in the world passing from one cave to another. Tours are first-come, first-served, so plan to arrive early, especially on weekends, when locals join the crowds. There's a picnic area, cafeteria, and gift shop. ⊠ *Rte. 129, Km 18.9* ☎ *787/898–3100* ⊕ *www. parquesnacionalespr.com* ⊠ *$15* ⊙ *Wed.–Sun. 8–3:30; last tour at 3:30.*

Rincón. Jutting out into the ocean along the rugged western coast, Rincón, meaning "corner" in Spanish, may have gotten its name because of how it is nestled in a corner of the coastline. The town jumped into the surfing spotlight after hosting the World Surfing Championship in 1968. Although the beat here picks up from October through April, when the waves are the best, Rincón, basically laid-back and unpretentious, is seeing a lot of development. If you visit between December and February, you might get a glimpse of the humpback whales that winter off the coast. Because of its unusual setting, Rincón's layout can be a little disconcerting. The main road, Route 413, loops around the coast, and many beaches and sights are on dirt roads intersecting it.

WHERE TO EAT

Your palate will be delighted by the range of dining choices available in Puerto Rico. In San Juan you can find restaurants serving everything from Italian to Thai, as well as superb local eateries serving comida criolla (traditional home-style Puerto Rican food). No matter your price range or taste, San Juan is a great place to eat.

WHAT TO WEAR

Dress codes vary greatly, though a restaurant's price category is a good indicator of its formality. For less expensive places, anything but beachwear is fine. Ritzier eateries will expect collared shirts for men (jacket and tie requirements are rare) and chic attire for women. When in doubt, do as the Puerto Ricans often do and dress up.

OLD SAN JUAN

$$$
SEAFOOD
★

✕ **Aguaviva.** The name means "jellyfish," which explains why this ultra-cool, ultramodern place has dim blue lighting like a tranquil ocean, and lamps shaped like jellyfish floating overhead. Elegantly groomed oysters and clams float on cracked ice along the raw bar. Eating here is like submerging oneself into the ocean. The extensive and regularly changing menu is alive with inventive ceviches, some with coconut or roasted red peppers. For something more filling, try seared jumbo shrimp with yuca gnocchi or grilled mahimahi with guava balsamic glaze. You could also empty out your wallet for one of the *torres del mar,* or "towers of the sea." This gravity-defying dish comes hot or cold and includes oysters, mussels, shrimp—you name it. Oh, and don't pass up the lobster mashed potatoes. Those alone are worth the trip—and the wait. ✉ *364 Calle Fortaleza, Old San Juan* ☎ *787/722–0665* ⊕ *www.oofrestaurants. com* ⚑ *Reservations not accepted* ⊘ *No lunch weekdays.*

\$\$–\$\$\$
ECLECTIC
✕ **Barú.** A global menu has earned Barú a solid reputation among *sanjuaneros*, so this stylishly contemporary restaurant in a colonial town home with original tile floor is often crowded. The dishes, some served in medium-size portions so you can order several and share, range from Middle Eastern to Asian to Caribbean. Favorites include almond-crusted goat cheese with mango sauce and yuca chips, and carpaccio made from beef, tuna, or salmon. More substantial fare includes risotto with porcini mushrooms and goat cheese, filet mignon with horseradish mashed potatoes, and pork ribs with a ginger-tamarind glaze. The dining room, in a beautifully renovated colonial house, is dark and mysterious. You can dine on high stools at the bar. Wine servings here are generous. ✉ *150 Calle San Sebastián, Old San Juan* ☎ *787/977–7107* ⊕ *www.barupr.com* ⊘ *No lunch.*

\$\$–\$\$\$
ASIAN
✕ **Dragonfly.** It's not hard to find this little restaurant—it's the one with waitresses in Chinese blouses beckoning you in off the sidewalk. If you can stand the wait on weekends—as you undoubtedly will have to, because reservations aren't accepted—you'll get to sample chef Severo Duran's Latin Asian cuisine. (The best way to avoid a frustrating wait is to come midweek, or when it opens at 6 pm.) The *platos* (plates) are meant to be shared, so order several for your table. Favorites include criollo barbecue steamed buns, Peking duck nachos, and Szechuan glazed ribs. There's sushi, but at exorbitant prices. Budget hounds should stick to the delicious chicken and vegetable lo mein. The two-tier dining room, all done up in Chinese red, resembles an opium den. Note that there's a dress code: no shorts allowed. ✉ *364 Calle Fortaleza, Old San Juan* ☎ *787/977–3886* ⊕ *www.oofrestaurants.com* ⚑ *Reservations not accepted* ⊘ *No lunch.*

\$\$\$
SPANISH
✕ **El Picoteo.** You could make a meal of the small dishes that dominate the menu at this tapas restaurant, on a mezzanine balcony at the Hotel El Convento. You won't go wrong ordering the sweet sausage in brandy or the grilled cuttlefish and passing them around the table. If you're not into sharing, there are two different kinds of paella that arrive on huge plates. There's a long, lively bar inside; one dining area overlooks a pleasant courtyard, whereas the other looks out onto Calle Cristo. Even if you have dinner plans elsewhere, consider stopping here for a nightcap or a midday pick-me-up. ✉ *Hotel El Convento, 100 Calle Cristo, Old San Juan* ☎ *787/723–9202* ⊕ *www.elconvento.com.*

\$\$–\$\$\$
SPANISH
✕ **El Toro Salao.** The name means "The Salty Bull," and there's something about this place that makes its moniker entirely appropriate. (And it's not just the bullfighting posters that decorate one of the two-story-high walls.) This popular tapas restaurant was opened by Emilio Figueroa, who helped turn the southern end of Calle Fortaleza into the city's top dining destination: he owns three other restaurants at the east end of Calle Fortaleza and around the corner on Plaza Somohano. There are plenty of small dishes to share, like the cocas (Spanish flat-bread pizzas), as well as heartier fare such as seared lamb chops in a Rioja wine sauce. The dining room, with a bar illuminated in lusty red, is pleasant

17

enough, but the tables that spill onto the adjacent cobblestone square are even better. ⊠ *367 Calle Tetuán, Old San Juan* ☎ *787/722–3000* ⊕ *www.oofrestaurants.com.*

$–$$
CARIBBEAN
Fodor'sChoice
★

✕ **La Fonda del Jibarito.** The menus are handwritten and the tables wobble, but sanjuaneros have favored this casual, no-frills, family-run restaurant—tucked away on a quiet cobbled street—for years. The shrimp with garlic sauce, goat fricassee, and shredded beef stew are among the specialties on the menu of typical Puerto Rican comida criolla dishes. The tiny back porch is filled with plants, and the dining room is filled with fanciful depictions of life on the street outside. The ever-present owner, Pedro J. Ruíz, is filled with the desire to ensure that everyone is happy. ⊠ *280 Calle Sol, Old San Juan* ☎ *787/725–8375* ⊕ *www. eljibaritopr.com* ⌕ *Reservations not accepted.*

$$–$$$
LATIN AMERICAN

✕ **La Mallorquina.** Dating from 1848, La Mallorquina is thought to be the island's oldest restaurant. The menu is heavy on such basic Puerto Rican and Spanish fare as *asopao* and paella, but the old-fashioned atmosphere is what really recommends the place. Nattily attired staffers zip between tables set against peach-color walls and beneath the whir of ceiling fans. They can be a bit short with tourists, however. Note that it's closed during the low-season (and peak-hurricane season) month of September. ⊠ *207 Calle San Justo, Old San Juan* ☎ *787/722–3261* ⊕ *www.mallorquinapr.com* ☾ *Closed Sun.*

$$–$$$
CONTEMPORARY
Fodor'sChoice
★

✕ **Marmalade.** "Wow!" could well be your first reaction to entering Old San Juan's hippest and finest restaurant. U.S.-born owner-chef Peter Schintler has created a chic class act, famous for its überhip lounge bar. The restaurant's sensuous and minimalist orange-and-white decor features high-back chairs and corner-cushion banquettes beneath recessed halogens. The menu features local ingredients prepared in California–French fashion, resulting in complex flavors full of explosive fragrance. Begin with the scallop mojito with rum, mint, and fresh coconut and lime; then move to the honey-and-lime shrimp with baked jalapeño with sweet corn sauce and shellfish emulsion, or perhaps the braised Colorado lamb shank with Lebanese tabbouleh, pomegranate, and minted yogurt. Leave room for the chocolate mousse—a divine work of art. Schintler, who apprenticed with Raymond Blanc and Gordon Ramsay, offers a monthly four-, five-, or six-course tasting menu and an 11-course dinner with wine pairings. ⊠ *317 Calle Fortaleza, Old San Juan* ☎ *787/724–3969* ⊕ *www.marmaladepr.com* ☾ *No lunch.*

$$$–$$$$
ECLECTIC

✕ **Panza.** Tucked discreetly within the lobby of Chateau Cervantes, this restaurant recently reopened after a total remake, with a new chef and menu that is a wonderful mix of different-size dishes, so you can have your own or share a few with friends. Some favorites include arugula salad with blue cheese and pears, and lemon and herb-roasted chicken over butternut squash risotto. The half-moon banquettes in the front window are the perfect place to sample any of the 200 wines from the eatery's extensive cellars, or opt for a high stool at the bar with an oval recessed ceiling lighted by hidden orange lamps. Nice! ⊠ *Chateau Cervantes, 329 Calle Recinto Sur, Old San Juan* ☎ *787/724–7722* ⊕ *www.cervantespr.com* ⌕ *Reservations essential* ☾ *No lunch Fri. and Sat. Closed Sun.*

GREATER SAN JUAN

$$–$$$ ✕**Ajili-Mójili.** A Puerto Rico landmark with a noble objective: cook
CARIBBEAN like Grandma used to, largely with locally sourced ingredients. Gone
★ are the white tablecloths, and the high prices that discouraged many.
The food, however, is still executed with a flourish. The menu is a
catalog of local favorites, including terrific piononos (meat or fish
rolled in a sweet plantain with cheese), shrimp smothered in coconut,
and mofongo with chorizo. Wash it all down with a delicious mangó
bajito (rum with fresh mango juice). During the summer or fall the
restaurant offers a taste of various Puerto Rican towns (El Sabor de
los Pueblos), on a rotating two-week schedule. (By local demand, it
repeats Loíza, known for its fritters.) ✉ *1006 Av. Ashford, Condado*
☎ *787/725–9195* ⊕ *www.ajilimojilipr.com.*

$$$–$$$$ ✕**Budatai.** You'll feel like you're entering a secret club when you arrive
ASIAN at this stylish spot on the third floor in Condado's poshest shopping
★ district. The restaurant is decked out in rich, dark colors with Chi-
nese lanterns that look like they were designed by Salvador Dalí. The
attentive service and the elegantly dressed crowd, however, never feel
stuffy, and the menu doesn't shirk on substance either. The brainchild
of noted chef Roberto Treviño, it's a seamless mix of Latin-accented
Pan-Asian food, including duck fried rice with sweet plantains and
halibut sashimi with coconut, yuzu, and toasted garlic. We couldn't
get enough of the calamari, fried for a few seconds in hot oil, then
quickly sautéed with sweet onions. For a more casual experience,
head upstairs to the rooftop bar, where you'll find smaller dim sum–
style dishes and live music on weekends. ✉ *1056 Av. Ashford, Con-
dado* ☎ *787/725–6919* ⊕ *www.budatai.com.*

$$$–$$$$ ✕**Il Mulino New York.** You'll want for nothing at the San Juan outpost
ITALIAN of the famed Manhattan restaurant, where a team of tuxedoed waiters
Fodor's Choice effortlessly coordinates your entire meal experience. The dark-wood-
★ paneled walls and heavy velvet drapes are an odd juxtaposition with the
tropical climate, but everything about this place is elegant and tasteful.
Garlic bread and antipasti arrive moments after you sit down, though
you'll want to pace yourself and leave room for the mammoth entrées
to come. Standouts include rigatoni Bolognese, stuffed whole branzino
(deboned table-side), and fresh pappardelle with sausage. A side of fried
zucchini is a must. There's no fusion or haute cuisine here, just solid
Italian dishes, painstakingly executed to perfection. All this perfection
comes at a price, though the shot of homemade grappa offered at the
end might help ease the shock. ✉ *The Ritz-Carlton, San Juan, 6991 Av.
de los Gobernadores, Isla Verde* ☎ *787/791–8632* ⊕ *www.ilmulino.com*
⊘ *Reservations essential* ⊙ *No lunch.*

$$–$$$ ✕**Kasalta.** Those who think coffee can never be too strong should make
CAFÉ a beeline to Kasalta, which has an amazing pitch-black brew that will
knock your socks off. Make your selection from the display cases full
of luscious pastries, particularly the famous *quesito* (cream-cheese-filled
puff pastry) and other tempting treats. Walk up to the counter and
order a sandwich, such as the savory Cubano, or other items such as
octopus salad. For dinner there are fish dishes and other, more substan-
tial fare. Occasionally quality can be uneven, though, and some staff

17

members are curt with tourists. ✉ *1966 Calle McLeary, Ocean Park* ☎ *787/727–7340* ⊕ *www.kasalta.com.*

$$$
SPANISH

✕ **Miró.** Like its namesake, the painter Joan Miró, this small restaurant draws its inspiration from the Catalan region of Spain, where the cuisine is heavy on seafood and hearty tapas. Start with steamed clams with garlic or braised chorizo and peppers. Main courses include sizzling lamb chops, as well as grilled tuna with anchovy and caper butter or codfish in a red-pepper and eggplant sauce. Prints by the artist hang on the walls, adding an authentic touch to the maze of tiny dining rooms. Its location, on busy Avenida Ashford across from the San Juan Marriott Resort, means that the place is always packed. ✉ *1214 Av. Ashford, Condado* ☎ *787/723–9593.*

$$$–$$$$
CARIBBEAN
Fodor'sChoice
★

✕ **Pamela's.** If you've always dreamed of a table for two on the beach, only steps from where crashing waves meet the shore, head to this local favorite in Ocean Park. If you prefer air-conditioning, an elegant glassed-in solarium awaits, complete with black cobblestone floors and slow-turning ceiling fans. The menu is a contemporary, creative mix of Caribbean spices and other tropical ingredients. The restaurant prides itself on its fresh seafood; we liked the artfully plated crabmeat Napoleon, served with avocado, chayote, and black beans as an appetizer. But the real showstopper is the entrée: codfish with a spicy shrimp sofrito. ✉ *Numero Uno Guesthouse, 1 Calle Santa Ana, Ocean Park* ☎ *787/726–5010* ⊕ *www.numero1guesthouse.com.*

$$$–$$$$
ECLECTIC
Fodor'sChoice
★

✕ **Pikayo.** Celebrity chef and Puerto Rico native Wilo Benet's flagship restaurant has moved from its Santurce location in the Museo de Arte de Puerto Rico to this more accessible spot (for tourists and locals alike) at the Conrad San Juan Condado Plaza hotel. At 10,000 square feet, it's twice as large, and the impressive new digs are already drawing a big crowd. Works from local artists line the walls, and the atmosphere is elegant and formal, but never hushed. The menu offers a twist on traditional Puerto Rican classics as well as more international flavors. Start with a glass of Benet's own wine, either a simple *tempranillo* (red) or an *albariño* (white). Then try some of the starters; particularly good are the pork belly burgers and the spicy tuna on crispy rice (known here as pegao). For main courses, Benet offers veal tenderloin wrapped in bacon with zucchini pappardelle and halibut with wild mushrooms in a crabmeat sauce. Don't be surprised if Benet himself stops by your table to make sure everything is just to your liking. ✉ *Conrad San Juan Condado Plaza, 999 Av. Ashford, Condado* ☎ *787/721–6194* ⊕ *www.wilobenet.com* ☽ *No lunch.*

EASTERN PUERTO RICO

$$$–$$$$
SEAFOOD

✕ **Calizo.** There's a string of seafood shacks on the island's northeastern coast, all serving delicious fried fish. This open-air eatery, one of the best in the village of Las Croabas, takes things up a notch or two. Look for dishes like conch salad in a spicy vinaigrette, mahimahi in a honey-and-white-wine sauce, or chunks of lobster sautéed in garlic. Wash it all down with an icy-cold beer on tap. It's almost across from the Balneario Seven Seas, making it a great place to refuel after a day at the beach.

The only drawback is that it's a bit on the pricey side. ⊠ *Rte. 987, Las Croabas* ☎ *787/863–3664* ⊗ *No lunch weekdays.*

$$$–$$$$
CARIBBEAN

✕ **Pasión por el Fogón.** The name refers to the passion that chef Myrta Pérez Toledo possesses for taking traditional dishes and making them into something special. Pérez loves to present her dishes in unexpected ways—for example, the flank steak is rolled into a cylinder and stands on one end. But what makes this dish remarkable is the slightly sweet tamarind sauce that brings out the meat's earthy flavors. If you're a seafood lover, start with the lemony ceviche, and then move on to the lobster medallions broiled in butter. Owner Norma Guadaloupe, who will no doubt greet you at the door, often wears a brilliant shade of red that matches the main dining room's walls. It seems to be a case of a food lover wearing her heart on her sleeve. ⊠ *Rte. 987, Km 2.3* ☎ *787/315–9820* ⊕ *www.pasionporelfogon.net* ⊗ *No lunch weekdays.*

VIEQUES AND CULEBRA

$$$–$$$$
ECLECTIC
Fodor's Choice
★

✕ **El Quenepo.** Elegant yet unpretentious, this newcomer was the hottest act in town during our last visit, adding fine dining and a touch of class to the Esperanza waterfront. Local produce such as quenepos and breadfruit find their way into the lively, work-of-art nouvelle dishes that owners Scott and Kate Cole call "fun, funky island food." He plays chef while she plays consummate hostess. Kate likes to wear full-length dresses but says the dress code is "wet bikinis to wet ball gowns." Try some of the sensational seafood such as mofongo stuffed with shrimp and lobster in sweet-and-spicy criollo sauce. They're also very vegetarian and gluten-free friendly. Oenophiles will appreciate the large, varied wine list, and the sangria is delicious. ⊠ *148 Calle Flamboyan, Esperanza* ☎ *787/741–1215* ⌕ *Reservations essential* ⊗ *Closed Mon. No lunch.*

$–$$
CONTINENTAL

✕ **Mamacita's.** Watching iguanas plodding along the dock is reason enough to dine at this simple open-air, tin-roofed restaurant on a rough-plank deck beside the Dewey canal. Tarpon cruise past in the jade waters below, and the to and fro of boaters also keeps patrons amused. Those are all good reasons why this is the gringo hangout in town, although we suspect that Mamacita's down-home dishes play a part. The menu is heavy on burgers, but seafood dishes include an excellent mahimahi. And do try the killer smoothies. You'll dine at tables painted in a rainbow of pastels adorned with floral motifs. ⊠ *64 Calle Castelar, Dewey* ☎ *787/742–0322* ⊕ *www.mamacitasguesthouse.com.*

$$$–$$$$
ECLECTIC

✕ **Mix on the Beach.** The überhip W Retreat & Spa has taken local dining to divine heights courtesy of celebrated chef Alain Ducasse, who graces Vieques with his luminous presence at the hotel's Mix on the Beach. You'll need a fat wallet to dine here, but you can reliably expect Ducasse's artful French-Caribbean-Latino cuisine to be worth every penny. After all, he was the youngest chef ever to be honored with three Michelin stars and the only chef to earn the honor at three separate restaurants. Food aside, we're enamored of its romantic dining terraces overlooking a sensational swimming pool complex. ⊠ *Rte. 200, Km 3.2, Isabel Segunda* ☎ *787/741–4100* ⊕ *www.whotels.com/vieques* ⌕ *Reservations essential* ⊗ *No lunch.*

17

SOUTHERN PUERTO RICO

$$–$$$
ECLECTIC
★

✕**Cabuqui.** On sweltering hot days, it takes a lot to make *ponceños* leave their homes. Yet they come out in droves to the tree-shaded courtyard of the Cubuqui in the Ponce center. When a breeze shakes the flower-covered branches, things cool down considerably. And if nature doesn't cooperate, there are always the three air-conditioned dining rooms. The menu is extremely well traveled, stopping in Argentina (*churrasco*, or skirt steak, served with homemade chimichurri) and France (veal fillet in a red wine sauce) before heading back to Puerto Rico for such dishes as *masitas de cerdo* (chunks of perfectly seasoned pork). The wine list, which includes many bottles from Spain and Chile, is quite reasonable. There's always live music, whether it's a small band playing jazz or a single accordionist losing himself in a tango. ✉ *32 Calle Isabel, Ponce Centro* ☎ *787/984–5696.*

$$–$$$
SEAFOOD

✕**El Ancla.** Families favor this laid-back restaurant, whose dining room sits at the edge of the sea. The kitchen serves generous and affordable plates of fish, crab, and other fresh seafood with *tostones* (fried plantains), french fries, and garlic bread. Try the shrimp in garlic sauce, salmon fillet with capers, or the delectable mofongo stuffed with seafood. Finish your meal with one of the fantastic flans. The piña coladas—with or without rum—are exceptional. ✉ *805 Av. Hostos, Ponce Playa* ☎ *787/840–2450* ⊕ *www.restauranteelancla.com.*

WESTERN PUERTO RICO

$$–$$$
SEAFOOD

✕**El Bohío.** Watch seagulls dive for their dinner while you dine on a covered deck extending out into the bay. The long list of seafood is prepared in a variety of ways: shrimp comes breaded, stewed, or skewered; conch is served as a salad or cooked in a butter-and-garlic sauce. And the lobster can be prepared in just about any way you can imagine. ✉ *Rte. 102, Km 13.9, Joyuda* ☎ *787/851–2755.*

$–$$
CARIBBEAN

✕**Rincón Tropical.** Don't be scared off by the cheap plastic tables and chairs. What you should notice is that they're almost always full of locals enjoying the area's freshest seafood. The kitchen keeps it simple, preparing dishes with the lightest touch. Highlights include the mahimahi with onions and peppers, or fried red snapper with beans and rice. Fried plantains make a nice accompaniment to almost anything. ✉ *Rte. 115, Km 12* ☎ *787/823–2017.*

$$
CARIBBEAN

✕**Tamboo.** A bar and grill that doesn't fall too much into either category, this restaurant with an open-air kitchen prepares any number of tempting items, from king crab sandwiches to baby back ribs in a guava barbecue sauce. The bar, also open to the elements, serves a mean margarita. The deck is a great place to watch novice surfers wipe out on the nearby beach. An added plus: free Wi-Fi. ✉ *Beside the Pointe, Rte. 413, Km 4.7, Rincón* ☎ *787/823–8550* ⊕ *www.besidethepointe.com.*

WHERE TO STAY

In San Juan, the best beaches are in Isla Verde, though Condado is more centrally located. Old San Juan offers easy access to dining and nightlife. Outside San Juan, particularly on the east coast, you can find self-contained luxury resorts that cover hundreds of acres. Around the island, government-sponsored *paradores* are rural inns, others offer no-frills apartments, and some are large hotels close to either an attraction or beach.

VILLAS AND CONDOS

In the west, southwest, and south—as well as on the islands of Vieques and Culebra—smaller inns and condominiums for short-term rentals are the norm. Villa rentals are increasingly popular. **Island West Properties & Beach Rentals** (⊠ *Rte. 413, Km 1.3, Box 700, Rincón* ☎ *787/ 823–2323* ⊕ *www.islandwestrentals.com*) can help you rent villas in Rincón by the day, week, or month. **Puerto Rico Vacation Apartments** (⊠ *Calle Marbella del Caribe Oeste S-5, Isla Verde* ☎ *787/727–1591 or 800/266–3639* ⊕ *www.sanjuanvacations.com*) represents some 200 properties in San Juan's Condado and Isla Verde sections. For condos or villas on Vieques, contact **Rainbow Realty** (⊠ *Rte. 996, Esperanza, Vieques* ☎ *787/741–4312* ⊕ *www.viequesrainbowrealty.com*).

The following reviews have been condensed for this book. Please go to Fodors.com for full reviews of each property.

17

OLD SAN JUAN

$
HOTEL
★

Chateau Cervantes. Decorated by local fashion icon Nono Maldonado, this luxury lodging has a look that's completely au courant. **Pros:** gorgeous rooms; luxurious bathrooms; great restaurant. **Cons:** no views; very pricey; some rooms get street noise. ⊠ *329 Calle Recinto Sur, Old San Juan* ☎ *787/724–7722* ⊕ *www.cervantespr.com* ⇥ *6 rooms, 6 suites* ⌂ *In-room: a/c, safe, Wi-Fi (some). In-hotel: restaurant, room service, bar* ⫶⊙⫶ *No meals.*

$-$$
HOTEL
★

Gallery Inn. Nothing like this eclectic, artsy hotel exists anywhere else in San Juan—or Puerto Rico, for that matter. **Pros:** one-of-a-kind lodging; ocean views; wonderful classical music concerts. **Cons:** no restaurant; an uphill walk from rest of Old San Juan; sometimes raucous pet macaws and cockatoos. ⊠ *204–206 Calle Norzagaray, Old San Juan* ☎ *787/722– 1808* ⊕ *www.thegalleryinn.com* ⇥ *13 rooms, 10 suites* ⌂ *In-room: a/c, safe (some), no TV, Internet, Wi-Fi. In-hotel: room service, pool, business center, parking (some), some pets allowed* ⫶⊙⫶ *Breakfast.*

$$
HOTEL
Fodor's Choice
★

Hotel El Convento. The accommodations in this 350-year-old convent beautifully combine the old and the new. **Pros:** lovely building; atmosphere to spare; plenty of nearby dining options. **Cons:** near some noisy bars. ⊠ *100 Calle Cristo, Old San Juan* ☎ *787/723–9020*

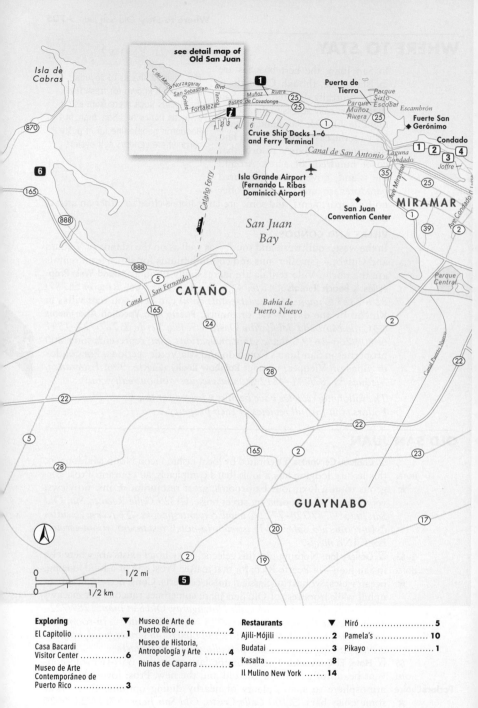

see detail map of Old San Juan

Isla de Cabras

Isla de Cabras

870

6

165

888

888

5

165

CATAÑO

24

22

5

28

28

22

165

165

20

2

19

5

C del Morro
Norzagaray Blvd
San Sebastien
Cristo
Fortaleza
Tanca
Fortaleza
Paseo de Covadonga

1

i

7 5 3 2 4 6

**Cruise Ship Docks 1–6
and Ferry Terminal**

Muñoz Rivera

25
25

1

**Puerta de
Tierra**

Parque
Sixto
Escobar
Escambrón

Parque
Muñoz
Rivera

25

**Fuerte San
Gerónimo**

Canal de San Antonio

Laguna
Condado

Condado

1 2
3 4

Joffre

**Isla Grande Airport
(Fernando L. Ribas
Dominicci Airport)**

35

1

Ave Miramar

25

MIRAMAR

1

39

2

San Juan
Bay

**San Juan
Convention Center**

Parque
Central

Bahía de
Puerto Nuevo

2

Canal Puerto Nuevo

22

22

2

23

GUAYNABO

17

Canal San Fernando

Cataño Ferry

2

5

0 ___ 1/2 mi
0 ___ 1/2 km

5

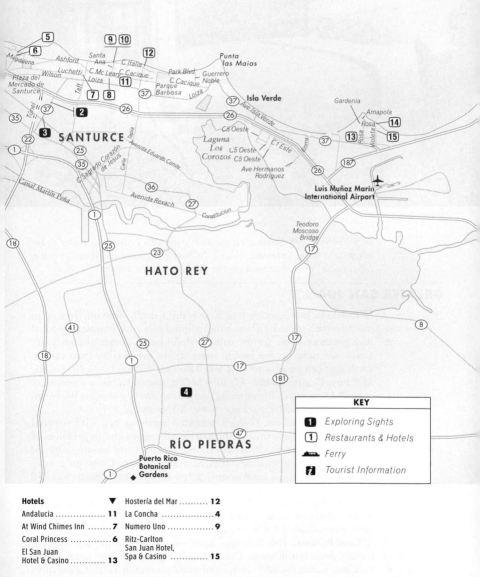

Greater San Juan

ATLANTIC OCEAN

Isla Verde

SANTURCE

HATO REY

RÍO PIEDRAS

Luis Muñoz Marín International Airport

Teodoro Moscoso Bridge

Laguna Los Corozos

Canal Martin Peña

Puerto Rico Botanical Gardens

KEY

1 Exploring Sights
1 Restaurants & Hotels
Ferry
Tourist Information

Hotels ▼	
Andalucia **11**	Hostería del Mar **12**
At Wind Chimes Inn **7**	La Concha **4**
Coral Princess **6**	Numero Uno **9**
El San Juan Hotel & Casino **13**	Ritz-Carlton San Juan Hotel, Spa & Casino **15**

El Convento Hotel.

or 800/468–2779 ⊕ *www.elconvento.com* ➯ *63 rooms, 5 suites* ⚥ *In-room: a/c, safe, Internet, Wi-Fi. In-hotel: restaurants, room service, bars, pools, gym, business center, parking* ¶O¶ *No meals.*

GREATER SAN JUAN

¢ ⊞ **Andalucía.** In a Spanish-style house, this friendly little inn lives up to
INN its name with such details as hand-painted tiles and ceramic pots filled
★ with greenery. **Pros:** terrific value; helpful hosts; gorgeous courtyard.
Cons: not right on the beach; some rooms are smaller than others; small sign can be easy to miss when you are driving by. ⊠ *2011 Calle McLeary, Ocean Park*☎ *787/309–3373* ⊕ *www.andalucia-puertorico. com* ➯ *11 rooms* ⚥ *In-room: a/c, no phone, kitchen (some), Wi-Fi. In-hotel: business center, parking (some)* ¶O¶ *No meals.*

¢ ⊞ **At Wind Chimes Inn.** Hidden behind a whitewashed wall covered
HOTEL with bougainvillea, this Spanish-style villa gives the impression of
an exclusive retreat. **Pros:** charming architecture; on the edge of Condado; can use facilities at Acacia Seaside Inn. **Cons:** on a busy street; old-fashioned rooms; only a few rooms have closets. ⊠ *1750 Av. McLeary, Condado*☎ *787/727–4153 or 800/946–3244* ⊕ *www. atwindchimesinn.com* ➯ *17 rooms, 5 suites* ⚥ *In-room: a/c, safe (some), kitchen (some). In-hotel: room service, bar, pool, parking, some pets allowed* ¶O¶ *No meals.*

$ ⊞ **Coral Princess.** This boutique hotel—set in one of the few remain-
HOTEL ing art deco buildings in Condado—has personality to spare. **Pros:**
★ excellent value; friendly staff; comfortable common areas. **Cons:** short
walk to the beach. ⊠ *1159 Av. Magdalena, Condado*☎ *787/977–7700*

⊕ *www.coralpr.com* ☞ *25 rooms* ৬ *In-room: a/c, Internet, Wi-Fi. In-hotel: bar, pool* ⊚ *Breakfast.*

$ ⊞ **El San Juan Hotel & Casino, The Waldorf Astoria Collection.** This iconic resort is widely considered the don't-miss destination in Isla Verde. **Pros:** beautiful pool; great dining options in and near hotel; on a fantastic beach. **Cons:** noise in the lobby from bars and casino; self-parking lot is a long walk from the hotel entrance. ⊠ *6063 Av. Isla Verde, Isla Verde* ☎ *787/791–1000* ⊕ *www.elsanjuanhotel.com* ☞ *386 rooms, 57 suites* ৬ *In-room: a/c, safe, Internet, Wi-Fi. In-hotel: restaurants, room service, bars, tennis court, pools, gym, spa, beach, water sports, children's programs, business center, parking* ⊚ *No meals.*

RESORT

☺

Fodor's Choice

★

¢ ⊞ **Hostería del Mar.** This simple breezy inn tucked away in residential Ocean Park is the place to go if you want to be right on a quiet beach and far from the big-name Isla Verde and Condado hotels. **Pros:** right on the beach; lovely building; great on-site dining. **Cons:** rooms could use some updating; a long walk to other restaurants. ⊠ *1 Calle Tapia, Ocean Park* ☎ *787/727–3302* ⊕ *www.hosteriadelmarpr.com* ☞ *21 rooms, 2 suites* ৬ *In-room: a/c, safe, kitchen (some). In-hotel: restaurant, bar, beach* ⊚ *Breakfast.*

INN

$$ ⊞ **La Concha—A Renaissance Resort.** A stunning example of tropical modernist architecture, La Concha has become the envy of the hospitality industry and the center of social life in San Juan for travelers and locals (including politicians and celebrities) alike. **Pros:** stunning tropical modernist architecture; most rooms have ocean views; numerous on-site social activities. **Cons:** noise from lobby and bar can be heard from nearby rooms. ⊠ *1077 Av. Ashford, Condado* ☎ *787/721–7500* ⊕ *www.laconcharesort.com* ☞ *232 rooms, 250 suites* ৬ *In-room: a/c, safe, kitchen (some), Internet, Wi-Fi. In-hotel: restaurants, room service, bars, pools, gym, beach* ⊚ *No meals.*

RESORT

$ ⊞ **Numero Uno.** Although the name refers to the hotel's address, Numero Uno is how guests rate this small, sleek hotel. **Pros:** friendly atmosphere; great restaurant; good value. **Cons:** a long walk to other restaurants; small pool. ⊠ *1 Calle Santa Ana, Ocean Park* ☎ *787/726–5010 or 866/726–5010* ⊕ *www.numero1guesthouse.com* ☞ *11 rooms, 4 apartments* ৬ *In-room: a/c, safe, kitchen (some), Internet. In-hotel: restaurant, room service, bar, pool, beach, some pets allowed* ⊚ *Breakfast.*

HOTEL

★

BEST BETS FOR LODGING
Best for Romance
Hotel El Convento
Numero Uno
The Ritz-Carlton, San Juan
Best Beachfront
El San Juan Hotel & Casino
The Ritz-Carlton, San Juan
Best Pool
El San Juan Hotel & Casino
Gallery Inn
The Ritz-Carlton, San Juan

17

El San Juan Hotel & Casino.

$$$$ RESORT Fodor'sChoice ★ **The Ritz-Carlton, San Juan.** Elegant marble floors and fountains won't undermine the feeling that this is a true beach getaway. **Pros:** top-notch service; excellent restaurant options; pretty pool area. **Cons:** not much is within walking distance; very expensive for San Juan lodging. ✉ *6961 Av. de los Gobernadores, Isla Verde* ☎ *787/253–1700 or 800/241–3333* 🌐 *www.ritzcarlton.com/sanjuan* *416 rooms, 11 suites* *In-room: a/c, safe (some), Internet, Wi-Fi. In-hotel: restaurants, room service, bars, tennis courts, pool, gym, spa, beach, water sports, children's programs, parking* *No meals.*

EASTERN PUERTO RICO

$$$ RESORT Fodor'sChoice ★ **El Conquistador Resort & Golden Door Spa.** Perched on a bluff overlooking the ocean, El Conquistador is one of Puerto Rico's loveliest destination resorts. **Pros:** some of the island's best rooms; unbeatable views of the nearby islands; good dining options in and near hotel. **Cons:** must take a boat to the beach; long waits at the funicular taking guests between levels; self-parking lot is a long distance from the front door. ✉ *1000 Av. El Conquistador, Fajardo* ☎ *787/863–1000 or 800/468–0389* 🌐 *www.elconresort.com* *750 rooms, 17 suites, 157 villas with 234 rooms* *In-room: a/c, safe, Wi-Fi. In-hotel: restaurants, bars, golf course, tennis courts, pools, gym, spa, beach, water sports, children's programs, parking* *No meals.*

$ RESORT **Gran Meliá Golf Resort Puerto Rico.** On an enviable stretch of pristine coastline is this massive resort that boasts two 18-hole golf courses. **Pros:** beautiful setting; lovely pool area; short walk to the beach. **Cons:** parking spots are scarce; facade is blank and uninviting; rooms are temperature controlled and tend to be on the chilly side. ⊠ *Rte. 968, Km 5.8, Coco Beach* ☎ *787/657–1026 or 800/336–3542* ⊕ *www.gran-melia-puerto-rico.com* ⟱ *500 suites* ♿ *In-room: a/c, safe, Internet, Wi-Fi. In-hotel: restaurants, room service, bars, golf courses, tennis courts, pool, gym, spa, beach, water sports, children's programs, business center, some pets allowed* ◯ *No meals.*

$$$$
RESORT
★

Rio Mar Beach Resort & Spa, a Wyndham Grand Resort. On more than 500 acres, this sprawling resort is geared toward outdoor activities. **Pros:** on one of the island's best beaches; great restaurants in and near the hotel; plenty of outdoor activities. **Cons:** dark parking garage; long lines at check-in desk. ⊠ *6000 Río Mar Blvd., Río Grande* ☎ *787/888–6000 or 877/636–0636* ⊕ *www.wyndhamriomar.com* ⟱ *528 rooms, 72 suites, 59 villas* ♿ *In-room: a/c, safe (upon request), Internet, Wi-Fi. In-hotel: restaurants, bars, golf courses, tennis courts, pools, gym, spa, beach, water sports, children's programs, business center* ◯ *No meals.*

VIEQUES AND CULEBRA

$
HOTEL

Club Seabourne. The prettiest place to stay in Culebra, this cluster of plantation-style cottages sits on a hilltop overlooking Fulladoza Bay, a five-minute drive south of Dewey. **Pros:** lovely cottages; well-regarded restaurant; lush gardens. **Cons:** staff can seem overworked; some steps to negotiate and no elevator. ⊠ *Calle Fulladoza, Km 1.5* ✉ *Box 357, Culebra 00775* ☎ *787/742–3169* ⊕ *www.clubseabourne.com* ⟱ *3 rooms, 8 villas, 1 cottage* ♿ *In-room: no phone, a/c, kitchen (some), Wi-Fi. In-hotel: restaurant, bar, pool, parking* ◯ *Breakfast.*

$
B&B
Fodor's Choice
★

Hacienda Tamarindo. The 250-old tamarind tree rising through the center of the main building gives this plantation-style house, one of the most beautiful hotels in Vieques, its name. **Pros:** beautiful views; nicely designed rooms; excellent breakfasts. **Cons:** drive to beaches; small parking lot; no full-service restaurant; no elevator. ⊠ *Rte. 996, Km 4.5, Barrio Puerto Real* ✉ *Box 1569, Vieques 00765* ☎ *787/741–8525* ⊕ *www.haciendatamarindo.com* ⟱ *17 rooms* ♿ *In-room: no phone, a/c, no TV, Wi-Fi. In-hotel: pool, parking, some age restrictions* ◯ *Breakfast.*

$
HOTEL
Fodor's Choice
★

Hix Island House. Constructed entirely of concrete—wait, keep reading!—this award-winning ecochic hotel on 13 secluded acres is one of the most striking in Puerto Rico. **Pros:** eye-popping architecture; secluded setting; friendly staff. **Cons:** no windows means some bugs in the rooms; no elevator; far from restaurants. ⊠ *Rte. 995, Km 1.5, Vieques* ☎ *787/741–2302* ⊕ *www.hixislandhouse.com* ⟱ *13 rooms* ♿ *In-room: no a/c, no phone, kitchen, no TV. In-hotel: pool, parking, some pets allowed, some age restrictions* ◯ *Breakfast.*

$
B&B/INN

Inn on the Blue Horizon. This inn, consisting of six Mediterranean-style villas, was the tiny island's first taste of luxury. **Pros:** eye-popping view; elegant accommodations; good dining options. **Cons:** aloof staff and inattentive management; pricey for what you get; no elevator.

17

✉ *Rte. 996, Km 4.3, Esperanza, Vieques* ✆ *Box 1556, Vieques 00765* ☎ *787/741–3318* ⊕ *www.innonthebluehorizon.com* 🖧 *10 rooms* ✎ *In-room: no phone, a/c, safe, no TV. In-hotel: restaurant, bar, tennis court, pool, beach, parking, some pets allowed, some age restrictions in high season (Dec. 15–Easter)* ▯Ⓞ❙ *Breakfast.*

$$$$
RESORT
★
❑ **W Retreat & Spa—Vieques Island.** Hovering over two gorgeous beaches (one topless and adults-only), the überhip W Retreat & Spa is the island's hot spot for urbane fashionistas. **Pros:** sensational decor; full-service spa; five-minute drive from the airport. **Cons:** high prices even in low season. ✉ *Rte. 200, Km 3.2, Isabel Segunda* ☎ *787/741–4100* ⊕ *www.whotels.com/vieques* 🖧 *157 rooms* ✎ *In-room: a/c, safe, Internet (some), Wi-Fi (some). In-hotel: restaurants, room service, bars, tennis courts, pools, gym, spa, beach, water sports, business center, parking, some pets allowed* ▯Ⓞ❙ *No meals.*

SOUTHERN PUERTO RICO

$
RESORT
❑ **Copamarina Beach Resort.** Without a doubt the most beautiful resort on the southern coast, the Copamarina is set on 16 palm-shaded acres facing the Caribbean Sea. **Pros:** tropical decor; plenty of activities; great dining options. **Cons:** sand at the beach has a gummy feel; noise from the many kids. ✉ *Rte. 333, Km 6.5, Box 805, Guánica* ☎ *787/821–0505* or *800/468–4553* ⊕ *www.copamarina.com* 🖧 *102 rooms, 2 suites, 2 villas* ✎ *In-room: a/c, safe, Internet, Wi-Fi. In-hotel: restaurants, bars, tennis courts, pools, gym, spa, beach, water sports, laundry facilities, business center, parking* ▯Ⓞ❙ *No meals.*

$
RESORT
❑ **Hilton Ponce Golf & Casino Resort.** The south coast's biggest resort sits on a black-sand beach about 4 mi (6 km) south of Ponce. **Pros:** good golf; large casino. **Cons:** isolated location; bland rooms. ✉ *1150 Av. Caribe, La Guancha Ponce* ☎ *787/259–7676* or *800/445–8667* ⊕ *www.ponce.hilton.com* 🖧 *255 rooms* ✎ *In-room: a/c, safe, Wi-Fi. In-hotel: restaurants, room service, bars, golf course, tennis courts, pool, gym, spa, beach, children's programs, business center, parking* ▯Ⓞ❙ *No meals.*

¢
HOTEL
❑ **Hotel Meliá.** In the heart of the city, this family-owned hotel has long been a local landmark. **Pros:** great location on the main square; walking distance to downtown sites; good dining options near hotel. **Cons:** rooms are somewhat outdated; front rooms are a bit noisy. ✉ *75 Calle Cristina, Ponce Centro* ✆ *Box 1431, Ponce 00733* ☎ *787/842–0260* or *800/448–8355* ⊕ *www.hotelmeliapr.com* 🖧 *72 rooms, 6 suites* ✎ *In-room: a/c, Wi-Fi. In-hotel: pool, business center, parking* ▯Ⓞ❙ *Breakfast.*

$–$$
RENTAL
Fodor's Choice
★
❑ **Mary Lee's by the Sea.** This meandering cluster of apartments sits upon quiet grounds full of brightly colored flowers. **Pros:** feels like a home away from home; warm and friendly owner; near pristine beaches and forests. **Cons:** weekly maid service unless requested daily; no nightlife options. ✉ *Rte. 333, Km 6.7* ✆ *Box 394, Guánica 00653* ☎ *787/821–3600* ⊕ *www.maryleesbythesea.com* 🖧 *10 apartments* ✎ *In-room: no phone, a/c, kitchen, no TV (some). In-hotel: laundry facilities, parking, some pets allowed* ▯Ⓞ❙ *No meals.*

Tres Sirenas.

WESTERN AND CENTRAL PUERTO RICO

¢
HOTEL
Fodor's Choice
★

Casa Grande Mountain Retreat. Here you'll come as close as you can to sleeping in a tree house. **Pros:** unspoiled setting with spectacular views; accessible for people with disabilities; plentiful outdoor activities. **Cons:** no air-conditioning; long drive to other sights, restaurants. ⊠ *Rte. 612, Km 0.3, Utuado*☎ *787/894–3939 or 888/343–2272* ⊕ *www. hotelcasagrande.com* ⤳ *20 rooms* ♿ *In-room: no a/c, no phone, no TV. In-hotel: restaurant, bar, pool, parking* ⍟*No meals.*

$
HOTEL

Casa Isleña. With its barrel-tile roofs, wall-enclosed gardens, and open-air dining room, Casa Isleña might remind well-traveled souls of a villa on the coast of Mexico. **Pros:** secluded setting; beautiful beach; eye-catching architecture. **Cons:** restaurant closed during low season (May–November); books up quickly; management seldom on-site. ⊠ *Rte. 413 Interior, Km 4.8, Barrio Puntas*☎ *787/823–1525 or 888/289–7750* ⊕ *www. casa-islena.com* ⤳ *9 rooms* ♿ *In-room: a/c, no phone, Internet, Wi-Fi. In-hotel: restaurant, bar, pool, beach, parking* ⍟*No meals.*

$$$$
RESORT
Fodor's Choice
★

Horned Dorset Primavera. Thirty-nine whitewashed villas and suites comprise what is, without a doubt, the most luxurious property in Puerto Rico. **Pros:** unabashed luxury; unmatched meals; lovely setting. **Cons:** on a very slender beach; staff is sometimes haughty; morning light floods through small shadeless windows near the ceiling. ⊠ *Rte. 429, Km 3, Box 1132, Rincón* ☎ *787/823–4030 or 800/633–1857* ⊕ *www.horneddorset.com* ⤳ *22 villas, 17 suites* ♿ *In-room: a/c, safe, kitchen, no TV (villas). In-hotel: restaurants, bar, pools, gym, beach, some age restrictions (villas), parking, some pets allowed* ⍟*No meals.*

¢ HOTEL **Lazy Parrot.** Painted in eye-popping tropical hues, this mountainside hotel doesn't take itself too seriously. **Pros:** whimsical design; lush setting; friendly staff. **Cons:** not on the beach; stairs to climb. *Rte. 413, Km 4.1, Rincón 787/823–5654 or 800/294–1752 www.lazyparrot.com 21 rooms In-room: a/c, Wi-Fi. In-hotel: restaurants, bars, pool, parking Breakfast.*

$ RENTAL **LemonTree Oceanfront Cottages.** Sitting right on the beach, this pair of lemon-yellow buildings holds six apartments named after such fruits as Mango, Cocoa, Banana, and Piña. **Pros:** far from the crowds; on-call massage therapist; spacious balconies. **Cons:** beach is very narrow; must drive to shops and restaurants; no elevator. *Rte. 429, Km 4.1, Box 200, Rincón 787/823–6452 www.lemontreepr.com 6 apartments In-room: a/c, kitchen, Wi-Fi. In-hotel: beach No meals.*

$ RESORT **Rincón Beach Resort.** It's a bit off the beaten path, but that's part of the allure of this oceanfront resort. **Pros:** beautiful setting; gorgeous pool area; laid-back vibe. **Cons:** far from dining options; lacks a Puerto Rican flavor; decor is slightly dated; halls echo. *Rte. 115, Km 5.8, Añasco 787/589–9000 www.rinconbeach.com 112 rooms In-room: a/c, safe, kitchen (some), Wi-Fi. In-hotel: restaurant, bars, pool, gym, beach, water sports, parking No meals.*

$ HOTEL Fodor's Choice ★ **Tres Sirenas.** Waves gently lap against the shores at this luxurious boutique hotel named "Three Mermaids" in honor of the owners' daughters. **Pros:** in-room massages available; discounted low-season rates (May 1–December 15); resident owner. **Cons:** usually booked; set breakfast hour. *26 Seabeach Dr., Rincón 787/823–0558 www.tressirenas.com 3 rooms, 1 apartment In-room: a/c, no phone, kitchen (some). In-hotel: pool, beach, water sports, parking Breakfast.*

NIGHTLIFE AND THE ARTS

Qué Pasa, the official visitor's guide, has listings of events in San Juan and out on the island. For daily listings, pick up a copy of the English-language edition of the *San Juan Star.* The Thursday edition's weekend section is especially useful. For the gay scene, check out the monthly *Puerto Rico Breeze*; the free newspaper is found in many businesses, especially in the Condado area.

NIGHTLIFE

Wherever you go, dress to impress. Puerto Ricans have flair, and both men and women love getting dressed up to go out. Bars are usually casual, but if you have on jeans, sneakers, and a T-shirt, you may be refused entry at swankier nightclubs and discos.

In Old San Juan, Calle San Sebastián is lined with bars and restaurants. Salsa music blaring from jukeboxes in cut-rate pool halls competes with mellow Latin jazz in top-flight nightspots. Evenings begin with dinner and stretch into the late hours (often until 3 or 4 in the morning) at the bars of the more upscale, so-called SoFo (south of Fortaleza) end of Old San Juan. An eclectic crowd heads to the Plaza del Mercado in Santurce after work to hang out in the plaza or enjoy drinks and food in one of the small establishments skirting the farmers' market. Condado and Ocean Park have their share of nightlife, too. Most are restaurant-and-bar environments.

Just east of San Juan along Route 187, funky Piñones has a collection of open-air seaside eateries that are popular with locals. On weekend evenings, many places have merengue combos, Brazilian jazz trios, or reggae bands. In the southern city of Ponce, people embrace the Spanish tradition of the *paseo*, an evening stroll around the Plaza de las Delicias. The boardwalk at La Guancha in Ponce is also a lively scene. Live bands often play on weekends. Elsewhere *en la isla*, nighttime activities center on the hotels and resorts.

OLD SAN JUAN AND GREATER SAN JUAN

BARS AND MUSIC CLUBS

The wildly popular **El Batey** (✉ *101 Calle Cristo, Old San Juan, San Juan* ☎ *787/725–1787*) won't win any prizes for its decor. Grab a marker to add your own message to the graffiti-covered walls, or add your business card to the hundreds that cover the light fixtures. The jukebox, packed with vintage 45s, has one of the best music selections on the island.

★ **Nuyorican Café.** There's something interesting happening at this hipper-than-hip, no-frills, wood-paneled performance space nearly every night, be it an early-evening play, poetry reading, or talent show or, later on, a band playing Latin jazz, Cuban son, Puerto Rican salsa, or even rock. During breaks between performances the youthful, creative set converses in an alley outside the front door. It's usually closed on Monday. ✉ *312 Calle San Francisco (entrance on Callejón de la Capilla), Old San Juan* ☎ *787/977–1276* ⊕ *www.nuyoricancafepr.com.*

Wet. On the roof of the San Juan Water & Beach Club Hotel, this sexy spot offers some of the best ocean views anywhere in Isla Verde. On the weekends there's a DJ, and locals pack in to relax at the bar. At this writing, it was under construction and due to reopen in early 2011. ✉ *San Juan Water & Beach Club, 2 Calle Tartak, Isla Verde* ☎ *787/725–4664.*

CASINOS

By law, all casinos are in hotels, primarily in San Juan. The government keeps a close eye on them. Dress for the larger casinos is on the formal side, and the atmosphere is refined, particularly in the Isla Verde resorts. Casinos set their own hours but are generally open from noon to 4 am. In addition to slot machines, typical games include blackjack, roulette, craps, Caribbean stud (a five-card poker game), and *pai gow* poker (a combination of American poker and the Chinese game pai gow). Hotels with casinos have live entertainment most weekends, as well as restaurants and bars. The minimum age to gamble (and to drink) is 18.

You may feel as if you're in Las Vegas when you step into the **Inter-Continental San Juan Resort & Casino** (✉ *5961 Av. Isla Verde, Isla Verde, San Juan* ☎ *787/791–6100*). A torch singer warms up the crowd at a lounge-bar just outside the gaming room. Inside, a garish chandelier, dripping with strands of orange lights, runs the length of a mirrored ceiling. The casino at the **Ritz-Carlton San Juan Hotel, Spa & Casino** (✉ *6961 Av. Las Gobernadores, Isla Verde, San Juan* ☎ *787/253–1700*) is refined by day or night. There's lots of activity, yet everything is hushed.

17

The only place to gamble in Old San Juan is at the **Sheraton Old San Juan Hotel & Casino** (✉ *101 Calle Brumbaugh, Old San Juan, San Juan* ☎ *787/721–5100*). You can see the gaming room from the hotel's main stairway, from the balcony above, and from the lobby. Light bounces off the Bahía de San Juan and pours through its many windows; passengers bound off their cruise ships and pour through its many glass doors.

DANCE CLUBS

Blend. This hip SoFo nightspot draws fashionistas enamored of the black walls, neon-blue lighting, and eye-candy female waitstaff. You can settle in at the marble-top bar, nestle cozily in a banquet sofa, or dance to salsa, techno, and world beat music in the dance hall to the rear. It serves late-night nouvelle native cuisine. ✉ *309 Calle Fortaleza, Old San Juan* ☎ *787/360–3681.*

Club Lazer. This multilevel club has spots for quiet conversation, spaces for dancing to loud music, and a landscaped roof deck overlooking San Juan. The crowd changes every night; Saturday is ladies' night, when male strippers sometimes perform. ✉ *251 Calle Cruz, Old San Juan* ☎ *787/725–7581* ⊕ *www.clublazer.com.*

Rumba. The air-conditioning blasts, the music thumps, and the under-30s crowd pretends not to notice how hip the place has become. With a large dance and stage area and smokin' Afro-Cuban bands, it's one of the best parties in town. Things cool down for jazz on Wednesday night. ✉ *152 Calle San Sebastián, Old San Juan* ☎ *787/725–4407.*

THE ARTS

The **Museo de Arte de Ponce** (✉ *2325 Av. Las Américas, Sector Santa María, Ponce* ☎ *787/840–1510*) occasionally sponsors chamber music concerts and recitals by members of the Puerto Rico Symphony Orchestra.

Check for theater productions and concerts at the **Teatro La Perla** (✉ *Calle Mayor at Calle Cristina, Ponce Centro, Ponce* ☎ *787/843–4322*).

Named for Puerto Rican playwright Alejandro Tapia, **Teatro Tapia** (✉ *Calle Fortaleza at Plaza Colón, Old San Juan, San Juan* ☎ *787/722–0247*) hosts theatrical and musical productions.

SHOPPING

San Juan has the island's best range of stores, but it isn't a free port, so you won't find bargains on electronics and perfumes. You can, however, find excellent prices on china, crystal, clothing, and jewelry. Shopping for local crafts can also be gratifying: you'll run across a lot that's tacky, but you can also find treasures, and in many cases you can watch the artisans at work. Popular items include *santos* (small carved figures of saints or religious scenes), hand-rolled cigars, handmade *mundillo* lace from Moca, *vejigantes* (colorful masks used during Carnival and local festivals) from Loíza and Ponce, and fancy men's shirts called guayaberas.

In Old San Juan—especially on Calles Fortaleza and Cristo—you can find everything from T-shirt emporiums to selective crafts stores, bookshops, art galleries, jewelry boutiques, and even shops that specialize in made-to-order Panama hats. Calle Cristo has a number of factory-outlet stores, including Coach and Ralph Lauren.

With many stores selling luxury items and designer fashions, the shopping spirit in the San Juan neighborhood of Condado is reminiscent of that in Miami. Avenida Ashford is considered the heart of San Juan's fashion district, and you'll find plenty of high-end clothing stores here.

OLD SAN JUAN AND GREATER SAN JUAN
SPECIALTY STORES

ART
★ **Galería Botello** (⊠ 208 Calle Cristo, Old San Juan, San Juan ☎ 787/723–9987), a gorgeous gallery, displays the works of the late Angel Botello, who as far back as 1943 was hailed as the "Caribbean Gauguin." His work, which often uses the bright colors of the tropics, often depicts island scenes. There are pieces on display here by other prominent local artists as well. Among those who have displayed their works at **Galería Petrus** (⊠ 726 Calle Hoare, Miramar, San Juan ☎ 787/289–0505 ⊕ www. petrusgallery.com) are Dafne Elvira, whose surreal oils and acrylics tease and seduce; Marta Pérez, another surrealist, whose bewitching paintings examine such themes as how life on a coffee plantation might have been; and Elizam Escobar, a former political prisoner whose oil paintings convey the often-intense realities of human experience.

CLOTHES **Clubman** (⊠ 1351 Av. Ashford, Condado, San Juan ☎ 787/722–1867), after many years of catering to a primarily local clientele, is still the classic choice for gentlemen's clothing.

Prolific designer **David Antonio** (⊠ 69 Av. Condado, Condado, San Juan ☎ 787/725–0600) runs a small shop that's full of surprises. His joyous creations range from updated version of the men's classic guayabera shirt to fluid chiffon tunics for women.

Lisa Cappalli (⊠ 151 Av. José de Diego, Condado, San Juan ☎ 787/724–6575) sells her lacy designs from a boutique in Condado.

The window displays at **Nativa** (⊠ 55 Calle Cervantes, Condado, San Juan ☎ 787/724–1396) are almost as daring as the clothes its sells.

★ **Nono Maldonado** (⊠ 1112 Av. Ashford, Condado ☎ 787/721–0456) is well known for his high-end, elegant linen designs. He should know a thing or two about style—he worked for many years as the fashion editor of *Esquire*.

Otto (⊠ 69 Av. Condado, Condado, San Juan ☎ 787/722–4609), owned by local designer Otto Bauzá, stocks his own line of casual wear for younger men.

GIFTS Exotic *mariposas* cover the walls of **Butterfly People** (⊠ 257 Calle de la Cruz, Old San Juan ☎ 787/723–2432 ⊕ www.butterflypeople.com). Clear plastic cases hold everything from a pair of common butterflies to dozens of rare specimens in this lovely shop. Only the "You break it, you bought it" signs detract from the colorful display. You can find many unique spices and sauces from around the Caribbean, kitchen

17

items, and cookbooks at **Spicy Caribbee** (✉ *154 Calle Cristo, Old San Juan* ☎ *888/725–7259* ⊕ *www.spicycaribbee.com*).

JEWELRY   For a wide array of watches and jewelry, visit the two floors of **Bared** (✉ *154 Calle Fortaleza, Old San Juan* ☎ *787/724–4811*), with a charmingly old-fashioned ambience. Look for the massive clock face on the corner. **Joyería Cátala** (✉ *152 Calle Rafael Cordero, Plaza de Armas, Old San Juan, San Juan* ☎ *787/722–3231*) is distinguished for its large selection of pearls. **Joyería Riviera** (✉ *Caribe Hilton San Juan, 1 San Gerónimo Grounds, Puerta de Tierra, San Juan* ☎ *787/725–4000*) sells fine jewelry by David Yurman and Rolex watches.

SPORTS AND ACTIVITIES

BOATING AND SAILING

Aqua Frenzy Kayaks (✉ *At dock area below Calle Flamboyán, Esperanza* ☎ *787/741–0913* ⊕ *www.aquafrenzy.com*) rents kayaks and arranges kayak tours of Puerto Mosquito bioluminescent bay and other areas. Reservations are required for the excursion to the bio bay; the evening kayak trip costs $65 for two people. Make reservations at least 24 hours in advance. **Blue Caribe Kayaks** (✉ *149 Calle Flamboyán, Esperanza* ☎ *787/741–2522* ⊕ *www.bluecaribekayaks.com*) offers kayak trips to Puerto Mosquito for about $25, as well as trips to deserted parts of the coast and nearby islets. You can also rent a kayak and set off on your own.

★   **East Island Excursions** (✉ *At dock area of Marina Puerto Del Rey, Fajardo* ☎ *787/860–3434* ⊕ *www.eastwindcats.com*) can accommodate those who prefer to see Puerto Mosquito bioluminescent bays and return to the mainland on the same evening. Transportation to Vieques is provided and dinner at a local restaurant included before you board an electrically powered pontoon boat for a tour of Puerto Mosquito. Bring a towel, because you can leap into the bio bay, where the outline of your body will be eerily illuminated. Flotation belts are provided. The cost is about $110 per person. Reservations are required. Transportation from your hotel can be arranged for a fee.

DIVING AND SNORKELING

The diving is excellent off Puerto Rico's south, east, and west coasts, as well as its nearby islands. Particularly striking are dramatic walls created by a continental shelf off the south coast near La Parguera and Guánica. There's also some fantastic diving near Fajardo and around Vieques and Culebra, two small islands off the east coast. It's best to choose specific locations with the help of a guide or outfitter. Escorted half-day dives range from $65 to $120 for one or two tanks, including all equipment; in general, double those prices for night dives. Packages that include lunch and other extras are more. Snorkeling excursions, which include transportation, equipment rental, and sometimes lunch, start at $50. Equipment rents for about $5 to $10.

At **Aquatic Adventures** (☎ 787/209–3494 ⊕ *www.diveculebra.com*) in Culebra, Captain Taz Hamrick will take you out snorkeling, on dolphin trips, or to the surrounding cays. **Culebra Divers** (✉ *4 Calle Pedro Marquez, Dewey, Culebra* ☎ 787/742–0803 ⊕ *www.culebradivers.com*), run by Monica and Walter Rieder, caters to those who are new to scuba diving. You travel to dive sites on one of the company's pair of 26-foot cabin cruisers. One-tank dives are $65, and two-tank dives are $95. The office is in downtown Dewey, across from the ferry terminal.

At **Sea Ventures Pro Dive Center** (✉ *Puerto del Rey Marina, Rte. 3, Km 51.4, Fajardo* ☎ 787/863–3483 ⊕ *www.divepuertorico.com*) you can get PADI certified, arrange dive trips from either Fajardo or Palmas del Mar, or organize boating and sailing excursions. A two-tank dive for certified divers, including equipment, is $119.

FISHING

Puerto Rico's waters are home to large game fish such as marlin, wahoo, dorado, tuna, and barracuda; as many as 30 world records for catches have been set off the island's shores.

Half-day and full-day excursions can be arranged through **Mike Benítez Sport Fishing** (✉ *Club Náutico de San Juan, 480 Av. Fernández Juncos, Miramar* ☎ 787/723–2292 ⊕ *www.mikebenitezsportfishing.com*). From the 45-foot *Sea Born* you can fish for sailfish, white marlin, and blue marlin.

17

GOLF

Aficionados may know that Puerto Rico is the birthplace of golf legend Chi Chi Rodríguez—and he had to hone his craft somewhere. Currently, you can find nearly 20 courses on the island, including many championship links. Be sure to call ahead for tee times; hours vary, and several hotel courses give preference to guests. Greens fees start at about $20 and go up as high as $165. The **Puerto Rican Golf Association** (✉ *58 Calle Caribe, San Juan* ☎ 787/793–3444 ⊕ *www.prga.org*) is a good source for information on courses and tournaments.

The 18-hole Arthur Hills–designed course at **El Conquistador Resort & Golden Door Spa** (✉ *1000 Av. El Conquistador, Fajardo* ☎ 787/863–6784) is famous for its 200-foot changes in elevation. The trade winds make every shot challenging.

Palmas del Mar Country Club (✉ *Rte. 906, Humacao* ☎ 787/285–2700 ⊕ *www.palmasdelmar.com*) has two good golf courses: the Rees Jones–designed Flamboyán course, named for the nearly six dozen flamboyant trees that pepper its fairway, winds around a lake, over a river, and to the sea before turning toward sand dunes and wetlands. The older, Gary Player–designed Palm course has a challenging par 5 that scoots around wetlands.

★ The spectacular **Río Mar Country Club** (✉ *Rio Mar Beach Resort & Spa, a Wyndham Grand Resort, 6000 Río Mar Blvd., Río Grande* ☎ 787/888–7060 ⊕ *www.wyndhamriomar.com*) has a clubhouse with a pro shop, two restaurants between two 18-hole courses, and a recently added fire pit that doubles as a place to grab a quick beverage and bite. The River Course, designed by Greg Norman, has challenging fairways that skirt the Mameyes River. The Ocean Course, designed by Tom and George Fazio, has slightly wider fairways than its sister; iguanas can usually be spotted sunning themselves near its fourth hole. If you're not a resort guest, be sure to reserve tee times at least 24 hours in advance. Greens fees for hotel guests range from $50 to $150, depending on tee time and time of year. Fees for walk-ins range from $60 to $165.

HORSEBACK RIDING

Horseback riding is a well-established family pastime in Puerto Rico, with *cabalgatas* (group day rides) frequently organized on weekends through mountain towns.

★ **Hacienda Carabalí** (⊠ *Rte. 992, Km 4, north of entrance to El Yunque* ☎ *787/690–3781* ⊕ *www.haciendacarabalipuertorico.com*), a family-run operation, is a good place to jump in the saddle and ride one of Puerto Rico's Paso Fino horses. Hour-long rides ($60) take you around the 600-acre ranch, and two-hour treks take you to a river where you and your horse can take a dip.

SURFING

The very best surfing beaches are along the northwestern coast from Isabela south to Rincón, which gained notoriety by hosting the World Surfing Championship in 1968. Today the town draws surfers from around the globe, especially in winter, when the waves are at their best.

East of the city, in Piñones, the Caballo has deep- to shallow-water shelf waves that require a big-wave board known as a gun. Playa La Pared, near Balneario de Luquillo, is a surfer haunt with medium-range waves. Numerous local competitions are held here throughout the year. **Desecheo Surf & Dive Shop** (⊠ *Rte. 413, Km 2.5, Rincón* ☎ *787/823–0390* ⊕ *www.desecheosurfshop.com*) rents a variety of short and long surfboards ($25 to $30 a day), snorkeling gear, and Jet Skis. **Mar Azul** (⊠ *Carr. 413, Km 4.4, Rincón* ☎ *787/823–5692 or 787/214–7224* ⊕ *www.puertoricosurfinginfo.com*) has Rincón's best selection of performance surfboards ($40–$60 a day) and stand-up paddleboards to buy or rent ($25 a day). Paddleboard lessons ($40) are also available. **Rincón Surf School** (⊠ *Rte. 413, Rincón* ☎ *787/823–0610* ⊕ *www. rinconsurfschool.com*) offers full-day lessons that include board rental and transportation. You can also arrange two-, three-, and five-day surfing seminars. Boards can be rented for $20 without a lesson.

Saba

WORD OF MOUTH

"Saba is a total gem of an island. Once on it, you can hike/climb
Mt. Scenery. I don't know about snorkeling but understand it's a
GREAT place to go scuba diving."

—BellaClaire

WELCOME TO SABA

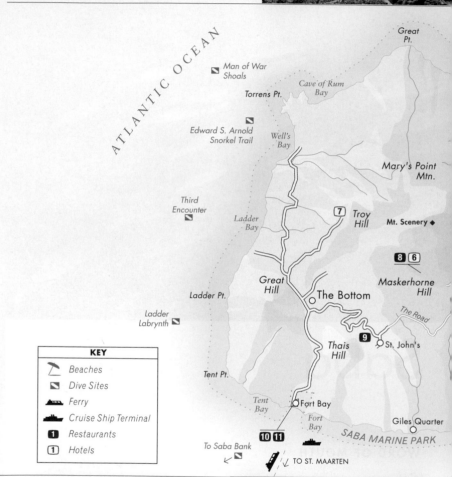

KEY

Beaches	
Dive Sites	
Ferry	
Cruise Ship Terminal	
1 Restaurants	
(1) Hotels	

ATLANTIC OCEAN

Great Pt.

Man of War Shoals

Torrens Pt.

Cave of Rum Bay

Edward S. Arnold Snorkel Trail

Well's Bay

Mary's Point Mtn.

Third Encounter

Ladder Bay

7 Troy Hill

Mt. Scenery ◆

8 **6**

Great Hill

The Bottom

Maskerhorne Hill

Ladder Pt.

The Road

Ladder Labrynth

9 St. John's

Thais Hill

Tent Pt.

Tent Bay

Fort Bay

Fort Bay

Giles Quarter

SABA MARINE PARK

10 **11**

To Saba Bank

TO ST. MAARTEN

Mountainous Saba's precipitous terrain allows visitors to choose between the heights and the depths. The Bottom, the island's capital, was once thought to be the crater of a dormant volcano, from which a trail of 400 rough-hewn steps drops to the sea. Divers can take a different plunge to view the pristine reef.

THE UNSPOILED QUEEN

Tiny Saba—an extinct volcano that juts out of the ocean to a height of 2,855 feet—is just 5 square mi (13 square km) in size and has a population of about 1,500. Part of the Dutch Caribbean, it's 28 mi (45 km) south of St Maarten and surrounded by some of the richest dive sites in the Caribbean.

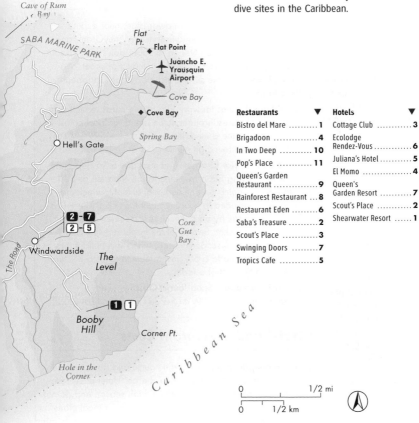

Restaurants ▼		Hotels ▼	
Bistro del Mare	1	Cottage Club	3
Brigadoon	4	Ecolodge Rendez-Vous	6
In Two Deep	10	Juliana's Hotel	5
Pop's Place	11	El Momo	4
Queen's Garden Restaurant	9	Queen's Garden Resort	7
Rainforest Restaurant	8	Scout's Place	2
Restaurant Eden	6	Shearwater Resort	1
Saba's Treasure	2		
Scout's Place	3		
Swinging Doors	7		
Tropics Cafe	5		

18

SABA

TOP REASONS TO VISIT SABA

1 Diving: Divers flock to Saba because of the clear water and spectacular ocean life.

2 Hiking: Hikers can climb the island's pinnacle, Mt. Scenery, but the less intense trails offer many sweeping vistas as well.

3 Authenticity: Saba reminds you of what the Caribbean used to be: locals are genuine and tourist traps are nonexistent.

4 Ecotourism: Several hotels cater to ecotourists with resident nature pros who can tell you everything about local flora and fauna.

SABA PLANNER

Fast Facts

Banks and Exchange Services: U.S. dollars are accepted everywhere, but Saba's official currency is the Netherlands Antilles florin (NAf; also called the guilder). The exchange rate is fixed at NAf 1.79 to US$1. Both First Caribbean International Bank and the Royal Bank of Trinidad and Tobago are in Windwardside and provide foreign-exchange services. The Windward Island Bank in the Bottom offers full banking services, weekdays 8:30–3:30.

Electricity: 110 volts/60 cycles; visitors from North America should have no trouble using their travel appliances.

Emergency Services: Ambulance (☎ 599/416–3288 or 599/416–3289). **Fire** (☎ 599/416–3710 or 599/416–3737). **Police** (✉ The Bottom ☎ 599/416–3237).

Passport Requirements: Visitors must carry a valid passport and have an ongoing or return ticket.

Weddings: If you choose to be married somewhere other than in the courtroom at the Government Building, you must submit a written request to the **Lt. Governor of Saba** (✉ Census Offices, The Bottom ☎ 599/416–3497, 599/416–3311, or 599/416–3312).

Essentials

Mail: The post office is in Windwardside, near Scout's Place, and offers express-mail service, MoneyGram, and E Zone services. When writing to Saba, don't worry about addresses without post-office-box numbers or street locations. However, make sure to include "Dutch Caribbean" in the address.

Telephones: Phones take prepaid phone cards, which can be bought at stores throughout the island, or local coins. To call Saba from the United States, dial 011 + 599 + 416, followed by the four-digit number.

Taxes and Service Charges: You must pay a $5 departure tax when leaving Saba by plane for St. Maarten or $20 if you're continuing on an international flight, which may already be included in your international ticket. There is a $5 departure tax by boat, which is sometimes covered in the cost of the ticket. Several of the larger hotels will tack on a 10% to 15% service charge; others will build it into the rates. Hotels add a 5% government tax plus a 3% turnover tax to the cost of a room.

Visitor Information: Saba Tourist Office (⊕ www.sabatourism.com ☎ 599/416–2231 or 599/416–2322).

Hotel and Restaurant Costs

Restaurant prices are for a main course and do not include the customary 10%–15% service charge. Hotel prices are for two people in a double room in high season and do not include 8% tax, 10%–15% service charge, or meal plans.

WHAT IT COSTS IN U.S. DOLLARS					
	¢	$	$$	$$$	$$$$
Restaurants	under $8	$8–$12	$12–$20	$20–$30	over $30
Hotels	under $150	$150–$275	$276–$375	$376–$475	over $475

Getting to and Around Saba

Hassle Factor: Medium–high.

Nonstops: None.

Air Travel: Only **Winair** (☎ 599/416-2255 or 800/634-4907 ⊕ www.fly-winair.com) flies to Saba (SAB), and then only from St. Maarten

The approach to Saba's tiny airstrip is as thrilling as a roller-coaster ride, but no need to worry, because the de Havilland Twin Otter aircraft are built for it. In fact, the pilot needs only half the length of the runway to land properly. (If you're nervous, don't sit on the right. The wing seems almost to scrape against the cliff side on the approach.) Once you've touched down on the airstrip, the pilot taxis an inch or two, turns, and deposits you just outside **Juancho E. Yrausquin Airport** (☎ 599/416-2255).

Boat and Ferry Travel: *The Edge* (☎ 599/544-2640 ⊕ www.stmaarten-activities.com), a high-speed ferry, leaves St. Maarten's Pelican Marina in Simpson Bay for Fort Bay on Saba every Wednesday through Sunday at 9 am and boards for the return trip about 3:45 pm. The trip, which can be rough, takes just over an hour each way. Round-trip fare is $75 per person for a Saba day trip, plus a $12 port fee, and 5% extra if you pay by credit card. Passports are necessary for travel.

Another option for a trip to or from St. Maarten is the *Dawn II* (☎ 599/416-3671 ⊕ www.sabactransport.com), a 65-foot aluminum vessel that holds 50 people and runs on Tuesday, Thursday, and Saturday between Philipsburg and Fort Bay. *Dawn II* departs Saba at 6:30 am, arriving at St. Maarten at 8:30 am, and departs St. Maarten at 5 pm, arriving at Fort Bay at 7 pm. The fare is $45 one-way or $68 for same-day return ticket; a $5 harbor fee is additional. Call ahead to check current schedules.

Car Travel: You won't need long to tour the island by car—you can cover the entire circuitous length of the Road in the space of a morning. If you want to shop, have lunch, and do some sightseeing, plan on a full day. If you rent a car, try **Caja's Car Rental** (✉ The Bottom ☎ 599/416-2388) and remember that the island's only gas station, in Fort Bay, closes at 3 pm.

Taxi Travel: Taxis charge a set rate for up to four people per taxi, with an additional cost for each person more than four. The fare from the airport to Hell's Gate is $10, to Windwardside it's $12.50, and to the Bottom it's $20. The fare from the Fort Bay ferry docks to Windwardside is $15. A taxi from Windwardside to the Bottom is $10.

Island Activities

Forget the beach, because there is only Cove Bay, which is more of picnic area than a bona fide beach, and Wells Bay, which has strong undertows and disappears at summer's end. Abundant **reefs**, however, are a different story. The island is surrounded by—and zealously preserves—myriad extraordinary **dive sites.** If you don't dive, there are plenty of shallow reefs you can explore by **snorkel.**

If you're not into the briny deep, there's always the **hike** to the top of Mt. Scenery, a breathtaking trip to an even better view, assuming the top isn't shrouded in cloud cover.

Otherwise, it's a quiet and peaceful place with some good restaurants, and a pleasant destination if all you want to do is relax and chat with the ever-friendly locals.

18

Language

Saba's official language is Dutch, but everyone on the island speaks English. Sabans are always willing to help, and they enjoy conversation. If you're open to chatting, you may get some good local advice.

By Roberta Sotonoff

One of the Dutch Caribbean islands, tropical Saba (pronounced *say*-ba) explodes out of the Caribbean Sea. Though just south of St. Maarten (if you've seen the original *King Kong*, you'll recognize its majestic silhouette from the beginning of the film), the island couldn't be more different. Whereas St. Maarten is all beaches, gambling, and duty-free shopping, Saba is ecotourism, diving, and hiking.

Nearly half of Saba's 5 square mi (13 square km) is covered in verdant tropical rain forest; the other half is sprinkled with petite hamlets composed of white, green-shuttered houses trimmed in gingerbread, roofed in red, and built on grades so steep they seem to defy physics. Flower-draped walls and neat picket fences border narrow paths among the bromeliads, palms, hibiscus, orchids, and Norfolk Island pines. The land dips and climbs à la San Francisco and eventually drops off into sheer cliffs that fall right into the ocean, the fodder for some of the world's most striking dive sites and the primary reason for Saba's cultlike following. Divers seem to relish the fact that they're in on Saba's secret.

But word is slowly getting out. Every year, more tourists are turned on to Saba's charms and make the 11-minute, white-knuckle flight from St. Maarten into the tiny airport (barely the size of an aircraft carrier's and one of the shortest in the world). Indeed, traffic jams along the winding, narrow road (yes, there's really just one) are seldom, unless the driver in front of you stops to chat. The past few years have seen more restaurants (big advances considering around-the-clock electricity was established only in 1970). But don't fear you will find a booming metropolis; even as it changes, Saba retains an old-world charm.

A major point of local pride is that many Saban families can be traced all the way back to the island's settlement in 1640 (the surnames Hassell, Johnson, and Peterson fill the tiny phone book). And Sabans hold their traditions dear. Saba lace—a genteel art that dates back to the 1870s—is still hand-stitched by local ladies who, on the side, also distill potent, 151-proof Saba Spice, which is for sale in most of the island's mom-and-pop shops. And, families follow the generations-old tradition of burying their dead in their neatly tended gardens.

Like the residents of most small towns, the Sabans are a tight-knit group; nothing happens without everyone hearing about it, making crime pretty much a nonissue. But they are eager to welcome newcomers and tend to make travelers feel less like tourists and more like old friends. After all, they're proud to show off their home, which they lovingly call "the unspoiled queen."

EXPLORING SABA

Getting around the island means negotiating the narrow, twisting roadway that clings to the mountainside and rises from sea level to almost 2,000 feet. Although driving isn't difficult, be sure to go slowly and cautiously. If in doubt, leave the driving to a cabbie so you can enjoy the scenery.

The Bottom. Sitting in a bowl-shaped valley 820 feet above the sea, this town is the seat of government and the home of the lieutenant governor. The gubernatorial mansion, next to Wilhelmina Park, has fancy fretwork, a steeply pitched roof, and wraparound double galleries. Saba University School of Medicine runs a **medical school** in the Bottom, at which about 400 students are enrolled.

On the other side of town is the Wesleyan Holiness Church, a small stone building with white fretwork. Though it's been renovated and virtually reconstructed over the years, its original four walls date from 1919; go inside and look around. Stroll by the church, beyond a place called the Gap, to a lookout point where you can see the 400 rough-hewn steps leading down to Ladder Bay. This and Fort Bay were the two landing sites from which Saba's first settlers had to haul themselves and their possessions up to the heights. Sabans sometimes walk down to Ladder Bay to picnic. Think long and hard before you do: climbing back requires navigating the same 400 steps.

18

Cove Bay. Near the airport on the island's northeastern side, a 20-foot-long strip of rocks and pebbles laced with gray sand is really the only place for sunning. There's also a small tide pool here for swimming.

Flat Point. This is the only place on the island where planes can land. The runway here is one of the world's shortest, with a length of approximately 1,300 feet. Only STOL (short takeoff and landing) prop planes dare land here, as each end of the runway drops off more than 100 feet into the crashing surf below.

Fort Bay. The end of the Road is also the jumping-off place for all of Saba's dive operations and the location of the St. Maarten ferry dock. The island's only gas station is here, as is a 277-foot pier that accommodates the tenders from ships. On the quay is a decompression chamber, which at this writing is not in use, and three dive shops. Deep End Bar and Grill and Pop's Place are two good places to catch your breath while enjoying some refreshments and the view of the water.

Established in 1987 to preserve and manage the island's marine resources, the **Saba National Marine Park** encircles the entire island,

CLOSE UP

Engineering Feats

To view Saba from a distance is to be baffled: the island soars out of the Caribbean Sea. Steep, rocky shores, on the conical volcano that formed it, provide a seemingly impassable barrier to the outside world. How anyone saw this land as inhabitable is a mystery. But Sabans are a tenacious lot, and they were bound and determined to make this island theirs.

Among the sheer rock walls that surround Saba, at what is now Fort Bay, settlers found a tiny cove where entrance was possible. They navigated rowboats in between the crashing waves, steadied themselves against the swell, and then, waist-deep in water, pulled their boats to shore. Nothing got onto the island without coming this way, not a person, or a set of dishes, or a sofa. From there, supplies were hauled up a steep path composed of more than 200 steps (all of different heights and widths) in the hands or on the heads of Sabans. The trail had been carved into the mountain and climbed 820 feet above sea level to the Bottom through a grand crevice. Visitors who were unable to climb were carried to the top at a cost of 30 guilders.

For nearly 300 years after Saba was settled, this was how it was done. Then, in the early 1900s, the locals decided to build a road. They first approached the Dutch government for help. Legend has it that the Dutch said the grade was too steep, that it could not be done. But the Sabans, in particular, Josephus Lambert Hassell, would not be deterred. He took a correspondence course in road building, and in 1938, with no trained engineers, road construction began. The road took about 15 years to complete and now climbs 653 feet out of Fort Bay.

The next feat of engineering came in 1956, when the Technical Economic Counsel of Dutch Caribbean deemed tourism Saba's only marketable resource and decided a pier and an airport had to be built. With only one place flat enough for an airstrip, the airport was built on Flat Point, a solidified lava flow. In 1959, the first conventional single-engine aircraft landed on the 1,300-foot aircraft carrier–size strip, the shortest international one in the world. The airport itself opened in 1963. Engineers first tried to build a pier in 1934, but the perpetual waves destroyed it almost immediately. In 1972, the Sabans tried again and were able to build a short, 277-foot-long pier (the sea was simply too deep for anything longer). Unfortunately, it is too small to accommodate cruise ships, a major thorn in the tourism industry's side.

---

dipping down to 200 feet, and is zoned for diving, swimming, fishing, boating, and anchorage. One of the unique aspects of Saba's diving is the submerged pinnacles at about the 70-foot depth mark. Here all forms of sea creatures rendezvous. The information center offers talks and slide shows for divers and snorkelers and provides literature on marine life. (Divers are required to contribute $3 a dive to help maintain the park facilities.) Before you visit, call first to see if anyone is around. ⊠ *Saba Conservation Foundation/Marine Park Visitors Center, Fort Bay* ☎ *599/416–3295* ⊕ *www.sabapark.org* ☉ *Weekdays 8–5.*

Looking down from Mt. Scenery.

Hell's Gate. The Road makes 14 hairpin turns up nearly 2,000 vertical feet to Hell's Gate. Holy Rosary Church, on Zion's Hill, is a stone structure that looks medieval but was built in 1962. In the community center behind the church, village ladies sell their intricate lace. The same ladies make the potent rum-based Saba Spice, each according to her old family recipe. The intrepid can venture to Lower Hell's Gate, where the Old Sulphur Mine Walk leads to bat caves (with a sulfuric stench) that can—with caution—be explored.

18

Fodor's Choice
★ **Mt. Scenery.** Stone and concrete steps—1,064 of them—rise to the top of Mt. Scenery. En route to the mahogany grove at the summit, the steps pass giant elephant ears, ferns, begonias, mangoes, palms, and orchids; there are six identifiable ecosystems in all. The staff at the Trail Shop in Windwardside can provide a field guide. Have your hotel pack a picnic lunch, wear sturdy shoes, and take along a jacket and a canteen of water. The round-trip excursion will take about three hours and is best begun in the early morning.

Windwardside. The island's second-largest village, perched at 1,968 feet, commands magnificent views of the Caribbean. Here amid the oleander bushes are rambling lanes and narrow alleyways winding through the hills, and clusters of tiny, neat houses and shops as well as the Saba Tourist Office. At the village's northern end is the Church of St. Paul's Conversion, a colonial building with a red-and-white steeple.

★ Small signs mark the way to the **Harry L. Johnson Museum.** This 150-year-old former sea captain's home surrounds itself with lemon-grass and clover. Period pieces on display include a handsome mahogany four-poster bed, an antique organ, and, in the kitchen, a rock oven.

You can also look at old documents, such as a letter a Saban wrote after the hurricane of 1772, in which he sadly says, "We have lost our little all." Don't miss the delightful stroll to the museum down the stone-walled Park Lane, one of the prettiest walks in the Caribbean. ⊠ *Windwardside* ☎ *No phone* ⌦ *$2* ☉ *Weekdays 10–noon and 1–4.*

WHERE TO EAT

The island might be petite, but there's no shortage of mouthwatering fare from French to fresh seafood to Caribbean specialties. Reservations are necessary, as most of the restaurants are quite small. In addition, some places provide transportation.

WHAT TO WEAR

Restaurants are informal. Shorts are fine during the day, but for dinner you may want to put on slacks or a casual sundress. Just remember that nights in Windwardside can be cool because of the elevation.

$$$

ITALIAN

✕ **Bistro del Mare.** While dining alongside the pool at the Shearwater Resort, savor the sounds of the sea, soft jazz, and a panorama from 2,000 feet above sea level. The evolving but pricey menu offers a good wine selection. Specialties include tomato-basil soup, calamari fritti, and lobster ravioli. Fresh seafood is a given. ⊠ *Shearwater Resort, Booby Hill* ☎ *599/416–2498* ⊕ *shearwater-resort.com* ⌦ *Reservations essential* ☉ *No dinner Sun. and Mon.*

$$$

ECLECTIC

★

✕ **Brigadoon.** Just as many people visit this local favorite for the exceptional fare as for the entertaining atmosphere, which stars eccentric co-owner Trish Chammaa, who hosts with jokes and brassy banter. Trish's husband toils over supper in the back, and the result is a perfect gastronomic experience. The venue sports glass-top tables accented with Caribbean runners. The varied menu includes vegetarian entrées, fresh Saban lobster, sesame- and coriander-encrusted yellowfin tuna, and baby back ribs. Thursday and Saturday are prime rib and shawarma (a Middle Eastern meat-based wrap sandwich like gyros) nights. The homemade desserts are decadent.⊠ *Windwardside* ☎ *599/416–2380* ☉ *Closed Sept. and Tues. No lunch.*

¢–$$

ECLECTIC

✕ **Deep End Bar and Grill.** The owners of the Saba Deep dive shop run this lively harborside spot, with its stained-glass window, mahogany bar, and newly refinished furniture and floors. The soups and sandwiches (especially the Reuben) are excellent, and the customers are usually high-spirited—most have just come from a dive. Dinner is served only on holidays. ⊠ *Fort Bay* ☎ *599/416–3438 or 599/416–3397* ☉ *No dinner.*

¢–$

CARIBBEAN

✕ **Pop's Place.** Directly on the water overlooking the pier in Fort Bay is this itty-bitty come-as-you-are, Caribbean-flavor shack. Inside you'll find three tables, a tiny bar, and reggae music to really put you in the mood. Watch the divers come in as you eat lobster sandwiches, the absolute best on the island. ⊠ *Fort Bay* ☎ *599/416–3640* ⊟ *No credit cards* ☉ *Closed Mon.*

$$$–$$$$

ECLECTIC

Fodor'sChoice

★

✕ **Queen's Garden Restaurant.** Set in a lovely garden and showcasing sweeping views of the Bottom, this dimly lighted venue is the perfect place for a romantic meal. Diners can expect to sup on superb Saban lobster or some tasty menu offering, or the chef will create something to your liking. The smoked-duck-breast salad starter is mouthwatering. Service is excellent. Come early for cocktails at the outdoor bar, which overlooks the pool—and, below that, the ocean—then stay late and be awed by the array of stars above you. Poolside parties, musical events, and theme nights with international flavors spice things up.✉ *1 Troy Hill Dr., Troy Hill* ☎ *599/416–3494* ⊕ *www.queensaba.com/theresort/ dining* ☾ *Closed Tues.*

$$–$$$
SEAFOOD
★
✗ **Rainforest Restaurant** You might need a flashlight for the five-minute hike down the Crispeen Track, by way of the Mt. Scenery Trail, to find this restaurant in the middle of the rain forest. Once you arrive, you'll feel you're truly away from it all. Fresh seafood is always available, vegetables are picked fresh from the restaurant's own garden, and though the steaks are huge, locals usually opt for red curry shrimp and apple pie for dessert. On Wednesday, a slide show depicts the ecological aspects of the island. And every night you are surrounded by music—the lilting sound of the tree frogs.✉ *Ecolodge Rendez-Vous, Crispeen Track, Windwardside* ☎ *599/416-3888* ☾ *Closed Mon.*

$$$
ECLECTIC
Fodor's Choice
★
✗ **Restaurant Eden.** Chef Norbert Schippers has concocted an eclectic menu that might include anything from Italian risotto to seafood and steaks. Sample the Chèvre Normandy, a puff pastry filled with baby lettuce, goat cheese, and accented with caramelized apple and balsamic syrup. Dinner (5:30–9:30) is on the rooftop amid a lovely garden setting. ✉ *Lambee's Place Windwardside* ☎ *599/416-2539* ⊕ *www. edensaba.com* ⚴ *Reservations required* ☾ *Closed Tues.*

$$–$$$
ECLECTIC
✗ **Saba's Treasure.** Right in the heart of Windwardside sits this relaxed restaurant whose interior is crafted to look like the inside of a ship. Outside you practically sit on the street (grab one of these chairs for maximum local flavor). Go for a quick meal of stone-oven pizza, the best on the island, or linger over a drink at the tiny bar. ✉ *Windwardside* ☎ *599/416-2819* ⊕ *www.sabastreasure.com* ☾ *No dinner Sun.*

$$–$$$
ECLECTIC
✗ **Scout's Place.** At this spacious, oft-hopping restaurant and bar, the food, which runs the gamut from goat stew to spit-roasted chicken, is even better than in years past. Theme nights include Friday fish-and-chips or chicken ($14) and Saturday barbecue ($16). And, there's another great reason to come here: the atmosphere. Locals flock to Scout's Place on Friday for karaoke, but there's bound to be a group looking for fun every other night of the week. Sit on the outdoor verandah, which has stunning views of the water, the tiny houses, and the lush forest that make Saba so picturesque. ✉ *Scout's Place, Windwardside* ☎ *599/416-2740 or 599/416-2205.*

$–$$
BARBECUE
★
✗ **Swinging Doors.** A cross between an English pub and an Old West saloon (yes, there are swinging doors), this lively watering hole serves not-to-be-missed barbecue on Tuesday and Friday nights. Pick from ribs, chicken, or ribs and chicken ($12), and don't forget to ask for peanut sauce—you'll be glad you did. Steak night is Sunday ($16–$18). The rest of the week it's just libations. Expect plenty of conversation, including some local gossip. ✉ *Windwardside* ☎ *599/416-2506* ▭ *No credit cards.*

$$$
ECLECTIC
✗ **Tropics Café.** Breakfast, lunch, and dinner are served poolside at Juliana's Hotel in the cabana-style, open-air dining room or in the small dining room, which is dominated by a bar. The café is owned by the

18

same couple who own the hotel. Sandwiches, salads, and fresh fish dominate the menu. Nightly specials include, Wednesday and Sunday, "Grill Night," and on Friday, "Movie Night." The movie is projected onto a sheet strung up just beyond the pool and a chicken or burger dinner is just $12. ⊠ *Windwardside* ☎ *599/416–2469* ⊙ *Closed Mon.*

WHERE TO STAY

Saba's few hotel rooms are primarily in a handful of friendly, tidy inns or guesthouses perched on ledges or tucked into tropical gardens. Because the island is so small, it doesn't much matter where you stay. Among the choices are a couple of delightful small inns and splendid, small ecoresorts. There are also more than a dozen apartments, cottages, and villas for rent. Cable TV is common, but air-conditioning is a rarity.

The following reviews have been condensed for this book. Please go to Fodors.com for full reviews of each property.

¢   ▥ **Cottage Club.** Form follows function at these gingerbread bun-
RENTAL galows, where the price is right and the proximity to downtown is ideal. **Pros:** walking distance to Windwardside; lushly landscaped pool with a gorgeous view; majestic lobby–reception room. **Cons:** stark suites; no on-site dining; some of the walks to the rooms are steep; no a/c.⊠ *Windwardside* ☎ *599/416–2486 or 599/416–2386* ⊕ *www. cottage-club.com* ↝ *10 cottages, some wheelchair accessible* ♿ *In-room: no a/c, kitchen. In-hotel: pool* ⫱◯⫲ *No meals.*

¢   ▥ **Ecolodge Rendez-Vous.** If you like hiking and getting back to nature,
RENTAL this lodge, a five-minute walk deep in the rain forest, is for you.**Pros:** Candlelit Rainforest Restaurant serves three meals a day; nature-theme cottages. **Cons:** hike to get here; only three cottages have ocean views; no electricity (good for ecotourists); no Internet; steep climb to rooms. ⊠ *Crispeen Track, Windwardside* ☎ *599/416–3348* ⊕ *www. ecolodge-saba.com* ↝ *12 cottages* ♿ *In-room: no a/c, no phone, kitchen (some), no TV. In-hotel: restaurant* ⫱◯⫲ *No meals.*

¢   ▥ **El Momo.** If you want to feel as if you're doing your ecological
RENTAL part without giving up every modern convenience, consider these tiny cottages.**Pros:** snack bar–lounge with hammock; cottages buried in the woods; smoke-free property; Wi-Fi. **Cons:** tiny accommodations; strenuous hike to get here; no a/c. ⊠ *Booby Hill* ⌀ *Box 542, Windwardside* ☎ *599/416–2265* ⊕ *www.elmomocottages.com* ↝ *7 cottages* ♿ *In-room: no a/c, kitchen (some), no TV, Wi-Fi. In-hotel: pool* ⫱◯⫲ *No meals.*

¢–$ ▥ **Juliana's Hotel.** Reasonable, in town, great views, and accommoda-
HOTEL tions from good to luxurious—it's all here. **Pros:** across the street from
ⓒ   Tropics Café; outdoor, in-rock shower in Orchid Cottage; two on-site
★   computers with free Internet and full breakfast. **Cons:** close quarters; a hike to get off the property; no a/c in ocean-view rooms. ⊠ *Windward-side* ☎ *599/416–2269 or 866/783–3319* ⊕ *www.julianas-hotel.com* ↝ *9 rooms, 1 apartment, 3 cottages* ♿ *In-room: Wi-Fi, no a/c (some). In-hotel: restaurant, pool* ⫱◯⫲ *Breakfast.*

$$$ 🏨 **Queen's Garden Resort.** At this romantic getaway a quaint stone stair-
HOTEL   way winds up past the largest pool on the island, all the way to the patio
Fodor'sChoice   in front of the main building, which houses the lovely Queen's Garden
★   restaurant.**Pros:** pool bar; private Jacuzzis with sweeping views. **Cons:**
occasional parties can equal loud and crowded; ever-changing manage-
ment and restaurant staff; not wheelchair accessible. ✉ *1 Troy Hill Dr.,
Box 4, Troy Hill ☎ 599/416–3494 ⊕ www.queenssaba.com ↪ 12 1- or
2-bedroom suites ♿ In-room. safe, kitchen (some). In-hotel: restaurant,
bar, pool, gym* ⊘ *No meals.*

¢   🏨 **Scout's Place.** Owned by dive masters Wolfgang and Barbara Tooten,
HOTEL   this all-in-one, no-frills dive resort is especially good for the diver on
a tight budget. **Pros:** on-site dive shop; multilingual owners; karaoke
on Friday. **Cons:** smallish rooms; some don't get much sunlight; kara-
oke on Friday. ✉ *Windwardside ☎ 599/416–2740 or 599/416–2205,
866/656–7222 for reservations ⊕ www.scoutsplace.com ↪ 10 rooms,
1 2-bedroom cottage ♿ In-room: no a/c, kitchen (some), Wi-Fi. In-hotel:
restaurant, bar, pool* ⊘ *Breakfast.*

$ 🏨 **Shearwater Resort.** Formerly Willard's of Saba, this boutique hotel,
RESORT   2,000 feet above the sea, is so romantic, secluded and peaceful, you
may never want to leave. **Pros:** upscale with one of the best views on
the island. **Cons:** the road is very steep and it's a schlep to get here.
✉ *Booby Hill, Windwardside ☎ 599/416–2498 ⊕ shearwater-resort.
com ↪ 9 suites or cottage rooms with balcony ♿ In-room: safe, Wi-Fi,
no a/c. In-hotel: restaurant, bar, business center, pool, gym, tennis court,
spa* ⊘ *Breakfast.*

NIGHTLIFE

Guido's (✉ *Windwardside* ☎ *599/416–2230*) has dancing on weekends.
Lollipops (✉ *St. John's* ☎ *599/416–3330*) is the place to find locals and
med students, especially for weekend parties. Check the bulletin board
in each village for a list of events, which often include parties. **Scout's
Place** (✉ *Windwardside* ☎ *599/416–2740*) is a popular evening gather-
ing place. The convivial bar can get crowded, and sometimes there's
dancing. Go on Friday for karaoke night, when people swarm the spa-
cious dining area.

18

SHOPPING

The history of Saba lace, one of the island's most popular goods, goes
back to the late 19th century. Gertrude Johnson learned lace making
at a Caracas convent school. She returned to Saba in the 1870s and
taught the art that has endured ever since. Saban ladies display and sell
their creations at the community center in Hell's Gate and from their
houses; just follow the signs. Collars, tea towels, napkins, and other
small articles are relatively inexpensive; larger ones, such as tablecloths,
can be pricey. The fabric requires some care—it's not drip-dry. Saba
Spice is another island buy. Although it *sounds* as delicate as lace and
the aroma is as sweet as can be, the base for this liqueur is 151-proof

rum. You can find souvenirs, gifts, and *Saban Cottages: A Book of Watercolors,* in almost every shop.

El Momo Folk Art (✉ *Windwardside* ☎ *599/416–2518*) shelves overflow with regional crafts, local postcards, handmade jewelry, knickknacks, and anything else El Momo can find a spot for.

JoBean Glass (✉ *Windwardside* ☎ *599/416–2490*) sells intricate handmade glass-bead jewelry as well as sterling silver and gold pieces by artist-owner Jo Bean. She also offers workshops in beadwork.

★ From watercolors of local houses to ocean-inspired sculpture, the **Peanut Gallery** (✉ *Windwardside* ☎ *599/416–2509*) offers the island's best selection of local and Caribbean art. Take time to browse through the offerings, and you might just walk away with something better than a refrigerator magnet with which to remember your trip.

★ The **Saba Artisan Foundation** (✉ *The Bottom* ☎ *599/416–3260*) turns out hand-screened fabrics that you can buy by the yard or that are already made into resort clothing. It's also a central location where you can buy the famous Saba lace as well as T-shirts and spices.

Sea Saba (✉ *Windwardside* ☎ *599/416–2246*) carries T-shirts, diving equipment, clothing, and books.

SPORTS AND ACTIVITIES

DIVING AND SNORKELING

Fodor's Choice
★ Saba is one of the world's premier scuba-diving destinations. Visibility is extraordinary, and dive sites are alive with corals and other sea creatures. Within ½ mi (¾ km) of shore, seawalls drop to depths of more than 1,000 feet. The Saba National Marine Park, which includes shoals, reefs, and seawalls alive with corals and other sea creatures, is dedicated to preserving its marine life.

Divers have a pick of 28 sites, including **Third Encounter,** a top-rated pinnacle dive (usually to about 110 feet) for advanced divers, with plentiful fish and spectacular coral; **Man of War Shoals,** another hot pinnacle dive (70 feet), with a myriad of fish and coral; and **Ladder Labyrinth,** a formation of ridges and alleys (down to 80 feet), where likely sightings include grouper, sea turtles, and sharks.

Snorkelers need not feel left out: the marine park has several marked spots where reefs or rocks sit in shallow water. Among these sites is **Torrens Point** on the northwest side of the island. Waterproof maps are available from the marine park, the Saba Conservation Foundation, or dive shops.

Expect to pay about $50 for a one-tank dive, around $90 for a two-tank dive. There is also a mandatory $3 dive fee imposed by the Saba Marine Park plus a $1 per night nature fee and a $1 charge for the hyperbaric chamber per dive.

If you're looking for a more intimate dive experience, try **Saba Deep** (✉ *Fort Bay* ☎ *599/416–3347* ⊕ *www.sabadeep.com*), which tends to take out smaller groups. The company offers PADI- and/

Divers will find spectacular marine life and coral in Saba's 28 dive sites.

or NAUI-certified instructors. Owned by German divers, **Saba Divers** (✉ *Windwardside* ☎ *599/416–2740* ⊕ *www.sabadivers.com*) offers multilingual instruction, making this a great option for anyone interested in meeting international divers or in practicing their language skills. It's the only outfit on the island that allows its customers to dive Nitrox for free. **Sea Saba** (✉ *Windwardside* ☎ *599/416–2246* ⊕ *www.seasaba.com*) will take up to 10 divers out on one of two 40-foot boats; each excursion is accompanied by at least two dive instructors. The staff is both knowledgeable and jovial, making a day on the boat an illuminating and enjoyable experience for any diver.

☽ Every October since 2003, local dive operator Lynn Costenaro, of Sea Saba, orchestrates an event that has become an international attraction. **Sea and Learn** (☎ *599/416–2246* ⊕ *www.seaandlearn.org*) is when pharmacologists, biologists, and other nature experts from all over the world descend on Saba to give presentations, lead field trips, and show off research projects, all of which are designed to increase environmental awareness. Past events have included monitoring undersea octopus checkpoints and studying the medicinal value of indigenous plants. There are even special events for kids. And best of all, it's free. You can sign up online.

GUIDED TOURS

The taxi drivers who meet the planes at the airport or the boats at Fort Bay conduct tours of the island. Tours can also be arranged by dive shops or hotels. A full-day trek costs $50 for one to four passengers and $12.50 per person for groups larger than four. If you're in from

St. Maarten for a day trip, you can do a full morning of sightseeing, stop off for lunch (have your driver make reservations before starting), complete the tour afterward, and return to the airport in time to make the last flight back to St. Maarten. Guides are available for hiking; arrangements may be made through the tourist office or the Trail Shop in Windwardside. Or check out the island in a guided boat tour available for groups of up to 10 on Tuesday and Wednesday. In an hour and a half you will circle the island while learning about its history, its indigenous seabird population, and its coral reefs.

HIKING

On Saba you can't avoid hiking, even if you just go to mail a postcard. The big deal, of course, is Mt. Scenery, with 1,064 steps leading to its top. For information about Saba's 18 recommended botanical hikes, check with the **Saba Conservation Foundation** (⊠ *Fort Bay* ☎ *599/416–3295* ⊠ *Trail Shop, Windwardside* ☎ *599/416–2630* ⊕ *www.sabapark.org*), which maintains trails, or at the foundation's shop in Windwardside. Botanical tours are available on request. The charges for trail use are a voluntary $1 per day or $3 per stay. Crocodile James (James Johnson) will explain the local flora and fauna. A guided, strenuous, full-day hike through the undeveloped back side of Mt. Scenery costs about $50.

St. Barthélemy

WORD OF MOUTH

"If you've been to France and like the culture then I'm sure you will enjoy St. Barth. It's France in the tropics."

—Sharona

WELCOME TO
ST. BARTHÉLEMY

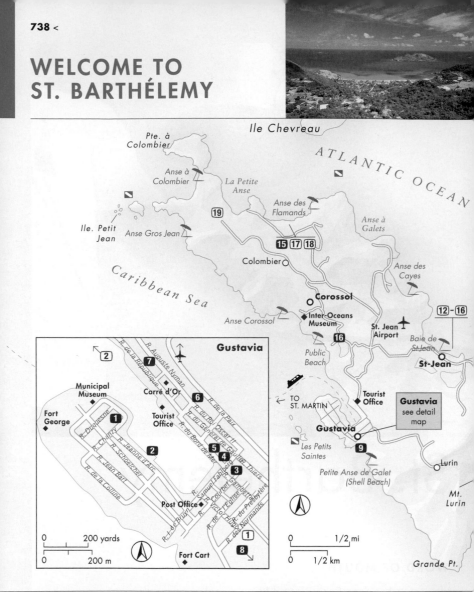

Ile Chevreau

ATLANTIC OCEAN

Pte. à Colombier

Anse à Colombier

La Petite Anse

Anse des Flamands

Anse à Galets

Ile. Petit Jean

Anse Gros Jean

19

15 17 18

Colombier

Anse des Cayes

Caribbean Sea

Anse Corossol

Corossol

Inter-Oceans Museum

St. Jean Airport

12 - 16

16

Public Beach

Baie de St-Jean

St-Jean

Gustavia

2

7

R. de la République

R. Auguste Nyman

Carré d'Or

6

R. de la Paix

R. du Roi Oscar II

R. du Général de Gaulle

R. du Bord de Mer

Municipal Museum

1

R. Duquesne

Fort George

R. Cherry

R. Jeanne d'Arc

Tourist Office

2

R. Schoelcher

5

4

R. Jean Bart

R. de la Colline

3

R. Samuel Fahlberg

R. Courbet Gambier

R. de l'Église

R. de Presbytère

Post Office

R. du Roi

R. de Bruyn

R. des Normands

1

0   200 yards

0   200 m

Fort Cart

8

TO ST. MARTIN

Gustavia

9

Les Petits Saints

Petite Anse de Galet (Shell Beach)

Tourist Office

Gustavia see detail map

Lurin

Mt. Lurin

0   1/2 mi

0   1/2 km

Grande Pt.

Chic travelers put aside their cell phones long enough to enjoy the lovely beaches—long, surf-pounded strands; idyllic crescents crowned by cliffs or forests; glass-smooth lagoons perfect for windsurfing. Nothing on St. Barth comes cheap. But on a hotel's awning-shaded terrace, St. Barth's civilized ways seem worth every penny.

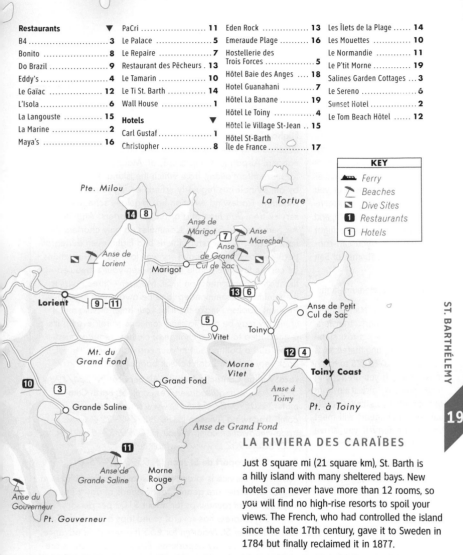

KEY

🚢 Ferry
➤ Beaches
◣ Dive Sites
🔳 Restaurants
① Hotels

ST. BARTHÉLEMY

19

LA RIVIERA DES CARAÏBES

Just 8 square mi (21 square km), St. Barth is a hilly island with many sheltered bays. New hotels can never have more than 12 rooms, so you will find no high-rise resorts to spoil your views. The French, who had controlled the island since the late 17th century, gave it to Sweden in 1784 but finally reclaimed it in 1877.

TOP REASONS TO VISIT ST. BARTHÉLEMY

1 **The Scene:** The island is active, sexy, hedonistic, and hip, and the human scenery is as beautiful as the sparkling blue sea vistas.

2 **Super Chic:** St. Barth continues to change and evolve, becoming ever more chic.

3 **Great Dining:** New restaurants continue to tempt gourmets and gourmands.

4 **Shopping Galore:** If you're a shopper, you'll find bliss stalking the latest in clothes and accessories in dozens of the Caribbean's best boutiques.

5 **Getting Out on the Water:** Windsurfing and other water sports make going to the beach more than just a lounging experience.

ST. BARTHÉLEMY PLANNER

Logistics

Getting to St. Barth: There are no direct flights to St. Barth (SBH). You must fly to another island and then catch a smaller plane for the hop over, or you can take a ferry. Most Americans fly first to St. Maarten, and then take the 10-minute flight to St. Barth, but you can connect through St. Thomas or San Juan as well.

Hassle Factor: Medium–high.

On the Ground: Many hotels offer free airport transfers. Otherwise, there's a taxi stand at the airport; unmetered taxis cost about €10 to €25 to reach most hotels. If you are renting a car, you may pick it up from the airport; if you have a reservation, rental agents will meet you at the ferry if you arrive by boat.

Getting Around the Island: Most people coming to St. Barth rent a car. Taxis are expensive and virtually disappear at night, making dinners out a burden rather than an adventure. Otherwise, there is no other transportation option on the island. It's also possible to rent a motorbike, but steep roads can make driving a stressful experience if you aren't experienced.

Getting to St. Barthélemy

Flights: There are no direct flights to St. Barth. Most North Americans fly first into St. Maarten's Queen Juliana International Airport (⇨ Chapter 23, St. Maarten/St. Martin for more information), from which the island is 10 minutes by air. Winair has regularly scheduled flights from St. Maarten. Tradewind Aviation has regularly scheduled service from San Juan and also does charters. Anguilla Air Services and St. Barth Commuter do only charters. You must reconfirm your return interisland flight, even during off-peak seasons, or you may very well lose your reservations. Be certain to leave ample time between your scheduled flight and your connection in St. Maarten—three hours is the minimum recommended (and be aware that luggage frequently doesn't make the trip; your hotel or villa-rental company may be able to send someone to retrieve it). It's a good idea to pack a change of clothes, required medicines, and a bathing suit in your carry-on—or better yet, pack very light and don't check baggage at all.

Local Airline Contacts: Anguilla Air Services (📞 264/498–5922 ⊕ www.anguillaairservices.com). **St. Barth Commuter** (📞 0590/27–54–54 ⊕ www.stbarthcommuter.com). **Tradewind Aviation** (📞 800/376–7922 ⊕ www.tradewindaviation.com). **Winair** (📞 0590/27–61–01 or 800/634–4907 ⊕ www.fly-winair.com).

Airports: Aéroport de St-Jean (📞 0590/27–75–81).

Ferries: All service is to and from Quai de la République in Gustavia. Ferries are geared to the needs of day-trippers. Voyager offers round-trips for about $100 per person. Great Bay Express has several round-trips a day from Bobby's Marina in St. Maarten for €55 if reserved in advance, or €60 for same-day departures. Private boat charters are also available, but they are very expensive; Master Ski Pilou is one of the companies that offer the service.

Ferry Companies: Great Bay Express Ferry (📞 590/52–45–06 ⊕ www.st-barths.com/great-bay-express). **Master Ski Pilou** (📞 0590/27–91–79 ⊕ www.st-barths.com/master-ski-pilou). **Voyager** (📞 0590/87–10–68 ⊕ www.voy12.com).

Getting Around St. Barthélemy

Driving: Roads are sometimes unmarked, so get a map and look for signs pointing to a destination. These will be nailed to posts at all crossroads. Roads are narrow and sometimes very steep, so check the brakes and gears of your rental car before you drive away, and make a careful inventory of the existing dents and scrapes on the vehicle. Maximum speed on the island is 30 mph (50 kph). Driving is on the right, as in the United States and Europe. Parking is an additional challenge. There are two gas stations on the island, one near the airport and one in Lorient. They aren't open after 5 pm or on Sunday, but you can use the one near the airport at any time with some credit cards, including Visa. Considering the short distances, a full tank of gas should last you most of a week.

Car Rentals: You must have a valid driver's license and be 25 or older to rent, and in high season there may be a three-day minimum. During peak periods, such as Christmas week and February, be sure to arrange for your car rental ahead of time. When you make your hotel reservations, ask if the hotel has its own cars available to rent; some hotels provide 24-hour emergency road service—something most rental companies don't offer. A tiny but powerful Smart car is a blast to buzz around in, and also a lot easier to park than larger cars. Expect to pay at least $55 per day.

Car-Rental Agencies: Avis (🖀 *0590/27–71–43*). **Budget** (🖀 *0590/27–66–30*). **Europcar** (🖀 *0590/27–74–34* ⊕ *www.st-barths.com/europcar/index.html*). **Gumbs** (🖀 *0590/27–75–32*). **Gust Smart of St-Barth** (🖀 *0690/41–66–72*). **Hertz** (🖀 *0590/27–71–14*). **Turbe** (🖀 *0590/27–71–42* ⊕ *www.saint-barths.com/turbecarrental/*).

Taxis: Taxis are expensive and not particularly easy to arrange, especially in the evening. There's a taxi station at the airport and another in Gustavia; from elsewhere you must contact a dispatcher in Gustavia or St-Jean. Technically, there's a flat rate for rides up to five minutes long. Each additional three minutes is an additional amount. In reality, however, cabbies usually name a fixed rate—and will not budge. Fares are 50% higher from 8 pm to 6 am and on Sunday and holidays. If you go out to dinner by taxi, let the restaurant know if you will need a taxi at the end of the meal, and they will call one for you.

Taxi Companies: Gustavia taxi dispatcher (🖀 *0590/27–66–31*). **St-Jean taxi dispatcher** (🖀 *0590/27–75–81*).

Mopeds and Scooters

Several companies rent motorbikes, scooters, mopeds, and mountain bikes. Motorbikes go for about $30 per day and require a $100 deposit. Helmets are required. Scooter and motorbike rental places are mostly along rue de France in Gustavia and around the airport in St-Jean. They tend to shift locations slightly.

Rental Companies: Barthloc Rental (✉ *Rue de France, Gustavia* 🖀 *0590/27–52–81*). **Chez Béranger** (✉ *Rue de France, Gustavia* 🖀 *0590/27–89–00*). **Ets Denis Dufau** (✉ *St-Jean* 🖀 *0590/27–70–59*).

Fast Facts

Banks and Exchange Services: Legal tender is the euro, but U.S. dollars are widely accepted. ATMs are common and dispense only euros.

Electricity: Voltage is 220 AC/60 cycles, as in Europe. You'll need a converter and perhaps a transformer for electronic devices.

Emergencies: Ambulance and Fire (🖀 *0590/27–62–31*). **Police** (🖀 *17 or 0590/27–66–66*).

Language: French, but English is widely spoken.

Passport Requirements: All visitors must carry a valid passport and have a return or ongoing ticket.

19

ST. BARTHÉLEMY PLANNER

Essentials

Mail: Mail is slow and can take up to three weeks to arrive. The main post office is in Gustavia, but smaller post offices are in St-Jean and Lorient. DHL, FedEx, and UPS all provide service to the island.

Safety: There's relatively little crime on St. Barth. Visitors can travel anywhere on the island with confidence. Most hotel rooms have safes for your valuables. As anywhere, don't tempt loss by leaving cameras, laptops, or jewelry out in plain sight in your hotel room or villa or in your car. Don't walk barefoot at night. There are venomous centipedes that can inflict a remarkably painful sting.

Taxes and Service Charges: The island charges a $5 departure tax when your next stop is another French island, $10 to anywhere else payable in cash only (dollars or euros). Some hotels add a 10% service charge. There is a 5% room tax on hotels and villa rentals.

Visitor Information: Office du Tourisme (⊠ *Quai Général-de-Gaulle* ☎ *0590/27-87-27* ⊕ *www.saintbarth-tourisme. com*).

Weddings: Because of the long legal residency requirement, it's not really feasible to get married on St. Barth unless you're a French citizen.

Essentials

Telephones: Many hotels will provide or rent you a cell phone to use during your stay. Some U.S. cell companies work in St. Barth. The country code for St. Barth is 590. Thus, to call St. Barth from the United States, dial 011 + 590 + 590 and the local six-digit number. Some cell phones use the prefix 690. For calls on St. Barth, you must dial 0590 plus the six-digit local number. Public telephones on the island require a *télécartes*, which you can buy at a gas station or post office.

Tipping: Restaurants include a 15% service charge in their published prices, but it's common French practice to leave 5% to 10% more in cash, even if you have paid by credit card. Most taxi drivers don't expect a tip.

Where to Stay

Most hotels on St. Barth are small (the largest has fewer than 60 rooms) and stratospherically expensive, but there are some reasonable options. About half of the accommodations on St. Barth are in private villas. Prices drop dramatically after March, and summer is a great time for a visit. Check hotel Web sites for updates of discounts and special offers that seem to be becoming more common with the current economy.

Hotel and Restaurant Costs: Restaurant prices are for a main course at dinner and include a 15% service charge. Hotel prices are per night for a double room in high season, excluding taxes, 10%–15% service charge, and meal plans. A 5% room tax may be added to your bill but could also be included in the rate.

WHAT IT COSTS IN EUROS

	¢	€	€€	€€€	€€€€
Restaurants	under €8	€8–€12	€12–€20	€20–€30	over €30
Hotels	under €150	€151–€275	€276–€375	€376–€475	over €475

DID YOU KNOW?

The largest hotel on St. Barth has just over 60 rooms, which means you get a great deal of personal service and attention wherever you stay.

ST. BARTHÉLEMY BEACHES

There is a beach in St. Barth to suit every taste. Whether you are looking for wild surf, a dreamy white-sand strand, or a spot at a chic beach club close to shopping and restaurants, you will find it within a 20-minute drive.

(Above) Snorkeling at Anse à Colombier. (Opposite page bottom) Anse à Colombier. (Opposite page top) Anse des Flamands.

There are many *anses* (coves) and nearly 20 *plages* (beaches) scattered around the island, each with a distinctive personality; all are open to the public, even if the beach fronts the toniest of resorts. Because of the variety and number of beaches, even in high season you can find a nearly empty beach, despite St. Barth's tiny size. That's not to say that all the island's beaches are equally good or even equally suitable for swimming, but each beach has something unique to offer. Unless you are having lunch at a beachfront restaurant that has lounging areas set aside for its patrons, you should bring your own umbrella, beach mat, and water (all of which are easily obtainable all over the island if you haven't brought yours with you on vacation). Topless sunbathing is common, but nudism is supposedly forbidden—although both Grande Saline and Gouverneur are de facto nude beaches. Shade is scarce.

THE RIGHT BEACH

For long stretches of talcum-soft pale sand choose La Saline, Gouverneur, or Flamands. For seclusion in nature, pick the tawny grains of Corossol. But the most remarkable beach on the island, Shell Beach, is right in Gustavia and hardly has sand at all! Millions of tiny pink shells wash ashore in drifts, thanks to an unusual confluence of ocean currents, sea-life beds, and hurricane action.

Anse à Colombier. The beach here is the least accessible, thus the most private, on the island; to reach it you must take either a rocky footpath from Petite Anse or brave the 30-minute climb down (and back up) a steep, cactus-bordered trail. But this is a good place to snorkel. Boaters favor this beach and cove for its calm anchorage.

Anse de Grand Cul de Sac. The shallow, reef-protected beach is nice for small children, fly-fishermen, kayakers, and windsurfers—and for the amusing pelicanlike frigate birds that dive-bomb the water fishing for their lunch.

Anse de Grande Saline. Secluded, with its sandy ocean bottom, this is just about everyone's favorite beach and is great for swimmers, too. However, there can be a bit of wind here, so you can enjoy yourself more if you go on a calm day. In spite of the prohibition, young and old alike go nude. The beach is a 10-minute walk up a rocky dune trail, so be sure to wear sneakers or water shoes. Although there are several good restaurants for lunch near the parking area, once you get here, the beach is just sand, sea, and sky.

Anse de Lorient. This beach is popular with St. Barth families and surfers, who like its rolling waves and central location. Be aware of the level of the tide, which can come in very quickly. Hikers and avid surfers like the walk over the hill to Point Milou in the late afternoon sun when the waves roll in.

Anse des Flamands. This is the most beautiful of the hotel beaches—a roomy strip of silken sand. Come here for lunch and then spend the afternoon sunning, taking a long beach walk, and swimming in the turquoise water. From the beach, you can take a brisk hike along a paved sidewalk to the top of the now-extinct volcano believed to have given birth to St. Barth.

★ **Anse du Gouverneur.** Because it's so secluded, this beach is a popular place for nude sunbathing. It is truly beautiful, with blissful swimming and views of St. Kitts, Saba, and St. Eustatius. Venture here at the end of the day and watch the sun set behind the hills. The road here from Gustavia also offers spectacular vistas. Legend has it that pirates' treasure is buried in the vicinity. There are no restaurants or other services here, so plan accordingly.

Baie de St-Jean. Like a mini–Côte d'Azur—beachside bistros, terrific shopping, bungalow hotels, bronzed bodies, windsurfing, and day-trippers who tend to arrive on BIG yachts—the reef-protected strip is divided by Eden Rock promontory. You can rent chaises and umbrellas at La Plage restaurant or at Eden Rock, where you can lounge for hours over lunch.

19

By Elise Meyer   St. Barthélemy blends the respective essences of the Caribbean, France, and *Architectural Digest* in perfect proportions. A sophisticated but unstudied approach to relaxation and respite prevails: you can spend the day on a beach, try on the latest French fashions, and watch the sunset while nibbling tapas over Gustavia Harbor, then choose from nearly 100 excellent restaurants for an elegant evening meal. You can putter around the island, scuba dive, windsurf on a quiet cove, or just admire the lovely views.

A mere 8 square mi (21 square km), St. Barth is a hilly island, with many sheltered inlets providing visitors with many opportunities to try out picturesque, quiet beaches. The town of Gustavia wraps itself around a modern harbor lined with everything from size-matters megayachts to rustic fishing boats to sailboats of all descriptions. Red-roofed villas dot the hillsides, and glass-front shops line the streets. Beach surf runs the gamut from kiddie-pool calm to serious-surfer dangerous, beaches from deserted to packed. The cuisine is tops in the Caribbean, and almost everything is tidy, stylish, and up-to-date. French *savoir vivre* prevails throughout the island.

Christopher Columbus discovered the island—called "Ouanalao" by its native Caribs—in 1493; he named it for his brother Bartholomé. The first group of French colonists arrived in 1648, drawn by the ideal location on the West Indian Trade Route, but they were wiped out by the Caribs, who dominated the area. Another small group from Normandy and Brittany arrived in 1694. This time the settlers prospered—with the help of French buccaneers, who took advantage of the island's strategic location and protected harbor. In 1784 the French traded the island to King Gustav III of Sweden in exchange for port rights in Göteborg. The king dubbed the capital Gustavia, laid out and paved streets, built three forts, and turned the community into a prosperous free port. The island thrived as a shipping and commercial center until the 19th century, when earthquakes, fires, and hurricanes brought financial ruin. Many residents fled for newer lands of opportunity, and Oscar II of Sweden decided to return the island to France. After briefly considering selling it to America, the French took possession of St. Barthélemy again on August 10, 1877.

Today the island is a free port, and in 2007 it became a Collectivity, a French-administered overseas territory outside of continental France. Arid, hilly, and rocky, St. Barth was unsuited to sugar production and thus never developed an extensive slave base. Some of today's 3,000 current residents are descendants of the tough Norman and Breton settlers of three centuries ago, but you are more likely to encounter attractive French twenty- and thirtysomethings from Normandy and Provence who are friendly, English speaking, and here for the sunny lifestyle.

EXPLORING ST. BARTHÉLEMY

With a little practice, negotiating St. Barth's narrow, steep roads soon becomes fun. Recent infrastructure upgrades and the prevalence of small, responsive cars have improved things a lot. Free maps are everywhere, roads are smooth and well marked, and signs will point the way. Parking in Gustavia is still a challenge, especially during busy vacation times.

Corossol. The island's French provincial origins are most evident in this two-street fishing village with a little rocky beach.

Ingenu Magras's **Inter Oceans Museum** has more than 9,000 seashells and an intriguing collection of sand samples from around the world. You can buy souvenir shells. ✉ *Corossol* ☎ *0590/27–62–97* 💰 *€3* ⊙ *Tues.–Sun. 9–12:30 and 2–5.*

Gustavia. You can easily explore all of Gustavia during a two-hour stroll. Most shops close from noon to 2 or 3, so plan lunch accordingly, but stores stay open past 7 in the evening.

A good spot to park your car is rue de la République, alongside the catamarans, yachts, and sailboats. The **tourist office** on the pier can provide maps and a wealth of information. During busier holiday periods, the office may be open all day. ✉ *Rue de la République, Gustavia* ☎ *0590/27–87–27* ⊕ *www.saintbarth-tourisme.com* ⊙ *Mon. 8:30– 12:30, Tues.–Fri. 8–noon and 2–5, Sat. 9–noon.*

On the far side of the harbor known as La Pointe is the charming **Municipal Museum**, where you can find watercolors, portraits, photographs, and historic documents detailing the island's history, as well as displays of the island's flowers, plants, and marine life. ✉ *La Pointe, Gustavia* ☎ *599/29–71–55* 💰 *€2* ⊙ *Mon., Tues., Thurs., and Fri. 8:30– 12:30 and 2:30–6, Sat. 9–12:30.*

Lorient. Site of the first French settlement, Lorient is one of the island's two parishes; a restored church, a school, and a post office mark the spot. Note the gaily decorated graves in the cemetery.

St-Jean. There is a monument at the crest of the hill that divides St-Jean from Gustavia. Called *The Arawak*, it symbolizes the soul of St. Barth.

19

A warrior, one of the earliest inhabitants of the area (AD 800–2,500), holds a lance in his right hand and stands on a rock shaped like the island; in his left hand he holds a conch shell, which sounds the cry of nature; perched beside him are a pelican (which symbolizes the air and survival by fishing) and an iguana (which represents the earth). The half-mile-long crescent of sand at St-Jean is the island's most popular beach. A popular activity is watching and photographing the hair-raising airplane landings, but be sure to not stand in the area at the beach end of the runway, where someone was seriously injured. You'll also find some of the best shopping on the island here, as well as several restaurants.

Toiny Coast. Over the hills beyond Grand Cul de Sac is this much-photographed coastline. Stone fences crisscross the steep slopes of Morne Vitet, one of many small mountains on St. Barth, along a rocky shore that resembles the rugged coast of Normandy. Nicknamed the "washing machine" because of its turbulent surf, it is not recommended even to expert swimmers because of the strong undertow.

WHERE TO EAT

Dining on St. Barth compares favorably to almost anywhere in the world. Varied and exquisite cuisine, a French flair in the decor, sensational wine, and attentive service make for a wonderful epicurean experience in almost any of the more than 80 restaurants. On most menus, freshly caught local seafood mingles on the plate with top-quality provisions that arrive regularly from Paris.

Most restaurants offer a chalkboard full of daily specials that are usually a good bet. But even the pickiest eaters will find something on every menu. Some level of compliance can be paid to dietary restrictions within reason, and especially if explained in French; just be aware that French people generally let the chef work his or her magic. Expect your meal to be costly; however, you can dine superbly and somewhat economically if you limit pricey cocktails, watch wine selections, share appetizers or desserts, and pick up snacks and picnic meals from one of the well-stocked markets. Or you could follow the locals to small *crêperies*, cafés, sandwich shops, and pizzerias in the main shopping areas. Lunch is usually less costly than dinner. *Ti Creux* means "snack" or "small bite."

The small *Ti Gourmet Saint-Barth* is a free pocket-size guidebook that's invaluable for addresses and telephone numbers of restaurants and services. Look for the annual *Saint-Barth Tables* for full restaurant menus.

Reservations are strongly recommended and, in high season, essential. However, except during the Christmas–New Year's season it's not usually necessary to book far in advance. A day's—or even a few hours'—notice is usually sufficient. At the end of the meal, as in France, you must request the bill. Until you do, you can feel free to linger at the table and enjoy the complimentary vanilla rum that's likely to appear.

Check restaurant bills carefully. A *service compris* (service charge) is always added by law, but you should leave the server 5% to 10% extra in cash. You'll usually come out ahead if you charge restaurant meals on a credit card in euros instead of paying with American currency, as your credit card might offer a better exchange rate than the restaurant (though since most credit cards nowadays have conversion surcharges of 3% or more, the benefit of using plastic is rapidly disappearing). Many restaurants serve locally caught *langouste* (lobster); priced by weight, it's usually the most expensive item on a menu and, depending on its size and the restaurant, will range in price from $40 to $60. *In menu prices below, it has been left out of the range.*

WHAT TO WEAR

A bathing suit and *pareu* (sarong) are acceptable at beachside lunch spots. Most women will top it off with a T-shirt or tank top. Jackets

BACK-UP FERRY

Even if you are planning to fly to St. Barth, it's a good idea to keep the numbers and schedules for the two ferry companies handy in case your flight is delayed. An evening ferry could save you having to scramble for a hotel room in St. Maarten. If you are planning to spend time in St. Maarten before traveling on to St. Barth, the ferry is half the cost and somewhat more reliable than the puddle-jumper, and you can leave from Marigot, Oyster Pond, or Philipsburg.

are never required and rarely worn by men, but most people do dress fashionably for dinner. Casual chic is the idea; women wear whatever is hip, current, and sexy. You can't go wrong in a tank dress or anything clingy and ruffly with tight jeans and high sandals. The sky is the limit for high fashion at nightclubs and lounges in high season, when you might (correctly) think everyone in sight is a model. Nice shorts (not beachy ones) at the dinner table may label a man *américain*, but many locals have adopted the habit, and nobody cares much. Pack a light sweater or shawl for the occasional breezy night.

ANSE DE TOINY

19

$$$$
FRENCH
Fodor's Choice
★

✕ **Le Gaïac.** Chef Stéphane Mazières is the only person in the Caribbean to share the Grand Chef designation of the Relais & Châteaux organization with the likes of Daniel Boulud and Thomas Keller. The new management of Hôtel Le Toiny (which includes Francophile Lance Armstrong) has fine-tuned the dramatic, tasteful, cliff-side dining porch to showcase his gastronomic art, and this is one dinner that you won't want to miss. Less stuffy than you might remember from seasons past, the food is notable for its innovation and extraordinary presentation, and the warm but consummately professional service, overseen by maître d' Philippe Casadumont, sets a glorious standard. Rare ingredients and unique preparations delight, gossamer sheets of beet encase tuna tartare "cannelloni"; veal is spiked with truffles and salt-roasted with purple artichokes; date fritters garnish rosy slices of lamb from the Pyrenees. A greenhouse has even been installed on this former pineapple field to grow organic produce for the restaurant. The menu changes frequently, evolving and refining ideas. On Tuesday's special Fish Market Night, you choose your own fish to be grilled; there's a €43 buffet brunch on Sunday. This is one restaurant that is a true hedonistic experience, but you're on

Le Gaïac, Anse de Toiny.

vacation, after all. ⊠ *Hôtel Le Toiny* ☎ *0590/29–77–47* ⊕ *www.letoiny. com* ⊘ *Closed Sept.–mid-Oct.*

FLAMANDS

$$$ ✕ **La Langouste.** This tiny beachside restaurant in the pool courtyard of
SEAFOOD Hôtel Baie des Anges is run by Anny, the hotel's amiable, ever-present
proprietor. It lives up to its name by serving fantastic, fresh-grilled lob-
ster at a price that is somewhat gentler than at most other island ven-
ues. Simple, well-prepared fish, pastas, and an assortment of refreshing
cold soups, including a corn-and-coconut soup perfumed with lemon-
grass, are also available. Be sure to try the warm goat cheese in pastry
served on a green salad with a fruity salsa. ⊠ *Hôtel Baie des Anges*
☎ *0590/27–63–61* ⊕ *www.hotelbaiedesanges.fr* ⊿ *Reservations essen-
tial* ⊘ *Closed May–Oct.*

GRAND CUL DE SAC

$$$$ ✕ **Restaurant des Pêcheurs.** From fresh, morning beachside brioche to
SEAFOOD a final evening drink in the sexy lounge, you can dine all day in this
soaring thatch pavilion that is the epitome of chic. The restaurant at Le
Sereno, like the Christian Liaigre–designed resort, is serenity itself. Each
menu item is a miniature work of art, beautifully arranged and amiably
served. Each day there is a different €44 three-course menu. "Authen-
tic" two-course bouillabaisse *à l'ancienne,* the famous French seafood
stew, is served every Friday, and the chef even gives a class in its prepa-
ration, but the menu also lists daily oceanic arrivals from Marseille and

Quiberon on France's Atlantic coast: roasted, salt-crusted, or grilled to your personal perfection. Fans of Provence will love the aioli special on Wednesday. For splurges, there is a caviar and foie-gras menu. This—and sand between your toes—is heaven. ⊠ *Le Sereno* ☎ *0590/29–83–00* ⊕ *www.lesereno.com* ⌖ *Reservations essential.*

GRANDE SALINE

$$$ ✗ **Le Tamarin.** A leisurely lunch here en route to Grande Saline beach is a
FRENCH   St. Barth *must.* But new management makes it tops for dinner too. Sit on
★   one of the licorice-colored Javanese couches in the lounge area and nibble excellent sushi, or settle at a table under the wondrous tamarind tree for which the restaurant is named. A unique cocktail each day, ultrafresh fish provided by the restaurant's designated fisherman, and gentle prices accommodate local residents as well as the holiday crowd. The restaurant is open year-round. ⊠ *Grande Saline* ☎ *0590/27–72–12* ☉ *Closed Tues.*

$$$ ✗ **PaCri.** An adorable young husband-and-wife team (she is the chef)
ITALIAN   serve delicious, huge portions of house-made pasta, wood-oven pizza (at lunch only), and authentic Italian main courses, including chicken Milanese, on a breezy open terrace right near Saline Beach. The menu—handwritten on a chalkboard—changes daily. Don't miss the softball size hunk of the best artisanal mozzarella you've ever had, flown in from Italy and garnished with prosciutto or tomato and basil. The eggplant Parmesan appetizer is delicious and more than enough for a meal. Like the pastas, the bread and the desserts are made in-house, and *Torta al ciocolato di Cristina* (Cristina's chocolate cake) is only one of the winners. Gorgeous waitstaff of both sexes add to the general air of voluptuousness. ⊠ *Rte. de Saline* ☎ *0590/29–35–63* ⊕ *www.pacristbarth.com* ⌖ *Reservations essential.*

GUSTAVIA

$$$ ✗ **B4.** Pronounced *before,* this newcomer in 2009 occupies the central
FRENCH   former location of longtime St. Barth mainstay Le Sapotillier. Offering lighter French cuisine (scallop sashimi, citrus duck, sole meunière, simply prepared turbot) in one half, and a lounge with music, bar, and flat-screen TVs in the other, it's designed to fill up the pocket time after dinner and *before* you head to your other late-night activities. ⊠ *13 rue Samuel Fahlberg* ☎ *590/52–45–31.*

$$$ ✗ **Bonito.** The former Mandala space has been completely transformed
LATIN AMERICAN   into a chic beach house, with big, white, canvas couches in the center, tables around the sides, an open kitchen, and three bar areas. The young Venezuelan owners go to great lengths to see that guests are having as much fun as they are. There is a ceviche bar with eight different varieties, not to mention combos that are prettily arrayed on poured-glass platters for culinary experimentation. Try octopus and shrimp, or wahoo garnished with sweet potatoes and popcorn. Traditionalists might like the fricassee of escargots, or foie gras served with mango, soy, and preserved lemon. Carnivores will love the Angus steaks. ⊠ *Rue Loubin Brin* ☎ *590/27–96–96* ⊕ *www.ilovebonito.com* ⌖ *Reservations essential* ☉ *Closed Mon. No lunch.*

19

$$$ ✕ **Do Brazil**. This restaurant is open every day for breakfast, lunch, and
ECLECTIC dinner, and offers live music for sundown cocktail hour on Thursday,
Friday, and Saturday evenings, as well as top DJs spinning the latest club
mixes for the evening events that are listed in the local papers. Right
on Gustavia's Shell Beach, you'll find tasty light fare like chilled soups,
fruit-garnished salads with tuna, shrimp, and chicken, plus sandwiches,
burgers, pastas, and grilled fresh fish for lunch. At dinner there is also a
€29 three-course prix fixe with a dozen choices, including lobster pasta,
steaks, ribs, and some of the lunchtime soups and salads, that can help
keep the bill in line. The extensive cocktail menu tempts, but at €12
each, your bar bill can quickly exceed the price of dinner. ⊠ *Shell Beach*
☎ *0590/29–06–66* ⊕ *www.dobrazil.com.*

$$$ ✕ **Eddy's**. By local standards, dinner in the pretty, open-air, tropical gar-
PAN-ASIAN den here is reasonably priced. The cooking is French-creole-Asian. Fish
specialties, especially the sushi tuna sampler, are fresh and delicious, and
there are always plenty of notable daily specials. Just remember some
mosquito repellent for your ankles. ⊠ *Rue du Centenaire* ☎ *0590/27–
54–17* ⌂ *Reservations not accepted* ۞ *Closed Sun. No lunch.*

$$$$ ✕ **La Marine**. This St. Barth harborside classic is run by Carole Gruson,
SEAFOOD who has created a spiffy decor to match and meld into her hot next-
door nightclub, Le Yacht Club (which, despite the ads, is not really
"private"). The traditional Thursday- and Friday-night mussels for €25
are always a hit, along with lots of other seafood choices. Tuesday is
Caribbean barbecue night, featuring all-you-can-eat grilled spiny lobster
along with ribs, side dishes, and desserts. It's a good choice for lunch,
too. ⊠ *Rue Jeanne d'Arc* ☎ *0590/27–68–91* ⊕ *www.caroleplaces.com.*

$$$ ✕ **Le Palace**. Tucked into a tropical garden, this popular in-town restaurant
CARIBBEAN known for its barbecued ribs, beef fillet, and rack of lamb is consistently
one of our absolute favorites. Fish-market specialties like red snapper
cooked in a banana leaf or grilled tuna are good here, as are grilled duck
with mushroom sauce and a skewered surf-and-turf with a green curry
sauce. The blackboard lists daily specials that are usually a great choice,
like a salad of tomato, mango, and basil. Pierrot, the friendly owner, is
sure to take good care of you. ⊠ *Rue Général-de-Gaulle* ☎ *0590/27–53–
20* ⌂ *Reservations essential* ۞ *Closed Sun. and mid-June–July.*

$$ ✕ **Le Repaire**. This friendly brasserie overlooks Gustavia's harbor, and
ECLECTIC is a popular spot from its opening at noon to its late-night closing. The
☾ flexible hours are great if you arrive midafternoon and need a substantial snack before dinner. Grab a cappuccino, pull a captain's chair up
to the street-side rail, and watch the pretty girls. The menu ranges from
cheeseburgers, which are served only at lunch along with the island's
best fries, to simply grilled fish and meat, pastas, and risottos. The composed salads always please. Wonderful ice-cream sundaes round out the
menu. ⊠ *Quai de la République* ☎ *0590/27–72–48.*

$$$ ✕ **L'Isola**. St. Barth's chic sister to the Santa Monica (California) favorite,
ITALIAN Via Veneto, is packing in happy guests for Italian classic dishes, dozens
of house-made pasta dishes, prime meats, and the huge, well-chosen
wine list. Restaurateur Fabrizio Bianconi wants it all to feel like a big
Italian party, and with all the celebrating you can hear at dinner, it sure

sounds like success. ⊠ *Rue du roi Oscar II* ☎ *590/51–00–05* ⊕ *www. lisolastbarth.com* ⚔ *Reservations essential* ☾ *Closed Sept. and Oct.*

$$$$
FRENCH

✕ **Maya's.** New Englander Randy Gurley and his wife Maya (the French-born chef) provide a warm welcome and a very pleasant dinner on their cheerful dock decorated with big, round tables and crayon-colored canvas chairs, all overlooking Gustavia Harbor. A market-inspired menu of good, simply prepared and garnished dishes like mahimahi in creole sauce, shrimp scampi, and pepper-marinated beef fillet changes daily, assuring the ongoing popularity of a restaurant that seems to be on everyone's list of favorites. ⊠ *Public* ☎ *0590/27–75–73* ⊕ *www.mayasstbarth.com* ⚔ *Reservations essential.*

$$$
ECLECTIC

✕ **Wall House.** The food is excellent—and the service is always friendly—at this restaurant on the far side of Gustavia Harbor. The snail and spinach ravioli are out of this world, and the rotisserie duck marinated in honey from the rotisserie is a universal favorite. Local business-people crowd the restaurant for the bargain €10.50 prix-fixe lunch menu. An old-fashioned dessert trolley showcases some really yummy sweets. ⊠ *La Pointe* ☎ *0590/27–71–83* ⊕ *www.wallhouserestaurant. com* ⚔ *Reservations essential* ☾ *Closed Sun. and Sept. and Oct.*

POINTE MILOU

$$$$
ECLECTIC
Fodor's Choice
★

✕ **Le Ti St. Barth Caribbean Tavern.** Chef-owner Carole Gruson captures the funky, sexy spirit of the island in her wildly popular hilltop hot spot. We always come here to dance to great music with the attractive crowd lingering at the bar, lounge at one of the pillow-strewn banquettes, or chat on the torch-lighted terrace. By the time your appetizers arrive, you'll be best friends with the next table. The menu includes Thai beef salad, lobster ceviche, rare grilled tuna with Chinese noodles, and the best beef on the island. Provocatively named desserts, such as Nymph Thighs (airy lemon cake with vanilla custard) and Daddy's Balls (passion-fruit sorbet and ice cream) end the meal on a fun note. Around this time someone is sure to be dancing on top of the tables. There's an extensive wine list. The famously raucous full-moon parties are legendary. ⊠ *Pointe Milou* ☎ *0590/27 97–71* ⊕ *www.letistbarth. com* ⚔ *Reservations essential.*

19

WHERE TO STAY

There's no denying that hotel rooms and villas on St. Barth carry high prices. You're paying primarily for the privilege of staying on the island, and even at $800 a night the bedrooms tend to be small. Still, if you're flexible—in terms of timing and in your choice of lodgings—you can enjoy a holiday in St. Barth and still afford to send the kids to college.

The most expensive season falls during the holidays (mid-December to early January), when hotels are booked far in advance, may require a 10- or 14-day stay, and can be double the high-season rates. At this writing, some properties are reconsidering minimum stays, and there are concessions to the current *crise* (economic downturn). A 5% govern-

St. Barth's Spas

Visitors to St. Barth can enjoy more than the comforts of home by taking advantage of any of the myriad spa and beauty treatments that are available on the island. Three major hotels, the Isle de France, the Guanahani, and the Carl Gustav, have beautiful, comprehensive, on-site spas. Others, including the Hôtel le Village St-Jean and Le Toiny, have added spa cottages, where treatments and services can be arranged on-site. Depending on availability, all visitors to the island can book services at all of these. In addition, scores of independent therapists will come to your hotel room or villa and provide any therapeutic discipline you can think of, including yoga, Thai massage, shiatsu, reflexology, and even manicures, pedicures, and hairdressing. You can find current therapists listed in the local guide, *Ti Gourmet*, or get up-to-date recommendations at the tourist office in Gustavia.

ment tourism tax on room prices (excluding breakfast) went into effect in 2008; be sure to ask if it is included in your room rate or added on.

When it comes to booking a hotel on St. Barth, the reservation manager can be your best ally. Rooms within a property can vary greatly. It's well worth the price of a phone call or the time investment of an email correspondence to make a personal connection, which can mean a lot when it comes to arranging a room that meets your needs or preferences. Details of accessibility, views, recent redecorating, meal options, and special package rates are topics open for discussion. Most quoted hotel rates are per room, not per person, and include service charges and airport transfers.

VILLAS AND CONDOMINIUMS

On St. Barth, the term *villa* is used to describe anything from a small cottage to a luxurious, modern estate. Today almost half of St. Barth's accommodations are in villas, and we recommend considering this option, especially if you're traveling with friends or family. Ever more advantageous to Americans, villa rates are usually quoted in dollars, thus bypassing unfavorable euro fluctuations. Most villas have a small private swimming pool and maid service daily except Sunday. They are well furnished with linens, kitchen utensils, and such electronic playthings as CD and DVD players, satellite TV, and broadband Internet. Weekly in-season rates range from $1,400 to "oh-my-gosh." Most villa-rental companies are based in the United States and have extensive Web sites that allow you to see pictures of the place you're renting; their local offices oversee maintenance and housekeeping and provide concierge services to clients. Just be aware that there are few beachfront villas, so if you have your heart set on "toes in the sand" and a cute waiter delivering your Kir royale, stick with the hotels or villas operated by hotel properties.

VILLA RENTAL COMPANIES

Marla (☎ 0590/27–62–02 ⊕ *www.marlavillas.com*) is a local St. Barth villa-rental company that represents more than 100 villas, many of which are not listed with other companies. **St. Barth Properties, Inc.**

(☎ *508/528–7727 or 800/421–3396 ⊕ www.stbarth.com*), owned by American Peg Walsh—a regular on St. Barth since 1986—represents more than 120 properties here and can guide you to the perfect place to stay. Weekly peak-season rates range from $1,400 to $40,000, depending on the property's size, location, and amenities. The excellent Web site offers virtual tours of most of the villas and even details of availability. An office in Gustavia can take care of any problems you may have and offers some concierge-type services. **Wimco** (☎ *800/932–3222 ⊕ www. wimco.com*), which is based in Rhode Island, oversees bookings for more than 230 properties on St. Barth. Rents range from $2,000 to $10,000 for two- and three-bedroom villas; larger villas rent for $7,000 per week and up. Properties can be previewed and reserved on Wimco's Web site (which occasionally lists last-minute specials), or you can obtain a catalog by mail. The company will arrange for babysitters, massages, chefs, and other in-villa services for clients, as well as private air charters.

The following reviews have been condensed for this book. Please go to Fodors.com for expanded reviews of each property.

ANSE DE TOINY

$$$$
HOTEL
Fodor'sChoice
★

Hôtel Le Toiny. When perfection is more important than price, choose Le Toiny's romantic villas with mahogany furniture and divine white linens with crisp, colorful, striped accents, all new in 2008. **Pros:** extremely private; luxurious rooms; flawless service; environmental awareness. **Cons:** not on the beach; isolated (at least half an hour's drive from town). ⊠ *Anse de Toiny* ☎ *0590/27–88–88 ⊕ www.letoiny. com* ➫ *14 1-bedroom villas, 1 3-bedroom villa* ⚥ *In-room: a/c, safe, kitchen, Wi-Fi. In-hotel: restaurant, bar, pools* ☻ *Closed Sept.–late Oct.* ⏏ *Breakfast.*

19

COLOMBIER

$
HOTEL

Le P'tit Morne. Each of the modestly furnished but freshly decorated and painted mountainside studios has a private balcony with panoramic views of the coastline. **Pros:** reasonable rates; great area for hiking. **Cons:** rooms are basic; remote location. ⊠ *Box 14, Colombier 97133* ☎ *0590/52–95–50 ⊕ www.timorne.com* ➫ *14 rooms* ⚥ *In-room: a/c, kitchen. In-hotel: pool* ⏏ *Breakfast.*

FLAMANDS

$–$$
HOTEL
☙
★

Hôtel Baie des Anges. Everyone is treated like family at this casual retreat. **Pros:** on St. Barth's longest beach; family-friendly; excellent value. **Cons:** the area is a bit remote from the town areas, necessitating a car. ⊠ *Anse des Flamands* ☎ *0590/27–63–61 ⊕ www.hotelbaiedesanges. fr* ➫ *10 rooms* ⚥ *In-room: a/c, safe, kitchen. In-hotel: restaurant, pool* ☻ *Closed Sept.* ⏏ *No meals.*

$$$$
RESORT
Fodor'sChoice
★

Hotel St-Barth Isle de France. An obsessively attentive management team ensures that this intimate, casually refined resort remains among the very best accommodations in St. Barth—if not the entire Caribbean. **Pros:** prime beach location; terrific management; great spa; excellent

Hotel Guanahani and Spa, Grand Cul de Sac.

restaurant. **Cons:** garden rooms—though large—can be dark; unfortunately, the day will come when you will have to leave this paradise. ✉ *B.P. 612 Baie des Flamands* ☎ *0590/27–61–81* ⊕ *www.isle-de-france. com* ↳ *32 rooms, 2 villas* ⚐ *In-room: a/c, Internet, Wi-Fi. In-hotel: restaurant, tennis court, bar, pools, gym, spa, water sports* ☉ *Closed Sept.–mid-Oct.* ⊚ *Breakfast.*

GRAND CUL DE SAC

$$$$ ☷ **Hotel Guanahani and Spa.** The largest full-service resort on the island
RESORT has lovely rooms and suites (14 of which have private pools) and
☖ impeccable personalized service, not to mention one of the island's
Fodor'sChoice only children's programs (though it's more of a nursery). **Pros:** fantastic
★ spa; beachside sports; family-friendly; great service. **Cons:** lots of cats;
steep walk to beach. ✉ *Grand Cul de Sac* ☎ *0590/27–66–60* ⊕ *www. leguanahani.com* ↳ *33 rooms, 28 suites, 1 3-bedroom villa* ⚐ *In-room: a/c, Wi-Fi. In-hotel: restaurants, tennis courts, bar, children's programs, pools, spa, water sports* ☉ *Closed Sept.* ⊚ *Breakfast.*

$$$$ ☷ **Le Sereno.** A St. Barth classic on a beautiful stretch of beach was
RESORT reborn as a sexy, ultrachic retreat in 2005 (designed by Parisian archi-
Fodor'sChoice tect Christian Liaigre). **Pros:** romantic rooms; beach location; superchic
★ comfort; fun atmosphere. **Cons:** no a/c in bathrooms; lots of construction planned for this part of the island over next few years. ✉ *B.P. 19 Grand-Cul-de-Sac* ☎ *0590/29–83–00* ⊕ *www.lesereno.com* ↳ *37 suites and villas* ⚐ *In-room: a/c, safe, Wi-Fi. In-hotel: restaurant, bar, pool, gym, water sports* ⊚ *No meals.*

Le Sereno, Grand Cul de Sac.

GRANDE SALINE

¢–$
VACATION
RENTAL

🏠 **Salines Garden Cottages**. Budget-conscious beach lovers need look no further than these small garden cottages, a short stroll from what is arguably St. Barth's best beach. **Pros:** only property walkable to Salines Beach; quiet; reasonable rates. **Cons:** far from town; not very private. ⊠ *Grand Saline* 🕿 *0590/51-04-44* ⊕ *www.salinesgarden.com* 🛏 *5 cottages* ⚐ *In-room: a/c, safe, kitchen (some), Wi-Fi. In-hotel: bar, pool* ☉ *Closed mid-Aug.–mid-Oct.* ¶❍¶ *Breakfast.*

19

GUSTAVIA

¢¢¢¢
HOTEL
Fodor'sChoice
★

🏠 **Carl Gustaf**. This sophisticated hotel right in Gustavia received a welcome overhaul in 2006, and its new incarnation is the last word in luxury. **Pros:** luxurious decor; in-town location; loads of in-room gadgets; excellent restaurant; beautiful spa. **Cons:** not on the beach; outdoor space limited to your private plunge pool. ⊠ *Rue des Normands, Box 700, Gustavia* 🕿 *0590/29-79-00* ⊕ *www.hotelcarlgustaf.com* 🛏 *14 suites* ⚐ *In-room: a/c, kitchen, Wi-Fi. In-hotel: restaurant, bar, pool, gym, parking* ☉ *Closed May–Oct.* ¶❍¶ *Breakfast.*

¢
HOTEL

🏠 **Sunset Hotel**. Ten simple, utilitarian rooms (one can accommodate three people) right in Gustavia sit across from the harbor and offer an economical and handy, if not luxurious, accommodation option for those who want to stay in town. **Pros:** reasonable rates; in town. **Cons:** no elevator; not resortlike in any way. ⊠ *Rue de la Républic* 🕿 *590/27-77-21* ⊕ *www.saint-barths.com/sunset-hotel/* 🛏 *10 rooms* ⚐ *In-room: a/c, safe, Wi-Fi (some)* ¶❍¶ *No meals.*

LORIENT

$$$$
HOTEL

Hotel La Banane. A young vibe and a sociable attitude attract chic visitors to the nine smallish pavilion rooms with Euro-style contemporary furnishings, white-draped four-poster beds, and pale aqua walls. **Pros:** short walk to beach; friendly and social atmosphere at pool areas; great baths. **Cons:** rooms are small; location of entrance through parking lot is not attractive. ⊠ *Lorient* ☎ *0590/52–03–00* ⊕ *www.labanane. com* ⟟ *9 rooms* ⅄ *In-room: a/c, Wi-Fi. In-hotel: restaurant, bar, pools* ⊙ *Closed Sept.–Oct. 15* ¶O¶ *Breakfast.*

$
B&B/INN
★

Le Normandie. Wendy and Dennis Carlton, longtime St. Barth visitors, have renovated this eight-room inn in a Euro-meets-nautical theme, reflecting the eponymous art-deco ocean liner. **Pros:** friendly management; pleasant atmosphere; good value. **Cons:** tiny rooms. ⊠ *Lorient* ☎ *0590/27–61–66* ⊕ *www.normandiehotelstbarts.com* ⟟ *8 rooms (7 double, 1 single)* ⅄ *In-room: a/c, Wi-Fi. In-hotel: bar, pool* ¶O¶ *Breakfast.*

¢–$
RENTAL
☾

Les Mouettes. This guesthouse offers clean, simply furnished, and economical bungalows that open directly onto the beach. **Pros:** right on the beach; family-friendly. **Cons:** rooms are basic; right near the road; takes only cash. ⊠ *Lorient Beach* ☎ *0590/27–77–91* ⊕ *www.st-barths. com/hotel-les-mouettes* ⟟ *7 bungalows* ⅄ *In-room: a/c, kitchen. In-hotel: beach* ▭ *No credit cards* ¶O¶ *No meals.*

POINTE MILOU

$$–$$$$
RESORT
☾

Christopher. This longtime St. Barth favorite of European families underwent a thoughtful and stylish transformation in 2009. **Pros:** comfortable elegance; family-friendly; reasonable price; updated rooms. **Cons:** resort is directly on the water but not on a beach. ⊠ *Pointe Milou* ☎ *590/27–63–63* ⊕ *www.hotelchristopher.com* ⟟ *41 rooms* ⅄ *In-room: a/c, safe, Internet (some), Wi-Fi. In-hotel: restaurants, bars, pool, gym, spa, business center, water sports, parking, some pets allowed* ⊙ *Closed Sept.–mid-Oct.* ¶O¶ *Breakfast.*

ST-JEAN

$$$$
RESORT
☾
Fodor's Choice
★

Eden Rock. St. Barth's first hotel opened in the 1950s on the craggy bluff that splits Baie de St-Jean. Extensive renovations and an expansion in 2005 raised it into the top category of St. Barth properties. **Pros:** chic clientele; beach setting; can walk to shopping and restaurants. **Cons:** some suites are noisy because of proximity to street. ⊠ *Baie de St-Jean* ☎ *0590/29–79–99, 877/563–7015 in U.S.* ⊕ *www.edenrockhotel.com* ⟟ *32 rooms, 2 villas* ⅄ *In-room: a/c, Internet. In-hotel: restaurants, bars, pool, water sports* ¶O¶ *Breakfast.*

$$$–$$$$
HOTEL
☾
★

Emeraude Plage. Right on the beach of Baie de St-Jean, this petite resort consists of small but immaculate bungalows and villas with modern, fully equipped outdoor kitchenettes on small patios; nice bathrooms add to the comfort. **Pros:** beachfront and in-town location; good value; cool kitchens on each porch. **Cons:** smallish rooms. ⊠ *Baie de St-Jean* ☎ *0590/27–64–78* ⊕ *www.emeraudeplage.com* ⟟ *28 bungalows* ⅄ *In-room: a/c, safe, kitchen, Wi-Fi. In-hotel: restaurant, bar, beach* ⊙ *Closed Sept.–mid-Oct.* ¶O¶ *No meals.*

Eden Rock, St-Jean

$-$$
HOTEL
Fodor's Choice
★

☒ **Hôtel le Village St-Jean.** For two generations, the Charneau family has offered friendly service and reasonable rates at its small hotel, making guests feel like a part of the family. Recent upgrades have raised the bar, but not the prices. **Pros:** great value; convenient location; wonderful management. **Cons:** somewhat old-fashioned; can be noisy, depending on how close your room is to the street below. ⌂ *Box 623, Baie de St-Jean 97133*☎*0590/27–61–39 or 800/651–8366* ⊕*www. villagestjeanhotel.com* ⇆*5 rooms, 20 cottages, 1 3-bedroom villa, 2 2-bedroom villas* ⚬ *In-room: a/c, kitchen (some), no TV. In-hotel: restaurant, bar, pool, spa* ⓧ*No meals.*

$$$-$$$$
RENTAL
🄲

☒ **Les Îlets de la Plage.** On the far side of the airport, tucked away at the far corner of Baie de St-Jean, these well-priced, comfortably furnished island-style one-, two-, and three-bedroom bungalows (four right on the beach, seven up a small hill) have small kitchens, pleasant open-air sitting areas, and comfortable bathrooms. **Pros:** beach location; apartment conveniences; front porches. **Cons:** no a/c outside bedrooms; right next to the airport. ⊠ *Plage de St-Jean* ☎ *0590/27–88–57* ⊕ *www.lesilets. com* ⇆ *11 bungalows* ⚬ *In-room: a/c, safe, kitchen, Wi-Fi. In-hotel: pool, gym, beach, business center* ☻ *Closed Sept.–Nov. 1* ⓧ *No meals.*

$$$-$$$$
HOTEL

☒ **Le Tom Beach Hôtel.** This chic but casual boutique hotel right on busy St-Jean beach is fun for social types, and the nonstop house party often spills out onto the terraces and lasts into the wee hours. **Pros:** party central at beach, restaurant, and pool; in-town location. **Cons:** trendy social scene is not for everybody, especially light sleepers. ⊠ *Plage de St-Jean* ☎ *0590/27–53–13* ⊕ *www.st-barths.com/tom-beach-hotel* ⇆ *12 rooms* ⚬ *In-room: a/c, safe, Wi-Fi. In-hotel: restaurant, bar, pool, beach* ⓧ *Breakfast.*

VITET

$
B&B/INN

Hostellerie des Trois Forces. For the young, the spiritual, and the cost-conscious, a respite at one of the seven tiny bungalows at the very top of the highest peak on the island at this so-called "New Age Inn" might be your karmic destiny. **Pros:** far from the hustle and bustle of cosmopolitan St. Barth. **Cons:** remote and a tough drive up the mountain (rent a four-wheel-drive vehicle); rooms and baths are clean but basic. ⊠ *Vitet* ☎ *590/27–61–25* ⊕ *www.3forces.net* ⤺*7 rooms* ⚘ *In-room: a/c, no phone, safe (some), kitchen (some), no TV. In-hotel: restaurant, pool, parking, some pets allowed* ⍾ *No meals.*

NIGHTLIFE

Most of the nightlife in St. Barth is centered in Gustavia, though there are a few places to go outside of town. "In" clubs change from season to season, so you might ask around for the hot spot of the moment. There's more nightlife than ever in recent memory, and a late (10 pm or later) reservation at one of the club-restaurants will eventually become a front-row seat at a party. *Saint-Barth Leisures* contains current information about sports, spas, nightlife, and the arts.

GUSTAVIA

Bar de l'Oubli. This is where young locals gather for drinks. ⊠ *Rue du Roi Oscar II, Gustavia* ☎ *0590/27–70–06.*

Carl Gustaf. This hotel lures a more sedate crowd, namely those in search of quiet conversation and sunset watching. ⊠ *Rue des Normands, Gustavia* ☎ *0590/27–82–83.*

Le Repaire. This restaurant lures a crowd for cocktail hour and its pool table. ⊠ *Rue de la République, Gustavia* ☎ *0590/27–72–48.*

Le Sélect. This is St. Barth's original hangout, commemorated by Jimmy Buffett's "Cheeseburger in Paradise." The boisterous garden is where the barefoot boating set gathers for a brew. ⊠ *Rue du Centenaire, Gustavia* ☎ *0590/27–86–87.*

Le Yacht Club. At this writing, the hot spot in St. Barth is Le Yacht Club; although ads call it a private club, you can probably get in anyway. ⊠ *Rue Jeanne d'Arc, Gustavia* ☎ *0690/49–23–33.*

ST-JEAN

Le Nikki Beach. This place rocks on weekends during lunch, when the scantily clad young and beautiful lounge on the white canvas banquettes. ⊠ *St-Jean* ☎ *0590/27-64-64* ⊕ *www.nikkibeach.com.*

SHOPPING

Fodor'sChoice
★
St. Barth is a duty-free port, and with its sophisticated crowd of visitors, shopping in the island's 200-plus boutiques is a definite delight, especially for beachwear, accessories, jewelry, and casual wear. It would be no overstatement to say that shopping for fashionable clothing, accessories, and decorative items for the home is better in St. Barth than anywhere else in the Caribbean. New shops open all the time, so there's always something new to discover. Stores often close for lunch from noon to 2, and many on Wednesday afternoon as well, but they are open until about 7 in the evening. A popular afternoon pastime is strolling about the two major shopping areas in Gustavia and St-Jean.

In Gustavia, boutiques line the three major shopping streets. Quai de la République, which is right on the harbor, rivals New York's Madison Avenue or Paris's avenue Montaigne for high-end designer retail, including shops for **Louis Vuitton, Bulgari, Cartier, Chopard,** and **Hermès.** These shops often carry items that are not available in the United States. The Carré d'Or plaza is great fun to explore. Shops are also clustered in **La Savane Commercial Center** (across from the airport), **La Villa Créole** (in St-Jean), and **Espace Neptune** (on the road to Lorient). It's worth working your way from one end to the other at these shopping complexes—just to see or, perhaps, be seen. Boutiques in all three areas carry the latest in French and Italian sportswear and some haute couture. Bargains may be tough to come by, but you might be able to snag that *pochette* that is sold out stateside, and in any case, you'll have a lot of fun hunting around.

Shopping for up-to-the-minute fashions is as much a part of a visit to St. Barth as going to the beach. Shops change all the time, both in ownership and in the lines that are carried. Current listings are just a general guide. The best advice is simply to go for a long stroll and check out all the shops on the way.

If you are looking for locally made art and handicrafts, call the tourist office, which can provide information about the studios of some of the island artists, including Christian Bretoneiche, Robert Danet, Nathalie Daniel, Patricia Guyot, Rose Lemen, Aline de Lurin, and Marion Vinot.

19

GUSTAVIA

CLOTHING

Black Swan. Black Swan has an unparalleled selection of bathing suits. The wide range of styles and sizes is appreciated. ⊠ *Le Carré d'Or, Gustavia.*

Blanc Bleu. This boutique carries classy and comfortable linen and cotton separates for men, women, and kids, mostly in white, blue, and a wonderful soft gray. There are also outposts in St-Jean and at Le Sereno hotel. ⊠ *Gustavia Harbor, Gustavia* ☎ *590/27–99–53.*

Boutique Lacoste. This store has a huge selection of the once-again-chic alligator-logo wear, as well as a shop next door with a complete selection of the Petit Bateau line of T-shirts popular with teens. ⊠ *Rue Du Bord de Mer, Gustavia* ☎ *0590/27–66–90.*

Café Coton. Café Coton is a great shop for men, especially for long-sleeve linen shirts in a rainbow of colors and Egyptian cotton dress shirts. ⊠ *Rue du Bord du Mer, Gustavia* ☎ *0590/52–48–42.*

Calypso. Calypso carries sexy resort wear that fits the island sensibility. ⊠ *Le Carré d'Or, Gustavia* ☎ *0590/27–95–82.*

EuroPann. EuroPann has tailored linen shirts for men in a rainbow of soft colors, and soft slip-on driving mocs in classic styles are a St. Barth must. ⊠ *Rue Lafayette, Gustavia* ☎ *0590/27–54–26.*

Hermès. The Hermès store in St. Barth is an independently owned franchise, and prices are slightly below those in the States. ⊠ *Rue de la République, Gustavia* ☎ *0590/27–66–15.*

jee's. Jee's is an excellent source if you are looking for accessories. ⊠ *Rue Samuel Fahlberg, Gustavia* ☎ *No phone.*

Kokon. Kokon offers a nicely edited mix of designs for on-island or off, including the bo'em, Lotty B. Mustique, and Day Birger lines, and cute shoes to go with them by Heidi Klum for Birkenstock. ⊠ *Rue Fahlberg, Gustavia* ☎ *0590/29–74–48.*

Linde Gallery. Linde sells vintage sunglasses, accessories, vintage ready-to-wear from the 1970s and '80s, as well as books, CDs, and DVDs. ⊠ *Les Hauts de Carré d'Or, Gustavia* ☎ *590/29–73–86* ⊕ *www.lindegallery.com.*

Lolita Jaca. Don't miss this store for trendy, tailored sportswear. ⊠ *Le Carré d'Or, Gustavia* ☎ *0590/27–59–98* ⊕ *www.lolitajaca.com.*

Longchamp. Fans of the popular travel bags, handbags, and leather goods will find a good selection at about 20% off stateside prices. ⊠ *Le Carré d'Or, Gustavia* ☎ *0590/52–00–94.*

Made in Saint Barth. This is the largest of the three shops that stock the chic, locally made T-shirts, totes, and beach wraps that have practically become the logo of St. Barth. The newest styles have hand-done graffiti-style lettering. The shop also has some handicrafts, and other giftable items. ⊠ *Rue Du Bord de Mer, Gustavia* ☎ *0590/29–78–04* ⊕ *www.madeinstbarth.com.*

Poupette. All the brilliant color-crinkle silk and chiffon batik and embroidered peasant skirts and tops are designed by the owner. There also are great belts and beaded bracelets. ⊠ *Rue de la République, Gustavia* ☎ *0590/27–94–49* ⊕ *www.poupette-st-barth.com.*

Saint-Barth Stock Exchange. On the far side of Gustavia Harbor is the island's consignment and discount shop. ⊠ *La Pointe-Gustavia, Gustavia* ☎ *0590/27–68–12.*

Stéphane & Bernard. This store stocks a well-edited, large selection of superstar French fashion designers, including Rykiel, Tarlazzi, Kenzo,

Shops on rue de la France, Gustavia.

Féraud, and Mugler, and Eres beachwear. ⊠ *Rue de la République, Gustavia* ☎ *0590/27-65-69* ⊕ *www.stephaneandbernard.com.*

Vanita Rosa. This store showcases beautiful lace and linen sundresses and peasant tops, with accessories galore. ⊠ *Rue Oscar II, Gustavia* ☎ *0590/52-43-25* ⊕ *www.vanitarosa.com.*

FOODSTUFFS

A.M.C. This supermarket is a bit older than Match in St-Jean but able to supply anything you might need for housekeeping in a villa or for a picnic. ⊠ *Quai de la République, Gustavia.*

La Rotisserie. For exotic groceries or picnic fixings, stop by St. Barth's gourmet *traiteur* (takeout shop) for salads, prepared meats, groceries from Fauchon, and Iranian caviar. ⊠ *Rue du Roi Oscar II, Gustavia* ☎ *0590/27-63-13.*

HANDICRAFTS

Fabienne Miot. Look for unusual jewelry, including original designs and modern baubles by Tamara Comolli at this shop. ⊠ *Rue de la République, Gustavia* ☎ *0590/27-73-13.*

JEWELRY

Bijoux de la Mer. This store carries beautiful and artistic jewelry made of South Sea pearls in wonderful hues strung in clusters on leather to wrap around the neck or arms. ⊠ *Rue de la République, Gustavia* ☎ *590/52-37-68* ⊕ *www.bijouxdelamerstbarth.com.*

Carat. Carat has Chaumet and a large selection of Breitling watches. ⊠ *Quai de la République, Gustavia* ☎ *No phone.*

Donna del Sol. Next door to Cartier, Donna del Sol carries beautiful Tahitian pearl pieces, and baubles in multicolor diamonds. ⊠ *Quai de la République, Gustavia* ⊕ *www.donnadelsol.com.*

Sindbad. This is a tiny shop with funky, unique couture fashion jewelry by Gaz Bijou of St-Tropez, crystal collars for your pampered pooch, chunky ebony pendants on silk cord, and other reasonably priced, up-to-the-minute styles. ⊠ *Carré d'Or, Gustavia* ☎ *0590/27–52–29.*

LORIENT

COSMETICS
Ligne de St. Barth. Don't miss the superb skin-care products made on-site from local tropical plants by this St. Barth company. ⊠ *Rte. de Saline, Lorient* ☎ *0590/27–82–63.*

FOODSTUFFS
JoJo Supermarché. JoJo is the well-stocked counterpart to Gustavia's large supermarket and gets daily deliveries of bread and fresh produce. ⊠ *Lorient.*

ST-JEAN

CLOTHING
Black Swan. Black Swan has an unparalleled selection of bathing suits. The wide range of styles and sizes is appreciated. ⊠ *La Villa Créole, St-Jean.*

Iléna. This boutique has incredible beachwear and lingerie by Chantal Thomas, Sarda, and others, including Swarovski crystal–encrusted bikinis for the young and gorgeous. ⊠ *Villa Creole, St-Jean* ☎ *0590/29–84–05.*

Lili Belle. Check out Lili Belle for a nice selection of wearable and current styles. ⊠ *Pelican Plage, St-Jean* ☎ *0590/87–46–14.*

Morgan. Morgan has a line of popular casual wear in the trendy vein. ⊠ *La Villa Créole, St-Jean* ☎ *0590/27–71–00.*

St. Tropez KIWI. Look to this popular boutique with two branches (one in Gustavia and one in St-Jean) for resort wear. ⊠ *St-Jean* ☎ *0590/27–57–08.*

SUD SUD.ETC.Plage. This store stocks everything for the beach: inflatables, mats, bags, and beachy shell jewelry. ⊠ *Galerie du Commerce, St-Jean* ☎ *0590/27–90–56.*

COSMETICS
The Beauty Spot. This boutique offers a great selection of makeup and skin-care products, sun-care products, and beauty accessories. The store will also do makeup application for events. ⊠ *La Savane Shopping Center, St-Jean* ☎ *590/51–11–75* ⊕ *www.skinsuncare.com.*

FOODSTUFFS
La Rotisserie. For exotic groceries or picnic fixings, stop by St. Barth's gourmet *traiteur* (takeout) for salads, prepared meats, groceries from Fauchon, and Iranian caviar. ⊠ *Centre Vaval, St-Jean* ☎ *0590/29–75–69.*

Match. This fully stocked supermarket across from the airport has a wide selection of French cheeses, pâtés, cured meats, produce, fresh bread, wine, and liquor. ✉ *St-Jean* ☎ *0590/27–68–16.*

Maya's to Go. This is the place to go for prepared picnics, meals, salads, rotisserie chickens, and more from the kitchens of the popular restaurant in Gustavia. ✉ *Galleries du Commerce, St-Jean* ☎ *0590/29–83–70* ⊕ *mayastogo.com.*

SPORTS AND ACTIVITIES

BOATING AND SAILING

St. Barth is a popular yachting and sailing center, thanks to its location midway between Antigua and St. Thomas. Gustavia's harbor, 13 to 16 feet deep, has mooring and docking facilities for 40 yachts. There are also good anchorages available at Public, Corossol, and Colombier. You can charter sailing and motorboats in Gustavia Harbor for as little as a half day. Stop at the tourist office in Gustavia for an up-to-the minute list of recommended charter companies.

Jicky Marine Service (✉ *Ferry dock, Gustavia* ☎ *0590/27–70–34* ⊕ *www.jickymarine.com*) offers full-day outings, either on a variety of motorboats, or 42- or 46-foot catamaran, to the uninhabited Île Fourchue for swimming, snorkeling, cocktails, and lunch. The cost starts at about $100 per person; an unskippered motor rental runs about $260 a day.

Yellow Submarine (✉ *Ferry dock, Gustavia* ☎ *0590/52–40–51* ⊕ *www. yellow-submarine.fr*) takes you "six feet under" (the surface of the sea) for a close-up view of St. Barth's coral reefs through large glass portholes. Once a week you can go at night. It costs €40. Trips depart daily in the morning and in the afternoon, but more often depending on demand, so call first.

19

DIVING AND SNORKELING

Several dive shops arrange scuba excursions to local sites. Depending on weather conditions, you may dive at **Pain de Sucre, Coco Island,** or toward nearby **Saba.** There's also an underwater shipwreck to explore, plus sharks, rays, sea tortoises, coral, and the usual varieties of colorful fish. The waters on the island's leeward side are the calmest. For the uncertified who still want to see what the island's waters hold, there's an accessible shallow reef right off the beach at Anse de Cayes that you can explore if you have your own mask and fins.

Most of the waters surrounding St. Barth are protected in the island's **Réserve Marine de St-Barth** (✉ *Gustavia* ☎ *0590/27–88–18*), which also provides information at its office in Gustavia. The diving here isn't nearly as rich as in the more dive-centered destinations like Saba and St. Eustatius, but the options aren't bad either, and none of the smaller islands offer the ambience of St. Barth.

Plongée Caraïbe (📠 *0590/27–55–94* ⊕ *www.plongee-caraibes.com*) is recommended for its up-to-the-minute equipment and dive boat.

Splash (✉ *Gustavia* ☏ *0690/56–90–24*) does scuba, snorkeling, and fishing, too.

Marine Service operates the only five-star, PADI-certified diving center on the island, called **West Indies Dive** (☏ *0590/27–70–34*). Scuba trips, packages, resort dives, night dives, and certifications start at $90, including gear.

FISHING

Most fishing is done in the waters north of Lorient, Flamands, and Corossol. Popular catches are tuna, marlin, wahoo, and barracuda. There's an annual St. Barth Open Fishing Tournament, organized by Ocean Must, in mid-July.

Jicky Marine Service (✉ *Gustavia* ☏ *0590/27–70–34* ⊕ *www.boatrentalstbarth.com/*) arranges ocean-fishing excursions.

Océan Must Marina (✉ *Gustavia* ☏ *0590/27–62–25* ⊕ *www.oceanmust.com*) arranges deep-sea fishing expeditions as well as bareboat and staffed boat charters.

GUIDED TOURS

You can arrange island tours by minibus or car at hotel desks or through any of the island's taxi operators in Gustavia or at the airport. The tourist office runs a variety of tours with varying itineraries that run about €46 for a half day for up to eight people. You can also download up-to-the-minute walking and driving tour itineraries from the Tourist Board's Web site.

Mat Nautic (✉ *Quai du Yacht Club, Gustavia* ☏ *0690/49–54–72*) can help you arrange to tour the island by water on a Jet Ski or WaveRunner.

St-Barth Tours & Travel (✉ *Rue Jeanne d'Arc, Gustavia* ☏ *0590/27–52–14*) will customize a tour of the island.

Wish Agency (☏ *0590/29–83–74* ✎ *wishagency@saint-barths.com*) can arrange customized tours as well as take care of airline ticketing, event planning, maid service, and private party arrangements.

St. Eustatius

WORD OF MOUTH

"Ever considered Saint Eustatius? A real Caribbean island. No high-rise buildings. You [can] get there from St. Martin with an 18-minute flight. A real gem!"

—pechtold

WELCOME TO ST. EUSTATIUS

FRIENDLY TRANQUILLITY

A tiny part of the Dutch Caribbean, St. Eustatius (often just called "Statia") is just under 12 square mi (30 square km), making it twice as large as Saba. The island, which is 38 mi (63 km) south of St. Maarten, has a population of 3,400. Although there are three beaches, they are better for strolling than swimming.

Boven Bay

Cocoluch Bay

Jenkins Bay

Boven

Little Mountain

Tumble Down Dick Bay

Signal Hill

Interlopers Pt. ◆ **Ft. Royal**

Stenara ◢
Reef

Smoke Alley Beach (Oranje Beach)

Hotels ▼
Country Inn **1**
Statia Lodge **2**

Gallows Bay

◢
Double Wreck

Crooks ◢
Castle

KEY	
➤	*Beaches*
◢	*Dive Sites*
🌴	*Rain Forest*
①	*Hotels*

Barracuda Reef ◢

Like Saba, tiny Statia is a quiet Caribbean haven for scuba divers and hikers. When the island was called the Emporium of the Western World, warehouses stretched for miles along the quays, and 200 merchant ships could anchor at its docks. These days it's the day-trippers from St. Martin who walk the quays.

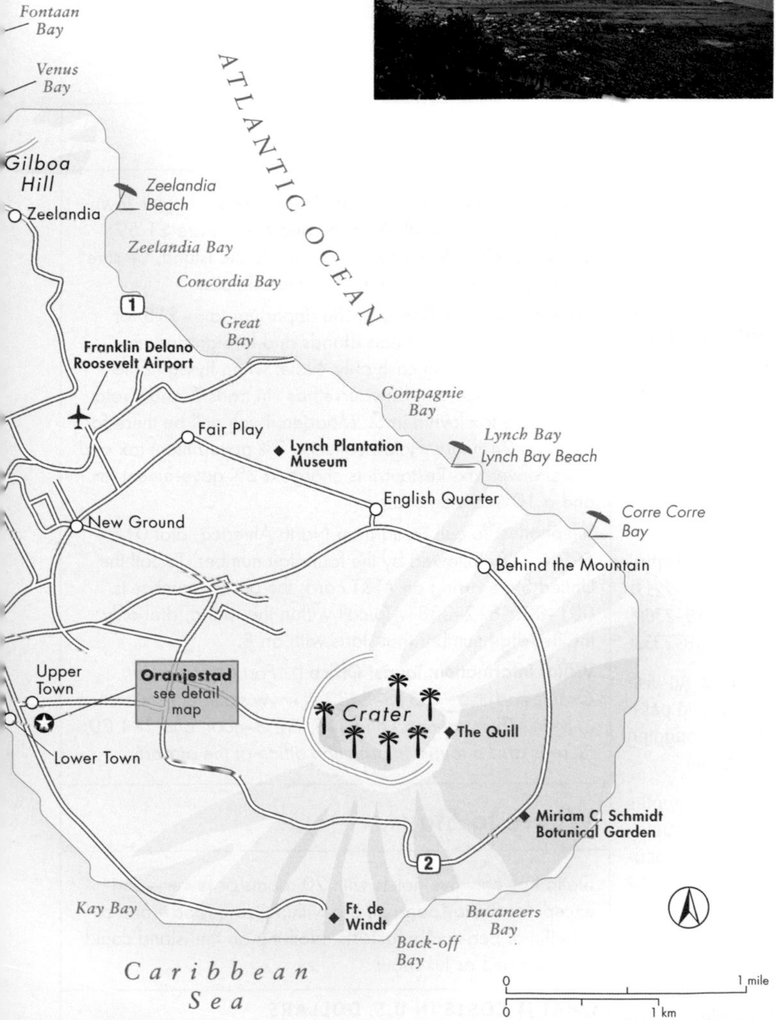

Fontaan
Bay

Venus
Bay

*Gilboa
Hill*
○ Zeelandia

ATLANTIC OCEAN

Zeelandia
Beach

Zeelandia Bay

Concordia Bay

[1]

*Great
Bay*

**Franklin Delano
Roosevelt Airport**

Fair Play

◆ **Lynch Plantation
Museum**

*Compagnie
Bay*

Lynch Bay
Lynch Bay Beach

○ New Ground

English Quarter

Corre Corre
Bay

○ Behind the Mountain

Upper
Town

Oranjestad
see detail
map

Crater

◆ The Quill

Lower Town

◆ Miriam C. Schmidt
Botanical Garden

[2]

Kay Bay

◆ **Ft. de
Windt**

*Bucaneers
Bay*

*Back-off
Bay*

*C a r i b b e a n
S e a*

0 ——— 1 mile
0 ——— 1 km

ST. EUSTATIUS

20

TOP REASONS TO VISIT ST. EUSTATIUS

1 Diving: Diving—particularly to its modern and archaeological wrecks—is a highlight in Statia's protected waters.

2 Hiking: Hiking the Quill, an extinct volcano that holds a primeval rain forest, is the top activity for landlubbers.

3 Welcoming: When you're not diving, you'll be overwhelmed by the genuine friendliness of the people.

4 History: For anyone interested in 18th-century history, even a day trip from St. Maarten is a satisfying experience.

ST. EUSTATIUS

Fast Facts

Banks and Currency Exchange: As of January 1, 2011 the U.S. dollar is the legal tender, replacing the Dutch Caribbean guilder (NAf or ANG). **First Caribbean International Bank** (☎ 599/318-2392) in Upper Town provides exchange services. There is an ATM at **Windward Islands Bank** (☎ 599/318-2846 or 599/318-2847), as well as exchange services.

Emergency Services: Ambulance (☎ 912 or 599/318-2211). **Fire** (☎ 913 or 599/318-2360). **Police** (☎ 911 or 599/318-2333).

Passports and Visas: All visitors must present a valid passport and a return or ongoing ticket for entry to Statia.

Weddings: Foreign couples must be at least 21 and Dutch nationals at least 18. Documents should be submitted 14 days before the wedding date. The application requires notarized original documents, including birth certificates, passports (for non-Dutch people), divorce decrees, and death certificates of deceased spouses. Fee is $213.

Essentials

Mail: The post office is on Ruby Hassell Road, Upper Town. Airmail letters to North America and Europe are $1.59, postcards 92¢. When sending letters to the island, be sure to include " Dutch Caribbean" in the address.

Taxes and Service Charges: The departure tax—$18 for flights to Dutch Caribbean islands and foreign destinations—is payable in cash only. Note: when flying home through St. Maarten, list yourself as "in transit" and avoid paying the tax levied in St. Maarten if you will be there for less than 24 hours. Hotels collect a 7% government tax and 3% turnover tax. Restaurants charge a 3% government tax and a 10% service charge.

Telephones: To call Statia from North America, dial 011 + 599 + 318, followed by the four-digit number. To call the United States using an AT&T card, the access number is 001–800–872–2881. To call within the island, dial only the five-digit number that starts with an 8.

Visitor Information: Tourist Office (✉ Fort Oranjestraat, Oranjestad ☎ 599/318-2433 ⊕ www.statiatourism.com ⊙ Mon.–Thurs. 8–noon and 1–5, Fri. 8–noon and 1–4:30; there is also a tourist information office at the airport).

Where to Stay

Statia has only five hotels with 20 rooms or fewer—and except for Statia Lodge all are within Oranjestad—and a handful of bed-and-breakfasts. Nothing on the island could be described as luxurious.

WHAT IT COSTS IN U.S. DOLLARS

	¢	$	$$	$$$	$$$$
Restaurants	under $8	$8–$12	$12–$20	$20–$30	over $30
Hotels	under $80	$80–$150	$150–$250	$250–$350	over $350

Restaurant prices are for a main course at dinner and include any taxes or service charges. Hotel prices are per night for a double room in high season, excluding taxes, service charges, and meal plans.

Getting to and Around St. Eustatius

Hassle Factor: Medium to High.

Nonstops: None.

Air Travel: The only way to get to Statia (EUX) is on one of the regularly scheduled **Winair** (☎ 599/318–3291, or 800/634–4907 ⊕ www.fly-winair.com) flights from Saba or St. Maarten; you'll have to book this flight yourself, directly with Winair, or online. Winair has six daily flights from St. Maarten to St. Eustatius. Flights to Statia from St. Maarten are timed to coincide with the arrival of international flights. There is no regularly scheduled ferry service. The flight from St. Maarten to Statia's **Franklin Delano Roosevelt Airport** (☎ 599/318–2620) takes 16 minutes. Reconfirm your flight, because schedules can change abruptly. The departure fee from the island is $18. If flying out of St. Maarten, check to see if the international departure fee has already been added into your airline ticket.

Car Travel: Driving in Statia is not difficult, mostly because there are not that many places to go. Street signs are not plentiful, but anyone you ask for directions will be more than happy to help you. The roads are generally in good condition. Daily rates for a car rental begin at $35.

ARC Car Rental (⊠ Oranjestad ☎ 599/318–2595). **Brown's** (⊠ White Wall Rd. 8, Oranjestad ☎ 599/318–2266). **Rainbow Car Rental** (⊠ Statia Mall, Oranjestad ☎ 599/318–2811). **Walter's** (⊠ Chapel Piece, Oranjestad ☎ 599/318–2719).

Scooters: Zipping around by scooter is another option. Scooter rentals run about $38 per day including insurance.

L.P.N. Scooter Rentals (☎ 599/318–1476).

Taxis: You could literally walk from the airport runway into town; one or two taxis are usually waiting for arriving passengers at the airport, and you'll be whisked into Oranjestad for about $8.

Island Activities

St. Eustatius's **beaches** are fairly rocky. The Caribbean side is much better suited for swimming, whereas the Atlantic side is better for walking, beachcombing, and sunning. The more interesting action is below the waves. Along with Saba, which helps to administer its dive sites as part of the Saba Marine Park, Statia is a major **diving** destination. It has good wreck diving, coral- and sponge-covered walls and pinnacles, and volcanic fissures and canyons. If you want to keep your head above water, then the Quill, Statia's extinct volcano, which holds a primeval rain forest, is well worth your time; a guided **hike** here will bring you face-to-face with all manner of exotic tropical flora and even some fauna.

Language

Statia's official language is Dutch (it's used in government documents), but everyone speaks English. Dutch is taught as the primary language in the schools, and street signs are in both Dutch and English.

20

Updated by Roberta Sotonoff

The stars are ablaze, but it's dark on the road between the Blue Bead Bar & Restaurant and the Old Gin House hotel. A chicken running across the road constitutes all the traffic, and except for the sound of crickets, there is silence. The island of St. Eustatius, commonly called Statia (pronounced *stay*-sha), is safe. How safe? The scuttlebutt is that a St. Maarten police officer sent to serve on the island thinks he is being punished because there is nothing for him to do.

With a population of almost 3,400, it's difficult for someone to commit a crime—or do most anything else—without everyone finding out. Everyone knows everyone, and that's also a blessing. Statians are friendly; they beep their horns and say hello to anyone they see. Even day-trippers are warmly welcomed as friends. There are no strangers here.

Think of this tiny Dutch Caribbean island and envision quiet times, strolls through history, and awesome diving and hiking. While many of its neighbors are pursuing the tourist business big-time, Statia just plods along. That's its charm.

During the late 18th century, the island in the Dutch Windward Triangle was a hub for commerce between Europe and the Americas. When ships carrying slaves, sugar, cotton, ammunition, and other commodities crowded its harbor, it was known as the Emporium of the Western World and the Golden Rock.

With an 11-gun salute to the American Stars and Stripes on the brig-of-war Andrew Doria on November 16, 1776, Statia's golden age ended. Statia's noteworthy role as the first country to recognize U.S. independence from Great Britain was not a gesture appreciated by the British. In 1781, British Admiral George Rodney looted and economically destroyed the island. It has never really recovered.

Indeed, chaos ensued between 1781 and 1816 as the Dutch, English, and French vied for control of the island. It changed hands 22 times.

The Netherlands finally won out, and Statia has been a Dutch possession since 1816.

Remnants of those bygone days are evident around the island. Hanging off the cliff at the only village, Oranjestad, is the nearly 370-year-old Ft. Oranje, the site from where the famous shots were fired. The original Dutch Reformed Church, built in 1755, sits in its courtyard. Oranjestad itself, on a ridge above the sea, is lush with greenery and bursting with bougainvillea, oleander, and hibiscus. The rest of the island is rather pristine. The eastern side, bordered by the rough waters of the Atlantic, has an untamed quality to it, and extinct volcanoes and dry plains anchor the north end. Statia's crown is the Quill, a 1,968-foot extinct volcano, its verdant crater covered with a primeval rain forest. Hiking to the peak is a popular pastime.

Beaches on the island come and go as the waters see fit, but first-class dive sites lure most visitors to the island. Wrecks and old cannons are plentiful at archaeological dive sites, and modern ships, such as the cable-laying *Charles L. Brown*, have been sunk into underwater craters. Stingrays, eels, turtles, and barracudas live in the undersea Caribbean neighborhood where giant pillar coral, giant yellow sea fans, and reef fingers abound. The sea has reclaimed the walls of Dutch warehouses that have sunk into the Caribbean over the past several hundred years, but these underwater ruins serve as a day-care center for abundant schools of juvenile fish.

On land, beachcombers hunt for blue beads. The 17th-century baubles, found only on Statia, were used to barter for rum, slaves, tobacco, and cotton. The chance of finding one is slim unless you visit the St. Eustatius Historical Foundation Museum. Pre-Columbian artifacts, dating back to 500 BC, are also on display there.

Statia is mostly a short-flight day-trip destination from nearby St. Maarten. That might be just enough for some visitors. But those who linger can appreciate the unspoiled island, its history, and its peacefulness. Most of all, it's the locals who make a visit to the island special.

EXPLORING ST. EUSTATIUS

20

Statia is an arid island with a valley between two mountain peaks. Most sights lie in the valley, making touring the island easy. From the airport you can rent a car or take a taxi and be in historic Oranjestad in minutes; to hike the Quill, Statia's highest peak, you can drive to the trailhead in less than 15 minutes from just about anywhere. Other trails with their breathtaking views include Boven, 450 feet elevation, Gilboa, 400 feet, and Venus Bay.

Lynch Plantation Museum. Also known as the Berkel Family Plantation, or the Berkel's Domestic Museum, these two one-room buildings show what life was like almost 100 years ago. A remarkable collection preserves this family's history—pictures, eyeglasses, original furnishings, and farming and fishing implements—and gives a detailed perspective of life on Statia. Call ahead to arrange a private tour. Since it's on the northeast side of the island, you need either a taxi or a car to get there. ✉ *Lynch Bay* ☎ *599/318–2338* ⊡ *Free* ⊙ *By appointment only.*

Ⓒ **Miriam C. Schmidt Botanical Garden.** As if Statia were not tranquil enough, now comes this peaceful 52-acre park. The botanical park is a place where relaxation and quiet abound. It has a greenhouse, a palm garden, a kitchen garden, and an observation bird trail. Its location, on the Atlantic side of the Quill on a plot called Upper Company, reveals a superb view of St. Kitts. For a picnic, there's no better place, but the only way to get there is by car or taxi, and some of the road is not well paved. ☎ *599/318–2284* ⊕ *www.statiapark.org* ⊡ *Suggested donation $5* ⊙ *Sunrise–sunset.*

ORANJESTAD

Ⓒ
Fodor'sChoice
★

Statia's capital and only town, **Oranjestad** sits on the west coast facing the Caribbean. Both Upper Town—with its new cobblestone streets that designate its historic section—and Lower Town are easy to explore on foot.

Ft. Oranje. Three bastions have clung to these cliffs since 1636. In 1976, Statia participated in the U.S. bicentennial celebration by restoring the fort, and now the black cannons extend beyond the ramparts. In the parade grounds a plaque, presented in 1939 by Franklin D. Roosevelt, reads "Here the sovereignty of the United States of America was first formally acknowledged to a national vessel by a foreign official."

Built in 1775, the partially restored **Dutch Reformed Church,** on Kerkweg (Church Way), has lovely stone arches that face the sea. Ancient tales can be read on the gravestones in the adjacent 18th-century cemetery where people were often buried atop one another. On Synagogepad (Synagogue Path), off Kerkweg, is **Honen Dalim** ("She Who Is Charitable to the Poor"), one of the Caribbean's oldest synagogues. Dating from 1738, its exterior is partially restored.

Lower Town sits below Fort Oranjestraat (Fort Orange Street) and some steep cliffs. It is accessible from Upper Town on foot via the zigzagging, cobblestone Fort Road or by car via Van Tonningenweg. Warehouses and shops that were piled high with European imports in the 18th century are either abandoned or simply used to store local fishermen's equipment. One of them is being restored to become a branch of **Mazinga Gift Shop.**

Along the waterfront is a lovely park with palms, flowering shrubs, and benches—the work of the historical foundation. Peeking out from the shallow waters are the crumbling ruins of 18th-century buildings, from Statia's days as the merchant hub of the Caribbean. The sea has slowly advanced since then, and it now surrounds many of the stone-and-brick ruins, making for fascinating snorkeling.

St. Eustatius Historical Foundation Museum. In the center of Upper Town is the former headquarters of Lord George Rodney, a British admiral during the American Revolution. While here, Rodney confiscated everything from gunpowder to wine in retaliation for Statia's gallant support of the fledgling country. The completely restored house is Statia's most important intact 18th-century dwelling. Exhibits, which were renovated in 2007, trace the island's history from the pre-Columbian 6th century to the present. Statia is the only island thus far where ruins

St. Eustatius Historical Foundation Museum.

and artifacts of the Saladoid, a newly discovered ancient tribe, have been excavated. ⌧ *Doncker House, 3 Wilhelminaweg, Upper Town, Oranjestad* ☎ *599/318–2288* ✉ *$3* ⊙ *Weekdays 9–5, weekends 9–noon.*

Fodor's Choice
★

The Quill. This extinct, perfectly formed, 1,968-foot volcano has a primeval rain forest in its crater. Hike and be surrounded with giant elephant ears, ferns, flowers, wild orchids, and fruit trees, and maybe if you're lucky, glimpse the elusive and endangered *iguana delicatissima* (a large—sometimes several feet long—greenish-gray creature with spines down its back). The volcanic cone rises 3 mi (5 km) south of Oranjestad on the main road. Local boys go up to the Quill by torchlight to catch delectable land crabs. The tourist board or Statia Marine Park will help you make hiking arrangements. Figure on two to four hours to hike the volcano. Purchase the required $6 permit at the **St. Eustatius National Parks, office the tourist the information booth at the airport or at your hotel.** (⌧ *Gallows Bay, Lower Town* ☎ *599/318–2884* ⊕ *www. statiapark.org*) before you begin.

BEACHES

If you desire a white sandy beach, calm waters, and a place to cool yourself off with a quick dip, you're looking at the wrong island. Statia's beaches are mostly deserted, rocky stretches of pristine shoreline. Many of the beaches on the Caribbean side are here today and reclaimed by the sea tomorrow, and the Atlantic side is an untamed mass of wild swells and vicious undertow. Walking, shelling, and searching for the elusive blue beads are popular pastimes for beachgoers. It's more likely,

DID YOU KNOW?

The Quill's peak is known as Manzinga. The last eruption of the now-dormant volcano dates back to 400 AD.

however, that the only place you will find real blue beads is in the St. Eustatius Historical Foundation.

Lynch Bay Beach. Just two bends north of Corre Corre Bay on the island's Atlantic side, light-brown sand and rock cover this small beach, which is really an extension of Zeelandia Beach. Opt for walking instead of swimming here. There are turbulent swells and there's a strong undertow. ⊠ *Lynch Bay.*

Smoke Alley Beach (*Oranje Beach*). The color of the sand varies from light beige to black at this beach on the Caribbean side near Gallows Bay. Sometimes, much of the beach is claimed by ebb and flow. The waters are sometimes calm, so snorkeling is possible, but it's usually a better place for a swim or sunning. ⊠ *Oranjestad, north end.*

Zeelandia Beach. Walking, shelling, and sunbathing are popular pastimes on this 2-mi (3-km) stretch of black-and-tan sand. Its Atlantic-side location makes it a dangerous place to put even one piggy in the water. ⊠ *Oranjestad.*

WHERE TO EAT

It's surprising that on such a small island, you can find such a wide range of cuisines: Italian, German, French, Chinese, Indonesian, international, as well as Caribbean. What you won't find is anything very fancy. As with most everything on the island, low-key and casual is the name of the game.

$$–$$$
ECLECTIC
Fodor's Choice
★

✕ **Blue Bead Bar & Restaurant.** This delightful little restaurant with its cheerful blue-and-yellow decor is a favorite with locals and the perfect place to watch the sunset. It is one of those places where everyone talks to everyone. There are always daily specials, and the menu has an array of choices that include pizza and seafood. ⊠ *Bay Rd., Gallows Bay, Lower Town, Oranjestad* ☎ 599/318–2873 ☒ *Closed Mon. and Tues.*

$–$$
ASIAN

✕ **Chinese Bar & Restaurant.** Unless you're into Formica, don't expect to be wowed by the atmosphere at this simple spot. What you will find are large portions of dishes such as *bami goreng* (Indonesian-style noodles with bits of beef, pork, or shrimp as well as tomatoes, carrots, bean sprouts, cabbage, soy sauce, and spices); or pork chops with spicy sauce. It's do-it-yourself table hauling if you want to eat outside. ⊠ *Queen Beatrix Rd., Upper Town, Oranjestad* ☎ 599/318–2389 ▭ *No credit cards.*

$–$$
CARIBBEAN

✕ **Golden Era Hotel Restaurant.** Don't pass up this restaurant just because it's completely nondescript. Concentrate instead on the tasty seafood and fine creole fare. It has another thing going for it: it's alongside the water, so the sound of the Caribbean is always playing in the background. ⊠ *Golden Era Hotel, Bay Rd., Lower Town Oranjestad* ☎ 599/318–2445, 599/318–2345, or 599/318–2355 ⊕ *goldenerahotel.com.*

$–$$
CHINESE

✕ **Grillhouse/San Yen Chinese Bar & Restaurant.** Here is yet another Chinese restaurant that is short on decor—a few tables and a bar on the verandah—but long on taste. Its special—a dish combining chicken, scallops, shrimp, beef, and sausage with vegetables—is delicious, filling, and well worth the trip. ⊠ *White Wall* ☎ 599/318–2915 ▭ *No credit cards.*

20

$$–$$$ **✗ King's Well Restaurant.** It's like watching Mom and Dad make dinner to
ECLECTIC see owners Win and Laura Piechutzki scurry around their open kitchen
preparing the night's meal. And don't expect to eat alone, because a
meal at this breezy terrace overlooking the sea makes you part of
the family. The *rostbraten* (roast beef) and schnitzels are authentic,
as Win is German. The fresh lobster is a good choice. ✉ *King's Well
Resort, Bay Rd., Lower Town, Oranjestad* ☎ *599/318-2538* ⊕ *www.
kingswellstatia.com.*

¢–$ **✗ Ocean View Terrace.** This spot in the courtyard overlooking the historic
ECLECTIC Ft. Oranje is a favorite for those who like to watch the sunset. It hasn't
changed over the years. Owner Lauris Redan serves sandwiches and
burgers for lunch and local cuisine—baked snapper with shrimp sauce,
spicy chicken, tenderloin steak—at dinner. Every now and then there's
a succulent barbecue. ✉ *Fort Oranjestraat, Upper Town, Oranjestad*
☎ *599/318-2934* ⊟ *No credit cards* ⊗ *No lunch Sun.*

$$$ **✗ The Old Gin House Main Dining Room.** Though the setting—a comfort-
FRENCH able dining room that borders a flower-filled courtyard—remains the
same, this bistro has reinvented itself yet again. It now serves a very
basic menu of fish, lobster, and steak. Chocolate Thunder Cake and
crème brûlée cheesecake are specialty desserts. Gourmet private dining
for 6 to 12 guests is the restaurants newest option (advanced reserva-
tions necessary). ✉ *Old Gin House, Bay Rd., Lower Town, Oranjestad*
☎ *599/318-2319* ⊗ *Closed Wed. No lunch.*

¢ **✗ Sand Box Tree Bakery.** This is the perfect spot for a quick sandwich; to
CAFÉ satisfy your sweet tooth; or to order a wedding, birthday, or other spe-
cial-occasion cake. It's opposite the Dutch Reformed Church. ✉ *Kerk-
weg, Upper Town, Oranjestad* ☎ *599/318-2469* ⊟ *No credit cards.*

$–$$ **✗ Seaside Bar & Grill.** This extension of the Gin House faces the water.
ECLECTIC The simple menu includes great scrambled eggs for breakfast, sand-
wiches and tasty salads for lunch, and a Wednesday night barbecue
with live music. It's not open for dinner any other night. Service is
slow, but on this island there is no reason to rush. ✉ *Old Gin House
Hotel, Bay Rd., Lower Town, Oranjestad* ☎ *599/318-2319* ⊗ *No dinner Thurs.–Tues.*

$$–$$$ **✗ Smoke Alley Bar & Grill.** Owner Michelle Balelo cooks Tex-Mex, Ital-
ECLECTIC ian, Caribbean, and American food to order at this beachfront hangout.
The open-air eatery, famous for its happy hour, is the only place on the
island where you can get draft beer. There's live music and barbecue
every Friday night. Tuesday is "two for Tuesday." You get two meals
for $22. ✉ *Gallows Bay, Lower Town, Oranjestad* ☎ *599/318-2002*
⊟ *No credit cards* ⊗ *Closed Sun.*

¢–$ **✗ Superburger.** Statia's version of fast food comes from this little hang-
BURGER out, which serves burgers, shakes, and ice cream as well as local West
Indian dishes. It's a local favorite for lunch. ✉ *Graaffweg, Upper Town,
Oranjestad* ☎ *599/318-2412* ⊟ *No credit cards* ⊗ *No dinner weekends.*

WHERE TO STAY

Renting an apartment is an alternative to staying in a hotel. Although Statia has only a handful of them, several are available for $60 or less per night, but don't expect much beyond cable TV, a bathroom, and a kitchenette. Check with the tourist office for options.

The following reviews have been condensed for this book. Please go to Fodors.com for full reviews of each property.

¢

B&B/INN

⚏ **Country Inn.** Facing Zeelandia Bay and close to the airport, this folksy little inn is surrounded by a lush tropical garden. **Pros:** very homey; tropical garden is lovely. **Cons:** not on the water and a 15-minute walk to town; a vehicle is recommended. ✉ *3 Passionfruit Rd., Concordia* ☎ *599/318–2484* ⬛ *6 rooms* ⚭ *In-room: a/c* ⬛ *No credit cards* ⎟⊚⎟ *No meals.*

¢

HOTEL

⚏ **Golden Era Hotel.** On the waterfront across the street from the Old Gin House, this property has a funky, retro-1960s feel. **Pros:** friendly staff; right on the waterfront; dive shop is next door; breakfast included. **Cons:** no-frills rooms are dark. ✉ *Bay Rd., Lower Town, Box 109, Oranjestad* ☎ *599/318–2545* ⬛ *19 rooms, 1 suite* ⚭ *In-hotel: restaurant, bar, pool* ⎟⊚⎟ *No meals.*

¢

B&B/INN

⚏ **King's Well Resort.** Win and Laura Piechutzki, along with their macaws, iguanas, fishponds, cats, and Great Danes, warmly welcome visitors to their little inn. **Pros:** eclectic and unusual furnishings; good view of the bay; breakfast included; observatory with 800x telescope. **Cons:** not a place for non-animal-loving guests, especially iguanas; not on the water or in town; one room doesn't have a/c. ✉ *On curve of Van Tonningenweg, Smoke Alley, Oranjestad* ☎ *599/318–2538* ⊕ *www.kingswellstatia.com* ⬛ *14 rooms, 1 with kitchenette* ⚭ *In-room: no a/c (some), Wi-Fi (some). In-hotel: restaurant, bar, pool* ⎟⊚⎟ *Breakfast.*

$–$$

HOTEL

★

⚏ **Old Gin House.** Built from 17th- and 18th-century cobblestones, this old cotton warehouse is now a hotel and restaurant. **Pros:** conveniently located; American breakfast at the Seaside Bar is included. **Cons:** rooms are dark; hotel could use some sprucing up. ✉ *Bay Rd., Lower Town, Oranjestad* ☎ *599/318–2319* ⊕ *www.oldginhouse.com* ⬛ *18 rooms, 2 suites* ⚭ *In-hotel: restaurants, bar, pool* ⎟⊚⎟ *Breakfast.*

¢

RENTAL

☾

Fodor'sChoice

★

⚏ **Statia Lodge.** Look out from your cottage patio of the island's best digs and enjoy drop-dead-gorgeous views of St. Kitts and Nevis. **Pros:** the best views and most modern accommodations on the island; landscaping is lovely; French, English, and German spoken. **Cons:** no a/c; not near the water or town (which is why the car or scooter is necessary); not accessible for people with disabilities. ✉ *White Wall* ☎ *599/318–1900* ⊕ *www.statialodge.com* ⬛ *10 1-bedroom cottages, 2 2-bedroom cottages* ⚭ *In-room: no a/c, no phone, Wi-Fi, kitchen, no TV. In-hotel: bar, pool* ☾ *Closed Sept.* ⎟⊚⎟ *No meals.*

20

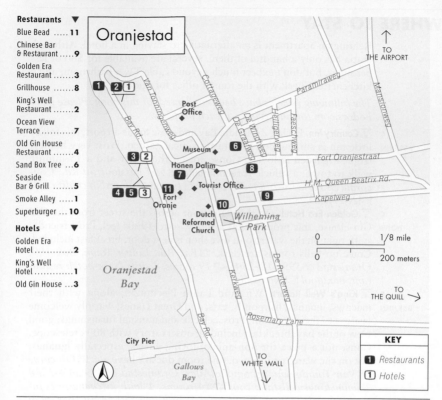

Restaurants ▼

Blue Bead **11**

Chinese Bar
& Restaurant **9**

Golden Era
Restaurant **3**

Grillhouse **8**

King's Well
Restaurant **2**

Ocean View
Terrace **7**

Old Gin House
Restaurant **4**

Sand Box Tree ...**6**

Seaside
Bar & Grill **5**

Smoke Alley **1**

Superburger ... **10**

Hotels ▼

Golden Era
Hotel **2**

King's Well
Hotel **1**

Old Gin House ...**3**

NIGHTLIFE

Statia's nightlife consists of local bands playing weekend gigs and quiet drinks at hotel bars. The island's oldest bar, tiny **Kool Korner** (✉ *Wilhelminaweg, Upper Town, Oranjestad* ☎ *599/318–2523*) is temporarily closed for renovation but reopens in January 2011, across from the St. Eustatius Historical Foundation Museum, is a lively after-work and weekend hangout.

Local. Statia's new nightspot with a white lattice fence over a red, yellow, and blue metal fence at the entrance. Locals find it a fun, happening hang out. ✉ *Oranjestad* ☎ *599/318–5811* ☉ *Fri. and Sat. 10 pm to 5 am; Sun. 8 pm to 2 am.*

Smoke Alley Bar & Grill (✉ *Lower Town, Gallows Bay* ☎ *599/318–2002*) has live music on Friday night.

SHOPPING

The limited shopping here is all duty-free. But other than the predictable souvenirs, there's not much to buy. Several shops carry Dutch cheeses and chocolates and an interesting book by Heleen Cornett called *St. Eustatius: Echoes of the Past.* **Mazinga Gift Shop** (✉ *Fort Oranjestraat,*

Upper Town, Oranjestad ☎ *599/318–2245*) is a small department store that sells the basic necessities. An old seaside warehouse across from the Gin House is being refurbished for a second Mazinga Gift Shop on Gallows Bay. The **Paper Corner** (✉ *Van Tonningenweg, Upper Town, Oranjestad* ☎ *599/318–2208*) sells magazines, a few books, computers, computer accessories, and stationery supplies.

SPORTS AND ACTIVITIES

DIVING AND SNORKELING

Fodor's Choice
★
Forget about glitz and nightlife. Statia is the quintessential low-key island. Finding an elusive *iguana delicatissima* on the Quill is probably the most exciting thing you can do on land. Statia's real thrills are underwater.

Long ago, the ocean reclaimed the original seawall built by the Dutch in the 1700s. The sunken walls, remnants of old buildings, cannons, and anchors are now part of an extensive reef system populated by reef fingers, juvenile fish, and other sea creatures.

Statia has more than 30 dive sites protected by the Statia Marine Park, which has an office on Bay Road in Lower Town. Barracuda swim around colorful coral walls at **Barracuda Reef,** off the island's southwest coast. At **Double Wreck,** just offshore from Lower Town, you can find two tall-masted ships that date from the 1700s. The coral has taken on the shape of these two disintegrated vessels, and the site attracts spiny lobsters, stingrays, moray eels, and large schools of fish. About 100 yards west of Double Wreck is the Japanese ship Cheng Tong, which sank in 2004. Off the south end of the island, the sinking of the Charles L. Brown, a 1957 cable-laying vessel, which was once owned by AT&T, created another artificial reef when it was sunk in a 135-foot underwater crater. Off the island's western shore, **Stenapa Reef** is an artificial reef created from the wrecks of barges, a harbor boat, and other ship parts. Large grouper and turtles are among the marine life you can spot here. For snorkelers, **Crooks Castle** has several stands of pillar coral, giant yellow sea fans, and sea whips just southwest of Lower Town.

The island's three dive shops along Bay Road in Lower Town rent all types of gear (including snorkeling gear for about $10 a day), offer certification courses, and organize dive trips. One-tank dives start at $40; two-tank dives are about $80. Both the Saba Marine Park and Quill National Park are under the supervision of **Statia National Parks** (☎ *599/318–2884* ⊕ *www.statiapark.org*). The marine tag fee, which all divers must buy, is used to help offset the costs of preserving the coral and other sea life here; the cost is $4 per day or $30 annually. There are two decompression chambers on the island, and the University of St. Eustatius, a medical school, offers technical training in undersea and hyperbaric medicine.

Dive Statia (✉ *Bay Rd., Lower Town, Oranjestad* ☎ *599/318–2435 or 866/614–3491* ⊕ *www.divestatia.com*), a fully equipped and PADI-certified dive shop, has earned PADI's five-star Gold Palm designation.

20

Owners Rudy and Rinda Hees operate the shop out of an old warehouse. In addition to the standard courses, Dive Statia also offers underwater photography courses, Nitrox diving, and DVPs—diver propulsion vehicles—for diving or snorkeling. **Golden Rock Dive Center** (✉ *Gallows Bay, Lower Town, Oranjestad* ☎ *599/318–2964* ⊕ *www.goldenrockdive. com*), operated by Glenn and Michele Faires, also boasts PADI's Gold Palm designation. In addition to certification courses, the shop offers a National Geographic program that emphasizes conservation. **Scubaqua** (✉ *Gallows Bay behind Blue Bead Restaurant, Lower Town, Oranjestad* ☎ *599/318–5450* ⊕ *www.scubaqua.com*) caters to Europeans as well as Americans. Dive courses are offered in various languages.

GUIDED TOURS

Statia's three taxis and two large buses are available for island tours. A 2½-hour outing costs $40 per vehicle for five people (extra people are $5 each), usually including airport transfer.

The **St. Eustatius Historical Foundation Museum** (✉ *3 Wilhelminaweg, Oranjestad* ☎ *599/318–2288*) sells a booklet detailing a self-guided walking tour of the sights for $10. The tour begins in Lower Town at the marina and ends at the museum.

HIKING

Trails range from the easy to the "Watch out!" The big thrill here is the Quill, the 1,968-foot extinct volcano with its crater cradling a rain forest. Give yourself two to four hours to complete the hike. The tourist office has a list of 12 marked trails and can put you in touch with a guide. Quill National Park includes a trail into the crater, which is a long, winding but safe walk. Maps and the necessary $6 permit, which is good for a year, are available at the Statia Marine Park headquarters on Bay Road. Wear layers: it can be cool on the summit and steamy in the interior.

KAYAKING

One excellent way to tour the island is by kayak. Two-person kayaks are available at **Dive Statia** (✉ *Bay Rd., Lower Town, Oranjestad* ☎ *599/318–2435 or 866/614–3491* ⊕ *www.divestatia.com*) at $15 for a single and $20 for a double per hour. Guided tours take paddlers to Black Rock Reef and Jenkins Bay.

St. Kitts and Nevis

WORD OF MOUTH

"If it's not a beach day, do go to Brimstone Hill. It's a wonderful excursion and is a World Heritage Site. All the islands have beaches but Brimstone Hill is worth the trip, even if it is a beach day."

—CW

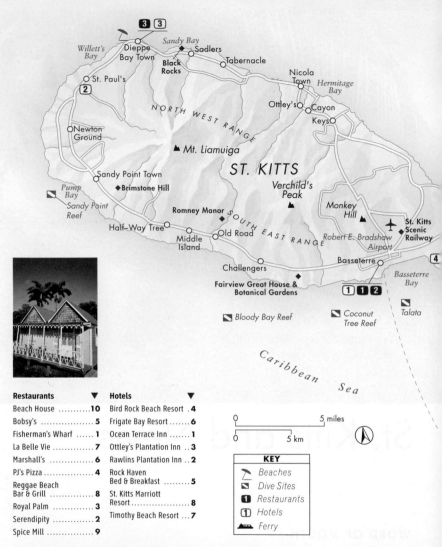

3 **3**

Willett's Bay
Dieppe Bay Town
Sandy Bay
Sadlers
Black Rocks
Tabernacle
St. Paul's **2**
Nicola Town
Hermitage Bay
Ottley's
Cayon
Keys
N O R T H W E S T R A N G E
Newton Ground
▲ Mt. Liamuiga
ST. KITTS
Sandy Point Town
◆ Brimstone Hill
Verchild's Peak ▲
Monkey Hill
St. Kitts Scenic Railway
Pump Bay
Sandy Point Reef
Romney Manor
S O U T H   E A S T   R A N G E
Half-Way Tree
Middle Island
Old Road
Robert E. Bradshaw Airport
Basseterre
4
Challengers
Fairview Great House & Botanical Gardens
1 **1** **2**
Basseterre Bay
Bloody Bay Reef
Coconut Tree Reef
Talata

C a r i b b e a n   S e a

Restaurants ▼		Hotels ▼	
Beach House	**10**	Bird Rock Beach Resort	**4**
Bobsy's	**5**	Frigate Bay Resort	**6**
Fisherman's Wharf	**1**	Ocean Terrace Inn	**1**
La Belle Vie	**7**	Ottley's Plantation Inn	**3**
Marshall's	**6**	Rawlins Plantation Inn	**2**
PJ's Pizza	**4**	Rock Haven Bed & Breakfast	**5**
Reggae Beach Bar & Grill	**8**	St. Kitts Marriott Resort	**8**
Royal Palm	**3**	Timothy Beach Resort	**7**
Serendipity	**2**		
Spice Mill	**9**		

5 miles
5 km

KEY
⌐ Beaches
◣ Dive Sites
1 Restaurants
1 Hotels
⛴ Ferry

TOP REASONS TO VISIT ST. KITTS AND NEVIS

1 History: Both St. Kitts and Nevis are steeped in history; Brimstone Hill Fortress is a man-made UNESCO World Heritage site.

2 Landscape: Both islands have extinct volcanoes and luxuriant rain forests ideal for hikes, as well as fine diving and snorkeling sites.

3 Unspoiled: You'll find less development—particularly on Nevis—and more cordial islanders than on more touristy islands.

4 Water Activities: Both islands feature aquatic activities aplenty, with fine sailing, deep-sea fishing, diving (especially off St. Kitts), and windsurfing (especially around Nevis).

WELCOME TO
ST. KITTS AND NEVIS

THE MOTHER COLONY AND HER SISTER

St. Kitts, a 65-square-mi (168-square-km) island is 2 mi (3 km) from smaller Nevis, about 40 square mi (121 square km). The two former British colonies are joined in a sometimes strained independence. St. Kitts is often called "The Mother Colony," because it is the first permanent English settlement in the Caribbean.

A yucca watches over North Friar's Bay on St. Kitts's narrow peninsula where Nevis, its diminutive companion, looms on the horizon. On both islands, green fields of sugarcane run to the sea, once-magnificent plantation houses are now luxurious inns, and lovely stretches of uncrowded beach stretch before you.

ST. KITTS AND NEVIS PLANNER

Island Activities

Both St. Kitts and Nevis have good but not great **beaches** (Friar's or Frigate Bay are the best choices on St. Kitts, Pinney's, Newcastle or Oualie Beach on Nevis).

St. Kitts offers a wider range of activities, including good **diving, horseback riding**, and **hiking** tours in the rain forest, and **boat rides**.

Nevis has fewer organized activities, but they run the gamut from **windsurfing** to **deep-sea fishing** to **kayaking** to **horseback riding**.

The **Royal St. Kitts Golf Club** was renovated in 2004; other golf courses are being developed at this writing, including a Tom Fazio–designed beaut at Christophe Harbour.

The Four Seasons Resort Nevis has one of the Caribbean's finest **golf courses** and remains a strong draw for the resort.

Both St. Kitts and Nevis have good **restaurants**; the fine plantation inn eateries provide some of the best dining experiences on either island.

Getting to St. Kitts and Nevis

Hassle Factor: medium for St. Kitts, medium to high for Nevis.

Nonstops: Flights to St. Kitts from Atlanta (Delta), Charlotte (US Airways), Miami (American), and New York–JFK (American). There are no nonstops from the U.S. to Nevis.

Air Travel: Many travelers connect in Antigua, San Juan, St. Maarten, or St. Thomas. To Nevis, it's almost always cheaper to fly into St. Kitts and then take a sea taxi or regularly scheduled ferry, but check the schedules or book your sea taxi in advance.

American/American Eagle (☎ 869/465–2273 or 869/469–8995) has daily flights into St. Kitts and thrice-weekly flights to Nevis from San Juan; Miami is another option. Other major domestic airlines (US Airways once weekly nonstop from Charlotte and Delta once weekly from Atlanta) fly from their eastern hubs either into Antigua, St. Maarten, San Juan, or St. Thomas, where connections to St. Kitts (and, less frequently, to Nevis) can be made on **LIAT** (☎ 869/465–1330 ⊕ www.liatairline.com). Nevis connections can also be made from St. Maarten on **Winair** (☎ 869/469–5302 ⊕ www.fly-winair.com).

St. Kitts' airport (SKB) is **Robert L. Bradshaw International Airport** (⊠ Golden Rock, St. Kitts ☎ 465–8013). The Nevis airport (NEV) is **Vance W. Amory International Airport** (⊠ Newcastle, Nevis ☎ 869/469–9343).

Boat and Ferry Travel: There are several ferry services between St. Kitts and Nevis, all with schedules that are subject to abrupt change. Most companies make two or three daily trips. All the ferries take about 30 to 45 minutes and cost $8–$10. Up-to-date information is available at **Leyton Ferry Schedule** (☎ 869/466–6734, 869/662–9811, or 869/469–0403 ⊕ boatschedule.leytonms.com).

Sea-taxi service between the two islands is operated by **Kenneth's Dive Centre** (☎ 869/465–2670). **Leeward Island Charters** (☎ 869/465–7474) also schedules sea taxis. **Nevis Water Sports** (☎ 869/469–9060) provides sea-taxi service. Auston Macleod of **Pro-Divers** (☎ 869/465–3223) is a recommended sea-taxi service. Each operator charges about $20 one way in summer, $25 in winter, with a four-person minimum.

Getting Around St. Kitts and Nevis

Car Travel: You can get by without a car if you are staying in the Frigate Bay–Basseterre area, but elsewhere you'll need to rent a car. On Nevis, it's often easier to just take taxis and guided tours. On St. Kitts, present your valid driver's license and $24 at the police station on Cayon Street in Basseterre to get a temporary driving permit (on Nevis the car-rental agency will help you obtain the $24 local license at the police station). The license is valid for three months on both islands. On either island, car rentals start at about $45 per day for a compact; expect to pay a few extra bucks for air-conditioning. Most agencies offer substantial multiday discounts.

Avis (✉ *South Independence Sq., Basseterre, St. Kitts* ☎ *869/465–6507* ⊕ *www.avisstkitts.com*) has the best selection of Suzuki and Daihatsu four-wheel-drive vehicles on St. Kitts, as well as rental exchange on Nevis and complimentary pickup. **Delisle Walwyn** (✉ *Liverpool Row, Basseterre, St. Kitts* ☎ *869/465–8449*) provides an excellent selection and the option of a replacement car for one day on Nevis if you rent for three days or more on St. Kitts. **Funky Monkey Tours & Rentals** (✉ *Nelson Springs, Nevis* ☎ *869/665–6045*) lets you ride on the wild side in Polaris Ranger and Razor 4x4s; prices start at $95 per half day. You can also rent Vespas for $60–$75 per day, as well as Sea-Doo wave runners. Or follow in their tire tracks, off-roading through the island on a three-hour Funky Monkey tours. **Nevis Car Rentals** (✉ *Newcastle, Nevis* ☎ *869/469–9837*) is a recommended agency. **Noel's Courtesy Garage** (✉ *Farms Estate, Nevis* ☎ *869/469–5199* ⊕ *www.noelcarrental.com*) offers a wide variety of cars and jeeps for Nevis. **Striker's Car Rental** (✉ *Hermitage Rd., Gingerland, Nevis* ☎ *869/469–2654*) has a good selection of vehicles. **TDC/Thrifty Rentals** (✉ *Central St., West Independence Square, Basseterre, St. Kitts* ☎ *869/465–2991* ✉ *Bay Rd., Charlestown, Nevis* ☎ *869/469–5690 or 869/469–1005*) has a wide selection of vehicles and outstanding service; it offers a three-day rental that includes a car on both islands.

Taxi Travel: Taxi rates are government regulated and are posted at the airport, the dock, and in the free tourist guide. Be sure to clarify whether fare is in EC or U.S. dollars. There are fixed rates to and from all the hotels and to and from major points of interest. **St. Kitts Taxi Association** (☎ *869/465–8487 or 869/465–4253, 869/465–7818 after hrs*). **Nevis Taxi Service** (☎ *869/469–5631 or 869/469–1483, 869/469–9790 for the airport, 869/469–5515 after dark*)

Driving Tips

One well-kept main road circumnavigates St. Kitts and is usually clearly marked, making it difficult to get lost, though the northeast can get a bit bumpy, and the access roads to the plantation inns are notoriously rough.

The roads on Nevis are fairly new and generally smooth, at least on the most traveled north, west, and south sides of the island.

The east coast has some potholes, and pigs, goats, and sheep still insist on the right-of-way all around the island.

Drivers on both islands tend to travel at a fast clip and pass on curves, so drive defensively. Driving is on the left, British-style, though you will probably be given an American-style car.

21

ST. KITTS AND NEVIS PLANNER

Fast Facts

Banks and Exchange Services: Legal tender is the Eastern Caribbean (EC) dollar. The rate of exchange at this writing is EC$2.70 to US$1. U.S. dollars are accepted practically everywhere, but change is usually EC currency. Most large hotels, restaurants, and shops accept major credit cards, but small inns and shops often do not. All banks, including the Royal Bank of St. Kitts and Scotia Bank, have ATMs. There are ATMs on Nevis at the airport, Bank of Nova Scotia, First Caribbean International Bank, and St. Kitts–Nevis National Bank.

Electricity: 110 volts, 60 cycles.

Emergency Services: Ambulance and Emergencies (☎ 911). **Police** (☎ 869/465–2241 on St. Kitts, 869/469–5391 on Nevis).

Passport Requirements: All travelers must have a valid passport and a return or ongoing ticket.

Weddings: Two-day residency requirement. License is $80, application $20. Valid passport or birth certificate required; if divorced, a divorce decree; if widowed, a death certificate of the deceased spouse.

Essentials

Mail: Airmail letters to the United States and Canada cost EC90¢ per half ounce; postcards require EC80¢; to the United Kingdom letters cost EC$1.20, postcards EC$1; to Australia and New Zealand, letters cost EC$1.60, postcards EC$1.20. Mail takes at least 7 to 10 days to reach the United States. St. Kitts and Nevis issue separate stamps, but each honors the other's.

Taxes: The departure tax is US$22, payable in cash only. There's no sales tax on either St. Kitts or Nevis. Hotels collect a 9% government tax.

Telephones: Phone cards, which you can buy in denominations of EC$5, $10, and $20, are handy for making local phone calls, calling other islands, and accessing U.S. direct lines. Many private lines and hotels charge access rates if you use your AT&T, Sprint, or MCI calling card; there's no regularity, so phoning can be frustrating. Pay phones, usually found in major town squares, take EC coins or phone cards. Port Zante has banks of "international" phones that accept credit and, erratically, calling cards. To make a local call, dial the seven-digit number. To call St. Kitts and Nevis from the United States, dial area code 869, then access code 465, 466, 468, or 469 and the local four-digit number.

Tipping: Hotels add a 10%–12% service charge to your bill. Restaurants occasionally do the same; ask if it isn't printed on the menu; a 15% tip is appropriate when it isn't included. Taxi drivers typically receive a 10% tip, porters and bellhops $1 per bag; housekeeping staff, $2 to $3 per night.

Visitor Information: Nevis Tourism Authority (✉ Elm House, Park La., Lower Froyle, Alton, Hampshire, U.K. ☎ 01420/520810 ⊕ www.nevisisland.com). **St. Kitts Tourism Authority** (☎ 212/535–1234 in New York City, 800/582–6208, 866/556–3847 for Nevis alone ⊕ www.stkittstourism.kn). **St. Kitts–Nevis Hotel and Tourism Association** (✉ Liverpool Row, Box 438, Basseterre, St. Kitts ☎ 869/465–5304 ⊕ www.stkittsnevishta.org).

Where to Stay

St. Kitts has a wide variety of places to stay—beautifully restored plantation inns, full-service affordable hotels, simple beachfront cottages, and all-inclusive resorts. One large resort—the Marriott—is more midrange than upscale and attracts large groups and package tourists. Choose St. Kitts if you want a wider choice of activities and accommodations (you can always do Nevis as a day trip). Nevis is a small island with no large resorts, and most accommodations are upscale—primarily plantation inns and the luxurious Four Seasons. It's much quieter than St. Kitts, so choose it if you want to get away from the hectic island scene and simply relax in low-key comfort and surprisingly high style.

Four Seasons Nevis: Really in a class by itself, the Four Seasons is the only lavish, high-end property on either island. If you can afford it, the resort is certainly one of the Caribbean's finest; recent post-hurricane renovations improved on near-perfection.

Plantation Inns: St. Kitts and Nevis feature renovated, historic plantation houses that have been turned into upscale inns. On Nevis, the inns are the most distinctive form of lodging. They are usually managed by hands-on owner–operators and offer fine cuisine and convivial hospitality; though not usually on a beach, most of these inns have beach clubs with free private shuttle service.

Hotel and Restaurant Costs

Restaurant prices are for a main course at dinner and include any taxes or service charges. Hotel prices are per night for a double room in high season, excluding taxes, service charges, and meal plans (except at all-inclusives).

WHAT IT COSTS IN U.S. DOLLARS

	¢	$	$$	$$$	$$$$
Restaurants	under $8	$8–$12	$12–$20	$20–$30	over $30
Hotels		under $150	$150–$275	$276–$375	$376–$475	over $475

When to Go

The high season is relatively short, starting in mid-December and stretching into early or mid-April. The shoulder season (roughly April to mid-June and November to mid-December) offers lower rates. Rates are lower still from mid-June through November, but some establishments close for a month or longer.

FESTIVALS AND EVENTS

Carnival on St. Kitts is celebrated during the 10 days right after Christmas.

The **St. Kitts Music Festival** in late June or early July is the biggest event on the island and draws international singing stars from Michael Bolton to Boyz II Men.

September on St. Kitts is devoted to **independence festivals.**

Nevis calls its summer carnival **Culturama,** and it's celebrated in late July and early August.

The **Nevis International Culinary Heritage Exposition** brings in guest chefs for cooking demonstrations and wine tastings the third week of October.

Taking a page from the Cayman Islands book, Nevis introduced the weeklong **Peppered Pickled Pirate Party**, held twice during the last week of both October and November, celebrating the likes of William Kidd and Black Bart with an "invasion," regattas, cooking and cocktail competitions, treasure hunts, and more.

ST. KITTS AND NEVIS BEACHES

St. Kitts and Nevis aren't noted for endless sensuous strands, yet beachcombers will find enough variety during their holiday. The finest beaches are fairly developed (Frigate Beach on the Caribbean side, with one bar after another, is a party-hearty destination on weekends), but both islands offer surf-lashed Atlantic stretches fine for R&R à deux if not swimming.

(Above) Pinney's Beach, Nevis. (Opposite page bottom) Friar's Bay, St. Kitts. (Opposite page top) Frigate Bay, St. Kitts.

Beaches on St. Kitts are free and open to the public (even those occupied by hotels). The best beaches, with powdery white sand, are in the Frigate Bay area or on the lower peninsula. The Atlantic waters are rougher, and many black-sand beaches northwest of Frigate Bay double as garbage dumps.

All beaches on Nevis are free to the public (the plantation inns cordon off "private" areas on Pinney's Beach for guests), but there are no changing facilities, so wear a swimsuit under your clothes.

THE SAND

Both islands have appealing beige-hue beaches, such as Pinney's or those garlanding St. Kitts's Southeast Peninsula. Many abutting the Atlantic feature earthier colors, ranging from warm mocha to taupe-gray. Some Atlantic beaches are wind-whipped and wilder, such as Conaree, ideal for bodysurfing, though they're not regularly maintained so otherwise soft sand competes with seaweed, shells, and driftwood.

ST. KITTS

Banana/Cockleshell Bays. These twin connected eyebrows of glittering champagne-color sand—stretching nearly 2 mi (3 km) total at the southeastern tip of the island—feature majestic views of Nevis and are backed by lush vegetation and coconut palms. The first-rate restaurant–bar Spice Mill (next to Rasta-hue Lion Rock Beach Bar—order the knockout Lion Punch) and Reggae Beach Bar & Grill bracket either end of Cockleshell. As of this writing, a 125-room mixed-use Park Hyatt (with additional residential condos and villas) will commence building for an anticipated late 2013 opening. The water is generally placid, ideal for swimming. The downside is irregular maintenance, with seaweed (particularly after rough weather) and occasional litter, especially on Banana Bay. Follow Simmonds Highway to the end and bear right, ignoring the turnoff for Turtle Beach. ⊠ *Banana Bay.*

Friar's Bay. Locals consider Friar's Bay, on the Caribbean (southern) side, the island's finest beach. It's a long, tawny scimitar where the water always seems warmer and clearer. Unfortunately, the new Marine World development has co-opted nearly half the strand. Still, several happening bars, including Shipwreck, Mongoose, and Sunset Grill, serve terrific, inexpensive local food and cheap, frosty drinks. Chair rentals cost around $3, though if you order lunch,

you can negotiate a freebie. Friar's is the first major beach along Southeast Peninsula Drive (aka Simmonds Highway), approximately a mile (1½ km) southeast of Frigate Bay. ⊠ *Friar's Bay.*

Frigate Bay. The Caribbean side offers talcum-powder-fine beige sand framed by coconut palms and sea grapes, and the Atlantic side—sometimes called North Frigate Bay—is a favorite with horseback riders. South Frigate Bay is bookended by Sunset Café and Buddies Beach Hut. In between are several other lively beach spots, including Cathy's (fabulous jerk ribs), the Monkey Bar, Elvis Love Shack, and Mr. X Shiggidy Shack. Most charge $3 to $5 to rent a chair, though they'll often waive the fee if you ask politely and buy lunch. Locals barhop late into Friday and Saturday nights. Waters are generally calm for swimming; the rockier eastern end offers fine snorkeling. The incomparably scenic Atlantic side is dominated by the Marriott (plentiful dining options), attracting occasional pesky vendors. The surf is choppier and the undertow stronger here. On cruise-ship days, groups stampede both sides. Frigate Bay is easy to find, just less than 3 mi (5 km) from downtown Basseterre. ⊠ *Frigate Bay.*

Sand Bank Bay. A dirt road, nearly impassable after heavy rains, leads to a long mocha crescent on the Atlantic. The shallow coves are protected here,

WELCOME

About 4 miles long, Pinney's Beach is one of the best on Nevis.

making it ideal for families, and it's usually deserted. The rocky far left area can have fierce sudden swells and currents. This exceptionally pretty beach lacks shade; Christophe Harbour has constructed several villas and a beach club. As you drive southeast along Simmonds Highway, approximately 10 mi (16 km) from Basseterre, look for an unmarked dirt turnoff to the left of the Great Salt Pond. ⊠ *Sand Bank Bay*.

White House Bay. The beach is rocky, but the snorkeling is superb. It's usually deserted, though the calm water (and stunning scenery) makes it a favorite anchorage of yachties. There are no facilities and little shade, but there's also little seaweed. A dirt road skirts a hill to the right off Simmonds Highway approximately 2 mi (3 km) after Friar's. ⊠ *White House Bay*.

NEVIS

Newcastle Beach. This broad swath of soft ecru sand shaded by coconut palms is near Nisbet Plantation, on the channel between St. Kitts and Nevis. It's popular with snorkelers, but beware stony sections and occasional strong currents that kick up seaweed and roil the sandy bottom. ⊠ *Newcastle*.

Oualie Beach. This beige-sand beach lined with palms and sea grapes is where the folks at Oualie Beach Hotel can mix you a drink and fix you up with water-sports equipment. There's excellent snorkeling and fantastic sunset views with St. Kitts silhouetted in the background. Several beach chairs and hammocks (free with lunch, $3 rental without) line the sand and the grassy "lawn" behind it. Oualie is at the island's northwest tip, approximately 3 mi (5 km) west of the airport. ⊠ *Oualie Beach*.

Pinney's Beach. The island's showpiece has soft, golden sand on the calm Caribbean, lined with a magnificent grove of palm trees. The Four Seasons Resort is here, as are the plantation inns' beach clubs and casual beach bars such as Sunshine's, Chevy's, and the Double Deuce. Regrettably, the waters can be murky and filled with kelp if the weather has been inclement anywhere within a hundred miles, depending on the currents. ⊠ *Pinney's Beach*.

By Jordan
Simon

These idyllic sister islands, 2 mi (3 km) apart at their closest point, offer visitors a relatively authentic island experience. Both have luxuriant mountain rain forests; uncrowded beaches; historic ruins; towering, long-dormant volcanoes; charming if slightly dilapidated Georgian capitals in Basseterre (St. Kitts) and Charlestown (Nevis); intact cultural heritage; friendly if shy people; and restored, 18th-century sugar plantation inns run by elegant, if sometimes eccentric, expatriate British and American owners.

The islands' history follows the usual Caribbean route: Amerindian settlements, Columbus's voyages, fierce colonial battles between the British and French, a boom in sugar production second only to that of Barbados. St. Kitts became known as the mother colony of the West Indies: English settlers sailed from there to Antigua, Barbuda, Tortola, and Montserrat, and the French dispatched colonists to Martinique, Guadeloupe, St. Martin, and St. Barths.

St. Kitts and Nevis, in addition to Anguilla, achieved self-government as an associated state of Great Britain in 1967. Anguillians soon made their displeasure known, separating immediately, whereas St. Kitts and Nevis waited until 1983 to become an independent nation. The two islands, despite their superficial similarities, have taken increasingly different routes regarding tourism. Nevis received an economic boost from the Four Seasons, which helped establish it as an upscale destination. St. Kitts, however, has yet to define its identity at a time when most islands have found their tourism niche. A fierce sibling rivalry has ensued.

Though its comparative lack of development is a lure, the Kittitian government is casting its economic net in several directions. Golf, eco-tourism, and scuba diving are being aggressively promoted. And the government hopes the number of available rooms will increase roughly

30% by 2013 to more than 2,000, according to the "build it and they will come" philosophy. But is St. Kitts ready to absorb all this? The island offers a surprisingly diverse vacation experience while retaining its essential Caribbean flavor. Divers have yet to discover all its underwater attractions, and nature lovers will be pleasantly surprised by the hiking. There's now every kind of accommodation, as well as gourmet dining, golf, and gaming.

Meanwhile, Nevis seems determined to stay even more unspoiled (there are still no traffic lights). Its natural attractions and activities certainly rival those of St. Kitts, from mountain biking and ecohiking to windsurfing and deep-sea fishing, though lying in a hammock and dining on romantic candlelit patios remain cherished pursuits. Pinney's Beach, despite occasional hurricane erosion, remains a classic Caribbean strand. Its historic heritage, from the Caribbean's first hotel to Alexander Hamilton's childhood home, is just as pronounced, including equally sybaritic plantation inns that seem torn from the pages of a romance novel.

Perhaps it's a warning sign that many guests call the catamaran trip to Nevis the high point of their stay on St. Kitts—and many Kittitians build retirement and second homes on Nevis. The sister islands' relationship remains outwardly cordial if slightly contentious. Nevis papers sometimes run blistering editorials advocating independence, though one plebiscite has already failed. St. Kitts and Nevis may separate some day, but for now their battles are confined to ad campaigns and political debates. Fortunately, well-heeled and barefoot travelers alike can still happily enjoy the many energetic and easygoing enticements of both blissful retreats.

ST. KITTS

EXPLORING ST. KITTS

You can explore Basseterre, the capital city, in a half hour or so, and should allow four hours for an island tour. Main Road traces the northwestern perimeter of the island through seas of sugarcane and past breadfruit trees and stone walls. Villages with tiny pastel-color houses of stone and weathered wood are scattered across the island, and the drive back to Basseterre around the island's other side passes through several of them. The most spectacular stretch of scenery is on Dr. Kennedy Simmonds Highway, which goes to the tip of the Southeast Peninsula. This modern road twists and turns through the undeveloped grassy hills that rise between the calm Caribbean and the windswept Atlantic, passing the shimmering pink Great Salt Pond, a volcanic crater, and seductive beaches. Major developments are under way, including the Beaumont Park Racetrack near Dieppe Bay. The 6-furlong racetrack and state-of-the-art stables opened in December 2009. Cards include some stakes races with horses from as far afield as France and Ireland competing; admission and parking are free; up to 9,000 spectators converge on the site, enhancing the exciting equine environment. At this writing an entertainment complex with fine-dining restaurant as well as polo grounds, go-karts, retail complex, and bird and butterfly parks are slated to follow by late 2012. Construction starts and stops on Marine World at South Friar's Bay, a 4-acre theme park with dolphin encounter, stingray lagoon, ecofriendly water-sports center, beach bar, upscale restaurant (Carambola Beach Club, whose opening has been repeatedly delayed), nature trail, and aviary.

WHAT TO SEE

Basseterre. On the south coast, St. Kitts's walkable capital is graced with tall palms and flagstone sidewalks; although many of the buildings appear run-down, there are interesting shops, excellent art galleries, and some beautifully maintained houses. Duty-free shops and boutiques line the streets and courtyards radiating from the octagonal **Circus**, built in the style of London's famous Piccadilly Circus.

There are lovely gardens on the site of a former slave market at **Independence Square** (⊠ *Off Bank St., Basseterre*). The square is surrounded on three sides by 18th-century Georgian buildings.

St. George's Anglican Church (⊠ *Cayon St., Basseterre*) is a handsome stone building with a crenellated tower originally built by the French in 1670 and called Nôtre-Dame. The British burned it down in 1706 and rebuilt it four years later, naming it after the patron saint of England. Since then it has suffered a fire, an earthquake, and hurricanes and was once again rebuilt in 1869.

Port Zante (⊠ *Waterfront, behind Circus, Basseterre*) is an ambitious, ever-growing 27-acre cruise-ship pier and marina in an area that has been reclaimed from the sea. The domed welcome center is an imposing neoclassical hodgepodge, with columns and stone arches, shops, walkways, fountains, and West Indian–style buildings housing luxury shops, galleries, restaurants, and a small casino. A second pier, 1,434 feet long, has a draft that accommodates even leviathan cruise ships. The selection of shops and restaurants (Tiffany Bar and Deli is a find for fantastic local fare, Twist for global fusion cuisine) is expanding as well.

In the restored former Treasury Building, the **National Museum** presents an eclectic collection reflecting the history and culture of the island. ⊠ *Bay Rd., Basseterre* ☎ *869/465–5584* ☎ *EC$1 residents, US$1 nonresidents* ☉ *Weekdays 9–5, Sat. 9 1.*

NEED A BREAK?

The tropically themed second-floor terrace eatery **Ballahoo** (⊠ *Fort St., Basseterre* ☎ *869/465–4197*) draws a crowd for breakfast, lunch, and dinner. Specialties include chili shrimp, Madras beef curry, and a toasted rum-and-banana sandwich topped with ice cream. At lunchtime, you can watch the bustle of the Circus and enjoy special prices on such dishes as roti bursting with curried chicken or vegetables. Grab fresh local juices (tamarind, guava) if you can. Though the service is lackadaisical bordering on rude, the food is at least plentiful, the daiquiris are killer, the Wi-Fi free, and the people-watching delightful.

Black Rocks. This series of lava deposits was spat into the sea ages ago when the island's volcano erupted. It has since been molded into fanciful shapes by centuries of pounding surf. ⊠ *Atlantic coast, outside town of Sadlers, Sandy Bay.*

★ **Brimstone Hill.** This 38-acre fortress, a UNESCO World Heritage Site, is part of a national park dedicated by Queen Elizabeth in 1985. After routing the French in 1690, the English erected a battery here; by 1736 the fortress held 49 guns, earning it the moniker Gibraltar of the West Indies. In 1782, 8,000 French troops laid siege to the stronghold, which was defended by 350 militia and 600 regular troops of the Royal Scots and East Yorkshires. When the English finally surrendered, they were allowed to march from the fort in full formation out of respect for their bravery (the English afforded the French the same honor when they surrendered the fort a mere year later). A hurricane severely damaged the fortress in 1834, and in 1852 it was evacuated and dismantled. The beautiful stones were carted away to build houses.

The citadel has been partially reconstructed and its guns remounted. It's a steep walk up the hill from the parking lot. A seven-minute orientation film recounts the fort's history and restoration. You can see remains of the officers' quarters, redoubts, barracks, ordnance store, and cemetery. Its museum collections were depleted by hurricanes, but some pre-Columbian artifacts, objects pertaining to the African heritage of the island's slaves (such as masks and ceremonial tools), weaponry, uniforms, photographs, and old newspapers remain. The spectacular view includes Montserrat and Nevis to the southeast; Saba and St. Eustatius to the northwest; and St. Barth and St. Maarten to the north. Nature trails snake through the tangle of surrounding hardwood forest and savanna (a fine spot to catch the green vervet monkeys—inexplicably brought by the French and now outnumbering the residents—skittering about). ⊠ *Main Rd., Brimstone Hill* 🕾 *869/465-2609* ⊕ *www. brimstonehillfortress.org* 🖅 *$8* ⊘ *Daily 9:30–5:30.*

Fairview Great House & Botanical Gardens. Parts of this French colonial greathouse set on more than 2 lush tropical acres date back to 1701, including original ipe beams. The interior has been impeccably restored in period fashion, with each room painted in different colors from pomegranate to lemon. Furnishings include a 16-seat mahogany dinner table set with china and silver; docents relate fascinating factoids (chaises were broadened to accommodate petticoats—or "can-can skirts," in local parlance). Cross the cobblestone courtyard to the original kitchen, replete with volcanic stone and brick oven, and bathing room (heated rocks warmed spring water in the tub). The fieldstone cellar now contains the gift shop, offering local pottery, art, and honey harvested onsite at the apiary. You can wander meticulously maintained gardens with interpretive signage, filled with chattering birds and monkeys. The Nirvana restaurant offers worthy local food (lunch buffets, creative Mediterranean-tinged fare for dinner); dips in the pool are a bonus. ⊠ *Artist's Level Hill, Boyd's* 🕾 *869/465-3141* ⊕ *www.stkittstourism. kn/plantations.html* 🖅 *$10* ⊘ *Daily 9–5 (last entrance 4:30).*

Old Road. This site marks the first permanent English settlement in the West Indies, founded in 1624 by Thomas Warner. Take the side road toward the interior to find some Carib petroglyphs, testimony of even earlier habitation. The largest depicts a female figure on black volcanic rock, presumably a fertility goddess. Less than a mile east of Old Road along Main Road is **Bloody Point,** where French and British soldiers

Cannons at Brimstone Hill, a UNESCO World Heritage Site on St. Kitts.

joined forces in 1629 to repel a mass Carib attack; reputedly so many Caribs were massacred that the stream ran red for three days. ✛ *Main Rd. west of Challengers.*

★ **Romney Manor.** The ruins of this somewhat restored house (reputedly once the property of Thomas Jefferson) and surrounding replicas of chattel-house cottages are set in 6 acres of glorious gardens, with exotic flowers, an old bell tower, and an enormous, gnarled 350-year-old saman tree (sometimes called a rain tree). Inside, at **Caribelle Batik,** you can watch artisans hand-printing fabrics by the 2,500-year-old Indonesian wax-and-dye process known as batik. Look for signs indicating a turnoff for Romney Manor near Old Road. ✉ *Old Road* ☎ *869/465–6253* ⊕ *www.caribellebatikstkitts.com* ✆ *Free* ⊘ *Daily 9–5.*

St. Kitts Scenic Railway. The old narrow-gauge train that had transported sugarcane to the central sugar factory since 1912 is all that remains of the island's once-thriving sugar industry. Two-story cars bedecked in bright Kittitian colors circle the island in just under four hours. Each passenger gets a comfortable, downstairs air-conditioned seat fronting vaulted picture windows and an upstairs open-air observation spot. The conductor's running discourse embraces not only the history of sugar cultivation but also the railway's construction, local folklore, island geography, even other agricultural mainstays from papayas to pigs. You can drink in complimentary tropical beverages (including luscious guava daiquiris) along with the sweeping rain-forest and ocean vistas, accompanied by an a cappella choir's renditions of hymns, spirituals, and predictable standards like "I've Been Workin' on the Railroad." ✉ *Needsmust* ☎ *869/465-7263* ⊕ *www.stkittsscenicrailway.com* ✆ *$89, children 4–12*

$44.50 ⊙ Departures vary according to cruise-ship schedules (call ahead, but at least once daily Dec.– Apr., usually 8:30 am).

WHERE TO EAT

St. Kitts restaurants range from funky beachfront bistros to elegant plantation dining rooms (most with prix-fixe menus); most fare is tinged with the flavors of the Caribbean. Many restaurants offer West Indian specialties such as curried mutton, pepper pot (a stew of vegetables, tubers, and meats), and Arawak chicken (seasoned and served with rice and almonds on breadfruit leaf).

WHAT TO WEAR

Throughout the island, dress is casual at lunch (but no bathing suits). Dinner, although not necessarily formal, definitely calls for long pants and sundresses.

$$–$$$
ECLECTIC
Fodor's Choice
★

✕ **Beach House.** Executive chef Lionel Garnier (formerly of Taos, New Mexico) and staff put the sin in scintillating at this outpost of chic on Turtle Beach. The opening salvo of the überluxurious Christophe Harbour development on the island's Southwest Peninsula, the Beach House preens like an advance scout for the army of chic. The tiered 60-seat restaurant and oversize 30-seat lounge wouldn't be out of place in L.A., featuring a rich color palette, plush yet comfy furnishings, hardwood floors, sea grass carpets, billowing white draperies forming cozy nooks, and romantically lighted lanterns throughout. Lionel's eclectic menu showcases the Caribbean's sultry melting pot of culinary traditions—Spanish, Asian, French, and African, taking the confusion out of fusion cuisine. Stunners such as poached mahimahi with parsnip-cassava mash, wilted zucchini leekoven-dried tomato jam, and wild mushroom-roast garlic sauce provide textbook examples of how to juxtapose textures, flavors, even colors. The island's finest wine list runs from Argentina to Alsace to Australia; bracket your evening with trendy cocktails with *cojones* and the extensive postprandial selection of aged rums and Cuban cigars. Lunch is less expensive and varied but equally hedonistic; try the killer lobster avocado salad or conch fritters reinvented with lime-cilantro-thyme tartar sauce. ⊠ *Turtle Beach* ☎ *869/469–5299* ⊕ *www.stkittsbeachhouse.com* ⚖ *Reservations essential* ⊙ *Closed Sun. No lunch Mon.*

$$$
CARIBBEAN

✕ **Bobsy's.** Locals flock to this semi-alfresco terrace eatery for lively happy hours and, on weekends, for karaoke, sizzling salsa, live bands, and a DJ spinning favorite dance tunes. Vivid colors (scarlet linens, orange walls with mauve and lime trim, turquoise rafters), African masks, and autographed photos of reggae stars attest to the authentic island ambience, as do such fine specialties as pumpkin soup, glazed passion-fruit ribs, and shrimp in tamarind-ginger sauce (you can also

Beach House.

get hefty burgers, gourmet pizzas, and such Continental standbys as chicken fettuccine Alfredo and rack of lamb). At this writing it is slated to move to new quarters by late fall 2011, closer to the beach, but maintain the decor and menu. ⊠ *Sugar's Complex, Frigate Bay* ☎ *869/466–6133* ⊕ *www.bobsysbarandgrill.com* ⊗ *No lunch Sun. and Mon.*

$$–$$$
SEAFOOD

✕ **Fisherman's Wharf.** Part of the Ocean Terrace Inn, this extremely casual waterfront eatery is decorated in swaggering nautical style, with rusty anchors, casks, buoys, and walls splashed with aqua waves and wild, psychedelically hued murals of fishing boats and their catch. Try the excellent conch chowder, followed by fresh grilled lobster or other shipshape seafood, and finish off your meal with a slice of the memorable banana cheesecake. The place is generally hopping, especially on weekend nights when live bands often jam atop the split-level, breeze-swept bar. ⊠ *Ocean Terrace Inn, Fortlands, Basseterre* ☎ *869/465–2754* ⊕ *www.oceanterraceinn.com* ⊗ *No lunch.*

$$$
FRENCH

✕ **La Belle Vie.** This très sympa nod to St. Kitts' French heritage is aptly titled "the good life." The cozy antiques-strewn lobby–bar leads to the semi-enclosed garden dining patio. Everything brims with brio from the brioches baked on-site to Brel and Aznavour on the soundtrack (accompanied by tree frogs). Nantes-born Fabien Richard deftly executes bistro fare at fair prices. You could feast on appetizers alone: salad *chabichoux* (warm goat cheese, *lardons*, mesclun) or velvety tomato *bavarois* with prosciutto. But opt for the bargain $38 three-course prix fixe; main courses might include salmon in aniseed sauce, duck sautéed with honey and lime, or olive-and-balsamic-crusted rack of lamb. Even the old-fashioned veggies delight, including smashing potatoes *dauphinoise*. Save room for an unimpeachable peach sable (tart) with crème anglaise. A few minor complaints include: mosquitoes on still nights, limited wine selection, and the occasional overcooked if tasty entrée. ⊠ *19 Golf View, Frigate Bay* ☎ *869/465–5216 or 869/764–6035* ⊕ *www.labellevie-stkitts.com* ☞ *Reservations essential* ☺ *No lunch.*

$$–$$$$ ✕ **Marshall's.** The pool area of Horizons Villa Resort is transformed
ECLECTIC into a stylish eatery thanks to smashing ocean views, potted plants, serenading tree frogs, and elegant candlelit tables. Jamaican chef Verral Marshall fuses ultrafresh local ingredients with global influences. Recommended offerings include conch cutlets with remoulade, pan-seared duck breast with raspberry-ginger sauce, or homemade sorbets. Most dishes are regrettably orthodox (rack of lamb in port reduction), and the execution is uneven, especially since Verral opened a branch of Marshall's on Nevis. ⊠ *Horizons Villa Resort, Frigate Bay* ☎ *869/466–8245* ⊕ *www.marshalls-stkitts.com* ⚓ *Reservations essential* ☺ *No lunch.*

$$–$$$ ✕ **PJ's Pizza.** "Garbage pizza"—topped with everything but the kitchen
ITALIAN sink—is a favorite, or you can create your own pie at this longtime hangout owned by three expats (two Canadians and a Texan: Pat, Jude, and Janet). Sandwiches, calzones, simple but lustily flavored pastas (try the goat cheese ravioli in sun-dried tomato sauce or spaghetti with humongous garlicky meatballs), and mamma-mia classics (eggplant Parmesan to chicken piccata) are also served. Finish your meal with delicious, moist rum cake. This casual spot, bordering the golf course and open to cooling breezes, is always boisterous (especially during the 9–10 pm happy hour, overseen with good spirits by bartending fixture Ashton), despite—or perhaps because of—its ironic location beside the Frigate Bay police station. ⊠ *Frigate Bay* ☎ *869/465–8373* ⊕ *www.pjsrestaurantstkitts.com* ☺ *Closed Mon. and Sept. No lunch.*

$$$ ✕ **Reggae Beach Bar & Grill.** Treats at this popular daytime watering hole
ECLECTIC include honey-mustard ribs, coconut shrimp, grilled lobster, decadent banana bread pudding with rum sauce, and an array of tempting tropical libations. Business cards and pennants from around the world plaster the bar, and the open-air space is decorated with a variety of nautical accoutrements, from fishnets and turtle shells to painted wooden crustaceans. You can snorkel here, spot hawksbill turtles and the occasional monkey, visit the enormous house pig Wilbur (who once "ate" beer cans whole, then moved to "lite" beers—but feeding is no longer encouraged), laze in a palm-shaded hammock, or rent a kayak, Hobie Cat or snorkeling gear. Beach chairs are free. Locals come Sunday afternoons for dancing to live bands. ⊠ *S.E. Peninsula Rd., Cockleshell Beach* ☎ *869/762–5050* ⊕ *www.reggaebeachbar.com* ☺ *No dinner.*

$$$$ ✕ **Royal Palm.** A 65-foot, spring-fed pool bisects the elegant restaurant at
ECLECTIC Ottley's Plantation Inn into a semi-enclosed lounge with sea views and a
★ breezy alfresco stone patio. Four-course extravaganzas (dishes are also available à la carte) blend indigenous ingredients with Asian, Mediterranean, Southwestern, and Latin touches: for example, pumpkin-chèvre ravioli in hazelnut brown butter; lobster Bambaya swirled with ginger, tomato, tamarind, key lime, white wine, and cream over coconut rice;

or marinated, grilled, flat-iron steak Bayamon with chipotle drizzle, African cream polenta, and avocado salsa. Finish with simple yet sinful indulgences such as coconut cream cheesecake or mango mousse with raspberry coulis. The combination of superb food, artful presentation, romantic setting, and warm bonhomie is unbeatable. ⊠ *Ottley's Plantation Inn, Ottley's* ☎ *869/465–7234* ⊕ *www.ottleys.com* ⌲ *Reservations essential.*

$$$–$$$$
ECLECTIC
★

✕ **Serendipity.** This stylish restaurant occupies an old Creole home whose deck offers lovely views of Basseterre and the bay. As charming as the enclosed patio is, the interior lounge is more conducive to romantic dining, with cushy sofas, patterned hardwood floors, porcelain lamps, and African carvings. The menu reflects co-owner–chef Alexander James's peripatetic postings: you might start with wonderfully crispy fried Brie with sweet-and-sour blackberry sauce or beautifully presented spring rolls with plum-soy dipping sauce. Mahimahi crusted with cheddar, Parmesan, basil, and garlic floating on pools of creole and saffron cream sauces; or bacon-wrapped beef tenderloin topped with pâté, prosciutto slice, and Madeira sauce paired with tiger shrimp in garlic sauce typify the ambitious main courses. The wine list is well considered; vegetarians will be delighted by the many creative options; and very affordable lunches feature gargantuan tapas-style selections. ⊠ *3 Wigley Ave., Fortlands, Basseterre* ☎ *869/465–9999* ⊕ *www.serendipitystkitts.com* ⌲ *Reservations essential* ⊘ *Closed Mon. No lunch weekends.*

$$$
ECLECTIC
★

✕ **Spice Mill.** This beachfront beauty references the Caribbean's multiethnic cuisine, a melting pot of African, French, English, Iberian, Indian, Chinese, and Dutch influences. But the kitchen also stays home in proper locavore fashion, sourcing as much local produce as possible from Kittitian farmers and fishermen (who might troop through the restaurant with 30 just-caught snapper for "De Bossman"). Spice Mill merrily marries those gastronomic traditions with fresh ingredients, juxtaposing colors, tastes, and textures right from the dips served with scrumptious homemade breads. Grilled spiny lobster might be plated with green banana ratatouille, ginger-scented jasmine rice, and curry butter—or cherry tomatoes, breadfruit hash, spinach, and chive-butter sauce. Confit of duck leg brilliantly contrasts sweet and savory: pumpkin, braised celery, and orange sauce. The culinary globe-trotting approach also dictates the decor—a mix of regional (coconut-wood-top bar, Carib canoe, and crayfish baskets from Dominica) and cosmopolitan (white beach beds, cushioned couches) elements, making even the bar (open daily and serving light snacks) a barefoot-chic hangout. ⊠ *Cockleshell Bay* ☎ *869/465–6455* ⊕ *www.spicemillrestaurant.com* ⌲ *Reservations essential* ⊘ *Closed Sun. No dinner Mon.*

$–$$
SEAFOOD
★

✕ **Sprat Net.** This simple cluster of picnic tables—sheltered by a brilliant-turquoise corrugated-tin roof and decorated with driftwood, life preservers, photos of coastal scenes, and fishnets—sits on a sliver of sand. Nonetheless, it's an island hot spot. There's nothing fancy on the menu: just grilled fish, lobster, ribs, and chicken served with mountains of coleslaw and peas and rice. But the fish is amazingly fresh: the fishermen–owners heap their catches on a center table from which you choose your own dinner, then watch it grilled to your specification before dining family-style on paper plates. An adjacent hut serves up the final food group: pizza, Wednesday–Sunday. Sprat Net offers old-style Caribbean flavor, with the cheapest drinks and best bands on weekends. No wonder cars line up along the road, creating an impromptu jump-up. ⊠ *Main Road, Old Road Town* ☎ *869/466–7535* ▭ *No credit cards* ☉ *Closed Sept. No lunch.*

WHERE TO STAY

St. Kitts has an appealing variety of places to stay—beautifully restored plantation inns (where a Modified American Plan, including afternoon tea in addition to breakfast and dinner, is the norm), full-service affordable hotels, simple beachfront cottages, and all-inclusive resorts. There are also several guesthouses and self-serve condos. Increasing development has been touted (or threatened) for years. At this writing, the ultraritzy Park Hyatt is planning to debut its first Caribbean property in 2013 on Cockleshell Bay, alongside oft-delayed upmarket villa compounds such as the culture-oriented, ecocentric Kittitian Hills (architect Bill Bensley designed some of Thailand's most remarkable resorts), a major marine theme park, several golf courses, and the $17 million Beaumont Park horse-racing venue (itself part of a megadevelopment on the island's northwest end). The island's first large hotel, the St. Kitts Marriott Resort, plans to add 270 condos by late 2012, but any upcoming developments are all fewer than 300 units, including the sparkling 185-unit Ocean's Edge condo complex on Frigate Bay and deluxe properties such as the grand Christophe Harbour development that will sprawl elegantly across the Southeast Peninsula replete with spectacular villas, beach clubs, celebrity restaurants, megayacht marina, Tom Fazio–designed golf course, and boutique hotels (perhaps a Mandarin Oriental).

The following reviews have been condensed for this book. Please go to Fodors.com for full reviews of each property.

¢
RESORT
Bird Rock Beach Resort. This basic scuba-set resort crowns a bluff above Basseterre, delivering amazing views of the town, sea, and mountains from every vantage point. **Pros:** exuberant, friendly clientele; great diving; excellent value; superb views. **Cons:** small man-made beach; insufficient parking; difficult for physically challenged to maneuver; several rooms leased longterm to students; poor lighting; dilapidated decor. ⊠ *Basseterre Bay, 2 mi (3 km) east of Basseterre* ⊕ *Box 227, Basseterre* ☎ *869/465–8914 or 800/621–1270* ⊕ *www.birdrockbeach. com* ↪ *31 rooms, 19 studios* ☖ *In-room: kitchen (some), Internet. In-hotel: restaurants, tennis court, bars, pools, beach, business center, water sports* ❘O❘ *No meals.*

¢–$
HOTEL
Frigate Bay Resort. This cheery property's combination of location, value, and polite service compensates for dowdy decor and dire need for minor repairs throughout (new ownership as of early 2011 vows to freshen the rooms and replace appliances). **Pros:** terrific value; easy walk to beaches; pretty pool spanned by gazebo and bridge; plentiful year-round deals; sofa beds and easily combined units ideal for families. **Cons:** no direct beachfront; slightly dilapidated; occasionally

Ottley's Plantation Inn.

noisy; uneven food; Wi-Fi signal intermittent. ☐ *Box 137, Frigate Bay* ☎ *869/465-8935 or 800/266-2185* ⊕ *www.frigatebay.com* ⌨ *40 rooms, 24 studios* ⚐ *In-room: kitchen (some), Internet, Wi-Fi (some). In-hotel: restaurant, bar, pool, business center* ⏀ *No meals.*

¢–$
HOTEL
▣ **Ocean Terrace Inn.** Referred to by locals as OTI, this is a rarity: a smart, intimate business hotel that nonetheless appeals to vacationers. **Pros:** excellent service; fine facilities for a small hotel; good restaurants; walking distance to Basseterre attractions and restaurants; suites represent excellent value for families. **Cons:** must drive to beaches; sprawling layout; some rooms need sprucing up; difficult for physically challenged to navigate. ☒ *Wigley Ave., Box 65, Fortlands* ☎ *869/465-2754 or 800/524-0512* ⊕ *www.oceanterraceinn. com* ⌨ *69 rooms, 8 condos* ⚐ *In-room: safe (some), kitchen (some), Wi-Fi (some). In-hotel: restaurants, bars, pools, gym, business center, water sports* ⏀ *No meals.*

$$$–$$$$
HOTEL
Fodor'sChoice
★
▣ **Ottley's Plantation Inn.** You're treated like a beloved relative rather than a commercial guest at this quintessential Caribbean hotel, formerly a sugar plantation, at the foot of Mt. Liamuiga. **Pros:** posh yet unpretentious luxury; wonderfully helpful staff and owners; gorgeous gardens; excellent dining. **Cons:** no beach; bumpy access road; long walk from farthest cottages to office. ☒ *Ottley's, southwest of Nicola Town* ☎ *869/465-7234 or 800/772-3039* ⊕ *www.ottleys. com* ⌨ *24 rooms* ⚐ *In-room: safe, no TV (some), Internet, Wi-Fi (some). In-hotel: restaurant, tennis court, bar, pool, spa, business center* ⏀ *No meals.*

$$–$$$ ⚏ **Rawlins Plantation Inn.** Civilized serenity awaits at this remote plan-
B&B/INN   tation inn between verdant Mt. Liamuiga and the cobalt Caribbean.
Pros: utter tranquillity; exquisite setting; fine kitchen; no TV. Cons: no
beach; uneven service; no TV. ⌦ *Box 340, St. Paul's* ☎ *869/465–6221
or 888/790–5264* ⊕ *www.rawlinsplantation.com* ↄ *12 rooms* & *In-
room: no a/c, no phone, no TV. In-hotel: restaurant, tennis court, bar,
pool, business center* ⊙ *Closed Aug. and Sept.* ⊺⊙⊺ *Breakfast.*

$ ⚏ **Rock Haven Bed & Breakfast.** This restful, cozy bed-and-breakfast,
B&B/INN   a two-minute drive from Frigate Bay beaches (airport transfers are
included), provides true local warmth, courtesy of Judith and Keith
Blake. Pros: genuine island hospitality; immaculately maintained; delicious breakfasts. Cons: long walk to beach; car recommended to get
around. ⌦ *Box 821, Frigate Bay* ☎ *869/465–5503* ⊕ *www.rock-haven.
com* ↄ *2 rooms* & *In-room: no a/c (some), kitchen (some), Wi-Fi. In-
hotel: laundry facilities, Wi-Fi* ⊺⊙⊺ *Breakfast.*

$$–$$$ ⚏ **St. Kitts Marriott Resort.** Although this big, bustling beachfront resort
RESORT   offers something for everyone from families to conventioneers, golfers
to gamblers, it's overscaled for tiny, quiet St. Kitts and almost devoid of
Caribbean charm and flair, save for a jungle mural behind reception, an
odd pirate ship replica, and craft market hidden in the basement. Pros:
great range of activities; good bars; plentiful on-site duty-free shopping;
enormous main pool. Cons: impersonal, sometimes inefficient service;
surprise extra charges; mostly mediocre food; not enough units feature
ocean views. ⊠ *858 Frigate Bay Rd., Frigate Bay* ☎ *869/466–1200 or
800/223–6388* ⊕ *www.stkittsmarriott.com* ↄ *393 rooms, 76 suites*
& *In-room: safe, Wi-Fi (some), Internet. In-hotel: golf course, restaurants, room service, tennis courts, bars, children's programs, pools,
gym, spa, beach, business center, water sports* ⊺⊙⊺ *No meals.*

¢–$ ⚏ **Timothy Beach Resort.** The only St. Kitts resort sitting directly on a
RENTAL   Caribbean beach is incomparably located and restful, a great budget find thanks to smiling service and simple but sizable apartments.
Pros: unbeatable location; close to the beach action; pleasant on-site
restaurant and bar; plentiful deals. Cons: occasionally worn decor;
can hear beach bar music weekend nights; no view from most bedrooms. ⊠ *1 South Frigate Bay Beach, Frigate Bay* ☎ *869/465–8597
or 877/942–3224* ⊕ *www.timothybeach.com* ↄ *60 apartments* & *In-
room: kitchen (some), Wi-Fi. In-hotel: restaurant, bar, pool, beach,
business center* ⊺⊙⊺ *No meals.*

NIGHTLIFE

Most nightlife revolves around the hotels, which host folkloric shows
and calypso and steel bands of the usual limbo-rum-and-reggae variety. The growing Frigate Bay "strip" of beach bars, including Monkey
Bar, Rainbow, Mr. X Shiggidy Shack, Inon's, Elvis Love Shack, Buddies
Beach hut, and Ziggy's, is the place to party hearty on weekend nights.
A wild, wacky evening is promised by **Bob & Elvis The Party Bus** (⊠ *Frigate
Bay* ☎ *869/466–8110* ⊕ *www.caribbeanjourneymasters.com/BobElvis.
cfm*) as they escort an increasingly raucous crowd via their psychedelically hued bus Wednesday and Friday to four of the island's top liming

spots. Look for such hard-driving local exponents of soca music as Nu-Vybes, Grand Masters, Small Axe, and Royalton 5; and "heavy dancehall" reggae group, House of Judah. The Marriott's large, glitzy casino has table games and slots.

BARS AND CLUBS

A favorite happy-hour watering hole is the **Circus Grill** (✉ *Bay Rd., Basseterre* ☎ *869/465–0143*), a second-floor eatery whose verandah offers views of the harbor and the activity on the Circus.

Club Kactus (✉ *Lighthouse, outside Basseterre by Bird Rock Beach Resort* ☎ *869/466–9016*) is jammed and jamming on most weekend nights, especially when respected Jamaican musical acts perform live. Its kitchen also turns out local fare with surprising flair.

★ **Keys Cigar Bar** (✉ *St. Kitts Marriott Resort, Frigate Bay* ☎ *869/466– 1200*) is a surprisingly low-key, classy hangout, with jazz–salsa duos, cushy sofas, high-back straw chairs, chess-set tables, and a superlative selection of aged rums and *Cubanos* (as well as top Dominican and Nicaraguan brands). If it's packed, try the hotel's Blue Martini, for piano stylings and 'tinis with 'tude.

★ **Mr. X Shiggidy Shack** (✉ *Frigate Bay* ☎ *869/762–3983 or 869/465–0673* ⊕ *www.mrxshiggidyshack.com*) is known for its sizzling Thursday-night bonfire parties replete with fire-eaters, raucous karaoke Saturday, and Sunday dinners accompanied by the MRT band; it's also a must-stop on locals' unofficial Friday-night liming circuit of Frigate Bay bars.

SHOPPING

St. Kitts has limited shopping, but several duty-free shops offer good deals on jewelry, perfume, china, and crystal. Numerous galleries sell excellent paintings and sculptures. The batik fabrics, scarves, caftans, and wall hangings of Caribelle Batik are well known. British expat Kate Spencer is an artist who has lived on the island for years, reproducing its vibrant colors on everything from silk pareus (beach wraps) to note cards to place mats. Other good island buys include crafts, jams, and herbal teas. Don't forget to pick up some CSR (Cane Spirit Rothschild), which is distilled from fresh wild sugarcane right on St. Kitts. The Brinley Gold company has made a splash among spirits connoisseurs for its coffee, mango, coconut, lime, and vanilla rums (there is a tasting room at Port Zante).

AREAS AND MALLS

Most shopping plazas are in downtown Basseterre, on the streets radiating from the Circus. **All Kind of Tings**, a peppermint-pink edifice on Liverpool Row at College Street Ghaut, functions as a de facto vendors' market, where several booths sell local crafts and cheap T-shirts. Its courtyard frequently hosts folkloric dances, fashion shows, poetry readings, and steel-pan concerts. The **Pelican Mall** —a shopping arcade designed to look like a traditional Caribbean street—has 26 stores, a restaurant, tourism offices, and a bandstand near the cruise-ship pier. Directly behind Pelican Mall, on the waterfront, is **Port Zante**, the deep-water cruise-ship pier where a much-delayed upscale shopping–dining complex is becoming a 25-shop area (including the usual ubiquitous large jewelry concerns like Aboott's, Diamonds International, and Kay Jewelers); the **Amina Market** here is a fine source for cheap local crafts. If you're looking for inexpensive, island-y T-shirts and souvenirs, check out the series of vendors' huts behind Pelican Mall to the right of Port Zante as you face the sea. **Shoreline Plaza** is next to the Treasury Building, right on Basseterre's waterfront. **TDC Mall** is just off the Circus in downtown, with a few boutiques and Chef's Garden for great local food in the a courtyard setting adorned with gingerbread and sports photos.

SPECIALTY ITEMS

ART **Booyork Gallery** (⊠ *Sir Lee Moore's Bldg., College St., Basseterre* ☎ *869/ 466–9159*) is the atelier of Dennis Richards, who works in a remarkable range of media from pastels to papier-mâché, ceramics to collages: creative Carnival-inspired accessories (incorporating coconut husks, painted ostrich feathers, spangles, and beads), paintings on packed black sand, and wondrous watercolors, both figurative and abstract. Call ahead for appointments.

Spencer Cameron Art Gallery (⊠ *10 N. Independence Sq., Basseterre* ☎ *869/465–1617*) has historical reproductions of Caribbean island charts and prints, in addition to owner Rosey Cameron's popular Carnevale clown prints and a wide selection of exceptional artwork by Caribbean artists. It also showcases the work of Glass Island (exquisite Italianate art glass from frames to plates in sinuous shapes and seductive colors) and various local craftspeople. The gallery will mail anywhere. Rosey and Kate Spencer also run a new offshoot in the Marriott called the Art Cooperative.

HANDICRAFTS **Caribelle Batik** (⊠ *Romney Manor, Old Road Town* ☎ *869/465–6253*)
★ sells gloriously colored batik wraps, kimonos, caftans, T-shirts, dresses, wall hangings, and the like.

The **Crafthouse** (⊠ *Bay Rd., Southwell Industrial Site, ½ mi [1 km] east of Shoreline Plaza, Basseterre* ☎ *869/465–7754*) is one of the best sources for local dolls, wood carvings, and straw work.

Island Hopper (⊠ *The Circus, Basseterre* ☎ *869/465–2905*) is a good place for island crafts, especially wood carvings, pottery, textiles, and colorful resort wear, as well as humorous T-shirts and trinkets.

Fodor's Choice **Kate Design** (⊠ *Mount Pleasant House, St. Paul's* ☎ *869/465–7740*)
★ showcases the highly individual style of Kate Spencer, whose original paintings, serigraphs, note cards, and other pieces are available from her studio outside Rawlins Plantation.

The **Potter's House** (⊠ *Camps Estate House, Camps Village* ☎ *869/465– 5947*) is the atelier-home of Carla Astaphan, whose beautifully glazed ceramics and masks celebrate Afro-Caribbean heritage; she also carries marvelous Haitian pieces.

SPORTS AND ACTIVITIES

BOATING AND FISHING

Most operators are on the Caribbean side of Frigate Bay, known for its gentle currents. Turtle Bay offers stronger winds and stunning views of Nevis. Though not noted for big-game fishing, several steep offshore drop-offs do lure wahoo, barracuda, shark, tuna, yellowtail snapper, and mackerel. Rates are occasionally negotiable; figure approximately $350 for a four-hour excursion with refreshments. The knowledgeable Todd Leypoldt of **Leeward Island Charters** (✉ *Basseterre* ☎ *869/465–7474* ∰ *www.stkittsleewardislandcharters.com*) takes you out on his charter boats, *Caona* and *Eagle*. He's also available for snorkeling charters, beach picnics, and sunset-moonlight cruises. **Mr. X Watersports** (✉ *Frigate Bay* ☎ *869/465–0673* ∰ *www.mrxshiggidyshack.com*), located within Mr. X Shiggidy Shack (⇨ *see Nightlife above*) rents small craft, including motorboats (waterskiing and jet skiing are available). Paddleboats are $15 per hour, sailboats (with one free lesson) $25 per hour. Deep-sea fishing charters, snorkeling tours, water taxis, sunset dinner cruises, and private charters with captain and crew are available. Mr. X and his cohorts are usually hanging out at the adjacent open-air Monkey Bar. **Reggae Beach Bar & Grill** (✉ *Cockleshell Beach* ☎ *869/762–5050* ∰ *www. reggaebeachbar.com*) rents kayaks from the restaurant, offers sailing lessons, and can also arrange fishing trips.

DIVING AND SNORKELING

Though unheralded as a dive destination, St. Kitts has more than a dozen excellent sites, protected by several new marine parks. The surrounding waters feature shoals, hot vents, shallows, canyons, steep walls, and caverns at depths from 40 to nearly 200 feet. The St. Kitts Maritime Archaeological Project, which surveys, records, researches, and preserves the island's underwater treasures, has charted several hundred wrecks of galleons, frigates, and freighters dating back to the 17th century. **Bloody Bay Reef** is noted for its network of underwater grottoes daubed with purple anemones, sienna bristle worms, and canary-yellow sea fans that seem to wave you in. **Coconut Tree Reef,** one of the largest in the area, includes sea fans, sponges, and anemones, as well as the Rocks, three enormous boulders with impressive multilevel diving. The only drift dive site, **Nags Head** has strong currents, but experienced divers might spot gliding rays, lobsters, turtles, and reef sharks. Since it sank in 50 feet of water in the early 1980s, the *River Taw* makes a splendid site for less experienced divers. **Sandy Point Reef** has been designated a National Marine Park and includes Paradise Reef, with swim-through 90-foot sloping canyons, and Anchors Away, where anchors have been encrusted with coral formations. The 1985 wreck of the *Talata* lies in 70 feet of water; barracudas, rays, groupers, and grunts dart through its hull.

Dive St. Kitts (✉ *2 mi [3 km] east of Basseterre, Frigate Bay* ☎ *869/465–1189* ∰ *www.divestkitts.com*), a PADI–NAUI facility, offers competitive prices, computers to maximize time below, wide range of courses from refresher to technical, and friendly, laid-back dive masters. The Bird Rock location features superb shore diving (unlimited when you book packages): common sightings 20 to 30 feet out include octopuses, nurse sharks, manta and spotted eagle rays, sea horses, even barracudas George and Georgianna. It also offers kayak and snorkeling tours. Kenneth Samuel of **Kenneth's Dive Center** (✉ *Bay Rd., Newtown* ☎ *869/465-2670* ⊕ *www.kennethsdivecenter.com*), a PADI company, takes small groups of divers with C cards to nearby reefs. Rates average $70 for single-tank dives, $95 for double-tank dives; add $10 for equipment. Night dives, including lights, are $80–$90, and snorkeling trips (four-person minimum) are $40, drinks included. After 25 years' experience, former fisherman Samuel is considered an old pro (Jean-Michel Cousteau requested his guidance upon his first visit in the 1990s) and strives to keep groups small and prices reasonable. **Pro-Divers** (✉ *Ocean Terrace Inn, Basseterre* ☎ *869/466-3483* ⊕ *www.prodiversstkitts.com*) is owned by Auston Macleod, a PADI-certified dive master–instructor, and offers resort and certification courses running $125–$420. Dive computers are included gratis. He offers free introductory scuba courses twice weekly at Ocean Terrace Inn. He also takes groups to snorkeling sites accessible only by boat via his custom-built 38-foot Cat.

GOLF

St. Kitts hopes to market itself as a golf destination with the remodeling of the Royal St. Kitts Golf Course and two upcoming resort and villa developments that include 18-hole courses, one designed by Tom Fazio (which promises to be one of the Caribbean's most spectacular, with huge elevation drops, ruins, extraordinary sweeping vistas, carries over ravines: "Scottsdale meets Pebble Beach"), another by Ian Woosnam. The **Royal St. Kitts Golf Club** (✉ *St. Kitts Marriott Resort, Frigate Bay* ☎ *869/466-2700 or 866/785-4653* ⊕ *www.royalstkittsgolfclub.com*) is an 18-hole, par-71 links-style championship course that underwent a complete redesign by Thomas McBroom to maximize Caribbean and Atlantic views and increase the challenge (there are 12 lakes and 83 bunkers). Holes 15 through 17 (the latter patterned after Pebble Beach No. 18) skirt the Atlantic in their entirety, lending new meaning to the term sand trap. The sudden gusts, wide but twisting fairways, and extremely hilly terrain demand pinpoint accuracy and finesse, yet holes such as 18 require pure power. Greens fees are $150 for Marriott guests in high season, $180 for nonguests, with twilight and super-twilight discounts. The development includes practice bunkers, a putting green, a short-game chipping area, and the fairly high-tech Royal Golf Academy.

GUIDED TOURS

The taxi driver who picks you up will probably offer to act as your guide to the island. Each driver is knowledgeable and does a three-hour tour of Nevis for $75 or a four-hour tour of St. Kitts for $80. He can also make a lunch reservation at one of the plantation restaurants, and you can incorporate this into your tour.

On St. Kitts, **Kantours** (☎ *869/465-2098, 869/465-3054 in St. Kitts, 869/469-0136 in Nevis* ⊕ *www.kantours.com*) offers comprehensive general island tours, as well as a variety of specialty excursions, including ATV expeditions. The friendly guides at **Tropical Tours** (☎ *869/465-4167* ⊕ *www.tropicalstkitts-nevis.com*) can run you around St. Kitts (from $27 per person), arrange kayaking and snorkeling, deep-sea fishing ($135 per person), and take you to the volcano or rain forest for $52 per person and up.

HIKING

Trails in the central mountains vary from easy to don't-try-it-by-yourself. Monkey Hill and Verchild's Peak aren't difficult, although the Verchild's climb will take the better part of a day. Don't attempt Mt. Liamuiga without a guide. You'll start at Belmont Estate—at the west end of the island —on horseback, and then proceed on foot to the lip of the crater, at 2,600 feet. You can go down into the crater—1,000 feet deep and 1 mi (1½ km) wide, with a small freshwater lake—clinging to vines and roots and scaling rocks, even trees. Expect to get muddy. There are several fine operators (each hotel recommends its favorite); tour rates generally range from $50 for a rain-forest walk to $95 for a volcano expedition and usually include round-trip transportation from your hotel and picnic lunch.

★ Earl of **Duke of Earl's Adventures** (☎ 869/465–1899 or 869/663–0994) is as entertaining as his nickname suggests—and his prices are slightly cheaper ($45 for a rain-forest tour includes refreshments, $70 volcano expeditions add lunch; hotel pickup and drop-off is complimentary). He genuinely loves his island and conveys that enthusiasm, encouraging hikers to swing on vines or sample unusual-looking fruits during his rain-forest trip. He also conducts a thorough volcano tour to the crater's rim and a drive-through ecosafari tour ($50 with lunch). Greg Pereira of **Greg's Safaris** (☎ 869/465–4121 ⊕ www.gregsafaris.com), whose family has lived on St. Kitts since the early 19th century, takes groups on half-day trips into the rain forest and on full-day hikes up the volcano and through the grounds of a private 18th-century greathouse. The rain-forest trips include visits to sacred Carib sites, abandoned sugar mills, and an excursion down a 100-foot coastal canyon containing a wealth of Amerindian petroglyphs. The Off the Beaten Track 4x4 Plantation Tour provides a thorough explanation of the role sugar and rum played in the Caribbean economy and colonial wars. He and his staff relate fascinating historical, folkloric, and botanical information.

HORSEBACK RIDING

Wild North Frigate Bay and desolate Conaree Beach are great for riding, as is the rain forest. Guides from **Trinity Stables** (☎ 869/465–3226) offer beach rides ($50) and trips into the rain forest ($60), both including hotel pickup. The latter is intriguing, as guides discuss plants' medicinal properties along the way (such as sugarcane to stanch bleeding) and pick oranges right off a tree to squeeze fresh juice. Otherwise, the staffers are cordial but shy; this isn't a place for beginners' instruction.

SEA EXCURSIONS

In addition to the usual snorkeling, sunset, and party cruises (ranging in price from $40 to $95), most companies offer whale-watching excursions during the winter migrating season, January through April. **Blue Water Safaris** (✉ Basseterre ☎ 869/466–4933 ⊕ www.bluewatersafaris. com) offers half-day snorkeling trips or beach barbecues on deserted cays, as well as sunset and moonlight cruises on its 65-foot catamarans

Irie Lime and *Swaliga*, and the smaller *Falcon*. It also runs kayaking tours. **Leeward Island Charters** (⊠ *Basseterre* 🖀 *869/465–7474* ⊕ *www. stkittsleewardislandcharters.com*) offers day and overnight charters on two catamarans—the 67-foot *Eagle* and 78-foot *Spirit of St. Kitts*. Day sails are from 9:30 to 4:30 and include a barbecue, an open bar, and use of snorkeling equipment. The Nevis trip stops at Pinney's Beach for a barbecue and at Shooting Bay, a tiny cove in the bullying shadow of a sheer cliff, where petrels and frigate birds inspect your snorkeling skills. The crews are mellow, affable, and knowledgeable about island life.

ZIP-LINING

🕉 **Sky Safari Tours** (⊠ *Wingfield Estate* 🖀 *869/466–4259 or 869/465–4347* ⊕ *www.skysafaristkitts.com*) whisks would-be Tarzans and Janes through the "Valley of the Giants" (so dubbed for the towering trees) at speeds up to 50 mph (80 kph along five cable lines); the longest (nicknamed "The Boss") stretches 1,350 feet through towering turpentine and mahogany trees draped thickly with bromeliads, suspended 250 feet above the ground. Following the Canadian-based company's mantra of "faster, higher, safer," it uses a specially designed trolley with secure harnesses attached. Many of the routes afford unobstructed views of Brimstone Hill and the sea beyond. The outfit emphasizes environmental and historic aspects. Guides provide nature interpretation and commentary, and the office incorporates Wingfield Estate's old sugar plantation, distillery, and church ruins, which visitors can explore. Admission is usually $65–$75, depending on the tour chosen. It's open daily 9–6, with the first and last tours departing at 10 and 3.

NEVIS

Nevis's charm is its rusticity: there are no traffic lights, goats still amble through the streets of Charlestown, and local grocers announce whatever's in stock on a blackboard (anything from pig snouts to beer).

EXPLORING NEVIS

Nevis's Main Road makes a 21-mi (32-km) circuit through the five parishes; various offshoots of the road wind into the mountains. You can tour Charlestown, the capital, in a half hour or so, but you'll need three to four hours to explore the entire island.

Bath Springs. The Caribbean's first hotel, the Bath Hotel, built by businessman John Huggins in 1778, was so popular in the 19th century that visitors, including such dignitaries as Samuel Taylor Coleridge and Prince William Henry, traveled two months by ship to "take the waters" in the property's hot thermal springs. It suffered extensive hurricane and probably earthquake damage over the years and languished in disrepair until recently. Local volunteers have cleaned up the spring and built a stone pool and steps to enter the waters; now residents and visitors enjoy the springs, which range from 104°F to 108°F, though signs still caution that you bathe at your own risk, especially if you have heart problems. The development houses the Nevis Island Administration offices; there's still talk of adding massage huts, changing rooms, a restaurant, and a cultural center and historic exhibit on the original hotel property. Follow Main Street south from Charlestown. ⊠ *Charlestown outskirts* ☎ *No phone.*

★ **Botanical Gardens of Nevis.** In addition to terraced gardens and arbors, this remarkable 7.8-acre site in the glowering shadow of Mt. Nevis has natural lagoons, streams, and waterfalls, superlative bronze mermaids, egrets and herons, and extravagant fountains. You can find a proper rose garden, sections devoted to orchids and bromeliads, cacti, and flowering trees and shrubs—even a bamboo garden. The entrance to the Rain Forest Conservatory—which attempts to include every conceivable Caribbean ecosystem and then some—duplicates an imposing Maya temple. A splendid re-creation of a plantation-style greathouse contains a café with sweeping sea views, and the upscale Galleria shop selling art, textiles, jewelry, and Indonesian teak furnishings sourced during the owners' world travels. ⊠ *Montpelier Estate* ☎ *869/469–3509* ⊕ *www. botanicalgardennevis.com* 🎫 *$10, children 6–12 $7* ⊙ *Mon.–Sat. 9–5.*

★ **Charlestown.** About 1,200 of Nevis's 10,000 inhabitants live in the capital. If you arrive by ferry, as most people do, you'll walk smack onto Main Street from the pier. It's easy to imagine how tiny Charlestown, founded in 1660, must have looked in its heyday. The weathered buildings still have fanciful galleries, elaborate gingerbread fretwork, wooden shutters, and hanging plants. The stone building with the clock tower (1825, but mostly rebuilt after a devastating 1873 fire) houses the courthouse and second-floor **library** (a cool respite on sultry days). The little park next to the library is Memorial Square, dedicated to the fallen of World Wars I and II. Down the street from the square, archaeologists have discovered the remains of a Jewish cemetery and synagogue (Nevis reputedly had the Caribbean's second-oldest congregation), but there's little to see.

The **Alexander Hamilton Birthplace**, which contains the Hamilton Museum, sits on the waterfront. This bougainvillea-draped Georgian-style house is a reconstruction of what is believed to have been the American patriot's original home, built in 1680 and likely destroyed during a mid-19th earthquake. Born here in 1755, Hamilton moved to St. Croix when he was about 12. He moved to the American colonies to continue his education at 17; he became George Washington's Secretary of the Treasury and died in a duel with political rival Aaron Burr in 1804. The Nevis House of Assembly occupies the second floor; the museum downstairs contains Hamilton memorabilia, documents pertaining to the island's history, and displays on island geology, politics, architecture, culture, and cuisine. The gift shop is a wonderful source for historic maps, crafts, and books on Nevis. ⊠ *Low St., Charlestown* ☎ *869/469–5786* ⊕ *www.nevis-nhcs.org* 🎫 *$5, with admission to Nelson Museum $7* ⊙ *Weekdays 9–4, Sat. 9–noon.*

Eden Brown Estate. This government-owned mansion, built around 1740, is known as Nevis's haunted house, or haunted ruins. In 1822 a Miss Julia Huggins was to marry a fellow named Maynard. However, come wedding day, the groom and his best man killed each other in a duel. The bride-to-be became a recluse, and the mansion was closed down.

Mt. Nevis rising behind the Botanical Gardens of Nevis.

Local residents claim they can feel the presence of "someone" whenever they go near the eerie old house with its shroud of weeds and wildflowers. Though memorable more for the story than the hike or ruins, it's always open, and it's free. ⊠ *East Coast Rd., between Lime Kiln and Mannings, Eden Brown Bay* ☎ *No phone.*

Mansa's Farm. Anyone who wants a real sense of island daily life and subsistence should call Mansa. He'll take you past his fruit trees and herb gardens through rows of tomatoes, cucumbers, string beans, eggplant, zucchini, sweet pepper, melons, and more. Discussing the needs for at least partial organic growing practices, he passionately explains how he adapted traditional folk pesticides and describes the medicinal properties of various plants, cultivated and wild. He'll prepare a lunch using his produce, including delectable refreshing fruit drinks at his Mansa's Last Stand grocery across from the beach. Weekend barbecues are a highlight. All in all, this agritourism foray redefines food for thought. ⊠ *Cades Bay* ☎ *869/469–8520* 🍽 *Varies* ⊗ *Call for appointment.*

Nelson Museum. Purportedly this is the Western Hemisphere's largest collection of Lord Horatio Nelson memorabilia, including letters, documents, paintings, and even furniture from his flagship. Nelson was based in Antigua but came on military patrol to Nevis, where he met and eventually married Frances Nisbet, who lived on a 64-acre plantation here. Half the space is devoted to often-provocative displays on island life, from leading families to vernacular architecture to the adaptation of traditional African customs, from cuisine to Carnival. The shop is an excellent source for gifts, from homemade soaps to historical guides. ⊠ *Bath Rd. out-*

side Charlestown ☎ *869/469–0408* ⊕ *www.nevis-nhcs.org* ⊠ *$5, with Museum of Nevis History $7* ☉ *Weekdays 9–4, Sat. 9–noon.*

St. John's Figtree Church. Among the records of this church built in 1680 is a tattered, prominently displayed marriage certificate that reads "Horatio Nelson, Esquire, to Frances Nisbet, Widow, on March 11, 1787." ⊠ *Church Ground* ☎ *No phone.*

WHERE TO EAT

Dinner options range from intimate meals at plantation guesthouses (where the menu is often prix fixe) to casual eateries. Seafood is ubiquitous, and many places specialize in West Indian fare. The island is trying to raise its profile as a fine-dining destination by holding NICHE (Nevis International Culinary Heritage Exposition), a gastronomic festival with guest chefs and winemakers offering cooking seminars and tastings during the second half of October. Despite the difficult economy, a few promising eateries debuted the past two years.

WHAT TO WEAR

Dress is casual at lunch, although beach attire is unacceptable. Dress pants and sundresses are appropriate for dinner.

$$–$$$
ECLECTIC
★
✕ **Bananas.** Peripatetic English owner Gillian Smith has held jobs with Disney and Relais & Châteaux, and everything about Bananas (read lovably nuts) borrows from her wildly diverse experiences. Even the setting is delightfully deceptive: the classic stone, brick, and wood plantation greathouse nestled amid extravagant gardens was painstakingly built by Gillian herself in 2006. Her fun, funky, shabby-chic sensibility informs every aspect of the restaurant. The colonial look (pith helmets, steamer trunks, beamed ceiling, white wicker, chandeliers dangling from the corrugated tin roof) contrasts with Turkish kilims, Moroccan lamps, and whimsical touches like a lighted tailor's dummy and antique tennis rackets. The food is equally eclectic and globe-trotting, running from bourbon-glazed ribs to lobster tails with pineapple-ginger salsa. Despite the improvisational ambience, there's no monkeying around with quality at Bananas. ⊠ *Upper Hamilton Estate* ☎ *869/469–1891* ⊕ *www.bananasrestaurantnevis. com* ⬧ *Reservations essential* ☉ *Closed Sun. and Thurs.*

$$$–$$$$
ECLECTIC
★
✕ **Coconut Grove.** This thatched-palm roof–and–rough timber structure sports a sensuous South Seas look, best appreciated on the deck as the sun fireballs across the Caribbean. Inside, handsome teak furnishings are animated by Buddhas, parrot-hue throw pillows, batik hangings, and gauzy curtains. The service is warm, the champagne is properly chilled, and the splendid Pacific Rim–Mediterranean fusion fare seems designed to complement the admirable wine selection—with 8,000 bottles it is second on the sister islands only to that of the Four Seasons—rather than the other way around. Owners Gary and Karin Colt often bring winemaker friends in from Europe for tastings and dinners. Stephen "Chef Steve" Smith, a CIA grad and registered dietitian, introduced heart-healthier options such as curry-scented pumpkin soup with fat-free soy cream, grilled line-catch-of-the-day with pumpkin mash and sour-orange beurre-blanc foam, and a miraculously fiber-licious 100-calorie whole-wheat-flour–and–black-bean brownie sweetened

with agave syrup. Nonetheless, Gary (who likes his indulgences) laughs, "We're not the food police"; hence the menu includes the likes of burger en brioche with homemade duck foie gras and baby Camembert baked in pear brandy with cranberry confiture. Happy hour, 11 pm–midnight, often ushers in impromptu dancing, continuing the "Bali high" theme. The downstairs "Coco Beach" is hip-hopping and happening with infinity pool for use, sensational St. Kitts views, affordable, creative, lighter daytime fare (try ceviche made—and caught—by sous chef Matt Lloyd, or wondrous watermelon gazpacho goosed with basil), and live music many evenings. ⌖ *Nelson's Spring, Pinney's Beach* ☎ *869/469–1020* ⊕ *www.coconutgroverestaurantnevis.com* ⌖ *Reservations essential* ⊘ *Closed Aug.–Oct.*

$$$–$$$$
STEAKHOUSE
Fodor's Choice
★
✕ **Coral Grill.** The most ambitious aspect of the Four Seasons' renovation was the "de-formalizing" of its restaurants, most notably the unlikely but wildly successful conversion of its former haute Dining Room into a stunning steak house. Yet it eschews the genre's typical men's-club decor, lightening and brightening the original's imposing space. The graceful patio, beamed cathedral ceilings, flagstone hearth, and parquet floors remain; yet an open contemporary lounge that wouldn't be out of place in SoHo or Santa Monica now bisects the vast interior. Exquisite, deceptively simple appetizers include popcorn shrimp with red pepper dip or by-the-book beef tartare. But you're here for the grilled items, from Wagyu steak that dissolves in your mouth to intensely flavored yet meltingly tender Berkridge Kurobata pork chops to gossamer lobster tails. Corn-fed USDA prime cuts are Black Diamond–labeled, sourced from select Midwest farms. Meats are served with a choice of Shiraz reduction, béarnaise, or chimichurri; seafood with saffron sauce, lemongrass-coriander vinaigrette, or citrus hollandaise. Or dip into one of several flavored butters. The must extravagance is the Parillada, $65 for person for two (enough to feed a family). The hotel can arrange a unique interactive dive-and-dine experience, plunging you into the deep to pluck lobster and other marine creatures that the chefs will cook for you later. The phone-book-size wine list is admirably comprehensive with some surprisingly fair prices. Friday-night beach barbecues are deliciously hedonistic. ⌖ *Four Seasons Nevis, Pinney's Beach* ☎ *869/469–1111 or 869/469–6238* ⊕ *www.fourseasons.com/nevis* ⌖ *Reservations essential* ⊘ *No lunch.*

$–$$$
SEAFOOD
★
✕ **Double Deuce.** Mark Roberts, the former chef at Montpelier, decided to chuck the "five-star lifestyle" and now co-owns this jammed, jamming beach bar, which lures locals with fine, fairly priced fare, creative cocktails, and a Hemingway-esque feel (the shack is plastered with sailing and fishing pictures, as well as Balinese masks, steer horns, license plates, and wind chimes). Peer behind the ramshackle bar and you'll find a gleaming modern kitchen where Mark (and fun-loving firebrand partner Lyndeta) prepare sublime seafood he often catches himself, as well as organic beef burgers, velvety pumpkin soup, creative pastas, and lip-smacking ribs. The "DD" is as cool and mellow as it gets. Stop by for free Wi-Fi and proper espresso, a game of pool, riotous Thursday-night karaoke, or just to hang out with a Double Deuce Stinger (Lyndy's answer to Sunshine's Killer Bee punch). You'll find more than 5,000

songs on the "jukebox"—Akon to ZZ Top, Sarah Vaughan to Van Morrison; if you can't find your favorite, the "DJ" will download it for you while you take a quick dip. Dinner can be arranged for parties of 6 to 10. ⊠ *Pinney's Beach* ☎ *869/469–2222* ⊕ *www.doubledeucenevis.com* ⚑ *Reservations essential* ▭ *No credit cards* ⊘ *Closed Mon.*

$$–$$$
SEAFOOD

✗ **Gallipot.** Gallipot attracts locals with ultrafresh seafood at reasonable prices, marvelous views of St. Kitts across the road, and sensational sunsets. Large Sunday lunches with ample portions (musts are lobster eggs Benedict and classic roast beef and Yorkshire pudding) are a big draw. The Fosberys originally built the octagonal bar as an addition to their small beach house down the road, and their daughter and son-in-law, Tracy and Julian Rigby, provide the catch (fishnets and photos from their sportfishing championships grace the bar). Julian built a smoker (Tracy dubs it "the eyesore"), where he cures melt-in-your-mouth wahoo, kingfish, and sailfish carpaccio. Those seeking land specialties can happily tuck into the smoked duck, steak-and-kidney pie, or chicken korma curry, seasoned with herbs from Tracy's garden. ⊠ *Jones Bay* ☎ *869/469–8230* ⊕ *www.gallipotnevis.com* ⊘ *Closed Mon.–Wed. No dinner Sun.*

$$$–$$$$
ECLECTIC
★

✗ **Hermitage Plantation Inn.** After cocktails in the inn's antiques-filled parlor (the knockout rum punches are legendary), dinner is served on the verandah. Many ingredients are harvested from the inn's herb garden, fruit trees, piggery, and livestock collection; the scrumptious cured meats, baked goods, preserves, and ice creams are homemade. Sumptuous three- and five-course set menus lovingly prepared by the incomparable (and delightfully named) chef Lovey Boddie and team might include breadfruit-cheddar soufflé, seafood quenelles in gossamer curry cream, lobster with tomato-basil butter and conch stuffing, and passion fruit–ginger cheesecake. You can also order signature favorites such as lemongrass-lime fish cakes with ginger aioli or herb-crusted lamb with rosemary and guava à la carte. Wednesday night pig roasts are an island must. The ever-growing wine list is exceptionally priced. Bon mots and bonhomie serve as prelude, intermezzo, and coda for a lively evening. ⊠ *Gingerland* ☎ *869/469–3477* ⊕ *www.hermitagenevis.com* ⚑ *Reservations essential.*

$$–$$$
CARIBBEAN

✗ **Mango.** This casual beach bar at the Four Seasons is a perennial hot spot for locals and visitors, thanks to a gorgeous outdoor deck overlooking the illuminated water, sizzling music, fab drinks, hip decor, and fairly reasonable menu showcasing local ingredients, many grown by the staff. You can savor artfully presented, robustly flavored Caribbean classics such as calamari or conch fritters with curry remoulade; mouth- and eye-watering lamb curry with cardamom-scented basmati rice, fried okra, and papaya chutney; and barbecued baby back ribs. The kitchen also delights with updated twists, such as ethereal coconut foam floating in silken, roasted butternut-squash soup infused with ginger and cinnamon. ⊠ *Four Seasons Resort, Pinney's Beach* ☎ *869/469–1111 or 869/469–6238.*

$$$$
CARIBBEAN
★

✗ **Miss June's Cuisine.** Dinner with Miss June Mestier, a dynamo originally from Trinidad, could never be called ordinary. The all-inclusive experience (held only once weekly, usually Wednesday) begins with cocktails in the ornate living room, followed by dinner in an elegant dining room where tables are set with mismatched china and crystal. Hors d'oeuvres and three courses, including soup and fish, are served. "Now that you've had dinner," Miss June proclaims, "let's have fun," and she presents a grand multidish feast highlighting her Trinidadian curries, local vegetable preparations, and meats. "I invite people into my home for dinner and then my manager has the audacity to charge them as they leave!" quips Miss June, who joins guests (diners have included Oprah Winfrey, John Grisham, and members of Aerosmith) after dinner for coffee and brandy. Miss June won't kick you out, but she may ask you to turn the lights out as you leave. ⊠ *Jones Bay* ☎ *869/469–5330* ⚏ *Reservations essential* ☉ *Closed Thurs.–Tues. No lunch.*

$$$$ ✕ **Montpelier Plantation.** The Hoffman family (Muffin, son Tim, and
ECLECTIC daughter-in-law Meredith) presides over a scintillating evening, start-
★ ing with canapés and cocktails in the civilized Great Room. Dinner is served on the breezy west verandah, which gazes serenely upon the lights of Charlestown and St. Kitts. The inventive executive chef, Kosta Staicoff, uses the inn's organic herb gardens and fruit trees to full advantage, while experimenting with molecular gastronomy to create playful foam and froth. The changing three-course menu might present lemongrass consommé with spiny lobster salpicon, braised pork shoulder with onion confit and coconut jus, and guava tartlet with carrot froth. Meredith has crafted an exemplary wine list perfectly matched to the cuisine. The Mill opens nightly with sufficient reservations, offering a different set four-course menu accompanied by champagne and sorbets. Torches light cobblestone steps up to this theatrical faux sugar mill with crystal sconces, floating candles, and an antique mahogany gear wheel suspended from the ceiling. Simpler lunches (order the lobster salad from the constantly changing menu) are served on the refreshing patio, while a tapestry of tapas is on tap for $4 to $15 per dish at the poolside Indigo. ⊠ *Montpelier Estate* ☎ *869/469–3462* ⊕ *www.montpeliernevis. com* ⚏ *Reservations essential* ☉ *Closed late Aug.–early Oct.*

$$$ ✕ **Mount Nevis Hotel & Beach Club.** Savor cocktails in the distinctive lounge
ECLECTIC (accented by sisal rugs, mosaic tiles, towering bamboo stalks, and flowers floating in crystal bowls). Then repair to the sublime open-air dining room, where a pianist holds forth on an illuminated stage by the pool with a splendid view of St. Kitts. The elegant yet light menu deftly blends local ingredients with a cornucopia of Caribbean-Continental cuisines, artfully presented by Acapulco-born chef Vicente Zaragoza. Sterling starters on the ever-changing menu might be goat cheese and fire-roasted peppers on jerk foccacia or homemade conch ravioli in tomato-basil sauce. Worthy main courses include roast Cornish hen in caper-lime beurre blanc with polenta and grilled local tomatoes, or blackened red snapper in mango gastrique. There's always a fine vegetarian choice such as fresh mozzarella ovoline and tomato stack over local hydroponic greens. Finish with tropical variations on classics such as ginger crème brûlée or passion fruit cheesecake. Vicente also runs the new, more affordable alfresco grill whose convection oven turns out marvelous baked goods in minutes. ⊠ *Shaws Rd., Mt. Nevis Estates* ☎ *869/469–9373* ⊕ *www.mountnevishotel.com* ⚏ *Reservations essential.*

$$$ ✕ **Neve.** It's difficult for a three-meal all-purpose resort restaurant to
ITALIAN provide sophisticated ambience, but come evening Neve triumphantly
★ transforms into a sleek, but not slick, Italian trattoria. The antipasti are
superb, from a classic caprese salad with homemade mozzarella and
eggplant roulade to textbook tuna carpaccio. The kitchen scales the
heights with its pizzas and pastas: gnocchi in sage butter sauce; black
squid risotto with garlic-fried baby squid, pinot grigio reduction, and
citrus gremolata; or a perfectly crispy *quattro stagioni* pie (double-
smoked ham, marinated artichokes, white anchovies, black olives) that
would be the envy of Chicago and Napoli. The fun, hip wine program
showcases affordable Italian offerings on a cart: 14 reds, 14 whites,
five Proseccos by the bottle, carafe, or glass. Finish with a tiramisu that
would bring any Tuscan Mamma to tears. ⊠ *Four Seasons Nevis, Pin-
ney's Beach* ☎ *869/469–1111 or 869/469–6238* ⊕ *www.fourseasons.
com/nevis* ☞ *Reservations essential.*

$$$$ ✕ **Nisbet Plantation Beach Club.** The blissfully air-conditioned greathouse
ECLECTIC is an oasis of polished hardwood floors, mahogany and cherrywood
furnishings, equestrian bronzes, antique hurricane lamps, wicker fur-
nishings, portraits by famed Nevisian artist Eva Wilkin, and stone
walls. Tables on the verandah look down the palm-tree-lined fairway
to the sea. The four-course menu combines Continental, Pacific Rim,
and Caribbean cuisines with local ingredients. The more mature clien-
tele dictates less complex options from house-cured gravlax to three-
cheese tortellini marinara. But Filipino-born executive chef Antonio
Piani might sneak in chicken-and-coconut dumpling soup, lobster ravi-
oli in seafood Nantua sauce, and lemon-and-vanilla mascarpone mousse
with hazelnut praline. Enjoy an impressively cosmopolitan selection of
cocktails or coffee with silky-soft live music in the civilized front bar.
Witty, dapper maître d' Patterson Fleming (his cravat collection, more
than 1,000 augmented by guests over the years, is enviable!) ensures
a smooth, swank experience. ⊠ *Newcastle* ☎ *869/469–9325* ⊕ *www.
nisbetplantation.com* ☞ *Reservations essential.*

$$ ✕ **Riviere House.** Labor of love is redefined at this carefully restored and
ECLECTIC expanded colonial home with stately colonnades, gingerbread trim,
★ and luscious hues from lemon to lavender. Prices remain affordable to
entice islanders; 20% of profits go to the local hospital—eat well and
feel good about yourself. It doubles as de facto entertainment center,
starting with live music on the brick patio. One wall pays tribute to
great African(-American) leaders: Bob Marley, Mandela, Marcus Garvey, Martin Luther King Jr. The cinema, decorated with original posters
and soundtrack LPs, features fantastic acoustics and regular screenings
of classics. Another front room acts as gallery, including recycled-plastic
mosaics and magnificent painterly photographs of Namibia by co-owner
Annie. Meals are attractively presented, perhaps garnished with edible
tarragon florets or swirls of balsamic vinaigrette. Among the standouts
are splendidly chunky conch-corn chowder; braised free-range mutton (a
revelation) over sautéed forest-grown breadfruit; and wonderfully aromatic portobello mushrooms served with roasted red pepper, polenta,
and three-bean ragout, drizzled with cream-cashew sauce. Stewed for
five hours, the meaty texture would convert even the most confirmed

carnivore. Superlative lunch options range from curried chicken wrap with guacamole to lobster-spinach quiche. ⊠ *Government Rd., Charlestown* 🕾 *869/469–7117* ☞ *Reservations essential* ⊘ *Closed Sun. and Mon.*

$$$–$$$$ ✕ **The Rocks at Golden Rock.** Merely calling this glam eatery's tiered set-
ECLECTIC ting dramatic doesn't do justice to a genuine artistic and engineering masterpiece. Glass panels and ceilings (displaying the night sky while reflecting patio lights) open up the existing stone-and–ipe hardwood great house. A series of cascading waterfalls, chutes, limpid pools, lily ponds, and fountains filigree the surrounding civilized jungle with liquid silver. Strategically placed boulders resemble hulking Henry Moore sculpture; even the cut stone was painstakingly joined without mortar. Decor playfully contrasts classic and modern. A stone gazebo recalls an upside-down plantation-era copper boiler (the patio's barrel-vaulting also slyly mimics sugar equipment). Twisted metal chairs provide conversation pieces (not seating); splashes of red, orange, yellow, and slate blue enliven the chairs and long banquette. Contemporary and colonial artworks from Mali and Afghanistan grace the interior. Sadly the kitchen doesn't quite match the setting's splendor or creativity. But the atmosphere more than compensates, and solid choices include jerk pork with pineapple relish or pan-roasted snapper with crispy risotto cake and red-pepper coulis. ⊠ *Gingerland* 🕾 *869/469–3346* ⊕ *www. golden-rock.com* ☞ *Reservations essential* ⊘ *No lunch.*

$$ ✕ **Sunshine's.** Everything about this shack overlooking (and spilling
CARIBBEAN onto) the beach is larger than life, including the Rasta man Llewelyn "Sunshine" Caines himself. Flags and license plates from around the world complement the international patrons (including an occasional movie or sports star wandering down from the Four Seasons). Picnic tables are splashed with bright sunrise-to-sunset colors; even the palm trees are painted, though "it gone upscaled," as locals say, with VIP cabanas. Fishermen cruise up with their catch—you might savor lobster rolls or snapper creole. Don't miss the lethal house specialty, Killer Bee rum punch. As Sunshine boasts, "One and you're stung, two, you're stunned, three, it's a knockout." ⊠ *Pinney's Beach* 🕾 *869/469–5817.*

WHERE TO STAY

Most lodgings are in restored manor or plantation houses scattered throughout the island's five parishes (counties). The owners often live at these inns, and it's easy to feel as if you've been personally invited down for a visit. Before dinner you may find yourself in the drawing room having a cocktail and conversing with the family, other guests, or visitors who have come for a meal. Meal plans for most inns include breakfast and dinner (including afternoon tea) and offer a free shuttle service to their "private" stretch of beach. If you require TVs and air-conditioning, you're better off staying at hotels and simply dining with the engaging inn owners. A collection of 24 smart, spacious, two- to four-bedroom units called Nelson Spring Beach Villas & Spa (at the eponymous historic site, just north of Pinney's Beach) is a worthy addition, though rentals are usually by the week. All units include washer/dryer, kitchen, private garage, and modern amenities; the property features a small spa and the reasonably priced, festive Yachtsman

Four Seasons Resort Nevis.

Grill restaurant (though ownership squabbles may force it to move). Other small upmarket compounds are in various stages of development, including the overhauled Cliffdwellers at Tamarind Bay (site of Marshall's Nevis restaurant) and the Zenith Beach houses, connected with the delightful Chrishi Beach Club on Cades Bay.

The following reviews have been condensed for this book. Please go to Fodors.com for full reviews of each property.

$$$$ **Four Seasons Resort Nevis.** This beachfront beauty impeccably combines
RESORT world-class elegance with West Indian hospitality, while scrupulously
☾ maintaining and upgrading facilities. **Pros:** luxury without attitude;
★ superlative service; marvelous food; dazzling golf and spa; each building block has a washer/dryer and room amenities include free detergent. **Cons:** pricey; sometimes overrun by conventions, incentive groups (off-season mainly), and families; long walk from farthest rooms to lobby and restaurants; berms added as secondary defense against storm surges impede some beachfront room views; inconveniently placed electrical outlets. ⊠ *Pinney's Beach* ✆ *Box 565, Charlestown* ☎ *869/469–1111 or 869/469–6238, 800/332–3442 in U.S., 800/268–6282 in Canada* ⊕ *www.fourseasons.com* ↘ *179 rooms, 17 suites, 61 villas* ☾ *In-room: safe, Internet, Wi-Fi (some). In-hotel: golf course, restaurants, room service, tennis courts, bars, children's programs, pools, gym, laundry facilities, spa, beach, business center, water sports* ⏐⏐ *No meals.*

$–$$ **Golden Rock Plantation Inn.** Pam Barry's great-great-great-grandfather
HOTEL built this hillside estate in the early years of the 19th century; Pam has
★ imbued the inn with her love of Nevisian heritage and nature, and co-owners, acclaimed artists Brice Marden and wife Helen Harrington,

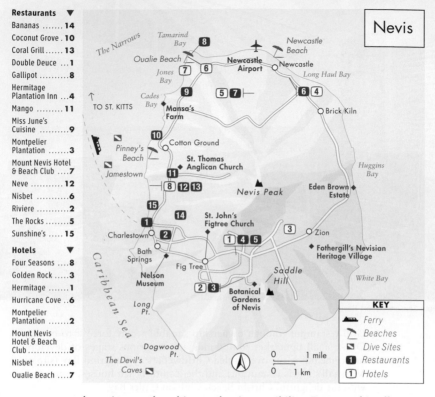

have imparted a chic, modernist sensibility. **Pros:** ecofriendly; arty crowd; glorious grounds. **Cons:** no actual beach though there are two beach clubs; lack of air-conditioning can be a problem on still days. ✉ *Gingerland* ⏱ *Box 493, Charlestown* ☎ *869/469–3346* ⊕ *www. golden-rock.com* ⮒ *16 rooms, 1 suite* ⚐ *In-room: no a/c, no TV (some), Wi-Fi. In-hotel: restaurants, bar, pool, business center* ☾ *Closed mid-Aug.–mid-Oct.* ¶○¶ *No meals.*

$$$–$$$$
HOTEL
Fodor'sChoice
★

⛶ **Hermitage Plantation Inn.** A snug 1670 greathouse—reputedly the Caribbean's oldest surviving wooden building—forms the heart of this breeze-swept hillside hideaway. **Pros:** wonderful sense of history; delightful owners and clientele; delicious food. **Cons:** long drive to beach; hillside setting difficult for physically challenged to negotiate. ✉ *Gingerland* ☎ *869/469–3477 or 800/682–4025* ⊕ *www.hermitagenevis. com* ⮒ *8 rooms, 8 cottages, 1 house* ⚐ *In-room: no a/c (some), safe, kitchen (some), no TV (some), Wi-Fi. In-hotel: restaurant, tennis court, bar, pool* ¶○¶ *Breakfast.*

$$$
RENTAL

⛶ **Hurricane Cove Bungalows.** These dramatically set one-, two-, and three-bedroom bungalows (cleverly designed and imported from Finland) cling like glorified tree houses to a cliff overlooking several glittering beaches. **Pros:** sensational views; good value for one-bedroom cottages; free use of snorkeling equipment. **Cons:** no air-conditioning for the rare stifling day; minuscule pool; hike back up from beach; kitchens need

CLOSE UP

Nevis's Day at the Races

21

One of the Caribbean's most festive, endearingly idiosyncratic events is the Nevis Turf and Jockey Club's Day at the Races, held 9 to 12 times a year on the wild and windswept Indian Castle course. I first experienced the event in the mid-1990s, when I met club president Richard "Lupi" Lupinacci, owner of the Hermitage Plantation Inn. Before even introducing himself, Richard sized me up in the driveway: "You look about the right size for a jockey. How's your seat?" His equally effervescent wife, Maureen, then interceded, "Darling, if you loathe horses, don't worry. In fact, Lupi and I have an agreement about the Jerk and Turkey Club. I get major jewels for every animal he buys."

Since my riding skills were rusty, it was decided that I should be a judge (despite questionable vision, even with glasses). "If it's really by a nose, someone will disagree with you either way," I was reassured. The next day presented a quintessential Caribbean scene. Although a serious cadre of

aficionados (including the German consul) talked turf, the rest of the island seemed more interested in liming and enjoying lively music. Local ladies dished out heavenly barbecued chicken and devilish gossip. Sheep and cattle unconcernedly ambled across the course. But when real horses thundered around the oval, the wooden stands groaned under the weight of cheering crowds, and bookies hand-calculated the payouts.

The irregularly scheduled races continue, albeit now on a properly sodded track, as does the equine hospitality. The **Hermitage Stables** (✉ *Gingerland* ☎ *869/469–3477*) arranges everything from horseback riding to jaunts in hand-carved mahogany carriages. The **Nevis Equestrian Centre** (✉ *Cotton Ground, Pinney's Beach* ☎ *869/662–9118* ⊕ *www.nevishorseback.com*) offers leisurely beach rides as well as more demanding canters through the lush hills.

—Jordan Simon

upgrading. ✉ *Hurricane Hill, Oualie Beach* ☎ *869/469–9462* ⊕ *www.hurricanecove.com* ⇆ *13 cottages* & *In-room: no a/c, kitchen, no TV, Wi-Fi. In-hotel: pool, business center* ☉ *Closed Sept.* �𝍢 *No meals.*

$$$$
RESORT
Fodor'sChoice
★

⬚ **Montpelier Plantation.** This Nevisian beauty—a Relais & Châteaux property—epitomizes understated elegance and graciously updated plantation living, courtesy of the congenial, cultured Hofmann family. **Pros:** impeccable service; lovely cuisine; exquisite gardens; trendily minimalist decor. **Cons:** some may find it a little stuffy; no beach on-site. ✉ *Montpelier Estate* ✇ *Box 474, Charlestown* ☎ *869/469–3462* ⊕ *www.montpeliernevis.com* ⇆ *17 rooms, 2 1-bedroom villas, 1 2-bedroom villa* & *In-room: kitchen (some), no TV, Wi-Fi (some). In-hotel: restaurants, tennis court, bars, pool, beach, spa, business center, water sports, some age restrictions* ☉ *Closed mid-Aug.–early Oct.* ⯑ *Breakfast.*

$$$$
HOTEL
★

⬚ **Mount Nevis Hotel & Beach Club.** The personable, attentive Meguid family blends the intimacy of the plantation inns, contemporary amenities of the Four Seasons, and typical Nevisian warmth in this hilltop aerie. **Pros:** friendly staff; fantastic views; comforts of home at comparatively affordable prices; complimentary cell phone (pay for card). **Cons:** lacks beach; long drive to many island activities; occasional plane noise. ✉ *Shaw's Rd., Mount Nevis* ✆ *Box 494, Newcastle* ☎ *869/469–9373 or 800/756–3847* ⊕ *www.mountnevishotel.com* ⟿ *8 rooms, 8 junior suites, 16 suites, 10 villas* ♿ *In-room: kitchen (some), Wi-Fi. In-hotel: restaurants, bar, pool, gym, business center, Wi-Fi* ⎸◯⎹ *Breakfast.*

$$$$
RESORT
★

⛱ **Nisbet Plantation Beach Club.** At this beachfront plantation inn, pale yellow cottages face a regal, palm-lined grass avenue that sweeps like a bridal gown's train to the champagne-hue beach. **Pros:** glorious setting; the definition of casual elegance; environmentally conscious practices; plentiful recreational options such as mountain bikes, kayaks, even Vespa scooters; extras such as free use of digital video recorders and handheld GPS locators. **Cons:** long drive to most activities on island; airplanes occasionally whoosh by; food is variable; occasionally dodgy Wi-Fi signal. ✉ *Newcastle* ☎ *869/469–9325 or 800/742–6008* ⊕ *www. nisbetplantation.com* ⟿ *36 rooms* ♿ *In-room: safe, no TV, Internet, Wi-Fi. In-hotel: restaurants, tennis court, bars, pool, gym, spa, beach, business center, water sports* ⎸◯⎹ *Some meals.*

$$–$$$
RENTAL

⛱ **Oualie Beach Hotel.** These cozy Creole-style gingerbread cottages daubed in cotton-candy colors sit just steps from a hammock-strewn taupe beach overlooking St. Kitts and are carefully staggered to ensure sea views from every room. **Pros:** fantastic water-sports operations; affordable (especially with recreational packages); appealing beach. **Cons:** showing some wear; not ideal for less active types. ✉ *Oualie Beach* ☎ *869/469–9735* ⊕ *www.oualiebeach.com* ⟿ *32 rooms* ♿ *In-room: safe, kitchen (some), Wi-Fi. In-hotel: restaurant, bar, spa, beach, business center, water sports* ⎸◯⎹ *No meals.*

NIGHTLIFE

In season it's usually easy to find a local calypso singer or a steel or string band performing at one of the hotels, notably the Four Seasons and Oualie Beach (which also features string musicians on homemade instruments Tuesday evening), as well as at the Pinney's bars. Scan the posters plastered on doorways announcing informal jump-ups. Though Nevis lacks high-tech discos, many restaurants and bars have live bands or DJs on weekends.

★ Though more a daytime hangout (especially Sunday when Nevisian movers and shakers descend on the lovely beach with their families— and act like overgrown kids themselves), **Chrishi Beach Club** (✉ *Main St. Cades Bay* ☎ *869/469/662–3958 or 3959* ⊕ *www.chrishibeachclub. com*) remains hip and happening through sunset thanks to vivacious Norwegian expats Hedda and Christian "Chrishi" Wienpahl. You can sprawl on comfy chaises and thatched, white, beach waterbeds (exemplifying the couple's wit and whimsy). Enjoy the righteous lounge mix (and mixology) and the glorious St. Kitts views (even the hideous Sea Bridge car ferry looks like an art installation from this vantage point), and what Hedda calls "European café-style" food (salads, pizzas, sandwiches like Brie with sun-dried tomatoes and cranberries). Kids have their own club with fresh-fruit smoothies, and Hedda's fun funky HWD jewelry line (incorporating leather, coins, found objects) is on sale. **Eddy's Bar & Restaurant** (⊠ *Main St., Memorial Sq.,* *Charlestown* ☎ 869/ 469–5958) has traditionally been the place to go on Wednesday night for a raucous West Indian happy hour. Burgers, shepherd's pie, quesadillas, and a variety of well-prepared food will get you prepared for the long night ahead. The evening will go on and on to the wee hours with karaoke and dancing to a local DJ. The **Water Department Barbecue** (⊠ *Pump Rd., Charlestown* ☎ *No phone*) is the informal name for a lively Friday-night jump-up that's run by two fellows from the local water department to raise funds for department trips. Friday afternoons the tents go up and the grills are fired. Cars line the streets and the guys dish up fabulous barbecue ribs and chicken—as certain customers lobby to get their water pressure adjusted. It's a classic Caribbean scene.

SHOPPING

Nevis is certainly not the place for a shopping spree, but there are some unusual and wonderful surprises, notably the island's stamps, pottery, hand-embroidered clothing, and dolls by Jeannie Rigby. Honey is another buzzing biz. Quentin Henderson, the amiable former head of the **Nevis Beekeeping Cooperative,** will even arrange trips by appointment to various hives for demonstrations of beekeeping procedures. Other than a few hotel boutiques and isolated galleries, virtually all shopping is concentrated on or just off Main Street in Charlestown. The lovely old stonework and wood floors of the waterfront Cotton Ginnery Complex make an appropriate setting for stalls of local artisans.

SPECIALTY ITEMS

ART Nevis has produced one artist of some international repute, the late Dame Eva Wilkin, who for more than 50 years painted island people, flowers, and landscapes in an evocative art naïf style. Her originals are now quite valuable, but prints are available in some local shops. The **Eva Wilkin Gallery** (⊠ *Clay Ghaut, Gingerland* ☎ 869/469–2673) occupies her former atelier (hours are very irregular, so call ahead). If the paintings, drawings, and prints are out of your price range, consider buying the lovely note cards based on her designs; the new owners are also promoting promising regional artists. **Robert Humphreys** (⊠ *Zetlands* ☎ *869/469–3326 or 869/469–6217*) sells his work, flowing bronze sculptures of pirouetting marlins and local birds and animals, at his home, where it's possible to watch the artist at work in his studio.

CLOTHING Most hotels have their own boutiques. **Island Fever** (⊠ *Main St., Charlestown* ☎ *869/469–0867*) has become the island's classiest shop, with an excellent selection of everything from bathing suits and dresses to straw bags and jewelry.

HANDICRAFTS Cheryl "Cherrianne" Liburd's **Bocane Ceramics** (⊠ *Main St., Stoney* ★ *Grove* ☎ *869/469–5437*) stocks beautifully designed and glazed local pottery, which she dubs "functional art," such as platters painted with marine life, pineapple tea sets, and coffee tables topped with mosaic depictions of chattel houses.

The **CraftHouse** (✉ *Pinney's Rd.*, *Charlestown* ☎ *869/469–5505*) is a marvelous source for local specialties from vetiver mats to leather moccasins; there's a smaller branch in the Cotton Ginnery.

Mish Mash (✉ *Hunkins Plaza, Charlestown* ☎ *869/469–3626*) offers more than just a garage-sale jumble, highlighting fine island and regional crafts from potpourri to pottery.

The **Nevis Handicraft Co-op Society** (✉ *Main St.*, *Charlestown* ☎ *869/469–1746*), next to the tourist office, offers works by local artisans (clothing, ceramic ware, woven goods) and locally produced honey, hot sauces, and jellies (try the guava and soursop).

★ **Newcastle Pottery** (✉ *Main Rd.*, *Newcastle* ☎ *869/469–9746*), a cooperative, has continued the age-old tradition of hand-built red-clay pottery fired over burning coconut husks. It's possible to watch the potters and purchase wares at their small Newcastle factory.

★ The **Philatelic Bureau** (✉ *Cotton Ginnery, Charlestown* ☎ *869/469–0617*), opposite the tourist office, is the place to go for stamp collectors. St. Kitts and Nevis are famous for their decorative, and sometimes valuable, stamps. Real beauties include the butterfly, hummingbird, and marine-life series.

SPORTS AND ACTIVITIES

BIKING

Windsurfing Nevis/Wheel World (✉ *Oualie Beach* ☎ *869/469–9682* ⊕ *www.bikenevis.com*) offers mountain-bike rentals as well as specially tailored tours on its state-of-the-art Gary Fisher, Trek, and Specialized bikes. The tours ($55–$75), led by Winston Crooke, a master windsurfer and competitive bike racer, encompass lush rain forest, majestic ruins, and spectacular views. Costs vary according to itinerary and ability level but are aimed generally at experienced riders. Winston and his team delight in sharing local knowledge, from history to culture. For those just renting (rates from $25 daily), Winston and Reggie determine your performance level and suggest appropriate routes.

DAY SAILS

Sea Nevis Charters (✉ *Tamarind Bay* ☎ *869/469–9239*) offers its 44-foot *Sea Dreamer* for snorkeling and island sunset cruises. Captain Les Windley takes you to less-trammeled sites and is a font of information on marine life.

DIVING AND SNORKELING

The **Devil's Caves** are a series of grottoes where divers can navigate tunnels, canyons, and underwater hot springs while viewing lobsters, sea fans, sponges, squirrelfish, and more. The village of **Jamestown,** which washed into the sea around Ft. Ashby, just south of Cades Bay, makes for superior snorkeling and diving. Reef-protected Pinney's Beach offers especially good snorkeling. Single-tank dives are usually $70, two-tank dives $100; packages provide deep discounts.

☼ **Scuba Safaris** (✉ *Oualie Beach* ☎ *869/469–9518* ⊕ *www.scubanevis.com*)
★ is a PADI five-star facility, NAUI Dream Resort, and NASDS Examining Station, whose experienced dive masters offer everything from a resort

course to full certification. Their equipment is always state-of-the-art, including new underwater scooters. It also provides a snorkeling learning experience that enables you not only to see but to listen to sea life, including whales and dolphins, as well as an exhilarating underwater scooter safari, night dives, and kids' bubblemakers.

FISHING

Fishing here focuses on kingfish, wahoo, grouper, tuna, and yellowtail snapper, with marlin occasionally spotted. The best areas are Monkey Shoals and around Redonda. Charters cost approximately $450–$500 per half day, $850–$1,000 per full day, and usually include an open bar. **Deep Venture** (✉ *Oualie Beach* ☎ *869/469–5110*), run by fisherman–chef Matt Lloyd, does day-fishing charters (he keeps the catch), providing a real insight into both commercial fishing and the Caribbean kitchen. **Nevis Water Sports** (✉ *Oualie Beach* ☎ *869/469–9060* ⊕ *www. fishnevis.com*) offers sportfishing aboard the 31-foot *Sea Brat* under the supervision of tournament-winning captain Ian Gonzaley. The company helps organize the annual Nevis Yacht Club Sports Fishing Tournament, which reels in competitors from all over the Caribbean.

GOLF

Fodor's Choice ★ Duffers doff their hats to the beautiful, impeccably maintained Robert Trent Jones Jr.–designed **Four Seasons Golf Course** (⛳ *18 holes, par 72, 6,766 yd* ✉ *Four Seasons Resort Nevis, Pinney's Beach* ☎ *869/469– 1111*): the virtual botanical gardens surrounding the fairways almost qualify as a hazard in themselves. The front 9 holes are fairly flat until Hole 8, which climbs uphill after your tee shot. Most of the truly stunning views are along the back 9. The signature hole is the 15th, a 660-yard monster that encompasses a deep ravine; other holes include bridges, steep drops, rolling pitches, extremely tight and unforgiving fairways, sugar-mill ruins, and fierce doglegs. Attentive attendants canvas the course with beverage buggies, handing out chilled, peppermint-scented towels and preordered Cubanos that help test the wind. Greens fees per 18 holes are $190 for hotel guests, $290 for nonguests.

GUIDED TOURS

Fitzroy "Teach" Williams (☎ *869/469–1140*) is a recommended guide. He's the former president of the taxi association—even older cabbies call him "the Dean." TC, a Yorkshire lass who used to drive a double-decker bus in England and has been married to a Nevisian for more than a decade, offers entertaining explorations via **TC's Island Tours** (☎ *869/469–2911*).

HIKING

The center of the island is Nevis Peak—also known as Mt. Nevis— which soars 3,232 feet and is flanked by Hurricane Hill on the north and Saddle Hill on the south. If you plan to scale Nevis Peak, a daylong affair, it's highly recommended that you go with a guide. Your hotel can arrange it (and a picnic lunch) for you. The **Upper Round Road Trail** is a 9-mi (15-km) road constructed in the late 1600s that was cleared and restored by the Nevis Historical and Conservation Society. It connects the Golden Rock Plantation Inn, on the east side of the island, with Nisbet Plantation Beach Club, on the northern tip. The trail encompasses numerous vegetation zones, including pristine rain forest, and impressive plantation ruins. The original cobblestones, walls, and ruins are still evident in many places.

★ **Peak Heaven at Herbert Heights** (☎ 869/469–2856 or 869/665–6926 *www. peakheavennevis.com*) is run by the Herbert family, who lead four-hour nature hikes up to panoramic Herbert Heights, where you drink in fresh local juices and the views of Montserrat; the powerful telescope, donated by Greenpeace, makes you feel as if you're staring right into that island's simmering volcano (or staring down whales during their migratory season). The trail formed part of an escape route for runaway slaves, and you can also inspect recent archaeological excavations providing insight into the indigenous peoples. Numerous hummingbirds, doves, and butterflies flit and flutter through the rain forest. The Herberts painstakingly reconstructed thatched cottages that offer a glimpse of village life a century ago, dubbed Peak Heaven, at Nelson's Lookout. These include a small, poignant, history museum; shop selling local crafts; gallery; and massage room. The solar-powered Coal Pot restaurant offers heaping helpings of affordable island fare (try any soup, the thyme-seared snapper, and scrumptious homemade ice creams) alongside the splendid vistas. There's even a small playground at the entrance. Hike prices start at $25. **Sunrise Tours** (☎ 869/469–2758 ⊕ *www.nevisnaturetours.com*), run by Lynell and Earla Liburd, offers a range of hiking tours, but their most popular is Devil's Copper, a rock configuration full of ghostly legends. Local people gave it its name because at one time the water was hot—a volcanic thermal stream. The area features pristine waterfalls and splendid bird-watching. They also do a Nevis village walk, a Hamilton Estate Walk, an Amerindian walk along the wild southeast Atlantic coast, and trips to the rain forest and Nevis Peak. They love highlighting Nevisian heritage, explaining time-honored cooking techniques, the many uses of dried grasses, and medicinal plants. Hikes range from $20 to $40 per person, and you receive a certificate of achievement. **Top to Bottom** (☎ 869/469–9080 ⊕ *www.walknevis.com*) offers ecorambles (slow tours) and hikes that emphasize Nevis's volcanic and horticultural heritage (including pointing out bat caves and folkloric herbal and "murderous" medicines). Kayaks are available for rent, and Lynne conducts tours in Long Haul Bay. Three-hour rambles or hikes are $20 per person (snacks and juice included); it's $40 for more strenuous climbs (two are offered) up Mt. Nevis.

WINDSURFING

★ Waters are generally calm and northeasterly winds steady yet gentle, making Nevis an excellent spot for beginners and intermediates. **Windsurfing Nevis** (⊠ *Oualie Beach* ☎ 869/469–9682) offers top-notch instructors (Winston Crooke is one of the best in the islands) and equipment for $30 per hour. Beginners get equipment and two-hour instruction for $55. Groups are kept small (eight maximum), and the equipment is state-of-the-art from Mistral, North, and Tushingham. It also offers kayak rentals and tours along the coast, stopping at otherwise inaccessible beaches.

St. Lucia

WORD OF MOUTH

"St. Lucia . . . is very lush with mountains, flora, fauna, plantations, and waterfalls. Reminded us of Jamaica and Hawaii . . . Driving can be a little difficult and everything is quite spread out. The beaches are made up of coarse brownish/beige sand and the water is a dark blue. There are a few black sand beaches also."
—KVR

WELCOME TO ST. LUCIA

THE CARIBBEAN'S TWIN PEAKS

St. Lucia, 27 mi (43.5 km) by 14 mi (22.5 km), is a volcanic island covered to a large extent by a lush rain forest, much of which is protected as a national park. The most notable geological features are the twin Pitons, some 2,600 feet high.

KEY	
⟁	*Beaches*
◩	*Dive Sites*
⛴	*Ferry*
🚢	*Cruise Ship Terminal*
1	*Restaurants*
①	*Hotels*
⍦	*Rain Forest*

Explorers, pirates, soldiers, sugar planters, and coal miners have made their mark on this lovely landfall, and the lush tropical peaks known as the Pitons (Gros and Petit) have witnessed them all. Today's visitors come to snorkel and scuba dive in St. Lucia's calm cobalt-blue waters, sun themselves on its multihued beaches, or sail off tiny Pigeon Island.

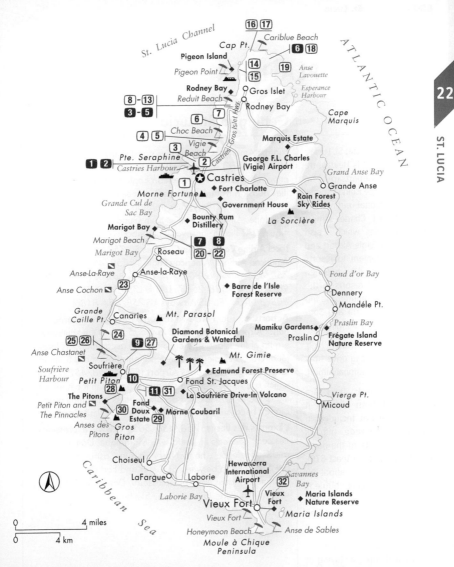

St. Lucia Channel

ATLANTIC OCEAN

16 17

Cap Pt.

Cariblue Beach

Pigeon Island

6 18

Pigeon Point

14

19

Anse Lavouette

15

Rodney Bay

Esperance Harbour

8 - 13

Reduit Beach

Gros Islet

3 - 5

Rodney Bay

Cape Marquis

6

7

4 5

Choc Beach

Vigie Beach

Marquis Estate

3

George F.L. Charles (Vigie) Airport

Grand Anse Bay

1 2

Pte. Seraphine

2

Castries Harbour

Castries/Gros Islet Hwy.

1

Castries

Grande Anse

Fort Charlotte

Grande Anse

Morne Fortune

Rain Forest Sky Rides

Grande Cul de Sac Bay

Government House

Bounty Rum Distillery

La Sorcière

Marigot Bay

Marigot Beach

7 8

Marigot Bay

Roseau

20 - 22

Anse-La-Raye

Anse-La-Raye

Fond d'or Bay

Anse Cochon

23

Barre de l'Isle Forest Reserve

Dennery

Grande Caille Pt.

Canaries

Mt. Parasol

Mandéle Pt.

Praslin Bay

24

Mamiku Gardens

Anse Chastanet

25 26

9 27

Diamond Botanical Gardens & Waterfall

Praslin

Frégate Island Nature Reserve

Soufrière Harbour

Soufrière

Mt. Gimie

Edmund Forest Preserve

Petit Piton

10

Fond St. Jacques

The Pitons

28

11 31

La Soufrière Drive-In Volcano

Vierge Pt.

Petit Piton and The Pinnacles

30

Fond Doux Estate

Morne Coubaril

Micoud

29

Anses des Pitons

Gros Piton

Choiseul

Hewanorra International Airport

Savannes Bay

LaFargue

Laborie

32

Vieux Fort

Maria Islands Nature Reserve

Laborie Bay

Vieux Fort

Vieux Fort

Maria Islands

0   4 miles

Honeymoon Beach

Anse de Sables

0   4 km

Caribbean Sea

Moule à Chique Peninsula

TOP REASONS TO VISIT ST. LUCIA

1 The Beauty: Magnificent, lush scenery makes St. Lucia one of the most beautiful Caribbean islands.

2 The Romance: A popular honeymoon spot, St. Lucia is filled with romantic retreats.

3 Indulgent Accommodations: Sybaritic lodging options include an all-inclusive spa resort, a posh dive resort, and two

picturesque resorts optimally positioned between the Pitons.

4 The St. Lucia Jazz Festival: Performers and fans come from all over the world for this musical event.

5 The Welcome: The friendly St. Lucians love sharing their island and their cultural heritage with visitors.

ST. LUCIA PLANNER

Logistics	Getting to St. Lucia

Logistics

Getting to St. Lucia: St. Lucia's primary gateway is Hewanorra International Airport (UVF) in Vieux Fort, on the island's southern tip. Regional airlines fly into George F. L. Charles Airport (SLU) in Castries, which is also referred to as Vigie Airport and is more convenient to resorts in the north. The drive between Hewanorra and resorts in the north takes 90 minutes; the trip between Hewanorra and Soufrière takes about 30 minutes.

Hassle Factor: Medium to high, because of the long drive from Hewanorra International Airport.

On the Ground: Taxis are available at both airports if transfers are not included in your travel package, but it's an expensive ride to the north from Hewanorra (at least $70); the transfer time is about 90 minutes. A helicopter shuttle is available but costly ($145 per person); it cuts the transfer time to about 10 minutes.

Getting Around: A car is more important if you are staying at a small inn or hotel away from the beach. If you're staying at an all-inclusive beach resort, taxis are a better bet.

Getting to St. Lucia

Flights: American Airlines flies nonstop from Miami and New York (JFK) and connecting service from New York and other major cities via American Eagle from San Juan. Delta flies nonstop from Atlanta. JetBlue flies nonstop from New York (JFK). US Airways flies nonstop from Philadelphia and Charlotte. Air Caraïbes flies from Guadeloupe and Martinique; LIAT flies from several neighboring islands.

Local Airline Contacts: Air Caraïbes (☎ 758/453–0357). **American Airlines/American Eagle** (☎ 758/452–1820, 758/454–6777, or 800/744–0006). **JetBlue** (☎ 877/766–9614 or 800/538–2583). **LIAT** (☎ 758/452–3056 or 888/844–5428). **US Airways** (☎ 758/454–8186).

Airports: St. Lucia has two airports: **Hewanorra International Airport** (UVF ☎ 758/454–6355) is at the southeastern tip of the island in Vieux Fort and accommodates large jet aircraft, including all nonstop flights from the U.S. mainland. **George F. L. Charles Airport** (SLU ☎ 758/452–1156), which is also referred to as Vigie Airport, is in the north of the island in Castries and accommodates only small prop aircraft because of its location and runway limitations. **L'Express des Iles** (☎ 758/456–5022 ⊕ www.express-des-iles.com) connects St. Lucia with Martinique, Dominica, and Guadeloupe. The fast ferry calls in Castries four days a week. The trip between St. Lucia and Fort de France, Martinique, takes 1½ hours; Roseau, Dominica, 3½ hours; and Point-à -Pitre, Guadeloupe, 5½ hours.

Getting Around St. Lucia

Buses: Privately owned and operated minivans constitute St. Lucia's bus system, an inexpensive and efficient means of transportation used primarily by local people. Buses are a good way to travel between Castries and the Rodney Bay area. Fares in the north range from EC$1.25 to EC$2.25 (ideally payable in local currency). But you can also travel to Vieux Fort (two-plus hours, EC$7) or Soufrière (even longer, EC$10). Wait at a marked stop and hail the passing minivan. If you tell the conductor or driver where you need to go, he'll stop at the appropriate place.

Driving: Roads in much of St. Lucia are winding and mountainous, making driving a challenge for timid or apprehensive drivers. You drive on the left, British-style. Seat belts are required, and speed limits are enforced, especially in Castries.

Car Rentals: To rent a car you must be at least 25 years old and provide a valid driver's license and a credit card. If you don't have an international driver's license, you must buy a temporary St. Lucia driving permit ($20 [EC$54]) at the car-rental office, the immigration office at either airport, or the Gros Islet police station. Rates are usually quoted in U.S. dollars and range from $50 to $80 per day or $300 to $425 per week.

Car-Rental Agencies: Avis (⌧ Vide Bouteille, Castries ☎ 758/452-2700 ⌧ Vieux Fort ☎ 758/454-6325 ⌧ Vigie ☎ 758/452-2046 ⊕ www.avisstlucia.com). **Cool Breeze Jeep/Car Rental** (⌧ Soufrière ☎ 758/459-7729 ⊕ www.coolbreezecarrental.com). **Courtesy Car Rental** (⌧ Bois d'Orange, Gros Islet ☎ 758/452-8140 ⊕ www.courtesycarrentals.com). **Hertz** (⌧ Castries ☎ 758/452-0679 ⌧ Vieux Fort ☎ 758/454-9636 ⌧ Vigie ☎ 758/451-7351 ⊕ www.hertz.com).

Air Transfers: You can reduce travel time from the airport from about 90 minutes to 10 minutes by taking **St. Lucia Helicopters** (⌧ Pointe Seraphine, Castries ☎ 758/453-6950 ⊕ www.stluciahelicopters.com), but the price is high (starting at $145 per person).

Ferries: When cruise ships are in port in Castries, a water taxi shuttles back and forth between Pointe Seraphine on the north side of the harbor and Place Carenage on the south side of the harbor for $1 per person each way. For those arriving at Rodney Bay Marina, **Rodney Bay Ferry** (☎ 758/452-8816) travels between the marina and the Rodney Bay shopping complex daily on the hour, from 9 to 4, for $5 per person round-trip.

Taxis

Taxis are unmetered, although fares are fairly standard. Sample fares for up to four passengers are Castries to Rodney Bay, $20; Rodney Bay to Cap Estate, $10; Castries to Cap Estate, $25; Castries to Marigot Bay, $30; Castries to Anse La Raye, $40; Castries to Soufrière, $80. Always ask the driver to quote the price *before* you get in, and be sure that you both understand whether it's quoted in EC or U.S. dollars. Drivers are generally careful, knowledgeable, and courteous.

Island Activities

St. Lucia has excellent **diving** along its entire southwest coast from Soufrière northwards. One upscale resort, Anse Chastanet, specializes in diving from its base near the Pitons.

Deep-sea **fishing** is also good. A **day sail** is one of the best ways to see a good bit of the island and a good way to travel from Castries to Soufrière, or vice versa.

However, St. Lucia's crown jewel is its well-preserved **rain forest**, which is best explored on a guided hike.

Climbing one of the twin **Pitons** is a rewarding—if arduous—experience and can be done without any special mountain- or rock-climbing experience (though that never hurts). You must hire a guide, however.

22

ST. LUCIA PLANNER

Fast Facts	Essentials

Banks and Exchange Services: The official currency is the Eastern Caribbean dollar (EC$), but U.S. dollars are usually accepted. Major credit cards and traveler's checks are widely accepted. ATMs dispense only local currency. Major banks on the island include Bank of Nova Scotia, FirstCaribbean International Bank, and Royal Bank of Canada.

Electricity: The electric current on St. Lucia is 220 volts, 50 cycles, with a square, three-pin plug (U.K. standard). A few large hotels have 110-volt outlets for electric razors only. To use most North American appliances, you'll need a transformer to convert voltage and a plug adapter; dual-voltage computers or appliances will still need a plug adapter, which you can often borrow from the hotel.

Emergency Services: Ambulance and Fire (☎ 911). **Police** (☎ 999).

Passport Requirements: U.S. and Canadian citizens must have a valid passport to enter St. Lucia and a return or ongoing ticket.

Weddings: Wedding licenses require either a three-day waiting period ($125) or none ($200). Some resorts offer free weddings.

Mail: The General Post Office is on Bridge Street in Castries and is open weekdays from 8:30 to 4:30; all towns and villages have branches. Postage for airmail letters to the United States, Canada, and the United Kingdom is EC95¢ per half ounce; postcards are EC65¢. Airmail can take two or three weeks to be delivered.

Safety: Although crime isn't a significant problem, take the same precautions you would at home—lock your door, secure your valuables, and don't carry too much money or flaunt expensive jewelry on the street or at the beach.

Taxes: The departure tax of $26 (EC$68) is incorporated into the price of your airfare. A government tax of 8% is added to all hotel and restaurant bills. There's no sales tax on goods purchased in shops. Most restaurants and some hotels add a service charge of 10% in lieu of tipping.

Telephones: The area code for St. Lucia is 758. You can make direct-dial overseas and interisland calls from St. Lucia, and the connections are excellent. You can charge an overseas call to a major credit card with no surcharge. From public phones and many hotels, dial 811 and charge the call to your credit card. Phone cards can be purchased at many retail outlets and used for either local or international calls from any touch-tone telephone (including pay phones) in St. Lucia. You can dial local calls throughout St. Lucia directly from your hotel room by connecting to an outside line and dialing the seven-digit number. Some hotels charge a small fee (usually about EC$1) for local calls. Pay phones accept EC25¢ and EC$1 coins. Cell phones may be rented from LIME offices in Castries, Gablewoods Mall, Rodney Bay Marina, and Vieux Fort; or you can purchase a local SIM card for $20 (which includes an $8 call credit) at Digicel offices in those same areas. The cards can be topped up at hundreds of business locations around the island.

Visitor Information: St. Lucia Tourist Board (☎ 212/867–2950 in New York, 800/456–3984 ⊕ www.stlucianow.com).

Where to Stay

Nearly all St. Lucia's resorts and small inns are tucked into lush surroundings on secluded coves, unspoiled beaches, or forested hillsides in three locations along the calm Caribbean (western) coast. They're in the greater Castries area between Marigot Bay, a few miles south of the city, and Choc Bay in the north; in and around Rodney Bay and north to Cap Estate; and in and around Soufrière on the southwest coast near the Pitons. There's only one resort in Vieux Fort, near Hewanorra. New resort development is underway on the Atlantic (east) coast. The advantage of being in the north is that you have easier access to a wider range of restaurants and nightlife; in the south you are limited to your hotel's offerings and a few other dining options, albeit some of the best, in and around Soufrière.

Big Beach Resorts: Most people choose to stay in one of St. Lucia's many beach resorts, the majority of which are upscale and fairly pricey. Several are all-inclusive, including three Sandals resorts, two Sunswept resorts (Body Holiday at LeSPORT and Rendezvous), Almond Morgan Bay, and Smugglers Cove Resort & Spa.

Small Inns: If you are looking for something more intimate and perhaps less expensive, a locally owned inn or small hotel is a good option, but it may not be directly on the beach.

Villas: Luxury villa communities and independent private villas are a good alternative for families. Many of these are in the north in or near Cap Estate.

HOTEL AND RESTAURANT COSTS

Restaurant prices are for a main course at dinner and do not include the 8% tax or customary 10% service charge. Hotel prices are per night for a double room in high season, excluding 8% tax and meal plans (except at all-inclusives).

WHAT IT COSTS IN U.S. DOLLARS

	¢	$	$$	$$$	$$$$
Restaurants	under $8	$8–$12	$12–$20	$20–$30	over $30
Hotels	under $150	$150–$275	$276–$375	$376–$475	over $475

When to Go

The high season runs from mid-December through mid-April and during the annual St. Lucia Jazz Festival and Carnival events; at other times of the year, hotel rates can be significantly cheaper.

FESTIVALS AND EVENTS

In April, the **St. Lucia Golf Open** is an amateur tournament at the St. Lucia Golf Club in Cap Estate.

The **St. Lucia Jazz Festival** in early May is the year's big event; during that week, you may have trouble finding a hotel room at any price.

St. Lucia's summer **Carnival** is held in Castries beginning in late June and continuing into July.

The **St. Lucia Billfishing Tournament**, which attracts anglers from far and wide, is held in late September or early October.

October is Creole Heritage Month, which culminates in **Jounen Kwéyòl Entenasyonal** (International Creole Day) on the last Sunday of the month.

In late November or early December, the finish of the **Atlantic Rally for Cruisers,** the world's largest ocean-crossing race, is marked by a week of festivities at Rodney Bay.

22

ST. LUCIA BEACHES

The sand on St. Lucia's beaches ranges from golden to black, but the island has some of the best off-the-beach snorkeling in the Caribbean, especially along the southwest coast.

(Above) Reduit Beach at Rodney Bay Village. (Opposite page bottom) Anse des Pitons on Jalousie Bay. (Opposite page top) Marigot Bay

St. Lucia's longest, broadest, and most popular beaches are in the north, which is also the flattest part of this mountainous island and the location of most resorts, restaurants, and nightlife. Most of the island's biggest resorts front the beaches in the Rodney Bay area, extending north to Cap Estate. Elsewhere, tiny coves with inviting crescents of sand offer great swimming and snorkeling opportunities. Beaches are all public, but hotels flank many along the northwest coast. A few secluded stretches of beach on the west coast south of Marigot Bay are accessible primarily by boat and are popular swimming and snorkeling stops on catamaran or powerboat sightseeing trips. Don't swim along the windward (east) coast; the Atlantic Ocean is too rough—but the views are spectacular. There's only one resort facing the Atlantic at this writing: the Coconut Bay Resort, which is next to Hewanorra Airport. Although it has a beautiful beach, the surf is really too rough for swimming.

GOLDEN SAND

Reduit Beach at Rodney Bay Village is considered St. Lucia's finest, with golden sand and lots of water sports. Farther south, tiny beaches have sand ranging in color from gold to gray, becoming darker as you head south; one, magnificently located right between the Pitons, has imported white sand on top of the natural black. Marigot Bay, a little peninsula of golden sand studded with palm trees, is particularly lovely.

22

Anse Chastanet. In front of the resort of the same name, just north of the city of Soufrière, this palm-studded dark-sand beach has a backdrop of green hills, brightly painted fishing skiffs bobbing at anchor, and the island's best reefs for snorkeling and diving. The resort's gazebos are nestled among the palms; its dive shop, restaurant, and bar are on the beach and open to the public. ⊠ *1 mi (1½ km) north of Soufrière.*

Anse Cochon. This remote dark-sand beach is reached only by boat or via Ti Kaye Village's mile-long access road. The water and adjacent reef are superb for swimming, diving, and snorkeling. Moorings are free, and boaters can enjoy refreshments at Ti Kaye's beach bar. ⊠ *3 mi (5 km) south of Marigot Bay.*

Anse des Pitons (*Jalousie Beach*). The white sand on this crescent beach, snuggled between the Pitons, was imported and spread over the natural black sand. Accessible through the Jalousie Plantation Sugar Beach resort property or by boat, the beach offers good snorkeling, diving, and breathtaking scenery. ⊠ *1 mi (1½ km) south of Soufrière.*

Marigot Beach (*Labas Beach*). Calm waters rippled only by passing yachts lap a sliver of sand studded with palm trees on the north side of Marigot Bay. The beach is accessible by a ferry that operates continually from one side of the bay to the other, and you can find

refreshments at adjacent restaurants. ⊠ *Marigot Bay.*

Pigeon Point. At this small beach within Pigeon Island National Park ($5 admission), on the northwestern tip of St. Lucia, a restaurant serves snacks and drinks, but this is also a perfect spot for picnicking. ⊠ *Pigeon Island.*

Reduit Beach. This long stretch of golden sand frames Rodney Bay and is within walking distance of many hotels and restaurants in Rodney Bay Village. The Rex St. Lucian hotel, which faces the beach, has a water-sports center, where you can rent sports equipment and beach chairs and take windsurfing or waterskiing lessons. Many feel that Reduit (pronounced red-wee) is the island's finest beach. ⊠ *Rodney Bay.*

Vigie Beach. This 2-mi (3-km) strand runs parallel to the George F. L. Charles Airport runway in Castries and continues on past the Rendezvous resort, where it is called Malabar Beach. ⊠ *Castries, next to airport.*

By Jane E. Zarem

All eyes focus on St. Lucia for 10 days each May, when the St. Lucia Jazz Festival welcomes renowned international musicians who perform for enthusiastic fans at Pigeon Island National Park and other island venues. St. Lucians themselves love jazz—and the beat of Caribbean music resonates through their very souls.

A lush, mountainous island between Martinique and St. Vincent, St. Lucia (pronounced *loo*-sha) easily earns the moniker "Helen of the West Indies." The capital city of Castries and nearby villages in the northwest are home to 40% of the population and, along with Rodney Bay farther north and Marigot Bay just south of the capital, are generally the destinations of most vacationers. In the central and southwestern parts of the island, dense rain forest, jungle-covered mountains, and vast banana plantations dominate the landscape. A tortuous road follows most of the coastline, bisecting small villages, cutting through mountains, and passing by fertile valleys. On the southwest coast, Petit Piton and Gros Piton, the island's unusual twin peaks that rise out of the sea to more than 2,600 feet, are familiar navigational landmarks for sailors and aviators alike. Divers are attracted to the reefs found just north of Soufrière, which was the capital during French colonial times. Most of the natural tourist attractions are in this area, along with several more fine resorts and inns. "If you haven't been to Soufrière," St. Lucians will tell you, "you haven't been to St. Lucia."

St. Lucia has evolved over the years into one of the Caribbean's most popular vacation destinations—particularly for honeymooners and other romantics enticed by the island's striking natural beauty, its many splendid resorts and appealing inns, and its welcoming atmosphere. And the evolution continues. Renewed emphasis from both the public and private sectors is being placed on enhancing the island's tourism product and supporting new and renewed lodgings, activities, and attractions. That's great news for visitors, who already appear delighted with St. Lucia.

The pirate François Le Clerc, nicknamed Jambe de Bois (Wooden Leg) for obvious reasons, was the first European "settler" in St. Lucia. In the late 16th century, Le Clerc holed up on Pigeon Island, just off the island's northernmost point, and used it as a staging ground for attacking passing ships. Now Pigeon Island is a national park, a playground for locals and visitors alike, and, as mentioned, a performance venue for the annual St. Lucia Jazz Festival. Several years ago, a man-made causeway attached Pigeon Island to the mainland; today, Sandals Grande St. Lucian Spa & Beach Resort, one of the largest resorts in St. Lucia, and The Landings, a luxury villa community with an 80-slip marina, are sprawled along that causeway.

22

Like most of its Caribbean neighbors, Arawaks and then the Carib Indians first inhabited St. Lucia. British settlers attempted to colonize the island twice in the early 1600s, but it wasn't until 1651, after the French West India Company secured the island from the Caribs, that Europeans gained a foothold. For 150 years, battles for island possession were frequent between the French and the British, with a dizzying 14 changes in power before the British finally took possession in 1814. The Europeans established sugar plantations, using slaves from West Africa to work the fields. By 1838, when the slaves were emancipated, more than 90% of the population was of African descent—also the approximate proportion of today's 170,000 St. Lucians. Indentured East Indian laborers were brought over in 1882 to help bail out the sugar industry, which collapsed when slavery was abolished and then all but died in the 1960s, when bananas became the major crop.

On February 22, 1979, St. Lucia became an independent state within the British Commonwealth of Nations, with a resident governor-general appointed by the queen. Still, the island appears to have retained more relics of French influence—notably the island patois, cuisine, village names, and surnames—than of the British. Most likely, that's because the British contribution primarily involved the English language, the educational and legal systems, and the political structure, whereas the French culture historically had more influence on the arts—culinary, dance, and all that jazz!

EXPLORING ST. LUCIA

Except for a small area in the extreme northeast, one main route circles all of St. Lucia. The road snakes along the coast, cuts across mountains, makes hairpin turns and sheer drops, and reaches dizzying heights. It takes at least four hours to drive the whole loop. Even at a leisurely pace with frequent sightseeing stops, the curvy roads make it a tiring drive in a single outing.

The West Coast Road between Castries and Soufrière (a 1½- to 2-hour journey) has steep hills and sharp turns, but it's well marked and incredibly scenic. South of Castries, the road tunnels through Morne Fortune, skirts the island's largest banana plantation (more than 127 varieties of bananas, called "figs" in this part of the Caribbean, grow on the island), and passes through tiny fishing villages. Just north of Soufrière the road negotiates the island's fruit basket, where most of the mangoes,

CLOSE UP

Embracing Kwéyòl

English is St. Lucia's official language, but most St. Lucians speak and often use Kwéyòl—a French-based Creole language—for informal conversations between and among themselves. Primarily a spoken language, Kwéyòl in its written version doesn't look at all like French; pronounce the words phonetically, though—*entenasyonnal* (international), for example, or the word *Kwéyòl* (Creole) itself—and you indeed sound as if you're speaking French.

Pretty much the same version of the Creole language, or patois, is spoken in the nearby island of Dominica. Otherwise, the St. Lucian Kwéyòl is quite different from that spoken in other Caribbean islands that have a French and African heritage, such as Haiti, Guadeloupe, and Martinique—or elsewhere, such as Louisiana, Mauritius, and Madagascar. Interestingly, the Kwéyòl spoken in St. Lucia and Dominica is mostly unintelligible to people from those other locations—and vice versa.

St. Lucia embraces its Creole heritage by devoting the month of October each year to celebrations that preserve and promote Creole culture, language, and traditions. In selected communities throughout the island, events and performances highlight Creole music, food, dance, theater, native costumes, church services, traditional games, folklore, native medicine—a little bit of everything, or *tout bagay*, as you say in Kwéyòl.

Creole Heritage Month culminates at the end of October with all-day events and activities on Jounen Kwéyòl Entenasyonnal, or International Creole Day, which is recognized by all countries that speak a version of the Creole language.

---

breadfruit, tomatoes, limes, and oranges are grown. In the mountainous region that forms a backdrop for Soufrière, you will notice 3,118-foot Mt. Gimie (pronounced Jimmy), St. Lucia's highest peak. Approaching Soufrière, you'll have spectacular views of the Pitons; and that spume of smoke wafting out of the thickly forested mountainside just east of Soufrière emanates from La Soufrière Drive-In Volcano.

The landscape changes dramatically between the Pitons and Vieux Fort on the island's southeastern tip. Along the South Coast Road traveling southeasterly from Soufrière, the terrain starts as steep mountainside with dense vegetation, progresses to undulating hills, and finally becomes rather flat and comparatively arid. Anyone arriving at Hewanorra International Airport, which is in Vieux Fort, and staying at a resort near Soufrière will travel along this route, a journey of about 30 minutes.

From Vieux Fort north to Castries, a 1½-hour drive, the East Coast Road twists through Micoud, Dennery, and other coastal villages. It then winds up, down, and around mountains, crosses Barre de l'Isle Ridge, and slices through the rain forest. Much of the scenery is breathtaking. The Atlantic Ocean pounds against rocky cliffs, and acres and acres of bananas and coconut palms blanket the hillsides. If you arrive at Hewanorra and stay at a resort near Castries or Rodney Bay, you'll travel along the East Coast Road.

CASTRIES AND THE NORTH

Castries, the capital city, and the area north and just south of it are the island's most developed areas. The roads are straight, mostly flat, and easy to navigate. The beaches are some of the island's best. Rodney Bay Marina and most of the resorts, restaurants, and nightspots are north of Castries. Pigeon Island, one of the important historical sites, is at the island's northwestern tip. About 15 minutes south of Castries, lovely Marigot Bay is both a yacht haven and a picture-pretty destination for landlubbers.

22

WHAT TO SEE

Bounty Rum Distillery. St. Lucia Distillers, which produces the island's own Bounty Rum, offers 90-minute Rhythm and Rum tours of its distillery, including information on the history of sugar, the background of rum, a detailed description of the distillation process, colorful displays of local architecture, a glimpse at a typical rum shop, Caribbean music, and a chance to sample the company's rums and liqueurs. The distillery is at the Roseau Sugar Factory in the Roseau Valley, on the island's largest banana plantation, a few miles south of Castries and not far from Marigot. Reservations for the tour are essential. ⊠ *Roseau Sugar Factory, West Coast Rd., Roseau* ☎ *758/451–4258* ⊕ *www.saintluciarums. com* ⊠ *$5* ⊙ *Weekdays 9–3.*

Castries. The capital, a busy commercial city of about 65,000 people, wraps around a sheltered bay. Morne Fortune rises sharply to the south of town, creating a dramatic green backdrop. The charm of Castries lies in its liveliness rather than its architecture, since four fires that occurred between 1796 and 1948 destroyed most of the colonial buildings. Freighters (exporting bananas, coconut, cocoa, mace, nutmeg, and citrus fruits) and cruise ships come and go frequently, making Castries Harbour one of the Caribbean's busiest ports. Pointe Seraphine is a duty-free shopping complex on the north side of the harbor, about a 20-minute walk or two-minute cab ride from the city center; a launch ferries passengers across the harbor when cruise ships are in port. Pointe Seraphine's attractive Spanish-style architecture houses more than 20 upscale duty-free shops, a tourist information kiosk, a taxi stand, and car-rental agencies. **La Place Carenage,** on the south side of the harbor near the pier and markets, is another duty-free shopping complex with a dozen or more shops and a café. **Derek Walcott Square** (formerly Columbus Square), a green oasis bordered by Brazil, Laborie, Micoud, and Bourbon streets, was renamed to honor the hometown poet who won the 1992 Nobel Prize in Literature—one of two Nobel laureates from St. Lucia (the late Sir W. Arthur Lewis won the 1979 Nobel in economic science). Some of the few 19th-century buildings that survived fire, wind, and rain can be seen on Brazil Street, the square's southern border. On the Laborie Street side, there's a huge, 400-year-old samaan (monkeypod) tree with leafy branches that shade a good portion of the square. Directly across Laborie Street from Derek Walcott Square is the Roman Catholic **Cathedral of the Immaculate Conception,** which was built in 1897. Though it's rather somber on the outside, its interior walls are decorated with colorful murals reworked in 1985, just before Pope John Paul II's visit, by St. Lucian artist Dunstan St. Omer. This church has an active parish and is open daily for both public viewing and religious services. At the corner of Jeremie and Peynier streets, spreading beyond its brilliant orange roof, is the **Castries Market**. Full of excitement and bustle, the market is open every day except Sunday. It's liveliest on Saturday morning, when farmers bring their fresh produce and spices to town, as they have for more than a century. Next door to the produce market is the **Craft Market**, where you can buy pottery, wood carvings, and hand-woven straw articles. At the Vendor's Arcade, across Peynier Street from the Craft Market, you'll find still more handicrafts and souvenirs.

> ## ST. LUCIA LINGO
>
> As in many Caribbean islands, to "lime" is to hang out and a "jump-up" is a big party with lots of dance music (often in the street, as in the village of Gros Islet every Friday night). North American women, especially, will find it charming to be called "milady." And don't be surprised when people in St. Lucia call you "darling" instead of "ma'am" or "sir"—they're being friendly, not forward.

Ft. Charlotte. Begun in 1764 by the French as the Citadelle du Morne Fortune, Ft. Charlotte was completed after 20 years of battling and changing hands. Its old barracks and batteries are now government buildings and local educational facilities, but you can drive around and look at the remains, including redoubts, a guardroom, stables, and cells. You can also walk up to the Inniskilling Monument, a tribute to the 1796 battle in which the 27th Foot Royal Inniskilling Fusiliers wrested the Morne from the French. At the military cemetery, which was first used in 1782, faint inscriptions on the tombstones tell the tales of French and English soldiers who died here. Six former governors of the island are buried here, as well. From this point atop Morne Fortune, you can view Martinique to the north and the twin peaks of the Pitons to the south. ⊠ *Morne Fortune.*

Government House. The official residence of the governor-general of St. Lucia, one of the island's few remaining examples of Victorian architecture, is perched high above Castries, halfway up Morne Fortune—the "Hill of Good Fortune"—which forms a backdrop for the capital city. Morne Fortune has also overlooked more than its share of *bad* luck over the years, including devastating hurricanes and four fires that leveled Castries. Within Government House itself is **Le Pavillon Royal Museum,** which houses important historical photographs and documents, artifacts, crockery, silverware, medals, and awards; original architectural drawings of Government House are displayed on the walls. However, you must make an appointment to visit. ⊠ *Morne Fortune, Castries* 🕾 *758/452–2481* 🕾 *Free* ☉ *Tues. and Thurs. 10–noon and 2–4, by appointment only.*

Fodor'sChoice ★ **Marigot Bay.** This is one of the prettiest natural harbors in the Caribbean. In 1778, British admiral Samuel Barrington sailed into this secluded bay-within-a-bay and, the story goes, covered his ships with palm fronds to hide them from the French. Today this small community—where parts of the original movie *Doctor Dolittle* were filmed in the late 1960s—is a favorite anchorage for boaters and a peaceful destination for landlubbers. The **Marigot Bay Hotel**—a luxury resort (formerly Discovery at Marigot Bay), marina, and marina village with restaurants, bars, grocery store, bakery, boutiques, and other services and activities—has totally revitalized the area, yet great pains were taken to protect both the beauty and the ecology of Marigot Bay. A 24-hour ferry ($2 round-trip) connects the bay's two shores—a voyage that takes about a minute each way.

22

☺ **Pigeon Island National Park.** Jutting out from the northwest coast, Pigeon
★ Island is connected to the mainland by a causeway. Tales are told of the pirate Jambe de Bois (Wooden Leg), who once hid out on this 44-acre hilltop islet—a strategic point during the French and British struggles for control of St. Lucia. Now it's a national park and a venue for concerts, festivals, and family gatherings. There are two small beaches with calm waters for swimming and snorkeling, a restaurant, and picnic areas. Scattered around the grounds are ruins of barracks, batteries, and garrisons that date from 18th-century French and English battles. In the Museum and Interpretative Centre, housed in the restored British officers' mess, a multimedia display explains the island's ecological and historical significance. ✉ *Pigeon Island, St. Lucia National Trust, Rodney Bay* ☎ *758/452–5005* ⊕ *www.slunatrust.org* 🎫 *$5* ⊗ *Daily 9–5.*

☺ **Rain Forest Sky Rides.** Ever wish you could get a bird's-eye view of the
★ rain forest or experience it without hiking up and down miles of mountain trails? Here's your chance. Depending on your athleticism, choose the two-hour aerial tram ride, the zip-line experience, or both. Either guarantees a magnificent view as you peacefully slip above or actively zip through the canopy of the 3,442-acre Castries Waterworks Rain Forest in Babonneau, 30 minutes east of Rodney Bay. On the tram ride, eight-passenger gondolas glide slowly among the giant trees, twisting vines, and dense thickets of vegetation accented by colorful flowers as a tour guide explains and shares anecdotes about the various trees, plants, birds, and other wonders of nature found in the area. The zip line, on the other hand, is a thrilling experience in which you're rigged with a harness, helmet, and clamps that attach to cables strategically strung through the forest. Short trails connect the 10 lines, so riders come down to earth briefly and hike to the next station before speeding through the forest canopy to the next stop. Bring binoculars and a camera. ✉ *Chassin, Babonneau* ☎ *758/458–5151* ⊕ *www.rfat.com* 🎫 *Tram $72, zip line $69, combo $85* ⊗ *Tues.–Sun. 9–4.*

Rodney Bay. About 15 minutes north of Castries, the natural bay and an 80-acre man-made lagoon—surrounded by hotels and many popular restaurants—are named for Admiral George Rodney, who sailed the British Navy out of Gros Islet Bay in 1780 to attack and ultimately decimate the French fleet. With 232 slips, Rodney Bay Marina is one of the Caribbean's premier yachting centers and the destination of the Atlantic Rally for Cruisers (transatlantic yacht crossing) each December. Yacht charters and sightseeing day trips can be arranged at the marina. The Rodney Bay Ferry makes hourly crossings between the marina and the shopping complex, as well as daily excursions to Pigeon Island.

SOUFRIÈRE

Soufrière is the destination of most sightseeing trips. This is where you can get up close to the landmark Pitons and explore the French colonial capital of St. Lucia, with its drive-in volcano, botanical gardens, working plantations, waterfalls, and countless other examples of the natural beauty for which St. Lucia is deservedly famous.

WHAT TO SEE

Fodor'sChoice
★

Diamond Botanical Gardens and Waterfall. These splendid gardens are part of Soufrière Estate, a 2,000-acre land grant presented by King Louis XIV in 1713 to three Devaux brothers from Normandy in recognition of their services to France. The estate is still owned by their descendants; Joan Du Bouley Devaux maintains the gardens. Bushes and shrubs bursting with brilliant flowers grow beneath towering trees and line pathways that lead to a natural gorge. Water bubbling to the surface from underground sulfur springs streams downhill in rivulets to become Diamond Waterfall, deep within the botanical gardens. Through the centuries, the rocks over which the cascade spills have become encrusted with minerals and tinted yellow, green, and purple. Near the falls, curative mineral baths are fed by the underground springs. King Louis XVI of France provided funds in 1784 for the construction of a building with a dozen large stone baths to fortify his troops against the St. Lucian climate. It's claimed that Joséphine Bonaparte bathed here as a young girl while visiting her father's plantation nearby. During the Brigand's War, just after the French Revolution, the bathhouse was destroyed. In 1930 André Du Boulay had the site excavated, and two of the original stone baths were restored for his use. Outside baths were added later. For a small fee, you can slip into your swimsuit and soak for 30 minutes in one of the outside pools; a private bath costs slightly more. ⊠ *Soufrière Estate, Diamond Rd., Soufrière* 🕾 *758/452–4759 or 758/454–7565* ⊕ *www.diamondstlucia.com* ✉ *$5, outside bath $4, private bath $6* ☾ *Mon.–Sat. 10–5, Sun. 10–3.*

Edmund Forest Reserve. Dense tropical rain forest stretches from one side of the island to the other, sprawling over 19,000 acres of mountains and valleys. It's home to a multitude of exotic flowers and plants, as well as rare birds—including the brightly feathered Jacquot parrot. The Edmund Forest Reserve, on the island's western side, is most easily accessible from just east of Soufrière, on the road to Fond St. Jacques. A trek through the lush landscape, with spectacular views of mountains, valleys, and the sea beyond, can take three or more hours. It takes an hour or so just to reach the reserve by car from the north end of the island. It's a strenuous hike, so you need plenty of stamina and sturdy hiking shoes. Permission from the Forest & Lands Department is required to access reserve trails, and the department requires that a naturalist or forest officer guide you because the vegetation is so dense. ⊠ *East of Fond St. Jacques* 🕾 *758/450–2231, 758/450–2078 for Forest & Lands Department* ✉ *Guide $10, guided tours that include round-trip transportation from your hotel $55–$85* ☾ *Daily by appointment only.*

DID YOU KNOW?

The Devaux family has owned Diamond Botanical Gardens since 1713; the sulfurous water has stained the surrounding rocks different colors.

Ⓒ **Fond Doux Estate.** One of the earliest French estates established by land
★ grant (1745 and 1763), this plantation still produces cocoa, citrus,
bananas, coconut, and vegetables on 135 hilly acres; the restored 1864
plantation house is still in use, as well. A 30-minute walking tour begins
at the cocoa fermentary, where you can see the drying process under
way. You then follow a trail through the lush cultivated area, where a
guide points out the various fruit- or spice-bearing trees and tropical
flowers. Additional trails lead to old military ruins, a religious shrine,
and another vantage point for viewing the spectacular Pitons. Cool
drinks and a creole buffet lunch are served at the restaurant. Souvenirs,
including just-made chocolate balls, are sold at the boutique. ⊠ *Chateaubelair, Soufrière* ☎ *758/459–7545* ⊕ *www.fonddouxestate.com*
🎫 *Estate $30, includes buffet lunch* ⊙ *Daily 9–4.*

Ⓒ **La Soufrière Drive-In Volcano.** As you approach, your nose will pick up
the strong scent of the sulfur springs—more than 20 belching pools of
muddy water, multicolor sulfur deposits, and other assorted minerals
baking and steaming on the surface. Actually, you don't drive in. You
drive up within a few hundred feet of the gurgling, steaming mass and
then walk behind your guide—whose service is included in the admission price—around a fault in the substratum rock. It's a fascinating,
educational half hour, though it can also be pretty stinky on a hot day.
⊠ *Bay St., Soufrière* ☎ *758/459–5500* 🎫 *$2* ⊙ *Daily 9–5.*

Ⓒ **Morne Coubaril.** On the site of an 18th-century estate, a 250-acre land
grant by Louis XIV of France in 1713, the original plantation house
has been renovated and a farm worker's village has been re-created to
show visitors what life was like for both the owners (a single family
who owned the land until 1960) and those who did all the hard labor
over the centuries producing cotton, coffee, sugarcane, and cocoa.
Cocoa, coconuts, and manioc are still grown on the estate using traditional agricultural methods. Guides show how coconuts are opened
and roasted for use as oil and animal feed and how cocoa is fermented,
dried, crushed by dancing on the beans, and finally formed into chocolate sticks. Manioc roots (also called cassava) are grated, squeezed of
excess water, dried, and turned into flour used in baking. The grounds
are lovely for walking or hiking, and the views of mountains and
sea beyond are spellbinding. The Pitt, a large, open-air restaurant,
serves a creole buffet at lunchtime by reservation only. ⊠ *Soufrière*
☎ *758/459–7340* ⊕ *www.mornecoubarilestate.com* 🎫 *$8, with lunch
$15* ⊙ *Daily 9–4:30.*

Fodor'sChoice **The Pitons.** These two unusual mountains, which are, in fact, a symbol
★ of St. Lucia and were named a UNESCO World Heritage Site in 2004,
rise precipitously from the cobalt-blue Caribbean Sea just south of Soufrière. Covered with thick tropical vegetation, the massive outcroppings were formed by lava from a volcanic eruption 30 to 40 million
years ago. They are not identical twins since—confusingly—2,619-foot
Petit Piton is taller than 2,461-foot Gros Piton, though Gros Piton is,
as the word translates, broader. It's possible to climb the Pitons as
long as you have permission and use a guide, but it's a strenuous trip.
Gros Piton is the easier climb, though the trail up even this shorter
Piton is one very tough trek and requires the permission of the Forest

& Lands Department and a knowledgeable guide. ☎ *758/450–2231, 758/450–2078 for St. Lucia Forest & Lands Department, 758/459–9748 for Pitons Tour Guide Association* ⌲ *Guide services $45* ⊙ *Daily by appointment only.*

Soufrière. The oldest town in St. Lucia and the former French colonial capital, Soufrière was founded by the French in 1746 and named for its proximity to the volcano of the same name. The wharf is the center of activity in this sleepy town (which currently has a population of about 9,000), particularly when a cruise ship is moored in pretty Soufrière Bay. French colonial influences can be noticed in the architecture of the wooden buildings, with second-story verandahs and gingerbread trim that surround the market square. The market building itself is decorated with colorful murals. The **Soufrière Tourist Information Centre** (✉ *Bay St., Soufrière* ☎ *758/459–7200*) provides information about area attractions. Outside some of the popular attractions in and around Soufrière, souvenir vendors can be persistent. Be polite but firm if you're not interested in their wares.

VIEUX FORT AND THE EAST COAST

Vieux Fort is on the southeast tip of St. Lucia and the location of Hewanorra International Airport, which serves all commercial jet aircraft arriving and departing St. Lucia. Although less developed for tourism than the island's north and west (although that may change in coming years), the area around Vieux Fort and along the east coast is home to some of St. Lucia's unique ecosystems and interesting natural attractions.

WHAT TO SEE

Barre de l'Isle Forest Reserve. St. Lucia is divided into eastern and western halves by Barre de l'Isle ridge. A mile-long (1½-km-long) trail cuts through the reserve, and four lookout points provide panoramic views. Visible in the distance are Mt. Gimie, immense green valleys, both the Caribbean Sea and the Atlantic Ocean, and coastal communities. The reserve is about a half-hour drive from Castries; it takes about an hour to walk the trail—an easy hike—and another hour to climb Mt. La Combe Ridge. Permission from the St. Lucia Forest & Lands Department is required to access the trail in Barre de l'Isle; a naturalist or forest officer guide will accompany you. ✉ *Trailhead on East Coast Rd., near Ravine Poisson, midway between Castries and Dennery* ☎ *758/450–2231 or 758/450–2078* ⌲ *Guide services $10* ⊙ *Daily by appointment only.*

Frégate Island Nature Reserve. A mile-long (1½-km) trail encircles the nature reserve, which you reach from the East Coast Road near the fishing village of Praslin. In this area, boat builders still fashion traditional fishing canoes, called *gommiers* after the trees from which the hulls are made. The Amerindian people, who originally populated the Caribbean, used the ancient design. A natural promontory at Praslin provides a lookout from which you can view the two small islets, Frégate Major and Frégate Minor, and—with luck—the frigate birds that nest here from May to July. The only way to visit is on a guided tour, which includes a ride in a gommier to Frégate Minor for a picnic lunch and a swim; all trips are by reservation only and require a minimum of two people. Arrange visits through your hotel, a tour operator, or the St. Lucia National Trust; many tours include round-trip transportation from your hotel, as well as the tour cost. ⊠ *Praslin* ☎ *758/452–5005 or 758/453–7656, 758/454–5014 for tour reservations* ⊕ *www.slunatrust. org* ⌑ *$18* ⊘ *Daily by appointment only.*

Mamiku Gardens. One of St. Lucia's largest and loveliest botanical gardens surrounds the hilltop ruins of the Micoud Estate. Baron Micoud, an 18th-century colonel in the French Army and governor general of St. Lucia, deeded the land to his wife, Madame de Micoud, to avoid confiscation by the British during one of the many times when St. Lucia changed hands. Locals abbreviated her name to "Ma Micoud," which, over time, became "Mamiku." Nevertheless, the estate did become a British military outpost in 1796 but, shortly thereafter, was burned to the ground by slaves during the Brigand's War. The estate is now primarily a banana plantation, but the gardens themselves—including several secluded or "secret" gardens—are filled with tropical flowers and plants, delicate orchids, and fragrant herbs. ⊠ *Vieux Fort Hwy., Praslin* ☎ *758/455–3729* ⌑ *$6; guided tour, $8* ⊘ *Daily 9–5.*

Maria Islands Nature Reserve. Two tiny islands in the Atlantic Ocean off St. Lucia's southeast coast make up the reserve, which has its own interpretive center. The 25-acre Maria Major and the 4-acre Maria Minor, its little sister, are inhabited by two rare species of reptiles (the colorful Zandoli Terre ground lizard and the harmless Kouwes grass snake) that share their home with frigate birds, terns, doves, and other wildlife. There's a small beach for swimming and snorkeling, as well as an undisturbed forest, a vertical cliff covered with cacti, and a coral reef for snorkeling or diving. The St. Lucia Trust offers tours, including the boat trip to the islands, by appointment only; bring your own picnic lunch, as there are no facilities. ⊠ *St. Lucia National Trust Regional Office, Vieux Fort* ☎ *758/452–5005 or 758/453–7656, 758/454–5014 for tour reservations* ⊕ *www.slunatrust.org* ⌑ *$35* ⊘ *Aug.–mid-May, Wed.–Sun. 9:30–5, by appointment only.*

Vieux Fort. St. Lucia's second-largest town is where you'll find Hewanorra International Airport. From the Moule à Chique Peninsula, the island's southernmost tip, you can see all of St. Lucia to the north and the island of St. Vincent 21 mi (34 km) south. This is where the waters of the clear Caribbean Sea blend with those of the deeper blue Atlantic Ocean.

WHERE TO EAT

Bananas, mangoes, passion fruit, plantains, breadfruit, okra, avocados, limes, pumpkins, cucumbers, papaya, yams, christophenes (also called chayote), and coconuts are among the fresh local fruits and vegetables that grace St. Lucian menus. The French influence is strong, and most chefs cook with a creole flair. Resort buffets and restaurant fare run the gamut, from steaks and chops to pasta and pizza. Every menu lists fresh fish along with the ever-popular lobster. Caribbean standards include callaloo, stuffed crab back, pepper-pot stew, curried chicken or goat, and *lambi* (conch). The national dish of salt fish and green fig—a stew of dried, salted codfish and boiled green banana—is, let's say, an acquired taste. Soups and stews are traditionally prepared in a coal pot, a rustic clay casserole on a matching clay stand that holds the hot coals. Chicken and pork dishes and barbecues are also popular here. Fresh lobster is available in season, which lasts from August through March. As they do throughout the Caribbean, local vendors set up barbecues along the roadside, at street fairs, and at Friday-night "jump-ups" and do a land-office business selling grilled fish or chicken legs, bakes (fried biscuits), and beer—you can get a full meal for less than $10. Most other meats are imported—beef from Argentina and Iowa, lamb from New Zealand. Piton is the local brew; Bounty, the local rum.

With so many popular all-inclusive resorts, guests take most meals at hotel restaurants—which are generally quite good and, in some cases, exceptional. It's fun when vacationing, however, to try some of the local restaurants, as well—for lunch when sightseeing or for a special night out.

WHAT TO WEAR

Dress on St. Lucia is casual but conservative. Shorts are usually fine during the day, but bathing suits and immodest clothing are frowned upon anywhere but at the beach. In the evening the mood is casually elegant, but even the fanciest places generally expect only a collared shirt and long pants for men and a sundress or slacks for women.

NORTH OF VIGIE TO POINTE DU CAP

$$$$ ✕ **The Edge.** Innovative Swedish chef Bobo Bergstrom, formerly the culi-
ECLECTIC nary director at Windjammer Landing and chef de cuisine at the famed
Fodor'sChoice Operakallaren in Stockholm, has brought "Eurobbean" cuisine to his
★ own fine-dining establishment overlooking the harbor at Harmony Suites hotel. St. Lucian locals and visitors alike rave about chef Bobo's culinary feats, the excellent wine list, and the island's first sushi bar. The contemporary fusion style combines the chef's European heritage, Caribbean traditions and ingredients, and a touch of Asian influence. Among the dozen starters is a dreamy lobster bisque scented with saffron and paprika. Follow that with snapper braised in fennel bouillon, jerk-marinated-and-grilled beef tenderloin, or spice-glazed rabbit roulade. You might want to consider the five-course tasting menu. There's sure to be a dish on the extensive menu (or at the sushi bar) that suits everyone in your party, but be sure to leave room for a fabulous dessert. ⌧ *Harmony Suites, Rodney Bay* ☎ *758/450–3343* ⊕ *www. edge-restaurant.com* ⌔ *Reservations essential.*

$$ ✕ **The Lime on the Bay.** A casual bistro with lime-green gingham curtains,
ECLECTIC straw hats decorating the ceiling, and hanging plants, the Lime special-
☾ izes in local dishes such as spicy jerk chicken or pork and breadfruit
★ salad—as well as char-grilled steak and fresh-caught fish. The portions are plentiful, and the prices are reasonable, which is perhaps why you often see St. Lucians and visitors alike "liming" (an island term that

means something akin to hanging around and relaxing) all day and most of the night at this popular restaurant. The Late Lime, a club where the crowd gathers as night turns to morning, is next door. ⊠ *Rodney Bay* ☎ *758/452–0761* ⊗ *Closed Tues.*

$$$ ✕ **Tao.** For exquisite dining, head for Tao at the Body Holiday at
ASIAN LeSPORT. Perched on a second-floor balcony at the edge of Cariblue
Fodor'sChoice Beach, you're guaranteed a pleasant breeze and a starry sky while you
★ enjoy fusion cuisine—a marriage of Asian tastes and a Caribbean touch. Choose from appetizers such as seafood dumplings, sashimi salad, or miso-eggplant timbale, followed by tender slices of pork loin teriyaki, twice-cooked duck, wok-seared calves' liver, or tandoori chicken—the results are mouthwatering. Fine wines accompany the meal, desserts are extravagant, and service is superb. Seating is limited; hotel guests have priority, so reserve early. ⊠ *The Body Holiday at LeSPORT, Cap Estate* ☎ *758/450–8551* ⊕ *www.thebodyholiday.com* ⚶ *Reservations essential* ⊗ *No lunch.*

$$$$ ✕ **Ti Bananne.** Poolside at the Coco Palm hotel in Rodney Bay, Ti
CARIBBEAN Bananne is an airy Caribbean-style bistro and bar that serves break-
Fodor'sChoice fast, lunch, and dinner daily. Breakfast attracts mostly hotel guests,
★ but the elegant yet casual restaurant has been positioned as an independent restaurant to attract both guests and nonguests for lunch and dinner. Lunch is a good bet if you're poking around Rodney Bay, need a break from Reduit Beach, or are just looking for a good meal in a friendly spot. On Wednesday there's a special creole lunch buffet; for Sunday brunch, a barbecue buffet. In the evening, stop first at the bar for a fruity rum drink, cold Piton beer, or something stronger—but the open-to-the-breeze dining room is where the magic really comes through. Executive chef Richardson Skinner and head chef Giancarlo Crumps, both natives of Trinidad and Tobago with extensive experience throughout the Caribbean, conjure up exquisite French-inspired, creole-influenced dishes such as panfried snapper with orange and butter sauce and green fig Lyonnaise. Leave room for dessert—the trio of crèmes brûlées (mango and ginger, coconut, and seamoss and cinnamon) is the showstopper. And speaking of the show, a live band entertains every evening. ⊠ *Coco Palm, Rodney Bay, Gros Islet* ☎ *758/456–2828* ⊕ *www.coco-resorts.com* ⚶ *Reservations essential.*

CASTRIES

$$$ ✕ **Coal Pot.** Popular since the early 1960s, this tiny (only 10 tables)
FRENCH waterfront restaurant overlooking pretty Vigie Cove is managed by
Fodor'sChoice local artist Michelle Elliott and her French husband, Xavier Ribot,
★ who is also the chef. For a light lunch, opt for a Greek or shrimp salad or, perhaps, broiled fresh fish with creole sauce. Dinner might start with divine lobster bisque, followed by fresh seafood accompanied by one (or more) of the chef's fabulous sauces—ginger, coconut-curry, lemon-garlic butter, or wild mushroom. Hearty eaters may prefer duck, lamb, beef, or chicken laced with peppercorns, red wine, and onion or Roquefort sauce. ⊠ *Vigie Marina, Castries* ☎ *758/452–5566* ⊕ *www.coalpotrestaurant.com* ⚶ *Reservations essential* ⊗ *Closed Sun. No lunch Sat.*

$$$ ✗ **Jacques Waterfront Dining.** Chef–owner Jacky Rioux creates magical
ECLECTIC dishes in his open-air garden restaurant (known for years as Froggie
Fodor's Choice Jack's) overlooking Vigie Cove. The cooking style is decidedly French,
★ as is Rioux, but fresh produce and local spices create a fusion cuisine
that's memorable at either lunch or dinner. You might start with a bowl
of creamy tomato-basil or pumpkin soup, a grilled portobello mush-
room, or octopus and conch in curried coconut sauce. Main courses
include fresh seafood, such as oven-baked kingfish with a white wine–
and–sweet pepper sauce, or breast of chicken stuffed with smoked
salmon in a citrus-butter sauce. The wine list is also impressive. ⊠ *Vi-
gie Marina, Castries* ☎ *758/458–1900* ⊕ *www.jacquesrestaurant.com*
⚖ *Reservations essential* ☾ *Closed Sun.*

22

BETWEEN CASTRIES AND CANARIES

$$–$$$ ✗ **Chateau Mygo.** Walk down a garden path to Chateau Mygo (a cor-
SEAFOOD ruption of the word Marigot), pick out a table on the dockside din-
☺ ing deck, pull up a chair, and soak up the waterfront atmosphere of
★ what is arguably the prettiest bay in the Caribbean. The tableau is
mesmerizing—and that's at lunch, when you can order a sandwich,
burger, fish- or chicken-and-chips, salads, or grilled fish or chicken
with peas and rice and vegetables. At dinner, chef–owner Doreen
Rambally—whose family has owned and operated this place since
the mid-1970s—draws on three generations of East Indian and creole
family recipes. Beautifully grilled fresh tuna, red snapper, kingfish,
mahimahi, and local lobster are embellished with flavors such as gin-
ger, mango, papaya, or passion fruit, and then dished up with regional
vegetables—perhaps callaloo, okra, dasheen, breadfruit, christophene,
or yams. Of course, you can also have roast pork, beef, a chicken
dish, or even pizza, if you wish. This is a very casual restaurant where
locals, yachties, and frequent visitors know they'll get a delicious,
reasonably priced meal right on the waterfront. And oh, that view!
⊠ *Marigot Bay* ☎ *758/451–4772.*

$$$–$$$$ ✗ **Rainforest Hideaway.** Fabulous fusion fare—in this case, the exotic
ECLECTIC tastes and flavors influencing classical French cuisine—is presented by
Fodor's Choice chef Myron at this romantic fine-dining hideaway on the north shore of
★ pretty Marigot Bay. It's definitely worth the 20-minute-or-so drive from
Castries. A little ferry whisks you to the alfresco restaurant, perched on
a dock, where you're greeted with complimentary champagne. You'll
be duly impressed by entrées such as balsamic-glazed roast quail, five-
spice roast fillet of beef, or citrus-marinated wild salmon, accompanied
by rich sauces, exotic vegetables, and excellent wines—not to mention
the blanket of stars in the sky overhead and the live jazz several times a
week. Sunday brunch is a special treat in this lovely setting on the bay.
⊠ *Marigot Bay* ☎ *758/286–0511* ⊕ *www.rainforesthideawaystlucia.*
com ⚖ *Reservations essential* ☾ *No lunch.*

Amazing views at Dasheene Restaurant in the Ladera Resort.

SOUFRIÈRE AND VICINITY

$$$
CARIBBEAN
Fodor'sChoice
★

✕ **Dasheene Restaurant and Bar.** The terrace restaurant at Ladera resort has breathtakingly close-up views of the Pitons and the sea between them, especially beautiful at sunset. It's casual by day and magical at night. Executive-chef Orlando Satchell describes his creative West Indian menu as "sexy Caribbean." Appetizers may include grilled crab claws with a choice of dips or silky pumpkin soup with ginger. Typical entrées are triggerfish seasoned and soaked in lime and fish stock and cooked in banana leaves, shrimp Dasheene (panfried with local herbs), seared duck breast with passion-fruit jus, or baron fillet of beef with sweet potato and green-banana mash. Light dishes, fresh salads, and sandwiches are served at lunchtime. ☒ *Ladera resort, 2 mi (3 km) south of Soufrière* ☎ *758/459–7323* ⊕ *www.ladera.com.*

$$–$$$
CARIBBEAN
★

✕ **Lifeline Restaurant at the Hummingbird.** The chef at this cheerful restaurant-bar in the Hummingbird Beach Resort specializes in French-creole cuisine, starting with fresh seafood or chicken seasoned with local herbs and accompanied by a medley of vegetables just picked from the Hummingbird's garden. Sandwiches and salads are also available. If you stop for lunch, sit outside by the pool for a magnificent view of the Pitons (you can also take a dip), and be sure to visit the batik studio and art gallery of proprietor Joan Alexander-Stowe, adjacent to the dining room. ☒ *Hummingbird Beach Resort, Anse Chastanet Rd., Soufrière* ☎ *758/459–7232* ⊕ *www.istlucia.co.uk.*

$$
CARIBBEAN
★

✕ **The Still.** When you're visiting Diamond Waterfall, this is a great lunch spot. The two dining rooms seat up to 400 people, so it's a popular stop for tour groups and cruise passengers. The emphasis is on local cuisine using vegetables such as christophene, breadfruit, yam, and callaloo along with grilled fish or chicken, but there are also pork and beef dishes. All fruits and vegetables used in the restaurant are organically grown on the estate. ⊠ *The Still Plantation, Sir Arthur Lewis St., Soufrière* ☎ *758/459–7261.*

22

WHERE TO STAY

Most people—particularly honeymooners—choose to stay in one of St. Lucia's many beach resorts, most of which are upscale and pricey. Several are all-inclusive, including the three Sandals resorts, two resorts owned or managed by Sunswept (the Body Holiday at LeSPORT and Rendezvous), Almond Morgan Bay, and Smugglers Cove Resort & Spa.

If you're looking for lodgings that are more intimate and less expensive, St. Lucia has dozens of small inns and hotels that are primarily locally owned, always charming, and often less expensive but may or may not be directly on the beach.

Luxury villa communities and independent private villas are another alternative in St. Lucia. Most of the villa communities are in the north near Cap Estate.

VILLAS AND CONDOS

Luxury villa communities are an important part of the accommodations mix on St. Lucia, as they can be an economical option for families, other groups, or couples vacationing together. Several villa communities have opened in recent years, and more are on the way. The villa units themselves are privately owned, but nonowners can rent individual units directly from the property managers for a vacation or short-term stay, the same as reserving hotel accommodations. Units with fully equipped kitchens, up to three bedrooms, and as many baths run $200 to $2,500 per night, depending on the size and the season.

PRIVATE VILLAS AND CONDOS

Local real estate agencies will arrange vacation rentals of privately owned villas and condos that are fully equipped. Most private villas are in the hills of Cap Estate in the very north of the island, at Rodney Bay or Bois d'Orange, or in Soufrière among St. Lucia's natural treasures. Some are within walking distance of a beach.

All rental villas are staffed with a cook who specializes in local cuisine and a housekeeper; in some cases, a caretaker lives on the property and a gardener and night watchman are on staff. All properties have telephones, and some have Internet access and fax machines. Telephones may be barred against outgoing overseas calls; plan to use a phone card or calling card. Most villas have TVs, DVDs, and CD players. All private villas have a swimming pool; condos share a community pool. Vehicles are generally not included in the rates, but rental cars can be arranged and delivered to the villa upon request. Linens and basic supplies (such as bath soap, toilet tissue, dish-washing detergent) are included. Pre-arrival grocery stocking can be arranged.

Units with one to nine bedrooms and as many baths run $200 to $2,000 per night, depending on the size of the villa, the amenities, the number of guests, and the season. Rates include utilities and government taxes. Your only additional cost will be for groceries and staff gratuities. A security deposit is required upon booking and refunded after departure less any damages or unpaid miscellaneous charges.

RENTAL AGENCIES

Discover Villas of St. Lucia (✉ *Cap Estate, Gros Islet* ☎ *758/484–3066* ⊕ *www.a1stluciavillas.com*). **Island Villas St. Lucia** (✉ *Rodney Bay, Gros Islet* ☎ *758/458–4903* ⊕ *www.island-villas.com/stlucia.php*). **Tropical Villas** (✉ *Cap Estate, Gros Islet* ☎ *758/452–8240* ⊕ *www.tropicalvillas.net*).

The following reviews have been condensed for this book. Please go to Fodors.com for expanded reviews of each property.

NORTH OF VIGIE TO POINTE DU CAP

$$$$
RESORT
☺
★
🖼 **Almond Morgan Bay Beach Resort.** An all-inclusive resort appropriate for singles, couples, and families alike, Almond Morgan Bay offers both quiet seclusion on 22 acres surrounding a stretch of white-sand beach and tons of free sports and activities. **Pros:** family-friendly; lots to do; three complimentary rounds of golf included; great atmosphere at Morgan's Pier. **Cons:** resort is huge and can be very busy, especially when all rooms are filled; beach is small. ✉ *Choc Bay, Gros Islet* ⌂ *Box 2167, Castries* ☎ *758/450–2511* ⊕ *www.almondresorts.com* ⇗ *340 rooms* ⚖ *In-room: safe. In-hotel: restaurants, room service, bars, tennis courts, pools, gym, spa, beach, water sports, children's programs, business center* ⟨○⟩ *All-inclusive.*

$
RESORT
☺
Fodor's Choice
★
🖼 **Bay Gardens Beach Resort.** One of three Bay Gardens properties in Rodney Bay Village, the family-friendly beach resort has a prime location directly on beautiful Reduit Beach. **Pros:** idyllic beachfront location; excellent value; stay at one, play at three resorts. **Cons:** popular place, so you need to book far in advance in season. ✉ *Reduit Beach, Rodney Bay, Gros Islet* ⌂ *Box 1892, Gros Islet* ☎ *758/457–8500* ⊕ *www.baygardensbeachresort.com* ⇗ *36 rooms, 36 suites* ⚖ *In-room: safe, kitchen (some), Internet. In-hotel: restaurants, room service, bars, pool, gym, spa, beach, water sports, children's programs, business center* ⟨○⟩ *No meals.*

¢
HOTEL
★
🖼 **Bay Gardens Hotel.** Independent travelers and regional businesspeople swear by this cheerful, well-run boutique hotel at Rodney Bay Village. **Pros:** excellent service; unusual value; Croton suites are a best bet. **Cons:** not beachfront; heavy focus on business travelers, so it's not exactly a vacation environment. ✉ *Rodney Bay* ⌂ *Box 1892, Castries* ☎ *758/452–8060* ⊕ *www.baygardenshotel.com* ⇗ *59 rooms, 28 suites* ⚖ *In-room: safe, kitchen (some), Internet, Wi-Fi (some). In-hotel: restaurant, room service, bar, pools, business center* ⟨○⟩ *No meals.*

$$$$
RESORT
Fodor's Choice
★
🖼 **Body Holiday at LeSPORT.** Even before you leave home, you can customize your own "body holiday" online—from robe size to tee time—at this adults-only resort in luxurious tropical surroundings. **Pros:** daily spa treatment included; excellent dining; unusual activities such as archery. **Cons:** pleasant but unremarkable rooms; small bathrooms with skimpy towels; lots of steps to get to the spa. ✉ *Cariblue Beach, Cap Estate, Gros Islet* ⌂ *Box 437, Castries* ☎ *758/450–8551* ⊕ *www.thebodyholiday.com*

Cotton Bay Village.

152 rooms, 2 suites ⌂ In-room: safe, no TV, Internet. In-hotel: restaurants, bars, tennis courts, pools, gym, spa, beach, water sports, business center, some age restrictions ⌁ All-inclusive.

$$$–$$$$
RESORT
Fodor's Choice
★

Cap Maison. This boutique villa community built on a seaside bluff has 22 units that can be configured as up to 49 rooms, junior suites, and oversize one-, two-, or three-bedroom villa suites. **Pros:** golf and tennis privileges nearby; private and elegant; those rooftop plunge pools. **Cons:** a/c in bedrooms only; beach access (62 steps) is strenuous. ⊠ *Smugglers Cove, Cap Estate, Gros Islet ⌂ Box 2188, Gros Islet ☎758/457–8678 ⊕ www.capmaison.com ☞ 10 rooms, 39 suites in 22 villas ⌂ In-room: safe, kitchen (some), Internet. In-hotel: restaurant, room service, bars, pool, gym, spa, beach, water sports, laundry facilities, business center ⌁ Breakfast.*

$–$$
HOTEL
☺
Fodor's Choice
★

Coco Palm. This stylish boutique hotel in Rodney Bay Village also includes Coco Kreole, a cozy guesthouse at the edge of the property, and is right in the middle of the Rodney Bay Village action. **Pros:** excellent value; feng-shui designed, fabulous swim-up rooms; family suites. **Cons:** not directly on the beach; nightly entertainment can get noisy. ⊠ *Reduit Beach Ave., Rodney Bay ⊠ Box GM605, Rodney Bay ☎758/456–2800 ⊕ www.coco-resorts.com ☞ 80 rooms, 12 suites ⌂ In-room: safe, Wi-Fi. In-hotel: restaurants, bars, pools, business center ⌁ No meals.*

$$–$$$
RESORT
☺
Fodor's Choice
★

Cotton Bay Village. Wedged between a quiet ocean beach and the St. Lucia Golf Club, luxurious, individually designed and decorated colonial-style town houses and chateau-style villas surround a village center and a free-form lagoon pool. **Pros:** truly luxurious accommodation; privacy; family-friendly. **Cons:** a/c in bedrooms only; bathrooms have showers only; rental car advised if you plan to leave the property. ⊠ *Cotton Bay, Cap Estate, Gros Islet* ☏ *758/456–5700* ⊕ *www.cottonbayvillage.com* ↩ *206 suites in 74 villas* ⚴ *In-room: safe, kitchen, Wi-Fi. In-hotel: restaurants, room service, bars, pool, gym, spa, beach, water sports, children's programs, laundry facilities* ⏀ *No meals.*

$$$–$$$$
RESORT
☺
Fodor'sChoice
★

The Landings. On 19 acres along the Pigeon Point Causeway at the northern edge of Rodney Bay, the Landings is so called because the property surrounds a private, 80-slip yacht harbor where residents can dock their own yachts literally at their doorstep. **Pros:** spacious, beautifully appointed units; perfect place for yachties to come ashore; personal chef service. **Con:** $30 per day activities fee in addition to the room rate. ⊠ *Pigeon Island Causeway, Gros Islet* ☏ *758/458–7300* ⊕ *www. landings.rockresorts.com* ↩ *80 units* ⚴ *In-room: safe, kitchen, Internet. In-hotel: restaurants, room service, bars, tennis courts, pools, gym, spa, beach, water sports, children's programs, business center* ⏀ *No meals.*

$$$$
RESORT
☺
Fodor'sChoice
★

Royal St. Lucia by Rex Resorts. This luxurious all-suites resort on St. Lucia's best beach caters to every whim. **Pros:** great beachfront; roomy accommodations; convenient to Rodney Bay Village. **Cons:** dated guest rooms and baths. ⊠ *Reduit Beach, Rodney Bay, Gros Islet* ⏍ *Box 977, Castries* ☏ *758/452–9999* ⊕ *www.rexcaribbean.com* ↩ *96 suites* ⚴ *In-room: safe, Wi-Fi. In-hotel: restaurants, room service, bars, tennis courts, pool, gym, spa, beach, water sports, children's programs, business center* ⏀ *No meals.*

$$$$
RESORT
Fodor'sChoice
★

Sandals Grande St. Lucian Spa & Beach Resort. Grand, indeed! And busy, busy, busy. Couples love this place—particularly young honeymooners and those getting married here—the biggest and splashiest of the three Sandals resorts on St. Lucia. **Pros:** excellent beach; lots of activities; lovely spa; airport shuttle. **Cons:** the really long ride to and from Hewanorra; buffet meals are uninspired. ⊠ *Pigeon Island causeway, Gros Islet* ⏍ *Box 2247, Castries* ☏ *758/455–2000* ⊕ *www. sandals.com* ↩ *271 rooms, 11 suites* ⚴ *In-room: safe, Internet, Wi-Fi (some). In-hotel: restaurants, room service, bars, tennis courts, pools, gym, spa, beach, water sports, business center, some age restrictions* ⏀ *All-inclusive.*

$$$$
RESORT
Fodor'sChoice
★

Sandals Halcyon Beach St. Lucia. This is the most intimate and low-key of the three Sandals resorts on St. Lucia. Like the others, though, it's beachfront, all-inclusive, for couples only, and loaded with amenities and activities. **Pros:** all the Sandals amenities in a more intimate setting; lots of dining and activity choices; exchange privileges (including golf) at two other Sandals properties. **Cons:** it's Sandals, so it's a theme property after all. ⊠ *Choc Bay, Castries* ⏍ *GM910, Castries* ☏ *758/453–0222 or 800/223–6510* ⊕ *www.sandals.com* ↩ *169 rooms* ⚴ *In-room: safe, Internet, Wi-Fi. In-hotel: restaurants, room service, bars, tennis courts, pools, gym, spa, beach, water sports, business center, some age restrictions* ⏀ *All-inclusive.*

$$$$
RESORT
Fodor'sChoice
★

Sandals Regency St. Lucia Golf Resort & Spa. One of three Sandals resorts on St. Lucia, this is the second-largest and distinguishes itself with its own 9-hole golf course (for guests only). **Pros:** lots to do; picturesque location; on-site golf; airport shuttle. **Cons:** somewhat isolated location; expert golfers will prefer St. Lucia Golf Club in Cap Estate. ⊠ *La Toc Rd.* ⏍ *Box 399, Castries* ☏ *758/452–3081* ⊕ *www.*

Sandals Grande St. Lucian Spa & Beach Resort.

sandals.com ⇌ *212 rooms, 116 suites* ♿ *In-room: safe, Internet, Wi-Fi (some). In-hotel: restaurants, room service, bars, golf course, tennis courts, pools, gym, spa, beach, water sports, business center, some age restrictions* ⦿ *All-inclusive.*

$$$$
RESORT
☺
★

⛳ **Smugglers Cove Resort & Spa.** This huge, all-inclusive, village-style resort has more food, fun, and features than you and your family will have time to enjoy in a week. **Pros:** family rooms sleep five; excellent children's program; superlative tennis facilities; nightly entertainment is family-friendly. **Cons:** busy, busy, busy; not the place for a quiet getaway; guest rooms are spread far and wide on the hillside. ✉ *Smugglers Cove, Cap Estate, Gros Islet* ☎ *758/450–0551* ⊕ *www.almondresorts.com* ⇌ *257 rooms, 100 suites* ♿ *In-room: safe. In-hotel: restaurants, room service, bars, tennis courts, pools, gym, spa, beach, water sports, children's programs, business center* ⦿ *All-inclusive.*

$$
RENTAL
☺
★

⛳ **Windjammer Landing Villa Beach Resort.** Windjammer Landing's Mediterranean-style villas climb the hillside on one of St. Lucia's prettiest bays. As perfect for families as for a romantic getaway, the resort offers lots to do yet still affords everyone plenty of privacy. **Pros:** lovely, spacious units; beautiful sunset views; family-friendly, in-unit dining. **Cons:** some units have living rooms with no a/c; you'll need to rent a car if you plan to leave the property, as it's far from the main road. ✉ *Labrelotte Bay* ⌂ *Box 1504, Castries* ☎ *758/456–9000* ⊕ *www.windjammer-landing.com* ⇌ *41 suites, 72 villas* ♿ *In-room: kitchen (some), Internet. In-hotel: restaurants, room service, bars, tennis courts, pools, gym, spa, beach, water sports, children's program, business center* ⦿ *No meals.*

Sandals Halcyon Beach, the Pierhouse Restaurant.

GREATER CASTRIES

$$$$ RESORT ★ **Rendezvous.** Romance is alive and well at this easygoing, all-inclusive, couples resort (for male-female couples only), which stretches along the dreamy white sand of Malabar Beach opposite the George F. L. Charles Airport runway. **Pros:** convenient to Castries and Vigie Airport; great beach; romance in the air. **Cons:** no room TVs; occasional flyover noise. *Malabar Beach, Vigie Box 190, Castries 758/457–7900 www.theromanticholiday.com 21 rooms, 35 suites, 8 cottages In-room: safe, no TV. In-hotel: restaurants, bars, tennis courts, pools, gym, spa, beach, business center, some age restrictions All-inclusive.*

SOUFRIÈRE AND VICINITY

$$$–$$$$ RESORT Fodor's Choice ★ **Anse Chastanet Beach Hotel.** Anse Chastanet is magical, if you don't mind the bone-crushing dirt road between the town and the resort and the steep climb to most rooms. **Pros:** great for divers; Room 14B with the tree growing through the bathroom; the Piton views. **Cons:** no pool; entrance road is difficult to negotiate; steep hillside certainly not conducive to strolling; some may miss in-room TVs, phones, and a/c. *Anse Chastanet Rd., Soufrière Box 7000, Soufrière 758/459–7000 www.ansechastanet.com 49 rooms In-room: no a/c, no phone, safe, no TV. In-hotel: restaurants, room service, bars, tennis court, spa, beach, water sports, business center, some age restrictions No meals.*

¢–$ INN **Hummingbird Beach Resort.** Unpretentious and welcoming, this delightful little inn on Soufrière Harbour has simply furnished rooms—a traditional motif emphasized by four-poster beds and African wood sculptures—in small seaside cabins. **Pros:** local island hospitality; small and quiet; good food; batik studio on-site. **Cons:** few resort amenities— but that's part of the charm. ⊠ *Anse Chastanet Rd., Soufrière* ⌂ *Box 280, Soufrière* ☎ *758/459–7232* ⊕ *www.istlucia.co.uk* ⌁ *9 rooms, 2 with shared bath; 1 suite; 1 cottage* ⌂ *In-room: no a/c (some), no phone (some), Wi-Fi. In-hotel: restaurant, bars, pool, beach* ⏺ *Breakfast.*

22

$$$$
RESORT
Fodor'sChoice
★

⊡ **Jade Mountain Club.** This premium-class and premium-priced hotel is a five-level behemoth looming out of the side of a mountain that slopes down to the sea. **Pros:** amazing accommodations; huge in-room pools; incredible Piton views. **Cons:** sky-high rates; lack of in-room communication and a/c; not appropriate for anyone with disabilities. ⊠ *Anse Chastanet, Soufrière* ⌂ *Box 7000, Soufrière* ☎ *758/459–4000* ⊕ *www.jademountainstlucia.com* ⌁ *28 suites* ⌂ *In-room: no a/c, no phone, no TV. In-hotel: restaurant, room service, bar, gym, spa, beach, water sports, business center, some age restrictions* ⏺ *No meals.*

$$$$
RESORT
⟳
Fodor'sChoice
★

⊡ **The Jalousie Plantation, Sugar Beach.** Located on the most dramatic 192 acres in St. Lucia, this resort flows down Val des Pitons—the steep valley smack between the Pitons—on the remains of an 18th-century sugar plantation 2 mi (3 km) south of Soufrière. **Pros:** incomparable scenery; in-room iPod stations and DVD players; lots of water sports, including complimentary scuba diving; the spa's tree-house treatment gazebos. **Cons:** fairly isolated, so a meal plan makes sense; cottages are surrounded by thick foliage, so bring mosquito spray. ⊠ *Val des Pitons, Soufrière* ⌂ *Box 251, Soufrière* ☎ *800/544–2883 or 758/459–7666* ⊕ *www.jalousieplantation.com* ⌁ *11 rooms, 100 villas* ⌂ *In-room: safe, Internet, Wi-Fi. In-hotel: restaurants, room service, bars, golf course, tennis courts, pool, gym, spa, beach, water sports, children's programs, business center* ⏺ *No meals.*

$$$$
HOTEL
Fodor'sChoice
★

⊡ **Ladera.** One of the most sophisticated small inns in the Caribbean, the elegantly rustic Ladera is perched 1,100 feet above the sea directly between the two Pitons. **Pros:** breathtaking Pitons vista; in-room pools; excellent cuisine. **Cons:** the hotel's single pool is not very big; open fourth walls and steep drops make this inappropriate for children (and also means no a/c); rental car advised. ⊠ *Val de Pitons, Soufrière* ⌂ *Box 225, Soufrière* ☎ *758/459–6600* ⊕ *www.ladera.com* ⌁ *23 suites, 9 villas* ⌂ *In-room: no a/c, no phone, no TV, Wi-Fi. In-hotel: restaurant, bars, pool, gym, spa, business center, some age restrictions (except during Christmas and Easter holidays)* ⏺ *Breakfast.*

$$$-$$$$
RENTAL
★

⊡ **Stonefield Estate Villa Resort & Spa.** One 18th-century plantation house and several gingerbread-style cottages dot this 26-acre property. All accommodations have oversize, handcrafted furniture and one or two bathrooms; some also have garden showers, and each has its own secluded plunge pool. **Pros:** very private; beautiful pool; great sunset views from villa decks; lovely wedding venue. **Cons:** a rental car is recommended; you have to drive to restaurants. ⊠ *1 mi (1½ km) south of Soufrière* ⌂ *Box 228, Soufrière* ☎ *758/459–5648 or 758/459–7037* ⊕ *www.stonefieldvillas.com* ⌁ *17 villas* ⌂ *In-room: no a/c (some), safe, kitchen (some), no TV. In-hotel: restaurant, room service, bar, pool, gym, spa, business center, some age restrictions* ⏺ *Breakfast.*

Small Hotels and Inns in St. Lucia

Choose one of these seven smaller properties if you're looking for something more intimate than the typical beach resort.

GREATER CASTRIES

$ **Auberge Seraphine** (⊠ *Vielle Bay, Pointe Seraphine, Castries* ⮌ *Box 390, Castries* ☎ *758/453-2073* ⊕ *www.aubergeseraphine.com*) is convenient to town and a good choice for independent travelers who don't require a beachfront location or a breadth of activities. Excellent restaurant, and all but six rooms have a water view. A broad sundeck surrounds a small pool.

$$ **Villa Beach Cottages** (⊠ *Choc Bay, Castries* ☎ *758/450-2884* ⊕ *www.villabeachcottages.com*) line the beach at this family establishment—a favorite of Nobel laureate Sir Derek Walcott. Units are cozy and fairly close together, but each has a balcony facing the water, guaranteeing glorious sunset viewing every evening.

MARIGOT BAY

$$ **Inn on the Bay** (⊠ *Marigot Bay* ☎ *758/451-4260* ⊕ *www.saint-lucia.com*) has five rooms (for adults only), and owners Normand Viau and Louise Boucher treat you as their personal guest. Cool sea breezes obviate the need for a/c, and the stunning views of Marigot Bay are absolutely enchanting from the balcony outside your room and from the pool deck.

$$ **Mango Beach Inn** (⊠ *Marigot Bay* ☎ *758/451-4872* ⊕ *www.mangobeachmarigot.com*) is a family-friendly bed-and-breakfast perched on the hillside above Rainforest Hideaway and overlooking pretty Marigot Bay. The four guest rooms are comfortable but small, though the living–dining room, to which you're always invited, is huge and has large windows open to the view—beautiful day or night.

RODNEY BAY VILLAGE

$$ **Ginger Lily** (⊠ *Rodney Bay* ☎ *758/458-0300* ⊕ *www.thegingerlilyhotel.com*), a small, modern enclave of 11 rooms, has its own restaurant and a swimming pool. It is across the street from Reduit Beach and perfectly situated in Rodney Bay Village.

$$ **Harmony Suites** (⊠ *Rodney Bay* ☎ *758/452-8756* ⊕ *www.harmonysuites.com*) guests (adults only) are scuba divers, boaters, or people who just like being close to Rodney Bay Marina. Of the 30 large suites cloistered around the swimming pool, the eight waterfront suites are the largest. Reduit Beach is across the road.

SOUFRIÈRE

$$-$$$ **Fond Doux Holiday Plantation** (⊠ *Soufrière* ☎ *758/459-7545* ⊕ *www.fonddouxestate.com*) is a collection of 10 historic homes salvaged from around the island and rebuilt in a rain-forest setting on an active 18th-century agricultural estate. The private, beautifully furnished cottages provide a truly ecofriendly vacation experience.

$$-$$$ **La Haut Plantation** (⊠ *Soufrière* ⮌ *Box 304, Soufrière* ☎ *758/459-7008* ⊕ *www.lahaut.com*) is an intimate, affordable, family-run inn that boasts a spectacular view of the Pitons. Guests are encouraged to roam the 52-acre mountaintop estate, and kids get a kick out of the resident goats, cows, birds, and donkeys.

$$$–$$$$
RESORT
Fodor's Choice
★

🏨 **Ti Kaye Village.** There is a specialness to this aerie overlooking Anse Cochon beach and down a mile-long dirt road off the main highway. Gingerbread-style cottages facing the ocean are surrounded by lush greenery and furnished with handcrafted furniture. Pros: perfect for a honeymoon or private getaway; garden showers are fabulous; excellent restaurant. Cons: far from anywhere; all those steps to the beach; not a good choice for anyone with physical challenges. ⊠ Anse Cochon ☎ Box GM669, Castries 🖀 758/456–8101 ⊕ www.tikaye.com ⇥ 33 rooms ⬩ In-room: safe, no TV, Wi-Fi. In-hotel: restaurants, bars, pool, gym, spa, beach, water sports, business center, some age restrictions ⦿ Breakfast.

22

VIEUX FORT

$$$$
RESORT
☯
★

🏨 **Coconut Bay Beach Resort & Spa.** The only resort in Vieux Fort, Coconut Bay is a sprawling (85 acres) seaside retreat minutes from St. Lucia's Hewanorra International Airport. Pros: great for families; perfect for windsurfers; friendly and sociable atmosphere. Cons: bathrooms have showers only; rough surf precludes ocean swimming; close to the airport but far from everything else. ⊠ Vieux Fort ⊠ Box 246, Vieux Fort 🖀 758/459–6000 ⊕ www.cbayresort.com ⇥ 254 rooms ⬩ In-room: safe, Wi-Fi. In-hotel: restaurants, bars, tennis courts, pools, gym, spa, beach, water sports, children's programs, business center ⦿ All-inclusive.

NIGHTLIFE AND THE ARTS

THE ARTS

Fodor's Choice
★

In early May, the weeklong **St. Lucia Jazz Festival** (⊕ www.stluciajazz.org) is one of the premier events of its kind in the Caribbean. International jazz greats perform at outdoor venues on Pigeon Island and at various hotels, restaurants, and nightspots throughout the island; free concerts are also held at Derek Walcott Square in downtown Castries.

THEATER

The small, open-air **Derek Walcott Center Theatre** (⊠ Cap Estate, Gros Islet 🖀 758/450–0551, 758/450–0450 for the Great House), next to The Great House restaurant in Cap Estate, seats 200 people for monthly productions of music, dance, and drama, as well as Sunday brunch programs. The Trinidad Theatre Workshop also presents an annual performance here. For schedule and ticket information, contact The **Great House** restaurant.

NIGHTLIFE

Most resort hotels have entertainment—island music, calypso singers, and steel bands, as well as disco, karaoke, and talent shows—every night in high season and a couple of nights per week in the off-season. Otherwise, Rodney Bay is the best bet for nightlife. The many restaurants and bars there attract a crowd nearly every night.

BARS

Jambe de Bois (✉ *Pigeon Island, Rodney Bay* ☎ *758/450–8166*) is a cozy Old English–style pub with live jazz on Sunday and violin on Thursday. **J. J.'s Paradise** (✉ *Marigot Bay* ☎ *758/451–0476*) has limbo and fire-eating shows Tuesday through Friday and karaoke on Saturday night.

DANCE CLUBS

Rodney Bay has the most bars and clubs. Most dance clubs with live bands have a cover charge of $10 to $12 (EC$25 to EC$30), and the music usually starts at 11 pm.

At **Delirius** (✉ *Rodney Bay* ☎ *758/451–3354*), visitors and St. Lucians alike "lime" over cocktails at the horseshoe-shaped bar and at tables in the garden; the atmosphere is casual, the decor is contemporary, and the music (live bands or DJ) from the 1960s, '70s, and '80s.

Doolittle's (✉ *Marigot Bay* ☎ *758/451–4974*) has live bands and dance music—calypso, soul, salsa, steel band, reggae, and limbo—that changes nightly.

The Lime on the Bay (✉ *Rodney Bay* ☎ *758/452–0761*) is a particular favorite of St. Lucians; upstairs above the restaurant of the same name, it's air-conditioned and intimate, with live music, a DJ, or karaoke every night until the last patron leaves.

STREET PARTIES

☾ For a taste of St. Lucian village life, head for **Anse La Raye "Seafood Fri-**
★ **day"** (✉ *Anse La Raye*), a street festival held every Friday night. Beginning at 6:30 pm, the main street in this tiny fishing village—about halfway between Castries and Soufrière—is closed to vehicles, and the residents prepare what they know best: fish cakes, grilled or stewed fish, hot bakes (biscuits), roasted corn, boiled crayfish, even grilled-before-your-eyes lobster. Prices range from a few cents for a fish cake or bake to $10 or $15 for a whole lobster, depending on its size. Walk around, eat, chat with the local people, and listen to live music until the wee hours of the morning.

Fodor's Choice A Friday-night ritual for locals and visitors alike is to head for the **Gros**
★ **Islet Jump-Up** (✉ *Gros Islet*), the island's largest street party. Huge speakers are set up on the village's main street and blast out Caribbean music all night long. Sometimes there are live bands. When you take a break from dancing, you can buy barbecued fish or chicken, rotis, beer, and soda from villagers who set up cookers right along the roadside. It's the ultimate "lime" experience.

SHOPPING

The island's best-known products are artwork and woodcarvings, clothing and household articles made from batik and silk-screened fabrics that are designed and produced in island workshops, straw mats, and clay pottery. You can also take home straw hats and baskets and locally grown cocoa, coffee, and spices.

AREAS AND MALLS

★ Along the harbor in Castries, the rambling structures with bright-orange roofs house several markets that are open from 6 am to 5 pm Monday through Saturday. Saturday morning is the busiest and most colorful time to shop.

22

Bay Walk Shopping Mall, at Rodney Bay, is a 60-store complex with boutiques, restaurants, banks, a beauty salon, jewelry and souvenir stores—and the island's first (and, so far, only) casino.

For more than a century, farmers' wives have gathered at the **Castries Market** to sell produce—which, alas, you can't import to the United States. But you can bring back spices (such as cocoa, turmeric, cloves, bay leaves, ginger, peppercorns, cinnamon sticks, nutmeg, mace, and vanilla essence), as well as bottled hot pepper sauces—all of which cost a fraction of what you'd pay back home.

The **Craft Market,** adjacent to the produce market, has aisles and aisles of baskets and other handmade straw work, rustic brooms made from palm fronds, woodcarvings, leather work, clay pottery, and souvenirs—all at affordable prices.

Gablewoods Mall, on the Gros Islet Highway in Choc Bay, a couple of miles north of downtown Castries, has about 35 shops that sell groceries, wines and spirits, jewelry, clothing, crafts, books and overseas newspapers, music, souvenirs, household goods, and snacks.

Along with 54 boutiques, restaurants, and other businesses that sell services and supplies, a large supermarket is the focal point of each **J. Q.'s Shopping Mall;** one is at Rodney Bay and another is at Vieux Fort.

Marigot Marina Village on Marigot Bay has shops and services for boaters and landlubbers alike, including a bank, grocery store, business center, art gallery, an assortment of boutiques, and a French bakery and café.

The duty-free shopping areas are at **Pointe Seraphine,** an attractive Spanish-motif complex on Castries Harbour with more than 20 shops, and **La Place Carenage,** an inviting three-story complex on the opposite side of the harbor. You can also find duty-free items in a few small shops at the arcade at the Royal St. Lucia hotel in Rodney Bay and, of course, in the departure lounge at Hewanorra International Airport. You must present your passport and airline ticket to purchase items at the duty-free price.

The **Vendor's Arcade,** across the street from the Craft Market, is a maze of stalls and booths where you can find handicrafts among the T-shirts and costume jewelry.

Vieux Fort Plaza, near Hewanorra International Airport in Vieux Fort, is the main shopping center in the southern part of St. Lucia. You'll find a bank, supermarket, bookstore, toy shop, and several clothing stores there.

SPECIALTY ITEMS

ART

Art & Antiques (✉ *Pointe Seraphine, Castries* ☎ *758/451–4150*) is a museum-type shop opened by artist Llewellyn Xavier and his wife, where you'll find fine art, antique maps and prints, sterling silver and crystal, rich linens, objets d'art, and mere collectibles.

Artsibit Gallery (✉ *Brazil and Mongiraud Sts., Castries* ☎ *758/452–7865*) exhibits and sells moderately priced pieces by St. Lucian painters and sculptors.

Caribbean Art Gallery (✉ *Rodney Bay Yacht Marina, Rodney Bay* ☎ *758/452–8071*) sells original artwork by local artists, along with antique maps and prints and hand-painted silk.

World-renowned St. Lucian artist **Llewellyn Xavier** (✉ *Mount du Cap, Cap Estate* ☎ *758/450–9155* ⊕ *www.llewellynxavier.com*) creates modern art, ranging from vigorous oil abstracts that take up half a wall, to small objects made from beaten silver and gold. Much of his work has an environmental theme and is created from recycled materials. Xavier's work is on permanent exhibit at major museums in New York and Washington, D.C. Others are sold in gift shops throughout the island. Call to arrange a visit to his studio.

GIFTS AND SOUVENIRS

Caribbean Perfumes (✉ *Jacques Waterfront Dining, Vigie Marina, Castries* ☎ *758/453–7249*) blends a half-dozen lovely scents for women and two aftershaves for men from exotic flowers, fruits, tropical woods, and spices. Fragrances are all made in St. Lucia, reasonably priced, and available at the perfumery (in the garden adjacent to the restaurant) and at many hotel gift shops.

Noah's Arkade (✉ *Jeremie St., Castries* ☎ *758/452–2523* ✉ *Pointe Seraphine, Castries* ☎ *758/452–7488*) has hammocks, wood carvings, straw mats, T-shirts, books, and other regional goods.

HANDICRAFTS

On the southwest coast, halfway between Soufrière and Vieux Fort, you can find locally made clay and straw pieces at the **Choiseul Arts & Crafts Centre** (✉ *La Fargue* ☎ *758/454–3226*). Many of St. Lucia's artisans come from this area.

Eudovic Art Studio (✉ *Morne Fortune, Castries* ☎ *758/452–2747* ⊕ *www.eudovicart.com*) is a workshop and studio where you can buy trays, masks, and abstract figures sculpted by Vincent Joseph Eudovic from local mahogany, red cedar, and eucalyptus wood.

At **Zaka** (✉ *Malgretoute, Soufrière* ☎ *758/457–1504* ⊕ *www.zaka-art.com*), you may get a chance to talk with artist and craftsman Simon Gajhadhar, who fashions totems and masks from driftwood and other environmentally friendly sources of wood—taking advantage of all the natural nibs and knots that distinguish each piece. Once the "face" is carved, it is painted in vivid colors to highlight the exaggerated features and provide expression. Each piece is unique.

DID YOU KNOW?

The large Castries Market sells fresh local produce and spices at bargain prices; next door is the large Craft Market, aimed at the tourist trade.

SPORTS AND ACTIVITIES

BIKING

Although the terrain is pretty rugged, two tour operators have put together fascinating bicycle and combination bicycle-hiking tours that appeal to novice riders as well as those who enjoy a good workout. Prices range from $60 to $100 per person.

★ **Bike St. Lucia** (✉ *Anse Chastanet, Soufrière* ☎ *758/451–2453* ⊕ *www. bikestlucia.com*) takes small groups of bikers on Jungle Biking tours along trails that meander through the remnants of an 18th-century plantation near Soufrière. Stops are made to explore the French colonial ruins, study the beautiful tropical plants and fruit trees, enjoy a picnic lunch, and take a dip in a river swimming hole or a swim at the beach. If you're staying in the north, you can arrange a tour that includes transportation to the Soufrière area.

Palm Services Bike Tours (✉ *Castries* ☎ *758/458–0908* ⊕ *www. adventuretoursstlucia.com*) is suitable for all fitness levels. Jeep or bus transportation is provided across the central mountains to Dennery, on the east coast. After a 3-mi (5-km) ride through the countryside, bikes are exchanged for shoe leather. The short hike into the rain forest ends with a picnic and a refreshing swim next to a sparkling waterfall—then the return leg to Dennery. All gear is supplied.

BOATING AND SAILING

Rodney Bay and Marigot Bay are centers for bareboat and crewed yacht charters. Their marinas offer safe anchorage, shower facilities, restaurants, groceries, and maintenance for yachts sailing the waters of the eastern Caribbean. Charter prices range from $400 to $500 per overnight or $1,750 to $10,000 per week, depending on the season and the type and size of vessel, plus $250 extra per day if you want a skipper and cook.

Bateau Mygo (✉ *Marigot Bay* ☎ *758/451–4772* ⊕ *www.bateaumygo.com*) specializes in customized, crewed charters on its 40- to 44-foot yachts for either a couple of days or a week. **Destination St. Lucia (DSL) Ltd.** (✉ *Rodney Bay Marina, Gros Islet* ☎ *758/452–8531* ⊕ *www.dsl-yachting.com*) offers bareboat yacht charters; vessels range in length from 38 to 51 feet. The **Moorings Yacht Charters** (✉ *Marigot Bay* ☎ *758/451–4357 or 800/535–7289* ⊕ *www.moorings.com*) rents bareboat and crewed yachts ranging from Beneteau 39s to Morgan 60s.

DIVING AND SNORKELING

Depending on the season and the particular trip, prices range from about $40 to $60 for a one-tank dive to $175 to $260 for a six-dive package over three days and $265 to $450 for a 10-dive package over five days. Dive shops provide instruction for all levels (beginner, intermediate, and advanced). For beginners, a resort course (pool training), followed by one open-water dive, runs from $90 to $120. Snorkelers are generally welcome on dive trips and usually pay $50 to $65, which includes equipment and sometimes lunch and transportation.

Fodor's Choice **Anse Chastanet,** near the Pitons on the southwest coast, is the best beach-★ entry dive site. The underwater reef drops from 20 feet to nearly 140 feet in a stunning coral wall.

22

A 165-foot freighter, *Lesleen M,* was deliberately sunk in 60 feet of water near **Anse Cochon** to create an artificial reef; divers can explore the ship in its entirety and view huge gorgonians, black coral trees, gigantic barrel sponges, lace corals, schooling fish, angelfish, sea horses, spotted eels, stingrays, nurse sharks, and sea turtles.

Anse La Raye, midway up the west coast, is one of St. Lucia's finest wall and drift dives and a great place for snorkeling.

At the base of **Petit Piton** a spectacular wall drops to 200 feet. You can view an impressive collection of huge barrel sponges and black coral trees; strong currents ensure good visibility.

At the **Pinnacles,** four coral-encrusted stone piers rise to within 10 feet of the surface.

DIVE OPERATORS

Buddies (✉ *Rodney Bay Marina, Rodney Bay* ☎ *758/452–9086*) offers wall, wreck, reef, and deep dives; resort courses and open-water certification with advanced and specialty courses are taught by PADI-certified instructors.

Dive Fair Helen (✉ *Vigie Marina, Castries* ☎ *758/451–7716, 888/855–2206 in U.S. and Canada* ⊕ *www.divefairhelen.com*) is a PADI center that offers half- and full-day excursions to wreck, wall, and marine reserve areas, as well as night dives.

Scuba St. Lucia (✉ *Anse Chastanet Resort, Anse Chastanet Rd., Soufrière* ☎ *758/459–7755* ⊕ *www.scubastlucia.com*) is a PADI five-star training facility. Daily beach and boat dives and resort and certification courses are offered; underwater photography and snorkeling equipment are available. Day trips from the north of the island include round-trip speedboat transportation.

FISHING

Among the deep-sea creatures you can find in St. Lucia's waters are dolphin (also called dorado or mahimahi), barracuda, mackerel, wahoo, kingfish, sailfish, and white and blue marlin. Sportfishing is generally done on a catch-and-release basis, but the captain may permit you to take a fish back to your hotel to be prepared for your dinner. Neither spearfishing nor collecting live fish in coastal waters is permitted. Half- and full-day deep-sea fishing excursions can be arranged at either Vigie Marina or Rodney Bay Marina. A half day of fishing on a scheduled trip runs about $75–$85 per person or $450 to $550 for a private charter for up to six or eight persons, depending on the size of the boat. Beginners are welcome.

Captain Mike's (✉ *Vigie Marina, Castries* ☎ *758/452–1216 or 758/452–7044* ⊕ *www.captmikes.com*) has a fleet of Bertram powerboats (31 to 38 feet) that accommodate as many as eight passengers; tackle and cold drinks are supplied.

Hackshaw's Boat Charters (✉ *Vigie Marina, Castries* ☎ *758/453–0553 or 758/452–3909* ⊕ *www.hackshaws.com*), in business since 1953, runs charters on boats ranging from the 31-foot *Blue Boy* to the 50-foot, custom-built *Lady Hack*.

Mako Watersports (✉ *Rodney Bay Marina, Rodney Bay* ☎ *758/452–0412*) takes fishing enthusiasts out on the well-equipped six-passenger *Annie Baby*.

GOLF

Although St. Lucia has only one 18-hole championship course at this writing, two more are on the drawing board. One will be in Praslin, on the east coast, as part of a new resort development; the other will be near the existing course in Cap Estate. **Sandals Regency Golf Resort and Spa** has a 9-hole course for its guests. **Jalousie Plantation** has a par-3 executive course.

St. Lucia and Country Golf Club (✉ *Cap Estate* ☎ *758/452–8523* ⊕ *www. stluciagolf.com*), the island's only public course, is at the northern tip and offers panoramic views of both the Atlantic and the Caribbean. It's an 18-hole championship course (6,836 yards, par 71). The clubhouse has a fine-dining restaurant called the Cap Grill that serves breakfast, lunch, and dinner; the Sports Bar is a convivial meeting place any time of day. You can rent clubs and shoes and arrange lessons at the pro shop and perfect your swing at the 350-yard driving range. Depending on the season, greens fees range from $95 for 9 holes to $145 for 18 holes; carts are required and included in the greens fee; club and shoe rentals are available. Reservations are essential. Complimentary transportation from your hotel or cruise ship is provided for parties of three or more people. The St. Lucia Golf Open, a two-day spring tournament, is open to amateurs; it's a handicap event, and prizes are awarded.

GUIDED TOURS

Taxi drivers are well informed and can give you a full tour and often an excellent one, thanks to government-sponsored training programs. From the Castries area, full-day island tours cost $35 to $70 per person for up to four people, depending on the route and whether entrance fees and lunch are included. If you plan your own day, expect to pay the driver $35 per hour plus tip.

Jungle Tours (✉ *Cas en Bas, Gros Islet* ☎ *758/450–0434*) specializes in rain-forest hiking tours for all levels of ability. You're required only to bring hiking shoes or sneakers and have a willingness to get wet and have fun. The cost is $95 per person and include lunch, fees, and transportation via open Land Rover truck.

St. Lucia Helicopters (✉ *Pointe Seraphine, Castries* ☎ *758/453–6950* ⊕ *www.stluciahelicopters.com*) offers a bird's-eye view of the island. A 10-minute North Island tour ($85 per person) leaves from Pointe Seraphine, in Castries, continues up the west coast to Pigeon Island, then flies along the rugged Atlantic coastline before returning inland over Castries. The 20-minute South Island tour ($145 per person) starts at Pointe Seraphine and follows the western coastline, circling beautiful Marigot Bay, Soufrière, and the majestic Pitons before returning inland over the volcanic hot springs and tropical rain forest. A complete island tour combines the two and lasts 30 minutes ($175 per person).

St. Lucia Heritage Tours (*⊠ Pointe Seraphine, Castries* ☎ *758/451–6058* ⊕ *www.heritagetoursstlucia.org*) has put together an "authentic St Lucia experience," specializing in the local culture and traditions. Groups are small, and some of the off-the-beaten-track sites visited are a 19th-century plantation house surrounded by nature trails, a 20-foot waterfall hidden away on private property, and a living museum presenting Creole practices and traditions. Plan on paying $75 per person for a full-day tour.

Sunlink Tours (*⊠ Reduit Beach Ave., Rodney Bay* ☎ *758/452–8232 or 800/786–5465* ⊕ *www.sunlinktours.com*) offers dozens of land, sea, and combination sightseeing tours, as well as shopping tours, plantation, and rain-forest adventures via jeep safari, deep-sea fishing excursions, and day trips to other islands. Prices range from $35 for a half-day shopping tour to $140 for a full-day land-and-sea jeep safari to Soufrière.

HIKING

The island is laced with trails, but you shouldn't attempt the more challenging ones on your own.

Seasoned hikers may aspire to climb the Pitons, the two volcanic cones rising 2,461 feet and 2,619 feet, respectively, from the ocean floor just south of Soufrière. Hiking is recommended only on Gros Piton, which offers a steep but safe trail to the top. The first half of the hike is moderately difficult; reaching the summit is challenging and should be attempted only by those who are physically fit. The view from the top is spectacular. Tourists are permitted to hike Petit Piton, but the second half of the hike requires a good deal of rock climbing, and you'll need to provide your own safety equipment. Hiking the Pitons requires the permission of the St. Lucia Forest & Lands Department and a knowledgeable guide ($25) from the **Pitons Tour Guide Association** (☎ *758/459–9748*).

The **St. Lucia Forest & Lands Department** (☎ *758/450–2231 or 758/450–2078*) manages trails throughout the rain forest and provides guides who explain the plants and trees you'll encounter and keep you on the right track for a small fee.

The **St. Lucia National Trust** (☎ *758/452–5005* ⊕ *www.slunatrust.org*) maintains two trails: one is at Anse La Liberté, near Canaries on the Caribbean coast; the other is on the Atlantic coast, from Mandélé Point to the Frégate Island Nature Reserve. Full-day excursions with lunch cost about $50 to $85 per person and can be arranged through hotels or tour operators.

HORSEBACK RIDING

Creole horses, a breed indigenous to South America and popular on the island, are fairly small, fast, sturdy, and even-tempered animals suitable for beginners. Established stables can accommodate all skill levels and offer countryside trail rides, beach rides with picnic lunches, plantation tours, carriage rides, and lengthy treks. Prices run about $50 for one hour, $65 for two hours, and $80 for a three-hour beach ride and barbecue. Transportation is usually provided between the stables and nearby hotels. Local people sometimes appear on beaches with their steeds and offer 30-minute rides for $10 to $15; ride at your own risk.

International Riding Stables (⊠ *Beauséjour Estate, Gros Islet* ☎ *758/452–8139 or 758/450–8665*) offers English- and Western-style riding. The beach-picnic ride includes time for a swim—with or without your horse. **Trim's National Riding Stable** (⊠ *Cas-en-Bas, Gros Islet* ☎ *758/452–8273* ⊕ *www.trimsnationalridingacademy.com*), the island's oldest riding stable, offers four sessions per day, plus beach tours, trail rides, and carriage tours to Pigeon Island.

SEA EXCURSIONS

Fodor'sChoice
★
A day sail or sea cruise from Rodney Bay or Vigie Cove to Soufrière and the Pitons is a wonderful way to see St. Lucia and a great way to get to the island's distinctive natural sites. Prices for a full-day sailing excursion to Soufrière run about $90 to $110 per person and include a land tour to the Diamond Botanical Gardens, lunch, a stop for swimming and snorkeling, and a visit to pretty Marigot Bay. Two-hour sunset cruises along the northwest coast cost $45 to $60 per person.

Ⓒ The 140-foot tall ship **Brig Unicorn** (⊠ *Vigie Marina, Castries* ☎ *758/452–8644*), used in the filming of the TV miniseries *Roots* and more recently the movie *Pirates of the Caribbean*, is a 140-foot replica of a 19th-century sailing ship. Day trips along the coast are fun for the whole family. Several nights each week a sunset cruise, with drinks and a live steel band, sails to Pigeon Point and back.

Customized sightseeing or whale-watching trips can be arranged for small groups (four to six people) through **Captain Mike's** (⊠ *Vigie Marina, Castries* ☎ *758/452–0216 or 758/452–7044* ⊕ *www.captmikes.com*). On **Endless Summer** (⊠ *Rodney Bay* ☎ *758/450–8651* ⊕ *www.stluciaboattours.com*), a 56-foot "party" catamaran, you can take a day trip to Soufrière or a half-day swimming and snorkeling trip. For romantics, there's a weekly sunset cruise, with dinner and entertainment. **Mystic Man Tours** (⊠ *Bay St., Soufrière* ☎ *758/459–7783* ⊕ *www.mysticmantours.com*) operates whale- and dolphin-watching tours, which are great family excursions.

For a boat trip to Pigeon Island, the **Rodney Bay Ferry** (⊠ *Rodney Bay Marina, Rodney Bay* ☎ *758/452–8816*) departs the ferry slip adjacent to the Lime restaurant twice daily for $50 round-trip, which includes the entrance fee to Pigeon Island and lunch; snorkeling equipment can be rented for $12.

St. Maarten/ St. Martin

WORD OF MOUTH

"[A] don't-miss activity would be an afternoon on Maho Beach watching the planes come in. [It's the o]nly place in the world where planes land and take off so close over your head. There are two bars and chairs to rent on the beach. If you go, I promise that you will always remember it as a high point of your [trip]."

—riverbirch

WELCOME TO ST. MAARTEN/ST. MARTIN

TO ANGUILLA

Bell Pt.

Baie de Grand Case

⑨ ⑩ 24 - 30

Grand Case

Baie de Friar

Aeroport de l'Espérance

Pt. Arago

Baie de la Potence

Colombier

ST. MARTIN

Pte. du Bluff

Pt. du Plum

Baie Rouge

Pte. des Pierres à Chaux

Baie Nettlé

Le Fort Louis

Baie de Marigot

Marigot

Terres Basses

Sandy Ground

Musée de Saint-Martin

18

19 - 22

⑧

17

Simpson Bay Lagoon

Sentry Hill

Baie Longue

13 - 16

Dutch Cul-de-Sac

Cupecoy Beach

Mullet Bay

Juliana International Airport

⑨ ⑩

ST. MAARTEN

⑦

12 11

6 5

Koolbaai

Maho Bay

Simpson Bay

⑧

Annie

④

Great Bay

KEY

- ⅂ Beaches
- ⚓ Cruise Ship Terminal
- ◪ Dive Sites
- ⛴ Ferry
- ❶ Restaurants
- ① Hotels

Cole Bay

Little Bay | Great Bay

3

Caribbean Sea

TWO NATIONS, ONE ISLAND

St. Maarten/St. Martin is home to approximately 77,000 people from some 70 different countries, but governance of the 37-square-mi (96-square-km) island is split between France and the Netherlands. It's the smallest island in the world divided between two ruling powers. The Dutch capital is Philipsburg; the French capital is Marigot.

St. Maarten/St. Martin, a half-Dutch, half-French island, is a place where gastronomy flourishes, where most resorts are large rather than small, where casinos draw gamblers, where sporting opportunities are plentiful, and where the sunning, as on the south end of Orient Beach, is au naturel.

TO ST. BARTHÉLEMY →

Creole Rock

Anse Marcel

Pt. des Froussards

Red Rock

Grandes Cayes

Ile Tintamarre →

11 – 13

French Cul de Sac

Ilet Pinel

31

14

Baie Orientale

32 33

Green Key

15

16

Pic du Paradis

23

17 ◆ Butterfly Farm

Galion Beach

Orléans

Etang aux Poissons

Baie de L. Embouchure

18

Boven Prinsen

19

Babit Pt.

Beneden Prinsen

20

St. Maarten Park

21 Dawn Beach

Mt. Flagstaf

Sucker Garden Rd.

◆ Guana Bay Point

Philipsburg

Geneve Bay

Pelican Key

2

1 – 7 1

Salt Pond

ATLANTIC OCEAN

Pt. Blanche

0 ___ 2 miles
0 ___ 3 km

Proselyte Reef

TO ST. BARTHÉLEMY →

Restaurants ▼

Antoine	1
Bacchus	27
Bamboo Bernies	11
Chesterfield's	7
Claude Mini-Club	20
Enoch's Place	21
Green House	6
Hidden Forest Café	23
Kangaroo Court Café	3
La Belle Epoque	19
La Cigale	17
La Gondola	15
La Vie en Rose	22
L'Astrolabe	32
L'Auberge Gourmande	30
L'Estaminet	24
Le Montmartre	14
Le Pressoir	25
Le Tastevin	29
L'Escargot	2
Mario's Bistro	18
Ocean Lounge	5
Palm Beach	33
Pizza Past Trattoria Italiana	12
Rare	16
Saratoga	9
Sol é Luna	31
Spiga	26
Talk of the Town	28
Taloula Mango's	4
Temptation	13
Top Carrot	8
Zee Best	10

Hotels ▼

Alamanda Resort	15
Bleu Emeraude	10
Captain Oliver's Resort	18
Divi Little Bay Beach Resort	3
Esmeralda	14
Holland House Beach Hotel	1
The Horny Toad	5
Hotel La Plantation	16
Hotel Le Marquis	12
La Samanna	8
La Vista	4
Le Domaine de Lonvilliers Hotel	11
Le Petit Hotel	9
Mary's Boon Beach Plantation	6
Oyster Bay Beach Resort	19
Palm Court	17
Princess Heights	21
Radisson Blu	13
Sonesta Great Bay	2
Sonesta Maho Beach Resort	7
Westin St. Maarten, Dawn Beach Resort & Spa	20

TOP REASONS TO VISIT ST. MAARTEN/ST. MARTIN

1 Great Food: Good food seeps from almost every island pore.

2 Lots of Shops: Philipsburg is one of the best shopping spots in the Caribbean, and Marigot is still chock-full of interesting stores.

3 Beaches Large and Small: Thirty-seven picture-perfect beaches are spread out all over the island.

4 Water Sports Galore: The wide range of water sports will meet almost any need.

5 Nightlife Every Night: There is a wide variety of nightlife: shows, discos, beach bars, and casinos.

ST. MAARTEN/ST. MARTIN PLANNER

Logistics

Getting to St. Maarten/St. Martin:
There are nonstop flights to St. Maarten from the United States, as well as connecting service through San Juan. Further, St. Maarten is a hub for smaller, regional airlines. The island's main airport is Princess Juliana International Airport (SXM), on the Dutch side. Aeroport de L'Espérance (SFG), on the French side, is small and handles only small planes.

Hassle Factor: Low to medium.

On the Ground: Most visitors rent a car upon arrival, but taxi service is available at the airport with fixed fares to all hotels on the island, and you'll be able to pay the fare in U.S. dollars. Although the island is small, it's still a long drive to many hotels on the French side, and the fares will add up.

Getting Around: Most visitors rent a car because rates are fairly cheap and the island is easy to navigate. It's possible to get by with taxis if you are staying in a major hub like Philipsburg or Baie Orientale, but you may spend more money than if you rented a car.

Getting to St. Maarten/St. Martin

Flights: There are nonstop flights from Atlanta (Delta), Charlotte (US Airways), Miami (American), New York–JFK (American, JetBlue), New York–Newark (Continental), Philadelphia (US Airways), Boston (JetBlue). There are also some nonstop charter flights (including GWV/Apple Vacations from Boston). You can also connect in San Juan, primarily on American. Many smaller Caribbean-based airlines, including Air Caraïbes, Caribbean Airlines, Dutch Antilles Express, Insel, LIAT, and Winair (Windward Islands Airways) offer service from other islands in the Caribbean.

Local Airline Contacts: Air Caraïbes (☎ 590/546–7663). **American Airlines** (☎ 599/545–2040). **Caribbean Airlines** (☎ 599/546–7610). **Continental Airlines** (☎ 599/546–7671). **Delta Airlines** (☎ 599/546–7615). **Dutch Antilles Express** (☎ 599/546–7842). **Insel Air** (☎ 599/546–7690). **JetBlue** (☎ 599/546–7664 or 599/546–7663). **LIAT** (☎ 599/546–7677). **St. Barths Commuter** (☎ 599/546–7698). **US Airways** (☎ 599/546–7683). **Winair** (☎ 599/546–7690). **Windward Express Airways** (☎ 599/545–2001).

Airports: Aéroport de L'Espérance (*SFG Route l'Espérance* ✉ *Grand Case* ☎ 590/87–53–03), on the French side, is small and handles only island-hoppers. **Princess Juliana International Airport** (*SXM* ☎ 599/546–7542 ⊕ *www.pjiae.com*) on the Dutch side handles all the large jets.

Ferries: You can take ferries to St. Barth (30–40 minutes, €67–€93 from the Dutch or French side); to Anguilla (20 minutes, $25 from the French side); and Saba (one to two hours, $90–$100 from the Dutch side). For more information, see the respective chapters.

Ferry Companies: *Dawn II* (*Saba* ☎ 599/416–2299 ⊕ *www.sabactransport.com*). ***Edge I and Edge II*** (*St. Barth, Saba, St. Eustatius* ☎ 599/544–2640 or 599/544–2631 ⊕ *www.stmaarten-activities.com*). **Link Ferries** (*Anguilla* ☎ 264/497–2231 or 264/497–3290 ⊕ *www.link.ai*). ***Shauna*** (*Anguilla* ☎ 264/772–2031). ***Voyager II*** (*St. Barth* ☎ 590/87–10–68 ⊕ *www.voy12.com*).

Getting Around St. Maarten/St. Martin

Driving: It's easy to get around the island by car. Most roads are paved and in generally good condition. However, they can be crowded, especially when the cruise ships are in port; you might experience traffic jams, particularly around Marigot and Philipsburg. Be alert for potholes and speed bumps, as well as the island tradition of stopping in the middle of the road to chat with a friend or yield to someone entering traffic. Few roads are identified by name or number, but most have signs indicating the destination. Driving is on the right. There are gas stations in Simpson Bay near the airport.

Car Rentals: You can book a car at Juliana International Airport, where all major rental companies have booths. They provide a shuttle to the rental-car lot. Rates are among the best in the Caribbean, as little as $20 per day. You can rent a car on the French side, but this rarely makes sense for Americans because of the unfavorable exchange rates.

Car Rental Agencies: Avis (☎ 599/545-2847 or 590-0690-634-947 on the French side). **Budget** (☎ 599/545-4030 or 599/55-40-30). **Dollar/Thrifty Car Rental** (☎ 599/545-2393). **Empress Rent-a-Car** (☎ 599/545-2067). **Golfe Car Rental** (☎ 0590/51-94-81 on the French side ⊕ www.golfecarrental.com). **Hertz** (☎ 599/545-4541). **Panoramic** (☎ 599/520-5650 ⊕ www.panoramiccarrental.com). **Unity** (☎ 599/545-2513 ⊕ www.unitycars.com).

Taxis: There is a government-sponsored taxi dispatcher at the airport and at the harbor. Posted fares are for one or two people. Add $5 for each additional person, $1 to $2 per bag, $1 for a box or bundle. It costs about $18 from the airport to Philipsburg or Marigot, and about $30 to Dawn Beach. After 10 pm fares go up 25%, and after midnight 50%. Licensed drivers can be identified by the "taxi" license plate on the Dutch side, and the window sticker on the French. You can hail cabs on the street or call the taxi dispatch to have one sent for you. Fixed fares apply from Juliana International Airport and the Marigot ferry to the various hotels around the island.

Taxi Contacts: Airport Taxi Dispatch (☎ 9247). **Philipsburg dispatch** (☎ 599/543-7815, 599/543-7814, or 590/542-2359).

Scooters

Though traffic can be heavy, speeds are generally slow, so a moped can be a good way to get around. Scooters rent for as low as €25 per day and motorbikes for €37 a day at Eugene Moto, on the French side. The Harley-Davidson dealer, on the Dutch side, rents hogs for $150 a day or $900 per week.

Contacts: Eugene Moto (✉ Sandy Ground Rd., Sandy Ground ☎ 590/87-13-97). **Harley-Davidson** (✉ 71 Union Rd., Cole Bay ☎ 599/544-2704 ⊕ www.h-dstmartin.com).

Island Activities

On the dozens of pristine beaches—some quiet and remote, others bustling—you can choose pounding surf or wading-pool calm; you can **snorkel** right off shore or walk for miles. The island is highly developed and offers a particularly broad range of **activities**.

The island is known for its cuisine, and you'll find some 200 **restaurants**, from simple roadside barbecue stands to upscale gourmet dining rooms.

Shopping is terrific, especially for tax-free jewelry and watches.

And for **nightlife**, there's an array of **clubs, bars,** and a baker's dozen of **casinos**.

ST. MAARTEN/ST. MARTIN PLANNER

Fast Facts

Banks and Exchange Services: Legal tender on the Dutch side is the Netherlands Antilles florin, but almost everyone accepts dollars. On the French side, the currency is the euro, but some establishments still accept dollars. ATMs dispense dollars or euros, depending on where you are.

Electricity: Generally, 110 volts AC (60-cycle) on the Dutch side, just as in the United States. The French side operates on 220 volts AC (60-cycle), with round-prong plugs; there, you'll need an adapter (many hotels can supply these for you).

Emergency Services: Dutch-side emergencies (☎ 911 or 599/542-2222). **French-side emergencies** (☎ 17 or 590/52-25-52).

Language: Dutch is the official language of St. Maarten, and French is the official language of St. Martin, but almost everyone speaks English.

Passport Requirements: A valid passport is required for all visitors.

Weddings: There's a 3-day waiting period on the Dutch side.

Essentials

Mail: Letters from the Dutch side to North America and Europe cost ANG2.85; postcards to all destinations are ANG1.65. From the French side, letters up to 20 grams and postcards are €1 to North America. Postal codes are used only on the French side.

Taxes and Service Charges: Departure tax from Juliana Airport is $10 to destinations within the Netherlands Antilles and $30 to all other destinations. It is usually included in your air ticket. It will cost you €3 (usually included in the ticket price) to depart by plane from Aéroport de L'Espérance and $5 (the rate can change) by ferry to Anguilla from Marigot's pier. Hotels on the Dutch side add a 15% service charge to the bill as well as a 5% government tax. Hotels on the French side add 10%–15% and generally 5% tax.

Telephones: Calling from one side of the island to another is an international call. To phone from the Dutch side to the French, you first must dial 00–590–590 for local numbers, or 00–590–690 for cell phones, then the number. To call from the French side to the Dutch, dial 00–599, then the local number. To call a local number on the French side, dial 0590 plus the six-digit number. On the Dutch side, just dial the seven-digit number with no prefix. Any of the local carriers—and most hotel concierges—can arrange for a prepaid rental phone for your use while you are on the island for $15 to $20 a week plus a per-minute charge.

Tipping: Service charges may be added to hotel and restaurant bills on the Dutch side (otherwise tip 15%–18%). On the French side, a service charge is customary; on top of the included service it is customary to leave an extra 5%–10% *in cash* for the server. Taxi drivers, porters, and maids depend on tips. Give 10% to 15% to cabbies, $1 per bag for porters, and $2 to $5 per night per guest for chambermaids.

Visitor Information: Dutch-side Tourist Information Bureau (✉ *Vineyard Park Bldg., 33 W. G. Buncamper Rd., Philipsburg* ☎ *599/542–2337* ⊕ *www.st-maarten.com*). **French-side Office de Tourisme** (✉ *Rte. de Sandy Ground near Marina de la Port-Royale, Marigot* ☎ *590/87–57–21* ⊕ *www.st-martin.org*).

Where to Stay

The island, though small, is well developed—some say overdeveloped—and offers a wide range of lodging. The larger resorts and time-shares are mostly on the Dutch side; the French side has more intimate properties. Just keep in mind that the popular restaurants around Grand Case, on the French side, are a long drive from most Dutch-side hotels. French-side hotels often charge in euros. Be wary of some of the very lowest-priced alternatives, as some of these can be very run-down time-shares, or properties that function as short-term housing for temporary workers or tourists with very low-end tour companies. Additionally, make note of locations of properties very close to the airport, to avoid unpleasant surprises related to noise. In general, the newer a property the better off you will be.

Resorts and Time-Shares: In general, many of the older properties, especially the time-shares, are suffering from the wear-and-tear of multiple owners, and it is hard to recommend them because of great variances from unit to unit.

Small Inns: Small guesthouses and inns can be found on both sides of the island. It is worth exploring these, especially if you are not the big-resort type.

Villas and Condos: Both sides of the island have a wide variety of villas and condos for every conceivable budget. Some of the resorts offer villa alternatives, which make for a good compromise. In addition, some of the high-end condo developments are offering unsold units as rentals, and some are brand-new and terrific bargains.

HOTEL AND RESTAURANT COSTS

Restaurant prices are for a main course, excluding taxes and service charges. Hotel prices are for two people in a double room in high season, excluding taxes, service charges, and meal plans (except at all-inclusive hotels).

WHAT IT COSTS IN U.S. DOLLARS

	¢	$	$$	$$$	$$$$
Restaurants	under $8	$8–$12	$12–$20	$20–$30	over $30
Hotels	under $150	$151–$275	$276–$375	$376–$475	over $475

When to Go

The high season begins in December and runs through the middle of April. During the off-season, hotel rooms can be had for as little as half the high-season rates.

The French side's **Carnival** is a pre-Lenten bash of costume parades, music competitions, and feasts. Carnival takes place after Easter on the Dutch side—the last two weeks of April—with a parade and music competition.

On the French side, parades, ceremonies, and celebrations commemorate **Bastille Day** on July 14, and there's more revelry later in the month on **Grand Case Day.**

The Dutch side hosts the **Heineken Regatta** in early March, with as many as 300 sailboats competing from around the world. (For the experience of a lifetime, you can sometimes purchase a working berth aboard a regatta vessel.) Other local holidays include November 11 (St. Martin Day), and April 30, the birthday of Queen Juliana.

23

ST. MAARTEN/ST. MARTIN BEACHES

For such a small island, St. Maarten/St. Martin has a wide array of beaches, from the long expanse of Baie Orientale on the French side to powdery-soft Mullet Bay on the Dutch side.

(Above) Beachgoers watching the Heineken Regatta. (Opposite page bottom) The cliffs at Cupecoy Beach. (Opposite page top) Mullet Bay Beach.

Warm surf and a gentle breeze can be found at the island's 37 beaches, and every one of them is open to the public. What could be better? Each is unique: some bustling and some bare, some refined and some rocky, some good for snorkeling and some for sunning. Whatever you fancy in the beach landscape department, it's here, including a clothing-optional one at the south end of Baie Orientale, one of the Caribbean's most beautiful beaches. The key to enjoying beach life on St. Maarten and St. Martin is to try out several beaches; one quickly discovers that several of the island's gems don't have big hotels lining their shores. Petty theft from cars in beach parking lots is an unfortunate fact of life in St. Maarten and St. Martin. Leave nothing in your parked car, not even in the glove compartment or the trunk.

THE SAND

Although the best beaches, including Baie Orientale, Mullet Bay, Anse Marcel, and Ilet Pinel, are lined with soft, white sand, some of the nicer beaches have small rocks, including Happy Bay and Baie des Péres. Atlantic-facing Le Galion has soft sand and gentle surf because it is protected by a reef, but soft sand (in the case of Guana Bay and Cupecoy) can also be accompanied by heavy surf.

DUTCH SIDE

Several of the best Dutch-side beaches are developed and have large-scale resorts. But others, including Simpson Bay and Cupecoy, have little development. You'll sometimes find vendors or beach bars to rent chairs and umbrellas (but not always).

Cupecoy Beach. This picturesque area of sandstone cliffs, white sand, and shoreline caves is a necklace of small beaches that come and go according to the whims of the sea. Even though the western part is more developed, the surf can be rough. It's popular with gay locals and visitors. Break-ins have been reported in cars, so don't leave anything at all in your vehicle. ⊠ *Cupecoy, between Baie Longue and Mullet Bay.*

★ Dawn Beach. True to its name, Dawn Beach is the place to be at sunrise. On the Atlantic side of Oyster Pond, just south of the French border, this is a first-class beach for sunning and snorkeling. It's not usually crowded, and there are several good restaurants nearby. To find it, follow the signs to Mr. Busby's restaurant. ⊠ *South of Oyster Pond, Dawn Beach.*

Great Bay. This is probably the easiest beach to find because it curves around Philipsburg. A bustling, white-sand beach, Great Bay is just behind Front Street. Here you'll find boutiques, eateries, and a pleasant boardwalk. Busy with cruise-ship passengers, the beach is best west of Captain Hodge Pier or around Antoine Restaurant. ⊠ *Philipsburg.*

Little Bay. Despite its popularity with snorkelers and divers as well as kayakers and boating enthusiasts, Little Bay isn't usually crowded. Maybe the gravelly sand is the reason. But, it does boast panoramic views of St. Eustatius, Philipsburg, the cruise-ship terminal, Saba, and St. Kitts. The beach is west of Fort Amsterdam and accessible via the Divi Little Bay Beach Resort. ⊠ *Little Bay Rd., Little Bay.*

Mullet Bay Beach. Many believe that this mile-long, powdery white-sand beach near the medical school is the island's best. Swimmers like it because the water is usually calm. When the swell is up, the surfers hit the beach. ⊠ *South of Cupecoy, Mullet Bay.*

Simpson Bay Beach. This secluded, half moon stretch of white-sand beach on the island's Caribbean side is a hidden gem. It's mostly surrounded by private residences. There are no big resorts, no Jet Skiers, no food concessions, and no crowds. Southeast of the airport, follow the signs to Mary's Boon and the Horny Toad guesthouses. ⊠ *Simpson Bay.*

FRENCH SIDE

Almost all the French-side beaches, whether busy Baie Orientale or less busy Baie des Pères (Friars Bay), have beach clubs and restaurants. For about

Baie Orientale, the island's longest beach.

$25 a couple you get two chaises (*transats*) and an umbrella (*parasol*) for the day, not to mention chair-side service for drinks and food. Only some beaches have bathrooms and showers, so if that is your preference, inquire.

Anse Heureuse (*Happy Bay*). Not many people know about this romantic, hidden gem. Happy Bay has powdery sand, gorgeous luxury villas, and stunning views of Anguilla. The snorkeling is also good. To get here, turn left on the rather rutted dead-end road to Baie des Péres (Friars Bay). The beach itself is a 10- to 15-minute walk from the last beach bar. ⊠ *Happy Bay.*

Baie de Grand Case. Along this skinny stripe of a beach bordering the culinary capital of Grand Case, the old-style gingerbread architecture sometimes peeps out between the bustling restaurants. The sea is calm, and there are tons of fun lunch options from bistros to beachside barbecue stands (called *lolos*). Several of the restaurants rent chairs and umbrellas; some include their use for lunch patrons. ⊠ *Grand Case.*

Baie des Péres (*Friars Bay*). This quiet cove close to Marigot has beach grills and bars, with chaises and umbrellas, calm waters, and a lovely view of Anguilla. Kali's Beach Bar, open daily for lunch and (weather permitting) dinner, has a Rasta vibe and color scheme—it's the best place to be on the full moon, with music, dancing, and a huge bonfire, but you can get lunch, beach chairs, and umbrellas there in any moon phase. To get to the beach, take National Road 7 from Marigot, go toward Grand Case to the Morne Valois hill, and turn left on the dead-end road at the sign. ⊠ *Friar's Bay.*

Baie Longue (*Long Bay*). Though it extends over the French Lowlands, from the cliff at La Samanna to La Pointe des Canniers, the island's longest beach has no facilities or vendors. It's the perfect place for a romantic walk. But car break-ins are a particular problem here. To get here, take National Road 7 south of Marigot. The entrance marked "La Samanna" is the first entrance to the beach. For a splurge, lunch at the resort or sunset drinks are a must. ⊠ *Baie Longue.*

Baie Orientale (*Orient Bay*). Many consider this the island's most beautiful

23

beach, but its 2 mi (3 km) of satiny white sand, underwater marine reserve, variety of water sports, beach clubs, and hotels also make it one of the most crowded. Lots of "naturists" take advantage of the clothing-optional policy, so don't be shocked. Early-morning nude beach walking is de rigueur for the guests at Club Orient, at the southeastern end of the beach. Plan to spend the day at one of the clubs; each bar has different color umbrellas, and all boast terrific restaurants and lively bars. You can have an open-air massage, try any sea toy you fancy, and stay until dark. To get to Baie Orientale from Marigot, take National Road 7 past Grand Case, past the Aéroport de L'Espérance, and watch for the left turn. ⊠ *Baie Orientale.*

Baie Rouge (*Red Bay*). At this home to a couple of beach bars, complete with chaises and umbrellas, you can bask with the millionaires renting the big-ticket villas in the "neighborhood" and take advantage of the gorgeous beach they came for. Baie Rouge and its salt ponds make up a nature preserve, the location of the oldest habitations in the Caribbean. This area is widely thought to have the best snorkeling beaches on the island. You can swim the crystal waters along the point and explore a swim-through cave. The beach is fairly popular with gay men in the mornings and early afternoons. There are two restaurants here; only Chez Raymond is open every day, and cocktail hour starts when the conch shell blows, so keep your ears open. There is a sign and a right turn after you leave Baie Nettlé. ⊠ *Baie Rouge.*

Ilet Pinel. A protected nature reserve, this kid-friendly island is a five-minute ferry ride from French Cul de Sac ($7 per person round-trip). The ferry runs every half hour from midmorning until dusk. The water is clear and shallow, and the

shore is sheltered. If you like snorkeling, don your gear and paddle along both coasts of this pencil-shaped speck in the ocean. You can rent equipment on the island or in the parking lot before you board the ferry for about $10. Plan for lunch any day of the week at the water's edge at a palm-shaded beach hut at **Karibuni** (except in September, when it's closed) for the freshest fish, great salads, tapas, and drinks—try the frozen mojito for a treat. ⊠ *Ilet Pinel.*

Le Galion. A coral reef borders this quiet beach, part of the island's nature preserve, which is paradise if you are traveling with children. The water is calm, clear, and quite shallow, so it's a perfect place for families with young kids. It's a full-service place, with chair rentals, restaurants, and water-sports operators. Kite-boarders and windsurfers like the trade winds at the far end of the beach. On Sunday there are always groups picnicking and partying. To get to Le Galion, follow the signs to the unmissable Butterfly Farm and continue toward the water. ⊠ *Quartier d'Orleans.*

Rouge Bay, St. Maarten

Updated by
Elise Meyer

St. Maarten/St. Martin is virtually unique among Caribbean destinations. The 37-square-mi (96-square-km) island is a seamless place (there are no border gates), but it is governed by two nations—the Netherlands and France—and has residents from 70-some different countries. A call from the Dutch side to the French is an international call, currencies are different, and the vibe is even different. Only the island of Hispaniola, which encompasses two distinct countries, Haiti and the Dominican Republic, is in even a similar position in the Caribbean.

Happily for Americans, who make up the majority of visitors to St. Maarten/St. Martin, English works in both nations. Dutch St. Maarten might feel particularly comfortable for Americans, the prices are lower (not to mention in U.S. dollars), the big hotels have casinos, and there is more nightlife. Huge cruise ships disgorge masses of shoppers into the Philipsburg shopping area at midmorning, when roads can quickly become overly congested. But once you pass the meandering, unmarked border into the French side, you will find a bit of the ambience of the south of France: quiet countryside, fine cuisine, and in Marigot, a walkable harbor area with outdoor cafés, outdoor markets, and plenty of shopping and cultural activities.

Almost 4,000 years ago, it was salt and not tourism that drove the little island's economy. Arawak Indians, the island's first known inhabitants, prospered until the warring Caribs invaded, adding the peaceful Arawaks to their list of conquests. Columbus spotted the isle on November 11, 1493, and named it after St. Martin (whose feast day is November 11), but it wasn't populated by Europeans until the 17th century, when it was claimed by the Dutch, French, and Spanish. The Dutch and French finally joined forces to claim the island in 1644, and the Treaty of Concordia partitioned the territory in 1648. According to

St. Maarten/St. Martin Top Reasons to Go

A two-nation vacation is what you get with St. Maarten/St. Martin. But the island has much more going for it than that.

■ Philipsburg is one of the best shopping spots in the Caribbean; though it has fewer bargains these days with the growing strength of the euro, Marigot (the capital of French St. Martin) is still chock-full of interesting stores.

■ Grand Case is the island's gastronomic capital, but there are good restaurants all over the French side. You'll find plenty of great restaurants in Philipsburg and Simpson Bay as well.

■ Thirty-seven perfect beaches are spread out all over the island (and most of the island's hotels are not on the best beaches, one reason so many people choose to rent a car). Whether you are looking for the busy scene at Baie Orientale or the deserted stretches of sand at Simpson Bay, each is unique.

■ The wide range of water sports—from sailing to waterskiing, snorkeling to deep-sea fishing—will meet almost any need.

23

legend the border was drawn along the line where a French man and a Dutch man, running from opposite coasts, met.

Both sides of the island offer a touch of European culture along with a lot of laid-back Caribbean ambience. Water sports abound—diving, snorkeling, sailing, windsurfing, and in early March, the Heineken Regatta. With soft trade winds cooling the subtropical climate, it's easy to while away the day relaxing on one of the 37 beaches, strolling Philipsburg's boardwalk, and perusing the shops on Philipsburg's Front Street or the *rues* (streets) of the very French town of Marigot. Although luck is an important commodity at St. Maarten's 13 casinos, chance plays no part in finding a good meal at the excellent eateries or after-dark fun in the subtle to sizzling nightlife. Still, the isle's biggest assets are its friendly residents.

Although the island has been heavily developed—especially on the Dutch side—somehow the winding, unmarked roads escaped improvement. When cruise ships are in port (and there can be as many as seven at once), shopping areas are crowded and traffic moves at a snail's pace. We suggest spending the days on the beach or the water, and planning shopping excursions for the early morning or at cocktail hour, after "rush hour" traffic calms down. Still, these are minor inconveniences compared with the feel of the sand between your toes or the breeze through your hair, gourmet food sating your appetite, or having the ability to crisscross between two nations on one island.

EXPLORING ST. MAARTEN/ST. MARTIN

The best way to explore St. Maarten/St. Martin is by car. Though often congested, especially around Philipsburg and Marigot, the roads are fairly good, though narrow and winding, with some speed bumps, potholes, roundabouts, and an occasional wandering goat herd. Few roads are marked with their names, but destination signs are common. Besides, the island is so small that it's hard to get really lost—at least that is what locals tell you.

A scenic "loop" around the island can take most of a day but gives you time to make plenty of stops. If you head up the east shoreline from Philipsburg, follow the signs to Dawn Beach and Oyster Pond. The road winds past soaring hills, turquoise waters, quaint West Indian houses, and wonderful views of St. Barth. As you cross over to the French side, turn into Le Galion for a stop at the beach, the stables, the butterflies, or the windsurf school, then keep following the road around Orient Bay, the St-Tropez of the Caribbean. Continue to Anse Marcel, Grand Case, Marigot, and Sandy Ground. From Marigot, the flat island of Anguilla is visible. Completing the loop brings you past Cupecoy Beach, through Maho and Simpson Bay, where Saba looms in the horizon, and back over the mountain road into Philipsburg.

DUTCH SIDE

Guana Bay Point. On the rugged, windswept east coast about 10 minutes north of Philipsburg, Guana Bay Point is an isolated, untended beach with a spectacular view of St. Barth. Undercurrents make it more a turf than a surf destination, and locals favor the area for hiking.

Philipsburg. The capital of Dutch St. Maarten stretches about a mile (1½ km) along an isthmus between Great Bay and the Salt Pond and has five parallel streets. Most of the village's dozens of shops and restaurants are on Front Street, narrow and cobblestone, closest to Great Bay. It's generally congested when cruise ships are in port, because of its many duty-free shops and several casinos. Little lanes called *steegjes* connect Front Street with Back Street, which has fewer shops and considerably less congestion. Along the beach is a ½-mi-long (1-km-long) boardwalk with restaurants and several Wi-Fi hot spots.

Wathey Square (pronounced watty) is in the heart of the village. Directly across from the square are the town hall and the courthouse, in the striking white building with the cupola. The structure was built in 1793 and has served as the commander's home, a fire station, a jail, and a post office. The streets surrounding the square are lined with hotels, duty-free shops, fine restaurants, and cafés. The **Captain Hodge Pier**, just off the square, is a good spot to view Great Bay and the beach that stretches alongside.

The **Sint Maarten Museum** hosts rotating cultural exhibits and a permanent historical display called Forts of St. Maarten–St. Martin. Artifacts range from Arawak pottery shards to objects salvaged from the wreck of the HMS *Proselyte*. ⊠ *7 Front St., Philipsburg* ☎ *599/542–4917* w*ww.speetjens.com/museum* ⊠ *$1* ☉ *Weekdays 10–4, Sat. 10–2.*

CLOSE UP

Concordia

The smallest island in the world to be shared between two different countries, St. Maarten/St. Martin has existed peacefully in its subdivided state for more than 360 years. The Treaty of Concordia, which subdivided the island, was signed in 1648 and was really inspired by the two resident colonies of French and Dutch settlers (not to mention their respective governments) joining forces to repel a common enemy, the Spanish, in 1644. Although the French were promised the side of the island facing Anguilla and the Dutch the south side of the island, the boundary itself wasn't firmly established until 1817 and then after several disputes (16 of them, to be exact).

Visitors to the island will likely not even notice that they have passed from the Dutch to the French side unless they notice that the roads on the French side feel a little smoother. In 2003, the population of St. Martin (and St. Barthélemy) voted to secede from Guadeloupe, the administrative capital of the French West Indies. That detachment became official in February 2007, and St. Martin is now officially known as the Collectivité de Saint-Martin.

23

☙ **St. Maarten Park.** This delightful little enclave houses animals and plants indigenous to the Caribbean and South America, including many birds that were inherited from a former aviary. There are also a few strays from other parts of the world and a snake house with boa constrictors and other slithery creatures. The zoo's lone male collared peccary now has a female to keep him company. A family of cotton-topped tamarins also have taken residence at the zoo. All the animals live among more than 100 different plant species. The Monkey Bar is the zoo's charming souvenir shop, and sells Caribbean and zoo mementos. This is a perfect place to take the kids when they need a break from the sand and sea. ⊠ *Madame Estate, Arch Rd., Philipsburg* ☎ *599/543–2030* ☞ *$10* ⊙ *Mid-Dec. mid-Apr., daily 9–5; mid-Apr.–mid-Dec., daily 9:30–6.*

FRENCH SIDE

☙
Fodor's Choice
★

Butterfly Farm. If you arrive early in the morning when the butterflies first break out of their chrysalis, you'll be able to marvel at the absolute wonder of dozens of butterflies and moths from around the world and the particular host plants with which each evolved. At any given time, some 40 species of butterflies—numbering as many as 600 individual insects—flutter inside the lush screened garden and hatch on the plants housed there. Butterfly art and knickknacks are for sale in the gift shop. In case you want to come back, your ticket, which includes a guided tour, is good for your entire stay. ⊠ *Le Galion Beach Rd., Quartier d'Orléans* ☎ *590/87–31–21* ⊕ *www.thebutterflyfarm.com* ☞ *$12* ⊙ *Daily 9–3:30.*

French Cul de Sac. North of Orient Bay Beach, the French colonial mansion of St. Martin's mayor is nestled in the hills. Little, red-roof houses look like open umbrellas tumbling down the green hillside. The area is peaceful and good for hiking. From the beach here, shuttle boats make

The view from Fort Louis, high above Marigot.

the five-minute trip to **Ilet Pinel**, an uninhabited island that's fine for picnicking, sunning, and swimming. There are full-service beach clubs there, so just pack the sunscreen and head over.

Grand Case. The Caribbean's own Restaurant Row is the heart of this French side town, a ten-minute drive from either Orient Bay or Marigot, stretching along a narrow beach overlooking Anguilla. You'll find a first-rate restaurant for every palate, mood, and wallet. At lunchtime, or with kids, head to the casual lolos (open-air barbecue stands) and feet-in-the-sand beach bars. Twilight drinks and tapas are fun. At night, stroll the strip and preview the sophisticated offerings on the menus posted outside before you settle in for a long and sumptuous meal. If you still have the energy, there are lounges with music (usually a DJ) that get going after 11 pm.

Fodor's Choice
★

Marigot. It is great fun to spend a few hours exploring the bustling harbor, shopping stalls, open-air cafés, and boutiques of St. Martin's biggest town, especially on Wednesday and Saturday, when the daily open-air craft markets expand to include fresh fruits and veggies, spices, and all manner of seafood. The market might remind you of Provence, especially when aromas of delicious cooking waft by. Be sure to climb up to the fort for the panoramic view, stopping at the museum for an overview of the island. Marina Port La Royale is the shopping–lunch-spot central to the port, but rue de la République and rue de la Liberté, which border the bay, have duty-free shops, boutiques, and bistros. The West Indies Mall offers a deluxe (and air-conditioned) shopping experience, with such shops as Lacoste. There's less bustle here than in Philipsburg, but the open-air cafés are still tempting places to sit and people-watch. Marigot is fun into the night, so you might wish to linger through dinnertime. From the harborfront you can catch ferries for Anguilla and St. Barth. Parking can be a real challenge during the business day, and even at night during the high season.

Though not much remains of the structure itself, **Fort Louis**, which was completed by the French in 1789, is great fun if you want to climb the 92 steps to the top for the wonderful views of the island and neighboring Anguilla. On Wednesday and Saturday there is a market in the square at the bottom. ⊠ *Marigot.*

23

The **Saint Martin Museum** is a model example of how a small museum can make an impact. This historic building (near the Catholic Church) explores the archaeology, anthropology, geology, marine life, and history of St. Martin in attractive displays that offer explanations in both French and English. ⊠ *7 Fichot St., Marigot* ☎ *0690/56–78–92* ⊠ *$5* ☉ *Daily 9–1 and 3–5.*

Orléans. North of Oyster Pond and the Étang aux Poissons (Fish Lake) is the island's oldest settlement, also known as the French Quarter. You can find classic, vibrantly painted West Indian–style homes with the original gingerbread fretwork, and large areas of the nature and marine preserve that is actively working to save the fragile ecosystem of the island.

Fodor's Choice
★
Pic du Paradis. Between Marigot and Grand Case, "Paradise Peak," at 1,492 feet, is the island's highest point. There are two observation areas. From them, the tropical forest unfolds below, and the vistas are breathtaking. The road is quite isolated and steep, best suited to a four-wheel-drive vehicle, so don't head up here unless you are prepared for the climb. There have also been some problems with crime in this area, so it might be best to go with an experienced local guide.

Halfway up the road to Pic du Paradis is **Loterie Farm**, a peaceful 150-acre private nature preserve opened to the public in 1999 by American expat B. J. Welch. There are hiking trails and maps, so you can go on your own (€5) or arrange a guide for a group (€25 for six people). Along the marked trails you will see native forest with tamarind, gum, mango, and mahogany trees, and wildlife including greenback monkeys if you are lucky. Don't miss a treetop lunch or dinner at **Hidden Forest Café** (⇨ *Where to Eat, below*), Loterie Farm's restaurant, where Julie, B. J.'s wife, cooks. If you are brave—and over 4 feet 5 inches tall—try soaring over trees on one of the longest zip lines in the Western Hemisphere. ⊠ *Rte. de Pic du Paradis 103* ☎ *590/87–86–16 or 590/57–28–55* ⊕ *www.loteriefarm.net* ⊠ *€35–€55* ☉ *Tues.–Sun. 9–4.*

WHERE TO EAT

Although most people come to St. Maarten/St. Martin for sun and fun, they leave praising the cuisine. On an island that covers only 37 square mi (96 square km), there are more than 400 restaurants from which to choose. You can sample the best dishes from France, Thailand, Italy, Vietnam, India, Japan, and, of course, the Caribbean.

Many of the best restaurants are in Grand Case (on the French side), but you should not limit your culinary adventures to that village. Great dining

BEST BETS FOR DINING

Fodor's Choice ★
Bacchus, Mario's Bistro, La Cigale, L'Astrolabe, Le Pressoir, Le Tastevin, Talk of the Town, Temptation

MOST ROMANTIC
Antoine, Le Pressoir, Sol é Luna, La Samanna, Le Domaine de Lonvilliers, Temptation

BEST VIEW
Sol é Luna, La Cigale, Taloula Mango's

BEST LOCAL FOOD
Chesterfield's, Claude Mini-Club

BEST FOR FAMILIES
Kangaroo Court, Taloula Mango's

BEST FOR A SPECIAL OCCASION
La Samanna (especially the wine dinner in the cellar)

HIP AND YOUNG
Treelounge/Hidden Forest Café, La Gondola, Palm Beach, Temptation

thrives throughout the island, from the bistros of Marigot to the hopping restaurants of Cupecoy to the low-key eateries of Simpson Bay. Whether you enjoy dining on fine china in one of the upscale restaurants or off a paper plate at the island's many lolos (roadside barbecue stands), St. Maarten/St. Martin's culinary options are sure to appeal to every palate.

ABOUT THE RESTAURANTS

During high season, it's essential to make reservations, and making them a month in advance is advisable for some of the best places. Dutch-side restaurants sometimes include a 15% service charge, so check your bill before tipping. On the French side, service is always included, but it is customary to leave 5% to 10% extra in cash for the server. Keep in mind that you can't always leave tips on your credit card (and it's customary to tip in cash, anyway), so carry enough cash. A taxi is probably the easiest solution to the parking problems in Grand Case, Marigot, and Philipsburg. Grand Case has two lots—each costs $4—at each end of the main boulevard, but they're often packed.

WHAT TO WEAR

Although appropriate dining attire ranges from swimsuits to sport jackets, casual dress is usually appropriate throughout restaurants on the island. For men, a jacket and khakis or jeans will take you anywhere; for women, dressy pants, a skirt, or even fancy shorts are usually acceptable. Jeans are fine in the less formal eateries. In the listings below, dress is casual (albeit chic) unless otherwise noted, but ask when making reservations if you're unsure.

DUTCH SIDE

CUPECOY

$$$
ITALIAN
✕ **La Gondola.** Owner Davide Foini started out by selling just his home-made pasta, which proved to be so popular that he opened this authentic trattoria that has found its way onto many "best bets" lists of island regulars. The kitchen still rolls out the dough for the dozens of pasta dishes on the encyclopedic Italian menu, which also includes favorites

like veal parmigiana, chicken piccata in marsala sauce, and osso buco Milanese. Save room for desserts like the *fantasia di dessert del Carnevale di Venezia* (a warm chocolate tart and frozen nougat served with raspberry sauce) or tiramisu. The service is professional and high-tech—the waiters take orders with earpieces and handheld computers. ⊠ *Atlantis World Casino, Rhine Rd. 106, Cupecoy* ☎ *599/544–3938* ⊕ *www.lagondola-sxm.com* ☾ *No lunch.*

$$$
FRENCH
✕ **Le Montmartre.** Newly refurbished, Montmarte has a new look and a whole new menu, Cane-back chairs, white tablecloths, and mir-rored white walls have a cozy look about them. French specialties like traditional onion soup, sautéed sole, and truffled eggs are joined by Caribbean-tinged specials. The lounge stays open well past 11, when the kitchen closes. ⊠ *Atlantis World Casino, Rhine Rd. 106, Cupecoy* ☎ *599/545–3939* ☾ *No lunch.*

$$$$
STEAK
✕ **Rare.** Within an intimate, clubby setting, a guitarist provides background music while carnivores delight in chef Dino Jagtiani's creative menu. The focus is steak: certified Angus prime cuts topped with chimichurri, béarnaise, horseradish, peppercorn, or mushroom sauce. Not into red meat? You can also choose from seafood, pork, lamb, or veal. Sample some delicious sides like truffled mashed potatoes or cultivated mushroom sauté (a tasty fungi variety). Luscious desserts will make you forget that you will want to look good in your bathing suit tomorrow morning. ⊠ *Atlantis World Casino, Rhine Rd. 106, Cupecoy* ☎ *599/545–5714* ☾ *Closed Sept. and Mon. June–Oct. No lunch.*

$$$$
ECLECTIC
Fodor's Choice
★
✕ **Temptation.** Supercreative chef Dino Jagtiani, who trained at the Culinary Institute of America, is the mastermind behind dishes like seared foie gras PB and J (melted foie gras accented with peanut butter and homemade port-wine fig jam) and herb-crusted Chilean sea bass. The chef, who compares dessert to lovemaking ("both intimate, and not to be indulged in lightly"), offers a crème brûlée tasting, as well as Granny Smith apple tempura with cinnamon ice cream and caramel sauce for the sweet tooth. The wine list is extensive, and features a number of reasonably priced selections. There are also many inventive cocktails, such as the St. Maartini—a refreshing blend of coconut rum, guava puree, passion-fruit juice, and peach schnapps. The dining room is pretty and intimate, in spite of its location behind the casino. There's outdoor seating as well. ⊠ *Atlantis Casino Courtyard, Rhine Rd. 106, Cupecoy* ☎ *599/545–5741* ⊕ *www.chefdino.com/* ☾ *Closed Sun. June–Oct. No lunch.*

MAHO

$$
ECLECTIC
✕ **Bamboo Bernies.** This dramatic and hip addition to the top level of the Maho central shopping area features red lacquer walls, lounging tables, Indonesian art, a first-rate bar, and electro-house tunes. You can get terrific sushi and sashimi, both the classic Japanese varieties and the Americanized ones (California roll, for example). All are good, as are the Asian hot appetizers and exotic cocktails like the Tranquillity (citrus vodka and smoky oolong tea). If you're not into Asian fare, try the salmon, ribs, or beef. The young crowd keeps this place hopping way past midnight. ⊠ *Sonesta Maho Beach Resort & Casino, Rhine Rd., Maho* ☎ *599/545–3622* ⊕ *www.bamboobernies.net* ☾ *No lunch weekdays.*

23

$$$ ✗ **Pizza Pasta Trattoria Italiana.** Tucked away on a quiet street near Casino
ITALIAN Royale, this Italian eatery is extremely popular with locals. The menu
includes favorites like penne Bolognese and eggplant Parmesan, but
the real winners are the thin-crust pizzas. The freshly brewed iced tea
is great on a hot day. With its laid-back atmosphere and friendly staff,
this is a cozy spot for families with small children or a place where
you just run in and grab a quick bite. ⊠ *Maho Shopping Plaza, Maho*
☎ *599/545–4034* ▭ *No credit cards* ☉ *No lunch Sun.*

PHILIPSBURG

$$$ ✗ **Antoine.** You'd be hard-pressed to find a more enjoyable evening in
FRENCH Philipsburg. Owner Jean Pierre Pomarico's warmth shines through as he
★ greets guests and ushers them into the comfy seaside restaurant. Low-key,
blue-accented decor, white bamboo chairs, watercolors lining the walls,
and candles—along with the sound of the nearby surf—create a relaxing
atmosphere. The lobster thermidor (a succulent tail oozing with cream
and Swiss cheese) is a favorite, but other specialties include lobster bisque,
seafood linguine, and a beef fillet with béarnaise sauce. At $35, the prix-
fixe menu is a great deal. ⊠ *119 Front St., Philipsburg* ☎ *599/542–2964*
⊕ *www.antoinerestaurant.com* ⌕ *Reservations essential.*

$$ ✗ **Chesterfield's.** On the Great Bay waterfront, this is an excellent place
CARIBBEAN for a cocktail, a beer, or a relaxed meal on the open-air deck. Both the
locals and tourists seem to love it. Seafood is the main focus, but steaks,
burgers, and pasta and poultry are not wanting. ⊠ *Great Bay Marina,*
Philipsburg ☎ *599/542–3484* ⊕ *www.chesterfields-restaurant.com.*

$$ ✗ **The Green House.** The famous happy hour is just one of the reasons
ECLECTIC people flock to the Green House. This waterfront restaurant balances
a relaxed atmosphere, reasonable prices, and quality food with a just-
right, flavorful bite. All the beef served is Black Angus, and some people
say the burgers and steaks are the best on the island. If you're seeking something spicy, try the creole shrimp. The daily specials, like the
Friday-night Lobster Mania, are widely popular. ⊠ *Bobby's Marina,*
Philipsburg ☎ *599/542–2941* ⊕ *www.thegreenhouserestaurant.com.*

$$ ✗ **Kangaroo Court Café.** Grab a table on the lovely back patio of this little
CAFÉ café. Almond trees shade it so well that nets are installed to keep nuts
and leaves from hitting diners. Although it's best known for coffees, ⊕
the café also serves great sandwiches, salads, and pizzas. Wash it all
down with a fruit frappé or a selection from one of the island's larg-
est selections of wines by the glass. Incidentally, the odd name comes
from the location, next to the courthouse in Philipsburg. ⊠ *6 Front St.,*
Philipsburg ☎ *599/542–7557* ☉ *Closed Sun. No dinner.*

$$$ ✗ **L'Escargot.** The wraparound verandah, the bunches of grapes hanging
FRENCH from the chandeliers, and the Toulouse-Lautrec–style murals add to the
colorful atmosphere of this restaurant in a 150-year-old, gingerbread,
Creole house. As the name suggests, snails are a specialty, and are
offered several ways. But the menu also includes many other French
standards like onion soup, crispy duck, and veal cordon bleu. There's a
Friday night cabaret show, complete with cancan in the tradition of *La
Cage aux Folles.* ⊠ *96 Front St., Philipsburg* ☎ *599/542–2483* ⊕ *www.*
lescargotrestaurant.com ☉ *Closed Sun. June–Oct. No lunch weekends.*

$$$ ✗**Ocean Lounge.** An airy modern verandah perched on the Philipsburg
ECLECTIC boardwalk gives Ocean Lounge its distinct South Beach vibe. You'll
want to linger over fresh fish and steaks, as you watch the scene with
tourists of all varieties passing by two-by-two on romantic evening
strolls, or determined cruise-ship passengers surveying the surround-
ing shops by day. The daily tasting menu at $39 ($47 with two glasses
of good wine) offers a chance to sample the cuisine. ⊠ *Holland House
Beach Hotel, 43 Front St., Philipsburg* ☎ *599/542–2572.*

$$ ✗**Taloula Mango's.** Ribs are the specialty at this casual beachfront res-
ECLECTIC taurant, but the jerk chicken and thin-crust pizza, not to mention a
few vegetarian options like the tasty falafel, are not to be ignored. On
weekdays lunch is accompanied by live music; every Friday during
happy hour a DJ spins tunes. In case you're wondering, the restaurant
got its name from the owner's golden retriever. ⊠ *Sint Rose Shopping
Mall, off Front St. on beach boardwalk, Philipsburg* ☎ *599/542–1645*
⊕ *www.taloulamango.com.*

SIMPSON BAY

$$$ ✗**Saratoga.** At Simpson Bay Yacht Club you can choose to be inside or
ECLECTIC on the waterside terrace. The menu changes daily, but you can never
★ go wrong with one of chef John Jackson's fish specialties, including red
snapper with white wine reduction or yellowfin tuna "filet mignon"
with miso-roasted veggies. You might start with oysters flown in from
France, or sesame seaweed salad. The wine list includes 150 different
bottles, including many by the glass. ⊠ *Simpson Bay Yacht Club, Air-
port Blvd., Simpson Bay* ☎ *599/544–2421* ⊕ *www.sxmsaratoga.com*
☖ *Reservations essential* ☉ *Closed Sun., Aug., and Sept. No lunch.*

$ ✗**Top Carrot.** Open from 7 am to 6 pm, this café and juice bar is a popu-
VEGETARIAN lar breakfast and lunch stop. It features vegetarian entrées, sandwiches,
salads, homemade pastries, and, more recently, fresh fish. Favorites
include a pastry stuffed with pesto, avocado, red pepper, and feta
cheese, or a cauliflower, spinach, and tomato quiche. The house-made
granola and yogurt are local favorites, but folks also drop in just for
espresso and the large selection of teas. Adjacent to the restaurant is
a gift shop with Asian-inspired items and spiritual books. ⊠ *Airport
Rd., near Simpson Bay Yacht Club, Simpson Bay* ☎ *599/544–3381*
☉ *Closed Sun. No dinner.*

$ ✗**Zee Best.** This friendly bistro serves one of the best breakfasts on the
CAFÉ island. There's a huge selection of fresh-baked pastries—try the almond
croissants—plus sweet and savory crepes, omelets, quiches, and freshly
baked croissants and other treats from the oven. Specialties include the
St. Martin omelet, filled with ham, cheese, mushrooms, onions, green
peppers, and tomatoes. Best of all, breakfast is served until 2 pm—
perfect for late risers. Lunch includes sandwiches, salads, and the chef's
famous spaghetti Bolognese. Grab a table in the dining room or on
the terrace; it's a good place to relax with a newspaper and a cup of
cappuccino. Zee Best turns into Piccolo restaurant for dinner. There is
another location at Port de Plaisance. ⊠ *Plaza del Lago, Simpson Bay*
☎ *599/544–2477* ▭ *No credit cards* ☉ *No dinner Sun.*

23

FRENCH SIDE

BAIE NETTLÉ

$$$-$$$$
FRENCH
Fodor'sChoice
★

✕ **La Cigale.** On the edge of Baie Nettlé, La Cigale has wonderful views of the lagoon from its dining room and its open-air patio, but the charm of the restaurant comes from the devoted attention of adorable owner Olivier, helped by his mother and brother, and various cousins, too. Stephane Istel's delicious food is edible sculpture: ravioli of lobster with wild mushrooms and foie gras is poached in an intense lobster bisque, and house-smoked swordfish and salmon is garnished with goat cheese and seaweed salad drizzled with dill-lime vinaigrette. ✉ *101 Laguna Beach, Baie Nettlé* ☎ *599/87–90–23* ⊕ *www.restaurant-lacigale.com* ☾ *Closed Sun. in Sept. and Oct. No lunch.*

BAIE ORIENTALE

$$$
FRENCH
Fodor'sChoice
★

✕ **L'Astrolabe.** Chef Stephan Decluseau gets raves for his modern interpretations of classic French cuisine served around the pool at this cozy, relaxed restaurant in the Esmeralda Resort. Corn soup; foie gras terrine with apricot and quince jam; an amazing roast duck with pineapple-ginger sauce; and deliciously fresh fish dishes are just some of the offerings. There are lots of choices for vegetarians, a three-course prix fixe for €44, a €15 children's menu, and a lobster party with live music every Friday night. ✉ *Esmeralda Resort, Box 5141, Baie Orientale* ☎ *0590/87–11–20* ⊕ *www.esmeralda-resort.com* ☾ *No lunch. No dinner Wed.*

$$$
AMERICAN

✕ **Palm Beach.** The newest addition to the Baie Orientale beach clubs is as stylish as its Florida namesake. Balinese art and furniture, big comfy chaises on the beach, and an active bar set the stage. Pretty girls are the decor. There are three big tree-house-like lounges for lunch or if you are looking for a place to spend the afternoon. The menu of salads, grills, and brochettes is served in a pavilion shaded by sail-like awnings. Take the exit to BooBoo Jam after the gas station. ✉ *Baie Orientale* ☎ *690/35–99–06* ⊕ *www.palmbeachsxm.net* ☾ *No dinner.*

FRENCH CUL DE SAC

$$$
CARIBBEAN

✕ **Sol é Luna.** Charming and romantic, this restaurant puts its best tables on the balcony, from which you can best appreciate the great views. Begin your meal with an appetizer like the roasted vegetables with goat cheese, lobster ravioli, or tuna carpaccio, then move on to the lamb shank with date-ginger puree or the filet mignon with mashed potatoes. Don't be surprised if you see a proposal or two during your meal, as this is one of the most romantic restaurants on the island. ✉ *61 Rte. de Mont Vernon, French Cul de Sac* ☎ *590/29–08–56* ⊕ *www.solelunarestaurant.com* ☾ *Closed mid-June–early July and Sept.–early Oct.*

GRAND CASE

$$
FRENCH
Fodor'sChoice
★

✕ **Bacchus.** If you want to lunch with the savviest locals, you have to scrape yourself from the beach and head into the industrial park outside Grand Case, where Benjamin Laurent, the best wine importer in the Caribbean, has built this lively, deliciously air-conditioned, reconstruction of a wine cellar. He serves up first-rate starters, salads, and main courses made from top ingredients brought in from France, lovingly prepared by top chefs. Shop here for gourmet groceries for your villa, or hang in the new cigar–rum lounge. The wines are sublime, and you will get an amazing education along with a great lunch. You won't mind eating indoors here—just think of it as the perfect sunblock. Enter at the "Hope Estate" sign in the roundabout across from the road that leads to the Grand Case Airport.

✉ *Hope Estate 18–19, Grand Case Rd., Grand Case* ☎ *0590/87–15–70* ⊕ *www.bacchussxm.com* ◔ *No dinner. Closed Sun.*

$$$ ✕ **L'Auberge Gourmande.** A fixture of Boulevard Grand Case, L'Auberge
FRENCH Gourmande is in one of the oldest Creole houses in St. Maarten/St. Martin. The formal dining room is framed by elegant arches. The light Provençal cuisine is a delight, with menu choices like roasted rack of lamb with an herb crust over olive mashed potatoes, Dover sole in lemon butter, and pork tenderloin stuffed with apricots and walnuts. There are vegetarian options, a kids' menu for €13, and a good selection of wines. ✉ *89 bd. de Grand Case, Grand Case* ☎ *590/87–73–37* ⊕ *www.laubergegourmande.com* ◔ *Closed Sept. No lunch.*

$$$ ✕ **L'Estaminet.** The name of this restaurant is an old-fashioned word for
FRENCH "tavern" in French, but the food is anything but archaic. The creative, upscale cuisine served in this modern, clean space is fun and surprising, utilizing plenty of molecular gastronomy. This means that intense liquid garnishes might be inserted into your goat cheese appetizer or perhaps given to you in a tiny toothpaste tube, or even a plastic syringe. The bright flavors, artistic plating, and novelty make for a lively meal that will be remembered fondly. Under no circumstances should you pass up the chocolate tasting for dessert. ✉ *139 bd. de Grand Case, Grand Case* ☎ *590/29–00–25* ⊕ *www.lestaminetsxm.blogspot.com* ◔ *Closed Mon. in June–Nov.*

$$$–$$$$ ✕ **Le Pressoir.** In a carefully restored West Indian house painted in
FRENCH brilliant reds and blues, Le Pressoir has charm to spare. The name
Fodor's Choice comes from the historic salt press that sits opposite the restaurant,
★ but the thrill comes from the culinary creations of chef Franc Mear and the hospitality of his beautiful wife Melanie. If you are indecisive, or just plain smart, try any (or all) of the degustations (tastings) of four soups, four foie gras preparations, or four fruit desserts, each showcasing sophisticated preparations with adorable presentations. Foie gras is served in a dollhouse-size terrine, with a teensy glass of Sauternes. ✉ *30 bd. de Grand Case, Grand Case* ☎ *590/87–76–62* ⊕ *www.lepressoir-sxm.com* ◔ *Closed mid-Sept.–mid-Oct. and Sun. in May–Dec. No lunch.*

$$$
FRENCH
Fodor's Choice
★

✕ **Le Tastevin.** In the heart of Grand Case, Le Tastevin is on everyone's list of favorites. The attractive wood-beamed room is the "real" St. Martin style, and the tasty food is enhanced by Joseph, the amiable owner, who serves up lunch and dinner every day on a breezy porch over a glittering blue sea. The menu changes frequently, and includes fusion treatments of local ingredients such as mahimahi in a pineapple-tomato sauce, and rack of lamb with glazed garlic and rosemary. There are two tasting menus, one at €45 that includes a half bottle of wine, and another at €75 that offers special wine pairings. ✉ 86 bd. de Grand Case, Grand Case ☎ 590/87–55–45 ⊕ www.letastevin-restaurant.com ⚱ Reservations essential ♥ Closed mid-Aug.–Sept.

$$$
ITALIAN

✕ **Spiga.** In a beautifully restored Creole house, Spiga's tasty cuisine fuses Italian and Caribbean ingredients and cooking techniques Look for dishes like lamb with tagliatelle, or crab cakes on peas. Save room for the lemon-ricotta cake and try the selection of grappas. ✉ 4 Rte. de L'Esperance, Grand Case ☎ 590/52–47–83 ⊕ www.spiga-sxm. com ♥ Closed mid-Sept.–late Oct. and Tues. in June–mid-Sept. No lunch Sun.

$
CARIBBEAN
Fodor's Choice
★

✕ **Talk of the Town.** Although St. Martin is known for its upscale dining, each town has its roadside barbecue stands, called lolos, including the island's culinary capital of Grand Case. They are open from lunchtime until evening, but earlier in the day you'll find fresher offerings. Locals flock to the square of a half-dozen stands in the middle of Grand Case, on the water side. Not to say that these stands offer haute or fine cuisine, but they are fun, relatively cheap, and offer an iconic St. Martin meal. Talk of the Town is one of the most popular. With plastic utensils and paper plates, it couldn't be more informal. The menu includes everything from succulent grilled ribs to stewed conch, fresh snapper, and grilled lobster at the most reasonable price on the island. Don't miss the johnnycakes and side dishes like plantains, curried rice, beans, and coleslaw that come with your choice. The service is friendly, if a bit slow, but sit back with a beer and enjoy the experience. On weekends there is often live music. **Sky's the Limit** is another iconic lolo, just two picnic tables over. At this writing the lolos are still offering a one-to-one exchange between euros and dollars. ✉ Bd. de Grand Case, Grand Case ☎ No phone ⊟ No credit cards.

MARIGOT

$$$
CARIBBEAN

✕ **Claude Mini-Club.** An island institution, Claude Mini-Club has delighted patrons with its blend of creole and French food since 1969. The whole place is built tree-house style around the trunks of coconut palms, and the lofty perch means you have great views of Marigot Harbor. The chairs and tablecloths are a mélange of sunny yellows and oranges. The €40 dinner buffet on Wednesday and Saturday nights is legendary. It includes more than 30 dishes, often including conch soup, roast leg of lamb, Black Angus roast beef, and roast pig. Fresh snapper is one of the excellent specialties on the à la carte menu. There's live music nightly. ✉ 49 bd. de France, Marigot ☎ 590/87–50–69 ♥ Closed Sun.

$
CARIBBEAN

✕ **Enoch's Place.** The blue-and-white-striped awning on a corner of the Marigot Market makes this place hard to miss. But Enoch's cooking is what draws the crowds. Specialties include garlic shrimp, fresh lobster, and rice and beans (like your St. Martin mother used to make). Try the saltfish and fried johnnycake—a great breakfast option. The food more than makes up for the lack of decor, and chances are you'll be counting the days until you can return. ⊠ *Marigot Market, Front de Mer, Marigot* ☎ *590/29–29–88* ▭ *No credit cards* ☉ *Closed Sun. No dinner.*

$$ ✕ **Lu Belle Epoque.** A favorite among locals, this brasserie is a good choice
ECLECTIC at the Marigot marina. Whether you stop for a drink or a meal, you'll soon discover that it's a great spot for boat- and people-watching. The menu has a bit of everything: big salads, pizza, and seafood are always good bets. There's also a good wine list. And it's open nonstop seven days a week for breakfast through late dinner. ⊠ *Marina de la Port Royale, Marigot* ☎ *590/87–87–70.*

$$$ ✕ **La Vie en Rose.** This restaurant on the quiet side of Marigot's harbor-
FRENCH front is all about romance. It's like Paris with palm trees. Start with the goat cheese salad or the famous lobster bisque, then enjoy a main course of fresh fish or a more traditional French entrée like roast veal and rack of lamb. Desserts are delightful, especially the trio of crème brûlées. The service is polite and professional. ⊠ *Front de Mer, Marigot* ☎ *590/87–54–42.*

PIC DU PARADIS

$$$ ✕ **Hidden Forest Café.** Schedule your trip to Loterie Farm to take advan-
ECLECTIC tage of the lovely tree-house pavilions where lunch or dinner has a safari vibe and where the yummy food is inventive and fresh, with touches of Asia. Curried-spinach chicken with banana fritters is a popular pick, but there are great choices for vegetarians, too, including cumin lentil balls; those with stouter appetites dig into the massive Black Angus tenderloin. Loterie Farm's other eatery, Treelounge, is open for lunch and dinner Monday–Saturday, and stays open late with a band on Saturday nights. ⊠ *Route du Pic Paradis, Pic Paradis* ☎ *590/87–86–16* ⊕ *www. loteriefarm.net* ☉ *Closed Mon.*

SANDY GROUND

$$$ ✕ **Mario's Bistro.** Don't miss dinner at this romantic eatery, a perennial
ECLECTIC favorite for its ravishing cuisine, romantic ambience, and most of all
Fodor's Choice the marvelously friendly owners. Didier Gonnon and Martyne Tardif
★ are out front, while chef Mario Tardif is in the kitchen creating dishes such as sautéed sea scallops with crab mashed potatoes and truffle oil, baked mahimahi with a macadamia-nut crust, orange-endive confit, and fennel salsa, and rack of lamb with caramelized onions and goat cheese. ⊠ *Sandy Ground Bridge, Marigot, Saint-Martin FWI* ☎ *590/87–06–36* ⊕ *www.mariosbistro.com* ⚠ *Reservations essential* ☉ *Closed Sun., Aug., and Sept. No lunch.*

23

St. Maarten vs. St. Martin

If this is your first trip to St. Maarten/St. Martin, you're probably wondering which side will better suit your needs. That's hard to say, because in some ways the difference between the two can seem as subtle as the hazy boundary line dividing them. But there are some major differences.

St. Maarten, the Dutch side, has the casinos, more nightlife, and bigger hotels. St. Martin, the French side, has no casinos, less nightlife, and hotels that are smaller and more intimate.

Many have kitchenettes, and most include breakfast. There are many good restaurants on the Dutch side, but if fine dining makes your holiday, the French side rules.

The biggest difference might be currency—the Netherlands Antilles guilder on the Dutch side, the euro on the French side. And the relative strength of the euro can translate to some expensive surprises. Many establishments on both sides (even the French) accept U.S. dollars.

WHERE TO STAY

St. Maarten/St. Martin accommodations range from modern mega-resorts like the Radisson and the Westin St. Maarten to condos and small inns. On the Dutch side many hotels cater to groups, and although that's also true to some extent on the French side, you can find a larger collection of intimate accommodations there. ■ TIP→ Off-season rates (April through the beginning of December) can be as little as half the high-season rates.

TIME-SHARE RENTALS

Time-share properties are scattered around the island, mostly on the Dutch side. There's no reason to buy a share, as these condos are rented out whenever the owners are not in residence. If you stay in one, be prepared for a sales pitch. Most rent by the night, but there's often substantial savings if you secure a weekly rate. Not all offer daily maid service, so make sure to ask before you book.

PRIVATE VILLAS

Villas are a great lodging option, especially for families who don't need to keep the kids occupied, or groups of friends who just like hanging out together. Since these are for the most part freestanding houses, their greatest advantage is privacy. These properties are scattered throughout the island, often in gated communities or on secluded roads. Some have bare-bones furnishings, whereas others are over-the-top luxurious, with gyms, theaters, game rooms, and several different pools. There are private chefs, gardeners, maids, and other staffers to care for both the villa and its occupants.

Villas are secured through rental companies. They offer properties with weekly prices that range from reasonable to more than many people make in a year. Check around, as prices for the same property vary from agent to agent. Because of the economy, many villas are now offered by the night rather than by the week, so it's often possible to

BEST BETS FOR LODGING

Fodor's Choice★

Holland House Beach Hotel, the Horny Toad, La Samanna, Palm Court, Westin St. Maarten Dawn Beach Resort & Spa

BEST FOR ROMANCE

La Samanna, Le Domaine de Lonvilliers, Palm Court, Princess Heights

BEST BEACHFRONT

The Horny Toad, La Samanna, Le Domaine de Lonvilliers

BEST POOL

Radisson Blu St. Martin, Westin St. Maarten Dawn Beach Resort & Spa

BEST SERVICE

La Samanna, Le Domaine de Lonvilliers

BEST FOR KIDS

Alamanda Resort, Divi Little Bay Beach Resort, Radisson St. Martin, Sonesta Great Bay Beach Resort and Casino

23

book for less than a full week's stay. Rental companies usually provide airport transfers and concierge service, and for an extra fee will even stock your refrigerator.

VILLA RENTAL AGENTS

French Caribbean International (⌂ *5662 Calle Real, Suite 333, Santa Barbara, CA* ☎ *805/967–9850 or 800/322–2223* ⊕ *www.frenchcaribbean. com*) offers rental properties on the French side of the island. **Island Hideaways** (⌂ *3843 Highland Oaks Dr., Fairfax, VA 22033* ☎ *800/832– 2302 or 703/378–7840* ⊕ *www.islandhideaways.com*), the island's oldest rental company, rents villas on both sides. **Island Properties** (⌂ *62 Welfare Rd., Simpson Bay, St. Maarten* ☎ *599/544–4580 or 866/978– 5852* ⊕ *www.islandpropertiesonline.com*) has properties scattered around the island. **Jennifer's Vacation Villas** (⌂ *Plaza Del Lago, Simpson Bay Yacht Club, St. Maarten* ☎ *631/546–7345 or 011–599/544– 3107* ⊕ *www.jennifersvacationvillas.com*) rents villas on both sides of the island. **Pierrescaraïbes** (⌂ *Plaza Caraibes, Bldg. A rue Kennedy, Marigot97150* ☎ *866/978–5795 or 590/51–02–85* ⊕ *www. pierrescaraibes.com*), owned by American Leslie Reed, has been renting and selling upscale St. Martin villas to satisfied clients for more than a decade. The company's well-designed Web site makes it easy to get a sense of the first-rate properties available in all sizes and prices. The company is associated with Christies Great Estates. **Romac Southeby's International Realty** (⌂ *54 Simpson Bay Rd., St. Maarten* ☎ *599/544– 2924 or 877/537–9282* ⊕ *www.romacsothebysrealty.com*) rents luxury villas, many in gated communities. **Villas of Distinction** (⌂ *951 Transport Way, Petaluma, CA94954* ☎ *800/289–0900* ⊕ *www.villasofdistinction. com*) is one of the oldest villa-rental companies on the French side of the island. **WIMCO** (⌂ *Box 1461, Newport, RI 02840* ☎ *401/849–8012 or 866/449–1553* ⊕ *www.wimco.com*) has more hotel, villa, apartment, and condo listings in the Caribbean than just about anyone else.

The following reviews have been condensed for this book. Please go to Fodors.com for expanded reviews of each property.

La Samanna.

DUTCH SIDE

BAIE ORIENTALE

$$$–$$$$
RESORT
☺
▦ **Alamanda Resort.** One of the few resorts directly on the white-sand beach of Orient Bay, this hotel has a funky feel and spacious, colonial-style suites with terraces that overlook the pool, beach, or ocean. **Pros:** pleasant property; friendly staff; right on Orient Beach. **Cons:** some rooms are noisy; could use some updating. ⊠ *Baie Orientale ⌂ BP 5166, Grand Case 97071* ☎ *590/52–87–40 or 800/622–7836* ⊕ *www.alamanda-resort. com* ⇨ *42 rooms* △ *In-room: a/c, safe, kitchen. In-hotel: restaurants, tennis courts, pool, gym, business center, water sports* ⏃*Breakfast.*

$$$–$$$$
RESORT
☺
▦ **Esmeralda Resort.** Almost all of these traditional Caribbean-style, kitchen-equipped villas, which can be configured to meet the needs of different groups, have their own private pool, and the fun of Orient Beach, where the hotel has its own private beach club, is a two-minute walk away. **Pros:** beachfront location; private pools; plenty of activities; frequent online promotions. **Cons:** rooms are very dark, some really need updating; water-pressure complaints; need a car to get around. ⌂ *Box 5141, Baie Orientale 97071* ☎ *590/87–36–36 or 800/622–7836* ⊕ *www.esmeralda-resort.com* ⇨ *65 rooms* △ *In-room: a/c, safe, kitchen (some). In-hotel: restaurants, tennis courts, pools, beach, business center, water sports* ⊙ *Closed Sept. and Oct.* ⏃*No meals.*

$$$–$$$$
HOTEL
▦ **Hotel La Plantation.** Perched high above Orient Bay, this colonial-style hotel is a charmer, and guests give high marks to the recent renovations. **Pros:** relaxing atmosphere; eye-popping views. **Cons:** small pool; beach is a 10-minute walk away. ⊠ *C5 Parc de La Baie Orientale, Baie Orientale* ☎ *590/29–58–00* ⊕ *www.la-plantation.com* ⇨ *17 suites, 34*

Palm Court Hotel.

studios ⚡ *In-room: a/c, safe, kitchen (some). In-hotel: restaurant, tennis courts, pool, gym* ☯ *Closed Sept.–mid-Oct.* ⚏ *Breakfast.*

$$
HOTEL
Fodor's Choice
★

🎬 **Palm Court.** Completely renovated in 2007 by a Parisian travel pro, the romantic beachfront units of this *hotel de charme* are steps from the fun of Orient Beach yet private, quiet, and stylishly up-to-date. **Pros:** big rooms; fresh and new; nice garden. **Cons:** across from, but not on the beach; some complaints about the a/c. ⊠ *Parc de la Baie Orientale, Baie Orientale* ☎ *590/87–41–94* ⊕ *www.sxm-palm-court.com* ⤙ *24 rooms* ⚡ *In-room: a/c, safe, Wi-Fi. In-hotel: restaurant, pool, parking, some pets allowed* ☯ *Closed Sept.* ⚏ *Breakfast.*

GRAND CASE

$–$$
RENTAL
☾

🎬 **Bleu Emeraude.** Brand-new in 2009, the 11 apartments in this tidy complex sit right on a sliver of Grand Case Beach. **Pros:** brand-new; walk to restaurants; attractive decor. **Cons:** it's not resort-y at all. ⊠ *240 bd. de Grand Case, Grand Case* ☎ *0590/87–27–71* ⊕ *www. bleuemeraude.com* ⤙ *4 studios, 6 1-bedroom apartments, 1 2-bedroom apartment* ⚡ *In-room: a/c, safe, kitchen, Wi-Fi (some). In-hotel: beach, parking, some pets allowed* ⚏ *Breakfast.*

$$–$$$
RESORT
☾

🎬 **Grand Case Beach Club.** This popular beachfront property on a cove at the east end of Grand Case has a friendly staff and spectacular sunset views. **Pros:** reasonable price; comfortable rooms; walking distance to restaurants. **Cons:** small beach; dated buildings. ⊠ *21 rue de Petit Plage, at north end of bd. de Grand Case, Box 339, Grand Case* ☎ *590/87–51–87 or 800/344–3016* ⊕ *www.grandcasebeachclub.com* ⤙ *72 apartments* ⚡ *In-room: a/c, safe, kitchen. In-hotel: restaurant, tennis court, bar, pool, gym, laundry facilities, beach, water sports* ⚏ *Breakfast.*

$$$
HOTEL
★

⊞ **Le Petit Hotel.** Surrounded by some of the best restaurants in the Caribbean, this beachfront boutique hotel, sister hotel to Hotel L'Esplanade, oozes charm and has the same caring, attentive management. **Pros:** walking distance to everything in Grand Case; friendly staff; clean, updated rooms. **Cons:** many stairs to climb; no pool. ⊠ *248 bd. de Grand Case, Grand Case* 🕾 *590/29–09–65* ⊕ *www.lepetithotel.com* ↘*9 rooms, 1 suite* ⚮ *In-room: a/c, safe, kitchen. In-hotel: beach* ⦿*Breakfast.*

OYSTER POND

$–$$
RESORT

⊞ **Captain Oliver's Resort.** This cluster of pink bungalows is perched high on a hill above a lagoon. **Pros:** restaurant is reasonably priced; ferry trips leave from the hotel. **Cons:** not on the beach. ⊠ *Oyster Pond* 🕾 *590/87–40–26 or 888/790–5264* ⊕ *www.captainolivers.com* ↘ *50 suites* ⚮ *In-room: a/c, safe. In-hotel: restaurants, bars, pool, business center* ⊘ *Closed Sept. and Oct.* ⦿*Breakfast.*

NIGHTLIFE

★ St. Maarten has lots of evening and late-night action. To find out what's doing on the island, pick up *St. Maarten Nights, St. Maarten Quick Pick Guide,* or *St. Maarten Events,* all of which are distributed free in the tourist office and hotels. The glossy *Discover St. Martin/St. Maarten* magazine, also free, has articles on island history and on the newest shops, discos, and restaurants. Or buy a copy of Thursday's *Daily Herald* newspaper, which lists all the week's entertainment.

DUTCH SIDE

BARS
MAHO

Bamboo Bernies. Bamboo Bernies is a sophisticated club-restaurant with soft techno music. ⊠ *Sonesta Maho Beach Resort & Casino, 1 Rhine Rd., Maho* 🕾 *599/545–3622.*

Soprano's. Starting each night at 8, the pianist at Soprano's takes requests for oldies, romantic favorites, or smooth jazz. ⊠ *Sonesta Maho Beach Resort & Casino, 1 Rhine Rd., Maho* 🕾 *599/545–2485* ⊕ *www. sopranospianobar.com.*

Sunset Beach Bar. This popular spot offers a relaxed, anything-goes atmosphere. Enjoy live music Wednesday through Sunday as you watch planes from the airport next door fly directly over your head. ⊠ *Maho Beach, Maho* 🕾 *599/545–3998* ⊕ *www.sunsetbeachbar.com.*

PHILIPSBURG

Axum Café. This 1960s-style coffee shop offers local cultural activities as well as live jazz and reggae. It's open daily, 11:30 am until the wee hours. ⊠ *7L Front St., Philipsburg* 🕾 *599/52–0547.*

Ocean Lounge. Ocean Lounge is the quintessential people-watching venue. Sip a Guavaberry colada and point your chair toward the boardwalk. ⊠ *Holland House Hotel, 43 Front St., Philipsburg* 🕾 *599/542–2572.*

Gambling, the most popular indoor activity in St. Maarten.

SIMPSON BAY

Bliss. The open-air nightclub and lounge, which is good for dancing, rocks till late. ⊠ *Caravanserai Resort, Simpson Bay* ☎ *599/545–3996.*

Buccaneer Bar. Buccaneer Bar is the place to enjoy a BBC (Bailey's banana colada), a slice of pizza, and a nightly bonfire. ⊠ *Behind Atrium Beach Resort, Simpson Bay* ☎ *599/544–5876* ⊕ *sxmbuccaneerbar.com.*

Cheri's Café. Across from Maho Beach Resort and Casino, Cheri's features Sweet Chocolate, a lively band that will get your toes tapping and your tush twisting. Snacks and hearty meals are available all day long on a cheerful verandah decorated with thousands of inflatable beach toys. ⊠ *Airport Rd., Simpson Bay* ☎ *599/545–3361.*

Lady C. A 70-year-old sailboat has been transformed into a floating party bar. It sits in Simpson Bay Lagoon, making it very convenient for the yachties. ⊠ *Simpson Bay* ☎ *599/544–4710* ⊕ *www.ladycfloatingbar.com.*

Pineapple Pete. At Pete's you can groove to live music or visit the game room for a couple of rounds of pool. ⊠ *Airport Rd., Simpson Bay* ☎ *599/544–6030* ⊕ *www.pineapplepete.com.*

Red Piano. The Red Piano has live music and tasty cocktails. ⊠ *Hollywood Casino, Simpson Bay* ☎ *599/580–1841* ⊕ *www.simpsonbayresort.com.*

CASINOS

The island's casinos—all 13 of them—are found only on the Dutch side. All have craps, blackjack, roulette, and slot machines. You must be 18 years or older to gamble. Dress is casual (but excludes bathing suits or skimpy beachwear). Most casinos are found in hotels, but there are also some independents.

COLE BAY

Princess Casino. One of the island's largest gaming halls, Princess Casino has a wide array of restaurants and entertainment options. ⊠ *Port de Plaisance, Union Rd., Cole Bay* ☎ *599/544–4311* ⊕ *www. princessportdeplaisance.com.*

CUPECOY

Atlantis World Casino. With some of the best restaurants on the island, Atlantis World is a popular destination even for those who don't gamble. It has more than 500 slot machines and gaming tables offering roulette, baccarat, three-card poker, Texas Hold'em poker, and Omaha high poker, not to mention some of the best restaurants on the Dutch side of the island. ⊠ *106 Rhine Rd., Cupecoy* ☎ *599/545–4601* ⊕ *www. atlantisworld.com or www.beachplazasxm.com.*

MAHO

Casino Royale. One of the island's largest gambling joints, Casino Royale is in bustling Maho, near plenty of restaurants, bars, and clubs. ⊠ *Maho Beach Resort & Casino, Maho Bay* ☎ *599/545–2590* ⊕ *www. playmaho.com.*

PHILIPSBURG

Beach Plaza Casino. Beach Plaza Casino, in the heart of the shopping area, has more than 180 slots and multigame machines with the latest in touch-screen technology. Because of its location, it is popular with cruise-ship passengers. ⊠ *Front St., Philipsburg* ☎ *599/543–2031.*

SIMPSON BAY

Dolphin Casino. The Dolphin, near the airport, has a giant slot machine at the entrance. ⊠ *Simpson Bay* ☎ *599/544–3411.*

Paradise Plaza Casino. Paradise Plaza has 250 slots and multigame machines. Betting on sporting events is a big thing here, which explains the 20 televisions tuned to whatever game happens to be on at the time. ⊠ *Airport Rd., Simpson Bay* ☎ *599/543–4721* ⊕ *www. paradisecasinosxm.com.*

DANCE CLUBS

MAHO

Tantra. Tantra is the eastern Caribbean's largest nightclub (the former Q Club), an Asian-inspired disco at the Casino Royale with a mix of music sure to please everyone. ⊠ *Sonesta Maho Beach Resort & Casino, Maho Bay* ☎ *599/545–2861* ⊕ *www.tantrasxm.com.*

PHILIPSBURG

Greenhouse. Greenhouse plays soca, merengue, zouk, and salsa, and has a two-for-one happy hour that lasts all night Tuesday. A second branch has opened in Simpson Bay. ⊠ *Bobby's Marina Philipsburg* ☎ *599/542–2941* ⊕ *www.thegreenhouserestaurant.com.*

SIMPSON BAY

Greenhouse. Greenhouse plays soca, merengue, zouk, and salsa, and has a two-for-one happy hour that lasts all night Tuesday. The original is in Philipsburg. ⊠ *Billy's Folly Rd., just past Atrium Beach Resort, Simpson Bay* ☎ *599/544–4173* ⊕ *www.thegreenhouserestaurant.com.*

FRENCH SIDE

BAIE DES PÈRES

BARS

Kali's Beach Bar. On the French side, Kali's is a happening spot with live music until midnight. On the night of the full moon and on every Friday night the beach bonfire and late-night party here is the place to be. ✉ *Baie des Pères* ☎ 690/49–06–01.

BAIE ORIENTALE

DANCE CLUBS

Boo Boo Jam. This club is a jumping joint with a mix of calypso, meringue, salsa, and other beats open only on Friday and Sunday nights, and every day for lunch. ✉ *Baie Orientale* ☎ 690/75–21–66.

La Chapelle. This sports bar transforms itself into a disco at night, right in the little village of Baie Orientale. ✉ *Baie Orientale* ☎ 590/52–38–90.

GRAND CASE

DANCE CLUBS

Calmos Café. Calmos Café draws a young local crowd. Just walk through the boutique and around the back to the sea and pull up a beach chair or park yourself at a picnic table. It's open all day, but the fun really begins at the cocktail hour, when everyone enjoys tapas. The little covered deck at the end is a perfect for romance. On Sundays there is often live reggae on the beach. ✉ *40 bd. de Grand Case, Grand Case* ☎ *0590/29–01–85* ⊕ *www.calmoscafe.com.*

La Noche. La Noche may tempt you during your after-dinner stroll in Grand Case; consider continuing your evening at this sexy lounge decorated in red, where the house music starts at 11 (or later) and continues until the last reveler quits. The dress code is "chic and sexy." ✉ *147 bd. de Grand Case, Grand Case* ☎ *0590/29–72–89.*

SHOPPING

It's true that the island sparkles with its myriad outdoor activities—diving, snorkeling, sailing, swimming, and sunning—but shopaholics are drawn to the sparkle in the jewelry stores. The huge array of such stores is almost unrivaled in the Caribbean. In addition, duty-free shops can offer substantial savings—about 15% to 30% below U.S. and Canadian prices—on cameras, watches, liquor, cigars, and designer clothing. It's no wonder that many cruise ships make Philipsburg a port of call. Stick with the big vendors that advertise in the tourist press, and you will be more likely to avoid today's ubiquitous fakes and replicas. On both sides of the island, be alert for idlers. They can snatch unwatched purses. Just be sure to know the U.S. prices of whatever you plan on buying in St. Maarten so you know if you're getting a deal or just getting dealt a bad hand.

Prices are in dollars on the Dutch side, in euros on the French side. As for bargains, there are more to be had on the Dutch side, where prices are in dollars; prices on the French side may sometimes be higher than those you'll find back home and are in euros, which compounds the difficulties with affordability. Merchandise may not be from the newest collections, especially with regard to clothing, but there are items available on the French side that are not available on the Dutch side. Finally, remember the important caveat about shopping anywhere: if it sounds too good to be true, it usually is.

DUTCH SIDE

PHILIPSBURG

Philipsburg's **Front Street** has reinvented itself. Now it's mall-like, with a redbrick walk and streets, palm trees lining the sleek boutiques, jewelry stores, souvenir shops, outdoor restaurants, and the old reliables, like McDonald's and Burger King. Here and there a school or a church appears to remind visitors there's more to the island than shopping. Back Street is where you'll find the **Philipsburg Market Place,** a daily open-air market where you can haggle for bargains on items such as handicrafts, souvenirs, and beachwear. **Old Street,** near the end of Front Street, has stores, boutiques, and open-air cafés offering French crepes, rich chocolates, and island mementos.

HANDICRAFTS

Guavaberry Emporium. Visitors to the Dutch side of the island come for free samples at the the small factory where the Sint Maarten Guavaberry Company makes its famous liqueur. You'll find a multitude of versions, including one made with jalapeño peppers. Check out the hand-painted bottles. ⊠ *8–10 Front St., Philipsburg* ☎ *599/542–2965 wwww.guavaberry.com.*

Shipwreck Shop. Shipwreck Shop has outlets all over the island that stock a little of everything: colorful hammocks, handmade jewelry, and lots of the local Guavaberry liqueur, but the main store on Front Street in Philipsburg has the largest selection of wares. ⊠ *42 Front St., Philipsburg* ☎ *599/542–2962 or 599/542–6710* ⊕ *www.shipwreckshops.com.*

JEWELRY AND GIFTS

Jewelry is big business on both the French and Dutch sides of the island, and many stores have outlets in both places. The so-called duty-free prices, however, may not give you much saving (if anything) over what you might pay at home, and sometimes prices are higher than you would pay at a shop back home. Compare prices in a variety of stores before you buy, and if you know you want to search for an expensive piece of jewelry or high-end watch, make sure you price your pieces at home and bargain hard to ensure you get a good deal.

Little Europe. Little Europe sells fine jewelry, crystal, and china in its two branches in Philipsburg. ⊠ *80 Front St., Philipsburg* ☎ *599/542–4371* ⊕ *www.littleeuropejewellers.com* ⊠ *2 Front St., Philipsburg* ☎ *599/542–3153* ⊕ *www.littleeuropejewellers.com.*

Little Switzerland. The large Caribbean duty-free chain sells watches, fine crystal, china, perfume, and jewelry. ⊠ *52 Front St., Philipsburg* ☎ *599/542–2523* ⊕ *www.littleswitzerland.com* ⊠ *Harbor Point Village, Pointe Blanche* ☎ *599/542–7785* ⊠ *Westin Dawn Beach Resort & Spa, Dawn Beach* ☎ *599/643–6451.*

Oro Diamante. Oro Diamante carries loose diamonds, jewelry, watches, perfume, and cosmetics. ⊠ *62-B Front St., Philipsburg* ☎ *599/543–0342 or 800/635–7950* ⊕ *www.oro-diamante.com.*

FRENCH SIDE

GRAND CASE

ART GALLERIES

Atelier des Tropismes. Contemporary Caribbean artists, including Paul Elliot Thuleau, who is a master of capturing the unique sunshine of the islands, are showcased at Atelier des Tropismes. ⊠ *107 bd. de Grand Case, Grand Case* ☎ *590/29–10–60* ⊕ *tropismesgallery.com.*

MARIGOT

On the French side, wrought-iron balconies, colorful awnings, and gingerbread trim decorate Marigot's smart shops, tiny boutiques, and bistros in the **Marina Port La Royale** complex and on the main streets, **Rue de la Liberté** and **Rue de la République.** Also in Marigot is the pricey **West Indies Mall** and the **Plaza Caraïbes,** which house designer shops, although some shops are closing in the economic downturn.

ART GALLERIES

Gingerbread Galerie. This gallery on the far side of the marina specializes in Haitian art and sells both expensive paintings and more reasonably priced decorative pieces of folk art. ⊠ *Marina Port La Royale, Marigot* ☎ *590/87–73–21* ⊕ *www.gingerbread-gallery.com.*

CLOTHING

On the French side, the best luxury-brand shops are found either in the modern, air-conditioned West Indies Mall or the Plaza Caraïbes center across from Marina Port La Royale in Marigot. There is also a small center in Grand Case, called La Petite Favorite, with four shops and a café.

JEWELRY AND GIFTS

Artistic Jewelers. Artistic Jewelers carries the work of David Yurman, among many others, as well as high-end designer watches. ⊠ *8 rue du Général de Gaulle, Marigot* ☎ *590/52–24–80.*

Manek's. Manek's sells, on two floors, luggage, perfume, jewelry, Cuban cigars, duty-free liquors, and tobacco products. ⊠ *Rue de la République, Marigot* ☎ *590/87–54–91.*

SPORTS AND ACTIVITIES

BOATING AND SAILING

The island is surrounded by water, so why not get out and enjoy it? The water and winds are perfect for skimming the surf. It'll cost you around $1,200 to $1,500 per day to rent a 28- to 40-foot powerboat, considerably less for smaller boats or small sailboats. Drinks and sometimes lunch are usually included on crewed day charters.

DUTCH SIDE

Lagoon Sailboat Rental (✉ *Airport Rd., near Uncle Harry's, Simpson Bay* ☎ *599/557–0714* ⊕ *www.lagoonsailboatrental.com*) has 20-foot day sailers for rent within Simpson Bay Lagoon for $150 per day, with a half day for $110. Either explore on your own or rent a skipper to navigate the calm, sheltered waters around Simpson Bay Yacht Club and miles of coastline on both the French and Dutch sides of the islands.

Random Wind (✉ *Ric's Place, Simpson Bay* ☎ *599/587–5742* ⊕ *www.randomwind.com*) offers full-day sailing and snorkeling trips on a traditional 54-foot clipper. Charter prices depend on the size of the group and whether lunch is served. The regularly scheduled Paradise Daysail costs $95 per person and includes food and drink. Departures are on the Dutch side, from Skipjack's at Simpson Bay, at 8:30 am Tuesday through Friday.

Sailing experience is not necessary for the **St. Maarten 12-Metre Challenge** (✉ *Bobby's Marina, Philipsburg* ☎ *599/542–0045* ⊕ *www.12metre.com*), one of the island's most popular activities. Participants compete on 68-foot racing yachts, including Dennis Connor's *Stars and Stripes* (the actual boat that won the America's Cup in 1987) and the *Canada II*. Anyone can help the crew grind winches, trim sails, and punch the stopwatch, or you can just sit back and watch everyone else work. The thrill of it is priceless, but book well in advance; this is the most popular shore excursion offered by cruise ships in the Caribbean. It's offered four times daily; the entire experience lasts about three hours. Only children over 12 are allowed.

FRENCH SIDE

MP Yachting (✉ *Marina Port La Royale, Marigot* ☎ *0690/53–37–98* ⊕ *www.mpyachting.com*) rents boats of all sizes, with or without a crew, and it's located conveniently at Marina Port La Royale in Marigot.

Sun Evasion (✉ *Marina Port La Royale, Marigot* ☎ *0690/35–03–19* ⊕ *www.the-argonauts.net*) is a charter company with locations all over the world, including St. Martin. You can take a half- or full-day charter to Tintamarre, St. Barth, or Ilet Pinel on a mono- or multihull powerboat, available with or without a skipper.

FISHING

You can angle for yellowtail snapper, grouper, marlin, tuna, and wahoo on deep-sea excursions. Costs range from $150 per person for a half day to $250 for a full day. Prices usually include bait and tackle, instruction for novices, and refreshments. Ask about licensing and insurance.

DUTCH SIDE

Lee's Deepsea Fishing (✉ *Welfare Rd. 82, Simpson Bay* ☎ *599/544–4233* ⊕ *www.leesfish.com*) organizes excursions, and when you return, Lee's Roadside Grill will cook your tuna, wahoo, or whatever else you catch and keep. Rates start at $150 per person for a half day.

Rudy's Deep Sea Fishing (✉ *14 Airport Rd., Simpson Bay* ☎ *599/545–2177* ⊕ *www.rudysdeepseafishing.com*) has been around for years, and is one of the more experienced sport-angling outfits.

FRENCH SIDE
Private Yacht Charter (✉ *Great House Marina, Oyster Bay* ☎ *0690/83–53–05* ⊕ *www.privateyachtcharter-sxm.com*) offers deep-sea fishing, snorkeling trips, and catamaran trips including snacks and drinks.

GOLF

DUTCH SIDE
St. Maarten is not a golf destination. Although **Mullet Bay Golf Course** (✉ *Airport Rd.*, *north of airport, Mullet Bay* ☎ *599/545–3069*), on the Dutch side, is an 18-hole course, it's the island's only one. At this writing, only 9 holes are open, as the beach side was damaged in 2008 by Hurricane Omar. But the course is serviceable, if you are really desperate for a golf fix. Otherwise, take the ferry from Marigot over to Anguilla for the top-notch (albeit expensive) Temenos course.

23

HORSEBACK RIDING

Island stables offer riding packages for everyone from novices to experts. A 90-minute ride along the beach costs $50 to $70 for group rides and $70 to $90 for private treks. Reservations are necessary. You can arrange rides directly or through most hotels.

FRENCH SIDE
Bayside Riding Club (✉ *Galion Beach Rd., Baie Orientale* ☎ *590/87–36–64* ⊕ *www.baysideridingclub.com*), on the French side, is a long-established outfit that can accommodate all levels of riders. Group beach rides of one to 1½ hours around a nature preserve are €65–€80 per person. Other rides can be arranged with prior contact.

KAYAKING

Kayaking is becoming very popular and is almost always offered at the many water-sports operations on both the Dutch and the French sides. Rental starts at about $15 per hour for a single and $19 for a double.

DUTCH SIDE
On the Dutch side, **Blue Bubbles** (✉ *Dawn Beach Resort, Oyster Pond* ☎ *599/542–2502* ⊕ *www.bluebubblessxm.com*) offers lagoon paddles and snorkeling tours by kayak.

TriSports (✉ *Airport Rd. 14B, Simpson Bay* ☎ *599/545–4384* ⊕ *www.trisportsxm.com*) organizes similar kayaking and snorkeling excursions.

FRENCH SIDE
On the French side, kayaks are available at **Kali's Beach Bar** (✉ *Friars Bay* ☎ *690/49–06–81* ✎ *kali.beach.bar@domaccess.com*).

Near Le Galion Beach, **Wind Adventures** (✉ *Orient Bay* ☎ *590/29–41–57* ⊕ *www.wind-adventures.com*) offers rentals and instruction in kayaking, kitesurfing, windsurfing, Hobie cats, and stand-up paddle surfing.

SCUBA DIVING

Diving in St. Maarten/St. Martin is mediocre at best, but those who want to dive will find a few positives. The water temperature here is rarely below 70°F (21°C). Visibility is often 60 to 100 feet. The island has more than 30 dive sites, from wrecks to rocky labyrinths. Right outside of Philipsburg, 55 feet under the water, is the HMS *Proselyte,* once explored by Jacques Cousteau. Although it sank in 1801, the boat's cannons and coral-encrusted anchors are still visible.

Off the north coast, in the protected and mostly current-free Grand Case Bay, is **Creole Rock.** The water here ranges in depth from 10 feet to 25 feet. Other sites off the north coast include **Ilet Pinel,** with its good shallow diving; **Green Key,** with its vibrant barrier reef; and **Tintamarre,** with its sheltered coves and geologic faults. On average, one-tank dives start at $55; two-tank dives are about $100. Certification courses start at about $400.

The Dutch side offers several full-service outfitters and SSI (Scuba Schools International) and/or PADI certification. There are no hyperbaric chambers on the island.

DUTCH SIDE

Blue Bubbles (⊠ *Dawn Beach Resort, Oyster Pond* ☎ *599/542–2502* ⊕ *www.bluebubblessxm.com*) offers Snuba, a shallow-water diving technique that is a great way to try undersea exploring.

Dive Safaris (⊠ *La Palapa Marina, Simpson Bay* ☎ *599/545–3213* ⊕ *www.divestmaarten.com*) has a shark-awareness dive on Friday where participants can watch professional feeders give reef sharks a little nosh.

Ocean Explorers Dive Shop (⊠ *113 Welfare Rd., Simpson Bay* ☎ *599/544–5252* ⊕ *www.stmaartendiving.com*) is St. Maarten's oldest dive shop, and offers different types of certification courses.

FRENCH SIDE

Neptune (⊠ *Plage d'Orient Bay, Baie Orientale* ☎ *690/50–98–51* ⊕ *www.neptune-dive.com*) is a PADI-certified outfit and very popular for its friendly owners Fabien and Sylvie, whose extensive experience thrills happy clients of reef, wreck, and cove dives. There is also an extensive program for beginners.

Octopus (⊠ *15 bd. de Grand Case, Grand Case* ☎ *590/29–11–27* ⊕ *www.stmartinscuba.com*) offers PADI diving certification courses and all-inclusive dive packages, using the latest equipment and a 30-foot power catamaran called *Octopussy.* The company also offers private and group snorkel trips starting at $40, including all necessary equipment.

At Marina Ft. Louis, **O2 Limits** (⊠ *Bd. de Grand Case, Grand Case* ☎ *690/34–14–00*) offers a full menu of diving options and the only Nitrox technology on St. Martin.

SEA EXCURSIONS

DUTCH SIDE

The 50-foot catamaran ***Bluebeard II*** (⊠ *Simpson Bay* ☎ *599/587–5935* ⊕ *www.bluebeardcharters.com*) sails around Anguilla's south and northwest coasts to Prickly Pear Cay, where there are excellent coral reefs for snorkeling and powdery white sands for sunning.

For low impact sunset and dinner cruises, try the catamaran ***Celine*** (⊠ *Skip Jack's Restaurant, Simpson Bay* ☎ *599/526–1170 or 599/552 1335* ⊕ *www.sailstmaarten.com*).

The sleek 76-foot catamaran ***Golden Eagle*** (☎ *599/542–3323* ⊕ *www. sailingsxm.com*) takes day-sailors to outlying islets and reefs for snorkeling and partying.

FRENCH SIDE

A cross between a submarine and a glass-bottom boat, the 34-passenger ***Seaworld Explorer*** (⊠ *Bd. de Grand Case, Grand Case* ☎ *599/542–4078* ⊕ *www.atlantisadventures.com*) offers a 1½-hour excursion that crawls along the water's surface from Grand Case to Creole Rock. While seated below the waterline, passengers view marine life and coral through large windows. Divers jump off the boat and feed the fish and eels. The excursion costs $39.

SNORKELING

Some of the best snorkeling on the Dutch side can be found around the rocks below Fort Amsterdam off Little Bay Beach, in the west end of Maho Bay, off Pelican Key, and around the reefs off Oyster Pond Beach. On the French side, the area around Orient Bay—including Caye Verte, Ilet Pinel, and Tintamarre—is especially lovely and is officially classified and protected as a regional underwater nature reserve. Sea creatures also congregate around Creole Rock at the point of Grand Case Bay. The average cost of an afternoon snorkeling trip is about $45 to $55 per person.

DUTCH SIDE

Aqua Mania Adventures (⊠ *Pelican Marina, Simpson Bay* ☎ *599/544–2640 or 599/544–2631* ⊕ *www.stmaarten-activities.com*) offers a variety of snorkeling trips. The newest activity, called Rock 'n Roll Safaris, lets participants not only snorkel, but navigate their own motorized rafts.

Blue Bubbles (⊠ *Dawn Beach Resort, Oyster Pond* ☎ *599/542–2502* ⊕ *www.bluebubblessxm.com*) has both boat and shore snorkel excursions.

Eagle Tours (⊠ *Bobby's Marina, Philipsburg* ☎ *599/542–3323* ⊕ *www. sailingsxm.com*) is geared more to cruise groups, but anyone can sign on for the four-hour power rafting, or sailing trips that include snorkeling, a beach break, and lunch. The sailing trips are done aboard a 76-foot catamaran. Some cruises stop in Grand Case or Marigot for a bit of shopping.

23

FRENCH SIDE

Arrange equipment rentals and snorkeling trips through **Kontiki Watersports** (✉ *Northern beach entrance, Baie Orientale* ☎ 590/87–46–89).

WINDSURFING

The best windsurfing is on Galion Bay on the French side. From November to May, trade winds can average 15 knots.

FRENCH SIDE

Wind Adventures (✉ *Northern beach entrance, Baie Orientale* ☎ 590/29–41–57 ⊕ *www.wind-adventures.com*) offers rentals and lessons in both windsurfing and kitesurfing. One-hour lessons are about €40.

Windy Reef (✉ *Galion Beach, past Butterfly Farm* ☎ 690/34–21–85 ⊕ *www.windyreef.fr*) has offered windsurfing lessons and rentals since 1991.

St. Vincent and the Grenadines

WORD OF MOUTH

"My husband and I went to St. Vincent & Bequia for a week . . . it was probably the most relaxing trip we've ever taken."

—ChrisAroundTheWorld

"Life was too short, the world too big [to visit the same place twice]. Then I discovered Bequia. Now I visit at least twice a year."

—ElwoodKitten

WELCOME TO ST. VINCENT AND THE GRENADINES

A STRING OF PEARLS

St. Vincent, which is 18 mi (29 km) long and 11 mi (18 km) wide, is the northernmost and largest of the chain of 32 islands that make up St. Vincent and the Grenadines and extend 45 mi (72 km) southwest toward Grenada. What these islands all have in common is a get-away-from-it-all atmosphere and a virtual lack of large-scale development.

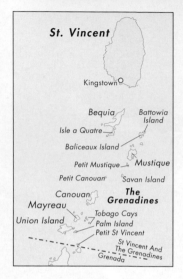

St. Vincent

Kingstown

Bequia   Battowia Island
Isle a Quatre
Baliceaux Island
Petit Mustique   Mustique
Petit Canouan   Savan Island
Canouan   **The Grenadines**
Mayreau
Union Island   Tobago Cays
        Palm Island
        Petit St Vincent
          St Vincent And The Grenadines
          Grenada

Restaurants ▼
Basil's Bar & Restaurant **2**
Cobblestone Roof-Top ...**3**
The French Verandah **5**
Grenadine House **1**
Wallilabou Anchorage ..**4**
Young Island Resort **6**

Grenadine House **1**
Mariners Hotel **9**
Rosewood
Apartment Hotel **8**
Sunsest Shores
Beach Hotel **6**
Villa Lodge Hotel **4**
Young Island Resort **7**

Hotels ▼
Beachcombers Hotel **5**
Buccament Bay Resort **10**
Cobblestone Inn **2**
Grand View
Beach Hotel **3**

KEY	
⌁	Beaches
⏴	Cruise Ship Terminal
◪	Dive Sites
⏴	Ferry
❶	Restaurants
①	Hotels

There are 32 perfectly endowed Grenadine islands and cays in this archipelago that provide some of the Caribbean's best anchorages and prettiest beaches.

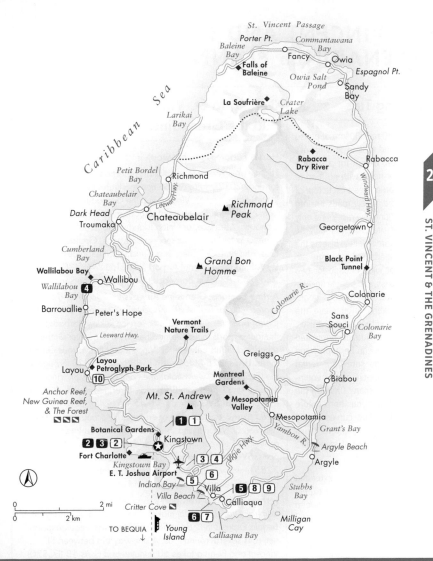

St. Vincent Passage

Porter Pt.
Commantawana Bay
Baleine Bay
Fancy
Owia
Espagnol Pt.
Falls of Baleine
Owia Salt Pond
Sandy Bay
La Soufrière
Crater Lake
Larikai Bay

Caribbean Sea

Rabacca Dry River
Rabacca

Petit Bordel Bay
Richmond
Windward Hwy.

Chateaubelair Bay
Richmond Peak
Leeward Hwy.
Dark Head
Chateaubelair
Troumaka
Georgetown

Cumberland Bay
Grand Bon Homme
Black Point Tunnel

Wallilabou Bay
Wallilabou Bay **4**
Wallibou
Colonarie R.
Colonarie

Barrouallie
Peter's Hope
Sans Souci
Colonarie Bay

Leeward Hwy.
Vermont Nature Trails
Greiggs

Layou Petroglyph Park **10**
Layou
Montreal Gardens
Biabou

Anchor Reef, New Guinea Reef, & The Forest
Mt. St. Andrew
Mesopotamia Valley
Mesopotamia
Grant's Bay

Botanical Gardens
1 **1**
Kingstown
Yambou R.
Argyle Beach

2 **3** **2**
Fort Charlotte
3 **4**
Vigie Hwy.
Argyle

E. T. Joshua Airport
6
Kingstown Bay
Indian Bay
5
Villa
Stubbs Bay
5 **8** **9**

Villa Beach
Calliaqua
Critter Cove
6 **7**
Milligan Cay

TO BEQUIA
Young Island
Calliaqua Bay

0   2 mi
0   2 km

TOP REASONS TO VISIT ST. VINCENT & THE GRENADINES

1 Diverse Landscape: St. Vincent offers a lush landscape, extraordinary hiking trails, remarkable botanical gardens, majestic waterfalls, and intriguing dive sites.

2 Tranquillity: With few large resorts and no crowds, you're guaranteed peace and quiet.

3 Sail Away: Island-hopping sailing charters are the premier way to travel through the beautiful Grenadines.

4 Beach Paradise: Grenadine beaches have brilliant white and powdery soft sand, washed by gentle waves in several shades of blue.

ST. VINCENT AND THE GRENADINES PLANNER

Driving Tips

About 360 mi (580 km) of paved roads wind around St. Vincent's perimeter, except for a section in the far north with no road at all that precludes a circle tour of the island. A few roads jut into the interior a few miles, and only one east–west road (through the Mesopotamia Valley) bisects the island. Roads in the country are often not wide enough for two cars to pass, and people (including schoolchildren), dogs, goats, and chickens often share the roadway with cars, minibuses, and trucks. Outside populated areas, roads can be bumpy and potholed; be sure your rental car has tire-changing equipment and a spare. Drive on the left, and toot your horn before you enter blind curves out in the countryside, where you'll encounter plenty of steep hills and hairpin turns.

If you're planning an extended stay on St. Vincent and expect to travel frequently between Kingstown and, say, the Villa Beach area, a rental car might be useful although not necessary, as both taxis and buses are inexpensive and readily available. On Bequia, a rental car will be handy if you're staying for several days in a remote location—that is, anywhere beyond Port Elizabeth.

Getting to St. Vincent and the Grenadines

Hassle Factor: High, but worth it.

Flights: Until Argyle International Airport opens (scheduled for early 2012), there are no nonstop flights between the United States and St. Vincent and the Grenadines. Travelers from North America arrive at airports in St. Vincent, Bequia, Canouan, Mustique, or Union Island via regional airlines that connect to major airlines serving Barbados, Grenada, Puerto Rico, and St. Lucia. There is a tourist information desk at **Grantley Adams International Airport** (✉ BGI ☎ 246/428–0961 or 246/233–8746) in Barbados to assist passengers in transit.

Airline Contacts: Grenadine Airways (☎ 246/418–1654 for shared–charter flights, 784/456–6793 for inter–Grenadine flights) operates shared–charter service linking Barbados with the four airports in the Grenadines, as well as inter-Grenadine scheduled flights between St. Vincent and the various Grenadines. **LIAT** (☎ 784/458–4841, 888/844–5428 throughout the Caribbean ⊕ www.liatairline.com) connects St. Vincent, Bequia, and Union with Barbados, Grenada, Puerto Rico, and St. Lucia. **SVG Air** (☎ 784/457–5124 or 800/744–7285 ⊕ www.svgair.com) operates daily scheduled flights between St. Vincent and St. Lucia's Hewanorra International, as well as between St. Vincent and the four Grenadine airports. **SVG Air (Grenada)** (☎ 473/444–3549 or 800/744–7285 ⊕ www.svgair.com/grenada) operates scheduled flights between Grenada and Union Island and St. Vincent.

Ferries: Admiralty Transport (☎☎ 784/458–3348 ⊕ www.admiralty-transport.com) makes several round-trips daily. **M/V Bequia Express** (☎ 784/458–3472 ⊕ www.bequiaexpress.net) runs several round-trips. A one-way trip between St. Vincent and Bequia takes 60 minutes and costs $8 (EC$20) each way or $14 (EC$35) round-trip with the same ferry company. **Jaden Sun** (☎ 784/451–2192 ⊕ www.jadeninc.com) is a fast-ferry service that offers reliable, comfortable service between mainland St. Vincent and Bequia (25 minutes), Canouan (1½ hours), and Union islands (2 hours), with an "as needed" stop in Mayreau. There is no service on Tues., Wed. afternoons, or public holidays and on Sat. in the low season only. The one-way fare between Kingstown and Canouan is $26; between Kingstown and Union, $28.

Getting Around St. Vincent and the Grenadines

Driving: Car rental is available on St. Vincent, Bequia, or Mustique. Rental cars in St. Vincent and Bequia cost about $55 to $85 per day or $300 to $400 a week. Unless you already have an international driver's license, you'll need to buy a temporary driving permit for $24 (EC$65), valid for six months. To get one, present your valid driver's license at the police station on Bay Street or the Licensing Authority on Halifax Street, both in Kingstown, St. Vincent, or the Revenue Office in Port Elizabeth, Bequia.

St. Vincent Contacts: Avis (✉ Airport, Arnos Vale, St. Vincent ☎ 784/456–6861 ⊕ www.avis.com) is the one international agency represented on St. Vincent. **Ben's Auto Rental** (✉ Arnos Vale, St. Vincent VC0110 ☎ 784/456–2907) is reliable and offers comparable rates. **David's Auto Clinic** (✉ Sion Hill, St. Vincent ☎ 784/457–1116) is a recommended local agency in St. Vincent. **Star Garage** (✉ Grenville St., Kingstown, St. Vincent ☎ 784/456–1743) provides good service in St. Vincent.

Bequia Contacts: You can rent a four-wheel-drive vehicle from **B & G Jeep Rental** (✉ Port Elizabeth, Bequia ☎ 784/458–3760 ⊕ www.bequiajeeprentals.com). **Challenger** (✉ Port Elizabeth, Bequia ☎ 784/458–3811) is a local taxi and tour-guide operation that also rents four-wheel-drive vehicles.

Mustique Contacts: Mustique Mechanical Services (✉ Britannia Bay, Mustique ☎ 784/488–8555) is a Mustique Company subsidiary that rents cars, Mokes, and motor scooters.

Taxis: Taxis are not metered. Settle on the price before entering the taxi—and the currency. Taxis are always available at the airport in St. Vincent; the fare from the airport to Kingstown is $12 (EC$30); to Villa, $10 (EC$25). In Bequia, the taxis—usually pickup trucks, with their beds fitted with seats and an awning—will take you to Port Elizabeth, to the various hotels, or on a day of sightseeing. On Canouan, the resorts generally provide airport transfers, although taxis are available. On Mustique, either transfers are provided or taxis are available. On Union Island, Clifton—the main town—is a short walk or jitney ride from the airport to the dock (a two-minute trip) to meet the launch from Palm Island or Petit St. Vincent; taxis are also available for the brief ride into town.

Island Activities

Beautiful **beaches** and excellent waters for **sailing** can be found throughout the Grenadines. The beaches on St. Vincent have mostly dark, volcanic sand and, although often beautiful, are less than excellent for swimming and sunbathing. You come to this part of the world to really get away from it all and for **relaxation**, but don't miss the opportunity to do some easy **island-hopping.**

The reef system surrounding the uninhabited Tobago Cays offers some of the best **snorkeling** in the world. Around St. Vincent itself, the waters are rich with marine life, offering **divers** abundant places to explore.

On land, you can **hike** through St. Vincent's verdant forests or **climb** its volcano, La Soufrière. But if you are staying at one of the excellent, luxurious resorts on an isolated Grenadine island, you may be tempted to lie back, immerse yourself in the moment, and do little more than raise a flag to request another rum punch.

24

ST. VINCENT AND THE GRENADINES PLANNER

Fast Facts

Banks and Exchange Services: ATMs can be found at banks in Kingstown and their branches. U.S. dollars are accepted nearly everywhere, although you'll receive change in Eastern Caribbean currency (EC$), which is the preferred currency. U.S. coins are not accepted anywhere. The exchange rate is fixed at EC$2.67 to US$1. Hotels, car-rental agencies, and most shops and restaurants accept major credit cards and traveler's checks.

Electricity: Generally 220–240 volts, 50 cycles. Some resorts, such as Petit St. Vincent, have 110 volts, 60 cycles (U.S. standard); most have 110-volt shaver outlets.

Passports Requirements: You need a valid passport and an ongoing or return ticket.

Weddings: 24-hour residency is a requirement. A special Governor General's marriage license must be obtained in person from the Ministry of Justice at the Registrar's Office in St. Vincent. Bring valid passports, return or ongoing plane tickets, certified and notarized divorce decrees, and an appropriate death certificate if either party is widowed. An official marriage officer, priest, or minister registered in St. Vincent and the Grenadines must officiate at the ceremony, and two witnesses must be present.

Essentials

Dress: Don't pack camouflage clothing. It is illegal to wear any form of camouflage clothing in St. Vincent and the Grenadines, as that pattern is reserved for the local police. The law is strictly enforced.

Mail: The General Post Office is on Halifax Street in Kingstown, St. Vincent. Most villages on St. Vincent have branch offices. Bequia's post office is in Port Elizabeth, across from the jetty. Airmail postcards cost EC60¢ to the United States, Canada, and the United Kingdom; airmail letters cost EC90¢ per ounce to the United States and Canada, EC$1.10 to the United Kingdom. When writing to a location in the Grenadines, the address on the envelope should always indicate the specific island name followed by "St. Vincent and the Grenadines, West Indies."

Taxes and Service Charges: The departure tax from St. Vincent and the Grenadines is $16 (EC$40), payable at the airport in cash in either U.S. or EC currency; children under 12 are exempt. Increasingly, departure taxes are incorporated into the price paid for airfare, although St. Vincent is currently an exception. A government tax of 10% is added to the room cost on hotel bills, a 15% V.A.T. (value-added tax) is added to restaurant checks and other purchases, and a 10% service charge is often added to hotel bills and restaurant checks.

Telephones: The area code is 784. Pay phones are readily available and best operated with prepaid phone cards. You'll see "top up here" signs, indicating places where you can add minutes to your prepaid cell phone or phone card. Local calls are free from private phones and most hotels.

Tipping: If a 10% service charge has not been added to your restaurant tab, a gratuity at that rate is appropriate. Otherwise, tipping is expected only for special service. Bellmen and porters, $1 per bag: housekeeping, $2 per day; taxi drivers and tour guides, 10%.

Visitor Information: St. Vincent and the Grenadines Tourist Office (☎ 212/687–4981 in New York City, 800/729–1726 ⊕ www.discoversvg.com). **St. Vincent & The Grenadines Hotel & Tourism Association** (⊕ www.svghotels.com).

Where to Stay

Mass tourism hasn't come to St. Vincent and the Grenadines, but that is likely to change after the Argyle International Airport opens in early 2017. With only one or two exceptions, hotels and inns on St. Vincent are small and simple. Look to one of the exclusive resorts in the Grenadines if you want luxury and privacy, where both can be found in great abundance. If you have the time, it's easy to island-hop by air or ferry, staying in simple guesthouses to maximize both your budget and experiences.

Luxury Resorts: On Young Island, just a stone's throw from St. Vincent's shore, at Buccament Bay on St. Vincent, and scattered throughout the Grenadines, fine, luxury resorts offer a laid-back vacation experience without sacrificing important comforts. Formalities tend to be few, but you will pay handsomely for service, comfort, and privacy.

Simple Resorts and Guesthouses: Most lodgings in St. Vincent are simple, small, and relatively inexpensive. You'll also find inexpensive small hotels and guesthouses throughout the Grenadines—on Bequia and Union, in particular.

Villas: Luxurious villas make up the majority of accommodations on Mustique, and they offer every amenity you can imagine. Private villas are also available for rent on St. Vincent, Bequia, and Canouan.

HOTEL AND RESTAURANT COSTS

Restaurant prices are for a main course at dinner and include any taxes or service charges. Hotel prices are per night for a double room in high season, excluding taxes, service charges, and meal plans (except at all-inclusives).

WHAT IT COSTS IN U.S. DOLLARS

	¢	$	$$	$$$	$$$$
Restaurants	under $8	$8–$12	$12–$20	$20–$30	over $30
Hotels	under $150	$150–$275	$276–$375	$376–$475	over $475

When to Go

High season runs from mid-December through mid-April; in the off-season, rates at larger resorts may be reduced by up to 40%. Seasonal discounts vary dramatically by resort and by island, with some of the luxury resorts offering specials periodically throughout the year; the most luxurious resorts, however, are always expensive. Inexpensive small hotels and guesthouses have little or no seasonal variation in their rates.

FESTIVALS AND EVENTS

The **SVG Gospelfest** is held throughout the month of April. Vincy Mas, the St. Vincent **Carnival** celebration, is the island's biggest cultural festival, beginning at the end of June and culminating in a huge street party in July.

Bequia has its own Bequia **Blues Festival** in late January or early February. An **Easter Regatta** on Easter weekend brings everyone out to watch boat races. The Bequia **Carnival** is a summer celebration in late June or early July.

The **Canouan Regatta** is held in May, and the **Canouan Carnival** is held at the end of July. The **Easterval Regatta** on Union Island is held on Easter weekend. The two-week Mustique **Blues Festival** begins in late January and ends in early February.

24

ST. VINCENT AND THE GRENADINES BEACHES

St. Vincent has a dramatic coastline with pretty coves, but its beaches, by and large, are not the primary reason to visit this interesting volcanic island. On the other hand, all the Grenadines have stunning beaches.

(Above) A fence-through view of Friendship Bay, Bequia. (Opposite page bottom) A sandbar in the Tobago Cays. (Opposite page top) Macaroni Beach, Mustique.

Although you'll find some of the most exclusive and expensive resorts in the Caribbean in the Grenadines, most of the island chain is relatively untouched and undeveloped. Many beaches on larger islands such as St. Vincent and Bequia are completely wild and rarely visited. Other beaches, such as the dozens of sugar-white sandy beaches on Mustique and those on Canouan, Mayreau, Palm Island, and Petit St. Vincent, look as if they jumped right off the pages of a fashion-magazine photo shoot—and in some cases they have been used as backdrops. But the Grenadines also include the chain of uninhabited, completely undeveloped islands known as the Tobago Cays, five islands that make up the Tobago Cays Marine Park, each with a pristine beach. Not all the beaches in the Grenadines are equally beautiful, but none are crowded.

VOLCANIC SAND

St. Vincent's origin is volcanic, so the sand on its beaches—the remnants of past volcanic eruptions —ranges in color from golden brown to black. On the windward coast, near Argyle, rolling surf breaks onto a broad expanse of black-sand beach—a beautiful view but dangerous for swimming. Indian Bay Beach has fairly light sand and is best for swimming.

ST. VINCENT

Aside from the beach on the private Young Island, just off shore, all beaches on St. Vincent are public. Indian Bay is a popular bathing and snorkeling spot. Villa Beach, on the mainland opposite Young Island, is really more of a waterfront area than a beach. The strip of sand is sometimes so narrow that it becomes nonexistent; nevertheless, boats bob at anchor in the channel and dive shops, inns, and restaurants line the shore, making this an interesting place to be. On the windward coast, dramatic swaths of broad black sand are strewn with huge black boulders, but the water is rough and unpredictable. On the leeward coast, swimming is recommended only in the lagoons, rivers, and bays.

24

BEQUIA

Bequia has clean, uncrowded white-sand beaches. Some are a healthy trek by foot or a short water-taxi ride from the jetty at Port Elizabeth; others require land transportation.

CANOUAN

Though only 3½ mi (5½ km) long, Canouan faces a mile-long coral reef—one of the longer barrier reefs in the Caribbean—that offers excellent diving and snorkeling opportunities. In addition, the island also has four exquisite white-sand beaches. Two-thirds of the island is set aside for a luxury resort and golf club. Its proximity to several of the other Grenadines (Mayreau and the Tobago Cays in particular) makes excursions to other beautiful beaches relatively easy.

MAYREAU

Mayreau's primary beach, Saltwhistle Bay, is unique because the calm water of the Caribbean is on one side, while the more powerful Atlantic surf is on the other; this narrow strip of white beach is all that separates them.

MUSTIQUE

For a relatively small island, Mustique has a large number of beautiful white-sand beaches at the foot of each of its lovely green valleys, perhaps one reason for its appeal to the private-jet set. Villas are strung out along the northern half of the island, but the best beach, picture-perfect Macaroni Beach, is on the south side.

PALM ISLAND

The beach on tiny Palm Island is beautiful, white, and powdery. Offshore, between Palm Island and its neighbor Petit St. Vincent, a sandbar with a single palapa offers an isolated spot in mid-ocean for a beach picnic.

Word of Mouth. "Palm Island is something special. It has thousands of palm trees. There is a large beach that just curls right around when you're walking. If you are looking for the Caribbean's prime place to lay out in the sun, this is it." —Knowing

Beautiful Macaroni Bay, Mustique

PETIT ST. VINCENT

This tiny private resort island has beautiful white-sand beaches on its western end; the sand here is particularly soft and free of most rocks, but there's a drop-off in the water. The beaches on the north shore, while beautiful, are fairly rocky. There's also a small, rocky beach on the south shore. Since the island is private, there are never any crowds.

TOBAGO CAYS

The five uninhabited Tobago Cays are known for their colorful reefs full of tropical fish and many green sea turtles that can be spotted on almost any visit. Four of the five islands—Petit Rameau, Petit Bateau, Jamesby, and Baradal—are enclosed within Horseshoe Reef; the fifth, Petit Tabac, stands separately to the east. All of the islands have gorgeous white-sand beaches that are the most pristine in the Grenadines, since they are completely unmarred by development (the Tobago Cays make up a marine sanctuary). A wreck just off the tip of Baradal offers good snorkeling. The Tobago Cays, in fact, are one of the top snorkeling destinations in the Caribbean.

UNION ISLAND

Although it's an important hub for travelers heading to some of the smaller islands in the Grenadines (especially the private retreats such as Petit St. Vincent and Palm Island and also Mayreau, which does not have an airstrip), the hilly, volcanic island has few beaches that compare with those on its closest neighbors. The best beach, Bigsand Beach, is on the north shore and has powdery white sand.

Updated by
Jane E. Zarem

A string of 32 islands and cays makes up the single nation of St. Vincent and the Grenadines. St. Vincent is one of the least touristy islands in the Caribbean—an unpretentious and relatively quiet island, where fishermen get up at the crack of dawn to drop their nets into the sea, working people conduct business in town, and farmers work their crops in the countryside.

Hotels and inns on St. Vincent are almost all small, locally owned and operated, and definitely not glitzy. So far, there are only two resorts—one on a bay north of Kingstown and another on a separate island, 600 feet from the mainland. Restaurants serve mainly local food—grilled fish, stewed or curried chicken, rice, and root vegetables (called "provisions"). And the beaches are either tiny crescents of black or brown sand on remote leeward bays or sweeping expanses of the same black sand pounded by Atlantic surf.

Independent travelers interested in active, ecofriendly vacations are discovering St. Vincent's natural beauty, its sports opportunities on land and sea, and the richness of its history They spend their vacation walking or hiking St. Vincent's well-defined jungle trails, catching a glimpse of the rare St. Vincent parrot in the Vermont Valley, exploring exotic flora in the Botanical Garden and in Montreal Gardens, delving into history at Ft. Charlotte, trekking to the spectacular Trinity Falls or the Falls of Baleine, and climbing the active volcano La Soufrière. Beneath the surface, snorkeling and scuba landscapes are similarly intriguing.

The Grenadines on the other hand dazzle vacationers with amazing inns and resorts, fine white-sand beaches, excellent sailing waters, and a get-away-from-it-all atmosphere.

Bequia, just south of St. Vincent and a pleasant hour's voyage by ferry, has a large complement of inns, hotels, restaurants, shops, and activities and, therefore, is a popular vacation destination in its own right. Its Admiralty Bay is one of the prettiest anchorages in the Caribbean. With superb views, snorkeling, hiking, and swimming, the island has much to offer the international mix of backpackers, landlubbers, and luxury-yacht owners who frequent its shores.

South of Bequia, on the exclusive, private island of Mustique, elaborate villas are tucked into lush hillsides. Mustique does not encourage wholesale tourism, least of all to those hoping for a glimpse of the rich and famous who own or rent villas here. The appeal of Mustique is its seclusion.

Boot-shape Canouan, mostly quiet and unspoiled and with only 1,200 or so residents, accommodates the well-heeled guests of the Canouan Resort. The posh, full-service resort takes up the entire northern third of the island and boasts one of the Caribbean's most challenging and scenic golf courses and a European-style casino, along with an incredibly inviting spa.

> **DOLLAR BUSES**
>
> Public buses, or "dollar buses," on St. Vincent are privately owned, brightly painted minivans, and fares range from EC$1 to EC$6 (40¢ to $2.25). Routes are indicated on the windshield, and the bus will stop on demand. Just wave from the road or point your finger to the ground as a bus approaches. When you want to get out, signal by tapping your knuckles twice above the window by your seat or ask the conductor, usually a young boy who rides along to open the door and collect fares; it's helpful to have the correct change in EC coins. In Kingstown, the central departure point is the bus terminal at the New Kingstown Fish Market.

Tiny Mayreau has fewer than 200 residents and one of the area's most beautiful (and unusual) beaches. At Saltwhistle Bay, the Caribbean Sea is often mirror calm while, just yards away, the rolling Atlantic surf washes the opposite shore. Otherwise, Mayreau has a single unnamed village, one road, rain-caught drinking water, and a couple of inns—but no airport, no bank, and no problems!

Union Island, with its dramatic landscape punctuated by Mt. Taboi, is the transportation center of the southern Grenadines. Its small but busy airport serves landlubbers, and its yacht harbor and dive operators serve sailors and scuba divers. Clifton, the quaint main town, has shops, restaurants, and a few guesthouses. Ashton, the second significant town, is mainly residential.

Meanwhile, it took decades to turn the 100-acre, mosquito-infested mangrove swamp called Prune Island into the upscale private resort now known as Palm Island. Today, vacationers (who can afford it) lounge in luxury on the island's five palm-fringed white-sand beaches.

Petit St. Vincent is another private, single-resort island, reclaimed from the overgrowth by the late Hazen K. Richardson II. The luxury resort's cobblestone cottages are so private that, if you wish, you could spend your entire vacation completely undisturbed.

And finally, the Tobago Cays, five uninhabited islands south of Canouan and east of Mayreau, draw snorkelers, divers, and boaters who are equally impressed with the sheer beauty of the area. Surrounded by a shallow reef, the tiny islands have rustling palm trees, pristine beaches with powdery sand, the clearest water in varying shades of brilliant blue—and plenty of resident fish and sea turtles.

The various islands of St. Vincent and the Grenadines are fairly close together. Whether you go by boat or by plane, traveling between them is not difficult. In fact, St. Vincent and each of the Grenadines are all quite unique. Once there, you'll definitely want to sample more than one.

ST. VINCENT

EXPLORING ST. VINCENT

24

Kingstown's shopping and business district, historic churches and cathedrals, and other points of interest can easily be seen in a half day, with another half day for the Botanical Garden. The coastal roads of St. Vincent offer spectacular panoramas and scenes of island life. The Leeward Highway follows the scenic Caribbean coastline; the Windward Highway follows the more dramatic Atlantic coast. A drive along the windward coast or a boat trip to the Falls of Baleine requires a full day. Exploring La Soufrière or the Vermont Trails is also a major undertaking, requiring a very early start and a full day of strenuous hiking.

Barrouallie. Once an important whaling village, Barrouallie (*bar*-relly) today is home to anglers earning their livelihoods trawling for blackfish, which are actually small pilot whales. The one-hour drive north from Kingstown, on the Leeward Highway, takes you along ridges that drop to the sea, through small villages and lush valleys, and beside bays with black-sand beaches and safe bathing.

Black Point Tunnel. In 1815, under the supervision of British colonel Thomas Browne, Carib and African slaves drilled a 300-foot tunnel through solid volcanic rock—an engineering marvel at the time—to facilitate the transportation of sugar from estates in the north to the port in Kingstown. Today, Jasper Rock Tunnel is the centerpiece of Black Point Historic & Recreation Park, which also has an interpretation center, children's playground, and washrooms. The tunnel, just off beautiful black-sand Black Point Beach, links Grand Sable with Byrea Bay, just north of Colonarie (pronounced con-a-*ree*).

☺
Fodor'sChoice
★

Botanical Gardens. A few minutes north of downtown by taxi is St. Vincent's famous Botanical Gardens. Founded in 1765, it's the oldest botanical garden in the Western Hemisphere. Captain Bligh—of *Bounty* fame—brought the first breadfruit tree to this island for landowners to propagate. The prolific bounty of the breadfruit trees was used to feed the slaves. You can see a direct descendant of this original tree among the specimen mahogany, rubber, teak, and other tropical trees and shrubs in the 20 acres of gardens. Two dozen rare St. Vincent parrots, confiscated from illegal collections, live in the small aviary. Guides explain all the medicinal and ornamental trees and shrubs; they also appreciate a tip at the end of the tour. ⊠ *Off Leeward Hwy., Montrose* ☎ *784/457–1003* 🎫 *Free* ☻ *Daily 6–6.*

St. Vincent's Complex History

Historians believe that the Ciboney were the first to journey from South America to St. Vincent, which they called Hairoun (Land of the Blessed). The Ciboney ultimately moved on to Cuba and Haiti, leaving St. Vincent to the agrarian Arawak tribes that journeyed north from coastal South America. Not long before Columbus sailed by in 1492, the Arawaks succumbed to the powerful Caribs, who had also paddled north from South America, conquering one island after another en route.

St. Vincent's mountains and forests thwarted European settlement, so as colonization advanced elsewhere in the Caribbean, many Caribs fled to St. Vincent. In 1626, the French did establish a colony, but their success was short-lived; England took over a year later. As "possession" of the island seesawed between France and England, the Caribs continued to make complete European colonization impossible. Ironically, a rift in the Carib community itself enabled the Europeans to gain a foothold.

In 1675, African slaves who had survived a Dutch shipwreck were welcomed into the Carib community. Over time, the Carib nation became, for all intents and purposes, two nations—one composed of the original Yellow Caribs; the other, the so-called Black Caribs or Garifuna. Relations between the two groups were often strained. In 1719, tensions rose so high that the Yellow Caribs united with the colonial French against the Black Caribs in what is called the First Carib War. The Black Caribs ultimately retreated to the hills but continued to resist the Europeans.

The French established plantations, importing African slaves to work the fertile land. In 1763, the British claimed the island yet again, and a wave of Scottish slave masters arrived with indentured servants from India and Portugal. Communities of direct descendants of the Scots still live near St. Vincent's Dorsetshire Hill and on Bequia.

Meanwhile, the determined French backed the Black Caribs, their previous foe, against the British in 1795 in the Second Carib War (also known as the Brigands War), during which British plantations were ravaged and burned on the island's windward coast. Black Carib chief Chatoyer managed to push the British troops down the leeward coast to Kingstown. Subsequently, on Dorsetshire Hill high above the town, Chatoyer lost a duel with a British officer. The 5,000 surviving Black Caribs were rounded up and shipped off to Honduras—present-day Belize—where their Garifuna descendants remain to this day. The few remaining Yellow Caribs retreated to the remote northern tip of St. Vincent, near Sandy Bay, where many of their descendants now live. A monument to Chatoyer has been erected on Dorsetshire Hill, where there's a magnificent westward view over Kingstown and the Caribbean.

The issue of "possession" of St. Vincent has long since been resolved; the nation has been fully independent since 1979 (but remains a part of the British Commonwealth). The various ethnic groups have mixed considerably over the years, creating a unique heritage simply described today as "Vincentian."

Fodor'sChoice **Falls of Baleine.** The falls are impossible to reach by car, so book an
★ escorted, all-day boat trip from Villa Beach or the Lagoon Marina. The
boat ride along the coast offers scenic island views. When you arrive,
you have to wade through shallow water to get to the beach. Then local
guides help you make the easy five-minute trek to the 60-foot falls and
the rock-enclosed freshwater pool the falls create—wear a bathing suit
so you can take a dip.

✪ **Ft. Charlotte.** Started by the French in 1786 and completed by the British
★ in 1806, the fort was named for Queen Charlotte, wife of King George
III. It sits on Berkshire Hill, a dramatic promontory 2 mi (3 km) north
of Kingstown and 636 feet above sea level, with a stunning view of the
capital city and the Grenadines. Interestingly, cannons face inward—the
fear of attack by the French and their native allies was far greater than
any threat approaching from the sea, though, truth be told, the fort saw
no action. Nowadays, the fort serves as a signal station for ships; its
ancient cells house historical paintings of the island by Lindsay Prescott.

24

Georgetown. St. Vincent's second-largest city (and former capital), halfway up the island's east coast, is surrounded by acres and acres of
coconut groves. This is also the site of the now-defunct Mount Bentinck
sugar factory. A tiny, quiet town—with a few streets, small shops, a
restaurant or two, and modest homes—it's completely unaffected by
tourism. It's a convenient place to stop for a cool drink or snack or other
essential shopping while traveling along the windward coast.

Kingstown. The capital city of St. Vincent and the Grenadines is on the
island's southwestern coast. The town of 13,500 residents wraps around
Kingstown Bay; a ring of green hills and ridges, studded with homes,
forms a backdrop for the city. This is very much a working city, with
a busy harbor and few concessions to tourists. Kingstown Harbour is
the only deepwater port on the island.

A few gift shops can be found on and around **Bay Street,** near the harbor. Upper Bay Street, which stretches along the bay front, bustles with
daytime activity—workers going about their business and housewives
doing their shopping. Many of Kingstown's downtown buildings are
built of stone or brick brought to the island in the holds of 18th-century
ships as ballast (and replaced with sugar and spices for the return trip to
Europe). The Georgian-style stone arches and second-floor overhangs
on former warehouses create shelter from midday sun and the brief,
cooling showers common to the tropics.

Grenadines Wharf, at the south end of Bay Street, is busy with schooners loading supplies and ferries loading people bound for the Grenadines. The **cruise-ship complex,** just south of the commercial wharf,
has a mall with a dozen or more shops, plus restaurants, a post office,
communications facilities, and a taxi-minibus stand.

An almost infinite selection of produce fills the **Kingstown Produce
Market,** a three-story building that takes up a whole city block on
Upper Bay, Hillsboro, and Bedford streets in the center of town. It's
noisy, colorful, and open Monday through Saturday—but the busiest
times (and the best times to go) are Friday and Saturday mornings. In

A waterfall near Waillabou Bay, St. Vincent.

the courtyard, vendors sell local arts and crafts. On the upper floors, merchants sell clothing, household items, gifts, and other products.

Little Tokyo, so called because funding for the project was a gift from Japan, is a waterfront shopping area with a bustling indoor fish market and dozens of stalls where you can buy inexpensive homemade meals, drinks, ice cream, bread and cookies, clothing, trinkets, and even get a haircut.

St. George's Cathedral, on Grenville Street, is a pristine, creamy yellow Anglican church built in 1820. The dignified Georgian architecture includes simple wooden pews, an ornate chandelier, and beautiful stained-glass windows; one was a gift from Queen Victoria, who actually commissioned it for London's St. Paul's Cathedral in honor of her first grandson. When the artist created an angel with a red robe, she was horrified by the color and sent it abroad. The markers in the cathedral's graveyard recount the history of the island. Across the street is **St. Mary's Roman Catholic Cathedral of the Assumption,** built in stages beginning in 1823. The strangely appealing design is a blend of Moorish, Georgian, and Romanesque styles applied to black brick. Nearby, freed slaves built the **Kingstown Methodist Church** in 1841. The exterior is brick, simply decorated with quoins (solid blocks that form the corners), and the roof is held together by metal straps, bolts, and wooden pins. **Scots Kirk** was built from 1839 to 1880 by and for Scottish settlers but became a Seventh-Day Adventist church in 1952.

La Soufrière. This towering volcano, which last erupted in 1979, is 4,000 feet high and so huge in area that its surrounding mountainside covers virtually the entire northern third of the island. The eastern trail to the rim of the crater, a two-hour ascent, begins at Rabacca Dry River.

Layou Petroglyph Park. Just beyond the small fishing village of Layou, about 45 minutes north of Kingstown, petroglyphs (rock carvings) were carved into a giant boulder by pre-Columbian inhabitants in the 8th century. Arrange a visit through the Layou Tourism and Heritage Organization (☎ 784/454–8686). For $2, you will be escorted along the nature trail to the site. ⊠ *Layou* ☎ *784/451 8686* 🖼 *$2* 𝄐 *Daily 8–5.*

Mesopotamia Valley. The rugged, ocean-lashed scenery along St. Vincent's windward coast is the perfect counterpoint to the lush, calm leeward coast. In between, the fertile Mesopotamia Valley (nicknamed Mespo) has a view of dense rain forests, streams, and endless banana and coconut plantations. Breadfruit, sweet corn, peanuts, and arrowroot also grow in the rich soil here. Mountain ridges, including 3,181-foot Grand Bonhomme Mountain, surround the valley.

Fodor's Choice
★

Montreal Gardens. Welsh-born landscape designer Timothy Vaughn renovated 7½ acres of neglected commercial flower beds and a falling-down plantation house into a stunning yet informal garden spot. Anthurium, ginger lilies, birds-of-paradise, and other tropical flowers are planted in raised beds; tree ferns create a canopy of shade along the walkways. The gardens are in the shadow of majestic Grand Bonhomme Mountain, deep in the Mesopotamia Valley, about 12 mi (19 km) from Kingstown. ⊠ *Montreal St., Mesopotamia* ☎ *784/458–1198* 🖼 *$2* 𝄐 *Dec.–Aug., weekdays 9–5.*

Owia. The Carib village of Owia, on the island's far northeast coast about two hours from Kingstown, is the home of many descendants of the Carib people of St. Vincent. It's also the home of the **Owia Arrowroot Processing Factory.** Used for generations to thicken sauces and flavor cookies, arrowroot is now also used in pharmaceutical products and as a finish for high-quality computer paper. St. Vincent produces 90% of the world's supply of arrowroot, but that is only a tiny fraction of the maximum levels exported in the 1960s. Close to the village is the **Owia Salt Pond,** created by the pounding surf of the Atlantic Ocean, which flowed over a barrier reef of lava rocks and ridges. Picnic and take a swim before the long return trip to Kingstown.

Rabacca Dry River. This rocky gulch just north of Georgetown was carved from the earth by lava flow from the 1902 eruption of nearby **La Soufrière.** When it rains in the mountains, the riverbed changes from dry moonscape to a trickle to a gushing river within minutes.

☺
★

Wallilabou Bay. The *Pirates of the Caribbean* left its mark at Wallilabou (pronounced wally-la-*boo*), a location used for filming the opening scenes of "The Curse of the Black Pearl" film in 2003. Many of the buildings and docks built as stage sets remain, giving the pretty bay (a port of entry for visiting yachts) an intriguingly historic appearance. You can sunbathe, swim, picnic, or buy your lunch at Wallilabou Anchorage. This is a favorite stop for day-trippers returning from the Falls of Baleine and boaters anchoring for the evening. Nearby, at Wallilabou Heritage Park, there's a river with a small waterfall and pool, where you can take a freshwater plunge.

BEACHES

Argyle. Though this spectacular black-sand beach on St. Vincent's southeast (windward) coast is not safe for swimming, you'll love to watch the surf crashing here.

Indian Bay. South of Kingstown and just north of Villa Beach, this beach has golden sand but is slightly rocky; it's good for snorkeling.

Villa Beach. The long stretch of sand in front of the row of hotels and restaurants along the Young Island Channel varies from 20 to 25 feet wide to practically nonexistent. The broadest, sandiest part is in front of Beachcombers Hotel, which is also the perfect spot for sunbathers to get lunch and liquid refreshments.

WHERE TO EAT

Nearly all restaurants in St. Vincent specialize in local West Indian cuisine, although you can find chefs with broad culinary experience at a few hotel restaurants. Local dishes to try include callaloo (similar to spinach) soup, curried goat or chicken, rotis (turnovers filled with curried meat or vegetables), fresh-caught seafood (lobster, kingfish, snapper, and mahimahi), local vegetables (squashlike christophene, breadfruit, and pumpkin) and "provisions" (roots such as yams and dasheen), and tropical fruit (from avocados, breadfruit, mangoes, and soursop to pineapples and papaya). Fried or baked chicken is available everywhere, often accompanied by "rice 'n' peas" or *pelau* (seasoned rice). The local beer, Hairoun, is brewed according to a German recipe at Campden Park, just north of Kingstown. Sunset is the local rum.

WHAT TO WEAR

Restaurants are casual. You may want to dress up a little—long pants and collared shirts for gents, summer dresses or dress pants for the ladies—for an evening out at a pricey restaurant , *but none of the places listed below require gentlemen to wear a jacket or tie.* Beachwear, however, is never appropriate in restaurants.

$$–$$$
CARIBBEAN

✕ **Basil's Bar and Restaurant.** It's not just the air-conditioning that makes this restaurant cool. Downstairs at the Cobblestone Inn, Basil's is owned by Basil Charles, whose Basil's Beach Bar on Mustique is a hangout for the vacationing rich and famous. This is the Kingstown power-lunch venue. Local businesspeople gather for the daily buffet (weekdays) or full menu of salads, sandwiches, barbecued chicken, or fresh seafood platters. Dinner entrées of pasta, local seafood, and chicken are served at candlelit tables. There's a Chinese buffet on Friday, and takeout is available that night only. ⊠ *Cobblestone Inn, Upper Bay St., Kingstown* ☎ *784/457–2713* ☼ *Closed Sun.*

$–$$
CARIBBEAN
★

✕ **Cobblestone Roof-Top Bar & Restaurant.** To reach what is perhaps the most pleasant, the breeziest, and the most satisfying breakfast and luncheon spot in downtown Kingstown, diners must climb the equivalent of three flights of interior stone steps within the historic Cobblestone Inn. But getting to the open-air rooftop restaurant is half the fun, as en route diners get an up-close view of the 19th-century sugar (and later arrowroot) Georgian warehouse that is now a very appealing boutique inn. A full breakfast menu is available to hotel guests and the public alike. The luncheon menu ranges from homemade soups, salads (tuna, chicken, fruit, or tossed), sandwiches, or burgers and fries to full meals of roast beef, stewed chicken, or grilled fish served with rice, plantains, macaroni pie, and fresh local vegetables. Dee-licious! ⊠ *Upper Bay St., Kingstown* ☎ *784/456–1937* ⊗ *No dinner.*

$$$–$$$$
FRENCH
Fodor's Choice
★

✕ **The French Verandah.** Dining by candlelight on the waterfront terrace of Mariners Hotel means exquisite French cuisine with Caribbean flair—and one of the best dining experiences on St. Vincent. Start with a rich soup—traditional French onion, fish with aioli, or callaloo and conch—or escargots, stuffed crab back, or conch salad. Main courses include fresh fish and shellfish grilled with fresh herbs, garlic butter and lime, or creole sauce. Landlubbers may prefer beef bourguignonne, *suprème de poulet* (stuffed chicken breast), or beef tenderloin with béarnaise, Roquefort, or mushroom sauce. For dessert, the *mi-cuit,* a warm chocolate delicacy with vanilla ice cream, is to die for. Lighter, equally delicious fare is served at lunch. ⊠ *Mariners Hotel, Villa Beach* ☎ *784/453–1111* ⊕ *www.marinershotel.com* ⚓ *Reservations essential.*

$$–$$$
CONTINENTAL
★

✕ **Grenadine House.** The Sapodilla Room at Grenadine House is a hidden gem. Whet your appetite with a fruity cocktail at the West Indies Bar—the actual bar is from an old English pub, and a gallery of classic black-and-white stills of movie stars graces the walls. Move inside to the dining room and enjoy light and delicious seafood dishes; creamy pasta concoctions; and tasty beef, lamb, and chicken entrées that reflect Caribbean flavors. Local people come here for special occasions and business dinners, as this is one of the finest—certainly the most elegant—dining spots on St. Vincent. They also enjoy the live jazz in the bar on Friday night. ⊠ *Kingstown Park, Kingstown* ☎ *784/456–1800* ⊕ *www.grenadinehouse.com* ⚓ *Reservations essential.*

$–$$
CARIBBEAN
☾

✕ **Wallilabou Anchorage.** Halfway up the Caribbean coast of St. Vincent, this is a favorite luncheon stop for folks sailing the Grenadines, for day-trippers returning from a visit to the Falls of Baleine, and for landlubbers touring the leeward coast. The picturesque view of the bay is enhanced by the period stage sets left behind by the *Pirates of the Caribbean* filmmakers. Open all day (from 8 am), the bar-and-restaurant serves snacks, sandwiches, tempting West Indian dishes, and lobster in season. Ice, telephones, business services, and shower facilities are available to boaters. ⊠ *Leeward Hwy., Wallilabou Bay* ☎ *784/458–7270.*

$$$$
CONTINENTAL
Fodor's Choice
★

✕ **Young Island Resort Restaurant.** Take the ferry (a two-minute ride from Villa Beach) to Young Island for a delightful lunch or a very special romantic evening. Stone paths lead to candlelit tables, some in breezy, thatch-roof kiosks. Tiny waves lap against the shore. Five-course, prix-fixe dinners of grilled seafood, roast pork, succulent beef tenderloin, duck breast, and sautéed chicken are accompanied by local vegetables. Two or three choices are offered for each course, and a board of freshly made breads (coconut, raisin, banana, country white, cinnamon, or whole-grain wheat) is offered for your selection. Lunch is à la carte—soups, salads, grilled meats, or fish—and served on the beachfront terrace. ⊠ *1 Young Island Crossing, Young Island* ✉ *Box 211, St. Vincent VC0100* ☎ *784/458–4826* ⊕ *www.youngisland.com* ⚓ *Reservations essential.*

24

WHERE TO STAY

With a few exceptions—most notably, the enormous Buccament Bay Resort north of the capital city—tourist accommodations and facilities on St. Vincent are in either Kingstown or the Villa Beach area. All guest rooms have air-conditioning, TV, and phone, unless stated otherwise.

PRIVATE VILLAS

Since the island's air service has been limited to small planes operated by regional carriers, huge villa communities and condo complexes have been late to arrive in St. Vincent—though the international airport set to open in early 2012 likely will change that. The island's first villa community at Buccament Bay opened in summer 2010; many of the one- and two-bedroom town houses are available for vacation rentals.

The following reviews have been condensed for this book. Please go to Fodors.com for expanded reviews of each property.

¢
HOTEL
★
Beachcombers Hotel & Spa. At one of the most popular hotels in St. Vincent, guests are attracted by the great beachfront, comfortable rooms, friendly service, and lively atmosphere both day and night. **Pros:** great value and location; best beachfront in the area. **Cons:** popular with small groups so book well ahead; standard rooms are rather "standard" (upgrade to deluxe or penthouse rooms for a relatively insignificant extra fee). ⊠ *Villa Beach* ☎ *784/458–4283* ⊕ *www.beachcombershotel. com* ⊃ *27 rooms, 4 suites* ♿ *In-room: safe, kitchen (some), Internet, Wi-Fi. In-hotel: restaurant, room service, bar, pool, spa, business center* ⊺◯⊦ *Breakfast.*

$$$$
RESORT
✪
Fodor's Choice
★
Buccament Bay Resort. This luxury villa community, by far the largest resort in St. Vincent, with a full menu of activities and amenities, is on a pretty bay about a half-hour north of Kingstown. **Pros:** beautiful accommodations; lots of amenities; food and service are very good; great spot for soccer-playing kids. **Cons:** very expensive; ongoing construction (into 2012 and perhaps beyond) could be a distraction. ⊠ *Buccament Bay* ☎ *784/457–4100* ⊕ *www.buccamentbay.com* ⊃ *438 units* ♿ *In-room: safe, Wi-Fi. In-hotel: restaurants, bars, tennis courts, pools, gym, spa, beach, water sports, children's programs, business center* ⊺◯⊦ *All-inclusive.*

¢
INN
★
Cobblestone Inn. Near the waterfront in "the city," as Vincentians call Kingstown, this boutique hotel is cozy, convenient, inexpensive, and loaded with historic charm—but it's nowhere near a beach. **Pros:** convenient for an overnight stay if you're taking an early ferry to the Grenadines; historical atmosphere; fascinating architecture. **Cons:** mostly tiny rooms; wandering around the downtown streets at night is not recommended. ⊠ *Upper Bay St., Box 867, Kingstown* ☎ *784/456– 1937* ⊕ *www.thecobblestoneinn.com* ⊃ *20 rooms, 6 suites* ♿ *In-room: Internet, Wi-Fi. In-hotel: restaurant, bar* ⊺◯⊦ *No meals.*

$
HOTEL
★
Grand View Beach Hotel. The unobstructed view of the Grenadines from this stylish, family-run hotel on a very private promontory is very grand indeed. **Pros:** friendly, family-run boutique vibe; beautiful (grand) sunset views; lots of on-site amenities—including a squash court. **Cons:** that hike down to the beach; a rental car would be handy; a few rooms don't have air-conditioning. ⊠ *Villa Point* ☎ *784/458–4811* ⊕ *www.*

grandviewhotel.com ⟳ *19 rooms, 2 suites* ♿ *In-room: no a/c (some), safe, Internet, Wi-Fi. In-hotel: restaurants, room service, tennis court, bars, pool, gym, water sports* ❑ *No meals.*

$–$$
INN
★

⊞ **Grenadine House.** Favored by business travelers, this Victorian-style boutique inn is also perfect for vacationers who want modern comforts in an elegant setting but don't require planned activities or beachfront resort features. Pros: friendly atmosphere; very attractive rooms with both 110v and 220v electric outlets; excellent dining. Cons: quiet, residential area far from any beach and a $4 taxi ride to town. ⌂ *Box 2523, Kingstown Park, Kingstown VC0100* ☎ *784/458–1800, 866/659–8351, or 919/439–4227* ⊕ *www.grenadinehouse.com* ⟳ *20 rooms* ♿ *In-room: safe, Wi-Fi. In-hotel: restaurant, room service, bar, pool, gym, business center* ❑ *Breakfast.*

24

$
HOTEL

⊞ **Mariners Hotel.** This pleasant, small hotel on the Villa Beach waterfront, opposite Young Island, has large rooms, and each has a balcony or terrace facing the water or overlooking the small pool. Pros: restaurant's French cuisine; you may use lovely Young Island beach; many water sports available nearby. Cons: rooms large but rather simply decorated; bathrooms have showers, no tubs; pool small but refreshing. ✉ *Mariners Hotel, Villa Beach* ⌂ *Box 859, St. Vincent VC0100* ☎ *784/457–4000* ⊕ *www.marinershotel.com* ⟳ *21 rooms* ♿ *In-room: safe, Internet, Wi-Fi. In-hotel: restaurant, bar, pool, business center* ❑ *No meals.*

¢
RENTAL

⊞ **Rosewood Apartment Hotel.** Perched high on a hillside overlooking Villa Beach and Young Island, the view of the Grenadines from the patio or terrace of any of these self-contained apartments is mesmerizing—particularly at sunset. Pros: accommodating management, and what a view! Cons: not on the beach; steep driveway and hillside location may complicate casual strolls. ✉ *Rose Cottage, Villa* ☎ *784/457–5051* ⊕ *www.rosewoodsvg.com* ⟳ *9 rooms, 1 suite* ♿ *In-room: kitchen (some), Internet, Wi-Fi (some). In-hotel: restaurant, room service, business center* ❑ *No meals.*

$
HOTEL
★

⊞ **Sunset Shores Beach Hotel.** Down a long, steep driveway off the main road, this lemon-yellow, low-rise, family-owned hotel faces a narrow curve of Villa beachfront. Pros: picturesque location opposite Young Island; pool–bar area lovely at sundown; the price is right. Cons: room decor is attractive but undistinguished; beach is narrow and sometimes next-to-nothing. ✉ *Villa Beach* ⌂ *Box 849, St. Vincent VC0100* ☎ *784/458–4411* ⊕ *www.sunsetshores.com* ⟳ *32 rooms* ♿ *In-room: safe, Wi-Fi. In-hotel: restaurant, room service, bars, pool, beach, business center, water sports* ❑ *No meals.*

¢
INN

⊞ **Villa Lodge Hotel.** The venerable Villa Lodge has been welcoming guests since 1961, when a private hillside home was first transformed into a family-operated inn. Pros: inexpensive; catch a minibus at the door to go to town or Villa Beach; rooms have both 110v and 220v outlets; restaurant is very good. Cons: rooms are large but not fancy; street noise may be an issue in front rooms. ✉ *Indian Bay* ⌂ *Box 1191, St. Vincent VC0100* ☎ *784/458–4641* ⊕ *www.villalodgehotel.com* ⟳ *11 rooms, 8 apartments* ♿ *In-room: safe, Internet. In-hotel: restaurant, bars, pool, business center* ❑ *No meals.*

Young Island Resort.

$$$$
RESORT
☕
Fodor's Choice
★

🔲 **Young Island Resort.** One of St. Vincent's two true resorts is 200 yards offshore (a three-minute ride from Villa Beach by hotel launch) on its own, exclusive 35-acre island, where 29 elegant, airy cottages dot the hillside. **Pros:** St. Vincent's best (white-sand) beach; casually elegant environment; great honeymoon choice or wedding venue; also appropriate for families. **Cons:** no a/c in some rooms; other than Wi-Fi, no in-room communication devices (unless that appeals to you). ✉ *1 Young Island Crossing, Young Island ☎ Box 211, St. Vincent VC0100* ☎ *784/458–4826* ⊕ *www.youngisland.com* ⤴ *23 cottage rooms, 6 cottage suites* ♿ *In-room: no a/c (some), no phone, safe, no TV, Wi-Fi. In-hotel: restaurant, room service, tennis court, bars, pool, spa, beach, business center, water sports* ⏀ *Some meals.*

NIGHTLIFE

Nightlife in St. Vincent consists mostly of once-a-week (in season) hotel barbecue buffets with a steel band or a local string band (usually older gents who play an assortment of string instruments). Jump-ups, so called because the lively calypso music makes listeners jump up and dance, happen around holidays, festivals, and Vincy Mas—St. Vincent's Carnival—which begins in late June and is the biggest cultural event of the year. At a couple of nightspots in Kingstown and at Villa Beach, you can join Vincentians for late-night dancing to live or recorded reggae, hip-hop, and soca music.

DANCE AND MUSIC CLUBS

Dance clubs generally charge a cover of $10 (EC$25), slightly more for headliners. The **Aquatic Club** (✉ *Villa Beach* ☎ 784/458–4205) features live local music on most Friday and Saturday nights. The **Attic Sports Bar** (✉ *1 Melville St., Kingstown* ☎ 784/457–2558) is above the KFC; you'll hear international jazz and blues on Sunday night.

SHOPPING

The 12 small blocks that hug the waterfront in **downtown Kingstown** compose St. Vincent's main shopping district. Among the shops that sell goods to fulfill household needs are a few that sell local crafts, gifts, and souvenirs. Bargaining is neither expected nor appreciated. The **cruise-ship complex,** on the waterfront in Kingstown, has a collection of a dozen or so boutiques, shops, and restaurants that cater primarily to cruise-ship passengers but welcome all shoppers. The best souvenirs of St. Vincent are intricately woven straw items, such as handbags, hats, slippers, baskets, and grass mats that range in size from place mats to room-size floor mats. If you're inclined to bring home a floor mat, pack a few heavy-duty plastic bags and some twine. The mats aren't heavy and roll or fold rather neatly; wrapped securely and tagged, they can be checked or carried on board as luggage for the flight home. Otherwise, local artwork and carvings are available in galleries, from street vendors, and in shops at the cruise-ship complex.

24

ANTIQUES AND FURNITURE

At **Basil's** (✉ *Villa* ☎ 784/456–2602), near the Young Island ferry dock and Mariners Hotel, is St. Vincent's only antiques and furniture store. Specializing in 200-year-old Asian pieces and the latest creations from Bali, India, and Africa, Basil's collection appeals to fine-furniture collectors as well as anyone seeking interesting, affordable objets d'art for either home or garden. Even if you're just looking, you might be smitten by the French wines, chocolates, and cheeses.

DUTY-FREE GOODS

At **Gonsalves Duty-Free Liquor** (✉ *Airport Departure Lounge, Arnos Vale* ☎ 784/456–4781), spirits and liqueurs are available at discounts of up to 40%. **Voyager** (✉ *R. C. Enterprises Ltd. Halifax St., Kingstown* ☎ 784/456–1686), one of the few duty-free shops in St. Vincent, has a very small selection of cameras, electronics, watches, china, and jewelry.

FOOD

Whether you're putting together a picnic, stocking your kitchenette, provisioning a yacht, looking for locally made seasoning sauces, or just want some snacks, **C. K. Greaves Supermarket** (✉ *Upper Bay St., Kingstown* ☎ 784/457–1074) is the main supermarket and your best bet. **Sunrise Supermarket** in Arnos Vale, across the road from the airport, is owned by the same company. Both can be reached by the same phone number, and either store will deliver your order to the dock. **Gourmet Food** (✉ *Calliaqua* ☎ 784/456–2987 ⊕ *www.gourmetfoodsvg.com*) specializes in delicious breads and imported cheeses and meats, as well as a full range of deli items and other tasty tidbits.

Don't miss visiting **Market Square** (⊠ *Bay and Bedford Sts., Kingstown* ☏ *No phone*). The market is a three-story enclosed building open daily (except Sunday), but really bustles on Friday and Saturday mornings when vendors bring their produce, meats, and fish to market.

LOCAL ART AND HANDICRAFTS

★ The **Little Art Gallery** (⊠ *Downstairs, Grand View Grill, Indian Bay* ☏ *784/458–4811*) is owned and operated by Caroline Sardine, an accomplished artist and daughter of the owners of Grand View Beach Hotel. Many of her paintings are on display in the hotel; in the gallery, she offers original art (her own and that of others), along with handcrafted items such as pottery, ceramics, coconut toys, handmade dolls, painted calabashes ("bashees"), goatskin drums, and mahogany carvings. The gallery is in the hotel's beachfront restaurant and is open daily (except Monday) from 2 pm. **Nzimbu Browne** (⊠ *McKie's Hill, Kingstown* ☏ *784/457–1677* ⊕ *www.nzimbu-browne.com*) is a self-taught Vincentian craftsman, artist, musician, and drum maker. He is best known for his original banana art, which he creates from dried banana leaves, carefully selecting and snipping varicolored bits and arranging them on pieces of wood to depict local scenes. Prices range from $15 or $20 for smaller items to several thousands of dollars for larger works sold in galleries. Browne has a kiosk in front of his home but often sets up shop on Bay Street, near the Cobblestone Inn. **St. Vincent Craftsmen's Centre** (⊠ *Frenches St., Kingstown* ☏ *784/457-2516*), three blocks from the wharf, sells locally made grass floor mats, place mats, and other straw articles, as well as batik cloth, handmade West Indian dolls, hand-painted calabashes, and framed artwork. No credit cards are accepted. On the leeward coast about a half-hour's drive north of Kingstown, **Wallilabou Craft Centre** (⊠ *Leeward Hwy., Wallilabou* ☏ *784/456–0078*) was established in 1986 as a local cooperative where villagers can learn various techniques for weaving straw and other natural fibers. Workers create baskets, handbags, hats, toys, and other items that are sold in the Kingstown market and make good souvenirs of a visit to St. Vincent.

SPORTS AND ACTIVITIES

BICYCLING

Bicycles can be rented for about $25 per day, but roads aren't conducive to leisurely cycling. Serious cyclists, however, will enjoy mountain biking in wilderness areas. **Sailor's Wilderness Tours** (⊠ *Middle St., Kingstown* ☏ *784/457–1712, 784/457–9207 after hours* ⊕ *www.sailortours.com*) takes individuals or groups on half-day bike tours for $50 per person (which includes 21-speed mountain-bike rental).

BOATING AND FISHING

Fodor's Choice From St. Vincent you can charter a monohull or catamaran (bare-
★ boat or complete with captain, crew, and cook) to weave you through the Grenadines for a day or a week of sailing—or a full-day fishing trip. One of the most spectacular cruising areas in the world, particularly for sailing, the Grenadines are close enough to allow landfall at a different island nearly every day, yet far enough apart, in some

cases, to experience true blue-water sailing. Bequia and Union Island have excellent yacht services and waterfront activity. Mustique is a dream destination, as is Mayreau. Visitors on yachts are welcome to dine at the private Palm Island and Petit St. Vincent resorts. Canouan has come alive in the past few years, and the Tobago Cays are a don't-miss destination for snorkeling and diving. Boats of all sizes and degrees of luxury are available. Bareboat charter rates in high season start at about $260 per day for monohull sailing yachts and $600 per day for catamarans; add $120 per day for a captain and $110 per day for a chef. Rates for a crewed luxury sailing yacht begin at about $7,800 per week for two guests up to $30,000 or more for boats that accommodate 8 or 10 guests. Fishing trips cost about $400 for a half day and $600 for a full day. **Barefoot Yacht Charters** (⊠ *Blue Lagoon, Ratho Mill* ☎ *784/456–9526* ⊕ *www.barefootyachts.com*) has a fleet of catamarans and monohulls in the 32- to 50-foot range. **Crystal Blue Sportfishing Charters** (⊠ *Indian Bay* ☎ *784/457–4532*) offers sportfishing charters on a 34-foot pirogue for both amateur and serious fishermen. **Sunsail** (⊠ *Blue Lagoon, Ratho Mill* ☎ *784/458–4308* ⊕ *www.sunsail.com*) charters bareboat and crewed yachts ranging from 30 feet to 50 feet. **TMM Yacht Charters** (⊠ *Blue Lagoon, Ratho Mill* ☎ *784/456–9608* ⊕ *www.sailtmm.com*) offers fully equipped yachts and catamarans that range from 38 to 51 feet, either bareboat or crewed.

DIVING AND SNORKELING

Fodor's Choice ★ Novices and advanced divers alike will be impressed by the marine life in the waters around St. Vincent—brilliant sponges, huge deep-water coral trees, and shallow reefs teeming with colorful fish. Many sites in the Grenadines are still virtually unexplored. Most dive shops offer three-hour beginner "resort" courses, full certification courses, and excursions to reefs, walls, and wrecks throughout the Grenadines. A single-tank dive costs about $65; a two-tank, $115; a 10-dive package, $550. All prices include equipment. It can't be emphasized enough, however, that the coral reef is extremely fragile, and you must only look and never touch.

St. Vincent, "the critter capital of the Caribbean," is ringed by one long, almost continuous reef. The best dive spots are in the small bays along the western coast between Kingstown and Layou; many are within 20 yards of shore and only 20 to 30 feet down. **Anchor Reef** has excellent visibility for viewing a deep-black coral garden, schools of squid, sea horses, and maybe a small octopus. **Critter Corner**, just 600 feet off Indian Bay beach, is St. Vincent's hallmark "muck" dive site—a wealth of marine life lurks in and among the sand, silt, sea grass, and boulders. The **Forest**, a shallow dive, is still dramatic, with soft corals in pastel colors and schools of small fish. **New Guinea Reef** slopes to 90 feet and can't be matched for its quantity of corals and sponges. The pristine waters surrounding the **Tobago Cays**, in the southern Grenadines, will give you a world-class diving or snorkeling experience.

Dive Fantasea (⊠ *Villa Beach* ☎ *784/457–5560 or 784/457–5577*) offers dive and snorkeling trips to the St. Vincent coast and the Tobago Cays. **Dive St. Vincent** (⊠ *Young Island Dock, Villa Beach* ☎ *784/457–4714 or 784/457–4928* ⊕ *www.divestvincent.com*) is where NAUI- and

PADI-certified instructor Bill Tewes and his two certified dive masters offer beginner and certification courses for ages eight and up, advanced water excursions along the St. Vincent coast and to the southern Grenadines for diving connoisseurs, and an introductory scuba lesson for novices. **Indigo Dive** (⊠ *St. Vincent Yacht Club, Ratho Mill* ☎ *784/493–9494* ⊕ *www.indigodive.com*) tailors dive experiences for divers of all experience levels.

GUIDED TOURS

Several operators on St. Vincent offer sightseeing tours on land or by sea. Per-person prices range from $25 for a two-hour tour to the Botanical Garden to $150 for a day sail to the Grenadines. A full-day tour around Kingstown and either the leeward or windward coast, including lunch, will cost about $65 per person. You can arrange for informal land tours through taxi drivers, who double as knowledgeable guides. Expect to pay $20 to $25 per hour for up to four people.

Fantasea Tours (⊠ *Villa Beach, St. Vincent* ☎ *784/457–5555* ⊕ *www.fantaseatours.com*) will take you on one of a fleet of powerboats to the Falls of Baleine, Bequia, and Mustique, or to the Tobago Cays for snorkeling. For bird-watchers, hikers, and ecotourists, **HazECO Tours** (⊠ *Kingstown, St. Vincent* ☎ *784/457–8634* ⊕ *www.hazecotours.com*) offers wilderness tours, bird-watching expeditions, and hikes to explore the natural beauty and see historic sites throughout St. Vincent. **Sailor's Wilderness Tours** (⊠ *Middle St., Kingstown, St. Vincent* ☎ *784/457–1712*) runs the gamut, from a comfortable sightseeing drive (by day or by moonlight) to mountain biking on remote trails to a strenuous hike up La Soufrière volcano—usually under the expert guidance of Trevor "Sailor" Bailey himself. **Sam's Taxi Tours** (⊠ *Cane Garden, St. Vincent* ☎ *784/456–4338, 784/458–3686 in Bequia*) offers half- and full-day tours of St. Vincent, as well as hiking tours to La Soufrière and scenic walks along the Vermont Nature Trails. Sam's also operates a tour on Bequia that includes snorkeling at Friendship Bay.

HIKING

St. Vincent offers hikers and trekkers a choice of experiences: easy, scenic walks near Kingstown; moderately difficult nature trails in the central valleys; and exhilarating climbs through a rain forest to the rim of an active volcano. Bring a hat, long pants, and insect repellent if you plan to hike in the bush.

Fodor's Choice
★ **La Soufrière**, the queen of climbs, is St. Vincent's active volcano (which last erupted in April 1979). Approachable from either the windward or leeward coast, this is *not* a casual excursion for the inexperienced—the massive mountain covers nearly the entire northern third of the island. Climbs are all-day excursions. You'll need stamina and sturdy shoes to reach the top and peek into the mile-wide (1½-km-wide) crater at just over 4,000 feet. Be sure to check the weather before you leave; hikers have been disappointed to find a cloud-obscured view at the summit. You can arrange for a guide ($25 to $30) through your hotel, the Tourism Authority, or tour operators. The eastern approach is most popular. In a four-wheel-drive vehicle you pass through Rabacca Dry River, north of Georgetown, and the Bamboo

Forest; then it's a two-hour, 3½-mi (5½-km) hike to the summit. If you're approaching from the west, near Châteaubelair, the climb is longer—6 mi (10 km)—and rougher, but even more scenic. If you hike up one side and down the other, you must arrange in advance to be picked up at the end.

Trinity Falls, in the north, requires a trip by a four-wheel-drive vehicle from Richmond Bay to the interior, then a steep two-hour climb to a crystal-clear river and three waterfalls, one of which forms a whirlpool where you can take a refreshing swim.

Vermont Nature Trails are two hiking trails that start near the top of the Buccament Valley, 5 mi (8 km) north of Kingstown. A network of 1½-mi (2½-km) loops passes through bamboo, evergreen forest, and rain forest. In the late afternoon you may be lucky enough to see the rare St. Vincent parrot, *Amazona guildingii*.

24

THE GRENADINES

The Grenadine Islands are known for great sailing, excellent scuba diving and snorkeling, magnificent beaches, and unlimited chances to relax with a picnic, watch the sailboats, and wait for the sun to set. Each island has a different appeal. Whether you like quiet, nonstop activity, or socializing (as long as you're not looking for wild nightlife), the Grenadines may be your thing.

BEQUIA

Bequia (pronounced *beck*-way) is a Carib word meaning "island of the cloud." Hilly and green, with several gold-sand beaches, Bequia is 9 mi (14½ km) south of St. Vincent's southwestern shore; with a population of 5,000, it's the largest of the Grenadines. Although boatbuilding, whaling, and fishing have been the predominant industries here for generations, sailing has now become almost synonymous with Bequia. Picturesque Admiralty Bay is a favored anchorage for both privately owned and chartered yachts. Lodgings range from comfortable resorts and villas to cozy West Indian–style inns. Bequia's airport and frequent ferry service from St. Vincent make this a favorite destination for day-trippers, as well. The ferry docks in Port Elizabeth, a tiny town with waterfront bars, restaurants, and shops where you can buy handmade souvenirs, including the exquisitely detailed model sailboats for which Bequia has become famous. The Easter Regatta is held during the four-day Easter weekend, when revelers gather to watch boat races and celebrate Bequia's seafaring traditions with food, music, dancing, and competitive games.

EXPLORING BEQUIA

To see the views, villages, beaches, and boatbuilding sites around Bequia, hire a taxi at the jetty in Port Elizabeth. Several usually line up under the almond trees to meet each ferry from St. Vincent. The driver will show you the sights in a couple of hours, point out a place for lunch, and drop you (if you wish) at a beach for swimming and snorkeling and pick you up later on. Negotiate the fare in advance, but expect

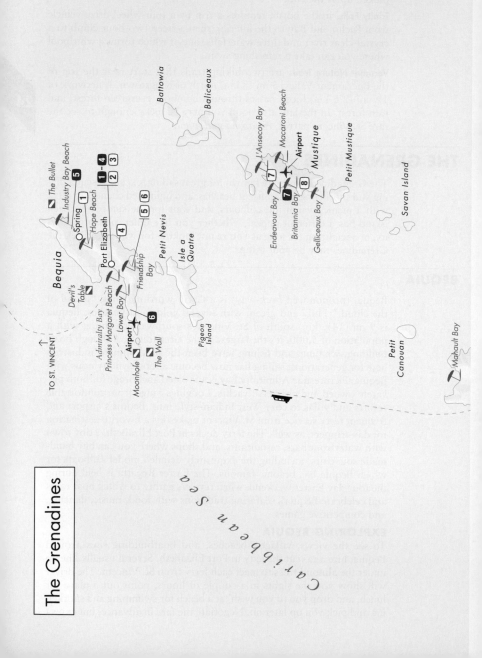

The Grenadines

Caribbean Sea

TO ST. VINCENT

Bequia

The Bullet

Industry Bay Beach

Spring

Hope Beach

Port Elizabeth

Devil's Table

Admiralty Bay

Princess Margaret Beach

Lower Bay

Moonhole

Airport

The Wall

Friendship Bay

Petit Nevis

Isle a Quatre

Pigeon Island

Petit Canouan

Mahault Bay

Battowia

Baliceaux

L'Ansecoy Bay

Macaroni Beach

Airport

Mustique

Endeavour Bay

Britannia Bay

Gelliceaux Bay

Petit Mustique

Savan Island

1 – 4

1 2 3

4

5

5 6

6

7

7

8

to pay about $25 per hour for the tour. Water taxis are available for transportation between the jetty in Port Elizabeth and the beaches. The cost is $6 (EC$15) per person each way, but keep in mind that most of these operators are not regulated: ride at your own risk.

Admiralty Bay. This huge sheltered bay on the leeward side of Bequia is a favorite anchorage of yachters. Year-round it's filled with boats; in season they're moored cheek by jowl. It's the perfect spot for watching the sun dip over the horizon each evening—either from your boat or from the terrace bar of one of Port Elizabeth's bay-front hotels.

Hamilton Battery/Ft. Hamilton. Just north of Port Elizabeth, high above Admiralty Bay, the 18th-century fort was built to protect the harbor from marauders. Today it's a place to enjoy a magnificent view.

Mt. Pleasant. Bequia's highest point (an elevation of 881 feet) is a reasonable goal for a hiking trek. Alternatively, it's a pleasant drive. The reward is a stunning view of the island and surrounding Grenadines.

★ **Old Hegg Turtle Sanctuary.** In the far northeast of the island, Orton "Brother" King, a retired skin-diving fisherman, tends to more than 200 endangered hawksbill turtles until they can be released back into the sea. He'll be glad to show you around and tell you how his project is increasing the turtle population in Bequia. ⊠ *Park Beach, Industry* ☎ *784/458–3245* ⊕ *www.turtles.bequia.net* ⊠ *$5 donation requested* ⊙ *By appointment only.*

★ **Port Elizabeth.** Bequia's capital, referred to locally as "the harbour," is on the northeastern side of Admiralty Bay. The ferry from St. Vincent docks at the jetty in the center of the tiny town, which is only a few blocks long and a couple of blocks deep. Walk north along Front Street, which faces the water, to the open-air market, where you can buy local fruits and vegetables and some handicrafts; farther along, you can find the model-boat-builders' workshops for which Bequia is renowned. Walking south from the jetty, Belmont Walkway meanders along the bay front past shops, cafés, restaurants, bars, and small hotels.

BEACHES

Friendship Bay. This horseshoe-shape, mile-long (1½-km-long), protected
Fodor's Choice beach on Bequia's midsouthern coast can be reached by land taxi. It's a
★ great beach for swimming, snorkeling, and windsurfing.

Hope Bay. Getting to this beach facing Bequia's windward side involves a long taxi ride (about $10) and a mile-long (1½-km-long) walk downhill on a semipaved path. Your reward is a magnificent crescent of white sand, total seclusion, and—if you prefer—nude bathing. Be sure to ask your taxi driver to return at a prearranged time. Bring your own lunch and drinks; there are no facilities. Even though the surf is fairly shallow, swimming may be dangerous because of the undertow.

Industry Bay. This nearly secluded beach is fringed with towering palms on the northeastern (windward) side of the island; getting here requires transportation from Port Elizabeth. This beach is good for snorkelers, but there could be a strong undertow. Bring a picnic; the nearest facilities are at Firefly Bequia resort, about a 10- to 15-minute walk.

Port Elizabeth, Bequia.

☾ **Lower Bay.** This broad, palm-fringed beach south of Port Elizabeth and
Fodor'sChoice Princess Margaret Beach is reachable by land or water taxi or a healthy
★ hike from town. It's an excellent beach for swimming and snorkeling.
There are restaurants here (Mango's Beach Bar, De Reef), as well as
facilities to rent water-sports equipment.

☾ **Princess Margaret Beach.** Quiet and wide, with a natural stone arch at
★ one end, the beach is not far from Port Elizabeth's Belmont Walkway
but access will require a water- or land-taxi ride. It's a popular spot for
swimming, snorkeling, or snoozing under the palm and sea grape trees.
Plan to have lunch at Max's Bar.

WHERE TO EAT

Dining on Bequia ranges from casual local-style meals to more elaborate
cuisine, and the food and service are both consistently good. Barbecues
at Bequia's hotels mean spicy West Indian seafood, chicken, and beef,
plus a buffet of side salads, vegetable dishes, and sweet desserts.

$$ ✕ **Dawn's Creole.** It's worth the trip to Industry for the delicious West
CARIBBEAN Indian food and the view. Lunch options include sandwiches, rotis,
fresh mutton, "goat water" (a savory soup with bits of goat meat and
root vegetables), fresh fish, and conch. At dinner (by reservation only),
the five-course creole seafood, lobster, or vegetarian specials include
the christophene (chayote) and breadfruit accompaniments for which
Dawn's is known. Barbecue is always available on request. There's
live music at Sunday brunch; full-moon grill parties feature country-
and-western music. ✉ *Creole Garden Hotel, Industry* ☎ *784/458–3715*
✍ *Reservations essential.*

¢–$ ✕**De Reef.** This café-restaurant on Lower Bay is the primary feeding
CARIBBEAN station for long, lazy beach days. When the café closes at dusk, the restaurant takes over—if you've made reservations, that is. For breakfast (from 7) or a light lunch, the café bakes its own breads, croissants, coconut cake, and cookies—and blends fresh juices to accompany them. For a full lunch or dinner, conch, lobster, whelk, and shrimp are treated the West Indian way, and the mutton curry is famous. Every other Saturday in season there's a seafood buffet dinner accompanied by live music; on Sunday afternoon there's a music jam. ✉ *Lower Bay* ☎ *784/458–3958* ⚓ *Reservations essential* ▭ *No credit cards.*

$$–$$$ ✕**Frangipani.** It's a perfect spot for a harborside breakfast or lunch; but
CARIBBEAN just before sunset, the yachting crowd comes ashore to what is argu-
★   ably the most popular gathering spot in Bequia—the Frangipani Hotel's waterfront bar. After a drink and a chat, the mood turns romantic, with candlelight and excellent Caribbean cuisine in the open-air dining room. The à la carte menu emphasizes seafood and local dishes. On Monday night in high season, a local string band plays catchy tunes; on Friday night, folksingers entertain. The Thursday Frangi barbecue buffet (about $30) is accompanied by steel-band music and a jump-up. ✉ *Frangipani Hotel, Belmont Walkway, Admiralty Bay, Port Elizabeth* ☎ *784/458–3255* ⊕ *www.frangipanibequia.com* ⚓ *Reservations essential.*

$$–$$$ ✕**Gingerbread.** The airy dining verandah at the Gingerbread Hotel
ECLECTIC offers all-day dining and a panoramic view of Admiralty Bay and all
☾   the waterfront activity. The lunch crowd enjoys barbecued beef kebabs
★   or chicken with fried potatoes or onions, grilled fish, homemade soups, salads, and sandwiches. In the evening, steaks, seafood, and curries are specialties of the house. Save room for warm, fresh gingerbread— served here with lemon sauce. In season, dinner is often accompanied by live music. ✉ *Gingerbread Hotel, Belmont Walkway, Admiralty Bay, Port Elizabeth* ☎ *784/458–3800* ⊕ *www.gingerbreadhotel.com* ⚓ *Reservations essential.*

$$–$$$ ✕**L'Auberge des Grenadines.** Owned by the French-born Jacques
FRENCH Thevenot and his Vincentian wife, Eileen, this fine French restaurant
★   on the north shore of Admiralty Bay is convenient for the yachting crowd, day-trippers, and anyone staying awhile. The extensive menu marries French and West Indian cuisines: seafood and local vegetables prepared with a French twist. Lobster is a specialty; select your own from the lobster pool. Light salads and sandwiches are available at lunch. Choose dinner from either the à la carte or prix-fixe ($30) menu. Delicious baguettes and delicate pastries round out any meal. ✉ *Hamilton, Admiralty Bay, Port Elizabeth* ☎ *784/458–3555* ⊕ *www. caribrestaurant.com* ⚓ *Reservations essential.*

$–$$ ✕**Mac's Pizzeria.** Overheard at the dock in Mustique: "We're sailing
PIZZA over to Bequia for pizza." The two-hour sunset sail to Admiralty Bay
☾   is worth the trip to Mac's, which has been serving brick-oven pizza in
★   Bequia since 1980. Choose from 17 mouthwatering toppings (including lobster), or select homemade quiche, conch fritters, pita sandwiches, lasagna, or soups and salads. Mac's home-baked cookies, muffins, and banana bread (by the slice or the loaf) are great for dessert or a snack. Or top off your meal with a scoop or two of Marianne's homemade

ice cream in tropical flavors. The outdoor terrace has water views. ⊠ *Belmont Walkway, Admiralty Bay, Port Elizabeth* ☎ *784/458–3474* ⚑ *Reservations essential* ☾ *Closed Mon.*

WHERE TO STAY

In addition to several small hotels and inns, a number of villas are available for vacation rental in Spring, Friendship Bay, Lower Bay, and other scenic areas of Bequia. They're suitable for two people or for as many as a dozen, and the weekly rentals in high season run from as low as $560 a week for a "sweet and simple" villa to $9,000 or more for an elaborate villa with an Italian-style courtyard, gardens, and pool. **Grenadine Island Villas** (⊠ *Belmont, Port Elizabeth* ☎ *784/457–3739 or 784/457–3888* ⊕ *www.grenadinevillas.com*).

The following reviews have been condensed for this book. Please go to Fodors.com for expanded reviews of each property.

24

$$–$$$
RENTAL
☾

⌘ Bequia Beachfront Villas. Perfectly situated on mile-long (1½-km-long) Friendship Bay beach, this is an excellent alternative for couples traveling together, a group, or a family. **Pros:** perfect for families or small groups; villas are 20 feet from the water; huge accommodations; all the comforts of home. **Cons:** far from town; rent a jeep to get around; steep hill to road might be difficult for those with disabilities. ⊠ *Friendship Bay* ☎ *784/457–3423* ⊕ *www.fortrecoverybequia.com* ↪ *4 villas* ⚐ *In-room: kitchen, Wi-Fi. In-hotel: beach* ⟊ *No meals.*

$–$$
HOTEL
☾
Fodor's Choice
★

⌘ Bequia Beach Hotel & Villas. This three-story boutique hotel has 12 rooms that surround a pool and are furnished in contemporary style, with family suites that accommodate four. **Pros:** everything's brand-new; fabulous beach; great for families. **Cons:** lots of steps up to the restaurant and street level from beachfront suites; no TV except in villas—is that a problem? ⊠ *Box 225, Friendship Bay* ☎ *784/458–1600* ⊕ *www.bequiabeach.com* ↪ *11 rooms, 41 suites, 6 villas* ⚐ *In-room: safe, kitchen (some), no TV (some), Internet, Wi-Fi (some). In-hotel: restaurants, bars, pools, gym, spa, beach, water sports, business center* ⟊ *Breakfast.*

¢–$
HOTEL

⌘ Frangipani Hotel. The venerable Frangipani, a historic sea captain's home and also the birthplace of James Mitchell, former prime minister of St. Vincent and the Grenadines, is known for its welcoming waterfront bar and restaurant. **Pros:** great waterfront location; beautiful harbor view from hillside rooms; lively bar and restaurant at night. **Cons:** steep hillside not easy for anyone with disabilities; no air-conditioning in most rooms. ⊠ *Admiralty Bay, Belmont Walkway, Box 1, Port Elizabeth* ☎ *784/458–3255* ⊕ *www.frangipanibequia.com* ↪ *15 rooms, 10 with bath* ⚐ *In-room: no a/c (some), no phone, no TV (some), Wi-Fi. In-hotel: restaurant, room service, tennis court, bar, business center* ☾ *Closed Sept.* ⟊ *No meals.*

$
HOTEL
☾

⌘ Gingerbread Hotel. The breezy waterfront suites—each suitable for three guests—are large, modern, and stylishly decorated, with bedroom alcoves, adjoining salons, and full kitchens—but no air-conditioning. **Pros:** right in the middle of all the action; lovely waterfront suites suitable for three people; good casual restaurant; weekly rates available. **Cons:** you might miss air-conditioning if the breeze isn't brisk enough; no TV; skip the economy hillside apartments, even though they have a/c. ✉ *Belmont Walkway, Admiralty Bay, Box 191, Port Elizabeth* ☎ *784/458–3800* ⊕ *www.gingerbreadhotel.com* ⤳ *7 suites, 3 apartments* ♿ *In-room: no a/c (some), no phone, safe, kitchen, no TV, Wi-Fi. In-hotel: restaurant, bar, tennis court, water sports, business center* ⍩ *No meals.*

$ 🏚 **The Old Fort.** This stone greathouse of a former sugar estate is the
RENTAL   only fully restored historic plantation house in St. Vincent and the Grenadines. **Pros:** stunning location; attentive hosts; complimentary vehicle when booking the entire property. **Cons:** minimum stay one week; somewhat isolated; no beach for swimming. ✉ *Mt. Pleasant* ☎ *784/458–3440* ⊕ *www.theoldfort.com* ⤳ *6 rooms* ♿ *In-room: refrigerator (some), no TV, Wi-Fi. In-hotel: restaurant, bar, pool, business center* ⍩ *All-inclusive.*

$$$$ 🏚 **Spring House.** A long and winding ride up a dirt road to the top of
RENTAL   the Spring Estate brings you to Spring House, a magnificent villa that
★   can accommodate up to 16 guests in eight private suites arranged in two separate wings of the building. **Pros:** perfect for large families or wedding parties; extreme privacy; beautiful design and decor, fabulous gardens and sea views; beach transportation provided. **Cons:** isolated; bumpy dirt access road requires a jeep. ✉ *Spring* ☎ *784/493–7333* ⊕ *www.springhousebequia.com* ⤳ *8 rooms* ♿ *In-room: no phone, safe, Internet, Wi-Fi. In-hotel: pool* ⍩ *No meals.*

SHOPPING

Long renowned for their boatbuilding skills, Bequians have translated that craftsmanship to model-boat building. In their workshops in Port Elizabeth, you can watch as hair-thin lines are attached to delicate sails or individual strips of wood are glued together for decking. Other Bequian artisans create scrimshaw, carve wood, crochet, or work with fabric—designing or handpainting it first, then creating clothing and gift items for sale. Bequia's shops are mostly on Front Street and Belmont Walkway, its waterfront extension, just steps from the jetty where the ferry arrives in Port Elizabeth. North of the jetty, there's an open-air market; farther along the road, you'll find the model-boat-builders' shops. Opposite the jetty, at Bayshore Mall, shops sell ice cream, baked goods, stationery, gifts, and clothing; there's also a grocery, liquor store, pharmacy, travel agent, and bank. On Belmont Walkway, south of the jetty, shops and studios showcase gifts and handmade articles. Shops are open weekdays from 8 to 5, Saturday 8 to noon.

Bequia Bookshop (✉ *Belmont Walkway, Port Elizabeth* ☎ *784/458–3905*) has Caribbean literature, plus cruising guides and charts, Caribbean flags, beach novels, souvenir maps, and exquisite scrimshaw and whalebone penknives hand-carved by Bequian scrimshander Sam McDowell. You can visit the studio of French artist **Claude Victorine** (✉ *Lower Bay* ☎ *784/458–3150*) and admire her delicate, hand-painted, silk wall hangings and scarves. Her studio is open from noon to 7 pm; it's closed Friday. **Local Color** (✉ *Belmont Walkway, Port Elizabeth* ☎ *784/458– 3202*), above the Porthole restaurant—near the jetty—has an excellent and unusual selection of handmade jewelry, wood carvings, scrimshaw, and resort clothing; it's closed in October.

Fodor's Choice
★ **Mauvin's Model Boat Shop** (⊠ *Front St., Port Elizabeth* ☎ *784/458–3669*) is where you can purchase the handmade model boats for which Bequia is known. You can even special-order a replica of your own yacht. They're incredibly detailed and quite expensive—from a few hundred to several thousand dollars. The simplest models take about a week to make. **Noah's Arkade** (⊠ *Frangipani Hotel, Belmont Walkway, Port Elizabeth* ☎ *784/458–3424*) sells gifts, souvenirs, and contemporary arts and crafts from all over the Caribbean.

Fodor's Choice
★ **Sargeant Brothers Model Boat Shop** (⊠ *Front St., Port Elizabeth* ☎ *758/458–3344*) sells handcrafted, expertly rigged and authentically detailed model boats and will build custom models on commission.

SPORTS AND ACTIVITIES

24

BOATING AND SAILING

Fodor's Choice
★ With regular trade winds, visibility for 30 mi (48 km), and generally calm seas, Bequia is the primary venue for those sailing the Grenadines—which easily rates among the best blue-water sailing found anywhere in the world. At Port Elizabeth, you'll find all kinds of options: day sails or weekly charters, bareboat or fully crewed, monohulls or catamarans—whatever your pleasure. Prices for day trips start at about $125 per person.

Friendship Rose (⊠ *Port Elizabeth* ☎ *784/458–0886* ⊕ *www.friendshiprose. com*), an 80-foot schooner that spent its first 25 years ferrying both passengers and mail between Bequia and neighboring islands, was refitted in the late 1960s to take passengers on day trips from Bequia to Mustique, the Tobago Cays, and along the St. Vincent coast.

DIVING AND SNORKELING

About 35 dive sites around Bequia and nearby islands are accessible within 15 minutes by boat. The leeward side of the 7-mi (11-km) reef that fringes Bequia has been designated a marine park. The **Bullet,** off Bequia's northeast point, has limited access because of rough seas but is a good spot for spotting rays, barracuda, and the occasional nurse shark. **Devil's Table** is a shallow dive at the northern end of Admiralty Bay that's rich in fish and coral and has a sailboat wreck nearby at 90 feet. The **Wall** is a 90-foot drop, off West Cay. Expect to pay dive operators $70 for a one-tank and $106 for a two-tank dive, including equipment. Dive boats welcome snorkelers for about $20 per person, but for the best snorkeling in Bequia, take a water taxi to the bay at Moonhole and arrange a pickup time.

Bequia Dive Adventures (⊠ *Belmont Walkway, Admiralty Bay, Port Elizabeth* ☎ *784/458–3826* ⊕ *www.bequiadiveadventures.com*) offers PADI instruction courses and takes small groups on three dives daily; harbor pickup and return is included for customers staying on yachts. **Dive Bequia** (⊠ *Belmont Walkway, Admiralty Bay, Port Elizabeth* ☎ *784/458–3504* ⊕ *www.bequiadive.com*), based at the Gingerbread Hotel, offers dive and snorkel tours, night dives, and full equipment rental. Resort and certification courses are available.

The Canouan Resort.

CANOUAN

Halfway down the Grenadines chain, this tiny boot-shape island—3½ mi (5½ km) long and 1¼ mi (2 km) wide—has only about 1,200 residents. But don't let its historically slow pace and quiet ways fool you. Canouan (pronounced *can*-o-wan), which is the Carib word for "turtle," has a modern airport with an extended runway suitable for small to midsize jets. The island boasts one of the region's largest and most exquisite resorts, with a championship golf course and a world-class spa. It also claims four of the most pristine white-sand beaches in the Caribbean, and it's a busy port for yacht charters and diving expeditions to the Tobago Cays. Mt. Royal, the highest point on the island at 900 feet, offers panoramic 360-degree views of St. Vincent, all the Grenadines, and even St. Lucia on a clear day.

BEACHES

Godahl Beach. This lovely stretch of white-sand beach (pronounced *gud*-ul) is at the southern end of Carenage Bay and surrounded by The Canouan Resort property, including the resort's beach bar and restaurant and its spa. For beach access, nonguests must purchase a day package at The Canouan Resort front office.

Grand Bay. In the center of Canouan on the leeward side, Grand Bay is the island's longest beach and the site of Charlestown, the largest town, where ferries dock; it's also called Charlestown Bay.

Mahault Bay. This lovely but remote expanse of beach (pronounced *ma*-ho) is at the northern tip of the island, surrounded by Mt. Royal;

the beach is accessible through the Canouan Resort property or by sea. There are no changing, restroom, or refreshment facilities.

South Glossy Bay. This and other Glossy Bay beaches along the southwest (windward) coast of Canouan are absolutely spectacular. South Glossy Bay is within walking distance of the airport. There are no changing, restroom, or refreshment facilities.

WHERE TO STAY

The following reviews have been condensed for this book. Please go to Fodors.com for expanded reviews of each property.

$$$$
RESORT
C
Fodor's Choice
★

☒ The Canouan Resort. The guest accommodations at this full-service beach resort are in roomy villas that are sprinkled, amphitheater-style, around 300 acres of the resort's 1,200-acre property. **Pros:** beautiful accommodations; lots of activities for the entire family; and ahh, the spa! **Cons:** very expensive; everything is à la carte (except breakfast). ☒ *Carenage Bay, Canouan* ☎ *784/458–8000* ☞ *30 suites, 13 villas* ⌖ *In-room: safe, kitchen (some), Internet, Wi-Fi. In-hotel: restaurants, room service, bars, tennis courts, golf course, pool, gym, spa, beach, children's programs, business center, water sports* ❢❍❢ *Breakfast.*

$$$$
HOTEL
C
★

☒ Tamarind Beach Hotel & Yacht Club. Thatched roofs are a trademark of this low-rise beachfront hotel, owned by the same Italian consortium that owns the nearby superluxe Raffles property. **Pros:** good value on Canouan; excellent setting for diving and boating enthusiasts. **Cons:** no pool; standard rooms are small. ☒ *Charlestown* ☎ *784/458–8044* ⊕ *www.tamarindbeachhotel.com* ☞ *32 rooms, 8 suites* ⌖ *In-room: safe, kitchen (some), Wi-Fi. In-hotel: restaurants, bars, spa, beach, business center, water sports* ❢❍❢ *Breakfast.*

SPORTS AND ACTIVITIES

Fodor's Choice
★

BOATING

The Grenadines has some of the most superb cruising waters in the world. Canouan is at the midpoint of the Grenadines, an easy sail north to St. Vincent, Bequia, and Mustique or south to Mayreau, the Tobago Cays, and beyond. The **Moorings** (☒ *Charlestown* ☎ *784/482–0653* ⊕ *www.moorings.com*) operates next to Tamarind Beach Hotel & Yacht Club. It has bareboat and crewed yacht charters of monohulls and catamarans ranging in size from 38 to 52 feet.

DIVING AND SNORKELING

The mile-long (1½-km-long) reef and waters surrounding Canouan offer excellent snorkeling as well as spectacular sites for both novice and experienced divers. **Gibraltar,** a giant stone almost 30 feet down, is a popular site; plenty of colorful fish and corals are visible. **Windward Bay,** on Canouan's southeast coast, is a large lagoon protected by a barrier reef, making it perfect for snorkeling. The crystalline waters surrounding the nearby **Tobago Cays** offer marvelous diving and snorkeling.

One-tank dives cost $110 per dive; two-tank dives, $175 per dive; night dives, $130 per dive. A full range of PADI courses are offered; novices can take a Discover Scuba Diving course for $175. Three-hour snorkeling trips to the Tobago Cays cost $110 per person, including equipment.

Canouan Dive Center (✉ *Tamarind Beach Hotel, Charlestown* ☎ *784/528–8030* ⊕ *www.canouandivecenter.com*) is a full-service PADI facility that offers resort and certification courses and specializes in taking small groups of divers, whether beginners or experts, to the Tobago Cays and other nearby sites.

GOLF

The only 18-hole, championship golf course in St. Vincent and the Grenadines is also one of the best in the Caribbean. Located on The Canouan Resort property, it's operated by Trump Enterprises.

Fodor's Choice
★
Trump International Golf Club (✉ *The Canouan Resort, Carenage Bay* ☎ *784/458–8000*) is an 18-hole, par-72 championship course spread over 60 acres with unparalleled views. The first 9 holes of the Jim Fazio–designed course, along with holes 10 and 18, are in a pretty, green plain that stretches down to the sea. The rest have been carved into the mountainside, affording spectacular views of Canouan Island, the resort itself, and the surrounding Grenadines. The 13th hole offers a wraparound view of the Grenadines; it's also the most challenging, as its unforgiving green is at the edge of a cliff. Greens fees for 18 holes are $220 for resort guests, $300 for nonguests; for 9 holes, $135 (for resort guests only). Greens fees include a golf cart. Golf instruction and rental clubs are available, and a pro shop and lounge are in the resort.

MAYREAU

Mayreau (pronounced *my*-row) is minuscule—1½ square mi (4 square km). With the exception of 22 acres at its northern tip that was purchased in 1977 by a German-Canadian family and 21 acres that comprise the island's single (unnamed) village and were acquired by St. Vincent and the Grenadines, Mayreau is privately owned by heirs of the original French plantation owners. Only about 250 residents live in the hilltop village, and there are no proper roads. Guests at the resort on Saltwhistle Bay enjoy these natural surroundings in one of the prettiest locations in the Grenadines—one of the few spots where the calm Caribbean is separated from the Atlantic surf by only a narrow strip of beach. It's a favorite stop for boaters as well, who anchor in Saltwhistle Bay and come ashore for lunch or dinner. Except for water sports and hiking, there's not much to do—but everyone prefers it that way. For a day's excursion, you can hike up Mayreau's only hill (wear sturdy shoes) for a stunning view of the Tobago Cays. Then stop for a drink at Dennis' Hideaway and enjoy a swim at Saline Bay beach, where you may be joined by a boatload of cruise-ship passengers. This pretty little island is a favorite stop for small ships that ply the waters of the Grenadines and anchor just offshore for the day. The only access to Mayreau is by boat (ferry, private, or hired), which you can catch or arrange for at Union Island.

BEACHES

Saline Bay Beach. This beautiful 1-mi (1½-km) crescent of sand on the southwest coast has no facilities, but you can walk up the hill to Dennis' Hideaway for lunch or drinks. The adjacent dock is where the ferry that travels between St. Vincent and Union Island ties up, and small cruise ships occasionally anchor offshore to give passengers a beach break.

Fodor'sChoice
★
Saltwhistle Bay Beach. This beach at the northwestern tip of the island takes top honors—it's an exquisite crescent of powdery white sand, shaded by perfectly spaced palms, sea grape trees, and flowering bushes. It's also a popular anchorage for the yachting crowd, who stop for a swim and lunch or dinner at the beachfront Saltwhistle Bay Club.

WHERE TO STAY

The following reviews have been condensed for this book. Please go to Fodors.com for expanded reviews of each property.

¢
INN
▣ **Dennis' Hideaway.** Each room in this hilltop guesthouse has a private balcony with a perfect view of the sun as it sets over Saline Bay. **Pros:** great value; friendly atmosphere; good restaurant; good base for boaters and divers. **Cons:** no frills or amenities. ⊠ *Saline Bay* ☎ *784/458–8594* ⊕ *www.dennis-hideaway.com* ⇨ *5 rooms* ⚐ *In-room: no phone, no TV. In-hotel: restaurant, bar, pool* ▤ *No credit cards* ⑩ *Breakfast.*

$$$$
RESORT
★
▣ **Saltwhistle Bay Club.** Tom and Undine Potter purchased this idyllic spot in 1977, cleared the land just enough to build four double bungalows out of locally quarried stone and natural wood, and opened for business in 1979. **Pros:** delightfully natural; great anchorage; excellent all-day dining; fabulous beach. **Cons:** extremely remote—especially for landlubbers. ⊠ *Saltwhistle Bay* ☎ *784/458–8444* ⊕ *www.saltwhistlebay.com* ⇨ *8 units* ⚐ *In-room: safe, no TV. In-hotel: restaurant, bar, beach, business center, water sports* ☒ *Closed Sept. and Oct.* ⑩ *Some meals.*

SPORTS AND ACTIVITIES

BOATING AND FISHING

Yacht charters, drift-fishing trips, dive trips, and day sails can be arranged at **Dennis' Hideaway** (⊠ *Saline Bay* ☎ *784/458–8594* ⊕ *www. dennis-hideaway.com*). Expect to pay $40 per person for drift fishing for 1½ hours and $75–$100 per person (depending on the number of passengers) for a full day of sailing, swimming, and snorkeling—lunch included.

MUSTIQUE

This upscale haven, 18 mi (29 km) southeast of St. Vincent, is 3 mi (5 km) by 1¼ mi (2 km) at its widest point. The island is hilly and has several green valleys, each with a sparkling white-sand beach facing an aquamarine sea. The permanent population is about 300. Britain's late Princess Margaret put this small, private island on the map after owner Colin Tennant (Lord Glenconner) presented her with a 10-acre plot of land as a wedding gift in 1960 (Tennant had purchased the entire 1,400-acre island in 1958 for $67,500). The Mustique Company—which Tennant formed in 1968 to develop the copra, sea-island cotton, and sugarcane estate into the glamorous hideaway it has become—now manages the privately owned villas, provides housing for all island employees, and operates Mustique Villa Rentals. Arrangements must

Cotton House.

be made about a year in advance to rent one of the luxury villas that now pepper the northern half of the island.

Sooner or later, stargazers see the resident glitterati at Basil's Bar, the island's social center. Proprietor Basil Charles also runs a boutique crammed with clothes and accessories specially commissioned from Bali. A pair of cotton-candy-color, gingerbread-style buildings, the centerpiece of the tiny village, houses a gift shop and clothing boutique. There's a delicatessen–grocery to stock yachts and supply residents with fresh Brie and Moët; an antiques shop is filled with fabulous objets d'art to decorate those extraordinary villas—or to bring home.

The Mustique Blues Festival, held during the first two weeks of February, features artists from North America, Europe, and the Caribbean; shows occur nightly at Basil's Bar. The festival is quite a draw.

BEACHES

Endeavour Bay. This is the main beach used by guests of the Cotton House. Swimming and snorkeling are ideal, and a dive shop with watersports equipment rental is available on-site. The resort's Beach Café restaurant and bar are convenient for lunch or snacks.

Gelliceaux Bay. One of 10 marine conservation areas designated by St. Vincent and the Grenadines, this beach on the southwest coast is a perfect spot for snorkeling.

L'Ansecoy Bay. At the island's very northern tip, this broad crescent of white sand fringes brilliant turquoise water. Just offshore, the French liner *Antilles* went aground in 1971.

Macaroni Beach. Macaroni is Mustique's most famous stretch of fine white sand—offering swimming (no lifeguards) in moderate surf that's several shades of blue, along with a few palm huts and picnic tables in a shady grove of trees.

Fodor's Choice
★

WHERE TO EAT

$$$–$$$$
SEAFOOD
★

✗ **Basil's Bar.** Basil's is *the* place to be—and only partly because it's the *only* place to be in Mustique. This rustic eatery is simply a wood deck perched on bamboo stilts over the waves; there's a thatched roof, a congenial bar, and a dance floor that's open to the stars—in every sense. You never know what celebrity may show up at the next table. The food is simple and good—mostly seafood, homemade ice cream, burgers, and salads, great French toast and banana pancakes, the usual cocktails, and unusual wines. Wednesday is Jump Up & Barbecue Night, with live music; Sunday is Locals Night, with a buffet of local dishes. ⊠ *Britannia Bay* ☎ *784/488–8350* ⊕ *www.basilsmustique.com* ⚮ *Reservations essential.*

24

WHERE TO STAY

Except for the Cotton House and Firefly hotels, Mustique is an island of villas—74 of them, in fact. Villa rentals are arranged solely through **Mustique Villa Rentals** (⌂ *The Mustique Co., Ltd., Box 349, St. Vincent VC0100* ☎ *784/458–4621* ⊕ *www.mustique-island.com*), even though the villas are privately owned. Villas are all architecturally unique, with two to nine bedrooms. Rentals include a full staff (with a cook), laundry service, and a vehicle or two. Houses range from "rustic" (albeit with en suite bathrooms for every bedroom, phones, pools, and other amenities) to extravagant, expansive, faux-Palladian follies with resident butler. All are elegant and immaculately maintained. Weekly rentals run from $5,000 for a two-bedroom villa in the off-season to $55,000 for a palatial seven-bedroom villa in winter.

The following reviews have been condensed for this book. Please go to Fodors.com for expanded reviews of each property.

$$$$
RESORT
Fodor's Choice
★

Cotton House. Mustique's grand hotel, the main building of which was once an 18th-century cotton warehouse, has oceanfront rooms and suites with private walkways leading to the beach, a quartet of elegant ocean-view suites, and three poolside cottages. **Pros:** beautiful rooms; great attention to detail; the pillow menu; excellent dining. **Cons:** madly expensive; more sedate atmosphere than, say, Firefly. ⊠ *Endeavor Bay* ⌂ *Box 349, St. Vincent VC0100* ☎ *784/456–4777* ⊕ *www.cottonhouse.net* ⥹ *12 rooms, 5 suites, 3 cottages* ⚴ *In-room: no phone, safe, Wi-Fi. In-hotel: restaurants, tennis courts, bars, pool, gym, spa, beach, water sports, business center* ⊙ *Closed Sept. and Oct.* ⓄⓁ *Breakfast.*

$$$$
INN
★

Firefly Mustique. Tiny and charming, this exclusive, reclusive three-story aerie is wedged into dense tropical foliage on a steep hillside above Britannia Bay. **Pros:** relaxed and friendly spot; great ocean views from each room; the bar—a hangout for guests and visiting celebrities—features martini and champagne menus. **Cons:** very expensive; house-party atmosphere at the bar can get noisy at night. ⊠ *Britannia Bay* ⌂ *Box 349, St. Vincent VC0100* ☎ *784/488–8414* ⊕ *www.*

mustiquefirefly.com ⤴5 *rooms* ⚄ *In-room: safe, no TV, Wi-Fi. In-hotel: restaurant, room service, bar, pools, water sports, some age restrictions* ⍟ *Breakfast.*

SPORTS AND ACTIVITIES

Water-sports facilities are available at the Cotton House, and most villas include sports equipment. Four floodlighted tennis courts are near the airport for those whose villa lacks its own; there's a cricket field for the Brits (matches on Sunday afternoon), and motorbikes or "mules" (beach buggies) to ride around the bumpy roads rent for $75 per day.

DIVING AND SNORKELING

Mustique is surrounded by coral reefs, and nearly 20 dive sites are nearby. **Mustique Watersports** (⊠ *Cotton House, Endeavour Bay* ☎ *784/456–3486* ⊕ *www.mustique-island.com*) offers PADI instruction and certification and has a 28-foot, fully equipped dive boat. Rates are $110 for an introductory course, $85 for a one-tank dive, and $350 for a five-dive package. A special "bubble maker" introduction-to-diving course for children ages 8–11 costs $40. Snorkelers can rent a mask and fins for $10 per hour or $25 per day; snorkeling trips are $40 per person, with a two-person minimum.

HORSEBACK RIDING

Mustique is the only island in the Grenadines where you can find a fine thoroughbred horse or pony to ride. Daily excursions leave from the **Mustique Equestrian Centre** (☎ *784/488–8000* ⊕ *www.mustique-island. com*), which is one block from the airport. Rates are $65 per hour for an island trek; private lessons begin at $50. All rides are accompanied, and children over five years are allowed to ride.

PALM ISLAND

A private speck of land (only 135 acres), exquisite Palm Island used to be an uninhabited, mosquito-infested swamp called Prune Island. One intrepid family put heart and soul—as well as muscle and brawn—into taking the wrinkles out of the prune and rechristened it Palm Island. The Caldwell family cleaned up the five surrounding beaches, built bungalows, planted palm trees, and irrigated the swamp with seawater to kill the mosquitoes. The rustic getaway existed for 25 years before Palm Island's current owners, Elite Island Resorts, dolled up the property, and now it's one of the finest resorts in the Caribbean. Other than the resort, the island is populated only by a handful of privately owned villas. Access is via Union Island, 1 mi (1½ km) to the west and a 10-minute ride in the resort's launch.

WHERE TO STAY

The following review has been condensed for this book. Please go to Fodors.com for an expanded review.

Continued on page 956

GOLF IN THE CARIBBEAN

Is there anything better than sinking a 25-foot putt where palm trees sway and turquoise waves meet cerulean sky? Golfers love playing the first-rate Caribbean courses, where stunning views come with comfortable and luxurious resorts. Let the duffers lounge by the pool while you head off for a morning round before the sun gets too hot. You can always meet up on the 19th hole. Mild weather year-round means you can be digging out of a sand trap in the Dominican Republic or Barbados instead of digging out of a snowstorm back home.

With more than three dozen terrific courses from which to choose, golfers of all ages and abilities can find Nirvana, or at least a couple of fun holiday rounds in the Caribbean. The combination of high-end development and advances in lower-maintenance, drought-tolerant turf hybrids has sparked a boom for golf tourism. You will find iconic courses designed by top celebrities like Nicklaus, Player, Norman, Fazio, Dye, and a couple of Joneses. Every course isn't for every player—some are a bit worse for the wear, some are killer-tough, and others are quite costly. Look for golf packages, promotions, all-inclusives, and learning programs that include greens fees and equipment rentals to lessen the bite.

BEST CARIBBEAN GOLF COURSES

(A) Four Seasons Golf Course, Nevis

Majestic scenery, lush landscaping, and a $10 million renovation bring this Robert Trent Jones, Jr. up to par. The wicked layout winds through ravines and sugar mills, and is home to a monkey colony on the back nine, where the land elevates 400 feet to offer views of the 36-square-mile paradise.

(B) Temenos Golf Club, Anguilla

One of the finest golf experiences in the Caribbean has been re-opened and is now managed by Cap Juluca. Anguilla's first and only course, a $50 million creation of golf legend Greg Norman, was first opened in 2006 and offers dramatic elevation changes and water features on 13 holes. In planning the course, significant environmental efforts were undertaken to preserve and to enhance the island's natural habitats, protecting mangroves, salt marshes, dunes and an historic salt pond.

(C) Sandy Lane, Barbados

45 blissful holes on three spectacular courses. There are only 112 guest rooms at this superluxe enclave. The original "Old Nine" winds through the estate gardens, The "Country Club" has five lakes for challenge and pristine fairways, but it's Tom Fazio's famed "Green Monkey" that gets the bragging rights. It's strictly state of the art. The golf carts, included in the green fees of the Country Club and Green Monkey courses, are fitted with a GPS device to show your location on the green. It reveals hazards such as bunkers and provides tips on the best way to play the hole. You can even use it to order light refreshments.

(D) Teeth of the Dog, Casa de Campo, DR

The "teeth" of Teeth of the Dog is a local nickname for the island's jagged-edge coral reefs, visible along the breathtaking beachside holes. *Golf Magazine* calls it the #1 Caribbean Course. Its superstar designer, Pete Dye, calls it a "a masterpiece, with seven holes created by God." Signature Dye challenges and obstacles abound, as do the fans, amateur and pro, of this classic beauty. Pack your camera for this one, at least you will have some shots to show off.

(E) Trump International Golf Club, Grenadines

This was designed by Jim Fazio and has astounding views. Created to be fun for golfers of all levels, the front nine is shorter, flatter and protected from the winds that pick up on the challenging back nine, where the holes get longer, as the course winds its way around 877 ft. high Mount Royal, providing stunning panoramas of the Grenadines and the Blue Caribbean.

Punta Espada Golf Course, Dominican Republic

The first of what will be three Jack Nicklaus—designed courses at the new Cap Cana development in Punta Cana has already hosted one PGA championship event. Stunning bluffs and lush tropical vegetation along three miles of white-sand beach make for a breathtaking par 72 round of play for golfers at all levels of play. But don't trust us, *Golfweek* named it "Best Course in the Caribbean and Mexico."

Tobago Plantations Golf & Country Club, Trinidad and Tobago

The ocean-side course—the newest on the island—has amazing views, not to mention challenging greens and fairways.

BEST CARIBBEAN TEACHING PROGRAMS

Casa de Campo Resort, Dominican Republic

Let's face it, a shot glass is a far less useful souvenir than a precision chip shot. If you're looking to polish your golf skills along with your tan, there are fine teaching programs offered at some of the premier Caribbean courses.

JAMAICA

Two prime courses in the Montego Bay area provide terrific teaching programs.

The Half Moon Golf Academy (⊕ *www. halfmoongolf.com* ♟ *from $100/hr. to $150/hr.*)offers a variety of instructional programs individually tailored for beginners through professionals. Individuals or family groups can take hour-long private lessons or multi-lesson introductory clinics focusing on the fundamentals. Seasoned players will enjoy the two-hour lessons to work on club and shot selection as well as course management skills. Head Pro Ewan Peebles, who runs the program, is a PGA player from Scotland with more than 10 years of teaching experience. He is currently Jamaica's top-ranked professional golfer.

At **Kevyn Cunningham's** eponymous **Golf Academy** (⊕ *www.caribbeangolfschool. com* ♟ *$625 2-day school; $975 3-day school; $175/person for lessons*) at the Ritz Carlton, the "classroom" is the famously difficult White Witch course. An effective and popular instructor, he directed the David Leadbetter program in the Caribbean for 10 years before starting his own school. There are one-, two-, and three-day programs focusing on swing mechanics, complete with high-tech computer analysis. Book a full-day private lesson if, perish the thought, you need to shake the yips or the shanks—or just want to spend 8 hours (and $1,500) with a top pro. You'll go home with a complete analysis and a plan for ongoing improvements on a DVD. It's easy to arrange customized programs for families or groups here as well.

THE DOMINICAN REPUBLIC

Casa de Campo is home to the **David Leadbetter Golf Academy** (⊕ *http://davidleadbetter.com* ♟ *$650 2-day school; $975 3-day school; $225/hr. for lessons*) and its respected teaching curriculum. PGA Pro Tim Vickers, Sr., heads the various workshops, which vary in length and subject matter; but we know more than one golfer who credits his terrific short game (chipping and putting) to a course here. One-, two-, and three-day customized programs include, video analysis, club-fitting, course management, and skills development.

PRACTICAL INFORMATION

Golf field on the Bavaro area, DR

PACKING

A little forethought will keep you safe and keep expensive resort pro-shop purchases to a minimum. Pack for tropical heat and blazing sun with wicking, breathable golf attire. Seek sun-protective sportswear such as Golf-wear with an SPF of up to 50. It blocks more than 90% of the sun's harmful rays. Light colors are cooler, and you will undoubtedly want a brimmed hat and UV-protective sunglasses.

Most clubs maintain strict dress codes. In general: denim, cut-offs, sneakers, gym/running shorts, and tank tops are prohibited. Both men and women are expected to wear soft-spike golf shoes (these can be rented at most courses). Men wear collared shirts with sleeves. Women may wear sleeveless sport shirts (not tank tops) with Bermuda-length shorts, capris, or skirts no shorter than about 5 inches above the knee.

Accessories such as gloves, tees, golf balls, markers, repair tools for greens and the like are available at the pro shops but will prove costly. Don't forget to stash a golf towel or two, insect repellent, and sunscreen. Power bars, Band-aids, and small packets of pain relievers are light to carry and invaluable when you need them.

SHIPPING

Be sure to check with your airline for the latest guidelines, but generally, major carriers allow a passenger to check in one hard-sided golf bag of up to 50 pounds. Heavier than that, and you'll likely incur extra baggage fees. This will be enough for 14 clubs, a dozen balls, a pair of shoes, accessories, and a lightweight stand bag. A soft-sided bag is not advisable; in fact the airline will usually require a damage waiver. Connecting flights can mean lost or delayed luggage, especially on smaller planes. Consider renting equipment at your destination, but keep in mind that new clubs at high-end pro shops can top $60 per round, and older courses may have older equipment.

Golfers (and other sports-enthusiasts too) have good experiences using reliable, if pricy, door-to-door luggage delivery services such as **Golf Bag Shipping** (⊕ *www.golfbagshipping.com*) or **Luggage Forward** (⊕ *www.luggageforward.com*). Prices range from $350 to $500 round trip to Dominican Republic or Barbados. Plan ahead: it takes up to 10 business days. If you are going to Puerto Rico or the U.S. Virgin Islands you can ship by UPS Ground or FedEx for about $200 to $300 each way, depending delivery speed. In any case, include durable identification, insure the delivery, and address it to the hotel concierge, being sure to notify the concierge, also.

$$$$
RESORT
Fodor's Choice
★
 ⊡ **Palm Island Resort.** Perfect for a honeymoon, rendezvous, or luxurious escape, this palm-studded resort offers peace and tranquillity, along with five dazzling white-sand beaches, a calm aquamarine sea for swimming and enjoying water sports, nature trails for quiet walks, a pool with waterfall, a 9-hole golf course, sophisticated dining, impeccable service, and exquisite accommodations (though not touted as luxurious, except for the villas). **Pros:** private and romantic; fabulous beach; great snorkeling right outside beachfront cottages 15 and 16; free scuba resort course; personal welcome by the general manager upon arrival at the dock. **Cons:** quiet nights (early to bed and early to rise); fairly isolated. ⊠ *Palm Island* ☎ *784/458–8824* ⊕ *www.palmislandresortgrenadines. com* ⟿ *33 rooms, 8 suites, 2 villas* ⚒ *In-room: no phone, safe, kitchen (some), no TV. In-hotel: restaurants, bars, golf course, tennis court, pool, gym, spa, beach, water sports, business center, some age restrictions (Dec. 15.–Apr. 15)* ¶⊙¶ *All-inclusive.*

PETIT ST. VINCENT

The southernmost of St. Vincent's Grenadines, tiny (113 acres), private Petit St. Vincent—pronounced "Petty" St. Vincent and affectionately called PSV—is ringed with white-sand beaches and covered with tropical foliage. Hazen Richardson, who passed away in 2008, created the resort in 1968. New owners (as of December 2010) are making extensive renovations to the property (cottage upgrades, a new casual beachside restaurant, an air-conditioned fitness and yoga center, an open-air spa, an air-conditioned library with a TV and Internet access, a new children's center, and landscaping upgrades), with a promise to not to change the design and nature of the property. To get to PSV, you fly from Barbados to Union Island, where the resort's motor launch meets you for the 30-minute voyage.

WHERE TO STAY

The following review has been condensed for this book. Please go to Fodors.com for an expanded review.

$$$$
RESORT
Fodor's Choice
★
 ⊡ **Petit St. Vincent.** No phones, no room TVs, no outside interferences, and no planned activities are particularly appealing when you can indulge your desert-island fantasies without forgoing luxury. **Pros:** beautifully secluded; roomy and comfortable accommodations; excellent cuisine. **Cons:** you're pretty much a captive audience here; some of the beaches are rocky; no pool. ⊠ *Petit St. Vincent* ⌖ *PSV, Box 841338, Pembroke Pines, FL 33084* ☎ *784/458–8801* ⊕ *www.psvresort.com* ⟿ *22 cottages* ⚒ *In-room: no phone, no TV. In-hotel: restaurants, room service, tennis court, bar, beach, spa, water sports* ⊗ *Closed Sept. and Oct.* ¶⊙¶ *All meals.*

TOBAGO CAYS

Fodor's Choice
★
 Tobago Cays Marine Park is a small group of uninhabited islands just east of Mayreau in the southern Grenadines. It was declared a wildlife reserve in 2006 by the St. Vincent and the Grenadines government to preserve the natural beauty and biodiversity of the cays, allowing you

to experience some of the best snorkeling in the world. The sparkling clear water is studded with sponges and coral formations and populated by countless colorful fish and turtles. All the major dive operators and sailing and snorkeling day trips go here. It's one unforgettable place.

UNION ISLAND

Union is a popular anchorage for vacationers sailing the Grenadines and a crossroads for others heading to surrounding islands. Clifton, the main town and a port of entry for yachts, is small and commercial, with a bustling harbor, a few simple beachfront inns and restaurants, businesses that cater to yachts, and the regional airstrip—perhaps the busiest in the Grenadines. Hugh Malzac Square, in the center of town, honors the first black man to captain a merchant marine ship. The ship was the *Booker T. Washington*; the time was 1942. Malzac was from Union Island. Taxis and minibuses are available to get around the island, and water taxis go between islands—including Happy Island, a man-made islet in the harbor where you can get a good stiff rum punch and even some grilled lobster or fish. The Easterval Regatta occurs during the Easter weekend with festivities that include boat races, sports and games, a calypso competition, a beauty pageant, and a cultural show featuring the Big Drum Dance (derived from French and African traditions). Union Island has several small inns and hotels, some directly on the waterfront and others inland.

24

BEACHES

🌊 **Bigsand.** Union has relatively few good beaches, but this one at Richmond Bay on the north shore, a five-minute drive from Clifton, is a pretty crescent of powdery white sand, protected by reefs and with lovely views of Mayreau and the Tobago Cays.

Chatham Bay. The desolate but lovely golden-sand beach at Chatham Bay offers good swimming.

WHERE TO EAT

$$–$$$

SEAFOOD

🌊

✕ **Anchorage Yacht Club.** You can't get much closer to waterfront dining than here at AYC. This is the yachting crowd's favorite stop for landside meals—breakfast, lunch, or dinner. It's also a perfect alternative for guests at Palm Island Resort to get the opposite perspective in terms of the view (and, let's face it, the environment). Freshly baked croissants and other pastries, along with pitchers of fresh-squeezed juice and piping-hot coffee, present the perfect wake-up. At lunch, sandwiches, salads, burgers, grilled fish, and more are served with a view. And at dinner, the place comes alive with weekend entertainment (more often in season) as you enjoy fresh seafood cooked to order or, perhaps, a lobster prepared to your liking. ✉ *Dockside, Clifton* ☎ *784/458–8824* ⊕ *www.anchorage-union.com* ⚓ *Reservations essential.*

$

CARIBBEAN

✕ **Lambi's.** During high season (November to May), Lambi's, which overlooks the waterfront in Clifton, offers a daily buffet for each meal. The dinner buffet includes some 50 dishes, including the specialty, delicious conch creole. In the low season (June to October), dining is à la carte, and you can choose from a menu of fish, chicken, conch, pork, lobster, shrimp, and beef dishes. Lambi is Creole patois for "conch," and the restaurant's walls are even constructed from conch shells. Yachts and dinghies can tie up at the wharf, and there's steel-band music and limbo dancing every night in season. ⊠ *Clifton* ☎ *784/458–8549.*

WHERE TO STAY

The following reviews have been condensed for this book. Please go to Fodors.com for expanded reviews of each property.

$
HOTEL

⛅ Anchorage Yacht Club. Reopened as a hotel in 2010 after a several-year hiatus, the popular AYC is immediately across the channel from Palm Island, which shares the same ownership. **Pros:** two minutes from airport via jitney; convenient for all boating activities, good restaurant; convivial atmosphere **Cons:** rooms are comfortable but definitely not luxurious; entrance into beach bungalows is (oddly enough) through the bathroom! ⊠ *Clifton* ☎ *784/458–8824* ⊕ *www.anchorage-union. com* ⤢ *10 rooms, 1 suite* �� *In-room: no phone, no TV, Wi-Fi. In-hotel: restaurant, bar, beach, water sports* ⦿ *No meals.*

¢
HOTEL

⛅ Kings Landing Hotel. Divers flock to Kings Landing, because Grenadines Dive—the biggest operator in the region—is based at the hotel. **Pros:** great for divers; excellent waterfront location; good value. **Cons:** tiny beach; bathrooms have showers only. ⊠ *Clifton* ☎ *784/485–8823* ⊕ *www.kingslandinghotel.com* ⤢ *15 rooms, 2 cottages* ⅅ *In-room: no phone, kitchen (some), Internet, Wi-Fi. In-hotel: restaurant, bar, pool, beach* ⦿ *Breakfast.*

¢
VACATION
CONDOS
☙

⛅ St. Joseph's House. Quaint and colorful St. Joseph's Catholic Church, which the apartments overlook, operates this small hostelry—actually a training and meeting complex for the community. **Pros:** very inexpensive; dorm room is great for young kids and teenagers; good for brief stays or overnights. **Cons:** taxi or minibus required to get to town. ⊠ *Clifton* ☎ *784/458–8405* ⤢ *3 apartments, 1 cottage, 1 dorm room* ⅅ *In-room: no phone, kitchen (some), no TV (some). In-hotel: Laundry service* ⦿ *No meals.*

SPORTS AND ACTIVITIES

BOATING AND SAILING

Union is a major base for yacht charters and sailing trips. At the Union Island airstrip, you can arrange a day sail throughout the lower Grenadines: Palm Island, Mayreau, the Tobago Cays, Petit St. Vincent, and Carriacou. A full day of snorkeling, fishing, and swimming costs about $75 per person for a scheduled sail or $750 for up to four passengers on a private charter—lunch and drinks included. **Yannis Sail** (⊠ *Anchorage Yacht Club Dock, Clifton* ☎ *784/458–8513* ⊕ *www.yannissail.com*) has two 60-foot catamarans. Snorkeling gear, drinks, and a buffet lunch are included in a day sail.

DIVING AND SNORKELING

Grenadines Dive (⊠ *Kings Landing Hotel, Clifton* ☎ *784/458–8138* ⊕ *www.grenadinesdive.com*) offers Tobago Cays snorkeling trips and wreck dives at the *Purina,* a sunken World War I English gunboat. Single-tank dives cost $60; multidive packages are discounted. Glenroy Adams, a Bequia native who claims to "know every dive site in the Grenadines," is the dive master and an environmentalist. Beginners can take a four-hour resort course, which includes a shallow dive, for $85. Certified divers can rent equipment by the day or week.

Trinidad and Tobago

WORD OF MOUTH

"The most relaxing, peaceful week of my entire life was on vacation in Tobago."

—tejana

WELCOME TO TRINIDAD AND TOBAGO

Caribbean Sea

Blanchisseuse Bay

11

Cyril Bay
Chupara Pt.
Tyrico Bay
Maracas Bay
La Vache Bay
Las Cuevas Bay
Saddle Rd.
El Tucuche
Asa Wright Nature Centre
Lopinot Complex

Dragon's Mouth

Chaguaramas
9
8
12
Tunapuna
Eastern
Arima

Port of Spain ★
San Juan
10
Piarco International Airport

1 - **11**
1 - **7**
Caroni Bird Sanctuary ◆

Chaguaramas Military History & Aerospace Museum ◆
Chaguanas
Dattareya Yoga Centre ◆
Flanigin Town

California
Couva
Tabaquite

Gulf of Paria

San Fernando
Tableland
Oropuche Lagoon
Princes Town
New Grant

Irois Bay
La Brea

Cedros Bay
Point Fortin
Penal
Pointe-a-Pierre

Fullarton
Basse Terre

Icacos Pt.
Islote Pt.
Erin Bay
San Francique
Moruga
Erin Pt.

KEY	
🚢	*Ferry*
⌐	*Beaches*
1	*Restaurants*
1	*Hotels*

```
0            10 mi
|-----|-----|
0            10 km
```

The most southerly of the Caribbean islands, Trinidad is also the most colorful. Islanders trace their roots to Africa, India, China, and Madeira, and they speak English, Spanish, Hindi, and French patois. On much quieter Tobago the most exciting event is often the palm trees swaying high above a gentle arc of a beach.

Scarborough

TO TOBAGO

Grande Rivière
Madamas Bay
Toco
Salibea Bay
Galera Pt.
Matelot
Sans Souci
Point Galera Lighthouse
Mt. Oropuche
Redhead
El Cerro del Aripo
Balandra Bay
Matura
Saline Bay
Main Rd.
Valencia
Sangre Grande
Churchill-Roosevelt Hwy.
Matura Bay
Manzanilla Beach

ATLANTIC OCEAN

Cocos Bay

Guataro Pt.
Rio Claro
Pierreville
Mayaro Bay
Guayaguayare
Galeota Pt.
Guayaguayare Bay

BUSINESS AND PLEASURE

The two-island republic is the southern-most link in the Antillean island chain, some 7 mi (11 km) off the coast of Venezuela, but Tobago's Main Ridge and Trinidad's Northern Range are believed to represent the farthest reaches of the Andes Mountains. Trinidad is a large petroleum and natural-gas producer. Tiny Tobago is known more for its quiet atmosphere and gorgeous, wild beaches.

Tobago

Scarborough

25

TRINIDAD AND TOBAGO

Restaurants	▼
Angelo's	6
Apsara	7
Chaud	10
Il Colosseo	3
Joseph's	5
Mélange	9
Prime Restaurant	1
Tiki Village	2
Trotters	11
Veni Mangé	4
The Verandah	8
Wings Restaurant	12

Hotels	▼
Asa Wright Nature Centre Lodge	11
Carlton Savanna	7
Coblentz Inn	3
Courtyard by Marriott	8
Crews Inn	9
Crowne Plaza	4
Hilton Trinidad	1
Holiday Inn Express	10
Hyatt Regency Trinidad	6
Kapok Hotel	2
Le Grande Almandier	12
Monique's	5

TOP REASONS TO VISIT TRINIDAD AND TOBAGO

1 Carnival: Trinidad's Carnival is the Caribbean's biggest and best party, but nightlife is hopping the rest of the year, too.

2 Bird-Watching: Both Trinidad and Tobago are major bird-watching destinations; Trinidad itself has more resident species than any other Caribbean island.

3 Culture Sharing: A melding of many cultures means lively festivals year-round and excellent multicultural cuisine.

4 Music: The steel pan was invented in Trinidad, and excellent bands play all over the island.

TRINIDAD AND TOBAGO PLANNER

Driving Tips

Major highways are good, but bumper-to-bumper traffic is the norm during large parts of the day, and smaller roads can be in poor condition. During the rainy season roads often flood. Never drive into downtown Port of Spain during afternoon rush hour (generally from 3 to 6:30), when traffic is at its heaviest. In Tobago, many roads, particularly in the interior or on the coast near Speyside and Charlotteville, are bumpy, pitted, winding, and steep.

Safety

Travelers should exercise caution in Trinidad, especially in the highly populated east–west corridor and downtown Port of Spain, where walking on the streets at night is not recommended unless you're with a group. Trinidad has recorded over 400 homicides annually for the past few years but these do not generally involve tourists. As a general rule, Tobago is safer than its larger sister island. There is little visible police presence in most areas of Trinidad. Petty theft occurs on both islands, so don't leave cash in bags that you check at the airport, and use hotel safes for valuables.

Getting to Trinidad and Tobago

Hassle Factor: Medium to high.

Flights: There are nonstops to Trinidad from Houston (Continental), Miami (American, Caribbean Airlines), New York–JFK (American, Caribbean Airlines), and New York–Newark (Continental). There are no nonstop flights to Tobago from the United States; to get to Tobago, you will have to hop over from Trinidad on LIAT or Caribbean Airlines.

Local Airline Contacts: American Airlines (☎ 868/664–4661). **Caribbean Airlines** (☎ 868/625–1010 or 868/669–3000). **Continental Airlines** (☎ 800/461–2744). **LIAT** (☎ 868/627–2942 or 868/623–1838).

Airports: Piarco International Airport (✉ POS ☎ 868/669–4101 ⊕ www.tntairports.com), about 30 minutes east of Port of Spain (take Golden Grove Road north to the intersection with the Churchill-Roosevelt Highway and then follow it west for about 10 mi [16 km] to Port of Spain), is a thoroughly modern facility complete with 14 air bridges. Tobago's small **Crown Point Airport** (✉ TAB ☎ 868/639–0509) is the gateway to the island.

Ferries: The **Port Authority of Trinidad & Tobago** (☎ 868/625–2901 in Port of Spain, 868/639–2181 in Scarborough ⊕ www.patnt.com) maintains ferry service every day between Trinidad and Tobago. Flying, however, is preferable because the seas can be very rough. The trip is made on one of the two high-speed CAT ferries. The ferries leave twice a day (from the jetty at the foot of Independence Square in Port of Spain and three times a day from the cruise-ship complex in Scarborough); the trip on the high-speed CAT takes 2½ hours. The round-trip fare is TT$100. There is also a water-taxi service that travels between Port of Spain and San Fernando in Southern Trinidad for TT$15 each way.

Getting Around Trinidad and Tobago

Driving: Don't rent a car if you're staying in Port of Spain, but if you're planning to tour Trinidad, you'll need some wheels, as you will if you end up staying out on the island. In Tobago you're better off renting a four-wheel-drive vehicle than relying on expensive taxi service. On either island, driving is on the left, British-style. Be aware that Tobago has very few gas stations—the main ones are in Crown Point and Scarborough. Be cautious driving on either island, as the country has very lax and seldom-enforced drinking-and-driving laws, and erratic driving is the norm rather than the exception.

Trinidad Car Rentals: Auto Rentals (⊠ *Piarco International Airport, Piarco, Trinidad* ☎ *868/669–2277*). **Southern Sales Car Rentals** (⊠ *Piarco International Airport, Piarco, Trinidad* ☎ *868/669–2424, 269 from courtesy phone in airport baggage area*). **Thrifty** (⊠ *Piarco International Airport, Piarco, Trinidad* ☎ *868/669–0602*).

Tobago Car Rentals: Baird's Rentals (⊠ *Crown Point Airport, Crown Point, Tobago* ☎ *868/639–7054*). **Rattan's Car Rentals** (⊠ *Crown Point Airport, Crown Point, Tobago* ☎ *868/639–8271*). **Rollock's Car Rentals** (⊠ *Crown Point Airport, Crown Point, Tobago* ☎ *868/639–0328*). **Thrifty** (⊠ *Rex Turtle Beach Hotel, Great Courland Bay, Black Rock, Tobago* ☎ *868/639–8507*).

Taxis: In Trinidad, taxis are readily available at Piarco Airport; the fare to Port of Spain is set at $50 ($100 after 10 pm). In Tobago the fare from Crown Point Airport to Scarborough or Grafton Beach is about $65. Taxis in Trinidad and Tobago are easily identified by their license plates, which begin with the letter *H*. Passenger vans, called Maxi Taxis, pick up and drop off passengers as they travel (rather like a bus) and are color-coded according to which of the six areas they cover. Rates are generally less than $1 per trip. (Yellow is for Port of Spain, red for eastern Trinidad, green for south Trinidad, and black for Princes Town. Brown operates from San Fernando to the southeast—Erin, Penal, Point Fortin. The only color for Tobago is blue.) They're easy to hail day or night along most of the main roads near Port of Spain. For longer trips you need to hire a private taxi. Cabs aren't metered, and hotel taxis can be expensive.

Island Activities

Trinidad has some good **beaches**—the best being Maracas Bay—but none is as picture-perfect as those on Tobago.

Though they don't have the manicured, country-club elegance you will find on many islands, the **beaches** on **Tobago** feel wilder and hark back to a time when towering hotels didn't line every picturesque Caribbean crescent.

Bird-watching is one of the highlights of a trip to either Trinidad or Tobago; both islands have reserves where you'll see a wide variety of species.

Diving is good off the shores of Tobago, particularly around Arnos Vale Reef, off the island's west coast.

Golfers will do better on Tobago, which has one excellent course and two other good ones.

Nightlife is much better in Port of Spain, with live music being a particular highlight, but Tobago as a whole is much quieter after dark.

25

TRINIDAD AND TOBAGO PLANNER

Fast Facts

Banks and Exchange Services: At this writing, the exchange rate for the Trinidadian dollar (TT$) is about TT$6.40 to US$1. Most businesses on the islands will accept U.S. currency. Credit cards and ATM cards are almost universally accepted. Cash is necessary only in the smallest neighborhood convenience shops and roadside stalls. Trinidad has ATMs in all but the most remote areas. In Tobago there are only a few in Scarborough and at the airport in Crown Point. Be aware that there are far fewer bank branches in Tobago than in Trinidad.

Electricity: 110 volts/60 cycles (U.S. standard).

Emergency Services: Ambulance and Fire (☎ 990). **Police** (☎ 999).

Passport Requirements: Everyone coming into Trinidad and Tobago must have a valid passport.

Weddings: There is a three-day residency requirement. A passport, airline ticket, and proof of divorce (if you've been married before) are all required, as is a $55 license fee. **Registrar General** (✉ Jerningham St., Scarborough, Tobago ☎ 868/639-3210 ✉ 72-74 South Quay, Port of Spain, Trinidad ☎ 868/624-1660).

Essentials

Mail: Postage to the United States and Canada is TT$3.45 for first-class letters and TT$2.25 for postcards; prices are slightly higher for other destinations. The main post offices are on Wrightson Road (opposite the Crowne Plaza) in Port of Spain and in the N.I.B. Mall on Wilson Street (near the docks) in Scarborough. There are no zip codes on the islands. To write to an establishment here, you simply need its address, town, and "Trinidad and Tobago, West Indies."

Taxes: The departure tax is TT$100 but is required by law to be included in the ticket price. All hotels add a 10% government tax. Prices for almost all goods and services include a 15% V.A.T. (value-added tax).

Telephones: The area code for both islands is 868 ("TNT" if you forget). This is also the country code if you're calling to Trinidad and Tobago from another country. From the United States, just dial "1" plus the area code and number. To make a local call to any point in the country simply dial the seven-digit local number. Most hotels and guesthouses will allow you to dial a direct international call. To dial a number in North America or the Caribbean simply dial "1" and the U.S. or Canadian area code before the number you're calling, but be warned that most hotels add a hefty surcharge for overseas calls.

Tipping: Almost all hotels will add a 10% to 15% service charge. Most restaurants include a 10% service charge, which is considered standard on these islands. If it isn't on the bill, tip according to service: 10% to 15% is fine. Tip taxi drivers 10%; housekeeping staff $1 to $2 per night.

Visitor Information. Tourism Hotline (☎ 888/595-4868). **Trinidad and Tobago Tourism Office** (☎ 800/748-4224 ⊕ www.gotrinidadandtobago.com). **TDC** (✉ Maritime Centre, Level 1, 9 10th Ave., Barataria ☎ 868/638-7962 ✉ Piarco International Airport, Piarco ☎ 868/669-5196). **Tobago Division of Tourism** (✉ N.I.B. Mall, Wilson St., Level 3, Scarborough ☎ 868/639-2125 ✉ Crown Point Airport, Crown Point ☎ 868/639-0509).

Where to Stay

Trinidad isn't a top tourist destination, so resorts are few and far between, and many are a long drive from Port of Spain and the airport. However, a few ecoconscious options are worth the hassle, particularly if you are a bird-watcher. Tobago has a wide array of lodging options, and it's a much smaller island with better beaches, so your choice of resort is driven more by the amenities you want and your budget than by the resort's location.

Beach Resorts: Tobago has a nice mix of midsize resorts, including several offering a fair degree of luxury, but there are also many choices for budget-oriented tourists, as is the case in Trinidad, where fewer tourists mean better value at the small beach resorts that cater primarily to locals. Few hotels on either island offer anything but room-only rates, though there are now two all-inclusive resorts on Tobago.

Ecoresorts: Nature lovers, particularly bird-watchers, have an especially good option in Trinidad in the Asa Wright Nature Centre Lodge. Several of Tobago's small resorts are particularly ecoconscious.

Hotels: Though they have nice pools and other resort-type amenities, Trinidad's hotels are geared more for business travelers. Options for beachgoers are more limited and farther removed from Port of Spain.

HOTEL AND RESTAURANT PRICES

Restaurant prices are for a main course at dinner and include any taxes or service charges. Hotel prices are per night for a double room in high season, excluding taxes, service charges, and meal plans (except at all-inclusives).

WHAT IT COSTS IN U.S. DOLLARS

	¢	$	$$	$$$	$$$$
Restaurants	under $8	$8–$12	$12–$20	$20–$30	over $30
Hotels	under $150	$150–$275	$276–$375	$376–$475	over $475

When to Go

Trinidad is more of a business destination than a magnet for tourists, so hotel rates (particularly in Port of Spain) are fairly stable year-round, nevertheless, you can usually get a price break during the traditional Caribbean low season (from May to December). Carnival (in January or February) brings the highest rates.

Tobago is much more of a tourist destination, but busy periods on Tobago—since it is still more popular with Europeans than Americans—can sometimes differ from the typical vacation periods in the United States.

FESTIVALS AND EVENTS

Trinidad's **Carnival** in January, February, or March is the biggest and best celebration in the Caribbean.

The **Tobago Heritage Festival** is usually held in late July.

Divali, held in October or November and called the Festival of Lights, is one of the more popular Hindu festivals in Trinidad.

TRINIDAD AND TOBAGO BEACHES

Trinidad and Tobago offer two completely different beach experiences. Tobago attracts thousands of international visitors with a choice of white or honey-color beaches. Big sister Trinidad has a few good beaches on the north coast and sightseeing on the island's east coast.

(Above) Sarongs for sale on Turtle Beach, Tobago. (Opposite page bottom) Manzanilla Beach, Trinidad. (Opposite page top) A lifeguard tower at Maracas Bay, Trinidad.

Trinidad has some good beaches for swimming and sunning, though none as picture-perfect as those in Tobago. Although popular with some locals, the beaches of the western peninsula (such as Maqueripe) are not particularly attractive, and the water in this area is often polluted by sewage. All beaches on Trinidad are free and open to the public. Many locals are fond of playing loud music wherever they go, and even the most serene beach may suddenly turn into a seaside disco.

You won't find manicured country-club sand in Tobago. But those who enjoy feeling as though they've landed on a desert island will relish the untouched quality of these shores.

BAKE AND SHARK

Maracas Bay in Trinidad is famous for its bake and shark (about $5), a deep-fried piece of shark stuffed into fried batter. To this, you can add any of dozens of toppings, such as tamarind sauce and coleslaw. There are dozens of beach huts serving the specialty, as well as stands in the nearby parking lot (Richard's is by far the most popular).

TRINIDAD

Balandra Bay. On the northeast coast, the beige-sand beach—popular with locals on weekends—is sheltered by a rocky outcropping and is a favorite of bodysurfers. Much of this beach is suitable for swimming. The noise level on weekends can be a problem for those seeking solitude. Take the Toco Main Road from the Valencia Road, and turn off at the signs indicating Balandra (just after Salybia). ⊠ *Off Valencia Rd. near Salybia.*

Blanchisseuse Bay. On North Coast Road you can find this narrow, palm-fringed beach. Facilities are nonexistent, but it's an ideal spot for a romantic picnic. A lagoon and river at the east end of the beach allow you to swim in freshwater, but beware of floating logs in the river, as they sometimes contain mites that can cause a body rash (called *bete rouge* locally). You can haggle with local fishermen to take you out in their boats to explore the coast. This beach is about 14 mi (23 km) after Maracas; just keep driving along the road until you pass the Arima turnoff. The coastal and rain-forest views here are spectacular. ⊠ *North Coast Rd. just beyond Arima turnoff.*

Grande Riviere. On Trinidad's rugged northeast coast, Grande Riviere is well worth the drive. Swimming is good, and there are several guesthouses nearby for refreshments, but the main attractions

here are turtles. Every year up to 500 giant leatherback turtles come onto the beach to lay their eggs. If you're here at night, run your hand through the black sand to make it glow—a phenomenon caused by plankton. ⊠ *Toco Main Rd. at end of road.*

Las Cuevas Bay. This narrow, picturesque strip on North Coast Road is named for the series of partially submerged and explorable caves that ring the beach. A food stand offers tasty snacks, and vendors hawk fresh fruit across the road. You can also buy fresh fish and lobster from the fishing depot near the beach. You have to park your car in the small parking lot and walk down a few steps to get to the beach, so be sure to take everything from the car (which is out of sight once you are on the beach). There are basic changing and toilet facilities. It's less crowded here than at nearby Maracas Bay and seemingly serene, although, as at Maracas, the current can be treacherous. ⊠ *North Coast Rd., 7 mi (11 km) east of Maracas Bay.*

Manzanilla Beach. You can find picnic facilities and a pretty view of the Atlantic here, though the water is occasionally muddied by Venezuela's Orinoco River. The Cocal Road running the length of this beautiful beach is lined with stately palms, whose fronds vault like the arches at Chartres. This is where many well-heeled Trinis have vacation homes. The Nariva River, which enters

Beach-goers relaxing on Turtle Beach, Tobago

the sea just south of this beach and the surrounding Nariva Swamp, is home to the protected manatee and many other rare species, including the much-maligned anaconda. To get to this beach take the Mayaro turnoff at the town of Sangre Grande. Manzanilla is where this road first meets the coast. ⊠ *Southeast of Sangre Grande.*

Maracas Bay. This long stretch of sand has a cove and a fishing village at one end. It's *the* local favorite, so it can get crowded on weekends. Lifeguards will guide you away from strong currents. Parking sites are ample, and there are snack bars (selling the famous bake and shark) and restrooms. Take the winding North Coast Road from Maraval (it intersects with Long Circular Road right next to KFC Maraval) over the Northern Range; the beach is about 7 mi (11 km) from Maraval. ⊠ *North Coast Rd.*

Salibea Bay (*Salybia Bay*). This gentle beach has shallows and plenty of shade—perfect for swimming. Snack vendors abound in the vicinity. Like many of the beaches on the northeast coast, this one is packed with people and music trucks blaring soca and reggae on weekends. It's off the Toco Main Road, just after the town of Matura. ⊠ *Off Toco Main Rd. south of Toco.*

TOBAGO

Bacolet Beach. This dark-sand beach was the setting for the films *Swiss Family Robinson* and *Heaven Knows, Mr. Allison.* Though used by the Blue Haven Hotel, like all local beaches it's open to the public. If you are not a guest at the hotel, access to the beach is down a track next door to the hotel. The bathroom and changing facilities on the beach are for hotel guests only. ⊠ *Windward Rd. east of Scarborough.*

Great Courland Bay. Near Ft. Bennett, the bay has clear, tranquil waters. Along the sandy beach—one of Tobago's longest—you can find several glitzy hotels. A marina attracts the yachting crowd. ⊠ *Leeward Rd. northeast of Black Rock, Courland.*

King's Bay. Surrounded by steep green hills, this is the most visually satisfying of the swimming sites off the road from Scarborough to Speyside—the bay hooks around so severely, you can feel like you're in a lake. The crescent beach is easy to find because it's marked by a sign about halfway between the two towns. Just before you reach the bay, there's a bridge with an unmarked turnoff that leads to a gravel parking lot; beyond that, a landscaped path leads to a waterfall with a rocky pool. You'll likely meet locals who can offer to guide you to the top of the falls; however, you may find the climb not worth the effort. ⊠ *Delaford.*

Lovers Beach. So called because of its pink sand and its seclusion—you have to hire a local to bring you here by boat—it's an isolated and quiet retreat. Ask one of the fishermen in Charlotteville to arrange a ride for you, but be sure to haggle. It should cost you no more than TT$25 a person for a return ride (considerably less sometimes). ⊠ *North coast, reachable only by boat from Charlotteville.*

Mt. Irvine Beach. Across the street from the Mt. Irvine Bay Hotel is this unremarkable beach, but it has great surfing in July and August; the snorkeling is excellent, too. It's also ideal for windsurfing in January and April. There are picnic tables surrounded by painted concrete pagodas, and there's a snack bar. ⊠ *Shirvan Rd., Mt. Irvine.*

Parlatuvier. On the north side of the island, the beach is best approached via the road from Roxborough. It's a classic Caribbean crescent, a scene peopled by villagers and fishermen. ⊠ *Parlatuvier.*

Pigeon Point Beach. This stunning locale is often displayed on Tobago travel brochures. The white-sand beach is lined with swaying coconut trees, and there are changing facilities and food stalls nearby. Although the beach is public, it abuts part of what was once a large coconut estate, and you must pay a token admission (about TT$18) to enter the grounds and use the facilities. ⊠ *Pigeon Point.*

Sandy Point Beach. Situated at the end of the Crown Point Airport runway, this beach is abutted by several hotels, so you won't lack for amenities around here. The beach is accessible by walking around the airport fence to the hotel area. ⊠ *At Crown Point Airport.*

Stone Haven Bay. A gorgeous stretch of sand is across the street from the Grafton Beach Resort. ⊠ *Shirvan Rd., Black Rock.*

Store Bay. The beach, where boats depart for Buccoo Reef, is little more than a small sandy cove between two rocky breakwaters, but the food stands here are divine: several huts licensed by the tourist board to local ladies who sell roti, *pelau* (meat stewed in coconut milk with peas and rice), and the world's messiest dish—curried crab and dumplings. Near the airport, just walk around the Crown Point Hotel to the beach entrance. ⊠ *Crown Point.*

Turtle Beach. Named for the leatherback turtles that lay their eggs here at night between February and June, it's on Great Courland Bay. (If you're very quiet, you can watch; the turtles don't seem to mind.) It's 8 mi (13 km) from the airport between Black Rock and Plymouth. ⊠ *Southern end of Great Courland Bay between Black Rock and Plymouth.*

25

Pigeon Point, Tobago

EATING AND DRINKING WELL IN TRINIDAD AND TOBAGO

The truly multicultural-crossroads local fare, symbolic of Trinidad and Tobago's dual island status, blends Amerindian, British, French, Spanish, African, South American, East Indian, Chinese, and even Middle Eastern influences.

(Above) Curried crab. (Opposite page bottom) Ingredients for a roti. (Opposite page top) Creole-style pelau.

Referencing the national dish, acclaimed second-generation chef Debra Sardinha-Metivier notes, "We are a callaloo in people form. Maybe you had a Chinese grandmother or Indian grandfather who helped broaden, sophisticate your palate." Today there's a growing awareness, pun intended, of returning to roots: "Everything comes full circle; organic-farm-to-table sustainability was always a necessity. More people then had a backyard garden . . . and shared. If I had a mango tree, and my neighbor had a coconut, we would barter. . . . Adapting to modern life while creatively meeting the needs of three square meals (including a rushed lunch for workers) began fusion cuisine." It's the fusion (particularly of Indian and Caribbean) that sets Trinidad apart.

—Jordan Simon

STREET FOOD

Although much of the fare resembles variations on Caribbean standards, the street food, which rules rushed Trini life, is virtually unique. You'll find fresh rotis (akin to wraps) stuffed with curried meat, seafood, or chicken; chicken *geera* (a cumin-scented Indian dish); pies—beef, cheese, fish, *aloo* (Indian potato); and *pows* (from the Cantonese *pao-tzu*, steamed wrapped buns with savory or sweet filling, typically pork).

CALLALOO

Callaloo is the national dish (variants are found throughout the islands), exhibiting a pronounced African influence. This thick sultry stew is simmered from okra, chili peppers, coconut milk, *chadon bene*, garlic, onion, crab, tubers (including dasheen, whose leaves, resembling a slightly bitter spinach, are also called callaloo), and sometimes various meats. It's often served with macaroni pie (essentially pasta baked with cheese and eggs).

CRAB AND DUMPLING

Tobagonian cuisine mimics Trinidad's, for the most part, but its signature dish is messy, marvelous curried crab with dumpling. The sweet blue crabs and dumplings are simmered in a rich coconut sauce. Tobago is also celebrated for its sumptuously prepared provisions, soups, and stews, sometimes known as blue food (for the color of boiled dasheen) across the country.

PELAU

Pelau is another mainstay, its roots dating back to 5th-century BC Mesopotamia and brought to Europe by Alexander the Great's army. International variations run from rice pilaf to Spain's paella; Trinidad's version borrows from several cultures. Chicken, beef, pork, or goat is cooked down with rice, pigeon peas, pumpkin, brown sugar, onions, garlic, and often the ubiquitous curry

(which Trinis consider a metaphor for the spiciness of their lives).

ROTI

One of the great Indian contributions to Trinidad, this is unleavened flatbread cooked on an iron griddle called a *tawa/tava* and stuffed with a variety of filling fillings. *Sada* roti is the simplest kind, filled with curried lentils, fire-roasted tomato, eggplant, potato, and other vegetables. It's a popular breakfast option, along with *paratha* roti (aka "Buss-Up-Shut"), rubbed with clarified butter to enhance flavor and grilled until crisp, brown, and crumbly, and usually served with fried eggs. The classic roti, *dhalpuri,* is stuffed with ground yellow split peas, garlic, cumin, and pepper; meats are often added.

SWEETS

Guava paste, sticky-sweet but delectable candied tamarind or papaya balls, and Indian staples like *gulab jamon* (creamy dough fried in sugar syrup scented with cardamom and rosewater) are common. Popular pone, which is similar to bread pudding, derives its consistency from ground provisions such as cassava (manioc), sweet potato, or pumpkin. Grated cinnamon, nutmeg, raisins, coconut, and sugar are added and baked in a casserole. Tobago chefs often add a pinch of black pepper to provide an edgy counterpoint.

25

Updated by Vernon O'Reilly-Ramesar

These lush islands lay claim to being the economic powerhouse of the Caribbean. Vast oil and gas reserves have led to a high standard of living, where tourism is not the mainstay of the economy. Indeed, the word tourist is seldom mentioned here; the preference is for the much friendlier visitor. Trinidad's Northern Range is thought to be part of the Andes in South America (connected to the mainland as recently as the last Ice Age). This geological history helps explain why the range of flora and fauna is much greater than on other Caribbean islands.

The two islands have very different histories. Sadly, the Amerindian populations of both islands were virtually wiped out by the arrival of Europeans. After Columbus landed in Trinidad in 1498, the island came under Spanish rule. In an attempt to build the population and provide greater numbers to fend off a potential British conquest, the government at the time encouraged French Catholics from nearby islands to settle in Trinidad. This migration can be seen in the large number of French place-names scattered around the island. Despite this effort, the British conquered the island in 1797.

Tobago had a much more turbulent history. Named after the tobacco that was used by the native Amerindian population, it was settled by the British in 1508. The island was to change hands at least 22 times before eventually returning to Britain in 1814.

The two islands were merged into one crown colony in 1888, with Tobago being made a ward of Trinidad. Independence was achieved in 1962 under the leadership of Dr. Eric Williams, who became the first prime minister. The islands became an independent republic in 1976 with a bicameral Parliament and an appointed president.

Trinidad's capital city, Port of Spain, is home to some 300,000 of the island's 1.3 million inhabitants. Downtown Port of Spain is a bustling commercial center complete with high-rise office buildings and seemingly perpetual traffic. Happily, the northern mountain range rises just behind the city and helps to take much of the edge off the urban clamor.

Much of the charm of Trinidad lies in the ethnic mix of the population. The majority of the population is of either African or East Indian background—the descendants of African slaves and indentured East Indian laborers, who came to work the plantations in the 19th century. The island is always buzzing with a variety of celebrations and arts performances that can range from African drumming to classical Indian dance. The national cuisine has also absorbed the best of both cultures. Although these two groups compose more than 80% of the population, other groups such as the French, Spanish, Chinese, and even Lebanese have left their mark.

Many of the art forms that are considered synonymous with the Caribbean were created on this relatively small island. Calypso was born here, as were soca, limbo, and the steel pan (steel drum). The island can also claim two winners of the Nobel Prize in Literature—V. S. Naipaul (2001), who was born in Trinidad and wrote several of his earlier books about the island, and Derek Walcott (1992), a St. Lucian who moved to Trinidad in 1953. Many tourists make a pilgrimage simply to trace the places mentioned in Naipaul's magnum opus, *A House for Mr. Biswas*.

Physically, the island offers an exact parallel to the rain forests of South America, which allows for interesting—and sometimes challenging—ecological adventures. Beach lovers accustomed to the electric blue water and dazzling white sand of coral islands may be disappointed by the beaches on Trinidad. The best beaches are on the north coast, with peach sand, clean blue-green water, and the forest-covered Northern Range as a backdrop. Beaches are almost completely free of hotel development.

Tobago is 23 mi (37 km) northeast of Trinidad. The population here is much less ethnically diverse than that of Trinidad, with the majority being of African descent. Tobagonians have their own dialect and distinct culture. Tourism is much more a part of the island's economy, and you can find excellent resorts and facilities. Tobago also has pretty white-sand beaches.

TRINIDAD

EXPLORING TRINIDAD

The intensely urban atmosphere of Port of Spain belies the tropical beauty of the countryside surrounding it. You'll need a car and three to eight hours to see all there is to see. Begin by circling the Queen's Park Savannah to Saddle Road, in the residential district of Maraval. After a few miles the road begins to narrow and curve sharply as it climbs into the Northern Range and its undulating hills of dense foliage. Stop at the lookout on North Coast Road; a camera is a must-have here. You pass a series of lovely beaches, starting with Maracas. From the town of Blanchisseuse there's a winding route to the Asa Wright Nature Centre that takes you through canyons of towering palms, mossy grottoes, and

East Indians in Trinidad

With the abolition of slavery in the British colonies in 1838, many plantation economies like Trinidad were left looking for alternative sources of cheap labor. Trinidad tried to draw Europeans, but the heat made them ineffective. Attention finally turned to the Indian subcontinent, and in 1845 the first ship of Indian laborers arrived in Trinidad. These workers were hired indentured and came mainly from the poorer parts of Uttar Pradesh. They undertook the three-month journey to the New World with the understanding that after their five-year work stint was over, they could reindenture themselves or return to India. The system stayed in place until 1917.

The Indians proved effective on the sugarcane and cocoa plantations, helping them return to prosperity. In an effort to discourage the Indians from returning home, the colony eventually offered a land grant as an incentive for those who chose to stay. Many took up the offer and stayed to make new lives in their adopted homeland. Their descendants still maintain many traditions and, to some extent, language. East Indian culture is a vibrant component of T&T's national culture, and you can find Indian festivals and music sharing center stage at all national events. East Indians actually compose about half the islands' population and are an integral part of Trinidad and Tobago society.

imposing bamboo. In this rain forest keep an eye out for vultures, parakeets, hummingbirds, toucans, and, if you're lucky, maybe red-bellied, yellow-and-blue macaws. Trinidad also has more than 600 native species of butterflies and far more than 1,000 varieties of orchids.

Fodor's Choice ★ **Asa Wright Nature Centre.** Nearly 200 acres here are covered with plants, trees, and multihued flowers, and the surrounding acreage is atwitter with more than 200 species of birds, from the gorgeous blue-crowned motmot to the rare (and protected) nocturnal oilbird. If you stay at the center's inn for two nights or more, take one of the guided hikes (included in your room price if you are staying here) to the oilbirds' breeding grounds in Dunston Cave (reservations for hikes are essential). Those who don't want to hike can relax on the inn's verandah and watch birds swoop about the porch feeders—an armchair bird-watcher's delight. You are also more than likely to see a variety of other animal species, including agoutis and alarmingly large golden tegu lizards. This stunning plantation house looks out onto the lush, untouched Arima Valley. Even if you're not staying over, book ahead for lunch (TT$140), offered Monday through Saturday, or for the noontime Sunday buffet (TT$200). The center is an hour outside Blanchisseuse. ✉ Box 4710, Arima Valley 🕾 868/667–4655 ⊕ www.asawright. org 🖾 $10 ☉ Daily 9–5. Guided tours at 10:30 and 1:30.

☉ **Caroni Bird Sanctuary.** This large swamp with mazelike waterways is bordered by mangrove trees, some plumed with huge termite nests. If you're lucky, you may see lazy caimans idling in the water and large snakes hanging from branches on the banks, taking in the sun. In the middle of the sanctuary are several islets that are home to Trinidad's national

The visitor center and lodge at Asa Wright Nature Centre, Trinidad.

bird, the scarlet ibis. Just before sunset the ibis arrive by the thousands, their richly colored feathers brilliant in the gathering dusk, and as more flocks alight, they turn the mangrove foliage a brilliant scarlet. Bring a sweater and insect repellent. The sanctuary's only official tour operator is Winston Nanan (⇨ *Bird-watching in Sports and Activities*). ⊠ *½ hr from Port of Spain; take Churchill Roosevelt Hwy. east to Uriah Butler south; turn right and in about 2 mins, after passing Caroni River Bridge, follow sign for sanctuary* ▨ *$10* ⊙ *Daily dawn–dusk.*

Chaguaramas Military History & Aerospace Museum. On the former U.S. military base, this is a must-see for history buffs. The exhibits are in a large hangarlike shed without air-conditioning, so dress appropriately. Exhibits cover everything from Amerindian history to the Cold War, but the emphasis is on the two World Wars. There's a decidedly charming and homemade feel to the place; in fact, most exhibits were made by the curator and founder, Commander Gaylord Kelshall of the T&T Coast Guard. The museum is set a bit off the main road but is easily spotted by the turquoise BWIA L1011 jet parked out front (Trinidad and Tobago's former national airline). ⊠ *Western Main Rd., Chaguaramas* ☎ *868/634–4391* ▨ *TT$20* ⊙ *Mon.–Sat. 9–5.*

Dattatreya Yoga Centre. This impressive temple site was constructed by artisans brought in from India. It is well worth a visit to admire the intricate architectural details of the main temple, learn about Trinidad Hinduism, and marvel at the towering 85-foot statue of the god Hanuman. Krishna Ramsaran, the compound manager, is extremely helpful and proud to explain the history of the center and the significance of the various *murtis* (sacred statues). Kids are welcome, so this makes for a pleasant and educational family outing (kids seem especially interested in the giant elephant statues that guard the temple doors). This is a religious site, so appropriate clothing is required (no shorts), and shoes must be left outside the temple door. It's fine to take pictures of the statue and the temple exterior and grounds, but permission is required to take pictures inside, as it's an active place of worship. The temple is half an hour from Port of Spain; take Churchill Roosevelt Highway east to Uriah Butler south; turn right until the Chase Village flyover; follow the signs south to Waterloo; then follow signs to the temple. ⊠ *Datta Dr. at Orangefield Rd., Carapichaima* ☎ *868/673–5328* ☎ *Free* ☉ *Daily dawn–dusk, services daily.*

Lopinot Complex. It's said that the ghost of the French count Charles Joseph de Lopinot prowls his former home on stormy nights. Lopinot came to Trinidad in 1800 and chose this magnificent site to plant cocoa. His restored estate house has been turned into a museum—a guide is available from 10 to 6—and a center for *parang*, the Venezuelan-derived folk music. Although worthwhile for those interested in the finer points of Trinidad history, this may not be worth the long and winding drive for most visitors. ⊠ *Take Eastern Main Rd. from Port of Spain to Arouca; look for sign that points north* ☎ *No phone* ☎ *Free* ☉ *Daily 6–6.*

☾ **Point Galera Lighthouse.** An essential stop when touring the northeast, this lighthouse was constructed in 1897 on a stunning cliff and is still actively used to warn ships about the rough waters below, the point where the Atlantic Ocean and Caribbean Sea meet. You can walk out onto a nearby rocky outcropping that marks Trinidad's easternmost point. On most days Tobago is clearly visible from here. A local legend (unprovable) tells that a group of Arawaks jumped off this point to their deaths rather than be captured by the Spanish. You'll pass several beautiful beaches on the drive from Toco to the lighthouse. The journey from Port of Spain takes about two hours; take Churchill Roosevelt Highway east to Valencia Road; follow the road east to Toco Main Road sign; take this road all the way to Toco; from the Toco intersection, follow the sign to Point Galera. ⊠ *Galera Rd., 3 mi (5 km) from triangular Toco intersection* ☎ *Free* ☉ *Daily dawn–dusk.*

NEED A BREAK?

On the long drive to Point Galera, be sure to stop at **Kay's Pot** (⊠ *Toco Main Rd., Rampanalgas* ☎ *No phone*) for a great meal en route. Many consider it worth the drive all by itself. In a corner of the front parking lot of Arthur's Grocery and Bar, Kay serves an incredible array of local food such as souse (pickled pigs' feet in a lime-and-cucumber sauce), curried crab, and a variety of grilled and jerk meats. The informal atmosphere, low prices, and music pouring out of the bar make for a fun and unusual dining experience.

Port of Spain. Most organized tours begin at the port. If you're planning to explore on foot, which will take two to four hours, start early in the day; by midday the port area can be as hot and packed as Calcutta. It's best to end your tour on a bench in the Queen's Park Savannah, sipping a cool coconut water bought from one of the vendors operating out of flatbed trucks. For about 75¢ he'll lop the top off a green coconut with a deft swing of the machete and, when you've finished drinking, lop again, making a bowl and spoon of coconut shell for you to eat the young pulp. As in most cities, take extra care at night; women should not walk alone. Local police advise tourists and locals to avoid the neighborhoods just east of Port of Spain.

The town's main dock, **King's Wharf,** entertains a steady parade of cruise and cargo ships, a reminder that the city started from this strategic harbor. When hurricanes threaten other islands, it's not unusual to see as many as five large cruise ships taking advantage of the safety of the harbor. It's on Wrightson Road, the main street along the water on the southwest side of town. The national government has embarked on a massive development plan, which means that most of the wharf area is an active construction zone. The plan is to turn the area into a vibrant and attractive commercial and tourism zone. Many spanking-new high-rises have already been built, but the area is likely to be a work in progress for several years.

Across Wrightson Road and a few minutes' walk from the south side of King's Wharf, the busy **Independence Square** has been the focus of the downtown area's major gentrification. Flanked by government buildings and the familiar twin towers of the Financial Complex (they adorn all T&T dollar bills), the square (really a long rectangle) is a lovely park with trees, flagstone walkways, chess tables, and the Brian Lara Promenade (named after Trinidad's world-famous cricketer). On its south side is the International Waterfront Centre, with its gleaming skyscrapers and fast-ferry dock. On the eastern end of the square is the Cathedral of the Immaculate Conception; it was by the sea when it was built in 1832, but subsequent landfill around the port gave it an inland location. The imposing Roman Catholic structure is made of blue limestone from nearby Laventille.

Frederick Street, Port of Spain's main shopping drag, starting north from the midpoint of Independence Square, is a market street of scents and sounds—perfumed oils sold by sidewalk vendors and music tapes being played from vending carts—and crowded shops. Although it may be tempting to purchase CDs from these street vendors, they are selling pirated material, and doing so robs local artists of their livelihood.

At Prince and Frederick streets, **Woodford Square** has served as the site of political meetings, speeches, public protests, and occasional violence. It's dominated by the magnificent Red House, a Renaissance-style building that takes up an entire city block. Trinidad's House of Parliament takes its name from a paint job done in anticipation of Queen Victoria's Diamond Jubilee in 1897. The original Red House was burned to the ground in a 1903 riot, and the present structure was built four years later. The chambers are open to the public.

The view of the south side of the square is framed by the Gothic spires of Trinity, the city's Anglican cathedral, consecrated in 1823; its mahogany-beam roof is modeled after that of Westminster Hall in London. On the north are the impressive Public Library, the Hall of Justice, and City Hall.

25

If the downtown port area is the pulse of Port of Spain, the great green expanse of **Queen's Park Savannah,** roughly bounded by Maraval Road, Queen's Park West, Charlotte Street, and Saddle Road, is the city's soul. You can walk straight north on Frederick Street and get there within 20 minutes. Its 2-mi (3-km) circumference is a popular jogger's track. The northern end of the Savannah is devoted to plants. A rock garden, known as the Hollows, and a fishpond add to the rusticity. In the middle of the Savannah you will find a small graveyard where members of the Peschier family—who originally owned the land—are buried. Although the perimeter of the Savannah is busy and safe, you shouldn't walk across the park, as there have been occasional reports of muggings. The sheer size of the Savannah makes it difficult for local authorities to patrol, so it is best avoided altogether at night.

A series of astonishing buildings constructed in several 19th-century styles—known collectively as the **Magnificent Seven**—flanks the western side of the Savannah. Notable are Killarney, patterned (loosely) after Balmoral Castle in Scotland, with an Italian-marble gallery surrounding the ground floor; Whitehall, constructed in the style of a Venetian palace by a cacao-plantation magnate and, until recently, the office of the prime minister; Roomor (named for the Roodal and Morgan families—it's still occupied by the Morgans), a flamboyantly baroque colonial house with a preponderance of towers, pinnacles, and wrought-iron trim that suggests an elaborate French pastry; and the Queen's Royal College, in German Renaissance style, with a prominent tower clock that chimes on the hour. Sadly, several of these fine buildings have fallen into advanced decay.

Head over to the southeast corner of the Savannah, which is dominated by the shiny new **National Academy for the Performing Arts.** It opened in 2009 in time to host the opening ceremony for the Commonwealth Heads of Government Meeting. The structure looks something like a rounded glass-and-metal version of Sydney's famous opera. Be sure to walk a few yards farther south to see the **National Museum & Art Gallery** (⊠ *117 Upper Frederick St., Port of Spain* ☎ *868/623–5941* ⬚ *Free* ⊙ *Tues.–Sat. 10–6, Sun. 2–6*), especially its Carnival exhibitions, the Amerindian collection and historical re-creations, and the fine 19th-century paintings of Trinidadian artist Cazabon.

The cultivated expanse of parkland north of the Savannah is the site of the president's and prime minister's official residences and also the **Emperor Valley Zoo & Botanical Gardens** (⊠ *Northern side of Queen's Park Savannah, Port of Spain* ☎ *868/622–3530 or 868/622–5343* ⬚ *Zoo TT$4, gardens free* ⊙ *Daily 9–6*) A meticulous lattice of walkways and local flora, the parkland was first laid out in 1820 for Governor Ralph Woodford. In the midst of the serene wonderland is the 8-acre zoo, which exhibits mostly birds and animals of the region—from the brilliantly plumed scarlet ibis to slithering anacondas and pythons; you can also see (and hear) the wild parrots that breed in the surrounding foliage. The zoo draws a quarter of a million visitors a year. The admission price is a steal, and tours are free.

WHERE TO EAT

The food on T&T is a delight to the senses and has a distinctively creole touch, though everyone has a different idea about what creole seasoning is (just ask around, and you'll see). Bountiful herbs and spices include bay leaf, chadon beni (similar in taste to cilantro), nutmeg, turmeric, and different varieties of peppers. The cooking also involves a lot of brown sugar, rum, plantain, and local fish and meat. If there's fresh juice on the menu, be sure to try it. You can taste Asian, Indian, African, French, and Spanish influences, among others, often in a single meal. Indian-inspired food is a favorite: rotis (ample sandwiches of soft dough with a filling, similar to a burrito) are served as a fast food; a mélange of curried meat or fish and vegetables frequently makes an appearance, as do vindaloos (spicy meat, vegetable, and seafood dishes). Pelau (meat stewed in coconut milk with peas and rice), a Spanish-influenced dish, is another local favorite. Crab lovers will find large bluebacks curried, peppered, or in callaloo (Trinidad's national dish), a stew made with green dasheen leaves, okra, and coconut milk. Shark and bake (lightly seasoned, fried shark meat) is the sandwich of choice at the beach.

25

WHAT TO WEAR

Restaurants are informal: you won't find any jacket-and-tie requirements. Beachwear, however, is too casual for most places. A nice pair of shorts is appropriate for lunch; for dinner you'll probably feel most comfortable in a pair of slacks or a casual sundress.

$$$–$$$$
ITALIAN

✕ **Angelo's.** Calabrian chef Angelo Cofone married a Trinidadian and soon found himself in the restaurant business. He has opened his own restaurant, and it is already proving popular with locals and visiting businesspeople alike. His trademark innovative Italian menu changes regularly, and there is always a daily special. The restaurant is on Ariapita Avenue, which locals now refer to as the restaurant strip. ⊠ *38 Ariapita Ave., Woodbrook, Port of Spain* ☎ *868/628–5551.*

$$$–$$$$
INDIAN

✕ **Apsara.** This upscale Indian eatery is one of the few in Trinidad that features genuine Indian cuisine and not the local (though equally tasty) version. The name means "celestial dancer," and the food here is indeed heavenly. The inviting terra-cotta interior is decorated with hand-painted interpretations of Moghul art. Choosing dishes from the comprehensive menu is a bit daunting, so don't be afraid to ask for help. The *Husseini boti kebab* (lamb marinated in poppy seeds and masala) is an excellent choice. Service can be a bit slow at times, and those used to dining at Indian establishments in other parts of the world may find the prices comparatively high. ⊠ *13 Queen's Park E, Belmont, Port of Spain* ☎ *868/627–7364 or 868/623–7659* ☺ *Closed Sun.*

$$$–$$$$
ECLECTIC
Fodor'sChoice
★

✕ **Chaud.** Style meets substance at veteran chef Khalid Mohammed's latest gift to the local dining scene. Set in a restored house opposite the Queen's Park Savannah, the restaurant offers expansive views of Port of Spain's largest park, and local artwork adorns the walls. Famous for his extravagance, Mohammed presents food that rises off the plate like a Manhattan skyscraper. There is an obsession with freshness here, and

The Steel Pan

The sound of a steel band playing poolside has become emblematic of the Caribbean. What you may not know is that the fascinating instrument has an interesting and humble history that began in Trinidad.

In 1883 the British government banned the playing of drums on the island, fearful that they were being used to carry secret messages. Enterprising Afro-Trinidadians immediately found other means of creating music. Some turned to cut bamboo poles beaten rhythmically on the ground; these were called Tambu Bamboo bands, and they soon became a major musical force on the island. With the coming of industry, new materials such as hubcaps and biscuit tins were added as "instruments" in the bands. These metal additions were collectively known as "pan." Later, after the Americans established military bases on the islands during World War II, empty oil drums became available and were quickly put to musical use.

At some point it was discovered that these drums could be cut down, heated in a fire, and beaten into a finely tuned instrument. The steel pan as we know it was thus born. Soon there were entire musical bands playing nothing but steel pans. For years the music gestated in the poorer districts of Port of Spain and was seen as being suitable only for the lower classes of society, a reputation not helped by the fact that the loyal followers of early steel bands sometimes clashed violently with their rivals. Eventually, the magical sound of the "pan" and its amazing ability to adapt to any type of music won it widespread acceptance.

Today the government recognizes the steel pan as the official musical instrument of Trinidad and Tobago. It's played year-round at official functions and social gatherings, but the true time for the steel pan is Carnival. In the annual Panorama festival, dozens of steel bands from around the country compete for the "Band of the Year" title. Some have fewer than a dozen steel pans, whereas others number in the hundreds. The performance of the larger bands creates a thunderous wall-of-sound effect.

satisfaction is virtually guaranteed. It's a bit pricey for frequent visits but well worth it for a special romantic evening. ⊠ *2 Queen's Park W, Port of Spain* ☎ *868/623–0375* ⊕ *www.chaudkm.com* ⌕ *Reservations essential* ⊘ *Closed Sun. No lunch Sat.*

$$–$$$ ✕ **Joseph's.** Lebanese-born chef Joseph Habr has been serving fine cui-
ECLECTIC sine at his Maraval location for nine years but has 20 years of experi-
Fodor's Choice ence under his belt. The restaurant is a lovely open affair with a dining
★ room that looks out on a lush garden—complete with the sound of flowing water. Joseph visits every table and is always happy to offer helpful advice. The menu is comprehensive, and somehow there seems to be an Arabic element in even seemingly conventional dishes. If in doubt, it's impossible to go wrong with any of the lamb offerings. ⊠ *3A Rookery Nook, Maraval; the restaurant is a little out of the way; take Saddle Rd. into Maraval and follow it to RBTT Bank. Rookery Nook is on left.* ☎ *868/622–5557* ⊘ *Closed Sun. No lunch Sat.*

$$$–$$$$ ✕ **Mélange.** Some of the finest and most imaginative food on the island
ECLECTIC is to be found at this elegant establishment on restaurant row. Chef and owner Moses Ruben uses his years of experience as head chef at the Hilton to create delightfully balanced meals. His imaginative curried-crab-and-dumplings appetizer, which consists of delicately curried crab-meat served on a shell full of miniature dumplings, is an exceptional treat. ⊠ *40 Ariapita Ave., Woodbrook, Port of Spain* ☎ *868/628–8687* ⊘ *Closed Sun. No lunch Sat. No dinner Mon.*

$$$$ ✕ **Prime Restaurant.** Occupying the ground floor of the BHP Billiton
ECLECTIC tower, this upscale establishment caters to the business set with large expense accounts and demanding tastes. The subtle lighting, under-stated decor, and attentive staff also make this the ideal spot for a romantic dinner or a special-occasion splurge. Though a variety of options are available, most diners come for the excellent Angus steaks, and not without reason. The wine cellar is one of the best on the island, and a well-chosen vintage may help take some of the edge off the inevi-tably large bill. The restaurant is behind the Marriott and next door to the Movietowne complex. ⊠ *Ground fl., BHP Billiton Bldg., Invaders Bay* ☎ *868/624–6238* ⊕ *www.trentrestaurants.com/prime* ⌕ *Reservations essential* ⊘ *Closed Sun.*

$$$ ✕ **Tiki Village.** Port of Spainers in the know flock to the eighth floor of
ASIAN the Kapok Hotel, where the views of the city day and night are sim-
★ ply spectacular and the food is usually dependable. The dining room is lined with teak, and the menu includes the best of Polynesian and Asian fare. The Sunday dim sum—with tasting-size portions of dishes such as pepper squid and tofu-stuffed fish—is very popular. ⊠ *Kapok Hotel, 16–18 Cotton Hill, St. Clair, Port of Spain* ☎ *868/622–5765* ⌕ *Reservations essential.*

$$–$$$ ✕ **Trotters.** Although Trinidad has numerous examples of American
AMERICAN sports-bar chain restaurants, this local version beats them at their own game. There is often a lively crowd watching the more than 20 giant screens featuring all the latest in soccer and international sports. The huge square bar in the middle of the restaurant is where folks gather. Dining areas branch off from the bar area, and though some are more isolated than others, it is virtually impossible to escape the cheers of

25

the throng of sports enthusiasts. The food ranges from excellent burgers and hearty salads to Italian favorites and steaks. The standard is consistently excellent, and the servers, bedecked in pins and wearing safari hats, are always efficient and attentive. ⊠ *Corner of Maraval Rd. and Sweetbriar Rd., St. Clair* ☎ *868/627–8768.*

$$–$$$
CARIBBEAN
♨
FodorśChoice
★

✕ **Veni Mangé.** The best lunches in town are served in this traditional West Indian house. Credit Allyson Hennessy—a Cordon Bleu–trained chef and local television celebrity—and her friendly, flamboyant sister and partner, Rosemary (Roses) Hezekiah. Despite Allyson's training, home cooking is the order of the day here. The creative creole menu changes regularly, but there's always an unusual and delicious vegetarian entrée. Veni's version of Trinidad's national dish, callaloo, is considered one of the best on the island. The *chip chip* (a small local clam) cocktail is deliciously piquant and is a restaurant rarity. The restaurant's signature dish, stewed oxtail with dumplings, is not served every day but is worth ordering if it's available. ⊠ *67A Ariapita Ave., Woodbrook, Port of Spain* ☎ *868/624–4597* ⊕ *www.venimange.com* ⌲ *Reservations essential* ⊘ *Closed weekends. No dinner Mon., Tues., or Thurs.*

$$–$$$
CARIBBEAN
FodorśChoice
★

✕ **The Verandah.** Owner and hostess Phyllis Vieira has been hosting diners since the 1980s and prides herself on her "free-style Caribbean" menu, which is one of the best-kept secrets on the island. But the reasonable prices and consistently excellent cuisine make this a secret we can no longer keep. The open verandah, interior, and courtyard of this beautiful gingerbread-style colonial house provide a suitable setting for the menu, which changes weekly and is brought to you on a blackboard by the attentive, white-garbed staff. ⊠ *10 Rust St., St. Clair, Port of Spain* ☎ *868/622–6287* ⌲ *Reservations essential* ⊘ *Closed Sun. No dinner Mon.–Wed. and Fri. No lunch Sat.*

¢–$
CARIBBEAN

✕ **Wings Restaurant & Bar.** Rum shops and good food are an intrinsic part of Trinidad life, and both are combined in this colorful eatery, which is open only from 10 to 6. Regulars from the nearby university and industrial park flock here at lunchtime to enjoy a wide selection of local Indian food. It can get a bit loud, but at least fans keep the heat under control—just barely. To get here, turn off the Churchill Roosevelt Highway at the FedEx building (north side of the highway) in Tunapuna, and take the first left. ⊠ *16 Mohammed Terr., Tunapuna* ☎ *868/645–6607* ▭ *No credit cards* ⊘ *Closed Sun. No dinner.*

WHERE TO STAY

Because Trinidad is primarily a business destination, most accommodations are in or near Port of Spain. Standards are generally good, though not lavish. Port of Spain has a small downtown core—with a main shopping area along Frederick Street—and is surrounded by inner and outer suburbs. The inner areas include Belmont, Woodbrook, Newtown, St. Clair, St. Ann's, St. James, and Cascade. The nearest beach to most hotels is Maracas Bay, which is a half-hour drive over the mountains. Carnival visitors should book many months in advance and be prepared to pay top dollar for even the most modest hotel. The opening in 2008 of the new 428-room Hyatt Regency on the Port of Spain waterfront has added room capacity and means the Hilton Trinidad is no longer the only big international-class hotel on the island.

The following reviews have been condensed for this book. Please go to Fodors.com for expanded reviews of each property.

$$$
HOTEL

⬚ **Asa Wright Nature Centre Lodge.** This hotel, designed for serious bird-watchers, is surrounded by 200 acres of wilderness and by streams, waterfalls, and natural pools an hour's drive from the nearest beach or town. **Pros:** best bird-watching on the island; main house has a wonderful colonial feel; peaceful setting. **Cons:** miles from anything else on the island; no dining choices; the lack of entertainment options at night can be unnerving. ⬚ *Box 4710, Arima Valley* ☎ *868/667–4655 or 800/426–7781* ⊕ *www.asawright.org* ⬚ *24 rooms* ⬚ *In-room: no TV. In-hotel: restaurant, some age restrictions* ⦿ *All meals.*

$
HOTEL
Fodor's Choice
★

⬚ **The Carlton Savannah.** Those looking for a boutique hotel without compromising service and quality come to the Carlton. **Pros:** convenient and quiet location; free Wi-Fi; stylish, modern feeling; excellent restaurants. **Cons:** not within walking distance of shopping. ⬚ *2–4 Coblentz Ave., Cascade* ☎ *868/621–5000* ⊕ *www.thecarltonsavannah.com* ⬚ *155 rooms, 10 suites* ⬚ *In-room: safe, Wi-Fi. In-hotel: restaurants, room service, bar, pool, gym, spa, parking, some pets allowed* ⦿ *No meals.*

¢
B&B/INN

⬚ **Coblentz Inn.** Just a short drive from downtown in the quiet suburb of Cascade, this small boutique hotel offers peace, quiet, and style at a relatively affordable price. **Pros:** rooms have genuine charm; small but attentive staff; common areas are relaxing and great for catching up on reading. **Cons:** restaurant has wildly unreliable food quality; small compound can feel cramped. ⬚ *44 Coblentz Ave., Cascade, Port of Spain* ☎ *868/621–0541* ⊕ *www.coblentzinn.com* ⬚ *17 rooms* ⬚ *In-room: Wi-Fi. In-hotel: restaurant, bar, room service* ⦿ *Breakfast.*

$
HOTEL
★

⬚ **Courtyard by Marriott.** This large hotel in the capital offers excellent facilities and a great location. **Pros:** excellent location for shopping and dining; large and airy rooms; high service standards. **Cons:** just off busy highway; the many business travelers can make it feel a bit uncomfortable for leisure guests. ⬚ *Invaders Bay, Audrey Jeffers Hwy., Port of Spain* ☎ *868/627–5555* ⊕ *www.marriott.com* ⬚ *116 rooms, 3 suites* ⬚ *In-room: safe, Internet, Wi-Fi. In-hotel: restaurant, room service, bar, pool, gym, laundry facilities* ⦿ *No meals.*

¢–$
HOTEL

⬚ **Crews Inn Hotel & Yachting Centre.** On Trinidad's western peninsula, this hotel is about 20 minutes from downtown but smack in the middle of the island's most popular nightlife area. **Pros:** great view of marina; airy rooms are tastefully decorated; great for yachting enthusiasts. **Cons:** far from Port of Spain; very limited shopping and dining nearby. ⬚ *Point Gourde, Chaguaramas* ☎ *868/634–4384* ⊕ *www.crewsinn.com* ⬚ *42 rooms, 4 suites* ⬚ *In-room: kitchen, Internet. In-hotel: restaurant, room service, bars, pool, gym, laundry facilities* ⦿ *No meals.*

$
HOTEL

⬚ **Crowne Plaza Trinidad.** Proximity to the port and Independence Square is both the draw and the drawback here. **Pros:** close to downtown and the business core; revolving restaurant has wonderful views; much cheaper than the Hyatt for a similar downtown location. **Cons:** there's traffic noise by the pool area; hasn't kept pace with the higher standards offered by new hotels on the scene. ⬚ *Wrightson Rd., Box 1017, Port*

25

Hyatt Regency Trinidad.

of Spain ☎ 868/625–3361 *or* 800/227–6963 ⊕ *www.ichotelsgroup.com* 📠 *243 rooms, 5 suites* & *In-room: safe, Internet, Wi-Fi. In-hotel: restaurants, room service, bars, pool, gym* ⦿ *Breakfast.*

$ ⊞ **Hilton Trinidad & Conference Centre.** The Hilton was the most upscale
HOTEL hotel on the island before the arrival of the Hyatt Regency, and it still
★ commands a loyal following. **Pros:** great view; full range of hotel services; reliable and consistent service; the thrill of saying you stayed at the hotel where the U.S. president stayed. **Cons:** no longer the best luxury choice on the island; pool area can be very noisy when parties are going on—especially at Carnival time. ✉ *Lady Young Rd., Box 442, Port of Spain* ☎ 868/624–3211, 800/445–8667 *in U.S.* ⊕ *www.hiltoncaribbean.com* 📠 *385 rooms, 27 suites* & *In-room: safe, Internet. In-hotel: restaurants, room service, tennis courts, bars, pool, gym, business center* ⦿ *No meals.*

$ ⊞ **Holiday Inn Express & Suites Trincity.** Just five minutes from the air-
HOTEL port and with a complimentary shuttle service, this fairly new hotel
is popular with short-stay travelers. **Pros:** convenient to the airport;
close to Trincity Mall. **Cons:** not close to the major urban centers;
nearby traffic can be horrendous; has that bland chain-hotel feeling.
✉ *1 Exposition Dr., Trincity* ☎ 868/669–6209 ⊕ *www.ichotelsgroup. com* 📠 *62 rooms, 20 suites* & *In-room: safe, Internet, Wi-Fi. In-hotel: bar, pool* ⦿ *Breakfast.*

$ ⊞ **Hyatt Regency Trinidad.** Trinidad's only full-service hotel on the water-
HOTEL front is a striking high-rise structure and part of the government's dra-
Fodor'sChoice matic makeover of the Port of Spain waterfront. **Pros:** spanking new
★ and easily the most upscale full-service hotel on the island; view from
the rooftop pool is unbeatable; convenient to downtown and shopping.

Cons: right on the city's busiest commuter road; waterfront area is usually teeming with people; the smell of the nearby wharf can be unpleasant. ⊠ *1 Wrightson Rd., Port of Spain* ☎ *868/623–2222* ⊕ *trinidad. hyatt.com* ⟿ *418 rooms, 10 suites* ⟨ *In-room: safe, Wi-Fi. In-hotel: restaurants, room service, bars, gym, spa* ⦿ *No meals.*

$ ⚏ **Kapok Hotel.** This hotel in a good neighborhood just off Queen's Park
HOTEL   Savannah is a good all-around value if you want to stay in the city; it offers a high level of comfort and service. **Pros:** great location away from downtown noise; more intimate alternative to Hilton and Hyatt; one of the best restaurants on the island. **Cons:** lacks some of the services of larger hotels; some rooms are much smaller than others; pool is a bit small. ⊠ *16–18 Cotton Hill, St. Clair, Port of Spain* ☎ *868/622–5765 or 800/344–1212* ⊕ *www.kapokhotel.com* ⟿ *73 rooms, 12 suites, 9 studios* ⟨ *In-room: safe, kitchen (some), Internet. In-hotel: restaurants, room service, pool, gym, laundry facilities* ⦿ *No meals.*

¢   ⚏ **Le Grande Almandier.** This low-priced hotel is on Trinidad's remote
HOTEL   and beautiful northeast coast in an area that is a popular weekend
★   escape for locals who go to experience the lush rain-forest backdrop and expansive beach. **Pros:** right on the beach; great for turtle-watching in season; small with a friendly-family vibe. **Cons:** the northeast coast is at least two hours from the capital; limited shopping and dining options; car is definitely required for any exploring. ⊠ *2 Hosang St., Grande Riviere* ☎ *868/670–1013* ⊕ *www.legrandealmandier.com* ⟿ *10 rooms* ⟨ *In-room: no a/c (some). In-hotel: restaurant, room service, bar* ⦿ *Breakfast.*

¢   ⚏ **Monique's.** Spacious but simple rooms and proximity to Port of Spain
B&B/INN   ensure the popularity of this guesthouse, which consists of two separate buildings. **Pros:** huge rooms; in a generally quiet area; family ownership shows in the concern for the comfort of guests; on the main road to Maracas Beach. **Cons:** room decor feels very dated; not within walking distance of shopping or dining. ⊠ *114–116 Saddle Rd., Maraval, Port of Spain* ☎ *868/628–3334 or 868/628–2351* ⊕ *www.moniquestrinidad. com* ⟿ *20 rooms* ⟨ *In-room: kitchen (some), Internet. In-hotel: bar* ⦿ *Breakfast.*

NIGHTLIFE AND THE ARTS

NIGHTLIFE

There's no lack of nightlife in Port of Spain, and spontaneity plays a big role—around Carnival time look for the handwritten signs announcing the "Panyard," where the next informal gathering of steel-drum bands is going to be. Gay and lesbian travelers can take advantage of an increasingly lively gay scene in Trinidad, with parties drawing upward of 200 people on most weekends.

★   **51° Lounge** (⊠ *51 Cipriani Blvd., Woodbrook, Port of Spain* ☎ *868/627–0051*) is where the smart set hangs out. There's entertainment on most nights, and though admission is often free, it's advisable to call to confirm. Thursday night is always packed to the rafters, but go after 11 if you want to avoid the karaoke crowd. Don't even think about showing up in shorts, as there's a strict "elegant casual" dress code and an age limit of 25 years and older. Two of the island's top nightspots are on a former American army base in Chaguaramas. The **Anchorage/Tsunami Beach Club** (⌷ *Point Gourde Rd., Chaguaramas* ☎ *868/634–4334*) is a good spot for early-evening cocktails and snacks. **Coco Lounge** (⌷ *35 Carlos St., Woodbrook, Port of Spain* ☎ *868/622–6137*), a busy hangout on the popular Ariapita Avenue strip, caters to an upscale set who enjoy sipping cocktails in the elegant, modern-plantation-style interior or watching the world go by from the huge verandah. **Drink! Wine Bar** (⌷ *63 Rosalino St., Woodbrook, Port of Spain* ☎ *868/622–2895* ☉ *Closed Mon.*) has a cozy lounge atmosphere and a large and varied selection of wines, which makes this hangout popular with locals and visitors alike. There are snacks on offer and frequent performances from visiting DJs and musicians. This is a great place to meet members of the local arts community.

★   **More Vino** (⌷ *23 O'Connor St., Woodbrook, Port of Spain* ☎ *868/622–8466*) attracts a crowd of young professionals who come to network while sipping one of the more than 100 varieties of wine. Although most people choose to sit outside during the evening, seating is also available in the air-conditioned interior. Inside, you will also find an astonishing number of bottles on display for consumption on the premises or to take away. Cheeses and other items for nibbling are available, but no proper meals. **Pier 1** (⌷ *Western Main Rd., Chaguaramas* ☎ *868/634–4426*) is *the* place for lively late-night action. You can dance through the night on a large wooden deck jutting into the ocean with gentle sea breezes to cool you down. It's about 20 minutes west of Port of Spain, so get a party together from your hotel and hire a cab. It opens at 9 pm Wednesday through Sunday. **Sky Bar & Lounge** (⌷ *46 Ariapita Ave., Woodbrook, Port of Spain*) pulls a lively crowd on Friday and Saturday that parties until 5 am. The renovated rooftop setting is free of walls and offers dazzling views of Port of Spain harbor. There are occasional live performances, and there's always a large crowd on weekends. A nominal admission price of $7 is charged on Friday, when the bar is packed with a mostly gay crowd after 10 pm. **Trotters** (⌷ *Maraval and Sweet Briar Rd., St. Clair, Port of Spain* ☎ *868/627–8768*) is a sports bar in a two-story atrium. You can find an abundance of TV monitors as well as more than 30 varieties of beer from around the globe. It's incredibly popular on weekends despite the pricey drinks. **Zen** (⌷ *9–11 Keate St., Port of Spain* ☎ *868/625–9936*) is a very popular club in a former cinema with a stylish interior and a varied crowd. The cinema balcony has been transformed into a VIP area (open to anyone who pays the extra admission charge) where the well-heeled keep track of the action on the dance floor below. The action goes on until the sun comes up.

CARNIVAL

Trinidad always seems to be anticipating, celebrating, or recovering from a festival. Visitors are welcome at these events, which are a great way to explore the island's rich cultural traditions.

Fodor's Choice
★   Trinidad's version of the pre-Lenten bacchanal is reputedly the oldest in the Western Hemisphere; there are festivities all over the country, but the most lavish are in Port of Spain. Trinidad's Carnival has the warmth

and character of a massive family reunion and is billed by locals (not unreasonably) as "The Greatest Show on Earth." The season begins right after Christmas, and the parties, called *fêtes,* don't stop until Ash Wednesday. Listen to a radio station for five minutes, and you can find out where the action is. The Carnival event itself officially lasts only two days, from *J'ouvert* (2 am) on Monday to midnight the following day, Carnival Tuesday. If you really want to *experience* Carnival, then you need to arrive in Trinidad a week or two early to enjoy the preliminary events. (Hotels fill up quickly, so be sure to make reservations months in advance, and be prepared to pay premium prices for a minimum five-night stay. Even private homes have been known to rent bedrooms for as much as $300 per night.) If you visit during Carnival, try to get tickets to one of the all-inclusive parties where thousands of people eat and drink to the sound of music all night long. And while the festivities are mostly of the adult variety, children can parade in a kiddie carnival that takes place on the Saturday morning the week before the official events.

Carnival is a showcase for performers of calypso, which mixes dance rhythms with social commentary—sung by characters with such evocative names as Shadow, the Mighty Sparrow, and Black Stalin—and soca, which fuses calypso with a driving dance beat. As Carnival approaches, many of these singers perform nightly in calypso tents around the city. Many hotels also have special concerts by popular local musicians. You can also visit the city's "panyards," where steel orchestras such as the Renegades, Desperadoes, Neal and Massy All-Stars, Invaders, and Phase II rehearse their musical arrangements (most can also be heard during the winter season).

From the Sunday before Lent until midnight on Carnival Tuesday, when Port of Spain's exhausted merrymakers finally go to bed, it's basically one big nonstop party. The next day, feet are sore, but spirits have been refreshed. Lent (and theoretical sobriety) takes over for a while.

SHOPPING

Good buys in Trinidad include Angostura bitters, Old Oak or Vat 19 rum, and leather goods, all widely available throughout the country. Thanks in large part to Carnival costumery, there's no shortage of fabric shops. The best bargains for Asian and East Indian silks and cottons can be found in downtown Port of Spain, on Frederick Street and around Independence Square. Recordings of local calypsonians and steel-pan performances as well as *chutney* (a local East Indian music) are available throughout the islands and make great gifts.

AREAS AND MALLS

Downtown Port of Spain, specifically **Frederick, Queen,** and **Henry streets,** is full of fabrics and shoes. **Ellerslie Plaza** is an attractive outdoor mall well worth a browse. **Excellent City Centre** is set in an old-style oasis under the lantern roofs of three of downtown's oldest commercial buildings. Look for cleverly designed keepsakes, trendy cotton garments, and original artwork. The upstairs food court overlooks bustling Frederick Street.

The **Falls at West Mall,** just west of Port of Spain, is a dazzling temple to upscale shopping that could easily hold its own anywhere in the world. **Long Circular Mall** has upscale boutiques that are great for window-shopping. The **Market at the Normandie Hotel** is a small collection of shops that specialize in indigenous fashions, crafts, jewelry, basketwork, and ceramics. You can also have afternoon tea in the elegant little café.

SPECIALTY ITEMS

CLOTHING

A fine designer shop, **Meiling** (⊠ *Kapok Hotel, St. Clair Maraval, Port of Spain* ☎ *868/627–6975*) sells classically detailed Caribbean resort clothing. **Radical** (⊠ *The Falls at West Mall, Western Main Rd., Westmoorings* ☎ *868/632–5800* ⊠ *Long Circular Mall, Long Circular Rd., St. James, Port of Spain* ☎ *868/628–5693* ⊠ *Excellent City Centre, Independence Sq., Port of Spain* ☎ *868/627–6110*) carries T-shirts and original men's and women's casual clothing.

DUTY-FREE GOODS

Duty-free goods are available only at the airport upon departure or arrival. **De Lima's** (⊠ *Piarco International Airport, Piarco* ☎ *868/669–4738*) sells traditional duty-free luxury goods. **Stecher's** (⊠ *Piarco International Airport, Piarco* ☎ *868/669–4793*) is a familiar name for those seeking to avoid taxes on fine perfumes, china, crystal, handcrafted pieces, and jewelry. The branch at Ellerslie Plaza in Maraval carries only perfumes and cosmetics. **T-Wee Liquor Store** (⊠ *Piarco International Airport, Piarco* ☎ *868/669–4748*) offers deals on alcohol that you probably won't find in many other places around the world.

HANDICRAFTS

★ The tourism office can provide a list of local artisans who specialize in everything from straw and cane work to miniature steel pans. For painted plates, ceramics, aromatic candles, wind chimes, and carved-wood pieces and instruments, check out **Cockey** (⊠ *Long Circular Mall, Long Circular Rd., St. James, Port of Spain* ☎ *868/628–6546*). The **101 Art Gallery** (⊠ *Art Society of Trinidad and Tobago Bldg., Jamaica Blvd. and St. Vincent Ave., Federation Park, Port of Spain* ☎ *868/628–4081*) is Trinidad's foremost gallery, showcasing local artists such as Jackie Hinkson (figurative watercolors), Peter Sheppard (stylized realist local landscapes in acrylic), and Sundiata (semi-abstract watercolors). Openings are usually held Tuesday evening; the gallery is closed Sunday and Monday. **Poui Boutique** (⊠ *Ellerslie Plaza, Long Circular Rd., Maraval, Port of Spain* ☎ *868/622–5597*) has stylish handmade batik articles, Ajoupa ware (an attractive, local terra-cotta pottery), and many other gift items. The miniature ceramic houses and local scenes are astoundingly realistic, and are all handcrafted by owners Rory and Bunty O'Connor.

MUSIC

Just CDs and Accessories (⊠ *Long Circular Mall, Long Circular Rd., St. James, Port of Spain* ☎ *868/622–7516*) has a good selection of popular local musicians as well as other music genres. **Rhyner's Record Shop** ⊠ *Piarco International Airport, Piarco* ☎ *868/669–3064*) has a decent (and duty-free) selection of calypso and soca music.

SPORTS AND ACTIVITIES

BIRD-WATCHING

★ Trinidad and Tobago are among the top 10 spots in the world in terms of the number of species of birds per square mile—more than 430, many living within pristine rain forests, lowlands and savannahs, and fresh- and saltwater swamps. If you're lucky, you might spot the collared trogon, Trinidad piping guan (known locally as the common pawi), or rare white-tailed Sabrewing hummingbird. Restaurants often hang feeders outside on their porches, as much to keep the birds away from your food as to provide a chance to see them. Both the Asa Wright Nature Centre and Caroni Bird Sanctuary (⇨ *Exploring Trinidad*) are major bird-watching destinations.

Winston Nanan (☎ *868/645–1305*) is a self-taught ornithologist who knows the local fauna as well as his own children. He will arrange personal tours in his own car anywhere on the island. His business is based at the Caroni Bird Sanctuary, but his expertise makes a trip with him to the Northern Range or the northeast a must for any true bird-watcher. It won't be cheap, but the personal attention and his willingness to try to find rare species are well worth the expense.

FISHING

The islands off the northwest coast of Trinidad have excellent waters for deep-sea fishing; you may find wahoo, kingfish, and marlin, to name a few. The ocean here was a favorite angling spot of Franklin D. Roosevelt. Through **Bayshore Charters** (✉ *29 Sunset Dr., Bayshore, Westmoorings* ☎ *868/637–8711*) you can fish for an afternoon or hire a boat for a weekend; the *Melissa Ann* is fully equipped for comfortable cruising, sleeps six, and has an air-conditioned cabin, refrigerator, cooking facilities, and fishing equipment. Captain Sa Gomes is one of the most experienced charter captains on the islands. Members of the **Trinidad & Tobago Yacht Club** (✉ *Western Main Rd., Bayshore, Westmoorings* ☎ *868/637–4260*) may be willing to arrange a fishing trip for you.

GOLF

The best course in Trinidad is the 18-hole course at **St. Andrew's Golf Club** (✉ *Moka, Saddle Rd., Maraval, Port of Spain* ☎ *868/629–0066*), just outside Port of Spain. Greens fees are approximately $40 for 9 holes, $75 for 18 holes. The most convenient tee times are available on weekdays. Golf shoes with soft spikes are required.

GUIDED TOURS

Although any taxi driver in Trinidad or Tobago can take visitors to the major attractions, using a tour company allows for a more leisurely and educational adventure. Tour operators are also more mindful of the sensitivities of tourists and are much less likely to subject passengers to breakneck speeds and "creative" driving.

Caribbean Discovery Tours Ltd. (✉ *9B Fondes Amandes, St. Ann's, Port of Spain* ☎ *868/624–7281 or 868/620–1989* ⊕ *www.caribbeandiscoverytours. com*) is operated by Stephen Broadbridge. His tours are completely personalized and can include both on- and offshore activities. Tours can range from the strenuous to the leisurely, with prices based on the

25

duration of the expedition and the number of participants. **Kalloo's** (✉ *Piarco International Airport, Piarco* ☎ *868/669–5673 or 868/622–9073* ⊕ *www.kalloos.com*) offers tours ranging from a fascinating three-hour tour of Port of Spain to an overnight turtle-watching tour. **Sensational Tours & Transport** (✉ *47 Reservoir Rd., La Pastora, Santa Cruz* ☎ *868/702–4129 or 868/315–3652*) comes highly recommended and is your best choice for island tours. Owner Gerard Nicholas worked for the tourist board for many years and knows the island intimately. He is a complete delight to be with, and his tour prices are the lowest on the island by far.

TOBAGO

EXPLORING TOBAGO

A driving tour of Tobago, from Scarborough to Charlotteville and back, can be done in about four hours, but you'd never want to undertake this spectacular, and very hilly, ride in that time. The switchbacks can make you wish you had motion-sickness pills (take some along if you're prone). Plan to spend at least one night at the Speyside end of the island, and give yourself a chance to enjoy this largely untouched country and seaside at leisure.

Charlotteville. This delightful fishing village in the northeast is enfolded in a series of steep hills. Fishermen here announce the day's catch by sounding their conch shells. A view of Man O' War Bay with Pigeon Peak (Tobago's highest mountain) behind it at sunset is an exquisite treat.

Flagstaff Hill. One of the highest points on the island sits at the northern tip of Tobago. Surrounded by ocean on three sides and with a view of other hills, Charlotteville, and St. Giles Island, this was the site of an American military lookout and radio tower during World War II. It's an ideal spot for a sunset picnic. The turnoff to the hill is at the major bend on the road from Speyside to Charlotteville. It's largely unpaved, so the going may be a bit rough.

Ft. King George. On Mt. St. George, a short drive up the hill from Scarborough, Tobago's best-preserved historic monument clings to a cliff high above the ocean. Ft. King George was built in the 1770s and operated until 1854. It's hard to imagine that this lovely, tranquil spot commanding sweeping views of the bay and landscaped with lush tropical foliage was ever the site of any military action, but the prison, officers' mess, and several stabilized cannons attest otherwise. Just to the left of the tall wooden figures dancing a traditional Tobagonian jig is the former barrack guardhouse, now housing the small **Tobago Museum.** Exhibits include weapons and other pre-Columbian artifacts found in the area; the fertility figures are especially interesting. Upstairs are maps and photographs of Tobago's past. Be sure to check out the gift display cases for the perversely fascinating jewelry made from embalmed and painted lizards and sea creatures; you might find it hard to resist a pair of bright-yellow shrimp earrings. The **Fine Arts Centre** at the foot of the Ft. King George complex shows the work of local artists. ✉ *84 Fort St., Scarborough* ☎ *868/639–3970* 🎫 *Fort free, museum TT$5* ☉ *Weekdays 9–5.*

A cannon at Ft. King George, Tobago.

★ **Kimme Sculpture Museum.** The diminutive and eccentric German-born sculptress Luise Kimme fell in love with the form of Tobagonians and has devoted her life to capturing them in her sculptures. Her pieces can exceed 12 feet in height and are often wonderfully whimsical. Much of her work is done in wood (none of it local), but there are many bronze pieces as well. The museum itself is a turreted structure with a commanding view of the countryside. Most locals refer to it as "The Castle." There are numerous signs in Mt. Irvine directing visitors to the museum. ⊠ *Mt. Irvine* ☎ *868/639–0257* ⊕ *www.luisekimme.com* ⊠ *TT$20* ☉ *Sun. 10–2 or by appointment.*

Scarborough. Around Rockley Bay on the island's leeward hilly side, this town is both the capital of Tobago and a popular cruise-ship port, but it conveys the feeling that not much has changed since the area was settled two centuries ago. It may not be one of the delightful pastel-color cities of the Caribbean, but Scarborough does have its charms, including several interesting little shops. Whatever you do, be sure to check out the busy Scarborough Market, an indoor and outdoor affair featuring everything from fresh vegetables to live chickens and clothing. Note the red-and-yellow Methodist church on the hill, one of Tobago's oldest churches.

NEED A BREAK? **Ciao Café** (⊠ *20 Burnett St., Scarborough* ☎ *868/639–3001*) is an essential stop on any visit to the capital and offers a selection of more than 20 flavors of gelato, as well as the usual complement of coffees. You can also get pizza slices and sandwiches if you're looking for a quick snack. There's seating in the air-conditioned interior and a lovely outdoor perch from which to absorb the downtown action sheltered from the blazing sun. Stronger cocktails are also available.

Speyside. At the far reach of Tobago's windward coast, this small fishing village has a few lodgings and restaurants. Divers are drawn to the unspoiled reefs in the area and to the strong possibility of spotting giant manta rays. The approach to Speyside from the south affords one of the most spectacular vistas of the island. Glass-bottom boats operate between Speyside and **Little Tobago Island,** one of the most important seabird sanctuaries in the Caribbean.

St. Giles Island. The underwater cliffs and canyons here off the northeastern tip of Tobago draw divers to this spot where the Atlantic meets the Caribbean. ⊠ *Take Windward Rd. inland across mountains from Speyside.*

WHERE TO EAT

Curried crab and dumplings is a Sunday-dinner favorite in Tobago. *Oil-down*—a local dish—tastes better than it sounds: it's a gently seasoned mixture of boiled breadfruit and salt beef or pork flavored with coconut milk. Mango ice cream or a sweet-and-sour tamarind ball makes a tasty finish. You may want to take home some hot-pepper sauce or chutney to a spice-loving friend or relative.

$$–$$$
CARIBBEAN
Fodor's Choice
★

✕**Blue Crab Restaurant.** The Sardinha family have been serving the best local lunches at their home since the 1980s. The ebullient Alison entertains and hugs diners while her husband, Ken, does the cooking. The food is hearty and usually well seasoned in the creole style. The only bad news here is that the restaurant is rarely open for dinner; the good news is that you may not have room for dinner after lunch. ⊠ *Robinson and Main Sts., Scarborough* ☎ *868/639–2737* ⊕ *www.tobagobluecrab. com* ⊘ *Closed weekends. No dinner.*

$$–$$$
ECLECTIC

✕**Bonkers.** Despite the rather odd name, this restaurant at the Toucan Inn is atmospheric and excellent. Designed by expat British co-owner Chris James, the architecture is a blend of Kenyan and Caribbean styles, executed entirely in local teak and open on all sides. The menu is huge; Chris claims it pains him to remove any items, so he just keeps adding more. You can savor your lobster Rockefeller while enjoying the nightly entertainment. Open for breakfast and lunch seven days a week, this is the busiest eatery on the island. ⊠ *Toucan Inn, Store Bay Local Rd., Crown Point* ☎ *868/639–7173* ⊕ *www.toucan-inn.com.*

$$–$$$
ECLECTIC

✕**Café Coco.** This smart eatery seats 200, but it's divided into multiple levels, so there's still a sense of intimacy. Statuary is strewn about with carefree abandon, and the sound of flowing water permeates the room. Reasonably priced by Tobago standards, the main courses range from Cuban stewed beef to shrimp tempura. The restaurant is seldom full, so getting a table is usually not a problem. ⊠ *TTEC Substation Rd. off Crown Point Rd., Crown Point* ☎ *868/639–0996* ⊕ *www.cocoreef.com/cafecoco.*

$$$–$$$$
ECLECTIC

✕**Café Iguana.** This funky little restaurant and art gallery is a popular gathering place evenings, as it serves some of the best cocktails on the island. The menu is eclectic, but there is a distinct Tobago touch to everything and an emphasis on local ingredients. The crayfish, though messy to eat, is not to be missed. The art on the walls is available for sale—you might want to exercise restraint with the cocktails before deciding to become an art investor. ⊠ *Store Bay Local Rd. at Milford Rd., Crown Point* ☎ *868/631–8205* ⊕ *www.iguanatobago. com* ☉ *Closed Wed.*

$$$–$$$$
CARIBBEAN
★

✕ **Kariwak Village Restaurant.** Recorded steel-band music plays gently in the background at this romantic, candlelit spot in the Kariwak Village complex. In a bamboo pavilion that resembles an Amerindian round hut, Cynthia Clovis orchestrates a very original menu. Whatever the dish, it will be full of herbs and vegetables picked from her organic garden. Be sure to try the delicious homemade ice cream. Friday and Saturday buffets, with live jazz or calypso, are a Tobagonian highlight. ⊠ *Crown Point* ☎ *868/639–8442* ⊕ *www.kariwak.com.*

$$–$$$
ITALIAN

✕ **La Tartaruga.** Milanese owner Gabriele de Gaetano has created the island's most prominent Italian eatery. Over the years the restaurant has made its menu much less expensive, making it a bargain by island standards. Sitting on the large patio surrounded by lush foliage with Gabriele rushing from table to table chatting in Italian-laced English is all the entertainment you'll need. An impressive cellar is stocked solely with Italian wines. ⊠ *Buccoo Rd., Buccoo* ☎ *868/639–0940* ⌂ *Reservations essential* ☉ *Closed Sun. No lunch.*

$$$–$$$$
ECLECTIC

✕ **MeShell's.** This pretty little restaurant housed in a pink building on the road to Mt. Irvine may not always be consistent with the food, but it more than makes up for it with atmosphere. Most diners choose to dine on the covered patio surrounded by a tropical garden. The main focus here is seafood and steaks, and the daily panfried catch of the day in a creole sauce is a popular favorite. Though this is a fairly expensive establishment, don't expect towering exotic presentations. Regulars rave about the Death by Chocolate dessert. ⊠ *Corner of Shirvan Rd. and Old Buccoo Rd., Mt. Pleasant* ☎ *868/631–0353* ☉ *Closed Sun. No lunch.*

¢
CAFÉ
Fodor'sChoice
★

✕ **Shore Things Café & Craft.** With a dramatic setting over the ocean on the Milford Road between Crown Point and Scarborough, this is a good spot to stop for a lunch or coffee break. Survey the view from the deck tables while enjoying a variety of freshly prepared juices (the tamarind is particularly refreshing) and nibbling on excellent sandwiches. The whole-wheat pizza here may well be the best on the island. While waiting for your meal, you can shop for local crafts in the lovely and comprehensive gift shop. ⊠ *25 Old Milford Rd., Lambeau* ☎ *868/635–1072* ☉ *Closed Sun. No dinner.*

$$–$$$
CARIBBEAN
★

✕ **Shutters on the Bay.** In the stylish Blue Haven Hotel, this restaurant is sure to please even the most discerning diners. The warm-yellow dining area is on the second floor of a colonial-style building and is surrounded by white push-out shutters that afford a magical view of Bacolet Bay. The menu features a variety of dishes, all with a contemporary Caribbean twist. If crayfish is on the menu, get it, as it's a sure pleaser. ⊠ *Blue Haven Hotel, Bacolet Bay, Scarborough* ☎ *868/660–7500* ⌂ *Reservations essential.*

25

$$$ ✕ **Tamara's.** At the elegant Coco Reef Resort you can dine on con-
ECLECTIC temporary cuisine with an island twist. The peach walls and white-
washed wooden ceiling make the resort's restaurant feel airy and
light, and island breezes waft through the palm-lined terrace. The
prix-fixe menu changes seasonally, but the fish dishes are sure to
please. A full tropical buffet breakfast is served daily; dinner is served
nightly. There is a prix-fixe choice of one, two, or three courses.
⊠ *Coco Reef Resort, Crown Point, Scarborough* ☎ *868/639–8571*
⚐ *Reservations essential.*

WHERE TO STAY

Tobago is much more of a tourist destination than Trinidad, and this
is reflected in the range of accommodations. Those seeking luxury can
find a number of upscale resorts and villas, and the budget-minded can
take advantage of several smaller and more intimate establishments.

*The following reviews have been condensed for this book. Please go to
Fodors.com for expanded reviews of each property.*

¢ ⛨ **Arnos Vale Hotel.** On 450 hillside acres, this hotel is the perfect retreat
HOTEL for nature lovers and lovers in general. **Pros:** complete peaceful set-
ting; beautifully landscaped grounds; large and immaculate rooms;
stay where The Beatles stayed. **Cons:** miles away from dining or shop-
ping; some rooms are quite a hike away from the beach. ⊠ *Arnos Vale
and Franklin Rds., Box 208, Scarborough* ☎ *868/639–2881* ⊕ *www.
arnosvalehotel.com* ⤳ *29 rooms, 3 suites* ⚒ *In-room: no TV. In-hotel:
restaurant, tennis court, bars, pool, water sports* ⦿| *No meals.*

$ ⛨ **Blue Haven Hotel.** Justifiably celebrated, this 1940s-era luxury hotel
HOTEL overlooks a spectacular secluded beach on Bacolet Bay just outside
Fodor's Choice Scarborough. **Pros:** historic charm; beautiful beach; more European
★ flair than any other hotel on the island. **Cons:** lacks the range of ser-
vices of the larger hotels; far from the attractions of Crown Point;
beach is a short walk down a hillside. ⊠ *Bacolet Bay, Scarborough*
☎⛨ *868/660–7400* ⊕ *www.bluehavenhotel.com* ⤳ *43 rooms, 8 suites,
1 villa* ⚒ *In-room: Internet. In-hotel: restaurant, tennis court, bars,
pool, gym, laundry facilities, spa, beach* ⦿| *No meals.*

$ ⛨ **Blue Waters Inn.** A tropical rain forest creeps up behind this sprawl-
HOTEL ing ecofriendly hotel, which sits on sheltered, turquoise Batteaux Bay
★ with a white-sand beach just east of Speyside. **Pros:** rooms open onto
the beach and are near water; enthusiastic and friendly staff; simple
but delicious food. **Cons:** long drive from the nearest town. ⊠ *Bat-
teaux Bay, Speyside* ☎ *868/660–4077* ⊕ *www.bluewatersinn.com*
⤳ *31 rooms, 3 suites, 4 bungalows* ⚒ *In-room: kitchen (some), no
TV. In-hotel: restaurant, tennis court, bar, beach, business center, water
sports* ⦿| *Breakfast.*

$$$$ ⛨ **Coco Reef Resort.** This expansive enclave is just a short distance from
RESORT the airport but somehow seems miles away, its pink buildings sprawled
☾ along a perfect stretch of coast. **Pros:** beautifully appointed rooms; the
★ only private beach on the island; impeccable and understated service.
Cons: pool area can get a bit too animated; no Wi-Fi; some rooms
are quite far from the beach and reception. ⊠ *Coconut Bay, Box 434,*

Crown Point ☎ *868/639–8571 or 800/221–1294* ⊕ *www.cocoreef.com* ⇱ *100 rooms, 27 suites, 8 villas* ☪ *In-room:. In-hotel: restaurants, room service, tennis courts, bars, pool, gym, spa, beach, water sports* ¶◯*Breakfast.*

¢–$
RESORT
☪

🔳 **Grafton Beach Resort.** The first all-inclusive in Tobago now only offers the package as an $80 per person option—it remains a very popular choice for young couples. **Pros:** large rooms; lively pool area. **Cons:** mediocre food offerings, those on the free drinks plan can sometimes make for a rowdy crowd. ⊠ *Shirvan Rd., Black Rock* ☎ *868/639–0191* ⇱ *102 rooms, 4 suites* ☪ *In-room: safe. In-hotel: restaurants, bars, pool, beach, water sports* ¶◯*Breakfast.*

$
HOTEL
★

🔳 **Kariwak Village.** Alan and Cynthia Cloves have created an intimate, tranquil oasis for their loyal guests who return year after year to this holistic retreat. **Pros:** cozy and intimate throughout; excellent restaurant; beautiful grounds. **Cons:** the New Age concept may not be to all tastes, but it isn't imposed on guests; no beach. ✇ *Box 27, Crown Point* ☎ *868/639–8442* ⊕ *www.kariwak.com* ⇱ *24 rooms* ☪ *In-room: no TV, Wi-Fi. In-hotel: restaurant, bar, pool* ¶◯*No meals.*

$$$
RESORT

🔳 **Le Grand Courlan Resort & Spa.** This resort is more upscale than its sister property, the Grafton Beach Resort, with rooms that have large balconies overlooking one of the best beaches on the island. **Pros:** beautiful beach; perfect for those who want to get away from screaming children. **Cons:** other hotels offer better rooms and services for the same price or less; restaurants are mediocre. ⊠ *Shirvan Rd., Black Rock* ☎ *868/639–9667* ⊕ *www.legrandtobago.com* ⇱ *80 rooms, 3 suites* ☪ *In-room: safe. In-hotel: restaurants, tennis courts, bars, pool, gym, spa, beach, water sports, some age restrictions* ¶◯*All-inclusive.*

$–$$
HOTEL

🔳 **Mt. Irvine Bay Hotel.** Although the hotel lacks some of the fancier amenities, there's still something magical about its air of 1970s grandeur, which cannot be found at the flashy new resorts. **Pros:** beautiful grounds; perfect for the golf lover; access to one of the prettiest beaches. **Cons:** public spaces feel dated; poor restaurant service. ⊠ *Shirvan Rd., Box 222, Mt. Irvine* ☎ *868/639–8871* ⊕ *www.mtirvine.com* ⇱ *53 rooms, 6 suites, 46 cottages* ☪ *In-room: safe. In-hotel: golf course, restaurants, tennis courts, bars, pool, beach, water sports* ¶◯*No meals.*

$
RENTAL

🔳 **Plantation Beach Villas.** If you're looking for luxury living in a well-appointed Caribbean villa, you should be blissfully happy here. **Pros:** an engaging alternative to a hotel room; on the beach; all the comforts of home and maid service. **Cons:** no restaurant for dinner; lacks the diversions of a large hotel. ⊠ *Stone Haven Bay Rd., Black Rock* ✇ *Box 434, Scarborough* ☎ *868/639–9377* ⊕ *www.plantationbeachvillas.com* ⇱ *6 3-bedroom villas* ☪ *In-room: safe, kitchen, Wi-Fi. In-hotel: bar, pool, laundry facilities, beach* ¶◯*No meals.*

¢
HOTEL

🔳 **Toucan Inn.** This budget hotel near the airport offers simple, clean rooms and a lively social scene. **Pros:** great value; good restaurant. **Cons:** pool and bar area can be a bit raucous on weekends; rooms are serviceable but spartan; no beach. ⊠ *Store Bay Local Rd., Crown Point* ☎ *868/639–7173* ⊕ *www.toucan-inn.com* ⇱ *20 rooms* ☪ *In-hotel: restaurant, bar, pool* ¶◯*No meals.*

25

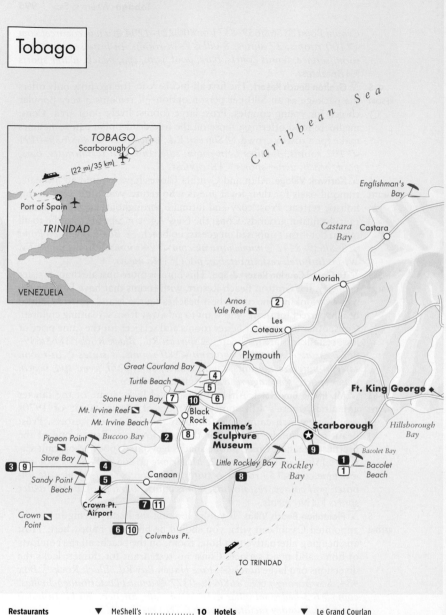

Tobago

TOBAGO

Scarborough

(22 mi/35 km)

Port of Spain ✈

TRINIDAD

VENEZUELA

Caribbean Sea

Englishman's Bay

Castara Bay — Castara

Moriah

Arnos Vale Reef [2]

Les Coteaux

Plymouth

Great Courland Bay [4]

Turtle Beach [5]

Stone Haven Bay [7] [10] [6]

Mt. Irvine Reef

Mt. Irvine Beach — Black Rock [8]

Kimme's Sculpture Museum

Ft. King George

Scarborough [9]

Hillsborough Bay

Bacolet Bay

Pigeon Point

Buccoo Bay [2]

Store Bay [3] [9]

Sandy Point Beach [4] [5]

Crown Pt. Airport [7] [11]

Crown Point

Canaan

Little Rockley Bay [8]

Rockley Bay

[1] [1] *Bacolet Beach*

[6] [10]

Columbus Pt.

TO TRINIDAD

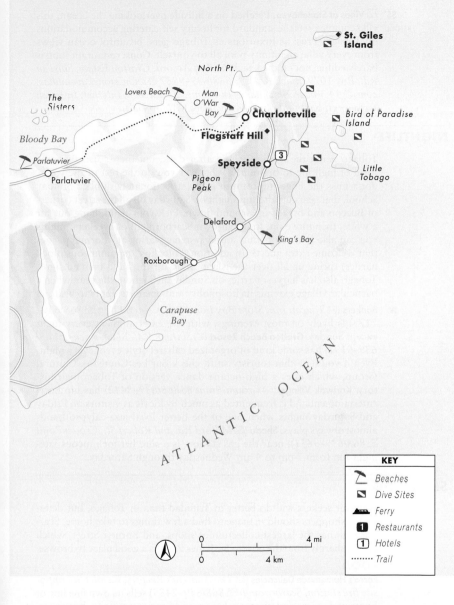

St. Giles
Island

North Pt.

Lovers Beach

Man
O'War
Bay

Charlotteville

Flagstaff Hill

The
Sisters

Bloody Bay

Parlatuvier

Parlatuvier

Pigeon
Peak

Speyside

3

Bird of Paradise
Island

Little
Tobago

Delaford

King's Bay

Roxborough

Carapuse
Bay

ATLANTIC OCEAN

KEY

⚲ Beaches

◥ Dive Sites

⛴ Ferry

1 Restaurants

① Hotels

⋯⋯⋯ Trail

0   4 mi

0   4 km

$$ **Villas at Stonehaven.** Perched on a hillside overlooking the ocean, this
RENTAL villa complex sets the standard for luxury self-catering accommodations
on Tobago. **Pros:** as luxurious as Tobago gets; beautiful ocean views
from every villa; an infinity pool all to yourself. **Cons:** restaurant food is
barely edible; not on the beach. ✉ *Bon Accord, Grafton Estate, Shirvan
Rd., Box 1079, Black Rock* ☎ *868/639–9887* ⊕ *www.stonehavenvillas.
com* ⇨ *14 3-bedroom villas* ⚷ *In-room: safe, kitchen, Internet. In-hotel:
restaurant, bar, pool, laundry facilities* ⓧ *No meals.*

NIGHTLIFE

Tobago is not the liveliest island after dark, but there's usually some
form of nightlife to be found. Whatever you do the rest of the week,
don't miss the huge impromptu party, affectionately dubbed Sunday
School, that gears up after midnight on Saturday on all the street corners
of Buccoo and breaks up around dawn. Pick your band, hang out for
a while, then move on. In downtown Scarborough on weekend nights
you can also find competing sound systems blaring at informal parties
that welcome extra guests. In addition, "blockos" (spontaneous block
parties) spring up all over the island; look for the hand-painted signs.
Tobago also has harvest parties on Sunday throughout the year, when a
particular village extends its hospitality and opens its doors to visitors.

★ **Bonkers** (✉ *Toucan Inn, Store Bay Local Rd., Crown Point* ☎ *868/639–
7173*) is lively on most evenings, with live entertainment every night
except Sunday. **Grafton Beach Resort** (✉ *Shirvan Rd., Black Rock* ☎ *868/
639–0191*) has some kind of organized cabaret-style event every night.
Even if you hate that touristy stuff, check out Les Couteaux Cultural
Group, which does a high-octane dance version of Tobagonian his-
tory. **Kariwak Village** (✉ *Crown Point* ☎ *868/639–8442*) has hip hotel
entertainment and is frequented as much by locals as visitors on Friday
and Saturday nights when one of the better local jazz-calypso bands
almost always plays. **Shade** (✉ *Milford Rd. and Robert St., Crown Point*
☎ *868/639–9651*), near the gas station, is a sure bet for raucous late-
night fun from 7 pm to 4 am Wednesday through Saturday.

SHOPPING

Souvenir seekers will do better in Trinidad than in Tobago, but deter-
mined shoppers should manage to find a few things to take home. Scar-
borough has the largest collection of shops, and Burnett Street, which
climbs sharply from the port to St. James Park, is a good place to browse.

FOOD

Forro's Homemade Delicacies (✉ *The Andrew's Rectory, Bacolet St., oppo-
site fire station, Scarborough* ☎ *868/639–2485*) sells its own fine line of
homemade tamarind chutney, lemon and lime marmalade, hot sauce,
and guava and golden-apple jelly. Eileen Forrester, wife of the Angli-
can archdeacon of Trinidad and Tobago, supervises a kitchen full of
good cooks who boil and bottle the condiments and pack them in little
straw baskets—or even in bamboo. Most jars are small, easy to carry,
and inexpensive.

Continued on page 1002

CARNIVAL IN TRINIDAD
Vernon O'Reilly Ramesar

The "Greatest Show on Earth" is also the best party in the Caribbean, and it's not brought to you by Barnum & Bailey but by the people of Trinidad. The island's pre-Lenten Carnival is rooted in Trinidad's African and French-Creole cultures and is more spontaneous than similar celebrations in Latin America; its influence reaches as far as Miami, Toronto, and London.

Trinidad's celebration has evolved through the years. What was once a two-day affair has turned into a lengthy party season starting in early January and lasting until Ash Wednesday. The biggest and best parties are held in and around Port of Spain, where locals max out their credit cards and even take out bank loans to finance their costumes and attend as many parties as possible.

On Carnival Monday and Tuesday the traffic lights of Port of Spain are turned off and the streets are turned over to a human traffic jam of costumed revelers.

They jump and dance to the pounding sound of music trucks—featuring huge speakers and either live music or a DJ—and turn Port of Spain into a pulsing celebration of island life that they call the *mas*.

Mas bands—some with thousands of members, others with a mere handful—must follow a route and pass judging points to win a prize, but increasingly, they simply don't bother. They're in it for the fun. To grease the wheels, makeshift bars are set up along all the city's streets.

Children stiltwalkers in colorful Carnival costumes, Queens Park Savannah, Port of Spain

CARNIVAL 101

THE FETE

Huge outdoor parties (called *fetes*) are held in the months before Carnival; during the final week, there are usually several fetes every day. You can get tickets for many of them through the major hotels, but some exclusive fetes may require an invitation from a well-connected Trinidadian.

THE PANORAMA

While fetes are important to Carnival, the Panorama Steelpan Preliminaries and finals are essential. Two weeks before Carnival, the "Prelims" are held, when dozens of steel drum orchestras compete for a place in the finals held on Carnival Saturday. Music lovers go to hear the throbbing sound of hundreds of steelpans beating out a syncopated rhythm, and the rum-fueled party often rivals even the best fetes.

DIMANCHE GRAS

On Carnival Sunday, top calypsonians compete to be Calypso Monarch, and this offers you an especially good opportunity to experience Carnival in one easy shot. The show was once held in Queen's Park Savannah, but the location now varies.

THE COSTUMES

To be a true part of Carnival, you need a costume. Every mas band has its own costumes, which must be reserved months in advance (these days online). You pick up yours at the band's mas "camp" and find out where and when to meet your band. Then all you have to do is jump, walk, or wave in the Carnival procession as the spirit moves you. Drinks and food may be included.

(top) Trinidad Carnival celebrations during Junior Parade of the Bands, (bottom) masquerader in a colorful costume.

MUSIC

Carnival is powered by music, and though the steelpan still plays a big part, it is the *soca* performers who draw the biggest crowds. Some of the big names include Machel Montano, Shurwayne Winchester, and Allyson Hinds. You can hear the most popular performers at the bigger fetes and at the Soca Monarch competition held on Carnival Friday before the more prestigious Calypso Monarch contest.

THE MAS BANDS

Trinis are passionate about their favorite mas band. The most popular have costumes largely comprised of beaded bikinis and feathered headdresses and are called "pretty mas." Very large bands such as Tribe, Island People, and Hart's fall into this category. If you're not willing to show that much skin or want more theater, then choose a band like MacFarlane, which offers more elaborate costumes with a thematic story. As has always been the case, women greatly outnumber men in the bands.

Carnival costumes are usually colorful—and skimpy.

TOP FETES

Safety is an increasing concern in Trinidad, especially at Carnival time. Fetes that attract a better heeled crowd offer more security and sufficient bars to cater to the thousands of revelers who attend. They usually command higher prices but are worth the cost.

Kama Sutra is held at the Trinidad Country Club on the Saturday before Carnival weekend. It is all-inclusive and features a good selection of food and premium drinks.

Eyes Wide Shut is held at The Oval (home of Trinidad cricket) and tends to attract a younger crowd.

Insomnia is an overnight fete held in Chaguaramas, just West of Port of Spain, on Carnival Saturday, and the partying doesn't stop till sunrise.

The Brian Lara and Moka all-inclusive fetes are both held on the afternoon of Carnival Sunday. Tickets for both are highly sought. Brian Lara is considered the most exclusive of all fetes and is the most expensive.

HANDICRAFTS

Cotton House (⊠ *Bacolet St., Scarborough* ☎ 868/639–2727) is a good bet for jewelry and imaginative batik work. Paula Young runs her shop like an art school. You can visit the upstairs studio; if it's not too busy, you can even make a batik square at no charge. **Shore Things Café & Crafts** (⊠ *25 Old Milford Rd., Lambeau* ☎ 868/635–1072) has a wide variety of souvenir items ranging from masks to music—and everything in between. **Store Bay** (⊠ *Store Bay, Crown Point*) has a variety of stalls offering everything from T-shirts to local handicrafts and is convenient to the airport for any last-minute purchases.

SPORTS AND ACTIVITIES

BIRD-WATCHING

★ Some 200 varieties of birds have been documented on Tobago: look for the yellow oriole, scarlet ibis, and the comical motmot—the male of the species clears sticks and stones from an area and then does a dance complete with snapping sounds to attract a mate. The flora is as vivid as the birds. Purple-and-yellow *poui* trees and spectacular orange immortelles splash color over the countryside, and something is blooming virtually every season. Pat Turpin and Renson Jack at **Pioneer Journeys** (☎ 868/660–4327 *or* 868/660–5175 ✆ *pturpin@tstt.net.tt*) can give you information about their bird-watching tours of Bloody Bay rain forest and Louis d'Or River valley wetlands. Naturalist and ornithologist David Rooks operates **Rooks Nature Tours** (⊠ *462 Moses Hill, Lambeau* ☎ 868/756–8594), offering bird-watching walks inland and trips to offshore bird colonies. He's generally considered the best guide on the island.

BOAT TOURS

Tobago offers many wonderful spots for snorkeling. Although the reefs around Speyside in the northeast are becoming better known, **Buccoo Reef**, off the island's southwest coast, is still the most popular—perhaps too popular. Over the years the reef has been badly damaged by the ceaseless boat traffic and by the thoughtless visiting divers who take pieces of coral as souvenirs. Still, it's worth experiencing, particularly if you have children. Daily 2½-hour tours by glass-bottom boats let you snorkel at the reef, swim in a lagoon, and gaze at Coral Gardens—where fish and coral are as yet untouched. Most dive companies in the Black Rock area also arrange snorkeling tours. There's also good snorkeling near the **Arnos Vale Hotel** and the **Mt. Irvine Bay Hotel**.

Hew's Glass Bottom Boat Tours (⊠ *Pigeon Point* ☎ 868/639–9058) are perfect excursions for those who neither snorkel nor dive. Boats leave daily at 11:30 am.

DIVING

An abundance of fish and coral thrives on the nutrients of Venezuela's Orinoco River, which are brought to Tobago by the Guyana current. Off the west coast is **Arnos Vale Reef**, with a depth of 40 feet and several reefs that run parallel to the shore. Here you can spot French and queen angelfish, moray eels, southern stingrays, and even the Atlantic torpedo ray. Much of the diving is drift diving in the mostly gentle current. **Crown Point**, on the island's southwest tip, is a good place for exploring the Shallows—a plateau at 50 to 100 feet that's favored by turtles, dolphins, angelfish, and nurse sharks. Just north of Crown Point on the southwest coast, **Pigeon Point** is a good spot to submerge. North of Pigeon Point, long, sandy beaches line the calm western coast; it has a gradual offshore slope and the popular **Mt. Irvine Wall,** which goes down to about 60 feet.

A short trip from Charlotteville, off the northeast tip of the island, is **St. Giles Island.** Here are natural rock bridges— London Bridge, Marble Island, and Fishbowl—and underwater cliffs. The **waters off Speyside** on the east coast draw scuba-diving aficionados for the many manta rays in the area. Exciting sites in this area include Batteaux Reef, Angel Reef, Bookends, Blackjack Hole, and Japanese Gardens—one of the loveliest reefs, with depths of 20 to 85 feet and lots of sponges.

Tobago is considered a prime diving destination, as the clear waters provide maximum visibility. Every species of hard coral and most soft corals can be found in the waters around the island. Tobago is also home to the largest-known brain coral. Generally, the best diving is around the Speyside area. Many hotels and guesthouses in this area cater to the diving crowd with minimalist accommodations and easy access to the water. You can usually get the best deals with these "dive-and-stay" packages. **AquaMarine Dive Ltd.** (✉ *Blue Waters Inn, Batteaux Bay, Speyside* ☎ *868/639–4416* ⊕ *www.aquamarinedive.com*) is on the northeast coast at the Blue Waters Inn and offers a friendly and laid-back approach, which makes it popular with casual divers. World traveler Stuart Sampson decided to settle in Tobago and launch **CaribStu** (✉ *On the beach between the jetty and the gas station, Charlotteville* ☎ *868/733–1298* ⊕ *www.caribstu.com*), a completely personalized diving service for individuals or couples. **Tobago Dive Experience** (✉ *Manta Lodge, Speyside* ☎ *868/639–7034* ⊕ *www.tobagodiveexperience.com*) offers the most comprehensive range of courses, including PADI, NAUI, and BSAC. Prices are very competitive, and class sizes are kept small to ensure that all divers get the attention they need.

FISHING

Dillon's Deep Sea Charters (✉ *Crown Point* ☎ *868/639–9386*) is excellent for full- and half-day trips for kingfish, barracuda, wahoo, mahimahi, blue marlin, and others. A full day on the sea with either a beach stop for lunch or a cruise around the island runs about $700, including equipment. With **Hard Play Fishing Charters** (✉ *13 The Evergreen, Old Grange, Mt. Irvine Bay* ☎ *868/639–7108*), colorful skipper Gerard "Frothy" De Silva helps you bag your own marlin.

GOLF

★ The 18-hole, par-72 course at the **Mt. Irvine Golf Club** (✉ *Mt. Irvine Bay Hotel, Shirvan Rd., Mt. Irvine* ☎ *868/639–8871*) was once ranked among the top courses in the Caribbean and among the top 100 in the world, but course maintenance has suffered over the years. Greens fees are $30 for 9 holes, $48 for 18 holes. The 18-hole, PGA-designed championship par-72 course at **Tobago Plantations Golf & Country Club** (✉ *Lowlands* ☎ *868/631–0875*) is set amid rolling greens and mangroves. It offers some amazing views of the ocean as a bonus. Greens fees are $60 for one 18-hole round, $95 for two rounds (these rates include a golf cart and taxes). This is the newer of the two main courses on the island and is by far the most popular. The course is well maintained and contains areas of mangrove and forest that are home to many bird species.

GUIDED TOURS

Frank's Glass Bottom Boat & Birdwatching Tours (⊠ *Speyside* 🖼🖼 *868/660–5438*) offers glass-bottom-boat and snorkeling tours of the shores of Speyside; Frank also conducts guided tours of the rain forest and Little Tobago. As a native of Speyside, he's extremely knowledgeable about the island's flora, fauna, and folklore. **Tobago Travel** (⊠ *Scarborough* ☎ *868/639–8778*) is the island's most experienced tour operator, offering a wide variety of services and tours.

HIKING

Ecoconsciousness is strong on Tobago, where the rain forests of the Main Ridge were set aside for protection in 1764, creating the first such preserve in the Western Hemisphere. Natural areas include Little Tobago and St. Giles islands, both major seabird sanctuaries. In addition, the endangered leatherback turtles maintain breeding grounds on some of Tobago's leeward beaches.

Harris Jungle Tours (⊠ *Golden Grove Rd., Canaan* ☎ *868/639–0513* ⊕ *www.harris-jungle-tours.com*) is run by the knowledgeable Harris McDonald and offers a variety of tours ranging from strenuous to laid-back. The more adventurous might want to try the rain-forest-at-night tour, which promises the possibility of encounters with some of Tobago's folklore characters, including La Diablesse (a beautifully dressed she-devil with a cloven hoof). **Yes Tourism** (⊠ *Pigeon Point Rd., Crown Point* ☎ *868/631–0287* ⊕ *www.yes-tourism.com*) offers a comprehensive range of tours for individuals and groups. The Rain Forest tour is an excellent guided hike, and the off-road jeep safari is hair-raising but memorable. Sightseeing tours around Tobago as well as to Trinidad and the Grenadines are also possible.

Turks and Caicos Islands

WORD OF MOUTH

"If you like a gorgeous 12 mile beach, beautiful condo resorts, and the most amazing turquoise water—then check out Turks and Caicos and the main island of Providenciales. You can do great snorkeling right from the beach or take an excursion to other reefs, and even explore some of the other islands by boat."

—sunblockstock

WELCOME TO TURKS AND CAICOS ISLANDS

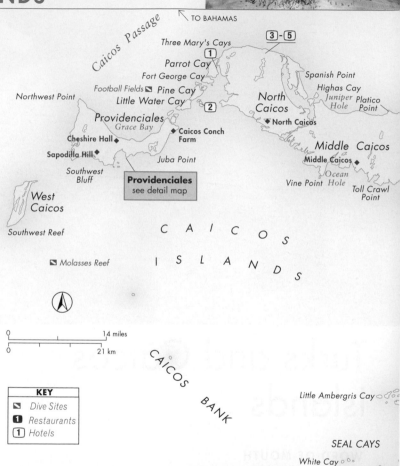

TO BAHAMAS

Caicos Passage

Three Mary's Cays

③-⑤

Parrot Cay ①

Fort George Cay

Football Fields ◩ Pine Cay

Little Water Cay ②

Spanish Point

Highas Cay

Juniper Platico
Hole Point

Northwest Point

Providenciales
Grace Bay

North
Caicos

◆ North Caicos

Cheshire Hall ◆

◆ Caicos Conch
Farm

Middle Caicos

Sapodilla Hill ◆

Middle Caicos ◆

Juba Point

Southwest
Bluff

Providenciales
see detail map

*Ocean
Hole*

Vine Point

Toll Crawl
Point

West
Caicos

C A I C O S

Southwest Reef

I S L A N D S

◩ Molasses Reef

| | 0 | | 14 miles |
| 0 | | 21 km | |

CAICOS BANK

Little Ambergris Cay ◌

SEAL CAYS

White Cay ◌

KEY	
◩	Dive Sites
❶	Restaurants
①	Hotels

Only 10 of these 40 islands between the Bahamas and Haiti are inhabited. Divers and snorkelers can explore one of the world's largest coral reefs. Land-based pursuits don't get much more taxing than teeing off at the Provo Golf and Country Club or sunset-watching from the seaside terrace of a laid-back resort.

GEOGRAPHICAL INFO

Though Providenciales is a major offshore banking center, sea creatures far outnumber humans in this archipelago of 40 islands, where the total population is a mere 25,000. From developed Provo to sleepy Grand Turk to sleepier South Caicos, the islands offer miles of undeveloped beaches, crystal-clear water, and laid-back luxury resorts.

Restaurants ▼
Island Thyme Bistro **1**
Pat's Place **2**

Hotels ▼
Blue Horizon Resort **6**
Caicos Beach Condos ...**4**

Meridian Club **2**
Parrot Cay Resort **1**
Pelican Beach Hotel **3**
Pirate's Hideaway **7**
Tradewinds
Guest Suites **9**
Villas of Salt Cay **8**

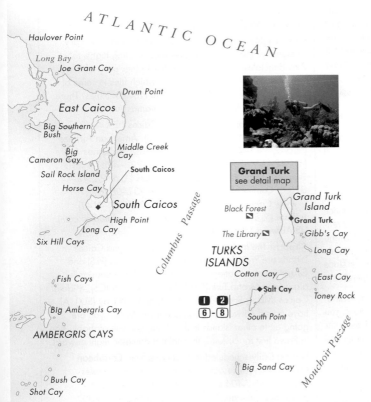

26

TURKS AND CAICOS ISLANDS

TOP REASONS TO VISIT TURKS AND CAICOS ISLANDS

1 Beautiful Beaches: Even on Provo, there are miles of deserted beaches without any beach umbrellas in sight.

2 Excellent Diving: The third-largest coral-reef system in the world is among the world's top dive sites.

3 Easy Island-Hopping: Island-hopping path will give you a feel for the islands.

4 The Jet Set: Destination spas, penthouse suites, and exclusive villas and resorts make celebrity-spotting a popular sport.

5 Exploring on the Sea: You'll find excellent fishing and boating among the uninhabited coves and cays.

TURKS AND CAICOS ISLANDS PLANNER

Logistics

Getting to the Turks and Caicos

Getting to the Turks and Caicos: Several major airlines fly nonstop to Providenciales from the United States. If you're going to one of the smaller islands, you'll usually need to make a connection in Provo. All international flights arrive at Providenciales International Airport (PLS), but you can hop over to the other islands from there.

Hassle Factor: Low–high, depending on the island and your home airport.

On the Ground: You can find taxis at the airports, and most resorts provide pickup service as well. Taxi fares are fairly reasonable on Provo and Grand Turk; on the smaller islands transfers can cost more since gas is much more expensive.

Getting Around on the Island: If you are staying on Provo, you may find it useful to have a car since the island is so large and the resorts so far-flung, if only for a few days of exploring or to get away from your hotel for dinner. On Grand Turk, you can rent a car, but you probably won't need to.

Nonstop Flights: You can fly nonstop from Atlanta (Delta), Boston (American and JetBlue), Charlotte (US Airways), Miami (American), New York–JFK (American and JetBlue), Newark–EWR(Continental), Philadelphia (US Airways).

Other Flights: Although carriers and schedules can vary seasonally, there are also several connecting flights to Providenciales as well as flights from other parts of the Caribbean on Air Turks & Caicos, which flies to some of the smaller islands in the chain from Providenciales. There are also flights from Nassau on Bahamas Air.

Local Airline Contacts: Air Turks & Caicos (☎ 649/941–5481 ⊕ www.airturksandcaicos.com). **American Airlines** (☎ 649/946–4948 or 800/433–7300). **Bahamas Air** (☎ 242/377–5505 in Nassau, 800/222–4262 ⊕ up.bahamasair.com). **Caicos Express** (☎ 649/243–0237). **Continental Airlines** (☎ 800/231–0856 ⊕ www.Continental.com). **Delta** (☎ 800/241–4141). **JetBlue** (☎ 800/Jetblue [538–2583] ⊕ www.JetBlue.com). **US Airways** (☎ 800/622–1015).

Airports: The main gateways into the Turks and Caicos Islands are Providenciales International Airport (PLS) and Grand Turk International Airport (GDT). There are smaller airports on Grand Turk (GDT), North Caicos (NCS), Middle Caicos (MDS), South Caicos (XSC), and Salt Cay (SLX). All have paved runways in good condition. Even if you are going on to other islands in the chain, you will probably stop in Provo first for customs, then take a domestic flight onward.

Ferries: Daily scheduled ferry service from **Caribbean Cruisin'** (✉ Walkin Marina, Leeward, Providenciales ☎ 649/946–5406 or 649/231–4191 ⊕ tcimall.tc/northcaicos/images/ferryservice.pdf) began in 2007 between Provo and North Caicos, with several departures from Walkin Marina in Leeward. **Salt Cay Ferry** (☎ 649/946–6909 ⊕ www.turksandcaicoswhalewatching.com) offers a twice-weekly ferry from Salt Cay to Grand Turk (weather permitting).

Getting Around the Turks and Caicos

Driving: Driving here is on the left side of the road, British-style; when pulling out into traffic, remember to look to your right. Give way to anyone entering a roundabout, as roundabouts are still a relatively new concept in the Turks and Caicos; stop even if you are on what appears to be the primary road. The maximum speed is 40 mph (64 kph), 20 mph (30 kph) through settlements, and limits, as well as the use of seat belts, are enforced.

Car Rentals: If you are staying on Provo, you may find it useful to have a car since the island is so large and the resorts are so far-flung, if only for a few days of exploring or to get away from your hotel for dinner. On Grand Turk, you can rent a car, but you probably won't need to. Car- and jeep-rental rates average $39 to $80 per day on Provo, plus a $15 surcharge per rental as a government tax. Reserve well ahead of time during the peak winter season. Most agencies offer free mileage and airport pickup service. Avis and Budget have offices on the islands. You might also try local agencies such as Grace Bay Car Rentals, Rent a Buggy, and Tropical Auto Rentals in Provo. Pelican Car Rentals is on North Caicos.

Car-Rental Agencies: Avis (✉ *Providenciales* ☎ *649/946–4705* ⊕ *www.avis.tc*). **Budget** (✉ *Providenciales* ☎ *649/946–4079* ⊕ *www.provo.net/Budget/*). **Grace Bay Car Rentals** (✉ *Providenciales* ☎ *649/941–8500* ⊕ *www.gracebaycarrentals.com*). **Pelican Car Rentals** (✉ *North Caicos* ☎ *649/241–8275*). **Rent a Buggy** (✉ *Providenciales* ☎ *649/946–4158* ⊕ *www.rentabuggy.tc*). **Scooter Bob's** (✉ *Turtle Cove, Providenciales* ☎ *649/946–4684* ⊕ *www.provo.net/Scooter/*). **Tony's Car Rental** (✉ *Grand Turk* ☎ *649/946–1879* ⊕ *www.tonyscarrental.com*). **Tropical Auto Rentals** (✉ *Providenciales* ☎ *649/946–5300* ⊕ *www.tropicalautorentaltci.com*).

Taxis: You can find taxis at the airports, and most resorts provide pickup service as well. A trip between Provo's airport and most major hotels runs about $12 per person. On Grand Turk a trip from the airport to Cockburn Town is about $8; it's $8 to $15 to hotels outside town on Grand Turk. Transfers can cost more on the smaller islands, where gas is much more expensive. Taxis (actually large vans) in Providenciales are metered, and rates are regulated by the government at $2 per person per mile traveled.

Taxi Companies: In Provo call the **Provo Taxi & Bus Group** (☎ *649/946–5481*) for more information. In the family islands, taxis may not be metered, so it's usually best to try to negotiate a cost for your trip in advance.

Guided Tours

Nell's Taxi (☎ *649/231–0051*) offers taxi tours of Provo, priced between $25 and $30 for the first hour and $25 for each additional hour.

You can independently arrange day trips to Grand Turk any day of the week on **Air Turks & Caicos** (☎ *649/946–5481 or 649/946–4181* ⊕ *www.airturksandcaicos.com*), and on Friday to Salt Cay.

Island Activities

The vast majority of people come to the Turks and Caicos to relax and enjoy the clear, **turquoise water.**

The Turks and Caicos Islands are known for **luxurious hotels.**

Provo has excellent **beaches,** particularly the long, soft beach along Grace Bay. If you can believe it, some of the smaller, more isolated islands have even better beaches.

Reefs are plentiful and are often close to shore, making **snorkeling** excellent. The **reef and wall diving** are among the best in the Caribbean.

The same reefs that draw colorful tropical fish draw big-game fish, so **deep-sea fishing** is also very good.

26

TURKS AND CAICOS ISLANDS PLANNER

Fast Facts

Banks and Exchange Services: The official currency on the islands is U.S. dollars. On Provo, there are ATMs at all bank branches (Scotiabank and First Caribbean), at the Graceway IGA Supermarket Gourmet, and at Ports of Call shopping center. There are also Scotiabank and First Caribbean branches on Grand Turk.

Electricity: Current is suitable for all U.S. appliances (120/240 volts, 60 Hz).

Emergencies: Emergency numbers in the Turks and Caicos are ☎ 999 or 911.

Passport Requirements: Valid passport is required to travel by air to the Turks and Caicos. Everyone must have an ongoing or return ticket.

Weddings: The residency requirement is 24 hours, after which you can apply for a marriage license to the registrar in Grand Turk. You must present a passport, original birth certificate, and proof of current marital status, as well as a letter stating both parties' occupations, ages, addresses, and fathers' full names. No blood tests are required. License fee is $50.

Contacts: Nila Destinations Wedding Planning (☎ 649/941–4375 ⊕ www. nilavacations.com).

Essentials

Mail: There is a post office in downtown Provo at the corner of Airport Road. Stamp collectors will be interested in the wide selection of stamps sold by the **Philatelic Bureau** (☎ 649/946–1534). You'll pay 50¢ to send a postcard to the United States; letters, per half ounce, cost 60¢ to the United States. When sending a letter to the Turks and Caicos Islands, be sure to include the specific island name and "Turks and Caicos Islands, BWI" (British West Indies). There is no home delivery of mail; everyone has a post-office box. Expect postcards to take a month to get to your friends and neighbors, if they get there at all. There's a **FedEx** (☎ 649/946–4682) service on Provo.

Taxes: The departure tax is $35 and is usually included in the cost of your airline ticket. If not, it's payable only in cash or traveler's checks. Restaurants and hotels add an 11% government tax. Hotels also typically add 11% to 15% for service.

Telephones: The country code for the Turks and Caicos is 649. To call the Turks and Caicos from the United States, dial 1 plus the 10-digit number, which includes 649. Be aware that this is an international call. Calls from the islands are expensive, and many hotels add steep surcharges for long distance.

Visitor Information: The tourist offices on Grand Turk and Providenciales are open daily from 9 to 5.

Contacts: Turks & Caicos Islands Tourist Board (☎ 954/568–6588 in Fort Lauderdale, 800/241–0824 ⊕ www.turksandcaicostourism.com). **Turks & Caicos Islands Tourist Board** (✉ Front St., Cockburn Town, Grand Turk ☎ 649/946–2321 ✉ Stubbs Diamond Plaza, The Bight, Providenciales ☎ 649/946–4970 ⊕ www.turksandcaicostourism.com).

Where to Stay

The Turks and Caicos can be a fairly expensive destination. Most hotels on Providenciales are pricey, but there are some moderately priced options; most accommodations are condo-style, but not all resorts are family-friendly. You'll find several upscale properties on the outer islands—including the famous Parrot Cay—but the majority of places are smaller inns. What you give up in luxury, however, you gain back tenfold in island charm. Though the smaller islands are relatively isolated, that's arguably what makes them so attractive in the first place.

Resorts: Most of the resorts on Provo are upscale; many are condo-style, so at least you will have a well-furnished kitchen for breakfast and a few quick lunches. There are two all-inclusive resorts on Provo. A handful of other luxury resorts are on the smaller islands.

Small Inns: Aside from the exclusive, luxury resorts, most of the places on the outlying islands are smaller, modest inns with relatively few amenities. Some are devoted to diving.

Villas and Condos: Villas and condos are plentiful, particularly on Provo, and usually represent a good value for families. However, you need to plan a few months in advance to get one of the better choices, less if you want to stay in a more developed condo complex.

HOTEL AND RESTAURANT PRICES

Restaurant prices are for a main course at dinner and include any taxes or service charges. Hotel prices are per night for a double room in high season, excluding taxes, service charges, and meal plans (except at all-inclusives).

WHAT IT COSTS IN U.S. DOLLARS

	¢	$	$$	$$$	$$$$
Restaurants	under $8	$8–$12	$12–$20	$20–$30	over $30
Hotels		under $150	$151–$275	$276–$375	$376–$475	over $475

When to Go

High season in Turks and Caicos runs roughly from January through March, with the usual extra-high rates during the Christmas and New Year's holiday period. Several hotels on Provo offer shoulder-season rates in April and May. During the off-season, rates are reduced substantially, as much as 40%. With bad world economies, you can find specials even during peak seasons or call resorts directly to negotiate.

There are two major festivals in the Turks and Caicos. At the end of November, the **Turks & Caicos Conch Festival** offers local boat races, live music, and conch recipe competitions.

At the end of December there is the annual **Maskanoo**, which offers live bands, street vendors, fireworks, and Junkanoo parades.

26

TURKS AND CAICOS BEACHES

If you're on a quest for the world's best beaches, then Turks and Caicos is your destination. They are blessed with stunning strands and shallow waters protected by outer reefs, a combination that makes for the most amazing turquoise water.

(Above) Beach palapas on Grace Bay, Providenciales. (Opposite page bottom) Half Moon Bay at Donna Cay, off Providenciales. (Opposite page top) Sapodilla Bay, Providenciales.

Grace Bay Beach in Providenciales has the best of the best, and most of the island's resorts clustered here. On the rare occasions that storms bring seaweed, it is quickly raked and buried. The water is protected by an outer reef, so it's often as still as glass. There is never an undertow or litter, and there are no beach vendors, so the opportunities for relaxation are optimal. Grand Turk is spoiled for choices when it comes to beach options: sunset strolls along miles of deserted beaches, picnics in secluded coves, beachcombing on the coralline sands, snorkeling around shallow coral heads close to shore, and admiring the impossibly turquoise-blue waters. There are also great beaches on several other less visited islands.

BEACH LOGISTICS

Although there is no charge for parking at any beach, come prepared. Umbrellas are provided by resorts for guests only, and resorts generally don't share with nonguests, even for a price. Grace Bay has the busiest sections of beachfront, especially at Beaches Resort and Club Med, but there are still plenty of secluded areas if you wish to explore beyond your own resort.

All the beaches of Turks and Caicos have bright white sand that's soft like baby powder. An added bonus is that no matter how hot the sun gets, your feet never burn. The sand is soft and clean, even in the water, so there is no fear of stepping on rocks or corals. Even the beach areas with corals for snorkeling have clean, clean sand for entry until you reach them.

THE CAICOS

PROVIDENCIALES

★ **Fodor's Choice** **Grace Bay.** The 12-mi (18-km) sweeping stretch of ivory-white, powder-soft sand on Provo's north coast is simply breathtaking, and home to migrating starfish as well as shallow snorkeling trails. The majority of Provo's beachfront resorts are along this shore, and it's the primary reason the Turks and Caicos is a world-class destination. ⊠ *Grace Bay Rd., on the north shore, Grace Bay.*

Half Moon Bay. A natural ribbon of sand linking two uninhabited cays is only inches above the sparkling turquoise waters and one of the most gorgeous beaches on the island. There are limestone cliffs to explore as well as small, private sand coves; there's even a small wreck offshore for snorkeling. It's only a short boat ride away from Provo, and most of the island's tour companies run excursions here or simply offer a beach drop-off.

These companies include Silverdeep and Caicos Dream Tours (⇨ *Boating and Sailing, in Sports and Activities).* ⊠ *15 mins from Leeward Marina, between Pine Cay and Water Cay, accessible only by boat, Big Water Cay.*

Malcolm's Beach. It's one of the most stunning beaches you'll ever see, but you'll need a high-clearance vehicle to reach it. Bring your own food and drinks, because it doesn't have any facilities or food service unless you have made a reservation with Amanyara to eat at the resort. ⊠ *Malcolm's Beach Rd., keep straight after passing the Amanyara turnoff.*

Sapodilla Bay. The best of the many secluded beaches and pristine sands around Provo can be found at this peaceful quarter-mile cove protected by Sapodilla Hill, with its soft strand lapped by calm waves, where yachts and small boats move with the gentle tide. ⊠ *North of South Dock, at end of South Dock Rd., Sapodilla Bay.*

NORTH CAICOS

The beaches of North Caicos are superb for shallow snorkeling and sunset strolls, and the waters offshore have excellent scuba diving. **Horse Stable Beach** is the main beach for annual events and beach parties. **Whitby Beach** usually has a gentle tide, and its thin strip of sand is bordered by palmetto plants and taller trees.

26

Pillory Beach, Grand Turk.

SOUTH CAICOS

The beaches at **Belle Sound** on South Caicos will take your breath away, with lagoonlike waters. Expect the beach to be natural and rustic—after storms you will see some seaweed. Due south of South Caicos is **Little Ambergris Cay**, an uninhabited cay about 14 mi (23 km) beyond the Fish Cays, with excellent bonefishing on the second-largest sandbar in the world. On the opposite side of the ridge from Belle Sound, **Long Bay** is an endless stretch of beach, but it can be susceptible to rough surf; however, on calmer days, you'll feel like you're on a deserted island.

THE TURKS

GRAND TURK

Governor's Beach. A beautiful crescent of powder-soft sand and shallow, calm turquoise waters front the official British governor's residence, called Waterloo, framed by tall casuarina trees that provide plenty of natural shade. To have it all to yourself, go on a day when cruise ships are not in port. On days when ships are in port, the beach is lined with lounge chairs.

Pillory Beach. With sparkling neon turquoise water, this is the prettiest beach on Grand Turk; it also has great off-the-beach snorkeling.

SALT CAY

Big Sand Cay. Accessible by boat with the on-island tour operators, Big Sand Cay, 7 mi (11 km) south of Salt Cay, is tiny and totally uninhabited; it's also known for its long, unspoiled stretches of open sand.

North Beach. The north coast of Salt Cay has superb beaches, with tiny, pretty shells and weathered sea glass, but North Beach is the reason to visit Salt Cay; it might be the finest beach in Turks and Caicos, if not the world. Part of the beauty lies not just in the soft, powdery sand and bright blue water but in its isolation; it's very likely that you will have this lovely beach all to yourself.

By Ramona
Settle

With water so turquoise that it glows, you may find it difficult to stray far from the beach in the Turks and Caicos. You may find no need for museums, and no desire to see ruins or even to read books. You may find yourself hypnotized by the water's many neon hues. And since the beaches are among the most incredible you will ever see, don't be surprised if you wake up on your last morning and realize that you didn't find a lot of time for anything else.

Although ivory-white, soft sandy beaches and breathtaking turquoise waters are shared among all the islands, the landscapes are a series of contrasts, from the dry, arid bush and scrub on the flat, coral islands of Grand Turk, Salt Cay, South Caicos, and Providenciales to the greener, foliage-rich undulating landscapes of Middle Caicos, North Caicos, Parrot Cay, and Pine Cay.

A much-disputed legend has it that Columbus first discovered these islands in 1492. Despite being on the map for longer than most other island groups, the Turks and Caicos Islands (pronounced *kay*-kos) still remain part of the less discovered Caribbean. More than 40 islands—only eight inhabited—make up this self-governing British overseas territory that lies just 575 mi (925 km) southeast of Miami on the third-largest coral-reef system in the world.

The political and historical capital island of the country is Grand Turk, but most of the tourism development, which consists primarily of boutique hotels and condo resorts, has occurred in Providenciales, thanks to the 12-mi (18-km) stretch of ivory sand that is Grace Bay. Once home to a population of around 500 people plus a few donkey carts, Provo has become a hub of activity, resorts, spas, restaurants, and water sports, with a population of around 25,000. It's the temporary home for the majority of visitors who come to the Turks and Caicos.

Despite the fact that most visitors land and stay in Provo, the Turks & Caicos National Museum is in the nation's administrative capital,

Grand Turk. The museum tells the history of the islands that have all, at one time or another, been claimed by the French, Spanish, and British as well as many pirates, long before the predominately North American visitors discovered its shores.

Marks of the country's colonial past can be found in the wooden and stone, Bermudian-style clapboard houses—often wrapped in deep-red bougainvillea—that line the streets on the quiet islands of Grand Turk, Salt Cay, and South Caicos. Donkeys roam free in and around the salt ponds, which are a legacy from a time when residents of these island communities worked hard as both slaves and then laborers to rake salt (then known as "white gold") bound for the United States and Canada. In Salt Cay the remains of wooden windmills are now home to large osprey nests. In Grand Turk and South Caicos, the crystal-edge tidal ponds are regularly visited by flocks of rose-pink flamingos hungry for the shrimp to be found in the shallow, briny waters.

Sea Island cotton, believed to be the highest quality, was produced on the Loyalist plantations in the Caicos Islands from the 1700s. The native cotton plants can still be seen dotted among the stone remains of former plantation houses in the more fertile soils of Middle Caicos and North Caicos. Here communities in tiny settlements have retained age-old skills using fanner grasses, silver palms, and sisal to create exceptional straw baskets, bags, mats, and hats.

In all, only 25,000 people live in the Turks and Caicos Islands; more than half are "Belongers," the term for the native population, mainly descended from African and Bermudian slaves who settled here beginning in the 1600s. The majority of residents work in tourism, fishing, and offshore finance, as the country is a haven for the overtaxed. Indeed, for residents and visitors, life in "TCI" is anything but taxing. But even though most visitors come to do nothing—a specialty in the islands—it does not mean there's nothing to do.

> **WHERE WHEN HOW**
>
> Check out ⊕ www.wherewhenhow. com, a terrific source with links to every place to stay, all the restaurants, excursions, and transportation. You can pick up the printed version of the magazine all around the island, or subscribe before you go so you know what do while in the Turks and Caicos.

THE CAICOS

PROVIDENCIALES

Passengers typically become oddly silent when their plane starts its descent, mesmerized by the shallow, crystal-clear turquoise waters of Chalk Sound National Park. This island, nicknamed Provo, was once called Blue Hills after the name of its first settlement. Just south of the airport and downtown area, Blue Hills still remains the closest thing you can get to a more typical Caicos island settlement on this, the most developed of the islands in the chain. Most of the modern resorts, exquisite spas, water-sports operators, shops, business plazas, restaurants, bars, cafés, and the championship golf course are on or close by the 12-mi (18-km) stretch of Grace Bay beach. In spite of the ever-increasing number of taller and grander condominium resorts—either completed or under construction—it's still possible to find deserted stretches on this priceless, ivory-white shoreline. For guaranteed seclusion, rent a car and go explore the southern shores and western tip of the island, or set sail for a private island getaway on one of the many deserted cays nearby.

Progress and beauty come at a price: there is considerable construction on the island. No worry here—it does not take away from the gorgeous beaches and wonderful dinners. Although you may start to believe that every road leads to a construction site (or is under construction itself), there are, happily, plenty of sections of beach where you can escape the din.

Although you may be kept quite content enjoying the beachscape and top-notch amenities of Provo itself, it's also a great starting point for island-hopping tours by sea or by air as well as fishing and diving trips. Resurfaced roads should help you get around and make the most of the main tourism and sightseeing spots.

26

EXPLORING PROVIDENCIALES

Cheshire Hall. Standing eerily just west of downtown Provo are the remains of a circa-1700 cotton plantation owned by Loyalist Thomas Stubbs. A trail weaves through the ruins, where a few inadequate interpretive signs tell the story of the island's doomed cotton industry with very little information about the plantation itself. A variety of local plants are also identified. To visit, you must arrange for a tour through the Turks & Caicos National Trust. The lack of context can be disappointing for history buffs; a visit to North Caicos Wades Green plantation or the Turks & Caicos National Museum could well prove a better fit. ⊠ *Leeward Hwy., behind Ace Hardware* ☎ *649/941–5710 for National Trust* ⊕ *www.tcinationaltrust.org* ✉ *$5* ☉ *Daily, by appointment.*

Sapodilla Hill. On this cliff overlooking the secluded Sapodilla Bay, you can discover rocks carved with the names of shipwrecked sailors and dignitaries from TCI's maritime and colonial past. There are carvings on the rocks that some claim are secret codes and maps to hidden treasures; many have tried in vain to find these treasures. The hill is known by two other names, Osprey Rock and Splitting Rock. The less adventurous can see molds of the carvings at Provo's International Airport. ⊠ *Off South Dock Rd., west of South Dock.*

WHERE TO EAT

There are more than 50 restaurants on Provo, from casual to elegant, with cuisine from Asian to European (and everything in between). You can spot the islands' own Caribbean influence no matter where you go, exhibited in fresh seafood specials, colorful presentations, and a tangy dose of spice. Pick up a free copy of *Where When How's Dining Guide* magazine, which you will find all over the island; it contains menus, Web sites, and pictures of all the restaurants.

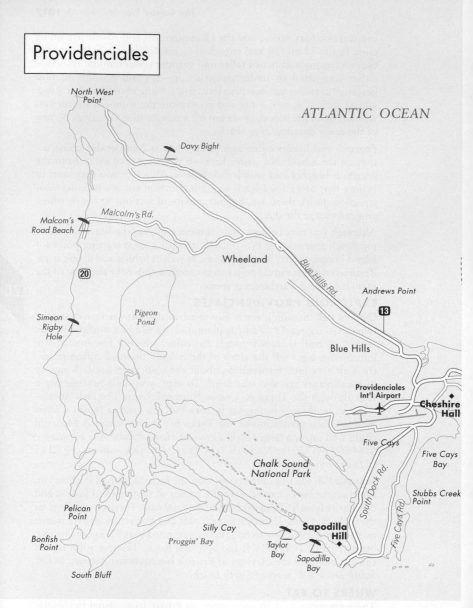

Providenciales

North West Point

Davy Bight

ATLANTIC OCEAN

Malcom's Road Beach

Malcom's Rd.

Wheeland

Blue Hills Rd.

20

Andrews Point

Simeon Rigby Hole

Pigeon Pond

13

Blue Hills

Providenciales Int'l Airport

Cheshire Hall

Five Cays

Five Cays Bay

South Dock Rd.

Chalk Sound National Park

Stubbs Creek Point

Pelican Point

Five Cays Rd.

Silly Cay

Sapodilla Hill

Bonfish Point

Proggin' Bay

Taylor Bay

Sapodilla Bay

South Bluff

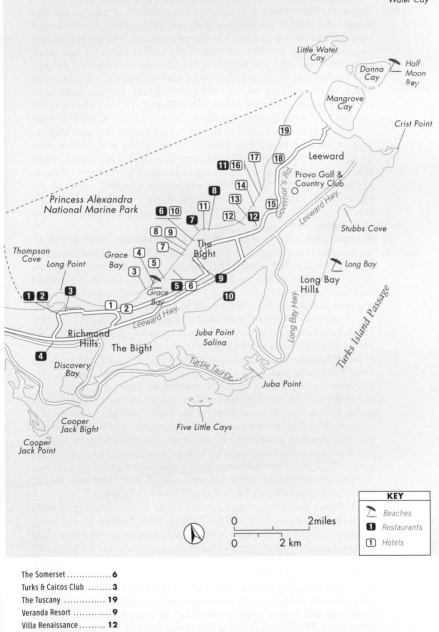

Water Cay

Little Water Cay

Donna Cay

Half Moon Bay

Mangrove Cay

Crist Point

Leeward

19

17

11 16

18

14

Provo Golf & Country Club

8

13

15

6 10

11

12 12

Princess Alexandra National Marine Park

8 9

7

The Bight

Stubbs Cove

7

4

Grace Bay

5

9

Long Bay

Thompson Cove

Long Point

3

5 6

Long Bay Hills

1 2

3

Grace Bay

10

1

2

Leeward Hwy.

Richmond Hills

Juba Point Salina

Long Bay Hwy.

Turks Island Passage

4

The Bight

Discovery Bay

Turtle Tail Dr.

Juba Point

Cooper Jack Bight

Five Little Cays

Cooper Jack Point

Governor's Rd.

Leeward Hwy.

0 ——— 2miles
0 ——— 2 km

KEY

Beaches
1 Restaurants
1 Hotels

$$$$ ✕**Anacaona.** At the Grace Bay Club, this palapa-shaded (thatch-roof)
ECLECTIC   restaurant has become a favorite of the country's chief minister. But
despite the regular presence of government bigwigs, the restaurant
continues to offer a memorable dining experience minus the tie, the
air-conditioning, and the attitude. Start with a bottle of fine wine;
then enjoy the light and healthful Mediterranean-influenced cuisine.
The kitchen uses the island's bountiful seafood and fresh produce. Oil
lamps on the tables, gently revolving ceiling fans, and the murmur of
the trade winds add to the Edenic environment. The entrancing ocean
view and the careful service make it an ideal choice when you want
to be pampered. It's a good thing the setting is amazing; portions are
tiny, so you're paying for ambience. Check out the world's first infinity bar, which seems to spill right into the ocean. The lighted menus
are a huge plus—no more squinting in the dark to read—yet they do
not take away from the romantic experience. Children under 12 are
not allowed. Long pants and collared shirts are required. ⊠ *Grace
Bay Club, Grace Bay* ☎ *649/946–5050* ⊕ *www.gracebayresorts.com*
⚷ *Reservations essential.*

$ ✕**Angela's Top o' the Cove New York Style Delicatessen.** Order deli sand-
AMERICAN   wiches, salads, enticingly rich desserts, and freshly baked pastries at this
island institution on Leeward Highway, just south of Turtle Cove. From
the deli case you can buy the fixings for a picnic; the shelves are stocked
with an eclectic selection of fancy foodstuffs, as well as beer and wine.
It's open at 6:30 am for a busy trade in coffees and cappuccinos. This
is a cheesesteak comparable to what you get in Philly, but the location
isn't where most tourists stay—it's worth the drive, though. ⊠ *Leeward
Hwy., Turtle Cove* ☎ *649/946–4694* ⊘ *No dinner.*

$$$ ✕**Baci Ristorante.** Aromas redolent of the Mediterranean waft from the
ITALIAN   open kitchen as you enter this intimate eatery east of Turtle Cove.
Outdoor seating is on a romantic canal-front patio, one of the love-
lier settings on Provo. The menu offers a small but varied selection of
Italian dishes. Veal is prominent on the menu, but main courses also
include pasta, chicken, fish, and brick-oven pizzas. You'll never see red-
der tomatoes than those in the tomato-and-mozzarella Caprese salad; a
standout entrée is the chicken with vodka-cream sauce. House wines are
personally selected by the owners and complement the tasteful wine list.
Try tiramisu for dessert with a flavored coffee drink. Wear bug spray at
night. ⊠ *Harbour Town, Turtle Cove* ☎ *649/941–3044.*

$$$$ ✕**Bay Bistro.** You simply can't eat any closer to the beach than here,
ECLECTIC   the only restaurant in all of Provo that is built directly on the sand.
⚙   Although service can be slow, the food and setting are excellent. You
dine on a covered porch surrounded by palm trees and the sound of lap-
ping waves. The spring-roll appetizer is delicious, and the oven-roasted
chicken is the best on the island. Junior, one of Provo's top bartend-
ers, might bring your drink balanced on the top of his head. Brunch
on weekends includes such favorites as eggs Benedict with mimosas
(included) and is very popular; lines can be long if you don't have a
reservation. ⊠ *Sibonné, Princess Dr., Grace Bay* ☎ *649/946–5396* ⊕ *si-
bonne.com/grace-bay-bistro/* ⊘ *No dinner Mon.*

$$$ ✗ **Caicos Café.** New owners have also brought a new menu focusing
ECLECTIC on island food with an Italian twist. The bruschetta that everyone gets
at the start of the meal is delicious enough that you may ask for sec-
onds, and the bread is baked fresh every day at the bakery next door.
Blackened fish and jerk chicken on top of pasta are popular with the
locals. Ravioli with cream sauce is the tastiest dish. On windy nights,
the inland setting offers protection from the breezes. Be sure to wear
bug spray at night. ✉ *Caicos Café Plaza, Grace Bay Rd., Grace Bay*
☎ *649/916-5278* ⊙ *Closed Sun.*

$$$$ ✗ **Coco Bistro.** With tables under palm trees, Coco Bistro has a divine
ECLECTIC setting, and the food is just as good. Though not directly on the beach,
★ the location under the tropical tree grove still reminds you that you are
on vacation. Main courses are complemented by both French flourishes
(served au poivre, for example) and West Indian (such as with mango
chutney) and are accompanied by fried plantains and mango slaw to
maintain a Caribbean flair. Consider conch soup, soft-shell-crab tem-
pura, and sun-dried tomato pasta from the internationally influenced
menu. This is one of the better restaurants on Provo. ✉ *Grace Bay
Rd., Grace Bay* ☎ *649/946-5369* ⊕ *www.CocoBistro.tc* ⌕ *Reservations
essential* ⊙ *Closed Mon. No lunch.*

$$$$ ✗ **Coyaba Restaurant.** Directly behind Grace Bay Club and next to
ECLECTIC Caribbean Paradise Inn, this posh eatery serves nostalgic favorites
Fodor's Choice with tempting twists in conversation-piece crockery and in a palm-
★ fringed setting. Chef Paul Newman uses his culinary expertise for
the daily-changing main courses, which include exquisitely presented
dishes such as crispy, whole, yellow snapper fried in Thai spices. One
standout is lobster thermidor in a Dijon-mushroom cream sauce.
Try several different appetizers instead of a single more expensive
entrée for dinner; guava-and-tamarind barbecue ribs and coconut-
shrimp tempura are two good choices if you go that route. If you
enjoy creative menus, this is the place for you. Chef Paul keeps
the resident expat crowd happy with traditional favorites such as
lemon meringue pie, albeit with his own tropical twist. Don't skip
dessert; Paul makes the most incredible chocolate fondant you
will ever have. The service here is seamless. ✉ *Off Grace Bay Rd.,
beside Caribbean Paradise Inn, Grace Bay* ⌂ *Box 459, Providencia-
les* ☎ *649/946-5186* ⊕ *www.coyabarestaurant.com* ⌕ *Reservations
essential* ⊙ *Closed Tues. No lunch.*

$$ ✗ **Da Conch Shack.** An institution in Provo for many years, this brightly
CARIBBEAN colored beach shack is justifiably famous for its conch and seafood.
The legendary specialty, conch, is fished fresh out of the shallows
and broiled, spiced, cracked, or fried to absolute perfection. On Friday night, you can dance in the sand after dinner. This is the freshest
conch anywhere on the island, as the staff dive for it only after you've
placed your order, but if you don't like seafood, there is chicken on the
menu. Thursday night, start rocking while you eat and mingle with
the locals; live bands have just been added as headliners to sing songs
that make everybody happy. ✉ *Blue Hills Rd., Blue Hills* ☎ *No phone*
⊕ *www.conchshack.tc/* ▭ *No credit cards* ⊙ *No lunch.*

26

$$$$ ✕ **Grace's Cottage.** At one of the prettiest dining settings on Provo, tables
ECLECTIC   are artfully set under wrought-iron cottage-style gazebos and around
the wraparound verandah, which skirts the gingerbread-covered main
building. In addition to such tangy and exciting entrées as panfried red
snapper with roasted-pepper sauce or melt-in-your-mouth grilled beef
tenderloin with truffle-scented mashed potatoes, the soufflés are well
worth the 15-minute wait and the top-tier price tag. Portions are small,
but the quality is amazing. Service is impeccable (ladies are given a small
stool so that their purses do not touch the ground). ✉ *Point Grace,
Grace Bay* ☎ *649/946–5096* ⌂ *Reservations essential* ⊘ *No lunch.*

$$$ ✕ **Hemingway's.** A casual and gorgeous setting, with a patio and deck
AMERICAN   offering views of Grace Bay, makes this one of the most popular res-
taurants that cater to tourists. At lunch do not miss the best fish tacos
with mango chutney. For dinner there is an excellent kids' menu and
something for everyone, including vegetarians. Order the popular "Old
Man of the Sea," which features the freshest fish of the day. It's known
for great sauces such as the wine reduction for the filet mignon, the
creole for fish dishes, and a delicious curry for chicken. If you're on a
budget, go right before 6 pm, when you can still order the less expensive
lunch menu items. Go on Thursday night when Quentin Dean plays
Caribbean versions of popular songs. ✉ *The Sands Resort, Grace Bay*
☎ *649/946–5199 Ext. 150* ⊕ *www.thesandsresort.com.*

$$$ ✕ **Magnolia Wine Bar and Restaurant.** Restaurateurs since the early 1990s,
ECLECTIC   hands-on owners Gianni and Tracey Caporuscio make success seem
★   simple. Expect well-prepared, uncomplicated choices that range from
European to Asian to Caribbean. You can construct an excellent meal
from the outstanding appetizers; do not miss the spring rolls and the
grilled-vegetable-and-fresh-mozzarella stack. Finish your meal with the
mouthwatering molten chocolate cake. The atmosphere is romantic,
the presentations are attractive, and the service is careful. It's easy to see
why the Caporuscios have a loyal following. The adjoining wine bar
includes a handpicked list of specialty wines, which can be ordered by
the glass. The marine setting is a great place to watch the sunset. ✉ *Miramar Resort, Turtle Cove* ☎ *649/941–5108* ⊘ *Closed Mon. No lunch.*

$$$$ ✕ **O'Soleil.** Located at the Somerset, this is one of Provo's few indoor,
ECLECTIC   air-conditioned restaurants, though you can also eat outside on the
★   terrace. White-on-white decor under vaulted ceilings gives it a Miami-
chic ambience. The executive chef mixes international styles, including
influences from the Caribbean, Asia, and Europe. Some of the standouts
include the best sea bass on the island, served with balsamic cherry
tomatoes; roasted Australian rack of lamb; and excellent risotto. You
can also order from the tapas menu—the presentations are as creative
as the food. Check out the conch spring rolls and shrimp tempura,
each with its own dipping sauce. Eat on a couch under the stars during
Friday-night happy hour while listening to live music from 7 until 10.
Ask for simpler off-the-menu options for the children. ✉ *The Somerset,
Princess Dr., Grace Bay* ☎ *649/946–5900* ⊕ *www.thesomerset.com.*

$$$ ✕ **Tiki Hut.** From its location overlooking the marina, the ever-popular
AMERICAN   Tiki Hut continues to serve consistently tasty, value-priced meals in a
ʘ   fun atmosphere. Locals take advantage of the Wednesday night $13

What Is a Potcake?

Potcakes are indigenous dogs of the Bahamas and Turks and Caicos Islands. Traditionally, the stray dogs would be fed from the leftover scraps of food that formed at the bottom of the pot; this is how they got their name. Much is being done these days to control the stray dog population. The TCSPCA and Potcake Place are two agencies working to adopt out the puppies. You can "travel with a cause" by adopting one of these gorgeous pups; they come with all the shots and all the papers required to bring them back home to the United States. Even if you don't adopt, you can help by volunteering as a carrier—bringing one back to its adopted family. Customs in the States is actually easier when you are bringing back a potcake! For more information on how you can help, check out the Web site for Potcake Place (⊕ *www.potcakeplace.com*).

this is one of Provo's few nightlife venues, Friday and Saturday nights can get a little too lively. ⊠ *Lower Bight Rd., Grace Bay, Providenciales, Turks and Caicos Islands, BWI* ☎ *649/941-7555* ⊕ *www. GansevoortTurksandCaicos.com* ⤳ *55 rooms, 32 suites, 4 penthouses* ⚘ *In-room: a/c, kitchen, Internet, Wi-Fi. In-hotel: restaurants, bars, children's programs, pool, gym, laundry facilities, spa, beach, parking, some pets allowed* ⅋⊘⅋ *Breakfast.*

$$$$
RESORT
☾
★
Grace Bay Club, Villas at Grace Bay Club, and the Estate at Grace Bay Club. This stylish resort retains a loyal following because of its helpful, attentive staff and unpretentious elegance. **Pros:** gorgeous pool and restaurant lounge areas with outdoor couches, daybeds, and fire pits; all guests receive a cell phone to use on the island. **Cons:** no children allowed at Anacaona restaurant; construction in front of the properties. ⊠ *Grace Bay Rd., behind Grace Bay Court, Grace Bay* ☎ *649/946–5050 or 800/946–5757* ⊕ *www.gracebayclub.com* ⤳ *59 suites* ⚘ *In-room: a/c, kitchen, Internet, Wi-Fi. In-hotel: restaurants, tennis courts, bar, pools, laundry facilities, spa, beach, business center, water sports* ⅋⊘⅋ *Breakfast.*

$$$–$$$$
RESORT
☾
★
Ocean Club Resorts. Enormous, locally painted pictures of hibiscus make a striking first impression as you enter the reception area at one of the island's most well-established condominium resorts. **Pros:** family-friendly resort with shuttles between the two shared properties; screened balconies and porches allow a respite from incessant air-conditioning. **Cons:** both resorts are showing their age. ⌂ *Box 240, Grace Bay* ☎ *649/946–5880 or 800/457–8787* ⊕ *www.oceanclubresorts.com* ⤳ *174 suites: 86 at Ocean Club East, 88 at Ocean Club West* ⚘ *In-room: a/c, kitchen (some), Wi-Fi. In-hotel: restaurants, tennis court, bars, pools, gym, laundry facilities, spa, beach, business center, water sports* ⅋⊘⅋ *No meals.*

$$$$
RESORT
Point Grace. Asian-influenced rooftop domes blend with Romanesque stone pillars and wide stairways in this plush resort, which offers spacious beachfront suites and romantic cottages surrounding the centerpiece: a turquoise infinity pool with perfect views of the beach. **Pros:** relaxing environment; beautiful pool. **Cons:** can be stuffy (signs around

the pool remind you to be quiet). ⌂ *Box 700, Grace Bay* ☎ *649/946–5096 or 888/924–7223* ⊕ *www.pointgrace.com* ➵ *23 suites, 9 cottage suites, 2 villas* ⟐ *In-room: a/c, kitchen. In-hotel: restaurants, bars, pool, spa, beach, business center, water sports* ⊙ *Closed Sept.* ⎮⊙⎮ *Breakfast.*

$$$$
RESORT
☾

⌂ **Regent Palms.** High on luxury and glitz, this is a place to see and be seen. **Pros:** great people-watching; lively atmosphere; one of the best spas in the Caribbean. **Cons:** some would say busy not lively; a little formal and stuffy (cover-ups are required when you go to the pool). ✉ *Grace Bay, Providenciales, Turks and Caicos Islands, BWI* ☎ *649/946–8666* ⊕ *www.regenthotels.com* ➵ *72 suites* ⟐ *In-room: a/c, kitchen (some), Wi-Fi. In-hotel: restaurants, tennis court, bar, children's programs, pool, gym, laundry facilities, spa, beach, water sports* ⎮⊙⎮ *Breakfast.*

$$$–$$$$
RESORT
★

⌂ **Royal West Indies Resort.** With a contemporary take on colonial architecture and the outdoor feel of a botanical garden, this unpretentious resort has plenty of garden-view and beachfront studios and suites for moderate self-catering budgets. **Pros:** the best bang for the buck on Provo; on one of the widest stretches of Grace Bay Beach. **Cons:** Club Med next door can be noisy. ⌂ *Box 482, Grace Bay* ☎ *649/946–5004 or 800/332–4203* ⊕ *www.royalwestindies.com* ➵ *99 suites* ⟐ *In-room: a/c, kitchen, Internet. In-hotel: restaurant, bar, pools, laundry facilities, beach, water sports* ⎮⊙⎮ *No meals.*

$$$–$$$$
RESORT
☾

⌂ **Sands at Grace Bay.** Spacious gardens and winding pools set the tone for one of Provo's most popular family resorts. **Pros:** one of the best places for families; central to shops and numerous restaurants; screened balconies and porches give an escape from incessant air-conditioning. **Cons:** a new wooden pool deck can cause splinters, so keep an eye on the kids; avoid courtyard rooms, which are not worth the price. ⌂ *Box 681, Grace Bay* ☎ *649/941–5199 or 877/777–2637* ⊕ *www.thesandsresort.com* ➵ *118 suites* ⟐ *In-room: a/c, kitchen (some), Internet, Wi-Fi. In-hotel: restaurant, tennis court, bar, pools, gym, laundry facilities, spa, beach, business center, water sports, some pets allowed* ⎮⊙⎮ *No meals.*

$$$–$$$$
RESORT

⌂ **Seven Stars.** The tallest property on the island is matched by the pure luxury it offers. **Pros:** gorgeous property in the center of the Grace Bay "hub" is walking distance to everything; terrific deck bar by the beach. **Cons:** some feel the proportions of the resort are too big for the rest of the island. ✉ *Grace Bay Rd.* ☎ *649/941–7777* ⊕ *www.SevenStarsGraceBay.com* ➵ *113 rooms* ⟐ *In-room: a/c, kitchen (some), Internet, Wi-Fi. In-hotel: restaurants, bars, tennis court, pool, gym, spa, beach, water sports, children's programs, laundry facilities, business center, parking* ⎮⊙⎮ *No meals.*

$–$$
HOTEL

⌂ **Sibonné.** Dwarfed by most of the nearby resorts, the smallest hotel on Grace Bay Beach has snug (by Provo's spacious standards) but pleasant rooms with Bermuda-style balconies and a completely circular but tiny pool. **Pros:** closest property to the beach; the island's best bargain directly on the beach. **Cons:** pool is small and dated. ✉ *Princess Dr., Box 144, Grace Bay, Providenciales, Turks and Caicos Islands, BWI* ☎ *649/946–5547 or 800/528–1905* ⊕ *www.sibonne.com* ➵ *29 rooms, 1 apartment* ⟐ *In-room: a/c. In-hotel: restaurant, bar, pool, beach, water sports* ⎮⊙⎮ *Breakfast.*

West Bay Club.

$$$$
RESORT
Fodor's Choice
★

⊡ **The Somerset.** This luxury resort has the "wow" factor, starting with the architecture, followed by the service, and ending in your luxuriously appointed suite. **Pros:** the most beautiful architecture on Provo; terrific service; Wednesday movie nights out on the lawn. **Cons:** the cheapest lock-out rooms are not worth the cost; can get noisy. ⊠ *Princess Dr., Grace Bay, Providenciales, Turks and Caicos Islands, BWI* ☎ *649/946–5900* ⊕ *www.thesomerset.com* ⇱ *53 suites* ⌂ *In-room: a/c, kitchen, Wi-Fi. In-hotel: restaurant, bar, children's programs, pool, gym, laundry facilities, beach, water sports* ¶⊙ *Breakfast.*

$$$–$$$$
RESORT
★

⊡ **Turks and Caicos Club.** On the quieter, western end of Grace Bay, this intimate all-suites hotel has a unique Caribbean bed-and-breakfast aura. The buildings are colonial-style with lovely gingerbread trim. **Pros:** incredible, lush grounds; on one of the best stretches of Grace Bay Beach; great snorkeling from the beach. **Cons:** small bathrooms. ⊠ *West Grace Bay Beach, Box 687, West Grace Bay, Providenciales, Turks and Caicos Islands, BWI* ☎ *649/946–5800 or 888/482–2582* ⊕ *www.turksandcaicosclub.com* ⇱ *21 suites* ⌂ *In-room: a/c, kitchen, Wi-Fi. In-hotel: restaurant, bar, pool, gym, laundry facilities, beach, water sports* ⊘ *Closed Sept.* ¶⊙ *Breakfast.*

$$$$
RENTAL

⊡ **The Tuscany.** This self-catering, quiet, upscale resort is the place for independent travelers to unwind around one of the prettiest pools on Provo. **Pros:** luxurious; all condos have ocean views; beautiful pool. **Cons:** no restaurant and far from the best restaurants; very expensive for self-catering. ⊲ *Box 623, Grace Bay* ☎ *649/941–4667* ⊕ *www. thetuscanyresort.com* ⇱ *30 condos* ⌂ *In-room: a/c, no safe, kitchen, Wi-Fi. In-hotel: tennis court, pool, gym, beach* ¶⊙ *No meals.*

$$$$
ALL-INCLUSIVE

⊡ **Veranda Resort.** And now for something completely different for Provo: an upscale, quiet, ultraluxury, all-inclusive resort. **Pros:** excellent service; top-shelf spirits included; unique clapboard architecture. **Cons:** included meals mean you may miss out on excellent independent restaurants; only two restaurants can mean a wait for a table at prime times. ⊠ *Princess Dr.* ☎ *649/339–5050* ⊕ *www.VerandaTCI.com* 🛏 *168 rooms* ⑂ *In-room: a/c, kitchen, Wi-Fi. In-hotel: restaurants, bar, tennis court, pools, gym, spa, beach, water sports, children's programs, laundry facilities, business center, parking* ¶⊖¶ *All-inclusive.*

$$$$
RENTAL

⊡ **Villa Renaissance.** Modeled after a Tuscan villa, this luxury property is for the self-catering tourist. **Pros:** luxury for less; one of the prettiest courtyards in Provo. **Cons:** no restaurant; not full-service resort. ⊕ *Box 592, Grace Bay* ☎ *649/941–5300 or 877/285–8764* ⊕ *www. villarenaissance.com* 🛏 *20 suites* ⑂ *In-room: a/c, kitchen. In-hotel: bar, pool, laundry facilities, spa, beach* ¶⊖¶ *No meals.*

$$$–$$$$
RESORT
Fodor'sChoice
★

⊡ **West Bay Club.** One of Provo's newest resorts has a prime location on a pristine stretch of Grace Bay Beach just steps away from the best off-the-beach snorkeling. **Pros:** all rooms have a beach view; new, clean, and sparkling; contemporary architecture makes it stand out from other resorts. **Cons:** a car is needed to go shopping and to the best restaurants. ⊠ *Lower Bight Rd., Lower Bight* ☎ *649/946–8550* ⊕ *www.TheWestBayClub.com* 🛏 *46 suites* ⑂ *In-room: a/c, kitchen, Internet, Wi-Fi. In-hotel: restaurant, bar, pool, gym, laundry facilities, spa, beach, water sports, parking* ¶⊖¶ *No meals.*

$$$–$$$$
RESORT
Fodor'sChoice
★

⊡ **Windsong Resort.** On a gorgeous beach lined with several appealing resorts, Windsong stands out for two reasons: an active Snuba program and a magnificent pool. **Pros:** the pool is the coolest; great Snuba program; gorgeous new resort. **Cons:** resort is experiencing some growing pains, so service can be lacking; studios have only a refrigerator and microwave; thinner stretch of beachfront here. ⊠ *Stubbs Rd., Lower Bight, Providenciales, Turks and Caicos Islands, BWI* ☎ *649/941–7700* ⊕ *www.windsongresort.com* 🛏 *16 studios, 30 suites* ⑂ *In-room: a/c, kitchen (some), Wi-Fi. In-hotel: restaurant, bars, children's programs, pool, gym, laundry facilities, beach, business center, water sports, parking* ¶⊖¶ *No meals.*

NIGHTLIFE

Although Provo is not known for its nightlife, there's still some fun to be found after dark. The best ambience can be found with live music from NaDa, a French-Canadian duo, so ask around to find out where they are playing and go! Normally, they appear Tuesday nights at Mango Reef, at Wednesday-night dinners at Parallel 23, and at fun "deck" parties on Thursday nights at The Deck at Seven Stars.

Thursday night through Saturday night, Danny Buoy's is a hot spot, as is Calico Jacks; both places usually have live bands. Somewhere On The Beach Restaurant has live bands—usually reggae and local music—on Tuesday, Thursday, and Saturday. There are live bands on Thursday nights at Da Conch Shack and Hemingway's. On Friday nights there is live music at O'Soleil and Anocaona. On Saturday nights Bagatelle at Gansevoort hosts live bands and DJs. Any night, you can also buy a pass to Club Med, which includes all your drinks, passes to the show, and the disco.

Keep abreast of events and specials by checking **TCI eNews** (⊕ *www.tcienews.com*).

Bagatelle. Bringing South Beach Miami chic to the beach, this is one of the few places that are "happening" on a Saturday night. Live bands, DJs, and celebrity sightings make the action. ⊠ *Gansevoort Wymara Resort, The Bight* ☎ *649/941–7555* ⊕ *www.gansevoortturksandcaicos. com/gansevoort-bagatelle-bistrot-beach-club.php.*

Calico Jack's Restaurant & Bar. On Friday night you can find a local band and lively crowd at this popular bar. ⊠ *Ports of Call, Grace Bay* ☎ *649/946–5129.*

Casablanca Casino. This casino has brought slots, blackjack, American roulette, poker, craps, and baccarat back to Provo. Open from 7 pm until 4 am, this is the last stop for the night. Grace Bay Club has introduced the infinity bar, the only one of its kind in the world, which gives the impression that it goes directly into the ocean. ⊠ *Grace Bay Rd., Grace Bay* ☎ *649/941–3737.*

Danny Buoy's. A popular Irish pub, Danny Buoy's has pool tables, darts, and big-screen TVs. It's a great place to watch sports from anywhere in the world. ⊠ *Grace Bay Rd., across from Carpe Diem Residences, Grace Bay* ☎ *649/946–5921.*

Somewhere . . . On The Beach. A Tex-Mex alternative that gives the wallet a break from fine dining becomes the hot spot on Thursday nights with live music. Three levels of outdoor decks add to the fun. ⊠ *Coral Gardens on Grace Bay, The Bight* ☎ *649/231–0590.*

SHOPPING

Handwoven straw baskets and hats, polished conch-shell crafts, paintings, wood carvings, model sailboats, handmade dolls, and metalwork are crafts native to the islands and nearby Haiti. The natural surroundings have inspired local and international artists to paint, sculpt, print, craft, and photograph; most of their creations are on sale in Providenciales.

★ **Anna's Art Gallery and Studio.** Anna's sells original artworks, silk-screen paintings, sculptures, and handmade sea-glass jewelry. ⊠ *The Saltmills, Grace Bay* ☎ *449/231–3293.*

ArtProvo. ArtProvo is the island's largest gallery of designer wall art; also shown are native crafts, jewelry, handblown glass, candles, and other gift items. Featured artists include Trevor Morgan, from Salt Cay, and Dwight Outten. ⊠ *Regent Village, Grace Bay* ☎ *649/941–4545.*

Caicos Wear Boutique. This store is filled with casual resort wear, including Caribbean-print shirts, swimsuits from Brazil, sandals, beach jewelry, and gifts. ⊠ *Regent Village, Grace Bay Rd., Grace Bay* ☎ *649/941–3346.*

Graceway IGA Supermarket Gourmet. With a large fresh-produce section, bakery, gourmet deli, and extensive meat counter, Provo's largest supermarket, is likely to have what you're looking for, and it's the most consistently well-stocked store on the island. It's got a good selection of prepared foods, including rotisserie chicken, pizza, and potato salad. But prices can be much higher than at home. ⊠ *Grace Bay Rd., Grace Bay* ☎ *649/941–5000.*

26

Greensleeves. This boutique offers paintings and pottery by local artists, baskets, jewelry, and sisal mats and bags. The proceeds from sales of works in the Potcake Corner help fund the Potcake Place rescue center for the islands' stray dogs. ⊠ *Central Sq., Leeward Hwy., Turtle Cove* ☎ *649/946–4147.*

Royal Jewels. This store sells gold and other jewelry, designer watches, perfumes, fine leather goods, and cameras—all duty-free—at several outlets. ⊠ *Providenciales International Airport* ☎ *649/941–4513* ⊠ *Arch Plaza* ☎ *649/946–4699* ⊠ *Beaches Turks & Caicos Resort & Spa, Grace Bay* ☎ *649/946–8285* ⊠ *Club Med Turkoise, Grace Bay* ☎ *649/946–5602.*

☺ ★ **Unicorn Bookstore.** If you need to supplement your beach-reading stock or are looking for island-specific materials, visit the Unicorn for a wide assortment of books and magazines, lots of information and guides about the Turks and Caicos Islands and the Caribbean, and a large children's section with crafts, games, and art supplies. ⊠ *In front of Graceway IGA Mall, Leeward Hwy., Discovery Bay* ☎ *649/941–5458.*

The Wine Cellar. This store has the best prices for alcohol and beer on the island. It's open Monday through Saturday from 8 to 6 (but closed Sunday and public holidays, when liquor sales aren't allowed). ⊠ *Leeward Hwy.* ☎ *649/946–4536* ⊕ *www.WineCellar.tc.*

SPORTS AND ACTIVITIES
BOATING AND SAILING

Provo's calm, reef-protected seas combine with constant easterly trade winds for excellent sailing conditions. Several multihull vessels offer charters with snorkeling stops, food and beverage service, and sunset vistas. Prices range from $39 per person for group trips to $600 or more for private charters.

For sightseeing below the waves, try the semisubmarine operated by **Caicos Tours** (⊠ *Turtle Cove Marina, Turtle Cove* ☎ *649/231–0006* ⊕ *www.caicostours.com*). You can stay dry within the small, lower observatory as it glides along on a one-hour tour of the reef, with large viewing windows on either side. The trip costs $39.

Sail Provo (☎ *649/946–4783* ⊕ *www.sailprovo.com*) runs 52-foot and 48-foot catamarans on scheduled half-day, full-day, sunset, and kid-friendly glowworm cruises, where underwater creatures light up the sea's surface for several days after each full moon.

Silverdeep (☎ *649/946–5612* ⊕ *www.silverdeep.com*) sailing trips include time for snorkeling and beachcombing at a secluded beach.

DIVING AND SNORKELING

Fodor's Choice ★ The island's many shallow reefs offer excellent and exciting snorkeling relatively close to shore. Try **Smith's Reef**, over Bridge Road east of Turtle Cove.

Scuba diving in the crystalline waters surrounding the islands ranks among the best in the Caribbean. The reef and wall drop-offs thrive with bright, unbroken coral formations and lavish numbers of fish and marine life. Mimicking the idyllic climate, waters are warm all year, averaging 76°F to 78°F in winter and 82°F to 84°F in summer. With

Diving with stingrays.

minimal rainfall and soil runoff, visibility is usually good and frequently superb, ranging from 60 feet to more than 150 feet. An extensive system of marine national parks and boat moorings, combined with an ecoconscious mind-set among dive operators, contributes to an uncommonly pristine underwater environment.

Dive operators in Provo regularly visit sites at **Grace Bay** and **Pine Cay** for spur-and-groove coral formations and bustling reef diving. They make the longer journey to the dramatic walls at **North West Point** and **West Caicos** depending on weather conditions. Instruction from the major diving agencies is available for all levels and certifications, even Technical diving. An average one-tank dive costs $45; a two-tank dive, $90. There are also two live-aboard dive boats available for charter working out of Provo.

☺ **Big Blue Unlimited** (✉ *Leeward Marina, Leeward, Providenciales* ☎ *649/946–5034* ⊕ *www.bigblue.tc*) has taken ecotouring to a whole new level with educational ecotours, including three-hour kayak trips and land-focused guided journeys around the family islands. Its Coastal Ecology and Wildlife tour is a kayak adventure through red mangroves to bird habitats, rock iguana hideaways, and natural fish nurseries. The Middle Caicos Bicycle Adventure gets you on a bike to explore the island, touring limestone caves in Conch Bar with a break for lunch with the Forbes family in the village of Bambarra. Packages are $255 for adults. No children under 12 are allowed.

Caicos Adventures (✉ *La Petite Pl., Grace Bay* ☎ *649/941–3346* ⊕ *www.tcidiving.com*), run by friendly Frenchman Fifi Kuntz, offers daily trips to West Caicos, French Cay, and Molasses Reef.

Diving the Turks and Caicos Islands

Scuba diving was the original water sport to draw visitors to the Turks and Caicos Islands in the 1970s. Aficionados are still drawn by the abundant marine life, including humpback whales in winter, sparkling clean waters, warm and calm seas, and the coral walls and reefs around the islands. Diving in the Turks and Caicos—especially off Grand Turk, South Caicos, and Salt Cay—is still considered among the best in the world.

Off Providenciales, dive sites are along the north shore's barrier reef. Most sites can be reached in anywhere from 10 minutes to 1½ hours. Dive sites feature spur-and-groove coral formations atop a coral-covered slope. Popular stops like **Aquarium, Pinnacles,** and **Grouper Hole** have large schools of fish, turtles, nurse sharks, and gray reef sharks. From the south side dive boats go to **French Cay, West Caicos, South West Reef,** and **Northwest Point.** Known for typically calm conditions and clear water, the West Caicos Marine National Park is a favorite stop. The area has dramatic walls and marine life, including sharks, eagle rays, and octopus, with large stands of pillar coral and huge barrel sponges.

Off Grand Turk, the 7,000-foot coral wall **drop-off** is actually within swimming distance of the beach. Buoyed sites along the wall have swim-through tunnels, cascading sand chutes, imposing coral pinnacles, dizzying vertical drops, and undercuts where the wall goes beyond the vertical and fades beneath the reef.

Caicos Dream Tours (☎ 649/243–3560 ⊕ *www.caicosdreamtours.com*), at the Alexandra Resort, offers several snorkeling trips, including one that has you diving for conch before lunch on a gorgeous beach. The company also offers private charters.

Dive Provo (✉ *Ports of Call, Grace Bay* ☎ 649/946–5040 *or* 800/234–7768 ⊕ *www.diveprovo.com*) is a PADI five-star operation that runs daily one- and two-tank dives to popular Grace Bay sites.

Provo Turtle Divers (✉ *Turtle Cove Marina, Turtle Cove* ☎ 649/946–4232 *or* 800/833–1341 ⊕ *www.provoturtledivers.com*), which also operates satellite locations at the Ocean Club East and Ocean Club West, has been on Provo since the 1970s. The staff is friendly, knowledgeable, and unpretentious.

FISHING

The islands' fertile waters are great for angling—anything from bottom- and reef-fishing (most likely to produce plenty of bites and a large catch) to bonefishing and deep-sea fishing (among the finest in the Caribbean). Each July the Caicos Classic Catch & Release Tournament attracts anglers from across the islands and the United States who compete to catch the biggest Atlantic blue marlin, tuna, or wahoo. For any fishing activity, you are required to purchase a $15 visitor's fishing license; operators generally furnish all equipment, drinks, and snacks. Prices range from $100 to $375, depending on the length of trip and size of boat. For deep-sea fishing trips in search of marlin, sailfish, wahoo, tuna, barracuda, and shark, look up **Grandslam Fishing Charters** (✉ *Turtle Cove Marina, Turtle Cove* ☎ *649/231–4420* ⊕ *www.GSFishing.com*).

Captain Arthur Dean at **Silverdeep** (✉ *Leeward Marina, Leeward* ☎ *649/946–5612* ⊕ *www.silverdeep.com*) is said to be among the Caribbean's finest bonefishing guides.

GOLF

Fodor's Choice
★ The par-72, 18-hole championship course at **Provo Golf and Country Club** (✉ *Governor's Rd., Grace Bay* ☎ *649/946–5991* ⊕ *www.provogolfclub. com*) is a combination of lush greens and fairways, rugged limestone outcroppings, and freshwater lakes, and is ranked among the Caribbean's top courses. Fees are $160 for 18 holes with shared cart. Premium golf clubs are available.

Turks & Caicos Miniature Golf (✉ *Long Bay Rd., Leeward* ☎ *649/231–4653*) is open every day and offers free shuttle service to most Grace Bay hotels. A round costs $15, and there is an on-site bar and grill where you can eat after your game.

HORSEBACK RIDING

Provo's long beaches and secluded lanes are ideal for trail rides on horseback. **Provo Ponies** (☎ *649/946–5252* ⊕ *www.provoponies.com*) offers morning and afternoon rides for all levels. A 45-minute ride costs $45; an 80-minute ride is $65. The rates include transportation from all major hotels.

PARASAILING

A 15-minute parasailing flight over Grace Bay is available for $70 (single) or $120 (tandem) from **Captain Marvin's Watersports** (☎ *649/231–0643*), who will pick you up at your hotel for your flight. The views as you soar over the bite-shaped Grace Bay area, with spectacular views of the barrier reef, are truly unforgettable.

TENNIS

You can rent tennis equipment at **Provo Golf and Country Club** (✉ *Grace Bay* ☎ *649/946–5991* ⊕ *www.provogolfclub.com*) and play on the two lighted courts, which are among the island's best. Nonmembers can play until 5 pm for $10 per hour (reservation required).

WATERSKIING AND KITESURFING

Nautique Sports (✉ *Ventura House West 101, Grace Bay Rd.* ☎ *649/941–7544* ⊕ *www.nautiquesports.com*) offers a water-sports dream. What better place to learn to ski than on the calm, crystal-clear waters of Providenciales. A great company for beginners, Nautique offers private instruction and will have you skiing in no time. Experts can try barefoot skiing. The company also rents kitesurfing equipment.

LITTLE WATER CAY

ꙮ
★ This small, uninhabited cay is a protected area under the Turks & Caicos National Trust. On these 150 acres are two trails, small lakes, red mangroves, and an abundance of native plants. Boardwalks protect the ground, and interpretive signs explain the habitat. The cay is home to about 2,000 rare, endangered rock iguanas. Experts say the iguanas are shy, but these creatures actually seem rather curious. They waddle

right up to you, as if posing for a picture. Several water-sports operators from Provo and North Caicos include a stop on the island as a part of their snorkeling or sailing excursions (it's usually called "Iguana Island"). There's a $5 fee for a permit to visit the cay, and the proceeds go toward conservation in the islands.

PARROT CAY

Once said to be a hideout for pirate Calico Jack Rackham and his lady cohorts Mary Read and Anne Bonny, the 1,000-acre cay, between Fort George Cay and North Caicos, is now the site of an ultraexclusive hideaway resort.

WHERE TO STAY

$$$$
RESORT
Fodor'sChoice
★

Parrot Cay Resort. This private paradise, on its own island, combines minimalist tranquillity with the best service in Turks and Caicos. **Pros:** impeccable service; gorgeous, secluded beach; the spa is considered one of the best in the world. **Cons:** only two restaurants on the entire island; it can be costly to get back and forth to Provo for excursions, as there is only private ferry service. ⊠ *Parrot Cay ⊕ Box 164, Providenciales* ☎ *649/946–7788* ⊕ *www.parrotcay.como.bz* ↪ *42 rooms, 4 suites, 14 villas* ⚐ *In-room: a/c, kitchen (some), Wi-Fi. In-hotel: restaurants, tennis courts, bars, pool, gym, spa, beach, business center, water sports* ❚❶ *Breakfast.*

PINE CAY

Pine Cay's 2½-mi-long (4-km-long) beach is among the most beautiful in the archipelago. The 800-acre private island is home to a secluded resort and around 37 private residences.

WHERE TO STAY

$$$$
ALL-INCLUSIVE
Fodor'sChoice
★

Meridian Club. A private club atmosphere on the prettiest beach in Turks and Caicos is *the* place to de-stress, with no phones, no TVs, no a/c, no worries. **Pros:** the finest beach in Turks and Caicos; rates include some of the best food in the Turks and Caicos as well as snorkeling trips. **Cons:** no TVs or phones, so you are really unplugged here; costly to get back to Provo for shopping or other Provo-based excursions or activities. ⊠ *Pine Cay, Turks and Caicos, BWI* ☎ *649/946–7758 or 866/746–3229* ⊕ *www.meridianclub.com* ↪ *12 rooms, 1 cottage, 7 villas* ⚐ *In-room: no a/c, no phone, no safe, no TV. In-hotel: restaurant, tennis court, bar, pool, beach, business center, water sports, some age restrictions* ☉ *Closed Aug.–Oct.* ❚❶ *All-inclusive.*

NORTH CAICOS

Thanks to abundant rainfall, this 41-square-mi (106-square-km) island is the lushest of the Turks and Caicos. Bird lovers can see a large flock of flamingos here, anglers can find shallow creeks full of bonefish, and history buffs can visit the ruins of a Loyalist plantation. Although there's no traffic, almost all the roads are paved, so bicycling is an excellent way to sightsee. The island is predicted to become one of the next tourism

Parrot Cay Resort.

hot spots, and foundations have been laid for condo resorts on Horse Stable Beach and Sandy Point. Even though it's a quiet place, you can find some small eateries around the airport and in Whitby, giving you a chance to try local and seafood specialties, sometimes served with homegrown okra or corn.

You can now reach North Caicos from Provo with a daily ferry from Walkin Marina in Leeward; the trip takes about 30 minutes. If you rent a car on North Caicos, you can even drive on the new causeway to Middle Caicos, a great day trip from Provo.

EXPLORING NORTH CAICOS

Flamingo Pond. This is a regular nesting place for the beautiful pink birds. They tend to wander out into the middle of the pond, so bring binoculars to get a better look.

Kew. This settlement has a small post office, a school, a church, and ruins of old plantations—all set among lush tropical trees bearing limes, papayas, and custard apples. Visiting Kew will give you a better understanding of the daily life of many islanders.

☺ **Wades Green.** Visitors can view well-preserved ruins of the greathouse, overseer's house, and surrounding walls of one of the most successful plantations of the Loyalist era. A lookout tower provides views for miles. Contact the National Trust for tour details. ⊠ *Kew* ☎ *649/941–5710 for National Trust* ⌨ *$5* ⊙ *Daily, by appointment only.*

Local Souvenirs

What should you bring home after a fabulous vacation in the Turks and Caicos Islands? Here are a few suggestions, some of which are free!

If you comb Pelican Beach or go on a conch-diving excursion, bring two conch shells (the maximum number allowed) home. Remember, only the shell, no living thing, is allowed.

The Middle Caicos Coop shop in Blue Hills sells carved wooden boats from Middle Caicos, and local straw hats and bags. You'll find locally made ceramics at Art Provo and at Turks & Caicos National Trust (at Town Center Mall or next to Island Scoop Ice Cream).

There are two cultural centers, one between Ocean Club East and Club Med, and the other next to Beaches Resort (there's a third one under construction between Aquamarine Beach Houses and Gansevoort). Here you'll find batik clothing and locally made jewelry. Custom-made pieces can be ordered.

The Conch Farm sells beautiful, affordable jewelry made from conch shells and freshwater pearls.

One of the best souvenirs is the hardcover coffee-table cookbook from the Red Cross. Not only is it gorgeous, featuring recipes from all the great chefs of the Turks and Caicos, but the proceeds help the Red Cross.

The best free souvenir—besides your phenomenal tan—is a potcake puppy. The puppy you adopt comes with carrier, papers, and all the shots—and will remind you year after year of your terrific vacation.

WHERE TO STAY

$–$$
RENTAL

⬜ **Caicos Beach Condos.** On Whitby Beach, this horseshoe-shape, two-story, solar-paneled hotel offers ocean views, comfortable and neatly furnished apartments, and a freshwater pool at quite reasonable rates. **Pros:** on the best beach of North Caicos; has the best restaurant on the island. **Cons:** you need a car to get anywhere on North Caicos; property is starting to age and could use some TLC. ⊠ *Whitby, North Caicos, Turks and Caicos, BWI* ☎ *649/946–7113 or 800/710–5204, 905/690–3817 in Canada* ⊕ *www.CaicosBeachCondos.com* ☞ *10 suites* ♿ *In-room: a/c, kitchen (some), no safe, no TV (some). In-hotel: restaurant, bar, pool, beach, business center, diving, water sports* ☉ *Closed June 15–Oct. 15* ⦿ *No meals.*

¢
HOTEL

⬜ **Pelican Beach Hotel.** North Caicos islanders Susan and Clifford Gardiner built this small, palmetto-fringed hotel in the 1980s on the quiet, mostly deserted Whitby Beach. **Pros:** the beach is just outside your room. **Cons:** location may be too remote and sleepy for some people; beach is in a "natural" state, meaning seaweed and pine needles. ⊠ *Whitby, North Caicos, Turks and Caicos, BWI* ☎ *649/946–7112* ⊕ *www.pelicanbeach.tc* ☞ *14 rooms, 2 suites* ♿ *In-room: a/c, no phone, no safe, no TV. In-hotel: restaurant, bar, beach, water sports* ☉ *Closed Aug. 15–Sept. 15* ⦿ *Some meals.*

MIDDLE CAICOS

At 48 square mi (124 square km) and with fewer than 300 residents, this is the largest and least developed of the inhabited islands in the Turks and Caicos chain. A limestone ridge runs to about 125 feet above sea level, creating dramatic cliffs on the north shore and a cave system farther inland. Middle Caicos has rambling trails along the coast; the **Crossing Place Trail,** maintained by the National Trust, follows the path used by the early settlers to go between the islands. Inland are quiet settlements with friendly residents. North Caicos and Middle Caicos are linked by a causeway; since they are now linked by a road, it's possible to take a ferry from Provo to North Caicos, rent a car, and explore both North Caicos and Middle Caicos.

EXPLORING MIDDLE CAICOS

Conch Bar Caves. These limestone caves have eerie underground lakes and milky-white stalactites and stalagmites. Archaeologists have discovered Lucayan Indian artifacts in the caves and the surrounding area. The caves are inhabited by some harmless bats. If you visit, don't worry—they don't bother visitors. It's best to get a guide. If you tour the caves, be sure to wear sturdy shoes, not sandals.

CAVE TOURS

Taxi driver and fisherman **Cardinal Arthur** (☎ 649/946–6107) can give you a good cave tour.

Local cave specialist and taxi driver **Ernest Forbes** (☎ 649/946–6140) can give you a cave tour and may even arrange for you to have a prix-fixe lunch at his house afterward if you ask nicely.

WHERE TO STAY

$–$$
RESORT
Blue Horizon Resort. At this property, undulating cliffs skirt one of the most dramatic beaches in the Turks and Caicos. **Pros:** breathtaking views of Mudjin Harbor from the rooms; lack of amenities and development make you feel like you're away from it all. **Cons:** lack of amenities and development; may be too isolated for some. ⊠ *Mudjin Harbor, Conch Bar, Middle Caicos, Turks and Caicos, BWI* ☎ *649/946–6141* ⊕ *www.bhresort.com* ➲ *5 cottages, 2 villas ⚒ In-room: a/c, no phone (some), kitchen (some), no safe, no TV (some). In-hotel: beach, water sports* ℮ *No meals.*

SOUTH CAICOS

This 8½-square-mi (21-square-km) island was once an important salt producer; today it's the heart of the fishing industry. Nature prevails, with long, white beaches, jagged bluffs, quiet backwater bays, and salt flats. Diving and snorkeling on the pristine wall and reefs are a treat enjoyed by only a few.

In September 2008, Hurricanes Hanna and Ike gave South Caicos a one-two punch, and many of the buildings at Cockburn Harbour received substantial damage; island residents had to wait more than a month to have power restored. The dive sights are fine, but the dive shops are gone, so you have to be an independent diver or take a diving excursion from another island. Also, there are four places to eat (with two of them open only occasionally for dinner).

26

EXPLORING SOUTH CAICOS

At the northern end of the island are fine white-sand beaches; the south coast is great for scuba diving along the drop-off; and there's excellent snorkeling off the windward (east) coast, where large stands of elkhorn and staghorn coral shelter several varieties of small tropical fish. A huge, sunken plane broken in pieces makes an excellent site. Spiny lobster and queen conch are found in the shallow Caicos Bank to the west and are harvested for export by local processing plants. The bonefishing here is some of the best in the West Indies.

Cockburn Harbour. The best natural harbor in the Caicos chain hosts the South Caicos Regatta, held each year in May.

THE TURKS

GRAND TURK

Just 7 mi (11 km) long and a little more than 1 mi (1½ km) wide, this island, the capital and seat of the Turks and Caicos government, has been a longtime favorite destination for divers eager to explore the 7,000-foot-deep pristine coral walls that drop down only 300 yards out to sea. On shore, the tiny, quiet island is home to white-sand beaches, the National Museum, and a small population of wild horses and donkeys, which leisurely meander past the white-walled courtyards, pretty churches, and bougainvillea-covered colonial inns on their daily commute into town. A cruise-ship complex that opened at the southern end of the island in 2006 brings about 300,000 visitors per year. Despite the dramatic changes this could make to this peaceful tourist spot, the dock is self-contained and is about 3 mi (5 km) from the tranquil, small hotels of Cockburn Town, Pillory Beach, and the Ridge and far from most of the western-shore dive sites. The influx has also pushed Grand Turk to open up a few new historic sites, including Grand Turk's Old Prison, and the Lighthouse.

EXPLORING GRAND TURK

Pristine beaches with vistas of turquoise waters, small local settlements, historic ruins, and native flora and fauna are among the sights on Grand Turk. Fewer than 5,000 people live on this 7½-square-mi (19-square-km) island, and it's hard to get lost, as there aren't many roads.

COCKBURN TOWN

The buildings in the colony's capital and seat of government reflect a 19th-century Bermudian style. Narrow streets are lined with low stone walls and old street lamps, which are now powered by electricity. The once-vital *salinas* (natural salt pans, where the sea leaves a film of salt) have been restored, and covered benches along the sluices offer shady spots for observing wading birds, including flamingos that frequent the shallows. Be sure to pick up a copy of the tourist board's *Heritage Walk* guide to discover Grand Turk's rich architecture.

Her Majesty's Prison. This prison was built in the 19th century to house runaway slaves and slaves who survived the wreck of the *Trouvadore* in 1841. After the slaves were granted freedom, the prison housed criminals and even modern-day drug runners until it closed in the 1990s.

CLOSE UP

All in the Family

Belongers, from the taxi driver meeting you to the chef feeding you, are often connected. "Oh, him?" you will hear. "He my cousin!" As development has been mercifully slow, such family connections, as well as crafts, bush medicine, ripsaw music, storytelling, and even recipes, have remained constant. But where do such traditions come from? Recently, researchers came closer to finding out. Many Belongers had claimed that their great-great-grandparents told them their forebears came directly from Africa. For decades their stories were ignored. Indeed, most experts believed that Belongers were descendants of mostly second-generation Bermudian and Caribbean slaves.

In 2005, museum researchers continued their search for a lost slave ship called *Trouvadore*. The ship, which wrecked off East Caicos in 1841, carried a cargo of 193 Africans, captured to be sold into slavery, almost all of whom miraculously survived the wreck. As slavery had been abolished in this British territory at the time, all the Africans were found and freed in the Turks and Caicos Islands. Since there were only a few thousand inhabitants in the islands at the time, these first-generation African survivors were a measurable minority (about 7% of the population then). Researchers have concluded that all the existing Belongers may be linked by blood or marriage to this one incident.

During one expedition, divers found a wrecked ship of the right time period. If these remains are *Trouvadore*, the Belongers may finally have a physical link to their past, to go with their more intangible cultural traditions. So while you're in the islands, look closely at the intricately woven baskets, listen carefully to the African rhythms in the ripsaw music, and savor the stories you hear. They may very well be the legacy of *Trouvadore* speaking to you from the past. For more information, check out the web site ⊕ *www.trouvadore.org*.

26

The last hanging here was in 1960. Now you can see the cells, solitary-confinement area, and exercise patio. The prison is open only when there is a cruise ship at the port. ⊠ *Pond St., Cockburn Town* ☎ No phone.

☾ ★ **Turks and Caicos National Museum.** In one of the oldest stone buildings on the islands, the national museum houses the Molasses Reef wreck, the earliest shipwreck—dating to the early 1500s—discovered in the Americas. The natural-history exhibits include artifacts left by Taíno, African, North American, Bermudian, French, and Latin American settlers. The museum has a 3-D coral reef exhibit, a walk-in Lucayan cave with wooden artifacts, and a gallery dedicated to Grand Turk's little-known involvement in the Space Race (John Glenn made landfall here after being the first American to orbit the Earth). An interactive children's gallery keeps knee-high visitors "edutained." The museum also claims that Grand Turk was where Columbus first landed in the New World. The most original display is a collection of messages in bottles that have washed ashore from all over the world. ⊠ *Duke St., Cockburn Town* ☎ *649/946–2160* ⊕ *www.tcmuseum.org* ⊑ *$5* ☉ *Mon., Tues., Thurs., and Fri. 9–4, Wed. 9–5, Sat. 9–1.*

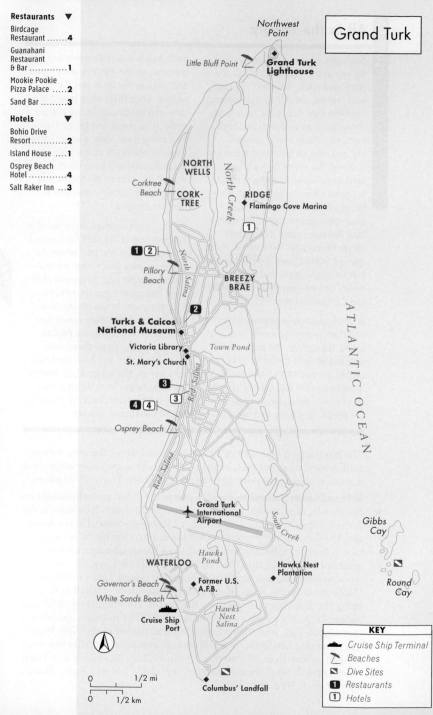

Grand Turk

Northwest
Point

Little Bluff Point
Grand Turk
Lighthouse

NORTH
WELLS

Corktree
Beach
CORK-
TREE

North Creek

RIDGE
Flamingo Cove Marina

1

1 2

Pillory
Beach

North Salina

BREEZY
BRAE

2

Turks & Caicos
National Museum

Victoria Library
St. Mary's Church

Town Pond

ATLANTIC OCEAN

3

3

4 4

Red Salina

Osprey Beach

Grand Turk
International
Airport

South Creek

Gibbs
Cay

Hawks
Pond

WATERLOO

Governor's Beach
White Sands Beach

Former U.S.
A.F.B.

Hawks Nest
Plantation

Round
Cay

Hawks
Nest
Salina

Cruise Ship Port

0   1/2 mi
0   1/2 km

Columbus' Landfall

KEY
⚓ Cruise Ship Terminal
🏖 Beaches
◩ Dive Sites
1 Restaurants
1 Hotels

BEYOND COCKBURN TOWN
Grand Turk Lighthouse. More than 150 years old, the lighthouse, built in the United Kingdom and transported piece by piece to the island, used to protect ships in danger of wrecking on the northern reefs. Use this panoramic landmark as a starting point for a breezy cliff-top walk by following the donkey trails to the deserted eastern beach. ⊠ *Lighthouse Rd., North Ridge.*

WHERE TO EAT
Conch in every shape and form, fresh grouper, and lobster (in season) are the favorite dishes at the laid-back restaurants that line Duke Street. Away from these more touristy areas, smaller and less expensive eateries serve chicken and ribs, curried goat, peas and rice, and other native island specialties. Prices are more expensive than in the United States, as most of the produce has to be imported.

$$$
CARIBBEAN
★
✕ Birdcage Restaurant. At the top of Duke Street, this has become the place to be on Sunday and Wednesday nights, when a sizzling barbecue of ribs, chicken, and lobster combines with live "rake-and-scrape" music from a local group called High Tide to draw an appreciative crowd. Arrive before 8 pm to secure beachside tables and an unrestricted view of the band; the location around the Osprey pool is lovely. The rest of the week, enjoy more elegant and eclectic fare accompanied by an increasingly impressive wine list. ⊠ *Osprey Beach Hotel, Duke St., Cockburn Town* ☎ 649/946–2666 ⊕ *www.ospreybeachhotel.com/dining/.*

$$$
ECLECTIC
★
✕ Guanahani Restaurant and Bar. Off the town's main drag, this restaurant sits on a stunning but quiet stretch of beach. The food goes beyond the usual Grand Turk fare, thanks to the talents of Canadian-born chef Zev Beck, who takes care of the evening meals. His pecan-crusted mahimahi and crispy sushi rolls are to die for. For lunch, Middle Caicos native Miss Leotha makes juicy jerk chicken to keep the crowd happy. The menu changes daily. The food is some of the best in Grand Turk. ⊠ *Bohio Dive Resort & Spa, Pillory Beach* ☎ 649/946–2135 ⊕ *www.bohioresort.com.*

$
ECLECTIC
✕ Mookie Pookie Pizza Palace. Local husband-and-wife team "Mookie" and "Pookie" have created a wonderful backstreet parlor that has gained well-deserved popularity over the years as much more than a pizza place. At lunchtime, the tiny eatery is packed with locals ordering specials such as steamed beef, curried chicken, and curried goat. You can also get burgers and omelets, but stick to the specials if you want fast service, and dine in if you want to get a true taste of island living. By night, the place becomes Grand Turk's one and only pizza take-out and delivery service, so if you're renting a villa or condo, put this spot on speed dial. ⊠ *Hospital Rd., Cockburn Town* ☎ 649/946–1538 ▭ *No credit cards* ۞ *Closed Sun.*

$$
AMERICAN
✕ Sand Bar. Run by two Canadian sisters, this popular beachside bar is a good value, though the menu is limited to fish-and-chips, quesadillas, and similarly basic bar fare. The tented wooden terrace jutting out onto the beach provides shade during the day, making it an ideal lunch spot, but it's also a great place to watch the sunset. The service is friendly, and the local crowd often spills into the street. ⊠ *Duke St., Cockburn Town* ☎ *No phone.*

26

Cockburn Town, Grand Turk.

WHERE TO STAY

Accommodations include original Bermudian inns, more modern but small beachfront hotels, and very basic to well-equipped self-catering suites and apartments. Almost all hotels offer dive packages, which are an excellent value.

The following reviews have been condensed for this book. Please go to Fodors.com for expanded reviews of each property.

$ ⌂ **Bohio Dive Resort and Spa.** Completely restored after two hurricanes in
RESORT September 2008, this basic yet comfortable hotel is the choice of divers. **Pros:** has the best restaurant in Grand Turk; on a gorgeous beach; steps away from awesome snorkeling. **Cons:** three-night minimum doesn't allow for quick getaways from Provo. ⊠ *Pillory Beach, Grand Turk, Turks and Caicos, BWI* ☎ *649/946–2135* ⊕ *www.bohioresort. com* ⌂ *12 rooms, 4 suites* ⌂ *In-room: a/c, no phone, no safe, kitchen (some). In-hotel: restaurant, bars, pool, spa, beach, business center, water sports* ⌂ *3-night minimum* ⍾○⍾ *No meals.*

$ ⌂ **Island House.** Years of business-travel experience have helped Colin
RENTAL Brooker create the comfortable, peaceful suites that overlook North
⌂ Creek. **Pros:** full condo units feel like a home away from home. **Cons:** not on the beach; you need a car to get around. ⊠ *Lighthouse Rd., Box 36, Grand Turk, Turks and Caicos, BWI* ☎ *649/946–1519* ⊕ *www. islandhouse.tc* ⌂ *8 suites* ⌂ *In-room: a/c, kitchen, no safe, Wi-Fi. In-hotel: pool, laundry facilities, water sports, some pets allowed* ⌂ *2-night minimum* ⍾○⍾ *No meals.*

¢–$

HOTEL

Fodor'sChoice

★

☷ **Osprey Beach Hotel.** Grand Turk veteran hotelier Jenny Smith has transformed this two-story oceanfront hotel with her artistic touches: palms, frangipani, and deep green azaleas frame it like a painting. **Pros:** renovated in 2007; best hotel on Grand Turk; walking distance to Front Street, restaurants, and excursions. **Cons:** three-night minimum; rocky beachfront. ✉ *Duke St., Cockburn Town, Grand Turk, Turks and Caicos, BWI* ☎ *649/946–2666* ⊕ *www.ospreybeachhotel.com* ⟻ *11 rooms, 16 suites* ⚐ *In-room: a/c, kitchen (some), no safe, Wi-Fi (some). In-hotel: restaurant, bar, pool, beach, water sports, some pets allowed* ⟳ *3-night minimum* ⊖ *No meals.*

¢–$

B&B/INN

☷ **Salt Raker Inn.** A large anchor on the sun-dappled pathway marks the entrance to this 19th-century house, which is now an unpretentious inn. **Pros:** excellent location that is an easy walk to Front Street, restaurants, and excursions. **Cons:** no no-smoking rooms. ✉ *Duke St., Box 1, Cockburn Town, Grand Turk, Turks and Caicos, BWI* ☎ *649/946–2260* ⊕ *www.hotelsaltraker.com* ⟻ *10 rooms, 3 suites* ⚐ *In-room: a/c, no safe, Wi-Fi. In-hotel: restaurant, bar, some pets allowed* ⊖ *No meals.*

NIGHTLIFE

Grand Turk is a quiet place where you come to relax and unwind, so most of the nightlife consists of little more than happy hour at sunset so you have a chance to glimpse the elusive green flash. Most restaurants turn into gathering places where you can talk with the new friends you have made that day, but there a few more nightlife-oriented places that will keep you busy after dark. On some evenings, you'll be able to catch Mitch Rollings of Blue Water Divers; he often headlines the entertainment at the island's different restaurants.

Nookie Hill Club. On weekends and holidays the younger crowd heads over to the Nookie Hill Club for late-night drinking and dancing. ✉ *Nookie Hill* ☎ *No phone.*

Osprey Beach Hotel. Every Wednesday and Sunday, there's lively rake-and-scrape music at the Osprey Beach Hotel. ✉ *Duke St., Cockburn Town* ☎ *649/946–2666.*

Salt Raker Inn. On Friday, rake-and-scrape bands play at the Salt Raker Inn. ✉ *Duke St., Cockburn Town* ☎ *649/946–2260.*

SPORTS AND ACTIVITIES

BICYCLING

The island's mostly flat terrain isn't very taxing, and most roads have hard surfaces. Take water with you: there are few places to stop for refreshments. Most hotels have bicycles available, but you can also rent them for $10 to $15 a day from **Oasis Divers** (✉ *Duke St., Cockburn Town* ☎ *649/946–1128* ⊕ *www.oasisdivers.com*).

DIVING AND SNORKELING

★ In these waters you can find undersea cathedrals, coral gardens, and countless tunnels, but note that you must carry and present a valid certificate card before you'll be allowed to dive. As its name suggests, the **Black Forest** offers staggering black-coral formations as well as the occasional black-tip shark. In the **Library** you can study fish galore, including large numbers of yellowtail snapper. At the Columbus Passage

26

separating South Caicos from Grand Turk, each side of a 22-mi-wide (35-km-wide) channel drops more than 7,000 feet. From January through March, thousands of Atlantic humpback whales swim through en route to their winter breeding grounds. **Gibb's Cay,** a small cay a couple of miles off of Grand Turk, where you can swim with stingrays, makes for a great excursion.

Blue Water Divers (✉ *Duke St., Cockburn Town, Grand Turk* 🖼🖼 *649/946–2432* ⊕ *www.grandturkscuba.com*) has been in operation on Grand Turk since 1983 and is the only PADI Gold Palm five-star dive center on the island. Owner Mitch will undoubtedly put some of your underwater adventures to music in the evenings when he plays at the Osprey Beach Hotel or Salt Raker Inn. **Oasis Divers** (✉ *Duke St., Cockburn Town* 🖼🖼 *649/946–1128* ⊕ *www.oasisdivers.com*) specializes in complete gear handling and pampering treatment. It also supplies Nitrox and rebreathers.

SALT CAY

Fewer than 100 people live on this 2½-square-mi (6-square-km) dot of land, maintaining an unassuming lifestyle against a backdrop of stucco cottages, stone ruins, and weathered wooden windmills standing sentry in the abandoned salinas. The beautifully preserved island is bordered by beaches where weathered green and blue sea glass and pretty shells often wash ashore. Beneath the waves, 10 dive sites are minutes from shore.

There are big plans for Salt Cay, which will change the small island forever, though probably not for several years. Gone will be the donkeys and chickens roaming the streets; in their place will be a luxurious resort and new golf course. If you want to see how the Caribbean was when it was laid-back, sleepy, and colorful, visit the island now before it changes.

EXPLORING SALT CAY

Salt sheds and salinas are silent reminders of the days when the island was a leading producer of salt. Now the salt ponds attract abundant birdlife. Island tours are often conducted by motorized golf cart. From January through April, humpback whales pass by on the way to their winter breeding grounds.

What little development there is on Salt Cay is found in its main community, Balfour Town. It's home to several small hotels and a few cozy stores, as well as the main dock and the Coral Reef Bar & Grill, where locals hang out with tourists to watch the sunset and drink a beer.

White House. The grand stone house, which once belonged to a wealthy salt merchant, is testimony to the heyday of Salt Cay's eponymous industry. Still privately owned by the descendants of the original family, it's sometimes opened up for tours. It's worth asking your guesthouse or hotel owner—or any local passerby—if Salt Cay islander "Uncle Lionel" is on-island, as he may give you a personal tour to see the still-intact, original furnishings, books, and medicine cabinet that date back to the early 1800s. ✉ *Victoria St., Balfour Town.*

WHERE TO EAT

$$$ ✕ **Island Thyme Bistro.** Owner Porter Williams serves potent alcoholic
ECLECTIC creations as well as fairly sophisticated local and international cui-
★ sine. Try steamed, freshly caught snapper in a pepper-wine sauce with
peas and rice, or spicy-hot chicken curry served with tangy chutneys.
Don't forget to order the "Porter" house steak. You can take cooking
lessons from the chef, enjoy the nightly Filipino fusion tapas during
happy hour, and join the gang for Friday-night pizza. This is a great
place to make friends and the best place to catch up on island gossip.
The airy, trellis-covered spot overlooks the salinas. There's a small
shop with gifts and tourist information; you can also get a mani-
cure or pedicure here. ✉ *North District* 🕿 *649/946–6977* ⊕ *www.*
islandthyme.tc/ ⚇ *Reservations essential* ⊗ *Closed Wed. mid-May–*
June and Sept.–late Oct.

$$ ✕ **Pat's Place.** Island native Pat Simmons can give you a lesson in the
CARIBBEAN medicinal qualities of her garden plants and periwinkle flowers, as
well as provide excellent native cuisine for a very reasonable price
in her typical Salt Cay home. Home cooking doesn't get any closer
to home than this. Try conch fritters for lunch and steamed grouper
with okra rice for dinner. Be sure to call ahead, as she cooks only when
there's someone to cook for. Pat also has a small grocery shop selling
staples. ✉ *South District* 🕿 *649/946–6919* ⚇ *Reservations essential*
⊟ *No credit cards.*

WHERE TO STAY

$ 🏠 **Pirates Hideaway and Blackbeard's Quarters.** Owner Candy Herwin—
HOTEL true to her self-proclaimed pirate status—has smuggled artistic treasures across the ocean and created her own masterpieces to deck out
this lair. **Pros:** artist workshops are offered during peak season. **Cons:**
rocky beachfront. ✉ *Victoria St., South District, Salt Cay, Turks and*
Caicos, BWI 🕿 *649/946–6909* ⊕ *www.saltcay.tc* ⛵ *2 suites, 1 house*
⚴ *In-room: no a/c, no phone, kitchen (some), no safe. In-hotel: beach,*
water sports ⏀ *No meals.*

$ 🏠 **Tradewinds Guest Suites.** Yards away from Dean's Dock, a grove of
RENTAL whispering casuarina trees surrounds these five single-story, basic apartments, which offer a moderate-budget option on Salt Cay with the
option of dive packages. **Pros:** walking distance to diving, fishing, dining, and dancing. **Cons:** a/c costs extra; some may feel isolated with
few nighttime activities and no TV. ✉ *Victoria St., Balfour Town, Salt*
Cay, Turks and Caicos, BWI 🕿 *649/946–6906* ⊕ *www.tradewinds.tc*
⛵ *5 apartments* ⚴ *In-room: no phone, kitchen (some), no TV, no safe.*
In-hotel: beach, water sports ⏀ *No meals.*

$$–$$$ 🏠 **Villas of Salt Cay.** One of the nicest and newest places to stay in
RENTAL Salt Cay is centrally located on Victoria Street, in the middle of everything. **Pros:** bedrooms are set up for extra privacy; on Victoria Street
within walking distance of everything; on a private stretch of beach.
Cons: not all rooms have a/c; cabanas don't have kitchens; shared pool.
✉ *Victoria St., Balfour Town, Salt Cay, Turks and Caicos, Islands, BWI*
🕿 *649/946–6909* ⊕ *www.villasofsaltcay.com* ⛵ *1 2-bedroom villa,*
1 1-bedroom cottage, 3 cabanas ⚴ *In-room: no a/c (some), kitchen*
(some), no safe, Wi-Fi. In-hotel: pool, beach ⏀ *No meals.*

26

SPORTS AND ACTIVITIES
DIVING AND SNORKELING
Scuba divers can explore the wreck of the *Endymion*, a 140-foot wooden-hull British warship that sank in 1790; you can swim through the hull and spot cannons and anchors. It's off the southern point of Salt Cay.

Salt Cay Divers (✉ *Balfour Town* ☎ *649/946–6906* ⊕ *www.saltcaydivers. tc*) conducts daily dive trips and rents all the necessary equipment. You'll pay around $80 for a two-tank dive.

WHALE-WATCHING
During the winter months (January through April), Salt Cay is a center for whale-watching, when some 2,500 humpback whales pass close to shore. Whale-watching trips can most easily be organized through your inn or guesthouse.

United States Virgin Islands

WORD OF MOUTH

"We always make it a point every trip to make it over to Jost Van Dyke and visit White Bay for the day whether by ferry or private charter [whenever we visit St. John]. Yes, there is enough to see on St John for sure. But we feel it is worth the day off island to experience White Bay."

—brendang

WELCOME TO UNITED STATES VIRGIN ISLANDS

AMERICA'S CARIBBEAN

About 1,000 mi (1,600 km) from the southern tip of Florida, the U.S. Virgin Islands were acquired from Denmark in 1917. St. Croix, at 84 square mi (218 square km), is the largest of the islands; St. John, at 20 square mi (52 square km), is the smallest. Together, they have a population of around 110,000, half of whom live on St. Thomas.

A perfect combination of the familiar and the exotic, the U.S. Virgin Islands are a little bit of home set in an azure sea. With hundreds of idyllic coves and splendid beaches, chances are that on one of the three islands you'll find your ideal Caribbean vacation spot.

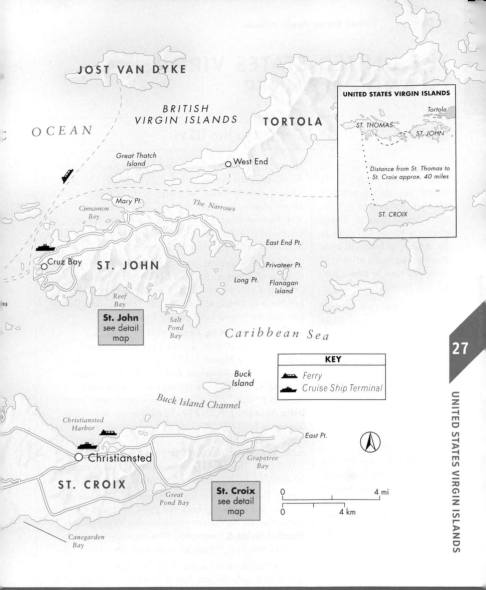

KEY

Ferry

Cruise Ship Terminal

TOP REASONS TO VISIT UNITED STATES VIRGIN ISLANDS

1 Incomparable Sailing: St. Thomas is one of the Caribbean's major sailing centers.

2 Great Hiking: Two-thirds of St. John is a national park that is crisscrossed by excellent hiking trails.

3 Beaches: Though Magens Bay on St. Thomas and Trunk Bay on St. John are two of the most perfect beaches you'll ever find,

St. Croix's West End beaches are fetching in their own way.

4 Shopping: Shopping on both St. Thomas and St. Croix is stellar.

5 Deep-Sea Fishing: St. Thomas is one of the best places to catch Atlantic blue marlin between the months of June and October.

THE UNITED STATES VIRGIN ISLANDS PLANNER

Logistics

Getting to the USVI: There are many nonstop flights to St. Thomas from the U.S., and there are a few nonstops to St. Croix; often, you'll have to change planes in Miami, San Juan, or St. Thomas to reach St. Croix. There are no flights at all to St. John; you have to take a ferry from St. Thomas.

Hassle Factor: Low to high, depending on your flight schedule.

On the Ground: Many travelers do just fine without a car in St. Thomas, but it's much harder if you are renting a villa; be aware, however, that taxis can be expensive when used every day. In St. John, you must rent a car if you are staying in a villa or in Coral Bay, but you might get by without one if you are staying elsewhere. A car is more of a necessity in St. Croix, regardless of where you stay.

Getting Around on the Islands: Frequent, convenient ferries connect St. Thomas and St. John. St. Croix is further removed, so a flight from St. Thomas is the most common mode of transport, but there is a ferry from St. Thomas several days a week.

Getting to the USVI

Nonstops: Fly nonstop to St. Thomas from Atlanta (Delta), Boston (US Airways), Charlotte (US Airways), Chicago (United), Detroit (Delta, seasonal), Fort Lauderdale (Spirit), Miami (American), New York–JFK (American), New York–Newark (Continental), Philadelphia (US Airways), or Washington, D.C.–Dulles (United). Fly nonstop to St. Croix from Atlanta (Delta) or Miami (American).

If you can't fly nonstop, then you can connect in San Juan. You can also take a seaplane between St. Thomas and St. Croix. The only option for St. John is a ferry from either Red Hook or Charlotte Amalie in St. Thomas. Both Caneel Bay and the Westin have private ferries.

Airports: Cyril E. King Airport (STT St. Thomas ☎ 340/774–5100) on the west end of the island. **Henry Rohlsen Airport** (STX St. Croix ☎ 340/778–1012). **Airlines: American Airlines/American Eagle** (☎ 800/433–7300 ⊕ www.aa.com). **Continental Airlines** (☎ 800/231–0856 ⊕ www.continental.com). **Delta Airlines** (☎ 800/221–1212 ⊕ www.delta.com). **Seaborne** (☎ 340/773–6442 ⊕ www.seaborneairlines. com). **Spirit Airlines** (☎ 800/772–7117 ⊕ www.spiritair. com). **United Airlines** (☎ 800/864–8331, 340/774–9190 in St. Thomas ⊕ www.united.com). **US Airways** (☎ 800/622–1015 ⊕ www.usairways.com).

Ferries: There's frequent service between St. Thomas and St. John and their neighbors, the BVI. Check with the ferry companies for the current schedules. The **Virgin Islands Vacation Guide & Community** (⊕ www.vinow.com) publishes current ferry schedules on its Web site.

There's frequent daily service from both Red Hook and Charlotte Amalie to Cruz Bay, St. John. About every hour, there's a car ferry; you should arrive at least 25 minutes before departure.

Ferry Companies: Inter-Island Boat Service (☎ 340/776–6597 in St. John). **Native Son** (☎ 340/774–8685 in St. Thomas ⊕ www.nativesonferry.com). **Smith's Ferry** (☎ 340/775–7292 in St. Thomas ⊕ www.smithsferry.com). **Speedy's** (☎ 284/494–6154 in Tortola ⊕ www. speedysbvi.com). **V.I. SeaTrans** (☎ 340/776–5494 in St. Thomas ⊕ www.goviseatrans.com).

Getting Around the USVI

Driving is on the left, British-style. The law requires that *everyone* wears a seat belt. Traffic can be bad during rush hour on all three islands.

Car Rentals in St. Thomas: Avis, Budget, and Hertz all have counters at Cyril E. King Airport, but there are some other offices as well; in addition, there are local companies. **Avis** (☎ *340/774–1468*). **Budget** (☎ *340/776–5774*). **Dependable Car Rental** (☎ *340/774–2253* or *800/522–3076*). **Discount** (☎ *340/776–4858*). **E-Z Car Rental** (☎ *340/775–6255* or *800/524–2027*). **Hertz** (☎ *340/774–1879*).

Car Rentals in St. John: All the car-rental companies in St. John are locally owned. Most companies are just a short walk from the ferry dock. Those a bit farther away will pick you up. **Best** (☎ *340/693–8177*). **Cool Breeze** (☎ *340/776–6588* ⊕ *www.coolbreezecarrental.com*). **Courtesy** (☎ *340/776–6650* ⊕ *www.courtesycarrental.com*). **Delbert Hill Taxi & Jeep Rental Service** (☎ *340/776–6637*). **Denzil Clyne** (☎ *340/776–6715*). **O'Connor Car Rental** (☎ *340/776–6343* ⊕ *www.oconnorcarrental.com*). **St. John Car Rental** (☎ *340/776–6103* ⊕ *www.stjohncarrental.com*). **Spencer's Jeep** (☎ *340/693–8784* or *888/776–6628* ⊕ *www.spencerjeeprentals.com*).

Car Rentals in St. Croix: There are both local and national companies on St. Croix; if your company doesn't have an airport location, you'll be picked up or a car will be delivered to you. **Atlas** (☎ *340/718–2886* or *800/426–6009*). **Avis** (☎ *340/778–9355*). **Budget** (☎ *340/778–9636*). **Judi of Croix** (☎ *340/773–2123* or *877/903–2123* ⊕ *www.judiofcroix.com*). **Midwest** (☎ *340/772–0438* or *877/772–0438* ⊕ *www.midwestautorental.com*). **Olympic** (☎ *340/773–8000* or *888/878–4227* ⊕ *www.stcroixcarrentals.com*).

Taxis: USVI taxis don't have meters; fares are per person, set by a schedule, and drivers usually take multiple fares, especially from the airport, ferry docks, and cruise-ship terminals. Many taxis are open safari vans, but some are air-conditioned vans.

St. Thomas: East End Taxi (☎ *340/775–6974*). **Islander Taxi** (☎ *340/774–4077*). **V.I. Taxi Association** (☎ *340/774–4550*).

St. John: Paradise Taxi (☎ *340/714–7913*).

St. Croix: Antilles Taxi Service (☎ *340/773–5020*). **St. Croix Taxi Association** (☎ *340/778–1088*).

Island Activities

St. Thomas is one of the Caribbean's most important centers for **sailing and sportfishing**.

Beaches are excellent on both St. Thomas and St. John, and good on St. Croix.

Of the three, St. Croix is more known for **diving**, particularly at Cane Bay. St. Croix's Buck Island and its surrounding reefs are also a protected part of the national park system and a great destination for **snorkeling**. The island also has a terrific **golf** course.

St. Thomas is the most developed of the three islands, but you'll find every imaginable kind of water- and land-based activity, **historic sights, golf, tennis**, and **horseracing** to mention but a few.

Since most of St. John is a national park, the island is in pristine condition, and its many **hiking** trails are well worth exploring on foot. Off-the-beach **snorkeling** is also a popular activity, though some prefer taking a snorkeling and sailing trip to enjoy hard-to-reach beaches in the U.S. and nearby British Virgin Islands.

27

THE UNITED STATES VIRGIN ISLANDS PLANNER

Fast Facts

Banks: The U.S. dollar is used throughout the U.S. Virgin Islands. All major credit cards are accepted by most hotels, restaurants, and shops. ATMs are common on St. Thomas. St. John has two banks in Cruz Bay. St. Croix has branches of Banco Popular in the Orange Grove and Sunny Isle. V.I. Community Bank is in Sunny Isle, Frederiksted, Estate Diamond, Orange Grove, and Christiansted. Scotia Bank has branches in Sunny Isle, Frederiksted, Christiansted, and Sunshine Mall.

Electricity: Electricity is the U.S. standard.

Emergencies: Dial 911 for all emergencies.

Weddings: Apply for a marriage license at the Superior Court. There's a $50 application fee and $50 license fee. You have to wait eight days after the clerk receives the application to get married, and licenses must be picked up in person weekdays, though you can apply by mail.

St. Croix Superior Court (✉ Box 929, Christiansted 00820 ☎ 340/778–9750).
St. Thomas Superior Court (✉ Box 70, St. Thomas, 00804 ☎ 340/774–6680).

Essentials

Mail: The main U.S. Post Office on St. Thomas is near the hospital, with branches in Charlotte Amalie, Frenchtown, Havensight, and Tutu Mall. Postal rates are the same as if you were in the mainland United States, but Express Mail and Priority Mail aren't as fast.

FedEx offers overnight service if you get your package to the office before 5 pm. Shipping services on St. Thomas are also available at Fast Shipping & Communications Nisky Mail Center and at Red Hook Mail Services. There's a post office in Cruz Bay, but the lines are often long.

There are post offices at Christiansted, Frederiksted, Gallows Bay, and Sunny Isle on St. Croix.

The FedEx office on St. Croix is in Peter's Rest Commercial Center; try to drop off your packages before 5:30 pm.

Safety: Keep your hotel or vacation villa door locked at all times and stick to well-lighted streets at night. Keep your rental car locked wherever you park, and lock possessions in the trunk. Don't leave valuables lying on the beach while you snorkel. Don't wander the streets of the main towns alone at night, whether you are in Charlotte Amalie, Cruz Bay, Christiansted, or Frederiksted.

Although crime is not as prevalent in St. John as it is on St. Thomas and St. Croix, it does exist. There are occasional burglaries at villas, even during daylight hours. Lock doors even when you're lounging by the pool. It's not a good idea to walk around Cruz Bay late at night. If you don't have a car, plan on taking a taxi. Since it can be hard to find a taxi in the wee hours of the morning, arrange in advance for a driver to pick you up.

Visitor Information: USVI Department of Tourism (☎ 340/774–8784 or 800/372–8784 ⊕ www.visitusvi.com).

Where to Stay

St. Thomas is the most developed of the Virgin Islands; choose it if you want extensive shopping opportunities and a multitude of activities and restaurants. St. John is the least developed of the three and has a distinct following; it's the best choice if you want a small-island feel and easy access to great hiking. However, most villas there aren't directly on the beach. St. Croix is a sleeper. With accommodations ranging from simple inns to luxury resorts, it's remarkably diverse, but none of the beaches is as breathtaking as those on St. Thomas and St. John.

Resorts: Whether you are looking for a luxury retreat or a moderately priced vacation spot, there's going to be something for you in the USVI. St. Thomas has the most options. St. John has only two large resorts, both upscale; others are small, but it has some unique eco-oriented camping options. St. Croix's resorts are more midsize.

Small Inns: Particularly on St. Croix, you'll find a wide range of attractive and accommodating small inns; if you can live without being directly on the beach, these friendly, homey places are a good option. St. Thomas also has a few small inns.

Villas: Villas are plentiful on all three islands, but they are especially popular on St. John, where they represent more than half the available lodging. They're always a good bet for families who can do without a busy resort environment.

HOTEL AND RESTAURANT PRICES

Restaurant prices are for a main course at dinner and include any taxes or service charges. Hotel prices are per night for a double room in high season, excluding taxes, service charges, and meal plans (except at all-inclusives).

WHAT IT COSTS IN U.S. DOLLARS

	¢	$	$$	$$$	$$$$
Restaurants	under $8	$8–$12	$12–$20	$20–$30	over $30
Hotels	under $150	$151–$275	$276–$375	$376–$475	over $475

When to Go

High season coincides with that on most other Caribbean islands, from December through April or May; before and after that time, rates can drop by as much as 25% to 50%, depending on the resort.

St. Thomas's **International Rolex Regatta** in March is a big draw. April is also a great time to visit St. Thomas, as the island comes alive for **Carnival.** The celebrations—steel-drum music, colorful costumes, and dancing in the streets—culminate on the last weekend of the month. The big **sportfishing tournaments** usually begin in July and go through the summer.

The **St. Croix Half Ironman Triathlon** attracts international-class athletes as well as amateurs every May. In February and March, the **St. Croix Landmarks Society House Tours** give you a chance to peek inside many historic homes that aren't usually open to the public.

There aren't too many big events on St. John, but **Carnival** tends to bring many people there as well as to the other two islands.

27

U.S. VIRGIN ISLANDS BEACHES

The beaches of the USVI are like pearly white smiles that outline the curve of the bays on both the Atlantic Ocean to the north and Caribbean Sea to the south. The brilliant sand provides a beaming contrast to the deep turquoise seas and the lush green palms and sea grape trees that line the shores.

(Above) Trunk Bay, St. John. (Opposite page bottom) Coki Beach, St. Thomas. (Opposite page top) Magens Bay, St. Thomas.

The three islands of the USVI offer a wide range of beach experiences and activities. St. Thomas and St. John are widely known for having the best beaches in the U.S. Virgin Islands, but there is one more island that you shouldn't miss if you're visiting St. Thomas. Water Island, a half-mile ferry ride from Crown Bay Marina on St. Thomas, has Honeymoon Beach, one of the most perfect powdery beaches you'll find (though some say that Sprat Beach, which is much farther away from the ferry dock, is better); there are restrooms on the beach as well as a restaurant that serves lunch, but it's a half-mile hike from the ferry dock (some of it up a rather steep hill).

DON'T MISS

St. Thomas is the busiest and most developed of the U.S. Virgin Islands. Don't miss watching the planes land from Brewer's Beach, eating fish and fungi (a cornmeal polenta-like side dish) at Coki Beach, renting a paddleboat at Magens Bay, bodysurfing in the winter at Hull Bay, and enjoying a rum and Coke from beachside bar service at Morningstar Beach.

For complete information on these beaches see individual beach sections within the chapter.

ST. THOMAS

All 44 St. Thomas beaches are open to the public, although you can reach some of them only by walking through a resort. Hotel guests frequently have access to lounge chairs and floats that are off-limits to nonguests; for this reason you may feel more comfortable at one of the beaches not associated with a resort, such as **Magens Bay** (which charges an entrance fee to cover beach maintenance) or **Coki Beach**, the latter abutting Coral World Ocean Park and offering the island's best off-the-beach snorkeling. **Morningstar Beach** sits between the twin Marriott Resorts on St. Thomas's south shore. **Sapphire Beach** is another of the island's better beaches, and it offers both soft, silky sand as well as access to a good reef for snorkeling.

ST. JOHN

St. John is blessed with many beaches, and all of them fall into the good, great, and don't-tell-anyone-else-about-this-place categories. Some are more developed than others—and many are crowded on weekends, holidays, and in high season—but by and large they're still pristine. Beaches along the south and eastern shores are quiet and isolated.

Two of the island's stand-out beaches can be found in the national park. **Trunk Bay** is the beach you often seen pictured on postcards from the Virgin Islands; a long, white sandy beach is fronted by a coral reef that makes waves smooth and steady. **Cinnamon Bay**, which is next to the national park campground, has a water sports center and excellent snorkeling; there are also a couple of hiking trails that start at the beach. St. John's other excellent beach is **Hawksnest Bay**. Close to Cruz Bay, it's often busy with locals and tourists alike, but it's a great spot for off-shore snorkeling.

ST. CROIX

St. Croix's beaches are not quite as spectacular as those on St. John or St. Thomas. But that's not to say you won't find some good places to spread out for a day on the water. The best beach is on nearby **Buck Island**, a national monument where a marked snorkeling trail leads you through an extensive coral reef while a soft, sandy beach beckons a few yards away. Other great beaches are the unnamed **west end beaches** both south and north of Frederiksted. You can park yourself at Sunset Grill, about a mile north of Frederiksted, where you can rent a lounger and get food and drinks from the restaurant.

27

Updated by
Carol M.
Bareuther and
Lynda Lohr

The U.S. Virgin Islands—St. Thomas, St. John, and St. Croix—may fly the American flag, but "America's Paradise" is in reality a delightful mix of the foreign and familiar that offers something for everyone to enjoy. The history, beautiful beaches, myriad activities, good food, and no-passport-required status make the Virgin Islands an inviting beach destination for many Americans.

With three islands to choose from, you're likely to find your piece of paradise. Check into a beachfront condo on the east end of St. Thomas; then eat burgers and watch football at a beachfront bar and grill. Or stay at an 18th-century plantation greathouse on St. Croix, dine on everything from local food to Continental cuisine, and go horseback riding at sunrise. Rent a tent or a cottage in the pristine national park on St. John; then take a hike, kayak off the coast, read a book, or just listen to the sounds of the forest. Or dive deep into "island time" and learn the art of limin' (hanging out, Caribbean-style) on all three islands.

History books give credit to Christopher Columbus for "discovering" the New World. In reality, the Virgin Islands, like the rest of the isles in the Caribbean chain, were populated as long ago as 2000 BC by nomadic waves of seagoing settlers as they migrated north from South America and eastward from Central America and the Yucatán Peninsula.

Columbus met the descendants of these original inhabitants during his second voyage to the New World, in 1493. He anchored in Salt River, a natural bay west of what is now Christiansted, St. Croix, and sent his men ashore in search of fresh water. Hostile arrows rather than welcoming embraces made for a quick retreat. In haste, Columbus named the island Santa Cruz (Holy Cross) and sailed north. He eventually claimed St. John, St. Thomas, and what are now the British Virgin Islands for Spain and at the same time named this shapely silhouette of 60-some islands Las Once Mil Virgenes, for the 11,000 legendary virgin followers of St. Ursula. Columbus believed the islands barren of priceless spices, so he sailed off, leaving more than a century's gap in time before the next Europeans arrived.

Pioneers, planters, and pirates from throughout Europe ushered in the era of colonization. Great Britain and the Netherlands claimed St. Croix in 1625. This peaceful coexistence ended abruptly when the Dutch governor killed his English counterpart, thus launching years of battles for possession that would see seven flags fly over this southernmost Virgin isle. Meanwhile, St. Thomas's sheltered harbor proved a magnet for pirates such as Blackbeard and Bluebeard. The Danes first colonized the island in 1666, naming their main settlement Taphus for its many beer halls. In 1691 the town received the more respectable name of Charlotte Amalie in honor of Danish king Christian V's wife. It wasn't until 1718 that a small group of Dutch planters raised their country's flag on St. John. As on its sibling Virgins, a plantation economy soon developed.

HOP ON THE BUS

On St. Thomas the island's large buses make public transportation a very comfortable—though slow—way to get from east and west to Charlotte Amalie and back (service to the north is limited). Buses run about every 30 minutes from stops that are clearly marked with "vitran" signs. Fares are $1 between outlying areas and town and 75¢ in town.

Plantations depended on slave labor, and the Virgin Islands played a key role in the triangular route that connected the Caribbean, Africa, and Europe in the trade of sugar, rum, and human cargo. By the early 1800s a sharp decline in cane prices because of competing beet sugar and an increasing number of slave revolts motivated Governor General Peter von Scholten to abolish slavery in the Danish colonies on July 3, 1848. This holiday is now celebrated as Emancipation Day.

After emancipation, the island's economy slumped. Islanders owed their existence to subsistence farming and fishing. Meanwhile, during the American Civil War, the Union began negotiations with Denmark for the purchase of the Virgin Islands in order to establish a naval base. However, the sale didn't happen until World War I, when President Theodore Roosevelt paid the Danes $25 million for the three largest islands; an elaborate Transfer Day ceremony was held on the grounds of St. Thomas's Legislature Building on March 31, 1917. A decade later, Virgin Islanders were granted U.S. citizenship. Today the U.S. Virgin Islands is an unincorporated territory, meaning that citizens govern themselves and vote for their own governors, but cannot vote for president or congressional representation.

Nowadays, Virgin Islanders hail from more than 60 nations. Descendants of African slaves are the largest segment of the population, so it's not surprising that they also provide the largest percentage of workers and owners of restaurants, resorts, and shops. The Danish influence is still strong in architecture and street names. Americana is everywhere, too, most notably in recognizable fast-food chains, familiar shows on cable TV, and name-brand hotels. Between this diversity and the wealth that tourism brings, Virgin Islanders struggle to preserve their culture.

Their rich, spicy West Indian–African heritage comes to full bloom at Carnival time, when celebrating and playing *mas* (with abandon) take precedence over everything else.

Although the idyllic images of a tropical isle are definitely here, there's evidence, too, of growing pains. Traffic jams are common, a clandestine drug trade fuels crime, and—particularly on St. Thomas—there are few beaches left that aren't fronted by a high-rise hotel. Despite fairly heavy development, wildlife has found refuge here. The brown pelican is on the endangered list worldwide but is a common sight in the USVI. The endangered native boa tree is protected, as is the hawksbill turtle, whose females lumber onto the beaches to lay eggs.

ST. THOMAS

By Carol M. Bareuther

If you fly to the 32-square-mi (83-square-km) island of St. Thomas, you land at its western end; if you arrive by cruise ship, you come into one of the world's most beautiful harbors. Either way, one of your first sights is the town of Charlotte Amalie. From the harbor you see an idyllic-looking village that spreads into the lower hills. If you were expecting a quiet hamlet with its inhabitants hanging out under palm trees, you've missed that era by about 300 years. Although other islands in the USVI developed plantation economies, St. Thomas cultivated its harbor, and it became a thriving seaport soon after it was settled by the Danish in the 1600s.

The success of the naturally perfect harbor was enhanced by the fact that the Danes—who ruled St. Thomas with only a couple of short interruptions from 1666 to 1917—avoided involvement in some 100 years' worth of European wars. Denmark was the only European country with colonies in the Caribbean to stay neutral during the War of the Spanish Succession in the early 1700s. Thus, products of the Dutch, English, and French islands—sugar, cotton, and indigo—were traded through Charlotte Amalie, along with the regular shipments of slaves. When the Spanish wars ended, trade fell off, but by the end of the 1700s Europe was at war again, Denmark again remained neutral, and St. Thomas continued to prosper. Even into the 1800s, while the economies of St. Croix and St. John foundered with the market for sugarcane, St. Thomas's economy remained vigorous. This prosperity led to the development of shipyards, a well-organized banking system, and a large merchant class. In 1845 Charlotte Amalie had 101 large importing houses owned by the English, French, Germans, Haitians, Spaniards, Americans, Sephardim, and Danes.

Charlotte Amalie is still one of the world's most active cruise-ship ports. On almost any day at least one and sometimes as many as eight cruise ships are tied to the docks or anchored outside the harbor. Gently rocking in the shadows of these giant floating hotels are just about every other kind of vessel imaginable: sleek sailing catamarans that will take you on a sunset cruise complete with rum punch and a Jimmy Buffett soundtrack, private megayachts that spirit busy executives away, and barnacle-bottom sloops—with laundry draped over the lifelines—that

Fort Christian (1672–80), the oldest surviving structure in St. Thomas.

are home to world-cruising gypsies. Huge container ships pull up in Sub Base, west of the harbor, bringing in everything from breakfast cereals to tires. Anchored right along the waterfront are down-island barges that ply the waters between the Greater Antilles and the Leeward Islands, transporting goods such as refrigerators, VCRs, and disposable diapers.

The waterfront road through Charlotte Amalie was once part of the harbor. Before it was filled in to build the highway, the beach came right up to the back door of the warehouses that now line the thoroughfare. Two hundred years ago those warehouses were filled with indigo, tobacco, and cotton. Today the stone buildings house silk, crystal, and diamonds. Exotic fragrances are still traded, but by island beauty queens in air-conditioned perfume palaces instead of through open market stalls. The pirates of old used St. Thomas as a base from which to raid merchant ships of every nation, though they were particularly fond of the gold- and silver-laden treasure ships heading to Spain. Pirates are still around, but today's versions use St. Thomas as a drop-off for their contraband: illegal immigrants and drugs.

EXPLORING ST. THOMAS

To explore outside Charlotte Amalie, rent a car or hire a taxi. Your rental car should come with a good map; if not, pick up the pocket-size "St. Thomas–St. John Road Map" at a tourist information center. Roads are marked with route numbers, but they're confusing and seem to switch numbers suddenly. Roads are also identified by signs bearing the St. Thomas–St. John Hotel and Tourism Association's mascot,

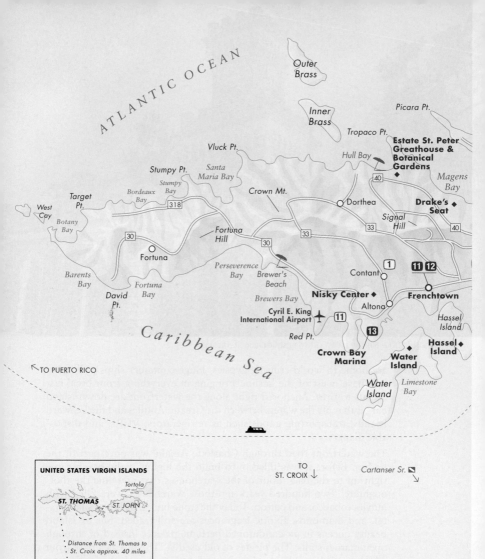

ATLANTIC OCEAN

Outer Brass

Inner Brass

Picara Pt.

Tropaco Pt.

Vluck Pt.

Hull Bay

Estate St. Peter Greathouse & Botanical Gardens

Magens Bay

Stumpy Pt.

Santa Maria Bay

Crown Mt.

Dorthea

Signal Hill

Drake's Seat

Bordeaux Bay

Stumpy Bay

318

Target Pt.

40

33

40

33

West Cay

Botany Bay

30

Fortuna Hill

30

Fortuna

Perseverence Bay

Brewer's Beach

Contant

1

11 12

Frenchtown

Barents Bay

Fortuna Bay

David Pt.

Brewers Bay

Nisky Center ◆

Altona

Hassel Island

Cyril E. King International Airport ✈

11

Red Pt.

13

Hassel Island ◆

Caribbean Sea

Crown Bay Marina

Water Island

Water Island

Limestone Bay

← TO PUERTO RICO

TO ST. CROIX ↓

Cartanser Sr. ◳

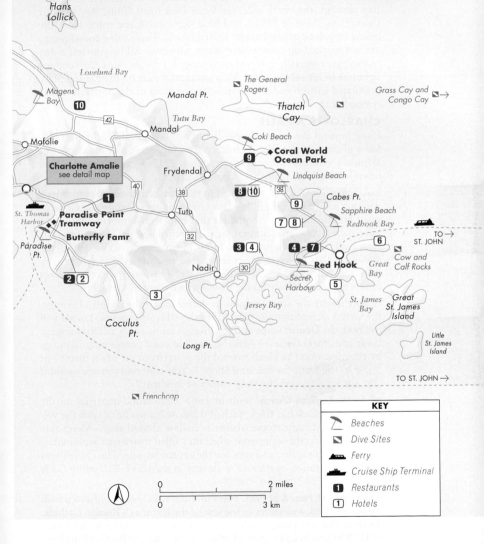

St. Thomas

Hans
Lollick

Lovelund Bay

Magens
Bay **10**

Mafolie

Mandal Pt.

Tutu Bay

Mandal

42

*The General
Rogers*

Grass Cay and
Congo Cay →

*Thatch
Cay*

Coki Beach

9 ◆ **Coral World
Ocean Park**

Charlotte Amalie
see detail map

40

Frydendal

8 **10**

38

Lindquist Beach

38

9

Cabes Pt.

1

St. Thomas
Harbor

◆ **Paradise Point
Tramway**

Butterfly Famr

Paradise
Pt.

38

Tutu

32

3 **4**

Nadir

30

Sapphire Beach

7 **8**

4 – 7

Redhook Bay

TO →
ST. JOHN

6

*Cow and
Calf Rocks*

● **Red Hook**

*Great
Bay*

2 **2**

Coculus
Pt.

*Secret
Harbour*

5

*St. James
Bay*

*Great
St. James
Island*

3

Jersey Bay

Long Pt.

*Little
St. James
Island*

TO ST. JOHN →

◹ *Frenchcap*

KEY	
⌒	Beaches
◹	Dive Sites
⛴	Ferry
🚢	Cruise Ship Terminal
1	Restaurants
1	Hotels

0   2 miles

0   3 km

Tommy the Starfish. More than 100 of these color-coded signs line the island's main routes. Orange signs trace the route from the airport to Red Hook, green signs identify the road from town to Magens Bay, Tommy's face on a yellow background points from Mafolie to Crown Bay through the north side, red signs lead from Smith Bay to Four Corners via Skyline Drive, and blue signs mark the route from the cruise-ship dock at Havensight to Red Hook. These color-coded routes are not marked on most visitor maps, however. Allow yourself a day to explore, especially if you want to stop to take pictures or to enjoy a light bite or refreshing swim. Most gas stations are on the island's more populated eastern end, so fill up before heading to the north side. And remember to drive on the left!

CHARLOTTE AMALIE

Look beyond the pricey shops, T-shirt vendors, and bustling crowds for a glimpse of the island's history. The city served as the capital of Denmark's outpost in the Caribbean until 1917, an aspect of the island often lost in the glitz of the shopping district.

Emancipation Gardens, right next to the fort, is a good place to start a walking tour. Tackle the hilly part of town first: head north up Government Hill to the historic buildings that house government offices and have incredible views. Several regal churches line the route that runs west back to the town proper and the old-time market. Virtually all the alleyways that intersect Main Street lead to eateries that serve frosty drinks, sandwiches, and West Indian fare. There are public restrooms in this area, too. Allow an hour for a quick view of the sights.

A note about the street names: In deference to the island's heritage, the streets downtown are labeled by their Danish names. Locals will use both the Danish name and the English name (such as Dronningens Gade and Norre Gade for Main Street), but most people refer to things by their location ("a block toward the waterfront off Main Street" or "next to the Little Switzerland Shop"). You may find it more useful if you ask for directions by shop names or landmarks.

All Saints Anglican Church. Built in 1848 from stone quarried on the island, the church has thick, arched window frames lined with the yellow brick that came to the islands as ballast aboard ships. Merchants left the brick on the waterfront when they filled their boats with molasses, sugar, mahogany, and rum for the return voyage. The church was built in celebration of the end of slavery in the USVI. ⊠ *Domini Gade* 🕾 *340/774–0217* ⊙ *Mon.–Sat. 9–3.*

Cathedral of St. Peter & St. Paul. This building was consecrated as a parish church in 1848, and serves as the seat of the territory's Roman Catholic diocese. The ceiling and walls are covered with a dozen murals painted in 1899 by two Belgian artists, Father Leo Servais and Brother Ildephonsus, and depict scenes from both the Old and New Testaments. The San Juan–marble altar and walls were added in the 1960s. ⊠ *Lower Main St.* 🕾 *340/774–0201* ⊙ *Mon.–Sat. 8–5.*

Danish Consulate Building. Built in 1830, this structure once housed the Danish Consulate. Although the Danish consul general, Søren Blak, has an office in Charlotte Amalie, the Danish Consulate is now in the

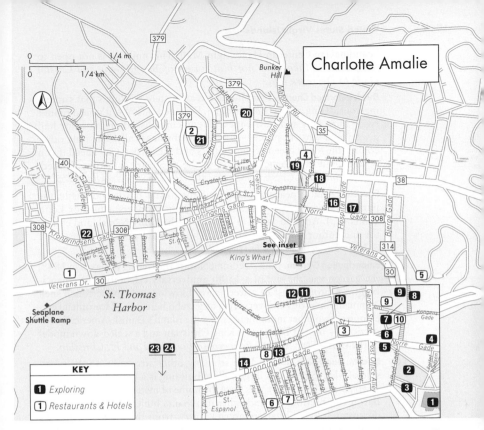

Charlotte Amalie

Scandinavian Center in Havensight Mall. This building is not open to the public. ⊠ *Take stairs north at corner of Bjerge Gade and Crystal Gade to Denmark Hill.*

Dutch Reformed Church. This church has an austere loveliness that's amazing considering all it's been through. Founded in 1744, it's been rebuilt twice after fires and hurricanes. The unembellished cream-color hall gives you a sense of peace—albeit monochromatically. The only other color is the forest green of the shutters and the carpet. Call ahead if you wish to visit at a particular time, as the doors are sometimes locked. ⊠ *Nye Gade and Crystal Gade* ☎ *340/776–8255* ⊙ *Weekdays 9–5.*

Educators Park. A peaceful place amid the town's hustle and bustle, the park has memorials to three famous Virgin Islanders: educator Edith Williams, J. Antonio Jarvis (a founder of the *Daily News*), and educator and author Rothschild Francis. The last gave many speeches here. ⊠ *Main St., across from post office.*

Ⅽ **Emancipation Garden.** Built to commemorate the freeing of slaves in 1848, the garden was the site of a 150th anniversary celebration of emancipation. A bronze bust of a freed slave blowing a symbolic conch shell commemorates this anniversary. The gazebo here is used for official ceremonies. Two other monuments show the island's Danish-American connection—a bust of Denmark's King Christian and a scaled-down model of the U.S. Liberty Bell. ⊠ *Between Tolbod Gade and Ft. Christian.*

Ⅽ **Enid M. Baa Public Library.** Like so many other structures on the north side of Main Street, this large yellow building is a typical 18th-century town house. The library was once the home of merchant and landowner Baron von Bretton. He and other merchants built their houses (stores downstairs, living quarters above) across from the brick warehouses on the south side of the street. This is the island's first recorded fireproof building, meaning it was built of ballast brick instead of wood. Its interior of high ceilings and cool stone floors is the perfect refuge from the afternoon sun. You can browse through historic papers or just sit in the breeze by an open window reading the paper. ⊠ *Main St.* ☎ *340/774–0630* ⊙ *Weekdays 9–6, Sat. 10–4.*

Ⅽ **Ft. Christian.** St. Thomas's oldest standing structure, this monument was built between 1672 and 1680 and now has U.S. National Landmark status. This remarkable building has, over time, been used as a jail, governor's residence, town hall, courthouse, and church. A multimillion-dollar renovation project was started in 2005 to stabilize the structure and halt centuries of deterioration. Delays have plagued the project, including the discovery of human skeletal remains buried in the walls from when the structure was used as a Lutheran church. You can see from the outside the four renovated faces of famous 19th-century clock tower. ⊠ *Waterfront Hwy. east of shopping district* ☎ *340/776–8605.*

Frederick Lutheran Church. This historic church has a massive mahogany altar, and its pews—each with its own door—were once rented to families of the congregation. Lutheranism is the state religion of Denmark, and when the territory was without a minister, the governor—who had his own elevated pew—filled in. ⊠ *Norre Gade* ☎ *340/776–1315* ⊙ *Mon.–Sat. 9–4.*

Government House. Built in 1867, this neoclassical white brick-and-wood structure houses the offices of the governor of the Virgin Islands. Inside, the staircases are of native mahogany, as are the plaques hand-lettered in gold with the names of the governors appointed and, since 1970, elected. Brochures detailing the history of the building are available, but you may have to ask for them. ⊠ *Government Hill* ☎ *340/774–0294* 🖅 *Free* ⊙ *Weekdays 8–5.*

Haagensen House. Behind Hotel 1829, this lovingly restored home was built in the early 1800s by Danish entrepreneur Hans Haagensen and is surrounded by an equally impressive cookhouse, outbuildings, and terraced gardens. A lower-level banquet hall showcases antique prints and photographs. Guided tours begin at Hotel 1829, then continue to Haagensen House. The tour includes stops at two other restored 119th-century homes, a rum factory, amber museum, and finally the lookout tour at Blackbeard's Castle. Tours are given between 9 am and 3 pm on days a cruise ship is in port ⊠ *Government Hill* ☎ *340/776–1234 or 340/776–1829* 🖅 *Tours $20 guided, $12 self-guided* ⊙ *Oct.–May, daily 9–3; June–Sept., by appointment only.*

Hassel Island. East of Water Island in Charlotte Amalie harbor, Hassel Island is part of the Virgin Islands National Park, as it has the ruins of a British military garrison (built during a brief British occupation of the USVI during the 1800s) and the remains of a marine railway (where ships were hoisted into dry dock for repairs). The island is accessible via daily guided kayak tours.

27

Hotel 1829. As its name implies, the hotel was built in 1829, albeit as the private residence of a prominent merchant named Alexander Lavalette. The building's coral-color facade is accented with fancy wrought-iron railings, and the interior is paneled in dark wood, which makes it feel delightfully cool. From the terrace there's an exquisite view of the harbor framed by brilliant orange bougainvillea. You can combine a visit to this hotel with a walking tour of Haagensen House, Villa Notman, Britannia House, rum factory, amber museum, and the lookout tower at Blackbeard's Castle just above the hotel. ⊠ *Government Hill* ☎ *340/776–1829 or 340/776–1234* ⊕ *www.hotel1829.com* 🖅 *Tour $20 guided, $12 self-guided* ⊙ *Oct.–May, daily 9–3; June–Sept., by appointment only.*

Legislature Building. Its pastoral-looking lime-green exterior conceals the vociferous political wrangling of the Virgin Islands Senate. Constructed originally by the Danish as a police barracks, the building was later used to billet U.S. Marines, and much later it housed a public school. You're welcome to sit in on sessions in the upstairs chambers. ⊠ *Waterfront Hwy. across from Ft. Christian* ☎ *340/774–0880* ⊙ *Daily 8–5.*

Memorial Moravian Church. Built in 1884, this church was named to commemorate the 150th anniversary of the Moravian Church in the Virgin Islands. ⊠ *17 Norre Gade* ☎ *340/776–0066* ⊙ *Weekdays 8–5.*

☾ **99 Steps.** This staircase "street," built by the Danes in the 1700s, leads to the residential area above Charlotte Amalie and to Blackbeard's Castle, a U.S. national historic landmark. The castle's tower, built in 1679, was once used by the notorious pirate Edward Teach. Today, it's home to the largest collection of life-size pirates crafted out of bronze and copper in the world. If you count the stairs as you go up, you'll discover, as have thousands before you, that there are more than the name implies. ⊠ *Look for steps heading north from Government Hill.*

Pissarro Building. Housing several shops and an art gallery, this was the birthplace and childhood home of Camille Pissarro, who later moved to France and became an acclaimed 19th-century impressionist painter. The art gallery contains three original pages from Pissarro's sketchbook and two pastels by Pissarro's grandson, Claude. ⊠ *Main St. between Raadets Gade and Trompeter Gade.*

☺ **Roosevelt Park.** First called Coconut Park, this park was renamed in honor of Franklin D. Roosevelt in 1945. It's a great place to put your feet up and people-watch. A renovation in 2007 added five granite pedestals representing the five branches of the military, bronze urns that can be lighted to commemorate special events, and bronze plaques inscribed with the names of the territory's veterans who died defending the United States. There's also a children's playground. ⊠ *Norre Gade.*

★ **Seven Arches Museum and Gallery.** This restored 18th-century home is a striking example of classic Danish–West Indian architecture. There seem to be arches everywhere—seven to be exact—all supporting a "welcoming arms" staircase that leads to the second floor and the flower-framed front doorway. The Danish kitchen is a highlight: it's housed in a separate building away from the main house, as were all cooking facilities in the early days (for fire prevention). Inside the house you can see mahogany furnishings and gas lamps and colorful abstract canvases painted by the museum's curator, a local artist. ⊠ *Government Hill, 3 buildings east of Government House* ☎ *340/774–9295* ⊕ *www.sevenarchesmuseum.com* ✉ *$5 donation* ⊙ *By appointment only.*

Synagogue of Beracha Veshalom Vegmiluth Hasidim. The synagogue's Hebrew name translates as the Congregation of Blessing, Peace, and Loving Deeds. The small building's white pillars contrast with rough stone walls, as does the rich mahogany of the pews and altar. The sand on the floor symbolizes the exodus from Egypt. Since the synagogue first opened its doors in 1833, it has held a weekly service, making it the oldest synagogue building in continuous use under the American flag and the second-oldest (after the one on Curaçao) in the Western Hemisphere. Guided tours can be arranged. Brochures detailing the key structures and history are also available. Next door the Weibel Museum showcases Jewish history on St. Thomas. ⊠ *15 Crystal Gade* ☎ *340/774–4312* ⊕ *www.onepaper.com/synagogue* ⊙ *Weekdays 9–4.*

U.S. Post Office. While you buy stamps, contemplate the murals of waterfront scenes by *Saturday Evening Post* artist Stephen Dohanos. His art was commissioned as part of the Works Project Administration in the 1930s. ⊠ *Tolbod Gade and Main St.*

☺ **Vendors Plaza.** Here merchants sell everything from T-shirts to African attire to leather goods. Look for local art among the ever-changing selections at this busy market. ⊠ *Waterfront, west of Ft. Christian* ⊙ *Weekdays 8–6, weekends 9–1.*

Weibel Museum. In this museum next to the synagogue, 300 years of Jewish history on St. Thomas are showcased. The small gift shop sells a commemorative silver coin celebrating the anniversary of the Hebrew congregation's establishment on the island in 1796. There are also tropically inspired items, such as menorahs painted to resemble palm trees. ✉ *15 Crystal Gade* ☎ *340/774–4312* 🎫 *Free* ⏰ *Weekdays 9–4.*

EAST END

Although the eastern end has many major resorts and spectacular beaches, don't be surprised if a cow or a herd of goats crosses your path as you drive through the relatively flat, dry terrain. You can pick up sandwiches from a deli in the Red Hook area if you want a picnic lunch.

☺ **Coral World Ocean Park.** This interactive aquarium and water-sports cen-
Fodor'sChoice ter lets you experience a variety of sea life and other animals up close
★ and personal. Coral World has an offshore underwater observatory, an 80,000-gallon coral reef exhibit, and 21 jewel aquariums displaying the Virgin Islands' coral reef habitats and unusual marine life. The park also has several outdoor pools where you can pet baby sharks, feed stingrays, touch starfish, and view endangered sea turtles. Daily feedings take place at most exhibits.

In addition, the park operates several activities, both above and below the water. The Sea Trek Helmet Dive allows you to walk along an underwater trail with a high-tech helmet that provides a continuous supply of air (and which keeps you head dry). Snuba, a cross between Scuba and snorkeling, allows you to snorkel deeper underwater connected to the top by an air hose rather than carrying your air on your back as you would when diving. Shark and Turtle Encounter programs let you observe these fascinating animals as they swim around you. Get a big, wet, whiskered kiss while taking a swim in the sea lion pool, or choose to have a personal encounter with a sea lion on dry land. Buy a cup of nectar and let the friendly, rainbow-colored lorikeets perch on your hand and drink. Finally, the Nautilus semi-submersible allows you to look at the abundant sea life and coral reefs around Coki Point from a depth of eight feet in air-conditioned comfort without ever leaving the vessel, which has underwater observation windows but stays on the surface. ✉ *Coki Point north of Rte. 38, Estate Frydendal* ☎ *340/775–1555* ⊕ *www.coralworldvi.com* 🎫 *$19, Sea Lion Swim $105, Sea Lion Encounter $65, Sea Trek $58, Snuba $52, Shark and Turtle Encounters $32, Nautilus $20* ⏰ *Daily 9–4. Off-season (May–Oct) hrs may vary so call to confirm.*

Red Hook. In this nautical center there are fishing and sailing charter boats, dive shops, and powerboat-rental agencies at the American Yacht Harbor marina. There are also several bars and restaurants, including Molly Molone's, Duffy's Love Shack, and the Caribbean Saloon. One grocery store and a deli offer picnic fixings—from sliced meats and cheeses to rotisserie-roasted chickens, prepared salads, burritos, and freshly baked breads. Ferries depart from Red Hook en route to St. John and the British Virgin Islands.

27

Coral World Ocean Park offers interactive sealife encounters.

SOUTH SHORE

Butterfly Garden. Coral World has reopened the former Butterfly Farm at Havensight, which had closed for the second half of 2010 for a renovation between owners. Take a guided tour through this tropical garden wonderland where hundreds of beautiful butterflies from around the world fly freely all around you. Discover the fascinating life cycle of the butterfly—from meandering caterpillar to fluttering, winged insect. Marvel at the beauty of their colorful winged markings and the uniqueness of their various shapes and sizes. A bird show is included in admission. The gift shop sells unique butterfly jewelry and souvenirs. ⊠ *Havensight Mall, adjacent to West Indian Company cruise ship dock, Havensight* ☎ *340/715–3366* ⊕ *www. butterflygardenvi.com* 🖃 *$15* ⊙ *Daily 8:30–4. Off-season (May–Oct.) hrs may vary so call to confirm.*

Frenchtown. Popular for its bars and restaurants, Frenchtown is also the home of descendants of immigrants from St. Barthélemy (St. Barths). You can watch them pull up their brightly painted boats and display their equally colorful catch of the day along the waterfront. If you chat with them, you can hear speech patterns slightly different from those of other St. Thomians. Get a feel for the residential district of Frenchtown by walking west to some of the town's winding streets, where tiny wooden houses have been passed down from generation to generation. ✛ *Turn south off Waterfront Hwy. at post office.*

French Heritage Museum. Next to Joseph Aubain Ballpark, the museum houses artifacts such as fishing nets, accordions, tambourines, mahogany furniture, and historic photographs that illustrate the lives of the French descendants during the 18th through 20th centuries. Admission is free, but donations are accepted. ⊠ *Intersection of Rue de St. Anne and Rue de St. Barthélemy* ☎ *340/774–2320* 🖼 *Free* ⊙ *Mon.–Sat. 9–6.*

⟳ **St. Thomas Skyride.** Fly skyward in a gondola to Paradise Point, an over-
★ look with breathtaking views of Charlotte Amalie and the harbor. There are several shops, a bar, a restaurant, and a wedding gazebo; kids enjoy the tropical bird show held daily at 10:30 am and 1:30 pm. A ¼-mi (½-km) hiking trail leads to spectacular views of St. Croix. Wear sturdy shoes, as the trail is steep and rocky. ⊠ *Rte. 30, across from Haven-sight Mall, Havensight* ☎ *340/774–9809* ⊕ *www.stthomasskyride.com* 🖼 *$21; Sky Jump $30* ⊙ *Thurs.–Tues. 9–5, Wed. 9–9.*

⟳ **Water Island.** This island, the fourth-largest of the U.S. Virgin Islands, floats about ¼ mi (½ km) out in Charlotte Amalie harbor. A ferry between Crown Bay Marina and the island operates several times daily from 6:30 am to 6 pm Monday through Saturday, and from 8 am to 5 pm on Sunday and holidays at a cost of $10 round trip. (On cruise-ship days, a ferry goes direct from the West India Company dock, but only for those passengers on the bike trip.) From the ferry dock, it's a hike of less than half-mile to Honeymoon Beach (though you have to go up a big hill), where Brad Pitt and Cate Blanchett filmed a scene of the movie *The Curious Case of Benjamin Button*. Get lunch from a mobile food van that pulls up on weekends. ⊠ *340/690–4159 for ferry information.*

27

WEST END

⟳ **Drake's Seat.** Sir Francis Drake was supposed to have kept watch over his fleet and looked for enemy ships from this vantage point. The panorama is especially breathtaking (and romantic) at dusk, and if you arrive late in the day, you can miss the hordes of day-trippers on taxi tours who stop here to take a picture and buy a T-shirt from one of the many vendors. ⊠ *Rte. 40, Estate Zufriedenheit.*

Estate St. Peter Greathouse and Botanical Gardens. This unusual spot is perched on a mountainside 1,000 feet above sea level, with views of more than 20 islands and islets. You can wander through a gallery displaying local art, sip a complimentary rum punch while looking out at the view, or follow a nature trail that leads you past nearly 70 varieties of tropical plants, including 17 varieties of orchids. ⊠ *Rte. 40, Estate St. Peter* ☎ *340/774–4999* ⊕ *www.greathousevi.com* 🖼 *$5* ⊙ *Mon.–Sat. 8–4.*

⟳ **Mountain Top.** Rebuilt and reopened in January 2011 after a devastat-
★ ing fire that destroyed the structure in May 2009, St. Thomas's famous viewpoint is once again a good place to sip a banana daiquiri and see spectacular views. Head out to the observation deck—more than 1,500 feet above sea level—to get a bird's-eye view that stretches from Puerto Rico's out-island of Culebra in the west all the way to the British Virgin Islands in the east. There's also a restaurant, restrooms, and shops that sell everything from Caribbean art to nautical antiques, ship models, and touristy T-shirts. Kids will like talking to the parrots–and hearing them answer back. ✢ *Head north off Rte. 33, look for signs, Mountain Top* ⊕ *www.greathouse-mountaintop.com* 🖼 *Free* ⊙ *Daily 8–5.*

BEACHES

Remember to remove all your valuables from the car and keep them out of sight when you go swimming. Unfortunately, break-ins have been reported on all three of the U.S. Virgin Islands; most locals recommend leaving your windows down and leaving absolutely nothing in your car.

EAST END

♻ **Coki Beach.** Funky beach huts selling local foods such as meat pate (fried
Fodor's Choice turnovers with a spicy ground-beef filling), picnic tables topped with
★ umbrellas sporting beverage logos, and a brigade of hair braiders and taxi men give this beach overlooking picturesque Thatch Cay a Coney Island feel. But this is the best place on the island to snorkel and scuba dive. Fish, including grunts, snappers, and wrasses, are like an effervescent cloud you can wave your hand through. Ashore you can find conveniences such as restrooms and changing facilities, both of which received a much-needed renovation in 2010. There are also beefed up security and regular police patrols in the area after a shooting incident in 2010 ⊠ *Rte. 388, next to Coral World Ocean Park.*

Lindquist Beach. The newest of the Virgin Islands' public beaches has a serene sense of wilderness that isn't found on the more crowded beaches. A lifeguard is on duty between 8 am and 5 pm. Picnic tables and restrooms are available. Try snorkeling over the offshore reef. There's a $2 per person entrance fee. ⊠ *Rte. 38, at end of a bumpy dirt road.*

★ **Sapphire Beach.** A steady breeze makes this beach a boardsailor's paradise. The swimming is great, as is the snorkeling, especially at the reef near Pettyklip Point. Beach volleyball is big on the weekends. Sapphire Beach Resort and Marina has a snack shop, bar, and water-sports rentals. ⊠ *Rte. 38, Sapphire Bay.*

Secret Harbour. Placid waters make it easy to stroke your way out to a swim platform offshore from the Secret Harbour Beach Resort & Villas. Nearby reefs give snorkelers a natural show. There's a bar and restaurant, as well as a dive shop. ⊠ *Rte. 32, Red Hook.*

Vessup Beach. This wild, undeveloped beach is lined with sea grape trees and century plants. It's close to Red Hook harbor, so you can watch the ferries depart. Calm waters are excellent for swimming. West Indies Windsurfing is here, so you can rent Windsurfers, kayaks, and other water toys. There are no restrooms or changing facilities. It's popular with locals on weekends. ⊠ *Off Rte. 322, Vessup Bay.*

SOUTH SHORE

Brewer's Beach. Watch jets land at the Cyril E. King Airport as you dip into the usually calm seas. Rocks at either end of the shoreline, patches of grass poking randomly through the sand, and shady tamarind trees 30 feet from the water give this beach a wild, natural feel. Civilization has arrived, as one or two mobile food vans park on the nearby road. Buy a fried-chicken leg and johnnycake or burgers and chips to munch on at the picnic tables. ⊠ *Rte. 30, west of University of the Virgin Islands.*

Morningstar Beach. Nature and nurture combine at this ¼-mi-long (½-km-long) beach between Marriott Frenchman's Reef and Morning Star Beach Resorts, where amenities range from water-sports rentals to beachside bar service. A concession rents floating mats, snorkeling equipment, sailboards, and Jet Skis. Swimming is excellent; there are good-size rolling waves year-round, but do watch the undertow. If you're feeling lazy, rent a lounge chair with umbrella and order a libation from one of two full-service beach bars. At 7 am and again at 5 pm, watch the cruise ships glide majestically out to sea from the Charlotte Amalie harbor. ⊠ *Rte. 315, 2 mi (3 km) southeast of Charlotte Amalie, past Havensight Mall and cruise-ship dock.*

WEST END

♺ Magens Bay. Deeded to the island as a public park, this heart-shape stretch of white sand is considered one of the most beautiful in the world. The bottom of the bay is flat and sandy, so this is a place for sunning and swimming rather than snorkeling. On weekends and holidays the sounds of music from groups partying under the sheds fill the air. There's a bar, snack shack, and beachwear boutique; bathhouses with restrooms, changing rooms, and saltwater showers are close by. Sunfish and paddleboats are the most popular rentals at the water-sports kiosk. East of the beach is Udder Delight, a one-room shop that serves a Virgin Islands tradition—a milk shake with a splash of Cruzan rum. Kids can enjoy virgin versions, which have a touch of soursop, mango, or banana flavoring. If you arrive between 8 am and 5 pm, you pay an entrance fee of $4 per person, $2 per vehicle; it's free for children under 12. ⊠ *Rte. 35, at end of road on north side of island.*

Fodor'sChoice
★

27

WHERE TO EAT

The beauty of St. Thomas and its sister islands has attracted a cadre of professionally trained chefs who know their way around fresh fish and local fruits. You can dine on everything from terrific cheap local dishes such as goat water (a spicy stew) and fungi (a cornmeal polentalike side dish) to imports such as hot pastrami sandwiches and raspberries in crème fraîche.

Restaurants are spread all over the island, although fewer are found on the west and northwest parts of the island. Most restaurants out of town are easily accessible by taxi and have ample parking. If you dine in Charlotte Amalie, take a taxi. Parking close to restaurants can be difficult to find, and walking around after dark isn't advisable for safety reasons.

If your accommodations have a kitchen and you plan to cook, there's good variety in St. Thomas's mainland-style supermarkets. Just be prepared for grocery prices that are about 20% to 30% higher than those in the United States. As for drinking, outside the hotels a beer in a bar will cost between $3 and $4 and a piña colada $6 or more.

WHAT TO WEAR

Dining on St. Thomas is informal. Few restaurants require a jacket and tie. Still, at dinner in the snazzier places shorts and T-shirts are inappropriate; men would do well to wear slacks and a shirt with buttons. Dress codes on St. Thomas rarely require women to wear skirts, but you can never go wrong with something flowing.

CHARLOTTE AMALIE

$$$$
ECLECTIC
Fodor'sChoice
★

✕ **Banana Tree Grille.** The eagle's-eye view of the Charlotte Amalie harbor from this breeze-cooled restaurant is as fantastic as the food. Linen tablecloths, china, and silver place settings combine with subdued lighting to create an elegant feel. To start, try the "seafood cocktail" of lobster, shrimp, scallops, and squid marinated in a savory herb vinaigrette. The signature dish here—and worthy of its fame—is Chef Patrick Bellantoni's New York sirloin seasoned simply with olive oil and garlic and grilled to order. Arrive before 6 pm and watch the cruise ships depart from the harbor while you enjoy a drink at the bar. ⌂ *Bluebeard's Castle, Bluebeard's Hill* ☎ *340/776–4050* ⊕ *www.bananatreegrille.com* ⌔ *Reservations essential* ⊗ *Closed Mon. No lunch.*

$$$
CARIBBEAN

✕ **Cuzzin's Caribbean Restaurant and Bar.** This is the place to sample bona fide Virgin Islands cuisine. For lunch, order tender slivers of conch stewed in a rich onion-and-butter sauce, savory braised oxtail, or curried chicken. At dinner the island-style mutton, served in thick gravy and seasoned with locally grown herbs, offers a tasty treat that's deliciously different. Side dishes include peas and rice, boiled green bananas, fried plantains, and potato stuffing. In a 19th-century livery stable on Back Street, this restaurant is hard to find but well worth it if you like sampling local foods. ⌂ *7 Wimmelskafts Gade, also called Back St.* ☎ *340/777–4711.*

$$
CARIBBEAN
Fodor'sChoice
★

✕ **Gladys' Cafe.** Even if the local specialties—conch in butter sauce, salt fish and dumplings, hearty red bean soup—didn't make this a recommended café, it would be worth coming for Gladys's smile. Her cozy alleyway restaurant is rich in atmosphere with its mahogany bar and native stone walls, making dining a double delight. While you're here, pick up a $5 or $10 bottle of her special hot sauce. There are mustard-, oil and vinegar–, and tomato-based versions; the tomato-based sauce is the hottest. Only Amex is accepted. ⌂ *Waterfront at Royal Dane Mall* ☎ *340/774–6604* ⊗ *No dinner.*

$$
AMERICAN
☽

✕ **Greenhouse Bar and Restaurant.** The hip and hip-at-heart come to this bustling waterfront restaurant to eat, listen to music, and play games, both video and pool. Even the most finicky eater should find something to please on the eight-page menu that offers burgers, salads, and pizza served all day long, along with more upscale entrées such as peel-and-eat shrimp, Maine lobster, Alaskan king crab, and Black Angus prime rib for dinner. This is generally a family-friendly place, though the Two-for-Tuesdays happy hour and Friday-night live reggae music that starts thumping at 10 pm draw a lively, sometimes rambunctious, young-adult crowd. ⌂ *Waterfront Hwy. at Storetvaer Gade* ☎ *340/774–7998* ⊕ *www.thegreenhouserestaurant.com.*

CLOSE UP

Where to Shop for Groceries

High food prices in Virgin Islands supermarkets are enough to dull anyone's appetite. According to a report by the U.S. Virgin Islands Department of Labor, food is significantly more expensive than on the mainland.

Although you'll never match the prices back home, you can shop around for the best deals. If you're traveling with a group, it pays to stock up on the basics at warehouse-style stores like Pricesmart (membership required) and Cost-U-Less. Even the nonbulk food items here are sold at lower prices than in the supermarkets or convenience stores. Good buys include beverages, meats, produce, and spirits.

After this, head to supermarkets such as Plaza Extra, Pueblo, and Food Center. Although the prices aren't as good as at the big-box stores, the selection is better.

Finally, if you want to splurge on top-quality meats, exotic produce, imported cheeses, exotic spices, and imported spirits, finish off your shopping at high-end shops such as Marina Market or Gourmet Gallery.

The Fruit Bowl is the place for fresh produce. The prices and selection are unbeatable.

For really fresh tropical fruits, vegetables, and seasoning herbs, visit the farmers' markets in Smith Bay (daily), at Market Square (daily), at Yacht Haven Grande (first and third Sunday of the month), and in Estate Bordeaux (last Sunday of every month).

27

$$$$
ITALIAN
★

✕ **Virgilio's.** For the island's best northern Italian cuisine, don't miss this intimate, elegant hideaway tucked on a quiet side street. Eclectic art covers the two-story brick walls, and the sound of opera sets the stage for a memorable meal. Come here for more than 40 homemade pastas topped with superb sauces—capellini with fresh tomatoes and garlic or peasant-style spaghetti in a rich tomato sauce with mushrooms and prosciutto. House specialties include osso buco and tiramisu—expertly crafted by chef Ernesto Garrigos, who has prepared these two dishes on the Discovery Channel's *Great Chefs of the World* series. ⊠ *18 Main St.* ☎ *340/776–4920* ⚛ *Reservations essential* ☉ *Closed Sun.*

EAST END

$$$$
SEAFOOD

✕ **Agave Terrace.** The freshest fish is what reels in the customers to this open-air restaurant in the Point Pleasant Resort. The catch of the day—a steak or a fillet—is served with choices of a dozen sauces, including teriyaki-mango and lime-ginger. If you get lucky on a sportfishing day charter, the chef will cook your fish if you bring it in by 3 pm. Come early and have a drink at the Lookout Lounge, which has breathtaking views of the British Virgins. ⊠ *Point Pleasant Resort, Rte. 38, Estate Smith Bay* ☎ *340/775–4142* ⊕ *www.agaveterrace.com* ☉ *No lunch.*

$$$
AMERICAN
☾

✕ **Blue Moon Café.** Watch the serene scene of sailboats floating at anchor while supping; sunsets are especially spectacular here. Enjoy French toast topped with toasted coconut for breakfast, a grilled mahimahi sandwich with black olive–caper mayonnaise at lunch, or grilled Long Island duck breast marinated in lime juice and Cruzan spiced rum for dinner.

No-see-ums, nearly invisible insects with a fierce bite, can be bothersome here at sunset, so bring bug spray. ⊠ *Secret Harbour Beach Resort, Rte. 32, Red Hook* ☎ *340/779–2080* ⊕ *www.bluemooncafevi.com.*

$$$
AMERICAN

✗ **Caribbean Saloon.** Dine casually, watch sports on wide-screen TVs, and listen to live music on the weekends at this hip sports bar that's in the center of the action in Red Hook. The menu ranges from finger-licking barbecue ribs to more sophisticated fare such has the signature filet mignon wrapped in bacon and smothered in melted Gorgonzola cheese. There's always a catch of the day; the fishing fleet is only steps away. A late-night menu is available from 10 pm until 4 am. ⊠ *Rte. 32 at American Yacht Harbor, Bldg B., Red Hook* ☎ *340/775–7060* ⊕ *www.caribbeansaloon.com.*

$$
ECLECTIC

✗ **Duffy's Love Shack.** If the floating bubbles don't attract you to this zany eatery, the lime-green shutters, loud rock music, and fun-loving waitstaff just might. It's billed as the "ultimate tropical drink shack," and the bartenders shake up such exotic concoctions as the Love Shack Volcano—a 50-ounce flaming extravaganza. The menu has a selection of burgers, tacos, burritos, and salads. Try the grilled mahimahi taco salad or jerk Caesar wrap. Wednesday night is usually a theme party complete with giveaways. ⊠ *Rte. 32, Red Hook* ☎ *340/779–2080* ⊕ *www.duffysloveshack.com* ▭ *No credit cards.*

$$$
IRISH
☾

✗ **Molly Molone's.** This dockside eatery has a devoted following among local boaters, who swear by the traditional American and Irish fare. Opt for eggs Benedict or rashers of Irish sausages and eggs for breakfast, or fork into fish-and-chips, Irish stew, or bangers and mash (sausage and mashed potatoes) for lunch or dinner. Beware: the resident iguanas will beg for table scraps—bring your camera. ⊠ *Rte. 32 at American Yacht Harbor, Bldg. D, Red Hook* ☎ *340/775–1270.*

$$$$
ECLECTIC
Fodor's Choice
★

✗ **Old Stone Farmhouse.** Dine in the splendor of a beautifully restored plantation house. Come early and sidle up to the beautiful mahogany bar, where you can choose from an extensive wine list. Then, spoon into French onion soup as an appetizer; move on to executive chef–owner Greg Engelhardt's braised Angus beef short ribs paired with a sautéed local Caribbean lobster tail; and finish with a decadent bananas Foster. Personalized attention makes dining here a delight. ⊠ *Rte. 42, 1 mi (1½ km) west of entrance to Mahogany Run Golf Course, Estate Lovenlund* ☎ *340/777–6277* ⊕ *www.oldstonefarmhouse.com* ⚞ *Reservations essential* ⊘ *Closed Mon.*

$$$$
ITALIAN
★

✗ **Romano's Restaurant and Art Gallery.** Inside this huge old stucco house, superb northern Italian cuisine is served in dining rooms where the walls are lined with whimsical works of art painted by doubly talented owner–chef Tony Romano. Try the pastas, either with a classic ragout or with one of Tony's more unique creations, such as a cream sauce with mushrooms, prosciutto, pine nuts, and Parmesan. There's classic osso buco and veal scaloppini, too. If you like the food here, know that Romano also offers his personal chef services at villas and condos. ⊠ *Rte. 388 at Coki Point, Estate Frydendal* ☎ *340/775–0045* ⊕ *www.romanosrestaurant.com* ⚞ *Reservations essential* ⊘ *Closed Sun. No lunch.*

SOUTH SHORE

$$$$
ECLECTIC
Fodor's Choice
★
✕ **Havana Blue.** The cuisine here is described as Cuban-Asian, but the dining experience is out of this world. A glowing wall of water meets you as you enter, and then you're seated at a table laid with linen and silver that's illuminated in a soft blue light radiating from above. Be sure to sample the mango mojito, made with fresh mango, crushed mint, and limes. Entrées include coconut-chipotle ceviche, sugarcane-glazed pork tenderloin medallions, and the signature dish, miso sea bass. Hand-rolled cigars and aged rums finish the night off in true Cuban style. For something really special, request an exclusive table for two set on Morning Star Beach—you get a seven-course tasting menu, champagne, and your own personal waiter, all for $350 for two. ✉ *Marriott Morningstar Beach Resort, Rte. 315, Estate Bakkeroe* ☎ *340/715–2583* ⊕ *www.havanabluerestaurant.com* ⌂ *Reservations essential* ☾ *No lunch.*

$$$$
ECLECTIC
★
✕ **Randy's Bar and Bistro.** There's no view here—even though you're at the top of a hill—but the somewhat hidden location has helped to keep this one of the island's best dining secrets. This wine shop and deli caters to a local lunch crowd. At night, you forget you're tucked into a nearly windowless building. The tableside bread for starters is a thick, crusty focaccia flavored with nearly 10 different vegetables. Try the Brie-stuffed filet mignon or the rack of lamb. After-dinner cigars and wine complete the experience. ✉ *Al Cohen's Plaza, atop Raphune Hill, ½ mi (¾ km) east of Charlotte Amalie* ☎ *340/777–3199.*

WEST END

$$$$
ECLECTIC
Fodor's Choice
★
✕ **Craig and Sally's.** In the heart of Frenchtown, culinary wizard Sally Darash shows off her tasty creativity by never duplicating a menu. Her inspiration is pure local; it may start when a French fisherman shows up on her doorstep with a fish wiggling at the end of his speargun or when a community matriarch brings by bunches of fresh basil and thyme. The result may be a yellowfin tuna ceviche or roasted eggplant cheesecake with a basil chiffonade. Husband Craig, who has a wry humor, maintains a 300-bottle wine list that's won accolades. ✉ *22 Honduras St., Frenchtown* ☎ *340/777–9949* ⊕ *www.craigandsallys.com* ☾ *Closed Mon. and Tues. No lunch weekends.*

$$$
SEAFOOD
☾
✕ **Hook, Line and Sinker.** Anchored right on the breezy Frenchtown waterfront, adjacent to the pastel-painted boats of the local fishing fleet, this harbor-view eatery serves high-quality fish dishes. The almond-crusted yellowtail snapper is a house specialty. Spicy jerk-seasoned swordfish and grilled tuna topped with a yummy mango-rum sauce are also good bets. This is one of the few independent restaurants serving Sunday brunch. ✉ *Frenchtown Mall, 2 Honduras St., Frenchtown* ☎ *340/776–9708* ⊕ *www.hooklineandsinkervi.com.*

$$
AMERICAN
☾
✕ **Tickle's Dockside Pub.** Nautical types as well as the local working crowd come here for casual fare with homey appeal: chicken-fried steak, meat loaf with mashed potatoes, and baby back ribs. Hearty breakfasts feature eggs and pancakes, and lunch is a full array of burgers, salads, sandwiches, and soups. From November through April, the adjacent marina is full of megayachts that make for some great eye candy while you dine. ✉ *Crown Bay Marina, Rte. 304, Estate Contant* ☎ *340/776–1595* ⊕ *www.ticklesdocksidepub.com.*

27

WHERE TO STAY

Of the USVI, St. Thomas has the most rooms and the greatest number and variety of resorts. You can let yourself be pampered at a luxurious resort—albeit at a price of $300 to more than $600 per night, not including meals. If your means are more modest, there are fine hotels (often with rooms that have a kitchen and a living area) in lovely settings throughout the island. There are also guesthouses and inns with great views (if not a beach at your door) and great service at about half the cost of what you'll pay at the beachfront pleasure palaces. Many of these are east and north of Charlotte Amalie or overlooking hills—ideal if you plan to get out and mingle with the locals. There are also inexpensive lodgings (most right in town) that are perfect if you just want a clean room to return to after a day of exploring or beach-bumming.

East End condominium complexes are popular with families. Although condos are pricey (winter rates average $350 per night for a two-bedroom unit, which usually sleeps six), they have full kitchens, and you can definitely save money by cooking for yourself—especially if you bring some of your own nonperishable foodstuffs. (Virtually everything on St. Thomas is imported, and restaurants and shops pass shipping costs on to you.) Though you may spend some time laboring in the kitchen, many condos ease your burden with daily maid service and on-site restaurants; a few also have resort amenities, including pools and tennis courts. The East End is convenient to St. John, and it's a hub for the boating crowd, with some good restaurants. The prices below reflect rates in high season, which runs from December 15 to April 15. Rates are 25% to 50% lower the rest of the year.

PRIVATE VILLAS AND CONDOMINIUMS

St. Thomas has a wide range of private villas, from modest two-bedroom houses to luxurious five-bedroom mansions. Most will require that you book for seven nights during high season, five in low season. A minimum stay of up to two weeks is often required during the Christmas season. You can arrange private villa rentals through various agents who represent luxury residences and usually have both Web sites and brochures that show photos of the properties they represent. Some are suitable for travelers with disabilities, but be sure to ask specific questions about your own needs. **Calypso Realty** (⌂ Box 12178, St. Thomas, USVI ☎ 340/774–1620 or 800/747–4858 ⊕ www.calypsorealty.com) specializes in rental properties around St. Thomas. **McLaughlin-Anderson Luxury Caribbean Villas** (⌂ 1000 Blackbeard's Hill, Suite 3, St. Thomas, USVI ☎ 340/776–0635 or 800/537–6246 ⊕ www.mclaughlinanderson. com) handles rental villas throughout the U.S. Virgin Islands, British Virgin Islands, and Grenada. Many villas and condominiums are in complexes on St. Thomas's East End.

The following reviews have been condensed for this book. Please go to Fodors.com for expanded reviews of each property.

CHARLOTTE AMALIE

Accommodations in town and near town offer the benefits of being close to the airport, shopping, and a number of casual and fine-dining restaurants. The downside is that this is the most crowded and noisy area of the island. Crime can also be a problem. Don't go for a stroll at night in the heart of town. Use common sense and take the same precautions you would in any major city. Properties along the hillsides are less likely to have crime problems, plus they command a steady breeze from the cool trade winds. This is especially important if you're visiting in summer and early fall.

¢
HOTEL
The Green Iguana. Atop Blackbeard's Hill, this value-priced small hotel offers the perfect mix of gorgeous harbor views, proximity to shopping (five-minute walk), and secluded privacy provided by the surrounding flamboyant trees and bushy hibiscus. **Pros:** personalized service; near the center of town; laundry on premises. **Cons:** need a car to get around; neighborhood is sketchy at night. ⊠ *37B Blackbeard's Hill* ☎ *340/776–7654 or 800/484–8825* ⊕ *www.thegreeniguana.com* ⤙ *6 rooms* ⚹ *In-room: a/c, no safe, kitchen (some), Wi-Fi. In-hotel: pool, laundry facilities* ⦿ *No meals.*

¢–$
B&B/INN
Hotel 1829. Antique charm—though some may simply call it old—is readily apparent in this rambling 19th-century merchant's house, from the hand-painted Moroccan tiles to a Tiffany window. **Pros:** close to attractions; budget-priced; breakfast served on the verandah. **Cons:** small rooms; tour groups during the day; neighborhood dicey at night. ⊠ *Government Hill, Box 1567* ☎ *340/776–1829 or 800/524–2002* ⊕ *www.hotel1829.com* ⤙ *15 rooms* ⚹ *In-room: a/c, no safe, Wi-Fi. In-hotel: bar, pool, some age restrictions* ⦿ *Breakfast.*

$
HOTEL
Fodor'sChoice
★
Villa Santana. Built by exiled General Antonio López Santa Anna of Mexico, this 1857 landmark provides a panoramic view of the harbor and plenty of West Indian charm, which will make you feel as if you're living in a charming slice of Virgin Islands history. **ros:** historic charm; plenty of privacy. **Cons:** not on a beach; no restaurant; need a car to get around. ⊠ *2D Denmark Hill* ☎ *340/776–1311* ⊕ *www.villasantana. com* ⤙ *6 rooms* ⚹ *In-room: a/c, no safe, kitchen (some), no TV (some), Wi-Fi. In-hotel: pool* ⦿ *No meals.*

$$
HOTEL
Windward Passage Hotel. Business travelers, those on their way to the British Virgin Islands, or laid-back vacationers who want the convenience of being able to walk to duty-free shopping, sights, and restaurants, stay at this harborfront hotel. **Pros:** walking distance to Charlotte Amalie; nice harbor views. **Cons:** basic rooms; on a busy street; no water sports, but dive shop is on property. ⊠ *Waterfront Hwy., Box 640* ☎ *340/774–5200 or 800/524–7389* ⊕ *www.windwardpassage.com* ⤙ *140 rooms, 11 suites* ⚹ *In-room: a/c, Wi-Fi. In-hotel: restaurant, bar, pool, gym* ⦿ *No meals.*

EAST END

You can find most of the large, luxurious beachfront resorts on St. Thomas's East End. The downside is that these properties are about a 30-minute drive from town and a 45-minute drive from the airport (substantially longer during peak hours). On the upside, they tend to be self-contained, plus there are a number of good restaurants, shops, and water-sports operators in the area. Once you've settled in, you don't need a car to get around.

$$$
RENTAL
☾

🖵 **The Anchorage Beach Resort.** A beachfront setting and homey conveniences that include full kitchens and washer–dryer units are what attract families to these two- and three-bedroom suites on Cowpet Bay next to the St. Thomas Yacht Club. **Pros:** on the beach; good amenities. **Cons:** small pool; noisy neighbors; need a car to get around. ⊠ *Rte. 317, Estate Nazareth ✆ Antilles Resorts, Box 24786, Christiansted, St. Croix 00824-0786* 🕾 *800/874–7897* ⊕ *www.antillesresorts.com* ⤳ *11 suites* ☾ *In-room: a/c, no safe, kitchen. In-hotel: bar, tennis courts, pool, gym, beach, laundry facilities* ¶◎¶ *No meals.*

$$
🖵 **Pavilions and Pools Villa Hotel.** Although the rates might lead you to believe you're buying resort ambience, the reality is that you get fairly basic accommodations here. **Pros:** intimate atmosphere; friendly host; private pools. **Cons:** some small rooms; on a busy road; long walk to beach. ⊠ *6400 Rte. 38, Estate Smith Bay* 🕾 *340/775–6110 or 800/524–2001* ⊕ *www.pavilionsandpools.com* ⤳ *25 1-bedroom villas* ☾ *In-room: a/c, kitchen. In-hotel: restaurant, pools* ¶◎¶ *Breakfast.*

$$$
RESORT

🖵 **Point Pleasant Resort.** Hilltop suites give you an eagle's-eye view of the East End and beyond, and those in a building adjacent to the reception area offer incredible sea views. **Pros:** lush setting; convenient kitchens; pleasant pools. **Cons:** steep climb from beach; need a car to get around; some rooms need refurbishing. ⊠ *6600 Rte. 38, Estate Smith Bay* 🕾 *340/775–7200 or 800/524–2300* ⊕ *www.pointpleasantresort. com* ⤳ *128 suites* ☾ *In-room: a/c, kitchen. In-hotel: restaurants, bar, tennis court, pools, gym, beach, laundry facilities, business center* ¶◎¶ *No meals.*

$$$$
RESORT
☾
Fodor's Choice
★

🖵 **Ritz-Carlton, St. Thomas.** Everything sparkles at the island's most luxurious resort, from the in-room furnishings and amenities to the infinity pool, white-sand beach, and turquoise sea beyond. **Pros:** gorgeous views; great water-sports facilities; beautiful beach; airport shuttle. **Cons:** service can sometimes be spotty for such an upscale hotel; food and drink can lack flair and are expensive ($15 hamburger, $9.75 piña colada); half-hour or more drive to town and airport. ⊠ *Rte. 317, Box 6900, Estate Great Bay* 🕾 *340/775–3333 or 800/241–3333* ⊕ *www.ritzcarlton.com* ⤳ *255 rooms, 20 suites, 2 villas, 81 condos* ☾ *In-room: a/c, Wi-Fi. In-hotel: restaurants, bars, tennis courts, pools, gym, spa, beach, water sports, children's programs, business center* ¶◎¶ *No meals.*

$$$–$$$$
RENTAL

🖵 **Sapphire Beach Condominium Resort and Marina.** A beautiful half-mile-long white-sand beach is the real ace here, because accommodations can be hit-or-miss depending on whether you book with a private condo owner (hit) or the management company (miss). **Pros:** beachfront location; water sports abound; near ferries. **Cons:** some rooms need refurbishing; restaurant fare limited; some construction noise. ⊠ *6720 Estate Smith Bay* 🕾 *800/524–2090, 340/773–9150, or 800/874–7897* ⊕ *www.antillesresorts.com* ⤳ *171 condos* ☾ *In-room: a/c, no safe, kitchen (some). In-hotel: restaurant, bar, tennis courts, pool, beach, water sports* ¶◎¶ *No meals.*

The Ritz-Carlton St. Thomas.

$$
RENTAL
🏨 **Sapphire Village.** These high-rise towers feel more like apartment buildings than luxury resorts, so if you're looking for a home away from home, this might be the place. **Pros:** within walking distance of Red Hook; nice views; secluded feel. **Cons:** small rooms; limited dining options; noisy neighbors. ⊠ *Rte. 38, Sapphire Bay 🕀 Antilles Resorts, Box 24786, Christiansted, St. Croix 00824-0786 ☎ 340/779–1540 or 800/874–7897 ⊕ www.antillesresorts.com ⤏ 15 condos ⚙ In-room: a/c, no safe, kitchen. In-hotel: restaurant, bar, tennis courts, pools, beach, water sports, laundry facilities* ⦿ *No meals.*

$$$–$$$$
RENTAL
🏨 **Secret Harbour Beach Resort.** There's not a bad view from these low-rise studio, one-, and two-bedroom condos, which are either beachfront or perched on a hill overlooking an inviting cove. **Pros:** beautiful beach and great snorkeling; good restaurant; secluded location. **Cons:** some rooms are small; car needed to get around; condo owners are territorial about beach chairs. ⊠ *Rte. 317, Box 6280, Estate Nazareth ☎ 340/775–6550 or 800/524–2250 ⊕ www.secretharbourvi.com ⤏ 49 suites ⚙ In-room: a/c, no safe, kitchen. In-hotel: restaurant, bar, tennis courts, pool, gym, beach, water sports* ⦿ *Breakfast.*

$$$$
ALL-INCLUSIVE
☕
Fodor's Choice
★
🏨 **Wyndham Sugar Bay Resort and Spa.** At the only full all-inclusive resort on St. Thomas, the terra-cotta high-rise buildings are surrounded by palm trees and lush greenery, but the rooms and the walkways between them have a bit of a generic feel. **Pros:** gorgeous pool area; full-service spa; on-site casino. **Cons:** some steps to climb; small beach; limited dining options. ⊠ *38 Smith Bay, Estate Smith Bay ☎ 340/777–7100 or 800/927–7100 ⊕ www.wyndham.com ⤏ 294 rooms, 7 suites ⚙ In-room: a/c. In-hotel: restaurants, bar, tennis courts, pool, gym, spa, beach, water sports, children's programs* ⦿ *All-inclusive.*

SOUTH SHORE

The south shore of St. Thomas connects town to the east end of the island via a beautiful road that rambles along the hillside with frequent peeks between the hills for a view of the ocean and, on a clear day, of St. Croix some 40 mi (64 km) to the south. The resorts here are on their own beaches. They offer several opportunities for water sports, as well as land-based activities, fine dining, and evening entertainment.

$-$$
ALL-INCLUSIVE
Bolongo Bay Beach Resort. All the rooms at this family-run resort tucked along a 1,000-foot-long palm-lined beach have balconies with ocean views; down the beach are 12 studio and two-bedroom condos with full kitchens. **ros:** family-run property; on the beach; water sports abound. **Cons:** a bit run-down; on a busy road; need a car to get around. ⊠ *Rte. 30, Box 7150, Estate Bolongo* ☎ *340/775–1800 or 800/524–4746* ⊕ *www.bolongobay.com* ⇨ *65 rooms, 12 condos* ⚐ *In-room: a/c, kitchen (some). In-hotel: restaurants, bar, tennis courts, pool, beach, water sports* ⛅ *Multiple meal plans.*

$$$-$$$$
RESORT
Marriott Frenchman's Reef and Morning Star Beach Resorts. Set majestically on a promontory overlooking the east side of Charlotte Amalie's harbor, Frenchman's Reef is the high-rise full-service superhotel, whereas Morning Star is the even more upscale boutique property nestled closer to the fine white-sand beach. **Pros:** beachfront location; good dining options; plenty of activities. **Cons:** musty smell on lower levels; long walk between resorts; a crowded cruise-ship feel. ⊠ *Rte. 315, Box 7100, Estate Bakkeroe* ☎ *340/776–8500 or 800/233–6388* ⊕ *www.marriott.com* ⇨ *479 rooms, 27 suites; 220 2- and 3-bedroom time-share units* ⚐ *In-room: a/c, Wi-Fi. In-hotel: restaurants, bar, tennis courts, pools, gym, spa, beach, children's programs* ⛅ *No meals.*

WEST END

A few properties are in the hills overlooking Charlotte Amalie to the west or near French Town, which is otherwise primarily residential.

$$-$$$
HOTEL
Best Western Emerald Beach Resort. You get beachfront ambience at this reasonably priced miniresort tucked beneath the palm trees, but the tradeoff is that it's directly across from a noisy airport runway. **Pros:** beachfront location; good value; great Sunday brunch. **Cons:** airport noise until 10 pm; on a busy road; limited water sports. ⊠ *8070 Lindberg Bay* ☎ *340/777–8800 or 800/780–7234* ⊕ *www.emeraldbeach. com* ⇨ *90 rooms* ⚐ *In-room: a/c, no safe. In-hotel: restaurant, bar, tennis courts, pool, gym, beach* ⛅ *Breakfast.*

¢-$
B&B/INN
Island View Guesthouse. Perched 545 feet up the face of Crown Mountain, this small inn has a homey feel; the hands-on owners can book tours or offer tips about the best sightseeing spots. **Pros:** spectacular views; friendly atmosphere; good value. **Cons:** small pool; need a car to

get around. ⊠ *Rte. 332, Box 1903, Estate Contant* ☎ *340/774–4270 or 800/524–2023* ⊕ *www.islandviewstthomas.com* ↪ *12 rooms, 10 with bath* ⚭ *In-room: a/c (some), no safe, kitchen (some). In-hotel: pool, laundry facilities* ⦿ *Breakfast.*

NIGHTLIFE AND THE ARTS

On any given night, especially in season, you can find steel-pan orchestras, rock and roll, piano music, jazz, broken-bottle dancing (actual dancing atop broken glass), disco, and karaoke. Pick up a free copy of the bright yellow *St. Thomas–St. John This Week* magazine when you arrive (it can be found at the airport, in stores, and in hotel lobbies). The back pages list who's playing where. The Friday edition of the *Daily News* carries complete listings for the upcoming weekend.

NIGHTLIFE
CHARLOTTE AMALIE
Greenhouse Bar and Restaurant. This restaurant closes for dinner at 10 pm. Once this favorite eatery puts away the salt-and-pepper shakers, it becomes a rock-and-roll club with a DJ or live reggae bands raising the weary to their feet six nights a week. ⊠ *Waterfront Hwy. at Storetvaer Gade, Charlotte Amalie* ☎ *340/774–7998.*

EAST END
Agave Terrace. This bar sometimes has an island-style steel-pan band, which is a treat that should not be missed. Steel-pan music resonates after dinner here on Tuesday and Thursday. ⊠ *Point Pleasant Resort, Rte. 38, Estate Smith Bay* ☎ *340/775–4142.*

Duffy's Love Shack. At this island favorite, a live band and dancing under the stars are the big draws for locals and visitors alike. ⊠ *Red Hook Plaza, Red Hook* ☎ *340/779–2080.*

SOUTH SIDE
Epernay Bistro. This place is an intimate nightspot with small tables for easy chatting, wine and champagne by the glass, and a spacious dance floor. Mix and mingle with island celebrities. The action runs from 4 pm until the wee hours Monday through Saturday. ⊠ *Frenchtown Mall, 24-A Honduras St., Frenchtown* ☎ *340/774–5348.*

Iggies Beach Bar. Bolongo Bay's beachside bar offers karaoke on Saturday nights, so you can sing along to the sounds of the surf or the latest hits at this beachside lounge. There are live bands on weekends, and you can dance inside or kick up your heels under the stars. Wednesday it's Carnival Night complete with steel-pan music, a limbo show and West Indian Buffet. ⊠ *Bolongo Bay Beach Club & Villas, Rte. 30, Estate Bolongo* ☎ *340/775–1800.*

THE ARTS
SOUTH SIDE
Pistarkle Theater. This theater in the Tillett Gardens complex is air-conditioned and has more than 100 seats; it hosts a dozen or more productions annually, plus a children's summer drama camp. ⊠ *Tillett Gardens, Rte. 38, across from Tutu Park Shopping Mall, Estate Tutu* ☎ *340/775–7877.*

27

Reichhold Center for the Arts. St. Thomas's major performing arts center has an amphitheater, and its more expensive seats are covered by a roof. Schedules vary, so check the paper to see what's on when you're in town. Throughout the year there's an entertaining mix of local plays, dance exhibitions, and music of all types. ⊠ *Rte. 30, across from Brewers Beach, Estate Lindberg Bay* ☏ *340/693–1559.*

SHOPPING

Fodor's Choice
★ St. Thomas lives up to its billing as a duty-free shopping destination. Even if shopping isn't your idea of how to spend a vacation, you still may want to slip in on a quiet day (check the cruise-ship listings—Monday and Sunday are usually the least crowded) to browse. Among the best buys are liquor, linens, china, crystal (most stores will ship), and jewelry. The amount of jewelry available makes this one of the few items for which comparison shopping is worth the effort. Local crafts include shell jewelry, carved calabash bowls, straw brooms, woven baskets, and dolls. Creations by local doll maker Gwendolyn Harley—like her costumed West Indian market woman—have been little goodwill ambassadors, bought by visitors from as far away as Asia. Spice mixes, hot sauces, and tropical jams and jellies are other native products.

On St. Thomas, stores on Main Street in Charlotte Amalie are open weekdays and Saturday 9 to 5. The hours of the shops in the Havensight Mall (next to the cruise-ship dock) and the Crown Bay Commercial Center (next to the Crown Bay cruise-ship dock) are the same, though occasionally some stay open until 9 on Friday, depending on how many cruise ships are anchored nearby. You may also find some shops open on Sunday if cruise ships are in port. Hotel shops are usually open evenings, as well.

There's no sales tax in the USVI, and you can take advantage of the $1,200 duty-free allowance per family member (remember to save your receipts). Although you can find the occasional salesclerk who will make a deal, bartering isn't the norm.

CHARLOTTE AMALIE
The prime shopping area in **Charlotte Amalie** is between Post Office and Market squares; it consists of two parallel streets that run east–west (Waterfront Highway and Main Street) and the alleyways that connect them. Particularly attractive are the historic **A.H. Riise Alley, Royal Dane Mall, Palm Passage,** and pastel-painted **International Plaza.**

Vendors Plaza, on the waterfront side of Emancipation Gardens in Charlotte Amalie, is a central location for vendors selling handmade earrings, necklaces, and bracelets; straw baskets and handbags; T-shirts; fabrics; African artifacts; and local fruits. Look for the many brightly colored umbrellas.

Made in St. Thomas

Date-palm brooms, frangipani-scented perfume, historically clad dolls, sun-scorched hot sauces, aromatic mango candles: these are just a few of the handicrafts made in St. Thomas.

Justin Todman, aka the Broom Man, keeps the dying art of broom making alive. It's a skill he learned at the age of six from his father. From the fronds of the date palm, Todman delicately cuts, strips, and dries the leaves. Then he creatively weaves them into distinctively shaped brooms with birch-berry wood for handles. There are feather brooms, cane brooms, multicolor-yarn brooms, tiny brooms to fit into a child's hand, and tall, long-handled brooms to reach cobwebs on the ceiling. Some customers buy Todman's brooms—sold at the **Native Arts & Crafts Cooperative**—not for cleaning but rather for celebrating their nuptials. It's an old African custom for the bride and groom to jump over a horizontally laid broom to start their new life.

Gail Garrison puts the essence of local flowers, fruits, and leaves into perfumes, powders, and body splashes. Her Island Fragrances line includes frangipani-, white ginger–, and jasmine-scented perfumes; aromatic mango, lime, and coconut body splashes; and bay rum aftershave for men. Garrison compounds, mixes, and bottles the products herself in second-floor offices on Charlotte Amalie's

Main Street. You can buy the products in the **Tropicana Perfume Shop**.

Gwendolyn Harley preserves Virgin Islands culture in the personalities of her hand-sewn, softly sculptured historic dolls for sale at the Native Arts & Crafts Cooperative. There are quadrille dancers clad in long, colorful skirts; French women with their neat peaked bonnets; and farmers sporting handwoven straw hats. Each one-of-kind design is named using the last three letters of Harley's first name; the dolls have names like Joycelyn, Vitalyn, and Iselyn.

Cheryl Miller cooks up ingredients such as sun-sweetened papayas, fiery Scotch bonnet peppers, and aromatic basil leaves into the jams, jellies, and hot sauces she sells under her Cheryl's Taste of Paradise line. Five of Miller's products—Caribbean Mustango Sauce, Caribbean Sunburn, Mango Momma Jam, Mango Chutney, and Hot Green Pepper Jelly—have won awards at the National Fiery Foods Show in Albuquerque, New Mexico. You can buy her products at Cost-U-Less, the Native Arts & Crafts Cooperative, and the farmers' market at Yacht Haven Grande on the first and third Sunday of each month.

Jason Budsan traps the enticing aromas of the islands such as Ripe Mango and Night Jasmine into sumptuous candles he sells at his **Tillett Gardens** workshop.

27

ART

Camille Pissarro Art Gallery. This second-floor gallery is actually in the birthplace of St. Thomas's famous artist, offering a fine collection of original paintings and prints by local and regional artists. ⊠ *14 Main St., Charlotte Amalie* ☎ *340/774–4621.*

Gallery St. Thomas. This gallery has a nice collection of fine art and collectibles in a charming space, including paintings, wood sculpture, glass, and jewelry that are from or inspired by the Virgin Islands. ⊠ *Palm Passage, Charlotte Amalie* ☎ *340/777–6363.*

CAMERAS AND ELECTRONICS

Boolchand's. This store sells brand-name cameras, audio and video equipment, and binoculars. ⊠ *31 Main St., Charlotte Amalie* ☎ *340/776–0794.*

Royal Caribbean. Royal Caribbean stocks a wide selection of cameras, camcorders, stereos, watches, and clocks. There are two branches near each other in Charlotte Amalie. ⊠ *23 Main St., Charlotte Amalie* ☎ *340/776–5449* ⊠ *33 Main St., Charlotte Amalie* ☎ *340/776–4110.*

CHINA AND CRYSTAL

Little Switzerland. This popular Caribbean chain carries crystal from Baccarat, Waterford, and Orrefors; and china from Kosta Boda, Rosenthal, and Wedgwood, among others in its two Charlotte Amalie stores. There's also an assortment of Swarovski cut-crystal animals, gemstone globes, and many other affordable collectibles. It also does a booming mail-order business; ask for a catalog. ⊠ *5 Dronningens Gade, across from Emancipation Garden, Charlotte Amalie* ☎ *340/776–2010* ⊠ *3B Main St., Charlotte Amalie* ☎ *340/776–2010.*

CLOTHING

☺ **Fresh Produce.** This clothing store doesn't sell lime-green mangoes, peachy-pink guavas, or sunny-yellow bananas. But you will find these fun, casual colors in the Fresh Produce clothing line. This is one of only 16 stores to stock 100% of this California-created, tropical-feel line of apparel for women. Find dresses, shirts, slacks, and skirts in small to plus sizes as well as accessories such as bags and hats. ⊠ *Riise's Alley, Charlotte Amalie* ☎ *340/774–0807.*

☺ **Local Color.** This St. Thomas chain has clothes for men, women, and children among its brand-name wear such as Jams World, Fresh Produce, and Urban Safari. There's also St. John artist Sloop Jones's colorful, hand-painted island designs on cool dresses, T-shirts, and sweaters. Find tropically oriented accessories such as big-brim straw hats, bold-color bags, and casual jewelry. ⊠ *Royal Dane Mall, at Waterfront, Charlotte Amalie* ☎ *340/774–2280.*

HANDICRAFTS

Native Arts and Crafts Cooperative. This crafts market is made up of a group of more than 40 local artists—including schoolchildren, senior citizens, and people with disabilities—who create the handcrafted items for sale here: African-style jewelry, quilts, calabash bowls, dolls, carved-wood figures, woven baskets, straw brooms, note cards, and cookbooks. This is also the site of the Virgin Islands Welcome Center. ⊠ *Tolbod Gade across from Emancipation Garden, Charlotte Amalie* ☎ *340/777–1153.*

JEWELRY

Cardow Jewelry. This store is a chain—with gold in several lengths, widths, sizes, and styles—along with diamonds, emeralds, and other precious gems. You're guaranteed 40% to 60% savings off U.S. retail prices or your money will be refunded within 30 days of purchase. ⊠ *33 Main St., Charlotte Amalie* ☎ *340/776–1140.*

Diamonds International. At this major chain shop with several outlets on St. Thomas, just choose a diamond, emerald, or tanzanite gem and a mounting, and you can have your dream ring set in an hour. Famous for having the largest inventory of diamonds on the island, this shop welcomes trade-ins, has a U.S. service center, and offers free diamond earrings with every purchase. ⊠ *31 Main St., Charlotte Amalie* ☎ *340/774–3707* ⊠ *3 Drakes Passage, Charlotte Amalie* ☎ *340/775– 2010* ⊠ *7AB Drakes Passage, Charlotte Amalie* ☎ *340/774–1516.*

H. Stern Jewelers. At this major Caribbean jeweler, the World Collection of jewels set in modern, fashionable designs and an exclusive sapphire watch have earned this Brazilian jeweler a stellar name. ⊠ *8 Main St., Charlotte Amalie* ☎ *340/776–1939.*

Jewels. This jewelry store sells name-brand jewelry and watches in abundance. Designer jewelry lines include David Yurman, Bulgari, Chopard, and Penny Preville. The selection of watches is extensive, with brand names including Jaeger le Coultre, Tag Heuer, Breitling, Movado, and Gucci. ⊠ *Main St. at Riise's Alley, Charlotte Amalie* ☎ *340/777–4222* ⊠ *Waterfront at Hibiscus Alley, Charlotte Amalie* ☎ *340/777–4222.*

Rolex Watches at A. H. Riise. A.H. Riise is the Virgin Islands' official Rolex retailer, and this shop offers one of the largest selections of these fine timepieces in the Caribbean. An After Sales Service Center assures that your Rolex keeps on ticking for a lifetime. ⊠ *37 Main St., at Riise's Alley, Charlotte Amalie* ☎ *340/776–2303.*

LEATHER GOODS

Coach Boutique at Little Switzerland. This designer leather store has a full line of fine leather handbags, belts, gloves, and more for women, plus briefcases and wallets for men. Accessories for both sexes include organizers, travel bags, and cell-phone cases. ⊠ *5 Main St., Charlotte Amalie* ☎ *340/776–2010.*

Zora's. This store specializes in fine, made-to-order leather sandals. There's also a selection of locally made backpacks, purses, and briefcases in durable, brightly colored canvas. ⊠ *Norre Gade across from Roosevelt Park, Charlotte Amalie* ☎ *340/774–2559.*

LINENS

Fabric in Motion. At Fabric in Motion, fine Italian linens share space with Liberty's of London silky cottons, colorful batiks, cotton prints, ribbons, and accessories at this small shop. ⊠ *Storetvaer Gade, Charlotte Amalie* ☎ *340/774–2006.*

Mr. Tablecloth. This store has prices to please, and the friendly staff here will help you choose from the floor-to-ceiling selection of linens, from Tuscany lace tablecloths to Irish linen pillowcases. ⊠ *6–7 Main St., Charlotte Amalie* ☎ *340/774–4343.*

LIQUOR AND TOBACCO

A.H. Riise Liquors and Tobacco. This giant duty-free liquor outlet offers a large selection of tobacco (including imported cigars), as well as cordials, wines, and rare vintage Armagnacs, cognacs, ports, and Madeiras. It also stocks fruits in brandy and barware from England. Enjoy rum

27

samples at the tasting bar. Prices are among the best in St. Thomas. ⊠ *37 Main St., at Riise's Alley, Charlotte Amalie* ☎ *340/776–2303.*

EAST END

Red Hook has **American Yacht Harbor,** a waterfront shopping area with a dive shop, a tackle store, clothing and jewelry boutiques, a bar, and a few restaurants.

ART

The Color of Joy. This gallery offers locally made arts and crafts, including pottery, batik, hand-painted linen-and-cotton clothing, glass plates and ornaments, and watercolors by owner Corinne Van Rensselaer. There are also original prints by many local artists. ⊠ *Rte. 317, about 100 yards west of Ritz-Carlton, Red Hook* ☎ *340/775–4020.*

FOODSTUFFS

Food Center. This supermarket sells fresh produce, meats, and seafood. There's also an on-site bakery and deli with hot-and-cold prepared foods, which are the draw here, especially for those renting villas, condos, or charter boats in the East End area. ⊠ *Rte. 32, Estate Frydenhoj* ☎ *340/777–8806.*

Marina Market. This market near the ferry to St. John has the best fresh meat and seafood on the island. ⊠ *Rte. 32 across from Red Hook ferry, Red Hook* ☎ *340/779–2411.*

HANDICRAFTS

Ⓒ **Dolphin Dreams.** This crafts store has gaily painted Caribbean-theme Christmas ornaments, art glass from the Mitchell-Larsen studio, and jewelry made from recycled coral. Signature clothing lines include Bimini Bay and Rum Reggae. This boutique is the exclusive Red Hook source for the famous Caribbean Hook Bracelet, originated by the Caribbean Bracelet Company on St. Croix. ⊠ *American Yacht Harbor, Bldg. C, Rte. 32, Red Hook* ☎ *340/775–0549.*

JEWELRY

Diamonds International. At this major chain shop with several outlets on St. Thomas, just choose a diamond, emerald, or tanzanite gem and a mounting, and you can have your dream ring set in an hour. Famous for having the largest inventory of diamonds on the island, this shop welcomes trade-ins, has a U.S. service center, and offers free diamond earrings with every purchase. ⊠ *Wyndham Sugar Bay Beach Club & Resort, Rte. 38, Estate Smith Bay* ☎ *340/714–3248.*

Jewels. This jewelry store sells name-brand jewelry and watches in abundance. Designer jewelry lines include David Yurman, Bulgari, Chopard, and Penny Preville. The selection of watches is extensive, with brand names including Jaeger le Coultre, Tag Heuer, Breitling, Movado, and Gucci. ⊠ *Ritz-Carlton St. Thomas, Rte. 322, Estate Nazareth* ☎ *340/776–7850.*

SOUTH SIDE

West of Charlotte Amalie, the pink-stucco **Nisky Center,** on Harwood Highway about ½ mi (¾ km) east of the airport, is more of a hometown shopping center than a tourist area, but there's a bank, clothing store, and Radio Shack.

At the Crown Bay cruise-ship pier, the **Crown Bay Center,** off the Harwood Highway in Sub Base about ½ mi (¾ km), has quite a few shops.

Havensight Mall, next to the cruise-ship dock, may not be as charming as downtown Charlotte Amalie, but it does have more than 60 shops. It also has an excellent bookstore, a bank, a pharmacy, a gourmet grocery, and smaller branches of many downtown stores. The shops at **Port of $ale,** adjoining Havensight Mall (its buildings are pink instead of brown), sell discount goods. Next door to Port of $ale is the **Yacht Haven Grande** complex, a stunning megayacht marina with beautiful, safe walkways and many upscale shops.

East of Charlotte Amalie on Route 38, **Tillett Gardens** is an oasis of artistic endeavor across from the Tutu Park Shopping Mall. The late Jim and Rhoda Tillett converted this Danish farm into an artists' retreat in 1959. Today you can watch artisans produce silk-screen fabrics, candles, pottery, and other handicrafts. Something special is often happening in the gardens as well: the Classics in the Gardens program is a classical music series presented under the stars, Arts Alive is a semiannual arts-and-crafts fair held in November and May, and the Pistarckle Theater holds its performances here from November through April.

Tutu Park Shopping Mall, across from Tillett Gardens, is the island's one and only enclosed mall. More than 50 stores and a food court are anchored by Kmart and Plaza Extra grocery store. Archaeologists have discovered evidence that Arawak Indians once lived near the grounds.

ART
Mango Tango. This gallery sells and displays works by popular local artists—originals, prints, and note cards. There's a one-person show at least one weekend a month, and the store also has the island's largest humidor and a brand-name cigar gallery. ⊠ *Al Cohen's Plaza, ½ mi [¾ km] east of Charlotte Amalie* ☎ *340/777–3060.*

BOOKS
Dockside Bookshop. This Havensight store is packed with books for children, travelers, cooks, and historians, as well as a good selection of paperback mysteries, best sellers, art books, calendars, and prints. It also carries a selection of books written in and about the Caribbean and the Virgin Islands. ⊠ *Havensight Mall, Bldg. VI, Rte. 30, Havensight* ☎ *340/774–4937.*

CAMERAS AND ELECTRONICS
Boolchand's. This store sells brand-name cameras, audio and video equipment, and binoculars. ⊠ *Havensight Mall, Bldg. II, Rte. 30, Havensight* ☎ *340/776–0302.*

CHINA AND CRYSTAL
Scandinavian Center. The Center has the best of Scandinavia, including Royal Copenhagen, Georg Jensen, Kosta Boda, and Orrefors. Owners Søren and Grace Blak make regular buying trips to northern Europe and are a great source of information on crystal. Online ordering is available if you want to add to your collection once home. ⊠ *Havensight Mall, Bldg. III, Rte. 30, Havensight* ☎ *340/777–8620 or 877/454–8377* ⊠ *Crown Bay Commercial Center, Rte. 30, Crown Bay* ☎ *340/777–8620.*

27

FOODSTUFFS

Fruit Bowl. This grocery store is the best place on the island to go for fresh fruits and vegetables. There's also many ethnic, vegetarian, and health-food items as well as a fresh meat and seafood department. ⊠ *Wheatley Center, Rtes. 38 and 313 intersection, Charlotte Amalie* ☎ *340/774–8565.*

Gourmet Gallery. This gourmet market is where visiting megayacht owners go to buy their caviar. There's also an excellent and reasonably priced wine selection, as well as specialty ingredients for everything from tacos to curries to chow mein. A full-service deli offers imported meats, cheeses, and in-store prepared foods that are perfect for a gourmet picnic. ⊠ *Crown Bay Marina, Rte. 304, Estate Contant* ☎ *340/776–8555* ⊠ *Havensight Mall, Bldg. VI, Rte. 30, Havensight* ☎ *340/774–4948.*

HANDICRAFTS

☪ **Caribbean Marketplace.** This is a great place to buy handicrafts from the Caribbean and elsewhere. Also look for Sunny Caribee spices, teas from Tortola, and coffee from Trinidad. ⊠ *Havensight Mall, Rte. 30, Havensight* ☎ *340/776–5400.*

JEWELRY

H. Stern Jewelers. At this major Caribbean jeweler, the World Collection of jewels set in modern, fashionable designs and an exclusive sapphire watch have earned this Brazilian jeweler a stellar name. (⊠ *Havensight Mall, Bldg. II, Rte. 30, Havensight* ☎ *340/776–1223.*

Jewels. This jewelry store sells name-brand jewelry and watches in abundance. Designer jewelry lines include David Yurman, Bulgari, Chopard, and Penny Preville. The selection of watches is extensive, with brand names including Jaeger le Coultre, Tag Heuer, Breitling, Movado, and Gucci. ⊠ *Havensight Mall, Bldg. II, Rte. 30, Havensight* ☎ *340/776–8590* ⊠ *Yacht Haven Grande, Rte. 38, Havensight* ☎ *340/776–1908.*

LIQUOR AND TOBACCO

Al Cohen's Discount Liquor. Cohen's has an extremely large wine selection in a warehouse-style store. ⊠ *Rte. 30 across from Havensight Mall, Havensight* ☎ *340/774–3690.*

Tobacco Discounters. This duty-free outlet carries a full line of discounted brand-name cigarettes, cigars, and tobacco accessories. ⊠ *Port of $ale Mall, Rte. 30, next to Havensight Mall, Havensight* ☎ *340/774–2256.*

MUSIC

Music Shoppe II. This is a good place to buy the latest Caribbean releases on CD—steel pan, reggae, and calypso. ⊠ *Rte. 30, Havensight Mall, Bldg. III, Havensight* ☎ *340/774–1900.*

TOYS

☪ **Kmart.** This giant discount chain store has five aisles of toys for boys and girls: Barbie dolls, hula hoops, computer games, dollhouses, talking teddies, and more. ⊠ *Tutu Park Shopping Mall, Rte. 38, Estate Tutu* ☎ *340/714–5839* ⊠ *Lockhart Gardens, Rte. 38, Estate Long Bay* ☎ *340/774–4046.*

Continued on page 1098

BELOW THE WAVES
By Lynda Lohr

Colorful reefs and wrecks rife with corals and tropical fish make the islands as interesting underwater as above. Brilliantly colored reef fish vie for your attention with corals in wondrous shapes. Scuba diving gets you up close and personal with the world below the waves.

Bright blue tangs and darting blue-headed wrasses. Corals in wondrous shapes—some look like brains, others like elk antlers. Colorful, bulbous sponges. All these and more can be spotted along the myriad reefs of the U.S. and British Virgin Islands. You might see a pink conch making its way along the ocean bottom in areas with seagrass beds. If you're really lucky, a turtle may swim into view, or a lobster may poke its antennac out of a hole in the reef or rocks. If you do a night dive, you might run into an octopus. But you may be surprised at how much you can see by simply hovering just below the surface, with nothing more than a mask and snorkel. It's a bird's-eye view, but an excellent one. Whether scuba diving or snorkeling, take along an underwater camera to capture memories of your exciting adventure. You can buy disposable ones at most dive shops or bring one from home.

DIVE AND SNORKELING SITES IN BRITISH VIRGIN ISLANDS

TORTOLA

Although a major base for dive operations in the BVI (due to its proximity to so many exceptional dive sites), Tortola itself doesn't have as much to offer divers. However, there are still some noteworthy destinations. The massive **Brewer's Bay Pinnacles** grow 70 feet high to within 30 feet of the surface; the rock mazes are only for advanced divers because of strong currents and they are not always acces-

sible. Abundant reefs close to shore make **Brewer's Bay** popular with snorkelers, as are **Frenchman's Cay** and **Long Bay Beef Island. Diamond Reef,** between Great Camanoe and Scrub Island, is a small wall about 200 yards long. **Shark Point,** off the northeast coast of Scrub Island, does have resident sharks. Though isolated in open ocean, the wreck of the *Chikuzen,* a Japanese refrigerator ship, is a popular site.

THE ISLANDS OF THE SIR FRANCIS DRAKE CHANNEL

Southeast of Tortola lie a string of islands with some of the BVI's finest dive sites, some world famous. The wreck of the royal mail ship *Rhone* is between Peter and Salt islands and is, perhaps, the most famous dive site in the BVI. **Wreck Alley,** consisting of three sunken modern ships, is between Salt and Cooper islands. At **Alice in Wonderland,** south of

Ginger Island, giant, mushroom-shaped corals shelter reef fish, moray eels, and crustaceans. **Alice's Backside,** off the northwestern tip of Ginger Island, is usually smooth enough for snorkeling and shallow enough so that beginner divers can get a good look at the myriad sealife and sponges.

The Chikuzen

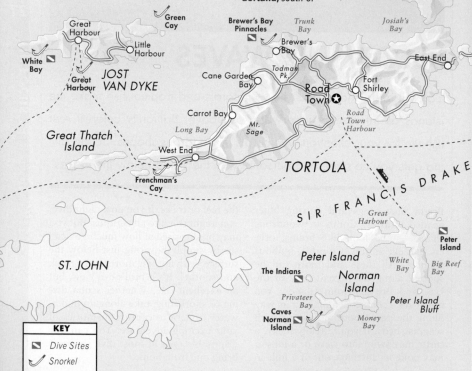

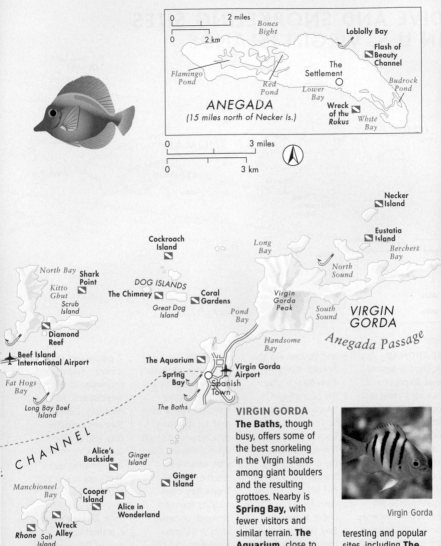

2 miles / 2 km

Bones Bight

Loblolly Bay

Flash of Beauty Channel

Flamingo Pond

The Settlement

Budrock Pond

Red Pond

Lower Bay

ANEGADA
(15 miles north of Necker Is.)

Wreck of the Rokus

White Bay

3 miles / 3 km

Necker Island

Eustatia Island

Berchers Bay

Long Bay

North Bay

Shark Point

Kitto Ghut

Scrub Island

North Sound

Cockroach Island

DOG ISLANDS

The Chimney

Great Dog Island

Coral Gardens

Virgin Gorda Peak

South Sound

VIRGIN GORDA

Anegada Passage

Diamond Reef

Pond Bay

Beef Island International Airport

Handsome Bay

The Aquarium

Virgin Gorda Airport

Fat Hogs Bay

Spring Bay

Spanish Town

Long Bay Beef Island

The Baths

CHANNEL

Alice's Backside

Ginger Island

Ginger Island

Manchioneel Bay

Cooper Island

Alice in Wonderland

Rhone

Salt Island

Wreck Alley

ANEGADA

Surrounded by the third-largest barrier reef in the world, Anegada has great snorkeling from virtually any beach on the island. But there are also some notable dive sites as well. The **Flash of Beauty Channel** on the north shore is a great open-water dive, but only suitable for experienced divers. But even novices can enjoy diving at the **Wreck of the *Rokus***, a Greek cargo ship off the Island's southern shore.

VIRGIN GORDA

The Baths, though busy, offers some of the best snorkeling in the Virgin Islands among giant boulders and the resulting grottoes. Nearby is **Spring Bay,** with fewer visitors and similar terrain. **The Aquarium,** close to Spanish Town and a good novice site, is so called because of the abundance of reef fish that swim around the submerged granite boulders that are similar to those of The Baths. Further west of Virgin Gorda, the Dog Islands have some in-

Virgin Gorda

teresting and popular sites, including **The Chimney,** a natural opening covered by sponges off Great Dog. South of Great Dog, **Coral Gardens** has a large coral reef with a submerged airplane wreck nearby. Fish are drawn to nearby **Cockroach Island.**

DIVE AND SNORKELING SITES IN U.S. VIRGIN ISLANDS

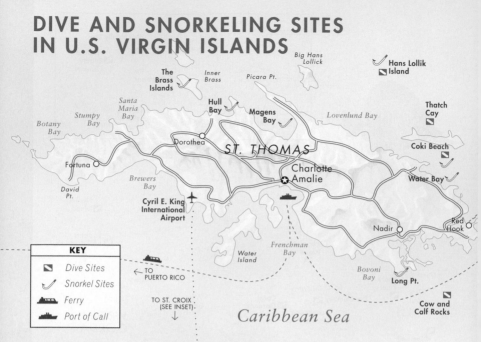

ST. THOMAS

St. Thomas has at least 40 popular dive sites, most shallow. Favorite reef dives off St. Thomas include **Cow and Calf Rocks,** which barely break water off the southeast coast of St. Thomas; the coral-covered pinnacles of **Frenchcap** south of St. Thomas; and tunnels where you can explore undersea from the Caribbean to the Atlantic at **Thatch Cay** (where the Coast Guard cutter *General Rogers* rests at 65 feet). **Grass Cay** and **Mingo Cay** between St. Thomas and St. John are also popular dive sites. **Coki Beach** offers the best off-the-beach snorkeling in St. Thomas. Nearby Coral World offers a dive-helmet walk for the untrained, and Snuba of St. Thomas has tethered shallow dives for non-certified divers. **Magens Bay,** the most popular beach on St. Thomas, provides lovely snorkeling if you head along the edges. You're likely to see some colorful sponges, darting fish, and maybe even a turtle if you're lucky. This is a stop on every island tour.

ST. JOHN

St. John is particularly known for its myriad good snorkeling spots—certainly more than for its diving opportunities, though there are many dive sites within easy reach of Cruz Bay. **Trunk Bay** often receives the most attention because of its underwater snorkeling trail created by the National Park Service; signs let you know what you're seeing in terms of coral and other underwater features. And the beach is easy to reach since taxis leave on demand from Cruz Bay.

A patchy reef just offshore means good snorkeling at **Hawksnest Beach.** Additionally, **Cinnamon Bay** and **Leinster Bay** also get their fair share of praise as snorkeling spots. That's not to say that you can't find good dive sites near St. John. **Deaver's Bay** is a short boat ride around the point from Cruz Bay, where you can see angelfish, southern stingrays, and triggerfish feeding at 30 to 50 feet. **The Leaf** is a large coral reef off St. John's southern shore.

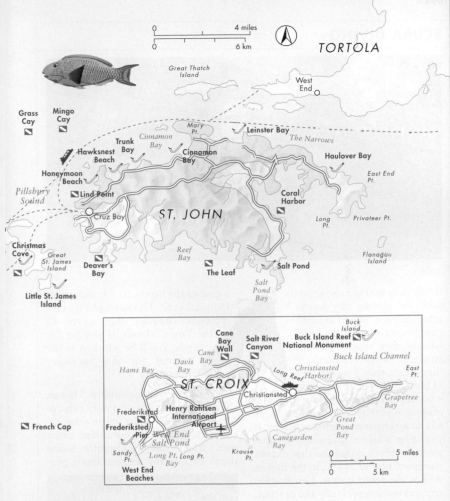

Coral near St. Croix

ST. CROIX

The largest of the U.S. Virgin Islands is a favorite of both divers and snorkelers and offers something for everyone. Snorkelers are often fascinated by the marked snorkeling trail at **Buck Island Reef,** which is a short boat ride from the island's east end; it's a U.S. national monument. Divers are drawn to the north shore, especially the **Cane Bay Wall,** a spectacular drop-off that's reachable from the beach, though usually reached by boat. Another north-shore site is the **Salt River Canyon,** where you can float downward through a canyon filled with colorful fish and coral. On the island's west end, **Frederiksted Pier** is home to a colony of sea horses, creatures seldom seen in the waters of the Virgin Islands. Casual snorkelers would also enjoy snorkeling at the **West End Beaches.**

SCUBA DIVING

St.Croix

If you've never been diving, start with an introductory lesson—often called a "resort course"—run by any one of the Virgin Islands' dive shops. All meet stringent safety standards. If they didn't, they'd soon be out of business. If you're staying at a hotel, you can often find the dive shop on-site; otherwise, your hotel probably has an arrangement with one nearby. If you're on a cruise, cruise-ship companies offer shore excursions that include transportation to and from the ship as well as the resort course. Certification requires much more study and practice, but it is required to rent air tanks, get air refills, and join others on guided dives virtually anywhere in the world.

The number one rule of diving is safety. The basic rules for safe diving are simple, and fools ignore them at their own peril. Serious diving accidents are becoming increasingly rare these days, thanks to the high level of diver training. However, they do still occur occasionally. Surfacing too rapidly without exhaling—or going too deep for too long—can result in an air embolism or a case of the bends. Roy L. Schneider Hospital in St. Thomas has a decompression chamber that serves all the Virgin Islands. If you get the bends, you'll be whisked to the hospital for this necessary treatment.

Fauna is another concern. Though sharks, barracuda, and moray eels are on the most-feared list, more often it's sea urchins and fire coral that cause pain when you accidentally bump them. Part of any scuba-training pro-

Divers learn how to jump in from a boat

St.Croix

gram is a review of sea life and the importance of respecting the new world you're exploring. Dive professionals recognize the value of protecting fragile reefs and ecosystems in tropical waters, and instructors emphasize look-don't-touch diving (the unofficial motto is: take only pictures, leave only bubbles). Government control and protection of dive sites is increasing, especially in such heavily used areas as the Virgin Islands.

While you can scuba dive off a beach—and you can find shops renting scuba equipment and providing airfills at the most popular beaches—a trip aboard a dive boat provides a more extensive glimpse into this wonderful undersea world. Since the dive shops can provide all equipment, there's no need to lug heavy weights and a bulky BC in your luggage. For the most comfort, you might want to bring your own regulator if you have one. The dive-boat captains and guides know the best dive locations, can find alternatives when the seas are rough, and will help you deal with heavy tanks and cumbersome equipment. Trips are easy to organize.

Dive shops on all islands make frequent excursions to a wide variety of diving spots, and your hotel, villa manager, or cruise-ship staff will help you make arrangements.

If you fly too soon after diving, you're at risk for decompression sickness, which occurs when nitrogen trapped in your bloodstream doesn't escape. This creates a painful and sometimes fatal condition called the bends, not a sickness you want to develop while you're winging your way home after a fun-filled beach vacation. Opinions vary, but as a rule of thumb, wait at least 12 hours after a single dive to fly. However, if you've made multiple dives or dived several days in a row, you should wait at least 18 hours. If you've made dives that required decompression stops, you should also wait at least 24 hours before flying. To be safe, consult with your physician.

The Virgin Islands offer a plethora of dive sites, and you'll be taken to some of the best if you sign on to a dive trip run by one of the many dive operations scattered around the islands.

DIVER TRAINING

Good to know: Divers can become certified through PADI *(www.padi.com)*, NAUI *(www.naui.org)*, or SSI *(www.divessi.com)*. The requirements for all three are similar, and if you do the classroom instruction and pool training with a dive shop associated with one organization, the referral for the open water dives will be honored by most dive shops. Note that you should not fly for at least 24 hours after a dive, because residual nitrogen in the body can pose health risks upon decompression. While there are no rigid rules on diving after flying, make sure you're well-hydrated before hitting the water.

Cost: The four-day cost for classroom dive training can range from $300 to $500, but be sure to ask if equipment, instruction manuals, and log books are extra. Some dive shops have relationships with hotels, so check for dive/stay packages. Referral dives (a collaborative effort among training agencies) run from $400 to $300 and discover scuba runs around $120 to $200.

SNUBA

Beyond snorkeling or the requirements of scuba, you also have the option of "Snuba." The word is a trademarked portmanteau or combo of snorkel and scuba. Marketed as easy-to-learn family fun, Snuba lets you breathe underwater via tubes from an air-supplied vessel above, with no prior diving or snorkel experience required.

NOT CERTIFIED?

Not sure if you want to commit the time and money to become certified? Not a problem. Most dive shops and many resorts will offer a discover scuba day-long course. In the morning, the instructor will teach you the basics of scuba diving: how to clear your mask, how to come to the surface in the unlikely event you lose your air supply, etc. In the afternoon, instructors will take you out for a dive in relatively shallow water—less than 30 feet. Be sure to ask where the dive will take place. Jumping into the water off a shallow beach may not be as fun as actually going out to the coral. If you decide that diving is something you want to pursue, the open dive may count toward your certification.

■**TIP→** You can often book discover dives at the last minute. It may not be worth it to go out on a windy day when the currents are stronger. Also the underwater world looks a whole lot brighter on sunny days.

(top) Underwater shot of tropical reef, (bottom) Diver silhouette, Cane Bay, St Croix

Sea Urchin	Tiger Grouper	Foureye Butterflyfish
Parrotfish	Blue Tang	Hogfish
Spotted Eagle Ray	Bonefish	Green Sea Turtle
Dolphin (mahi mahi)	Snook	French Angelfish

REEF CREATURES IN THE VIRGIN ISLANDS

From the striped sergeant majors to bright blue tangs, the reefs of the Virgin Islands are teeming with life, though not nearly as many as in eons past. Warming waters and pollution have taken their toll on both coral and fish species. But many reefs in the Virgin Islands still thrive; you'll also see sponges, crustaceans, perhaps a sea turtle or two, and bigger game fish like grouper and barracuda; sharks are seen but are rarely a problem for divers. Beware of fire corals, which are not really corals but rather a relative of the jellyfish and have a painful sting; if you brush up against a fire coral, spread vinegar on the wound as soon as possible to minimize the pain.

SPORTS AND ACTIVITIES

AIR TOURS

On the Charlotte Amalie waterfront next to Tortola Wharf, **Air Center Helicopters** (✉ *Waterfront, Charlotte Amalie* ☎ *340/775–7335 or 800/619–0013* ⊕ *www.aircenterhelicopters.com*) offers a minimum 30-minute tour that includes St. Thomas, St. John, and Jost Van Dyke priced at $750 for up to 6 people. If you can afford the splurge, it's a nice ride, but in truth, you can see most of the aerial sights from Paradise Point, and there's no place you can't reach easily by car or boat.

BOATING AND SAILING

Calm seas, crystal waters, and nearby islands (perfect for picnicking, snorkeling, and exploring) make St. Thomas a favorite jumping-off spot for day- or weeklong sails or powerboat adventures. With more than 100 vessels from which to choose, St. Thomas is the charter-boat center of the U.S. Virgin Islands. You can go through a broker to book a sailing vessel with a crew or contact a charter company directly. Crewed charters start at approximately $2,400 per person per week, and bareboat charters can start at $1,800 per person for a 50- to 55-foot sailboat (not including provisioning), which can comfortably accommodate up to six people. If you want to rent your own boat, hire a captain. Most local captains are excellent tour guides.

Single-day charters are also a possibility. You can hire smaller boats for the day, including the services of a captain if you wish to have someone take you on a guided snorkeling trip around the islands.

⟲ **Awesome Powerboat Rentals** (✉ *6100 Red Hook Quarter, Red Hook* ☎ *340/775–0860* ⊕ *www.powerboatrentalsvi.com*), at "P" dock offers 26-foot twin-engine catamarans for day charters. Rates range from $345 to $385 for a half or full day. A captain can be hired for $125 for a day.

Island Yachts (✉ *6100 Red Hook Quarter, 18B, Red Hook* ☎ *340/775–6666 or 800/524–2019* ⊕ *www.iyc.vi*) offers sail- or powerboats with or without crews.

Luxury is the word at **Magic Moments** (✉ *American Yacht Harbor, Red Hook* ☎ *340/775–5066* ⊕ *www.yachtmagicmoments.com*), where the crew of a 45-foot Sea Ray offers a pampered island-hopping snorkeling cruise. Nice touches include icy-cold eucalyptus-infused washcloths to freshen up with and a gourmet wine and lobster lunch.

Nauti Nymph (✉ *6501 Red Hook Plaza, Suite 201, Red Hook* ☎ *540/775–5066 or 800/734–7345* ⊕ *www.nautinymph.com*) has a large selection of 25- to 32-foot powerboats and power catamarans. Rates vary from $325 to $620 a day, including snorkeling gear, water skis, and outriggers, but not including fuel. You can hire a captain for $115 more.

Stewart Yacht Charters (✉ *6501 Red Hook Plaza, Suite 20, Red Hook* ☎ *340/775–1358 or 800/432–6118* ⊕ *www.stewartyachtcharters.com*) is run by longtime sailor Ellen Stewart, who is an expert at matching clients with yachts for weeklong crewed charter holidays.

Bareboat sail- and powerboats, including a selection of stable trawlers, are available at **VIP Yacht Charters** (✉ *South off Rte. 32, Estate Frydenhoj* ☎ *340/774–9224 or 866/847–9224* ⊕ *www.vipyachts.com*), at Compass Point Marina.

BICYCLING

Water Island Adventures (✉ *Water Island* ☎ *340/714–2186 or 340/775–5770* ⊕ *www.waterislandadventures.com*) offers a cycling adventure to the USVI's "newest" Virgin. You take a ferry ride from Crown Bay to Water Island before jumping on a Cannondale mountain bike for a 90-minute tour over rolling hills on dirt and paved roads. On cruise-ship days, a direct ferry goes from the West India Company Docks, but this is only for cruise passengers who have booked the bike tour. Explore the remains of the Sea Cliff Hotel, reputedly the inspiration for Herman Wouk's book *Don't Stop the Carnival*, and then take a cooling swim at beautiful Honeymoon Beach. Helmets, water, guides, and ferry fare are included in the $65 cost. Bike rentals are available on days when no tours are scheduled: call for details.

DIVING AND SNORKELING

Popular dive sites include such wrecks as the *Cartanser Sr.*, a beautifully encrusted World War II cargo ship sitting in 35 feet of water, and the *General Rogers*, a Coast Guard cutter resting at 65 feet. Here you can find a gigantic resident barracuda. Reef dives offer hidden caves and archways at **Cow and Calf Rocks**, coral-covered pinnacles at **Frenchcap**, and tunnels where you can explore undersea from the Caribbean to the Atlantic at **Thatch Cay, Grass Cay,** and **Congo Cay.** Many resorts and charter yachts offer dive packages. A one-tank dive starts at $80; two-tank dives are $99 and up. Call the USVI Department of Tourism to obtain a free eight-page guide to Virgin Islands dive sites. There are plenty of snorkeling possibilities, too.

↻ **Admiralty Dive Center** (✉ *Windward Passage Hotel, Waterfront Hwy., Charlotte Amalie* ☎ *340/777–9802 or 888/900–3483* ⊕ *www.admiraltydive.com*) provides boat dives, rental equipment, and a retail store. Four-tank to 12-tank packages are available if you want to dive over several days.

Blue Island Divers (✉ *Crown Bay Marina, Rte. 304, Estate Contant* ☎ *340/774–2001* ⊕ *www.blueislanddivers.com*) is a full-service dive shop that offers both day and night dives to wrecks and reefs and specializes in custom dive charters.

B.O.S.S. Underwater Adventure (✉ *Crown Bay Marina, Rte. 304, Charlotte Amalie* ☎ *340/777–3549* ⊕ *www.bossusvi.com*) offers an alternative to traditional diving in the form of an underwater motor scooter called BOSS, or Breathing Observation Submersible Scooter. A 3½-hour tour, including snorkel equipment, rum punch, and towels, is $100 per person.

↻ **Coki Beach Dive Club** (✉ *Rte. 388, at Coki Point, Estate Frydendal* ☎ *340/775–4220* ⊕ *www.cokidive.com*) is a PADI Gold Palm outfit run by avid diver Peter Jackson. Snorkeling and dive tours in the fish-filled reefs off Coki Beach are available, as are classes from beginner to underwater photography.

27

Snuba of St. Thomas (⊠ *Rte. 388, at Coki Point, Estate Smith Bay* ☎ *340/ 693–8063* ⊕ *www.visnuba.com*) offers something for nondivers, a cross between snorkeling and scuba diving: a 20-foot air hose connects you to the surface. The cost is $52. Children must be eight or older to participate.

St. Thomas Diving Club (⊠ *Bolongo Bay Beach Resort, Rte. 30, Box 7150, Estate Bolongo* ☎ *340/776–2381* ⊕ *www.stthomasdivingclub. com*) is another PADI five-star center that offers boat dives to the reefs around Buck Island and nearby offshore wrecks as well as multiday dive packages.

FISHING

★ Fishing here is synonymous with blue marlin angling—especially from June through October. Four 1,000-pound-plus blues, including three world records, have been caught on the famous North Drop, about 20 mi (32 km) north of St. Thomas. A day charter for marlin with up to six anglers costs $1,600 for the day. If you're not into marlin fishing, try hooking sailfish in winter, dolphin (the fish, not the mammal) in spring, and wahoo in fall. Inshore trips for four hours start at $600. To find the trip that will best suit you, walk down the docks at either American Yacht Harbor or Sapphire Beach Marina in the late afternoon and chat with the captains and crews.

� For marlin, Captain Red Bailey's **Abigail III** (⊠ *Rte. 38, Sapphire Bay* ☎ *340/775–6024* ⊕ *www.visportfish.com*) operates out of the Sapphire Beach Resort & Marina.

The **Charter Boat Center** (⊠ *6300 Red Hook Plaza, Red Hook* ☎ *340/775– 7990* ⊕ *www.charterboat.vi*) is a major source for sportfishing charters, both marlin and inshore.

For inshore or offshore trips, **Double Header Sportfishing** (⊠ *Sapphire Bay Marina, Rte. 38 Sapphire Bay* ☎ *340/775–5274* ⊕ *www. doubleheadersportfishing.net*) offers trips out to the North Drop on its 40-foot sportfisher and half-day reef and bay trips aboard its two speedy 35-foot center consoles.

Captain Eddie Morrison, aboard the 45-foot Viking **Marlin Prince** (⊠ *American Yacht Harbor, Red Hook* ☎ *340/693–5929* ⊕ *www. marlinprince.com*), is one of the most experienced charter operators in St. Thomas and specializes in fly-fishing for blue marlin.

GOLF

★ The **Mahogany Run Golf Course** (⊠ *Rte. 42, Estate Lovenlund* ☎ *340/777– 6006 or 800/253–7103* ⊕ *www.mahoganyrungolf.com*) attracts golfers for its spectacular view of the British Virgin Islands and the challenging three-hole Devil's Triangle. At this Tom and George Fazio–designed, par-70, 18-hole course, there's a fully stocked pro shop, snack bar, and open-air clubhouse. Greens fees and half-cart fees for 18 holes are $150. The course is open daily, and there are frequently informal weekend tournaments. It's the only course on St. Thomas.

GUIDED TOURS

VI Taxi Association St. Thomas City-Island Tour (✆ *340/774–4550* ⊕ *www. vitaxi.com*) gives a two-hour tour for two people in an open-air safari bus or enclosed van; aimed at cruise-ship passengers, this $29 tour includes stops at Drake's Seat and Mountain Top. Other tours include a three-hour trip to Coki Beach with a shopping stop in downtown Charlotte Amalie for $435 per person, a three-hour trip to the Coral World Ocean Park for $45 per person, and a five-hour beach tour to St. John for $75 per person. For $35 to $40 for two, you can hire a taxi for a customized three-hour drive around the island. Make sure to see Mountain Top, as the view is wonderful.

PARASAILING

The waters are so clear around St. Thomas that the outlines of coral reefs are visible from the air. Parasailers sit in a harness attached to a parachute that lifts them off a boat deck until they're sailing through the sky. Parasailing trips average a 10-minute ride in the sky that costs $75 per person. Friends who want to ride along pay $20 for the boat trip.

Caribbean Watersports and Tours (✉ *6501 Red Hook Plaza, Red Hook* ✆ *340/775–9360* ⊕ *www.viwatersports.com*) makes parasailing pick-ups from 10 locations around the island, including many major beach-front resorts. A parasail costs $75 per person. The company also rents Jet Skis, kayaks, and floating battery-power chairs.

SEA EXCURSIONS

Landlubbers and seafarers alike will enjoy the wind in their hair and salt spray in the air while exploring the waters surrounding St. Thomas. Several businesses can book you on a snorkel-and-sail to a deserted cay for a half day that starts at $85 per person or a full day that begins at $125 per person. An excursion over to the British Virgin Islands starts at $125 per person, not including customs fees. A luxury daylong motor-yacht cruise complete with gourmet lunch is $375 or more per person.

For a soup-to-nuts choice of sea tours, contact the **Adventure Center** (✉ *Marriott's Frenchman's Reef Hotel, Rte. 315, Estate Bakkeroe* ✆ *340/774–2992 or 866/868–7784* ⊕ *www.adventurecenters.net*).

The **Charter Boat Center** (✉ *6300 Red Hook Plaza, Red Hook* ✆ *340/775–7990* ⊕ *www.charterboat.vi*) specializes in day trips to the British Virgin Islands and day- or weeklong sailing charters.

Limnos Charters (✉ *Compass Point Marina, Rte. 32, Estate Frydenhoj* ✆ *340/775–3203* ⊕ *www.limnoscharters.com*) offers one of the most popular British Virgin Islands day trips, complete with lunch, open bar, and snorkeling gear. Destinations include the Baths in Virgin Gorda and the sparsely inhabited island of Jost Van Dyke.

Jimmy Loveland at **Treasure Isle Cruises** (✉ *Rte. 32, Estate Nadir* ✆ *340/ 775–9500* ⊕ *www.treasureislecruises.com*) can set you up with every-thing from a half-day sail to a seven-day U.S. and British Virgin Islands trip that combines sailing with accommodations and sightseeing trips onshore.

27

SEA KAYAKING

Ↄ Fish dart, birds sing, and iguanas lounge on the limbs of dense man-grove trees deep within a marine sanctuary on St. Thomas's southeast shore. Learn about the natural history here in a guided kayak-snorkel tour to Patricia Cay or via an inflatable boat tour to Cas Cay for snorkeling and hiking. Both are 2½ hours long. The cost is $75 per person.

Mangrove Adventures (✉ *Rte. 32, Estate Nadir* ☎ *340/779–2155* ⊕ *www. viecotours.com*) rents its two-person sit-atop ocean kayaks and inflatable boats for self-guided exploring as well as for a three-hour guided tour to historic Hassel Island, which includes a visit to some of the historic forts and military structures on the island, a short hike to a breathtaking vista and swim off a deserted beach. The cost is $89 per person. In addition, many resorts on St. Thomas's East End also rent kayaks.

WINDSURFING

Ↄ Expect some spills, anticipate the thrills, and try your luck clipping through the seas. Most beachfront resorts rent Windsurfers and offer one-hour lessons for about $120.

If you want to learn, try Paul Stoeken's **Island Sol** (✉ *Ritz-Carlton St. Thomas, Estate Nazareth* ☎ *340/776–9463* ⊕ *www.islandsol.net*). The two-time Olympic athlete charges $120 per hour for private lessons, $85 per hour for group lessons. There's a free windsurfing clinic every Tuesday at 9:30 am.

One of the island's best-known independent windsurfing companies is **West Indies Windsurfing** (✉ *Vessup Beach, No. 9, Estate Nazareth* ☎ *340/775–6530*). Owner John Phillips is the board buff who introduced the sport of kiteboarding to the USVI; it entails using a kite to lift a sailboard off the water for an airborne ride. A private kiteboarding lesson costs $100 per hour for the land portion and $200 for a two-hour private lesson on the water. Phillips also rents stand-up paddleboards (SUP), the latest water-sports rage, for $30 per hour or $175 to $225 per day based on the quality of the board. There's usually calm water, which is perfect for SUP right off Vessup Beach or around the peninsula in Great Bay.

ST. JOHN

By Lynda Lohr   St. John's heart is Virgin Islands National Park, a treasure that takes up a full two-thirds of St. John's 20 square mi (53 square km). The park helps keep the island's interior in its pristine and undisturbed state, but if you go at midday, you'll probably have to share your stretch of beach with others, particularly at Trunk Bay.

The island is booming (it receives more than 800,000 visitors each year), and it can get a tad crowded at the ever-popular Trunk Bay Beach during the busy winter season; parking woes plague the island's main town of Cruz Bay, but you won't find traffic jams or pollution. It's easy to escape from the fray, however: just head off on a hike or go early or late to the beach. The sun won't be as strong, and you may have that perfect crescent of white sand all to yourself.

Sugar Mill ruins at Annaberg Plantation.

St. John doesn't have a grand agrarian past like her sister island, St. Croix, but if you're hiking in the dry season, you can probably stumble upon the stone ruins of old plantations. The less adventuresome can visit the repaired ruins at the park's Annaberg Plantation and Caneel Bay Resort.

In 1675 Jorgen Iverson claimed the unsettled island for Denmark. By 1733 there were more than 1,000 slaves working more than 100 plantations. In that year the island was hit by a drought, hurricanes, and a plague of insects that destroyed the summer crops. With famine a real threat and the planters keeping them under tight rein, the slaves revolted on November 23, 1733. They captured the fort at Coral Bay, took control of the island, and held on to it for six months. During this period, about 20% of the island's total population was killed, the tragedy affecting both black and white residents in equal percentages. The rebellion was eventually put down with the help of French troops from Martinique. Slavery continued until 1848, when slaves in St. Croix marched on Frederiksted to demand their freedom from the Danish government. This time it was granted. After emancipation, St. John fell into decline, with its inhabitants eking out a living on small farms. Life continued in much the same way until the national park opened in 1956 and tourism became an industry.

Of the three U.S. Virgin Islands, St. John, which has 5,000 residents, has the strongest sense of community, which is primarily rooted in a desire to protect the island's natural beauty. Despite the growth, there are still many pockets of tranquillity. Here you can truly escape the pressures of modern life for a day, a week—perhaps forever.

EXPLORING ST. JOHN

St. John is an easy place to explore. One road runs along the northern shore, another across the center of the mountains. There are a few roads that branch off here and there, but it's hard to get lost. Pick up a map at the visitor center before you start out and you'll have no problems. Few residents remember the route numbers, so have your map in hand if you stop to ask for directions. Bring along a swimsuit for stops at some of the most beautiful beaches in the world. You can spend all day or just a couple of hours exploring, but be advised that the roads are narrow and wind up and down steep hills, so don't expect to get anywhere in a hurry. There are lunch spots at Cinnamon Bay and in Coral Bay, or you can do what the locals do—find a secluded spot for a picnic. The grocery stores in Cruz Bay sell Styrofoam coolers just for this purpose.

If you plan to do a lot of touring, renting a car will be cheaper and will give you much more freedom than relying on taxis; on St. John, taxis are shared safari vans, and drivers are reluctant to go anywhere until they have a full load of passengers. Although you may be tempted by an open-air Suzuki or Jeep, a conventional car will let you lock up your valuables. You can get just about everywhere on the paved roads without four-wheel drive unless it rains. Then four-wheel drive will help you get up the wet, hilly roads. You may be able to share a van or open-air vehicle (called a safari bus) with other passengers on a tour of scenic mountain trails, secret coves, and eerie bush-covered ruins.

WHAT TO SEE
CRUZ BAY

St. John's main town may be compact (it consists of only several blocks), but it's definitely a hub: the ferries from St. Thomas and the British Virgin Islands pull in here, and it's where you can get a taxi or rent a car to travel around the island. There are plenty of shops in which to browse, a number of watering holes where you can stop for a breather, many restaurants, and a grassy square with benches where you can sit back and take everything in. Look for the current edition of the handy, amusing "St. John Map" featuring Max the Mongoose.

Elaine Ione Sprauve Library. On the hill just above Cruz Bay is the Enighed Estate great house, built in 1757. *Enighed* is Danish for "concord" (unity or peace). The great house and its outbuildings (a sugar factory and horse-driven mill) were destroyed by fire and hurricanes, and the house sat in ruins until 1982. The library offers Internet access for $2 an hour. ⊠ *Rte. 104, make a right past Texaco station, Cruz Bay* ☎ *340/776–6359* ◱ *Free* ⊙ *Weekdays 9–5.*

V.I. National Park Visitors Center. To pick up a useful guide to St. John's hiking trails, see various large maps of the island, and find out about current Park Service programs, including guided walks and cultural demonstrations, stop by the park visitor center, which is open daily from 8 to 4:30. ⊠ *Near baseball field, Cruz Bay* ☎ *340/776–6201* ⊕ *www.nps.gov/viis.*

NORTH SHORE

Fodor'sChoice **Annaberg Plantation.** In the 18th century, sugar plantations dotted the
★ steep hills of this island. Slaves and free Danes and Dutchmen toiled to
harvest the cane that was used to create sugar, molasses, and rum for
export. Built in the 1780s, the partially restored plantation at Leinster
Bay was once an important sugar mill. Although there are no official
visiting hours, the National Park Service has regular tours, and some
well-informed taxi drivers will show you around. Occasionally you may
see a living-history demonstration—someone making johnnycake or
weaving baskets. For information on tours and cultural events, contact
the V.I. National Park Visitors Center. ⊠ *Leinster Bay Rd., Annaberg*
☎ *340/776–6201* ⊕ *www.nps.gov/viis* ⊠ *Free* ☉ *Daily dawn–dusk.*

Peace Hill. It's worth stopping at this spot just past the Hawksnest Bay
overlook for great views of St. John, St. Thomas, and the BVI. On the
flat promontory is an old sugar mill. ⊠ *Off Rte. 20, Denis Bay.*

MID ISLAND

★ **Bordeaux Mountain.** St. John's highest peak rises to 1,277 feet. Route
10 passes near enough to the top to offer breathtaking vistas. Don't
stray into the road here—cars whiz by at a good clip along this section.
Instead, drive nearly to the end of the dirt road that heads off next to
the restaurant and gift shop for spectacular views at Picture Point and
the trailhead of the hike downhill to Lameshur. Get a trail map from
the park service before you start. ⊠ *Rte. 10, Bordeaux.*

Catherineberg Ruins. At this fine example of an 18th-century sugar and
rum factory, there's a storage vault beneath the windmill. Across the
road, look for the round mill, which was later used to hold water.
In the 1733 slave revolt Catherineberg served as headquarters for the
Amina warriors, a tribe of Africans captured into slavery. ⊠ *Rte. 10,
Catherineberg.*

Fodor'sChoice **Reef Bay Trail.** This is one of the most interesting hikes on St. John, but
★ unless you're a rugged individualist who wants a physical challenge
(and that describes a lot of people who stay on St. John), you can probably get the most out of the trip if you join a hike led by a park service
ranger who can identify the trees and plants on the hike down, fill you
in on the history of the Reef Bay Plantation, and tell you about the
petroglyphs on the rocks at the bottom of the trail. A side trail takes
you to the plantation's greathouse, a gutted but mostly intact structure
that maintains vestiges of its former beauty. Take the safari bus from
the park's visitor center. A boat takes you from the beach at Reef Bay
back to the visitor center, saving you the uphill climb. You can make
advance reservations for this trip, and it's a good idea during the high
season. You should call a couple of weeks in advance, especially during
February and March, to make sure that the trips haven't filled up, but
a spot on the waiting list will suffice at most since since there are often
no-shows. ⊠ *Rte. 10, Reef Bay* ☎ *340/776–6201 Ext. 238 for reservations* ⊕ *www.nps.gov/viis* ⊠ *Free, safari bus $6, return boat trip to Cruz
Bay $15* ☉ *Tours at 9:30 am, days change seasonally.*

27

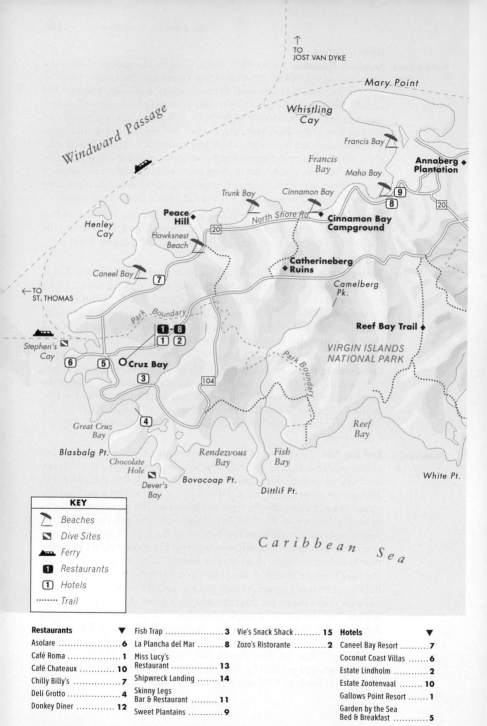

↑
TO
JOST VAN DYKE

Mary Point

Windward Passage

Whistling Cay

Francis Bay

Francis Bay

Annaberg Plantation ◆

Whistling Cay

Maho Bay

Cinnamon Bay

9

8

Trunk Bay

20

Peace Hill ◆

North Shore Rd ◆ **Cinnamon Bay Campground**

Henley Cay

Hawksnest Beach

20

Caneel Bay

7

Catherineberg Ruins ◆

Camelberg Pk.

←TO
ST. THOMAS

Park Boundary

Reef Bay Trail ◆

Stephen's Cay

6 **5** ○ **Cruz Bay**

1 **8**
1 **2**

VIRGIN ISLANDS NATIONAL PARK

3

104

Park Boundary

4

Great Cruz Bay

Reef Bay

Blasbalg Pt.

Chocolate Hole

Rendezvous Bay

Fish Bay

Dever's Bay

Bovocoap Pt.

Dittlif Pt.

White Pt.

C a r i b b e a n   S e a

KEY

⟍ *Beaches*

◻ *Dive Sites*

🚢 *Ferry*

1 *Restaurants*

① *Hotels*

······· *Trail*

Restaurants ▼	Fish Trap **3**	Vie's Snack Shack **15**	**Hotels** ▼
Asolare **6**	La Plancha del Mar **8**	Zozo's Ristorante **2**	Caneel Bay Resort **7**
Café Roma **1**	Miss Lucy's Restaurant **13**		Coconut Coast Villas **6**
Café Chateaux **10**	Shipwreck Landing **14**		Estate Lindholm **2**
Chilly Billy's **7**	Skinny Legs Bar & Restaurant **11**		Estate Zootenvaal **10**
Deli Grotto **4**	Sweet Plantains **9**		Gallows Point Resort **1**
Donkey Diner **12**			Garden by the Sea Bed & Breakfast **5**

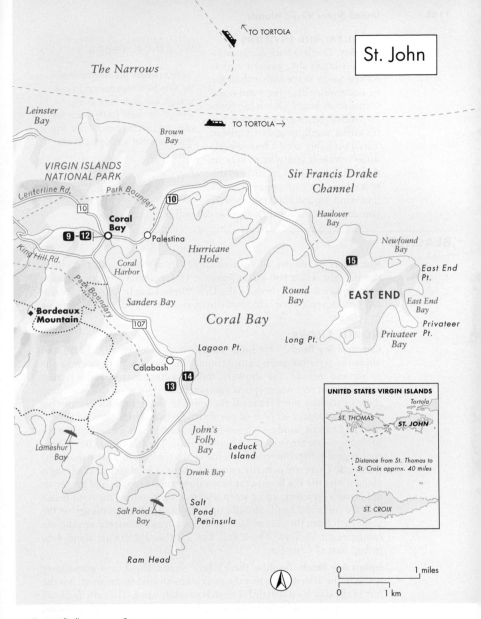

St. John

The Narrows

TO TORTOLA

Leinster
Bay

Brown
Bay

TO TORTOLA →

VIRGIN ISLANDS
NATIONAL PARK

Centerline Rd.   Park Boundary

10

10

**Coral
Bay**

9 -12   Palestina

King Hill Rd.

Coral
Harbor

**Bordeaux
Mountain**

Park Boundary

Sanders Bay

107

*Hurricane
Hole*

Sir Francis Drake
Channel

Haulover
Bay

Newfound
Bay

15

*East End
Pt.*

EAST END

*East End
Bay*

*Round
Bay*

Coral Bay

Long Pt.

*Privateer
Bay*

Privateer
Pt.

Lagoon Pt.

Calabash

14

13

*John's
Folly Bay*

Leduck
Island

Lameshur
Bay

Drunk Bay

Salt Pond
Bay

Salt
Pond
Peninsula

Ram Head

0   1 miles

0   1 km

CORAL BAY AND ENVIRONS

Coral Bay. This laid-back community at the island's dry, eastern end is named for its shape rather than for its underwater life—the word *coral* comes from *krawl,* Dutch for "corral." Coral Bay is growing fast, but it's still a small, neighborly place. You'll probably need a four-wheel-drive vehicle if you plan to stay at this end of the island, as some of the rental houses are up unpaved roads that wind around the mountain. If you come just for lunch, a regular car will be fine.

BEACHES

Remember to remove all your valuables from the car and keep them out of sight when you go swimming. Unfortunately, break-ins have been reported on all three of the U.S. Virgin Islands; most locals recommend leaving your windows down and leaving absolutely nothing in your car.

NORTH SHORE

Cinnamon Bay Beach. This long, sandy beach faces beautiful cays and abuts the national park campground. The facilities are open to the public and include cool showers, toilets, a commissary, and a restaurant. You can rent water-sports equipment here—a good thing, because there's excellent snorkeling off the point to the right; look for the big angelfish and large schools of purple triggerfish. Afternoons on Cinnamon Bay can be windy—a boon for windsurfers but an annoyance for sunbathers—so arrive early to beat the gusts. The Cinnamon Bay hiking trail begins across the road from the beach parking lot; ruins mark the trailhead. There are actually two paths here: a level nature trail (signs along it identify the flora) that loops through the woods and passes an old Danish cemetery, and a steep trail that starts where the road bends past the ruins and heads straight up to Route 10. Restrooms are on the main path from the commissary to the beach and scattered around the campground. ⊠ *North Shore Rd., Rte. 20, Cinnamon Bay, about 4 mi (6 km) east of Cruz Bay.*

Francis Bay Beach. Because there's little shade, this beach gets toasty warm in the afternoon when the sun comes around to the west, but the rest of the day it's a delightful stretch of white sand. The only facilities are a few picnic tables tucked among the trees and a portable restroom, but folks come here to watch the birds that live in the swampy area behind the beach. The park offers bird-watching hikes here on Sunday morning; sign up at the visitor center in Cruz Bay. To get here, turn left at the Annaberg intersection. ⊠ *North Shore Rd., Rte. 20, Francis Bay, ¼ mi (½ km) from Annaberg intersection.*

★ **Hawksnest Beach.** Sea grape and waving palm trees line this narrow beach, and there are restrooms, cooking grills, and a covered shed for

St. John Archaeology

Archaeologists continue to unravel St. John's past through excavations at Trunk Bay and Cinnamon Bay, both prime tourist destinations within Virgin Islands National Park.

Work began back in the early 1990s, when the park wanted to build new bathhouses at the popular Trunk Bay. In preparation for that project, the archaeologists began to dig, turning up artifacts and the remains of structures that date to AD 900. The site was once a village occupied by the Taino, a peaceful group that lived in the area for many centuries. A similar but not quite as ancient village was discovered at Cinnamon Bay.

By the time the Taino got to Cinnamon Bay—they lived in the area from about AD 1000 to 1500—their society had developed to include chiefs, commoners, workers, and slaves. The location of the national park's busy Cinnamon Bay campground was once a Taino temple that belonged to a king or chief. When archaeologists began digging in 1998, they uncovered several dozen *zemis*, which are small clay gods used in ceremonial activities, as well as beads, pots, and many other artifacts.

Near the end of the Cinnamon Bay dig archaeologists turned up another less ancient but still surprising discovery. A burned layer indicated that a plantation slave village had also stood near Cinnamon Bay campground; it was torched during the 1733 revolt because its slave inhabitants had been loyal to the planters. Since the 1970s, bones from slaves buried in the area have been uncovered at the water's edge by beach erosion.

27

picnicking. A patchy reef just offshore means snorkeling is an easy swim away, but the best underwater views are reserved for ambitious snorkelers who head farther to the east along the bay's fringes. Watch out for boat traffic—a channel guides dinghies to the beach, but the occasional boater strays into the swim area. It's the closest drivable beach to Cruz Bay, so it's often crowded with locals and visitors. ⊠ *North Shore Rd., Rte. 20, Hawksnest Bay, about 2 mi (3 km) east of Cruz Bay.*

Maho Bay Beach. This popular beach is below Maho Bay Camps, a wonderful hillside enclave of tent cabins. The campground offers breakfast and dinner at its Pavilion Restaurant, water-sports equipment rentals at the beach, and restrooms. After a five-minute hike down a long flight of stairs to the beach, snorkelers head off along rocky outcroppings for a look at all manner of colorful fish. Watch for a sea turtle or two to cross your path. Another lovely strip of sand with the same name sits right along the North Shore Road. Turn left at the Annaberg intersection and follow the signs about 1 mi (1½ km) for Maho Bay Camps. ⊠ *Off North Shore Rd., Rte. 20, Maho Bay.*

Fodor'sChoice **Trunk Bay Beach.** St. John's most-photographed beach is also the pre-
★ ferred spot for beginning snorkelers because of its underwater trail. (Cruise-ship passengers interested in snorkeling for a day flock here, so if you're looking for seclusion, arrive early or later in the day.) Crowded or not, this stunning beach is one of the island's most beautiful. There are changing rooms with showers, bathrooms, a snack bar,

picnic tables, a gift shop, phones, lockers, and snorkeling-equipment rentals. The parking lot often overflows, but you can park along the road. ⊠ *North Shore Rd., Rte. 20, Trunk Bay, about 2½ mi (4 km) east of Cruz Bay.*

CORAL BAY AND ENVIRONS

Lameshur Bay Beach. This sea grape–fringed beach is toward the end of a partially paved road on the southeast coast. The reward for your long drive is solitude, good snorkeling, and a chance to spy on some pelicans. The beach has a couple of picnic tables, rusting barbecue grills, and a portable restroom. The ruins of the old plantation are a five-minute walk down the road past the beach. The area has good hiking trails, including a trek (more than a mile) up Bordeaux Mountain before an easy walk to Yawzi Point. ⊠ *Off Rte. 107, about 1½ mi (2½ km) from Salt Pond, Lameshur Bay.*

Salt Pond Bay Beach. If you're adventurous, this rocky beach on the scenic southeastern coast—next to Coral Bay and rugged Drunk Bay—is worth exploring. It's a short hike down a hill from the parking lot, and the only facilities are an outhouse and a few picnic tables scattered about. Tide pools are filled with all sorts of marine creatures, and the snorkeling is good, particularly along the bay's edges. A short walk takes you to a pond where salt crystals collect around the edges. Hike farther uphill past cactus gardens to Ram Head for see-forever views. Leave nothing valuable in your car, as reports of thefts are common. ⊠ *Rte. 107, Salt Pond Bay, about 3 mi (5 km) south of Coral Bay.*

WHERE TO EAT

The cuisine on St. John seems to get better every year, with culinary-school-trained chefs vying to see who can come up with the most imaginative dishes. There are restaurants to suit every taste and budget—from the elegant establishments at Caneel Bay Resort (where men may be required to wear a jacket at dinner) to the casual in-town eateries of Cruz Bay. For quick lunches, try the West Indian food stands in Cruz Bay Park and across from the post office. The cooks prepare fried chicken legs, pâtés (meat- and fish-filled pastries), and callaloo.

Some restaurants close for vacation in September and even October. If you have your heart set on a special place, call ahead to make sure it's open during these months.

CRUZ BAY AND ENVIRONS

$$$$ ✗ **Asolare.** Contemporary Asian cuisine dominates the menu at this ele-
PAN-ASIAN   gant open-air eatery in an old St. John house. Come early and relax over
★   drinks while you enjoy the sunset lighting up the harbor. Start with an appetizer such as seared scallops with smoked bacon and a habanero vinegar sauce, then move on to entrées such as grilled pork tenderloin with a chipotle hoisin barbecue sauce or sesame-seared tuna served with a carrot ginger slaw. If you still have room for dessert, try the mimosa-poached pears with honey. ⊠ *Rte. 20 on Caneel Hill, Estate Lindholm* ☎ *340/779–4747* ☾ *No lunch.*

$$$
ITALIAN
☺ **✕ Café Roma.** This second-floor restaurant in the heart of Cruz Bay is *the* place for traditional Italian cuisine: lasagna, spaghetti and meatballs, and three-cheese manicotti. Small pizzas are available at the table, but larger ones are for takeout or at the bar. Rum-caramel bread pudding is a dessert specialty. This casual eatery can get crowded in winter, so show up early. ⊠ *Vesta Gade, Cruz Bay* ☎ *340/776–6524* ⊕ *www. stjohn-caferoma.com* ⊗ *No lunch.*

$
ECLECTIC **✕ Deli Grotto.** At this air-conditioned (but no-frills) sandwich shop you place your order at the counter and wait for it to be delivered to your table or for takeout. The portobello panini with savory sautéed onions is a favorite, but the other sandwiches such as the smoked turkey and artichoke get rave reviews. Order a delicious brownie or cookie for dessert. ⊠ *Mongoose Junction Shopping Center, North Shore Rd., Cruz Bay* ☎ *340/777–3061* ▤ *No credit cards* ⊗ *No dinner.*

$$$
ECLECTIC
☺ **✕ Fish Trap Restaurant and Seafood Market.** The main dining room here is open to the breezes and buzzes with a mix of locals and visitors, but the back room has air-conditioning. Start with a tasty appetizer such as conch fritters or fish chowder (a creamy combination of snapper, white wine, paprika, and secret spices). You can always find steak and chicken dishes, as well as the interesting fish of the day. ⊠ *Bay and Strand Sts., next to Our Lady of Mount Carmel Church, Cruz Bay* ☎ *340/693–9994* ⊕ *www.thefishtrap.com* ⊗ *Closed Mon. No lunch.*

$$$$
MEDITERRANEAN **✕ La Plancha del Mer.** Cooked on a searing hot iron grill called a *plancha*, the food at this restaurant takes its cues from Spain and southern France. The house specialty is steak with garlic herb fries, roasted red pepper coulis, and homemade chimichurri aioli. Locals and visitors come for the bargain-priced appetizers at happy hour at the bar. ⊠ *Rte. 104, Mongoose Junction Shopping Center, Cruz Bay* ☎ *340/777–7333* ⊕ *www.laplanchadelmar.com* ⊗ *Closed Sun.*

$$
CONTINENTAL **✕ Lime Inn.** Vacationers and mainland transplants who call St. John home flock to this alfresco spot for the congenial hospitality and good food, including all-you-can-eat shrimp on Wednesday night. Fresh lobster is the specialty, and the menu also includes shrimp-and-steak dishes and such specials as coconut-crusted chicken breast with plantains and a Thai curry–cream sauce. ⊠ *Lemon Tree Mall, King St., Cruz Bay* ☎ *340/776–6425* ⊕ *www.limeinn.com* ⊗ *No lunch Sat. No dinner Sun.*

$$$$
ITALIAN
Fodor's Choice
★ **✕ Zozo's Ristorante.** Creative takes on old standards coupled with lovely presentations draw the crowds to this restaurant at Gallows Point Resort. Start with crispy fried calamari served with a pesto mayonnaise. The chef dresses up roasted mahimahi with a pine-nut crust and serves it with a warm goat cheese–and-arugula salad. The slow-simmered osso buco comes with prosciutto-wrapped asparagus and saffron risotto. The sunset views will take your breath away. ⊠ *Gallows Point Resort, Bay St., Cruz Bay* ☎ *340/693–9200* ⊗ *No lunch.*

MID ISLAND

$
AMERICAN
★ **✕ Cafe Chateau.** Your hamburgers and sweet potato fries come with a side of fabulous views of Coral Bay and the British Virgin Islands. Located at the popular Bordeaux overlook, this restaurant also serves salads made with local greens and fish sandwiches. The adjacent

27

ice-cream shop blends up some delicious fruit smoothies. ⊠ *Rte. 10, Bordeaux* ☎ *340/776–6611* ⊘ *No dinner.*

CORAL BAY AND ENVIRONS

$$
ECLECTIC

✕ **Donkey Diner.** In an odd combination that works well for Coral Bay visitors and residents, this tiny spot along the main road through Coral Bay sells yummy breakfasts and pizza. Breakfasts can be as ordinary or as innovative as you like, with the menu running from fried eggs with bacon to blueberry pancakes to scrambled tofu served with home fries. Pizzas are equally eclectic, with toppings that include everything from the usual pepperoni and mushrooms to more exotic corn, raisins, and kalamata olives, but they are only available Wednesday through Friday and Sunday. ⊠ *Rte. 10, Coral Bay* ☎ *340/693–5240* ⊕ *www.donkeydiner.com* ▭ *No credit cards.*

$$$
CARIBBEAN
★

✕ **Miss Lucy's Restaurant.** Sitting seaside at remote Friis Bay, Miss Lucy's dishes up Caribbean food with a contemporary flair. Dishes such as tender conch fritters, a spicy West Indian stew called callaloo, and fried fish make up most of the menu, but you also find a generous paella filled with seafood, sausage, and chicken on the menu. Sunday brunches are legendary, and if you're around when the moon is full, stop by for the monthly full-moon party. The handful of small tables near the water is the nicest, but if they're taken or the mosquitoes are swarming, the indoor tables do nicely. ⊠ *Rte. 107, Friis Bay* ☎ *340/693–5244* ⊘ *Closed Mon. No dinner Sun.*

$
AMERICAN
★

✕ **Skinny Legs Bar and Restaurant.** Sailors who live aboard boats anchored offshore and an eclectic coterie of residents gather for lunch and dinner at this funky spot in the middle of a boatyard-cum–shopping complex. If owner Moe Chabuz is around, take a gander at his gams; you'll see where the restaurant got its name. It's a great place for burgers, fish sandwiches, and whatever sports event is on the satellite TV. ⊠ *Rte. 10, Coral Bay* ☎ *340/779–4982* ⊕ *www.skinnylegs.com.*

$$$
CARIBBEAN

✕ **Sweet Plaintains.** The food here is a sophisticated take on Caribbean cuisine. The fish of the day—it could be mahimahi or grouper—is served with a Caribbean flair and is always especially good, or try one of the curries if you don't want seafood. For a real local taste, start with the saltfish cakes served with shredded cabbage and mango puree. The coconut flan for dessert is another Caribbean favorite. ⊠ *Rte. 107, Coral Bay* ☎ *340/777–4653* ⊕ *www.sweetplaintains-stjohn.com* ⊘ *Closed Tues.*

$
CARIBBEAN
★

✕ **Vie's Snack Shack.** Stop by Vie's when you're out exploring the island. Although it's just a shack by the side of the road, Vie's serves up some great cooking. The garlic chicken legs are crisp and tasty, and the conch fritters are really something to write home about. Plump and filled with fresh herbs, a plateful will keep you going for the rest of the afternoon. Save room for a wedge of coconut pie—called a tart in this neck of the woods. When you're finished eating, a spectacular white-sand beach down the road beckons. ⊠ *Rte. 10, Hansen Bay* ☎ *340/693–5033* ▭ *No credit cards* ⊘ *Closed Sun. and Mon. No dinner.*

WHERE TO STAY

St. John doesn't have many beachfront hotels, but that's a small price to pay for all the pristine sand. However, the island's two excellent resorts—Caneel Bay Resort and the Westin St. John Resort & Villas—*are* on the beach. Sandy, white beaches string out along the north coast, which is popular with sunbathers and snorkelers and is where you can find the Caneel Bay Resort and Cinnamon and Maho Bay campgrounds. Most villas are in the residential south-shore area, a 15-minute drive from the north-shore beaches. If you head east, you come to the laid-back community of Coral Bay, where there are growing numbers of villas and cottages. Bands sometimes play at a couple of Coral Bay's nightspots, so if you're renting a villa in the hills above the village, you may hear music later than you'd like. A stay outside of Coral Bay will be peaceful and quiet.

If you're looking for West Indian village charm, there are a few inns in Cruz Bay. Just know that when bands play at any of the town's bars (some of which stay open until the wee hours), the noise can be a problem. Your choice of accommodations also includes condominiums and cottages near town; two campgrounds, both at the edges of beautiful beaches (bring bug repellent); ecoresorts; and luxurious villas, often with a pool or a hot tub (sometimes both) and a stunning view.

If your lodging comes with a fully equipped kitchen, you'll be happy to know that St. John's handful of grocery stores sell everything from the basics to sun-dried tomatoes and green chilies—though the prices will take your breath away. If you're on a budget, consider bringing some staples (pasta, canned goods, paper products) from home. Hotel rates throughout the island, though considered expensive by some, do include endless privacy and access to most water sports.

Many of the island's condos are just minutes from the hustle and bustle of Cruz Bay, but you can find more scattered around the island. St. John also has a handful of camping spots ranging from the basic Cinnamon Bay Campground to the more comfortable Maho Bay Camps. They appeal to those who don't mind bringing their own beach towels from home or busing their own tables at dinner. If you want your piña colada delivered beachside by a smiling waiter, you'd be better off elsewhere.

PRIVATE CONDOS AND VILLAS

Tucked here and there between Cruz Bay and Coral Bay are about 350 private villas and condos (prices range from $ to $$$$). With pools or hot tubs, full kitchens, and living areas, these lodgings provide a fully functional home away from home. They're perfect for couples and extended groups of family or friends. You need a car, since most lodgings are in the hills and very few are at the beach. Villa managers usually pick you up at the dock, arrange for your rental car, and answer questions upon arrival as well as during your stay. Prices drop in the summer season, which is generally after April 15. Some companies begin off-season pricing a week or two later, so be sure to ask.

If you want to be close to Cruz Bay's restaurants and boutiques, a villa in the Chocolate Hole and Great Cruz Bay areas will put you a few minutes away. The Coral Bay area has a growing number of villas, but

27

you'll be about 20 minutes from Cruz Bay. Beaches string out along the North Shore, so you won't be more than 15 minutes from the water no matter where you stay.

RENTAL AGENTS

Book-It VI (🖰 *5000 Estate Enighed, PMB 15, Cruz Bay 00831* ☎ *340/693– 8555 or 800/416–1205* ⊕ *www.bookitvi.com*) handles villas all across St. John.

Carefree Get-Aways (🖰 *Box 1626, Cruz Bay 00831* ☎ *340/779–4070 or 888/643–6002* ⊕ *www.carefreegetaways.com*) manages vacation villas on the island's southern and western edges.

Caribbean Villas & Resorts (🖰 *Box 458, Cruz Bay 00831* ☎ *340/776– 6152 or 800/338–0987* ⊕ *www.caribbeanvilla.com*) handles condo rentals for Cruz Views and Gallow's Point Resort, as well as for many private villas.

Caribe Havens (✉ *Box 455, Cruz Bay* ☎ *340/776–6518* ⊕ *www.caribehavens. com*) has mainly budget properties scattered around the island.

Catered to Vacation Homes (✉ *Marketplace Suite 206, 5206 Enighed, Cruz Bay* ☎ *340/776–6641 or 800/424–6641* ⊕ *www.cateredto.com*) has luxury homes, mainly in the middle of the island and on the west- ern edge.

Cloud 9 Villas (✉ *Box 102, Cruz Bay* ☎ *340/693–8495 or 866/693–8496* ⊕ *www.cloud9villas.com*) has several homes, with most in the Gifft Hill and Chocolate Hole area.

Great Caribbean Getaways (🖰 *Box 8317, Cruz Bay 00831* ☎ *340/693– 8692 or 800/341–2532* ⊕ *www.greatcaribbeangetaways.com*) handles private villas from Cruz Bay to Coral Bay.

Island Getaways (🖰 *Box 1504, Cruz Bay 00831* ☎ *340/693–7676 or 888/693–7676* ⊕ *www.islandgetawaysinc.com*) has villas in the Great Cruz Bay–Chocolate Hole area, with a few others scattered around the island.

On-Line Vacations (🖰 *Box 9901, Emmaus 00831* ☎ *340/776–6036 or 888/842–6632* ⊕ *www.onlinevacations.com*) books vacation villas around St. John.

Private Homes for Private Vacations (✉ *7605 Mamey Peak, Coral Bay* ☎🖰 *340/776–6876* ⊕ *www.privatehomesvi.com*) has homes across the island.

Seaview Vacation Homes (🖰 *Box 644, Cruz Bay 00831* ☎ *340/776–6805 or 888/625–2963* ⊕ *www.seaviewhomes.com*) handles homes with views of the ocean in the Chocolate Hole, Great Cruz Bay, and Fish Bay areas.

Star Villas (🖰 *1202 Gallows Point, Cruz Bay 00831* ☎ *340/776–6704* ⊕ *www.starvillas.com*) has cozy villas just outside Cruz Bay.

St. John Ultimate Villas (🖰 *Box 1324, Cruz Bay 00831* ☎ *340/776–4703 or 888/851–7588* ⊕ *www.stjohnultimatevillas.com*) manages villas across the island.

Vacation Vistas (✍ *Box 476, Cruz Bay 00831* ☎ *340/776–6462* ⊕ *www. vacationvistas.com*) manages villas mainly in the Chocolate Hole, Great Cruz Bay, and Rendezvous areas.

Windspree (✉ *7924 Emmaus, Cruz Bay* ☎ *340/693–5423 or 888/742– 0357* ⊕ *www.windspree.com*) handles villas mainly in the Coral Bay area.

The following reviews have been condensed for this book. Please go to Fodors.com for expanded reviews of each property.

CRUZ BAY AND ENVIRONS

$$–$$$
RENTAL
🏨 **Coconut Coast Villas.** This small condominium complex with studio, two-, and three-bedroom apartments is a 10-minute walk from Cruz Bay, but is insulated from the town's noise in a sleepy suburban neighborhood. **Pros:** good snorkeling; full kitchens; walk to Cruz Bay. **Cons:** small beach; some uphill walks; nearby utility plant can be noisy. ✉ *Turner Bay* ✍ *Box 618, Cruz Bay 00831* ☎ *340/693–9100 or 800/858–7989* ⊕ *www.coconutcoast.com* ↘ *9 units* ♿ *In-room: a/c, no safe, kitchen, Wi-Fi. In-hotel: pool, beach, business center* ⦿ *No meals.*

$$–$$$
B&B/INN
🏨 **Estate Lindholm Bed and Breakfast.** Built among old stone ruins on a lushly planted hill overlooking Cruz Bay, Estate Lindholm has an enchanting setting. **Pros:** lush landscaping; gracious host; pleasant decor. **Cons:** can be noisy; some uphill walks; on a busy road. ✉ *Rte. 20 on Caneel Hill, Estate Lindholm* ✍ *Box 1360, Cruz Bay 00831* ☎ *340/776–6121 or 800/322–6335* ⊕ *www.estatelindholm.com* ↘ *14 rooms* ♿ *In-room: a/c, no safe. In-hotel: restaurant, pool, gym, some age restrictions* ⦿ *Breakfast.*

$$$–$$$$
RESORT
🏨 **Gallows Point Resort.** You're a short walk from restaurants and shops at this waterfront location just outside Cruz Bay, but once you step into your condo, the hustle and bustle are left behind. **Pros:** walk to shopping; excellent restaurant; comfortably furnished rooms. **Cons:** some rooms can be noisy; mediocre beach; insufficient parking. ✉ *Gallows Point, Bay St., Box 58, Cruz Bay* ☎ *340/776–6434 or 800/323–7229* ⊕ *www.gallowspointresort.com* ↘ *60 units* ♿ *In-room: a/c, kitchen, Wi-Fi. In-hotel: restaurant, pool, beach, water sports, business center* ⦿ *No meals.*

$
B&B/INN
🏨 **Garden by the Sea Bed and Breakfast.** A stay here will allow you to live like a local in a middle-class residential neighborhood near a bird-filled salt pond. **Pros:** homey atmosphere; great breakfasts; breathtaking view from deck. **Cons:** noise from nearby power substation; some uphill walks; basic amenities. ✉ *Enighed* ✍ *Box 37, Cruz Bay 00831* ☎ *340/779–4731* ⊕ *www.gardenbythesea.com* ↘ *3 rooms* ♿ *In-room: a/c, no safe, no TV, Wi-Fi* ▭ *No credit cards* ⦿ *Breakfast.*

$–$$
RENTAL
🏨 **Serendip.** This complex offers modern apartments on lush grounds with lovely views and makes a great pick for a budget stay in a residential locale. **Pros:** comfortable accommodations; good views; nice neighborhood. **Cons:** no beach; need car to get around; nearby construction. ✉ *Off Rte. 104, Enighed* ✍ *Box 273, Cruz Bay 00831* ☎ *340/776– 6646 or 888/800–6445* ⊕ *www.serendipstjohn.com* ↘ *10 apartments* ♿ *In-room: a/c, no safe, kitchen, Wi-Fi. In-hotel: pool, laundry facilities* ⦿ *No meals.*

27

Caneel Bay Resort.

$$$$
RESORT

🏨 **Westin St. John Resort and Villas.** The island's largest resort provides a nice beachfront location and enough activities to keep you busy. **Pros:** entertaining children's programs; pretty pool area; many activities. **Cons:** mediocre beach; long walk to some parts of the resort; need car to get around. ✉ *Rte. 104, Great Cruz Bay* 🕮 *Box 8310, Cruz Bay 00831* 🖀 *340/693–8000 or 800/808–5020* ⊕ *www.westinresortstjohn. com* ⇆ *175 rooms, 146 villas* ⚭ *In-room: a/c, kitchen (some), refrigerator, Internet, Wi-Fi. In-hotel: restaurants, tennis courts, pool, gym, beach, water sports, children's programs* ❒ *No meals.*

NORTH SHORE

$$$$
RESORT
Fodor's Choice
★

🏨 **Caneel Bay Resort.** Well-heeled honeymooners, couples celebrating anniversaries, and extended families all enjoy Caneel Bay Resort's laid-back luxury. **Pros:** lovely beaches; gorgeous rooms; lots of amenities. **Cons:** staff can be chilly; isolated location; rates are pricey. ✉ *Rte. 20, Caneel Bay* 🕮 *Box 720, Cruz Bay 00831* 🖀 *340/776–6111 or 888/767–3966* ⊕ *www.caneelbay.com* ⇆ *166 rooms* ⚭ *In-room: a/c, no safe, no TV, Wi-Fi. In-hotel: restaurants, tennis courts, pool, spa, beach, water sports, children's programs, business center* ❒ *Breakfast.*

$
RESORT

🏨 **Harmony Studios.** An ecologically correct environment is one of the draws at these condominium-style units that sit hillside at Maho Bay. **Pros:** convivial atmosphere; near beach; comfortable units. **Cons:** lots of stairs; no air-conditioning; need car to get around. ✉ *Maho Bay* 🕮 *Box 310, Cruz Bay 00831* 🖀 *340/776–6240 or 800/392–9004* ⊕ *www. maho.org* ⇆ *12 units* ⚭ *In-room: no a/c, no safe, kitchen, no TV. In-hotel: restaurant, beach, water sports, children's programs, business center* ❒ *No meals.*

¢
RESORT
☺
Fodor'sChoice
★

🏨 **Maho Bay Camps.** Tucked into the greenery along the island's North Shore, eco-conscious Maho Bay Camps attracts a sociable crowd that likes to explore the undersea world off the campground's beach or attend on-site seminars. **Pros:** friendly atmosphere; tasty food; real eco-resort. **Cons:** many stairs to climb; can be buggy; need a car to get around. ⊠ *Maho Bay* 🐚 *Box 310, Cruz Bay 00831* ☎ *340/776–6240 or 800/392–9004* ⊕ *www.maho.org* 🛏 *114 tent cottages with shared baths* ♿ *In-room: no a/c, no safe, no TV. In-hotel: restaurant, beach, water sports, children's programs, business center* ⦿ *No meals.*

CORAL BAY AND ENVIRONS

$$$–$$$$
RENTAL

🏨 **Estate Zootenvaal.** Comfortable and casual, this small cottage colony gives you the perfect place to relax. **Pros:** quiet beach; private; near restaurants. **Cons:** some traffic noise; no air-conditioning. ⊠ *Rte. 10, Hurricane Hole, Zootenvaal* ☎ *340/776–6321* ⊕ *www.estatezootenvaal.com* 🛏 *4 units* ♿ *In-room: no a/c, no safe (some), kitchen, no TV (some). In-hotel: beach* ⊟ *No credit cards* ⦿ *No meals.*

27

NIGHTLIFE

St. John isn't the place to go for glitter and all-night partying. Still, after-hours Cruz Bay can be a lively little town in which to dine, drink, dance, chat, or flirt. Notices posted on the bulletin board outside the Connections telephone center—up the street from the ferry dock in Cruz Bay—or listings in the island's two small newspapers (the *St. John Sun Times* and *Tradewinds*) will keep you apprised of special events, comedy nights, movies, and the like.

CRUZ BAY

Fred's. There's calypso and reggae on Friday night at this popular nightspot. ⊠ *King St., Cruz Bay* ☎ *340/776–6363.*

Woody's. Young folks like to gather here, where sidewalk tables provide a close-up view of Cruz Bay's action. ⊠ *Near ferry dock and First Bank, Cruz Bay* ☎ *340/779–4625.*

Zozo's Ristorante. After a sunset drink at this restaurant, which is up the hill from Cruz Bay, you can stroll around town (much is clustered around the small waterfront park). Many of the young people from the U.S. mainland who live and work on St. John will be out sipping and socializing, too. ⊠ *Gallows Point Resort, Bay St., Cruz Bay* ☎ *340/693–9200.*

Maho Bay Camps & Estate Concordia Preserve.

CORAL BAY AND ENVIRONS

Island Blues. As its name implies, this is the hot place to go for music at the eastern end of the island. ⊠ *Rte. 107, Coral Bay* ☎ *340/776–6800.*

Skinny Legs Bar and Restaurant. On the far side of the island, landlubbers and old salts listen to music and swap stories at this popular casual restaurant and bar. ⊠ *Rte. 10, Coral Bay* ☎ *340/779–4982.*

FREE PARKING

Cruz Bay's parking problem is maddening. Your best bet is to rent a car from a company that allows you to park in their lot. Make sure you ask before you sign on the dotted line if you plan to spend time in Cruz Bay.

SHOPPING

CRUZ BAY

Luxury goods and handicrafts can be found on St. John. Most shops carry a little of this and a bit of that, so it pays to poke around. The Cruz Bay shopping district runs from **Wharfside Village,** just around the corner from the ferry dock, to **Mongoose Junction,** an inviting shopping center on North Shore Road. (The name of this upscale shopping mall, by the way, is a holdover from a time when those furry island creatures gathered at a nearby garbage bin.) Out on Route 104 stop in at the **Marketplace** to explore its gift and crafts shops. On St. John, store hours run from 9 or 10 to 5 or 6. Wharfside Village and Mongoose Junction shops in Cruz Bay are often open into the evening.

ART

Bajo el Sol. Bajo del Sol sells works by owner Livy Hitchcock, plus pieces from a roster of the island's best artists. Shop for oil and acrylics, sculptures, and ceramics. ✉ *Mongoose Junction Shopping Center, North Shore Rd., Cruz Bay* ☎ *340/693–7070.*

Caravan Gallery. This gallery owned by Radha Speer sells unusual jewelry that Radha has traveled the world to find. And the more you look, the more you see—wood carvings, tribal art, and masks for sale cover the walls and tables, making this a great place to browse. ✉ *Mongoose Junction Shopping Center, North Shore Rd., Cruz Bay* ☎ *340/779–4566.*

Coconut Coast Studios. This waterside shop is a five-minute walk from the center of Cruz Bay and showcases the work of Elaine Estern. She specializes in undersea scenes. ✉ *Frank Bay, Cruz Bay* ☎ *340/776–6944.*

BOOKS

National Park Headquarters Bookstore. The bookshop at Virgin Islands National Park Headquarters sells several good histories of St. John, including *St. John Back Time*, by Ruth Hull Low and Rafael Lito Valls, and, for intrepid explorers, longtime resident Pam Gaffin's *Feet, Fins and Four-Wheel Drive*. ✉ *Cruz Bay* ☎ *340/776–6201.*

CLOTHING

Big Planet Adventure Outfitters. You knew when you arrived that someplace on St. John would cater to the outdoor enthusiasts who hike up and down the island's trails. This store sells flip-flops and Reef footwear, along with colorful and durable cotton clothing and accessories by Billabong. The store also sells children's clothes. ✉ *Mongoose Junction Shopping Center, North Shore Rd., Cruz Bay* ☎ *340/776–6638.*

Bougainvillea Boutique. This store is your destination if you want to look as if you've stepped out of the pages of the resort-wear spread in an upscale travel magazine. Owner Susan Stair carries very chic men's and women's resort wear, straw hats, leather handbags, and fine gifts. ✉ *Mongoose Junction Shopping Center, North Shore Rd., Cruz Bay* ☎ *340/693–7190.*

St. John Editions. This boutique specializes in swimsuits and nifty cotton dresses that go from beach to dinner with a change of shoes and accessories. Owner Molly Soper also carries attractive straw hats and inexpensive jewelry. ✉ *North Shore Rd., Cruz Bay* ☎ *340/693–8444.*

FOOD

If you're renting a villa, condo, or cottage and doing your own cooking, there are several good places to shop for food; just be aware that prices are much higher than those at home.

★ **Starfish Market.** The island's largest store usually has the best selection of meat, fish, and produce. ✉ *The Marketplace, Rte. 104, Cruz Bay* ☎ *340/779–4949.*

27

GIFTS

Bamboula. This multicultural boutique carries unusual housewares, rugs, bedspreads, accessories, and men's and women's clothes and shoes that owner Jo Sterling has found on her world travels. ⊠ *Mongoose Junction Shopping Center, North Shore Rd., Cruz Bay* ☎ *340/693–8699.*

Best of Both Worlds. The store sells and displays the pricey metal sculptures and attractive artworks that hang from its walls; the nicest are small glass decorations shaped like mermaids and sea horses. ⊠ *Mongoose Junction Shopping Center, North Shore Rd., Cruz Bay* ☎ *340/693–7005.*

Donald Schnell Studio. You'll find unusual handblown glass, wind chimes, kaleidoscopes, fanciful fountains, and more in addition to pottery bowls and more here. Your purchases can be shipped worldwide. ⊠ *Amore Center, Rte. 104 near roundabout, Cruz Bay* ☎ *340/776–6420.*

Every Ting. As its name implies, the store at Gallows Point Resort has a bit of this and a bit of that. Shop for Caribbean books and CDs, picture frames decorated with shells, and T-shirts with tropical motifs. Residents and visitors also drop by to have a cup of coffee. ⊠ *Gallows Point Resort, Bay St., Cruz Bay* ☎ *340/693–5820.*

Fabric Mill. Fabric Mill has a good selection of women's clothing in tropical brights, as well as lingerie, sandals, and batik wraps. Or take home several yards of colorful batik fabric and make your own dress. ⊠ *Mongoose Junction Shopping Center, North Shore Rd., Cruz Bay* ☎ *340/776–6194.*

Nest and Company. This small shop carries perfect take-home gifts in colors that reflect the sea. Shop here for soaps in tropical scents, dinnerware, and much more. ⊠ *Marketplace Shopping Center, Rte. 108, Cruz Bay* ☎ *340/715–2552.*

★ **Pink Papaya.** Pink Papaya is where you can find the well-known work of longtime Virgin Islands resident M.L. Etre, plus a huge collection of one-of-a-kind gifts, including bright tableware, unusual trays, and unique tropical jewelry. ⊠ *Lemon Tree Mall, King St., Cruz Bay* ☎ *340/693–8535.*

JEWELRY

Free Bird Creations. This is your on-island destination for special handcrafted jewelry—earrings, bracelets, pendants, chains—as well as a good selection of water-resistant watches for your beach excursions. ⊠ *Dockside Mall, next to ferry dock, Cruz Bay* ☎ *340/693–8625.*

Jewels. A branch of the St. Thomas store, Jewels carries emeralds, diamonds, and other jewels in attractive yellow- and white-gold settings, as well as strings of creamy pearls, watches, and other designer jewelry. ⊠ *Mongoose Junction Shopping Center, North Shore Rd., Cruz Bay* ☎ *340/776–6007.*

R&I Patton Goldsmiths. This store is owned by Rudy and Irene Patton, who design most of the lovely silver and gold jewelry on display. The rest comes from various designer friends. Sea fans (those large, lacy plants that sway with the ocean's currents) in filigreed silver, starfish and hibiscus pendants in silver or gold, and gold sand-dollar-shape charms and earrings are choice selections. ⊠ *Mongoose Junction, North Shore Rd., Cruz Bay* ☎ *340/776–6548.*

Verace. This store is filled with jewelry from such well-known designers as Toby Pomeroy and Patrick Murphy. Murphy's stunning gold sailboats with gems for hulls will catch your attention. ⊠ *Wharfside Village, Strand St., Cruz Bay* ☎ *340/693–7599.*

CORAL BAY AND ENVIRONS

At the island's other end, there are a few stores—selling clothes, jewelry, and artwork—here and there from the village of **Coral Bay** to the small complex at **Shipwreck Landing.**

CLOTHING

Jolly Dog. Jolly Dog is a place where you can stock up on the stuff you forgot to pack. Sarongs in cotton and rayon, beach towels with tropical motifs, and hats and T-shirts sporting the "Jolly Dog" logo fill the shelves. ⊠ *Shipwreck Landing, Rte. 107, Sanders Bay* ☎ *340/693–5333* ⊠ *Skinny Legs Shopping Complex, Rte. 10, Coral Bay* ☎ *340/693–5900.*

Sloop Jones. This store is worth the trip all the way out to the island's east end to shop for made-on-the-premises clothing and pillows, in fabrics splashed with tropical colors. Fabrics are in cotton and linen, and are supremely comfortable. ⊠ *Off Rte. 10, East End* ☎ *340/779–4001.*

FOOD

Lily's Gourmet Market. This small store in Coral Bay carries the basics plus meat, fish, and produce. ⊠ *Cocoloba Shopping Center, Rte. 107, Coral Bay* ☎ *340/777–3335.*

Love City Mini Mart. The store may not look like much, but it's one of the very few places to shop in Coral Bay and has a surprising selection. ⊠ *Off Rte. 107, Coral Bay* ☎ *340/693–5790.*

GIFTS

Awl Made Here. This store on the East End specializes in locally made leather goods. Owner Tracey Keating creates lovely journal covers, wallets, and belts, but she also does special orders. The store carries other locally made items such as imaginative jewelry and hand-painted wineglasses. ⊠ *Skinny Legs Shopping Complex, Rte. 10, Coral Bay* ☎ *340/777–5757.*

Mumbo Jumbo. With what may be the best prices in St. John, Mumbo Jumbo carries everything from tropical clothing to stuffed sea creatures in a cozy little shop. ⊠ *Skinny Legs Shopping Complex, Rte. 10, Coral Bay* ☎ *340/779–4277.*

27

SPORTS AND ACTIVITIES

BOATING AND SAILING

If you're staying at a hotel or campground, your activities desk will usually be able to help you arrange a sailing excursion aboard a nearby boat. Most day sails leaving Cruz Bay head out along St. John's north coast. Those that depart from Coral Bay might drop anchor at some remote cay off the island's east end or even in the nearby British Virgin Islands. Your trip usually includes lunch, beverages, and at least one snorkeling stop. Keep in mind that inclement weather could interfere with your plans, though most boats will still go out if rain isn't too heavy.

★ **St. John Concierge Service** (✉ *Across from post office, Cruz Bay* ☎ *340/777–2665 or 800/808–6025* ⊕ *www.stjohnconciergeservice.com*). The capable staff can find a charter sail or power boat that fits your style and pocketbook. The company also books fishing and scuba trips.

For a speedier trip to the cays and remote beaches off St. John, you can rent a powerboat from **Ocean Runner** (✉ *On waterfront, Cruz Bay* ☎ *340/693–8809* ⊕ *www.oceanrunnerusvi.com*). The company rents one- and two-engine boats for $375 to $705 per day. Gas and oil will run you $100 to $300 a day extra, depending on how far you're going. It's a good idea to have some skill with powerboats for this self-drive adventure, but if you don't, you can hire a boat with a captain for $430 to $705 a day.

Even novice sailors can take off in a small sailboat from Cruz Bay Beach with **Sail Safaris** (✉ *On waterfront, Cruz Bay* ☎ *340/626–8181 or 866/820–6906* ⊕ *www.sailsafaris.net*) to one of the small islands off St. John. Guided half-day tours on small or large boats start at $70 per person. Rentals run $47 per hour.

DIVING AND SNORKELING

Although just about every beach has nice snorkeling—Trunk Bay, Cinnamon Bay, and Waterlemon Cay at Leinster Bay get the most praise—you need a boat to head out to the more remote snorkeling locations and the best scuba spots. Sign on with any of the island's water-sports operators to get to spots farther from St. John. If you use the one at your hotel, just stroll down to the dock to hop aboard. Their boats will take you to hot spots between St. John and St. Thomas, including the tunnels at **Thatch Cay,** the ledges at **Congo Cay,** and the wreck of the *General Rogers.* Dive off St. John at **Stephens Cay,** a short boat ride out of Cruz Bay, where fish swim around the reefs as you float downward. At **Devers Bay,** on St. John's south shore, fish dart about in colorful schools. **Carval Rock,** shaped like an old-time ship, has gorgeous rock formations, coral gardens, and lots of fish. It can be too rough here in winter, though. Count on paying $75 for a one-tank dive and $90 for a two-tank dive. Rates include equipment and a tour. If you've never dived before, try an introductory course, called a resort course. Or if certification is in your vacation plans, the island's dive shops can help you get your card.

Cruz Bay Watersports (✉ *Lumberyard Shopping Complex, Cruz Bay* ☎ *340/776–6234* ✉ *Westin St. John, Great Cruz Bay* ☎ *340/776–6234* ⊕ *www.divestjohn.com*) actually has two locations: in Cruz Bay at the Lumberyard Shopping Complex and at the Westin St. John Resort. Owners Marcus and Patty Johnston offer regular reef, wreck, and night dives and USVI and BVI snorkel tours. The company holds both PADI five-star-facility and NAUI-Dream-Resort status.

Low Key Watersports (⊠ *Wharfside Village, Strand St., Cruz Bay* ☎ *340/693–8999 or 800/835–7718* ⊕ *www.divelowkey.com*) offers two-tank dives and specialty courses. It's certified as a PADI five-star training facility.

FISHING

Well-kept charter boats—approved by the U.S. Coast Guard—head out to the north and south drops or troll along the inshore reefs, depending on the season and what's biting. The captains usually provide bait, drinks, and lunch, but you need to bring your own hat and sunscreen. Fishing charters run about $1,400 for the full day trip.

Captain Byron Oliver (☎ *340/693–8339*) takes you out to the north and south drops.

An excellent choice for fishing charters is **Captain Rob Richards** (⊠ *Westin, St. John, Great Bay* ☎ *340/513–0389* ⊕ *www.sportfishingstjohn.com*), who runs the 32-foot center console *Mixed Bag I* and 40-foot Luhrs Express *Mixed Bag II*, and who enjoys beginners—especially kids—as well as fishing with experienced anglers. He will pick up parties in St. Thomas even though he is based in St. John.

GUIDED TOURS

In St. John, taxi drivers provide tours of the island, making stops at various sites, including Trunk Bay and Annaberg Plantation. Prices run around $15 a person. The taxi drivers congregate near the ferry in Cruz Bay. The dispatcher will find you a driver for your tour. Along with providing trail maps and brochures about Virgin Islands National Park, the park service also gives several guided tours on- and offshore. Some are offered only during particular times of the year, and some require reservations. For more information, contact the **V.I. National Park Visitors Center** (⊠ *Cruz Bay* ☎ *340/776–6201* ⊕ *www.nps.gov/viis*).

HIKING

Although it's fun to go hiking with a Virgin Islands National Park guide, don't be afraid to head out on your own. To find a hike that suits your ability, stop by the park's visitor center in Cruz Bay and pick up the free trail guide; it details points of interest, trail lengths, and estimated hiking times, as well as any dangers you might encounter. Although the park staff recommends long pants to protect against thorns and insects, most people hike in shorts because it can get very hot. Wear sturdy shoes or hiking boots even if you're hiking to the beach. Don't forget to bring water and insect repellent.

Fodor's Choice
★ The **Virgin Islands National Park** (⊠ *1300 Cruz Bay Creek, St. John* ☎ *340/776–6201* ⊕ *www.nps.gov/viis*) maintains more than 20 trails on the north and south shores and offers guided hikes along popular routes. A full-day trip to Reef Bay is a must; it's an easy hike through lush and dry forest, past the ruins of an old plantation, and to a sugar factory adjacent to the beach. It can be a bit arduous for young kids, however. Take the $6 safari bus from the park's visitor center to the trailhead, where you can meet a ranger who'll serve as your guide. The park provides a boat ride back to Cruz Bay for $15 to save you the walk back up the mountain. The schedule changes from season to season; call for times and reservations, which are essential.

27

HORSEBACK RIDING

Clip-clop along the island's byways for a slower-pace tour of St. John. **Carolina Corral** (☎ 340/693–5778) offers horseback trips and wagon rides down scenic roads with owner Dana Barlett. She has a way with horses and calms even the most novice riders. Rates start at $65 for a one-hour ride.

SEA KAYAKING

Poke around crystal bays and explore undersea life from a sea kayak. Rates run about $110 for a full day in a double kayak. Tours start at $65 for a half day.

On the Cruz Bay side of the island, **Arawak Expeditions** (✉ *Mongoose Juction Shopping Center, North Shore Rd., Cruz Bay* ☎ *340/693–8312 or 800/238–8687* ⊕ *www.arawakexp.com*) has professional guides who use traditional and sit-on-top kayaks to ply coastal waters. The company also rents single and double kayaks, so you can head independently to nearby islands such as Stephen's Cay.

Explore Coral Bay Harbor and Hurricane Hole on the eastern end of the island in a sea kayak from **Crabby's Watersports** (✉ *Rte. 107, next to Cocoloba shopping center, Coral Bay* ☎ *340/714–2415* ⊕ *www. crabbyswatersports.com*). If you don't want to paddle into the wind to get out of Coral Bay Harbor, the staff will drop you off in Hurricane Hole so you can paddle downwind back to Coral Bay. Crabby's also rents snorkel gear, beach chairs, umbrellas, coolers, and floats.

Hidden Reef EcoTours (✉ *Rte. 10, Round Bay* ☎ *340/513–9613 or 877/ 529–2575* ⊕ *www.kayaksj.com*) offers two- and three-hour, full-day and full-moon kayak tours through Coral Reef National Monument and its environs. This pristine area is home to coral reefs, mangroves, and lush sea-grass beds filled with marine life.

WINDSURFING

Steady breezes and expert instruction make learning to windsurf a snap. Try **Cinnamon Bay Campground** (✉ *Rte. 20, Cinnamon Bay* ☎ *340/693– 5902 or 340/626–4769*), where rentals are $50 to $100 per hour. Lessons are available right at the waterfront; just look for the Windsurfers stacked up on the beach. The cost for a one-hour lesson starts at $60, plus the cost of the board rental. You can also rent kayaks, stand-up paddle boards, Boogie boards, small sailboats, and surfboards.

ST. CROIX

History is so popular in St. Croix that planes are filled with Danish visitors who, like other vacationers, come to sun at the island's powdery beaches, enjoy pampering at the hotels, and dine at interesting restaurants, but mainly wish to explore the island's colonial history.

Until 1917 Denmark owned St. Croix and her sister Virgin Islands, an aspect of the island's past that is reflected in street names in the main towns of Christiansted and Frederiksted as well as surnames of many island residents. Those early Danish settlers, as well as those from other European nations, left behind slews of 18th- and 19th-century ruins, all of them worked by slaves brought over on ships from Africa, their descendants, and white indentured servants lured to St. Croix to pay off their debt to society. Some of the ruins—such as the Christiansted National Historic Site, Whim Plantation, the ruins at St. George Village Botanical Garden, and those at Estate Mount Washington and Judith's Fancy—are open for easy exploration. Others are on private land, but a drive around the island reveals the ruins of 100 plantations here and there on St. Croix's 84 square mi (218 square km). Their windmills, greathouses, and factories are all that's left of the 224 plantations that once grew sugarcane, tobacco, and other agricultural products at the height of the island's plantation glory.

The downturn began in 1801 when the British occupied the island. The demise of the slave trade in 1803, another British occupation from 1807 to 1815, droughts, the development of the sugar beet industry in Europe, political upheaval, and a depression sent the island into a downward spiral.

St. Croix never recovered from these blows. The end of slavery in 1848, followed by labor riots, fires, hurricanes, and an earthquake during the last half of the 19th century, brought what was left of the island's economy to its knees. The start of prohibition in 1922 called a halt to the island's rum industry, further crippling the economy. The situation remained dire—so bad that President Herbert Hoover called the territory an "effective poorhouse" during a 1931 visit—until the rise of tourism in the late 1950s and 1960s. With tourism came economic improvements coupled with an influx of residents from other Caribbean islands and the mainland, but St. Croix depends partly on industries such as the huge oil refinery outside Frederiksted to provide employment.

Today suburban subdivisions fill the fields where sugarcane once waved in the tropical breeze. Condominium complexes line the beaches along the north coast outside Christiansted. Homes that are more elaborate dot the rolling hillsides. Modern strip malls and shopping centers sit along major roads, and it's as easy to find a McDonald's as it is Caribbean fare.

Although St. Croix sits definitely in the 21st century, with only a little effort you can easily step back into the island's past.

27

St. Croix

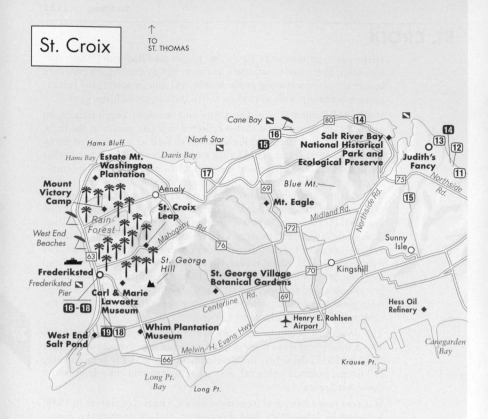

↑
TO
ST. THOMAS

Cane Bay

Hams Bluff

Hams Bay

Estate Mt. Washington Plantation

North Star

Davis Bay

Analy

80 14

16

15

Salt River Bay National Historical Park and Ecological Preserve

14

13 12

Judith's Fancy

11

Mount Victory Camp

Rain Forest

West End Beaches

St. Croix Leap

17

69

Blue Mt.—

♦ **Mt. Eagle**

Northside Rd.

75

Northside Rd.

15

Frederiksted

Frederiksted Pier

16 - 18

63

Mahogany Rd.

76

St. George Hill

72

Midland Rd.

70 Kingshill

Sunny Isle

Hess Oil Refinery ♦

Carl & Marie Lawaetz Museum

St. George Village Botanical Gardens

Centerline Rd.

69

West End Salt Pond

19 18

Whim Plantation Museum

Henry E. Rohlsen Airport

Canegarden Bay

Melvin H. Evans Hwy

66

Krause Pt.

Long Pt. Bay

Long Pt.

Canegarden Bay

KEY

⌐ *Beaches*

◣ *Dive Sites*

🚢 *Cruise Ship Terminal*

🌴 *Rain Forest*

1 *Restaurants*

1 *Hotels*

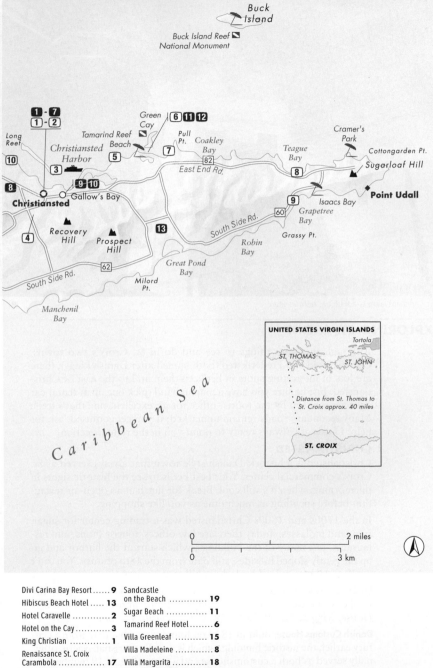

Fort Christiansvaern is a national historic site.

EXPLORING ST. CROIX

Although there are things to see and do in St. Croix's two towns, Christiansted and Frederiksted (both named after Danish kings), there are lots of interesting spots in between them and to the east of Christiansted. Just be sure you have a map in hand (pick one up at rental-car agencies, or stop by the tourist office for an excellent one that's free). Many secondary roads remain unmarked; if you get confused, ask for help. Locals are always ready to point you in the right direction.

CHRISTIANSTED

Christiansted is a historic Danish-style town that always served as St. Croix's commercial center. Your best bet is to see the historic sights in the morning, when it's still cool. Break for lunch at an open-air restaurant before spending as much time as you like shopping.

In the 1700s and 1800s Christiansted was a trading center for sugar, rum, and molasses. Today there are law offices, tourist shops, and restaurants, but many of the buildings, which start at the harbor and go up the gently sloped hillsides, still date from the 18th century. You can't get lost. All streets lead back downhill to the water.

St. Croix Visitor Center. If you want some friendly advice, stop by the weekdays between 8 and 5 for maps and brochures. ⊠ *Government House, King St.* ☎ *340/773–1404* ⊕ *www.visitusvi.com.*

Danish Customs House. Built in 1830 on foundations that date from a century earlier, the historic building, which is near Ft. Christiansvaern, originally served as both a customshouse and a post office. In 1926 it became the Christiansted Library, and it's been a national park facility since 1972.

CLOSE UP

Turtles on St. Croix

Like creatures from the prehistoric past, green, leatherback, and hawksbill turtles crawl ashore during the annual April-to-November turtle nesting season to lay their eggs. They return from their life at sea every two to seven years to the beach where they were born. Since turtles can live for up to 100 years, they may return many times to nest in St. Croix.

The leatherbacks like Sandy Point National Wildlife Refuge and other spots on St. Croix's western end, but the hawksbills prefer Buck Island and the East End. Green turtles are also found primarily on the East End.

All are endangered species that face numerous predators, some natural, some the result of the human presence. Particularly in the Frederiksted area, dogs and cats prey on the nests and eat the hatchlings. Occasionally

a dog will attack a turtle about to lay its eggs, and cats train their kittens to hunt at turtle nests, creating successive generations of turtle-egg hunters. In addition, turtles have often been hit by fast-moving boats that leave large slices in their shells if they don't kill them outright.

The leatherbacks are the subject of a project by the international group Earthwatch. Each summer teams arrive at Sandy Point National Wildlife Refuge to ensure that poachers, both natural and human, don't attack the turtles as they crawl up the beach. The teams also relocate nests that are laid in areas prone to erosion. When the eggs hatch, teams stand by to make sure the turtles make it safely to the sea, and scientists tag them so they can monitor their return to St. Croix.

27

It's closed to the public, but the sweeping front steps make a nice place to take a break. ⊠ *King St.* ☎ *340/773–1460* ⊕ *www.nps.gov/chri.*

🕐 **Ft. Christiansvaern.** The large yellow fortress dominates the waterfront.
Fodor'sChoice Because it's so easy to spot, it makes a good place to begin a walking
★ tour. In 1749 the Danish built the fort to protect the harbor, but the structure was repeatedly damaged by hurricane-force winds and had to be partially rebuilt in 1771. It's now a national historic site, the best preserved of the few remaining Danish-built forts in the Virgin Islands. The park's visitor center is here. Rangers are on hand to answer questions. ⊠ *Hospital St.* ☎ *340/773–1460* ⊕ *www.nps.gov/chri* 🎫 *$3 (includes Steeple Bldg.* 🕐 *Weekdays 8–4:30, weekends 9–4:30.*

Government House. One of the town's most elegant structures was built as a home for a Danish merchant in 1747. Today it houses offices. If you're here weekdays from 8 to 4:30, slip into the peaceful inner courtyard to admire the still pools and gardens. A sweeping staircase leads you to a second-story ballroom, still used for official government functions. ⊠ *King St.* ☎ *340/773–1404.*

Post Office Building. Built in 1749, Christiansted's former post office was once the Danish West India & Guinea Company warehouse. It now serves as the park's administrative building. ⊠ *Church St.*

Scale House. Constructed in 1856, this was once the spot where goods passing through the port were weighed and inspected. Park staffers now sell a good selection of books about St. Croix history and its flora and fauna. ⊠ *King St.* ☎ *340/773–1460* ⊕ *www.nps.gov/chri* ☉ *Weekdays 8–4:30, weekends 9–4:30.*

Steeple Building. Built by the Danes in 1753, the former church was the first Danish Lutheran church on St. Croix. It's now a museum containing exhibits on the island's Indian inhabitants. It's worth the short walk to see the building's collection of archaeological artifacts, displays on plantation life, and exhibits on the architectural development of Christiansted, the early history of the church, and Alexander Hamilton, the first secretary of the U.S. Treasury, who grew up in St. Croix. Hours are irregular, so ask at the visitor center. ⊠ *Church St.* ☎ *340/773–1460* ⊠ *$3 (includes Ft. Christiansvaern).*

EAST END

An easy drive (roads are flat and well marked) to St. Croix's eastern end takes you through some choice real estate. Ruins of old sugar estates dot the landscape. You can make the entire loop on the road that circles the island in about an hour, a good way to end the day. If you want to spend a full day exploring, you can find some nice beaches and easy walks with places to stop for lunch.

★ **Buck Island Reef National Monument.** Buck Island has pristine beaches that are just right for sunbathing, but there's also some shade for those who don't want to fry. The snorkeling trail set in the reef allows close-up study of coral formations and tropical fish. Overly warm seawater temperatures have led to a condition called coral bleaching that has killed some of the coral. The reefs are starting to recover, but how long it will take is anyone's guess. There's an easy hiking trail to the island's highest point, where you can be rewarded for your efforts by spectacular views of St. John. Charter-boat trips leave daily from the Christiansted waterfront or from Green Cay Marina, about 2 mi (3 km) east of Christiansted. Check with your hotel for recommendations. ⊠ *Off North Shore of St. Croix* ☎ *340/773–1460* ⊕ *www.nps.gov/buis.*

Point Udall. This rocky promontory, the easternmost point in the United States, is about a half-hour drive from Christiansted. A paved road takes you to an overlook with glorious views. More adventurous folks can hike down to the pristine beach below. On the way back, look for the castle, an enormous mansion that can only be described as a cross between a Moorish mosque and the Taj Mahal. It was built by an extravagant recluse known only as the Contessa. Point Udall is sometimes a popular spot for thieves. Residents advise taking your valuables with you and leaving your car unlocked so they won't break into it to look inside. ⊠ *Rte. 82, Et Stykkeland.*

MID ISLAND

A drive through the countryside between these two towns will take you past ruins of old plantations, many bearing whimsical names (Morningstar, Solitude, Upper Love) bestowed by early owners. The traffic moves quickly—by island standards—on the main roads, but you can pause and poke around if you head down some side lanes. It's easy to find your way west, but driving from north to south requires good navigation. Don't leave your hotel without a map. Allow an entire day for this trip, so you'll have enough time for a swim at a north-shore beach. Although you can find lots of casual eateries on the main roads, pick up a picnic lunch if you plan to head off the beaten path.

Cruzan Rum Distillery. A tour of the company's factory, established in 1760, culminates in a tasting of its products, all sold here at bargain prices. It's worth a stop to look at the distillery's charming old buildings even if you're not a rum connoisseur. ☒ *West Airport Rd., Estate Diamond* ☎ *340/692–2280* ⊕ *www.cruzanrum.com* ☒ *$5* ☉ *Weekdays 9–4.*

Fodor'sChoice **St. George Village Botanical Garden.** At this 17-acre estate, fragrant flora
★ grows amid the ruins of a 19th-century sugarcane plantation village. There are miniature versions of each ecosystem on St. Croix, from a semiarid cactus grove to a verdant rain forest. The small museum is also well worth a visit. ☒ *Rte. 70, turn north at sign, St. George* ☎ *340/692–2874* ⊕ *www.sgvbg.org* ☒ *$8* ☉ *Daily 9–5.*

☾ **Whim Plantation Museum.** The lovingly restored estate, with a windmill,
Fodor'sChoice cook house, and other buildings, will give you a sense of what life was
★ like on St. Croix's sugar plantations in the 1800s. The oval-shape greathouse has high ceilings and antique furniture and utensils. Notice its fresh, airy atmosphere—the waterless stone moat around the greathouse was used not for defense but for gathering cooling air. If you have kids, the grounds are the perfect place for them to run around, perhaps while you browse in the museum gift shop. It's just outside of Frederiksted. ☒ *Rte. 70, Estate Whim* ☎ *340/772–0598* ⊕ *www.stcroixlandmarks. com* ☒ *$10* ☉ *Mon.–Sat. 10–4.*

FREDERIKSTED AND ENVIRONS

St. Croix's second-largest town, Frederiksted, was founded in 1751. Whereas Christiansted is noted for its Danish buildings, Frederiksted is better known for its Victorian architecture. One long cruise-ship pier juts into the sparkling sea. It's the perfect place to start a tour of this quaint city. A stroll around its historic sights will take you no more than an hour. Allow a little more time if you want to duck into the few small shops.

Caribbean Museum Center for the Arts. Sitting across from the waterfront in a historic building, this small museum hosts an always-changing roster of exhibits. Many are cutting-edge multimedia efforts that you might be surprised to find in such an out-of-the-way location. The openings are popular events. ☒ *10 Strand St.* ☎ *340/772–2622* ⊕ *www.cmcarts. org* ☒ *Free* ☉ *Tues.–Sat. (and any cruise-ship day) 10–4.*

Estate Mount Washington Plantation. Several years ago, while surveying the property, the owners discovered the ruins of a sugar plantation beneath the rain-forest brush. The grounds have since been cleared and opened to the public. You can take a self-guided walking tour of the mill, the rum factory, and other ruins. ☒ *Rte. 63, Mount Washington* ☉ *Daily dawn–dusk.*

☾ **Fort Frederik.** On July 3, 1848, 8,000 slaves marched on this fort to demand their freedom. Danish governor Peter von Scholten, fearing they would burn the town to the ground, stood up in his carriage parked in front of the fort and granted their wish. The fort, completed in 1760, houses an art gallery and a number of interesting historical

27

exhibits, including some focusing on the 1848 Emancipation and the 1917 transfer of the Virgin Islands from Denmark to the United States. It's within earshot of the Frederiksted Visitor Center. ⊠ *Waterfront* ☎ *340/772–2021* ⌦ *$3* ☉ *Weekdays (and any cruise-ship day) 8:30–4.*

Frederiksted Visitor Center. Across from the pier, Frederiksted's visitor center has brochures from numerous St. Croix businesses, as well as a few exhibits about the island. You can stop in weekdays from 8 to 5. ⊠ *321 King St., Frederiksted Mall* ☎ *340/772–0357* ☉ *Weekdays 8–5.*

Fodor's Choice
★

Lawaetz Museum. For a trip back in time, tour this circa-1750 farm. Owned by the prominent Lawaetz family since 1896, just after Carl Lawaetz arrived from Denmark, the lovely two-story house is in a valley at La Grange. A Lawaetz family member shows you the four-poster mahogany bed Carl and Marie shared, the china Marie painted, the family portraits, and the fruit trees that fed the family for several generations. Initially a sugar plantation, it was subsequently used to raise cattle and grow produce. ⊠ *Rte. 76, Mahogany Rd., Estate Little La Grange* ☎ *340/772–1539* ⊕ *www.stcroixlandmarks.com* ⌦ *$10* ☉ *Tues., Thurs., Sat. (and any cruise-ship day) 10–4.*

St. Croix Leap. This workshop sits in the heart of the rain forest, about a 15-minute drive from Frederiksted. It sells mirrors, tables, breadboards, and mahogany jewelry boxes crafted by local artisans. ⊠ *Rte. 76, Brooks Hill* ☎ *340/772–0421* ☉ *Weekdays 9–5, Sat. 10–5.*

West End Salt Pond. A bird-watcher's delight, this salt pond attracts a large number of winged creatures, including flamingos. ⊠ *Veteran's Shore Dr., Hesselberg.*

NORTH SHORE

Judith's Fancy. In this upscale neighborhood are the ruins of an old greathouse and tower of the same name, both remnants of a circa-1750 Danish sugar plantation. The "Judith" comes from the first name of a woman buried on the property. From the guardhouse at the neighborhood entrance, follow Hamilton Drive past some of St. Croix's loveliest homes. At the end of Hamilton Drive the road overlooks Salt River Bay, where Christopher Columbus anchored in 1493. On the way back, make a detour left off Hamilton Drive onto Caribe Road for a close look at the ruins. The million-dollar villas are something to behold, too. ⊠ *Turn north onto Rte. 751, off Rte. 75, Judith's Fancy.*

Mt. Eagle. At 1,165 feet, this is St. Croix's highest peak. Leaving Cane Bay and passing North Star Beach, follow the coastal road that dips briefly into a forest; then turn left on Route 69. Just after you make the turn, the pavement is marked with the words "The Beast" and a set of giant paw prints. The hill you're about to climb is the famous Beast of the St. Croix Half Ironman Triathlon, an annual event during which participants must cycle up this intimidating slope. ⊠ *Rte. 69.*

Salt River Bay National Historical Park and Ecological Preserve. This joint national and local park commemorates the area where Christopher Columbus's men skirmished with the Carib Indians in 1493 on his second visit to the New World. The peninsula on the bay's east side is named for the event: Cabo de las Flechas (Cape of the Arrows). Although the park is just in the developing stages, it has several sights

Some of St. Croix's best beaches are on the west end of the island north and south of Frederiksted.

with cultural significance. A ball court, used by the Caribs in religious ceremonies, was discovered at the spot where the taxis park. Take a short hike up the dirt road to the ruins of an old earthen fort for great views of Salt River Bay. The area also encompasses a coastal estuary with the region's largest remaining mangrove forest, a submarine canyon, and several endangered species, including the hawksbill turtle and the roseate tern. A visitor center, open winter only, sits just uphill to the west. The water at the beach can be on the rough side, but it's a nice place for sunning. ⊠ *Rte. 75 to Rte. 80, Salt River* ☎ *340/773–1460* ⊕ *www.nps.gov/sari* ☉ *Nov.–June, Tues.–Thurs. 9–4.*

BEACHES

Remember to remove all your valuables from the car and keep them out of sight when you go swimming. Unfortunately, break-ins have been reported on all three of the U.S. Virgin Islands; most locals recommend leaving your windows down and leaving absolutely nothing in your car.

EAST END

Fodor's Choice ★ **Buck Island.** Part of Buck Island Reef National Monument, this is a must-see for anyone in St. Croix. The beach is beautiful, but its finest treasures are those you can see when you plop off the boat and adjust your mask, snorkel, and fins to swim over colorful coral and darting fish. Don't know how to snorkel? No problem—the boat crew will have you outfitted and in the water in no time. Take care not to step on those black-pointed spiny sea urchins or touch the mustard-color fire coral, which can cause a nasty burn. Most charter-boat trips start with a snorkel over the lovely reef before a stop at the island's beach.

An easy 20-minute hike leads uphill to an overlook for a bird's-eye view of the reef below. Find restrooms at the beach. ⊠ *5 mi (8 km) north of St. Croix* ☎ *340/773–1460* ⊕ *www.nps.gov/buis.*

NORTH SHORE

Cane Bay. On the island's breezy North Shore, Cane Bay does not always have gentle waters, but there are seldom many people around, and the scuba diving and snorkeling are wondrous. You can see elkhorn and brain corals, and less than 200 yards out is the drop-off called Cane Bay Wall. Cane Bay can be an all-day destination. You can rent kayaks and snorkeling and scuba gear at water-sports shops across the road, and a couple of casual restaurants beckon when the sun gets too hot. The beach has no public restrooms. ⊠ *Rte. 80, about 4 mi (6 km) west of Salt River, Cane Bay*

FREDERIKSTED

West End beaches. There are several unnamed beaches along the coast road north of Frederiksted, but it's best if you don't stray too far from civilization. For safety's sake, most vacationers plop down their towel near one of the casual restaurants spread out along Route 63. The beach at the Rainbow Beach Club, a five-minute drive outside Frederiksted, has a bar, a casual restaurant, water sports, and volleyball. If you want to be close to the cruise-ship pier, just stroll on over to the adjacent sandy beach in front of Ft. Frederik. On the way south out of Frederiksted, the stretch near Sandcastle on the Beach hotel is also lovely. ⊠ *Rte. 63, north and south of Frederiksted.*

WHERE TO EAT

Seven flags have flown over St. Croix, and each has left its legacy in the island's cuisine. You can feast on Italian, French, and American dishes; there are even Chinese and Mexican restaurants in Christiansted. Fresh local seafood is plentiful and always good; wahoo, mahimahi, and conch are most popular. Island chefs often add Caribbean twists to familiar dishes. For a true island experience, stop at a local restaurant for goat stew, curried chicken, or fried pork chops. Regardless of where you eat, your meal will be an informal affair. As is the case everywhere in the Caribbean, prices are higher than you'd pay on the mainland. Some restaurants may close for a week or two in September or October, so if you're traveling during these months, it's best to call ahead.

CHRISTIANSTED

$
ECLECTIC
✕ **Avocado Pitt.** Locals gather at this Christiansted waterfront spot for the breakfast and lunch specials as well as for a bit of gossip. Breakfast runs to stick-to-the-ribs dishes like oatmeal and pancakes. Lunches include such dressed-up basics as the Yard Bird on a Bun, a chicken-breast sandwich tarted up with a liberal dose of hot sauce. The yellow-fin tuna sandwich is made from fresh fish and gives a new taste to a standard lunchtime favorite. ⊠ *King Christian Hotel, 59 Kings Wharf* ☎ *340/773–9843* ☉ *No dinner.*

$$
FRENCH
★
✕ **Café Christine.** At this favorite with the professionals who work in downtown Christiansted the presentations are as dazzling as the food. The small menu changes daily, but look for dishes such as

shrimp-and-asparagus salad drizzled with a lovely vinaigrette or a vegetarian plate with quiche, salad, and lentils. Desserts are perfection. If the pear pie topped with chocolate is on the menu, don't hesitate. This tiny restaurant has tables in both the air-conditioned dining room and on the outside porch that overlooks historic buildings. ⊠ *Apothecary Hall Courtyard, 4 Company St.* ☎ *340/713–1500* ▭ *No credit cards* ⊘ *Closed weekends and July–mid-Nov. No dinner.*

$ ✕ **Harvey's.** The dining room is plain, even dowdy, and plastic lace tablecloths constitute the sole attempt at decor—but who cares? The food is delicious. Daily specials, such as mouthwatering goat stew and tender conch in butter, served with big helpings of rice and vegetables, are listed on the blackboard. Genial owner Sarah Harvey takes great pride in her kitchen, bustling out from behind the stove to chat and urge you to eat up. ⊠ *11B Company St.* ☎ *340/773–3433* ⊘ *Closed Sun. No dinner.*

CARIBBEAN

$$$$ ✕ **Kendricks.** The chef at this open-air restaurant—a longtime favorite among locals—conjures up creative contemporary cuisine. To start, try the Alaskan king crab cakes with habanero aioli or the warm chipotle pepper with a garlic and onion soup. Move on to the house specialty: herb-crusted rack of lamb with roasted garlic and fresh thyme sauce. ⊠ *Company St. and King Cross St.* ☎ *340/773–9199* ⊕ *www.kendricksdining.com* ⊘ *Closed Sun. No lunch.*

CONTINENTAL
★

$$$$ ✕ **Restaurant Bacchus.** On the chic side, this restaurant is as notable for its extensive wine list as it is for its food. The menu changes regularly, but often includes favorites such as chopped tuna in a soy-sesame dressing served over crispy wontons. Such entrées as local lobster and fresh fish, steak swimming in mushroom sauce, and the filet mignon with Gorgonzola and a foie gras butter are always popular. For dessert, try the rum-drenched sourdough bread pudding. ⊠ *Queen Cross St. off King St.* ☎ *340/692–9922* ⊕ *www.restaurantbacchus.com* ⊘ *Closed Mon. No lunch.*

CONTINENTAL
★

27

$$ ✕ **Rum Runners.** The view is as stellar as the food at this highly popular local standby. Sitting right on Christiansted boardwalk, Rum Runners serves everything, including a to-die-for salad of crispy romaine lettuce and tender grilled lobster drizzled with lemongrass vinaigrette. More hearty fare includes baby back ribs cooked with the restaurant's special spice blend and Guinness stout. ⊠ *Hotel Caravelle, 44A Queen Cross St.* ☎ *340/773–6585* ⊕ *www.rumrunnersstcroix.com.*

CONTINENTAL
☾
Fodor's Choice
★

$$$ ✕ **Savant.** Savant is one of those small but special spots that locals love. The cuisine is a fusion of Mexican, Thai, and Caribbean—an unusual combination that works surprisingly well. You can find anything from fresh fish to Thai curry with chicken to maple-teriyaki pork tenderloin coming out of the kitchen. With 20 tables crammed into the indoor dining room and small courtyard, this little place can get crowded. Call early for reservations. ⊠ *4C Hospital St.* ☎ *340/713–8666* ⊘ *Closed Sun. No lunch.*

ECLECTIC
★

WEST OF CHRISTIANSTED

$$$ ✕ **Breezez.** This aptly named restaurant is poolside at Club St. Croix condominiums. Visitors and locals are drawn by its reasonable prices and good food. This is *the* place on the island to be for Sunday brunch. Locals gather for lunch, when the menu includes everything from burgers

ECLECTIC
☾

to blackened prime rib with a horseradish sauce. For dessert, try the Amaretto cheesecake with either chocolate or fruit topping. ⊠ *Club St. Croix, 3220 Golden Rock, off Rte. 752, Golden Rock* ☎ *340/718–7077.*

$$$
ECLECTIC
Fodor's Choice
★

✕ **Elizabeth's at H2O.** With a lovely beachfront location and stellar food, this restaurant has developed quite a following. Lunch brings out lots of locals for the West Indian buffet that features mahimahi creole-style. Dinner entrées include surf and turf with mashed potatoes. ⊠ *Hibiscus Beach Resort, off Rte. 752, Estate Princess* ☎ *4131 La Grand Princess, Christiansted 00820* ☎ *340/718–0735* ⊕ *www.elizabethsath2o.com.*

$$$
ITALIAN

✕ **Salud Bistro.** This eatery's imaginative menu takes its cue from the fresh flavors of the Mediterranean. Start with the savory cheese plate served with homemade bread and crostini before moving on to fresh fish or the grilled duck with a hibiscus confit. ⊠ *Princess Shopping Center, Rte. 75, La Grande Princess* ☎ *340/718–7900* ⊕ *www.saludbistro. com* ⊘ *Closed Sun.*

EAST END

$$
ECLECTIC

✕ **The Deep End.** A favorite with locals and vacationers, this poolside restaurant serves up terrific crab-cake sandwiches, London broil with onions and mushrooms, and delicious pasta in various styles. To get here from Christiansted, take Route 82 and turn left at the sign for Green Cay Marina. ⊠ *Tamarind Reef Hotel, Annas Hope* ☎ *340/713–7071.*

$$$$
ECLECTIC

✕ **The Galleon.** This popular dockside restaurant is always busy. Start with the Caesar salad or perhaps a grilled lamb lollipop with a tamarind glaze. The chef's signature dish is a tender filet mignon topped with fresh local lobster. Fish lovers should try the grilled mahimahi with an artichoke and tomato salad. Take Route 82 out of Christiansted, and then turn left at the sign for Green Cay Marina. ⊠ *Green Cay Marina, Annas Hope* ☎ *340/773–9949* ⊕ *www.galleonrestaurant.com* ⊘ *No lunch.*

NORTH SHORE

$$
ECLECTIC

✕ **Off the Wall.** Divers fresh from a plunge at the North Shore's popular Cane Bay Wall gather at this breezy spot on the beach. If you want to sit a spell before you order, a hammock beckons. Deli sandwiches, served with delicious chips, make up most of the menu. Pizza and salads are also available. ⊠ *Rte. 80, Cane Bay* ☎ *340/778–4771* ⊕ *www.otwstx.com.*

FREDERIKSTED

$$
ECLECTIC

✕ **Beach Side Café.** Sunday brunch is big, but locals and visitors flock to this oceanfront bistro at Sandcastle on the Beach resort for lunch and dinner. Both menus include burgers and flatbread pizza, but at dinner the grilled pork chop with mango salsa shines. For lunch, the hummus plate is a good bet. ⊠ *Sandcastle on the Beach, 127 Smithfield* ☎ *340/772–1205* ⊕ *www.sandcastleonthebeach.com* ⊘ *Closed Tues.–Thurs.*

$$$
ECLECTIC
Fodor's Choice
★

✕ **Blue Moon.** This terrific little bistro, which has a loyal local following, offers a changing menu that draws on Cajun and Caribbean flavors. Try the spicy gumbo with andouille sausage or crab cakes with a spicy aioli for your appetizer. A grilled chicken breast served with spinach and artichoke hearts and topped with Parmesan and cheddar cheeses makes a good entrée. The Almond Joy sundae should be your choice for dessert. There's live jazz on Wednesday and Friday. ⊠ *7 Strand St.* ☎ *340/772–2222* ⊕ *www.bluemoonstcroix.com* ⊘ *Closed Mon.*

$ ✕**Turtles Deli.** You can eat outside at this tiny spot just as you enter
ECLECTIC downtown Frederiksted. Lunches are as basic as a corned beef on rye
♻ or as imaginative as the Raven (turkey breast with bacon, tomato, and
melted cheddar cheese on French bread). Also good is the Beast, named
after the grueling hill that challenges bikers in the annual triathlon.
It's piled high with hot roast beef, raw onion, and melted Swiss cheese
with horseradish and mayonnaise. Early risers stop by for cinnamon
buns and espresso. ✉ *38 Strand St., at Prince Passage* ☎ *340/772–3676*
⊕ *www.turtlesdeli.com* ⊟ *No credit cards* ⊘ *Closed Sun. No dinner.*

WHERE TO STAY

You can find everything from plush resorts to simple beachfront digs in
St. Croix. If you sleep in either the Christiansted or Frederiksted area,
you'll be closest to shopping, restaurants, and nightlife. Most of the
island's other hotels will put you just steps from the beach. St. Croix has
several small but special properties that offer personalized service. If you
like all the comforts of home, you may prefer to stay in a condominium
or villa. Room rates on St. Croix are competitive with those on other
islands, and if you travel off-season, you can find substantially reduced
prices. Many properties offer money-saving honeymoon and dive packages. Whether you stay in a hotel, a condominium, or a villa, you'll
enjoy up-to-date amenities. Most properties have room TVs, but at
some bed-and-breakfasts there might be only one, in the common room.

Although a stay right in historic Christiansted may mean putting up
with a little urban noise, you probably won't have trouble sleeping.
Christiansted rolls up the sidewalks fairly early, and humming air-con-
ditioners drown out any noise. Solitude is guaranteed at hotels and inns
outside Christiansted and those on the outskirts of sleepy Frederiksted.

PRIVATE CONDOMINIUMS AND VILLAS
St. Croix has villas scattered all over the island, but most are in the
center or on the East End. Renting a villa gives you all the convenience
of home as well as top-notch amenities. Many have pools, hot tubs, and
deluxe furnishings. Most companies meet you at the airport, arrange for
a rental car, and provide helpful information about the island.

If you want to be close to the island's restaurants and shopping, look for
a condominium or villa in the hills above Christiansted or on either side
of the town. An East End location gets you out of Christiansted's hustle
and bustle, but you're still only 15 minutes from town. North Shore
locations are lovely, with gorgeous sea views and lots of peace and quiet.

Vacation St. Croix (☎ *340/718–0361 or 877/788–0361* ⊕ *www.
vacationstcroix.com*) has villas all around the island.

*The following reviews have been condensed for this book. Please go to
Fodors.com for expanded reviews of each property.*

CHRISTIANSTED
$ ⊡ **Hotel Caravelle.** Near the harbor, at the waterfront end of a pleasant
HOTEL shopping arcade, the Caravelle's in-town location puts you steps away
from shops and restaurants. **Pros:** good restaurant; convenient location; convenient parking. **Cons:** no beach; busy in-town neighborhood.

27

✉ *44A Queen Cross St.* ☎ *340/773–0687 or 800/524–0410* 🌐 *www.hotelcaravelle.com* *43 rooms, 1 suite* *In-room: a/c, no safe, Wi-Fi. In-hotel: restaurant, bar, pool, business center* *No meals.*

$ RESORT **Hotel on the Cay.** Hop on the free ferry to reach this peaceful lodging in the middle of Christiansted Harbor. **Pros:** quiet atmosphere; convenient location; lovely beach. **Cons:** accessible only by ferry; no parking available; Wi-Fi in upstairs terrace only. ✉ *Protestant Cay* ☎ *340/773–2035 or 800/524–2035* 🌐 *www.hotelonthecay.com* *53 rooms* *In-room: a/c, no safe. In-hotel: restaurant, pool, beach, water sports, business center* *No meals.*

¢–$ HOTEL **King Christian Hotel.** A stay at the King Christian puts you right in the heart of Christiansted's historic district. **Pros:** rooms have ocean views; car rental in lobby; convenient location. **Cons:** no beach; need to take a taxi at night; no parking lot. ✉ *57 King St., Box 24467* ☎ *340/773–6330 or 800/524–2012* 🌐 *www.kingchristian.com* *39 rooms* *In-room: a/c, no safe (some), Wi-Fi (some). In-hotel: restaurant, pool, business center* *Breakfast.*

WEST OF CHRISTIANSTED

¢–$ B&B/INN Fodor's Choice ★ **Carringtons Inn.** Hands-on owners Claudia and Roger Carrington are the real reason to stay here, and they conjure up delicious breakfasts—rum-soaked French toast is a house specialty—dole out advice, and make you feel right at home. **Pros:** welcoming hosts; tasteful rooms; great breakfasts. **Cons:** no beach; need car to get around. ✉ *4001 Estate Hermon Hill, Christiansted* ☎ *340/713–0508 or 877/658–0508* 🌐 *www.carringtonsinn.com* *5 rooms* *In-room: a/c, no safe, no TV, Wi-Fi. In-hotel: pool, business center* *Breakfast.*

$–$$ RENTAL **Club St. Croix.** Sitting beachfront just outside Christiansted, this modern condominium complex faces a lovely sandy beach. **Pros:** beachfront location; good restaurant; full kitchens. **Cons:** need car to get around; sketchy neighborhood. ✉ *Rte. 752, Estate Golden Rock* ☎ *340/718–9150 or 800/524–2025* 🌐 *www.antillesresorts.com* *53 apartments* *In-room: a/c, no safe, kitchen, Wi-Fi. In-hotel: restaurant, tennis courts, pool, beach, business center* *No meals.*

$ RENTAL **Colony Cove.** In a string of condominium complexes, Colony Cove lets you experience comfortable beachfront living. **Pros:** beachfront location; comfortable units; good views. **Cons:** sketchy neighborhood; need car to get around. ✉ *Rte. 752, Estate Golden Rock* ☎ *340/718–1965 or 800/524–2025* 🌐 *www.antillesresorts.com* *62 apartments* *In-room: a/c, no safe, kitchen, Wi-Fi. In-hotel: pool, beach* *No meals.*

$ RESORT **Hibiscus Beach Hotel.** This hotel is on a lovely beach—the best reason to stay here. **Pros:** nice beach; good restaurant; close to Christiansted. **Cons:** dated decor; sketchy neighborhood; need car to get around. ✉ *4131 Estate La Grande Princesse, off Rte. 752, La Grande Princesse* ☎ *340/718–4042 or 800/442–0121* 🌐 *www.hibiscusbeachresort.com* *38 rooms* *In-room: a/c, Wi-Fi, In-hotel: restaurant, pool, beach, water sports, business center* *Breakfast.*

$$ RENTAL **Sugar Beach.** With all the conveniences of home, Sugar Beach has apartments that are immaculate and breezy. **Pros:** pleasant beach; full kitchens; space to spread out. **Cons:** sketchy neighborhood; need car to get around. ✉ *Rte. 752, Estate Golden Rock* ☎ *340/718–5345 or*

CAMPING IN ST. CROIX

Out on the west end, where few tourists stay, **Mount Victory Camp** (✉ *Creque Dam Rd., Frederiksted* ☎ *340/772-1651 or 866/772-1651* ⊕ *www.mtvictorycamp.com*) offers a remarkable quietude that distinguishes this out-of-the-way spread on 8 acres in the island's rain forest. If you really want to commune with nature, you'll be hard-pressed to find a better way to do it on St. Croix. Hosts Bruce and Mathilde Wilson are on hand to explain the environment. You sleep in screened-in tent-cottages ($95–$125) perched on a raised platform and covered by a roof. Each has electricity and a rudimentary outdoor kitchen. There are also some bare tent sites for $30 per night. The shared, spotlessly clean bathhouse is an easy stroll away. The location feels remote, but a lovely sand beach and the Sunset Grill restaurant are a 2-mi (3-km) drive down the hill. In another 10 minutes you're in Frederiksted. Reservations are essential, and this is a cash-only place.

800/524-2049 ⊕ *www.sugarbeachstcroix.com* ⟿ *46 apartments* ⚼ *In-room: a/c, no safe, kitchen, Wi-Fi (some). In-hotel: tennis courts, pool, beach, business center* ⦿ *No meals.*

EAST END

$$$–$$$$
RESORT
☾
☷ **The Buccaneer.** For travelers who want everything at their fingertips, this resort has sandy beaches, swimming pools, and extensive sports facilities. **Pros:** beachfront location; numerous activities; nice golf course. **Cons:** pricey rates; insular environment; need car to get around. ✉ *Rte. 82, Box 25200, Shoys* ☎ *340/712-2100 or 800/255-3881* ⊕ *www.thebuccaneer.com* ⟿ *138 rooms* ⚼ *In-room: a/c, Wi-Fi. In-hotel: restaurants, bar, golf course, tennis courts, pools, gym, spa, beach, water sports, children's programs, business center* ⦿ *Breakfast.*

$
RESORT
☾
☷ **Chenay Bay Beach Resort.** The seaside setting and complimentary tennis and water-sports equipment make this resort a real find, particularly for families with active kids. **Pros:** beachfront location; good children's program; wide array of water sports. **Cons:** need car to get around; lacks pizzazz; Wi-Fi in lobby and restaurant only. ✉ *Rte. 82, Green Cay* ⦿ *Box 24600, Christiansted00824* ☎ *340/773-2918 or 800/548-4457* ⊕ *www.chenaybay.com* ⟿ *50 rooms* ⚼ *In-room: a/c, no safe, kitchen. In-hotel: restaurant, bar, tennis courts, pool, beach, water sports, children's programs* ⦿ *No meals.*

$$–$$$
ALL-INCLUSIVE
☷ **Divi Carina Bay Resort.** An oceanfront location, the island's only casino, and plenty of activities make this resort a good bet. **Pros:** spacious beach; good restaurant; on-site casino. **Cons:** need car to get around; many stairs to climb; staff can seem chilly. ✉ *25 Rte. 60, Estate Turner Hole* ☎ *340/773-9700 or 877/773-9700* ⊕ *www.divicarina.com* ⟿ *146 rooms, 2 suites, 20 villas* ⚼ *In-room: a/c, Internet, Wi-Fi (some). In-hotel: restaurants, bars, golf course, tennis courts, pool, gym, beach, water sports, business center* ⦿ *All-inclusive.*

$–$$
HOTEL
☷ **Tamarind Reef Hotel.** Spread out along a sandy beach, these low-slung buildings offer casual comfort. **ros:** good snorkeling; tasty restaurant; rooms have kitchenettes. **Cons:** need car to get around; motel-style

Villa Greenleaf.

rooms. ✉ *5001 Tamarind Reef, off Rte. 82, Annas Hope* ☎ *340/773–4455 or 800/619–0014* ⊕ *www.tamarindreefhotel.com* ⇌ *39 rooms* ♿ *In-room: a/c, Wi-Fi (some). In-hotel: restaurant, pool, water sports* ⦿ *No meals.*

$$
RENTAL
★
🏨 **Villa Madeleine.** If you like privacy and your own private pool, you'll like Villa Madeleine. **Pros:** pleasant decor; full kitchens; private pools. **Cons:** lower units sometimes lack views; need car to get around; no beachfront. ✉ *Off Rte. 82, Teague Bay* ⌂ *5014 Villa Madeleine, Christiansted 00820* ☎ *340/718–0361 or 877/788–0361* ⊕ *www. vacationstcroix.com* ⇌ *43 villas* ♿ *In-room: a/c, no safe, kitchen, Internet (some), Wi-Fi (some). In-hotel: tennis court, pools* ⦿ *No meals.*

FREDERIKSTED

$
HOTEL
🏨 **Sandcastle on the Beach.** Right on a gorgeous stretch of white beach, this hotel caters primarily to gay men and lesbians, but everyone is welcome. **Pros:** lovely beach; close to restaurants; gay-friendly vibe. **Cons:** neighborhood sketchy at night; need car to get around; no children's activities. ✉ *127 Smithfield, Rte. 71, Frederiksted* ☎ *340/772–1205 or 800/524–2018* ⊕ *www.sandcastleonthebeach.com* ⇌ *8 rooms, 8 suites, 5 villas* ♿ *In-room: a/c, kitchen (some), Wi-Fi (some). In-hotel: restaurant, pools, gym, beach, water sports, laundry facilities, business center* ⦿ *Breakfast.*

NORTH SHORE

¢
🏨 **Arawak Bay: The Inn at Salt River.** With stellar views of St. Croix's North Shore and an affable host, this small inn allows you to settle into island life at a price that doesn't break the bank. **Pros:** 20 minutes from Christiansted; budget prices. **Cons:** no beach nearby; can be some road noise. ✉ *Rte. 80, Salt River* ⌂ *Box 3475, Kingshill 00851*

📠 *340/772–1684* ⊕ *www.arawakbaysaltriver.co.vi* ⤴ *14 rooms* ⚃ *In-room: a/c, no safe, Wi-Fi. In-hotel: pool, business center* ⦿ *Breakfast.*

$$$
RESORT
★

📺 **Renaissance St. Croix Carambola Beach Resort and Spa.** We like this resort's stellar beachfront setting and peaceful ambience. **Pros:** lovely beach; relaxing atmosphere; close to golf. **Cons:** ongoing renovation; still some dated rooms; need car to get around. ✉ *Rte. 80, Davis Bay* ⬠ *Box 3031, Kingshill 00851* 📠 *340/778–3800 or 888/503–8760* ⊕ *www.marriott.com* ⤴ *151 rooms* ⚃ *In-room: a/c, kitchen (some), Internet, Wi-Fi (some). In-hotel: restaurants, tennis courts, pool, gym, spa, beach, water sports, business center* ⦿ *No meals.*

$
RENTAL

📺 **Villa Margarita.** This quiet retreat provides a particularly good base if you want to admire the dramatic views of the windswept coast. **ros:** friendly host; great views; snorkeling nearby. **Cons:** isolated location; need car to get around; limited amenities. ✉ *Off Rte. 80, Salt River* ⬠ *9024 Salt River, Christiansted 00820* 📠 *340/713–1930* ⊕ *www.villamargarita.com* ⤴ *3 units* ⚃ *In-room: a/c, no safe, kitchen, Wi-Fi. In-hotel: pool, some age restrictions* ⦿ *No meals.*

$
HOTEL

📺 **Waves at Cane Bay.** St. Croix's famed Cane Bay Wall is just offshore from this hotel, giving it an enviable location. **Pros:** great diving; restaurants nearby; beaches nearby. **Cons:** need car to get around; on main road; bland decor. ✉ *Rte. 80, Cane Bay* ⬠ *Box 1749, Kingshill 00851* 📠 *340/718–1815 or 800/545–0603* ⊕ *www.canebaystcroix.com* ⤴ *12 rooms* ⚃ *In-room: a/c, no safe, kitchen, Wi-Fi. In-hotel: restaurant, bar, pool* ⦿ *No meals.*

MID ISLAND

$–$$
B&B/INN
Fodor's Choice
★

📺 **Villa Greenleaf.** This spacious B&B is all about the details—four-poster beds with elegant duvets, towels folded just so, hand-stenciled trim on the walls, and gardens tastefully planted. **Pros:** tasteful decor; convivial atmosphere; car included in rate. **Cons:** no beach; no restaurants nearby; need car to get around. ✉ *Island Center Rd., Montpelier* ⬠ *Box 675, Christiansted 00821* 📠 *340/719–1958 or 888/282–1001* ⊕ *www.villagreenleaf.com* ⤴ *5 rooms* ⚃ *In-room: a/c, Wi-Fi. In-hotel: pool* ⦿ *Breakfast.*

NIGHTLIFE AND THE ARTS

The island's nightlife is ever-changing, and its arts scene is eclectic—ranging from Christmastime performances of *The Nutcracker* to any locally organized shows. Folk-art traditions, such as quadrille dancers, are making a comeback. To find out what's happening, pick up the local newspapers—*V.I. Daily News* and *St. Croix Avis*—available at newsstands. Christiansted has a lively and eminently casual club scene near the waterfront. Frederiksted has a couple of restaurants and clubs offering weekend entertainment.

CHRISTIANSTED

Fort Christian Brew Pub. This pub is where locals and visitors listen to live music Wednesday, Friday, and Saturday. ✉ *Boardwalk at end of Kings Alley, Christiansted* 📠 *340/713–9820* ⊕ *www.fortchristianbrewpub.com.*

27

Hotel on the Cay. This off-shore resort hosts a West Indian buffet on Tuesday night in the winter season, when you can watch a broken-bottle dancer (a dancer who braves a carpet of shattered glass) and mocko jumbie (stilt-dancing) characters. ⊠ *Protestant Cay, Christiansted* ☎ *340/773–2035.*

EAST END

Divi Carina Bay Resort. Although you can gamble at the island's only casino, it's really the nightly music that draws big crowds to this resort. ⊠ *25 Rte. 60, Estate Turner Hole* ☎ *340/773–7529.*

MID ISLAND

Whim Plantation Museum. The museum outside Frederiksted hosts classical music concerts in winter. ⊠ *Rte. 70, Estate Whim* ☎ *340/772–0598.*

FREDERIKSTED

Fodor's Choice   **Blue Moon.** Blue Moon is a popular waterfront restaurant in Frederiksted, and it's the place to be for live jazz on Wednesday and Friday, one of the few nightlife options on this end of the island. ⊠ *7 Strand St., Frederiksted* ☎ *340/772–2222.*

Fodor's Choice   **Sunset Jazz.** This outdoor event has become the hot ticket in Frederiksted, drawing crowds of both visitors and locals at 6 pm on the third Friday of every month to watch the sun go down and hear good music. ⊠ *Waterfront, Frederiksted* ☎ *340/690–0617.*

SHOPPING

Although the shopping on St. Croix isn't as varied or extensive as that on St. Thomas, the island does have several small stores with unusual merchandise. St. Croix shop hours are usually Monday through Saturday 9 to 5, but there are some shops in Christiansted open in the evening. Stores are often closed on Sunday.

CHRISTIANSTED

In Christiansted the best shopping areas are the **Pan Am Pavilion** and **Caravelle Arcade,** off Strand Street, and along **King** and **Company streets.** These streets give way to arcades filled with boutiques. **Gallows Bay** has a blossoming shopping area in a quiet neighborhood.

ART

Danica Art Gallery. This gallery displays and sells the modernist paintings of owner Danica David; jewelry, pottery, and other works by various artists also fill this gallery. ⊠ *6 Company St., Christiansted* ☎ *340/719–6000.*

BOOKS

Undercover Books. This well-stocked independent bookseller sells Caribbean-themed books as well as the latest good reads. The store is across from the post office in the Gallows Bay shopping area. ⊠ *5030 Anchor Way, Gallows Bay* ☎ *340/719–1567.*

CLOTHING

Fodor's Choice   **Coconut Vine.** This is a great place to pop into at the start of your vacation. You'll leave with enough comfy cotton or rayon batik men's and women's clothes to make you look like a local. Although the tropical designs and colors originated in Indonesia, they're perfect for the Caribbean. ⊠ *1111 Strand St., Christiansted* ☎ *340/773–1991.*

From the Gecko. This store sells the hippest clothes on St. Croix, including superb island-style clothing and other items. ⊠ *1233 Queen Cross St., Christiansted* ☎ *340/778–9433.*

Hot Heads. This small store sells hats, hats, and more hats, which are often perched on top of cotton shifts, comfortable shirts, and other tropical wear. If you forgot your bathing suit, this store has a good selection. ⊠ *Kings Alley Walk, Christiansted* ☎ *340/773–7888.*

Pacificotton. Pacificotton will let you round out your tropical wardrobe with something new. Shifts, tops, and pants in Caribbean colors as well as bags and hats fill the racks. ⊠ *1110 Strand St., Christiansted* ☎ *340/773–2125.*

GIFTS

★ **Gone Tropical.** This store offers an eclectic collection of special gifts. On her travels about the world, Margo Meacham keeps her eye out for special delights for her shop—from tablecloths and napkins in bright Caribbean colors to unique fashion accessories. ⊠ *5 Company St., Christiansted* ☎ *340/773–4696.*

Many Hands. This shop sells pottery in bright colors, paintings of St. Croix and the Caribbean, prints, and maps—all made by local artists—and all making for perfect take-home gifts. If your purchase is too cumbersome to carry, the owners ship all over the world. ⊠ *21 Pan Am Pavilion, Strand St., Christiansted* ☎ *340/773–1990.*

Mitchell-Larsen Studio. This glass gallery offers an interesting amalgam of carefully crafted glass plates, sun-catchers, and more. All pieces are made on-site by a St. Croix glassmaker, and they are often whimsically adorned with tropical fish, flora, and fauna. ⊠ *200 Company St., Christiansted* ☎ *340/719–1000.*

Fodor's Choice
★ **Royal Poinciana.** An attractive shop, Royal Poinciana is filled with island seasonings and hot sauces, West Indian crafts, bath gels, and herbal teas. Shop here for tablecloths and paper goods in tropical brights. ⊠ *1111 Strand St., Christiansted* ☎ *340/773–9892.*

Tesoro. Tesoro is crowded with an eclectic range of colorful and boldly painted merchandise. Shop for metal sculptures made from retired steel pans, mahogany bowls, and hand-painted place mats in bright tropical colors. ⊠ *36C Strand St., Christiansted* ☎ *340/773–1212.*

HOUSEWARES

Designworks. This store and gallery sells furniture as well as one of the largest selections of local art, along with Caribbean-inspired bric-a-brac in all price ranges. If a mahogany armoire or cane-back rocker catches your fancy, the staff will arrange to have it shipped to your home at no charge from its mainland warehouse. ⊠ *6 Company St., Christiansted* ☎ *340/713–8102.*

JEWELRY

Crucian Gold. Crucian Gold carries the unique gold creations of St. Croix native Brian Bishop. His trademark piece is the Turk's Head ring (a knot of interwoven gold strands), but jewelry made of shards

27

of plantation-era china set in gold are just lovely. ⊠ *1112 Strand St., Christiansted* ☎ *340/773–5241.*

Gold Worker. This shop specializes in handcrafted jewelry in silver and gold that will remind you of the Caribbean. Hummingbirds dangle from silver chains, and sand dollars adorn gold necklaces. The sugar mills in silver and gold speak of St. Croix's past. ⊠ *3 Company St., Christiansted* ☎ *340/516–6042.*

ib Designs. This small shop showcases the handcrafted jewelry of local craftsman Whealan Massicott. In both silver and gold, the designs are simply elegant. ⊠ *Company St. at Queen Cross St., Christiansted* ☎ *340/773–4322.*

Nelthropp and Low. Nelthropp and Low specializes in gold jewelry but also carries diamonds, emeralds, rubies, and sapphires. Jewelers will create one-of-a-kind pieces to your design. ⊠ *1102 Strand St., Christiansted* ☎ *340/773–0365 or 800/416–9078.*

Sonya's. This store is owned and operated by Sonya Hough, who invented the popular hook bracelet. She has added an interesting decoration to these bracelets: the swirling symbol used in weather forecasts to indicate hurricanes. ⊠ *1 Company St., Christiansted* ☎ *340/778–8605.*

LIQUOR AND TOBACCO

Baci Duty Free Liquor and Tobacco (⊠ *1235 Queen Cross St., Christiansted* ☎ *340/773–5040*) has a walk-in humidor with a good selection of Arturo Fuente, Partagas, and Macanudo cigars. It also carries sleek Swiss-made watches and collectables.

WEST OF CHRISTIANSED

FOOD

Pueblo. This stateside-style market has two branches, though prices are still more than what you would pay back home. ⊠ *Orange Grove Shopping Center, Rte. 75, Christiansted* ☎ *340/773–0118.*

EAST END

FOOD

Schooner Bay Market. Although it's on the smallish side, this market has good-quality deli items. ⊠ *Rte. 82, Mount Welcome* ☎ *340/773–3232.*

MID ISLAND

FOOD

Cost-U-Less. This warehouse-type store is great for visitors because it doesn't charge a membership fee. It's east of Sunny Isle Shopping Center. ⊠ *Rte. 70, Sunny Isle* ☎ *340/719–4442.*

Plaza Extra. This supermarket chain has a good selection of Middle Eastern foods in addition to the usual grocery-store items. ⊠ *United Shopping Plaza, Rte. 70, Sion Farm* ☎ *340/778–6240* ⊠ *Rte. 70, Mount Pleasant* ☎ *340/719–1870.*

Pueblo. This stateside-style market has two branches, though prices are still more than what you would pay back home. ⊠ *Villa La Reine Shopping Center, Rte. 75, La Reine* ☎ *340/778–1272.*

Deep-sea fishing in St. Croix's costal waters.

LIQUOR AND TOBACCO

Kmart. The U.S. discount chain has two branches on St. Croix, both of which carry a huge line of deep discounted, duty-free liquor, among many other items. ⊠ *Sunshine Mall, Rte. 70, Frederiksted* ☎ *340/ 692–5848* ⊠ *Sunny Isle Shopping Center, Rte. 70, Sunny Isle* ☎ *340/ 719–9190.*

FREDERIKSTED

The best shopping in Frederiksted is along **Strand Street** and in the side streets and alleyways that connect it with **King Street.** Most stores close on Sunday, except when a cruise ship is in port. One caveat: Frederiksted has a reputation for muggings, so for safety's sake stick to populated areas of Strand and King streets, where there are few—if any—problems.

SPORTS AND ACTIVITIES

BOAT TOURS

Almost everyone takes a day trip to Buck Island aboard a charter boat. Most leave from the Christiansted waterfront or from Green Cay Marina and stop for a snorkel at the island's eastern end before dropping anchor off a gorgeous sandy beach for a swim, a hike, and lunch. Sailboats can often stop right at the beach; a larger boat might have to anchor a bit farther offshore. A full-day sail runs about $100, with lunch included on most trips. A half-day sail costs about $68.

Big Beard's Adventure Tours (⊠ *Christiansted* ☎ *340/773–4482* ⊕ *www. bigbeards.com*) takes you on catamarans, either the *Renegade* or the

Adventure, from the Christiansted waterfront to Buck Island for snorkeling before dropping anchor at a private beach for a barbecue lunch.

Caribbean Sea Adventures (✉ *Christiansted* ☎ *340/773–2628* ⊕ *www.caribbeanseaadventures.com*) departs from the Christiansted waterfront for half- and full-day trips.

Teroro Charters (✉ *Green Cay Marina, Annas Hope* ☎ *340/773–3161* ⊕ *www.gotostcroix.com/heinz/index.php*) offers charters on two trimarans, *Teroro II* and *Dragonfly,* which leave Green Cay Marina for full- or half-day sails. Bring your own lunch.

DIVING AND SNORKELING

At **Buck Island,** a short boat ride from Christiansted or Green Cay Marina, the reef is so nice that it's been named a national monument. You can dive right off the beach at **Cane Bay,** which has a spectacular drop-off called the Cane Bay Wall. Dive operators also do boat trips along the Wall, usually leaving from Salt River or Christiansted. **Frederiksted Pier** is home to a colony of sea horses, creatures seldom seen in the waters of the Virgin Islands. At **Green Cay,** just outside Green Cay Marina in the east end, you can see colorful fish swimming around the reefs and rocks. Two exceptional North Shore sites are **North Star** and **Salt River,** which you can reach only by boat. At Salt River you can float downward through a canyon filled with colorful fish and coral.

The island's dive shops take you out for one- or two-tank dives. Plan to pay about $65 for a one-tank dive and $95 for a two-tank dive, including equipment and an underwater tour. All companies offer certification and introductory courses called resort dives for novices.

Which dive outfit you pick usually depends on where you're staying. Your hotel may have one on-site. If so, you're just a short stroll away from the dock. If not, other companies are close by. Where the dive boat goes on a particular day depends on the weather, but in any case, all St. Croix's dive sites are special. All shops are affiliated with PADI, the Professional Association of Diving Instructors.

Folks staying in the Judith's Fancy area are closest to **Anchor Dive Center** (✉ *Salt River Marina, Rte. 80, Salt River* ☎ *340/778–1522 or 800/532–3483* ⊕ *www.anchordivestcroix.com*). The company also has facilities at the Buccaneer hotel. Anchor takes divers to more than 35 sites, including the Wall at Salt River Canyon.

Cane Bay Dive Shop (✉ *Rte. 80, Cane Bay* ☎ *340/773–9913 or 800/338–3843* ⊕ *www.canebayscuba.com*) is the place to go if you want to do a beach dive or boat dive along the North Shore. The famed Cane Bay Wall is 200 yards from the five-star PADI facility. This company also has shops at Pan Am Pavilion in Christiansted, on Strand Street in Frederiksted, at the Carambola Beach Resort, and at the Divi Carina Bay Resort.

If you're staying in Christiansted, **Dive Experience** (✉ *1111 Strand St., Christiansted* ☎ *340/773–3307 or 800/235–9047* ⊕ *www.divexp.com*) has PADI five-star status and runs trips to the North Shore walls and reefs in addition to offering the usual certification and introductory classes.

Horseback riding in the island's rain forest.

In Frederiksted, **N2 the Blue** (✉ *Frederiksted Pier, Rte. 631, Frederiksted* ☎ *340/772–3483 or 888/789–3483* ⊕ *www.n2theblue.com*) takes divers right off the beach near Coconuts restaurant, on night dives off the Frederiksted Pier, or on boat trips to wrecks and reefs.

St. Croix Ultimate Bluewater Adventures (✉ *Queen Cross St., Christiansted* ☎ *340/773–5994 or 877/567–1367* ⊕ *www.stcroixscuba.com*) can take you to your choice of more than 75 sites; it also offers a variety of packages that include hotel stays.

FISHING
Since the early 1980s, some 20 world records—many for blue marlin—have been set in these waters. Sailfish, skipjack, bonito, tuna (allison, blackfin, and yellowfin), and wahoo are abundant. A charter runs about $500 for a half day (for up to six people), with most boats going out for four-, six-, or eight-hour trips.

Caribbean Sea Adventures (✉ *59 Kings Wharf, Christiansted* ☎ *340/773–2628* ⊕ *www.caribbeanseaadventures.com*) will take you out on a 38-foot powerboat. **Gone Ketchin'** (✉ *Salt River Marina, Rte. 80, Salt River* ☎ *340/713–1175* ⊕ *www.goneketchin.com*) arranges trips with old salt Captain Grizz.

GOLF
Fodor'sChoice **Buccaneer Golf Course**. The Buccaneer Resort has an 18-hole course. It's
★ close to Christiansted, so it's convenient for those staying in or near town. Greens fees are $90, with an additional $20 for cart rental. ✉ *Rte. 82, Shoys* ☎ *340/712–2144* ⊕ *www.thebuccaneer.com*.

★ **Carambola Golf Club.** The spectacular 18-hole course at the Renaissance St. Croix Carambola Resort, in the northwest valley, was designed by Robert Trent Jones Sr. It sits near Carambola Beach Resort. Greens fees are $140 for 18 holes, which includes the use of a golf cart. ⊠ *Renaissance St. Croix Carambola Resort, Rte. 18, Davis Bay* ☎ *340/778–5638* ⊕ *www.golfcarambola.com.*

The Links at Divi St. Croix. This attractive minigolf course just across from the Divi Carina Bay Resort. ⊠ *Rte. 60, Turner Hole* ☎ *340/773–9700* ⊕ *www.divicarina.com* ⊠ *$8* ⊙ *Daily noon–8.*

Reef Golf Course. This public course on the island's east end has 9 holes. Greens fees are $20, and cart rental is $15. ⊠ *Teague Bay* ☎ *340/773–8844.*

GUIDED TOURS

St. Croix Safari Tours (☎ *340/773–6700* ⊕ *www.gotostcroix.com/safaritours*) offers van tours of St. Croix. Excursions depart from Christiansted and last about five hours. Costs run from $60 per person, including admission fees to attractions.

St. Croix Transit (☎ *340/772–3333*) offers van tours of St. Croix. Tours depart from Carambola Beach Resort, last about three hours, and cost from $65 per person, including the admission fees to all attractions visited on the tour.

HIKING

Although you can set off by yourself on a hike through a rain forest or along a shore, a guide will point out what's important and tell you why.

Ay-Ay Eco Hike and Tours Association (⊕ *Box 2435, Kingshill 00851* ☎ *340/772–4079*), run by Ras Lumumba Corriette, takes hikers up hill and down dale in some of St. Croix's most remote places, including the rain forest and Mt. Victory. Some hikes include stops at places such as the Lawaetz Museum and old ruins. The cost is $60 per person for a three- or four-hour hike. There's a three-person minimum. A full-day jeep tour through the rain forest runs $120 per person.

HORSEBACK RIDING

Well-kept roads and expert guides make horseback riding on St. Croix pleasurable. At Sprat Hall, just north of Frederiksted, Jill Hurd runs **Paul and Jill's Equestrian Stables** (⊠ *Rte. 58, Frederiksted* ☎ *340/772–2880 or 340/332–0417* ⊕ *www.paulandjills.com*). She will take you through the rain forest, across the pastures, along the beaches, and through valleys—explaining the flora, fauna, and ruins on the way. A 1½-hour ride costs $90.

KAYAKING

Caribbean Adventure Tours (⊠ *Salt River Marina, Rte. 80, Salt River* ☎ *340/778–1522* ⊕ *www.stcroixkayak.com*) takes you on trips through Salt River Bay National Historical Park and Ecological Preserve, one of the island's most pristine areas. All tours run $450

Virgin Kayak Tours (⊠ *Rte. 80, Cane Bay* ☎ *340/778–0071* ⊕ *www.virginkayaktours.com*) runs guided kayak trips on the Salt River and rents kayaks so you can tour around the Cane Bay area by yourself. All tours are $45. Kayak rentals are $40 for the entire day.

INDEX

PHOTO CREDITS

1, Timothy O'Keefe / age fotostock. 2, Alvaro Leiva / age fotostock. 5, Carlos Villoch - MagicSea.com / Alamy. Chapter 1 Experience the Caribbean: 10-11, Christian Goupi / age fotostock. 12, BVI Tourist Board. 13 (left), Holger W./Shutterstock. 13 (right), Diana Cochran Johnson/Shutterstock. 22, Peter Phipp/Peter Phipp/age fotostock. 23 (left), Philip Coblentz/Medioimages. 23 (right), TIDCO. 28 and 29 (right), Fabrice RAMBERT/Hostal Nicolas de Ovando. 29 (left), Tatiana Popova/Shutterstock. 30 (left), John A. Anderson/iStockphoto. 30 (top center), John A. Anderson/iStockphoto. 30 (bottom center), Michael DeFreitas / age fotostock. 30 (top right), DurdenImages/iStockphoto. 30 (bottom right), MeegsC/wikipedia.org. 31 (top left), The Dominican Republic Ministry of Tourism. 31 (bottom left), St Vincent & The Grenadines Tourist Office. 31 (center), Alvaro Leiva / age fotostock. 31 (right), Franz Marc Frei / age fotostock. 32, Grenada Board of Tourism. 33 (left and right), Casa de Campo. 34, St. Maarten Tourist Bureau. 35 (left), Denis Jr. Tangney/iStockphoto. 35 (right), Dominican Republic Ministry of Tourism. 36, Ramona Settle. 37, Jim Lopes/Shutterstock. 38, Olga Bogatyrenko/Shutterstock. 39, Christian Wheatley/Shutterstock. 40, nikitsin/Shutterstock. 41, Michael Macsuga/Shutterstock. 42, Aruba Tourism Authority. 43 (left), Brenda S and R Duncan Kirby. 43 (right), Coral World Ocean Park, St. Thomas. 44, Heeb Christian / age fotostock. 45 (top), Nico Tondini / age fotostock. 45 (bottom left and right), Dom/Shutterstock. 46 (top), Kobako/wikipedia.org. 46 (bottom), Rohit Seth/Shutterstock. 47 (top left), Karen Wunderman/Shutterstock. 47 (center left), Mulling it Over/Flickr. 47 (top right), Midori/wikipedia.org. 47 (center right), stu_spivack/Flickr. 47 (bottom), PL.Viel / age fotostock. 48 (top left), Arkady/Shutterstock. 48 (bottom left), Mlvalentin/wikipedia.org. 48 (top right), ahnhuynh/Shutterstock. 48 (bottom right), Sakurai Midori/wikipedia.org. 49 (top left), HLPhoto/Shutterstock. 49 (bottom left), Elena Elisseeva/Shutterstock. 49 (bottom right), Only Fabrizio/Shutterstock. 49 (top right), cck/Flickr. 50 (left), Ingolf Pompe / age fotostock. 50, (left center) yosoynuts/Flickr. 50 (right center), Charles Tobias. 50 (right), Knut.C/wikipedia.org. 51 (left), cogdogblog/Flickr. 51 (left center), NorthJoe/Flickr. 51 (top right), Robert S. Donovan/Flickr. 51 (right center), Granstrom/wikipedia.org. 51 (bottom right), pocketwiley/Flickr, 52, Gavin Hellier / age fotostock. Chapter 2 Anguilla: 53, Chris Caldicott / age fotostock. 54 (bottom), aturkus/Flickr. 54 (top), Philip Coblentz/Digital Vision. 59, Rick Strange / age fotostock. 60, Neil Emmerson / age fotostock. 61 (left), toddneville/Flickr. 61 (right), Steve Geer/iStockphoto. 62, Rick Strange / age fotostock. 63, Ku. 69, Straw Hat. 73, The Leading Hotels of the World. 75, Viceroy Hotel Group. Chapter 3 Antigua and Barbuda: 81, Philip Coblentz/Medioimages. 82 (top and bottom), Philip Coblentz/Digital Vision. 83, Philip Coblentz/Digital Vision. 87, Alvaro Leiva / age fotostock. 88, John Miller / age fotostock. 89 (left), Steve Geer/istockphoto. 89 (right), World Pictures / age fotostock. 90, Geoff Howes/Antigua & Barbuda Tourist Office. 92, Steve Geer/iStockphoto. 102, nik wheeler / Alamy. Chapter 4 Aruba: 115, Aruba Tourism Authority. 116 (bottom), Philip Coblentz/Medioimages. 116 (top), Aruba Tourism Authority. 121, Aruba Tourism Authority. 122, Famke Backx/iStockphoto. 123 (left), mbackx l/istock. 123 (right), angelo cavalli / age fotostock. 124, martinique/Shutterstock. 125, bert van wijk/iStockphoto. 134, Amsterdam Manor Beach Resort Aruba. 143, Aruba Tourism Authority. Chapter 5 Barbados: 147, John Miller / age fotostock.148, Doug Scott/age fotostock. 154, Barbados Tourism Authority/Jim Smith. 155 (left), Barbados Tourism Authority/Loralie Skeete. 155 (right), Barbados Tourism Authority. 156, Ingolf Pompe / age fotostock. 157, Barbados Tourism Authority/Mike Toy. 158, Barbados Tourism Authority/Andrew Hulsmeier. 163, Walter Bibikow / age fotostock. 167, St. Nicholas Abbey. 179, Addison Cumberbatch/Willie Alleyne Photography. 182, Coral Reef Club. 184, Roy Riley / Alamy. 191, Christian Goupi / age fotostock. 194 (left), Jose Gil/iStockphoto. 194 (right), Conway Bowman. 195, Nataliya Hora/Shutterstock. Chapter 6 Bonaire: 199, Philip Coblentz/Medioimages.200 (top), Tourism Corporation Bonaire. 200 (bottom), Suzi Swygert for the Bonaire Tourist Office. 201, Harry Thomas/istock. 204, travelstock44 / age fotostock. 205 (left), Harry Thomas/iStockphoto. 205 (right), Walter Bibikow / age fotostock. 206, Harbour Village Beach Club. 216, Harbour Village Beach Club. 222, Kees Opstal/istockphoto. Chapter 7 British Virgin Islands: 227, Alvaro Leiva / age fotostock. 228 (bottom), Joel Blit/Shutterstock. 228 (top), lidian neeleman/iStockphoto. 233, Jeff Leach/iStockphoto. 234, Kreder Katja / age fotostock. 235 (left), World Pictures / age fotostock. 235 (right), Ellen Rooney / age fotostock. 236, Ramunas Bruzas/Shutterstock. 241, Walter Bibikow / age fotostock. 250, Charles Krallman/Surfsong Villa Resort. 252, Alvaro Leiva / age fotostock. 257, Eric Sanford / age fotostock. 258 (top), Randy Lincks / Alamy. 258 (bottom), iStockphoto. 259 (top), Doug Scott / age fotostock. 259 (bottom), Slavoljub Pantelic/iStockphoto. 260, Doug Scott / age fotostock. 262, Giovanni Rinaldi/iStockphoto. 263, Walter Bibikow / age fotostock. 265, FB-Fischer/imagebroker.net/photolibrary.com. 275, Bitter End Yacht Club International, LLC. 277, Andre Jenny / Alamy. 282, Paul Zizka/Shutterstock. Chapter 8 Cayman Islands: 285, Peter Heiss/iStockphoto. 286 (top and bottom), Cayman Islands Department of Tourism. 287, Kevin Panizza/istockphoto. 292, The Ritz-Carlton, Grand Cayman. 293 (left), Cayman Islands Department of Tourism. 293 (right), Allister Clark/iStockphoto. 294, RENAULT Philippe / age fotostock. 295, Cayman Islands Department of Tourism. 297, Cayman Islands Department of Tourism. 314, Don McDougall/Cayman Islands Department of Tourism. 324, Corbis. 331, Durden-Images/iStockphoto. Chapter 9 Curaçao: 341, Philip Coblentz/Digital Vision. 342 (bottom), Fotoconcept Inc./ age fotostock. 342 (top), Curaçao Tourism. 347, Walter Bibikow / age fotostock. 348, Philip Coblentz/Digital Vision. 349 (left), Stuart Pearce / age fotostock. 349 (right), Curaçao Tourism. 350, Angels at Work/shutterstock. 351, Curaçao Tourism. 354, Curacao Tourist Board. 357, Walter Bibikow / age fotostock. Chapter 10 Dominica: 375, Xavier Font/age fotostock. 376, Dominica Tourist Office. 377 (top), John Anderson/istockphoto. 377 (bottom), Dominica Tourist Office. 380, Greg Johnston / age fotostock. 381 (left), Antoine Hubert/Flickr. 381 (right), Hans Hillewaert/wikipedia.org. 382, Buddy Mays / Alamy. 383 (left), John Gabriel Stedman/wikipedia.org. 383 (right), Peter Purchia viestiphoto.com. 384, Winston Davidian/istockphoto. 387, John A. Anderson/istockphoto. 395, Fort Young Hotel Dominica. 402, Reinhard Dirscherl / age fotostock. Chapter 11 Dominican Republic: 405, Doug Scott/age fotostock. 406 (bottom), Doug Scott/age fotostock. 406 (top), Guy Thouvenin/age fotostock. 412, RIEGER Bertrand / age fotostock. 413 (top and bottom), The Dominican Republic Ministry of Tourism. 414, The Dominican Republic Ministry of Tourism. 415, The Dominican Republic Ministry of Tourism. 418, Harry Pujols/Flickr. 425, The Dominican Republic Ministry of Tourism. 439, tedmurphy/Flickr. 441, Sanctuary Cap Cana Golf & Spa. 449 (background photo), Sailorr/Shutterstock. 449 (pirate flag), wikipedia.org. 450 (left), rj lerich/Shutterstock. 450 (top right), Photos 12 / Alamy. 450 (bottom right), Anguilla Tourist Board. 451 (left), Lonely Planet Images / Alamy. 451 (center), Nevis Pirate Festival. 451 (right), unforth/Flickr. 452 (top left), The Print Collector / age fotostock. 452 (top and bottom right), wikipedia.org. 453 (left and center), wikipedia.org. 453 (right), Public domain. Chapter 12 Grenada: 469, Doug Scott/age fotostock. 470 (top and bottom), Grenada Board of Tourism. 472, R Gombarik/shutterstock. 473, Grenada Board of Tourism. 474, SlidePix istock. 475, Grenada Board of Tourism. 476, PetePhipp/Travelshots / age fotostock. 477 (left), shaggyshoo/Flickr. 477 (right), Steven Allan/iStockphoto. 478, Grenada Board of Tourism. 484, Haltner Thomas / age fotostock. 501, Grenada Board of Tourism. Chapter 13 Guadeloupe: 503, Bruno Morandi/age fotostock. 504, Bruno Morandi/age fotostock. 510, Walter Bibikow / age fotostock. 511 (left), Ingolf Pompe 8 / Alamy. 511 (right), Walter Bibikow / age fotostock. 512, wikipedia.org. 513, Tristan Deschamps/F1 Online/age fotostock. 514, Susanne Kischnick / Alamy. 515 (left), wikipedia.org. 515 (right), Photocuisine / Alamy. 516, Holger W./shutterstock. 527, Philippe Michel / age fotostock. 533, La Toubana Hotel and Spa. 535, Philippe Giraud. 542, Sylvain Grandadam / age fotostock. Chapter 14 Jamaica: 549, Island Outpost. 550 (bottom), Torrance Lewis/Jamaica Tourist Board/Fotoseeker.com. 550 (top), Julian Love/Jamaica Tourist Board/Fotoseeker.com. 555, Breezes Runaway Bay. 556, Steve Sanacore/Sandals Resorts. 557 (left), Chee-Onn Leong/Shutterstock. 557 (right), newphotoservice/shutterstock. 558, Miranda van der Kroft/Shutterstock. 559, Chee-Onn Leong/shutterstock. 560, Brian Nejedly. 561 (left), LarenKates/Flickr. 561 (right), Jamaica Inn. 562, Jamaica Tourist Board. 567, Franz Marc Frei / age fotostock. 577, Torrance Lewis/Jamaica Tourist Board/Fotoseeker.com. 583, Sandals Resorts. 599, Tramonto / age fotostock. 600 (top and center), TimDuncan/wikipedia.org. 600 (bottom), wbrisco.skyrock.com. 601, Dave Saunders / age fotostock. 602, Doug Pearson / age fotostock. 603 (left), NawlinWiki/wikipedia.org. 603 (center), Philippe Jimenez/wikipedia.org. 603 (right), wikipedia.org. 607, Sergio Pitamitz / age fotostock. Chapter 15 Martinique: 609, P. Narayan / age fotostock. 610, Philip Coblentz/Medioimages. 611, Maison de la France/LEJEUNE Nicole. 612, ATOUT FRANCE/Patrice Thébault. 616, Guy Thouvenin / age fotostock. 617 (left), Luc Olivier for the Martinique Tourist Board. 617 (right), Pack-Shot/Shutterstock. 618, BarbachalNicolas BOUTHORS/wikipedia.org. 619, Luc Olivier for the Martinique Tourist Board. 622, GARDEL Bertrand / age fotostock. 626, ATOUT FRANCE/Patrice Thébault. 629, Walter Bibikow / age fotostock. 630, Luc Olivier for the Martinique Tourist Board. 642, Frameme/wikipedia.org. 647, Luc Olivier for the Martinique Tourist Board. Chapter 16 Montserrat: 651, John Cole. 652 (left), Igor Kravtchenko / KiMAGIC Photo and Design. 652 (right), Wailunip/wikipedia.org. 656, David Mac Gillivary -Montserrat Tourist Board. 657, David Mac Gillivary -Montserrat Tourist Board. Chapter 17 Puerto Rico: 669, Katja Kreder / age fotostock. 670 (bottom), John Rodriguez/iStockphoto. 670 (top), Morales/age fotostock. 673, Adam Bies/Shutterstock. 676, Julie Schwietert. 677 (left), Pavelsteidl/wikipedia.org. 677 (right), blucolt/Flickr. 678, Marlise Kast. 679, Katja Kreder / age fotostock. 680, steve bly / Alamy. 681 (left), Christian Sumner/iStockphoto. 681 (right), Steve Manson/iStockphoto. 682, Lori Froeb/Shutterstock. 688, Tomás Fano/Flickr. 689 (left), Franz Marc Frei/age fotostock. 689 (top right), Lawrence Robert/Shutterstock. 689 (bottom right), Franz Marc Frei/age fotostock. 690 (left) oStockphoto. 690 (right), Oquendo/ Flickr. 691 (top left) runneralan2004/Flickr. 691 (bottom left), runneralan2004/Flickr. 691 (top center), Franz Marc Frei/age fotostock. 691 (top right), Prknlot/Flickr. 697, Franz Marc Frei / age fotostock.

708, Hotel El Convento. 710, Thomas Hart Shelby. 713, Tres Sirenas Beach Inn. Chapter 18 Saba: 721, Michael S. Nolan/age fotostock. 722 (top), Simon Wong/wikipedia.org. 722 (bottom), Edwin van Wier/ Shutterstock. 726, Rutger Geerling / age fotostock. 729, Rutger Geerling / age fotostock. 735, Rutger Geerling / age fotostock. Chapter 19 St. Barthélemy: 737, Naki Kouyioumtzis / age fotostock. 738 (bottom), SuperStock / age fotostock. 738 (top), Philip Coblentz/Digital Vision (Own). 743, Christian Wheatley/iStockphoto. 744, Karl Weatherly / age fotostock. 745 (left), Jonathan Pozniak. 745 (right), Robert P Cocozza/iStockphoto. 746, Hotel Carl Gustaf. 750, Restaurant Le Gaiac. 756, Hotel Guanahani and Spa. 757, Le Sereno. 759, Eden Rock – St Barths. 763, Tibor Bognar / age fotostock. Chapter 20 St. Eustatius: 767, SuperStock /age fotostock. 768 (left), Hannah Madden/web.me.com/hannah. madden/Site/Welcome.html. 768 (right), Brenda S and R Duncan Kirby. 769, Hannah Madden/web. me.com/hannah.madden/Site/Welcome.html. 772, Hannah Madden/web.me.com/hannah.madden/Site/ Welcome.html. 775, Bob Turner / age fotostock. 776, Picture Contact / Alamy. Chapter 21 St. Kitts and Nevis: 783, Peter Phipp/Peter Phipp/age fotostock. 784, Doug Scott/age fotostock. 785, Peter Phipp/age fotostock. 787, Philip Coblentz/Medioimages. 790, Michael DeHoog /Cheryl Andrews Marketing Communications. 791 (left), World Pictures / age fotostock. 791 (right), maggiejp/Flickr. 792, Philip Coblentz/Digital Vision. 793, Lidian Neeleman/iStockphoto. 797, Roger Brisbane, Brisbane Productions. 799, Beach House. 803, Ottley's Plantation Inn. 812, Bob Turner / age fotostock. 819, Peter Peirce. Chapter 22 St. Lucia: 827, Colin Sinclair / age fotostock. 828 (left), Philip Coblentz/Medioimages. 828 (top right), Bruno Morandi/age fotostock. 828 (bottom right), Angelo Cavalli/age fotostock. 834, Benjamin Howell/iStockphoto. 835 (left), Christian Horan. 835 (right), Corinne Lutter/iStockphoto. 836, Saint Lucia Tourism Board. 843, Ian Cumming / age fotostock. 850, Ladera. 853, Cotton Bay Village. 855, Sandals Resorts. 856, Sandals Resorts. 863, Gavin Hellier / age fotostock. Chapter 23 St. Maarten/St. Martin: 869, Angelo Cavalli/age fotostock. 870, St Maarten Tourist Bureau. 871, Angelo Cavalli/age fotostock. 876, drewmon, Fodors.com member. 877 (top and bottom), St Maarten Tourist Bureau. 878, St Maarten Tourist Bureau. 879, St Maarten Tourist Bureau. 880, St Maarten Tourist Bureau. 884, alysta/Shutterstock. 896, Chris Floyd. 897, Palm Court Hotel & Caribbean Princess Suites. 899, St Maarten Tourist Bureau. Chapter 24 St. Vincent and the Grenadines: 909, Alvaro Leiva/age fotostock. 910 (bottom), St. Vincent Tourism. 910 (top), SuperStock/ age fotostock. 916, Hauke Dressler / age fotostock. 917 (bottom), Christian Goupi / age fotostock. 917 (top), Jason Pratt/ Flickr. 918, Jason Pratt/Flickr. 919, Raffles Hotels and Resorts. 924, Susan E. Degginger / Alamy. 930, Young Island Resort. 939, Christian Goupi / age fotostock. 944, Raffles Hotels and Resorts. 948, The Leading Hotels of the World. 951, AIC / age fotostock. 952 (top), Joy von Tiedemann. 952 (top center), pocketwiley/Flickr. 952 (bottom center), Tony Arruza. 952 (bottom), Raffles Hotels and Resorts. 952 (right), Casa de Campo. 953 (top and bottom), olly /Shutterstock. 954, Tony Arruza. 955, martinique/ Shutterstock. Chapter 25 Trinidad and Tobago: 959, Robert Harding Productions / age fotostock. 960 (bottom), Angelo Cavalli/age fotostock. 960 (top), Philip Coblentz/Digital Vision. 965, Trinidad & Tobago Tourism Development Company. 966, Michael Newton / age fotostock. 967 (left), ARCO/R Kiedrowski / age fotostock. 967 (right), PHB.cz (Richard Semik)/Shutterstock. 968, Gierth, F / age fotostock. 969, Philip Coblentz/Medioimages. 970, dbimages / Alamy. 971 (left), Paul Lowry/Flickr. 971 (right), Trinidad & Tobago Tourism Development Company. 972, Trinidad & Tobago Tourism Development Company. 975, Tereva/wikipedia.org. 980, Shanel/wikipedia.org. 984, Hyatt Regency Trinidad. 991, Bob Turner / age fotostock. 999, Blaine Harrington / age fotostock. 1000 (top and bottom), Blacqbook/Shutterstock, 1001, Peter Adams / age fotostock. Chapter 26 Turks and Caicos Islands: 1005, Takaji Ochi - VWPICS. 1006 (bottom), Angelo Cavalli/age fotostock. 1006 (top), Turks & Caicos Tourism. 1007, Turks & Caicos Tourism. 1011, Joaquin Palting/iStockphoto. 1012, Ramona Settle. 1013 (top and bottom), Ramona Settle. 1014, Ramona Settle. 1015, Ramona Settle. 1027, West Bay Club. 1031, Turks & Caicos Tourist Office. 1035, COMO Hotels and Resorts. 1042, Ian Cumming/ age fotostock. Chapter 27 United States Virgin Islands: 1047, U.S. Virgin Islands Department of Tourism. 1048 (bottom), Philip Coblentz/Medioimages. 1048 (top), U.S. Virgin Islands Dept. of Tourism. 1054, Ken Brown/iStockphoto. 1055, (left) Juneisy Q. Hawkins/Shutterstock. 1055 (right), cnabickum/Shutterstock. 1056, U.S. Virgin Islands Department of Tourism. 1059, SuperStock/age fotostock. 1068, Coral World Ocean Park, St. Thomas. 1079, The Ritz-Carlton, St. Thomas. 1089, Carlos Villoch - MagicSea.com / Alamy. 1091, Kendra Nielsam/Shutterstock. 1093, divemasterking2000/Flickr. 1094 (top), Shirley Vanderbilt / age fotostock. 1094 (center), Julie de Leseleuc/iStockphoto. 1094 (bottom), Marjorie McBride / Alamy. 1095, divemasterking2000/Flickr. 1096 (top), David Coleman/iStockphoto. 1096 (bottom), Steve Simonsen. 1103, Walter Bibikow / age fotostock. 1116, Caneel Bay/ Rosewood Hotels & Resorts. 1118, Maho Bay Camps & Estate Concordia Preserve. 1128, Walter Bibikow / age fotostock. 1133, Bill Ross/Flirt Collection/photolibrary.com. 1140, Villa Greenleaf. 1145, SuperStock / age fotostock. 1147, U.S. Virgin Islands Department of Tourism.

ABOUT OUR WRITERS

St. Thomas–based writer and dietitian **Carol M. Bareuther** writes for several regional and national magazines such as *Destinations, Discover St. Thomas-St. John,* and *St. Thomas-St. John This Week*. She's the author of two books, including *Virgin Islands Cooking*.

Long-time St. John resident **Lynda Lohr** lives above Coral Bay and writes for numerous publications as well as travel Web sites. She prefers swimming at Great Maho Bay and hiking the island's numerous trails. An inveterate traveler, she's logged many miles to beautiful spots around the world.

As a life-long resident of New England, **Elise Meyer** has always considered her trips to the Caribbean to be a wintertime necessity. St. Barth and Anguilla have been favored destinations for more than 20 years. Now that the two kids are off on their own adventures, she's been enjoying longer and more exotic trips with a husband who shares her wanderlust, as well as a firm resolve to never check in luggage. She maintains a blog at www.elisemeyer.blogspot.com.

Husband-wife team **Paris Permenter** and **John Bigley** have authored numerous guides to the Caribbean including Fodor's In Focus Jamaica. When they're not in the islands, they publish Lovetripper.com, focusing on romantic travel, and DogTipper.com, featuring tips for dog lovers, from their home base in Texas.

Vernon O'Reilly-Ramesar is a broadcaster and writer who divides his life between Trinidad and Canada. He spends much of his time exploring the wonders of the Southern Caribbean in his quest for the perfect beachside gin-martini.

Heather Rodino recently traded the island of Manhattan for the island of Puerto Rico, leaving behind a career in book publishing that included editorial positions at Barnes & Noble's publishing division and the Times Books imprint of Henry Holt. She is now a freelance editor and writer. She lives in the Condado neighborhood of San Juan and doesn't miss those long New York winters.

On a quest to find the best beaches in the world, **Ramona Settle** chose Providenciales in the Turks & Caicos Islands to be her second home. She has written articles on T&C for *Times of the Islands* and *Where When How* magazines, as well as has had pictures published in *Caribbean Travel & Life* and *Islands Magazine*.

Jordan Simon has written about nearly every Caribbean island for numerous national publications including *Cooking Light, Art & Antiques, Condé Nast Traveler, Modern Bride, Town & Country, American Way, Diversion,* Caribbean Travel & Life, and *Hamptons,* and serves as weekly columnist for AOL Travel and Lifestyle Editor for *Caribbean Living*. He has authored several books, including *Fodor's Colorado, Fodor's InFocus Cayman Islands,* and the *Gousha/USA Today Ski Atlas*.

Eileen Robinson Smith has lived in four of the Virgin Islands and is the former managing editor of the *Virgin Islander*. She has written about food and travel for many national magazines. A Fodor's veteran, she has written on the Dominican Republic for more than 15 years, on Martinique and Guadeloupe for more than a decade.

Chicago native **Roberta Sotonoff** is a confessed travel junkie who writes to support her habit. Her work has appeared in more than 75 domestic and international publications, Web sites, and guidebooks. She writes frequently about the Caribbean.

Jane E. Zarem travels frequently to the Caribbean from her Connecticut home. She has contributed to numerous Fodor's guides in addition to Caribbean, among them *New England, USA, Cape Cod, Bahamas,* and, most recently, authored *Barbados and St. Lucia InFocus*.